YEARBOOK
OF THE
UNITED
NATIONS

1957

OFFICE OF PUBLIC INFORMATION
UNITED NATIONS, NEW YORK

KRAUS REPRINT CO.
Millwood, N. Y.
1975

UNITED NATIONS PUBLICATIONS

SALES NO.: 58. I. 1

Reprinted with the permission of the United Nations
KRAUS REPRINT CO.
A U.S. Division of Kraus-Thomson Organization Limited

Printed in U.S.A.

Foreword

The opportunities and risks of the present age have made effective international co-operation essential for the security and well-being of all nations. The hope of progress depends largely upon public understanding of the problems involved.

This *Yearbook of the United Nations,* the eleventh of its kind, is offered as an aid to that understanding. It covers the year 1957, except for proceedings of the United Nations General Assembly in the early months of 1957, which were dealt with in the preceding *Yearbook.* It also contains comprehensive documentary references to the proceedings of the United Nations for the use of those who wish to go more fully into the subjects treated in this volume.

The present *Yearbook* and its predecessors show how the United Nations family contribute towards solutions of international problems which approach the goals of common interest as embodied in the aims and principles of the United Nations Charter. They indicate the ways in which the United Nations can serve Governments in efforts to control conflicts and reduce tensions and differences, thus at the same time opening the road to further advances. To understand this, and to act upon this understanding, is one important means of strengthening the role of the United Nations.

DAG HAMMARSKJOLD
Secretary-General

THE UNITED NATIONS AND RELATED AGENCIES

(As of 31 December 1957)

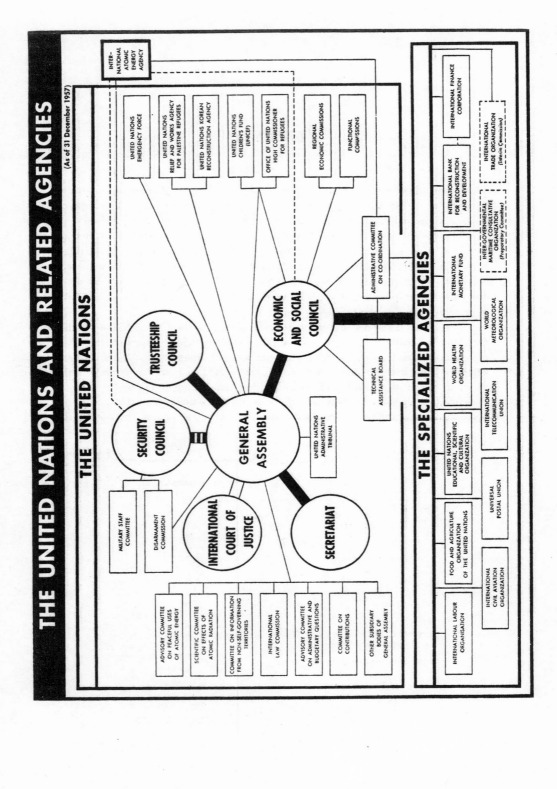

Contents

PART ONE. THE UNITED NATIONS

POLITICAL AND SECURITY QUESTIONS

ECONOMIC AND SOCIAL QUESTIONS

QUESTIONS CONCERNING NON-SELF-GOVERNING TERRITORIES AND THE INTERNATIONAL TRUSTEESHIP SYSTEM

LEGAL QUESTIONS

ADMINISTRATIVE AND BUDGETARY QUESTIONS

PART TWO. THE INTER-GOVERNMENTAL ORGANIZATIONS RELATED TO THE UNITED NATIONS

APPENDICES

INDEX 551

ILLUSTRATIONS AND CHARTS

STRUCTURE OF THE GENERAL ASSEMBLY
TWELFTH SESSION

GENERAL ASSEMBLY

MAIN COMMITTEES

- FIRST COMMITTEE: POLITICAL AND SECURITY (Including the regulation of armaments)
- SPECIAL POLITICAL COMMITTEE
- SECOND COMMITTEE: ECONOMIC AND FINANCIAL
- THIRD COMMITTEE: SOCIAL, HUMANITARIAN AND CULTURAL
- FOURTH COMMITTEE: TRUSTEESHIP (Including Non-Self-Governing Territories)
- FIFTH COMMITTEE: ADMINISTRATIVE & BUDGETARY
- SIXTH COMMITTEE: LEGAL

PROCEDURAL COMMITTEES

- GENERAL COMMITTEE
- CREDENTIALS COMMITTEE

STANDING COMMITTEES

- ADVISORY COMMITTEE ON ADMINISTRATIVE AND BUDGETARY QUESTIONS
- COMMITTEE ON CONTRIBUTIONS

Other Existing Bodies Set Up by General Assembly

Interim Committee of the General Assembly
Disarmament Commission
Sub-Committee of the Disarmament Commission
United Nations Emergency Force (UNEF)
Advisory Committee on UNEF
Committee on the Financing of UNEF
  (appointed under Assembly resolution 1089 (XI))
United Nations Conciliation Commission for Palestine
United Nations Relief and Works Agency
  for Palestine Refugees
Panel for Inquiry and Conciliation
Advisory Committee on the Peaceful Uses of Atomic Energy
Scientific Committee on the Effects of Atomic Radiation
Peace Observation Commission
Collective Measures Committee
Special Committee on the Problem of Hungary
General Assembly's Special Representative
  on the Hungarian Problem
United Nations Commission for the Unification
  and Rehabilitation of Korea
United Nations Korean Reconstruction Agency (UNKRA)
United Nations Children's Fund (UNICEF)
Office of the United Nations High Commissioner for Refugees
United Nations Refugee Fund Executive Committee
Preparatory Committee for the Special Fund
Ad Hoc Commission on Prisoners of War
United Nations Advisory Council for Somaliland
United Nations Commissioner for Supervision of Elections
  in Togoland under French Administration
Sub-Committee on the Revision of the Questionnaire
  (relating to Trust Territories)
Committee on South West Africa
Good Offices Committee on South West Africa
Committee on Information from Non-Self-Governing Territories
Advisory Committee for the United Nations
  Memorial Cemetery in Korea
Negotiating Committee for Extra-Budgetary Funds
United Nations Staff Pension Committee
Investments Committee
Board of Auditors
Committee on the Control and Limitation of Documentation
Expert Committee on United Nations Public Information
International Law Commission
United Nations Administrative Tribunal
Committee on Applications for Review of Administrative
  Tribunal Judgements
Committee on Arrangements for a Conference for the Purpose
  of Reviewing the Charter
Committee on Government Replies on the Question
  of Defining Aggression

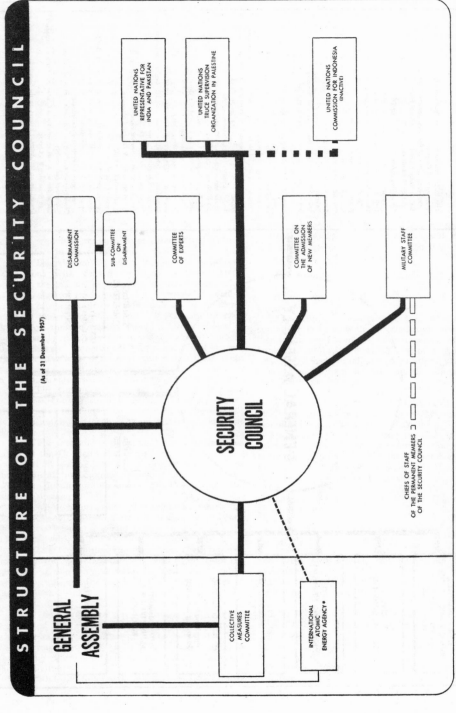

STRUCTURE OF THE SECURITY COUNCIL

(As of 31 December 1957)

GENERAL ASSEMBLY

SECURITY COUNCIL

DISARMAMENT COMMISSION

SUB-COMMITTEE ON DISARMAMENT

COMMITTEE OF EXPERTS

COMMITTEE ON THE ADMISSION OF NEW MEMBERS

MILITARY STAFF COMMITTEE

UNITED NATIONS REPRESENTATIVE FOR INDIA AND PAKISTAN

UNITED NATIONS TRUCE SUPERVISION ORGANIZATION IN PALESTINE

UNITED NATIONS COMMISSION FOR INDONESIA (INACTIVE)

COLLECTIVE MEASURES COMMITTEE

INTERNATIONAL ATOMIC ENERGY AGENCY *

CHIEFS OF STAFF OF THE PERMANENT MEMBERS OF THE SECURITY COUNCIL

* The International Atomic Energy Agency, an autonomous inter-governmental body under the aegis of the United Nations, reports annually on its activities to the General Assembly. It submits reports, when appropriate, to the Security Council and notifies the Council whenever, in connexion with the Agency's activities, questions within the Council's competence arise. In particular, Article XII of the Agency's Statute requires the Agency's Board of Governors to report cases of non-compliance with the safeguards provisions of the Statute to the Security Council.

Part One

THE UNITED NATIONS

EXPLANATORY NOTE ON DOCUMENTS

To assist readers who wish to make a more detailed study of subjects discussed in Part One, documentary references are provided at the end of each section. These references include the symbols and titles of documents of the principal organs and bodies of the United Nations, records of voting and texts of adopted resolutions. Also listed are the numbers of the meetings of the various organs at which the subject dealt with were discussed. These meeting numbers indicate the relevant discussion records.

For those unfamiliar with United Nations documentation, the following may serve as a guide to the principal document symbols:

A/ refers to documents of the General Assembly, A/C. documents are those of six of its seven Main Committees, e.g., A/C.1/777 is a document of the First Committee, A/C.2/189 of the Second Committee. The symbol for documents of the seventh Main Committee, the Special Political Committee, is A/SPC/. A/AC documents are those of *ad hoc* bodies of the Assembly, e.g., A/AC.73/L.8 is a document of the Committee on South West Africa, the "L" denoting limited circulation.

DC/ refers to documents of the Disarmament Commission.

S/ refers to documents of the Security Council.

E/ refers to documents of the Economic and Social Council. E/AC. and E/C. documents are those of the Committees of the Council, e.g., E/AC.6/L.136 is a document of the Economic Committee, and E/C.2/L.20 a document of the Council Committee on Non-Governmental Organizations. E/CN. documents are those of the Commissions of the Council, each of which also has its own number.

T/ refers to documents of the Trusteeship Council. T/COM. are communications; T/OBS., observations of the Administering Authorities on petitions and communications; and T/PET., petitions.

U.N.P. designates United Nations publications.

Full citations are given for documents of the International Court of Justice.

Y.U.N. stands for *Yearbook of the United Nations*.

Part One

THE UNITED NATIONS

EXPLANATORY NOTE ON DOCUMENTS

To assist readers who wish to make a more detailed study of subjects discussed in Part One, documentary references are provided at the end of each section. These references include the symbols and titles of documents of the principal organs and bodies of the United Nations, records of voting and texts of adopted resolutions. Also listed are the numbers of the meetings of the various organs at which the subject dealt with were discussed. These meeting numbers indicate the relevant discussion records.

For those unfamiliar with United Nations documentation, the following may serve as a guide to the principal document symbols:

A/ refers to documents of the General Assembly, A/C. documents are those of six of its seven Main Committees, e.g., A/C.1/777 is a document of the First Committee, A/C.2/189 of the Second Committee. The symbol for documents of the seventh Main Committee, the Special Political Committee, is A/SPC/. A/AC documents are those of *ad hoc* bodies of the Assembly, e.g., A/AC.73/L.8 is a document of the Committee on South West Africa, the "L" denoting limited circulation.

DC/ refers to documents of the Disarmamen Commission.

S/ refers to documents of the Security Council.

E/ refers to documents of the Economic and Social Council. E/AC. and E/C. documents are those of the Committees of the Council, e.g., E/AC.6/L.136 is a document of the Economic Committee, and E/C.2/L.20 a document of the Council Committee on Non-Governmental Organizations. E/CN. documents are those of the Commissions of the Council, each of which also has its own number.

T/ refers to documents of the Trusteeship Council. T/COM. are communications; T/OBS., observations of the Administering Authorities on petitions and communications; and T/PET., petitions.

U.N.P. designates United Nations publications.

Full citations are given for documents of the International Court of Justice.

Y.U.N. stands for *Yearbook of the United Nations*.

Political and Security Questions

CHAPTER I

DISARMAMENT

CONSIDERATION BY DISARMAMENT COMMISSION'S SUB-COMMITTEE

At its eleventh session, the Assembly, by resolution 1011(XI) of 14 February 1957, recommended: (1) that the Disarmament Commission and its Sub-Committee give prompt attention to various proposals that had been submitted to the Assembly at that session; and (2) that the Disarmament Commission ask the Sub-Committee to prepare a progress report for consideration by the Commission not later than 1 August 1957.

The Sub-Committee held 71 meetings in London, between 18 March and 6 September 1957. It adopted its fourth and fifth reports for submission to the Disarmament Commission on 1 August and 11 September 1957, respectively. The Sub-Committee having decided to make public the records of its meetings, the two reports were released on 8 August and 11 September, respectively. Annexed to the reports were the proposals, working papers, *notes verbales,* letters and memoranda submitted during the Sub-Committee's session (see DOCUMENTARY REFERENCES below).

The Sub-Committee had before it the following principal proposals: three USSR proposals, submitted on 18 March, 30 April and 14 June respectively, and two joint proposals by Canada, France, the United Kingdom and the United States, submitted on 2 August and 29 August, respectively.

USSR PROPOSAL OF 18 MARCH 1957

The USSR proposal of 18 March dealt with the reduction of armaments and armed forces, and the prohibition of nuclear weapons to be carried out in two stages, in 1957/1958 and in 1959. The proposal reiterated the points contained in a USSR statement of 17 November 1956 on disarmament and several points contained in earlier USSR proposals. In addition, it provided for a renunciation of the use of nuclear weapons, including rocket weapons with nuclear warheads, during the first stage of a disarmament agreement and for control over guided rockets during the second stage.

USSR PROPOSAL OF 30 APRIL 1957

On 30 April, the USSR Government, noting that the Western powers were not yet prepared to conclude an agreement on a comprehensive disarmament programme, and in order to facilitate progress on the disarmament issue, submitted a second set of proposals on the implementation of partial disarmament measures, with the following provisions:

(*a*) There should be a two-stage reduction of armed forces, as follows: for the United States and USSR, reductions to 2.5 million men each in the first stage, and then to 1–1.5 million men each in the second stage; for the United Kingdom and France, reductions to 750,000 men each in the first stage, and to 650,000 men each in the second stage.

(*b*) There should be a first-stage reduction of conventional armaments and military budgets by 15 per cent. The size of further reductions in armaments and budgets could be considered at a later stage.

(*c*) These reductions would be carried out under appropriate international control. During the first stage, a control organ, established within the framework of the Security Council, would examine information provided by States on their implementation of partial disarmament measures. Control posts would be established on the territory of States, on a basis of reciprocity, at large ports, railway junctions and on main motor highways. During the second stage, control posts would be established at airports and would be related to an agreement for the complete prohibition of nuclear weapons and their elimination from the armaments of States.

(d) States should undertake to renounce the use of nuclear weapons of all types, including aerial bombs, rockets carrying atomic and hydrogen warheads, irrespective of range, atomic artillery, etc. This undertaking should come into force from the beginning of the first stage. The States concerned should, furthermore, undertake to make every effort to conclude an agreement on the complete prohibition of nuclear weapons, their elimination from the arsenals of States, the cessation of their production and the destruction of their stockpiles.

(e) The discontinuance of tests of nuclear weapons should be dealt with independently of any other disarmament measures.

(f) Liquidation of foreign bases could be carried out by steps. Agreement should be sought, in the first instance, on those bases which could be liquidated during the period of one or two years.

(g) The armed forces of the United States, the USSR, the United Kingdom and France stationed in the territory of Germany should be reduced by one third as a means to ease international tension.

(h) Similarly, there should be a reduction of the armed forces of the United States, the United Kingdom and France stationed in the territory of the North Atlantic Treaty Organization (NATO) countries, and a reduction of the armed forces of the USSR stationed in the territory of the Warsaw Treaty countries. The size of the reductions could be determined in the course of subsequent negotiations.

(i) There should be aerial inspection for a sector in Europe bounded in the west by the Greenwich meridian, in the east by longitude 25° East, in the north by latitude 54° North and in the south by latitude 39° 38′ North. In the Far East, aerial inspection could be extended to the territories of the United States and the USSR east of longitude 108° East and west of longitude 90° West.

(j) Propaganda for war, particularly with regard to the use of atomic and hydrogen weapons, should be stopped.

USSR PROPOSAL OF 14 JUNE 1957

A third proposal was submitted by the USSR on 14 June, for the immediate cessation of all nuclear weapon tests for a period of two or three years. The USSR said it would agree to the institution of control over the cessation of these tests, and proposed the establishment of an international commission to supervise the fulfilment by States of their obligations. On a basis of reciprocity, control posts would be established in the territory of the Soviet Union, the United States and the United Kingdom, and in the Pacific Ocean area.

On 2 July, Canada, France, the United Kingdom and the United States welcomed the USSR's acceptance of the Western powers' requirement of inspection posts with appropriate scientific instruments, equipment and facilities, to be set up for the control and detection of nuclear weapon tests. Soviet acceptance of this principle, they declared, brought a temporary suspension of nuclear weapon tests within the realm of possibility, as a part of an agreement for a first step in disarmament. The four powers further declared that this temporary cessation of tests would be subject to precise agreement on its duration and timing, on the installation and location of the necessary controls, including inspection posts, and on its relationship to other provisions of a first-stage agreement such as reduction in armed forces and armaments and cessation of production of fissionable materials for weapons purposes.

WESTERN POWERS' PROPOSAL OF 2 AUGUST 1957

On 2 August, Canada, France, the United Kingdom and the United States submitted a working paper on systems of inspection to safeguard against the possibility of surprise attack. As a safeguard against the possibility of surprise attack, the inspection system would include: (a) aerial inspection; (b) ground observation posts at principal ports, railway junctions, main highways and important airfields; and (c) mobile ground teams with specifically defined authority.

The areas of inspection were described in the Western plan as follows: (1) All the territory of the continental United States, Alaska, including the Aleutian Islands, Canada and the USSR. Should, however, these limits be unacceptable to the USSR, the alternative would be an Arctic zone to include all of the USSR, Canada, Alaska, Greenland and Norway north of the Arctic Circle, in addition to a sector west of longitude 140° West, east of longitude 160° East and north of latitude 50° North, the remainder of Alaska, of the Aleutian and Kurile Islands and of the Kamchatka peninsula. (2) If the USSR were to accept either of these two zones, an area of inspection in Europe would be added to cover the territory bounded in the west by longitude 10° West, in the east by longitude 60° East and, in the south by latitude 40° North. If however the USSR were to reject this zone, a more limited inspection zone in Europe could be discussed on the understanding that this would include a significant part of the territory of the USSR, as well as the other countries of Eastern Europe.

WESTERN POWERS' PROPOSAL
OF 29 AUGUST 1957

On 29 August, Canada, France, the United Kingdom and the United States presented a further working paper consolidating various proposals for partial disarmament measures put forward by these powers in the course of the negotiations. The proposals were presented on the express understanding that they were inseparable. They included the following measures:

(a) Within one year after the disarmament convention entered into force, the USSR, the United States, the United Kingdom and France should each restrict or reduce their armed forces to the following maximum limits: 2.5 million men each for the USSR and the United States, and 750,000 men each for the United Kingdom and France.

(b) During the same period, the States should place a specific quantity of designated types of armaments to be agreed upon in storage depots, within their own territories and under the supervision of an international control organization (see k below).

(c) There would be a second-stage limitation of the armed forces of the United States and the USSR to 2.1 million men each and of those of the United Kingdom and France to 700,000 men each, on condition that compliance with the earlier provisions had been verified, that

there had been progress towards the solution of political issues, and that other essential States had become parties to the convention. This level could be further limited by negotiation to 1.7 million men each for the United States and the USSR and to 650,000 men each for the United Kingdom and France. The levels of other essential States would be specified at each stage through negotiations with them.

(d) In agreed relation to the armed forces and under appropriate control, France, the USSR, the United Kingdom and the United States should agree to make information available to the international control organization about their military budgets and expenditures for the year before the convention entered into force and for each year thereafter.

(e) In the field of nuclear armaments, each party should assume an obligation not to use nuclear weapons if an armed attack did not place the party in a situation of individual or collective self-defence.

(f) All future production of fissionable materials should be used at home or abroad under international supervision, exclusively for non-weapons purposes, including stockpiling, and equitable transfers of fissionable materials should be made, in successive increments, from previous production to non-weapons purposes, including stockpiling.

(g) Each party should further undertake not to transfer out of its control any nuclear weapons except in cases where they would be used in self-defence against armed attack.

(h) All parties to the convention would furthermore undertake to refrain from conducting nuclear test explosions for a period of 12 months from the date the convention came into force, provided that agreement had been reached on the installation and maintenance of the necessary control. If this inspection system operated to the satisfaction of each party concerned and if progress was achieved in the preparation of an inspection system for the cessation of the production of fissionable material for weapons purposes, all parties to the convention would undertake to refrain from conducting nuclear test explosions for a further period of 12 months. Testing could be resumed if the inspection system for the cessation of production of fissionable material for weapons purposes had not been installed at the end of 24 months.

(*i*) The parties should co-operate in the establishment of a technical committee to study the design of an inspection system which would make it possible to assure that the launching of objects through outer space would be exclusively for peaceful and scientific purposes.

(*j*) The limits of the areas of inspection to safeguard against the possibility of surprise attack were those proposed by the four Western powers on 2 August (see above). Any initial system of inspection designed to safeguard against the possibility of surprise attack might be extended by agreement of all concerned to the end that ultimately the system would deal with the danger of surprise attack from anywhere.

(*k*) An international control organization should be established within the framework of the Security Council. It should include, as its executive organ, a board of control, important decisions of which would require the affirmative vote of the representatives of the Governments represented on the Sub-Committee and of such other parties as might be agreed. In addition to other rights and responsibilities, the board of control should have the authority to study a system for regulating the export and import of designated armaments.

(*l*) Each party would have the right to suspend its obligations in the event of an important violation by another party prejudicing its security.

On 4 and 5 September, memoranda were submitted by the United States, the United Kingdom, France, Canada and the USSR, explaining the position of the respective Governments on the various proposals described above.

CONSIDERATION BY
DISARMAMENT COMMISSION

The fourth and fifth reports of the Sub-Committee were considered by the Disarmament Commission at two meetings on 30 September 1957.

After a debate in which the representatives of Australia, Canada, China, Colombia, France, Iraq, the United Kingdom, the USSR and the United States participated, the Disarmament Commission decided to take note of the reports of the Sub-Committee and to transmit them, together with the records and the relevant documents of the meetings of the Disarmament Com-

mission, for consideration by the General Assembly and the Security Council.

CONSIDERATION BY
GENERAL ASSEMBLY

The problem of disarmament was a main subject in the General Debate at the twelfth session of the General Assembly which took place between 19 September and 8 October 1957. Later, between 10 October and 6 November, it was discussed in the Assembly's First Committee. Some of the main points made in the General Debate are summarized below.

DISCUSSION DURING GENERAL DEBATE

During the General Debate, the Foreign Minister of the USSR referred to a memorandum of 20 September 1957 by the USSR Government on partial measures in the field of disarmament which have been submitted for the Assembly's consideration. These measures dealt with: the reduction of armed forces; the reduction of armaments and military budgets; the prohibition of atomic weapons; the suspension of nuclear weapon tests; international control; aerial photography; foreign military bases; the reduction of the armed forces of the United States, the USSR, the United Kingdom and France stationed in the territory of Germany and in the territories of NATO and Warsaw Treaty countries; the prohibition of war propaganda; and the composition of the Disarmament Commission and its Sub-Committee.

The USSR Foreign Minister announced that the Soviet Union was submitting a new proposal for the renunciation of the use of nuclear weapons for a period of five years, with the understanding that if no far-reaching agreement on disarmament was concluded during the period, it would be possible to revert to the consideration of that problem. The renunciation should be considered separately and made contingent on the solution of other aspects of disarmament.

He also repeated, with certain modifications, the USSR's general disarmament proposals of 30 April and its proposal of 14 June on the cessation of test explosions (see above). Thus, it was proposed that nuclear tests should be discontinued as of 1 January 1958 for two or three years, and that control bases to implement that suspension should be established in the territory of the Soviet Union, the United States, the

United Kingdom, and its possessions, and in the Pacific, including Australia. Further, the USSR favoured enlarging the Disarmament Commission and its Sub-Committee as it thought the membership of these bodies was not representative.

The Foreign Minister of Ireland urged the General Assembly to lay the political foundations of peace by a progressive elimination of areas of conflict between the great powers. This would provide a solid and lasting basis for agreements on the limitation of weapons. As far as Europe was concerned, progressive military disengagement would be a major contribution. In the Middle East, he added, progress could be made if the powers concerned agreed to respect the sovereignty of the weak countries, to harmonize their policies through the United Nations and to abate their diplomatic competition.

The Prime Minister of Canada drew attention to the particular danger of surprise attack as a result of the existence of nuclear weapons in large numbers together with bombers capable of delivering them and the development of intercontinental ballistic missiles. Canada, he said, was particularly interested in bringing about control of those weapons as a result of its geographical position between the United States and the USSR. He stressed the importance of diverting fissionable material from the manufacture of weapons to peaceful uses in order to prevent the continued stockpiling of nuclear weapons. He thought it essential that the Disarmament Commission and its Sub-Committee continue to operate in order to find an agreement on disarmament and on the prevention of surprise attack. The membership of the Sub-Committee might be broadened, he said, adding that Canada would be prepared to withdraw from the Sub-Committee if that would facilitate the solution of the disarmament problem.

The Foreign Secretary of the United Kingdom, explaining the Western powers' proposal submitted by Canada, France, the United Kingdom and the United States to the Disarmament Commission's Sub-Committee on 29 August, said that a comprehensive disarmament plan covering all stages was not yet practical. A first-stage disarmament agreement, however, was both desirable and possible, without being dependent upon political preconditions. It should encompass both the nuclear and conventional fields, and progress should extend as far as the area of control permitted.

Commenting on the USSR Foreign Minister's statement on the suspension of nuclear tests, he contended that the mere suspension of nuclear tests was not a disarmament measure, for it did not prevent the further stockpiling of nuclear weapons. Only the diversion of fissionable materials from armaments to peaceful uses would be meaningful. He then surveyed the areas of agreement or near-agreement between the Western powers and the USSR. As to the reduction of forces by stages, he felt that only a relaxation of international tension could facilitate the proposed second- or third-stage reductions. In any case, stress should be laid on the reduction of conventional armaments rather than on the number of men under arms, for the latter criterion had little meaning when the fire-power of a reduced force could be increased.

He also emphasized the importance of working out the technical details of disarmament and related control and inspection problems in advance—a view which, he said, the USSR refused to adopt. He proposed the appointment of a committee of experts to work out the relevant details on control over conventional armament, over nuclear weapons, the prohibition of nuclear tests, and the relevant details on safeguards against surprise attack.

The Foreign Minister of Belgium recognized that mutual confidence between East and West was lacking at present. In its absence, the only sure and permanent guarantee was that of international control. It was the resistance to control which had prevented agreement in the Sub-Committee. To overcome this obstacle, it was necessary to inform and enlighten the peoples of the world about the danger of the armaments race, and particularly about the destructive effects of nuclear weapons and the necessity of establishing control. Belgium had therefore proposed a draft resolution embodying a plan of action to provide the peoples of the world, through the United Nations, with a synthesis of information based on scientific and unchallengeable facts.

The Foreign Minister of Poland stated that the problem of disarmament was the key problem before the Assembly's twelfth session. He announced that, after consultations with other members of the Warsaw Pact, Poland was willing to accept a prohibition of production and stockpiling of nuclear weapons on its territory, should west Germany and east Germany express their consent to take, simultaneously, the same action on their own territory.

The Foreign Minister of Czechoslovakia welcomed Poland's initiative and declared that Czechoslovakia was willing to associate itself with it and to assume an obligation to renounce the production and stationing of atomic weapons on its territory, if both parts of Germany accepted the same obligation.

The Foreign Minister of Mexico recalled the establishment in 1951, upon Mexico's initiative, of a Sub-Committee of the Assembly's First Committee of which he, as President of the Assembly's sixth session, had been Chairman.

Stating that the work of that Sub-Committee had contributed to some progress in the negotiations on disarmament, he suggested that the Assembly should set up a similar body, consisting of the five members of the present Disarmament Sub-Committee and, perhaps, a president appointed by the Assembly. The Assembly should also consider the advisability of creating the new post of United Nations Commissioner for Disarmament, with the task of exploring any possibilities existing in the field of disarmament, to help the parties in their negotiations, and to submit privately for their consideration proposals that he might deem pertinent.

With regard to nuclear weapons, the Mexican Foreign Minister maintained that the idea of resorting to limited atomic war was wrong and dangerous. In addition, he thought it necessary for the United Nations to establish the responsibility of States for damage caused by nuclear tests to the populations of other countries.

India's representative recommended the establishment of a Disarmament Commission composed of an equal number of representatives of both power blocs and representatives of other States. It was for this reason, he said, that India had asked that the Assembly take up the question of expanding the membership of the Disarmament Commission and its Sub-Committee. The suggested new Commission would consider: the adoption of such measures as the suspension of nuclear weapon tests, under international control; the cessation of production of fissionable materials for weapons purposes; the renunciation of the use of nuclear weapons and

the dismantling of stocks of these weapons; and the implementation of an agreement on the reduction of conventional armaments.

CONSIDERATION BY FIRST COMMITTEE

The General Assembly's First Committee discussed the disarmament question at 28 meetings held between 10 October and 6 November 1957, when it dealt with the agenda item entitled "Regulation, limitation and balanced reduction of all armed forces and all armaments; conclusion of an international convention (treaty) on the reduction of armaments and the prohibition of atomic, hydrogen and other weapons of mass destruction: (a) Report of the Disarmament Commission; (b) Expansion of the membership of the Disarmament Commission and of its Sub-Committee; (c) Collective action to inform and enlighten the peoples of the world as to the dangers of the armaments race, and particularly as to the destructive effects of modern weapons; (d) Discontinuance under international control of tests of atomic and hydrogen weapons".

For convenience, some of the major comments in the First Committee are summarized below as follows: (1) remarks on the broader aspects of the disarmament question; (2) remarks on the question of halting atomic and hydrogen weapon tests; (3) remarks on the question of increasing the size of the Disarmament Commission and its Sub-Committee; and (4) remarks on collective action to inform and enlighten the peoples of the world about the dangers of the armaments race, particularly the destructive effects of modern weapons.

This is followed by a summary of the various proposals and decisions on these subjects.

Opening the debate in the First Committee, the United States representative stressed that the differences between the USSR and the Western powers had been narrowed by a number of steps taken by the USSR and Western representatives in the Disarmament Commission's Sub-Committee. The four Western members of the Sub-Committee had shown, no less than the USSR, a spirit of co-operation. In order to meet USSR objections, they had made a number of changes in their position. Their proposal of 29 August was aimed at: (1) putting an end to the production of fissionable materials for war purposes and making a start on a controlled transfer of fissionable materials from weapons

stockpiles to peaceful uses; (2) suspending nuclear tests immediately upon the entry into force
of an agreement, which was to be followed by
the prompt establishment of a monitoring system; (3) reducing the armaments and armed
forces of the great powers in three stages under
a minimum of inspection requirements; (4) preventing surprise attack by a system of progressive
ground and air inspection; and (5) controlling
outer-space weapons.

With regard to the last point, it was proposed
by the Western powers that a technical committee should be established to work out an inspection system which would ensure the use of outer
space exclusively for peaceful and scientific purposes. The United States stand was that if there
was general agreement to conduct such a study
on a multilateral basis, it would be prepared to
participate without awaiting the conclusion of
negotiations on the other substantive proposals.

The United States, however, did not think
that the prospects for agreement would be improved by enlarging the existing bodies dealing
with disarmament. The principle that progress
towards disarmament could be achieved only by
negotiation among the powers principally involved retained its full validity. This did not
mean that disarmament was the exclusive field
of competence of the great powers.

The United Kingdom representative noted
that the Western proposals made in the Sub-
Committee on 29 August were still valid. He
stressed the importance of setting up joint committees of experts to study inspection systems
and supported the United States proposal for
a multilateral study on the control of objects
entering outer space, pending full agreement on
a disarmament plan.

The Canadian representative also urged the
adoption of the measures proposed by the Western powers, but he pointed out that these proposals were not the only means by which progress could be made towards disarmament. He
felt that the sponsors of the proposals would be
ready to improve them in any possible way.

France's policy on the question of disarmament, said the representative of France, was
based on the principle that any disarmament
agreement, whether partial or general, must
have the unanimous support of the States concerned. The interests of security demanded that
disarmament, even if partial, should extend to

all fields simultaneously, for disarmament involving certain types of weapons only would
modify the relation of forces to the advantage
of some and the disadvantage of others. Current
international relations were marked by distrust.
Hence, the primary objective was the restoration
of confidence. This would be achieved only if
each Government was convinced that the others
were scrupulously fulfilling their obligations, in
other words, if there was effective control over
the execution of the agreements arrived at.

The need to restore confidence imposed limits
upon the measures of disarmament which could
be achieved at present. France was opposed to
uncontrolled disarmament or to control without
disarmament, since the former did not dissipate
doubts and the latter did not consolidate peace;
it preferred the progressive carrying out of such
disarmament as could at present be controlled,
by stages, each of which would consolidate
peace, restore some measure of confidence and
make subsequent progress easier. The ultimate
objective was to establish universal security
based on complete disarmament, fully controlled.
Pending the final stage, the independence of
France and its freedom must rest on defensive
alliances. The French Government could not
therefore accept the idea of regional disarmament, as favoured by the USSR, which was
aimed at disrupting those alliances. It could accept only global reductions.

The Western proposals were also endorsed
by the Netherlands representative, who felt
there was a possibility for successful negotiations
on those aspects of disarmament between the
powers concerned.

The specific concern of some of the smaller
countries with regard to the general disarmament question, said the representative of Australia, was that agreements developed mainly out
of concern for the security problems of the great
powers might require adjustment to take account of their effects on the security of smaller
countries in various parts of the world and on
the forces those countries would need to maintain. In particular, Australia felt that a disarmament agreement that would not impose suitable
obligations upon mainland China would have
little meaning in the Far East.

The representative of Pakistan urged the immediate conclusion of an agreement to reduce
armed forces substantially below existing levels,

to exchange lists of weapons to be set aside under international control and to set up depots under international supervision for the storage of designated types of armament to be mutually agreed upon. He urged the USSR to accept the Western proposal for such storage depots, and he appealed to the Western powers to agree to proceed to the second stage of the proposal, numely to reduce armed forces to lower numerical levels, without attaching conditions to the acceptance of those lower figures.

The representative of Israel stressed that the restoration of confidence in the world was a *sine qua non* for any hope of successful disarmament negotiations and that the cause of confidence was not served by the habit of "rocket rattling".

The Norwegian representative favoured an approach to disarmament which, through the achievement of some concrete limited measures, might establish a basis for further progress. He thought that complete prohibition of the use of nuclear weapons was a measure which could be realistically contemplated only at a later stage of disarmament, for no system for the control or elimination of existing stocks of nuclear weapons could be completely effective. He also dealt with the question of suspending nuclear weapon tests (see below for details).

The representative of Sweden thought that the "all-or-nothing" approach to disarmament had failed and that agreement on a more or less extensive programme of partial disarmament must be sought. However, there was still a danger that the "all-or-nothing" policy would be applied even to such partial disarmament by making the adoption of any one measure conditional upon acceptance of all the others.

While Sweden found the proposals of the four Western powers acceptable, it questioned the wisdom of making them an indivisible whole; each measure could be agreed upon without reference to the over-all plan of partial disarmament. Thus, the four powers had taken a realistic step when they had announced that they were prepared to begin a study of the control of outer space without awaiting agreement on the other points of their proposal.

Similarly, the transfer of stocks of fissionable materials from weapons to non-weapons purposes could be agreed upon without awaiting agreement on other measures. In fact, some transfers of such materials had already been announced. Obviously, when the agreement to transfer stocks would be supplemented by an agreement to cut off the production of fissionable materials for weapons purposes under effective international control, the amount of existing stocks transferred could be expected to increase substantially.

The Swedish representative also dealt with the USSR's objection that stopping the production of fissionable materials for weapons purposes would not prevent the continued production of nuclear weapons from existing stocks of materials. To meet that objection, the Swedish representative thought that a group of experts should be set up immediately to work out the necessary system of inspection.

Agreement on the reduction of armed forces, he added, was hardly possible without the cooperation of mainland China. Yet the four-power proposal omitted any reference to mainland China. If the great powers were to agree on an open inspection system with ground and aerial components to guard against the possibility of surprise attack, such a system could also be put into operation as a separate measure.

The USSR representative pointed out that the Soviet Union had proposed that the figures cited in the Western powers' proposal of 29 August for the maximum levels of forces of the great powers should be taken as the basis for agreement on the conventional armaments. Acceptance of these figures, together with the undertaking not to use nuclear weapons, would constitute an important step forward towards the settlement of the disarmament problem.

The Western position on the cessation of production of fissionable materials for war purposes, he said, was not acceptable to the USSR since the production of weapons from existing stockpiles would not be affected. Moreover, destruction of the stocks of weapons was not mentioned and the weapons would not be banned. The USSR, therefore, stood for the immediate suspension of nuclear weapon tests, for the renunciation of use of those weapons at least for a period of five years and for an undertaking to make efforts towards agreement on stopping production of these weapons, on destroying of the stockpiles of these weapons and eliminating them from armaments of States.

As to the question of control, the USSR representative noted that the methods of aerial survey could not achieve either the prevention of surprise attack or the control over disarmament. However, in an effort to clear the path to agreement, the USSR had submitted proposals regarding two aerial survey zones in Europe and in the Far East. The Western powers' answer to that proposal had been to suggest aerial photography of the Arctic. It was obvious that aerial survey in that region would be even more useless than in other areas.

One method of taking a forward step towards disarmament, added the USSR representative, was to implement regional disarmament measures. That was why the USSR had proposed reductions in the armed forces of France, the United Kingdom, the United States and the USSR stationed on German territory, the consideration of the question of dismantling bases on foreign territory, and the prohibition of the stationing of atomic units and atomic weapons outside national borders.

Among those who expressed general agreement with the USSR's views were the representatives of Bulgaria, Poland and Romania.

The Polish representative said that the organization of the armies of the great powers was increasingly adapted to the use of nuclear weapons. As a consequence, States which had hitherto used only conventional armaments would ultimately be obliged to re-equip their armies. This would increase the danger of destruction by nuclear weapons, even in local wars.

What was needed was a positive measure of mutual confidence such as the renunciation of the use of nuclear weapons, if only for a given period, as the Soviet Union had proposed. This would create an atmosphere of confidence propitious to the continuation of disarmament negotiations, particularly with regard to the total prohibition of manufacture of nuclear weapons and proper control measures. The prohibition of nuclear weapons would also lead towards the solution of the problem of intercontinental missiles or artificial satellites.

The Polish Government had announced its readiness to prohibit the production and stockpiling of nuclear weapons on its territory, provided that the two German States would agree to follow suit. The Polish delegation attached the greatest importance to a solution such as that of establishing a zone of limited armaments in Europe. Poland was ready to co-operate in drawing up plans for such a zone, to work towards securing an agreement and to impose within its territory the measures of control agreed upon, should the boundaries of the zone embrace its territory.

The representative of Romania suggested that the force levels of the United States and the USSR be reduced to 2.1 million men each, and that those of France and the United Kingdom be reduced to 700,000 each, without the reaching of an agreement on these levels being made conditional on political settlements (as provided for in the Western powers' proposal of 29 August).

The Yugoslav representative considered that an immediate halting of nuclear weapon tests would represent an advance in relation to the present state of affairs. In order to achieve the full prohibition and elimination of nuclear weapons, he also urged that agreement be reached on such measures as an undertaking not to transfer nuclear weapons or fissionable materials for military use to other countries, the cessation of the production of fissionable materials for weapons purposes, and arrangements whereby fissionable materials now stockpiled for military purposes should gradually be transferred to peaceful use. Renunciation of the use of nuclear weapons, as proposed by the USSR, would facilitate the efforts towards attaining their prohibition and elimination.

The representative of India, referring to the main disarmament problem, held that the most serious difference between the East and the West was the cut-off date for manufacture of fissionable materials. India, he said, was fully committed to the prohibition of production of fissionable materials for weapons purposes; no nuclear materials should be used for the manufacture of weapons. Bodies representing the three main groupings of States should take up the question of the cut-off date, for if it were possible to stop manufacture, it would also be possible to stop use.

The representative of India also urged measures to halt nuclear weapon tests (for further details, see below), as well as arrangements for inspection and control to implement agreements on conventional armaments so as to inspire confidence.

The Indonesian representative suggested a

programme for first steps towards disarmament, which would, among other things, provide for: total prohibition of the use and manufacture of nuclear and other mass-destruction weapons; conversion of existing nuclear weapon stocks to peaceful uses; the use of atomic energy for peaceful purposes; and effective international controls to guarantee observance of agreements on these matters as well as on conventional armaments.

He also expressed concern over the change in the position of some of the great powers, which now contended that the use of nuclear weapons should be permitted in cases of self-defence. Such a conditional prohibition of the use of nuclear weapons could be interpreted only as meaning that those weapons were to be used in local conflicts resulting from the power struggle between the two great blocs.

Mexico reiterated the proposal, made in the Assembly's General Debate for a United Nations Commissioner for Disarmament. This proposal was supported, in the First Committee, by Ecuador and El Salvador, among others.

The Japanese representative maintained that efforts to solve the problem of atomic weapons should be the major concern not only of the great military powers but of all nations, large or small, armed or unarmed. Modern nuclear weapons, when used or even tested, knew no national frontiers. As a peacetime problem, the effects of the radiation resulting from nuclear test explosions could not be ignored. Japan had, accordingly, submitted a draft resolution aimed at bringing about the early conclusion of a disarmament agreement and the suspension of nuclear test explosions. (For further details, see below, PROPOSALS AND DECISIONS.)

Various other speakers in the First Committee also discussed the question of suspending nuclear and thermonuclear tests. The following were among the points made:

The Indian representative pressed for the discontinuance of such tests, with appropriate supervision and control arrangement, and contended that supervision of such tests would help to lower world tensions and so pave the way for progress on further agreements for disarmament. The great powers, he observed, had supported the appointment of a United Nations Committee to study the effects of radiation, but they had not suspended test explosions. The Indian Government maintained that there was no insurmountable obstacle to the suspension of these explosions. For the last three years, the Indian Government had done its utmost to persuade the powers to accept that view. Suspension should not be regarded as a matter of partisan politics. (For further details, see below, PROPOSALS AND DECISIONS.)

The representative of Yugoslavia, as indicated above, made the point that an immediate cessation of these tests would make possible an advance in regard to the present state of affairs.

The USSR, as also indicated above, called for the immediate suspension of nuclear weapon tests and submitted a draft resolution in this connection. (For further details, see below, PROPOSALS AND DECISIONS.)

The subject of suspending test explosions was also dealt with in part of a draft resolution submitted by the following 24 Members: Argentina, Australia, Belgium, Brazil, Canada, Chile, Colombia, Cuba, Dominican Republic, Ecuador, France, Honduras, Italy, Laos, Liberia, Netherlands, Nicaragua, Panama, Paraguay, Peru, Philippines, Tunisia, United Kingdom and United States.

Their draft resolution called for priority efforts to reach a disarmament agreement which would, in part, provide for the immediate suspension of nuclear weapon tests, with effective international control measures. (For further details, see below, PROPOSALS AND DECISIONS.)

Others who commented on the matter included the representatives of Norway and Sweden. Norway, said the former, would welcome the suspension of nuclear tests because of the increasing apprehension of competent scientists about the possible effects of those tests on human beings.

However, much as it was concerned with the possible effects of nuclear tests on human health, the Norwegian delegation considered the continuing production of nuclear weapons a greater threat to mankind than radiation from the present tests. The prohibition of test explosions at present would in no way prevent the continued stockpiling of nuclear bombs, and an isolated suspension of tests would involve some risks for the Western powers without any compensation. Mere suspension of tests without cessation of production, he added, probably would not encourage other countries to refrain from preparations to produce their own nuclear weapons. But it was at least possible that a cessation of production by the three nuclear powers would encourage the others to refrain from such preparations.

The Swedish representative stated that it was for the powers conducting nuclear test explosions to agree among themselves on the question of the suspension of nuclear tests. Sweden, he added, continued to feel that a temporary moratorium, which it had proposed at the preceding Assembly session, would be extremely valuable; it would allow time for a thorough study of the dangers of tests and would constitute a first step towards the gradual elimination of nuclear weapons.

Another matter discussed in the First Committee during the disarmament debate was that of enlarging the Disarmament Commission and its Sub-Committee.

The USSR spokesman expressed dissatisfaction with the composition of the Commission as it was not representative, as it was too limited in membership and as it kept world public opinion in ignorance about its work. The USSR therefore proposed the establishment of a permanent Disarmament Commission consisting of all United Nations Members which would meet in public, its chairman and vice-chairmen to be responsible for co-operating with Members in organizing the necessary consultations.

The Yugoslav representative maintained that countries which did not form part of any bloc could play a useful role by helping the great powers to modify their opposing viewpoints. Yugoslavia therefore favoured enlarging the Disarmament Commission's Sub-Committee, in which case the greatest contribution could be expected from countries which did not belong to any of the present alignments of powers.

India thought it desirable, in regard to future negotiations on disarmament matters, to enlarge both the Commission and the Sub-Committee so as to permit non-committed countries to take part.

Others who favoured an increase in the size of the Commission (or its Sub-Committee) included the representatives of Egypt, Indonesia and Nepal.

The French representative, however, maintained that no way out of the present stalemate on disarmament matters was to be found by simple procedural measures. New steps towards peace could only be taken as a result of careful study by the Governments concerned. This could not be effected through changing the composition of the Disarmament Commission, the Sub-Committee or any other new organ which might be established.

The representatives of China, Cuba, Ecuador, the Netherlands, Norway, Pakistan and the United Kingdom were among the other speakers who thought that the present machinery provided a small working body that was best suited for delicate and detailed negotiations. Agreement, it was pointed out, was more likely to be achieved in a small working body. In any event, the basic problem was to be found at the substantive rather than at the procedural level. (For further details, see below, PROPOSALS AND DECISIONS.)

Also discussed was the Belgian proposal for a campaign to inform and enlighten the peoples of the world about the dangers of the armaments race, particularly the destructive effects of nuclear weapons. (For further details, see below, PROPOSALS AND DECISIONS.)

PROPOSALS AND DECISIONS

Eleven different draft resolutions bearing on various aspects of the disarmament question, and a number of amendments to them, were considered at the General Assembly's twelfth session. Not all of them, however, were voted on.

Some dealt with the broader aspects of the disarmament question. Others dealt more particularly with such specific matters as: the suspension of nuclear and thermonuclear weapon tests; an increase in the sizes of the Disarmament Commission and its Sub-Committee; and a world-wide publicity campaign to enlighten the peoples of the world about the dangers of the armaments race, especially the destructive effects of modern weapons.

For convenience, the various draft resolutions and amendments are grouped below under these four main subjects. Several of these draft resolutions, however, dealt with more than one of these subjects, as indicated in the text which follows.

The five following draft resolutions, and the amendments to them, related to the broader aspects of the disarmament question. Some of them also contained specific references to the suspension of nuclear weapon tests.

(1) Draft resolution submitted by Japan on 23 September (A/C.1/L.174). This draft called for: (i) further efforts by the Disarmament Commission's Sub-Committee to reach agreement without delay on unsettled points of the disarmament problem, particularly on initial disarmament measures, including the inspection system intended *(a)* to ensure that the manufacture of nuclear weapons was prohibited and that fissionable materials were devoted only to peaceful purposes and *(b)* to prevent surprise attack; and (ii) a suspension of nuclear weapon tests.

Japan, however, later withdrew the part of its proposal calling for further efforts by the Sub-Committee. The part on suspending nuclear tests was rejected by the First Committee on 6 November 1957, by a roll-call vote of 32 to 18, with 31 abstentions.

(2) Draft resolution, originally submitted by USSR on 24 September 1957 and later revised (A/C.1/L.175 and Rev.1). By the revised text, the Assembly would state its desire to facilitate agreement on: *(a)* the problem of the final prohibition of atomic and hydrogen weapons, together with their elimination from the armaments of States and the limitation of stockpiles of these weapons, and *(b)* the reduction of armed forces and conventional armaments. Accordingly, the Assembly would call on States possessing nuclear weapons to assume, as a first step, an obligation not to use atomic and hydrogen weapons, it being understood that if no comprehensive international agreement on the disarmament agreement had been reached at the end of five years, the United Nations would again consider the question of an obligation by States to renounce the use of nuclear weapons.

The First Committee rejected this draft resolution on 6 November by a roll-call vote of 45 to 11, with 25 abstentions.

(3) Draft resolution submitted by India on 26 September and later revised (A/C.1/L.178 and Revs. 1 and 2). In its final revised form, this text asked for recommendations on the following matters: *(a)* the time with effect from which future production of fissionable material in all countries would be available solely for peaceful purposes; *(b)* measures for refraining from the use of nuclear and thermonuclear weapons with a view to their eventual elimination; *(c)* the dismantling of stocks of these weapons and the conversion of the fissionable materials thus released to peaceful uses; and *(d)* arrangements for inspection and control required to implement agreements on conventional armaments, so as to inspire the necessary confidence. Appropriate recommendations on these matters, India proposed, should be made by representatives of States appointed forthwith by the Disarmament Commission, by agreement of the powers concerned. These representatives would consist of representatives of the States on the Commission holding the different views on nuclear and thermonuclear weapons, and representatives of other States, chosen by agreement between the aforementioned representatives of Commission members.

India later asked, however, that this draft resolution not be put to the vote. It was accordingly not voted on.

(4) Twenty-four-power draft resolution originally submitted on 11 October (A/C.1/L.179 and Corr.1 and Add.1). This draft resolution was submitted by the following 23 Members, who were later joined by Belgium: Argentina, Australia, Brazil, Canada, Chile, Colombia, Cuba, Dominican Republic, Ecuador, France, Honduras, Italy, Laos, Liberia, Netherlands, Nicaragua, Panama, Paraguay, Peru, Philippines, Tunisia, United Kingdom and United States.

By this text, the Assembly would urge the States concerned, especially those on the Disarmament Commission's Sub-Committee, to give priority to reaching a disarmament agreement which would provide for the following steps upon its entry into force: *(a)* the immediate suspension of nuclear weapon tests with the prompt installation of effective international control, including inspection posts equipped with appropriate scientific instruments located within the territories of the United States, the USSR, the United Kingdom, Pacific Ocean areas and other points as required; *(b)* the cessation of the production of fissionable materials for weapons purposes, future production of such materials to be devoted completely to non-weapons purposes under effective international control; *(c)* the reduction of nuclear weapon stocks through a programme for transferring, on an equitable and reciprocal basis and under international supervision, stocks of fissionable materials from weapons to non-weapons use; (d) reduction of armed forces and armaments through adequate safeguard arrangements; (e) the progressive establishment of open inspection with ground and aerial components to guard against the possibility of surprise attack; and (f) a joint study of an inspection system designed to ensure that objects sent through outer space were exclusively so sent for peaceful and scientific purposes. The draft resolution also asked that the Disarmament Commission's Sub-Committee be reconvened as soon as feasible with a view to reaching a disarmament agreement to these ends.

Three amendments to this 24-power text were proposed.

The first amendment was submitted on 31 October 1957 (and later revised) by Bolivia, Costa Rica, El Salvador and Uruguay, who were subsequently joined by Mexico. The revised amendment (A/C.1/L.181/Rev.1) was intended to add a paragraph by which the Assembly would invite the States concerned, particularly those on the Sub-Committee, to consider the possibility of devoting part of the savings from disarmament to the improvement of living conditions, throughout the world, especially in the less developed countries. The First Committee accepted this amendment on 6 November by 71 votes to 0, with 10 abstentions.

The second set of amendments to the 24-power draft was submitted by India (A/C.1/L.182) on 1 November 1957. By these amendments the Assembly would urge the States concerned, especially those on the Disarmament Commission's Sub-Committee: (1) to give priority to reaching agreement on the appointment of experts for recommending the control system and inspection arrangements envisaged in the 24-power draft with regard to an immediate suspension of nuclear weapon tests; and (2) to reach immediate agreement in principle and to make recommendations for measures on refraining from the use of nuclear and thermonuclear weapons with a view to their eventual elimination.

On 6 November, however, the First Committee rejected these amendments. But it agreed to another Indian amendment, to include a reference to a previous Assembly resolution of 4 November 1954 on disarmament.

The third amendment to the 24-power draft resolution was submitted jointly by Norway and Pakistan (A/C.1/L.184). It proposed that the Disarmament Commission's Sub-Committee establish a group or groups of technical experts to study and report on inspection systems for disarmament measures on which the Sub-Committee might agree. Each member of the Sub-Comittee was to provide such an expert. In addition, three other experts from other United Nations Member States would be designated by the Secretary-General in consultation with the Sub-Committee.

The amendment by Norway and Pakistan was accepted by the First Committee on 6 November 1957 by 61 votes to 9, with 10 abstentions.

On 6 November 1957, the First Committee adopted the 24-power draft resolution, as amended jointly by Bolivia, Costa Rica, El Salvador, Mexico, and Uruguay, by India, and jointly by Norway and Pakistan. It was approved in the First Committee, after a series of votes on individual paragraphs by a roll-call vote of 57 to 9, with 15 abstentions. Subsequently, it was approved at a plenary meeting of the Assembly on 14 November by a roll-call vote of 56 to 9, with 15 abstentions, in the form of resolution 1148(XII).

(5) Draft resolution submitted by Yugoslavia on 24 October (A/C.1/L.180). This text would have the Assembly urge that members of the Disarmament Commission's Sub-Committee, which was to meet at an early date, seek agreement or agreements on the following matters: (a) a reduction of armed forces, armaments and military expenditures; (b) measures contributing to the cessation of the nuclear armaments race such as an undertaking not to transfer nuclear weapons or fissionable materials for military use to other countries, a cessation of the production of fissionable materials for weapons purposes, and arrangements for gradually transforming fissionable materials now stockpiled for military use to non-weapons purposes; (c) measures to ensure that intercontinental ballistic missiles and all other devices for "outer-space" motion were used only for peaceful and scientific purposes; and (d) adequate and effective control and inspection measures for the implementation of the

agreement or agreements to be arrived at by the Sub-Committee.

This draft resolution, however, was not voted on in the First Committee in accordance with a request by Yugoslavia.

The following draft resolutions dealt more specifically with or contained some specific references to questions of suspending tests of atomic and hydrogen weapons.

(1) Draft resolution submitted by USSR on 20 September and later revised (A/3674 and Rev.1). By the revised text, the Assembly would call on those Governments carrying out tests of atomic and hydrogen weapons to reach an agreement forthwith on suspending such tests. This agreement would provide for: (i) the suspension of such tests for two to three years as of 1 January 1958; (ii) the creation of an international commission which would supervise the fulfilment by States of their obligations to discontinue these tests and also report to the Assembly and to the Security Council; (iii) the establishment of control posts, on a basis of reciprocity, in the USSR, in the United States, in the United Kingdom and its possessions, and in the Pacific Ocean area, including Australia. At the same time, the Assembly would call on other States to accede to the agreement on discontinuing tests of atomic and hydrogen weapons. The discontinuance of such tests, the draft resolution pointed out, would be an "important practical first step" towards the complete prohibition of atomic and hydrogen weapons and would constitute an obstacle to the development and production of new and even more destructive types of such mass-destruction weapons.

On 6 November 1957, however, the USSR asked that this draft resolution not be put to a vote.

(2) Draft resolution originally submitted by India on 21 September and later revised (A/C.1/L.176 and Revs.1, 2, and 4). The Assembly, by the final version of this text, would take the following steps, among others: (i) In view of the need to dispel doubts expressed about the detectability of explosions and to provide against possible evasions, it would ask the States concerned to agree forthwith to the nomination of a commission of experts representing the different views and with the participation of other

eminent scientific-technical experts to be agreed upon by the aforementioned representatives. (ii) This commission would recommend to the Disarmament Commission an adequate system of inspection arrangements in all the necessary territories of the world in order to supervise and render suspension of tests effective and to maintain the controls that would inspire the necessary confidence. (iii) The Assembly would appeal to the States concerned to agree without delay to suspend tests of nuclear and thermonuclear weapons and to inform the Secretary-General of their willingness to do so.

The draft resolution to this effect was rejected by the First Committee on 6 November 1957, by a roll-call vote of 38 to 22, with 20 abstentions. India resubmitted this draft resolution at a plenary meeting of the Assembly (A/L.232), where, on 19 November 1957, it was again rejected, by a roll-call vote of 34 to 24, with 20 abstentions.

Other draft resolutions which dealt in part with the question of suspending nuclear and thermonuclear weapon tests included one by Japan (A/C.1/L.174), originally introduced on 23 September, which would have the Assembly call on the States concerned to suspend all nuclear tests from the time an agreement was reached in principle on a supervision and inspection system to verify the suspension of tests until the next Assembly session in 1958. It would also call on them to negotiate immediately after the suspension of tests on the installation of the supervision system for verifying the suspension of tests. This proposal, however, was rejected by the First Committee on 6 November by a roll-call vote of 32 to 18, with 31 abstentions.

In addition, there was the Yugoslav draft resolution mentioned above (A/C.1/L.180) which contained references to an immediate halting of nuclear and thermonuclear tests. This, as already indicated, was not voted on.

The 24-power draft resolution, as approved by the First Committee in amended form on 6 November and later at a plenary meeting of the Assembly, also dealt with the question of suspending nuclear weapon tests. It urged the conclusion of a disarmament agreement providing in part for the immediate suspension of nuclear weapon tests, with prompt installation of effective international control including inspection posts within the USSR, the United States, the United Kingdom, the Pacific Ocean area and other points as required.

Other references as to the halting of nuclear weapon tests were contained in the amendments to the original version of the 24-power text which were submitted by India (A/C.1/L.182), and which were rejected by the First Committee.

The following draft resolutions and amendments to them dealt with the questions of enlarging the Disarmament Commission and/or its Sub-Committee.

(1) Draft resolution originally submitted by USSR on 28 October 1957 (A/C.1/797). By this text, the Assembly would establish a permanent Disarmament Commission consisting of all United Nations Member States, to meet in open and permanent session, with the task of examining all disarmament proposals submitted to the United Nations and to draft appropriate recommendations for the Assembly. This Commission would elect a chairman and vice-chairmen to direct the work of this body and to co-operate with United Nations Member States in organizing consultations and meetings on the disarmament problem. In setting up this permanent body, the Assembly would dissolve the existing 12-member Disarmament Commission and its five-member Sub-Committee.

On 6 November, the Ukrainian SSR submitted an amendment (A/C.1/L.186) whereby the Assembly would submit to the proposed permanent Commission all proposals and documents on the Disarmament Commission submitted at the Assembly's twelfth session.

The USSR draft, as thus amended, was rejected by the First Committee on 6 November 1957 by a roll-call vote of 51 to 9, with 21 abstentions. The rejected text was later resubmitted by the USSR at a plenary meeting (A/L.230), where, on 19 November, it was again rejected, by a roll-call vote of 46 to 9, with 24 abstentions.

(2) Draft resolution submitted by India on 25 September (A/C.1/L.177). By this text, the Assembly would increase the size of the present 12-member Disarmament Commission by an unspecified number of Member States to serve initially for two years. It would also add an unspecified number of States to the Commission's five-member Sub-Committee.

This text, however, was not voted on in the First Committee, in accordance with a request by India.

(3) Draft resolution originally submitted on 14 November by Canada and Japan, and later revised with Canada, India, Japan, Paraguay, Sweden and Yugoslavia[1] as co-sponsors (A/L.231 and Rev.1 and Add.1). By this revised text, introduced at a plenary meeting of the Assembly, the Assembly would increase the size of the existing Disarmament Commission by the following 14 members for the year 1 January 1958–1 January 1959: Argentina, Australia, Belgium, Brazil, Burma, Czechoslovakia, Egypt, India, Italy, Mexico, Norway, Poland, Tunisia and Yugoslavia. At the same time, the records of proceedings of the First Committee during the Assembly's twelfth session would be transmitted to this enlarged Commission.

By the draft resolution as originally introduced by Canada and Japan, the Commission membership would have been enlarged by 10 States. Egypt, Mexico, Norway, Poland were not included in the list as given above. Eighteen Latin American States, however, proposed an amendment (A/L.233) to add Mexico to the list. Another amendment (A/L.234) by India, Sweden and Yugoslavia proposed adding Egypt, Norway and Poland, to which Canada and Japan agreed.

Albania then proposed yet another amendment (A/L.236) to add Austria, Bulgaria, Ceylon, Finland, Indonesia, Romania and Sudan to the list, bringing the number of additional members of the Commission up to 21.

The Albanian amendment, however, was rejected by the Assembly on 19 November 1957 by a roll-call vote of 38 votes to 19, with 19 abstentions. Instead, the Assembly, by resolution 1150(XII) agreed to increase the size of the Disarmament Commission by the addition of the 14 members, as proposed by the sponsors of the joint draft resolution. It did so by a roll-call vote of 60 to 9, with 11 abstentions.

Prior to the vote in the First Committee on the various draft resolutions, the USSR representative announced that his Government would no longer participate in the work of either the

---

[1] Yugoslavia subsequently withdrew its sponsorship of this draft.

Disarmament Commission or its Sub-Committee as the bodies were presently composed.

On 19 November, at a plenary meeting of the Assembly, he said that if the Albanian amendment were adopted, the USSR would take part in the Commission's work.

Towards the close of the discussion in plenary meeting, Yugoslavia withdrew its sponsorship of the joint draft resolution before its adoption, as the proposed composition of the Commission was not acceptable to the USSR.

Another draft resolution discussed at the General Assembly's twelfth session dealt with the question of collective action to inform and enlighten the peoples of the world about the dangers of the armament's race especially the destructive effects of nuclear weapons. Originally proposed by Belgium on 12 August for the Assembly's agenda, and later revised, this text (A/3630/Corr.1) would have the Assembly state the desirability of seeking ways and means of organizing an effective and continuing world-wide publicity campaign under United Nations auspices and disregarding all ideological political considerations. The Assembly would accordingly ask the Disarmament Commission for recommendations on the nature of the information to be disseminated. It would also ask the Secretary-General to report to the Disarmament Commission on the means available for conducting such an international campaign and to give the Commission any assistance it may request for this. In addition, the Assembly would invite Member States to communicate to the Commission or the Secretary-General any views they might see fit to submit on the scope and content of this campaign.

Any agreement, whether partial or general, on the organization of armaments necessarily implied international control, the preamble to the Belgium draft stated. Consequently, it was necessary to make public opinion aware of (a) the effects of all kinds of modern weapons and (b) "the necessity for effective measures of control as part of a disarmament agreement". The latter phrase on the need for control measures was amended by Poland (A/C.1/L.185) to state the need for reaching a disarmament agreement providing effective measures of control.

The draft as thus amended was approved by the First Committee on 6 November by a roll-call vote of 70 to 9, with 2 abstentions. Eight days later, it was adopted at a plenary meeting of the Assembly, by a roll-call vote of 71 to 9, with 1 abstention, as resolution 1149(XII).

Rejected by the First Committee was a Polish amendment (A/C.1/L.185) to the preamble of the text. This was intended to make the point that an international agreement on the reduction of armaments and the prohibition of the use and manufacture of nuclear weapons should be reached. It would also state the urgent need for discontinuing further nuclear weapon tests as soon as possible. The wording to this effect was intended to replace the statement in the Belgian text that any agreement whatever, partial or general, on the regulation of armaments necessarily implied adequate international control.

DOCUMENTARY REFERENCES

CONSIDERATION BY DISARMAMENT COMMISSION'S SUB-COMMITTEE

SUB-COMMITTEE OF DISARMAMENT COMMISSION, meetings 87–142.

DC/112 (DC/SC.1/61). Fourth report of Sub-Committee of Disarmament Commission, containing following documents in Annexes 1–12:

DC/SC.1/49. USSR proposal of 18 March 1957 on reduction of armaments and armed forces and prohibition of atomic and hydrogen weapons.

DC/SC.1/50. *Note verbale* of 5 April 1957 from Permanent Representative of India.

DC/SC.1/51. *Note verbale* of 9 April 1957 from Japanese Ambassador in London.

DC/SC.1/52 and Add.1. *Notes verbales* of 10 April and 24 June 1957 from Yugoslav Ambassador in London.

DC/SC.1/53. United Kingdom working paper on relation of armaments to manpower—a suggested approach.

DC/SC.1/54. Letter of 26 April 1957 from Norwegian Chargé d'Affaires in London.

DC/SC.1/55. USSR memorandum of 30 April 1957. Proposals of Soviet Government on implementation of partial disarmament measures.

DC/SC.1/56. United Kingdom memorandum on nuclear test explosions.

DC/SC.1/57. United States memorandum on radioactive fall-out.

DC/SC.1/58. *Note verbale* of 21 May 1957 from Permanent Representative of India.

DC/SC.1/59. Joint statement of 2 July 1957 by Canada, France, United Kingdom and United States on temporary suspension of nuclear test explosions.

DC/SC.1/60. USSR proposal of 14 June 1957 on cessation of atomic and hydrogen weapon tests presented at Sub-Committee's meeting of 14 June 1957.

SUB-COMMITTEE OF DISARMAMENT COMMISSION, meetings 143–157.

DC/113. Fifth report of Sub-Committee of Disarmament Commission, containing the following documents in Annexes 1–13:

DC/SC.1/62/Rev.1. Canada, France, United Kingdom and United States working paper of 2 August 1957 on systems of inspection to safeguard against possibility of surprise attack.

DC/SC.1/63. Letter of 31 July 1957 from representative of USSR to Chairman of the Day of Sub-Committee concerning report of Sub-Committee of United Nations Disarmament Commission.

DC/SC.1/64. Letter of 1 August 1957 from representative of United States to representative of USSR concerning report of Sub-Committee of Disarmament Commission.

DC/SC.1/65/Rev.1. Statement of USSR Government with reference to disarmament talks.

DC/SC.1/66. Canada, France, United Kingdom and United States working paper of 29 August 1957 on proposals for partial measures of disarmament.

DC/SC.1/67. Statement of Chairman of United States delegation on 3 September 1957.

DC/SC.1/68. Statement of Chairman of French delegation on 29 August 1957.

DC/SC.1/69. Statement of Chairman of United Kingdom delegation on 29 August 1957.

DC/SC.1/70. Statement of Chairman of Canadian delegation on 29 August 1957.

DC/SC.1/71. Statement of Chairman of USSR delegation on 29 August 1957.

DC/SC.1/72. Statement of Chairman of USSR delegation on 4 September 1957.

DC/SC.1/73. Statement of Chairman of USSR delegation on 5 September 1957.

DC/SC.1/74. Statement of Chairman of French delegation on 5 September 1957.

CONSIDERATION BY DISARMAMENT COMMISSION

DISARMAMENT COMMISSION, meetings 63, 64.

DC/105. Letter of 20 February 1957 from Secretary-General to Chairman of Disarmament Commission.

DC/109. Letter of 18 March 1957 from Permanent Representative of Japan transmitting text of resolution of House of Councillors of Japan on prohibition of atom and hydrogen bombs, together with letter from Prime Minister and Minister for Foreign Affairs of Japan.

DC/114. Letter of 10 September 1957 from Secretary-General to Chairman of Disarmament Commission transmitting note of Permanent Representative of India.

DC/115. Letter of 11 September 1957 from Permanent Representative of USSR.

DC/121, 122, 123. Letters of 20 September, 20 November and 11 December 1957 from Secretary-General to Chairman of Disarmament Commission transmitting texts of resolutions adopted at 12th General Assembly session.

CONSIDERATION BY GENERAL ASSEMBLY

GENERAL ASSEMBLY—12TH SESSION
Plenary Meetings, 680–703, 715–719.
General Committee, meetings 111, 113.
First Committee, meetings 865–893.

REGULATION, LIMITATION AND BALANCED REDUCTION OF ALL ARMED FORCES AND ALL ARMAMENTS; CONCLUSION OF AN INTERNATIONAL CONVENTION (TREATY) ON THE REDUCTION OF ARMAMENTS AND THE PROHIBITION OF ATOMIC, HYDROGEN AND OTHER WEAPONS OF MASS DESTRUCTION

A/3685. Letter of 30 September 1957 from Chairman of Disarmament Commission transmitting report of Sub-Committee of Disarmament Commission.

A/C.1/793. Letter of 20 September 1957 from Head of USSR delegation transmitting memorandum of USSR Government on partial measures in field of disarmament.

A/C.1/L.174. Japan draft resolution (see also under SUSPENSION OF NUCLEAR WEAPON TESTS, below).

A/C.1/L.175 and Rev.1. USSR draft resolution and revision, rejected in First Committee, meeting 893, by roll-call vote of 45 to 11, with 25 abstentions, as follows:

In favour: Albania, Bulgaria, Byelorussian SSR, Cambodia, Czechoslovakia, Hungary, Poland, Romania, Ukrainian SSR, USSR, Yugoslavia.

Against: Argentina, Australia, Belgium, Brazil, Canada, Chile, China, Colombia, Costa Rica, Cuba, Denmark, Dominican Republic, Ecuador, El Salvador, France, Greece, Honduras, Iceland, Israel, Italy, Japan, Laos, Lebanon, Liberia, Luxembourg, Nicaragua, Norway, Pakistan, Panama, Paraguay, Federation of Malaya, Netherlands, New Zealand, Peru, Philippines, Portugal, Spain, Sweden, Thailand, Tunisia, Turkey, United Kingdom, United States, Uruguay, Venezuela.

Abstaining: Afghanistan, Austria, Bolivia, Burma, Ceylon, Egypt, Ethiopia, Finland, Ghana, Guatemala, Haiti, India, Indonesia, Iran, Iraq, Ireland, Jordan, Libya, Mexico, Morocco, Nepal, Saudi Arabia, Sudan, Syria, Yemen.

A/C.1/L.178 and Revs.1, 2. India draft resolution and revisions.

A/C.1/L.179 and Corr.1 and Add.1. Argentina, Australia, Belgium, Brazil, Canada, Chile, Colombia, Cuba, Dominican Republic, Ecuador, France, Honduras, Italy, Laos, Liberia, Netherlands, Nicaragua, Panama, Paraguay, Peru, Philippines, Tunisia, United Kingdom, United States draft resolution, adopted by First Committee, meeting 892, as amended by Bolivia, Costa Rica, El Salvador, Mexico and Uruguay, by India and by Norway and

Pakistan, by roll-call vote of 57 to 9, with 15 abstentions as follows:

In favour: Argentina, Australia, Austria, Belgium, Bolivia, Brazil, Cambodia, Canada, Chile, China, Colombia, Costa Rica, Cuba, Denmark, Dominican Republic, Ecuador, El Salvador, Ethiopia, France, Greece, Guatemala, Haiti, Honduras, Iceland, Iran, Iraq, Ireland, Israel, Italy, Jordan, Laos, Lebanon, Liberia, Libya, Luxembourg, Federation of Malaya, Mexico, Morocco, Netherlands, New Zealand, Nicaragua, Norway, Pakistan, Panama, Paraguay, Peru, Philippines, Portugal, Spain, Sweden, Thailand, Tunisia, Turkey, United Kingdom, United States, Uruguay, Venezuela.

Against: Albania, Bulgaria, Byelorussian SSR, Czechoslovakia, Hungary, Poland, Romania, Ukrainian SSR, USSR.

Abstaining: Afghanistan, Burma, Ceylon, Egypt, Finland, Ghana, India, Indonesia, Japan, Nepal, Saudi Arabia, Sudan, Syria, Yemen, Yugoslavia.

A/C.1/L.180. Yugoslavia draft resolution.

A/C.1/L.181 and Add.1. Bolivia, Costa Rica, El Salvador, Uruguay amendment to 24-power draft resolution, A/C.1/L.179.

A/C.1/L.181/Rev.1. Bolivia, Costa Rica, El Salvador, Mexico, Uruguay revised amendment to 24-power draft resolution, A/C.1/L.179.

A/C.1/L.182. India amendments to 24-power draft resolution, A/C.1/L.179.

A/C.1/L.184. Norway and Pakistan amendments to 24-power draft resolution, A/C.1/L.179.

A/3729 and Corr.1. Report of First Committee (draft resolution I).

RESOLUTION 1148(XII), as recommended by First Committee, A/3729, adopted by Assembly on 14 November 1957, meeting 716, by roll-call vote of 56 to 9, with 15 abstentions[2] as follows:

In favour: Argentina, Australia, Austria, Belgium, Bolivia, Brazil, Cambodia, Canada, Chile, China, Colombia, Cuba, Denmark, Dominican Republic, Ecuador, El Salvador, Ethiopia, France, Greece, Guatemala, Haiti, Honduras, Iceland, Iran, Iraq, Ireland, Israel, Italy, Jordan, Laos, Lebanon, Liberia, Libya, Luxembourg, Federation of Malaya, Mexico, Morocco, Netherlands, New Zealand, Nicaragua, Norway, Pakistan, Panama, Paraguay, Peru, Philippines, Portugal, Spain, Sweden, Thailand, Tunisia, Turkey, United Kingdom, United States, Uruguay, Venezuela.

Against: Albania, Bulgaria, Byelorussian SSR, Czechoslovakia, Hungary, Poland, Romania, Ukrainian SSR, USSR.

Abstaining: Afghanistan, Burma, Ceylon, Egypt, Finland, Ghana, India, Indonesia, Japan, Nepal, Saudi Arabia, Sudan, Syria, Yemen, Yugoslavia.

"*The General Assembly,*

"*Recalling* its resolution 808(IX) of 4 November 1954,

"*Emphasizing* the urgency of decreasing the danger of war and improving the prospects of a durable peace through achieving international agreement on reduction, limitation and open inspection of armaments and armed forces,

"*Welcoming* the narrowing of differences which has resulted from the extensive negotiations in the Sub-Committee of the Disarmament Commission,

"*Believing* that immediate, carefully measured steps, can be taken for partial measures of disarmament and that such steps will facilitate further measures of disarmament,

"1. *Urges* that the States concerned, and particularly those which are members of the Sub-Committee of the Disarmament Commission, give priority to reaching a disarmament agreement which, upon its entry into force, will provide for the following:

"(*a*) The immediate suspension of testing of nuclear weapons with prompt installation of effective international control, including inspection posts equipped with appropriate scientific instruments located within the territories of the United States of America, the Union of Soviet Socialist Republics, and the United Kingdom of Great Britain and Northern Ireland, in Pacific Ocean areas, and at other points as required;

"(*b*) The cessation of the production of fissionable materials for weapons purposes and the complete devotion of future production of fissionable materials to non-weapons purposes under effective international control;

"(*c*) The reduction of stocks of nuclear weapons through a programme of transfer, on an equitable and reciprocal basis and under international supervision, of stocks of fissionable material from weapons uses to non-weapons uses;

"(*d*) The reduction of armed forces and armaments through adequate, safeguarded arrangements;

"(*e*) The progressive establishment of open inspection with ground and aerial components to guard against the possibility of surprise attack;

"(*f*) The joint study of an inspection system designed to ensure that the sending of objects through outer space shall be exclusively for peaceful and scientific purposes;

"2. *Requests* the Disarmament Commission to reconvene its Sub-Committee as soon as feasible for this purpose;

"3. *Requests* the Disarmament Commission to invite its Sub-Committee to establish, as one of its first tasks, a group or groups of technical experts to study inspection systems for disarmament measures on which the Sub-Committee may reach agreement in principle and to report to it within a fixed period;

"4. *Recommends* that any such technical group or groups be composed of one expert from each of the States members of the Sub-Committee and one from each of three other States Members of the United Nations which shall be designated by the Secretary-General in consultation with the Sub-Committee;

"5. *Invites* the States concerned, and particularly those which are members of the Sub-Committee, to consider the possibility of devoting, out of the funds made available as a result of disarmament, as and when sufficient progress is made, additional resources

[2] The delegation of Costa Rica, which was absent at the time of the voting, subsequently informed the President that it would have cast its vote in favour of the draft resolution.

to the improvement of living conditions throughout the world and especially in the less developed countries;

"6. *Requests* the Sub-Committee to report to the Disarmament Commission by 30 April 1958 on the progress achieved."

SUSPENSION OF NUCLEAR WEAPON TESTS

A/3674 and Rev.1. Letter of 20 September 1957 from Chairman of USSR delegation containing draft resolution and request for inclusion of following item in agenda of 12th General Assembly session: Discontinuance under international control of tests of atomic and hydrogen weapons.

A/C.1/793. Letter of 20 September 1957 from Head of USSR delegation transmitting memorandum of USSR Government on partial measures in field of disarmament.

A/C.1/174. Japan draft resolution, as orally amended by sponsor, rejected in First Committee, meeting 893, by roll-call vote of 32 to 18, with 31 abstentions, as follows:

In favour: Bolivia, Burma, Ceylon, Ecuador, Egypt, El Salvador, Ghana, Indonesia, Iran, Iraq, Japan, Laos, Mexico, Morocco, Saudi Arabia, Sudan, Sweden, Yugoslavia.

Against: Albania, Argentina, Australia, Belgium, Brazil, Bulgaria, Byelorussian SSR, Canada, China, Colombia, Cuba, Czechoslovakia, France, Greece, Honduras, Hungary, Israel, Italy, Luxembourg, Netherlands, New Zealand, Nicaragua, Peru, Poland, Romania, Spain, Turkey, Ukrainian SSR, USSR, United Kingdom, United States, Venezuela.

Abstaining: Afghanistan, Austria, Cambodia, Chile, Costa Rica, Denmark, Dominican Republic, Ethiopia, Finland, Guatemala, Haiti, Iceland, India, Ireland, Jordan, Lebanon, Liberia, Libya, Federation of Malaya, Nepal, Norway, Pakistan, Panama, Paraguay, Philippines, Portugal, Syria, Thailand, Tunisia, Uruguay, Yemen.

A/C.1/L.176 and Rev.1, 2, 4. India draft resolution and revisions, rejected in First Committee, meeting 893, by roll-call vote of 38 to 22, with 20 abstentions, as follows:

In favour: Albania, Bulgaria, Burma, Byelorussian SSR, Ceylon, Czechoslovakia, Egypt, Finland, Ghana, Hungary, India, Indonesia, Iran, Mexico, Morocco, Nepal, Poland, Romania, Saudi Arabia, Ukrainian SSR, USSR, Yugoslavia.

Against: Argentina, Australia, Belgium, Brazil, Canada, Chile, China, Colombia, Costa Rica, Cuba, Denmark, Dominican Republic, Ecuador, El Salvador, France, Greece, Honduras, Iceland, Israel, Italy, Luxembourg, Netherlands, New Zealand, Nicaragua, Norway, Pakistan, Panama, Paraguay, Peru, Philippines, Portugal, Spain, Tunisia, Turkey, United Kingdom, United States, Uruguay, Venezuela.

Abstaining: Afghanistan, Austria, Bolivia, Cambodia, Ethiopia, Guatemala, Haiti, Iraq, Ireland, Japan, Jordan, Laos, Lebanon, Liberia, Libya, Federation of Malaya, Sudan, Sweden, Syria, Thailand.

See also following three documents which are listed in preceding section:

A/C.1/L.179 and Corr.1 and Add.1. Twenty-four power draft resolution.

A/C.1/L.180. Yugoslavia draft resolution.

A/C.1/L.182. India amendment to 24-power draft resolution.

A/3729 and Corr.1. Report of First Committee.

A/L.232. India draft resolution, rejected by Assembly on 19 November 1957, meeting 718, by 34 votes to 24, with 20 abstentions, as follows:

In favour: Albania, Bulgaria, Burma, Byelorussian SSR, Ceylon, Czechoslovakia, Egypt, Finland, Ghana, Guatemala, Hungary, India, Indonesia, Iran, Mexico, Morocco, Nepal, Poland, Romania, Sudan, Syria, Ukrainian SSR, USSR, Yugoslavia.

Against: Argentina, Australia, Belgium, Brazil, Canada, Chile, China, Colombia, Cuba, Denmark, Dominican Republic, Ecuador, El Salvador, France, Greece, Haiti, Honduras, Iceland, Israel, Italy, Luxembourg, Netherlands, New Zealand, Norway, Pakistan, Panama, Paraguay, Philippines, Portugal, Spain, Turkey, United Kingdom, United States, Venezuela.

Abstaining: Afghanistan, Austria, Bolivia, Cambodia, Iraq, Ireland, Japan, Jordan, Laos, Lebanon, Liberia, Libya, Federation of Malaya, Nicaragua, Peru, Saudi Arabia, Sweden, Tunisia, Uruguay, Yemen.

See also above, text of resolution 1148(XII), operative paragraph 1(*a*), in preceding section.

ENLARGEMENT OF DISARMAMENT COMMISSION AND ITS SUB-COMMITTEE

A/3657. Letter of 9 September 1957 from Permanent Representative of India requesting inclusion of following item in agenda of twelfth General Assembly session: Expansion of membership of Disarmament Commission and of its Sub-Committee.

A/C.1/793. Letter of 20 September 1957 from Head of USSR delegation transmitting memorandum from USSR Government on partial measures in the field of disarmament, including section on composition of Disarmament Commission and its Sub-Committee.

A/C.1/797. Letter of 27 October 1957 from Head of USSR delegation containing proposal and draft resolution on establishment of Permanent Disarmament Commission. Draft resolution, as amended by Ukrainian SSR, rejected by First Committee, meeting 893, by roll-call vote of 51 to 9, with 21 abstentions, as follows:

In favour: Albania, Bulgaria, Byelorussian SSR, Czechoslovakia, Hungary, Poland, Romania, Ukrainian SSR, USSR.

Against: Argentina, Australia, Belgium, Bolivia, Brazil, Canada, Chile, China, Colombia, Costa Rica, Cuba, Denmark, Dominican Republic, Ecuador, El Salvador, France, Ghana, Greece, Guatemala, Haiti, Honduras, Iceland, Iran, Ireland, Israel, Italy, Japan, Laos, Lebanon, Liberia, Luxembourg, Federation of Malaya, Netherlands, New Zealand, Nicaragua, Norway, Pakistan, Panama, Paraguay, Peru,

Philippines, Portugal, Spain, Sweden, Thailand, Tunisia, Turkey, United Kingdom, United States, Uruguay, Venezuela.

Abstaining: Afghanistan, Austria, Burma, Cambodia, Ceylon, Egypt, Ethiopia, Finland, India, Indonesia, Iraq, Jordan, Libya, Mexico, Morocco, Nepal, Saudi Arabia, Sudan, Syria, Yemen, Yugoslavia.

A/C.1/L.177. India draft resolution.

A/C.1/L.186. Ukrainian SSR amendment to USSR draft resolution, A/C.1/797.

A/3729 and Corr.1. Report of First Committee.

A/L.230. USSR draft resolution, rejected by Assembly on 19 November 1957, meeting 719, by roll-call vote of 46 to 9, with 24 abstentions as follows:

In favour: Albania, Bulgaria, Byelorussian SSR, Czechoslovakia, Hungary, Poland, Romania, Ukrainian SSR, USSR.

Against: Argentina, Australia, Belgium, Brazil, Canada, Chile, China, Colombia, Costa Rica, Cuba, Denmark, Dominican Republic, Ecuador, El Salvador, France, Greece, Guatemala, Haiti, Iceland, Iran, Ireland, Israel, Italy, Japan, Laos, Lebanon, Liberia, Luxembourg, Netherlands, New Zealand, Nicaragua, Norway, Pakistan, Panama, Paraguay, Peru, Philippines, Portugal, Spain, Sweden, Tunisia, Turkey, United Kingdom, United States, Uruguay, Venezuela.

Abstaining: Afghanistan, Austria, Bolivia, Burma, Cambodia, Ceylon, Egypt, Ethiopia, Finland, Ghana, India, Indonesia, Iraq, Jordan, Libya, Federation of Malaya, Mexico, Morocco, Nepal, Saudi Arabia, Sudan, Syria, Thailand, Yemen.

(Yugoslavia did not participate in the voting.)

A/L.231. Canada and Japan draft resolution.

A/L.231/Rev.1 and Add.1. Canada, India, Japan, Paraguay, Sweden, Yugoslavia[ᵃ] revised draft resolution.

A/L.233. Argentina, Bolivia, Brazil, Colombia, Costa Rica, Chile, Dominican Republic, Ecuador, El Salvador, Guatemala, Haiti, Honduras, Nicaragua, Panama, Paraguay, Peru, Uruguay, Venezuela amendment to joint draft resolution, A/L.231.

A/L.234. India, Sweden, Yugoslavia amendment to joint draft resolution, A/L.231.

A/L.236. Albania amendment to revised joint draft resolution, A/L.231/Rev.1 and Add.1.

RESOLUTION 1150(XII), as contained in A/L.231/Rev.1 and Add.1, adopted by Assembly on 19 November 1957, meeting 719, by roll-call vote of 60 to 9, with 11 abstentions, as follows:

In favour: Argentina, Australia, Austria, Belgium, Bolivia, Brazil, Burma, Canada, Ceylon, Chile, China, Colombia, Costa Rica, Denmark, Dominican Republic, Ecuador, Egypt, El Salvador, Ethiopia, France, Greece, Guatemala, Haiti, Honduras, Iceland, India, Indonesia, Iran, Iraq, Italy, Japan, Jordan, Laos, Lebanon, Libya, Luxembourg, Mexico, Nepal, Netherlands, New Zealand, Nicaragua, Norway, Panama, Paraguay, Peru, Philippines, Portugal, Saudi Arabia, Spain, Sudan, Sweden, Syria, Thailand, Tunisia, Turkey, United Kingdom, United States, Uruguay, Venezuela, Yemen.

Against: Albania, Bulgaria, Byelorussian SSR, Czechoslovakia, Hungary, Poland, Romania, Ukrainian SSR, USSR.

Abstaining: Afghanistan, Cambodia, Cuba, Finland, Ghana, Ireland, Israel, Liberia, Federation of Malaya, Morocco, Pakistan.

(Yugoslavia did not participate in the voting.)

"The General Assembly,

"Recalling its resolution 502(VI) of 11 January 1952 establishing the Disarmament Commission,

"1. *Decides* to enlarge the Disarmament Commission by the addition of fourteen Member States which, for the first year, from 1 January 1958 to 1 January 1959 shall be: Argentina, Australia, Belgium, Brazil, Burma, Czechoslovakia, Egypt, India, Italy, Mexico, Norway, Poland, Tunisia and Yugoslavia;

"2. *Transmits* to the Disarmament Commission the records of the proceedings of the First Committee during the twelfth session of the General Assembly at which disarmament was discussed."

COLLECTIVE ACTION TO INFORM AND ENLIGHTEN PEOPLES OF WORLD ABOUT DANGERS OF ARMAMENTS RACE, AND PARTICULARLY ABOUT DESTRUCTIVE EFFECTS OF MODERN WEAPONS

A/3630. Letter of 9 August 1957 from Permanent Representative of Belgium requesting inclusion in agenda of 12th General Assembly session of following item: "Collective action to inform and enlighten peoples of world as to dangers of armaments race, and particularly as to destructive effects of nuclear weapons."

A/3630/Corr.1. Belgium draft resolution, replacing draft resolution in A/3630, adopted, as amended by Poland, by First Committee, meeting 893, by roll-call vote of 70 to 9, with 2 abstentions, as follows:

In favour: Afghanistan, Argentina, Australia, Austria, Belgium, Bolivia, Brazil, Burma, Cambodia, Canada, Ceylon, Chile, China, Colombia, Costa Rica, Cuba, Denmark, Dominican Republic, Ecuador, Egypt, El Salvador, Ethiopia, Finland, France, Ghana, Greece, Guatemala, Haiti, Honduras, Iceland, India, Indonesia, Iran, Iraq, Ireland, Israel, Italy, Japan, Jordan, Laos, Lebanon, Liberia, Libya, Luxembourg, Federation of Malaya, Mexico, Morocco, Nepal, Netherlands, New Zealand, Norway, Pakistan, Panama, Paraguay, Peru, Philippines, Portugal, Saudi Arabia, Spain, Sudan, Sweden, Thailand, Tunisia, Turkey, United Kingdom, United States, Uruguay, Venezuela, Yugoslavia.

Against: Albania, Bulgaria, Byelorussian SSR, Czechoslovakia, Hungary, Poland, Romania, Ukrainian SSR, USSR.

Abstaining: Syria, Yemen.

A/C.1/L.185. Poland amendments to Belgium draft resolution, A/3630/Corr.1.

A/3729 and Corr.1. Report of First Committee (draft resolution II).

[ᵃ] Yugoslavia later withdrew its sponsorship of draft resolution A/L.231/Rev.1 and Add.1.

RESOLUTION 1149(XII), as recommended by First Committee, A/3729, adopted by Assembly on 14 November 1957, meeting 716, by roll-call vote of 71 to 9, with 1 abstention, as follows:

In favour: Afghanistan, Argentina, Australia, Austria, Belgium, Bolivia, Brazil, Burma, Cambodia, Canada, Ceylon, Chile, China, Colombia, Costa Rica, Cuba, Denmark, Dominican Republic, Ecuador, Egypt, El Salvador, Ethiopia, Finland, France, Ghana, Greece, Guatemala, Haiti, Honduras, Iceland, India, Indonesia, Iran, Iraq, Ireland, Israel, Italy, Japan, Jordan, Laos, Lebanon, Liberia, Libya, Luxembourg, Federation of Malaya, Mexico, Morocco, Nepal, Netherlands, New Zealand, Nicaragua, Norway, Pakistan, Panama, Paraguay, Peru, Philippines, Portugal, Saudi Arabia, Spain, Sudan, Sweden, Thailand, Tunisia, Turkey, United Kingdom, United States, Uruguay, Venezuela, Yemen, Yugoslavia.

Against: Albania, Bulgaria, Byelorussian SSR, Czechoslovakia, Hungary, Poland, Romania, Ukrainian SSR, USSR.

Abstaining: Syria.

"The General Assembly,

"Considering that the armaments race, owing to advances of nuclear science and other modern forms of technology, creates means whereby unprecedented devastation might be inflicted upon the entire world, and that peoples of all countries should be made to realize this,

"Considering that any agreement, whether partial or general, on the regulation of armaments necessarily implies adequate international control,

"Considering consequently that public opinion must be made aware both of the effects of modern weapons of all kinds and of the necessity of reaching a disarmament agreement providing effective measures of control,

"Considering that it is therefore desirable to seek ways and means of organizing an effective and continuing publicity campaign on a world-wide scale, under the auspices of the United Nations and disregarding all ideological or political considerations,

"1. Requests the Disarmament Commission to make recommendations on the nature of the information to be disseminated and requests the Secretary-General to report to the Commission on the means available for conducting such an international campaign;

"2. Requests the Secretary-General to furnish the Disarmament Commission whatever assistance it may request for this purpose;

"3. Invites Member States to communicate to the Disarmament Commission or to the Secretary-General in good time any views they may see fit to submit as to the scope and content of the proposed campaign."

OTHER DOCUMENTS

A/3804. Telegram of 4 October 1957 from Minister of Foreign Affairs of German Democratic Republic. Note by Secretary-General.

CHAPTER II

QUESTIONS RELATING TO ATOMIC ENERGY

EFFECTS OF ATOMIC RADIATION

CONSIDERATION BY
GENERAL ASSEMBLY

The question of the effects of atomic radiation was included in the agenda of the General Assembly's twelfth session at the request of Czechoslovakia.

The debate on this subject, in the Assembly's First Committee, was opened by the Minister for Foreign Affairs of Czechoslovakia on 7 November 1957. He pointed out that the question was one which directly affected people everywhere in the world, irrespective of their political, geographical, social or other conditions. Scientists, he said, agreed that radioactivity resulting from the use of atomic energy for peaceful purposes could be controlled, but that radioactivity resulting from test explosions of atomic and hydrogen weapons could not. "Delayed" or "global" fall-out, as distinguished from local fall-out, could be particularly dangerous.

The strontium-90 released into the stratosphere by a test explosion remained there for an average of 10 years and then gradually descended to earth, where it eventually penetrated into vegetable and human organisms. It was highly probable that as a result of nuclear tests in 1957, in addition to the tests of previous years, the strontium-90 content in some individuals might reach dangerous limits. Even small amounts of strontium-90 could cause cancer in the human body. Strontium irradiation also was harmful to bone marrow and might be the cause of leukaemia.

Radiation, he added, could also cause genetic

mutations and give rise to disorders such as blood diseases, blindness, deafness and dumbness, and defects in mental development. It might also cause premature death of the individual in either the pre-natal or post-natal period. Furthermore, there were strong grounds for believing that a small amount of radiation received by each of a large number of individuals could do an appreciable amount of damage to the population as a whole.

It had been argued, however, that a so-called "maximum permissible dose" of radiation produced no harmful effects, either immediately or in future generations. While opinions on this subject differed considerably, more and more scientists were coming around to the view that any dose of radiation was harmful, and that leukaemia and genetic mutations were to some extent the result of natural radiation. Any further increases in natural radiation levels should therefore be prevented.

The spokesman for Czechoslovakia also found it significant that during the past two decades, the tolerable dose of radiation for professional workers had been progressively lowered. Thus, while knowledge of the effects of atomic radiation was far from complete, it was safe to anticipate that future research would show that any exposure to radiative elements was dangerous. In the present stage of knowledge of the problem, it was pointless to speak of a maximum permissible dose.

Intensive scientific research on the effects of atomic radiation was necessary and it was no less important to ensure the proper co-ordination of such research activity. The establishment of the United Nations Scientific Committee on the Effects of Atomic Radiation was proof that the United Nations had realized the necessity of an expert judgement on the effects of atomic radiation. Now, as a result of a consistent rise in the levels of radiation, it was necessary to complete the work of that Committee with the help of the views of scientists of all parts of the world. The most appropriate forum for such an exchange of views would be a scientific conference convened under the auspices of the United Nations not later than the beginning of 1959.

Czechoslovakia accordingly submitted a draft resolution (on 2 November) recommending that a scientific conference on the effects of atomic radiation be held under United Nations auspices, and also that the Scientific Committee be asked: (1) to co-operate closely with the International Atomic Energy Agency; (2) to issue annual summary reports on the levels of ionizing radiation in the world and on the effects of radiation; and (3) to indicate research fields in which further study might be required.

Another draft resolution was submitted, on 8 November, by Argentina, Australia, Belgium, Brazil, France, Sweden, the United Kingdom and the United States. Mexico joined them in presenting a revised version three days later.

By this nine-power proposal, the Assembly would: (1) call on all concerned to continue their co-operation in making information available within the sphere of the Scientific Committee's terms of reference; (2) ask the Scientific Committee to complete its report as soon as possible and to make that report available to all Members of the United Nations, the specialized agencies and to the Second International Conference on the Peaceful Uses of Atomic Energy (scheduled to open in Geneva on 1 September 1958); and (3) to discuss the report of the Scientific Committee at the Assembly's thirteenth session in 1958.

The United States representative, pointing out that his country had long been concerned with the effects of atomic radiation, welcomed the opportunity to discuss the subject in the United Nations.

He summed up the position of his Government on the problem as follows: nuclear testing was one of the obligations imposed on the United States by its efforts to provide a strong defence for itself and other countries which relied on the United States for their security; it was well aware that there was some atmospheric contamination from all nuclear tests; because there was world concern over that fact, it wished to see tests stopped in the only way which would not endanger the defence of free countries, that is, as part of the first stage of an over-all disarmament programme; in its current testing activities, the United States was moving towards the development of nuclear weapons which produced much less radioactive fall-out; nuclear tests were only a minor source of the ionizing radiation which was harmful to human beings.

Human beings, the United States representative said, had always received a fairly constant amount of genetically harmful radiation from outer space, the earth's crust and even their own bodies. Radiation had always been an important cause of inherited physical defects. Weapons testing was only a minor element in a constantly changing situation in the field of radiation. The small reduction in radiation which would result from the cessation of tests could be more than offset by greater use of medical X-rays or by inadequately controlled industrial radiation. These facts suggested that radiation should not be a cause for panic. Rather, it was something to be watched and studied in an orderly scientific fashion so that whatever action was taken would be guided by scientific knowledge.

The United States considered that much further scientific work on radiation would have to be done by the United Nations, but it felt that the logical time for the General Assembly to decide on further steps in the field would be after it had received and studied the report of the Scientific Committee on the Effects of Atomic Radiation.

The USSR representative, supporting Czechoslovakia's position, pointed out that the peoples of the world, already conscious of the dangers involved in the stockpiling of weapons of mass destruction, were doubly concerned with the more imminent peril of radioactive fall-out from test explosions. It was very dangerous to belittle the importance of the increase in the level of radioactivity resulting from the explosions of nuclear weapons. Further, it was not true to say that the claimed decrease in the radioactive fall-out of the newer nuclear weapons would not significantly raise the world's level of radioactivity. In fact, radioactivity was increasing on the earth's surface because of the fall-out of strontium-90 which had accumulated in the upper strata of the atmosphere. So-called "clean" bombs would not improve the situation; the explosions would add considerably to the radioactivity of the environment. Serious thought should therefore be given to Czechoslovakia's constructive proposal for a conference which should be held no later than 1959.

The French representative, however, thought that such a conference would be necessary only if the results of atomic experiments were kept secret for military or technical reasons. In that case, an international conference would be a most valuable forum for the exchange of information, as the Geneva Conference on the Peaceful Uses of Atomic Energy had been. In the matter of atomic radiation, however, the Scientific Committee had, for 20 months, enabled experts throughout the world to meet and to exchange material involving neither military secrets nor industrial proprietary rights. The Scientific Committee, composed of representatives of the countries most advanced in nuclear physics, was in constant touch with all other relevant bodies and had already published a provisional report of great value to the specialized laboratories. This report was to be followed by a comprehensive report on the knowledge accumulated. There should be time to consider the data in the Scientific Committee's report before a large scientific gathering was scheduled. For the time being, a conference of the type envisaged by Czechoslovakia would be premature; it would not be conducive to scientific progress.

The United Kingdom representative considered that the Czechoslovak position was lacking in balance in that it gave almost exclusive attention to nuclear tests as a source of radiation and made little distinction between radioactive fall-out from tests and radiation in general. It ignored, for example, the fact that one of the causes of increased radiation was the greater medical use of radioactive material. It also ignored the fact that much larger amounts of radiation were released from the natural background, the peaceful uses of atomic energy, X-rays and other man-made sources than from test explosions. The genetic effects of fall-out from tests were insignificant in comparison with the effects from those other radioactive sources. The possible danger to individuals arose mainly from strontium-90, and the United Kingdom had on several occasions made it clear that the matter was being carefully watched.

In reply, the Czechoslovak representative pointed out that the Scientific Committee on the Effects of Atomic Radiation had been directly linked, in the Czechoslovak proposal, to the preparation of the proposed conference; indeed, the Scientific Committee's report was to be used as a basis for discussion. There was no conflict between the work of the Scientific Committee and the discussion of scientific findings on radiation in an international forum.

Other speakers on the subject included the

representatives of Albania, Austria, Belgium, Bulgaria, the Byelorussian SSR, Hungary, India, Japan, Poland, Sweden, the Ukrainian SSR and Yugoslavia.

The representative of Japan noted that there were certain difficulties connected with the submission of the report of the Scientific Committee either to an international scientific conference on the subject or to the Second International Conference on the Peaceful Uses of Atomic Energy to be held in Geneva in September 1958. A better approach might be to broaden the functions of the Scientific Committee. One way of doing that would be to increase its membership to include scientists of such countries as Norway, the Netherlands and Italy who were not now represented on it and who could make valuable contributions. It was already clear that thought should be given to strengthening the functions of the Scientific Committee and to placing it on a more permanent basis.

Japan accordingly proposed two amendments involving additions to the multiple-power draft resolution. By the first, the Assembly, in addition to calling on all concerned to continue making information available, within the sphere of the Scientific Committee's terms of reference, would call on them to include information on the levels of natural background radiation, exposure from the industrial uses of radiation and contamination of the environment by man-made radio-activity, including nuclear test explosions and radioactive waste from industries. The second Japanese amendment asked, in effect, that the Secretary-General study the need and method of strengthening the Scientific Committee's functions.

The Indian representative thought that it would be desirable to have a single text incorporating all the ideas put forth by the exponents of the two main schools of thought on the subject of radiation. At the same time, the terms of reference of the Scientific Committee might be broadened. The Secretary-General might be requested to consider these proposals in consultation with the Scientific Committee, taking into account the discussion and the proposals at the Assembly's twelfth session and to report thereon to the thirteenth session. India, however, would not go as far as to ask for any immediate decision on calling a conference. Its

suggestions were intended to pave the way for a unanimous Assembly proposal.

On 11 November, India introduced a draft resolution which was also sponsored by Argentina, Australia, Austria, Belgium, Brazil, Canada, Egypt, France, Japan, Mexico, Poland, Sweden, the United Kingdom, the United States and Yugoslavia. The General Assembly thereby would: (1) call upon all concerned to continue their co-operation in making available information within the sphere of the Scientific Committee's terms of reference; (2) ask the Scientific Committee to complete its report at the earliest possible date; (3) ask the Secretary-General, in consultation with the Scientific Committee, to consider the question of the strengthening and widening of scientific activities in this field, and to report to the Assembly's thirteenth session; (4) include in the agenda of its thirteenth session the report of the Scientific Committee; and (5) transmit to the Scientific Committee the record of the discussions in the First Committee on the effects of atomic radiation.

The 16-power draft resolution was approved unanimously by the First Committee, on 11 November. The nine-power draft resolution, at the request of its sponsors, was not put to the vote. Neither were the Japanese amendments to it, nor the Czechoslovak draft resolution.

On 14 November, the 16-power draft resolution, as recommended by the First Committee was approved—also unanimously—at plenary meeting of the General Assembly as resolution 1147(XII).

SCIENTIFIC COMMITTEE ON THE EFFECTS OF ATOMIC RADIATION

The 15-member Scientific Committee on the Effects of Atomic Radiation, established by General Assembly resolution 913(X), held one session in 1957 at the European Office of the United Nations, Geneva, from 8 April through 18 April. This was the third session of the Committee, and all meetings were closed. At this session Professor Zénon Bacq, of Belgium, was elected Chairman, and Dr. E. A. Watkinson, of Canada, was elected Vice-Chairman.

The two principal subjects for discussion at the third session were: (1) the genetic effects of radiation; (2) the form and general content of the comprehensive report which the Committee was due to complete by 1 July 1958. As a result of discussions by the Committee, working papers on the following subjects were prepared:

Genetic Aspects of Irradiation: (1) Genetic effects at the cellular level. (2) Mutation. (3) Selection. (4) Assessment of the social and biological consequences of mutation. (5) Genetic effects of multicellular organisms.

Preparation of the Report to Be Transmitted by the Scientific Committee on the Effects of Atomic Radiation to the General Assembly in 1958: (1) Introduction and general. (2) Radiological data. (3) Methods of measurements. (4) Fundamental cellular radiobiology. (5) Somatic effects on multicellular organisms. (6) Genetic effects on multicellular organisms. (7) Collected evaluations, conclusions and recommendations for the future.

Also studied were measurements of radiation levels, particularly with respect to radioactive fall-out and strontium-90. It was decided that it was desirable to make available, to nations requesting them, calibrated strontium-90 samples similar to those encountered in fall-out work. The United States agreed to furnish the calibrated samples. During 1957, four types of samples were received from the United States Atomic Energy Commission and were distributed to 26 countries.

In October 1957, the Committee submitted its second yearly progress report to the General Assembly's twelfth session. Following discussions by the Assembly on the agenda item entitled "Effects of Atomic Radiation" (see above), a resolution was adopted whereby the Assembly, among other things, asked the Secretary-General, in consultation with the Committee, to consider the question of the strengthening and widening of scientific activities in this field, and to report to the Assembly's thirteenth session.

The Scientific Committee co-operated closely with the Food and Agriculture Organization (FAO), the United Nations Educational, Scientific and Cultural Organization (UNESCO), the World Health Organization (WHO) and the World Meteorological Organization (WMO), and also with the International Commission on Radiological Protection and the International Commission on Radiological Units and Measurements.

As of 31 December 1957, the following Governments and international organizations and commissions had transmitted a total of 154 reports to the United Nations, 78 of which were submitted during the period between 9 March and 31 December 1957: Argentina, Australia, Austria, Belgium, Brazil, Canada, China, Czechoslovakia, Denmark, Egypt, France, Federal Republic of Germany, Hungary, India, Italy, Japan, Korea, Mexico, Netherlands, New Zealand, Norway, Poland, Romania, Sweden, Switzerland, Ukrainian SSR, Union of South Africa, USSR, United Kingdom and United States; FAO, UNESCO, WHO and WMO; and the International Commission on Radiological Protection and the International Commission on Radiological Units and Measurements.

The staff carrying out work for the Committee in 1957 continued to consist of a group of six scientists at United Nations Headquarters, working in close consultation with groups of delegates nominated by the Committee.

DOCUMENTARY REFERENCES

CONSIDERATION BY GENERAL ASSEMBLY

GENERAL ASSEMBLY—12TH SESSION
Plenary Meeting 715.
First Committee, meetings 894-898.

A/3659. Second yearly progress report of Scientific Committee on Effects of Atomic Radiation to General Assembly.
A/3614 and Add.1. Cable of 12 July 1957 and letter of 26 August 1957 from Minister for Foreign Affairs of Czechoslovak Republic, and Permanent Representative of Czechoslovakia, respectively, on inclusion in agenda of 12th Assembly session of item entitled "Effects of atomic radiation".

A/C.1/L.183. Czechoslovakia draft resolution.
A/C.1/L.187. Argentina, Australia, Belgium, Brazil, France, Sweden, United Kingdom, United States draft resolution.
A/C.1/L.187/Rev.1. Argentina, Australia, Belgium, Brazil, France, Mexico, Sweden, United Kingdom, United States revised draft resolution.
A/C.1/L.188. Japan amendments to joint draft resolution A/C.1/L.187.
A/C.1/L.189. Argentina, Australia, Austria, Belgium, Brazil, Canada, Egypt, France, India, Japan, Mexico, Poland, Sweden, United Kingdom, United States, Yugoslavia draft resolution adopted unanimously by First Committee.
A/3731. Report of First Committee.

RESOLUTION 1147(XII), as recommended by First Committee, A/3731, adopted unanimously by Assembly on 14 November 1957, meeting 715.

"*The General Assembly,*

"*Reaffirming* the importance of problems relating to the effects of ionizing radiation upon man and his environment,

"*Recalling* its resolution 913(X) of 3 December 1955 by which the General Assembly established a Scientific Committee on the Effects of Atomic Radiation and entrusted to it among others the task of collating in its report information on radiation effects on man and his environment,

"1. *Calls upon* all concerned to continue their co-operation in making available information within the sphere of the terms of reference of the Scientific Committee on the Effects of Atomic Radiation;

"2. *Requests* the Committee to complete its report at the earliest possible date and to make that report available to all Members of the United Nations and members of the specialized agencies and to the second conference on the peaceful uses of atomic energy;

"3. *Requests* the Secretary-General, in consultation with the Committee, to consider the question of the strengthening and widening of scientific activities in this field, taking into account in this connexion the discussion of this item at the twelfth session of the General Assembly, including the proposals submitted thereunder, and to report to the Assembly at its thirteenth session;

"4. *Decides* to include in the agenda of its thirteenth session the report of the Committee;

"5. *Transmits* to the Committee the records of the discussion in the First Committee of the item entitled 'Effects of atomic radiation'."

SCIENTIFIC COMMITTEE ON EFFECTS OF ATOMIC RADIATION

A/3659. Second yearly progress report of Scientific Committee on Effects of Atomic Radiation.

See also above, under CONSIDERATION BY GENERAL ASSEMBLY.

AGREEMENT BETWEEN UNITED NATIONS AND INTERNATIONAL ATOMIC ENERGY AGENCY

An Agreement bringing the International Atomic Energy Agency into relationship with the United Nations came into force on 14 November 1957 when the General Assembly unanimously approved this Agreement by resolution 1145(XII). The text of this Agreement was based upon a statement of the principles concerning the relationship between the Agency and the United Nations, as approved both by the Conference on the Statute of the Agency in October 1956[1] and later by the General Assembly at its eleventh session.

The draft of the Agreement was prepared by the United Nations Secretariat in consultation with the Secretariat of the Agency's Preparatory Commission. This draft text was considered by the Agency's Preparatory Commission, and, in the light of this discussion, the text, with revisions proposed by the Preparatory Commission, was considered by the Advisory Committee on the Peaceful Uses of Atomic Energy (acting on behalf of the General Assembly) on 29 May 1957.

At a joint meeting on 24 June, the Advisory Committee and the Preparatory Commission agreed upon a draft of the Agreement to be presented to the General Conference of the Agency and to the United Nations General Assembly for final approval. The Preparatory Commission had proposed the wording "primarily responsible" in article 1 of the Agreement. It was finally agreed, however, that the word "primarily" be dropped, subject to an exchange of letters between the Secretary-General of the United Nations and the President of the Preparatory Commission, setting forth a mutually acceptable interpretation of this article. (For final wording, see text of Agreement in DOCUMENTARY REFERENCES, below.)

The text of the agreed draft, together with the correspondence between the Secretary-General and the President of the Preparatory Commission, was transmitted to the Agency's Board of Governors (as Agency documents GOV.4 and GC.1/3 of 11 July) and to the General Assembly (as documents A/3620 and Corr.1 and Add.1).

The text of the Agreement was approved by the General Conference of the Agency on 23 October and by the General Assembly on 14 November, by resolution 1145(XII).

Also on 14 November, the General Assembly unanimously adopted a resolution (1146(XII)) authorizing the Agency to request advisory opinions from the International Court of Justice on legal questions arising within the scope of

[1] For text of the Agency's Statute, see below, PART II, CHAPTER I, THE INTERNATIONAL ATOMIC ENERGY AGENCY.

its activities other than questions concerning the relationship between the Agency and the United Nations or any specialized agency.

The Agreement recognized the Agency as the agency, under the aegis of the United Nations, responsible for international activities concerned with the peaceful uses of atomic energy in accordance with its Statute and without prejudice to the rights and responsibilities of the United Nations in this field under the Charter. In particular, the Agreement provides that the Agency shall report on its activities to the General Assembly at each regular session and shall submit reports, when appropriate, to the Security Council and notify the Council whenever, in connexion with its activities, questions within the competence of the Council arise. The Agency is also required to submit reports to the Economic and Social Council and other United Nations organs on matters falling within their respective spheres of competence. The Agency is to report to the Security Council and the General Assembly in case of non-compliance in relation to safeguards, as specified in article XII(C) of the Agency's Statute. It is also required to co-operate with the Security Council on matters pertaining to the maintenance or restoration of international peace and security.

The Agreement has provisions which are somewhat similar to those in the agreements between the United Nations and the specialized agencies on resolutions of the United Nations, the exchange of information, reciprocal representation and the inscription of agenda items. It also deals with co-ordination of activities and co-operation between the Secretariats of the Agency and the United Nations both on the administrative and on the substantive sides of the Agency's activities, including participation by the Agency in the work of the Administrative Committee on Co-ordination. It provides for close budgetary and financial relationships between the Agency and the United Nations, and for the use of uniform standards of international employment and personnel arrangements, to the extent that this is feasible.

The Agreement further entitles the members of the Agency's staff to use the United Nations *laissez-passer* and extends to the Agency certain administrative rights and facilities enjoyed by organizations within the United Nations system.

On 13 December 1957, the General Assembly approved without objection the admission of the Agency to the Joint Staff Pension Fund, by resolution 1201(XII). (For further details about the Joint Staff Pension Fund, see below, ADMINISTRATIVE AND BUDGETARY QUESTIONS, CHAPTER I, section on JOINT PENSION FUND.)

DOCUMENTARY REFERENCES

GENERAL ASSEMBLY—12TH SESSION
Plenary Meetings 714, 715.

A/3620 and Corr.1 and Add.1. Report of Advisory Committee on Peaceful Uses of Atomic Energy on its negotiations with Preparatory Commission of International Atomic Energy Agency and text of draft Agreement governing relationship between United Nations and International Atomic Energy Agency.
A/3713. Note by Secretary-General.
A/3747. Report of International Atomic Energy Agency to General Assembly. Note by Secretary-General.
A/L.228 and Add.1. Argentina, Australia, Belgium, Brazil, Canada, Czechoslovakia, Egypt, France, India, Indonesia, Japan, Pakistan, Peru, Portugal, Union of South Africa, USSR, United Kingdom, United States draft resolution.
RESOLUTION 1145(XII), as submitted by 18 powers, A/L.228 and Add.1, adopted unanimously by Assembly on 14 November 1957, meeting 715.

"*The General Assembly,*
"*Noting* the report of the Advisory Committee on the Peaceful Uses of Atomic Energy concerning its negotiations with the Preparatory Commission of the International Atomic Energy Agency, including the exchange of letters relating to the interpretation of article I, paragraph 1, of the Agreement governing the relationship between the United Nations and the International Atomic Energy Agency,
"*Noting* that the General Conference and the Board of Governors of the International Atomic Energy Agency have approved the above-mentioned Agreement,
"*Approves* the Agreement governing the relationship between the United Nations and the International Atomic Energy Agency, as set forth in the annex to the present resolution.

ANNEX
Agreement Governing the Relationship between the United Nations and the International Atomic Energy Agency
"*The United Nations and the International Atomic Energy Agency,*
"*Desiring* to make provision for an effective system of relationship whereby the discharge of their respective responsibilities may be facilitated,
"*Taking into account* for this purpose the provisions of the Charter of the United Nations and the statute of the Agency,

"Have agreed as follows:

ARTICLE I. PRINCIPLES

"1. The United Nations recognizes the International Atomic Energy Agency (hereinafter referred to as the Agency) as the agency, under the aegis of the United Nations as specified in the present Agreement, responsible for international activities concerned with the peaceful uses of atomic energy in accordance with its statute, without prejudice to the rights and responsibilities of the United Nations in this field under the Charter of the United Nations.

"2. The United Nations recognizes that the Agency, by virtue of its inter-governmental character and international responsibilities, will function under its statute as an autonomous international organization in the working relationship with the United Nations established by this Agreement.

"3. The Agency recognizes the responsibilities of the United Nations, in accordance with the Charter, in the fields of international peace and security and economic and social development.

"4. The Agency undertakes to conduct its activities in accordance with the Purposes and Principles of the Charter to promote peace and international co-operation, and in conformity with policies of the United Nations furthering the establishment of safeguarded world-wide disarmament and in conformity with any international agreements entered into pursuant to such policies.

ARTICLE II. CONFIDENTIAL INFORMATION

"The United Nations or the Agency may find it necessary to apply certain limitations for the safeguarding of confidential material furnished to them by their members or others, and, subject to the provisions of article IX below, nothing in the present Agreement shall be construed to require either of them to furnish any information the furnishing of which would, in its judgement, constitute a violation of the confidence of any of its members or anyone from whom it shall have received such information.

ARTICLE III. REPORTS OF THE AGENCY
TO THE UNITED NATIONS

"1. The Agency shall keep the United Nations informed of its activities. Accordingly it shall:

"(*a*) Submit reports covering its activities of the General Assembly at each regular session;

"(*b*) Submit reports, when appropriate, to the Security Council and to notify the Council whenever, in connexion with the activities of the Agency, questions within the competence of the Council arise;

"(*c*) Submit reports to the Economic and Social Council and to other organs of the United Nations on matters within their respective competences.

"2. The Agency shall report to the Security Council and the General Assembly any case of non-compliance within the meaning of article XII, paragraph C, of its statute.

ARTICLE IV. REPORT OF THE SECRETARY-GENERAL
OF THE UNITED NATIONS

"1. The Secretary-General of the United Nations shall report to the United Nations, as appropriate, on the common activities of the United Nations and the Agency and on the development of relations between them.

"2. Any written report circulated under paragraph 1 of the present article shall be transmitted to the Agency by the Secretary-General.

ARTICLE V. RESOLUTIONS OF THE UNITED NATIONS

"The Agency shall consider any resolution relating to the Agency adopted by the General Assembly or by a Council of the United Nations. Any such resolution shall be referred to the Agency together with the appropriate records. Upon request the Agency shall submit a report on any action taken, in accordance with the statute of the Agency, by it or by its members as a result of its consideration of any resolution referred to it under the present article.

ARTICLE VI. EXCHANGE OF
INFORMATION AND DOCUMENTS

"1. There shall be the fullest and promptest exchange between the United Nations and the Agency of appropriate information and documents.

"2. The Agency, in conformity with its statute and to the extent practicable, shall furnish special studies or information requested by the United Nations.

"3. The United Nations shall likewise furnish the Agency, upon request, with special studies or information relating to matters within the competence of the Agency.

ARTICLE VII. RECIPROCAL REPRESENTATION

"1. The Secretary-General of the United Nations shall be entitled to attend and participate without vote on matters of common interest in sessions of the General Conference and of the Board of Governors of the Agency. The Secretary-General shall also be invited as appropriate to attend and participate without vote in such other meetings as the Agency may convene at which matters of interest to the United Nations are under consideration. The Secretary-General may, for the purposes of the present paragraph, designate any person as his representative.

"2. The Director-General of the Agency shall be entitled to attend plenary meetings of the General Assembly of the United Nations for purposes of consultation. He shall be entitled to attend and participate without vote in meetings of the committees of the General Assembly, and meetings of the Economic and Social Council, the Trusteeship Council and, as appropriate, their subsidiary bodies. At the invitation of the Security Council, the Director-General may attend its meetings to supply it with information or give it other assistance with regard to matters within the competence of the Agency. The Director-General may, for the purposes of this present paragraph, designate any person as his representative.

"3. Written statements presented by the United Nations to the Agency for distribution shall be distributed by the Agency to all members of the appropriate organ or organs of the Agency. Written statements presented by the Agency to the United Nations for distribution shall be distributed by the Secretariat of the United Nations to all members of the appropriate organ or organs of the United Nations.

ARTICLE VIII. AGENDA ITEMS

"1. The United Nations may propose items for consideration by the Agency. In such cases, the United Nations shall notify the Director-General of the Agency of the item or items concerned, and the Director-General shall include any such item or items in the provisional agenda of the General Conference or Board of Governors or such other organ of the Agency as may be appropriate.

"2. The Agency may propose items for consideration by the United Nations. In such cases, the Agency shall notify the Secretary-General of the United Nations of the item or items concerned and the Secretary-General, in accordance with his authority, shall bring such item or items to the attention of the General Assembly, the Security Council, the Economic and Social Council or the Trusteeship Council, as appropriate.

ARTICLE IX. CO-OPERATION WITH
THE SECURITY COUNCIL

"The Agency shall co-operate with the Security Council by furnishing it at its request with such information and assistance as may be required in the exercise of its responsibility for the maintenance or restoration of international peace and security.

ARTICLE X. INTERNATIONAL COURT OF JUSTICE

"1. The United Nations will take the necessary action to enable the General Conference or the Board of Governors of the Agency to seek an advisory opinion of the International Court of Justice on any legal question arising within the scope of the activities of the Agency, other than a question concerning the mutual relationships of the Agency and the United Nations or the specialized agencies.

"2. The Agency agrees, subject to such arrangements as it may make for the safeguarding of confidential information, to furnish any information which may be requested by the International Court of Justice in accordance with the Statute of the Court.

ARTICLE XI. CO-ORDINATION

"The United Nations and the Agency recognize the desirability of achieving effective co-ordination of the activities of the Agency with those of the United Nations and the specialized agencies, and of avoiding the overlapping and duplication of activities. Accordingly, the Agency agrees to co-operate, in accordance with its statute, in measures recommended by the United Nations for this purpose. Furthermore, the Agency agrees to participate in the work of the Administrative Committee on Co-ordination and, as appropriate, of any other bodies which have been or may be established by the United Nations to facilitate such co-operation and co-ordination. The Agency may also consult with appropriate bodies established by the United Nations on matters within their competence and on which the Agency requires expert advice. The United Nations, on its part, agrees to take such action as may be necessary to facilitate such participation and consultation.

ARTICLE XII. CO-OPERATION BETWEEN SECRETARIATS

"1. The Secretariat of the United Nations and the staff of the Agency shall maintain a close working relationship in accordance with such arrangements as may be agreed upon from time to time between the Secretary-General of the United Nations and the Director-General of the Agency.

"2. It is recognized that similar close working relationships between the secretariats of the specialized agencies and the staff of the Agency are desirable and should be established and maintained in accordance with such arrangements as may be made between the Agency and the specialized agency or agencies concerned.

ARTICLE XIII. ADMINISTRATIVE CO-OPERATION

"1. The United Nations and the Agency recognize the desirability of co-operation in administrative matters of mutual interest.

"2. Accordingly, the United Nations and the Agency undertake to consult from time to time concerning these matters, particularly the most efficient use of facilities, staff and services and appropriate methods of avoiding the establishment and operation of competitive or overlapping facilities and services among the United Nations, the specialized agencies and the Agency, and with a view to securing, within the limits of the Charter of the United Nations and the statute of the Agency, as much uniformity in these matters as shall be found practicable.

"3. The consultations referred to in the present article shall be utilized to establish the most equitable manner in which any special services or assistance furnished by the Agency to the United Nations or by the United Nations to the Agency shall be financed.

ARTICLE XIV. STATISTICAL SERVICES

"The United Nations and the Agency, recognizing the desirability of maximum co-operation in the statistical field and of minimizing the burdens placed on national Governments and on organizations from which information may be collected, undertake to avoid undesirable duplication with respect to the collection, compilation and publication of statistics, and agree to consult with each other on the most efficient use of resources and of technical personnel in the field of statistics.

ARTICLE XV. TECHNICAL ASSISTANCE

"The United Nations and the Agency, recognize the desirability of co-operation concerning the provision of technical assistance in the field of atomic energy. They undertake to avoid undesirable duplication of activities and services relating to technical assistance and agree to take such action as may be necessary to achieve effective co-ordination of their technical assistance activities within the framework of existing co-ordination machinery in the field of technical assistance, and the Agency agrees to give consideration to the common use of available services as far as practicable. The United Nations will make available to the Agency its administrative services in this field for use as requested.

ARTICLE XVI. BUDGETARY AND
FINANCIAL ARRANGEMENTS

"1. The Agency recognizes the desirability of establishing close budgetary and financial relationships with the United Nations in order that the administrative operations of the United Nations, the Agency and the specialized agencies shall be carried out in the most efficient and economical manner possible, and that the maximum measure of co-ordination and uniformity with respect to these operations shall be secured.

"2. The Agency agrees to conform, as far as may be practicable and appropriate, to standard practices and forms recommended by the United Nations.

"3. The Agency agrees to transmit its annual budget to the United Nations for such recommendations as the General Assembly may wish to make on the administrative aspects thereof.

"4. The United Nations may arrange for studies to be undertaken concerning financial and fiscal questions of interest to the Agency and to the specialized agencies with a view to providing common services and securing uniformity in such matters.

ARTICLE XVII. PUBLIC INFORMATION

"The United Nations and the Agency shall co-operate in the field of public information with a view to avoiding overlapping or uneconomical services and, where necessary or appropriate, to establishing common or joint services in this field.

ARTICLE XVIII. PERSONNEL ARRANGEMENTS

"1. The United Nations and the Agency agree to develop, in the interests of uniform standards of international employment and to the extent feasible, common personnel standards, methods and arrangements designed to avoid unjustified differences in terms and conditions of employment, to avoid competition in recruitment of personnel, and to facilitate the interchange of personnel in order to obtain the maximum benefit from their services.

"2. The United Nations and the Agency agree:

"(a) To consult from time to time concerning matters of common interest relating to the terms and conditions of employment of the officers and staff, with a view to securing as much uniformity in these matters as may be feasible;

"(b) To co-operate in the interchange of personnel, when desirable, on a temporary or a permanent basis, making due provision for the retention of seniority and pension rights;

"(c) To co-operate, on such terms and conditions as may be agreed, in the operation of a common pension fund;

"(d) To co-operate in the establishment and operation of suitable machinery for the settlement of disputes arising in connexion with the employment of personnel and related matters.

"3. The terms and conditions on which any facilities or services of the Agency or the United Nations in connexion with the matters referred to in the present article are to be extended to the other shall, where necessary, be the subject of subsidiary agreements concluded for this purpose after the entry into force of the present Agreement.

ARTICLE XIX. ADMINISTRATION RIGHTS AND FACILITIES

"1. Members of the staff of the Agency shall be entitled, in accordance with such administrative arrangements as may be concluded between the Secretary-General of the United Nations and the Director-General of the Agency, to use the United Nations *laissez-passer* as a valid travel document where such use is recognized by States parties to the Convention on the Privileges and Immunities of the United Nations.

"2. Subject to the provisions of article XVIII above, the Secretary-General of the United Nations and the Director-General of the Agency shall consult, as soon as may be practicable after entry into force of the present Agreement, regarding the extension to the Agency of such other administrative rights and facilities as may be enjoyed by organizations within the United Nations system.

"3. The United Nations shall invite, and provide the necessary facilities to, any representative of a member of the Agency, representative of the Agency, or member of the staff of the Agency desiring to proceed to the United Nations Headquarters district on official business connected with the Agency, whether at the initiative of any organ of the United Nations, of the Agency or of the member thereof.

ARTICLE XX. INTER-AGENCY AND OTHER AGREEMENTS

"The Agency shall inform the United Nations before the conclusion of any formal agreement between the Agency and any specialized agency or inter-governmental organization or any non-governmental organization enjoying consultative status with the United Nations, of the nature and scope of any such agreement, and shall inform the United Nations of the conclusion of any such agreement.

ARTICLE XXI. REGISTRATION OF AGREEMENTS

"The United Nations and the Agency shall consult together as may be necessary with regard to the registration with the United Nations of agreements within the meaning of article XXII, paragraph B, of the statute of the Agency.

ARTICLE XXII. IMPLEMENTATION OF THE PRESENT AGREEMENT

"The Secretary-General of the United Nations and the Director-General of the Agency may enter into such arrangements for the implementation of the present Agreement as may be found desirable in the light of the operating experience of the two organizations.

ARTICLE XXIII. AMENDMENTS

"The present Agreement may be amended by agreement between the United Nations and the Agency. Any amendment so agreed upon shall enter into force on its approval by the General Conference of the Agency and the General Assembly of the United Nations.

ARTICLE XXIV. ENTRY INTO FORCE

"The present Agreement shall enter into force on its approval by the General Assembly of the United Nations and the General Conference of the Agency."

A/L.229. United States draft resolution.

RESOLUTION 1146(XII), as submitted by United States, A/L.229, adopted unanimously by Assembly on 14 November 1957, meeting 715.

"*The General Assembly,*

"*Recalling* the provisions of Article 96 of the Charter of the United Nations,

"*Noting* the provisions of article XVII of the statute of the International Atomic Energy Agency and of article X of the Agreement governing the relationship between the United Nations and the Agency,

"*Authorizes* the International Atomic Energy Agency to request advisory opinions of the International Court of Justice on legal questions arising within the scope of its activities other than questions concerning the relationship between the Agency and the United Nations or any specialized agency."

CHAPTER III

THE PALESTINE QUESTION

SYRIAN COMPLAINT ABOUT CONSTRUCTION OF BRIDGE IN DEMILITARIZED ZONE

On 20 April 1957, the Acting Chief of Staff of the United Nations Truce Supervision Organization in Palestine (UNTSO) reported that Syria had complained, late in March, to the Chairman of the Israel-Syrian Mixed Armistice Commission that Israel military forces had been building military fortifications and constructing a bridge of military value at the outlet of Lake Huleh in contravention of article V of the General Armistice Agreement establishing a Demilitarized Zone between Syria and Israel. Syria had asked for an immediate investigation by the Mixed Armistice Commission and for necessary action with the Israel authorities.

The Acting Chief of Staff stated that he had not been able to make an immediate investigation because Israel had refused to allow United Nations military observers to enter the Demilitarized Zone from Syrian territory and had refused to allow an investigation from its own side. Subsequently, however, while maintaining its opposition to what it considered Syrian interference in the Demilitarized Zone, Israel had ceased to object to inspection of the site of the bridge. On April 7, the Acting Chief of Staff found that there were no fortifications, but that an area on the western approaches to the bridge had been marked as mined. He said he was arranging to have any existing mines removed from the area.

Although stating that the bridge could be used for military purposes, he was satisfied that it had been erected in connexion with the Huleh reclamation project. Accordingly, he did not think that he would be justified in asking for its removal since such a request would have to be based on the assumption that the bridge would be used for military purposes in violation of the General Armistice Agreement, an assumption which he was not entitled to consider.

The Acting Chief of Staff also suggested that, in view of the difficulties which had occurred in the investigation, it would be advisable to reaffirm the special powers of the Chairman of the Mixed Armistice Commission and United Nations military observers in the Demilitarized Zone.

On 13 May 1957, the representative of Syria requested a meeting of the Security Council to consider the question. In a letter accompanying the request, he stated that while the Syrian Government would subscribe to most of the statements in the report of the Acting Chief of Staff, it could not concur in his conclusions.

The Council considered the Syrian complaint at three meetings between 23 and 28 May 1957 and invited the representatives of Syria and Israel to participate in the discussion.

The representative of Syria said, among other things, that the construction of the bridge had been accompanied by Israel military activity in the Demilitarized Zone which was explicitly prohibited by article V, paragraphs 5(a) and 5(b), of the General Armistice Agreement. The bridge was of military advantage to Israel, and thus represented a violation of the General Armistice Agreement. The intention of Israel not to avail itself of this military advantage, as referred to by the Acting Chief of Staff, was not relevant in determining any breach of the Agreement.

The Syrian representative urged the Council to condemn Israel for violation of the General Armistice Agreement, and to order removal of the bridge.

The representative of Israel maintained that the General Armistice Agreement had expressly provided for the restoration of normal civilian life in the Demilitarized Zone. For the past

six years, he said, Syria had constantly attempted to obstruct improvement schemes in the
Zone, but all its arguments against reclamation
work by Israel had been repeatedly rejected by
the Chief of Staff of UNTSO and the Security
Council.

The bridge in question had been constructed
by Israel solely for the transport of earth-moving
and dredging machinery for the completion of
the canal system to the River Jordan. All mines
near the western approaches to the bridge had
been removed and the Acting Chief of Staff
had been informed accordingly, the representative of Israel added.

Further, Israel would not interfere with the
movements of United Nations military observers
in the Demilitarized Zone when such movement was necessitated by their official functions.
It would not, however, agree to any investigations in the Demilitarized Zone based on Syrian
complaints.

On 28 May, summing up the debate, the
President said that all members of the Council
appeared to agree that the authority of the
Chief of Staff of UNTSO should be respected
and that the parties should co-operate with him.
In the present case, Council members had noted
that delay had been caused in his inspection of
the bridge and the discharge of his duties.

Some members of the Council, said the President, had made it clear that they did not agree
with the Acting Chief of Staff on Israel's right
to build the bridge. The majority of the members had, however, pointed out that it was for
the Chief of Staff to ensure full implementation
of the provisions of article V or the General
Armistice Agreement and had supported his decisions in that respect.

The President took note of a statement by
the Secretary-General that, in the light of the
Council's discussions, he would ask the Acting
Chief of Staff for an additional report within
a month.

On 27 June 1957, the Acting Chief of Staff
submitted an additional report on certain aspects of the work of United Nations organs in
the Demilitarized Zone, established under article
V of the General Armistice Agreement.

Until the beginning of June 1956, he stated,
United Nations military observers had generally
been able to circulate freely in the Zone either
on routine visits or for investigation purposes.

Subsequently, however, difficulties had been experienced in connexion with the investigation of
complaints of erection of fortifications in the
Israel settlements in the central and southern
sectors of the Demilitarized Zone. Since 30
October 1956, requests to enter the central
Demilitarized Zone had, for the most part, been
refused, and routine visits or investigations had
been stopped by Israel police.

The Acting Chief of Staff further stated that
the Syrian authorities had not refused United
Nations observers access to the Demilitarized
Zone for investigations or routine visits.

United Nations observers, he said, had been
prevented from investigating the present extent
of Israel fortifications in the central and southern sectors of the Demilitarized Zone. Israel
continued to object to the dismantling of these
fortifications which had been requested on the
ground that they went beyond what was required for protection of civilian life. Syria, on
the other hand, had expressed its willingness to
dismantle any fortifications which, upon investigation by United Nations observers, might
be revealed as encroaching on the Demilitarized
Zone.

The Acting Chief of Staff also reported that,
according to the information received from Israel authorities, mines had been removed from
the western approaches to the newly erected
Lake Huleh bridge and the Banat Yacoub
bridge. He believed that with the removal of
these mines, which were in contravention of the
General Armistice Agreement, no Israel mines
should remain in the Demilitarized Zone. He
had also been informed by the Israel Ministry
of Foreign Affairs that any mines which might
have been placed in the Demilitarized Zone at
the beginning of the military action against
Egypt had been removed.

In his conclusions, the Acting Chief of Staff
pointed out that the report raised the question
of the possibility of carrying out an investigation at any time, under article V of the General
Armistice Agreement, and of the enjoyment by
United Nations observers of full freedom of
movement in the Demilitarized Zone during an
investigation or during routine visits. That possibility was indispensable in order to exercise
responsibility for the general supervision of the
Demilitarized Zone. He thought it might be desirable, for the purpose of surveillance and more

rapid investigation, to have some observers remain on a 24-hour basis in portions of the Zone. (In an addendum to his report on 7 August, the Acting Chief of Staff reported that Israel had opposed establishment of an observation post in the area of the new Lake Huleh bridge.)

The Acting Chief added that he had been given to understand by the Israel Ministry of Foreign Affairs that Israel's objection to investigations of Syrian complaints had been of a purely formal nature and that Israel did not object to any investigations carried out by or on behalf of the Chairman on the basis of his authority under article V.

While it was a matter of satisfaction that Israel had agreed to clear the mines in the Demilitarized Zone, the Acting Chief of Staff noted, requests for the demolition of fortification works which exceeded those permissible for the protection of the civilian population had been rejected by Israel.

JORDAN AND ISRAEL COMPLAINTS ABOUT ZONE IN AREA OF GOVERNMENT HOUSE, JERUSALEM

On 4 September 1957, the representative of Jordan requested an urgent meeting of the Security Council to consider its complaint that a serious situation had arisen due to violations by Israel of the General Armistice Agreement in the no-man's-land between the Armistice Demarcation Lines in the area around Government House in Jerusalem.

On 5 September, Israel asked the Security Council to consider its complaint of violations by Jordan of the provisions of the General Armistice Agreement, particularly article VIII thereof.

On 6 September, both items were put on the Council's agenda. They were considered at five meetings, held on 6 September 1957, 22 November 1957 and 22 January 1958. The representatives of the parties concerned participated.

The representative of Jordan declared that, under the General Armistice Agreement, the important strategic Jabal El Mukkaber (Government House) area had the status of a no-man's-land between the Demarcation Lines and was under the supervision and control of the United Nations. The only exception related to the few Israelis and Arabs still there at the time of the signing of the Agreement. No one else was entitled to enter. Nor had one party the right to make use of the other party's properties. That arrangement in the area had never been modified by any partition or the drawing of a civilian line between the parties. Israeli labourers, he continued, had entered the no-man's-land area on 21 July 1957, under the protection of Israel military forces, and had then and subsequently exploited Arab properties there, by ploughing land and opening new roads in spite of the United Nations Chief of Staff's intervention. Such activities were violations of the General Armistice Agreement and the *status quo* and gave Israel evident political, economic and military advantages. In conclusion, the representative of Jordan requested re-establishment of the *status quo* and condemnation of Israel.

The representative of Israel charged that Jordan had violated fundamental provisions of the General Armistice Agreement, particularly article VIII, which, for Israel, was one of the crucial provisions of the Agreement. (Article VIII provided for a special committee to formulate arrangements to enlarge the scope of the Agreement in respect, among other things, to free movement of traffic on vital roads, resumption of normal functioning of institutions on Mount Scopus and free access to the Holy Places.) During the past eight years, the representative of Israel said, Jordan had refused to agree to the functioning of this special committee. As a result, rights which Israel regarded as being of cardinal religious, educational and practical importance had been gravely prejudiced.

Israel's representative further charged that Jordan had constantly violated the provisions of article I of the General Armistice Agreement calling for compliance with the fundamental principles of non-aggression, non-intimidation and the promotion of peace. He also referred to failure of the Secretary-General's efforts to secure Jordan's compliance with article XII, providing for review of the provisions of the Armistice Agreement.

With regard to the Jordan complaint, the Israel representative stated that there were no aggressive aspects to the work undertaken on the Israel side of the area between the Demarcation Lines preparatory to the planting of trees. The General Armistice Agreement, he said, did not define the rights and obligations of the parties in the area; and all subsequent arrangements concerning rights and duties of the parties in the area were the result of agreements of a formal nature or on the basis of tacit consent. Since a civilian line had been drawn eight years ago through the area dividing it between Jordan and Israel, civilians of both parties could and did perform civilian functions in their respective sectors. Planting trees was a purely civilian activity which did not violate any international agreement binding on the parties. He denied that any Israel military personnel had entered the area between the Lines during the period in question. The only violations of the Armistice Agreement, he declared, were those committed by Jordan in connexion with military fortifications erected in the area and military traffic on a highway constructed through it.

After discussing the course of action to be taken, the Security Council decided to request separate reports from the Chief of Staff in Palestine: one on the Jordanian complaint, to be submitted within two weeks, and one on the Israel complaint.

On 23 September 1957, the Acting Chief of Staff of UNTSO submitted a report on the area between the Lines (neutral zone) around the Government House area.

On 21 July 1957, he reported, Israel workmen had begun to stake out part of the neutral zone up to what Israel considered to be a *de facto* civilian line separating the civilian activities of both parties. Since then, work had been continued without interruption, the declared purpose of which was to prepare the land for afforestation as part of a beautification project.

After reviewing the origin and history of the neutral zone, the Acting Chief of Staff stated that the demilitarized character of the zone had been violated during the initial stages of Israel's afforestation project. Jordanian troops had been seen in the zone, trenches and positions had been renovated, and the Jerusalem-Bethlehem-Hebron highway, crossing one corner of the zone, was continually used for Jordanian military traffic. No Israel military personnel had been observed in the zone with the exception of several Israel army officers inspecting the area,

but armed Israel border police numbering up to about 15 men were in the zone with the stated purpose of providing protection for the labourers.

The Acting Chief of Staff reported that UNTSO considered itself competent to exercise surveillance over the zone in order to maintain its demilitarized status. It did not, however, have any specific authority or terms of reference with respect to civilian activities in the area.

A reading of the records, said the Acting Chief of Staff, showed that the status of the zone as regards civilian matters had been left regrettably vague for many years. Although some arguments advanced by the parties had merit and should be given due consideration, others did not appear to be fully supported.

Reviewing efforts of UNTSO to find a solution to the present controversy, the Acting Chief of Staff reported that UNTSO had been unable to arrange a meeting between the parties to discuss the dispute since neither party would attend the type of meeting desired by the other. In addition, Israel had been urged on several occasions to suspend the work complained of for the sake of maintaining the tranquillity which had prevailed in the area for many months. But Israel had indicated that it did not feel justified in suspending the work which, it claimed, was a permissible civilian activity on its side of the so-called civilian line.

The Acting Chief of Staff stated that there appeared to be three ways to approach the problem: (a) transform the area between the Lines into a no-man's-land and apply article IV(3) of the General Armistice Agreement prohibiting any person, except United Nations personnel, from crossing the Demarcation Line into the zone; (b) revert to the conditions existing on 3 April 1949; and (c) arrive at an arrangement which would, to some extent at least, take into account the changes which had taken place since 1949.

Only alternative (c) seemed to him to offer a reasonable basis for a solution. Civilian activities of both parties should continue but be kept separate. The ownership of land, as established by a thorough search of the land registries, should also be respected.

With a view to finding a solution along the lines of this third alternative, the Acting Chief of Staff made certain recommendations which were incorporated into the resolution eventually adopted by the Security Council on the question.

On 16 November, in an addendum to his report of 23 September, the Acting Chief of Staff stated that the United Nations military observers had not observed any work proceeding in the area in question since 8 November 1957.

On 31 October 1957, the Council received another report from the Acting Chief of Staff dealing primarily with the more specific aspects of Israel's complaint against Jordan, which had been submitted to the Council on 5 September. (This report was not considered by the Security Council during the period covered by the present Yearbook.)

On 22 November, the Council resumed consideration of the Jordan complaint and heard statements by the representatives of Jordan and Israel. Both reaffirmed the positions of their Governments and commented on the report of the Acting Chief of Staff, particularly on his proposals and recommendations.

The representative of Jordan also said that he had received information from his Government to the effect that Israel workers were still pursuing their unlawful activities in the area. The representative of Israel denied that any work had been proceeding in the area since 8 November.

The Council considered the Jordan complaint at two further meetings on 22 January 1958, when it unanimously adopted a draft resolution submitted by the United Kingdom and the United States.

By this resolution, the Council noted that the status of the zone between the Armistice Demarcation Lines in the area of Government House at Jerusalem was affected by the provisions of the General Armistice Agreement and that neither Israel nor Jordan enjoyed sovereignty over any part of the zone (which lay beyond the respective Demarcation Lines). By the operative part of the resolution, the Council took the following steps:

(1) It directed the Chief of Staff of UNTSO to regulate activities within the zone, subject to such arrangements as might be made pursuant to the provisions shown under (3) below, bearing in mind ownership of property there, it being understood that, unless otherwise mutually agreed, Israelis should not be allowed to use Arab-owned properties and Arabs should not be allowed to use Israeli-owned properties.

(2) It directed the Chief of Staff to conduct a survey of property records with a view to determining property ownership in the zone.

(3) It endorsed the recommendations made by the Acting Chief of Staff in his report of 23 September 1957 to the end that: (a) the parties should discuss, through the Mixed Armistice Commission, civilian activities in the zone; (b) in order to create an atmosphere which would be more conducive to fruitful discussion, activities in the zone, such as those initiated by Israelis on 21 July 1957, should be suspended until such time as the survey would have been completed and provisions made for the regulation of activities in the zone; (c) such discussions should be completed within a period of two months; and (d) the Security Council should be advised of the result of the discussions.

(4) The Council also called upon the parties to the Israel-Jordan General Armistice Agreement to co-operate with the Chief of Staff and in the Mixed Armistice Commission in carrying out the above recommendations.

(5) It further called on the parties to observe article III of the Agreement and prevent all forces referred to therein from passing over the Armistice Demarcation Lines and to remove or destroy all their respective military facilities and installations in the zone.

(6) The Council, in addition, called on the parties to use the machinery provided for in the General Armistice Agreement for the implementation of the provisions of that Agreement.

(7) The Council also asked the Chief of Staff to report on the implementation of this resolution.

The representatives of Jordan and Israel both commented on the draft resolution prior to its adoption. The former stated that, though the text only partly met Jordan's request, his Government accepted it because it contained a number of positive points. The representative of Israel declared that the first three operative paragraphs of the draft sought to amend, in certain important particulars, provisions of the Israel-Jordan General Armistice Agreement as they applied to the area between the Lines. Changes in the Agreement, he pointed out, could be made only with the joint consent of the signatories to the Agreement. Meanwhile, Israel would observe the Agreement as it stood.

THE PROBLEM OF MOUNT SCOPUS

Differences between Israel and Jordan regarding the Mount Scopus area within Jordan-held Jerusalem came to a head in November 1957 when Jordanian authorities raised objections to the inclusion of gasoline in the regular fortnightly Israel supply convoy to that area.

As a result, the Secretary-General visited the area and, on 1 December 1957, held an exchange of views with the Foreign Minister of Jordan in Amman on specific problems connected with the authority of the United Nations Truce Supervision Organization (UNTSO) in areas under United Nations responsibility, particularly in the Mount Scopus demilitarized area. The Secretary-General also discussed with the Israel Prime Minister main current problems affecting the armistice situation, including, in particular, the Mount Scopus problem. Before returning to New York on 7 December, he also held talks with the Syrian Foreign Minister

and visited Lebanon for a brief period.

On 4 December, it was announced that arrangements had been made for the resumption of the convoys to Mount Scopus. On the next day, it was announced that the Secretary-General had decided to assign a personal representative for negotiations with the Governments of Jordan and Israel with a view to full implementation of an agreement of 7 July 1948 for the demilitarization of the Mount Scopus area.

That agreement established the rules under which the area was to be maintained under United Nations protection until a new agreement was entered upon. Both Governments had stated to the Secretary-General that they were willing, on the basis of reciprocity, to give full implementation to the agreement and that they accepted, on that basis, the inspection of Mount Scopus by the United Nations, which was necessary in order to fulfil United Nations responsibility for checking on such implementation being established and maintained.

On 16 December, the Secretary-General designated Ambassador Francisco Urrutia of Colombia as his personal representative.

DOCUMENTARY REFERENCES

SYRIAN COMPLAINT ABOUT CONSTRUCTION OF BRIDGE IN DEMILITARIZED ZONE

SECURITY COUNCIL, meetings 780-782.

S/3815. Report by Acting Chief of Staff of UNTSO in Palestine, dated 20 April 1957, concerning a complaint by Syria under General Armistice Agreement between Israel and Syria.

S/3827. Letter of 13 May 1957 from Permanent Representative of Syria.

S/3844. Report by Acting Chief of Staff of UNTSO, dated 27 June 1957, relating to Demilitarized Zone established under article V of Israel-Syrian General Armistice Agreement.

S/3844/Add.1. Addendum to report of 27 June 1957. Note by Secretary-General, dated 7 August 1957.

JORDAN AND ISRAEL COMPLAINTS ABOUT ZONE IN AREA OF GOVERNMENT HOUSE, JERUSALEM

SECURITY COUNCIL, meetings 787, 788, 806, 809, 810

S/3878, S/3904, S/3907, S/3909, S/3914. Letters of 4 September, 4, 8, 11 and 18 November 1957 from Permanent Representative of Jordan.

S/3883, S/3910. Letters of 5 September and 14 November 1957 from Acting Permanent Representative of Israel and from Permanent Representative of Israel, respectively.

S/3892 and Adds.1, 2. Report by Acting Chief of Staff of UNTSO in Palestine, dated 23 September, 8 November and 16 November 1957, relating to area between Lines (neutral zone) around Government House area.

S/3913. Report by Acting Chief of Staff of UNTSO, dated 31 October 1957, relating to Israel, complaint dated 5 September 1957.

S/3942. Resolution, as proposed by United Kingdom and United States, unanimously adopted by Security Council on 22 January 1958, meeting 810.

"*The Security Council,*

"*Recalling* its consideration on 6 September 1957, of the complaint of the Hashemite Kingdom of Jordan concerning activities conducted by Israel in the zone between the armistice demarcation lines in the area of Government House at Jerusalem,

"*Having considered* the report relating to the zone dated 23 September 1957, submitted in response to the Council's request by the Acting Chief of Staff of the United Nations Truce Supervision Organization,

"*Noting* that the status of the zone is affected by the provisions of the General Armistice Agreement and that neither Israel nor Jordan enjoys sovereignty over any part of the zone (the zone being beyond the respective demarcation lines),

"*Motivated* by a desire to reduce tensions and avoid the creation of new incidents,

"1. *Directs* the Chief of Staff of the United Nations

Truce Supervision Organization to regulate activities within the zone subject to such arrangements as may be made pursuant to the provisions of the General Armistice Agreement and pursuant to paragraph 3 below, bearing in mind ownership of property there, it being understood that unless otherwise mutually agreed, Israelis should not be allowed to use Arab-owned properties and Arabs should not be allowed to use Israeli-owned properties;

"2. *Directs* the Chief of Staff to conduct a survey of property records with a view to determining property ownership in the zone;

"3. *Endorses* the recommendations of the Acting Chief of Staff to the end that:

"(*a*) The parties should discuss through the Mixed Armistice Commission civilian activities in the zone;

"(*b*) In order to create an atmosphere which would be more conducive to fruitful discussion, activities in the zone, such as those initiated by Israelis on 21 July 1957, should be suspended until such time as the survey will have been completed and provisions made for the regulation of activities in the zone;

"(*c*) Such discussions should be completed within a period of two months; and

"(*d*) The Security Council should be advised of the result of the discussions;

"4. *Calls upon* the parties to the Israel-Jordan General Armistice Agreement to co-operate with the Chief of Staff and in the Mixed Armistice Commission in carrying out these recommendations pursuant to this resolution;

"5. *Calls upon* the parties to the Israel-Jordan General Armistice Agreement to observe article 3 of the Agreement and prevent all forces referred to in article 3 of the Agreement from passing over the armistice demarcation lines and to remove or destroy all their respective military facilities and installations in the zone;

"6. *Calls upon* the parties to use the machinery provided for in the General Armistice Agreement for the implementation of the provisions of that Agreement; and

"7. *Requests* the Chief of Staff to report on the implementation of this resolution."

ASSISTANCE TO PALESTINE REFUGEES

REPORT OF DIRECTOR OF UNRWA

In his annual report to the General Assembly's twelfth session (for the 12 months ending 30 June 1957), the Director of the United Nations Relief and Works Agency for Palestine Refugees in the Near East (UNRWA) stated that the Agency had carried out its relief and rehabilitation work to the extent permitted by local conditions and available funds.

In the relief field, this meant in practice that despite an unprecedented series of operational difficulties, the Agency succeeded in maintaining its essential services (provision of food, public health services and shelter being most important).

In the rehabilitation field, political factors and opposition among refugees to large-scale self-support projects prevented any significant endeavours. But some progress was made in helping an appreciable number of refugees to become self-supporting—on the understanding that this did not affect their political rights or claims to repatriation or compensation.

The Agency, however, faced an extremely grave financial crisis which threatened its existence. This crisis had obliged it to halt, postpone or curtail a number of worthwhile activities and programmes in both fields.

To meet the financial crisis, the Director's report said, the following steps were required:

(*a*) Those of the regular contributors to its fund who had not as yet done so, should pay in contributions for the six-month period ending 31 December 1957 which would be at least equivalent to half the amounts contributed for the 12 months ending 30 June 1957.

(*b*) The Assembly should approve the UNRWA budget for 1958, as the minimum one consonant with the Agency's tasks.

(*c*) The sum of $25.7 million should be pledged and paid to meet the minimum relief expenditures in 1958, and $15 million should be pledged and paid to meet the rehabilitation budget for 1958.

(*d*) All contributions towards the 1958 budget should be paid in advance of expenditures, that is, one half before 1 January 1958 and the other half before 1 June 1958.

(*e*) The sum of $8 million should be paid in, to be used, with the Agency's small remaining reserve, to establish an appropriate working capital fund.

Another point made in the Director's report was that UNRWA had a continuous operating responsibility which could not be readily adjusted to suit financial circumstances. Most of the Agency's commitments were urgent and inescapable. If UNRWA failed to provide the daily food, medical care and shelter at the right times and in the right places to the hundreds of thousands of human beings depending on it, acute starvation and disease would become an immediate threat. Furthermore, grave social and political consequences would be expected to follow any curtailment of the general education programme. Such a curtailment would condemn the huge crowds of refugee children to frustrating idleness.

A further point was that only in the case of self-support projects could activities be postponed or stopped without immediately causing more human suffering. But when these were stopped, as most of them had been for lack of funds, the General Assembly missed an opportunity for the kind of endeavour to which it had once attached great importance.

Yet another point made was that the ultimate responsibility for the nature and extent of UNRWA's work rested with the Members of the General Assembly. The Agency was only its agent. It had no authority or power not granted by the Assembly.

As of 30 June 1957, the report said, 933,556 refugees were on the Agency's register, some 11,000 more than in the previous year. Of the refugees registered, 221,058 were in the Gaza Strip, 517,388 in Jordan, 102,586 in Lebanon and 92,524 in Syria.

The number of basic dry rations distributed monthly remained at about 830,000; they provided about 1,600 calories daily in winter and 1,500 a day in summer. An average of 23,000 pregnant and nursing mothers receiving additional rations. Some 44,000 hot mid-day meals a day were provided on the average to refugees needing them on doctors' orders. An average of 190,000 babies, children under 15, pregnant and nursing women and sick persons received daily milk rations.

About 38.9 per cent of the total refugee population still lived in camps, but the number of tents in camps had decreased from 14,000 to 8,000; the number of semi-permanent huts had risen from 83,000 to 90,000. One unfortunate result of the inadequacy of funds, the report added, was that the Agency could not provide new shelters to meet many of the needs resulting from marriages and increases in the sizes of families.

The health of the refugees in all areas continued to be satisfactory. The Agency's health services, which included the operation of 92 clinics and the provision of about 2,200 hospital beds, remained substantially unchanged. Shortage of funds had ended a programme providing some 402,000 refugee children under 15 with new outfits of clothes.

Although the basic essentials of the relief programmes were maintained, their standard, as regards food, shelter and clothing, remained inadequate, the Director's report stated. In spite of pressing appeals by the Director, supported by the host Governments and by many impartial observers, the Members of the United Nations had not been able to give the Agency an income sufficient to allow it to raise its present unsatisfactory standards of relief.

The annual report further pointed out that the absence of an acceptable solution to the Palestine question caused the great mass of the refugees to remain opposed to the development of large-scale projects for self-support, which they linked with permanent resettlement, and the abandonment of hopes for repatriation. It stressed, however, that there was an increasing realization on the part of refugees and host Governments that self-support was in the long-term interest of refugees and Governments alike and that there were signs among refugees of growing appreciation of the desirability of self-support and rehabilitation, in the broad sense of an improvement in their conditions of life and prospects for the future.

The Agency's financial difficulties, however, caused it to halt or defer some very important self-support projects. These, the Director's report said, had resulted in the termination of the very successful individual grants programmes in Jordan and Syria; the stoppage of the teachers' training schools in Jordan; the deferring of construction and equipment of new vocational and agricultural training centres; the deferring of the re-equipment of the agricultural training centre in the Gaza Strip (from which, as the Director of UNRWA later told the General Assembly's Special Political Committee, all equipment and livestock were looted during the military operations of November 1956); and the ending of all new project activities.

The annual report also pointed out that the Agency's educational system remained one of its most important means for preparing refugees to become self-supporting wherever they might ultimately live. There were 115,000 pupils and over 3,100 teachers in the 372 Agency schools, as well as 53,400 UNRWA-assisted refugee pupils in government and private schools. The Agency's two existing vocational training centres, at Gaza and at Kalandia, near Jerusalem in Jordan, continued their courses. But the shortage of funds made it necessary to suspend the construction of three vocational and two agricultural training centres, the planning of which was complete. Similarly, the closing down of UNRWA's teacher-training centres because of the shortage of funds had further aggravated the problem of the shortage of trained teachers which the Agency had been facing.

One of the most successful ways yet found by the Agency for helping refugees to become self-supporting had been the individual grants programmes in Jordan and Syria. The Agency had thereby given small grants to refugees desiring to establish themselves in economically sound ventures. More than 7,200 refugees (5,400 in Jordan and 1,800 in Syria) had been made self-supporting through this project until the lack of funds forced the Agency to bring it to an end.

Three of the Agency's small-scale agricultural projects became reasonably well established economically during the period covered by the report. The Director of UNRWA hoped that the host Government would be willing to assume responsibility for them. Two housing projects—one in Amman and one in Jerusalem —were completed and occupied by refugees who, when freed from the burden of rent payments, would become self-supporting.

CONSIDERATION BY GENERAL ASSEMBLY

The question of assistance to Palestine refugees was considered at the General Assembly's twelfth session by the Special Political Committee between 18 November and 6 December 1957.

In presenting his report, the Director of UNRWA again drew attention to the Agency's extremely serious financial situation. Even after cutting certain of its programmes, he said, the Agency would have spent, during the 18-month fiscal period ending 31 December 1957, $8.8 million more than it would have received, the difference being made up from its rapidly dwindling reserve of working capital. For the calendar year 1958, a minimum global budget of $40.7 million had been established. Of this,

$25.7 million was for relief (mainly food, shelter and health services) and $15 million for rehabilitation. In the rehabilitation budget, $7.2 million was to meet the estimated cost of continuing existing activities: mainly general education and the two vocational training centres. The balance ($7.8 million) was to meet the cost of resuming activities cut or deferred, such as the grants programmes and the construction and equipment of new training centres.

To meet its relief budget, the Director stated, the Agency required $2 million more than could at that time be reasonably foreseen. To carry on its minimum rehabilitation activities, it needed yet another $2 million more than could reasonably be foreseen. Meeting the full rehabilitation budget would require an additional $8 million. And another $8 million was needed to provide an adequate working capital fund.

Stressing the Agency's continuing operating responsibility, the Director pointed out that its programme could not readily be adjusted to suit fluctuating financial circumstances. If relief or education work financed by the Agency were to be stopped in 1958, he said, the host Governments must be informed very shortly in view of the impact of such decision on the economic and political conditions prevailing in the area.

In the course of discussion in the Assembly's Special Political Committee, some Members gave information about their Governments' contributions to UNRWA. Thus, Australia and the United States announced increases in their pledges towards the Agency's budget.

As regards a solution of the refugee problem, generally considered urgent, many representatives noted that the great majority of the refugees continued to express a desire for repatriation to their former homes. The representatives of Arab States maintained that a lasting solution of the problem lay in their repatriation in accordance with the Assembly's resolution 194(III), of 11 December 1948.

The representative of Israel, however, stated that repatriation was reckless and dangerous. It was unacceptable to his Government, which regarded the integration of the refugees into the Arab countries as the solution.

On 28 November, the Committee heard a statement by Dr. Izzat Tannous, Director of the Palestine Arab Refugee Office in New York and Beirut.

A draft resolution submitted by the Netherlands, New Zealand, the Philippines, the United Kingdom and the United States stressed the need for efforts to obtain additional funds to support the Agency's programme. Representatives of Arab States, however, found the draft unacceptable as they did not consider that it provided for the minimum needs of the refugees. The draft was thereupon revised to give still further emphasis to the question of obtaining additional contributions while not changing their voluntary character. It also proposed that the Secretary-General be asked to make a special effort to obtain the funds needed.

The draft resolution as amended on these lines, was adopted by the Special Political Committee on 6 December 1957 by a vote of 49 to 0, with 21 abstentions.

Before this vote was taken, the Director of UNRWA gave it as his understanding that, in approving the Special Committee's proposal, the Assembly would be expressing general approval of the programmes envisaged in the Agency's budget and of the estimates of money required for those programmes. He also understood that the Assembly would be deciding to make a determined effort to raise the funds UNRWA needed. Further, if the necessary funds were not made available, the Assembly would be deciding that UNRWA would be unable to resume its full-scale rehabilitation programme, that UNRWA would have to halt its education programme from the beginning of the 1958-1959 school year, and might be obliged to make cuts in some categories of its relief services. It was also his understanding that the Assembly, in approving the resolution, would be deciding, if the necessary working capital was not made available, to take the calculated risk that relief operations might be interrupted.

The Special Political Committee's resolution was given final approval at a plenary meeting of the Assembly on 12 December 1957, in the form of resolution 1191(XII), which was adopted by 52 votes to 0, with 19 abstentions.

After the adoption of the resolution, the President of the Assembly pointed out that the additional contributions needed by UNRWA over and above its reasonable expectations amounted to only about $19 million. Wholeheartedly endorsing the effort which the Secretary-General would be making, he declared that the Assembly's responsibility for finding the funds required to finance UNRWA's budget was urgent and inescapable. The United Nations could not allow NURWA's work to fail, he declared. Not only were the lives and future of the refugees at stake. The peace and stability of the Near East were also involved.

CONTRIBUTIONS PLEDGED IN 1957

Contributions totalling the equivalent of $42,255,315 were pledged by 38 Governments to finance UNRWA's activities during the 18 months ending 31 December 1957; the equivalent of $17,997,867 has been pledged by 31 Governments for programmes during the calendar year 1958.

These amounts include pledges announced at a meeting of the Ad Hoc Committee of the Whole Assembly on 4 October 1957. Of the total amount pledged during the 18 months period, $35,872,815 and $6,382,500 were earmarked for relief and rehabilitation activities, respectively. Of the total pledged for 1958, $14,831,200 was for relief and $3,166,667 for rehabilitation.

PLEDGES OF CONTRIBUTIONS TO UNWRA
(In U. S. Dollar Equivalents)

Pledging Government	FOR 18 MONTHS ENDING 31 DECEMBER 1957		FOR 12 MONTHS ENDING 31 DECEMBER 1958*	
	Relief	Rehabilitation	Relief	Rehabilitation
Australia	$ 212,000	—	$ 100,000	—
Austria	1,050	—	1,400	—
Bahrein	1,960	—	—	—
Belgium	50,000	—	20,000	—
Burma	2,972	—	—	—
Canada	772,500	—	2,040,000	—
Ceylon	1,400	—	—	—

Pledging Government	FOR 18 MONTHS ENDING 31 DECEMBER 1957		FOR 12 MONTHS ENDING 31 DECEMBER 1958*	
	Relief	Rehabilitation	Relief	Rehabilitation
Denmark	43,478	—	—	—
Egypt	182,182	—	184,000	—
Ethiopia	10,000	—	—	—
Finland	2,000	—	—	—
France	308,049	—	141,616	—
Greece	16,500	—	39,000	—
Gaza Authorities	19,157	—	14,000	—
Germany, Fed. Rep. of	24,997	—	190,476	$ 166,667
Indonesia	30,000	—	—	—
Iran	2,680	—	2,680	—
Israel	172,778	—	—	—
Japan	20,000	—	—	—
Jordan	54,003	—	70,000	—
Lebanon	11,652	—	8,000	—
Liberia	—	—	5,000	—
Libya	—	—	20,000	—
Luxembourg	2,000	—	2,000	—
Monaco	286	—	2,381	—
Morocco	5,714	—	4,762	—
Malaya, Federation of	1,500	—	—	—
Netherlands	64,474	—	32,895	—
New Zealand	238,000	—	—	—
Norway	63,202	—	42,075	—
Pakistan	41,964	—	21,000	—
Philippines	1,250	—	—	—
Qatar	—	$ 10,500	—	—
Saudi Arabia	172,421	—	212,420	—
Spain	—	—	23,810	—
Sudan	—	—	4,320	—
Sweden	86,872	—	57,915	—
Switzerland	—	—	70,093	—
Syria	110,415	—	74,000	—
Tunisia	—	—	2,000	—
Turkey	5,357	—	5,357	—
United Kingdom	6,600,002	1,500,000	2,400,000	500,000
United States	26,500,000	4,872,000	9,000,000	2,500,000
Yugoslavia	40,000	—	40,000	—
Total	$35,872,815	$6,382,500	$14,831,200	$3,166,667

* From reports as at 31 March 1958.

DOCUMENTARY REFERENCES

GENERAL ASSEMBLY—12TH SESSION
Plenary Meeting 728.
Special Political Committee, meetings 64-73, 75-79.
Ad Hoc Committee of the Whole Assembly, meeting 1.

A/3686 and Corr.1. Annual report of Director of UNRWA, 1 July 1956–30 June 1957.
A/3693. Statement by Director of UNRWA to Pledging Conference for Extra-Budgetary Funds (Ad Hoc Committee of Whole Assembly) on 4 October 1957.
A/3735. Letter of 12 November 1957 from Director of UNRWA.
A/SPC/20/Rev.1, A/SPC/23. Statements by Director of UNRWA before Special Political Committee on 18 November and 6 December 1957.
A/SPC/21. Letter of 25 November 1957 from Permanent Representative of Iraq.

A/SPC/L.21 and Rev.1. Netherlands, New Zealand, Philippines, United Kingdom, United States draft resolution and revision, adopted by Special Political Committee by 49 votes to 0, with 21 abstentions.
A/3776. Report of Special Political Committee.
RESOLUTION 1191(XII), as recommended by Special Political Committee, A/3776, adopted by Assembly on 12 December 1957, meeting 728, by 52 votes to 0, with 19 abstentions.

"The General Assembly,
"Recalling its resolutions 194(III) of 11 December 1948, 302(IV) of 8 December 1949, 393(V) of 2 December 1950, 513(VI) of 26 January 1952, 614 (VII) of 6 November 1952, 720(VIII) of 27 November 1953, 818(IX) of 4 December 1954, 916(X) of 3 December 1955 and 1018(XI) of 28 February 1957,

"*Noting* the annual report of the Director of the United Nations Relief and Works Agency for Palestine Refugees in the Near East and the report of the Advisory Commission of the Agency,

"*Having reviewed* the budget for relief and rehabilitation prepared by the Director of the Agency, and having noted the comment of the Advisory Commission to the effect that the budget is minimal,

"*Noting with grave concern* that contributions to the budget are not yet sufficient, that the financial situation of the Agency is serious, and that cuts have already had to be made in the rehabilitation programme,

"*Noting* that repatriation or compensation of the refugees, as provided for in paragraph 11 of resolution 194(III), has not been effected, that no substantial progress has been made in the programme endorsed in paragraph 2 of resolution 513(VI) for the reintegration of refugees and that, therefore, the situation of the refugees continues to be a matter of serious concern,

"*Noting* that the host Governments have expressed the wish that the Agency continue to carry out its mandate in their respective countries or territories and have expressed their wish to co-operate fully with the Agency and to extend to it every appropriate assistance in carrying out its functions, in accordance with the provisions of Articles 104 and 105 of the Charter of the United Nations, the terms of the Convention on the Privileges and Immunities of the United Nations, the contents of paragraph 17 of resolution 302(IV) and the terms of the agreements with the host Governments,

"1. *Draws the attention* of Governments to the critical financial position of the United Nations Relief and Works Agency for Palestine Refugees in the Near East, and urges them to consider to what extent they can contribute or increase their contributions in order that the Agency may carry out its budgeted relief and rehabilitation programmes and that cuts in services may be avoided;

"2. *Requests* the Secretary-General, in view of the critical financial position of the Agency, to make, as a matter of urgent concern, special efforts to secure the additional financial assistance needed to meet the Agency's budget and to provide adequate working capital;

"3. *Directs* the Agency to pursue its programme for the relief and rehabilitation of refugees, bearing in mind the response to paragraphs 1 and 2 above;

"4. *Requests* the host Governments to co-operate fully with the Agency and with its personnel and to extend to the Agency every appropriate assistance in carrying out its functions;

"5. *Requests* the Governments of the area, without prejudice to paragraph 11 of General Assembly resolution 194(III) of 11 December 1948, in co-operation with the Director of the Agency, to plan and carry out projects capable of supporting substantial numbers of refugees;

"6. *Requests* the Agency to continue its consultations with the United Nations Conciliation Commission for Palestine in the best interests of their respective tasks, with particular reference to paragraph 11 of resolution 194(III);

"7. *Expresses its thanks* to the Director and the staff of the Agency for their continued faithful efforts to carry out the mandate of the Agency and to the specialized agencies and the many private organizations for their valuable and continuing work in assisting the refugees;

"8. *Requests* the Director of the Agency to continue to submit the reports referred to in paragraph 12 of General Assembly resolution 1018(XI) of 28 February 1957."

CHAPTER IV

OTHER MIDDLE EAST MATTERS

THE SUEZ CANAL

In October 1956, the Security Council considered the situation created by the nationalization of the Suez Canal Company by Egypt in in July 1956, and unanimously adopted a resolution on 13 October whereby it was agreed that any settlement of the Suez question should meet the following six basic requirements:

(1) There should be free and open transit through the Canal without discrimination, overt or covert, this to cover both political and technical aspects. (2) The sovereignty of Egypt should be respected. (3) The operation of the Canal should be insulated from the politics of any country. (4) The manner of fixing tolls and charges should be decided by agreement between Egypt and the users. (5) A fair proportion of the dues should be allotted to development. (6) In case of disputes, unresolved affairs between the Suez Canal Company and the Egyptian Government should be settled by arbitration with suitable terms of reference and suitable provisions for the payment of sums found to be due.

Consideration of possible arrangements for

meeting those requirements was interrupted by the military action in Egypt of Israel and Anglo-French forces and by the blocking of the Canal.

The response of the General Assembly to these developments included its resolution (1121(XI)) of 24 November 1956 which authorized the Secretary-General to proceed with arrangements for clearing the Suez Canal. By mid-April 1957, the clearance operation was reported as completed.[1]

CONSIDERATION OF SUEZ CANAL QUESTION BY SECURITY COUNCIL

On 24 April 1957, the United States representative requested a meeting of the Security Council in order to resume discussion of the question and to take note of the situation with regard to passage through the Canal.

On the same day, Egypt's Minister for Foreign Affairs informed the Secretary-General that the Canal was now open again for normal traffic and transmitted a Declaration on the Suez Canal and the arrangements for its operation. The Declaration elaborated the principles set forth in an earlier Egyptian memorandum of 18 March 1957.

In his letter, the Egyptian Foreign Minister stated that the Declaration was made by the Government of Egypt in fulfilment of its participation in the Constantinople Convention of 1888, noting the Egyptian Government's understanding of the Security Council's resolution of 13 October 1956, and its statements before the Security Council relating to this resolution.

In the Declaration, the Government of Egypt stated its determination to continue to observe the 1888 Convention, and expressed its confidence that the other signatories and all others concerned would do the same. The Declaration further stated the Egyptian Government's determination: (1) to maintain free navigation for all nations within the limits of that Convention; (2) to limit any increase in tolls to 1 per cent within any 12 months, any increase beyond that level to be settled by negotiations and, failing agreement, by arbitration according to the procedure set forth elsewhere in the Declaration; and (3) to maintain and develop the Canal in accordance with the requirements of modern navigation.

Other points made in the Declaration included the following:

The Canal would be operated and managed by the autonomous Suez Canal Authority set up by Egypt on 26 July 1956; co-operation between the Authority and shipping and trade representatives would be encouraged with a view to increasing the usefulness of the Canal. Tolls would be payable in advance to the account of the Authority at an authorized bank. The Authority would pay 5 per cent of the gross receipts as royalty to the Government of Egypt and 25 per cent of the gross receipts would be paid into a Suez Canal Capital and Development Fund established by the Authority to assure adequate resources to meet development and capital expenditure needs.

Due notice, the Declaration added, would be given of any alteration of the Canal Code embodying the regulations governing operation of the Canal. Any challenges or complaints that an alteration of the Code affected commitments under the Declaration would be dealt with according to arbitration procedures as described immediately below.

Complaints of discrimination or violation of the Canal Code would be referred first to the Suez Canal Authority, and if not resolved, to an arbitration tribunal at the option of the complaining party or the Authority. The tribunal would consist of one nominee of the complaining party, one of the Authority and a third chosen by both. In case of disagreement, the third member would be chosen by the President of the International Court of Justice upon application of either party. A majority decision by the tribunal would be binding.

The question of compensation and claims connected with the nationalization of the Suez Canal Maritime Company, would, unless agreed between the parties concerned, be referred to arbitration according to established international practice.

Disputes arising in respect of the 1888 Convention or the present Declaration would be settled in accordance with the United Nations Charter. Differences arising between the parties to the Convention in respect of the interpretation or applicability of its provisions would be referred to the International Court, if not otherwise resolved. The Government of Egypt would

[1] For details about developments in 1956 and early 1957, see *Y.U.N., 1956,* pp. 19-25, 53-55, 61-62.

take the necessary steps to accept the compulsory jurisdiction of the Court under article 36 of the Court's Statute. In conclusion, the Government of Egypt stated that it made this Declaration which reaffirmed and was in full accord with the 1888 Convention, as an expression of its determination to enable the Canal to be an efficient and adequate waterway. The Declaration with the obligations therein, it was said, constituted an international instrument, and it would be deposited and registered with the United Nations Secretariat.

In a letter dated 24 April 1957, the Secretary-General acknowledged receipt of the original of the Declaration, which had been placed in the United Nations archives. He also said it had been registered with the United Nations Secretariat on his understanding that the Egyptian Government considered the Declaration to be an engagement of an international character coming within the scope of Article 102 of the United Nations Charter. (Article 102 provides for international agreements and treaties entered by any United Nations Member being registered with and published by the United Nations Secretariat. It further provides that no party to any such treaty or agreement not so registered may invoke it before any United Nations organ.)

At two meetings, on 26 April, the Council discussed the item. The representative of Egypt participated in the debate.

On 20 and 21 May 1957, the Council resumed its discussion at two further meetings, as requested on May 16 by the representative of France, who transmitted a *communiqué* of the Council of Ministers of France.

This *communiqué* expressed regret at the decisions of users of the Canal to make direct payment of tolls to Egypt without the minimum guarantees concerning free transit and the equitable distribution of the moneys collected. It further stated that the French Government could not regard as acceptable a solution of the Canal problem which was in contradiction with the six requirements set out in the Security Council decision of October 1956.

On 21 May 1957, at the close of the discussion, the United States representative, speaking as President of the Council, declared that a majority of the Council had shown awareness of the responsibilities of the United Nations by its adoption on 13 October 1956 of the six

requirements which should be met in any Suez Canal settlement. Although certain views had been expressed to the effect that the Egyptian Declaration and the present operation of the Suez Canal adequately implemented the six requirements of the Council, the majority opinion was that the requirements had not yet been met, that there were uncertainties requiring clarification and that the Egyptian position remained to be completed.

It had also been observed, the President added, that the Egyptian Government had not yet deposited its acceptance of the compulsory jurisdiction of the International Court in accordance with its statement of intention.

Questions had been raised, too, about the nature of the obligations which Egypt recognized under the Declaration, the way in which they had been put forward and whether Egypt considered it could amend or withdraw them at will. In that connexion, most Council members had qualified their acquiescence in the Egyptian Declaration as provisional. It had also been said that the United Nations must continue to seek a final solution while giving the interim arrangements a chance to work out without injury to the interests of any of the nations involved.

Doubts had been expressed, too, about the lack of provision in the Declaration for organized user co-operation, the President added. It had been pointed out that further clarification was required on the participation of the users implicit in various paragraphs of the Declaration, particularly those relating to arbitration and the fixing of tolls. Questions had also been raised about the compensation of claims in connexion with the nationalization of the Suez Canal Company and about the method of reaching agreement. Members had pointed out that the obligations which Egypt appeared to have assured required further initiative from Egypt if these obligations were to be carried out.

The insulation of the Canal from the politics of any nations, the President added, continued to be a matter of concern, and that concern was inherent in all the doubts expressed in the Council about the adequacy of the Egyptian Declaration.

The Egyptian Government would presumably wish as soon as possible to consider the concrete steps it could take to remove the doubts which had arisen. In the meantime, the President stated, the Council would remain seized of the question.

On 18 July, Egypt supplemented its Declaration of 24 April by accepting as compulsory the jurisdiction of the International Court of Justice in all legal disputes that might arise between the parties to the Constantinople Convention of 1888 regarding the interpretation or applicability of its provisions.

CLEARANCE OF SUEZ CANAL

In a memorandum of 16 September 1957, the Secretary-General proposed the inclusion of an item entitled "Clearance of the Suez Canal: report of the Secretary-General" in the agenda of the General Assembly's twelfth session. The item was subsequently allocated for discussion in plenary meeting.

On 1 November 1957, the Secretary-General submitted a report on the clearance of the Suez Canal. The report described the operations authorized under Assembly resolution 1121(XI) of 24 November 1956,[2] and the arrangements and agreements made in this connexion.

The report noted that the Secretary-General had appointed Lieutenant-General Raymond A. Wheeler as Special Representative in charge of technical operations and Mr. John J. McCloy as advisory on the business negotiations connected with the project. The plan to make possible the resumption of normal traffic provided for: clearance of obstructions from channels, ports and harbourages; rehabilitation of maintenance workshops; restoration of navigational lighting and telecommunication services; essential dredging; and the availability of operational craft for the handling of convoys.

On 10 April 1957, the United Nations salvage vessels completed the opening of ports and harbourages. This was some weeks earlier than had originally been predicted for the full clearance of the main shipping channel only. The expenditures and obligations incurred by the United Nations totalled approximately $8.4 million.

In conclusion, the Secretary-General reported that, after consideration of various possible alternatives for meeting the costs, he would recommend the payment of the sum of more than $11 million advanced during the actual operation by 11 contributing countries under which a levy of 3 per cent on Canal tolls would be paid. The procedures would be negotiated with the Egyptian Government and with the other parties to the payment. By that method it could be estimated that the costs would be reimbursed over a period of about three years.

The Assembly considered the report of the Secretary-General on 14 December. The Assembly also had before it a draft resolution, submitted by Brazil, Iran, the Philippines and Thailand. Mindful that the clearing of the Suez Canal was of direct and immediate benefit to all shipping and trade using the Canal, the Assembly would thereby: (1) authorize the Secretary-General to take the necessary steps to put into effect his recommendations for reimbursing the advances made by contributor countries; and (2) urge Member States to co-operate fully with the Secretary-General in these arrangements in order that the advances made to the United Nations for clearing the Suez Canal might be repaid.

During the debate, many speakers congratulated the Secretary-General and all those whose co-operation had brought about the clearance of the Canal rapidly and at less cost than originally anticipated.

The representatives of Australia, Denmark and the Netherlands said they would have preferred that the costs be borne by the United Nations itself in accordance with the normal scale of assessment. Some Members, including the USSR, which stated that it would abstain in the vote, objected to the proposed method of repayment. It held that the costs should not be shared by the Canal users but rather that all expenditures caused by the aggression of France, the United Kingdom and Israel against Egypt, including the expenditures connected with the clearance of the Canal, should be fully reimbursed by those States.

On 14 December 1957, the Assembly adopted the four-power draft resolution by 54 votes to 0, with 19 abstentions, as resolution 1212(XII).

[2] For earlier details, see *Y.U.N., 1956*, pp. 53-55.

DOCUMENTARY REFERENCES

*CONSIDERATION OF SUEZ CANAL
QUESTION BY SECURITY COUNCIL*

SECURITY COUNCIL, meetings 776-779.

S/3817 and Rev.1. Letter of 24 April 1957 from representative of United States relating to Suez Canal (item 28 of list of matters of which Security Council is seized).

S/3818 and Add.1 (A/3576 and Add.1). Declaration on Suez Canal and arrangements for its operation. Letters of 24 April and 18 July 1957 from Minister for Foreign Affairs of Egypt.

S/3819 (A/3577). Letter of 24 April 1957 from Secretary-General to Minister for Foreign Affairs of Egypt.

S/3829, S/3839/Rev.1. Letters of 15 May and 13 June 1957 from representative and Deputy Representative of France, respectively.

CLEARANCE OF SUEZ CANAL

A/3576 and Add.1 (S/3818 and Add.1). Declaration on Suez Canal and arrangements for its operation. Letters of 24 April and 18 July 1957 from Minister for Foreign Affairs of Egypt.

A/3577 (S/3819). Letter of 24 April 1957 from Secretary-General to Minister for Foreign Affairs of Egypt.

GENERAL ASSEMBLY—12TH SESSION
General Committee, meeting 112.
Plenary Meetings, 686, 696, 730.

A/3664. Memorandum by Secretary-General proposing inclusion in agenda of twelfth session of item entitled "Clearance of Suez Canal: report of Secretary General".

A/3719. Report of Secretary-General.

A/L.238. Brazil, Iran, Philippines, Thailand draft resolution.

RESOLUTION 1212(XII), as proposed by four powers, A/L.238, adopted by Assembly on 14 December 1957, meeting 730, by 54 votes to 0, with 19 abstentions.

"*The General Assembly,*

"*Recalling* its resolution 1121(XI) of 24 November 1956 regarding arrangements for clearing the Suez Canal,

"*Recalling further* that the Secretary-General, pursuant to that resolution, requested and received from various Governments as advances funds necessary to proceed with the clearing operation,

"*Having received* the report of the Secretary-General dated 17 November 1957,

"*Mindful* that the clearing of the Canal is of direct and immediate benefit to all shipping and trade using the Canal,

"*Expressing its appreciation* of the prompt and efficient manner in which the clearance operation was organized and completed,

"*Expressing its satisfaction* that the Canal is again serving world trade and international shipping,

"1. *Notes* the expenses and obligations that have been incurred by the United Nations in the clearing of the Suez Canal;

"2. *Endorses* the recommendation of the Secretary-General that, subject to reduction by such resources as might become otherwise available, reimbursement of the advances made by contributor countries to meet the costs of the operations be effected by the application of a surcharge on Canal traffic and that, under this arrangement, a surcharge of 3 per cent on Canal traffic would be paid by all shipping and trade using the Canal into a special United Nations account, the procedure to govern such payments to be negotiated with the Government of Egypt and with the other parties to the payments;

"3. *Authorizes* the Secretary-General to take the necessary steps to put this arrangement into effect;

"4. *Urges* the Governments of Member States to co-operate fully with the Secretary-General under the present resolution in order that advances made to the United Nations for the purpose of clearing the Canal may be repaid."

THE UNITED NATIONS EMERGENCY FORCE

Consequent upon the intervention in Egypt by Israel and by France and the United Kingdom in October 1956, the General Assembly established the United Nations Emergency Force (UNEF) "to secure and supervise the cessation of hostilities". The Force was set up by two resolutions, 1000(ES-I) and 1001(ES-I), which the Assembly adopted on 5 and 7 November 1956, respectively, thereby endorsing plans submitted by the Secretary-General, including guiding principles for its organization and functioning.

On 9 October 1957, the Secretary-General submitted a report at the Assembly's twelfth session, giving essential data about the Force, and appraising its functioning and the problem of its financing.[3] This report dealt particularly with the period since 8 March 1957. On that day, the withdrawal of all foreign troops from Egyptian territory in compliance with Assembly resolutions became complete when the Secretary-General informed the Assembly's eleventh session that there had been full compliance with

[3] For an account of the early history of UNEF and its origins, see *Y.U.N., 1956*, pp. 29-33, 39-43, 47-53, 55-56.

Assembly resolution 1124(XI) of 2 February 1957, which had called upon Israel to complete its withdrawal behind the Armistice Demarcation Lines between Egypt and Israel.

UNEF, the Secretary-General's report of 9 October said, had been maintained for 10 months, at a strength of about 6,000, with contingents from the 10 contributing countries: Brazil, Canada, Colombia, Denmark, Finland, India, Indonesia, Norway, Sweden and Yugoslavia. With its headquarters in Gaza, this international Force was subject to orders and instructions only from its Commander, Major-General E. L. M. Burns, and, through him, from the Secretary-General. A practice of rotation after six months of service had developed and a leave centre had been established in Beirut, the costs being met by the United Nations. The morale of the Force had been high. The crucial problem of logistics had been met quite satisfactorily. It was expected that the Force, soon to be reduced to about 5,600 men, would satisfy the minimum need.

In 10 months of duty, UNEF had undertaken important responsibilities involving a wide variety of tasks. The Force, however, had not been established to undertake enforcement action, the report pointed out. Nor did it use all normal military methods in achieving the objectives as defined for it by the Assembly. Its first detachment having entered Egyptian territory with the consent of the Egyptian Government on 15 November 1956, the Force had been concerned mainly with taking over from the foreign troops, following the successive stages of their withdrawals from the Suez Canal area, the Sinai Peninsula and the Gaza Strip. Since 6 March, the Force, interposed between the armed forces of Egypt and Israel, had concentrated on its basic function of maintaining quiet in the area through deployment and patrolling along lines totalling 273 kilometres in length in the Gaza Strip and along the eastern border of the Sinai Peninsula, as well as in the region of Sharm el Sheikh. Since the final withdrawals of Israel troops in March, the activities of the Force had centred on the fulfilment of Assembly resolution 1125(XI) of 2 February 1957. This resolution called for the placing of the Force on the Egyptian-Israel Armistice Demarcation Line. No UNEF unit, the Secretary-General's report of 9 October stated, had yet been stationed on the Israel side of the Line because of lack of consent by Israel.

The most difficult duties, it added, had been in the Gaza Strip. Here, if UNEF was to discharge its responsibilities effectively, it was essential to have the co-operation of the Gaza Administration and an awareness of the people in the area that the mission of UNEF was friendly and had the support of the Administration. Along the Gaza Line which was patrolled by UNEF alone, there had been a steady reduction in both the number and severity of incidents involving mines, crossings, attempted crossings and firing across the Line. Infiltrators whom UNEF was authorized to apprehend were handed over to the local police. There had been no raids from either side. As of 15 September, no reports of any serious incident had been received since 14 July. The Commander was of the view that the absence of incidents reflected more effective local police action. The relations between UNEF and the local population were reported to be good, generally speaking.

UNEF, continued the Secretary-General, was designed to meet a particular need in an acute emergency. The authority given to it was necessarily limited. But its basic purpose and role, as defined by the General Assembly, had been clear enough. In the course of its functioning, satisfactory solutions had been found for most of the many issues that had arisen. The Commander of UNEF had warned that there were a few unresolved issues which needed solution, when the time was propitious. These included: the completion of UNEF's deployment; authority for UNEF to fire during darkness at infiltrators approaching the Line from either direction, which would be somewhat broader than its unquestioned right to fire in self-defence—a right which it had, on occasion, exercised; and the idea of a protective fence along a part or the whole of the Demarcation Line.

There would seem to be no good reason to doubt that UNEF had been effective, the Secretary-General reported. It had earned acceptance as a significant pioneering effort in the evolution of methods of peace-making. However, the Line between Egypt and Israel was vulnerable under present conditions, and the quiet could at any moment be abruptly broken. Such quiet, in the Secretary-General's view, was indispensable to fruitful efforts towards removing the major obstacles to peace in the Near East.

With regard to the financial requirements of UNEF,[4] the Secretary-General's report estimated that the expenses for the 14-month period ending 31 December 1957 would total between $24 million and $30.5 million, depending on such arrangements as might be agreed on or confirmed by the General Assembly for reimbursement of special allowances paid to contingents in the initial emergency period of six months in the area and for all extra and extraordinary costs which Governments were obliged to incur in subsequently making contingents available for UNEF service. The expense figures excluded the value of the military contingents contributed, including basic salaries and equipment, and the materials and services provided without charge by Governments. Proposing that the United Nations assume responsibility for reimbursement of all extra and extraordinary costs, the Secretary-General considered that, beyond the limited emergency period, any arrangement under which a few Member States carried a disproportionate financial burden did not represent a sound or equitable basis on which to discharge a collective United Nations responsibility.

By 30 September 1957, only $6,330,000 had been paid into the UNEF Special Account. Of this, about $5,744,000 had been paid in towards the initial amount of $10 million, which, by resolution 1089(XI) of 21 December 1956, was to be apportioned among Member States in accordance with the scale of contributions to the annual United Nations budget. The balance of $586,000 had been paid in the form of contributions toward the additional expenditures of $6.5 million authorized by resolution 1090(XI) of 27 February 1957. A further amount of $3,213,000 had been pledged in voluntary contributions, but $2.7 million of this sum was dependent on the receipt of matching contributions from other United Nations Members.[5] Some Member States had notified the Secretary-General that they would not participate in the financing of the Force. The percentage assessments of these States amounted to about 20 per cent of the initial $10 million.

The wide disparity between the financial needs for the current period and the available cash resources, the report continued, made it imperative that the General Assembly, in addition to determining any costs to be reimbursed to Governments providing contingents to UNEF, should give urgent consideration to: (a) the granting of authority to the Secretary-General to incur expenses for the maintenance of the Force; and (b) the basis for financing UNEF costs. On the basis of the latest estimates of financial requirements, the Secretary-General asked that the Assembly authorize him to incur expenses for UNEF as follows: (a) up to $23,920,500 for the period ending 31 December 1957, and (b) for any 1958 period, not more than a total of $20 million, plus the additional amounts required for such reimbursements of costs as might be authorized, it being understood that as long as UNEF continued on its present basis, expenses of maintaining it would not normally exceed $2 million a month.

Perhaps the most important single issue, the Secretary-General's report said, resulted from the decision of the Assembly at its eleventh session (resolution 1090(XI)) to consider at its twelfth session the basis for financing any costs of the Force in excess of $10 million not covered by voluntary contributions. The Secretary-General held to his previously expressed view that Assembly decisions having important financial consequences carried with them an obligation on the part of all United Nations Members to make available the requisite resources or other means for their implementation.

In the light of the extremely limited response to the appeal for voluntary contributions and of the scope of UNEF operations, he questioned both the feasibility and the prudence of placing any undue reliance for the future on that method of obtaining the necessary budgetary provision. If the possibility of UNEF successfully completing its mission was not to be seriously jeopardized, he deemed it essential that this vital United Nations undertaking should be assured of the same degree and certainty of

[4] For earlier developments with regard to the financing of UNEF, see Y.U.N., 1956, pp. 42-43.

[5] By 31 December 1957, the final total of $1,841,700 in voluntary contributions had been paid by the Dominican Republic, France, Greece, New Zealand, Pakistan, The United States and the United Kingdom.

financial support as that afforded to other United Nations activities which had as their purpose the maintenance of security and peace.

On 19 November, the Secretary-General called the attention of the Assembly to an important new development: the United States and the United Kingdom, although considering that UNEF expenses were a United Nations obligation to be met by the regular scale of assessment, had offered $12 million and $1 million, respectively, as "special assistance" towards outstanding expenses for the period ending 31 December 1957. The offers, it was stated, were made on the assumption that any balance of 1957 expenses and all 1958 expenses of the Force would be assessed on the regular scale. Other such offers, in lesser amounts, he noted, had been, or appeared likely to be made. (By the end of 1957, Australia, Austria, Burma, Ceylon, Liberia, Mexico and the Netherlands had so contributed.)

When, on 22 November, the General Assembly considered its agenda item on the United Nations Emergency Force, it had before it the reports of the Secretary-General and a draft resolution submitted by the following 21 Members: Brazil, Canada, Ceylon, Colombia, Costa Rica, Denmark, Finland, India, Indonesia, Iran, Ireland, Italy, Japan, Liberia, Norway, Pakistan, Spain, Sweden, Thailand, Uruguay and Yugoslavia.

Mindful of the contribution of the Force to the maintenance of quiet in the area, the Assembly would, by this draft: express its appreciation of the assistance rendered to the Force by Members; approve the principles and proposals for allocation of costs between the Organization and Members contributing troops as set forth in the report of the Secretary-General; authorize an additional obligational authority up to $13.5 million for the period ending 31 December 1957 and, as necessary, an amount up to $25 million for the continuing operation of the Force; decide that the expenses authorized should be borne by Members in accordance with the regular scale of assessments; and ask its Fifth (Administrative and Budgetary) Committee to examine, with the assistance of the Advisory Committee on Administrative and Budgetary Questions, the cost estimates for maintaining the Force and make appropriate recommendations.

The Canadian representative introduced the 21-power draft resolution as a sound basis for the continued operation of UNEF. Expressing views shared by a large majority of the speakers supporting the draft, he stressed the significance of the establishment of UNEF and its valuable contribution to the maintenance of quiet and order in the area of its deployment and paid tribute to all Governments contributing to the Force and its personnel and to the Secretary-General and all those who had worked for its success.

The representatives of Chile, Ecuador, Guatemala and Mexico, while enthusiastically approving the creation and maintenance of the Force, opposed the 21-power draft resolution. They considered the scale of assessments neither equitable nor fair.

A number of Members opposing the draft resolution, including the USSR, reaffirmed the view they had expressed at the Assembly's eleventh session that the establishment of armed forces of the United Nations fell exclusively within the competence of the Security Council and that consequently the creation of UNEF was contrary to the Charter. The expenses of UNEF should be defrayed by the three States which had perpetrated armed aggression against Egypt, they declared, adding that they would not participate in the financing of the Force.

On 22 November, the 21-power draft resolution was adopted by the General Assembly by 51 votes to 11, with 19 abstentions. as resolution 1151(XII).

In accordance with that resolution, the Advisory Committee on Administrative and Budgetary Questions examined the UNEF cost estimates. Its report was principally concerned with the 1958 expenditures for the Force. It made various observations and recommendations for possible reduction of expenditures and considered that, in view of the lower rate of expenditure foreseen for many categories of expenses, the budget total for the first half-year should not exceed $9 to $10 million, exclusive of extra and extraordinary expenses as approved for reimbursement by resolution 1151(XII).

On 12 December, the Fifth Committee adopted a draft resolution, by 45 votes to 10, with 6 abstentions, whereby the Assembly would note with approval the Advisory Committee's observations and recommendations. The following day, this was approved at a plenary meeting of the Assembly, as resolution 1204(XII). The

vote for this in the Assembly was 45 in favour to 9 against, with 10 abstentions.

DOCUMENTARY REFERENCES

GENERAL ASSEMBLY—12TH SESSION
Plenary Meetings 686, 696, 720, 721, 729.
General Committee, meeting 112.
Fifth Committee, meetings 639, 646.

A/3665. Memorandum by Secretary-General requesting inclusion in agenda of 12th Assembly session of item entitled "United Nations Emergency Force: report of Secretary-General".
A/3694 and Add.1. United Nations Emergency Force. Report of Secretary-General.
A/3745. Note by Secretary-General.
A/L.235 and Add.1. Brazil, Canada, Ceylon, Colombia, Costa Rica, Denmark, Finland, India, Indonesia, Iran, Ireland, Italy, Japan, Liberia, Norway, Pakistan, Spain, Sweden, Thailand, Uruguay, Yugoslavia draft resolution.
RESOLUTION 1151(XII), as recommended by 21 powers, A/L.235 and Add.1, adopted by Assembly on 22 November 1957, meeting 721, by roll-call vote of 51 to 11, with 19 abstentions, as follows:
In favour: Afghanistan, Argentina, Australia, Austria, Belgium, Bolivia, Brazil, Burma, Canada, Ceylon, Colombia, Costa Rica, Cuba, Denmark, Dominican Republic, Finland, France, Ghana, Greece, Haiti, Honduras, Iceland, India, Indonesia, Iran, Ireland, Israel, Italy, Japan, Jordan,[6] Laos, Liberia, Luxembourg, Netherlands, New Zealand, Nicaragua, Norway, Pakistan, Paraguay, Peru, Philippines, Portugal, Spain, Sweden, Thailand, Turkey, United Kingdom, United States, Uruguay, Venezuela, Yugoslavia.
Against: Albania, Bulgaria, Byelorussian SSR, Chile, Czechoslovakia, Ecuador, Hungary, Poland, Romania, Ukrainian SSR, USSR.
Abstaining: Cambodia, China, Egypt, El Salvador, Ethiopia, Guatemala, Iraq, Lebanon, Libya, Federation of Malaya, Mexico, Morocco, Nepal, Panama, Saudi Arabia, Sudan, Syria, Tunisia, Yemen.

"*The General Assembly,*
"*Recalling* its resolutions 1000(ES-I) of 5 November 1956, 1001(ES-I) of 7 November 1956, 1089(XI) of 21 December 1956, 1125(XI) of 2 February 1957 and 1090(XI) of 27 February 1957 concerning the establishment, organization, functioning and financing of the United Nations Emergency Force,
"*Noting with appreciation* the report of the Secretary-General on the Force, dated 9 October 1957, and the effective assistance rendered by the Advisory Committee on the United Nations Emergency Force.
"*Mindful* of the contribution of the Force to the maintenance of quiet in the area,
"1. *Expresses its appreciation* of the assistance rendered to the United Nations Emergency Force by Members of the United Nations which have contributed troops and other support and facilities, and

expresses the hope that such assistance will be continued as necessary;
"2. *Approves* the principles and proposals for the allocation of costs between the organization and Members contributing troops as set forth in paragraphs 86, 88 and 91 of the report of the Secretary-General, and authorizes the Secretary-General in connexion therewith to enter into such agreements as may be necessary for the reimbursement of appropriate extra and extraordinary costs to Members contributing troops;
"3. *Authorizes* the Secretary-General to expend an additional amount for the Force, for the period ending 31 December 1957, up to a maximum of $13.5 million and, as necessary, an amount for the continuing operation of the Force beyond that date up to a maximum of $25 million, subject to any decisions taken on the basis of the review provided for in paragraph 5 below;
"4. *Decides* that the expenses authorized in paragraph 3 above shall be borne by the Members of the United Nations in accordance with the scales of assessments adopted by the General Assembly for the financial years 1957 and 1958 respectively, such other resources as may have become available for the purpose in question being applied to reduce the expenses before the apportionment for the period ending 31 December 1957;
"5. *Requests* the Fifth Committee to examine, with the assistance of the Advisory Committee on Administrative and Budgetary Questions and in the light of the present resolution, the cost estimates for maintaining the United Nations Emergency Force contained in the report of the Secretary-General, and to make such recommendations as it considers appropriate concerning the expenditure authorized under paragraph 3 above."

A/C.5/735. Statement of advances to working capital fund, contributions to budgets for financial years 1955, 1956 and 1957 and initial assessments for 1957 to UNEF Special Account as at 10 December 1957, Part V.
A/3761. Report of Advisory Committee on Administrative and Budgetary Questions.
A/3790. Report of Fifth Committee. Cost estimates for maintaining UNEF, containing draft resolution adopted by Fifth Committee by 45 votes to 10, with 6 abstentions.
RESOLUTION 1204(XII), as recommended by Fifth Committee, A/3790, adopted by Assembly on 13

[6] In a letter to the President of the General Assembly dated 26 November 1957, the delegation of Jordan stated that its affirmative vote should not be interpreted in any way as an acceptance by his Government of the financial commitment involved.

December 1957, meeting 729, by 45 votes to 9, with 10 abstentions.

"The General Assembly

"Takes note with approval of the observations and recommendations contained in the twenty-sixth report of the Advisory Committee on Administrative and Budgetary Questions to the twelfth session of the General Assembly."

OTHER DOCUMENTS

ST/SGB/UNEF/2. Provisional financial rules for Special Account for United Nations Emergency Force.

COMPLAINT ABOUT THREATS TO SECURITY OF SYRIA AND TO INTERNATIONAL PEACE

On 15 October 1957, Syria asked that an item entitled "Complaint about threats to the security of Syria and to international peace" be placed on the agenda of the General Assembly's twelfth session.

An explanatory memorandum accompanying the request stated that the concentration of several divisions of Turkish troops close to the Syrian-Turkish border had created an actual military threat to Syria. Acts of a provocative nature, such as violations of Syrian air space, armed raids into Syrian territory and shooting on the border had become frequent. These military pressures, it was claimed, were connected with foreign efforts to sway Syrian policy or to overthrow the Syrian Government. Since diplomatic and other efforts by the Syrian Government to prevent a deterioration of the situation had failed, the Syrian delegation deemed it necessary that the General Assembly should deal urgently with the proposed item and take such measures as were called for by the United Nations Charter. The Assembly should also set up a commission to investigate the situation on the Syrian-Turkish border and report to the Assembly.

On 16 October, in a letter to the President of the Assembly, the Head of the USSR delegation drew attention to the possibility that the situation might lead to an armed conflict at any moment. He contended that the Turkish General Staff, together with American military advisers, had worked out detailed plans for Turkey to attack Syria immediately after the Turkish elections on 27 October 1957. Syria would not remain alone in its struggle against aggression. The USSR, for its part, could not regard impassively the military provocations being planned in the immediate proximity of its southern frontiers.

The USSR Government, the letter added, favoured the Syrian request for a commission of investigation, and would also propose that United Nations Member States should immediately give armed aid to Syria if Turkey should attack Syria.

The Assembly's General Committee considered the Syrian request on 18 October, with the representatives of Syria and Turkey taking part in its discussions.

The Syrian representative reiterated the main points made in the request that the Assembly take up the matter. In appealing to the United Nations, Syria wished only to help lessen tension.

Turkey's representative recalled that his Government had repeatedly declared that it had no aggressive designs on Syria and that it had affirmed its respect for Syria's independence, sovereignty and territorial integrity. The USSR, however, had continued and intensified a propaganda and intimidation campaign against Turkey and its allies. The USSR had repeated the fictitious allegation that Turkey had been making plans to attack Syria, he said, and it had threatened to use rockets against Turkey and tried to interfere in the forthcoming Turkish elections. Since the increase of confusion and tension in the Middle East caused by increased Soviet efforts to intervene in that area was of profound concern to all peace-loving States, Turkey would welcome an item on the Middle East being placed on the Assembly's agenda.

The United States representative said that his Government had, for some time, been disturbed by the situation resulting from Soviet interference in the Middle East, but had deferred to the apparent desire of the Arab States to deal with the matter on a regional basis. However, now that Syria had raised the question, the United States delegation welcomed the opportunity to discuss the matter. He described the charges contained in the USSR delegation's letter as flagrant fabrications.

On 18 October, it was decided that the item

proposed by Syria be placed on the Assembly's agenda and discussed in plenary meeting.

On 22 October, when the Assembly met to consider the question, the representative of Turkey, on a point of order, announced that King Saud of Saudi Arabia had offered his good offices to mediate between Turkey and Syria. Turkey had accepted the offer and its Minister of State was on his way to Saudi Arabia. He suggested that the Assembly delay consideration of the item in order to allow these efforts to be fully explored. The Syrian representative, opposing a delay, said that although there might be some generous efforts by King Saud to ease some tensions in the area, there had been no mediation whatsoever. The USSR representative also opposed postponement.

Since the Turkish suggestion was not a formal proposal, the Assembly proceeded with the general debate.

The representative of Syria said that the massive concentration of Turkish troops near Syria's northern frontiers, and related activities, were closely connected with the policy pursued by the United States, certain Western colonial powers and World Zionism which sought to preserve the Middle East as an area of Western influence and attempted to maintain or establish political régimes in the region that would favour these powers and join military blocs to serve their objectives.

The Turkish military preparations, he claimed, had been supported by warlike dispositions such as the deployment of the United States Sixth Fleet. Turkish troop concentrations had been used since February 1955 as an instrument of pressure in order to force Syria to forsake its policy of positive neutrality and non-alignment and to participate in the Baghdad Pact.

Since the establishment of the Syrian National Front Cabinet in June 1956, he added, there had been a number of foreign attempts to overthrow the legally and democratically established Government of Syria. In 1957, the United States, implementing the "Eisenhower doctrine", had tried to rally other Arab States against Syria. In view of the failure of this effort, Turkey had been chosen as the instrument for carrying out the policy and had harboured certain reactionary Syrian elements which were plotting to set up a puppet Syrian government with the help of the Turkish armed forces.

The Syrian representative called for swift Assembly action to ensure the withdrawal of Turkish troop concentrations from Syria's borders and the ending of provocative acts along those borders. A commission of inquiry should be set up to investigate the facts and report to the Assembly within a short time, not more than 10 days.

Turkey's representative maintained that large-scale shipments of arms and equipment from the USSR to Syria and the construction of air and submarine bases were turning Syria into an arsenal, with far more arms supplies than it needed, so as to serve other countries. On 24 September, he added, Turkey's Prime Minister had warned world opinion that the situation in Syria was assuming a character which threatened the peace and security of the Middle East. On 30 September he had also drawn the attention of the Prime Minister of the USSR to the dangerous situation in that region.

Meanwhile, Turkey had repeatedly assured Syria of its sincere neighbourly goodwill and its desire for the inviolability of Syria's independence and territorial integrity. Syria, however, had vainly attempted to throw the responsibility for the tension in the Middle East on Turkey. It had made completely unfounded allegations of violations of air space, armed raids and frontier incidents. In actual fact, however, there had been only one frontier incident, and, in this case, the competent Turkish and Syrian frontier authorities had found a Syrian security officer to have been responsible. Further, the disposition of Turkish defence forces within the Turkish frontiers was a matter falling within Turkey's internal jurisdiction. Turkey had never massed any forces on any of its frontiers beyond the needs of defensive precautions.

While Turkey had no aggressive designs against anyone, the Turkish representative continued, the USSR had levelled unfounded accusations against Turkey and had threatened it with invasion involving the use of rockets. He therefore felt that it was necessary not only to investigate the situation in Syria but also to bring to light the true goals and aims of both Syria and the USSR.

The representatives of Czechoslovakia, Egypt and the USSR supported Syria's request for an investigation.

The United States representative welcomed

the mediation efforts of King Saud and Turkey's acceptance of mediation. He hoped that Syria would match this act of good faith by Turkey and suggested that the Assembly defer further consideration of the item pending the outcome of the mediation efforts. The representative of Afghanistan appealed to Turkey and Syria to try to persuade each other of their true purposes which, he was sure, were not hostile. Mediation efforts should be encouraged. He appealed to the great powers to exercise restraint in words and acts which might transform the present misunderstanding into a major conflict.

The representative of Paraguay proposed that further discussion in the Assembly be postponed until the results of King Saud's mediation were known.

The representative of Syria then moved an adjournment of the meeting, but this proposal was rejected by 36 votes to 30, with 6 abstentions. He then moved an amendment to the Paraguayan motion so that the debate would be adjourned for not more than three days. This amendment was adopted by a roll-call vote of 33 to 32, with 15 abstentions. The Paraguayan proposal, as amended, was then adopted by a roll-call vote of 39 to 10, with 32 abstentions.

The general debate on the question was resumed on 25 October and was continued on 28 and 29 October. The representative of Turkey stated that his Government's acceptance of King Saud's mediation offer and Syria's refusal thereof had already shown which side was interested in increasing tension. In view of the fantastic accusations and violent threats made against Turkey in a co-ordinated manner by its northern and southern neighbours, was it surprising, he asked, that Turkey had taken defensive precautions?

The Syrian representative regretted that several delegations had approached the question from the "cold war" angle. He claimed that the unfounded Turkish allegations about the construction of bases and arsenals in Syria and the subservience of its Government to international communism were intended as an excuse for attacking Syria and overthrowing its Government. The tremendous concentration of Turkish forces on the Syrian frontier—the cause of the Syrian complaint—had not been denied. Syria therefore had legitimate cause for concern.

Several representatives supported the Syrian request for an investigation commission. Several others welcomed King Saud's efforts at mediation and hoped that Syria would accept the offer. Some felt that the parties could use the good offices of the Secretary-General and that it was not necessary to create a new United Nations body. Several representatives considered that the charge of aggressive intensions levelled against Turkey was unfounded and that the problem before the Assembly had been artificially created with ulterior motives.

On 30 October, the Syrian representative submitted a draft resolution to set up a fact-finding commission to investigate the situation on both sides of the Syrian-Turkish border and submit a preliminary report to the Assembly and the Security Council within two weeks. The commission was to be composed of seven members: two to be designated by Syria, two by Turkey and three to be named by common agreement between Syria and Turkey.

The proposed commission, he said, would not only serve to establish the facts. It would also constitute a deterrent against adventurous actions and incidents which might provoke hostilities. The functioning of such a commission would not hinder any other efforts to relieve the existing tensions. The Syrian Government, however, could not encourage any effort to by-pass the United Nations, under the guise of a so-called regional initiative or in any other form.

Another draft resolution was also submitted on 30 October, by Canada, Denmark, Japan, Norway, Paraguay, Peru and Spain. The Assembly would thereby note that efforts consistent with Article 33 of the United Nations Charter were being made. Desiring to ease tension in the area, it would express its confidence that the Secretary-General, in the exercise of his responsibilities under the Charter, and without prejudice to efforts being made under Article 33, would be available to undertake discussions with the representatives of Syria and Turkey and could proceed, if necessary, to the countries concerned.

The sponsors, welcoming King Saud's efforts, said that their proposal was not to be regarded as a move to compete with the regional efforts to deal with the matter.

On 1 November, the Indonesian representative urged both parties to resolve their differences in an atmosphere of goodwill, mutual confidence and respect, in accordance with the purposes and principles of the Charter and the ten principles enunciated at the Bandung Conference of Asian and African States, and thus refrain from any actions likely to aggravate existing tensions. In that spirit of conciliation, he appealed to the sponsors of both draft resolutions not to press, at that particular juncture, for a vote on their respective draft resolutions.

The sponsors of the two drafts agreed to this.

Speaking for the sponsors of the seven-power draft, the Norwegian representative stated that the Indonesian suggestion corresponded with the basic purpose of these seven Members, namely, to reaffirm the Assembly's confidence in the usefulness and efficiency of the machinery already at the disposal of the parties.

The Syrian representative said that, in view of the difficulty of setting up a commission which required the fullest co-operation of the parties concerned, and in view of the Indonesian representative's appeal, he would not insist on a vote on his draft resolution, provided that the item remained on the agenda. He hoped, too, that Turkey would take all necessary measures to dispel the causes of tension and render further consideration of the Syrian complaint unnecessary.

Turkey's representative hoped that the debate in the Assembly and the awareness of world opinion might help to dissipate the real causes of concern regarding the Middle East and alleviate the existing tension. Turkey had accepted all peaceful proposals for solving the difficulties. But the Syrian Government's actions had not dispelled Turkey's concern. He hoped that United Nations Charter principles would serve as a guide for all efforts aimed at bringing tranquillity to the Middle East.

The President of the Assembly believed that the Assembly would regard the agreement not to ask for a vote as a satisfactory outcome of the debate.

On 6 November, the Acting Chargé d'Affaires of the Permanent Mission of Syria, in a letter to the Secretary-General, complained that foreign aircraft had violated Syrian air space on 4 November and that there had been a recurrence of provocative acts by Turkey along Syria's frontier. On 13 November, the Permanent Representative of Turkey, in a letter to the Secretary-General, stated that a thorough investigation by Turkish authorities had revealed that no Turkish aircraft had flown over any part of Syrian air space and that the allegations about frontier incidents were completely false.

DOCUMENTARY REFERENCES

GENERAL ASSEMBLY—12TH SESSION
Plenary Meetings 706, 708, 710-714.
General Committee, meeting 116.

A/3699. Letter of 15 October 1957 from Minister of Foreign Affairs and Chairman of delegation of Syria requesting that item entitled "Complaint about threats to security of Syria and to international peace" be put on agenda of 12th Assembly session.

A/3700. Letter of 16 October 1957 from Head of delegation of USSR.
A/3717, A/3724. Letters of 31 October and 6 November 1957 from Acting Chargé d'Affaires of Permanent Mission of Syria.
A/3739. Letter of 13 November 1957 from Permanent Representative of Turkey.
A/L.226. Syria draft resolution.
A/L.227. Canada, Denmark, Japan, Norway, Paraguay, Peru, Spain draft resolution.

COMMUNICATIONS RELATING TO OMAN AND MUSCAT

On 13 August 1957, Egypt, Iraq, Jordan, Lebanon, Libya, Morocco, Saudi Arabia, Sudan, Syria, Tunisia and Yemen requested an urgent meeting of the Security Council to consider the situation created by alleged acts of armed aggression by the United Kingdom against the Imamate of Oman. In a letter to the Council, their representatives stated that during the past few weeks the British Government had, in viola-

tion of its obligations under the United Nations Charter, engaged in attacks amounting to full-scale war, in an attempt to destroy the sovereignty of Oman. This country, they said, had long been independent and its independence had been reaffirmed in the Treaty of Sib of 1920.

On 17 August 1957, the Sultan of Muscat and Oman protested against the action requested by the 11 Arab States, and said the matters referred to in their letter lay exclusively within his internal jurisdiction.

On 20 August, the Council devoted two meetings to a debate on whether it should place the matter on its agenda.

Pressing for its inclusion in the agenda, the representative of Iraq contended that the United Kingdom, by its unilateral military action, endangered the maintenance of peace and security. This action was tantamount to a violation of the United Nations Charter in that it was an attack against an independent country.

Oman, he said, had enjoyed an independent status for a long time, and this status had been recognized by the Treaty of Sib in 1920. The large-scale military operations carried out by the United Kingdom, in collaboration with the forces of the Sultan of Muscat, were a violation of that status and were intended to subdue the people of Oman with a view to occupying their country.

The British action had not only disturbed the entire Arab people, the representative of Iraq added. It had also thrown in doubt the whole sense of security of small states. Further, as the British Foreign Secretary had admitted in the House of Commons, Britain was under no treaty obligation to come to the assistance of the Sultan. There was no justification, either under the United Nations Charter or under international law, for the United Kingdom to use its armed forces in a conflict between two States. It would be regrettable, if in a serious situation such as the present one, the Council did not take appropriate measures.

The representative of Iraq urged that the Oman question be included on the agenda under Articles 34 and 35 of the Charter. (Article 34 permits the Security Council to investigate a situation or dispute which might endanger the maintenance of international peace. Article 35 permits States to bring such a situation to the Council's attention.)

In asking for consideration of the item, those making the request asked merely that the Council first consider the matter, while reserving their position on the nature of the action which the Council should take.

The United Kingdom representative opposed inscription of the item on the Council's agenda. Although the representatives of the Arab States had accused the United Kingdom of armed aggression, he pointed out, they had nevertheless raised the matter under Article 35 of the Charter, as a dispute or situation, and not under Chapter VII, which dealt with aggression.

Further, the Arab States had assumed the existence of an independent State of Oman, whereas the fact was that there was no such independent sovereign State. The district of Oman was part of the dominions of the Sultan of Muscat and Oman, whose family had exercised sovereignty over Oman for the past two centuries. The sovereignty of the Sultan over the coastal areas of Muscat and the mountainous district of Oman had been recognized in various international treaties.

The Sib Agreement of 1920 was not an international treaty between two separate States, the United Kingdom representative added. It was an agreement concluded between the Sultan and a number of tribal leaders after certain troubles in the interior of Oman had been put down. The Treaty allowed the tribes a measure of autonomy but in no way recognized Oman as independent. Further, the military action of the United Kingdom had been undertaken at the request of the Sultan to help him restore order in the face of a revolt against his authority which had been encouraged and supported from without, and in the interest of the stability of that area where subversive forces had been known to be active for some time. If the disturbances in Oman had not been checked, the consequences might have been felt far beyond the Sultanate of Muscat and Oman.

The United Kingdom's position was supported by France and Australia. The French representative said that the Sultan had called upon his ally, the United Kingdom, for aid when the frontier of the Sultanate was illegally crossed by a certain rebel who was receiving outside military assistance. The rebels, defeated, were in flight. By a strange reversal of roles, some Member States had called the action of the United Kingdom armed aggression against the independence of Oman. The representative of Australia made the point that the representatives of Arab States had significantly omitted any mention of the Sultan of Muscat and Oman in their letter. The letter accused only the United Kingdom, and in the opinion of the Australian Government, this indicated that the real objective was to embarrass the United Kingdom.

The Cuban representative was also against placing the item on the Council's agenda. In his opinion, the question was a domestic problem, not an international one, and therefore did not fall within the competence of the Security Council. A study of the Treaty of Sib, he said, would show that although Oman had been given a measure of autonomy under the sovereignty of the Sultan of Muscat and Oman, the Imam of Oman had not signed the treaty as a representative of an independent State.

The representatives of the Philippines, Sweden and the USSR, however, were in favour of placing the item on the agenda.

The representative of the Philippines said that the nature of the complaint and the fact that military intervention had taken place left the Security Council with no alternative except to consider the item in order to determine whether or not an act of aggression had been committed. Moreover, complicated legal questions had been raised, particularly with reference to the status of the Treaty of Sib. These and other controversial points must be clarified so that the Council could act fairly and impartially.

The Swedish representative thought that the relationships between the Sultan and the Imam were so complex that the parties involved ought to be given a chance to clarify their positions. Although he saw no reason to dispute the United Kingdom's position that no illegal aggression had taken place, he considered that the Council was confronted not merely with the suppression of an internal revolt, but also with the intervention of a third power.

According to the USSR representative, the people of Oman were trying to free their country from foreign domination and achieve independence. The United Kingdom, however, had attempted to justify its military action by referring to old, traditional ties between Britain and the Sultan of Muscat But no colonial ties could justify the British intervention in Oman. All available information clearly showed that the British forces had conducted large-scale operations, using the most modern weapons. This action constituted a violation of the United Nations Charter. The Council should consider the events in Oman and take effective measures to put an end to the United Kingdom's aggression.

The United States representative said that his delegation did not have enough information to feel justified in voting either for or against inscription of the item and would therefore abstain. He nevertheless hoped that all concerned would take advantage of the relative calm in the area to settle any legitimate grievance peacefully.

China's representative said he would not take part in the voting. In view of the incomplete information on the relationship between the Sultan and the Imam and on other aspects of the case, he thought it would be premature for the Council to decide to place the item on the agenda.

When it came to voting on the question of inscribing the item on the agenda, four Council members voted in favour, five voted against, and one abstained. China did not vote.

The question was therefore not placed on the Council's agenda as the requested vote for it was not obtained.

DOCUMENTARY REFERENCES

SECURITY COUNCIL, meetings 783, 784.

S/3865 and Add.1. Letter of 13 August 1957 from Permanent Representatives of Egypt, Iraq, Jordan, Lebanon, Libya, Morocco, Saudi Arabia, Sudan, Syria, Tunisia and Yemen.

S/3866. Cable of 17 August 1957 received by President of Security Council.

S/3915. Letter of 21 November 1957 from representatives of Egypt, Iraq, Jordan, Lebanon, Libya, Morocco, Saudi Arabia, Sudan, Syria, Tunisia and Yemen.

COMMUNICATIONS CONCERNING GULF OF AQABA AREA

In May and June 1957, communications from Saudi Arabia to the Secretary-General complained of various violations of Saudi Arabian waters and air space in the Gulf of Aqaba area by Israel air and naval forces. Israel denied the allegations and stated that Israel forces were under strict instructions not to violate the territorial waters or air space of Saudi Arabia. Saudi Arabia submitted further charges of such violations in July and November 1957. Communications from Israel in November denied the charges as baseless.

DOCUMENTARY REFERENCES

A/3575. Question considered by 1st emergency special session of General Assembly from 1-10 November 1956. Letter of 12 April 1957 from Permanent Representative of Saudi Arabia.

S/3825, S/3833, S/3835, S/3841, S/3843, S/3846, S/3849. Letters from Permanent Representative of Saudi Arabia dated 7 and 27 May, 5, 19 and 24 June, 2 and 10 July 1957.

S/3905, S/3918. Letters from representative of Saudi Arabia dated 6 and 25 November 1957.

S/3838, S/3906, S/3919. Letters from Permanent Representative of Israel dated 10 June, 8 and 26 November 1957.

A/3648. Report of Security Council to General Assembly, covering period from 16 July 1956 to 15 July 1957. Chapter 15.

COMMUNICATIONS ABOUT SITUATION IN SOUTHERN PART OF ARABIAN PENINSULA

On 14 January 1957, the representative of Yemen, in a letter to the President of the Security Council, charged that British forces in Aden had committed acts of aggression against the territory of Yemen. He reported that on 8 January they had attacked the town of Sanah and bombarded the nearby town of Ka'ataba, and that on 9 January, Saum'a had been bombarded from the air and from the ground while aircraft had circled over the airfield of Hareeb. He reserved the right of his Government to ask the Council to consider its complaint.

With a letter dated 21 January, the representative of the United Kingdom transmitted to the President of the Council a memorandum on recent events in the neighbourhood of the Aden-Yemen frontier. The memorandum charged that rebels inspired by the Government of Yemen had, on 8 January, fired on guard posts of the Aden Protectorate, and that the security forces had pursued the rebels to the frontier post of Sanah. Investigation had revealed that the complaint of incidents on 9 January was unfounded, as no British aircraft or ground forces had been in action at Saum'a or had flown over the Hareeb airfield. The memorandum went on to charge that the Government of Yemen had for a long time encouraged its tribespeople to violate the frontier of the Aden Protectorate, and had subverted and armed the subjects of the rulers of the small Arab states under British protection. The United Kingdom Government, the memorandum added, was continuing its efforts to settle the outstanding frontier problems in direct talks with representatives of the Government of Yemen.

On 15 February, the United Kingdom representative sent another letter to the President of the Council, together with a memorandum charging that many fresh assaults had been made inside the Aden Protectorate by Yemen troops and tribesmen. The most serious of these incidents had begun in the Dhala area on 25 January, and, in the days that followed, the defending forces had pursued the raiders back towards the frontier in the area of Sanah and Ka'ataba.

As to the efforts to arrange direct talks with representatives of Yemen for a settlement of the problem, the United Kingdom memorandum stated that, according to recent Yemen statements, Yemen did not recognize any boundary between itself and the Aden Protectorate, and had made claims to all the territory of the Protectorate.

The United Kingdom Government had made a further approach to the Yemen Government on 12 February in urging it to agree to talks between representatives of the Yemen and Aden Governments, at which the Aden rulers concerned would be present. While hoping to receive an early reply to that invitation, the United Kingdom Government could not but be perturbed at the firm evidence that arms and military assistance were being supplied to Yemen by countries of the Soviet bloc and Egypt.

Yemen sources in Cairo, the memorandum added, had announced that $8.5 million worth of Czechoslovakian arms had already arrived in Yemen, and training centres staffed by Egyptian instructors had been established near Sanah and Hodeida to instruct the regular army of Yemen how to use these weapons.

No further communications were addressed to the Security Council with regard to this matter during the course of 1957.

DOCUMENTARY REFERENCES

S/3773. Letter of 14 January 1957 from representative of Yemen.
S/3777, S/3788. Letters of 21 January and 15 February 1957 from representative of United Kingdom.

A/3648 and Corr.1. Report of Security Council to General Assembly, covering period 16 July 1956 to 15 July 1957. Part V.

CHAPTER V

THE HUNGARIAN QUESTION

REPORT OF SPECIAL COMMITTEE ON THE PROBLEM OF HUNGARY

On 10 January 1957, at its eleventh session, the General Assembly set up at Special Committee on the Problem of Hungary, by resolution 1132(XI). The Assembly thereby charged the Special Committee with the duty of providing the Assembly and all United Nations Members with the fullest and best available information regarding the situation created by the intervention of the USSR, through its use of armed force and other means, in the internal affairs of Hungary, as well as regarding developments relating to the recommendations of the General Assembly on this subject.[1]

The Special Committee, consisting of representatives of Australia, Ceylon, Denmark, Tunisia and Uruguay, submitted an interim report to the General Assembly's eleventh session on 20 February 1957.[2] Its full report was circulated to United Nations Members on 12 June 1957.

In this report, the Committee expressed regret that, owing to the attitude of the Hungarian Government, it had not been in a position to establish and maintain direct observation in Hungary as enjoined by General Assembly resolution 1132(XI). After hearing witnesses at United Nations Headquarters in New York, the Committee had held hearings in Europe from 11 March to 16 April at the European Office of the United Nations, in Geneva, and thereafter in Rome, Vienna, London, and again in Geneva. The Committee heard 111 witnesses: 35 in New York, 21 in Geneva, 16 in Rome, 30 in Vienna, and 9 in London.

The main conclusions presented by the Committee were as follows:

(1) What had taken place in Hungary in October and November 1956 was a spontaneous national uprising, due to long-standing grievances such as the inferior status of Hungary with regard to the USSR. The system of government had, in part, been maintained by the weapon of terror, wielded by the AVH, or political police. USSR pressure had been resented in other respects also.

(2) The thesis that the uprising had been fomented by reactionary circles in Hungary and had drawn its strength from such circles and from Western "imperialists" had failed to survive the Committee's examination. From start to finish, the uprising had been led by students, workers, soldiers and intellectuals. Many of them had been Communists or former Communists. The majority of political demands put forward during the revolution had included one that democratic socialism should be the basis of the Hungarian political structure and that such social achievements as the land reform should be safeguarded. At no time had any proposal been made for the return to power, or to the Government, of any figure associated with pre-war days.

(3) The uprising had not been planned in advance, and events had actually taken participants by surprise.

[1] For an account of the consideration of the question by the Security Council, and at the General Assembly's second emergency special session and at its eleventh session between October 1956 and March 1957, see Y.U.N., 1956, pp. 67-89.
[2] See Y.U.N., 1956, p. 83.

(4) Although there was no evidence of advance planning, and although the whole course of the uprising bore the hallmark of continuous improvisation, it would appear that the USSR authorities had taken steps as early as 20 October 1956 to make armed intervention in Hungary possible. The evidence showed that Soviet troops from outside Hungary had been used even in the first intervention; it was also to be noted that the Warsaw Treaty contained no provision for intervention by armed forces of the USSR to dictate political developments within any signatory's frontiers.

(5) The demonstrations of 23 October 1956 had at first been entirely peaceable. No evidence had been discovered that any of those who had voiced political demands or had joined the demonstrators had had any intention to resort to force. The transformation of the demonstration into an armed uprising had been due to the action of the AVH in opening fire on the people outside the Radio Building in Budapest. Within a few hours, Soviet tanks had been in action against the Hungarians. The appearance of Russian soldiers in their midst, not as friendly allies, but as enemies in combat, had had the effect of still further uniting the people.

(6) Imre Nagy, the Prime Minister, had denied, with every appearance of truth, that he had issued any invitation to the USSR authorities to assist in quelling the uprising by force or had even been aware that such an invitation had been issued. Since Soviet tanks had appeared on the streets of Budapest at about 2 A.M. on 24 October 1956, it would have been impossible for him to have addressed any official message to the USSR authorities, since he had held no government post at the time when the tanks must have received their orders. Until further information came to light, the Special Committee said, it would be wise to suspend judgement as to whether an invitation had been issued at all. Similar considerations applied to the invitation allegedly addressed to the USSR authorities before the second intervention on 4 November.

Janos Kadar had remained a member of Mr. Nagy's Government when it was reconstituted on 3 November. The Committee was not aware of his having given any recorded indication of his disapproval of Mr. Nagy's policies. Mr. Kadar's movements at that time were not fully known, and his own claim to have called for Soviet help in the name of the Government could not be considered to have been substantiated. In any event, there was abundant evidence that USSR preparations for a further intervention, including the movement of troops and armour from abroad, had been under way since the last days of October. Mr. Kadar and his ministers had been absent from Budapest during the first few days after he had formed his Government, and administrative instructions to the people of Hungary had been issued by the commanders of the Soviet troops.

(7) Mr. Nagy had not at first been free to exercise the full powers of the premiership. Only when the grip of the AVH had been loosened by the victory of the insurgents had he been able to take an independent stand. Seeing that his countrymen were united in their desire for other forms of government and the departure of Soviet troops, he had thrown in his lot with the insurgents.

(8) The few days of freedom enjoyed by the Hungarian people had provided abundant evidence of the popular nature of the uprising. A free press and radio had come to life all over Hungary, and the disbanding of the AVH had been the signal for general rejoicing which revealed the degree of unity achieved by the people.

(9) There had been a number of lynchings and beatings by the crowds, concerning, in almost all cases, members of the AVH or those believed to have co-operated with them.

(10) Steps taken by the Workers' Council during that period had been aimed at giving the workers real control of nationalized industrial undertakings and abolishing unpopular institutions, such as the production norms. During the days of freedom, while negotiations had continued with the USSR authorities for the withdrawal of Russian troops, the Committee added, attempts had been made to clear the streets of Budapest and life had begun to return to normal.

(11) In contrast to demands put forward at that time for the re-establishment of political rights was the fact that basic human rights of the Hungarian people had been violated by the Hungarian Government prior to 23 October 1956, especially up to the autumn of 1955. Such violations were resumed after 4 November 1956.

The Committee was convinced that the numerous accounts of inhuman treatment and torture by the AVH were to be accepted as true. On the evidence, it was also convinced that, in an attempt to break the back of the revolution, numbers of Hungarians had been deported to the USSR and that some might not have been returned to their homes.

(12) Following the second USSR intervention on 4 November 1956, there had been no evidence of popular support for Mr. Kadar's Government. Mr. Kadar had successively abandoned most of the points from the revolutionary programme which he had at first promised to the Hungarian people. On the central question of the withdrawal of USSR troops, he had moved from complete acceptance of the nation's wishes to a refusal to discuss the subject in present circumstances. He had proceeded, step by step, to destroy the power of the workers. Strong repressive measures had been introduced and general elections had been postponed for two years. Only a small fraction of the 190,000 Hungarians who had fled the country had accepted his invitation to return.

(13) In the light of the extent of foreign intervention, the Special Committee concluded, consideration of the Hungarian question by the United Nations had been legally proper and, moreover, had been requested by a legal Government of Hungary. In the matter of human rights, Hungary had accepted specific international obligations in the Treaty of Peace. Accordingly, the Committee did not accept as valid the objections based on Article 2, paragraph 7, of the United Nations Charter (which precludes intervention in essentially domestic matters). A massive armed intervention by one power on the territory of another, with the avowed intention of interfering in its internal affairs, the Committee maintained, must, by the USSR's own definition of aggression, be a matter of international concern.

CONSIDERATION AT ASSEMBLY'S RESUMED ELEVENTH SESSION

On 10 September 1957, the eleventh session of the General Assembly was reconvened, in accordance with resolution 1119(XI) of 8 March 1957, to continue consideration of the Hungarian question. Nine plenary meetings were held between 10 and 13 September.

The Assembly had before it, in addition to the report of the Special Committee, a joint draft resolution submitted by 36 Members. Another delegation subsequently joined the sponsors, making a total of 37, as follows: Argentina, Belgium, Bolivia, Brazil, Canada, Chile, China, Colombia, Costa Rica, Cuba, Dominican Republic, Ecuador, El Salvador, France, Guatemala, Haiti, Honduras, Iceland, Ireland, Italy, Liberia, Luxembourg, Netherlands, New Zealand, Nicaragua, Norway, Pakistan, Panama, Paraguay, Peru, Philippines, Portugal, Spain, Turkey, United Kingdom, United States, Venezuela.

By this 37-power proposal, the Assembly, regretting that the USSR and the present authorities in Hungary had failed to co-operate in any way with the Special Committee, would endorse its unanimous report. It would also note the Committee's conclusion that the events which had taken place in Hungary in October and November 1956 constituted a spontaneous national uprising. Further, the Assembly would find that the Special Committee's conclusions (reached on the basis of all available evidence) confirmed that: (a) the USSR, in violation of of the Charter, had deprived Hungary of its liberty and political independence and the Hungarian people of the exercise of their fundamental human rights; (b) the present Hungarian régime had been imposed on the Hungarian people by the armed intervention of the USSR; (c) the USSR had carried out mass deportations of Hungarian citizens to the USSR; (d) the USSR had violated its obligations under the Geneva Convention of 1949; and (e) the present authorities in Hungary had violated the human rights and freedoms guaranteed by the Treaty of Peace with Hungary.

The Assembly, in addition, would: (1) condemn these acts and the continued defiance of its resolutions; (2) reiterate its concern with the continuing plight of the Hungarian people; (3) call upon the USSR and the present authorities in Hungary to desist from repressive measures against the Hungarian people, to respect the liberty and political independence of Hungary and the Hungarian people's enjoyment of fundamental human rights and freedoms, and to ensure the return to Hungary of those Hungarian citizens who had been deported to the USSR; (4) ask the President of its eleventh session, Prince Wan Waithayakon, acting as the General Assembly's special representative on the Hungarian problem, to take such steps as he deemed appropriate, in view of the findings of the Committee, to achieve the objectives of the United Nations in accordance with various specified resolutions of the Assembly and to report and make recommendations as he might deem advisable to the Assembly. The 37-power draft made provision, too, for placing the Hungarian item on the provisional agenda of the Assembly's twelfth session.

The Rapporteur of the Special Committee introduced the report at the beginning of the discussions at the resumed eleventh session. The report, he pointed out, was not based simply on the testimony of witnesses; equal weight had been given to contemporary documentation provided by the Hungarian press and radio during the uprising and to the statements of the present Hungarian Government. The Committee had also had access to information provided to it by Governments with diplomatic representatives in Budapest at the time. The Committee, he added, was confident that its account, while it might be supplemented on specific points, would stand the test of future investigations.

The representative of Hungary, speaking on a point of order, reiterated his Government's position that the events which had taken place in Hungary in October and November 1956 fell exclusively within the domestic jurisdiction of Hungary and that no organization or international committee could have any right to investigate the domestic affairs of sovereign and independent Hungary. The establishment of the Special Committee had been illegal. His Government protested against the activities it had undertaken. Moreover, the Special Committee had not followed the Assembly's directives to carry out an objective study. Instead, it had proved its hostility towards the People's Republic of Hungary and its social system. His Government therefore asked the General Assembly to condemn the Special Committee for its activity, to reject its report, which falsified the truth, and to delete the so-called Hungarian question from the Assembly's agenda.

This position was supported by the representative of the USSR. In his view, the urgent reconvening of the eleventh session of the Assembly to discuss the provocative so-called Hungarian question showed that the ruling circles of certain countries, particularly the United States, had not yet abandoned their attempts to carry out inadmissible intervention in Hungary's affairs. Nor had they abandoned their attempts to use the United Nations to increase international tension and to indulge in hostile propaganda against Hungary, the USSR and other socialist countries. They were seeking to divert the attention of world public opinion from their own aggressive acts in the Near and Middle East and other parts of the world. They were also trying to divert attention away from their refusal to reach agreement on the prohibition of atomic weapons, and from their unenviable position on a number of questions on the agenda of the twelfth Assembly session.

The President ruled that the General Assembly would proceed with the discussion.

Most representatives taking part in the debate endorsed the report of the Special Committee. Repression in Hungary was continuing, they stressed, and the General Assembly must continue its efforts. Among the other points they made were the following. The USSR and the régime which it had installed in Hungary had done their best to conceal the contents of the report from their own people. In view of the attitude adopted by the USSR and the Kadar Government towards the Special Committee, there were no grounds for complaint that the report did not take account of information which those Governments could have provided. Indeed, it was worthy of note that the report included a full summary of the official Soviet and Kadar Government version of the events. The Kadar Government should be judged by the fact it had broken, or failed to carry out, a series of promises made to the people of Hungary after the attack of 4 November 1956, including promises for withdrawal of USSR troops, promises that there would not be any reprisals against the freedom fighters and workers, promises for the establishment of a multi-party system, for free elections, for observance of the right to strike, for an end to Soviet economic exploitation, for freedom for writers and artists, and for freedom of religion. That record could not be passed off as a merely internal Hungarian affair, for it involved violations of human rights guaranteed by the Treaty of Peace as well as acts of a régime forcibly imposed on Hungary by the military forces of the USSR.

The representative of Hungary said that his Government, confronted by the inaccuracies and slanders contained in the Special Committee's report, considered it necessary to make the following points:

(1) The armed insurrection between 23 October and 4 November 1956 had been designed to overthrow by violence the constitutional and social order of the Hungarian Republic and to restore the old Horthyite fascist régime which had been directed against the social progress of the Hungarian people. Consequently, there had been a counter-revolution in Hungary during that interval. (2) The counter-revolutionary rebellion had been prepared, launched and maintained by Western imperialistic circles. (3) In Hungary, the organizers and leaders of the counter-revolution had been members of the former privileged classes and of the Horthyite fascist elements that had been driven from power. (4) The counter-revolutionary insurrection had been assisted by the traitorous and anti-constitutional activity of Imre Nagy and his group, which had also infiltrated the Government. (5) The measures taken by the Revolutionary Workers' and Peasants' Government during and after the counter-revolution had been based on the obligations that were made compulsory for any Government of the country in the Constitution which expressed and guaranteed the interests of the Hungarian people. Those measures served to protect legal order in the country. (6) The international obligations of the Hungarian Government, as embodied in article 4 of the Treaty of Peace, also required the Government to prevent the rebirth of fascism. (7) The United Nations Charter provided the same obligations for any Hungarian Government to prevent the rebirth of fascism. (8) In conformity with its obligations, the Revolutionary Workers' and Peasants' Government of Hungary, taking account of the fact that the counter revolutionary insurrection, instigated by Western imperialistic circles, constituted a serious threat to peace, had, as one of the signatories of the Warsaw Pact, asked the USSR Government to place at its disposal the USSR troops stationed in Hungary under that Pact. With the support of USSR troops, the Hungarian armed forces had

liquidated the counter-revolution and restored legal order in the country. The liquidation of the Hungarian counter-revolution was a domestic matter within the jurisdiction of Hungary. (9) In contrast to the distorted picture given by the Special Committee, the truth was that the Hungarian Government and the working people of Hungary had re-established the legal and constitutional order of the country. The political, cultural and economic life of the population had returned to normal.

Similar views were expressed by a number of other representatives, including the USSR representative. They described the 37-power draft resolution as an attempt to continue to use the United Nations for the purpose of crude interference in the internal affairs of Hungary.

Some representatives questioned the desirability of a further condemnatory resolution. Thus, the representative of Ceylon said that his Government regretted that, owing to lack of assistance from the USSR and Hungarian Governments, the report of the Special Committee might not be complete. Recalling that Ceylon had voted for the earlier General Assembly resolution involving condemnation (resolution 1131(XI), of 12 December 1956), he stated his Government's view that a renewed condemnation might not improve the situation and might even tend to hinder the emergence of a climate conducive to a speedy solution. Suggesting a number of changes in the 37-power draft resolution, he thought that, rather than place the President of the Assembly in the same situation as the Special Committee, the Assembly might ask the Secretary-General (who had been invited by the Hungarian Government to go to Budapest) to report on compliance with the requests envisaged in the joint draft.

Burma proposed three amendments. By the first, the Assembly would find that "the main conclusions" (rather than "the conclusions") of the Special Committee confirmed the various points set forth in the 37-power draft about the USSR's actions with regard to Hungary and about the violations by the present Hungarian authorities of the rights and freedoms guaranteed by the Treaty of Peace with Hungary. The Assembly rejected this amendment by 40 votes to 4, with 31 abstentions.

By the second amendment, the Assembly

would "deplore" rather than "condemn" the acts of the USSR and the present Hungarian authorities with regard to the situation in Hungary. This, too, was rejected, by a vote of 45 to 2, with 30 abstentions.

The third amendment was intended to delete the request in the 37-power draft that Prince Wan Waithayakon, as the Assembly's Special Representative on the Hungarian problem, should consult as appropriate with the Special Committee in the course of his endeavours. Forty-two Members voted against this amendment, 3 for, and 32 abstained.

On 14 September 1957, the day after it rejected Burma's amendments, the Assembly approved the text of the 37-power draft as resolution 1133(XI). It did so by a roll-call vote of 60 to 10, with 10 abstentions.

REPORT OF THE ASSEMBLY'S SPECIAL REPRESENTATIVE

On 9 December 1957, Prince Wan Waithayakon, the Special Representative of the General Assembly on the Hungarian Problem, reported to the Assembly's twelfth session on the steps which he had taken in connexion with the request made by the Assembly on 14 September.

He stated that he had tried to pursue the following objectives: (1) humanitarian treatment in Hungary; (2) return of deportees from the USSR; (3) withdrawal of Soviet troops from Hungary; and (4) free elections in Hungary. Aware of the difficulties of his task, he said, he had realized that he would have to proceed step by step. His first step was to concentrate on humanitarian treatment in Hungary; on 30 September, he contacted the Foreign Minister of the USSR and made an appeal in this connexion. The reply was that that matter did not concern the USSR Government. He then made a humanitarian appeal for the return of deportees from the USSR to Hungary. The USSR Foreign Minister replied that reports about the existence of deportees were fictitious, that the item on Hungary constituted an interference in internal affairs and was "illegitimate", and that he could, therefore, not discuss it.

The Special Representative added that he had made a similar approach to the Foreign Minister of Hungary on 10 October by appealing for more lenient treatment of prisoners, persons detained in concentration camps, and persons awaiting trial, and by appealing for due judicial process in trials, for admission of students to universities without discrimination, and so on, and, finally, for an amnesty for political offenders. The Foreign Minister replied that these were matters for the Hungarian Government to determine by virtue of its sovereign rights. The Special Representative then pointed out that this did not preclude an exchange of information and views in the United Nations, as a centre for harmonizing the actions of nations. Finally, the Hungarian Foreign Minister agreed to provide information on questions to be set forth by the Special Representative in a memorandum.

The Special Representative offered to proceed to Budapest to pursue the discussion, but was informed that the Hungarian Government could not give him a visa as it could not admit observers from the United Nations. Subsequently, on 15 November and on 2 December, the representative of Hungary informed the Special Representative that he had been instructed not to accept the memorandum of questions because the Hungarian Government could not negotiate on a matter which was an internal affair of Hungary.

The Special Representative also told the Assembly that he had had no occasion to consult with the Special Committee on the Problem of Hungary as no question involving it had arisen.

He regretted that he had been unable to find an opportunity for negotiations. He could not, however, believe that the Hungarian and USSR Governments would remain insensible to the voice of world opinion and the conscience of mankind which continued to make an insistent and righteous appeal for the freedom of the Hungarian people. He therefore hoped that, as international tension relaxed, he would be given an opportunity to help establish full international co-operation in promoting respect for human rights and fundamental freedoms in Hungary.

On 14 December, at the closing meeting of the Assembly's twelfth session, the President of the Assembly voiced the hope that the parties concerned would give the Special Representative the necessary co-operation if he continued his efforts.

In the discussion which ensued reference was made by the representatives of the Netherlands, the United States and Uruguay to reports of trials of participants in the 1956 uprising in Hungary, and it was urged that the work of the Special Committee should continue.

The representatives of Czechoslovakia, Hungary and the USSR, however, reiterated the view that Assembly discussion on Hungary's domestic matters was contrary to the Charter as were the appointment of the Special Representative and the activities of the Special Committee.

QUESTION OF CREDENTIALS

On 10 December 1957, at its twelfth session, the General Assembly considered the report of its Credentials Committee, which stated that it had adopted (by 6 votes to 1, with 2 abstentions) a United States motion to "take no decision regarding the credentials submitted on behalf of the representatives of Hungary". The representative of Hungary protested against what he termed a United States attempt at discrimination and interference. The credentials of his delegation, he declared, had been issued in conformity with the requirements of the Hungarian Constitution and the General Assembly's rules of procedure. Several other representatives expressed similar views.

Other speakers, however, contended that the General Assembly could not, in the light of the Special Committee's report and its own resolutions, accept the credentials of the Hungarian delegation.

The Assembly finally approved the report of the Credentials Committee by 77 votes to 1, by resolution 1183(XII).

LETTER FROM SPECIAL COMMITTEE TO HUNGARIAN FOREIGN MINISTER

On 20 December, the Special Committee on the Problem of Hungary approved a letter addressed to the Foreign Minister expressing its concern about continuing reports of trials

of participants in the 1956 uprising, and asking for further information and assurances that the highest humanitarian standards would be applied in the treatment of all who participated in the uprising. It had also decided to inform the Assembly's Special Representative of that action. In a press *communiqué* which it issued about this letter, the Special Committee said it had also decided to inform the Assembly's Special Representative about the decision to send the letter. The *communiqué* also said that the Special Committee would continue to watch the situation in Hungary under its mandate from the General Assembly.

On 21 December, the Permanent Representative of Hungary to the United Nations returned the letter. In doing so, he said that the Hungarian Government did not recognize the Special Committee, since the Assembly resolution setting it up was contrary to the United Nations Charter. The Permanent Representative said he was therefore in no position to transmit communications and requests by the Special Committee.

RELIEF TO THE HUNGARIAN PEOPLE

A programme of relief to the Hungarian people in Hungary was called for by the General Assembly in November 1956.[3] Such relief, in the form of food, clothing, medicine and other similar supplies to the value of $20,000,000 was distributed by the International Committee of the Red Cross, which acted as the sole agency for the distribution of aid furnished through the United Nations. This international relief programme was formally concluded on 30 September 1957.

For information about provision of assistance to Hungarian refugees throughout 1957, see below, ECONOMIC AND SOCIAL QUESTIONS, CHAPTER XI.

[3] See *Y.U.N., 1956*, pp. 89-92.

DOCUMENTARY REFERENCES

GENERAL ASSEMBLY—11TH SESSION (RESUMED)
Plenary Meetings 669-677.

A/3592. Report of Special Committee on Problem of Hungary.
A/3658 and Add.1. Argentina, Belgium, Bolivia, Brazil, Canada, Chile, China, Colombia, Costa Rica, Cuba, Dominican Republic, Ecuador, El Salvador, France, Guatemala, Haiti, Hounduras, Iceland, Ireland, Italy, Liberia, Luxembourg, Netherlands, New Zealand, Nicaragua, Norway, Pakistan, Panama, Paraguay, Peru, Philippines, Portugal, Spain, Turkey, United Kingdom, United States, Venezuela draft resolution.
A/L.223. Burma amendments to 37-power draft resolution (A/3658 and Add.1.).

RESOLUTION 1133(XI), as submitted by 37 powers, A/3658 and Add.1, adopted by Assembly on 14 September 1957, meeting 677, by roll-call vote of 60 to 10, with 10 abstentions, as follows:

In favour: Argentina, Australia, Austria, Belgium, Bolivia, Brazil, Burma, Cambodia, Canada, Chile, China, Colombia, Costa Rica, Cuba, Denmark, Dominican Republic, Ecuador, El Salvador, Ethiopia, France, Ghana, Greece, Guatemala, Haiti, Honduras, Iceland, Iran, Iraq, Ireland, Israel, Italy, Japan, Jordan, Laos, Lebanon, Liberia, Libya, Luxembourg, Mexico, Morocco, Netherlands, New Zealand, Nicaragua, Norway, Pakistan, Panama, Paraguay, Peru, Philippines, Portugal, Spain, Sudan, Sweden, Thailand, Tunisia, Turkey, United Kingdom, United States, Uruguay, Venezuela.

Against: Albania, Bulgaria, Byelorussian SSR, Czechoslovakia, Hungary, Poland, Romania, Ukrainian SSR, USSR, Yugoslavia.

Abstaining: Afghanistan, Ceylon, Egypt, Finland, India, Indonesia, Nepal, Saudi Arabia, Syria, Yemen.

"The General Assembly,

"Recalling its resolution 1132(XI) of 10 January 1957, establishing a Special Committee, consisting of representatives of Australia, Ceylon, Denmark, Tunisia and Uruguay, to investigate, and to establish and maintain direct observation in Hungary and elsewhere, taking testimony, collecting evidence and receiving information, as appropriate,

"Having now received the unanimous report of the Special Committee on the Problem of Hungary,

"Regretting that the Union of Soviet Socialist Republics and the present authorities in Hungary have failed to co-operate in any way with the Committee,

"1. *Expresses its appreciation* to the Special Committee on the Problem of Hungary for its work;

"2. *Endorses* the report of the Committee;

"3. *Notes* the conclusion of the Committee that the events which took place in Hungary in October and November of 1956 constituted a spontaneous national uprising;

"4. *Finds* that the conclusions reached by the Committee on the basis of its examination of all available evidence confirm that:

"(*a*) The Union of Soviet Socialist Republics, in violation of the Charter of the United Nations, has deprived Hungary of its liberty and political independence and the Hungarian people of the exercise of their fundamental human rights;

"(*b*) The present Hungarian régime has been imposed on the Hungarian people by the armed intervention of the Union of Soviet Socialist Republics;

"(*c*) The Union of Soviet Socialist Republics has carried out mass deportations of Hungarian citizens to the Union of Soviet Socialist Republics;

"(*d*) The Union of Soviet Socialist Republics has violated its obligations under the Geneva Conventions of 1949;

"(*e*) The present authorities in Hungary have violated the human rights and freedoms guaranteed by the Treaty of Peace with Hungary;

"5. *Condemns* these acts and the continued defiance of the resolutions of the General Assembly;

"6. *Reiterates its concern* with the continuing plight of the Hungarian people;

"7. *Considers* that further efforts must be made to achieve the objectives of the United Nations in regard to Hungary in accordance with the Purposes and Principles of the Charter and the pertinent resolutions of the General Assembly;

"8. *Calls upon* the Union of Soviet Socialist Republics and the present authorities in Hungary, in view of evidence contained in the report, to desist from repressive measures against the Hungarian people, to respect the liberty and political independence of Hungary and the Hungarian people's enjoyment of fundamental human rights and freedoms, and to ensure the return to Hungary of those Hungarian citizens who have been deported to the Union of Soviet Socialist Republics;

"9. *Requests* the President of the eleventh session of the General Assembly, H.R.H. Prince Wan Waithayakon, as the General Assembly's special representative on the Hungarian problem, to take such steps as he deems appropriate, in view of the findings of the Committee, to achieve the objectives of the United Nations in accordance with General Assembly resolutions 1004(ES-II) of 4 November 1956, 1005(ES-II) of 9 November 1956, 1127(XI) of 21 November 1956, 1131(XI) of 12 December 1956 and 1132(XI) of 10 January 1957, to consult as appropriate with the Committee during the course of his endeavours, and to report and make recommendations as he may deem advisable to the General Assembly;

"10. *Decides* to place the Hungarian item on the provisional agenda of the twelfth session of the General Assembly."

GENERAL ASSEMBLY—12TH SESSION
Plenary Meetings 678, 684, 726, 731.
General Committee, meeting 112.

A/3773. Report of Credentials Committee.
A/3774. Report of General Assembly's Special Representative on Hungarian Problem.
RESOLUTION 1183(XII), as recommended by Credentials Committee, A/3773, adopted by Assembly on 10 December 1957, meeting 726, by 77 votes to 1.

"The General Assembly
"Approves the report of the Credentials Committee."

OTHER DOCUMENTS

A/AC.88/1. Letter of 20 December 1957 from Special Committee on Problem of Hungary to Minister for Foreign Affairs of Hungarian People's Republic.
A/3571. Note by Secretary-General transmitting text of resolution and conclusions adopted by Governing Body of ILO.
A/3578 and Corr.1. Note by Secretary-General transmitting at request of Hungarian Minister of Foreign Affairs text of communication of 16 April

1957 concerning certain recommendations made by Governing Body of ILO.

A/3742. Note by Secretary-General transmitting text of conclusions adopted by Governing Body of ILO on 1 November 1957.

CHAPTER VI

THE QUESTION OF ALGERIA

On 16 July 1957, Afghanistan, Ceylon, Egypt, Ethiopia, India, Indonesia, Iran, Iraq, Japan, Jordan, Lebanon, Libya, Morocco, Nepal, Pakistan, the Philippines, Saudi Arabia, Sudan, Syria, Tunisia and Yemen asked that the question of Algeria be put on the agenda of the General Assembly's twelfth session. On 23 July 1957, Burma requested that it be included in the list of sponsoring States.

In an explanatory memorandum, the sponsors recalled that, on 15 February 1957, the General Assembly had unanimously adopted a resolution (1012(XI)) by which it had expressed the hope that, in a spirit of co-operation, a peaceful, democratic and just solution to the Algerian question would be found, through appropriate means, in conformity with the principles of the Charter of the United Nations.

The memorandum noted that despite the reasonable expectation that steps would be taken in pursuance of the resolution, there had been no indication to the United Nations from its Member States that any progress had been made in the period which had elapsed. On the contrary, there had been numerous reports that the situation in Algeria was deteriorating, contrary to the hope expressed by the Assembly.

The explanatory memorandum also pointed out that the continuing deterioration of the situation had been brought to the attention of the Secretary-General, and through him to all Member States, in a letter dated 15 April 1957, which had been signed by representatives of the following 19 Member States: Afghanistan, Burma, Ceylon, Egypt, Ethiopia, India, Indonesia, Iran, Iraq, Jordan, Libya, Morocco, Nepal, Pakistan, Saudi Arabia, Sudan, Syria, Tunisia and Yemen. This letter had contained excerpts from expressions of "responsible opinion" in France itself about developments in Algeria. It had also emphasized that the systematic application of violence and mass repression by French authorities had made a solution of the question even more remote.

On 20 September 1957 the General Assembly decided to include the item in its agenda. The matter was considered by the First Committee at 14 meetings between 27 November and 6 December 1957.

The representative of France stated that the fact that France had not objected to placing the question of Algeria on the Assembly's agenda should not be interpreted to mean that it had changed its position about United Nations intervention in the matter. The French delegation was participating in the discussion in order to make known the efforts that were being made to bring about a peaceful settlement and to refute the calumnies directed against France.

The French representative pointed out that Algeria had become a part of France with the adoption of the French Constitution of 1848. France had joined the United Nations with its recognized frontiers, which included Algeria. Consequently, the problems arising in Algeria, however complex they might be, fell within the framework of French sovereignty. The Algerian revolt, he insisted, was a political campaign organized by a minority. It would have failed had it not been supported by certain States which provided arms, money, directives and even bases of operations. Moral and material support came from Egypt, the Arab League, Morocco and Tunisia. The countries furnishing assistance were violating the United Nations Charter, the provisions of the Assembly's "Essentials of Peace" resolution, and the principles of peaceful co-existence adopted at the Bandung Conference in 1954.

The good offices offer from Morocco and Tunisia, the French representative said, could not be accepted because the sovereignty of these two countries was being threatened by the pressure of Algerian rebels, and they were not, therefore, sufficiently free to determine their own attitude regarding the rebels. Furthermore, the offer had stressed that the sovereignty of Algeria be recognized as a pre-condition. It also involved the claim that the National Liberation Front (F.L.N.) was the sole representative of the various segments of the Algerian population.

France's offers to negotiate, which were free of unacceptable pre-conditions, had consistently been rejected. France was still ready to negotiate a cease-fire with those who had taken up arms against it, and if the aim of the good offices offer had been only to obtain a cease-fire, France would have favoured Moroccan-Tunisian mediation.

The representative of France drew attention to antagonisms created by differences of race and language within Algeria and to the sharp division between the two major rebel groups, the Algerian National Movement (M.N.A.) and the National Liberation Front, which were waging both a propaganda and a military war against each other. He also referred to the role of Algerian Communism, whose terrorist organizations had merged with those of the National Liberation Front and had also infiltrated rebel bands. The terrorist groups in the cities had been successfully broken up, he said. The French Government had instructed its forces to refrain from reprisals and, he added, if occasionally these instructions had not been obeyed, the matter had been investigated and sanctions applied.

The representative of France, in addition, reviewed the social and political reforms, particularly communal reforms, which had been carried out by the French Administration.

The three pillars of French policy in Algeria, he noted, were: a cease-fire, elections and negotiations.

As to the holding of elections—under a single electoral college system—his Government would invite Governments of countries accustomed to democratic procedures to send observers. The enabling legislation (the *loi cadre*), which under the French system established principles but did not go into the details of implementation, was one of the instruments of French policy. The legislation was designed, first of all, to ensure absolute equality for citizens and communities through the institution of universal suffrage, under a single college, for elections to representative assemblies. A further aim, he said, was to ensure as great a measure of decentralization as possible by establishing legislative and executive organs in the various regions as well as for Algeria as a whole. The legislation provided for the development of Algerian institutions; the powers conferred on the various groups could be modified in the light of experience. The original text of the legislation had been amended without narrowing its scope to guarantee minority representation and make provision for community councils which were designed to eliminate all possibility of discriminatory practices. The legislation, including an electoral law, attested to the fact that France was determined to bring about conditions conducive to peace and stability and to set up the practical machinery required to attain the threefold aim of "cease-fire, elections, negotiations".

The French representative also stated that France desired more than ever to extend its co-operation with other countries, particularly with those of North Africa, for which a new economic era might dawn when the newly discovered wealth of the Sahara was developed.

To apply the principle of self-determination to Algeria in the existing circumstances, he continued, would result in splitting Algeria into two or more states. France believed that the principle should be applied only with due respect for individual freedom, the protection of minorities, the gradual preparation of an *élite* capable of making valid decisions, the exercise of true democracy and the maintenance of public order.

As the situation in Algeria had become much simpler with the military, psychological and political losses of the rebels, he added, any interference in the matter by the United Nations, besides being a violation of the Charter, would be likely only to delay the solution of the problem.

Several other representatives also argued that the United Nations was not competent to intervene in the question. It was pointed out *inter alia*, that Article 2(7) of the United Nations Charter (which precludes intervention in essentially domestic matters) applied to all United Nations organs and governed all Articles of the Charter, regardless of whether or not they bore upon the principle of self-determination. Furthermore, the United Nations could not revise the constitutional structure of any Member State; therefore, it was necessary to make a rigorous distinction between the discussion of a problem and United Nations intervention in the sphere of national sovereignty.

Among those who argued that the United Nations had no right to intervene in the matter were the representatives of Argentina, Australia, Cuba, Israel, the Netherlands, Peru, Portugal, Spain and the United Kingdom.

Several other representatives, however, contended that the United Nations was competent to deal with the Algerian problem. They pointed out that the question of competence could not be decided by the unilateral declaration of a Member State. As French rule in Algeria had originally been installed by military intervention, its present character could be regarded only as a colonial occupation maintained without regard for the wishes of the Algerian people. Furthermore, as the struggle in Algeria had developed into a war and had endangered peace and security in the area, it was both the right and the duty of the United Nations to continue its quest for an equitable solution.

It was also pointed out that the Algerian question had been the subject of diplomatic negotiation between France and other Governments, that the Algerian situation had been of great international importance for a long time and that it had been discussed at many international conferences. It was anachronistic to assert that matters regarding Algeria fell solely within the national competence of France. Moreover, the Algerian crisis was also prejudicial to good relations between France, on the one hand, and Tunisia and Morocco, on the other. It was therefore legitimate to invoke Article 14 of the Charter under which the General Assembly might recommend measures for the peaceful adjustment of any situation, regardless of origin, which it deemed likely to impair the general welfare or friendly relations among nations.

Further, Algeria had enjoyed full statehood as a national entity before the French occupation; the claim that Algeria was an integral part

of France was not only erroneous but also contradicted by the history and development of French policy in Algeria.

Among those presenting such views were the representatives of Albania, the Byelorussian SSR, Ceylon, Egypt, Guatemala, Haiti, Indonesia, Jordan, Lebanon, Morocco, Nepal, Pakistan, Romania, Saudi Arabia, Sudan, Syria, Tunisia, the Ukrainian SSR, Uruguay, the USSR and Yemen.

Representatives of Arab States, in addition, rejected French charges of intervention, and said that the state of affairs in Algeria resulted directly from French policy in that country.

A number of representatives also maintained that the Algerian liberation movement was genuinely representative of the Algerian people as a whole, and that Algerian rebels were actually administering a large part of the country. The *loi cadre* could not lead to a solution of the Algerian problem because it was a unilateral French action. In fact, the measures contained in the new legislation constituted a retreat from proposals which the French delegation had put forward at the preceding Assembly session, and the situation in Algeria had deteriorated since the adoption of the previous Assembly resolution on the matter (1012(X)). A peaceful settlement could only be achieved under the auspices of the United Nations, and the Assembly should therefore call for negotiations in order to arrive at a solution.

Furthermore, the Assembly should recognize that the principle of self-determination applied to the Algerian people. Also, unconditional recognition of the independence of Algeria was essential as a basis for a settlement of the Algerian question; the presence of one million French settlers could not be used as an argument for denying freedom to the Algerians.

Some other representatives, however, held that the will of the Algerian populations must be made manifest in order that their national aspirations might be satisfied. They thought it only natural that the French Government should demand an end to violence as a prerequisite for any negotiations, and that elections should be held to determine who were to be the authorized representatives of the Algerian people. It was also pointed out that the role of the United Nations was necessarily limited by legal considerations and by standards of prudence, and that the principle of self-determination could not be distorted in such a way as to ignore relevant historical, economic, political and social factors. In the view of these representatives, the General Assembly should avoid recommending steps which might prejudice prospects for a peaceful solution.

Several representatives welcomed the offer of good offices by the King of Morocco and the President of Tunisia and hoped that a peaceful solution would be found. Despite differences of opinion as to the way in which the parties concerned should proceed, they welcomed the recognition on all sides of the need to reach a solution in accordance with the principles of the United Nations Charter.

Two draft resolutions were submitted in the First Committee.

One was sponsored jointly by the following 17 powers: Afghanistan, Burma, Ceylon, Egypt, Ghana, Indonesia, Iraq, Jordan, Lebanon, Libya, Morocco, Nepal, Saudi Arabia, Sudan, Syria, Tunisia and Yemen. Under the terms of this draft resolution, the General Assembly would regret that the hope for a solution, as expressed in its resolution 1012(XI) of 15 February 1957, had not yet been realized. Recognizing that the principle of self-determination was applicable to the Algerian people and noting that the situation in Algeria continued to cause much suffering and loss of human life, the Assembly would call for negotiations in order to arrive at a solution in accordance with the principles and purposes of the United Nations Charter.

The second draft resolution was sponsored by Argentina, Brazil, Cuba, the Dominican Republic, Italy, Peru and Spain. Under its terms, the Assembly, bearing in mind the situation in Algeria which continued to cause much suffering and loss of life, would: (1) take note of the attempts which had been reported to the Assembly to settle the problem both through the good offices of Heads of State and by French legislative measures; and (2) express the hope once again that, in a spirit of co-operation, a peaceful, democratic and just solution would be found, through appropriate means, in conformity with the principles of the Charter of the United Nations.

Two amendments to the 17-power draft resolution were submitted jointly by Canada, Ireland, and Norway.

By the first amendment, the Assembly would recognize that the Algerian people were entitled to work out their own future in a democratic way (rather than recognize that the principle of self-determination was applicable to the Algerian people).

By the second amendment, the Assembly, instead of calling for negotiations for a solution in accordance with the purposes and principles of the Charter, would propose effective discussions in order to resolve the troubled situation and in order to reach a solution in accordance with the purposes and principles of the Charter.

The sponsors of the 17-power draft resolution said that they were unable to accept these amendments.

The 17-power draft resolution and the amendments thereto were put to the vote in the First Committee on 6 December 1957, the representative of France declaring that he would not participate in the voting. The amendments were voted on first and were adopted as a whole by a roll-call vote of 37 to 36, with 7 abstentions. The draft resolution, as amended, was then put to a roll-call vote. It was not adopted, the vote being 37 for, 37 against, with 6 abstentions.

The representative of Argentina, on behalf of the sponsors of the seven-power draft resolution, stated that this draft resolution would not be pressed to a vote, but the sponsors reserved the right to introduce it at a plenary meeting of the Assembly.

The First Committee was therefore unable to recommend to the General Assembly the adoption of any draft resolution on the question of Algeria.

On 10 December 1957, following presentation of the report of the First Committee at a plenary meeting, a joint draft resolution was submitted by Argentina, Brazil, Canada, Cuba, the Dominican Republic, India, Iran, Ireland, Italy, Japan, Mexico, Norway, Peru, Spain and Thailand. The Assembly adopted it by 80 votes to 0, as resolution 1184(XII). The Assembly thereby again expressed its concern over the situation in Algeria. It took note of the good offices offer made by the King of Morocco and the President of the Republic of Tunisia. And it expressed the wish that, in a spirit of effective co-operation, *pourparlers* would be entered into, and other appropriate means used, with a view to a solution, of the Algerian question, in conformity with the purposes and principles of the United Nations Charter.

DOCUMENTARY REFERENCES

GENERAL ASSEMBLY—12TH SESSION
Plenary Meetings 682, 726.
General Committee, meeting 111.
First Committee, meetings 913-926.

A/3617 and Add.1. Letter of 16 July 1957 from Permanent Representatives of Afghanistan, Ceylon, Egypt, Ethiopia, India, Indonesia, Iran, Iraq, Japan, Jordan, Lebanon, Libya, Morocco, Nepal, Pakistan, Philippines, Saudi Arabia, Sudan, Syria, Tunisia, and Yemen and letter of 23 July 1957 from Burma, requesting that question of Algeria be included in agenda of 12th Assembly session.

A/C.1/L.194. Afghanistan, Burma, Ceylon, Egypt, Ghana, Indonesia, Iraq, Jordan, Lebanon, Libya, Morocco, Nepal, Saudi Arabia, Sudan, Syria, Tunisia, Yemen draft resolution as amended by Canada, Ireland, Norway, A/C.1/L.196, failed of adoption on 6 December 1957 on a roll-call vote of 37 to 37, with 6 abstentions, as follows:

In favour: Argentina, Australia, Austria, Belgium, Brazil, Canada, Chile, China, Colombia, Costa Rica, Cuba, Denmark, Dominican Republic, Ecuador, El Salvador, Finland, Honduras, Iceland, Ireland, Israel, Italy, Laos, Luxembourg, Netherlands, New Zealand, Nicaragua, Norway, Panama, Paraguay, Peru, Portugal, Spain, Sweden, United Kingdom, United States, Uruguay, Venezuela.

Against: Afghanistan, Albania, Bulgaria, Burma, Byelorussian SSR, Ceylon, Czechoslovakia, Egypt, Ethiopia, Ghana, Greece, Haiti, Hungary, India, Indonesia, Iran, Iraq, Japan, Jordan, Lebanon, Liberia, Libya, Federation of Malaya, Morocco, Nepal, Pakistan, Poland, Romania, Saudi Arabia, Sudan, Syria, Thailand, Tunisia, Ukrainian SSR, USSR, Yemen, Yugoslavia.

Abstaining: Bolivia, Cambodia, Guatemala, Mexico, Philippines, Turkey.

A/C.1/L.195. Argentina, Brazil, Cuba, Dominican Republic, Italy, Peru, Spain draft resolution.

A/C.1/L.196. Canada, Ireland, Norway, amendments to 17-power joint draft resolution, A/C.1/L.194.

A/3772. Report of First Committee.

A/L.239. Argentina, Brazil, Canada, Cuba, Dominican Republic, India, Iran, Ireland, Italy, Japan, Mexico, Norway, Peru, Spain, Thailand draft resolution.

RESOLUTION 1184(XII), as recommended by 15 powers A/L.239, adopted by Assembly on 10 December 1957, meeting 726, by 80 votes to 0.

"*The General Assembly,*

"*Having discussed* the question of Algeria,

"*Recalling* its resolution 1012(XI) of 15 February 1957,

"1. *Expresses again its concern* over the situation in Algeria;

"2. *Takes note* of the offer of good offices made by His Majesty the King of Morocco and His Excellency the President of the Republic of Tunisia;

"3. *Expresses the wish* that, in a spirit of effective co-operation, *pourparlers* will be entered into, and other appropriate means utilized, with a view to a solution, in conformity with the purposes and principles of the Charter of the United Nations."

CHAPTER VII

THE QUESTION OF CYPRUS

On 12 July 1957, Greece requested that the question of Cyprus be included in the agenda of the twelfth session of the General Assembly under the title "Cyprus: (*a*) Application, under the auspices of the United Nations, of the principle of equal rights and self-determination of peoples in the case of the population of the island of Cyprus; (*b*) Violations of human rights and atrocities by the British Colonial Administration against the Cyprians".

A Greek explanatory memorandum of 13 September 1957 stated that no progress had been made since 26 February 1957—the date of the last Assembly resolution on the Cyprus question (1013(XI))—towards a solution of the main problem.

On 20 September 1957, the General Assembly decided to place the Cyprus question on its agenda, referring it to its First Committee.

Greece submitted a draft resolution whereby the Assembly would express the desire that the people of Cyprus be given the opportunity to determine their own future. In so doing, the Assembly would express its concern that no progress had been made towards solving the problem as the Assembly had hoped in its last resolution on the matter (1013(XI)). The Assembly would also state that the situation in Cyprus was still fraught with danger and that a solution at the earliest possible moment in conformity with the principles of the United Nations Charter was needed to preserve peace and stability in the area.

The United Kingdom representative stated that, while the Cyprus problem was an international one, the difficulties being encountered inside Cyprus fell exclusively within the domestic jurisdiction of his Government. A solution acceptable to all concerned was needed. The United Kingdom's policy over the years had been to promote self-government in Cyprus. The British Government had had several previous discussions with the Cypriot leaders on the problem, and its offers of discussion remained open.

The Cyprus question had also become an international matter affecting the relations between Greece, Turkey and the United Kingdom. The British Government was seeking a solution which should be acceptable to the three Governments concerned and to the people of Cyprus.

Outlining the steps which his Government had taken, the United Kingdom representative drew attention to the framing of a draft constitution by Lord Radcliffe, the release of Archbishop Makarios, the offer of safe conduct out of Cyprus to the terrorists, and the acceptance in March 1957 of the good offices offer to conciliation which the Secretary-General of the North Atlantic Treaty Organization (NATO) had made to each of the three Governments. The draft constitution, however, had been rejected. The good offices offer had not been accepted by the Greek Government. The British Government had then initiated talks with Greece and Turkey with the clear intention of inviting representatives of Cyprus to participate in the discussions as soon as any broad agreement could be reached. A scheme for partnership in Cyprus had been proposed, but it had been rejected. The United Kingdom Government had then reverted to discussions with representatives of Cyprus and had asked for the sympathetic assistance of the Greek and Turkish Governments. That procedure, too, had broken down.

At that point, the British Government had decided that the best hope of making progress lay in private discussions on the international aspects of the problem with the Greek and Turkish authorities, in order to prepare for a settlement of the internal problems with representatives of the population of the island. The Turkish Government had agreed to this procedure. But the Greek Government had insisted on prior agreement on the basic outlines of a solution through diplomatic channels. Owing to the Turkish elections at the end of October 1957, no suitable date for a meeting could be agreed upon, but exchanges of views between the three Governments had continued, which was a hopeful sign.

The United Kingdom representative regarded the renewal of terrorist activity in the island as a form of pressure put upon the General Assembly. He thought it would indeed be tragic if a resumption of widespread violence should intervene when a real prospect of making progress towards a solution was in sight.

The representative of Greece offered to have charges of Greek involvement in terrorist activity in Cyprus investigated. The Radcliffe constitution, he contended, was one designed to continue the colonial system. He thought it essential that Britain recognize the right of Cypriots to self-determination and to self-government, based on the territorial integrity of the island. Greece had made clear the principle that the Cyprus question was clearly one between the United Kingdom Government and the people of Cyprus.

Denying the allegation that Cypriots did not have an ethnic personality, he maintained that a plebiscite under United Nations supervision would show that 80 per cent were Greek in language, race, culture and feelings.

He also rejected the Turkish argument that the Lausanne Treaty precluded forever any change in the status of Cyprus. No people, he asserted, could be deprived of its freedom or its right to self-determination on the ground that the disposition of its territory would affect the security of several other States. In any event, Cyprus had deficiencies as a military base, and it could be demilitarized by agreement.

The Cypriots and their leaders had responded constructively to the important Assembly resolution 1013(XI) of 26 February 1957. Violence on the island had ended after the release of Archbishop Makarios from detention in the Seychelles. Colonial repression had, however, continued.

The Greek representative pointed out that unless there was a new policy leading towards self-determination for the people of Cyprus, there was a possibility that the struggle against colonialism might be resumed resulting in a renewal of repression. The British Government was responsible in law for the repressive measures being carried on in Cyprus by its agents, and it should take urgent action to end them quickly. The United Kingdom had made no serious effort to negotiate a solution of the issues involved since the adoption of the last Assembly resolution on the matter, on 26 February 1957. Subsequent appeals by Archbishop Makarios for a resumption of negotiations on the rights of the Cypriots to self-determination had fallen on deaf ears. The British had countered with a threat to partition the island.

The Greek spokesman further felt that the United Kingdom's formula of negotiation between Greece, Turkey and the United Kingdom was intended to by-pass the people of Cyprus, whose interests must predominate. The formula was also intended to isolate Greece and to compel it either to betray the Cypriots or else to take the responsibility of breaking off negotiations.

The Greek Government, he added, spoke for the Cypriots because they were unable to plead their own case before the United Nations, although their right to self-determination was recognized in the Charter. Greece, he stated, had no expansionist designs or intentions to seize Cyprus which belonged only to its own people. Greece, in fact, was the only country to declare that it had no claim on Cyprus. The United Kingdom, on the other hand, was trying to assert its colonial rights, and Turkey was striving to assert greater rights than were justified either by the existence of a Turkish-speaking minority or on strategic grounds.

Greece was willing in advance to accept any decision freely taken by the people of Cyprus.

The representative of Turkey emphasized there were two completely different peoples living in Cyprus and that Cyprus lacked the characteristics of a nation as well as of a juridical state organization. These facts, had to be given due consideration.

Turkey's direct interest in Cyprus was a valid one because Cyprus was an off-shore island of the Turkish mainland commanding Turkey's vital defence and trade communications.

Finally, he noted that the present status of Cyprus had been decided by mutual consent between Turkey, Greece and the United Kingdom under the Treaty of Lausanne which was still a valid international instrument to which due importance should be given. "Enosis" or any other unilateral solution would be unacceptable. The issue as posed by Greece was one of annexation and not one of colonialism versus the right of a people to self-determination. The minority in Cyprus did not ever wish to be placed under Greek rule.

The Turkish representative drew attention to some promising developments since the adoption of the Assembly resolution on 26 February 1957. Terrorism in Cyprus had decreased, although Colonel Grivas, a regular officer of the Greek Army, was still heading the terrorist activities. The United Kingdom had relaxed its security measures. It had released Archbishop Makarios from the Seychelles even though he had not denounced terrorism. Britain had accepted an offer of mediation—as had Turkey—and it had made efforts to resume negotiations. Only Greece stood against the offer of good offices, insisting that its aspirations concerning Cyprus be recognized in advance.

Neutral observers, the Turkish representative also noted, had established that the terrorists in Cyprus, had consistently committed crimes against the Turkish population, and against Greek Cypriots who opposed annexation by Greece. The Greek Government's wish to annex Cyprus, had been expressed in its first request for United Nations intervention in Cyprus, when the words "union with Greece" and "self-determination" had been used interchangeably. The final goal of Greece obviously remained total annexation of Cyprus.

Among the representatives, who expressed general support for the Greek draft resolution were those of Bolivia, the Byelorussian SSR, Ceylon, Colombia, Czechoslovakia, Egypt, Ethiopia, Guatemala, Haiti, Hungary, Ireland, the USSR, Uruguay and Yugoslavia.

Stressing the principle of the Cypriots' right to self-determination and advocating a peaceful solution of the problem in accordance with the Charter some of them insisted on the withdrawal of foreign troops and military bases from the island and asked that democratic freedoms be restored to the people. They recognized the need for adequate guarantees of protection for the interests of the minority element in Cyprus and for assurances to neighbouring States regarding their security. Many of those generally in favour of the Greek draft resolution regarded the problem as one between the United Kingdom Government and the people of Cyprus.

Other representatives held that a solution required "quiet" negotiations not only between the United Kingdom Government and the leaders of the people of Cyprus, but also between the Governments of the United Kingdom, Greece and Turkey, as the interests of all three were involved.

Some thought that the Cyprus question was a problem outside the competence of the United Nations and that direct United Nations intervention might complicate rather than ease a delicate and dangerous problem.

Afghanistan, Australia, Belgium, China, France, Iran, the Federation of Malaya, Nepal, the Netherlands, New Zealand, Pakistan, Portugal and the United States were among those who advocated resumption of negotiations between the parties concerned. They pointed out that some good had come of resolution 1013 (XI), of 26 February 1957; the Assembly would therefore do well to reiterate it.

Canada, Chile, Denmark and Norway jointly proposed amendments to the Greek draft resolution. One amendment was to have the Assembly reaffirm its resolution 1013(XI). By another, the Assembly would express its concern that more progress had not been made towards the solution of the problem instead of expressing concern that "no progress" had been made. Thirdly, the Assembly would state that a solution at the earliest possible time (rather than a solution at the earliest possible time "in conformity with the principles of the Charter") was required to preserve peace and stability in the area. By a fourth amendment, the Assembly would express its earnest hope that further negotiations and discussions between those concerned would be promptly undertaken in a spirit of co-operation with a view to finding a peaceful, democratic and just solution in conformity with the purposes and principles of United Nations Charter. This paragraph was intended to replace the paragraph in the Greek draft whereby the Assembly would express the wish that the people be given the opportunity to determine their own future by application of their right to self-determination.

Greece proposed revising the latter amendment so that the Assembly would express the earnest hope that further negotiations and discussions would be undertaken in a spirit of co-operation with a view to having the right of self-determination applied in the case of the people of Cyprus.

Spain proposed yet another revision of the fourth four-power amendment so that the Assembly would express the wish that further negotiations and discussions among those concerned be promptly undertaken. This change was accepted by Canada on behalf of the sponsors of the four-power amendments. The First Committee accepted the Greek proposal for revising the fourth four-power amendment, by a roll-call vote of 33 to 18, with 27 abstentions. (Greece accepted the other three amendments put forward by Canada, Chile, Denmark and Norway).

The Greek draft resolution, as amended, was adopted in the First Committee by a roll-call vote of 33 to 20, with 25 abstentions. However, it failed to secure the two-thirds majority required for final approval when it was voted on, by roll-call, at a plenary meeting of the Assembly on 14 December 1957. The vote then was 31 for, 23 against, with 24 abstentions.

DOCUMENTARY REFERENCES

GENERAL ASSEMBLY—12TH SESSION
Plenary Meetings, 682, 731.
General Committee, meeting 111.
First Committee, meetings 927-934.

A/3616 and Add.1. Letters of 12 July and 13 September 1957 from Permanent Representative of Greece requesting inclusion in agenda of twelfth Assembly session of item entitled "Cyprus: (a) Application under the auspices of the United Nations, of the principle of equal rights and self-determination of peoples in the case of the population of the island of Cyprus; (b) Violations of human rights and atrocities by the British Colonial Administration against Cyprians".

A/C.1/803. Letter of 5 December 1957 from Permanent Representative of Greece.

A/C.1/L.197. Greece draft resolution, as amended by Canada, Chile, Denmark and Norway, and by Greece and Spain, adopted by First Committee by roll-call vote of 33 to 20, with 25 abstentions, as follows:

In favour: Albania, Bolivia, Bulgaria, Byelorussian SSR, Costa Rica, Czechoslovakia, Ecuador, Egypt, El Salvador, Ethiopia, Ghana, Greece, Guatemala, Haiti, Hungary, Iceland, Indonesia, Iraq, Ireland, Lebanon, Morocco, Panama, Poland, Rumania, Saudi Arabia, Sudan, Syria, Tunisia, Ukrainian SSR, USSR, Uruguay, Yemen, Yugoslavia.

Against: Australia, Belgium, Canada, Chile, Colombia, Denmark, Dominican Republic, France, Iran, Italy, Luxembourg, Netherlands, New Zealand, Nicaragua, Norway, Pakistan, Portugal, Sweden, Turkey, United Kingdom.

Abstaining: Afghanistan, Argentina, Austria, Brazil, Burma, Cambodia, Ceylon, China, Finland, Honduras, India, Israel, Japan, Laos, Liberia, Federation of Malaya, Mexico, Nepal, Paraguay, Peru, Philippines, Spain, Thailand, United States, Venezuela.

A/C.1/L.199. Canada, Chile, Denmark, Norway amendments to Greece draft resolution.

A/C.1/L.200. Greece amendment to joint amendments, A/C.1/L.199.

A/C.1/L.201. Spain amendment to joint amendments, A/C.1/L.199.

A/3794. Report of First Committee.

DRAFT RESOLUTION, A/3794, as recommended by First Committee, having failed to obtain the required two-thirds majority, was not adopted by the Assembly, 14 December 1957, meeting 731. The vote by roll-call, was 31 in favour to 24 against, with 24 abstentions as follows:

In favour: Albania, Bolivia, Bulgaria, Byelorussian SSR, Costa Rica, Czechoslovakia, Ecuador, Egypt, El Salvador, Ethiopia, Ghana, Greece, Guatemala, Haiti, Hungary, Iceland, Indonesia, Ireland, Lebanon, Panama, Poland, Romania, Saudi Arabia, Sudan, Syria, Tunisia, Ukrainian SSR, USSR, Uruguay, Yemen, Yugoslavia.

Against: Argentina, Australia, Belgium, Canada, Chile, Colombia, Denmark, Dominican Republic, Ecuador, France, Iran, Italy, Luxembourg, Netherlands, New Zealand, Nicaragua, Norway, Pakistan, Portugal, Spain, Sweden, Turkey, Union of South Africa, United Kingdom.

Abstaining: Afghanistan, Austria, Brazil, Burma, Cambodia, Ceylon, China, Finland, Honduras, India, Iraq, Israel, Japan, Laos, Liberia, Federation of Malaya, Mexico, Nepal, Paraguay, Peru, Philippines, Thailand, United States, Venezuela.

CHAPTER VIII

THE QUESTION OF WEST IRIAN (WEST NEW GUINEA)

The dispute between Indonesia and the Netherlands over the political status of West Irian (West New Guinea) was considered at the ninth, tenth and eleventh sessions of the General Assembly. At the eleventh session, a resolution recommended by the First Committee was not adopted by the General Assembly for lack of the required two-thirds majority.

On 16 August 1957, the representatives of Afghanistan, Burma, Ceylon, Egypt, Ethiopia, India, Indonesia, Iran, Iraq, Jordan, Lebanon, Libya, Morocco, Nepal, Pakistan, the Philippines, Saudi Arabia, Sudan, Syria, Tunisia and Yemen, requested that the question of West Irian (West New Guinea) be put on the agenda of the Assembly's twelfth session. They explained that the failure of the Assembly at its previous session to recommend specifically a peaceful approach had not in fact helped to lessen tensions between Indonesia and the Netherlands. In their view, the continuance of the situation deterred the encouragement and improvement of friendlier relations between the two countries. Under these circumstances, they felt it incumbent on the General Assembly, utilizing adequate measures and machinery, to promote a peaceful solution of this long-standing political dispute.

On 18 September 1957, the Assembly's General Committee decided by 7 votes to 4, with 4 abstentions, to recommend that the item be put on the Assembly's agenda. The Assembly agreed to this at a plenary meeting on 20 September 1957, by a roll-call vote of 49 to 21, with 11 abstentions.

The item was referred to the First Committee where it was considered at eight meetings between 20 and 26 November 1957.

At the second meeting devoted to this question, the Committee received a joint draft resolution submitted by the following 19 Members: Afghanistan, Bolivia, Burma, Ceylon, Egypt, Ethiopia, India, Indonesia, Iraq, Jordan, Lebanon, Libya, Morocco, Nepal, Saudi Arabia, Sudan, Syria, Tunisia and Yemen. By this draft, the Assembly would: (1) invite both parties to pursue their attempts to find a solution of the dispute in conformity with the principles of the United Nations Charter; and (2) request the Secretary-General to assist the parties concerned as he deemed appropriate in the implementation of the resolution. The Secretary-General was to report on the progress made to the Assembly's next regular session.

During the debate, the Indonesian representative stated that the West Irian problem had not lost its urgency since it was first brought before the United Nations. The problem was a matter of emergency requiring prompt solution. It was a continuous source of tension between Indonesia and the Netherlands.

Instead of the United Nations being allowed to serve as an instrument for reconciling the differences between the two States, numerous pretexts were being invoked to prevent a peacefull settlement, notably the principle of "self-determination". The Indonesian representative found it curious that certain powers which had proclaimed their adherence to the principle of reunification of divided States were conducting a movement exactly in reverse of that principle with respect to West Irian. Indonesia was fighting against the amputation of West Irian from the rest of Indonesia and for the principle of reunification and national unity. Any thought of splitting Indonesia into several smaller States was illusory. If Indonesia were to disintegrate and if the present democratic character of the State were to come to an end and be re-placed by a different political system, it would not be a development designed to increase the stability or ensure the peace and security of South-East Asia.

Indonesia was still in favour of peaceful negotiations without adherence to rigid positions on the issue of sovereignty. If the Netherlands Government were prepared to consider the issue within the proper context of Netherlands-Indonesian relations and international relations in general, further negotiations would have some chance of success. If the Netherlands Government were to persist in its present position, confident in the superiority of its physical strength, Indonesia for its part would also have to concentrate on its physical defences. Such a development would replace the rule of international law by that of the jungle.

The Indonesian Government was deeply concerned by the joint statement of the Netherlands and Australia of 6 November 1957 with regard to their future policies in West Irian and East New Guinea. That statement might have been intended as an effective weapon to counter an Indonesian request in the United Nations for a peaceful settlement of the question of West Irian. The Indonesian Government feared, however, that the statement might also have military implications and that it was a foreboding of the formation of a military alliance directed against a country with which a dispute existed.

The Indonesian representative, while admitting that his country had internal difficulties, added that Indonesia had survived predictions of doom before. It was certainly in a position, however, to promote the educational and social advancement of West Irian.

Indonesia had once again come to the United Nations seeking a settlement. It was difficult to say whether it was its last effort, for the patience of the Indonesian people was not inexhaustible. The Indonesian Government, however, was ready to co-operate fully in an endeavour to reach a settlement consonant with the principles and purposes of the Charter.

The representative of the Netherlands summed up the basic position of his Government as follows: (1) The Netherlands, in accordance with Chapter XI of the United Nations Charter, was responsible for the administration of

Netherlands New Guinea and was fulfilling its obligations under Article 73. (2) If the Netherlands were to agree to transfer the territory to Indonesia without first ascertaining the wishes of the inhabitants, it would be forsaking its duty to them and to the United Nations. (3) The Netherlands had solemnly promised the territory's inhabitants that they would be granted the opportunity to decide their own political future as soon as they were able to express their will on this. (4) In the absence of such a decision, the Netherlands could not and would not comply with any Indonesian demands for the annexation of the territory. Nor would it enter into any negotiations about its future status.

The Agreement on Transitional Measures signed by Indonesia and the Netherlands at the Round Table Conference, the Netherlands representative continued, had established the right of territories to exercise self-determination with regard to their position within the federal Republic of Indonesia and with regard to the possibility of negotiating a special relationship outside the Republic. These provisions would have been applicable to New Guinea, in view of its particular circumstances and its stage of development. They had, however, remained a dead letter, particularly after the Republic of the United States of Indonesia had been replaced in 1950 by a unitary state, in which there was no place for federal states or territories, nor for any special relationship of any territory either with the Netherlands or with Indonesia. Moreover, Indonesia had unilaterally abrogated the Round Table Agreements in 1956. Thus, any possible relevant obligations on the part of the Netherlands under these Agreements had lapsed.

The Netherlands representative further stated that Indonesia was not really advocating negotiations with the Netherlands so as to reach a solution by common consent which would take the wishes of the territory's inhabitants into account. On the contrary, it was urging the General Assembly to advocate negotiations on the basis of two assumptions: (1) that Netherlands New Guinea was legally part of Indonesia and illegally occupied by the Netherlands, and (2) that the territory should be transferred to Indonesia without its population being previously consulted.

The Netherlands, he added, was willing to have the first assumption tested by the International Court of Justice. The second assumption, he thought, was a denial of the right of self-determination and thus contrary to the Charter.

There were indications that the Indonesian Government was trying to create a threat to international peace, even though it was clear that Western New Guinea posed no such threat. Outrages had been committed against Netherlands nationals in Indonesia and the Indonesian President had indicated that Indonesia would resort to methods which would startle the world if the United Nations did not comply with his Government's wishes.

The Netherlands representative explained that the joint Australian-Netherlands statement of 6 November 1957 clarified the aims and principles of the co-operation of the two Authorities administering the area. It did not prejudice the decision which the inhabitants of the two parts of the island would eventually have to make for themselves. It recognized their ethnological and geographical affinity and opened up possibilities for their future development along sound lines for their existence in the modern world.

The representative of Australia regretted that the Indonesian Government had again brought this question before the Assembly only eight months after the Assembly had rejected a draft resolution which advocated the Indonesian claim that there was a case for negotiations over Western New Guinea. The Netherlands Government, he felt, had attacked the task of promoting the territory's development with determination and in accordance with the principles and policies set forth in Chapter XI of the Charter. It was abiding by its obligations under Article 73. But these obligations would cease to exist if the territory became an integral part of the Republic of Indonesia, since the latter would then be in a position to reject any claim by the United Nations for information on conditions in West New Guinea.

The joint Netherlands-Australian statement of 6 November 1957 was fully consistent with the terms of Chapter XI of the Charter, the Australian representative said. It was a solemn undertaking by the two Governments that their policies would be such as to prepare the people of New Guinea for the time when they would be able to determine their own future. That statement had no military implications. It was not directed against the interests of the Indonesian people. Nor was it connected in any way with SEATO (the South-East Asia Treaty Organization).

Indonesia's claim for negotiations was purely political, the Australian representative continued, since it had refused to submit its case to the International Court of Justice and had unilaterally abrogated the very Agreements it sought to invoke. In Australia's view, adoption of the 19-power draft resolution would mean that the United Nations was implicitly supporting a unilateral claim of one Member State to some of the territory of another Member State.

Support for the 19-power draft resolution came, however, from the representatives of a number of Members, among them: Afghanistan, Bolivia, Bulgaria, Burma, the Byelorussian SSR, Ceylon, Costa Rica, Czechoslovakia, Egypt, Ethiopia, Ghana, Greece, Haiti, India, Iraq, Japan, Jordan, Laos, the Federation of Malaya, Nepal, Pakistan, the Philippines, Poland, Romania, Saudi Arabia, Sudan, Syria, Thailand, the Ukrainian SSR, the USSR and Yemen.

The arguments they advanced included one that a call for new negotiations could not prejudice the substance of the case, but might rather lead to a relaxation of tension between Indonesia and the Netherlands.

Opposition to the 19-power draft resolution came from the spokesmen for Argentina, Austria, Belgium, Brazil, China, Cuba, the Dominican Republic, France, Ireland, Israel, Italy, Mexico, New Zealand, Peru, Spain, Sweden, the United Kingdom, Uruguay and others.

One argument against the draft resolution was that the General Assembly, under Article 2, paragraph 7, of the United Nations Charter, was not competent to discuss the question. Another argument was that the Charter of Transfer of Sovereignty expressly provided that the *status quo* of New Guinea was to be maintained, thereby best protecting the right of the inhabitants to self-determination under the present circumstances.

Some representatives mentioned the possibility of establishing a United Nations Trusteeship for the entire island of New Guinea, in order that the population as a whole might in due course decide its own future.

On 26 November 1957, the First Committee approved the 19-power draft resolution by a roll-call vote of 42 to 28, with 11 abstentions. It failed to be adopted, however, when it came up for final approval at a plenary meeting of the Assembly, since it did not secure the required two-thirds majority. The vote in plenary, by roll-call, was taken on 29 November 1957. The result was 41 votes in favour, 29 against, with 11 abstentions.

DOCUMENTARY REFERENCES

GENERAL ASSEMBLY—12TH SESSION
Plenary Meetings 682, 724.
General Committee, meeting 111.
First Committee, meetings 905-912.

A/3644. Letter of 16 August 1957 from Permanent Representatives of Afghanistan, Burma, Ceylon, Egypt, Ethiopia, India, Indonesia, Iran, Iraq, Jordan, Lebanon, Libya, Morocco, Nepal, Pakistan, Philippines, Saudi Arabia, Sudan, Syria, Tunisia, Yemen requesting inclusion in agenda of 12th Assembly session of item entitled "Question of West Irian (West New Guinea)".
A/C.1/L.193. Afghanistan, Bolivia, Burma, Ceylon, Egypt, Ethiopia, India, Indonesia, Iraq, Jordan, Lebanon, Libya, Morocco, Nepal, Saudi Arabia, Sudan, Syria, Tunisia, Yemen draft resolution adopted by roll-call vote of 42 to 28, with 11 abstentions, as follows:
In favour: Afghanistan, Albania, Bolivia, Bulgaria, Burma, Byelorussian SSR, Ceylon, Costa Rica, Czechoslovakia, Egypt, El Salvador, Ethiopia, Ghana, Greece, Guatemala, Haiti, Hungary, India, Indonesia, Iran, Iraq, Japan, Jordan, Laos, Lebanon, Libya, Federation of Malaya, Morocco, Nepal, Pakistan, Philippines, Poland, Romania, Saudi Arabia, Sudan, Syria, Thailand, Tunisia, Ukrainian SSR, USSR, Yemen, Yugoslavia.
Against: Argentina, Australia, Austria, Belgium, Brazil, Canada, Chile, China, Colombia, Cuba, Denmark, Dominican Republic, France, Honduras, Iceland, Ireland, Israel, Italy, Luxembourg, Netherlands, New Zealand, Nicaragua, Norway, Peru, Portugal, Spain, Sweden, United Kingdom.
Abstaining: Cambodia, Ecuador, Finland, Liberia, Mexico, Panama, Paraguay, Turkey, United States, Uruguay, Venezuela.
A/3757. Report of First Committee.
Draft resolution, as recommended by First Committee, A/3757, having failed to obtain the required two-thirds majority, was not adopted by the Assembly on 29 November 1957, meeting 724. The vote by roll-call, was 41 to 29, with 11 abstentions as follows:

In favour: Afghanistan, Albania, Bolivia, Bulgaria, Burma, Byelorussian SSR, Ceylon, Costa Rica, Czechoslovakia, Egypt, El Salvador, Ethiopia, Ghana, Greece, Guatemala, Haiti, Hungary, India, Indonesia, Iran, Iraq, Japan, Jordan, Laos, Lebanon, Libya, Federation of Malaya, Morocco, Nepal, Pakistan, Poland, Romania, Saudi Arabia, Sudan, Syria, Thailand, Tunisia, Ukrainian SSR, USSR, Yemen, Yugoslavia.

Against: Argentina, Australia, Austria, Belgium, Brazil, Canada, Chile, China, Colombia, Cuba, Denmark, Dominican Republic, France, Honduras, Iceland, Ireland, Israel, Italy, Luxembourg, Netherlands, New Zealand, Nicaragua, Norway, Peru, Portugal, Spain, Sweden, Union of South Africa, United Kingdom.

Abstaining: Cambodia, Ecuador, Finland, Liberia, Mexico, Panama, Paraguay, Turkey, United States, Uruguay, Venezuela.

CHAPTER IX

THE INDIA-PAKISTAN QUESTION

COMMUNICATIONS FROM PAKISTAN TO THE SECURITY COUNCIL

On 16 November 1956, the representative of Pakistan informed the President of the Security Council by letter that, according to press reports, a constitution for the State of Jammu and Kashmir, framed by an assembly calling itself a Constituent Assembly and sitting at Srinagar, was due to come into force on 26 January 1957. Further, that part of the Constitution integrating the State into India would come into force on 17 November 1956. The move would nullify the Council's resolution of 30 March 1951 and the assurances given by the Indian representative at that time. It would also run counter to the Council's objective that the accession of the State to India or Pakistan should be decided by a plebiscite under United Nations auspices.

Any action by India aimed at integration of the State of Jammu and Kashmir into its territory, the representative of Pakistan said, would constitute a violation of United Nations resolutions and a repudiation of international agreements to which India was a party. India should be called upon to desist from such action.

On 26 November, in another letter, the representative of Pakistan reported to the Council that it had now been confirmed that the action which, according to Indian press reports, was to be taken on 17 November 1956 by the "so-called Constituent Assembly at Srinagar", had been taken. He asked the President of the Council to seek clarification from the Government of India.

On 2 January 1957, the Foreign Minister of Pakistan informed the Security Council, by letter, that India had refused, "on one pretext or another", to honour its international commitments accepted under the two resolutions of the United Nations Commission for India and Pakistan (UNCIP) adopted on 13 August 1948 and 5 January 1949 respectively. Pakistan was therefore forced to the conclusion that continuance of direct negotiations between the two Governments held no prospect of settling the dispute. Believing that the current situation called for firm and timely action by the Council, he requested an early meeting of the Council to consider the Kashmir question.

CONSIDERATION BY SECURITY COUNCIL

The Security Council considered the question at 14 meetings between 16 January and 21 February 1957.

In the discussion, the representative of Pakistan made the point that the dispute between his country and India involved, in essence, the right of the people of the State of Jammu and Kashmir to self-determination. Until a plebiscite had been held, he also contended, the territory was neither part of India nor of Pakistan, despite the *de facto* situation whereby India occupied part of the State and the authority of Azad Kashmir prevailed over the remaining portion of the State. On the basis of the two resolutions of UNCIP, which had been accepted by the parties, an international agreement bound India and Pakistan. No part of the agreement, which was an integral whole, could be used, repudiated or frozen unilaterally. He further questioned India's assertion that the State was legally part of the territory of the Indian Union.

The representative of India said that his

Government's approach to the Kashmir problem, since 1 January 1948, had been based on the following considerations, among others: The State had legally acceded to India. It was a constituent unit of the Union of India, and the only authority that could legally separate the State of Jammu and Kashmir from the Union was the sovereign Parliament of India. The territorial integrity of the State was inviolable, and Pakistan had committed an act of aggression against the State and therefore against India and must "vacate that aggression". India stood by its commitments under the UNCIP resolutions in the light of its understanding of them and of the explanations and assurances given to it by UNCIP as regards the provisions of the resolutions. In view of the changed conditions, which had altered the circumstances relating to the proposals, India could not forever regard these proposals as applicable or binding.

On 24 January, the Council adopted, by 10 votes to 0, with 1 abstention (USSR), a draft resolution sponsored by Australia, Colombia, Cuba, the United Kingdom and the United States. It thereby declared that the convening of a Constituent Assembly and any action it might have taken or might attempt to take to determine the future shape and affiliation of the State of Jammu and Kashmir or any action taken to support such action by that Assembly would not constitute a disposition of the State in accordance with the principle enunciated in earlier resolutions. In adopting this resolution, the Council also recalled its resolutions of 21 April and 3 June 1948, of 14 March 1950 and 30 March 1951, and the UNCIP resolutions of 13 August 1948 and 5 January 1949.

On 20 February, another draft resolution was submitted to the Council by Australia, Cuba, the United Kingdom and the United States. By this, the Council would voice concern at the lack of progress in settling the dispute and, considering the importance it had attached to the demilitarization of the State of Jammu and Kashmir preparatory to the holding of a plebiscite, would note Pakistan's proposal for the use of a temporary United Nations force in connexion with demilitarization and would state its belief that the use of such a force deserved consideration. By the operative part of the draft, the Security Council would ask its President (the representative of Sweden) to visit the sub-continent to examine with the Governments of India and Pakistan proposals which, in his opinion, would help to bring about demilitarization or further the settlement of the dispute. The President would be directed to take into account the previous resolutions of the Council and of UNCIP and to report to the Council not later than 15 April 1957.

The draft resolution received 9 votes in favour, 1 against (USSR), with 1 abstention (Sweden). It was not adopted as the negative vote was that of a permanent member of the Council. Amendments proposed by Colombia and the USSR also failed of adoption.

Following the rejection of the four-power draft resolution, Australia, the United Kingdom and the United States submitted another text. Recalling its resolution of 24 January 1957 and its previous resolutions, the Council would thereby ask its President: (1) to examine with the Governments of India and Pakistan any proposals which, in his opinion, were likely to contribute towards the settlement of the dispute, having regard to the previous resolutions of the Council and of UNCIP; (2) to visit the sub-continent for this purpose; and (3) to report to the Council not later than 15 April 1957. India and Pakistan were invited to co-operate with the President in his task.

On 21 February, the three-Power draft resolution was adopted by 10 votes to 0, with 1 abstention (USSR).

The President of the Council at the time this resolution was adopted was Gunnar V. Jarring of Sweden.

REPORT OF MR. JARRING

Mr. Jarring visited India and Pakistan between 14 March and 11 April 1957, and had a number of discussions with the two Governments. On 29 April, he submitted his report.

Mr. Jarring said that, in view of the statements made by the representatives of India and Pakistan to the Council that their Governments had accepted the UNCIP resolutions of 13 August 1948 and 5 January 1949, he had attempted to find out what was impeding the full implementation of those two resolutions, and to find a solution for the problems which had arisen in connexion with them.

The resolution of 5 January 1949 envisaged the holding of a plebiscite to decide the accession of the State of Jammu and Kashmir to India or Pakistan. In exploring this question, Mr. Jarring said he had been aware of the grave problems that might arise in connexion with, and as a result of, such a plebiscite. In consequence, he had made a number of suggestions to both Governments by which the difficulties could be met, or at least substantially mitigated, but they had not proved mutually acceptable.

According to India, Mr. Jarring reported, there were two factors which prevented the implementation of two UNCIP resolutions:

(1) Pakistan had not implemented Part I (entitled "Cease-fire order") of the resolution of 13 August 1948, particularly section B and E. (Under section B, the High Commands of the Indian and Pakistan forces agree to refrain from taking any measures that might augment the military potential of the forces under their control in the State of Jammu and Kashmir. Under section E the two Governments agree to appeal to their respective peoples to assist in creating and maintaining an atmosphere favourable to the promotion of further negotiations.) For that reason, India had considered it premature to discuss either implementing Parts II and III of that resolution or implementing the resolution of 5 January 1949. (Part II of the resolution of 13 August 1948 deals with the principles to serve as a basis for the formulation of a truce agreement. Part III contains: a reaffirmation by the two Governments of their wish that the future status of Jammu and Kashmir shall be determined in accordance with the will of the people; and an agreement to enter into consultations on plebiscite conditions. The resolution of 5 January 1949 sets forth details on the proposed plebiscite.)

(2) As to Part II of the resolution of 13 August 1948 (which deals with a truce agreement), it was India's view that it was incumbent on the Council to express itself on what India considered to be aggression committed by Pakistan against India and equally incumbent on Pakistan "to vacate the aggression". India had argued that, prior to the fulfilment of these requirements on the part of the Council and of Pakistan, India's commitments under the resolution could not reach the operative stage.

Mr. Jarring said he had explained to the Government of India that the Council had properly taken cognizance of India's original complaint, and that it was not for him to say whether the Council's resolutions on the matter had been adequate or not. He had pointed out that, regardless of the merits of the present position taken by India, it could not be overlooked that India had accepted the two UNCIP resolutions.

Pakistan, for its part, had maintained that it had implemented Part I of the resolution of 13 August 1948 fully and in good faith, and that the time had come to proceed to the implementation of Part II.

Mr. Jarring said that, under the circumstances, he had decided it might be appropriate to approach first the question of the implementation of Part I of the UNCIP resolution (of 13 August 1948). His impression was that India attached substantial weight to the absence of "an atmosphere favourable to the promotion of further negotiations" as envisaged in section E of that resolution, and it had repeatedly stressed that the military *status quo* envisaged in section B did not obtain, owing to the policies pursued by Pakistan.

In order to break the deadlock on the implementation of Part I, he said he had asked the two Governments whether they would be prepared to submit to arbitration the question of whether or not that part of the resolution in question had been implemented. He used the term "arbitration" largely in the sense of a determination of certain facts in question. In case the arbitrator or arbitrators found that the implementation had been incomplete, his suggestion envisaged that they would also be empowered to indicate the measures to be taken to attain full implementation of Part I. It was further envisaged that, after a given time-limit, they would determine whether the indicated measures had been followed and whether Part I of the UNCIP resolution of 13 August 1948 had been implemented.

Pakistan, after a certain amount of hesitation, had accepted his suggestion in principle, Mr. Jarring said. India, however, had considered arbitration as he had outlined it would not be appropriate. India explained that it was not against the principle of arbitration; but it felt that the issues in dispute in the present instance did not lend themselves to arbitration, as outlined by him, because such a procedure would be inconsistent with the sovereignty of Jammu and Kashmir and the rights and obligations of India in respect of this territory. India was also apprehensive that arbitration, even on an isolated part of the resolutions, might be interpreted as indicating that Pakistan had a *locus standi* in the question.

Mr. Jarring further reported that, in dealing as extensively as he had done with the problem, he could not but take note of the concern expressed in connexion with the changing political, economic and strategic factors surrounding the whole of the Kashmir question, together with the changing pattern of power relations in West and South Asia. The Council, he added, would be aware that the implementation of international agreements of an *ad hoc* character, if not achieved fairly speedily, might become progressively more difficult because the situation with which they were designed to deal tended to change.

While he felt unable to report to the Council any concrete proposals which, in his opinion, were at that time likely to contribute towards a settlement of the dispute, Mr. Jarring concluded that his examination of the situation as it then obtained would indicate that, despite the deadlock, both parties still wished to find a peaceful solution to the problem. They were willing to co-operate with the United Nations to this end.

FURTHER COMMUNICATIONS FROM INDIA AND PAKISTAN

In a letter sent to the President of the Security Council on 29 April 1957, the representative of Pakistan drew attention to a press report indicating closer association of Jammu and Kashmir with India's development programme, for which purpose the State had been made a member of the Northern Zonal Council of India. This new move, he commented, constituted a further step towards determining unilaterally the future shape and affiliation of the state. Pakistan took a grave view of the situation created by India's action and reserved its right to seek further action by the Security Council with regard to that matter.

On 5 August 1957, in another letter, the representative of Pakistan declared that it appeared that India had settled a large number of non-Muslims, who were not residents of the State of Jammu and Kashmir, in the area under its control and that it had also allotted property left behind by Muslin residents to such non-Muslim settlers. This action contravened the Security Council resolution of 17 January 1948 and was designed to enable India to assert later that the plebiscite had become more difficult because of changed circumstances. Moreover, India's move would also result in the harassment of the native population of the State, leading to an increased influx of Muslim refugees from the India-held zone into Pakistan or Azad Kashmir.

The representative of India, in a letter dated 9 August 1957, rejected the allegations in the Pakistan letter of 5 August as false and baseless. No non-resident, he said, was permitted to become a resident of Jammu and Kashmir and no evacuee property could be allotted to any non-resident. Evacuee properties in Jammu and Kashmir were being alloted to refugees driven from their homes in Pakistan-occupied areas of the State. Consequently, the allegation that India had contravened the Council's resolution of 17 January 1948 was without foundation.

The Indian representative stressed, too, that the increased movement of persons over the cease-fire line had been into Jammu and Kashmir rather than in the opposite direction.

Further, the term "India-held zone" had no sanction in the Security Council or UNCIP resolutions and was a patent misrepresentation of the facts. Pakistan, he said, was in occupation of the territory of the Union of India by aggression and continued to be in occupation of that territory in violation of the Council resolution of 17 January 1948 and the two UNCIP resolutions.

In another letter dated 21 August, the representative of India, referring to a press report on the subject, cited the execution of the Mangla Dam project by the Government of Pakistan as a further instance of Pakistan's consolidating its authority over the Indian territory of Jammu and Kashmir and of the exploitation of that territory to the disadvantage of the people of the States and for the benefit of the people of Pakistan. Pakistan's action, he added, was in violation of the Council resolution of 17 January 1948 and of the assurances given to India by the Chairman of UNCIP.

In a letter dated 3 October 1957, the representative of Pakistan stated that the Mangla Dam project was being carried out co-operatively by the Pakistan Government and the Azad Kashmir authorities. It would greatly strengthen the economy of the Azad Kashmir area and would in no way adversely affect any existing interests. India, he added, had carried out a number of projects on its side of the cease-fire line. If India's action could not be deemed to aggravate the situation in terms of the resolution of 17 January 1948, Pakistan failed to understand how a development project in the Azad Kashmir area could be described as a violation of that resolution.

COUNCIL'S CONSIDERATION OF MR. JARRING'S REPORT

On 21 August 1957, the representative of Pakistan asked that a meeting of the Council be called to discuss Mr. Jarring's report and to consider further action.

The Security Council took up consideration of the report on 24 September 1957 and held 14 meetings on the India-Pakistan question between 24 September and 2 December.

In the course of the discussion, the representatives of two parties concerned reiterated views expressed earlier in the year and made various observations on Mr. Jarring's report.

The representative of Pakistan, pointing out that his Government had accepted Mr. Jarring's suggestions, concluded that they were unacceptable only to India. He considered India's present refusal to enter into negotiations for implementation of Part II of the UNCIP resolution of 13 August 1948 (on the plea that Part I had not been implemented) was an excuse for reopening issues which had long been settled.

The charge of aggression levelled by India, he maintained, had been summarily dismissed by Mr. Jarring as irrelevant to his task. This position was in accordance with that taken on the issue both by UNCIP and the United Nations mediators.

The representative of India observed that Mr. Jarring had described the suggestions he had made to the parties as not having been "mutually acceptable"; this clearly meant that Mr. Jarring had been unable to find common ground.

The representative of India disagreed with the statement in the Jarring report that India's attitude had been negative on arbitration of the question as to whether Part I of the UNCIP resolution of 13 August 1948 had been implemented. Mr. Jarring's suggestion, he noted, had envisaged that the arbitrator should be empowered to indicate to the parties measures for full implementation. India's attitude had been positive from the beginning, but there was no need to arbitrate the obvious fact that Pakistan had increased its military potential and that an atmosphere in which a plebiscite might be held did not prevail. India could not accept arbitration on matters involving its honour and integrity.

The representative of Sweden thought that certain legal aspects of the Kashmir question might usefully, and at an appropriate time, be referred to the International Court of Justice for an advisory opinion. These aspects related to the legality of the accession of the State of Jammu and Kashmir and to the obligations of India and Pakistan in respect of a plebiscite if a confirming plebiscite was a condition for the accession.

The representative of India stated his Government's willingness to answer the question raised at an appropriate time.

The representative of Pakistan had no doubt that his Government would give due consideration at the appropriate time to the Swedish representative's suggestion. In his view, however, the issues involved were political rather than juridicial.

On 16 November 1957, the representatives of Australia, Colombia, the Philippines, the United Kingdom and the United States submitted a joint draft resolution to the Council.

By the preamble to this text, the Council would thank Mr. Jarring and make the observation that the Governments of India and Pakistan recognized and accepted the commitments undertaken by them in the two UNCIP resolutions of 13 August 1948 and 5 January 1949, which envisaged the determination of the future status of the State of Jammu and Kashmir in accordance with the will of the people through a free and impartial plebiscite. The Council would also take into consideration the importance it had attached to demilitarization of the State as one of the steps towards a settlement.

By the operative part of the draft resolution, the Council would in effect: (1) ask the two Governments in effect to avoid aggravation of the situation and to establish and maintain an atmosphere favourable to the promotion of further negotiations; (2) ask the United Nations Representative for India and Pakistan (Dr. Frank P. Graham) to make any recommendations to the parties for further action which he considered desirable in connexion with Part I of the UNCIP resolution of 13 August 1948, having regard to his third and fifth reports and to the report of Mr. Jarring, and to enter into negotiations with the two Governments in order to implement Part II of the 13 August 1948 resolution, and, in particular, to reach agreement on a reduction of forces on either side of the cease-fire line to a specific number, arrived at on the basis of the relevant Security Council resolutions and having regard to Dr. Graham's fifth report; and (3) call upon the Governments of India and Pakistan to co-operate with the United Nations Representative in order to formulate an early agreement on demilitarization procedures, which should be implemented within three months of such an agreement being reached.

On 27 November, Sweden submitted a number of amendments to the five-power draft resolution.

By one of them, the Council would make the observation that the Governments of India and Pakistan recognized and accepted the provisions in the Council's resolution of 17 January 1948 and in the UNCIP resolutions of 13 August 1948 and 5 January 1949 (rather than state that the two Governments recognized and accepted "the commitments undertaken by them" in these two UNCIP resolutions).

By another Swedish amendment, to the operative part of the draft resolution, the United Nations Representative would only be asked to make any recommendations to the parties for further appropriate action with a view to making progress toward the implementation of the UNCIP resolutions and towards a peaceful settlement. Sweden also proposed deleting the operative paragraph in the draft text which called upon the two Governments to co-operate in the formulation of an early agreement on demilitarization procedures.

On 2 December 1957, the sponsors of the joint draft resolution indicated that they welcomed the Swedish amendments in the hope that, while preserving the balance of the draft resolution, they might meet some of the difficulties which it had evidently created. The amendments were adopted by 10 votes to 0, with 1 abstention (USSR). The draft resolution as amended was then approved by an identical vote.

By the operative part of the resolution as adopted, the Security Council thus asked the Governments of India and Pakistan to refrain from making any statements and from doing or causing to be done or permitting any acts which might aggravate the situation, and to appeal to their respective peoples to help create and maintain an atmosphere favourable to the promotion of further negotiations. It asked the United Nations Representative for India and Pakistan to make any recommendations to the parties for further appropriate action with a view to making progress towards the implementation of the UNCIP resolutions of 13 August 1948 and 5 January 1949 and towards a peaceful settlement. The United Nations Representative was authorized to visit the subcontinent for these purposes, and was instructed to report on his efforts as soon as possible to the Council.

DOCUMENTARY REFERENCES

SECURITY COUNCIL meetings 761-775, 791, 795-805, 807, 808.

S/3744, S/3750. Letters of 16 and 26 November 1956 from representative of Pakistan.
S/3767. Letter of 2 January 1957 from Minister for Foreign Affairs of Pakistan.
S/3778. Australia, Colombia, Cuba, United Kingdom, United States draft resolution.

S/3779. Resolution, as submitted by 5 powers, S/3778, adopted by Security Council on 24 January 1957, meeting 765, by 10 votes to 0, with 1 abstention as follows:
In favour: Australia, China, Colombia, Cuba, France, Iraq, Philippines, Sweden, United Kingdom, United States.
Against: None.
Abstaining: USSR.

"*The Security Council,*

"*Having heard* statements from representatives of the Governments of India and Pakistan concerning the dispute over the State of Jammu and Kashmir,

"*Reminding* the Governments and Authorities concerned of the principle embodied in its resolutions of 21 April 1948, 3 June 1948, 14 March 1950 and 30 March 1951, and the United Nations Commission for India and Pakistan resolutions of 13 August 1948 and 5 January 1949, that the final disposition of the State of Jammu and Kashmir will be made in accordance with the will of the people expressed through the democratic method of a free and impartial plebiscite conducted under the auspices of the United Nations,

"*Reaffirms* the affirmation in its resolution of 30 March 1951 and declares that the convening of a Constituent Assembly as recommended by the General Council of the 'All Jammu and Kashmir National Conference' and any action that Assembly may have taken or might attempt to take to determine the future shape and affiliation of the entire State or any part thereof, or action by the parties concerned in support of any such action by the Assembly, would not constitute a disposition of the State in accordance with the above principle;

"*Decides* to continue its consideration of the dispute."

S/3781. Letter of 26 January 1957 from representative of Portugal.

S/3787. Australia, Cuba, United Kingdom, United States draft resolution.

S/3789. USSR amendments to joint draft resolution, S/3787.

S/3791 and Rev.1, Rev.1/Corr.1. Colombia amendments and revised amendments to joint draft resolution, S/3787.

S/3792 and Corr.1. Australia, United Kingdom, United States draft resolution.

S/3793. Resolution, as submitted by 3 powers, S/3792 and Corr.1, adopted by Security Council on 21 February 1957, meeting 774, by 10 votes to 0, with 1 abstention as follows:
In favour: Australia, China, Colombia, Cuba, France, Iraq, Philippines, Sweden, United Kingdom, United States.
Against: None.
Abstaining: USSR.

"*The Security Council,*

"*Recalling* its resolution of 24 January 1957, its previous resolutions and the resolutions of the United Nations Commission for India and Pakistan on the India-Pakistan question,

"1. *Requests* the President of the Security Council, the representative of Sweden, to examine with the Governments of India and Pakistan any proposals which, in his opinion, are likely to contribute towards the settlement of the dispute, having regard to the previous resolutions of the Security Council and of the United Nations Commission for India and Pakistan; to visit the sub-continent for this purpose; and to report to the Security Council not later than 15 April 1957;

"2. *Invites* the Governments of India and Pakistan to co-operate with him in the performance of these functions; and

"3. *Requests* the Secretary-General and the United Nations Representative for India and Pakistan to render such assistance as he may request."

S/3821. Report on India-Pakistan question submitted by representative of Sweden in pursuance of resolution of Security Council of 21 February 1957, S/3793.

S/3822, S/3860, S/3868. Letters of 29 April, 5 and 21 August 1957 from Permanent Representative of Pakistan.

S/3861. Letter of 9 August 1957 from Permanent Representative of India.

S/3869. Letter of 21 August from Permanent Representative of India (on Mangla Dam project).

S/3896. Letter of 3 October 1957 from representative of Pakistan (on Mangla Dam project).

S/3911. Australia, Colombia, Philippines, United Kingdom, United States draft resolution.

S/3920. Sweden amendments to joint draft resolution, S/3911.

S/3922. Resolution, as submitted by 5 powers, S/3911, and as amended by Sweden, S/3920, adopted by Security Council on 2 December 1957, meeting 808, by 10 votes to 0, with 1 abstention, as follows:
In favour: Australia, China, Colombia, Cuba, France, Iraq, Philippines, Sweden, United Kingdom, United States.
Against: None.
Abstaining: USSR.

"*The Security Council,*

"*Having received and noted with appreciation* the report of Mr. Gunnar V. Jarring, the representative of Sweden, on the mission undertaken by him pursuant to the Security Council resolution of 21 February 1957,

"*Expressing its thanks* to Mr. Jarring for the care and ability with which he has carried out his mission,

"*Observing with appreciation* the expressions made by both parties of sincere willingness to co-operate with the United Nations in finding a peaceful solution,

"*Observing further* that the Governments of India and Pakistan recognize and accept the provisions of its resolution dated 17 January 1948 and of the resolutions of the United Nations Commission for India and Pakistan dated 13 August 1948 and 5 January 1949, which envisage in accordance with their terms the determination of the future status of the State of Jammu and Kashmir in accordance with the will of the people through the democratic method of a free and impartial plebiscite, and that Mr. Jarring felt it appropriate to explore what was impeding their full implementation,

"*Concerned* over the lack of progress towards a settlement of the dispute which his report manifests,

"*Considering* the importance which it has attached to demilitarization of the State of Jammu and Kashmir as one of the steps towards a settlement,

"*Recalling* its previous resolution and the resolutions

of the United Nations Commission for India and Pakistan on the India-Pakistan question,

"1. *Requests* the Government of India and the Government of Pakistan to refrain from making any statements and from doing or causing to be done or permitting any acts which might aggravate the situation and to appeal to their respective peoples to assist in creating and maintaining an atmosphere favourable to the promotion of further negotiations;

"2. *Requests* the United Nations Representative for India and Pakistan to make any recommendations to the parties for further appropriate action with a view to making progress towards the implementation of the resolutions of the United Nations Commission for India and Pakistan of 13 August 1943 and 5 January 1949 and towards a peaceful settlement;

"3. *Authorizes* the United Nations Representative to visit the sub-continent for these purposes; and

"4. *Instructs* the United Nations Representative to report to the Security Council on his efforts as soon as possible."

OTHER DOCUMENTS

S/PV.761. Annexes I-III. Documents submitted by Pakistan delegation as annexes to statement by representative of Pakistan.

S/PV.762/Add.1. Documents submitted by Indian delegation as annexes to statement by representative of India at 762nd and subsequent meetings of Security Council.

CHAPTER X

THE KOREAN QUESTION

At the General Assembly's twelfth session, the First Committee considered the Korean question between 12 and 18 November 1957. There were two reports before the Committee: the seventh annual report of the United Nations Commission for the Unification and Rehabilitation of Korea (UNCURK) for the period between 24 August 1956 and 14 August 1957; and a report from the United States in its capacity as the Unified Command.

The UNCURK report stated that there had been no change in the prospects for realizing the United Nations objective of bringing about the establishment of a unified, independent and democratic government for all Korea, since there was no sign that the authorities in North Korea or the Central People's Government of the People's Republic of China were willing to negotiate a settlement on the basis of the principles laid down by the United Nations.

The report of the Unified Command noted that the Communist side had upset the relative military balance between the two sides, provided for by the Armistice Agreement, and upon which the maintenance of peace depended. It had done so by introducing, in violation of the Armistice Agreement, improved and different weapons, including combat aircraft.

Efforts to rectify the situation through the Military Armistice Commission and the Neutral Nations Supervision Commission (NNSC) having been of no avail, it had been announced after consultation with the other Governments which had contributed forces to repel the aggression in Korea, that the United Nations Command considered itself entitled to be relieved of its corresponding obligations under the Armistice Agreement. Thus, old weapons would be replaced with new ones currently available with the sole purpose of restoring the relative balance of military strength and thus to preserve the stability of the Armistice.

In early October, the Democratic People's Republic of Korea urged by cable that its representative be invited to participate in the Assembly's discussion of the Korean question. When, however, the First Committee took up the item, it approved a United States draft resolution to invite only the representative of the Republic of Korea to participate in the debate, without the right to vote. The vote for this was 44 to 15, with 16 abstentions.

Before taking this decision, the First Committee rejected an Indian amendment to invite representatives of both the Republic of Korea and the Democratic People's Republic of Korea. This was defeated by 36 votes to 20, with 20 abstentions.

Prior to the general debate, Australia, Ethiopia, France, Greece, Luxembourg, New Zealand, the Philippines, Thailand, Turkey, the United Kingdom and the United States submitted a draft resolution. By this, the Assembly would: (1) urge continuing efforts on behalf of the United Nations objective of bringing about by peaceful means the establishment of a unified, independent and democratic Korea; (2) call upon the Communist authorities concerned to accept these objectives in order to achieve a settlement in Korea based on the principles set forth by the nations participating on behalf of the United Nations at the Korean political conference at Geneva in 1954 as reaffirmed by the General Assembly; and (3) ask UNCURK to continue its work.

In support of the 11-power draft, the United States representative stated that the Communist aggression against the Republic of Korea and the gross violations by the Communist side of the 1953 Armistice Agreement had led to remedial action which the United Nations Command announced would take place. The Command had strictly observed the cease-fire and the other provisions of the Agreement, save to the extent that it was entitled to be relieved from compliance as a result of Communist violations.

Until the Communists showed a sincere desire to seek a solution, the United States representative said, there was little hope for a settlement of the Korean question. They had persistently rejected all proposals for an equitable solution. They still refused to discuss any settlement based on the two principles set forth at Geneva in 1954 and subsequently approved by the Assembly. Thus, they refused free and fair elections in Korea under United Nations supervision and even asserted that the United Nations was, in effect, the aggressor and therefore not competent to deal with a Korean settlement.

The North Korean and Communist Chinese authorities could demonstrate their sincerity by withdrawing the Chinese Communist troops still occupying North Korea in defiance of the Assembly's resolution of 1 February 1951, which called for their withdrawal. They could do so by responding to the United Nations proposals for peaceful unification set forth at the Geneva Conference in 1954, by accounting for the 2,720 military personnel whose fate was still unknown, and by returning to their homes the thousands of civilians abducted from South Korea or, at least, by disclosing their fate.

Among those voicing support for the 11-power draft resolution, were the representatives of Australia, Belgium, Canada, China, France,

Japan, the Netherlands, New Zealand, the Philippines, Sweden, Thailand, Turkey and the United Kingdom.

The points they made included the following. The recent action of the United Nations Command with regard to the introduction of new weapons was fully justified on both practical and legal grounds. Great importance was to be attached to the fact that the essential parts of the Armistice Agreement had been preserved. Whatever the difficulties, the United Nations must uphold its repeatedly affirmed objectives in Korea, and fulfil its obligations. Several speakers suggested that once the broad United Nations principles had been accepted, the practical details could be settled by negotiation.

The Australian representative rejected the Communist view that there were two States in Korea and that they should negotiate "without outside influence". There was only one Korean people, with one history and one heritage, he said. A political conference of both parts of Korea without United Nations "intervention" would leave South Korea alone to negotiate with the Communist authorities in North Korea behind whom stood the might of Communist China and the USSR.

The representative of the Republic of Korea declared that the longer the situation caused by aggression in Korea persisted, the worse it became. The belated steps taken by the United Nations Command had not yet rectified the dangerous military imbalance. After reviewing the great political, economic, social and educational progress made by the Republic despite formidable difficulties, he deplored the continued artificial division of a homogenous people. He called on the protagonists of "peaceful co-existence" to put their theory into immediate practice by withdrawing their forces from Northern Korea and by agreeing to hold genuinely free elections there under United Nations supervision for the unification of the country.

Opposition to the 11-power draft resolution came from the representatives of Albania, Bulgaria, the Byelorussian SSR, Czechoslovakia, Poland, the Ukrainian SSR and the USSR.

They criticized attempts which had been made for years to impose unrealistic, one-sided resolutions on the Assembly in order to secure the aggressive United States objective of forcing the Korean people to accept the South

Korean régime. The absence from the discussion of representatives of the People's Republic of Korea and of the People's Republic of China had prevented a constructive solution, they maintained. There was no hope of a settlement as long as the terms of the Geneva declaration of 1954 were insisted upon. National unity, they said, could only be achieved by recognizing the existence in Korea of two separate States with different social systems and by the gradual rapprochement of those States. Broad political, economic and cultural links would lay the groundwork for unification on a democratic basis by the Korean people themselves, without foreign intervention or pressure. A variety of proposals by the Democratic People's Republic of Korea had been categorically rejected by the régime in South Korea. These had included a proposal put forward jointly with the People's Republic of China in June 1957 for the immediate convening of an international conference of all the States involved to bring about a peaceful settlement. This joint proposal had also been rejected by the United States.

Those against the 11-power draft maintained that the main obstacles to a Korean settlement were the positions of the United States (which counted on South Korea as a strategic base) and the South Korean authorities (which had repeatedly called for annulment of the Armistice Agreement). While the Korean-Chinese side had complied strictly with the terms of that Agreement, the United States had flagrantly violated its commitments and had built up the South Korean armed forces while the forces in North Korea were being reduced. Its violations had been aggravated by the United Nations Command's declaration that it did not intend to abide by the provisions prohibiting the shipment of new weapons to Korea and by the United States announcement that its troops in South Korea were to be equipped with weapons capable of firing atomic warheads.

The USSR representative charged that UNCURK had, in a way, encouraged the aggressive tendencies of the South Korean régime and that its activities were designed to provide a cloak of United Nations respectability for the aggressive policy of the United States in Korea. The United States, he said, had made the same demands at previous sessions; it had demanded that Chinese volunteers be withdrawn from Korea without making any mention of the withdrawal of United States forces; it had demanded that the People's Republic of Korea acquiesce in the proposals of the Assembly while refusing to hear representatives of the Korean people; the United States had also demanded that the Korean People's Republic observe an Armistice Agreement which neither the United States nor South Korea considered binding. The USSR representative also said that the question of returning allegedly kidnapped South Korean citizens rested on a slanderous allegation.

The representatives of Ceylon, India and Nepal considered that the 11-power draft resolution could not help solve the Korean question.

The Indian representative supported the principle of holding elections under international supervision, but thought that national unity would be brought about more easily without outside interference. In his view, the proposals for the organization of free elections under international supervision and for the unification of the country, as submitted in 1954 by the French Minister of Foreign Affairs, were logical and constructive. The United Nations could be called on to give its approval and sanction both before and after such elections and the subsequent unification.

The First Committee, however, approved the 11-power draft resolution. It did so on 18 November by a roll-call vote of 53 to 9, with 15 abstentions. This decision was endorsed by a plenary meeting of the General Assembly on 29 November by a roll-call vote of 54 to 9, with 16 abstentions (resolution 1180(XII)).

DOCUMENTARY REFERENCES

SECURITY COUNCIL

S/3848. Note of 3 July 1957 from representative of United States concerning appointment of General George H. Decker as Commanding General of Military Forces made available to Unified Command pursuant to Security Council Resolution of 7 July 1950 (S/1588).

GENERAL ASSEMBLY—12TH SESSION
Plenary Meeting 724.
First Committee, meetings 899-904.

A/3631. Unified Command Report on United Nations Command Statement in Military Armistice Commission on 21 June 1957. Communication of 9 August 1957 from representative of United States.

A/3672. Report of United Nations Commission for Unification and Rehabilitation of Korea (UNCURK).

A/C.1/795. Text of cablegram of 3 October 1957 from Minister for Foreign Affairs of Democratic People's Republic of Korea.

A/C.1/L.190. United States draft resolution (on invitation to representative of Republic of Korea) adopted by First Committee, by 44 votes to 15, with 16 abstentions.

A/C.1/L.191. India amendments to United States draft resolution.

A/C.1/L.192. Australia, Ethiopia, France, Greece, Luxembourg, New Zealand, Philippines, Thailand, Turkey, United Kingdom, United States draft resolution adopted by First Committee by roll-call vote of 53 to 9, with 15 abstentions, as follows:

In favour: Argentina, Australia, Austria, Belgium, Bolivia, Brazil, Canada, Chile, China, Colombia, Costa Rica, Cuba, Denmark, Dominican Republic, Ecuador, Ethiopia, France, Greece, Guatemala, Honduras, Iceland, Iran, Iraq, Ireland, Israel, Italy, Japan, Laos, Lebanon, Liberia, Libya, Luxembourg, Federation of Malaya, Mexico, Netherlands, New Zealand, Nicaragua, Norway, Pakistan, Panama, Paraguay, Peru, Philippines, Portugal, Spain, Sweden, Thailand, Tunisia, Turkey, United Kingdom, United States, Uruguay, Venezuela.

Against: Albania, Bulgaria, Byelorussian SSR, Czechoslovakia, Hungary, Poland, Romania, Ukrainian SSR, USSR.

Abstaining: Afghanistan, Burma, Cambodia, Ceylon, Egypt, Finland, Haiti, Indonesia, Morocco, Nepal, Saudi Arabia, Sudan, Syria, Yemen, Yugoslavia.

A/3746. Report of First Committee.

RESOLUTION 1180(XII), as recommended by First Committee, A/3746, adopted by Assembly on 29 November 1957, meeting 724, by roll-call vote of 54 to 9, with 16 abstentions, as follows:

In favour: Argentina, Australia, Austria, Belgium, Bolivia, Brazil, Canada, Chile, China, Colombia, Costa Rica, Cuba, Denmark, Dominican Republic, El Salvador, Ethiopia, France, Greece, Guatemala, Haiti, Honduras, Iceland, Iran, Iraq, Ireland, Israel, Italy, Japan, Jordan, Laos, Liberia, Libya, Luxembourg, Federation of Malaya, Mexico, Nether-

lands, New Zealand, Nicaragua, Norway, Pakistan, Panama, Paraguay, Peru, Philippines, Portugal, Spain, Sweden, Thailand, Tunisia, Turkey, United Kingdom, United States, Uruguay, Venezuela.

Against: Albania, Bulgaria, Byelorussian SSR, Czechoslovakia, Hungary, Poland, Romania, Ukrainian SSR, USSR.

Abstaining: Afghanistan, Burma, Cambodia, Ceylon, Egypt, Finland, Ghana, India, Indonesia, Morocco, Nepal, Saudi Arabia, Sudan, Syria, Yemen, Yugoslavia.

"*The General Assembly,*

"*Having received and noted* the report of the United Nations Commission for the Unification and Rehabilitation of Korea,

"*Recalling* its resolutions 195(III) of 12 December 1948, 498(V) of 1 February 1951, 811(IX) of 11 December 1954, 910(X) of 29 November 1955 and 1010(XI) of 11 January 1957,

"*Noting* that the Armistice Agreement of 27 July 1953 remains in effect,

"1. *Reaffirms* that the objectives of the United Nations are to bring about by peaceful means the establishment of a unified, independent and democratic Korea under a representative form of government, and the full restoration of international peace and security in the area;

"2. *Urges* that continuing efforts be made to this end;

"3. *Calls upon* the communist authorities concerned to accept the established United Nations objectives in order to achieve a settlement in Korea based on the fundamental principles for unification set forth by the nations participating on behalf of the United Nations in the Korean Political Conference held at Geneva in 1954, and reaffirmed by the General Assembly;

"4. *Requests* the United Nations Commission for the Unification and Rehabilitation of Korea to continue its work in accordance with the relevant resolutions of the General Assembly;

"5. *Requests* the Secretary-General to place the Korean question on the provisional agenda of the thirteenth session of the General Assembly."

KOREAN RELIEF AND REHABILITATION

REPORT OF AGENT-GENERAL TO GENERAL ASSEMBLY

Successful completion of the United Nations Korean Reconstruction Agency's programme of economic assistance to the Republic of Korea by 30 June 1958, thus concluding a "most significant and highly successful chapter in United Nations history", was forecast in the seventh annual report of UNKRA's Agent-General to the United Nations General Assembly. The re-

port, covering the period 1 July 1956 to 30 June 1957, was supplemented by an addendum for the period 1 July to 31 October 1957.

The large majority of UNKRA projects, the Agent-General reported, had now been completed. Most of the remaining projects would be finished by the end of December 1957. Only a small number would carry over into the final quarter of 1958.

A total sum of $140 million, the Agent-

General recalled, had been made available by United Nations Members and by non-member States, for UNKRA's relief and rehabilitation programmes which were intended to supplement the general recovery efforts of the Korean people themselves. To this sum had been added miscellaneous income amounting to $7 million. These funds would be expended by 30 June 1958, except for the sum required for the final liquidation of the Agency's affairs and for certain necessary technical assistance.

The whole-hearted participation of the Korean Government and people had proved of further inestimable value during the period in expediting the remaining projects, the Agent-General declared. The most generous financial assistance of the contributing Governments had been turned into permanent capital assets. These now constituted a significant factor in the Korean economy. They also provided, for all nations, a visible and effective demonstration of United Nations action and accomplishment. A goodly and successful measure of assistance in the reconstruction of the Republic's industrial and social establishment and the restoration of its economy had been provided.

Reviewing over-all Agency accomplishments, the Agent-General said that by 30 June 1957 activities had been completed at 3,995 of 4,664 project sites provided with material or technical assistance. The total allocation for industrial projects had amounted to $27.5 million. This had been used mainly to increase cement, textile, paper and flat-glass production, and to provide effective financial assistance to small industries. The new 200,000-metric-ton cement plant at Mungyong had started operations in September 1957. The output of this plant, combined with that of an UNKRA-rehabilitated cement plant at Samchok, would meet a good part of the domestic requirements. The Agency's $9 million textile programme had been virtually completed. Five automatic cotton-opening and cotton-picking units, auxiliary spinning equipment and 1,025 cotton looms had arrived and been installed during the period. Since 1953, the cotton textile industry had been supplied with 55,440 spindles, 2,100 looms, much accessory equipment and eight large opening and picking units. These were considered adequate, with industry-rehabilitated or newly acquired equip-

ment, to meet present cotton textile requirements. A new worsted yarn plant, a woollen and worsted dyeing plant and rehabilitation and improvement of South Korea's only silk waste plant also had been completed. Work was proceeding on the only outstanding textile project, a flax, hemp and ramie spinning plant.

Korea's first flat-glass plant began operations in September 1957. Its annual capacity of 12 million square feet could meet normal demands, the Agent-General said. Rehabilitation activities had been concluded at the Korea Paper Manufacturing Company plant, the only present producer of newsprint in South Korea. Installations for Korea's first modern kraft paper plant and for a bond paper plant continued. Small private industrial establishments had received substantial further aid through the UNKRA Small Business Loan Fund. A total of 1,381 loans had been made between August 1954 and 30 June 1957, amounting to $2,090,280 in foreign exchange and hwan 1,409,599,000. The 1,162 separate enterprises which had received the loans represented almost one out of every seven small businesses in the Republic of Korea.

Total allocations in the mining field had amounted to $13 million. Of this sum, $8.6 million had been earmarked for restoring and expanding coal production, and $4.4 million for increasing metal- and mineral-mining operations. More equipment had arrived for Government and private coal mines. UNKRA aid had resulted in further substantial coal production gains. The Taechon-ni gold placer dredge had been assembled and extraction of gold had started. Mining equipment had arrived for the Chungju Iron Mine, and the new talc grinding plant at Chungju had begun operations. The major $1.46 million project to modernize the Changhang non-ferrous smelter and refinery was under way, and a new 200-ton-a-day mill was being installed at the Sihung crystalline graphite mine. The UNKRA Mine Loan Fund had lent an additional $198,500 and hwan 24,750,000, raising the total lent to $383,500 and hwan 39,750,000. Ten small mines with good development potentials had benefited.

The $3.4 million power programme had been completed, the Agent-General also noted. This included rehabilitation of Korea's main 550-kilometre-long 154 kilovolt transmission system, restoration and extension of 66 kilovolt-transmission lines in south-west Korea, repairs to war-damaged sub-stations on the mainland and the establishment of new power facilities on Cheju Island.

The $5.5 million transport and communications programme was fulfilled during the period, with the restoration of Kunsan-Changhang harbour to full operational condition. In addition, 310,000 ties had been provided for secondary rail lines in south-west Korea since 1953, almost 600 trucks had been added to Korea's civilian motor fleet, a large harbour dredge had been provided. Several engine houses and railroad backshops had been restored. Also restored were 44 vital navigational aids. In addition, replacement parts and new equipment had been supplied to the Korean national broadcasting system.

The fisheries programme, drawing rapidly to a close, had been an important factor in the recovery of the fisheries industry, the Agent-General added. Altogether, $3.6 million in fishing nets, gear, trawlers, boat-building materials, ice and cold storage facilities and cannery equipment had been supplied. Included under the programme were two modern fish canneries now being established. Built or under construction were 486 fishing craft. Close to 1,200 other vessels had been repaired. The UNKRA Fisheries Loan Fund had provided more than hwan 201 million in loans and credits to the Republic's fishermen and their fisheries guilds.

Reviewing over-all achievements in irrigation and forestry, the Agent-General noted that 111 irrigation projects had been fully completed. First-phase work had been carried out on 147 other, longer-range projects. Rice production had risen by 30,000 metric tons a year. A high potential for further increases in rice output was implicit in the continued use of UNKRA-provided capital equipment. The forestry programme had restored essential research and experimental facilities; research operations had now recovered to about the June 1950 level. Other aid in the forestry field had helped to re-establish teaching facilities, to provide trained forestry leadership, and to furnish equipment for effective forest management and reforestation activities.

Work at 59 flood control project sites and on 10 river and current gauge stations had been concluded during the period under review. Activities at an additional 14 sites were nearing completion. UNKRA materials still on hand would be used on 15 more projects to be finished during the financial year 1957-1958. On completion, the programme would give protection to 78,000 acres of land and about 98,000 persons.

Some 8,800 permanent-type housing units out of 9,850 had been completed under the Agency's $4.6 million housing programme. Constructed in Seoul, Pusan and 30 provincial cities and towns, they included single-family homes, two-story row-houses and a number of apartment buildings. Improved designs and building methods had been introduced and guidance provided for the establishment of a sound national housing scheme.

Allocation for education projects had totalled $11 million. Over 3,600 classrooms had been built to accommodate some 200,000 children. Four vocational training centres had been dedicated during the period under review, and three more would be ready by the end of December 1957, the Agent-General added.

In anticipation of the closing of the UNKRA programme, the Foreign Language Institute and the Fundamental Education Centre had been transferred to UNESCO. The Agent-General recalled that the Agency had also established a Merchant Marine Academy and a modern text-book printing plant, restocked college and university libraries, re-equipped laboratories and provided a foreign book retail store.

As to health and welfare projects, construction had started on the new $4.4 million National Medical Centre in Seoul. The National Rehabilitation Centre for the physically handicapped had been generally completed. The child welfare institutions programme had been concluded. Fifty-four orphanages had been expanded, 10 hostels built, and several special homes had been established to train social welfare workers. In July 1957, a site allowing for future expansion of the present National Vaccine Laboratory had been selected, and construction of a new laboratory had started. This would provide adequate facilities for producing vaccines and diagnostic biologicals. Rehabilitation work on the National Chemical Laboratory had been completed.

All but one of 156 voluntary agency projects

assisted with Agency grants had been completed. The grants, totalling almost $1 million since 1952, had helped to provide many new and valuable facilities for the Republic's health, welfare and educational services. A major start had been made on the country's fundamental education programme with the opening in November 1956 of the new UNKRA/UNESCO/Republic of Korea Fundamental Education Centre at Suwon. A regular two-year course was under way in 1957 for a capacity enrolment of 48 students. Noting that UNKRA's direct support for an internationally staffed community co-ordinated development programme had come to an end, the Agent-General said further efforts would now be carried out through the students and graduates of the Fundamental Education Centre.

Technical assistance activities carried out with UNKRA staff seconded to the United Nations Command had been concluded as of 30 June 1957. Since January 1952, these activities had provided a cadre of competent specialists and technicians to help develop and direct, as well as carry out in the field, the United Nations Command's health, welfare, sanitation and general relief and resettlement programmes, besides supplying other valuable specialist personnel. Most recently, this staff had worked with the Office of the Economic Co-ordinator of the United Nations Command in providing assistance for efficient functioning of the United States aid programme while replacement personnel for the latter were being recruited.

Reviewing the economic situation of the Republic of Korea, the Agent-General reported encouraging improvement during the financial year 1957. Industrial and mining production had further increased. More electric power was available. The previous year's more moderate trend in price and wage movements continued. Many of the production increases had resulted from the use of new equipment and facilities introduced through UNKRA and United States International Cooperation Administration (ICA) projects. Ultimately, the Agent-General observed, the over-all improvement had stemmed directly from the cumulative effects of the United Nations and United States aid programmes.

CONSIDERATION BY GENERAL ASSEMBLY

On 1 October 1957, the President of the Republic of Korea addressed a letter to the President of the General Assembly's twelfth session voicing appreciation for UNKRA's outstanding work. While noting that the Republic's need for aid still continued, he expressed thanks for the generous assistance already received. The memory of the nations who had contributed to the Agency's programme would remain. There was more to UNKRA than its effect on the Republic, the President's letter added. "Every Asian nation had marked what UNKRA had done."

The Agent-General's report was considered at the General Assembly's twelfth session by the Second (Economic and Financial) Committee on 15 November 1957. Also before the Committee were comments from the United Nations Commission for the Unification and Rehabilitation of Korea (UNCURK) on the Agency's programme.

The Commission expressed the opinion that UNKRA had contributed substantially to the recovery and reconstruction of the Republic of Korea. It also shared the Agent-General's view that UNKRA operations had provided further and valuable evidence of the possibilities of collective action through the United Nations in peace-time endeavours.

In the course of a statement to the Committee, the Agent-General observed that successful conclusion of the UNKRA programme, now in sight, would permit major changes in the Agency's organization effective 30 June 1958. Again commenting on the co-operation received from the Government and people of the Republic, and expressing gratitude for the financial support by United Nations Members, he pointed out that much more aid would be needed to repair fully the damage due to the fighting in Korea.

Favourable comments on UNKRA's work were made by the representatives of Belgium, Canada, China, Iran, Netherlands, New Zealand, Sweden, Turkey, the United Kingdom, the United States and Uruguay. Among the points made were the following. The available funds had been used in such a way as to bring the greatest possible economic and social benefit to the Republic of Korea and its people. UNKRA's achievements had covered every sector of the Korean economy. The United Nations had acted with striking success to aid a country devastated by war. The successful completion of this task would go down in history as one of the Organization's finest achievements.

Also favourably commented on was the fact that specialized agencies had taken over certain UNKRA projects which otherwise would terminate with the conclusion of UNKRA operations in the country. The representatives of China, the Netherlands and Sweden, in addition, observed that the large-scale efforts of the United States for Korean reconstruction had played a most important part in restoring the Korean economy.

The USSR representative, on the other hand, said that the Agent-General's report showed the economy of South Korea was still under great strain. This, in his view, was related to military expenditures. Foreign economic aid to South Korea had not resulted in any serious increase in its productive capacity, he added, introducing some statistics on North Korea.

Adopted by the Second Committee, and later endorsed at a plenary meeting of the General Assembly, was a resolution commending the Agent-General of UNKRA for the excellent work performed by the Agency in assisting the Korean people to relieve the sufferings and to repair the devastation caused by aggression. The Assembly thereby stated its conviction that the work of the Agency would have long-lasting and significant effects upon the Korean economy and the well-being of the Korean people, and expressed appreciation for the valuable assistance given to the Agency by specialized agencies and by voluntary non-governmental organizations. The Assembly also approved the Agent-General's recommendation that the Agency should cease as an operational organization on 30 June 1958. It further approved arrangements and procedures proposed by the Agent-General for the completion after 30 June 1958 of the residual responsibilities of the Agency and the liquidation of its accounts.

The draft resolution, sponsored by Canada, the United Kingdom, the United States and Uruguay, was approved by the Second Committee on 15 November by a vote of 44 to 0, with 18 abstentions. On 26 November it was adopted, without discussion, at a plenary meeting of the Assembly by 54 votes to 0, with 18 abstentions as resolution 1159(XII).

PLEDGES AND CONTRIBUTIONS TO UNKRA
(As of 31 December 1957; in U.S. Dollars)

United Nations Member States	Amount Pledged	Total Received	Balance Outstanding
Argentina	$ 500,000	$ 500,000	—
Australia*	3,616,446	3,616,446	—
Austria	179,474	179,474	—
Belgium	600,000	600,000	—
Burma	49,934	49,934	—
Cambodia	1,000	1,000	—
Canada	7,413,021	7,413,021	—
Chile	250,000	250,000	—
Denmark	860,000	336,615	$523,385†
Dominican Republic	10,000	10,000	—
Egypt	28,716	28,716	—
El Salvador	500	500	—
Ethiopia	40,000	40,000	—
France	142,857	142,857	—
Greece	18,063	18,063	—
Guatemala‡	7,704	7,704	—
Honduras	2,500	2,500	—
Indonesia	143,706	143,706	—
Israel	36,100	36,100	—
Italy	2,014,933	2,014,933	—
Lebanon	50,000	50,000	—

United Nations Member States	Amount Pledged	Total Received	Balance Outstanding
Liberia	15,000	15,000	—
Luxembourg	50,000	50,000	—
Mexico	40,000	40,000	—
Netherlands	1,052,632	1,052,632	—
New Zealand	836,850	836,850	—
Norway	1,725,323	1,725,323	—
Pakistan	315,000	315,000	—
Panama	3,000	—	3,000
Paraguay	10,000	10,000	—
Saudi Arabia	20,000	20,000	—
Sweden	988,904	974,167	14,737†
United Kingdom*	26,840,002	26,840,002	—
United States*	92,902,615	92,902,615	—
Venezuela	100,000	100,000	—
Total	$140,864,280	$140,323,158	$541,122
Non-Member States			
Liechtenstein	465	465	—
Monaco	1,144	1,144	—
Switzerland	313,954	313,954	—
The Vatican	10,000	10,000	—
Viet-Nam	10,000	10,000	—
Total	$ 335,563	$ 335,563	—
Grand Total	$141,199,843	$140,658,721	$541,122

* Previous contribution statements have shown pledges of $4,001,726 for Australia, $28,000,000 for the United Kingdom and $162,500,000 for the United States. At the time these pledges were made, the Governments concerned stipulated that payment of the full amounts was conditional upon certain matching contributions being received from other Governments, and in the case of Australia and the United States upon certain percentage limitations. In this statement these amounts have been adjusted to reflect the maximum contributions of these Governments in accordance with the terms of their pledges, on the basis of total contributions made by other Governments to the programme.

† To be settled under agreement of 31 March 1956 for the establishment and operation of a National Medical Centre in Korea.

‡ The contribution from the Government of Guatemala represents the proceeds of the sale of 15,000 pounds of coffee by the Government.

DOCUMENTARY REFERENCES

GENERAL ASSEMBLY—12TH SESSION
Plenary Meeting 723.
Second Committee, meetings 490, 491.

A/3651 and Corr.1 and Add.1. Report of Agent-General of United Nations Korean Reconstruction Agency for period 1 July 1956 to 30 June 1957, and addendum covering period 1 July to 1 October 1957.
A/3675. Comments of United Nations Commission for Unification and Rehabilitation of Korea (UNCURK) on report of Agent-General.
A/3697. Letter of 1 October 1957 from President of Republic of Korea.
A/C.2/L.350 and Corr.1. Memorandum by Agent-General regarding arrangements for termination of operational activities of UNKRA and for liquidation of Agency.
A/C.2/L.351. Memorandum by UNKRA Advisory Committee.

A/C.2/L.352 and Add.1. Canada, United Kingdom, United States, Uruguay draft resolution, adopted by Second Committee by 44 votes to 0, with 18 abstentions.
A/3748. Report of Second Committee.
RESOLUTION 1159(XII), as recommended by Second Committee, A/3748 adopted by Assembly on 26 November 1957, meeting 723, by 54 votes to 0, with 18 abstentions.

"The General Assembly,
"Recalling its resolutions 410(V) of 1 December 1950, 701(VII) of 11 March 1953, 725(VIII) of 7 December 1953, 828(IX) of 14 December 1954, 920 (X) of 25 October 1955 and 1020(XI) of 7 December 1956,
"Taking note of:
"(a) The report of the Agent-General of the United Nations Korean Reconstruction Agency on the work of the Agency for the period 1 July 1956

to 30 June 1957, and of the comments thereon by the United Nations Commission for the Unification and Rehabilitation of Korea,

"(b) The addendum to the Agent-General's report, dated 31 October 1957,

"(c) The memorandum of the Agent-General to the Advisory Committee of the Agency, dated 13 November 1957,

"*Recognizing* the especial importance of the Agency's programme for the relief and rehabilitation of the Republic of Korea,

"1. *Commends* the Agent-General of the United Nations Korean Reconstruction Agency for the excellent work performed by the Agency in pursuing its mission of assisting the Korean people to relieve the sufferings and to repair the devastation caused by aggression;

"2. *Expresses its conviction* that the work of the Agency will have long-lasting and significant effects upon the economy of Korea and upon the well-being of the Korean people;

"3. *Expresses its appreciation* for the valuable asssitance given to the Agency by specialized agencies of the United Nations and by voluntary non-governmental organizations;

"4. *Approves* the recommendation of the Agent-General that the Agency cease as an operational organization on 30 June 1958;

"5. *Further approves* the arrangements and procedures proposed by the Agent-General in his memorandum of 13 November 1957 for the completion, after 30 June 1958, of the residual responsibilities of the Agency and the subsequent liquidation of its accounts."

CHAPTER XI

THE QUESTION OF THE REPRESENTATION OF CHINA

On 13 September 1957, India asked that the question of the representation of China in the United Nations be put on the agenda for the General Assembly's twelfth session. A memorandum accompanying the request declared that a solution of this problem was important not only from the point of view of the legitimate rights of the Chinese people and Government, but also from the point of view of the effectiveness of the United Nations Organization itself, which was handicapped by the virtual absence of China.

The Assembly's General Committee considered India's request on 19 September.

The United States representative proposed a draft resolution whereby the Assembly would: (1) decide to reject the request for the inclusion of the item in the agenda; and (2) decide not to consider, at its twelfth session, any proposal to exclude the representatives of the Government of the Republic of China or to seat representatives of the Central People's Government of the People's Republic of China.

The representative of India, supported by the representatives of Ceylon, Czechoslovakia and the USSR, considered that the second part of the United States draft resolution was out of order, as it dealt with the merits of the case.

The United States representative disagreed. The proposal, he said, was not that the Committee should decide a political question, but that it should merely make a recommendation to the Assembly. Support in the General Committee for the United States draft resolution was voiced by the representatives of China, Iran, Thailand and the United Kingdom.

The General Committee decided by 10 votes to 3, with 2 abstentions, to vote first on the United States draft resolution. The first operative paragraph of the draft text was adopted by 10 votes to 4, with 1 abstention, and the second by 9 votes to 4, with 2 abstentions. The draft resolution as a whole was adopted by 9 votes to 4, with 2 abstentions.

When the General Assembly took up the General Committee's report on 24 September, it also had before it an Indian amendment to the draft resolution recommended by the Committee. By this amendment, the Assembly would, in effect: (1) accede to, rather than reject, the request that the item on the representation of China be put on its agenda, and (2) delete the provision not to consider any proposal to exclude the representatives of the Republic of China or to seat representatives of the People's Republic of China at the twelfth session.

The representative of India stated that the debate which had been provoked by the proposal to include the item in the Assembly's agenda in itself indicated that it would be far better for the Assembly to consider the matter fully and then to take whatever decision it wished. The question should not be disregarded as it involved 600 million people in a state of political maturity and great economic progress, with a Government which maintained trading relations with 68 other countries. The main point of India's proposal was that the representation of China should be discussed by the Assembly. If the item were to be placed on the agenda, the question of a change of representation might arise and might require consideration, but it would not be the only possibility. The Indian representative said that he would not press the second part of his amendment.

Among those supporting the Indian amendment were the representatives of Bulgaria, Hungary, Nepal and the Ukrainian SSR. One argument advanced was that the refusal to permit representatives of the People's Republic of China to participate in the work of the United Nations undermined its authority, hindered the attainment of universality by the Organization, and worked against a peaceful and just settlement of problems of concern to the Far East.

The United States representative, supported by the representatives of Guatemala, the Federation of Malaya, Mexico and Peru, advocated the adoption of the recommendation put forward by the General Committee. Some might term it realistic to recognize that the People's Republic of China was a fact, at least so far as internal affairs were concerned. But, he declared, it was quite proper for the United Nations to take into account what a country did outside its borders and to maintain a moral standard, including the United Nations Charter

provision that Member States should be "peace-loving". The Charter had not been amended, nor had the United Nations repealed its decision branding the Chinese Communists as aggressors in Korea. In his view, to admit the Chinese Communists would stultify the United Nations and thus destroy its usefulness; a debate on the question would only serve to divide the Organization.

The Assembly rejected the first Indian amendment, by a roll-call vote of 43 to 29, with 9 abstentions. The draft resolution recommended by the General Committee was then voted upon paragraph by paragraph, and was adopted as a whole by a roll-call vote of 47 to 27, with 7 abstentions. The question of the representation of China was thus not put on the agenda of the twelfth regular Assembly session.

The issue, however, was raised again in the course of the twelfth session, both at a meeting of the Credentials Committee on 8 December and at a plenary meeting of the General Assembly on 10 December at which the report of the Credentials Committee was considered. Although Albania, Bulgaria, Burma, Czechoslovakia, India, Nepal, Poland, Romania, the USSR and Yugoslavia, among others, registered reservations with regard to the question of Chinese representation, the Assembly approved the report of the Credentials Committee by a vote of 77 to 1.

The question of the representation of China was also raised in other United Nations organs and bodies during 1957 (see DOCUMENTARY REFERENCES below).

DOCUMENTARY REFERENCES

GENERAL ASSEMBLY—12TH SESSION
Plenary Meetings 684, 686, 726.
General Committee, meeting 112.

A/3663. Letter of 13 September 1957 from Permanent Representative of India requesting inclusion in agenda of 12th session of item entitled "Representation of China in United Nations".
A/3670. First report of General Committee, containing draft resolution as proposed orally by United States and adopted by General Committee, by 9 votes to 4 with 2 abstentions.
A/L.224. India amendments to draft resolution recommended by General Committee, A/3670, paragraph 7. First amendment rejected by Assembly on 24 September 1957, meeting 686, by roll-call vote of 43 against, to 29 in favour, with 9 abstentions, as follows:

In favour: Afghanistan, Albania, Bulgaria, Burma, Byelorussian SSR, Cambodia, Ceylon, Czechoslovakia, Denmark, Egypt, Ethiopia, Finland, Ghana, Hungary, India, Indonesia, Ireland, Morocco, Nepal, Norway, Poland, Romania, Sudan, Sweden, Syria, Ukrainian SSR, USSR, Yemen, Yugoslavia.
Against: Argentina, Australia, Austria, Belgium, Bolivia, Brazil, Canada, Chile, China, Colombia, Costa Rica, Cuba, Dominican Republic, Ecuador, El Salvador, France, Guatemala, Haiti, Honduras, Iceland, Iran, Iraq, Italy, Japan, Jordan, Lebanon, Liberia, Luxembourg, Federation of Malaya, Netherlands, New Zealand, Nicaragua, Panama, Paraguay, Peru, Philippines, Spain, Thailand, Turkey, United Kingdom, United States, Uruguay, Venezuela.
Abstaining: Greece, Israel, Laos, Libya, Mexico, Pakistan, Portugal, Saudi Arabia, Tunisia.
RESOLUTION 1135(XII), as proposed by General Com-

mittee, A/3670, adopted by Assembly on 24 September 1957, meeting 686, by roll-call vote of 47 to 27, with 7 abstentions, as follows:

In favour: Argentina, Australia, Austria, Belgium, Bolivia, Brazil, Canada, Chile, China, Colombia, Costa Rica, Cuba, Dominican Republic, Ecuador, El Salvador, Ethiopia, France, Greece, Guatemala, Haiti, Honduras, Iceland, Iran, Iraq, Italy, Japan, Jordan, Lebanon, Liberia, Libya, Luxembourg, Federation of Malaya, Mexico, Netherlands, New Zealand, Nicaragua, Panama, Paraguay, Peru, Philippines, Spain, Thailand, Turkey, United Kingdom, United States, Uruguay, Venezuela.

Against: Afghanistan, Albania, Bulgaria, Burma, Byelorussian SSR, Ceylon, Czechoslovakia, Denmark, Egypt, Finland, Ghana, Hungary, India, Indonesia, Ireland, Morocco, Nepal, Norway, Poland, Romania, Sudan, Sweden, Syria, Ukrainian SSR, USSR, Yemen, Yugoslavia.

Abstaining: Cambodia, Israel, Laos, Pakistan, Portugal, Saudi Arabia, Tunisia.

"The General Assembly
"1. *Decides* to reject the request of India for the inclusion in the agenda of its twelfth regular session of the additional item entitled 'The representation of China in the United Nations';
"2. *Decides* not to consider, at its twelfth regular session, any proposal to exclude the representatives of the Government of the Republic of China or to seat representatives of the Central People's Government of the People's Republic of China."

A/3773. Report of Credentials Committee.
RESOLUTION 1183(XII), approving report of Credentials Committee, as recommended by Credentials

Committee, A/3773, adopted by Assembly on 10 December 1957, meeting 726, by 77 votes to 1.

OTHER ORGANS OF UNITED NATIONS
COMMITTEE ON ARRANGEMENTS FOR CONFERENCE FOR PURPOSE OF REVIEWING CHARTER, meeting 1.
ECONOMIC AND SOCIAL COUNCIL—23RD *and* 24TH SESSIONS
Plenary Meetings 955, 971, 972.

E/L.753. Communication from delegation of USSR.
E/L.754, E/L.771. Communcations from delegation of China.
E/2990, E/3043. Report of President and Vice-Presidents on credentials of representatives to 23rd and 24th sessions of Council, respectively.

Commission on Human Rights, 13th session, meeting 547.
Social Commission, 11th session, meetings 261, 262, 268, 275.
Commission on Status of Women, 11th session, meeting 231.
Commission on Narcotic Drugs, 12th session, meeting 332.
Commission on International Commodity Trade, 5th session, meeting 71.
Economic Commission for Asia and Far East, 13th session, meeting 169; Committee on Industry and Trade (ECAFE), 9th session, meeting 125.
Council Committee on Non-Governmental Organizations, meeting 163.

TRUSTEESHIP COUNCIL, meetings 784, 836.

CHAPTER XII

QUESTIONS RELATING TO SOUTHERN AFRICA

THE QUESTION OF RACE CONFLICT IN THE UNION OF SOUTH AFRICA

In a letter dated 6 August 1957, the representatives of Bolivia, Costa Rica, Egypt, India, Indonesia, Liberia, Sudan and Uruguay asked that the question of race conflict in the Union of South Africa resulting from the Union Government's *apartheid* policies be placed on the agenda for the General Assembly's twelfth session. On 3 September 1957, Ceylon joined them in making this request.

The letter noted that, in disregard of the last Assembly resolution on the subject (1016(XI), of 30 January 1957), the Union Government had continued to adopt legislative and other

measures in implementation of its declared policy of *apartheid*. In these circumstances, the letter concluded, the Assembly would undoubtedly wish to give the matter its renewed consideration in order to prevent further deterioration of the situation and to bring about a settlement in accordance with the provisions of the United Nations Charter.

In the course of the discussion of this request in the General Committee, and later in the General Assembly itself, the representative of the Union of South Africa once again objected to the inclusion of the item in the agenda. He referred to the detailed statement on the matter made at the previous session by the South African Minister of External Affairs and to the action taken by his Government after the inscription of the item on the agenda for that session (i.e., to maintain only a token representation in the future at meetings of the Assembly and at United Nations Headquarters). The South African representative confined his participation in the proceedings at the twelfth session to a formal protest against the continued intervention of the United Nations in the domestic affairs of South Africa.

On 20 September 1957, on the recommendation of its General Committee, the Assembly decided to place the item on its agenda. It did so by a roll-call vote of 64 to 8, with 9 abstentions.

The question was referred to the Special Political Committee which considered it between 21 October and 1 November 1957.

During the general debate, the representative of India reviewed the relevant legislative measures recently enacted or proposed by the South African Government. She drew attention to three measures in particular. One was the 1957 Separate University Education Bill, the object of which was to enforce segregation on racial lines in the universities and to subject the higher education of African students to complete Government control. The second was the 1957 Native Laws Amendment Bill, which was designed to reduce social contacts between Africans and members of other groups to a minimum, and which could prohibit Africans from attending church services or functions within any urban area other than a native residential area. The Bill also authorized the Minister of Native Affairs to prohibit Africans from attending schools, hospitals and places of public entertainment. The third measure referred to by the Indian representative was the 1957 Nursing Act, which provided for segregation in the nursing profession.

As further evidence of the policy pursued by the Union Government in disregard of human rights, the representative of India cited the arrest in December 1956 of 140 persons on alleged charges of treason.

The failure of the South African Government to conform to its obligations under the Charter, she added, had compelled India to join with other Member States in bringing the matter to the Assembly's attention each year.

Discussion in the Special Political Committee broadly reflected the division of opinion which had revealed itself at the Assembly's eleventh session. However, several delegations—Argentina and Canada, for instance—took a somewhat different view of certain aspects of the matter from that taken by them at the previous session.

The majority of representatives who participated in the debate at the twelfth session maintained that the United Nations was competent to consider the question of race conflict in South Africa. That competence, they said, derived both from the Charter provisions dealing with human rights and fundamental freedoms and from the fact that the Assembly had considered the matter since 1952. Furthermore, the Assembly had repeatedly adopted resolutions condemning the racial policies pursued by the Union Government and calling upon it to reconsider its position and revise its policies in the light of its obligations under the Charter. The United Nations thus properly concerned itself with a situation arising from a policy of deliberate violation by a single Government of the universally recognized principle of respect for human rights and of that Government's continued failure to heed the Assembly's recommendations.

The representatives of Bulgaria, Hungary, Romania, the USSR, Yugoslavia and others thought that the United Nations should deal with the question of race conflict in South Africa because the *apartheid* policy pursued by the Union Government compromised its relations with other countries and thus endangered peace in that part of the world. Referred to in this regard were the implications of the *apartheid* policy in respect of developments on the African continent such as the emergence of new independent States. There was a possibility that the situation might degenerate into one threatening international peace.

Opinion was considerably divided on the question of the action which the Assembly could properly and effectively take in order to discharge its responsibility in the matter and promote respect for human rights.

Some representatives stressed the need for the Assembly to condemn the *apartheid* policy because it constituted a manifest violation of the provisions laid down in the Charter, the principles embodied in the Universal Declaration of Human Rights and the terms of previous Assembly resolutions. They thought the Assembly should take this stand regardless of the apparent failure of its previous resolutions on the matter to produce results.

Others, emphasizing the moral influence which the Assembly's resolutions were bound to exert in the field of human rights, believed that there was merit in the reiteration of universally recognized principles. Several representatives felt that failure by the Assembly to perform an act of conscience, as represented by the adoption of a resolution, would injure the United Nations much more than the repeated failure of its resolutions to bring about a settlement.

Some representatives who favoured the adoption of a resolution as evidence of the continued concern of the United Nations with the question of race conflict in South Africa, nevertheless had doubts as to the wisdom of resorting once more to a policy of condemnation, particularly in face of South Africa's virtual withdrawal from the Assembly. The Assembly, they suggested, might instead embark more profitably upon a policy of conciliation and persuasion, which might encourage the Union Government to reconsider its position. The representative of Syria suggested, for example, that the United Nations might request the assistance of three winners of the Nobel Peace Prize, Dr. Ralph Bunche, Dr. Albert Schweitzer and Mr. Lester B. Pearson, in an effort to further the solution of the problem. Another suggestion was that the Secretariat might be asked to prepare a factual report on developments in South Africa and report annually to the General Assembly.

The representatives of Australia, Belgium and the United Kingdom were against retaining the item on the Assembly's agenda. While conceding that the United Nations undoubtedly had the duty to promote respect for human rights, they maintained that it was specifically precluded from passing resolutions reflecting on the domestic policies of Member States, however objectionable those policies might be to other Members.

Agreeing with this point, the representatives of Argentina, Canada, New Zealand, Peru, Spain, the United States and others questioned the propriety or desirability of adopting new resolutions on the matter. While they agreed that it was within the scope of the responsibility of the United Nations to set general standards of conduct which Member States should strive to attain, they observed that Article 2, paragraph 7, of the Charter limited the authority of the United Nations with regard to promoting respect for human rights and fundamental freedoms. (This paragraph of the Charter, among other things, precludes United Nations intervention in matters essentially within the domestic jurisdiction of a State.) The United Nations, they argued, were not endowed with powers to indicate specific measures with regard to a given situation. Further, the record of the United Nations in dealing with race conflict in South Africa was not an encouraging one. Little, if anything, had been contributed towards improving the situation in the Union. The Union Government had withdrawn from the Assembly, and the prestige of the Organization had not been enhanced.

Under the circumstances, the representative of Argentine suggested the Assembly should seek to clarify the legal issue of competence through the International Court of Justice. The representatives of Canada, New Zealand and the United States thought it better to adopt a resolution of a general nature designed to remind all Member States of their obligations under the Charter in respect of the observance of human rights.

On 4 November 1957, the Special Political Committee adopted, by a roll-call vote of 59 to 5, with 10 abstentions, a draft resolution on the question, sponsored by 30 members. On 26 November, this resolution was approved at a plenary meeting of the Assembly by a roll-call vote of 59 to 6, with 14 abstentions, as resolution 1178(XII).

The Assembly thereby deplored the fact that the South African Government had not yet responded to the Assembly's call of 30 January 1957 under resolution 1016(XI), to "reconsider its position and revise its policies in the light of its obligations and responsibilites under the Charter and in the light of the principles subscribed to and the progress achieved in other contemporary multi-racial societies". It also deplored the fact that the Union had not yet responded to its invitation of 30 January 1957 for the Union Government "to co-operate in a constructive approach to this question, more particularly by its presence in the United Nations". It again drew the attention of the Union Government to the terms of the resolution of 30 January 1957. The Assembly also appealed to the Union Government in the interests of the common observance by United Nations Members of the high principles and purposes enshrined in the Charter (to which the Union Government had also subscribed and was as much committed as any other Member), to revise its policy in the light of

those principles and purposes and of world opinion, and to inform the Secretary-General of its response.

The 30 countries originally sponsoring the resolution adopted by the Assembly on 26 November 1957 were Afghanistan, Bolivia, Burma, Ceylon, Costa Rica, Ecuador, Egypt, Ethiopia, Ghana, Greece, Haiti, India, Indonesia, Iran, Iraq, Ireland, Jordan, Laos, Liberia, Libya, Morocco, Nepal, Pakistan, the Philippines, Saudi Arabia, Sudan, Syria, Tunisia, Uruguay, Yemen.

DOCUMENTARY REFERENCES

GENERAL ASSEMBLY—12TH SESSION
Plenary Meetings 682, 723.
General Committee, meeting 111.
Special Political Committee, meetings 50-57.

A/3628 and Add.1. Letter of 6 August 1957 from Permanent Representatives of Bolivia, Costa Rica, Egypt, India, Indonesia, Liberia, Sudan and Uruguay, and letter of 3 September 1957 from Permanent Representative of Ceylon, requesting inclusion of following item in agenda of 12th Assembly session "Question of race conflict in South Africa resulting from the policies of *apartheid* of the Government of the Union of South Africa".
A/3670. First report of General Committee.
Item, as recommended by General Committee, A/3670, placed on agenda by Assembly on 20 September 1957, plenary meeting 682, by roll-call vote of 64 to 8, with 9 abstentions, as follows:
In favour: Afghanistan, Albania, Bolivia, Brazil, Bulgaria, Burma, Byelorussian SSR, Cambodia, Ceylon, Chile, China, Colombia, Costa Rica, Cuba, Czechoslovakia, Denmark, Ecuador, Egypt, El Salvador, Ethiopia, Ghana, Greece, Guatemala, Haiti, Honduras, Hungary, Iceland, India, Indonesia, Iran, Iraq, Ireland, Israel, Japan, Laos, Lebanon, Liberia, Libya, Federation of Malaya, Mexico, Morocco, Nepal, Nicaragua, Norway, Pakistan, Panama, Paraguay, Peru, Philippines, Poland, Romania, Saudi Arabia, Sudan, Sweden, Syria, Thailand, Tunisia, Ukrainian SSR, USSR, United States, Uruguay, Venezuela, Yemen, Yugoslavia.
Against: Australia, Belgium, France, Luxembourg, Portugal, Spain, Union of South Africa, United Kingdom.
Abstaining: Argentina, Austria, Canada, Dominican Republic, Finland, Italy, Netherlands, New Zealand, Turkey.
A/SPC/L.18 and Add.1, 2. Afghanistan, Bolivia, Burma, Ceylon, Costa Rica, Ecuador, Egypt, Ethiopia, Ghana, Greece, Haiti, India, Indonesia, Iran, Iraq, Ireland, Jordan, Laos, Liberia, Libya, Morocco, Nepal, Pakistan, Philippines, Saudi Arabia, Sudan, Syria, Tunisia, Uruguay, Yemen

draft resolution, adopted by Special Political Committee, by roll-call vote of 59 to 5, with 10 abstentions, as follows:
In favour: Afghanistan, Albania, Austria, Bolivia, Brazil, Bulgaria, Burma, Byelorussian SSR, Cambodia, Ceylon, Chile, China, Colombia, Costa Rica, Cuba Czechoslovakia, Denmark, Ecuador, Egypt, Ethiopia, Ghana, Greece, Guatemala, Haiti, Hungary, Iceland, India, Indonesia, Iran, Iraq, Ireland, Israel, Japan, Jordan, Laos, Liberia, Libya, Federation of Malaya, Mexico, Morocco, Nepal, Norway, Pakistan, Panama, Philippines, Poland, Romania, Saudi Arabia, Sudan, Sweden, Syria, Thailand, Tunisia, Ukrainian SSR, USSR, Uruguay, Venezuela, Yemen, Yugoslavia.
Against: Australia,* Belgium, France, Portugal, United Kingdom.
Abstaining: Argentina, Canada, Dominican Republic, Finland, Italy, Netherlands, New Zealand, Peru, Spain, United States.
A/3722. Report of Special Political Committee.
RESOLUTION 1178(XII), as recommended by Special Political Committee, A/3722, adopted by Assembly on 26 November 1957, meeting 723, by roll-call vote of 59 to 6, with 14 abstentions, as follows:
In favour: Afghanistan, Albania, Bolivia, Brazil, Bulgaria, Burma, Byelorussian SSR, Cambodia, Ceylon, Chile, China, Colombia, Costa Rica, Cuba, Czechoslovakia, Denmark, Ecuador, Egypt, El Salvador, Ethiopia, Ghana, Greece, Guatemala, Haiti, Hungary, Iceland, India, Indonesia, Iran, Iraq, Ireland, Israel, Japan, Jordan, Laos, Liberia, Libya, Federation of Malaya, Mexico, Morocco, Nepal, Norway, Pakistan, Panama, Paraguay, Philippines, Poland, Romania, Saudi Arabia, Sudan, Sweden, Syria, Thailand, Tunisia, Ukrainian SSR, USSR, Uruguay, Venezuela, Yemen, Yugoslavia.
Against: Australia, Belgium, France, Luxembourg, Portugal, United Kingdom.
Abstaining: Argentina, Austria, Canada, Dominican Republic, Finland, Honduras, Italy, Netherlands, New Zealand, Nicaragua, Peru, Spain, Turkey, United States.

"*The General Assembly,*

"*Recalling* its previous resolutions, in particular resolutions 1016(XI) of 30 January 1957, on the question of race conflict in South Africa resulting from the policies of *apartheid* of the Government of the Union of South Africa,

"*Recalling in particular* paragraph 6 of its resolution 917(X) of 6 December 1955, calling upon the Government of the Union of South Africa to observe its obligations under the Charter of the United Nations,

"*Noting* that the General Assembly, in resolution 616 B (VII) of 5 December 1952, declared, *inter alia,* that governmental policies which are designed to perpetuate or increase discrimination are inconsistent with the Charter,

"*Further noting* that resolutions 395(V) of 2 December 1950, 511(VI) of 12 January 1952 and 616 A (VII) of 5 December 1952 have successively affirmed that a policy of 'racial segregation'

(*apartheid*) is necessarily based on doctrines of racial discrimination,

"1. *Deplores* that the Government of the Union of South Africa has not yet responded to the call and invitation conveyed in paragraphs 3 and 4 of General Assembly resolution 1016(XI) of 30 January 1957;

"2. *Again draws the attention* of the Government of the Union of South Africa to that resolution and, in particular, to paragraphs 3 and 4 thereof;

"3. *Appeals* to the Government of the Union of South Africa, in the interests of the common observance by Member States of the high purposes and principles enshrined in the Charter of the United Nations, to which the Government of the Union of South Africa has also subscribed and is as much committed as any other Member, to revise its policy in the light of those purposes and principles and of world opinion and to inform the Secretary-General of its response."

TREATMENT OF PEOPLE OF INDIAN ORIGIN IN THE UNION OF SOUTH AFRICA

The question of the treatment of people of Indian origin in the Union of South Africa was proposed for the agenda of the General Assembly's twelfth session by India and Pakistan.

In a letter of 16 August 1957 requesting the inclusion of the item, the representative of India recalled that, in a resolution adopted at its previous session (1015(XI)), the Assembly had urged the parties concerned to enter into negotiations to facilitate a settlement of the problem, and to report as appropriate, either jointly or separately, to the Assembly. In pursuance of that resolution, the Government of India had communicated to the Union Government its desire to enter into such negotiations with the Government of the Union of South Africa, but it had received no acknowledgement or reply to its communication. Since the Assembly's explicit wish had been frustrated while the position of persons of Indian origin in South Africa had continued to deteriorate, the Indian Government proposed to report to the Assembly at its twelfth session. It felt certain that the Assembly would wish to take further steps to implement its resolutions on the subject.

In a letter of the same day which also requested that the question be placed on the agenda, the representative of Pakistan explained that his Government had asked the Union Government to enter into negotiations, as recommended by the Assembly in resolution

1015(XI), but had received no reply. As the purposes of the Assembly's resolution had remained unfulfilled, the Government of Pakistan proposed to report on this matter to the Assembly at its twelfth session.

When the question of the inclusion of the item in the agenda was considered by the General Committee, and later by the General Assembly, the representative of the Union of South Africa once again protested that consideration of the item constituted an intervention in the domestic affairs of South Africa, in violation of the explicit provision in Article 2, paragraph 7, of the United Nations Charter. (This paragraph states, in part, that nothing in the Charter "shall authorize the United Nations to intervene in matters... essentially within the domestic jurisdiction of any State".)

On 20 September 1957, the General Assembly decided, by a roll-call vote of 63 to 2, with 16 abstentions, to include the item in its agenda. The Union of South Africa did not participate in the subsequent discussion (see also pages 98-99).

The Special Political Committee, to which the question was referred, considered it between 4 and 12 November 1957.

The Indian representative, opening the debate, recalled that the Assembly had tried, since its first session in 1946, to find a solution to the problem of the treatment of the people of Indian origin under South Africa's policy of racial discrimination. The Union Government, he said, continued in its policy of *apartheid,* contrary to the provisions of the Charter, the Universal Declaration of Human Rights, the Assembly resolutions and the international agreements entered into by India and South Africa. That policy had culminated in the Group Areas Act, which had resulted in grave injustices to the non-European population of South Africa, who included the inhabitants of Indian origin. To implement that Act, the South African authorities were now carrying out major population shifts which obliged large numbers of people to leave areas where they had long lived and worked and which entailed property losses and unemployment.

Pakistan's representative said his delegation was still prepared to explore all possible means for a peaceful settlement of the problem, including direct negotiation with the Union's representative. Responsibility for the settlement of the problem, he also believed, rested with the United Nations.

During the general debate, many references were made to the treatment of people of Indian origin being an aspect of the general policy of *apartheid* pursued by the South African Government.

The representative of China, who was among those subscribing to this view, thought there was little point in continuing to handle the question of the treatment of people of Indian origin in South Africa as a separate item now that the Assembly had, since 1952, become seized of the overriding question of *apartheid,* which concerned the treatment of all non-European racial groups in South Africa. Further, the record of the Assembly's previous efforts in dealing with the matter under consideration indicated that there was no way of solving the particular problem of the people of Indian origin in South Africa until the Union Government revised its general racial policy.

Several other representatives, though conceding that the item did in fact constitute one aspect of the *apartheid* question, insisted that it should continue to be discussed separately. This was because of its distinct history which antedated the introduction of the *apartheid* policy and existed independently of it, and also because it involved, in addition to the general problem of respect for human rights, the special rights of the Governments of India and Paki-

stan by virtue of existing international agreements.

Most representatives who participated in the debate expressly or implicitly endorsed the view that the Assembly was fully competent to deal with matters affecting human rights. Articles 1 (paragraph 3), 10, 13, 14, 55 and 56 of the United Nations Charter were cited to refute the contention that the Assembly was precluded, under Article 2, paragraph 7, from considering the item. Some representatives argued that the effect of the word "essentially" in Article 2, paragraph 7, was to limit the scope of domestic jurisdiction and to exclude those matters which the Charter deemed to be of international concern.

The representatives of Argentine, Australia, Belgium and the Dominican Republic, on the other hand, contested or had reservations about this argument.

The United States representative and others were of the opinion that the aim should be to create an atmosphere which would facilitate the resumption of negotiations between India, Pakistan and the Union of South Africa. It was therefore urged that moderate and conciliatory terms should be used in any resolution to be adopted, so as to encourage and promote a solution by negotiation.

The United Kingdom representative was not convinced by the argument that the United Nations was competent to intervene in the matter, even by discussion. He thought that the only way to solve the problem was by direct negotiation. He preferred direct talks outside the United Nations. Such talks would have more chance of success if the Assembly refrained from passing a resolution on the question.

A number of representatives maintained that the Assembly had no alternative but to reiterate its adherence to the purposes and principles of the Charter and to appeal once more to world opinion, irrespective of whether past resolutions to this effect had produced the desired results.

The representative of Peru suggested that the Assembly might meet the objections of some delegations as to its competence in the matter if it tried to bring about a settlement of the problem with the assistance of Member States not directly involved, or even with the aid of a State which was not a Member of the United

Nations. Such assistance might be acceptable to the parties concerned.

Although the idea of getting neutral advice did not evoke opposition in the Committee, it elicited little response. The representative of India noted that such an approach had been unsuccessfully tried in the past.

On 12 November 1957, the Special Political Committee approved a draft resolution submitted by Iran, Mexico, the Philippines and Yugoslavia. It was subsequently adopted at a plenary meeting of the Assembly on 26 November as resolution 1179(XII).

Noting thereby that the Governments of both India and Pakistan had reiterated their readiness to pursue negotiations with the Government of the Union of South Africa, the Assembly noted with regret that the Union Government had not agreed to carry forward the purposes of resolution 1015(XI) of 30 January 1957. It appealed to the Union Government to participate in negotiations with the Governments of India and Pakistan, with a view to solving the problem of the treatment of people of Indian origin in South Africa, in accordance with the purposes and principles of the Charter and the Universal Declaration of Human Rights. It also invited the parties concerned to report as appropriate, jointly or separately, to the Assembly on the progress of the negotiations.

The vote for this resolution in the Special Political Committee, following a paragraph-by-paragraph vote, was 63 to 0, with 14 abstentions, by roll-call. The vote in plenary, also by roll-call, was 64 to 0, with 15 abstentions.

DOCUMENTARY REFERENCES

GENERAL ASSEMBLY—12TH SESSION
Plenary Meetings 682, 723.
General Committee, meeting 111.
Special Political Committee, meetings 58-63.

A/3643. Letter of 16 August 1957 from Permanent Representative of India.
A/3645. Letter of 16 August 1957 from Permanent Representative of Pakistan.
Item, as recommended by General Committee, A/3670, placed on agenda by Assembly on 20 September 1957, meeting 682, by roll-call vote of 63 to 2, with 16 abstentions, as follows:
In favour: Afghanistan, Albania, Austria, Bolivia, Brazil, Bulgaria, Burma, Byelorussian SSR, Cambodia, Ceylon, Chile, Colombia, Costa Rica, Cuba, Czechoslovakia, Denmark, Ecuador, Egypt, El Salvador, Ethiopia, Ghana, Greece, Guatemala, Haiti, Honduras, Hungary, Iceland, India, Indonesia, Iran, Iraq, Ireland, Israel, Japan, Laos, Lebanon, Liberia, Libya, Federation of Malaya, Mexico, Morocco, Nepal, Norway, Pakistan, Panama, Paraguay, Peru, Philippines, Poland, Romania, Saudi Arabia, Sudan, Sweden, Syria, Thailand, Tunisia, Ukrainian SSR, USSR, United States, Uruguay, Venezuela, Yemen, Yugoslavia.
Against: France, Union of South Africa.
Abstaining: Argentina, Australia, Belgium, Canada, China, Dominican Republic, Finland, Italy, Luxembourg, Netherlands, New Zealand, Nicaragua, Portugal, Spain, Turkey, United Kingdom.
A/3670. First report of General Committee.
A/SPC/L.19. Iran, Mexico, Philippines, Yugoslavia draft resolution, adopted by Special Political Committee by roll-call vote of 63 to 0, with 14 abstentions, as follows:
In favour: Afghanistan, Albania, Austria, Bolivia, Brazil, Bulgaria, Burma, Byelorussian SSR, Cambodia, Ceylon, Chile, Colombia, Costa Rica, Cuba, Czechoslovakia, Denmark, Ecuador, Egypt, El Salvador, Ethiopia, Ghana, Greece, Guatemala, Haiti, Hungary, Iceland, India, Indonesia, Iran, Iraq, Ireland, Israel, Japan, Jordan, Laos, Lebanon, Liberia, Libya, Federation of Malaya, Mexico, Morocco, Nepal, Norway, Pakistan, Panama, Paraguay, Peru, Philippines, Poland, Romania, Saudi Arabia, Sudan, Sweden, Syria, Thailand, Tunisia, Turkey, Ukrainian SSR, USSR, United States, Uruguay, Venezuela, Yemen, Yugoslavia.
Against: None.
Abstaining: Argentina, Australia, Belgium, Canada, China, Dominican Republic, Finland, France, Italy, Netherlands, New Zealand, Portugal, Spain, United Kingdom.
A/3732. Report of Special Political Committee.
RESOLUTION 1179(XII), as recommended by Special Political Committee, A/3732, adopted by Assembly on 26 November 1957, meeting 723, by roll-call vote of 64 to 0, with 15 abstentions, as follows:
In favour: Afghanistan, Albania, Austria, Bolivia, Brazil, Bulgaria, Burma, Byelorussian SSR, Cambodia, Ceylon, Chile, Colombia, Costa Rica, Cuba, Czechoslovakia, Denmark, Ecuador, Egypt, El Salvador, Ethiopia, Ghana, Greece, Guatemala, Haiti, Honduras, Hungary, Iceland, India, Indonesia, Iran, Iraq, Ireland, Israel, Japan, Jordan, Laos, Liberia, Libya, Federation of Malaya, Mexico, Nepal, Nicaragua, Norway, Pakistan, Panama, Paraguay, Peru, Philippines, Poland, Romania, Saudi Arabia, Sudan, Sweden, Syria, Thailand, Tunisia, Turkey, Ukrainian SSR, USSR, United States, Uruguay, Venezuela, Yemen, Yugoslavia.
Against: None.
Abstaining: Argentina, Australia, Belgium, Canada, China, Dominican Republic, Finland, France, Italy, Luxembourg, Netherlands, New Zealand, Portugal, Spain, United Kingdom.

"*The General Assembly*,

"*Recalling* its resolution 1015(XI) of 30 January 1957,

"*Having considered* the reports of the Governments of India and of Pakistan,

"1. *Notes* that the Governments of both India and Pakistan have reiterated their readiness to pursue negotiations with the Government of the Union of South Africa in accordance with the expressed desires of the United Nations;

"2. *Notes with regret* that the Government of the Union of South Africa has not agreed to carry forward the purposes of General Assembly resolution 1015(XI) of 30 January 1957;

"3. *Appeals* to the Government of the Union of South Africa to participate in negotiations with the Governments of India and of Pakistan with a view to solving this problem in accordance with the purposes and principles of the United Nations Charter and the Universal Declaration of Human Rights;

"4. *Invites* the parties concerned to report to the General Assembly as appropriate, jointly or separately, regarding the progress of the negotiations."

CHAPTER XIII

THE QUESTION OF PEACEFUL CO-EXISTENCE AND PEACEFUL RELATIONS AMONG STATES

On 20 September 1957, the USSR asked, by letter, that an item entitled "Declaration concerning the peaceful co-existence of States" be placed on the agenda of the twelfth session of the General Assembly.

An explanatory memorandum attached to the letter stated that the policy of "negotiation from strength", pursued by certain States, had divided States into antagonistic military groupings. It had created a tense international situation, and intensified the threat of a new world war. It had also resulted in a serious disruption of economic relations among States, trade discrimination, and an almost complete cessation of business, scientific and cultural contacts between certain States. The situation thus created required effective measures by the United Nations to end the armaments race and to develop peaceful co-operation among States.

The proclamation of certain principles of peaceful co-existence, particularly at the Bandung Conference, had exerted a favourable influence on the development of relations among the countries recognizing these principles, the memorandum added. An appeal by the General Assembly that United Nations Members be guided in their mutual relations by these principles would improve the international situation markedly. It would strengthen the forces of peace, too, and help make the United Nations an effective instrument for the consolidation of peace.

The USSR also submitted a draft resolution with its request. By the preamble to this draft, the Assembly would note with satisfaction that many States had recently begun to base their relations with others upon the following principles: mutual respect for one another's territorial integrity and sovereignty; non-aggression; no intervention in one another's domestic affairs for any economic, political or ideological reasons; equality and mutual benefit; and peaceful co-existence. It would recognize that the application of these principles in relations among all States would be of exceptional importance in reducing international tension and extending international co-operation. By the operative paragraph of the draft, the Assembly would call upon States to be guided by these principles in their mutual relations and to settle any disputes that might arise between them solely by peaceful means.

On 1 October 1957, the General Assembly decided to include the item in the agenda and referred it to the First Committee, where it was considered between 12 and 14 December 1957.

In addition to the USSR draft resolution, the Committee had before it a draft resolution submitted by India, Sweden and Yugoslavia entitled "Peaceful and neighbourly relations among States", which had been circulated on 11 December.

By this draft, the Assembly would point out the urgency and importance of strengthening international peace and of developing peaceful and neighbourly relations among States irrespective of their divergencies or the relative stages and the nature of their political, economic and social development. The Assembly would also state the need: to promote the fundamental objectives of the Charter, which included the maintenance of international peace and security and friendly co-operation among States; to develop, in conformity with the Charter, peaceful and tolerant relations among States on the basis of mutual respect and benefit, non-aggression, respect for each other's sovereignty, equality and territorial integrity, and non-intervention in each other's internal affairs; and to fulfil the purposes and principles of the Charter. Further, the Assembly would recognize the need to broaden international co-operation, reduce tensions, and settle differences and disputes by peaceful means. By the operative part of the three-power draft, the Assembly would call upon all States to make every effort to strengthen international peace, and to develop friendly and co-operative relations and to settle disputes by peaceful means as enjoined in the Charter and as set forth in the draft resolution.

The ensuing debate centred largely on the reasons for the existing tension in international affairs and on means to relieve it. There was general agreement on the need for peaceful and harmonious relations among States. But opinion was divided on how to achieve this, on the utility and wisdom of the Assembly's restating principles already set forth in the Charter, as well as on the steps needed to give effect to the principle of peaceful co-existence. In this connexion there was discussion on the relationship between peaceful co-existence and the principle of respect for the territorial integrity and sovereignty of States.

There was much discussion on conduct not consonant with the principle of respect for the territorial integrity and sovereignty of States.

The representatives of the USSR and of some other Members contended that the Western countries, led by the United States, were trying to impose their will upon other nations— particularly the peoples of Asia and Africa who had recently emerged from a colonial régime— by means of colonial systems of exploitation and by the employment of force or the threat of force, as in the Middle East, when the internal régime or foreign policy of a country did not suit them. Under the guise of anti-communism, they had adopted aggressive monopolist policies of world domination aimed at acquisition and control of the sources of raw materials. Concomitants were: the establishment of military bases on foreign soil and of various regional military organizations; efforts to undermine and subvert socialist States, as in Hungary; and unwillingness to agree to the reduction of armed forces and the abolition of atomic weapons.

The representative of the United States and several other Members maintained that a tyrannical rule far worse than old-fashioned colonialism had been imposed by the USSR policies of infiltrating and subverting non-Soviet countries and of dominating sovereign States in Eastern Europe since 1939. More than any other country in the world, the USSR devoted its energies to the armaments race and sought to resolve its differences with others by means of force, as in Hungary, or the threat of force, as it had done in 1957 against 22 countries, including the United States.

The representative of Ceylon observed that the fear of a nation for its territorial integrity was not always the result of threats of violence and aggression. It might well be engendered by what were sometimes termed defensive alliances built around that nation. However defensive such alliances might be in origin or character, they hardly made for the peace and security of the nations surrounded by them. This last point was also supported by the representatives of Egypt, Indonesia, Saudi Arabia and Yugoslavia, among others.

As to the means of achieving peaceful coexistence, the USSR representative observed that the international situation, marked by the emergence of antagonistic military groupings, had been worsened by the race in the production of armaments for mass destruction. The USSR sought peaceful relations and constructive co-operation with all States, whatever their political and social systems. The success of the Allied coalition during the Second World War had shown that socialist and capitalist countries could co-operate successfully. Joint efforts, he said, must be made to avert another war.

The USSR was prepared to apply the principles of peaceful co-existence as the only basis for relations among States, especially between the United States and the USSR. It advocated the following steps: conclusion of an agreement of friendship and co-operation between the United States and the USSR; cessation of the current propaganda which created suspicion and distrust; restoration of normal economic, cultural and scientific relations between the two powers; conclusion of a disarmament agreement and a provisional undertaking by the United Kingdom, the USSR and the United States not to use nuclear weapons and to suspend tests of such weapons as of 1 January 1958 for a period of two or three years; a special régime of nuclear disarmament in Central Europe; a non-aggression pact between the countries of the North Atlantic Treaty Organization (NATO) and those of the Warsaw Treaty Organization; non-interference in the domestic affairs of States in the Near and Middle East; and a commitment not to use force in the settlement of questions arising in that area.

The United States representative envisaged the question as one of the building of peaceful relations among States on the basis of peaceful behaviour rather than words. He, too, stressed the need for wider economic, scientific and cultural contacts between States, and for disarmament, and expressed the hope that the Soviet Union would co-operate with the United Nations Disarmament Commission in fruitful discussions.

He noted that there was an appreciable gap between the professions and practices of the Soviet Union. Most of the propaganda which engendered mutual distrust originated in the USSR, which devoted more of its resources to the armaments race than perhaps any other country in the world. The phrase "peaceful co-existence", which had been successively used by Lenin, Stalin and Khrushchev, was merely a temporary tactical instrument in the Soviet communist struggle for world conquest. Hence, the United States would not agree that a system of peaceful co-existence could be achieved by words alone.

The United Kingdom representative noted that the principles in the USSR draft resolution were contained in the Charter and were, as such, unexceptionable. The difficulty with the USSR draft resolution, however, lay in the phrase "peaceful co-existence". Soviet policy since the war had shown that, to the USSR the phrase meant the opposite of what countries

desiring to practice tolerance and to live together as good neighbours thought it to mean. In addition, the USSR proposal was incomplete. It made no mention of the principles of justice and respect for international law contained in Article 1 of the Charter. Nor did it mention the idea of tolerance. These references, however, were included in the three-power draft resolution, which had the advantage also of leaving no doubt about the meaning attributed by the sponsors to the words they used.

In reply, the USSR representative said that an objective appraisal of the facts would show who was in favour of peace and who was against it. To the Soviet Union, "peaceful co-existence" meant not a phase but a cardinal principle of his country's foreign policy followed since the earliest days of the Soviet State when it had been first enunciated by Lenin.

Other representatives holding similar views maintained that only a policy of peaceful co-existence would prevent the holocaust of an atomic war, whereas armed co-existence, preventing the expansion of a peace zone, was fraught with immeasurable dangers for mankind.

The representative of Colombia who favoured the three-power draft held that the principle of co-existence as implied by the USSR was a venerable one and comprised the essence of international law. Moreover, the USSR version disassociated the principle from the Charter which it thus tended to supplant. He noted that the USSR appealed for peace at the same time that its instrument of permanent intervention in the political affairs of other States issued a call to war.

Some representatives found declarations of the kind proposed for adoption redundant since the Charter formulated these ideas better, more directly and more completely. Preferring a formulation in the language of the Charter which provided peaceful means for settling all disputes, the representatives of China, Peru, the Philippines and others warned against the danger that the idea of co-existence might will people into a false sense of security.

Others, however, thought it important to have a periodic re-affirmation of the Charter principles and thought circumstances were appropriate for this.

The representatives of the Byelorussian SSR,

Japan, Mexico, Poland and the Ukrainian SSR maintained that the need to re-affirm the purposes and principles of the Charter was particularly opposite in particular circumstances. The representative of the Ukrainian SSR observed also that a declaration on peaceful co-existence would not supplant the Charter, but would constitute a practical application thereof. There was no basis for the idea that the principles of peaceful co-existence involved a kind of compulsory neutrality aimed at destroying the Western world.

The representative of India said that the utility of the principles under discussion was shown by their inclusion in the Charter of the Organization of American States and in declarations signed by some 20 countries of Asia, Africa, Europe and America.

The representative of Syria thought that the USSR text stressed matters not emphasized enough in the Charter. Ceylon's representative considered that the USSR statement on the principle of mutual respect for the territorial integrity and sovereignty of States was an improvement on Article 2 of the Charter.

The representative of Sweden had some doubts as to the value of the Assembly's adopting the five principles in the USSR draft resolution. No problem would arise in accepting the principle of peaceful co-existence if all agreed that it meant recognition of the right of States to preserve their different political and ideological systems without outside interference. He thought, however, that the drafting of a declaration supplementing the Charter in this sense might present difficulty. The real value of a resolution on the subject lay in its acceptability to the principal powers, a requirement basic to the wording of the three-power draft resolution.

The representative of India noted a general desire to implement the purposes and principles of the Charter in more concrete terms. Many States—including the United States, the United Kingdom, the USSR and India—had on various occasions subscribed to the principles contained in the three-power draft resolution. These principles, he said, formed the basis of India's success in establishing friendly relations with countries of entirely different persuasions and divergent systems.

The three-power draft resolution was not an attempt at a limitative restatement of the purposes of the Charter, he pointed out. Its value lay in the indication of the correct way of approach to the deeds on which others had laid stress. Account had been taken of the views expressed in the First Committee, he added, by formulating the five principles somewhat differently from the USSR draft so as to go beyond the concept of merely existing side by side, for, as the representative of Peru had observed, it was necessary to do more than simply to co-exist.

Many representatives, in addition to warning against the false sense of security which might be engendered by unguarded trust in peaceful co-existence, stressed the need to make explicit the requirements for safe reliance on such a principle.

The representatives of Burma, Finland and Greece interpreted co-existence as the maintenance of friendly relations between sovereign States having different political, economic and social systems. Their respective relations with the USSR, the People's Republic of China and Yugoslavia were cited as examples.

The representative of Saudi Arabia maintained that the principle of peaceful co-existence did not apply to an ideology which was characterized by expansion and aggression. As for neighbourly relations among States, the concept of statehood had to be defined, for a declaration of the kind under discussion could apply only to States born in legitimacy, within their right, and in their own territory.

The representative of Israel supported the three-power draft resolution and regarded it as a commitment to respect the sovereignty, independence and integrity of all States, without exception, and to apply the principles of the Charter to all States, irrespective of historical controversies.

Yugoslavia's representative held that genuine peaceful co-existence involved constant practical efforts to dispel misunderstandings, increase confidence, reduce armaments and settle the problems at the root of difficulties. As did the representatives of Iraq and Peru, he believed that co-existence required co-operative efforts to develop and use the human and material resources of the world.

The representative of Iran, pointing out that his country had for two centuries endured the consequences of "cold war" and co-existence between the British and Russian Empires, said that non-intervention in the internal affairs of other States called for true and sincere mutual respect. Subversion, though not accompanied by force from without, should be dealt with as an act of aggression. Prerequisites for truly peaceful co-existence were: the will of the large and the small powers to abide by their obligations honestly and meticulously; and co-operation, based on well-defined principles recognized and respected by all.

On 14 December 1957, at the request of the representative of India and with the agreement of the USSR representative, the joint draft resolution was put to the vote first. The USSR representative thought that his draft resolution was more definite and logical than the joint draft resolution, but found nothing unacceptable in the three-power draft which expressed the same ideas.

The three-power draft resolution was then adopted by the First Committee by a roll-call vote of 75 to 0, with 1 abstention. The USSR did not press for a vote on its draft resolution.

The draft resolution recommended by the Committee was adopted at a plenary meeting of the Assembly on 14 December 1957 by a roll-call vote of 77 to 0, with 1 abstention, as resolution 1236(XII).

DOCUMENTARY REFERENCES

GENERAL ASSEMBLY—12TH SESSION
Plenary Meetings 697, 731.
General Committee, meeting 113.
First Committee, meetings 935-940.

A/3673. Letter of 20 September 1957, containing draft resolution, from Chairman of delegation of USSR requesting inclusion of following item in agenda of 12th Assembly session: Declaration concerning peaceful co-existence of States.

A/C.1/L.198. India, Sweden, Yugoslavia draft resolution adopted by First Committee by roll-call vote of 75 to 0, with 1 abstention as follows:
In favour: Afghanistan, Albania, Argentina, Australia, Austria, Belgium, Bolivia, Brazil, Bulgaria, Burma, Byelorussian SSR, Cambodia, Canada, Chile, Colombia, Costa Rica, Cuba, Czechoslovakia, Denmark, Dominican Republic, Ecuador, Egypt, El Salvador, Ethiopia, Finland, France, Ghana, Greece, Guatemala, Honduras, Hungary, Iceland, India, Indonesia, Iran, Iraq, Ireland, Israel, Italy, Japan, Jordan, Laos, Lebanon, Liberia, Libya, Luxembourg, Federation of Malaya, Mexico, Nepal, Netherlands, New Zealand, Nicaragua, Norway, Pakistan, Panama, Peru, Philippines, Poland, Portugal, Romania, Saudi Arabia, Spain, Sudan, Sweden, Syria, Thailand, Tunisia, Ukrainian SSR, USSR, United Kingdom, United States, Uruguay, Venezuela, Yemen, Yugoslavia.
Against: None.
Abstaining: China.

A/3802. Report of First Committee.

RESOLUTION 1236(XII), as recommended by First Committee, A/3802, adopted by Assembly on 14 December 1957, meeting 731, by roll-call vote of 77 to 0,[1] with 1 abstention as follows:
In favour: Afghanistan, Albania, Argentina, Australia, Austria, Belgium, Bolivia, Brazil, Bulgaria, Burma, Byelorussian SSR, Cambodia, Canada, Ceylon, Chile, Colombia, Costa Rica, Czechoslovakia, Denmark, Dominican Republic, Ecuador, Egypt, El Salvador, Ethiopia, Finland, France, Ghana, Greece, Guatemala, Haiti, Honduras, Hungary, Iceland, India, Indonesia, Iran, Iraq, Ireland, Israel, Italy, Japan, Jordan, Laos, Liberia, Libya, Luxembourg, Federation of Malaya, Mexico, Nepal, Netherlands, New Zealand, Nicaragua, Norway, Pakistan, Panama, Paraguay, Peru, Philippines, Poland, Portugal, Romania, Saudi Arabia, Spain, Sudan, Sweden, Syria, Thailand, Tunisia, Turkey, Ukrainian SSR, USSR, United Kingdom, United States, Uruguay, Venezuela, Yemen, Yugoslavia.
Against: None.
Abstaining: China.

"The General Assembly,

"Considering the urgency and the importance of strengthening international peace and of developing peaceful and neighbourly relations among States irrespective of their divergences or the relatives stages and nature of their political, economic and social development,

"Recalling that among the fundamental objectives of the Charter of the United Nations are the maintenance of international peace and security and friendly co-operation among States,

"Realizing the need to promote these objectives and to develop peaceful and tolerant relations among States, in conformity with the Charter, based on mutual respect and benefit, non-aggression, respect for each other's sovereignty, equality and territorial integrity and non-intervention in one another's internal affairs, and to fulfil the purposes and principles of the Charter,

"Recognizing the need to broaden international co-operation, to reduce tensions and to settle differences and disputes among States by peaceful means,

"Calls upon all States to make every effort to strengthen international peace, and to develop friendly and co-operative relations and settle disputes by peaceful means as enjoined in the Charter of the United Nations and as set forth in the present resolution."

[1] The representatives of Cuba and Lebanon, who were absent when the vote was taken, subsequently intimated that they had intended to vote in favour of the draft resolution.

CHAPTER XIV

THE ADMISSION OF NEW MEMBERS

ADMISSION OF THE FEDERATION OF MALAYA

By cablegram dated 31 August 1957, the Prime Minister and Minister of External Affairs of the Federation of Malaya submitted his country's application for admission to membership in the United Nations, as well as a declaration of acceptance of the membership obiligation set out in the United Nations Charter.

On 1 September 1957, Australia and the United Kingdom requested an early meeting of the Security Council to consider the question of the admission of the Federation of Malaya. On the following day, they submitted a joint draft resolution calling for a recommendation for its admission. This was adopted unanimously on 5 September 1957, all the members of the Council welcoming the application.

The Security Council's recommendation was considered by the General Assembly at the opening meeting of its twelfth session on 17 September. The Assembly unanimously adopted a resolution (1134(XII)) by roll-call to admit the Federation of Malaya. It did so by approving a draft resolution sponsored by Australia, Canada, Ceylon, Ghana, India, New Zealand, Pakistan and the United Kingdom.

APPLICATIONS OF REPUBLIC OF KOREA, DEMOCRATIC PEOPLE'S REPUBLIC OF KOREA, VIET-NAM, MONGOLIAN PEOPLE'S REPUBLIC

CONSIDERATION BY SECURITY COUNCIL

On 9 September 1957, Australia, China, Colombia, Cuba, France, the Philippines, the United Kingdom and the United States submitted a joint draft resolution to the Security Council recommending the admission of the Republic of Korea to membership in the United Nations. The USSR representative submitted an amendment by which the Council would recommend that the Democratic People's Republic of Korea and the Republic of Korea be admitted to membership simultaneously.

The same eight members of the Council who submitted the draft resolution on membership for the Republic of Korea also proposed another one whereby the Council would recommend the admission of Viet-Nam.

The USSR submitted yet another draft resolution, recommending the admission of the Mongolian People's Republic.

Most Council members supported the two eight-power draft resolutions. The General Assembly, various representatives pointed out, had repeatedly expressed its support for the admission of the Republic of Korea and Viet-Nam.

One point made against the USSR proposal for the simultaneous admission of North and South Korea was that the Assembly had recognized the Government of the Republic of Korea as the only lawful Government in Korea. In contrast, the North Korean régime had repeatedly demonstrated flagrant disregard of the United Nations. The USSR representative, on the other hand, emphasized that the Democratic People's Republic of Korea fully met the requirements of Article 4 of the Charter. The only possible way to solve the question of the admission of Korea at that time was to recommend that the two parts of the country be admitted simultaneously.

The USSR amendment, however, was rejected by 9 votes to 1 (USSR), with 1 abstention (Sweden).

The joint draft resolution on the Republic of Korea's application received 10 votes in favour and 1 against (USSR). It was not adopted since the negative vote had been cast by a permanent member of the Council.

As to Viet-Nam's application, the USSR representative proposed that consideration of the question of Viet-Nam's admission be postponed until that country had been unified. In doing so, he pointed out that the elections provided for in the Geneva Agreements of 1954 for unifying Viet-Nam had not yet been held. Other Council members, however, were against the USSR motion.

The USSR motion to postpone consideration of Viet-Nam's application was rejected by 10 votes to 1 (USSR). The joint draft resolution on Viet-Nam's application received 10 votes. The USSR voted against it. As this was the negative vote of a permanent member of the Council, the draft resolution was not adopted.

In urging membership for the Mongolian People's Republic, the USSR representative recalled that the Assembly had supported its admission in 1955. It remained a victim of a policy of discrimination, though there was no question that it fully met all the requirements of the Charter for membership.

Several representatives, however, opposed the USSR draft resolution, saying that the Mongolian People's Republic was neither a State nor independent. Others, having serious doubts about the qualifications of the Mongolian People's Republic, said that they would abstain in the voting on that proposal.

The USSR draft resolution to recommend admission of the Mongolian People's Republic was rejected by 5 votes against, to 2 in favour (Sweden, USSR), with 4 abstentions (Australia, France, Iraq, the United Kingdom).

The voting on the draft resolutions and amendments took place on 9 September 1957.

CONSIDERATION BY GENERAL ASSEMBLY

On 9 September 1957, the Security Council submitted a special report to the twelfth General Assembly session on its consideration of the question of admission of new Members. The Assembly, on 20 September, decided to place this question on its agenda, and referred it to its Special Political Committee, where it was considered at six meetings held between 10 and 17 October.

Three draft resolutions were submitted to the Special Political Committee.

Thirteen members—Australia, Chile, Colombia, Costa Rica, France, Iraq, Italy, Japan, the Netherlands, New Zealand, the Philippines, the United Kingdom and the United States—sponsored a joint draft resolution whereby the Assembly, recalling previous resolutions, finding the Republic of Korea qualified for membership, and noting with regret the continued inability of the Security Council to recommend admission of the Republic of Korea owing to the negative vote of a permanent member of the Council, would reaffirm that the Republic of Korea was fully qualified for membership in the United Nations.

The same 13 Members submitted a draft resolution providing for a similar reaffirmation about Viet-Nam.

The third draft resolution was submitted by India and Indonesia. By this, the General Assembly, considering that the question of admission of new Members required further examination, would (1) decide to transmit the relevant records and the proposals made during the Assembly's twelfth session to the Security Council, and (2) ask the Council to consider all applications for admission.

Most speakers in the discussions on these proposals supported the two 13-power draft resolutions. They deplored the failure of the Security Council, owing to the opposition of the USSR representative, to recommend admission of the Republic of Korea and of Viet-Nam, both of which, in their view, met the Charter requirements for membership.

Several representatives, however, were opposed to these two draft resolutions. Both the Democratic People's Republic of Korea and the Republic of Korea, they urged, should be admitted. They also wanted consideration of Viet-Nam's admission to be postponed until after the general elections stipulated in the Geneva Agreements had been held. In addition, they regretted the continued exclusion of the Mongolian People's Republic from membership, which they ascribed to the fact that its political régime was viewed with disfavour by the United States and its supporters.

A number of representatives indicated their intention of abstaining in the voting on the two 13-power draft resolutions. Apart from the questionable effects of admission of one part of a divided country on the problem of unification, they contended, resolutions of a declaratory nature were unlikely to produce a solution.

On 17 October, the Indian representative asked that the draft resolution submitted by India and Indonesia be voted upon first. The Committee agreed to this by 35 votes to 7, with 31 abstentions. The joint Indian-Indonesian draft resolution was then voted upon in part. The second operative paragraph, to ask the Security Council to consider all applications for membership, was rejected. The remainder of the draft, however, was approved. The Indian-Indonesian draft resolution, thus amended, was then voted on. It was rejected by a roll-call vote of 37 to 33, with 10 abstentions.

The 13-power joint draft resolution on the Republic of Korea was approved by a roll-call vote of 51 to 9, with 20 abstentions. The second 13-power joint draft resolution, on Viet-Nam, was approved by a roll-call vote of 49 to 9, with 22 abstentions.

The resolution, on the Republic of Korea, was finally adopted at a plenary meeting of the Assembly on 25 October, by 51 votes to 9, with 21 abstentions, as resolution 1144 A (XII). That on Viet-Nam was approved in plenary by 49 votes to 9, with 23 abstentions, as resolution 1144 B (XII).

DOCUMENTARY REFERENCES

ADMISSION OF FEDERATION OF MALAYA

SECURITY COUNCIL, meeting 786.

S/3872. Cablegram of 31 August 1957 from Prime Minister and Minister for External Affairs of Federation of Malaya.
S/3874. Letter of 1 September 1957 from Alternate Representative of Australia and Acting Permanent Representative of United Kingdom.
S/3876. Australia and United Kingdom draft resolution.
S/3882. Resolution, as submitted by Australia and United Kingdom, S/3876, adopted unanimously by Security Council on 5 September 1957, meeting 786.

"*The Security Council,*
"*Having examined* the application of the Federation of Malaya for membership in the United Nations,
"*Recommends* to the General Assembly that the Federation of Malaya be admitted to membership in the United Nations."

GENERAL ASSEMBLY—12TH SESSION
Plenary Meeting 678.

A/3652. Cable of 31 August 1957 from Prime Minister and Minister for External Affairs of Federation of Malaya.
A/3654. Letter of 5 September 1957 from President of Security Council, containing recommendation of Council.
A/3655 and Rev.1. Australia, Canada, Ceylon, Ghana, India, New Zealand, Pakistan, United Kingdom draft resolution and revision.
RESOLUTION 1134(XII), as submitted by 8 powers, A/3655/Rev.1, adopted unanimously by Assembly on 17 September 1957, meeting 678, by roll-call vote.

"*The General Assembly,*
"*Having received* the recommendation of the Security Council of 5 September 1957 that the Federation of Malaya should be admitted membership in the United Nations,
"*Having considered* the application for membership of the Federation of Malaya,
"*Decides* to admit the Federation of Malaya to membership in the United Nations."

REPUBLIC OF KOREA, DEMOCRATIC PEOPLE'S REPUBLIC OF KOREA, VIET-NAM, MONGOLIAN PEOPLE'S REPUBLIC

SECURITY COUNCIL, meetings 789, 790.

S/3803. Letter of 4 March 1957 from Secretary-General.
S/3880. Letter of 4 September 1957 from representative of United States concerning application of Republic of Korea for membership.
S/3884. Australia, China, Colombia, Cuba, France, Philippines, United Kingdom, United States draft resolution, recommending membership for Republic of Korea.
S/3887. USSR amendment to joint draft resolution, S/3884.
S/3881. Letter of 4 September 1957 from Representative of United States concerning application for membership of Viet-Nam.
S/3885. Australia, China, Colombia, Cuba, France, Philippines, United Kingdom, United States draft resolution, recommending membership for Viet-Nam.
S/3873 and Add.1. Cables of 1 and 7 September 1957 from Foreign Minister of Mongolian People's Republic and memorandum on its application for membership.
S/3877. Letter of 3 September 1957 from USSR representative and draft resolution recommending membership for Mongolian People's Republic.

GENERAL ASSEMBLY—12TH SESSION
Plenary Meeting 709.
Special Political Committee, meetings 44-49.

A/3662. Special Report of Security Council.
A/SPC/L.15 and Add.1, 2. Australia, Chile, Colombia, Costa Rica, France, Iraq, Italy, Japan, Netherlands, New Zealand, Philippines, United Kingdom, United States draft resolution (on admission of Republic of Korea), adopted by Special Political Committee (as draft resolution A) by roll-call vote of 51 to 9, with 20 abstentions, as follows: *In favour:* Argentina, Australia, Austria, Belgium, Bolivia, Brazil, Canada, Chile, China, Colombia, Costa Rica, Cuba, Denmark, Dominican Republic, Ecuador, El Salvador, Ethiopia, France, Greece, Guatemala, Haiti, Honduras, Iceland, Iran, Iraq, Ireland, Israel, Italy, Japan, Jordan, Lebanon,

Liberia, Luxembourg, Netherlands, New Zealand, Nicaragua, Norway, Pakistan, Panama, Paraguay, Peru, Philippines, Portugal, Spain, Sweden, Thailand, Turkey, United Kingdom, United States, Uruguay, Venezuela.

Against: Albania, Bulgaria, Byelorussian SSR, Czechoslovakia, Hungary, Poland, Romania, Ukrainian SSR, USSR.

Abstaining: Afghanistan, Burma, Cambodia, Ceylon, Egypt, Finland, Ghana, India, Indonesia, Libya, Federation of Malaya, Mexico, Morocco, Nepal, Saudi Arabia, Sudan, Syria, Tunisia, Yemen, Yugoslavia.

A/SPC/L.16 and Add.1, 2. Australia, Chile, Colombia, Costa Rica, France, Iraq, Italy, Japan, Netherlands, New Zealand, Philippines, United Kingdom, United States draft resolution (on admission of Viet-Nam), adopted by Special Political Committee (as draft resolution B) by roll-call vote of 49 to 9, with 22 abstentions, as follows:

In favour: Argentina, Australia, Austria, Belgium, Bolivia, Brazil, Chile, China, Colombia, Costa Rica, Cuba, Denmark, Dominican Republic, Ecuador, El Salvador, Ethiopia, France, Greece, Guatemala, Haiti, Honduras, Iceland, Iran, Iraq, Ireland, Israel, Italy, Japan, Jordan, Lebanon, Luxembourg, Netherlands, New Zealand, Nicaragua, Norway, Pakistan, Panama, Paraguay, Peru, Philippines, Portugal, Spain, Sweden, Thailand, Turkey, United Kingdom, United States, Uruguay, Venezuela.

Against: Albania, Bulgaria, Byelorussian SSR, Czechoslovakia, Hungary, Poland, Romania, Ukrainian SSR, USSR.

Abstaining: Afghanistan, Burma, Cambodia, Canada, Ceylon, Egypt, Finland, Ghana, India, Indonesia, Liberia, Libya, Federation of Malaya, Mexico, Morocco, Nepal, Saudi Arabia, Sudan, Syria, Tunisia, Yemen, Yugoslavia.

A/SPC/L.17. India and Indonesia draft resolution, rejected by roll-call vote of 37 to 33, with 10 abstentions, as follows:

In favour: Afghanistan, Albania, Bulgaria, Burma, Byelorussian SSR, Cambodia, Ceylon, Czechoslovakia, Egypt, Ethiopia, Finland, Ghana, Guatemala, Hungary, India, Indonesia, Iran, Israel, Jordan, Mexico, Morocco, Nepal, Poland, Romania, Saudi Arabia, Sudan, Sweden, Syria, Tunisia, Ukrainian SSR, USSR, Yemen, Yugoslavia.

Against: Argentina, Australia, Austria, Belgium, Brazil, Chile, China, Colombia, Costa Rica, Cuba, Denmark, Dominican Republic, El Salvador, France, Honduras, Iceland, Iraq, Italy, Japan, Liberia, Luxembourg, Netherlands, New Zealand, Nicaragua, Norway, Pakistan, Panama, Paraguay, Peru, Philippines, Portugal, Spain, Turkey, United Kingdom, United States, Uruguay, Venezuela.

Abstaining: Bolivia, Canada, Ecuador, Greece, Haiti, Ireland, Lebanon, Libya, Federation of Malaya, Thailand.

A/3712. Report of Special Political Committee (draft resolutions A and B).

RESOLUTION 1144 A and B (XII), as recommended by Special Political Committee, A/3712, adopted by Assembly on 25 October 1957, meeting 709 as follows: 1144 A (XII), by 51 votes to 9, with 21 abstentions, and 1144 B (XII), by 49 votes to 9, with 23 abstentions.

A

"The General Assembly,

"Recalling its resolutions 296 G (IV) of 22 November 1949 and 1017 A (XI) of 28 February 1957 finding the Republic of Korea qualified for membership in the United Nations,

"Noting with regret the continued inability of the Security Council to recommend the admission of the Republic of Korea to membership in the United Nations owing to the negative vote of a permanent member of the Council,

"Reaffirms that the Republic of Korea is fully qualified for and should be admitted to membership in the United Nations."

B

"The General Assembly,

"Recalling its resolutions 620 C (VII) of 21 December 1952 and 1017 B (XI) of 28 February 1957 finding Viet-Nam qualified for membership in the United Nations,

"Noting with regret the continued inability of the Security Council to recommend the admission of Viet-Nam to membership in the United Nations owing to the negative vote of a permanent member of the Council,

"Reaffirms that Viet-Nam is fully qualified for and should be admitted to membership, in the United Nations."

CHAPTER XV

QUESTIONS RELATING TO THE ORGANS OF THE UNITED NATIONS AND THE CHARTER

ARRANGEMENTS FOR CONFERENCE TO REVIEW THE UNITED NATIONS CHARTER

At its tenth session in 1955 the General Assembly decided, by resolution 992 (X), to appoint a Committee of all Members of the United Nations to consider, in consultation with the Secretary-General, the question of arrangements for a General Conference, to be held at an appropriate time, to review the Charter. The Committee was asked to report with its recommendations to the General Assembly's twelfth session.

This Committee on Arrangements for a Conference for the Purpose of Reviewing the Charter met on 3 June 1957. At the opening of its discussions, the Committee had before it a draft resolution sponsored by Brazil, Canada, Egypt, El Salvador, India, Indonesia, Ireland, Iran, Liberia and Panama. This draft resolution contained recommendations that the Committee be kept in being, that its report and recommendations be submitted to the Assembly not later than its fourteenth session, and that the Secretary-General be asked to continue the work on the preparation and publication of supplements to the *Repertory of Practice of United Nations Organs.*

Most delegations supported this draft resolution. They included some who had abstained in the vote on General Assembly resolution 992(X) (whereby the Committee was set up) on the ground that a General Conference for reviewing the Charter should not be convened unless there were prospects of general agreement on possible amendments.

Those in favour of the 10-power draft resolution felt that a review conference should take place, but that the fixing of a time and place for it should be deferred, for not more than two years, because the "appropriate time" and

"auspicious international circumstances" mentioned in resolution 992(X) had not yet materialized. They also hoped that the international climate would be more favourable in two years time, thus making it possible to set the time and place for a Charter review conference.

The representatives of the USSR, Yugoslavia, Hungary, Poland, Romania, Bulgaria, Albania, the Byelorussian SSR and the Ukrainian SSR were of the opinion that the Charter, as it stood, provided fully for the maintenance of peace, and the promotion of the political, economic and social advancement of all peoples. Any revision of the Charter, they felt, would hamper the attainment of those purposes, which could be realized if Member States fulfilled their Charter obligations. The will to make the Charter work, these delegations maintained, was more important than talking about how it ought to work.

The 10-power draft resolution was finally adopted by the Committee by 67 votes to 0, with 9 abstentions.

On 14 October, the Committee's report was taken up at a plenary meeting of the General Assembly. Before the Assembly was a draft resolution endorsing the Committee's recommendations. It was sponsored by Afghanistan, Argentina, Austria, Brazil, Canada, Egypt, El Salvador, India, Indonesia, Ireland, Liberia and Panama. The Assembly adopted it by 54 votes to 0, with 9 abstentions, as resolution 1136(XII).

DOCUMENTARY REFERENCES

GENERAL ASSEMBLY—12TH SESSION
Plenary Meeting 705.

A/AC.81/SR.1 and 2. Summary records of meetings of Committee on Arrangements for Conference for Purpose of Reviewing Charter.
A/3593. Report of Committee on Arrangements for Conference for Purpose of Reviewing Charter.
A/L.225 and Add.1. Afghanistan, Argentina, Austria, Brazil, Canada, Egypt, El Salvador, India, Indonesia, Ireland, Liberia, Panama, draft resolution.
RESOLUTION 1136(XII), as submitted by 12 powers, A/L.225 and Add.1, adopted by Assembly on 14 October 1957, meeting 705, by 54 votes to 0, with 9 abstentions.

"The General Assembly,
"Recalling the provisions of its resolution 992(X)

of 21 November 1955,
"Having considered the report of the Committee established by the above resolution,
"1. *Decides* to keep in being the Committee on arrangements for a conference for the purpose of reviewing the Charter, established by General Assembly resolution 992(X) and composed of all Members of the United Nations, and to request the Committee to report with recommendations, to the General Assembly not later than at its fourteenth session;
"2. *Requests* the Secretary-General to continue the work envisaged in paragraph 4 of General Assembly resolution 992(X)."

OTHER DOCUMENTS
Repertory of Practice of United Nations Organs. Table of Contents and Subject Index to Vols. I-V. U.N.P. Sales No.: 1955.V.2 (index).

QUESTIONS OF ENLARGING THE SECURITY COUNCIL, THE ECONOMIC AND SOCIAL COUNCIL AND THE INTERNATIONAL COURT OF JUSTICE

The questions of amending the United Nations Charter in order to increase the number of non-permanent members of the Security Council and the number of votes required for its decisions and in order to enlarge the Economic and Social Council were first discussed at the General Assembly's eleventh session. So was the question of amending the Statute of the International Court of Justice with respect to increasing the number of the Court's judges.

Consideration of these three items, however, was postponed to the Assembly's twelfth session, when they were assigned to the Special Political Committee.

At the opening of the debate, the Committee decided, on the proposal of India, to consider all three items together. Following this decision, the Indian representative said that the matter could not be usefully discussed until agreement could be foreseen on the question of amending the Charter accordingly, and until it was fairly certain that the permanent members of the Security Council would agree to accept any proposals that might be adopted by the Assembly. Subsequently, he introduced a draft resolution providing for the postponement of the matter until the thirteenth session. The draft was sponsored also by the following 16 Members: Argentina, Bolivia, Brazil, Ceylon, Chile, Colombia, Costa Rica, Ecuador, Egypt, Guatemala, Honduras, Indonesia, Nicaragua, Panama, Paraguay and Venezuela.

The representative of Ecuador said that a satisfactory settlement of the problem of increasing the membership of the principal organs of the United Nations was most desirable, and that it should not be endangered by premature discussion. Those who had joined with India in proposing postponement, he said, had done so in the hope that the atmosphere would be more favourable at the next Assembly session. The Ecuadorean representative made the statement to this effect on behalf of the delegations which had originally proposed the items for the Assembly's agenda. (The item relating to the Security Council had been proposed for the agenda of the Assembly's eleventh session by Argentina, Bolivia, Brazil, Chile, Colombia, Costa Rica, Cuba, Dominican Republic, Ecuador, El Salvador, Haiti, Honduras, Panama, Paraguay, Peru, Spain and Venezuela. The item relating to the Economic and Social Council had been proposed by these same 17 Members plus Mexico, and that relating to the Court by Costa Rica, Cuba, Dominican Republic, Ecuador, El Salvador, Haiti and Spain.)

The Committee adopted the draft resolution by 52 votes to 0. This was endorsed at a plenary meeting of the Assembly on 12 December 1957 by 65 votes to 0, as resolution 1190(XII). Consideration of the matter was thereby postponed until the Assembly's thirteenth session.

DOCUMENTARY REFERENCES

GENERAL ASSEMBLY—12TH SESSION
Plenary Meeting 728.
Special Political Committee, meetings 74, 75.

A/SPC/L.20. Argentina, Bolivia, Brazil, Ceylon, Chile, Colombia, Costa Rica, Ecuador, Egypt, Guatemala, Honduras, India, Indonesia, Nicaragua, Panama, Paraguay, Venezuela draft resolution, adopted by Special Political Committee by 52 votes to 0.

A/3765. Report of Special Political Committee.

RESOLUTION 1190(XII), as recommended by Special Political Committee, A/3765, adopted by Assembly on 12 December 1957, meeting 728, by 65 votes to 0.

"*The General Assembly,*

"1. *Decides* to give further consideration at its thirteenth session to items 19, 20 and 21[1] of the agenda of the twelfth session;

"2. *Requests* the Secretary-General to include these

items in the provisional agenda of the thirteenth session of the General Assembly."

[1] Item 19: Question of amending the United Nations Charter, in accordance with the procedure laid down in Article 108 of the Charter, to increase the number of non-permanent members of the Security Council and the number of votes required for decisions of the Council.

Item 20: Question of amending the United Nations Charter, in accordance with the procedure laid down in Article 108 of the Charter, to increase the membership of the Economic and Social Council.

Item 21: Question of amending the Statute of the International Court of Justice, in accordance with the procedure laid down in Article 108 of the Charter of the United Nations and Article 69 of the Statute of the Court, with respect to an increase in the number of judges of the International Court of Justice.

QUESTIONS RELATING TO SIZE AND COMPOSITION
OF ASSEMBLY'S GENERAL COMMITTEE

NINTH VICE-PRESIDENCY FOR ASSEMBLY'S TWELFTH SESSION

On 1 October 1957, Italy, Norway, Paraguay, the Philippines and the Netherlands asked that the "question of the establishment of a ninth Vice-Presidency for the twelfth session of the General Assembly" be put on the agenda for that session, as an urgent matter. They were later joined in this request by Japan. These States were of the opinion that the composition of the General Committee should have a representative character reflecting the membership of the Organization, and that the number of Vice-Presidencies should therefore be considered in the light of the increase in that membership (which had risen by 22 since 14 December 1955).

Aware that a permanent increase in the size of the General Committee might require further consideration, they proposed that a ninth Vice-Presidency be established as an *ad hoc* measure for the twelfth session.

Acting on the recommendation of its General Committee, the Assembly agreed to the request, and, on 7 October, it agreed to the proposal for a ninth Vice-Presidency. Spain was elected to this position on 8 October.

CHANGES IN COMPOSITION OF GENERAL COMMITTEE

On 4 October, Czechoslovakia asked that the question of the composition of the General Committee be placed on the agenda of the twelfth Assembly session as a matter of urgency.

In an explanatory memorandum, it said that *ad hoc* practices of enlarging the General Committee by increasing the number of the Assembly's Vice-Presidencies might lead to a violation of the principle that the General Committee should reflect an equitable geographical distribution in its membership. It was pointed out that there was a widely held view that the question of the composition of the General Committee and an increase in its size at future Assembly sessions should be considered in the light of the rise in the number of United Nations Members, due regard being paid to the principle of equitable geographical distribution. Czechoslovakia proposed an increase in the number of Vice-Presidents in accordance with this view.

The Assembly agreed to place the item proposed by Czechoslovakia on its agenda. It was referred to the Special Political Committee which considered it at five meetings held between 6 and 11 December 1957.

At the outset of the discussions, a draft resolution was proposed by the following 13 Members: Burma, Ceylon, Czechoslovakia, Egypt, Ethiopia, Ghana, India, Indonesia, Liberia, Saudi Arabia, Sudan, Syria and Thailand. Amendments to it were proposed by Costa Rica, Ecuador, El Salvador, Mexico, Peru and Uruguay. Accepted by the sponsors of the 13-power draft, these amendments were intended to confirm the established practice for the geographical distribution of the chairmanships of of the Assembly's Main Committees.

By the draft resolution so revised, the Assembly would: (1) confirm the already established practice of having two chairmen of Main Committees from Latin America, two from Asia and Africa, two from Western Europe and other countries, and one from Eastern Europe; (2) amend its rules of procedure (rules 31 and 38) so as to increase the number of Vice-Presidents from 8 to 13, and (3) to elect the 13 Vice-Presidents so that four would come from Asian and African States, one from Eastern Europe, two from Latin America, two from Western Europe and other States. The five permanent members of the Security Council would continue to serve as Vice-Presidents. The region from which the Assembly's President was elected would result in the number of Vice-Presidencies allocated to it being reduced by one.

The debate centred mainly on the two following points: (1) the principle of enlarging the composition of the Committee; and (2) the pattern proposed in the draft resolution for the allocation of Vice-Presidencies.

The representatives of Czechoslovakia, India, and Ceylon pointed out that the admission of 22 Member States since December 1955—mostly from Eastern Europe, Asia and Africa—meant that the General Committee's present composition no longer reflected an equitable geographical distribution of seats on that Committee. Its present composition had been set at a time when there were fewer Members and when the various areas of the world were not as widely represented as they were now. The change proposed in the draft resolution would ensure a more adequate representation and contribute to the smooth working of the United Nations.

It was felt important that arrangements on the new system should be set down in a written text, seeing that, in the past, unwritten agreements on geographical distribution had not been adhered to. It might be that certain countries had a special role in some United Nations bodies, but in the General Assembly all States were equal and sovereign and should be able to act as such with the assurances that the General Committee should reflect the views of the Assembly as a whole. It was necessary to remedy such glaring inequalities as the fact that the Asian-African group, which was composed of 29 States had only four representatives on the General Committee, while the Western European group and other States, with 22 Members, had seven seats.

These views were also shared by the other sponsors of the draft resolution, and of the amendments to it, and also by other delegations, including those of Afghanistan, Albania, Bulgaria, Iraq, Nepal, Poland, Romania, USSR. They, too deemed it necessary to enlarge the General Committee so as to keep its representative character.

Some other delegations, however, were opposed to the principle of enlarging the General Committee, or else, though in favour of this disapproved of the way proposed for making the Committee larger. Among them were Belgium, Canada, Denmark, France, Ireland, Italy, the Netherlands, Sweden and the United Kingdom.

Among the arguments advanced were the following: (1) The Assembly, with 82 Members, had one Vice-President for 10 Members, which seemed a reasonable ratio and was enough to ensure the representative character of the General Committee. (2) An increase in the membership of the General Committee in no way guaranteed an increase in efficiency and would lengthen its debates and increase the danger of a tendency to examine, in that procedural committee, the substance of proposed items. (3) There was no need to act hastily on the matter,

since the Special Political Committee had recently decided to postpone consideration of the question of enlarging the membership of the Security Council, the Economic and Social Council and the International Court of Justice. (4) The division into so-called geographical groups would make for dangerous rigidity. (5) The phrase "Western Europe and other countries" used in the draft resolution did not obviously refer to a geographical concept since it apparently included such countries as France, Canada, New Zealand and the Union of South Africa. Europe, however, was a geographical entity. There was thus a case for considering it as a single region irrespective of ideological differences. It was also considered regrettable that a functioning group such as the Commonwealth countries which were spread over the world should disappear from the groupings.

Delegations presenting these arguments also thought the matter should be postponed for further consideration.

On 10 December, however, the revised 13-power draft resolution was adopted by the Special Political Committee by a roll-call vote of 48 to 17, with 10 abstentions.

Two days later it came before a plenary meeting of the Assembly when eight Members—Burma, Ceylon, Ethiopia, Ghana, India, Liberia, Syria and Thailand—proposed an amendment providing for representation of a Commonwealth country.

The sponsors of the resolution in the Special Political Committee stressed the need for the proposed action and hoped for a unaminous vote for draft recommended by the Special Political Committee and for the eight-power amendment to it. Some Members, who had opposed the draft resolution in the Special Political Committee, considered that the proposed amendment was a valuable improvement. But they still questioned other provisions in the draft such as those which encouraged bloc voting. They said they would abstain in the vote.

The amendment, put to a roll-call vote, was adopted by 59 votes to 0, with 18 abstentions.

The draft resolution as amended was then adopted by a roll-call vote of 49 to 1, with 27 abstentions, as resolution 1192(XII).

NINTH VICE-PRESIDENCY FOR
ASSEMBLY'S TWELFTH SESSION

GENERAL ASSEMBLY—12TH SESSION
Plenary Meetings 702, 704.
General Committee, meetings 113, 114.

A/3687 and Add.1. Item proposed by Italy, Norway, Paraguay, Philippines, Netherlands, Japan.

CHANGES IN COMPOSITION
OF GENERAL COMMITTEE

GENERAL ASSEMBLY—12TH SESSION
Plenary Meeting 728.
General Committee, meeting 115.
Special Political Committee, meetings 79-83.

A/3692 and Corr.1. Letter of 4 October 1957 from Head of Czechoslovakia delegation, requesting inclusion in agenda of 12th session of item entitled "Question of composition of General Committee of General Assembly".
A/SPC/L.22 and Rev.1, 2. Burma, Ceylon, Czechoslovakia, Egypt, Ethiopia, Ghana, India, Indonesia, Liberia, Saudi Arabia, Sudan, Syria, Thailand draft resolution and revisions, adopted by Special Political Committee by roll-call vote of 48 to 17, with 10 abstentions, as follows:
In favour: Afghanistan, Albania, Argentina, Bolivia, Brazil, Bulgaria, Burma, Byelorussian SSR, Cambodia, Ceylon, Chile, Costa Rica, Czechoslovakia, Ecuador, Egypt, El Salvador, Ethiopia, Ghana, Guatemala, Haiti, Hungary, India, Indonesia, Iran, Iraq, Japan, Jordan, Laos, Liberia, Libya, Federation of Malaya, Mexico, Nepal, Pakistan, Peru, Poland, Romania, Saudi Arabia, Sudan, Syria, Thailand, Tunisia, Ukrainian SSR, USSR, Uruguay, Venezuela, Yemen, Yugoslavia.
Against: Australia, Belgium, Canada, China, Denmark, Finland, France, Ireland, Israel, Italy, Luxembourg, Netherlands, New Zealand, Norway, Portugal, Sweden, United Kingdom.
Abstaining: Austria, Colombia, Cuba, Dominican Republic, Greece, Nicaragua, Philippines, Spain, Turkey, United States.
A/SPC/L.23. Costa Rica, Ecuador, El Salvador, Mexico, Peru, Uruguay amendments to joint draft resolution.
A/3781. Report of Special Political Committee.
A/L.242. Burma, Ceylon, Ethiopia, Ghana, India, Liberia, Syria, Thailand amendment to draft resolution recommend by Special Political Committee, A/3781.
RESOLUTION 1192(XII), as recommended by Special Political Committee, A/3781, and as amended by 8-power amendment, A/L.242, adopted by Assembly on 12 December 1957, meeting 728, by roll-call vote of 49 to 1, with 27 abstentions, as follows:
In favour: Afghanistan, Albania, Argentina, Bolivia, Brazil, Bulgaria, Burma, Byelorussian SSR, Cambodia, Ceylon, Chile, Costa Rica, Czechoslovakia,

Ecuador, Egypt, El Salvador, Ethiopia, Ghana, Guatemala, Hungary, India, Indonesia, Iran, Iraq, Japan, Jordan, Laos, Lebanon, Liberia, Libya, Federation of Malaya, Mexico, Nepal, Panama, Paraguay, Peru, Poland, Romania, Saudi Arabia, Sudan, Syria, Thailand, Tunisia, Ukrainian SSR, USSR, Uruguay, Venezuela, Yemen, Yugoslavia.
Against: China.
Abstaining: Australia, Austria, Belgium, Canada, Colombia, Cuba, Denmark, Dominican Republic, Finland, France, Honduras, Ireland, Israel, Italy, Luxembourg, Netherlands, New Zealand, Nicaragua, Norway, Pakistan, Philippines, Portugal, Spain, Sweden, Turkey, United Kingdom, United States.

"The General Assembly,
"Taking into account the considerable increase in the membership of the United Nations,
"Taking also into account that the General Committee should be so constituted as to ensure its representative character on the basis of a balanced geographical distribution among its members,
"Believing that for these reasons it is desirable to enlarge the composition of the General Committee,
"Noting that the General Committee is composed of the President, the Vice-Presidents and the Chairmen of the Main Committees,
"1. Confirms the practice established with regard to the distribution of the chairmanships of the Main Committees, namely, two from Latin American States, two from Asian and African States, two from Western European and other States, and one from an Eastern European State;
"2. Decides to amend as follows rules 31 and 38 of its rules of procedure:

Rule 31
" 'The General Assembly shall elect a President and thirteen Vice-Presidents, who shall hold office until the close of the session at which they are elected. The Vice-Presidents shall be elected, after the election of the Chairmen of the seven Main Committees referred to in rule 101, on the basis of ensuring the representative character of the General Committee.'

Rule 38
" 'The General Committee shall comprise the President of the General Assembly, who shall preside, the thirteen Vice-Presidents and the Chairmen of the seven Main Committees. No two members of the General Committee shall be members of the same delegation, and it shall be so constituted as to ensure its representative character. Chairmen of other committees upon which all Members have the right to be represented and which are established by the General Assembly to meet during the session shall be entitled to attend meetings of the General Committee and may participate without vote in the discussions';
"3. Decides that the thirteen Vice-Presidents shall be elected as provided in the annex to the present resolution."

"1. The thirteen Vice-Presidents shall be elected according to the following pattern:

"(*a*) Four representatives from Asian and African States;

"(*b*) One representative from an Eastern European State;

"(*c*) Two representatives from Latin American States;

"(*d*) Two representatives from Western European and other States;

"(*e*) Five representatives from the permanent members of the Security Council.

"2. The region from which the President is elected will, however, reduce by one the number of vice-presidencies allocated in paragraph 1 of the present annex.

"3. At least one of the Vice-Presidents in categories (*a*) or (*d*) above, or the President or one of the Chairmen of the Main Committees, will be from a Commonwealth country, without altering the geographical distribution of seats in the General Committee, as defined in paragraphs 1 and 2 of this annex and in paragraph 1 of the resolution."

Rules of Procedure of General Assembly (A/520/ Rev.4/Corr.1). Amendments approved by General Assembly during its 11th session.

Rules of Procedure of General Assembly (embodying amendments and additions adopted by General Assembly up to and including its 11th session) (A/3660). U.N.P. Sales No.: 1957.I.24.

Rules of Procedure of General Assembly (A/3660/ Corr.1). Amendments approved by General Assembly during its 12th session.

APPOINTMENT OF THE SECRETARY-GENERAL OF THE UNITED NATIONS

On 10 April 1953, following his election by the General Assembly, Dag Hammarskjold took the oath of office as Secretary-General of the United Nations for a term of five years. On 26 September 1957, at a meeting held in private, the Security Council unanimously decided to recommend to the General Assembly that Mr. Hammarskjold be appointed as Secretary-General of the United Nations for a new five-year term of office.

In a letter dated 26 September, the President of the Security Council informed the President of the General Assembly of the Council's recommendation. He also addressed a letter to Mr. Hammarskjold conveying to him the decision of the Council, expressing sincere appreciation of the able and devoted manner in which he had been carrying out the great responsibilities entrusted to him under the Charter, and earnestly expressing the hope that he would agree to serve the United Nations as its Secretary-General for a second term, should the General Assembly proceed with re-appointment following the Council's recommendation.

On 26 September 1957, the General Assembly, by secret ballot, unanimously decided to appoint him for a new five-year term of office.

On 14 December, the Assembly unanimously decided, by resolution 1229(XII), that the terms of appointment for the Secretary-General's second term of office should be the same as for his first term.[2] This decision was taken on the basis of a proposal by Brazil, India and Italy.

[2] See *Y.U.N., 1946-1947*, pp. 82, 650, and *Y.U.N., 1953*, p. 44.

DOCUMENTARY REFERENCES

SECURITY COUNCIL, meeting 792 (in private).

GENERAL ASSEMBLY—12TH SESSION
Plenary Meetings 690, 731.

A/3682. Letter of 26 September 1957 from President of Security Council to President of General Assembly.

A/L.243. Brazil, India, Italy draft resolution.

RESOLUTION 1229(XII), as submitted by three powers,

A/L.243, adopted unanimously by Assembly on 14 December 1957, meeting 731.

"*The General Assembly*,

"*Recalling* its resolutions 11(I) of 24 January 1946, 13(I) (paragraph 32) of 13 February 1946 and 709 (VII) of 7 April 1953,

"*Decides* that the terms of appointment of the Secretary-General during his second term of office shall be the same as during his first term."

CHAPTER XVI

SITUATION BETWEEN HONDURAS AND NICARAGUA

In conformity with the provisions of Article 54 of the United Nations Charter, the Chairman of the Council of the Organization of American States (OAS) addressed communications to the Secretary-General on 3 May, 27 May, 8 July and 23 July 1957, to inform him and the Security Council of action taken by the Council of OAS in relation to a territorial dispute between Honduras and Nicaragua. The communications dealt with action in the fields of a cease-fire, and investigation and conciliation, culminating in the signature by both Honduras and Nicaragua of an agreement to submit their differences, arising over the interpretation of an Arbitral Award handed down by the King of Spain on 23 December 1906 to the International Court of Justice.

DOCUMENTARY REFERENCES

S/3824. Letter of 3 May 1957 from Chairman of Council of Organization of American States.
S/3856. Letter of 27 May 1957 from Chairman of Council of Organization of American States transmitting report of Investigating Committee.
S/3857/Rev.1. Letter of 8 July 1957 from Chairman of Council of Organization of American States transmitting resolution adopted on 5 July 1957.
S/3859. Letter of 23 July 1957 from Chairman of Council of Organization of American States transmitting text of Agreement signed by Ministers of Foreign Affairs of Honduras and Nicaragua on 21 July 1957.

Economic and Social Questions

CHAPTER I

THE WORLD ECONOMIC SITUATION

REVIEW OF TRENDS AND CONDITIONS

The Economic and Social Council's annual review of world economic conditions took place in 1957 at its mid-year, the twenty-fourth, session.

Among the main topics discussed were: recent developments; inflationary pressures; post-war balance-of-payments questions; measures for promoting international economic co-operation and international economic consultations (see INTERNATIONAL ECONOMIC CONSULTATIONS AND BASES FOR ECONOMIC CO-OPERATION below); the reduction of armaments expenditures; international machinery for trade co-operation and the expansion of world trade (see CHAPTER II, INTERNATIONAL TRADE, below); and economic development problems.

Reports and studies before the Council included the *World Economic Survey, 1956,* supplemented by reports on *Economic Developments in the Middle East, 1955–1956,* and on *Economic Developments in Africa, 1955–1956;* and a study entitled *Industrialization in Egypt, Israel and Turkey,* undertaken as part of the expanded programme of economic studies proposed by the Secretary-General and approved by the General Assembly in 1955.

In response to a previous request by the Council that the *World Economic Survey* should continue to focus attention upon long-term problems of general interest, the *Survey* carried an examination not only of recent economic currents but also of post-war balance-of-payments developments.

While for many of the industrial countries the balance-of-payments problem had lost much of the critical character which it possessed in the early post-war years, the *Survey* noted, it pressed increasingly upon many of the under-developed countries. For the industrial countries, adverse balances of payments had nevertheless often recurred, even though the domestic problem of excess demand, had ceased to overshadow the economic scene. While considerable flexibility had been shown in the adaptation of output to the changing pattern of domestic and foreign demand, insufficient growth in some key industries had, perhaps, had its most important consequence in the emergence of shortfalls in the balance of payments.

In many under-developed countries, the adaptation of resources to the changing pattern of domestic demand had been faced with much greater obstacles. The lack of balance in growth between various sectors of their economies had even more pronounced effects on their foreign-payments positions.

Economic growth in the under-developed countries depended heavily on rising imports of capital equipment. Their exports, however, tended to be limited to a narrow range of primary products. This, coupled with difficulties in adapting resources to the changing structure of world demand have usually restricted the ability of these countries to finance their rising demand for imports. Many under-developed countries were thus confronted with the dilemma that a rate of growth consistent with a state of equilibrium in their balance of payments was likely to widen the gap between their levels of living and those of industrial countries.

In reviewing recent economic developments, the *Survey* noted that economic activity in the industrially advanced countries of North America and Western Europe continued to increase in 1956, although more slowly than in the previous year. Industrial investment continued to be a dynamic factor in the upswing, but housing and the consumer durable industries had lost their expansive force. The advance in prices had nevertheless accelerated, and a number of countries had experienced some deterioration in their balance of payments. Restraint upon the current expansion continued to be the aim of economic policy.

In the primary-producing countries, the impact of changes in world commodity markets was much less decisive than in earlier years. Internal policies and events were therefore more conspicuous in shaping developments. Policies of restraint to moderate domestic demand and to ease pressure on the balance of payments were widespread.

According to replies to a questionnaire on full employment and the balance of payments sent by the Secretary-General in November 1956, most Governments in the developed private enterprise economies, in assessing the outlook for 1957, reported that they did not expect any acceleration in economic activity, but neither was any serious recession foreseen.

Some under-developed countries expected that the increase in foreign exchange reserves in 1956, which resulted from import restrictions, would permit some relaxation of these restrictions in 1957. Though a number of countries looked forward to a lessening of inflationary pressure through increasing production, much depended on favourable harvests.

In the centrally planned economies, industrial production continued to expand in 1956, but generally less rapidly than in 1955. In some countries, the advance of agricultural production was also lower. Plans for 1957 were strongly influenced by supply shortages in certain key sectors. A considerable decentralization of planning and management had recently taken place.

The report on *Economic Developments in the Middle East, 1955–1956* noted that the impact of the Suez crisis on the region's economy was strong but local and of very limited duration. Foreign trade increased appreciably during 1955 and the first half of 1956, with a small shift from Western Europe to the USSR and Eastern Europe.

Apart from the improved position of the petroleum producers, there was little change in the balance of payments, this report added. Much of the increase in exports was accounted

for by petroleum, but other products, notably cotton, also shared in the rise. Crude petroleum output increased by 13 per cent in 1954 and by 18 per cent in 1955, but because of the sharp decline in the last two months of 1956, the increase in 1956 over 1955 was little more than 5 per cent. The direc petroleum revenues received by the Middle Eastern Governments increased from $880 million in 1955 to about $940 million in 1956.

Industrial output continued to expand, but agricultural output fluctuated considerably. Crops in Turkey, which account for close to half the grain crop of the region, were poor in both 1955 and 1956. In the other countries, the very poor crops of 1955 were followed by fairly good crops in 1956. Most of the countries of the region experienced inflationary pressures, the active forces of which were internal in origin. Government expenditures on defence and development increased. This, together with greater private investment and limitations on imports of consumer goods, resulted in an upward pressure on price levels.

The report on *Economic Developments in Africa, 1955–1956* revealed a general slowing down of the expansion of economic activity noted in the previous year.

In the case of the Union of South Africa, the rate of increase in the national income was substantially lower than in 1954. The immediate causes of the change appeared to be: (1) a progressive tightness of money, resulting in part from anti-inflationary measures associated with a sharp drop in the net inflow of capital from abroad; and (2) a decline in prices of some of the Union's major agricultural products, notably wool and maize, combined, in the latter instance, with a smaller crop.

The physical volume of economic activity in Tunisia and Morocco was lower in 1956 than in the previous year. This also was probably true of Algeria, which in 1956 enjoyed good harvests. The result of the gains from these harvests, were, however, offset by a decline in mineral and industrial output.

In tropical Africa, the most significant developments, as far as exports were concerned, were the changes in world prices of primary commodities. Although the terms of trade of most countries deteriorated, the money income of many agricultural communities did not fully

STRUCTURE OF THE ECONOMIC AND SOCIAL COUNCIL

(As of 31 December 1957)

GENERAL ASSEMBLY

ECONOMIC AND SOCIAL COUNCIL

SESSIONAL COMMITTEES

AD HOC COMMITTEES

STANDING COMMITTEES
- Technical Assistance Committee
- Committee on Negotiations with Inter-Governmental Agencies
- Council Committee on Non-Governmental Organizations
- Interim Committee on Programme of Conferences

SECRETARIAT
UNDER THE SECRETARY-GENERAL

International Atomic Energy Agency

Administrative Committee on Co-ordination

Technical Assistance Board

SPECIALIZED AGENCIES

- International Labour Organisation
- Food and Agriculture Organization of the United Nations
- United Nations Educational, Scientific and Cultural Organization
- World Health Organization
- International Bank for Reconstruction and Development
- International Finance Corporation (Affiliate of Bank)
- International Monetary Fund
- International Civil Aviation Organization
- Universal Postal Union
- International Telecommunication Union
- World Meteorological Organization
- International Trade Organization (Interim Commission)
- Inter-Governmental Maritime Consultative Organization (Preparatory Committee)

COMMISSIONS

Regional Economic Commissions
- Economic Commission for Europe
- Economic Commission for Asia and the Far East
- Economic Commission for Latin America

- Transport and Communications
- Statistical
- Population
- Social
- Human Rights
- Status of Women
- Narcotic Drugs
- International Commodity Trade

Sub-commission
- Prevention of Discrimination and Protection of Minorities

Other Bodies
- United Nations Children's Fund (UNICEF)
- Office of the United Nations High Commissioner for Refugees
- Permanent Central Opium Board
- Drug Supervisory Body
- Interim Co-ordinating Committee for International Commodity Arrangements

reflect the fall in prices of their exports. This was due partly to an expansion in output and partly to the intervention of stabilization funds. The increased earnings of the few countries, particularly in Central Africa, which benefited from a rise in their export prices, accrued almost entirely to non-indigenous enterprises, so that generally they were not fully reflected in personal income.

CONSIDERATION BY THE ECONOMIC AND SOCIAL COUNCIL

Opening the Council's debate on the world economic situation, the Secretary-General said that the year 1956 had witnessed a continuation of the economic growth which had been so distinguishing a feature of the post-war decade. The rate of expansion, however, had slackened almost everywhere. Although the persistence of the rising post-war trend was gratifying, the past 18 months had been mainly significant in bringing to light the basic problems involved in the maintenance of long-term economic growth in every type of economy.

Council members, in general, noted that the post-war decade had been a period of unprecedented economic attainment in large areas of the world. It was emphasized, however, that Governments faced considerable difficulties in their attempts to achieve the multiple goals of full employment and economic development simultaneously with stability of price levels and of external balances of payments. A number of representatives commented on the heavy burden that armaments placed upon domestic economies, thus restricting the resources available for economic development.

The United States representative considered that the chief cause of current inflationary pressures was an excess of effective demand over available supply. He called attention to the conflicting demands for higher investment to speed up the rate of growth on the one hand and for increased current consumption on the other.

The United Kingdom representative regretted that many countries had been forced to use disinflationary measures which temporarily reduced the rate of expansion. He considered that the check placed upon expansion of investment was particularly unfortunate. It was noted, however, that the disinflationary policies had been applied with sufficient timeliness and skill to prevent the level of employment from being significantly affected.

The representative of the International Monetary Fund agreed with the stress placed by the *World Economy Survey, 1956,* on internal pressure of demand as the most important factor determining annual changes in the balance of trade and payments during the post-war decade.

The representatives of Egypt and Pakistan, among others, called attention to important differences between the economies of developed and those of under-developed countries. Despite the under-employment of resources in under-developed countries, it was pointed out, increased investment could quickly become inflationary unless there was a corresponding increase in the output of consumer goods.

Many representatives agreed that a distinction should be made between remedial measures possible in developed countries and those feasible in under-developed countries. It was easier to curtail expenditures in developed countries when they became excessive than to do so in the under-developed countries, where there was an overriding need for economic development.

The French and Polish representatives stressed the fact that economic balance, though dependent to a considerable degree on national policy, was at the same time an international matter.

Also referred to in the debate was the compartmentalization of the world economy that had become evident in the course of the post-war decade between countries with centrally planned systems and those with private enterprise economies, and between developed and under-developed countries. The USSR representative, however, thought that present circumstances offered every opportunity for promoting international economic co-operation; he observed that, with the rapid expansion of its economy, the USSR had been increasing the scope of its foreign trade.

One of the problems of international economic co-operation discussed at length by most representatives was the project for a European Common Market and European "free trade" area. The need to examine the probable effects of the establishment of the proposed European Common Market and European "free trade" area was stressed. It was generally considered that it was too early to estimate them accurately, and it was recognized that they would depend largely on the principles and practices developed.

In this connexion, the USSR proposed in the Council's Economic Committee, that the Council ask the Economic Commissions for Europe and for Asia and the Far East to study, as the Economic Commission for Latin America had decided to do, the possible repercussions of the creation of the European Common Market on their respective geographical regions. The USSR also proposed that the Council ask all three regional economic commissions to study the possible consequences of plans for setting up a European "free trade" area.

The general feeling among members of the Economic Committee was that developments resulting from implementation of the Treaty for a European Economic Community and the project for a European "free trade" area should normally be examined within the framework of the annual regional economic survey for each of the areas covered by the economic commissions as well as within the framework of the annual *World Economic Survey*.

The USSR did not press for a vote on its proposal.

Taking up another point, the representative of the Food and Agriculture Organization told Council members that the problem of surpluses of some agricultural commodities continued to be a potential danger to the stability of world agricultural markets.

Representatives of several non-governmental organizations were also heard by the Council.

On 30 July 1957, the Council unanimously adopted a resolution (654 B (XXIV)) recalling the continuing efforts being made through the United Nations Disarmament Commission to achieve agreement on the disarmament problem. At the same time, it hoped that these efforts might progress steadily towards the goal of internationally supervised disarmament, thus leading to a significant reduction in arms spending and thereby freeing additional resources which could be used to speed economic and social development, including the development of under-developed areas.

This resolution was adopted on the recommendation of the Economic Committee, which

approved it unanimously on the basis of a USSR proposal and amendments by Canada, France, the United Kingdom and the United States.

By another resolution (654 C (XXIV)), also adopted unanimously on 30 July, the Council reaffirmed its desire that the *World Economic Survey* continue to focus attention on long-term problems of general interest, and that it give special attention to problems of primary importance for the development of less developed economies and the economic progress of the world as a whole.

This resolution, too, was adopted on the recommendation of the Council's Economic Committee, which approved it unanimously, on the basis of a proposal by Argentina, Brazil, Canada, Dominican Republic, France, Greece and Mexico.

Yet another resolution unanimously adopted on 30 July (654 D (XXIV)) asked that account be taken, in preparing the next *World Economic Survey* (i.e., that for 1957), of the views expressed at the Council's twenty-fourth session about the importance of the inflation problem, the need for further study of the extent of inflation, its causes and impact on economic and social development and the measures used or contemplated by various countries for curbing it in future, bearing in mind the urgent need for the development of under-developed economies.

This resolution, too, was adopted on the unanimous recommendation of the Council's Economic Committee, which adopted it on the proposal of France and the United States.

Other Council resolutions arising out of the discussions on world economic conditions dealt with international economic consultations (for details, see section on this subject which follows) and international machinery for trade co-operation (for details, see CHAPTER II below).

Various matters bearing on the world economy were also discussed later in the year at the General Assembly's twelfth session. (For further details about this, see section below on INTERNATIONAL ECONOMIC CONSULTATIONS AND BASES FOR ECONOMIC CO-OPERATION; CHAPTER II, INTERNATIONAL TRADE; CHAPTER V, ACTIVITIES OF THE REGIONAL ECONOMIC COMMISSIONS.)

DOCUMENTARY REFERENCES

ECONOMIC AND SOCIAL COUNCIL—23RD SESSION
E/2987. Note by Secretary-General.

ECONOMIC AND SOCIAL COUNCIL—24TH SESSION
Plenary Meeting 973-979, 993.
Economic Committee, meetings 227-232.

World Economic Survey, 1956 (E/2982). U.N.P.
Sales No.: 1957.II.C.1.
Economic Developments in Middle East, 1955-1956
(E/2983). U.N.P. Sales No.: 1957.II.C.2.
Economic Developments in Africa, 1955-1956 (E/
2984 and Corr.1). U.N.P. Sales No.: 1957.II.C.3.
E/3016. *Industrialization in Egypt, Israel and Turkey.*
Part I: Growth and structure of manufacturing in-
dustry. Study by Secretary-General.

MATTERS CONCERNING EUROPEAN COMMON MARKET
E/AC.6/L.187. USSR draft resolution.
E/3036. Report of Economic Committee (paragraph
4).

REDUCTION OF ARMAMENTS EXPENDITURE
E/AC.6/L.179. USSR draft resolution.
E/AC.6/L.193. Canada, France, United Kingdom,
United States amendments to USSR draft resolution.
E/AC.6/L.196. Draft resolution consisting of texts
accepted by sponsors of proposals in E/AC.6/L.179
and E/AC.6/L.193 and presented orally, adopted
unanimously by Economic Committee, as amended.
E/3036. Report of Economic Committee (draft resolution B).
RESOLUTION 654 B (XXIV), as recommended by Economic Committee, E/3036, adopted unanimously
by Council on 30 July 1957, meeting 993.

"The Economic and Social Council,
"Noting that in many countries huge sums are currently being spent on armaments,
"Noting further that this expenditure imposes a
heavy economic and fiscal burden on many countries
and absorbs resources which might otherwise be devoted to peaceful uses,
"Recognizing that a concerted reduction in armaments would reflect a relaxation of international tension and could also facilitate the consolidation of
peace, a reduction in the burden of taxation imposed
on the peoples by the current levels of armament expenditure, and the development of economic relations
between States,
"Recalling that efforts are being continued through
the United Nations Disarmament Commission and its
Sub Committee to achieve agreement on the problem
of disarmament,
"Expresses the hope that these efforts may progress
steadily towards the goal of internationally supervised
disarmament, thus leading to a significant reduction
in armament expenditures and thereby freeing additional resources which could be used to accelerate
economic and social development, including the

economic development of under-developed countries
and areas."

WORLD ECONOMIC SURVEY AND FULL EMPLOYMENT
AND BALANCE-OF-PAYMENTS QUESTIONNAIRE
E/AC.6/L.185. Full employment and balance-of-pay-
ments questionnaire. Note by Secretary-General.
E/AC.6/L.188. Greece and France draft resolution.
E/AC.6/L.188/Rev.1, Rev.2, Rev.2/Add.1. Argentina,
Brazil, Canada, Dominican Republic, France,
Greece, Mexico revised draft resolutions and state-
ment of financial implications by Secretary-General.
Revision 2 of draft resolution adopted unanimously
by Economic Committee.
E/3036. Report of Economic Committee (draft reso-
lution C).
RESOLUTION 654 C (XXIV), as recommended by Eco-
nomic Committee, E/3036, adopted unanimously by
Council on 30 July 1957, meeting 993.

"The Economic and Social Council,
"Having examined the *World Economic Survey,*
1956, and the contents and uses of the full employment and balance-of-payments questionnaire through
which information is obtained for the World Economic Survey from Governments,
"Recalling the appropriate resolutions on the *World
Economic Survey* and the questionnaire on full employment and the balance of payments and the recommendations of the Co-ordination Committee,
"Bearing in mind the various opinions expressed at
the twenty-fourth session of the Council,

I

"1. *Takes note with satisfaction* of the *World
Economic Survey, 1956;*
"2. *Considers* that the *Survey* in its present form
is a most valuable document dealing with the current
economic situation and economic outlook and with
selected economic problems of long-term significance
to the world as a whole;
"3. *Reaffirms* the desirability of continuing to have
the *World Economic Survey* prepared with these objectives in mind, and with particular attention to the
analysis of economic problems of primary importance
for the economic development of less developed countries and areas and the economic progress of the world
as a whole;
"4. *Expresses the desire* that this information be
made available to Governments at the earliest possible
date, and in this regard *suggests* to the Secretary-
General that he should consider the feasibility of
issuing part I, dealing with selected long-term economic problems, in advance of part II;

II

"1. *Notes* that the information obtained through
the questionnaire is used fairly extensively in the
World Economic Survey;
"2. *Notes* that over the years the questionnaire has
been modified to elicit information relating more directly to the problems and developments covered in
the *World Economic Survey;*

"3. *Suggests* that the changed nature of the questionnaire should be reflected in its title."

WORLD ECONOMIC SURVEY, 1957

E/AC.6/L.197. France and United States draft resolution.

E/AC.6/L.199. Draft resolution consisting of texts accepted by sponsors of proposal contained in E/AC.6/L.197 or else orally presented, adopted unanimously by Economic Committee.

E/3036. Report of Economic Committee (draft resolution D).

RESOLUTION 654 D (XXIV), as recommended by Economic Committee, E/3036, adopted unanimously by Council on 30 July 1957, meeting 993.

"The Economic and Social Council,

"Recognizing that an upward movement of price levels is a problem affecting all countries of the world, both the more and the less developed,

"Taking account of the importance which many countries attach to the curbing of inflationary pressures as one of the primary aims of their domestic economic policy,

"Considering that both the economic and the social progress of the world would be impeded by continuing inflation of price levels,

"Bearing in mind that the Secretary-General has announced his intention to deal with a major topic of public policy in future *World Economic Surveys,*

"1. *Requests* the Secretary-General, in selecting a major topic for treatment in part I of the 'World Economic Survey, 1957', to take into account the views expressed during the twenty-fourth session of the Council on the importance of the problem of inflation and the need for further study of the extent of inflation, its causes, its impact on social and economic development, its international aspects, and measures used or contemplated by various countries for curbing inflation in the future, bearing in mind the urgent need for the economic development of the under-developed countries;

"2. *Urges* Governments of Member States to give the Secretary-General such assistance as he may require for the purpose of obtaining relevant information."

GENERAL ASSEMBLY—12TH SESSION

A/3613. Report of Economic and Social Council to General Assembly (Chapter II, Sections I, II).

A/C.2/L.329. Statement made by Under-Secretary for Economic and Social Affairs, 2 October 1957.

INTERNATIONAL ECONOMIC CONSULTATIONS AND BASES FOR ECONOMIC CO-OPERATION

INTERNATIONAL CONSULTATIONS ON WORLD ECONOMIC CONDITIONS

The question of international consultations on world economic conditions was considered at the Economic and Social Council's twenty-fourth session in mid-1957, in the course of its annual debate on the world economic situation (see section above).

In his statement opening the debate on the world economic situation, the Secretary-General drew attention to international repercussions of national policies and pointed out that the world economy might profit from more systematic consultations between countries on their general economic policies. In this way, he said, each Government would be enabled to act with more information on the international situation confronting it and of the probable effects thereon of its own actions.

Discussions in the Council on the world economic situation also brought out the similarity of certain economic problems faced by different countries, regardless of their specific institutions or stages of development. Consequently, Council members felt that countries could profit from a sharing of experience, although each country would choose the economic policies it wished to pursue in the light of its own particular situation and requirements. In this connexion, some representatives observed that there already was machinery for international economic consultations between Governments. Others, however, thought it necessary to strengthen the existing facilities and to use them more effectively (see also CHAPTER II, INTERNATIONAL TRADE, below).

In the course of debate in the Council's Economic Committee, the USSR proposed that the Council decide to convene an international conference of economists in 1958, within the United Nations framework, to consider new ways for the further development of economic relations between countries, regardless of their social system. It proposed at the same time that the Council ask the Secretary-General to set up a preparatory committee on the organization of the conference, in consultation with national economic institutes and associations of economists.

The draft resolution to this effect was not, however, pressed to a vote.

Egypt, Greece, Indonesia, Poland and Yugoslavia submitted another draft resolution—on international economic consultations. Amendments to this were proposed jointly by Brazil,

Canada, Mexico, the United Kingdom and the United States.

By the five-power draft resolution, the Council, stressing the need for an international exchange of views for any betterment of world economic conditions, would in effect take the following steps: (1) invite the Secretary-General to examine the various methods possible for developing international consultations in order to explore ways of improving international conditions necessary for a balanced growth of the world economy, particularly for speeding the development of under-developed economies; (2) authorize him, if he thought it advisable, to arrange for an *ad hoc* panel of experts from different regions to help him in this task; and (3) ask him to report on the result of these explorations to the Council's twenty-sixth session in mid-1958.

The Economic Committee, however, amended this draft resolution by incorporating the main points of revisions proposed jointly by Brazil, Canada, Mexico, the United Kingdom and the United States. It also agreed to some other amendments presented orally.

The final text was as approved unanimously both by the Economic Committee and by the Council, as resolution 654 E (XXIV) of 30 July 1957. Among the principal provisions of the resolution were the following:

The Council, recognizing that at present there were in existence various institutions and types of machinery for international economic consultations among United Nations Member States, stressed the desirability of a more effective international exchange of views, within the United Nations framework, on ways to improve international economic conditions.

Noting the Secretary-General's observations on the usefulness of such consultations, the Council asked him for a report on existing facilities and methods for the conduct and development of economic consultations between Governments in the economic field. This report was to be transmitted to Member States, who were invited to submit their comments to him at an early date on possible methods for making inter-governmental economic consultations more effective, with a view to promoting the balanced growth of world economy and, particularly, the acceleration of the economic development of the under-developed countries. The Council also

asked the Secretary-General to transmit to Member Governments, concurrently with his report, any observations and questions which he deemed appropriate. After receiving the comments of Member States, the Secretary-General was to submit a report to the Council's twenty-sixth session, in mid-1959, containing the information included in his own report to Member States, the comments received from the latter and his own observations on these comments. In addition, the Council authorized him to use experts or groups of experts from different regions to assist him in carrying out the tasks assigned to him by the resolution. Finally, the Council drew the attention of Governments to the desirability of encouraging informal contacts and meetings between economic experts of different countries so as to promote greater common understanding of national and international economic problems.

BASES FOR INTERNATIONAL ECONOMIC CO-OPERATION

Bases and principles for strengthening international economic co-operation were discussed at the General Assembly's twelfth session, during consideration of the Economic and Social Council's annual report.

Romania introduced a draft resolution in the Second Committee whereby the Assembly would, in effect, state its conviction that the development of mutually advantageous trade between countries, irrespective of their social and political systems and the level of their economic development, helped to strengthen peaceful relations among peoples.

By the Romanian draft, the Assembly would also agree that international economic relations should be based on: "(1) mutual respect for the economic independence of each State; (2) complete respect for the sovereign right of each State to dispose of its natural wealth and resources; (3) the observance, in international economic relations, of equality, equivalent exchanges and mutual advantages; (4) the granting of economic aid and technical assistance to the under-developed countries, free of any conditions which might impair the economic and political independence of these countries; (5) the maintenance of exchanges of experience and of wide contacts in the economic, scientific and technical fields".

Support for this proposal came from the representatives of Albania, Bulgaria, Czechoslovakia, Syria, the Ukrainian SSR, the USSR and others.

Among the points they made were the following: The Romanian proposal was a timely one. It would help to consolidate international relations and facilitate peaceful co-existence. Adoption of the proposed declaration of principles would serve the cause of the under-developed countries, would help to protect them from domination by richer countries, and would show that economic negotiations were being conducted between equals. It would also facilitate practical work.

Others, however, said they were unable to vote for the Romanian draft resolution. Among them were the representatives of Argentina, Bolivia, Brazil, Canada, China, Cuba, Mexico, Pakistan, Spain, Sweden, the United Kingdom, the United States and Uruguay.

While some of them were in general agreement with some or all of the five principles of co-operation set out in the draft, they thought that other equally important principles had been omitted. Another criticism was that further discussion would lead to discord and would only delay consideration of more practical and more urgent matters. Also, the proposed declaration might hamper rather than help the development of under-developed countries.

Mexico introduced another draft resolution. Recalling that both the Assembly and the Economic and Social Council had in the past adopted several resolutions embodying various principles of international economic co-operation, this draft would have the Assembly ask the Secretary-General to prepare a compendium of resolutions or extracts from them, with a subject index to facilitate study of the resolutions. This compendium would be sent to all United Nations Member States as soon as possible.

Romania subsequently withdrew its proposal and became a co-sponsor of the Mexican draft. India added a phrase whereby the Secretary-General would inform the Economic and Social Council during 1958 when he had prepared the compendium.

The draft resolution, as amended by India, was unanimously approved by the Second Committee.

On 26 November 1957, it was adopted, also unanimously, at a plenary meeting of the Assembly as resolution 1157(XII). (For final text, see DOCUMENTARY REFERENCES below.)

In recommending the resolution for approval by the full Assembly, the Committee agreed to a suggestion by Egypt and the United States that the Secretary-General be authorized to annex a few relevant documents other than Council and Assembly resolutions to the compendium, at his discretion.

DOCUMENTARY REFERENCES

INTERNATIONAL CONSULTATIONS ON WORLD ECONOMIC CONDITIONS

ECONOMIC AND SOCIAL COUNCIL—24TH SESSION
Plenary Meetings 973-979, 993.
Economic Committee, meetings 227-232.

E/AC.6/L.189. USSR draft resolution on convening of international conference of economists.
E/AC.6/L.195 and Corr.1. Egypt, Greece, Indonesia, Poland, Yugoslavia draft resolution on international consultations on world economic conditions.
E/AC.6/L.200. Brazil, Canada, Mexico, United Kingdom, United States amendments to joint draft resolution, E/AC.6/L.195 and Corr.1.
E/AC.6/L.202 and Corr.1, and Add.1. Note by Secretariat containing draft resolution consisting of texts, accepted by sponsors, of various proposals, E/AC.6/L.195 and Corr.1, E/AC.6/L.200 or made orally, and note on financial implications submitted by Secretary-General. Draft resolution adopted unanimously by Economic Committee.
E/3036. Report of Economic Committee (draft resolution E).

RESOLUTION 654 E (XXIV), as recommended by Economic Committee, E/3036, adopted unanimously by Council on 30 July 1957, meeting 993.

"*The Economic and Social Council,*
"*Recalling* its basic task of promoting international co-operation with a view to a steady and balanced growth of the world economy,
"*Recognizing* that despite the fact that in many countries economic activity has in recent years been advancing at a satisfactory rate, nevertheless large segments of the world did not show an adequate rate of growth,
"*Mindful* of the fact that an extremely important factor for the balanced growth of national economies is constituted by international economic conditions,
"*Recognizing* that there exist at present various institutions and forms of machinery which provide for international consultation in the economic field among Member States,
"*Stressing* the desirability for more effective international exchange of views within the framework of the United Nations regarding means of improving international economic conditions,

"Noting the observations of the Secretary-General in his opening statement to the present session of the Council regarding possible benefits that might flow from more systematic consultation between Governments on the general outlines of their economic policies,

"1. *Requests* the Secretary-General to prepare a report on the facilities and methods which now exist for the conduct and development of consultations between Governments in the economic field and to transmit this report to Member States, together with such observations and questions as he may deem appropriate in the light of paragraph 2 below;

"2. *Invites* Member States, taking into account the above-mentioned report, to submit to the Secretary-General at an early date comments on possible methods for ensuring more effective consultation between Governments, with a view to promoting a balanced growth of world economy and, in particular, the acceleration of the economic development of the underdeveloped countries;

"3. *Authorizes* the Secretary-General to use experts or groups of experts from different regions to assist him in carrying out the tasks assigned to him under the terms of the present resolution;

"4. *Requests* the Secretary-General to submit to the Council at its twenty-sixth session a report containing the information requested in operative paragraph 1 above, the comments received from Member States and his observations relating thereto;

"5. *Draws the attention* of Governments to the desirability of encouraging informal contacts and meetings between economic experts of different countries with a view to promoting greater common understanding of national and international economic problems."

BASES FOR INTERNATIONAL ECONOMIC CO-OPERATION

GENERAL ASSEMBLY—12TH SESSION
Plenary Meeting 723.
Second Committee, meetings 465, 466, 472, 475-477.

A/3613. Report of Economic and Social Council to General Assembly (Chapter II, Section I).

A/C.2/L.329. Statement by Under-Secretary for Economic and Social Affairs on 2 October 1957.

A/C.2/L.330. Romania draft resolution.

A/C.2/L.337 and Add.1. Mexico and Romania draft resolution, as amended orally by Egypt and United States, adopted unanimously by Second Committee, meeting 477.

A/C.2/L.342. India amendment to draft resolution, A/C.2/L.337.

A/C.2/L.346. Draft report of Second Committee.

A/C.2/L.349 and Rev.1. United Kingdom amendment and revised amendment to draft report, paragraph 26.

A/3740. Report of Second Committee (draft resolution III).

RESOLUTION 1157(XII), as recommended by Second Committee, A/3740, adopted unanimously by Assembly on 26 November 1957, meeting 723.

"The General Assembly,

"Considering that the strengthening and development of international economic co-operation is, under the Charter, one of the most important means available to the United Nations for the promotion of peaceful relations among peoples,

"Recalling that the General Assembly and the Economic and Social Council have on several occasions adopted resolutions embodying various principles relating to international economic co-operation,

"Taking into account the fact that a large number of countries have recently been admitted to membership in the United Nations and, consequently, were not represented in the debates on those resolutions,

"Considering also that, in view of the proposals and opinions submitted and expressed in the General Assembly at its twelfth session, it would be useful for all Member States to have at their disposal a compendium of those principles,

"Requests the Secretary-General to prepare such a compendium of resolutions or extracts from them, with a subject index, in order to facilitate the study of the resolutions, to transmit the compendium to all Member States as soon as it is prepared, and to inform the Economic and Social Council during 1958 that he has done so."

REPORT OF INTERNATIONAL MONETARY FUND

The Economic and Social Council, at its twenty-third session, considered the annual report of the International Monetary Fund for the fiscal year ending 30 April 1956, together with a supplement covering the period from 1 May 1956 to 31 January 1957.

In a statement to the Council, the Managing Director of the Fund characterized the period under review as exceptionally active; drawings had exceeded $1,000 million and stand-by agreements reached $1,105 million. The total value of operations since the inception of the Fund was over $3,000 million.

Pointing out that the purpose of the Fund was to assist members in meeting emergencies, he cited the aid given to sterling currency during the period of the Suez crisis. Owing to strengthened economies and monetary reserves, resulting from flexible credit and fiscal policies, the Managing Director said, the countries of the continent of Europe had been able to meet the increased cost of oil shipments during that period without aid from the Fund.

Membership applications, he added, had been received from Saudi Arabia, Libya and Morocco.

The Fund had concluded drawing and stand-by agreements with India, Chile, Peru and Bolivia to help them combat inflation and advance towards multilateral payment systems. Assistance had also been rendered to Nicaragua, Honduras, El Salvador and Cuba—all virtually dependent on one major export crop—to help tide them over seasonal deficits in their balance of payments.

There had been no grave monetary disturbances or serious set-backs to the liberalization of trade and payments. Belgium, Italy, the Netherlands and Sweden had extended the area of transferability of their currencies.

Notwithstanding strong inflationary pressures, private business investment had risen markedly, particularly in the United States and Western Europe. This type of investment, the Managing Director stressed, should be financed out of savings rather than through the creation of credit. He believed in the theory of compensatory fiscal policy to promote monetary stability.

The United States representative was gratified that progress had been maintained in extending multilateral trade and payments and that monetary and fiscal controls were replacing direct controls to an increasing extent in efforts to achieve and maintain financial stability. The Canadian representative considered that the Fund's periodic discussions on restrictive exchange control practices had been particularly useful and that the opportunities thus afforded for considering the economic and financial problems giving rise to such practices had helped to relax controls still further. The Argentine representative said that the Fund's readiness to extend assistance had enabled Latin American countries to render their exchange systems more flexible and realistic.

He also considered the problem of currency convertibility to be one of the major economic issues. The representative of France considered that, while convertibility should remain the long-term goal of every country, encouragement should in the meantime be given to every measure designed to bring about a gradual liberalization. He cited the Treaty establishing the European Economic Community as an excellent example of such an attempt.

The United Kingdom representative acknowledged the part which the Fund had played in reinforcing sterling during the latter half of 1956 and early 1957.

Praise for the Fund's measures to deal with the seasonal balance-of-payments deficits in countries whose exports were largely dependent on a single crop came from the representatives of France, Mexico, the United Kingdom, and other members.

The Greek representative pointed out that stability even in the economically advanced countries could be seriously threatened by lack of confidence or by inflation and that the smaller countries were almost defenceless against the latter danger; their only possible support was from the Fund. The Netherlands representative felt that the Fund should ensure that its resources were so used as not to cause inflationary pressures, by analysing the causes of inflation and by recommending the proper preventive or curative measures to combat monetary instability.

The spokesmen for Brazil, Egypt, Indonesia and Pakistan were among those who thought it most important that the Fund should help the under-developed countries in promoting their economic development. While the economically developed countries had progressed, it was noted, the situation in the under-developed countries had not shown any marked improvement. In fact, the gap between the two groups had widened. The Egyptian representative felt, in addition, that the price support policies of many highly developed countries obstructed the less developed countries in the disposal of their primary products and in their development plans.

Replying to various points raised in the Council's debate, the Managing Director of the Fund stated that the Fund always tried to ensure that its assistance should not contribute to inflation in the recipient country by increasing its expenditure. He observed that countries whose economy was based on the export of a single commodity needed long-term capital, which the Fund could not supply, to enable them to diversify their economy. In the case of short-term assistance, the Fund required adequate justifications from the applicant country, but experience showed that this policy did not give rise to prolonged difficulties.

On 17 April, the Economic and Social Council adopted a resolution (636(XXIII)) noting the Fund's annual report.

DOCUMENTARY REFERENCES

ECONOMIC AND SOCIAL COUNCIL—23RD SESSION
Plenary Meetings 956, 957.

E/2945 and Add.1. Report of International Monetary Fund for fiscal year ended 30 April 1956 and sum-

mary of activities of Fund from 1 May 1956 to 31 January 1957.
RESOLUTION 636(XXIII), taking note of International Monetary Fund report, adopted by the Council on 17 April 1957, meeting 957.

CHAPTER II

INTERNATIONAL TRADE

EXPANSION OF INTERNATIONAL TRADE AND TRADE CO-OPERATION

CONSIDERATION BY ECONOMIC AND SOCIAL COUNCIL

In discussing the world economic situation at its twenty-fourth session in mid-1957 (see CHAPTER I, above), the Economic and Social Council devoted considerable attention to problems of international trade.

Among the reports submitted to the Council was an analysis by the Secretary-General of comments from Governments on the international machinery for trade co-operation. (This analysis had been requested by the Council on 9 August 1956 by resolution 614 A(XXII).) The majority of Governments replying indicated satisfaction with the adequacy of current arrangements. Others, however, favoured the creation of a new international trade organization. Questions raised in the replies concerned the following, among others: the membership of existing organizations in the trade field, the scope of the activities of existing organizations, and the co-ordination of the work of the various bodies.

During the discussion at the Council's twenty-fourth session, the delegation of the USSR introduced a draft resolution to have immediate steps taken to establish an organization within the United Nations framework to deal with international trade questions. Most representatives felt that better use might be made of the facilities provided by existing international organizations. Amendments to the USSR proposal were submitted by Brazil, Canada and the Netherlands urging full co-operation under the present international machinery.

The need to increase international co-operation on trade matters was stressed by most representatives. Attention was given both to the pos-

sibility of establishing new machinery and to the alternative of improving the existing machinery. Several delegations thought that, before reaching a conclusion on the matter, the Council should have the views of Governments which had not so far given their comments on international machinery for trade co-operation, and that, in the meantime, the Secretary-General should report on further developments.

On 30 July 1957—by resolution 654 A (XXIV), which was adopted unanimously— the Council asked the Secretary-General to keep under review developments in the field of trade co-operation, particularly with respect to international machinery for trade co-operation. It also asked him to submit a further report to its twenty-sixth session (in mid-1958); taking into account both the replies already received and others that might be received. The Council expressed the hope, too, that Governments would co-operate fully in making the international machinery for trade co-operation as effective as possible.

Also adopted on 30 July was a resolution (654 E (XXIV)) on international economic consultations. (For further details, see CHAPTER I, above.)

CONSIDERATION BY GENERAL ASSEMBLY

Ways to expand international trade were again discussed at the twelfth session of the General Assembly.

In the Assembly's Second (Economic and Financial) Committee, Bulgaria proposed that a conference of experts of the countries concerned be convened in 1958 to assist the Secretary-General in preparing his report to the Council on international machinery for trade co-operation. The Bulgarian draft resolution to this effect also proposed obtaining the views from Governments on the establishment of an international trade organization, and on existing practical possibilities for developing international economic co-operation and for expanding international trade on the basis of equality and mutual benefit.

Another draft resolution was sponsored by the following seven members: Argentina, Australia, Denmark, Iceland, Japan, Norway and Pakistan. By this, the Assembly would urge Governments to continue their efforts to reduce existing barriers to international trade in a mutually satisfactory manner and to take action to approve the Agreement on the Organization for Trade Co-operation as soon as possible.

During the discussion, some delegations, including those of the United Kingdom and Japan, pointed out that there was no dearth of machinery for economic co-operation and that Governments should be persuaded to make better use of the existing machinery. They felt that the organization of GATT covered all aspects of trade and had a constantly widening membership. It was therefore ideally suited for expanding international trade.

The USSR representative and others, however, maintained that the Assembly could not be asked to approve the Organization for Trade Co-operation (OTC) proposed by GATT, since GATT was not a United Nations specialized agency and since the text of the Agreements for OTC has never been officially submitted to the United Nations.

Several delegations also had reservations about GATT and the OTC on the grounds that the membership of these bodies was restricted. They felt that all conditions for admission to these organizations should be removed.

There was general agreement on the need for a trade organization that would include as many countries as possible.

The draft resolution by Bulgaria was finally withdrawn.

Amendments to the seven-power draft resolution were proposed by France, Brazil and Greece and by Afghanistan.

The seven-power draft resolution was eventually approved in an amended form by the Second Committee by 42 votes to 7, with 21 abstentions, and then, on 26 November at a plenary meeting of the Assembly, by a vote of 51 to 7, with 19 abstentions.

By this resolution (1156(XII)), the Assembly in effect reaffirmed the requests it had made on 20 February 1957 by resolution 1027(XI), which urged Member Governments to continue their efforts to lower existing barriers to international trade in a mutually satisfactory manner so as to expand this trade at the fastest possible rate. Endorsing the Economic and Social Council's resolution of 30 July 1957 on international machinery for trade co-operation, the Assembly also urged Member Governments to take action with a view to approving the Agreement for the Organization for Trade Co-operation (OTC) as soon as possible. Establishment of OTC, it pointed out, would further strengthen the existing organizations and agreements concerned with international trade.

It recognized, too, that greater efforts should be made to promote free and fair international competition by eliminating or lowering unduly high tariffs and other unjustifiable barriers to international trade, with due regard paid to the special problems arising from the economic development needs of the less developed countries.

The Assembly also took into account its resolution 1028(XI) of 20 February 1957 about the needs of land-locked countries in the matter of transit facilities.

DOCUMENTARY REFERENCES

ECONOMIC AND SOCIAL COUNCIL—24TH SESSION
Plenary Meetings 973-979, 993.
Economic Committee, meetings 227-232.

E/3004 and Add.1-3. International machinery for trade co-operation. Report by Secretary-General and text of replies of Governments.
E/AC.6/L.178. USSR draft resolution.
E/AC.6/L.194 and Rev.1. Brazil, Canada, Nether-

lands amendment and revised amendment to USSR draft resolution.
E/AC.6/L.198. Note by Secretariat. Draft resolution (consisting of various texts accepted by sponsors of proposals in E/AC.6/L.178 and E/AC.6/L.194/Rev.1), adopted unanimously by Economic Committee.
E/3036. Report of Economic Committee (draft resolution A).

RESOLUTION 654 A (XXIV), as recommended by Economic Committee, E/3036, adopted unanimously by Council on 30 July 1957, meeting 993.

International Machinery for Trade Co-operation
"The Economic and Social Council,
"Recalling its resolution 614 A (XXII) of 9 August 1956 on measures for the development of trade co-operation, and *having considered* the report by the Secretary-General on the comments of Governments concerning international machinery for such co-operation,
"Recalling General Assembly resolution 1027(XI) of 20 February 1957, particularly in regard to the establishment of the Organization for Trade Co-operation,
"Recognizing the need for improved co-operation in questions of international trade in order more effectively to promote the development of international economic relations in accordance with the principles of the Charter of the United Nations,
"Further recognizing that opinions differ about specific ways and means of accomplishing this objective,
"Noting the report by the Secretary-General, and *noting further* that only twenty-one replies have been received to the invitation contained in paragraph 2 of resolution 614 A (XXII),
"1. *Requests* the Secretary-General to keep under review developments in the field of trade co-operation, in particular with respect to international machinery for trade co-operation, and to submit to the Council at its twenty-sixth session a further report pursuant to resolution 614 A (XXII), taking into account the replies already received and others that may be received;
"2. *Expresses* the hope that Governments will co-operate fully in making the international machinery for trade co-operation as effective as possible."

GENERAL ASSEMBLY—12TH SESSION
Plenary Meetings 722, 723.
Second Committee, meetings 454-480.

A/3613. Report of Economic and Social Council to General Assembly (Chapter II, Section II).
A/C.2/L.329. Statement by Under-Secretary for Economic and Social Affairs on 2 October 1957.
A/C.2/L.332. Bulgaria draft resolution.
A/C.2/L.335 and Rev.1. Argentina, Australia, Denmark, Iceland, Japan, Norway, Pakistan draft resolution and revision, adopted by Second Committee, as amended in Committee, by 42 votes to 7, with 21 abstentions.
A/C.2/L.336. France amendment to joint draft resolution.
A/C.2/L.340. Greece amendment to revised joint draft resolution.

A/C.2/L.343. Afghanistan amendment to revised joint draft resolution.
A/3740. Report of Second Committee (draft resolution II).
RESOLUTION 1156(XII), as recommended by Second Committee, A/3740, adopted by Assembly on 26 November 1957, meeting 723, by 51 votes to 7, with 19 abstentions.

Expansion of International Trade
"The General Assembly,
"Recalling its resolution 1027(XI) of 20 February 1957 and Economic and Social Council resolution 654 A (XXIV) of 30 July 1957,
"Recognizing that further expansion of international trade is necessary to full employment and the improvement of living standards of all countries, and especially to the economic development of the less developed countries,
"Recognizing further that, for achieving the above-mentioned objectives, greater efforts should be made to promote free and fair international competition by eliminating or lowering unduly high tariffs and other unjustifiable barriers to international trade, having due regard to the special problems arising from the economic development needs of the less developed countries,
"Taking into account its resolution 1028(XI) of 20 February 1957 concerning the needs of land-locked countries in the matter of transit facilities,
"Considering that, although existing organizations and agreements concerned with international trade have done valuable work in this field, establishment of the Organization for Trade Co-operation as a permanent international body in this field will further strengthen these organizations and agreements,
"Recalling that the Agreement on the Organization for Trade Co-operation makes provision with respect to membership for all countries which are or shall become contracting parties to the General Agreement for Tariffs and Trade or with respect to the association of countries invited by the Organization for Trade Co-operation to take part in its work,
"1. *Reaffirms* the requests contained in paragraph 1 of General Assembly resolution 1027(XI) of 20 February 1957, which urges the Governments of Member States to continue their efforts to reduce existing barriers to international trade in a mutually satisfactory manner for the purpose of expanding such trade at the fastest feasible rate;
"2. *Endorses* Economic and Social Council resolution 654 A (XXIV) of 30 July 1957, and urges the Governments of Member States to take action with a view to approving the Agreement on the Organization for Trade Co-operation at as early a date as possible."

INTERNATIONAL COMMODITY QUESTIONS

COMMISSION ON INTERNATIONAL COMMODITY TRADE

The Commission on International Commodity Trade (CICT) held its fifth session in May 1957, when it reviewed the current situation in international trade in primary commodities. It noted that during 1956 there had been considerable variation in the markets for primary products, some of which had been adversely affected by the fact that the rate of growth in industrial production in 1956 was somewhat slower than in 1955. Particular note was taken of the decline in prices of non-ferrous metals, the continued existence of large surplus stocks of certain agricultural commodities and the effect of the continued growth in the production of synthetic products.

The Commission asked that certain pilot studies be undertaken to assist in its consideration of the nature and the extent of short-term and long-term fluctuations in primary commodity prices and in the volume of trade in primary commodities. It also decided to review, at its sixth session, the methods which it might adopt in pursuing its studies.

In response to the Economic and Social Council's resolution 620(XXII) of 9 August 1956, the Commission also reported that the desired co-ordination existed between the Commission and other bodies active in the field of primary commodities, especially the Food and Agriculture Organization (FAO) and the Interim Co-ordinating Committee for International Commodity Arrangements. The Commission also recommended to the Council that its rules of procedure be amended to provide that the Commission normally hold only one regular session a year instead of two sessions as in the past. This was approved by the Council by resolution 656(XXIV) on 30 July 1957, by 16 votes to 0, with 2 abstentions.

INTERIM CO-ORDINATING COMMITTEE FOR INTERNATIONAL COMMODITY ARRANGEMENTS

During 1957 the Interim Co-ordinating Committee for International Commodity Arrangements (ICCICA) met twice, in April and in September. At these sessions, it considered its report to the Economic and Social Council and discussed the current situation in commodity markets. It also took note of inter-governmental consultations and action on commodities during that period. The Committee noted that there had been declines in the prices of a number of primary commodities in the last few months of 1957. It felt that some international action was needed, particularly in the case of three non-ferrous metals, namely, copper, lead and zinc, and recommended that informal soundings be made to determine whether the Governments most interested considered that exploratory meetings should be held with a view to arranging further consultations if these were found desirable.

The Committee's annual report to the twenty-fourth session of the Economic and Social Council described inter-governmental consultations and action during the previous year with regard to problems concerning certain individual commodities. It also contained observations and recommendations arising out of its review of developments in this period. The report further contained the views of the Committee (as requested by Council resolution 620(XXII) of 9 August 1956) on the organizational and procedural arrangements governing its activities and on the co-ordination of its functions within the framework of the United Nations.

CONSIDERATION BY THE ECONOMIC AND SOCIAL COUNCIL

At its twenty-fourth session, in mid-1957, the Economic and Social Council considered the report of the Commission on International Commodity Trade (CICT) covering its fourth and fifth sessions. The Council also had before it the *1957 Review of International Commodity Problems,* prepared by the Interim Co-ordinating Committee for International Commodity Arrangements (ICCICA). Other information on commodity trends was contained in the *World Economic Survey, 1957,* and the surveys of the regional economic commissions, also before the Council.

During discussion in the Council, reference was made to the need to avoid excessive fluctuations in the market prices of raw materials. The representative of the International Monetary Fund drew attention to the relationship between the payment difficulties of certain exporting countries and the fluctuations in world market prices for their exports. Such excessive fluctuations were considered to present one of the most difficult international economic problems.

Also before the Council were the views of CICT, ICCICA and FAO on existing organizational and procedural arrangements governing their activities in the field of international commodity problems and co-ordination of functions within the framework of the United Nations. These views were submitted in response to a request made by the Secretary-General of the United Nations (as authorized by Council resolution 620(XXII) of 9 August 1956). The replies of CICT, ICCICA, and FAO, it was pointed out during the Council's discussions, indicated that the organizations working in the commodity field were endeavouring to co-ordinate their activities and that no difficulties had arisen. Some representatives, however, thought that the position might be reviewed later in the light of further experience.

Problems arising from the replacement of natural by synthetic products were also dealt with in the debates. It was suggested that the Commission give attention to the repercussions of the development of synthetic products on markets for natural products.

Discussed, too, were the harmful effects, particularly on under-developed countries, of excessive fluctuations in the prices of primary products. The negotiation of individual commodity agreements, industrialization and greater diversification of production were among the ways of alleviating these difficulties cited by various representatives.

It was further suggested that the Commission might study short-term price fluctuations, since the sudden and sharp fluctuations which had occurred in recent years were particularly harmful.

Several representatives expressed the hope that all countries would be able to contribute to international collaboration in the commodity field within the framework of CICT.

On 30 July 1957 the Council adopted a resolution expressing the opinion that CICT's work programme and the procedural arrangements recommended by it should enable it to carry out the tasks assigned to it by the Council. The resolution also expressed the desire that CICT, FAO's Committee on Commodity Problems and ICCICA should continue to co-operate, within the framework of their respective terms of reference, in examining the problems coming within their purview. The Council decided, too, to examine international commodity problems again at its twenty-sixth session, in mid-1958. The resolution to this effect (656 (XXIV)), originally sponsored by Argentina, Brazil, the Dominican Republic and France, was adopted by the Council on 30 July 1957 by a vote of 16 to 0, with 2 abstentions.

CONSIDERATION BY GENERAL ASSEMBLY

International commodity problems were again discussed at the twelfth session of the General Assembly.

On the recommendation of its Second (Economic and Financial) Committee, the Assembly adopted a resolution endorsing the Economic and Social Council's decision to discuss international commodity problems at the Council's twenty-sixth session, and drawing the attention of United Nations Member Governments to the opportunity that existed under Council resolution 557 F(XVIII) for them to bring commodity problems to CICT. The Assembly, at the same time, drew the Council's attention to the importance of United Nations assistance in promoting international commodity agreements as an effective means of improving and stabilizing commodity prices. The Council was also asked to communicate the results of its action to the thirteenth session of the Assembly, due to be held in the latter quarter of 1958.

The resolution to this effect (1218(XII)) was approved in the Assembly's Second Committee by 60 votes to 0, with 5 abstentions, and later at a plenary meeting of the Assembly on 14 December 1957, by 75 votes to 0, with 3 abstentions.

This resolution was based on a proposal in the Second Committee sponsored by Brazil, Ceylon, Chile, Colombia, Costa Rica, Ecuador, Egypt, France, Indonesia, Iran, Iraq, Jordan, Liberia, Panama, Saudi Arabia, Sudan and Tunisia.

UNITED NATIONS MEETING ON OLIVE OIL

Conditions for the entry into force of the International Agreement on Olive Oil (prepared at the United Nations Olive Oil Conference in 1955) were not fulfilled by 1 October 1956 (the date set for the Agreement to come into force). A meeting of signatory Governments was therefore held late in 1956; it decided to explore

further the possibilities of reaching an agreement. A second session of signatories was held in Geneva on 19 and 20 July 1957, when the Secretary-General was asked to assist again in ascertaining the possibilities of bringing the Agreement into force.

DOCUMENTARY REFERENCES

ECONOMIC AND SOCIAL COUNCIL—24TH SESSION
Plenary Meeting 993.
Economic Committee, meetings 232, 233.

E/3000. Interim Co-ordinating Committee for International Commodity Arrangements. *1957 Review of International Commodity Problems.*

E/3003. Commission on International Commodity Trade. Report of fourth and fifth sessions, 28 November-7 December 1956, 6-17 May 1957.

E/3012 and Add.1. Organizational and procedural arrangements governing activities in field of international commodity problems and co-ordination of functions within framework of United Nations. Report by Secretary-General and statement by FAO.

E/AC.6/L.201. Argentina, Brazil, Dominican Republic, France draft resolution, as corrected, adopted by Economic Committee by 16 votes to 0, with 2 abstentions.

E/3038. Report of Economic Committee.

RESOLUTION 656(XXIV), as recommended by Economic Committee, E/3038, adopted by Council on 30 July 1957, meeting 993, by 16 votes to 0, with 2 abstentions.

"The Economic and Social Council,
"Having taken cognizance of the reports submitted by the Commission on International Commodity Trade and the Interim Co-ordinating Committee for International Commodity Arrangements,

"Having examined the report by the Secretary-General prepared in pursuance of its resolution 620 (XXII) of 9 August 1956 and the views submitted by the Food and Agriculture Organization of the United Nations in the addendum to that report,

"Considering that international co-operation in seeking fair and equitable solutions to commodity price problems is calculated to promote international economic relations and particularly the development of under-developed countries,

"1. *Takes note* of the above-mentioned reports;

"2. *Considers* that the work programme of the Commission on International Commodity Trade and the procedural arrangements recommended by it at its last session, should enable it to carry out its set tasks under Council resolutions 512 A (XVII) of 30 April 1954 and 557 F (XVIII) of 5 August 1954;

"3. *Expresses the desire* that the Commission on International Commodity Trade, the Committee on Commodity Problems of the Food and Agriculture Organization of the United Nations, and the Interim Co-ordinating Committee for International Commodity Arrangements, should continue to co-operate, within the framework of their respective terms of refer-

ence, in examining the problems coming within their purview;

"4. *Approves* the amendment to rule 1 of the rules of procedure of the Commission on International Commodity Trade;

"5. *Decides* to place the examination of international commodity problems on the agenda for its twenty-sixth session."

GENERAL ASSEMBLY—12TH SESSION
Plenary Meeting 730.
Second Committee, meetings 492-508.

A/3613. Report of Economic and Social Council to General Assembly (Chapter II, Section II).

A/C.2/L.357. Ceylon, Colombia, Egypt, India, Indonesia, Iran, Iraq, Liberia, Morocco, Saudi Arabia, Sudan, Tunisia draft resolution.

A/C.2/L.357/Rev.1. Ceylon, Colombia, Egypt, Indonesia, Iran, Iraq, Jordan, Liberia, Saudi Arabia, Sudan, Tunisia draft resolution.

A/C.2/L.358. Brazil, Chile, Colombia, Costa Rica, Ecuador, Panama draft resolution.

A/C.2/L.359. Brazil, Ceylon, Chile, Colombia, Costa Rica, Ecuador, Egypt, France, Indonesia, Iran, Iraq, Jordan, Liberia, Panama, Saudi Arabia, Sudan, Tunisia draft resolution (replacing draft resolutions A/C.2/L.357/Rev.1 and A/C.2/L.358) adopted by Second Committee, as amended orally by Belgium, by 60 votes to 0, with 5 abstentions.

A/3782. Report of Economic Committee (draft resolution II).

RESOLUTION 1218 (XII), as recommended by Second Committee, A/3782, adopted by Assembly on 14 December 1957, meeting 730, by 75 votes to 0, with 3 abstentions.

"The General Assembly,
"Considering that it is essential to the economic development of under-developed countries that they should be able to derive appreciable resources from their own national savings,

"Mindful that export revenues are basic for the economic development of many countries, and in particular of the under-developed countries,

"Noting that the general level of primary commodity prices continues to be unstable and has been falling during 1957,

"Considering that such conditions have harmful effects on the economy of countries exporting primary products, including their balance of payments, their programmes for economic development and their purchases from other countries,

"Bearing in mind the serious economic and social

effects which arise in both exporting and importing countries from excessive fluctuations in prices of primary products,

"1. *Endorses* the decision of the Economic and Social Council, in its resolution 656(XXIV) of 30 July 1957, to discuss the subject of international commodity problems at its twenty-sixth session;

"2. *Draws the attention* of the Governments of Member States to General Assembly resolution 1029 (XI) of 20 February 1957 and invites them, in terms of paragraph 1 of that resolution, to submit their commodity problems to the Commission on International Commodity Trade which, at it sixth session in May 1958, will prepare a report for consideration at the twenty-sixth session of the Economic and Social Council;

"3. *Draws the attention* of the Economic and Social Council to the importance of the United Nations assisting in the promotion of international commodity agreements as an effective means of improving and stabilizing commodity prices;

"4. *Requests* the Economic and Social Council to communicate to the General Assembly, at its thirteenth session, the conclusions drawn from its action under this resolution."

OTHER DOCUMENTS

United Nations Sugar Conference, 1956 Summary of Proceedings (E/CONF.22/7). U.N.P. Sales No.: 1957.II.D.2.

Recent commodity developments. Memoranda Nos. 16-18. January-March 1957.

E/CN.13/Ser.A/19-25. Recent commodity developments. April-November 1957.

E/CA/INF.9, 10. Calendar of international meetings relating directly or indirectly to commodities. March, June 1957.

CHAPTER III

THE ECONOMIC DEVELOPMENT OF UNDER-DEVELOPED COUNTRIES

PROPOSALS FOR A SPECIAL UNITED NATIONS FUND

REPORTS OF AD HOC COMMITTEE

In 1955 the General Assembly created the Ad Hoc Committee on the Question of the Establishment of a Special United Nations Fund for Economic Development (SUNFED). Consisting of 16 governmental representatives, it held two sessions in 1957, on 11 and 12 March and from 19 March to 22 May. At these sessions, the Committee adopted two reports.

One was a final report, as requested by the General Assembly on 9 December 1955, which contained a summary and analysis of the views of Governments on the establishment, role, structure and operations of SUNFED. This report consisted of a revision of the Committee's interim report, adopted in May 1956, and took into account information submitted by Governments to the Secretary-General since that time. It also embodied a set of conclusions which the Committee had drawn from the views sent in by Governments.

The second report, adopted by the Ad Hoc Committee in 1957, was a supplementary one as requested by the General Assembly on 26 February 1957. It outlined the different forms of legal framework on which a Special United Nations Fund for Economic Development might be established and statutes drafted. It also indicated the types of projects which could be financed by such a fund.

CONSIDERATION BY ECONOMIC AND SOCIAL COUNCIL

The Ad Hoc Committee's final and supplementary reports were considered at the Economic and Social Council's twenty-fourth session, in mid-1957.

Several representatives held that a wide area of agreement between Governments emerged from these reports; others, on the contrary, felt that there were still some fundamentally divergent views.

Most of the discussion dealt with the timing of the establishment of SUNFED and the types of action which could be recommended to the General Assembly.

Several representatives, particularly those of Brazil, Egypt, France, Greece, Indonesia, Mexico, the Netherlands, Poland, the USSR and Yugoslavia, again stressed how urgent were the needs of under-developed countries. They favoured immediate action by the Assembly to establish a Special Fund.

The representative of the Netherlands thought

that such action should be recommended by the Council even if this were not a unanimous recommendation. At various times in the past, he observed, compromise resolutions had been adopted in order to give the major potential contributors more time to decide on the establishment of the Special Fund. The time had now come, however, when a decision could not again be postponed.

Other representatives reaffirmed their Government's position that the establishment of the Special Fund should be contingent upon internationally supervised, world-wide disarmament.

The United States representative gave three main reasons why it would be untimely for the Council to recommend that the General Assembly take immediate steps to set up the Fund. First, if the Fund were to be established forthwith, it would only be set up on a minute scale that would be ineffective, lead to disillusionment and damage the United Nations' prestige. Second, until a substantial amount of additional resources could be released by an international agreement on a reduction of military expenditure, no meaningful fund could be established without increasing inflationary pressures. Third, private international capital movements had recently been increasing rapidly. Taking into account existing bilateral programmes of governmental aid and loans by existing international institutions, he observed, a substantial and rising volume of development financing was being furnished.

The United Kingdom representative felt that, pending the release of large-scale resources at present allocated to defence, all efforts to promote economic development should be directed through existing channels. If limited amounts of additional resources became available, they could be better spent on existing assistance programmes. He believed that action by the United Nations to embark forthwith on the establishment of a Special Fund without the United States and the United Kingdom was not likely to induce their legislatures to agree to their respective Governments joining the Fund. On the contrary, since neither Government would have played any part in drafting the statutes, the opposite would undoubtedly be the case. The representative of Canada believed that a recommendation for immediate action might well be interpreted by the legislative organs of those Member States whose full support was required as an attempt to compel their Governments to comply with such a recommendation.

The United Kingdom and the United States representatives both reaffirmed that their Governments were prepared, when sufficient progress had been made in internationally supervised world-wide disarmament, to ask their legislatures to devote a portion of the savings achieved through such disarmament to an international fund, within the framework of the United Nations, for the development of under-developed countries.

Several representatives, including those of Argentina, France and Pakistan, recognized that the Special Fund would be unable to make any real progress unless the great majority of Member States, especially the major industrial countries, participated in it.

The representative of Argentina recalled two earlier Argentinian proposals for immediate steps which were of a less ambitious nature than those involving establishment of the Special Fund. One proposal put forward—in mid-1956, at the Council's twenty-second session—was that a special fund be set up to finance regional centres for the surveying and study of natural resources and regional technological institutes. The other suggestion, made by Argentina at the General Assembly's eleventh session, was for the establishment of a small organization responsible to the Council and co-operating closely with the Technical Assistance Board, the International Bank and UNICEF. This would be charged with promoting the financing, by means of public funds provided by Member States, of basic projects in the under-developed countries which could not be financed by existing inter-governmental financial agencies. These two proposals by the Argentinian representative were favourably received by several representatives.

On the basis of a draft resolution introduced by Argentina, Egypt, Greece, Indonesia, Mexico, the Netherlands and Yugoslavia, the Council finally adopted a resolution (662 B (XXIV)) urging that the General Assembly decide at its twelfth session to establish the Special Fund and to take the necessary steps to that end. It also recommended that the Assembly set up a preparatory commission to prepare the necessary steps for the establishment of the Fund and select a limited number of projects to be financed through voluntary contributions on an experimental basis pending the full operation of the Fund. This resolution was approved on 31 July 1957 by a vote of 15 to 3.

CONSIDERATION BY GENERAL ASSEMBLY

At the General Assembly's twelfth session, debate on the SUNFED proposal took place in the Second (Economic and Financial) Committee. Among the documents before it were the Ad Hoc Committee's final and supplementary reports.

At the beginning of the debate, India introduced an 11-power draft resolution calling for the establishment, by 1 January 1960, of a United Nations fund for economic development to help the under-developed countries, either by loans or grants, in the financing of their economic and social infrastructure (i.e., health and educational facilities, power schemes, transport facilities, etc.). The other sponsors of this draft resolution were Argentina, Ceylon, Chile, Egypt, Greece, Indonesia, Mexico, the Netherlands, Venezuela and Yugoslavia. This draft resolution was supported by representatives of the less developed countries and a few of the industrialized countries. The latter, apart from the Netherlands, included the USSR.

Among the main arguments in favour of the early establishment of such a fund were the following. No one had disputed its necessity. It was essential for speeding the economic development of under-developed countries. Setting up a multilateral fund would be the best guarantee against the use of aid for political purposes and would enable smaller countries with limited financial resources to participate efficiently in the financing of economic development. Competing bilateral programmes would in the long run be harmful to balanced economic growth in the under-developed countries. Private capital alone could not satisfy all the investment needs of the under-developed countries. The fund would help to create the economic conditions necessary to attract private capital to under-developed countries. The proposal for a United Nations development fund had been carefully studied for years.

As for the contention that further large-scale financial assistance to economic development should be subordinated to disarmament, it was argued that the United Nations would reduce the causes of political tension by trying to decrease the widening gap in the economic development between the under-developed countries and the industrialized countries.

In answer to the argument that the establishment of a Special Fund on a minute scale would raise false hopes and eventually lead to disillusionment, the representatives of several of the less developed countries contended that these countries were too realistic to expect too much from such a fund whatever its size.

The United States representative said that his Government supported the idea of an international development fund whenever circumstances made it practicable. However, the resources which countries could make available at the time would not be sufficient to carry out the task. There were risks that it would raise hopes among the people of under-developed countries which could not be fulfilled and that the fund's limited resources would be dissipated on relatively minor projects. Taking this into account, the United States Government had reached the conclusion that it must continue to oppose the immediate establishment of SUNFED.

The United States would not only vote against the 11-power draft resolution. It would also refuse to participate in the work of any preparatory commission which might be appointed to draft the regulations of such a fund.

The problem of the economic development of under-developed countries, the United States representative believed, required a more constructive approach at present. He accordingly submitted a draft resolution calling for the establishment of a Special Projects Fund as an integral part of the Expanded Programme of Technical Assistance. He proposed that the annual voluntary contributions of Governments to the Expanded Programme be raised from $30 million to $100 million. The increase in financial resources of the programme would come from voluntary contributions on a matching basis. The projects to be aided by this Special Fund would be surveys of natural resources, industrial research, training of manpower, public administration and basic statistics.

The Indonesian and USSR representatives asked whether the fund proposed by the 11-power draft resolution and that proposed by the United States could develop side by side, or whether the United States regarded its own proposal as a substitute for SUNFED. The United States representative replied that since it was apparent that sufficient funds were not available to carry out both projects, it seemed wiser to concentrate on a realistic goal. The United States proposal, however, was not a substitute for SUNFED, he said. Nor was it an attempt to exclude the future development of SUNFED.

Opinions on the United States proposal varied.

The representatives of the Byelorussian SSR, Cambodia, Czechoslovakia, Egypt, Poland, Romania, the USSR and Yugoslavia had strong reservations about this proposal.

The following were among the points they made. The proposal should not be accepted unless it was linked with a decision to establish SUNFED. The United States proposal could not in any way help to solve the fundamental problem of the economic development of the under-developed countries. The expansion of the technical assistance programme could not be accepted as a substitute for setting up a multilateral economic development fund.

Other representatives, among them those of the United Kingdom and of Denmark, favoured the United States proposal.

The United Kingdom representative said his Government was not in a position to contribute to the economic development fund as envisaged in the 11-power draft resolution and would vote against this proposal. The United States draft resolution seemed to him to offer a generous and constructive approach, since technical knowledge and competence were a prerequisite to capital development.

The Danish representative, whose Government had consistently supported the early establishment of SUNFED, regretted to say that this fund could not be created at the present time as it would not receive enough resources without the support of the major capital-supplying countries—particularly the United States and the United Kingdom. Denmark would, however, support the United States proposal.

Another group of representatives still favoured the prompt establishment of a United Nations Development Fund but did not view the proposals as mutually exclusive. They were therefore prepared to support both resolutions.

Several representatives thought it possible for the sponsors of the two draft resolutions to work out a compromise proposal.

After extended negotiations, a compromise was arrived at in the form of a revision to the 11-power draft resolution. The compromise text retained some features which the sponsors of the latter considered essential, and also incorporated parts of the United States proposal.

After further amendment in the Second Committee, the compromise text was unanimously approved by the Second Committee. The Assembly also adopted it unanimously at a plenary meeting on 14 December 1957, as resolution 1219(XII).

The Assembly thereby decided to set up a separate Special Fund to provide systematic and sustained assistance in fields essential to the integrated technical, economic and social development of less developed countries. This Fund was to be an expansion of existing technical assistance and development activities of the United Nations and the specialized agencies.

Since the resources prospectively available at the time were not likely to exceed $100 million annually, the Assembly was agreed that the operations of the Special Fund would be directed towards enlarging the scope of the United Nations technical assistance programme so as to include special projects in certain basic fields to be defined by a 16-member Preparatory Committee, e.g., surveys of water, mineral and potential power resources, the establishment—including staffing and equipping—of training institutes in public administration, statistics and technology, and of agricultural and industrial research and productivity centres.

The Assembly at the same time charged the 16-member Preparatory Committee set up by the resolution with the following tasks: (a) to define the basic fields of assistance and types of eligible projects; (b) to define the administrative and operational machinery to be recommended for the Special Fund, including such changes as might be required in the present legislation and procedures of the Expanded Programme of Technical Assistance; (c) to find out to what extent the Governments would be willing to contribute to the Special Fund.

The Assembly looked forward to the Special Fund being established as of 1 January 1959.

It was also decided that as and when the resources prospectively available were considered by the Assembly to be sufficient to enter into the field of capital development, the Assembly would review the scope and future activities of the Special Fund and take such action as it might consider appropriate.

In an annex to the resolution, the Assembly indicated that the Special Fund should be a multilateral fund of the United Nations, deriving its finances mainly from voluntary contributions from Governments and others. The Fund would aid only those projects which would help in the economic development of the countries requesting aid from it. The operations of the Fund were to conform with the principles of the United Nations Charter and were not to be influenced by political considerations.

After the adoption of the resolution, the President of the Assembly appointed the following 16 United Nations Members to the Preparatory Committee: Canada, Chile, Denmark, Egypt, France, Ghana, India, Japan, Mexico, Netherlands, Pakistan, Peru, USSR, United Kingdom, United States and Yugoslavia.

DOCUMENTARY REFERENCES

SUNFED

ECONOMIC AND SOCIAL COUNCIL—24TH SESSION
Plenary Meetings 990-994.

E/2961 and Corr.1. and Add.1. Final report of Ad Hoc Committee on Question of Establishment of Special United Nations Fund for Economic Development, prepared in accordance with General Assembly resolution 923(X).
E/2999. Supplementary report of Ad Hoc Committee on Question of Establishment of Special United Nations Fund for Economic Development, prepared in accordance with General Assembly resolution 1030(XI).
E/L.764 and Rev.1 and Rev.1/Add.1. Argentina, Egypt, Greece, Indonesia, Mexico, Netherlands, Yugoslavia draft resolution and revision.
E/L.768. Canada amendments to revised joint draft resolution, E/L.764/Rev.1.
RESOLUTION 662 B (XXIV), as submitted by 7 powers, E/L.764/Rev.1 and Rev.1/Add.1, adopted by Council on 31 July 1957, meeting 994, by 15 votes to 3.

"The Economic and Social Council,
"Considering that both the Council and the General Assembly of the United Nations have on a number of occasions approved unanimously the principle of the establishment of a special United Nations Fund for the financing of the economic and social development of under-developed countries,
"Considering further that the final report of the Ad Hoc Committee on the Question of the Establishment of a Special United Nations Fund for Economic Development has again shown that a substantial majority of the States Members of the United Nations is in favour of the immediate establishment of such a fund,
"Convinced that the establishment of such a fund is economically desirable and possible, will strengthen the United Nations, will help the under-developed countries in their efforts towards economic development and social advancement, and will thus contribute to the stability and peace of the world,

I
"Commends the Ad Hoc Committee on the Question of the Establishment of a Special United Nations Fund for Economic Development for its work, and forwards to the General Assembly its final and supplementary reports prepared in accordance with General Assembly resolutions 923(X) of 9 December 1955 and 1030(XI) of 26 February 1957;
II
"Urges the General Assembly of the United Nations, at its twelfth session, to decide to establish this Fund and to take the steps necessary to this end;
III
"Recommends to the General Assembly to establish a preparatory commission entrusted with the tasks of:
"(a) Preparing the necessary steps for the establishment of the Fund, as mentioned in operative paragraph II above;
"(b) Selecting a limited number of projects to be financed through voluntary contributions on an experimental basis pending the full operation of the Fund."

SUNFED AND SPECIAL FUND

GENERAL ASSEMBLY—12TH SESSION
Plenary Meeting 730.
Second Committee, meetings 453, 492-504, 507-510.

A/3579 and Corr.1 and Add.1; A/3580 (submitted to 24th session of Economic and Social Council under document symbols E/2961 and E/2999, respectively, given above).
A/3613. Report of Economic and Social Council to General Assembly (Chapter III, Section A I).
A/3661. Questions relating to economic development. Memorandum by Secretary-General.
A/C.2/L.331 and Rev.1. Argentina, Ceylon, Chile, Egypt, Greece, India, Indonesia, Mexico, Netherlands, Venezuela, Yugoslavia draft resolution and revision. Revised draft resolution, as amended by United States, and orally by Iran and Iraq, and co-sponsored by United States, Canada and France, adopted by Second Committee by roll-call vote of 72 to 0, as follows:

In favour: Afghanistan, Albania, Argentina, Australia, Austria, Belgium, Brazil, Bulgaria, Burma, Byelorussian SSR, Cambodia, Canada, Ceylon, Chile, China, Colombia, Costa Rica, Cuba, Czechoslovakia, Denmark, Dominican Republic, Ecuador, Egypt, El Salvador, Ethiopia, Finland, France, Ghana, Greece, Guatemala, Haiti, Honduras, Hungary, Iceland, India, Indonesia, Iran, Iraq, Israel, Italy, Japan, Liberia, Libya, Luxembourg, Federation of Malaya, Mexico, Morocco, Nepal, Netherlands, New Zealand, Norway, Pakistan, Panama, Paraguay, Peru, Philippines, Poland, Portugal, Romania, Spain, Sudan, Sweden, Thailand, Tunisia, Turkey, Ukrainian SSR, USSR, United Kingdom, United States, Uruguay, Venezuela, Yugoslavia.

Against: None.

Abstaining: None.

A/C.2/L.354. United States draft resolution.

A/C.2/L.360. United States amendments to Part B of revised 11-power draft resolution.

A/3782. Report of Second Committee (draft resolution III).

RESOLUTION 1219(XII), as recommended by Second Committee, A/3782, adopted unanimously by Assembly on 14 December 1957, meeting 730.

"The General Assembly,

"In conformity with the determination of the United Nations, as expressed in its Charter, to promote social progress and better standards of life in larger freedom, and for these ends, to employ international machinery for the promotion of the economic and social advancement of all peoples,

"Conscious of the particular needs of the less developed countries for international aid in achieving accelerated development of their economic and social infrastructure,

"Recalling its resolutions on the establishment of an international fund for economic development within the framework of the United Nations and, in particular, reaffirming its unanimously adopted resolutions 724 A (VIII) and 724 B (VIII) of 7 December 1953,

"Noting the recommendation of the Economic and Social Council in its resolution 662 B (XXIV) of 31 July 1957,

"Recognizing that the United Nations Expanded Programme of Technical Assistance is of proven effectiveness in promoting the economic development of the less developed countries,

"Recognizing however that neither the Expanded Programme nor other existing programmes of the United Nations or the specialized agencies can now meet certain urgent needs which, if met, would advance the processes of technical, economic and social development of the less developed countries, and, in particular, would facilitate new capital investments of all types—private and public, national and international—by creating conditions which would make such investments either feasible or more effective,

"Convinced that a rapidly achieved enlargement in the financial resources and scope of technical assistance rendered by the United Nations and the specialized agencies to the less developed countries would constitute a constructive advance in United Nations assistance and would be of immediate significance in accelerating their economic development,

"Recognizing that, while long-term pledges are desirable, some Governments are unable to make financial commitments except with the approval of their legislatures and on an annual basis,

I

"Commends the *Ad Hoc* Committee on the Question of the Establishment of a Special United Nations Fund for Economic Development for the work embodied in its final and supplementary reports prepared in accordance with General Assembly resolutions 923 (X) of 9 December 1955 and 1030(XI) of 26 February 1957;

II

"1. Decides that, subject to the conditions prescribed hereunder, there shall be established as an expansion of the existing technical assistance and development activities of the United Nations and the specialized agencies a separate Special Fund which would provide systematic and sustained assistance in fields essential to the integrated technical, economic and social development of the less developed countries,

"2. Decides further that, in view of the resources prospectively available at this time, which are not likely to exceed $100 million annually, the operations of the Special Fund shall be directed towards enlarging the scope of the United Nations programmes of technical assistance so as to include special projects in certain basic fields to be defined by the Preparatory Committee provided for in paragraph 4 below, for example, intensive surveys of water, mineral and potential power resources, the establishment—including staffing and equipping—of training institutes in public administration, statistics and technology, and of agricultural and industrial research and productivity centres;

"3. Considers that while, without impairing the separate identity of the Special Fund, the fullest possible use should be made of the existing machinery of the United Nations, the specialized agencies—including the existing international financial institutions—and the Expanded Programme of Technical Assistance, the Special Fund will require some new administrative and operational machinery;

"4. Decides to establish a Preparatory Committee composed of representatives of sixteen Governments to do the following, taking into account the principles set out in the annex to the present resolution and the views and suggestions forwarded by Governments pursuant to paragraph 7 below:

"(a) Define the basic fields of assistance which the Special Fund should encompass and, within these fields, the types of projects which should be eligible for assistance;

"(b) Define in the light of paragraph 3 above the administrative and operational machinery to be recommended for the Special Fund, including such

changes as may be required in the present legislation and procedures of the Expanded Programme of Technical Assistance;

"(c) Ascertain the extent to which Governments would be willing to contribute to the Special Fund;

"5. *Invites* the President of the General Assembly to appoint the members of the Preparatory Committee;

"6. *Invites* the Secretary-General to provide the Preparatory Committee with all the necessary facilities, including the provision of such expert consultants as might be required;

"7. *Requests* Governments to assist the Preparatory Committee in its work by forwarding their views and suggestions to the Committee through the Secretary-General and, in particular, by indicating the extent to which they would be willing to contribute to the Special Fund;

"8. *Invites* the Secretary-General, the executive heads of the specialized agencies and the Executive Chairman of the Technical Assistance Board to forward their views and suggestions to the Preparatory Committee;

"9. *Requests* the Preparatory Committee to submit the results of its work in the form of a report and recommendations to the Economic and Social Council, at its twenty-sixth session;

"10. *Requests* the Economic and Social Council to transmit the Preparatory Committee's report, together with its own comments, to the General Assembly, at its thirteenth session, for final action;

"11. *Looks forward* to the establishment of the Special Fund as of 1 January 1959;

"12. *Appeals* to all States Members of the United Nations, in a spirit of co-operation and solidarity, to give the greatest possible assistance to the Special Fund;

III

"*Decides* that as and when the resources prospectively available are considered by the General Assembly to be sufficient to enter into the field of capital development, principally the development of the economic and social infrastructure of the less developed countries, the Assembly shall review the scope and future activities of the Special Fund and take such action as it may deem appropriate."

ANNEX

"1. The Special Fund shall be a multilateral fund of the United Nations, with financial resources principally derived from voluntary annual contributions of Governments and others in or transferable into currency usable by the Fund and, as much as possible, pledged or indicated for a number of years.

"2. Assistance from the Special Fund shall be given only to projects which would make a contribution to the economic development of the requesting country or countries. The operations of the Fund shall be in conformity with the principles of the Charter of the United Nations and shall not be influenced by political considerations.

"3. The Special Fund shall be administered by a chief executive officer under policies established by an executive body in accordance with such rules and principles as may be laid down by the General Assembly and the Economic and Social Council. The membership of the executive body shall be equally distributed between two groups, one consisting mainly of major contributing countries and the other consisting mainly of less developed countries. Each member of the executive body shall have one vote. Decisions of the executive body on questions of policy, including the allocation of funds, shall require a qualified majority vote."

INTERNATIONAL FLOW OF PRIVATE CAPITAL

The role of foreign private capital in financing the economic development of under-developed countries was again taken up by the Economic and Social Council at its twenty-fourth session in mid-1957.

Before the Council was a report entitled *The International Flow of Private Capital, 1956,* prepared by the Secretary-General as requested by General Assembly resolution 1035(XI) of 26 February 1957.

During 1956, the report indicated, the international flow of private long-term capital had attained the highest level of the post-war period, rising substantially above the volume of the preceding year. In large measure, this was due to greatly increased capital exports by the United States, but the outflow of capital from the United Kingdom and west Germany also rose

markedly. United States capital for direct investment abroad more than doubled; portfolio investments, made predominantly in Canada, also rose substantially. The strained conditions in the capital markets of several Western European countries caused some reduction in the flotation of new issues for foreign account.

The bulk of the funds absorbed by the less developed countries, the report added, continued to be directed into the extractive industries, particularly petroleum production, and included large payments for new concessions awarded. Nevertheless, there was also a significant expansion of investments in manufacturing, primarily in Latin America.

In the major capital-exporting countries, no significant changes occurred during 1956 in the framework of governmental measures affecting capital exports. Several countries, however, took steps in the field of taxation and exchange control which were expected to help stimulate or facilitate the export of capital.

In several capital-importing countries, there was a continuation of the tendency to liberalize, in various ways, restrictions on remittances of income and capital of non-resident investments and to provide assurances in this regard. Some countries, however, tightened restrictions on remittances while others reduced or postponed payments in order to deal with temporary balance-of-payments difficulties.

Several representatives who took part in the Council's debate noted the gratifying increase in the flow of private capital during 1956.

Thus, the United States representative observed that if governmental aid programmes and loans by existing international institutions were taken into account, a substantial and rising volume of development financing was being furnished. He believed that private investment was the most valuable and effective kind of development financing. He drew particular attention to the indirect benefits of foreign private investment in under-developed countries. Recent studies had shown that even the direct balance-of-payments effects of foreign investment had been considerably understated. Also to be taken into account, he added, were the tax revenues derived by capital-importing countries, the secondary effects of the activities of the investors on the economic environment in under-developed countries and the transfer of skills.

The Canadian representative cited Canada's success in finding adequate capital resources in the private market for its own development to show that there was still considerable scope for other countries to secure from private sources the capital they needed, and that they might find it fruitful to develop policies likely to encourage an increased flow of foreign investment.

A number of representatives (including those of Greece, Indonesia, the Netherlands and Pakistan) pointed out, on the other hand, that the flow of capital had been directed primarily towards Canada and Latin America. According to the Netherlands representative, much of that capital had, moreover, been directed into the extractive industries. This, he said, did not necessarily correspond to economic priorities, since foreign investments were determined by the profit motive rather than by the development needs of under-developed countries. The representative of Pakistan stated that the flow of capital to under-developed areas in Asia, the Far East, the Middle East and Africa had not increased significantly. He feared that tightness in the United States capital market might reduce the flow of private foreign investment to below the 1956 level. Under-developed countries, he nevertheless felt, should introduce measures to inspire confidence in those seeking to invest abroad.

Several representatives, gratified at the relaxation of restrictions affecting foreign capital, maintained that further liberalization would produce a still greater inflow of capital. Some thought that further action was called for. The representative of Brazil, for example, suggested that the International Bank for Reconstruction and Development be enabled to extend its activities so as to induce a greater and more regular flow of private capital.

The French representative stressed the need for more consistency between national laws governing private investments. He suggested that the Secretary-General be authorized to consult United Nations Member Governments to see how far they would be prepared to take part in preparing agreements specifying the guarantees to be offered both to capital-importing and capital-exporting countries. He also suggested that the United Nations Secretariat, together with the specialized agencies, continue to study various forms of technical machinery—such as investment corporations and special types of shares and bonds—for safeguarding the rights of the capital-importing countries and the interests of investors.

No resolution on the subject was adopted by the Council.

DOCUMENTARY REFERENCES

ECONOMIC AND SOCIAL COUNCIL—24TH SESSION
Plenary Meetings 990-994.

E/3021. International flow of private capital, 1956.
Report by Secretary-General.

REPORT OF INTERNATIONAL BANK FOR RECONSTRUCTION AND DEVELOPMENT

At its twenty-third session, the Economic and Social Council considered the annual report of the International Bank for Reconstruction and Development and a supplement to this report. These outlined the Bank's principal activities between 1 July 1956 and 31 January 1957.

In a statement to the Council, the President of the Bank observed that recent events had emphasized the need for unremitting efforts to raise living standards. The Bank was meeting the challenge by making modern techniques more widely available and by stimulating investment in under-developed areas. Its loans had reached a new record of $507 million in the past fiscal year. It had now made 166 loans to 44 countries, for a gross total exceeding $3,000 million. Its membership had increased to 60. By the second half of 1956, its income was 20 per cent higher than a year earlier. Reserves had reached $254 million. Despite tight money markets, in 1956 the Bank had been able to sell substantial portions of its loans without its guarantee. It had also succeeded in sponsoring further joint operations. It had continued to give technical assistance, and the International Finance Corporation and the Economic Development Institute, which it had helped to establish, were making encouraging progress.

The Bank was only authorized to make loans on the express condition that they would be serviced and would help establish an environment in which foreign capital could play a more effective role in the development of the less developed parts of the world.

The President of the Bank also referred to the advantages and disadvantages of loans as opposed to grants in economic assistance. He preferred loans repayable in the local currency of the borrower since they did not create fixed foreign exchange obligations for the borrower which might lower its international credit standing. Although grants had many advantages, they tended to create an atmosphere of unhealthy dependence.

During the subsequent debate in the Council all the representatives who spoke expressed their appreciation of the Bank's activities. Thus, the Yugoslav representative drew attention to the Bank's contribution towards creating better understanding between countries. Many representatives commented favourably on the substantial increase in the percentage of loans granted to under-developed countries and on the establishment of the International Finance Corporation and the Economic Development Institute.

The United States and Netherlands representatives made the point that the Bank had made an effective contribution towards the establishment of the basic facilities on which the diversification and industrialization of under-developed countries depended directly. The Netherlands representative made special mention of the fact that 70 per cent of the Bank's assistance had been for projects to develop electric power and improve transport. He also welcomed the action of Mexico in becoming the first Latin American country to release the entire remaining portion of its 18 per cent subscription. The United States representative was gratified to note—in the light of the increasing attention given in the United Nations to the industrialization of under-developed countries —that the Bank had granted the largest industrial development loan in its history to a project in India.

The representative of Mexico welcomed the Bank's success in securing additional funds from private investors in the face of keen competition. He also thought that the Bank's officers had acquired a marked ability to judge how the Bank could help meet the economic development needs of various countries without departing from standards dictated by common prudence.

Argentina's representative wanted more account taken of the capacity of the under-developed countries to absorb investment capital. This absorptive capacity, he said, involved cultural, economic and administrative factors.

The French representative welcomed the efforts being directed to the collective financing of a series of operations forming part of an overall long-term programme. As an example of this, he cited the project for the economic development of the southern part of Italy, which involved assistance from the Bank, national funds, private investors and other sources of international aid.

The Canadian representative regarded the

advice and technical aid given by the Bank as almost as important as its loans.

The United Kingdom representative felt that the soundness of the Bank's loans—evident from the fact that no country had ever defaulted on a loan—was important not only for its relations with countries to which loans were made but also for its standing in securing additional funds.

The representative of Pakistan, disagreeing with some of the conclusions in the Bank's report, cited the experience of his own country to show the need for large-scale investments in primary-producing countries to provide rural credit and to set up adequate machinery and marketing arrangements.

The Greek representative welcomed the Bank's policy of granting "follow-up loans" to countries in which a first investment had been made. But he felt that the Bank's not being active in some areas of the world had a harmful effect not only on the peoples and Governments of these areas but also on the Bank itself.

The Indonesian representative was gratified that the Bank had formed a new department to deal with operations for nine Far Eastern countries, including Indonesia. He thought it desir-

able, however, that the Bank should make a more dynamic evaluation of applications from the under-developed countries and that it should have a more favourable lending rate.

In reply to the various points raised in the debate, the President of the Bank stated that the Bank would do all in its power to provide additional investments for sound projects in under-developed countries, which were within their absorptive capacity. He regretted that the tightening of the capital market had necessitated the increase in the Bank's interest rate, and he gave assurances that the statutory commission would be reduced as soon as that was found possible. An increased flow of private investment capital, he stressed, depended not only on measures taken by the Governments of the capital-supplying countries but also on action by the capital-importing countries to provide a favourable investment climate. He also hoped that it would be possible for the Bank to make larger investments in Asia and Africa which were so urgently in need of capital.

On 18 April 1957, the Council adopted a resolution (637(XXIII)) taking note of the Bank's report.

DOCUMENTARY REFERENCES

ECONOMIC AND SOCIAL COUNCIL—23RD SESSION
Plenary Meetings 958, 959.

E/2944 and Add.1. Report of International Bank for Reconstruction and Development for fiscal year

ended 30 June 1956 and Summary of developments from 1 July 1956-31 January 1957.
RESOLUTION 637(XXIII), taking note of International Bank for Reconstruction and Development report, adopted by Council on 18 April 1957, meeting 959.

COLLECTION OF INFORMATION ON INTERNATIONAL ECONOMIC ASSISTANCE

In the course of the discussions at the General Assembly's eleventh session on the financing of economic development, reference was made to the fact that economic aid was being contributed to the less developed countries both through multilateral aid programmes and in the form of bilateral aid programmes. It was generally felt that consideration of the general problems of financing economic development would be assisted if there were available information showing the over-all size of international economic aid, and distinguishing the main categories of assistance being given to the less developed countries.

The Assembly therefore asked the Economic and Social Council (in February 1957) to consider at its twenty-fourth session the question

of the collection of such information on international economic aid programmes as would contribute to constructive consideration by the United Nations of assistance to less developed areas. In order that the Council might be aware of the dimensions of economic aid in recent years, the Secretary-General prepared a statistical report surveying the nature, magnitude and direction of the economic aid provided to the less developed areas by the main contributing countries through bilateral programmes and through various international agencies. It was estimated that in the three-year period 1954-1956 bilateral grants amounted to approximately $3,400 million, net bilateral loans to $1,200 million, and grants and net loans through international agencies to $266 million and $280 million.

In order to put the scale of assistance in perspective, the aid furnished to each self-governing country was related to the size of its population and to the level of its economic development. The Secretary-General's report showed, for the three-year period covered, that countries with an aggregate population of 665 million whose gross national product was less than $100 per head per year received about $2.5 per head; countries with an aggregate population of 122 million whose gross national product was between $100 and $200 per head per year received about $8.4 per head; countries with an aggregate population of 131 million whose gross national product was between $200 and $300 per head per year received about $5.1 per head; and countries with an aggregate population of 55 million whose gross national product was more than $300 per head per year received about $3.0 per head.

The survey also identified a number of major issues involved in compiling studies of international economic assistance and, for the Council's consideration, made proposals on definitions and methods to be employed in future surveys.

In the course of the Council's discussions, it was noted that, compared with other sources of international development financing, bilateral aid programmes were of major importance for many of the less developed countries. It was agreed that the report should be distributed to all Member States. On 30 July 1957 the Council adopted a resolution (662 A (XXIV)) asking the Secretary-General to submit information to it periodically on economic assistance to the less developed countries and urging Governments and international organizations to co-operate with the Secretary-General in the provision of appropriate information for future surveys.

DOCUMENTARY REFERENCES

ECONOMIC AND SOCIAL COUNCIL—24TH SESSION
Plenary Meetings 990-994.

E/3047 and Add.1. Financing of economic development. Information concerning international economic assistance for less developed countries. Report by Secretary-General.
E/L.767 and Add.1. Argentina, Canada, France draft resolution.
RESOLUTION 662 A (XXIV), as submitted by three powers, E/L.767 and Add.1, and as orally amended by the Netherlands, adopted by Council on 30 July 1957, meeting 993, by 11 votes to 0, with 7 abstentions.

Collection of Information concerning International Economic Assistance for the Less Developed Countries
"The Economic and Social Council,
"Recalling General Assembly resolution 1034(XI) of 26 February 1957 on the collection of information concerning international economic assistance for the less developed countries,
"Considering that such information will contribute to better understanding of the progress and problems

of economic development,
"Taking note of the document circulated by the Secretary-General as a preliminary survey of the economic assistance provided by Governments and public institutions of States Members of the United Nations both bilaterally and through the international agencies concerned with the development of the less developed countries,
"1. Expresses appreciation to the Secretary-General for his report which constitutes a useful source of information for States Members of the United Nations on the subject of the financing of economic development;
"2. Requests the Secretary-General to submit this survey on a periodic basis to the Council including such supplementary information as may be provided by contributing and recipient Governments, taking account of the comments of delegations at the twenty-fourth session of the Council;
"3. Urges Governments and international organizations concerned to co-operate with the Secretary-General in the provision of appropriate information for future surveys, including information on the economic utilization of aid."

INDUSTRIALIZATION AND PRODUCTIVITY

In 1957, the United Nations Secretariat began work on several projects dealing with industrialization and ways to increase productivity, particularly in under-developed areas. It did so in carrying out a work programme in these fields as approved in 1956 by the General Assembly

(resolution 1033(XI)) and the Economic and Social Council (resolutions 597(XXI) and 618(XXII)).

The first project undertaken was a general survey of the problem of capital intensity (that is, the problem of determining the best combination of the production factors—capital and labour) in developing industrial production in under-developed countries.

Two papers were prepared on this subject. The first, a general study by a consultant to the Secretariat, dealt with the theoretical aspects of the problem of choice among alternative techniques of production. It briefly reviewed the state of empirical research in this field and suggested a systematic approach to the question in future. The second paper, based on reports of United Nations technical assistance experts, dealt with the problem of capital intensity as it has actually arisen in countries in the process of economic development.

Work was also begun on the question of capital intensity as it relates to specific industries, studies on the construction industry being undertaken. One of them analysed the economic and technological factors involved in the choice of techniques for heavy-engineering projects, such as canals, dams and other extensive earth-moving operations for hydro-electric and multi-purpose water development. The material in this study was based for the most part on the experience of industrialized countries and was appraised in the light of conditions prevailing in under-developed countries.

The study was discussed by the conference on water resource development held by the Economic Commission for Asia and the Far East (ECAFE) in December 1957. A preliminary draft of it was submitted to the Committee on Electric Power of the Economic Commission for Europe (ECE). A questionnaire on construction costs of hydro-electric installations was prepared and circulated to Governments in the ECE region.

In connexion with the programme of economic integration in Central America, studies were being prepared by the United Nations Headquarters Secretariat during 1957, in collaboration with the Economic Commission for Latin America (ECLA), on the relationship between the cost of production and plant capacity in several selected industries in the region.

Preliminary work started on a number of questions relating to the promotion of small-scale industries. This involved, among other things, an analysis of reports by United Nations

technical assistance experts on Government measures for the encouragement of such enterprises.

A panel of experts on industrial management met at United Nations Headquarters from 24 September to 5 October 1957. The panel considered various economic and social aspects of industrial management in under-developed countries and recommended measures which might be taken by both government and private enterprise to improve the effectiveness of management in such countries. To help attain this aim, suggestions were also made for co-operation with international organizations, particularly with the United Nations Technical Assistance Administration (TAA).

A number of the studies mentioned above were completed or nearing completion by the end of 1957. Several of them were to be published in the first issue of the forthcoming *Bulletin on Industrialization and Productivity,* scheduled to appear in the early part of 1958. The report of the panel of experts on industrial management was to be published separately.

Steps were also taken by the Secretariat to carry out a number of studies on the social aspects of industrialization recommended by the Social Commission at its eleventh session, in 1957, as follows: (1) case studies on the relationship of community development and co-operatives to the process of industrialization; (2) a study on current trends in environmental planning; (3) a seminar on environmental planning and the location of industry for Asia and the Far East; and (4) a study of general social services in relation to industrialization. (See also below, CHAPTER XII, SOCIAL AND POPULATION QUESTIONS.)

CONSIDERATION BY THE ECONOMIC AND SOCIAL COUNCIL

At its twenty-third session in April 1957, the Economic and Social Council had before it a progress report by the Secretary-General describing the programme of work on industrialization and productivity up to that date, as requested by the Council in 1956 by resolution 597(XXI) and 618(XXII).

In the debate on the subject, there was a general agreement that efforts should be made to expand the scope of the programme and that the projects undertaken should provide practical assistance and guidance to under-developed countries.

The Netherlands representative considered that a project on the techniques of economic planning and programming was of practical importance. He suggested that the Secretariat should collect and disseminate information required for such programming, particularly data on international trends likely to influence the development of various countries. He also suggested studies on experience gained in the operation of public enterprises, and on the relationship between market prices for capital and labour, and their real prices.

The representative of France suggested early implementation of a project on environmental planning, and the Polish representative thought that high priority should be given to studies of resources needed for industrial development and the technology of raw materials.

Several representatives drew attention to the importance of studies on small-scale industries. Among the additional projects suggested for inclusion in the work programme was one mentioned by the spokesman for China on the construction of small-scale and medium-scale factories and another by the USSR representative on the relationship between prices of raw materials and industrial products.

Several Council members considered the problem of organizational machinery as extremely important in implementing the programme of work in industrialization. The representative of Yugoslavia suggested the establishment of a special United Nations body to deal with the problem, to take the form, for the present, of a functional commission of the Council. Pakistan's representative considered that it might be necessary to establish a permanent unit within the Secretariat. Several representatives, including those of Greece and the United Kingdom, noted that the programme of work was being implemented by the appropriate units of the Secretariat in close collaboration with the specialized agencies. They urged that such cooperation be continued in order to avoid any duplication of effort.

On 2 May 1957, the Council finally adopted a resolution looking forward to intensified implementation of the work programme which it had approved the year before, with special attention being given to the needs of the Middle East and Africa and to studies and projects that would provide practical help and guidance in the industrial progress of the under-developed countries.

At the same time, the Council made two requests of the Secretary-General: (1) to explore, in consultation with the appropriate specialized agencies, further possibilities of organizing seminars, consultations and training centres which would serve the practical application of the work programme on industrialization; and (2) to consider the possibility of collecting available up-to-date basic economic information (including that bearing on trends) of interest to public and private agencies concerned with economic programming.

The resolution to this effect (649(XXIII)) was approved unanimously on the recommendation of the Council's Economic Committee. It was based on a proposal put forward in the Committee by Canada, France, Indonesia, the Netherlands, Pakistan, and Yugoslavia, as amended orally by Argentina, Egypt, Pakistan and Yugoslavia.

DOCUMENTARY REFERENCES

ECONOMIC AND SOCIAL COUNCIL—23RD SESSION
Plenary Meetings 960-964, 971.
Second Committee, meetings 217-220.

E/2958. Industrialization: Progress report of Secretary-General on implementation of programme of work on industrialization and productivity.
E/AC.6/L.175. Canada, France, Indonesia, Netherlands, Pakistan, Yugoslavia draft resolution, as amended orally by Argentina, Egypt, Pakistan and Yugoslavia, adopted unanimously by Economic Committee.
E/2988. Report of Economic Committee (Section I).

RESOLUTION 649 A (XXIII), as recommended by Economic Committee, E/2988, adopted unanimously by Council on 2 May 1957, meeting 971.

"The Economic and Social Council,
"Taking note of the progress report on the implementation of the programme of work on industrialization and productivity,
"Recalling that, in accordance with General Assembly resolution 1033 B (XI) of 26 February 1957, the question of organizational and administrative machinery in the field of industrialization will be considered by the Council at its twenty-fifth session,

"*Bearing in mind* the importance of rapid industrialization in the less developed countries as a significant factor in the balanced development of their economies,

"*Recognizing* the role that the industrially advanced and the under-developed countries have to play in such a programme,

"1. *Looks forward* to intensified implementation of the programme of work contained in the report by the Secretary-General under Council resolution 597 A (XXI) of 4 May 1956, with special attention to the needs of the Middle East and Africa in accordance with paragraph 9 of the above-mentioned resolution, and with particular emphasis on such studies and projects as would provide practical assistance and guidance in the industrial progress of the under-developed countries;

"2. *Requests* the Secretary-General to explore, in consultation with the appropriate specialized agencies, further possibilities of organizing—in connexion with the studies on industrialization—seminars, consultations and training centres, which would serve the practical application of the programme;

3. *Requests* the Secretary-General to consider the possibility of collecting available up-to-date basic economic data, including those bearing on trends, which would be of interest to the public and private agencies concerned with economic programming."

LAND REFORM

Land reform questions were considered during 1957 by the Economic and Social Council at its twenty-third session, held between 16 April and 2 May.

Before it was a report entitled *Progress in Land Reform, Second Report,* prepared by the Secretary-General in collaboration with the Food and Agriculture Organization (FAO) and the International Labour Organisation (ILO) in compliance with resolution 370(XIII), adopted by the Council in 1951.

This report analysed the replies from Governments to a questionnaire on land reform (transmitted by the Secretary-General under the terms of resolution 370(XIII)) and a supplementary questionnaire requested under Council resolution 512 C (XVII), which was adopted in 1954. The second questionnaire dealt with the impact of land reform measures already undertaken on agricultural employment and output, production patterns in rural economy, standards of living of rural populations, and, economic development in general.

The report to the Council dealt mainly with general reform policies, agrarian structure and related land reform measures. Containing information on the impact of land reform measures already under way, it briefly summarized the progress achieved by Governments, reviewed the main obstacles to land reform measures and made recommendations for further international action. The relevant activities of the United Nations and the specialized agencies in the field were also surveyed.

In the course of the discussions in the Council's Economic Committee, several representatives referred to specific problems of land reform in their countries and in territories under their administration. One point frequently made was that land reform, being an aspect of economic development, should be studied and dealt with as part of comprehensive national and international efforts for both economic and social development. Many members emphasized the importance of employment for surplus rural populations, drew attention to the close link between land reform and industrialization, and pointed out the need for international action for the financing of agricultural development programmes and for further technical assistance, including the organization of training courses and the dissemination of information. Attention was also drawn to the close relationship between the use of co-operatives and land reform.

There was general agreement that the second report prepared by the Secretary-General was a useful reference work. However, some Council members and the representatives of the World Federation of Trade Unions and the International Confederation of Free Trade Unions maintained that the questionnaires and the report had not paid sufficient attention to various social aspects of land reform. Several representatives pointed out that no set pattern could be followed in carrying out land reform programmes or in their evaluation because conditions varied widely from country to country.

It was generally agreed that the periodic inquiries and reports by international organizations could be more usefully spread over longer intervals than was required under present arrangements.

As to the studies on the impact of land reform policies, there was general agreement that future reports by the Secretariat should be focused on specific problems, such as the effects of such policies on production, employment, living standards and general economic development. The representative of FAO suggested that such studies should also be undertaken by Governments. He added that FAO was prepared, in co-operation with other specialized agencies, to assist in organizing these studies.

The final outcome of the discussions was a unanimous resolution urging Governments to continue their efforts to implement the relevant Council and Assembly resolutions on land reform. The Council also suggested that they undertake specific studies on the implementation of land reform measures and their economic and social impacts, and it called attention to the availability of technical assistance from the United Nations and the specialized agencies. In adopting its resolution to this effect, the Council noted that progress in various aspects of land reform had been made in many countries, and recognized that further progress toward the solution of problems of land utilization, ownership and tenure was important both for the social advancement of low-income rural populations and over-all economic development.

The Council further invited the Secretary-General and the specialized agencies to give particular attention to such activities as the dissemination of information on the experience of individual countries, the organization of semi-nars and training courses, the promotion of pilot projects and the promotion of national and international collaboration in research. A report on these activities was requested for the Council's twenty-seventh session, to be held early in 1959.

The Council also renewed a previous recommendation that the International Bank for Reconstruction and Development give "sympathetic consideration" to loan applications for development projects designed to implement agrarian reform programmes.

In addition, the Secretary-General was asked to keep developments in land reform under review and to submit a further report to the Council in 1962, and, in this connexion, to prepare the prospectus for its twenty-seventh session describing the specific land reform problems to be taken up, and indicating the information available or required. Finally, the Council invited Governments to provide the Secretary-General and the specialized agencies with the information which might be needed.

The resolution to this effect (649 B (XXIII)) was unanimously adopted by the Council on 2 May 1957, on the unanimous recommendation of its Economic Committee. It was based on an amended proposal in the Economic Committee sponsored by Argentina, Egypt, Indonesia, Mexico, Poland and the United States.

DOCUMENTARY REFERENCES

ECONOMIC AND SOCIAL COUNCIL—23RD SESSION
Plenary Meetings 960-964, 971.
Economic Committee, meetings 217-220.

Progress in Land Reform, Second Report (E/2930). U.N.P. Sales No.: 1956.II.B.3.
E/AC.6/L.176. Argentina, Egypt, Indonesia, Mexico, Poland, United States draft resolution, as amended orally by Canada, adopted unanimously by Economic Committee.
E/2988. Report of Economic Committee (Section II).
RESOLUTION 649 B (XXIII), as recommended by Economic Committee, E/2988, adopted unanimously by Council on 2 May 1957, meeting 971.

"The Economic and Social Council,
"*Having examined* the second report on progress in land reform, prepared by the Secretary-General in co-operation with the International Labour Organisation and the Food and Agriculture Organization of the United Nations,
"*Taking into account* the views expressed on various aspects of land reform during the discussion on this subject at the twenty-third session of the Council,

"*Noting* from the analysis, contained in the above-mentioned report, of the replies to the questionnaire distributed by the Secretary-General that progress in various aspects of land reform has been made in many countries,
"*Recognizing* that, for many countries, further progress towards satisfactory solutions of problems of land utilization, ownership and tenure is important both for the social advancement of low-income rural populations and over-all economic development,
"1. *Urges* Governments to continue their efforts to implement the appropriate recommendations in Council resolutions 370(XIII) of 7 September 1951, 512 C I (XVII) of 30 April 1954 and General Assembly resolutions 625 A (VII) of 21 December 1952 and 826(IX) of 14 December 1954, suggests that Governments undertake specific studies of the implementation of land reform measures and their impact on production, living standards and economic and social development, and calls the attention of Governments to the availability of technical advice and assistance from the United Nations and specialized agencies;
"2. *Invites* the Secretary-General, the Food and Agriculture Organization of the United Nations, the

International Labour Organisation and other specialized agencies, in their respective fields of work for
advancement of land reform, to give particular attention to such activities as:

"(a) The dissemination of information regarding
the experience of individual countries with respect to
national measures of land reform;

"(b) The organization of seminars and training
courses on institutional problems to assist in the promotion of sound national land policies;

"(c) The promotion, with the aid of technical
assistance from the United Nations and the specialized
agencies, of appropriate pilot projects and studies in
individual countries;

"(d) The promotion, both nationally and internationally, of collaboration by institutions on research
related to land reform;

"3. Renews its recommendation that the International Bank for Reconstruction and Development give
sympathetic consideration to loan applications for development projects designed to implement programmes
of agrarian reform;

"4. Requests the Secretary-General to keep under

review developments in the field of land reform and
to prepare, in collaboration with the appropriate
specialized agencies, a further report on land reform
for submission to the Council in 1962;

"5. Requests the Secretary-General, in collaboration with the specialized agencies and recognizing the
major responsibilities in this field of the Food and
Agriculture Organization of the United Nations, to
present to the Council at its twenty-seventh session a
report on progress in the work referred to in paragraph 2 above, together with a prospectus of the
report referred to in paragraph 4 above which would
describe the specific land reform problems to which it
was planned to devote attention and indicate the information which would be available for such a report
as well as the kinds and sources of additional information which would be required;

"6. Decides that paragraphs 4 and 5 above super-
sede paragraph 8 of Council resolution 370(XIII);

"7. Invites Governments to provide the Secretary-
General and the specialized agencies with information
which may be needed for the implementation of the
present resolution."

CO-OPERATIVES

The question of co-operatives was considered
by the Economic and Social Council at its
twenty-third session, held between 16 April and
2 May 1957. Before it was a report on co-
operatives in the less developed economies, prepared by the Secretary-General in collaboration
with the International Labour Organisation
(ILO) and the Food and Agriculture Organization (FAO) in accordance with a Council resolution adopted in 1954. The report described
the various forms of assistance which might be
provided by Governments and other agencies,
and the sectors of economies suitable for the
co-operative form of organization. It also outlined the problems which arise in the development of co-operatives, particularly in under-
developed countries.

In the debate on the subject, Council members agreed generally that assistance to co-operative societies should consist primarily of training
staff and disseminating information on the
objectives, methods and advantages of co-operative organization. Several representatives
stressed the importance of these forms of aid.
They also called attention to the need for seminars, training facilities and other types of technical aid in promoting the development of
co-operatives. These points were further emphasized by the representative of the International Co-operative Alliance.

Some representatives felt that the relationship
between Governments and co-operatives should
be thoroughly explored. Several stated that
while it was difficult in most under-developed
countries to establish co-operative societies without Government support, it was desirable to
maintain their voluntary character and independence. Some doubted the usefulness of co-
operative organizations in promoting industrialization. But others were of the opinion that the
application of co-operative techniques could be
fruitful in this and in other fields. Some representatives also maintained that agricultural,
fisheries and housing co-operatives could make
an effective contribution in the earlier stages of
economic development. Stressed, too, was the
usefulness of this form of organization in community development schemes.

There was general agreement that future
studies by the United Nations and the specialized agencies should explore specific topics, such
as the role of co-operatives in community development and low-cost housing programmes,
the question of government participation in promoting co-operative societies, and the experience gained with co-operative projects for which
technical assistance has been provided.

The Council finally adopted a resolution recognizing that, while co-operatives were based
on the principle of voluntary association and

self-administration, they might benefit from Government support and advice in their organization and management. It noted that inadequate understanding of the purposes and ideals of co-operatives, and the lack of training for their management, made it difficult to establish these organizations and impaired their efficiency. It invited Governments to encourage, when appropriate, the organization of co-operatives, especially in agriculture, fisheries and community development, and to take suitable measures for both the elementary and advanced training of staff, bearing in mind the assistance available under various technical aid programmes.

In addition, the Council requested the Secretary-General of the United Nations and the specialized agencies concerned to give Member States all possible assistance and advice in carrying out these activities, including the establishment of training institutions.

The Secretary-General was also asked to ensure that appropriate attention would be given in studies on economic and social development

to co-operatives as a technique for development, and to continue specific studies on the role of co-operatives in community development and low-cost housing programmes. The Council recommended, too, that ILO and FAO continue to carry out studies on methods found to be most effective in developed and under-developed countries in the specific fields in which co-operatives could most usefully contribute to the promotion of modern techniques, particularly agriculture and fisheries.

The Secretary-General was asked to report on the implementation of this resolution at the Council's twenty-ninth session, in the earlier part of 1960.

The resolution (649 C (XXIII)), adopted by the Council unanimously on 2 May 1957, was based on a proposal introduced in the Council's Economic Committee by Canada, Finland, France, Mexico, Pakistan and Yugoslavia. The Economic Committee also adopted it unanimously.

DOCUMENTARY REFERENCES

ECONOMIC AND SOCIAL COUNCIL—23RD SESSION
Plenary Meetings 960-964, 971.
Second Committee, meetings 217-220.

E/2950. Co-operatives. Report of Secretary-General.
E/AC.6/L.177 and Rev.1. Canada, Finland, France, Mexico, Pakistan, Yugoslavia draft resolution and revision, as amended by sponsors in light of suggestions made by Egypt and Netherlands, adopted unanimously by Economic Committee.
E/2988. Report of Economic Committee (Section III).
RESOLUTION 649 C (XXIII), as recommended by Economic Committee, E/2988, adopted unanimously by Council on 2 May 1957, meeting 971.

"The Economic and Social Council,
"Having examined the report prepared by the Secretary-General in collaboration with the International Labour Organisation and the Food and Agriculture Organization of the United Nations, pursuant to Council resolution 512 C II (XVII) of 30 April 1954, and taking into account the opinions expressed at the twenty-third session of the Council,
"Recognizing that while co-operatives are based on the principle of voluntary association and self-administration, they may benefit from Governments' support and advice in organization and management,
"Considering that the Secretary-General and the specialized agencies have already completed many studies on the subject of co-operatives, particularly in the field of agriculture and fisheries,
"Considering that priority should be given to studies

and research on methods whereby the action of co-operatives in specific fields could most effectively contribute to the integrated economic and social development of under-developed areas,
"Noting that, particularly in the early stages of economic development, inadequate understanding of the purposes and ideals of co-operatives and the lack of appropriate training for management make co-operatives difficult to establish and impair their efficiency,
"1. Invites the Governments of Member States:
"(a) To encourage, when appropriate, the organization of co-operatives in the less developed areas, especially in the field of agriculture and fisheries and in the general field of community development, and to this end to take suitable measures, especially in respect of elementary and advanced training for their staff and information for their members, both in the preliminary and in the more advanced stages of their development;
"(b) To bear in mind that from various technical assistance programmes assistance is available to the Governments of under-developed countries for promoting the development of co-operatives;
"2. Requests the Secretary-General and the specialized agencies concerned, through their regional offices when appropriate, to give Member States all possible assistance and advice in carrying out the above activities, including the establishment of training institutions;
"3. Requests the Secretary-General to ensure that:
"(a) In studies on economic and social development, attention should be given when appropriate to

the place of co-operatives as a technique for development having important social as well as economic benefits;

"(b) Specific studies on the role of co-operatives in community development and low-cost housing programmes should be continued within the framework of programmes authorized by the Council at its twenty-second session;

"4. *Recommends* that the International Labour Organisation and the Food and Agriculture Organization of the United Nations should continue to carry out studies on the methods which experience in developed and under-developed countries has shown to be most effective in the various specific fields in which co-operatives can most usefully contribute to the promotion of modern techniques, especially in agriculture and fisheries;

"5. *Requests* the Secretary-General to report to the Council at its twenty-ninth session on the implementation of the above recommendations."

CONSERVATION AND USE OF NON-AGRICULTURAL RESOURCES

REPORT BY SECRETARY-GENERAL

A report on United Nations action for the conservation and use of non-agricultural resources was submitted by the Secretary-General of the United Nations for the Economic and Social Council's twenty-third session, held between 16 April and 2 May 1957. The tenth of its kind, it was prepared in accordance with Council resolution 345(XII), adopted in March 1951. It was not, however, discussed at the Council's twenty-third session.

Among other things, the report gave a brief account of work on mineral resources. A review, it said, had been made of: (a) requests for technical assistance in mining development and geological surveys which had been addressed to the United Nations Technical Assistance Administration and (b) reports by technical assistance experts in connexion with such aid. The review was intended as a guide for future technical assistance activities in mining development and geological surveys.

The report gave a brief account, too, of work of the United Nations regional economic commissions on the use and development of non-agricultural resources.

The report also described various activities for the use and development of water resources and preparations for studies on the use of atomic energy and other new sources of energy for furthering economic development, as requested by the Council by resolutions 597 B (XXI) and 598(XXI) both adopted on 4 May 1956.

WATER RESOURCES

Activities for the use and development of water resources, the Secretary-General's report stated, had been devoted mainly to meeting the requests made by the Council on 3 May 1956 (by resolution 599(XXI)) for (a) a preliminary inquiry into existing hydrologic services and plans and conditions for their extension and (b) the establishment of a panel of world-renowned experts to review the administrative, economic and social implications of integrated river-basin development and to advise on proper action to ensure a world-wide exchange of relevant experience and information.

In preparation for the study on hydrologic services, the report said, a questionnaire had been drawn up jointly by the World Meteorological Organization and the United Nations Secretariat, and addressed to the Members of the United Nations and the specialized agencies. Replies to the questionnaire were being received and processed. A report on this was to be submitted to the Council's twenty-fifth session in the early part of 1958.

In addition, a study on industrial uses of water was being prepared by the Secretariat.

The Secretary-General also informed the Council that a third inter-agency meeting on international co-operation on the development and use of water resources had been held in July 1956.[1]

FOURTH INTER-AGENCY MEETING ON
INTERNATIONAL CO-OPERATION IN THE
DEVELOPMENT AND USE OF WATER RESOURCES

The fourth inter-agency meeting on water resources was held at United Nations Headquarters in New York on 25-27 November 1957. It was attended by members of the Secretariats of the United Nations, the World Meteorological Organization, the World Health Organization, the United Nations Educational, Scientific and Cultural Organization and the Food and Agriculture Organization. Among the matters discussed were the possibilities of concerted action in the use and development of water re-

[1] See also *Y.U.N., 1956,* pp. 179-80.

sources in the light of Economic and Social Council resolution 665 A (XXIV) (see below, CHAPTER XV, QUESTIONS OF CO-ORDINATION AND RELATIONS OF THE UNITED NATIONS WITH THE SPECIALIZED AGENCIES). Examined, too, were questions dealing with the preparation of reports for the Council's twenty-fifth session, the Secretary-General's report on international co-operation on the development of water resources, the study on hydrologic services, and a progress report on work in respect of techniques of resources and requirements surveys as requested by the Economic and Social Council on 4 August 1956, by resolution 614 C (XXII). In addition, the meeting also discussed: current projects of common interest, such as the Mekong River project; recent developments in the appraisal of hydro-power resources in the regions covered by the regional economic commissions for Europe, for Asia and the Far East and for Latin America; preparatory work on drawing up a water resources terminology; bases and possible arrangements for collecting statistics dealing with the use and development of water resources.

USE OF NEW ENERGY SOURCES FOR ECONOMIC DEVELOPMENT

At its twenty-fourth session, in mid-1957, the Council had before it two studies on new energy resources and their use in furthering economic development.

One, entitled *Economic Applications of Atomic Energy: Power Generation and Industrial and Agricultural Uses,* analysed, in relation to probable trends in the demand for power and to conventional sources of power supply, the possibilities of using atomic energy to produce electric power. It also discussed the use of radioisotopes and radiation in industry and agriculture, the section on agricultural uses having been prepared by the Food and Agriculture Organization (FAO). A second part of the study presented supporting material, including a questionnaire sent by the Secretary-General to members of the United Nations Advisory Committee on the Peaceful Uses of Atomic Energy and the replies to it received from the Governments of Canada, France, the USSR, the United Kingdom and the United States. It also carried a statement on associated labour problems, prepared by the International Labour

Organisation, and a statement on facilities for technical training in the uses of atomic energy for peaceful purposes, prepared by UNESCO.

The second report was entitled *New Sources of Energy and Economic Development: Solar Energy, Wind Energy, Tidal Energy, Geothermic Energy and Thermal Energy of the Seas.* In preparing it, the Secretary-General had asked five specialists of international reputation each to send him a background study on one of these new sources of energy. The report briefly reviewed possible methods of controlling and using these five sources of energy for economic purposes. It also appraised their main characteristics, their possible role in the production of electric power and other uses to which they could be put. The second part of the report presented extracts from the experts' background studies in the form of five annexes. An annotated bibliography, prepared by UNESCO, constituted the third part of the report.

Debate in the Council and its Economic Committee revealed general agreement that, in relation to economic development, sources of energy, conventional and unconventional, whether of atomic or of other origin, should not be considered in isolation one from another. This basic importance of energy for economic development was fully recognized.

One question discussed was that of the desirability of devoting a substantial part of the Second International Conference on the Peaceful Uses of Atomic Energy (to be held in 1958) to an examination of the practical uses of nuclear energy for promoting the development of under-developed economies. In a report to the Council on this matter, the Secretary-General stated that his consultations with the Advisory Committee on the Peaceful Uses of Atomic Energy and the interested specialized agencies had led him to the view that the agenda prepared for the Conference would cover a wide range of topics with important implications for the economic development of under-developed countries. It was generally agreed that the agenda of the Conference would fully cover the subject in which the Council was interested and that there was no reason to organize a special conference to consider practical uses of nuclear energy for promoting the economic development of under-developed countries.

Several representatives stressed how important it was for all countries to be kept fully informed of progress made in the practical application of atomic energy. Many also pointed out the importance of providing more facilities for training scientific and technical personnel in related fields.

The USSR representative raised the question of the role which might be played by the regional economic commissions in furthering co-operation in using atomic energy for peaceful purposes. He proposed, in the Council's Economic Committee, that the commissions be asked to work out measures at the regional level (such as the establishment of committees or other bodies) for the exchange of scientific and technical information.

A number of other representatives, however, maintained that such measures could not be envisaged until the new International Atomic Energy Agency had been given enough time to develop its activities. The USSR proposal was rejected by the Economic Committee by a vote of 8 to 7, with 2 abstentions.

Also discussed were new energy sources other than the atomic. One point made was that while these sources could play an important role in some areas lacking conventional sources of energy, further technical developments were needed to make economic use of them. Special assistance could be given in that respect by such specialized agencies as UNESCO and FAO, it was maintained. Several representatives considered that an international conference on these new energy sources would be an effective way to promote research on them. Others, however, disagreed. They thought it would be premature to have such a conference in the near future.

The Council finally adopted a unanimous resolution on 26 July, on the unanimous recommendation of its Economic Committee. This commended the Secretary-General for the studies prepared in consultation with the specialized agencies and asked him to continue to follow the relationship of conventional, atomic and other sources of energy to economic development. It also asked him to review, in consultation with the appropriate specialized agencies, the work already being done in the field of energy resources, including technical assistance, and to make appropriate recommendations to its twenty-seventh session, due to be held in

the early part of 1959. The Council further recognized the interest of under-developed countries in being kept fully informed of possible applications of atomic energy, especially in the fields of power, industry and agriculture, and it invited Governments to make the fullest use of United Nations facilities, including technical assistance, for the training of scientific and technical personnel in the fields of the peaceful applications of atomic energy.

The Secretary-General was also asked: to transmit the study *Economic Applications of Atomic Energy* to the regional economic commissions and interested specialized agencies for their consideration and comment; to take the necessary steps to bring the report to the attention of the Second International Conference on the Peaceful Uses of Atomic Energy; and to transmit the study to the International Atomic Energy Agency (IAEA) for its examination and comments on the fields in which the United Nations and IAEA could act jointly. Noting also that further developments of a technical character were needed to bring new sources of energy other than the atom to a stage of wider economic application, the Council requested the Secretary-General to transmit the study *New Sources of Energy and Economic Development* to the appropriate specialized agencies, particularly UNESCO and FAO, and to appropriate non-governmental organizations with a view to encouraging further scientific and technological studies, especially with regard to solar and wind energy. In addition, it asked the Secretary-General for a progress report for the Council's twenty-seventh session on developments in these fields with recommendations about the agenda for an international conference on the economic applications of new sources of energy, to be convened as soon as feasible after the Council's twenty-seventh session. The progress report was to be prepared in collaboration with UNESCO and FAO.

The resolution to this effect (653(XXIV)) was based on the amended version of a proposal introduced in the Economic Committee by Argentina, Brazil, France, Indonesia, Mexico, the Netherlands and Yugoslavia.

Before giving final approval to the resolution, the Council, at a plenary meeting, rejected a USSR amendment asking the regional economic commissions to develop co-operation in the field of the peaceful use of atomic energy on a regional basis such as might ultimately contribute to the successful activities of the International Atomic Energy Agency. The Council rejected this amendment by 11 votes to 5, with 2 abstentions.

DOCUMENTARY REFERENCES

ECONOMIC AND SOCIAL COUNCIL—23RD SESSION

E/2981. Conservation and utilization of non-agricultural resources. Report of Secretary-General on action taken under Council resolution 345(XII).

ECONOMIC AND SOCIAL COUNCIL—24TH SESSION
Plenary Meeting 990.
Economic Committee, meetings 223-226.

New Sources of Energy and Economic Development: Solar Energy, Wind Energy, Tidal Energy, Geothermic Energy and Thermal Energy of the Seas (E/2997). U.N.P. Sales No.: 1957.II.B.1.

Economic Applications of Atomic Energy: Power Generation and Industrial and Agricultural Uses (E/3005). U.N.P. Sales No.: 1957.II.B.2.

E/3014. Sources of energy as a means of economic development. Report by Secretary-General under Council resolution 597 B (XXI), paragraph 4.

E/AC.6/L.184. USSR draft resolution (on regional co-operation in peaceful uses of atomic energy).

E/AC.6/L.186. Argentina draft resolution (on studies on uses of atomic energy for peaceful purposes).

E/AC.6/L.190 and Add.1, 2. Argentina, Brazil, France, Indonesia, Mexico, Netherlands, Yugoslavia draft resolution (on sources of energy as means of economic development), adopted unanimously by Economic Committee, as amended.

E/AC.6/L.191. United Kingdom amendments to joint draft resolution, E/AC.6/L.190.

E/AC.6/L.192. Egypt amendments to joint draft resolution, E/AC.6/L.190.

E/3032. Report of Economic Committee.

E/L.763. USSR amendment to draft resolution contained in Report of Economic Committee, E/3032.

RESOLUTION 653(XXIV), as recommended by Economic Committee, E/3032, adopted unanimously by Council on 26 July 1957, meeting 990.

"*The Economic and Social Council,*

"*Having considered* the reports presented by the Secretary-General on the economic applications of atomic energy pursuant to paragraph 1 of resolution 597 B (XXI) of 4 May 1956, on the new sources of energy other than the atom as a means of economic development in accordance with resolution 598(XXI) of 4 May 1956, and the report dealing specifically with paragraph 4 of resolution 597 B (XXI),

"*Taking into account* the basic importance of energy for economic development, for increasing productivity and for industrialization, and *recognizing* that sources of energy, conventional and non-conventional, cannot be considered in isolation one from another in relation to economic development,

"*Reaffirming* the interest of the Council 'in promoting the effective and sustained use of the world's natural resources as a means of furthering economic development' as expressed in its resolution 345 B (XII) of 9 March 1951,

"*Considering* the work already carried out in this field by the Secretary-General, particularly through the regional offices,

I

"1. *Commends* the Secretary-General for these studies prepared in consultation with the specialized agencies;

"2. *Requests* the Secretary-General to continue to follow the relationship of all forms of conventional and of atomic and other new sources of energy to economic development, particularly of the under-developed countries, as part of his continuing work in the field of conservation and utilization of non-agricultural resources pursuant to Council resolution 345 (XII);

"3. *Further requests* the Secretary-General to review, in consultation with the appropriate specialized agencies, the work already being done in the field of energy resources, including technical assistance activity, and to make to the Council at its twenty-seventh session such recommendations regarding future work, as he considers appropriate;

II

"*Recognizing* the interest of under-developed countries in being kept fully informed of the possible economic applications of atomic energy, especially in the fields of power, industry and agriculture,

"1. *Invites* Governments to make the fullest possible use of United Nations facilities, including those of the Expanded Programme of Technical Assistance, for the training of scientific and technical personnel in the fields of the peaceful applications of atomic energy;

"2. *Requests* the Secretary-General to transmit the above-mentioned report on the economic applications of atomic energy to the regional economic commissions and the interested specialized agencies for their consideration and comment as appropriate;

"3. *Further requests* the Secretary-General to take the necessary steps to bring this report to the attention of the second international conference on exchange of technical information regarding the peaceful uses of atomic energy;

"4. *Further requests* the Secretary-General to transmit this report to the International Atomic Energy Agency, upon its establishment, for examination and comments on the fields in which the United Nations and the International Atomic Energy Agency could act jointly to discharge their responsibilities in this regard according to both the Charter of the United Nations and the Statute of the Agency;

III

"*Noting also* that in regard to new sources of energy other than the atom, further developments of a technical character are needed to bring them to a stage of wider economic application,

"1. *Requests* the Secretary-General to transmit the report on new sources of energy to the appropriate specialized agencies, particularly the United Nations Educational, Scientific and Cultural Organization and the Food and Agriculture Organization of the United Nations, and to the appropriate non-governmental organizations in consultative status, with a view to encouraging further scientific and technological studies leading to wider economic applications of the new sources of energy other than the atom, especially solar and wind energy;

"2. *Further requests* the Secretary-General to pre-pare, in collaboration with the United Nations Educational, Scientific and Cultural Organization, the Food and Agriculture Organization of the United Nations and other appropriate specialized agencies, for the twenty-seventh session of the Council, a progress report on developments in these fields, together with recommendations regarding the agenda of an international conference on the new sources of energy other than the atom and their economic applications, to be convened as early as feasible thereafter."

CHAPTER IV

TECHNICAL ASSISTANCE FOR ECONOMIC DEVELOPMENT

THE TECHNICAL ASSISTANCE PROGRAMMES

ACTIVITIES DURING 1957

Eighty-four Governments pledged a total of $30,837,533 in some 52 different currencies to carry out operations under the Expanded Programme of Technical Assistance during 1957. Operations under this Programme are financed from voluntary contributions by Governments. The funds so obtained are shared among: the United Nations; the International Labour Organisation (ILO); the Food and Agriculture Organization (FAO); the United Nations Educational, Scientific and Cultural Organization (UNESCO); the World Health Organization (WHO); the International Civil Aviation Organization (ICAO); the International Telecommunication Union (ITU) and the World Meteorological Organization (WMO).

More than 100 countries and territories received aid by the end of 1957, for a total cost of $31,516,883. During the year, 2,612 experts from 67 countries and territories served in the field, 516 of them provided by the United Nations. They were assigned to 101 countries and territories. A total of 2,061 fellowships and study grants were awarded to the nationals of over 100 countries and territories, for study in almost 100 countries.

The major fields in which the United Nations and the specialized agencies advised and aided Governments during 1957 were: agricultural production, health services, economic planning, basic surveys of resources and building up of administrative services, industrial production, auxiliary services to industry and agriculture, education, public utilities, power, transport and communications, community development, and other social services such as housing and social security.

In addition to participating in the Expanded Programme, the United Nations, through its Technical Assistance Administration (TAA) also provided technical assistance in economic development, public administration and advisory social welfare. This was paid for out of funds from the regular United Nations budget.

During 1957, the United Nations, under the Expanded Programme as well as under its regular programme which is financed from the United Nations budget, sent out 785 experts drawn from 56 nations to 68 different countries and territories. A total of 752 fellowships and scholarships was awarded to nationals of 75 countries and territories for study abroad in 43 countries. It also provided limited quantities of supplies and equipment.

Expenditures incurred for all these United Nations operations in 1957 under both programmes totalled $7,940,092. This sum included $5,292,117 for economic development, $1,052,551 for public administration activities, and $1,308,380 for advisory social welfare services, plus $287,044 for TAA's share of local costs.

Of the experts supplied by the United Nations under both programmes, 504 gave help on economic development matters (including telecommunications and meteorology), 103 were provided for public administration projects, and

178 for advisory social welfare services. Fellowships and scholarships awarded in these three fields totalled 452, 130 and 170, respectively.

Expenditures under the regular United Nations programme in 1957 amounted to $1,704,400, of which $479,400 was for economic development, $300,000 for public administration and $925,000 for advisory social welfare services. The total number of experts provided under this particular programme came to 211. The total number of fellowships and scholarships awarded was 261.

MEMBERSHIP OF TECHNICAL ASSISTANCE COMMITTEE

On 1 May 1957, at its twenty-third session, the Economic and Social Council took steps to increase the membership of its Technical Assistance Committee (TAC) from 18 to 24, as recommended by the General Assembly on 26 February 1957. (For details of membership, see DOCUMENTARY REFERENCES below; see also APPENDIX II.)

CONSIDERATION OF EXPANDED PROGRAMME BY ECONOMIC AND SOCIAL COUNCIL

PLEDGING PROCEDURE

At its twenty-fourth session, in mid-1957, the Economic and Social Council noted the action taken by its Technical Assistance Committee (TAC) early in 1957 on the means of obtaining pledges of contributions for the Expanded Technical Assistance Programme. (The Committee had favoured the continuation of the system of holding a separate Technical Assistance Pledging Conference at which Governments could announce pledges of contributions to the Expanded Programme. The General Assembly then agreed to continuing this system by resolution 1091 (XI), adopted on 27 February 1957 at its eleventh session.) (See also below, FINANCING OF THE EXPANDED PROGRAMME FOR 1958.)

ANNUAL TAB REPORT FOR 1956

In its ninth annual report, which was considered both by the Council, at its twenty-fourth session, and by TAC, the Technical Assistance Board (TAB) described activities in 1956 as a "landmark in the history of the Expanded Programme".

The 1956 programme was the first to be based on the new country-programming procedure laid down by the Economic and Social Council.

The year 1956 also witnessed the highest level of aid given since the inception of the Expanded Programme in 1950; altogether, 104 countries and territories, including 47 Trust and Non-Self-Governing Territories, received assistance in 1956. The total expenditure reached $30.5 million. The number of experts in the field totalled 2,346, while 1,128 fellowships were awarded for training abroad. The cost of equipment and supplies provided for training and demonstration purposes in 1956 totalled $3.3 million. In addition to these expenditures by the international organizations, the TAB report indicated that the recipient Governments themselves were incurring expenditures in counterpart funds of some $77 million to provide national staffs, offices and other physical facilities, transport, local living allowances for experts, and equipment and supplies for project support. This estimate did not include the further long-term capital investments incurred by Governments in support of Expanded Programme projects.

The Technical Assistance Committee hoped that the downward trend in administrative costs of the Programme would continue in so far as it was consonant with efficient operations.

Members of TAC commented on the successful introduction of full-scale country programming.

The Committee again discussed "continuing projects", i.e., projects which involved Expanded Programme aid for two years or more. In its report, TAB calculated that, in terms of expenditure, continuing projects accounted for some 85 per cent of the total 1956 field programme. The Committee expressed concern at this high percentage. While recognizing that it was necessary to continue certain projects for several years, it asked that TAB keep the question under careful review.

In its annual report for 1956, TAB also included two new sections: one on evaluation, the other containing information on the regular programme activities of the organizations participating in or co-operating with the Expanded Programme.

The evaluation study reviewed some 710 projects in 30 countries on the basis of information supplied by the TAB Resident Representatives in consultation with officials of Governments receiving technical aid. TAC members felt that the study represented a notable attempt at objective appraisal. They also felt that further emphasis should be given to the views of recipient Governments, and that evaluation should be essentially an exercise of "self-appraisal" both by Governments and by the organizations participating in the Expanded Programme.

On 30 July, acting on the recommendation of TAC, the Council, unanimously took note with appreciation of TAB's ninth annual report (resolution 658 A I (XXIV)).

AID ON REIMBURSABLE BASIS

During the discussion of the TAB annual report, several references were made in TAC to the occasional practice of some participating organizations of accepting requests from Governments (e.g., Iran and Burma) for the provision of technical assistance on a reimbursable basis, in addition to assistance provided under the regular or expanded programmes.

On the recommendation of TAC, the Council unanimously adopted a resolution (658 B (XXIV) of 30 July 1957) calling on TAB to examine the question further, in consultation with the participating organizations and recipient Governments, and to report to TAC at its mid-1958 session.

EXPANSION OF ACTIVITIES IN EUROPE

The Technical Assistance Committee received a report by the Executive Chairman of TAB on the question of an increase in activities in Europe under the Expanded Programme. In view of the Expanded Programme's financial status at the time 1958 target figures were being established, he said, the Board had decided provisionally to consider further the question of expansion of activities in Europe before recommending, for 1958, any new programmes for European countries which had not received assistance in 1957. It had also decided to avoid any substantial increases in the existing programmes in European countries.

Some TAC members, supporting the TAB decision, stated that the needs of the various European countries were not as acute as those elsewhere. Others felt that the criterion for the allocation of Programme funds should simply be the degree of need, regardless of the location of the country concerned.

TAC finally approved a draft resolution endorsing the Board's efforts to make the most efficient use of the Expanded Programme's resources and accepting TAB's provisional decision about increasing assistance to new recipient countries for 1958. The draft, however, recognized the decision as a temporary measure which should not prejudice the basic principles governing the Programme. The draft resolution was adopted unanimously by the Council on 30 July 1957 as resolution 658 A II (XXIV).

"A FORWARD LOOK"

At the twenty-second session of the Council, in mid-1956, the Technical Assistance Committee had reviewed a TAB report entitled, *A Forward Look*.[1] The Committee had then asked TAB to invite comments from the participating Governments on the contents of the report. At its mid-1957 session, TAC considered these replies and further discussed the recommendations made in the report.

By a resolution, first proposed by TAC and later adopted unanimously on 30 July as resolution 659 B (XXIV), the Council concurred in the conclusion of the *Forward Look* report that the needs of under-developed countries and territories for technical assistance far exceeded current resources, and that these countries could use more assistance than was currently available. The Council therefore appealed to participating Governments to consider the possibility of increasing the Programme's resources. The Council also expressed the belief that the more important projects reviewed in the *Forward Look* report would help considerably in speeding the economic and social progress of under-developed countries. It recognized, however, that the desirable stepping-up of the work was not possible within the current scope of the Expanded Programme and would call for substantially increased resources. In addition, the Council asked TAB and Governments to suggest measures which would make it possible to carry out a substantially larger programme.

CO-ORDINATION OF ACTIVITIES

In its discussion on the *Forward Look* report, TAC also took up the question of co-ordination on the part of recipient Governments. Members of the Committee welcomed the fact reported

[1]See *Y.U.N., 1956*, p. 184.

by TAB that in 1956 the emphasis in matters of co-ordination had shifted from eliminating over-lapping efforts to combining the aid available from several sources. Recognizing the variety of national economic development programmes and bilateral and multilateral aid programmes, TAC stressed the role of recipient Governments in co-ordinating the facilities offered by these programmes.

On 30 July 1957, acting on the recommenda-tion of TAC, the Council asked Governments to continue their efforts to co-ordinate their tech-nical assistance programmes. It also recom-mended increased efforts to correlate the re-sources of the Expanded Programme with those of other programmes in an over-all integrated economic development programme.

The resolution to this effect (659 A (XXIV)) was approved by the Council by 14 votes to 0, with 4 absentions.

ADMINISTRATIVE AND FINANCIAL MATTERS

The Technical Assistance Committee took up a number of administrative and financial mat-ters in connexion with its over-all review of the activities of the Expanded Programme.

The Committee decided to continue its Ad-ministrative Review Group for another year. Composed of members of TAC, the Group was charged with reviewing the administrative and operational services costs estimates for the 1958 programme. It was to report thereon to the November 1957 session of TAC.

FINANCING OF THE EXPANDED PROGRAMME FOR 1958

CONTRIBUTION PLEDGES

Following the eighth Technical Assistance Pledging Conference in October 1957, contribu-tions totalling the equivalent of $32,317,900 were pledged by 82 Governments to finance operations under the Expanded Programme in 1958. The majority of these contributions, numbering 59, were pledged in the form of local currencies not convertible into dollars. Contributions were pledged as follows:

Country	Equivalent in U.S. Dollars	Country	Equivalent in U.S. Dollars
Afghanistan	$ 12,500	Bolivia	$ 20,800
Albania	2,000	Brazil	832,400
Argentina	360,000	Bulgaria	14,700
Australia	625,000	Burma	30,000
Austria	57,700	Byelorussian SSR	50,000
Belgium	437,500	Cambodia	6,200

Country	Equivalent in U.S. Dollars	Country	Equivalent in U.S. Dollars
Canada	$2,000,000	Libya	$ 6,000
Ceylon	20,000	Luxembourg	3,000
Chile	83,700	Malaya, Fed. of	20,000
China	20,000	Mexico	113,600
Colombia	100,000	Monaco	1,400
Costa Rica	10,000	Nepal	5,000
Cuba	25,000	Netherlands	1,092,500
Czechoslovakia	69,400	New Zealand	210,000
Denmark	579,100	Norway	408,800
Dominican Republic	33,000	Pakistan	166,200
Ecuador	11,300	Panama	3,000
Egypt	114,900	Paraguay	12,000
El Salvador	7,700	Peru	30,000
Ethiopia	20,000	Philippines	66,000
Finland	25,000	Poland	75,000
France	1,542,900	Portugal	15,000
Germany, Fed. Rep. of	952,400	Romania	16,700
Ghana	44,100	Spain	50,000
Greece	25,000	Sudan	157,400
Guatemala	10,000	Sweden	792,600
Haiti	14,400	Switzerland	350,500
Honduras	10,000	Syria	14,000
Hungary	42,600	Thailand	38,800
Iceland	3,900	Tunisia	2,000
India	525,000	Turkey	210,000
Indonesia	35,800	Ukrainian SSR	125,000
Iran	50,000	USSR	1,000,000
Iraq	56,000	United Kingdom	2,240,000
Ireland	10,200	United States	15,500,000*
Israel	50,000	Uruguay	120,000
Italy	112,000	Vatican City	2,000
Japan	135,000	Venezuela	100,000
Jordan	5,900	Viet-Nam	25,700
Laos	3,000	Yugoslavia	116,700
Lebanon	7,900		
Liberia	25,000	Total	$32,317,900

*Maximum contribution, subject to condition that it should not exceed 45 per cent of total.

REVIEW OF 1958 PROGRAMME
AND ALLOCATION OF FUNDS

After the eighth Pledging Conference, TAC met from 25 November to 4 December 1957 to review the activities under the Expanded Pro-gramme for 1958.

In presenting the 1958 programme, the Executive Chairman of TAB noted that a total project expenditure of $29,925,822 had been proposed for 1958, which was about $200,000 less than that for 1957. However, the recom-mended programme for 1958 still exceeded the funds expected to be on hand by about $1 million. He also said that there was a noticeable increase in assistance to be provided to countries and territories in Africa—and particularly to the four countries which had become independent since the beginning of 1957. This emphasis on newly independent countries and non-self-governing territories, combined with the over-all reduction in resources, had made it necessary, he said, to cut back somewhat on the extent of the activities in some of the major recipients.

The Technical Assistance Committee expressed particular satisfaction that the programme for 1958 had been prepared on the basis of a complete assimilation of all currencies pledged.

In reply to several comments, the Executive Chairman of TAB pointed out that, as the Programme was contracting in size, Governments in general seemed more inclined to forego fellowships and equipment than to cut down on the services of experts.

The Committee noted with approval that TAB had kept allocations for regional projects as close as possible to 10 per cent of total anticipated resources.

It also commented favourably on the report submitted by the Executive Chairman of TAB on his use of contingency authorizations in 1957. (These funds are for financing high-priority projects not generally foreseen at the time when Governments draw up their annual requests.) Examples of contingency projects in 1957 were: activities in the newly independent countries; technical assistance for narcotics control in Iran; and surveys related to the development of the Lower Mekong River in South-East Asia.

TAC established the limit for contingency authorizations in 1958 at $1.6 million.

The Committee also concurred with its Administrative Review Group in expressing concern about the proposed increase in administrative and operational services costs for 1958. It was recognized, however, that part of the increase was attributable to the establishment of new TAB field offices at the specific requests of Governments. But the Committee still felt that reduction of these costs should be further studied.

The Committee also asked for a further study on the allocation of administrative and operational services costs of the regular and Expanded Programme budgets.

The Committee decided to maintain the programme's Working Capital and Reserve Fund at its current level —$12 million— for 1958. On 29 November 1957, TAC unanimously approved the programme for 1958 and authorized the allocation of funds to the participating organizations, subject to confirmation by the General Assembly. The resolution to this effect was approved at a plenary meeting of the Assembly on 16 December as resolution 1216(XII). (For details of allocations, see DOCUMENTARY REFERENCES below.)

CONSIDERATION OF REGULAR UNITED NATIONS PROGRAMME BY ECONOMIC AND SOCIAL COUNCIL

At its twenty-fourth session, the Economic and Social Council, by resolution 657(XXIV), of 30 July 1957, took note with appreciation of a report by the Secretary-General on the United Nations regular technical assistance programme. Financed from the normal United Nations budget, this programme provides for aid in the fields of economic development, advisory social welfare services and public administration. The Council asked the Secretary-General to continue his efforts to extend technical assistance services along the lines indicated in his report.

ASSEMBLY CONSIDERATION OF THE TECHNICAL ASSISTANCE PROGRAMMES

Activities under both the Expanded Programme and the regular United Nations programme were also discussed in the Assembly's Second Committee, at the General Assembly's twelfth session.

So were questions of increasing the technical assistance activities of the United Nations and the specialized agencies; these were dealt with in connexion with debates in the Assembly's Second Committee on the financing of economic development. (For details, see above, CHAPTER III, THE ECONOMIC DEVELOPMENT OF UNDER-DEVELOPED COUNTRIES, section on PROPOSALS FOR A SPECIAL UNITED NATIONS FUND.)

The Executive Chairman of TAB pointed out that 'in view of the financial outlook, the activities for 1958 under the Expanded Programme, as already approved by TAC, represented a reduction over 1957, and that there was a possibility of further reduction in subsequent years.

On the other hand, there was a steady improvement in the calibre of the operations under the Expanded Programme. He recalled the forecast in the *Forward Look* report that activities under the Expanded Programme could be expanded over a period of years without loss of effectiveness or any appreciable increase in the present administrative establishment.

The Director-General of the United Nations Technical Assistance Administration (TAA) suggested several ways in which the United Nations might use its limited resources to the best advantage. These included the possibility of giving supplementary assistance to Governments on a reimbursable basis, co-operation with nongovernmental organizations and the possibility of obtaining short-term assistance on a voluntary basis from a small number of internationally known experts.

Members of the Second Committee paid tribute to the support for and achievements under the technical aid programmes of the United Nations and specialized agencies. There was general regret, however, that the Expanded Programme faced reductions in 1958 and possibly in subsequent years. The representatives of the Netherlands, New Zealand and Yugoslavia, among others, hoped that Governments would find it possible to reconsider their contributions and help prevent the threatened curtailment.

In view of the financial outlook, members of the Second Committee also paid special attention to the need for concentrating and conserving funds and stressed the need to keep administrative costs at the lowest possible level compatible with efficiency.

The representatives of Australia, Canada, Ceylon, France, Sweden and the United States stressed the need for recipient Governments to co-ordinate aid under the Expanded Programme with aid received from other sources.

The representatives of Ceylon, Greece, Iraq, Poland, Sweden, the United Kingdom and the United States were among those who expressed support of the plan for supplementary assistance under the Expanded Programme on a reimbursable basis, provided that this aid would in no way replace the normal assistance given under the Programme.

The representatives of Czechoslovakia, France, Indonesia, Poland and Yugoslavia regretted the need for the Economic and Social Council's decision temporarily to limit the increase of activities in Europe under the Expanded Programme. This, they stressed, should not be considered a precedent. Finland's representative was among those who preferred limiting the number of countries aided to those with the greatest need. The representatives of Canada, Iraq, and Mexico, however, favoured reducing the number of fields in which the Programme operated.

Three draft resolutions on the subject of technical assistance were submitted in the Second Committee, which recommended them for adoption by the Assembly. They were subsequently adopted at a plenary meeting of the Assembly on 14 December 1957.

One appealed to participating Governments to examine the financial situation of the Expanded Programme and to consider the possibility of increasing its financial resources. The resolution to this effect, adopted by the Committee by 59 votes to 0, with 6 abstentions, was approved at a plenary meeting of the Assembly by 75 votes to 0, with 4 abstentions, as resolution 1214(XII).

By the second resolution (1215(XII)), the Assembly asked the Economic and Social Council to study the desirability of promoting, with the co-operation of national Governments, increased use of regional and national training facilities available under the Expanded Programme. This was adopted unanimously both by the Second Committee and at a plenary meeting of the Assembly.

By the third resolution (1216(XII)), the Assembly confirmed the allocation of funds for 1958 to the organizations taking part in the Expanded Programme.

DOCUMENTARY REFERENCES

MEMBERSHIP OF TECHNICAL ASSISTANCE COMMITTEE

ECONOMIC AND SOCIAL COUNCIL—23RD SESSION AND RESUMED 24TH SESSION
Plenary Meetings 970, 971, 997.

E/L.750 and Add.1. Brazil, Canada, Indonesia, Netherlands, United States draft resolution.

E/L.775. Agenda of resumed 24th session. Note by Secretary-General.

RESOLUTION 647(XXIII), as submitted jointly by 5 powers, E/L.750 and Add.1, adopted by Council on 1 May 1957, meeting 970, by 16 votes to 0, with 2 abstentions.

"*The Economic and Social Council,*

"*Taking into consideration* General Assembly resolution 1036(XI) of 26 February 1957 on the membership of the Technical Assistance Committee,

"*Noting* the provisions of paragraph 6 of Council resolution 222 A (IX) of 15 August 1949,

"*Decides* that:

"1. The Technical Assistance Committee shall consist, as from 1 June 1957, of the following:

"(*a*) The members of the Council;

"(*b*) Six members to be elected by the Council from among the States Members of the United Nations or members of the specialized agencies, having due regard to geographical distribution and to the representation of contributing and recipient countries having an important interest in the Expanded Programme of Technical Assistance;

"2. The term of office of the members of the Technical Assistance Committee referred to under paragraph 1 (*b*) above shall be two years, except that at the initial election the Council shall elect six members, the term of office of three of which shall end on 31 December 1958, whereas the term of office of the other three shall end on 31 December 1959;

"3. In the event that a member of the Technical Assistance Committee referred to under paragraph 1 (*b*) above becomes a member of the Council, the Council shall elect another State to the membership of the Committee for the remainder of the term of office of that member."

CONSIDERATION OF EXPANDED PROGRAMME BY ECONOMIC AND SOCIAL COUNCIL

ECONOMIC AND SOCIAL COUNCIL—24TH SESSION
Plenary Meeting 993.
Technical Assistance Committee, meetings 126-149.

PLEDGING PROCEDURE

E/2952. Report of TAC.

ANNUAL TAB REPORT FOR 1956

E/2965. Annual report of TAB for 1956 to TAC.
E/TAC/REP/103. Addendum to annual report of TAB to TAC for 1956.
E/TAC/L.124. Note by Executive Chairman of TAB on project handbook.
E/TAC/L.126. Opening statement by Executive Chairman of TAB on 25 June 1957.
E/3041. Report of TAC (paragraphs 4-22 and Annex II A I).
RESOLUTION 658 A I (XXIV), as recommended by TAC, E/3041, adopted unanimously by Council on 30 July 1957, meeting 993.

"*The Economic and Social Council*

"*Takes note with appreciation* of the ninth report submitted by the Technical Assistance Board to the Technical Assistance Committee."

AID ON REIMBURSABLE BASIS

E/TAC/L.133 and Add.1, and Rev.1. Brazil, Netherlands, United States draft resolution and revision,

adopted by TAC, as amended, by roll-call vote of 22 to 1, with 1 abstention.
E/TAC/L.134. Pakistan amendments to joint draft resolution, E/TAC/L.133.
E/3041. Report of TAC (paragraphs 36-40 and Annex II B).
RESOLUTION 658 B (XXIV), as recommended by TAC, E/3041, adopted unanimously by Council on 30 July 1957, meeting 993.

"*The Economic and Social Council,*

"*Being impressed* by the evidence that the Expanded Programme of Technical Assistance has proved to be increasingly useful,

"*Believing* that all possible means of increasing the access of Governments to the technical resources of the Programme should be fully explored without impairing the efficiency of the regular and expanded programmes of technical assistance,

"*Considering* that in addition to technical assistance provided under the regular and expanded programmes, moderate amounts of technical assistance are also being provided to Governments on a payment basis, such as funds in trust arrangements, by the United Nations Technical Assistance Administration and the specialized agencies,

"1. *Requests* the Technical Assistance Board to examine, in consultation with the participating organizations and the recipient Governments, the provision of technical assistance under the Expanded Programme on a payment basis, it being understood that such assistance would be in addition to that already provided under the regular and expanded programmes of technical assistance;

"2. *Requests* the Technical Assistance Board to report on this matter to the Technical Assistance Committee at its summer session in 1958."

EXPANSION OF ACTIVITIES IN EUROPE

E/TAC/65. Report by Executive Chairman of TAB.
E/TAC/L.128 and Rev.1. Netherlands, Switzerland, United States draft resolution and revision, adopted, as amended by France, Pakistan and Egypt, by TAC by 21 votes to 0, with 3 abstentions.
E/TAC/L.129. France amendments to joint draft resolution, E/TAC/L.128.
E/TAC/L.131. Note by Secretariat on verbal amendments to revised joint draft resolution, E/TAC/L.128/Rev.1.
E/3041. Report of TAC (paragraphs 23-30 and Annex II A II).
RESOLUTION 658 A II (XXIV), as recommended by TAC, E/3041, adopted unanimously by Council on 30 July 1957, meeting 993.

"*The Economic and Social Council,*

"*Considering* the desirability of continuing to strive for the most effective utilization of the resources of the Expanded Programme of Technical Assistance,

"*Considering further* that requests for technical assistance currently exceed the resources available for meeting them,

"*Having in mind* the question raised by the Technical Assistance Board with respect to the concentration of future programme development,

"*Noting* that the accession of countries to independence normally leads to an increase in the technical assistance required by them,

"*Noting* the desirability of maintaining in the 1958 programme the highest possible level of technical assistance to such under-developed countries as are in a crucial stage of economic development,

"*Noting further* the provisional decision of the Technical Assistance Board to the effect that the question of expansion of technical assistance activities under the Expanded Programme in Europe should be further considered before any new programme is recommended for European countries for approval by the Technical Assistance Committee, and that substantial increases in the existing programmes of European countries should be similarly avoided,

"1. *Endorses* the efforts by the Technical Assistance Board to make the most efficient use of the resources of the Expanded Programme by giving priority to most urgent requirements;

"2. *Accepts* the provisional decision of the Technical Assistance Board concerning the programme for 1958 with respect to the question of the expansion of technical assistance activities in new beneficiary countries, as a temporary measure and without prejudice to the basic principles governing the Programme."

"A FORWARD LOOK"

E/TAC/64, Add.1-3 and Add.2/Corr.1. Replies from Governments.

E/TAC/L.135 and Rev.1. Argentina, Brazil, Canada, Egypt, Sweden, United States draft resolution and revision, adopted by TAC as orally amended by Egypt, by 14 votes to 0, with 9 abstentions.

E/TAC/L.137 and Rev.1, 2. Argentina, Brazil, Greece, India, Indonesia, Mexico, Pakistan, Sudan, Venezuela, Yugoslavia draft resolution and revisions, adopted unanimously by TAC.

E/TAC/L.138. Indonesia, Mexico, Pakistan, Sudan amendment to joint draft resolution, E/TAC/L.135.

E/TAC/L.139. Brazil draft resolution.

E/TAC/L.140. Canada, France, United States amendment to revised joint draft resolution, E/TAC/L.137/Rev.1.

E/3041. Report of TAC (Annex III A and B).

RESOLUTION 659 A and B (XXIV), as recommended by TAC, E/3041, adopted by Council on 30 July 1957, meeting 993, as follows: 659 A (XXIV) by 14 votes to 0, with 4 abstentions; 659 B (XXIV) unanimously.

A

"*The Economic and Social Council,*

"*Recalling* its resolution 542 B II (XVIII) of 29 July 1954, by which it established the country programming procedures for the Expanded Programme of Technical Assistance,

"*Recognizing* also that there exists a variety of national programmes of economic development and of bilateral and multilateral programmes of economic and technical assistance,

"*Believing* that careful co-ordination in planning as well as in implementing development programmes is essential to the most effective utilization of the available resources,

"*Being further convinced* that it is the role of the recipient Governments to co-ordinate their economic and social development programmes,

"*Noting* that the co-ordinating committees of several recipient Governments have established standard procedures whereby requests for assistance are accompanied by statements specifying the relationship, if any, of an Expanded Programme project to the projects in operation or planned under other programmes,

"1. *Notes with satisfaction* the conclusion stated by the Technical Assistance Board in its report for 1956 to the Technical Assistance Committee that 'the emphasis in co-ordination shifted from the negative aspect of elimination of over-lapping or duplication of efforts, to the more positive form of enhancing the value of projects through concerted effort to ensure the best timing of each action and the most effective combination of assistance coming from different sources';

"2. *Requests* the recipient Governments to continue their efforts to co-ordinate their technical assistance programmes in order to make them more effective;

"3. *Recommends* that, when formulating plans and projects, recipient Governments endeavour increasingly to correlate the resources of the Expanded Programme with other programmes of economic and technical assistance in over-all integrated economic development programmes;

"4. *Requests* the Technical Assistance Board to report to the Technical Assistance Committee, at its next summer session, on the implementation of the pertinent paragraphs of this resolution, particularly of paragraph 3 above."

B

"*The Economic and Social Council,*

"*Having examined with interest* the report of the Technical Assistance Board entitled 'Expanded Programme of Technical Assistance: A Forward Look' and having noted the observations on it submitted by Governments,

"*Concurring* in the conclusion of that report to the effect that the needs of under-developed countries and territories for technical assistance far exceed current resources,

"*Considering* that the countries and territories participating in the Expanded Programme of Technical Assistance are now in a position effectively to make use of technical assistance on a larger scale than is at present available,

I

"1. *Regrets* that the programme of operations for 1958 is to be planned on a somewhat lower level than that of 1957;

"2. *Appeals* to the participating Governments to consider, in the light of their economic conditions and particular circumstances, the possibility of increasing the financial resources of the Expanded Programme;

"3. *Requests* the Technical Assistance Board to inform the participating Governments on the financial position and outlook of the Expanded Programme;

II

"1. *Believes* that the implementation of the more important projects reviewed in the report would considerably assist in accelerating the economic and social progress of under-developed countries;

"2. *Recognizes,* however, that the desirable expansion of the work cannot be achieved with the present scope of the Expanded Programme but would call for substantially increased resources;

III

"*Requests* the Technical Assistance Board and *invites* the participating Governments to suggest measures which would make it possible to implement a substantially larger programme, including some of the more important projects described in the report, for discussion by the Technical Assistance Committee at the twenty-sixth session of the Council."

ADMINISTRATIVE AND FINANCIAL MATTERS

ECONOMIC AND SOCIAL COUNCIL—24TH SESSION
Plenary Meeting 993.
Technical Assistance Committee, meetings 127-149.

LOCAL COST ARRANGEMENTS
E/TAC/60. Report of TAB.
E/TAC/62. Resolution on local costs under technical assistance programme, adopted by WHO Executive Board at its 19th session.
E/3041. Report of TAC (paragraphs 31-33).

REGIONAL PROJECTS
E/TAC/66. Regional and inter-regional projects. Report of TAB.
E/3041. Report of TAC (Section IV).

APPOINTMENTS FOR EXPERTS AND TAB SECRETARIAT
E/TAC/61 and Corr.1. Appointments for experts and for secretariat of TAB. Report of TAB.
E/3041. Report of TAC (Section V).

ADMINISTRATIVE AND OPERATIONAL SERVICES COSTS
E/TAC/67. Report of TAB.
E/TAC/L.136. Note by Executive Chairman of TAB.
E/TAC/L.142. Apportionment of charges for administrative and operational services costs between Expanded Programme and regular budgets. Statement by Executive Chairman of TAB on 18 July 1957.
E/TAC/L.144. Egypt and Netherlands draft resolution, adopted unanimously.
E/3041. Report of TAC (Section VII).

SIZE OF WORKING CAPITAL AND RESERVE FUND
E/TAC/59. Report of TAB.
E/3041. Report of TAC (paragraph 81).

CONSOLIDATED COUNCIL RESOLUTION ON THE EXPANDED PROGRAMME
E/TAC/63 and Corr.1. Draft consolidated resolution on Expanded Programme.

E/3041. Report of TAC (paragraph 82).

REPORT ON STATUS OF PROJECTS
E/TAC/L.141. Note by Executive Chairman of TAB.
E/3041. Report of TAC (paragraph 88).

FINANCING OF THE EXPANDED PROGRAMME FOR 1958

EIGHTH UNITED NATIONS TECHNICAL ASSISTANCE CONFERENCE

A/CONF.14/SR.1, 2. Summary records of meetings on 10 October 1957.
A/CONF.14/L.1. Provisional agenda.
A/CONF.14/L.2. Draft final act of eighth United Nations Technical Assistance Conference.
A/CONF.14/L.3. Rules of procedure. Memorandum by Secretary-General.

REVIEW OF 1958 PROGRAMME AND ALLOCATION OF FUNDS

TECHNICAL ASSISTANCE COMMITTEE, meetings 150-154.

E/TAC/68. Budget estimates for secretariat of TAB for year 1958. Report of TAB.
E/TAC/69 and Add.1. Estimates of administrative and operational services costs of participating organizations for year 1958. Report of TAB.
E/TAC/70. Allocation of administrative and operational services costs between regular and expanded programme budgets. Interim report of TAB.
E/TAC/71. Transfer of allocations: 1957. Report of TAB.
E/TAC/72. Report of Administrative Review Group.
E/TAC/L.146. Programme for 1958. Category I programme recommended by TAB.
E/TAC/L.147. Programme for 1958. Category II programme recommended by TAB.
E/TAC/L.148. Programme for 1958. Recommendations of TAB.
E/TAC/L.148/Add.1. Programme for 1958. Treatment of local costs revenues. Recommendations of TAB.
E/TAC/L.149. Programme for 1958. Descriptive summary of category I programme.
E/TAC/L.150. Review of contingency authorizations made in 1957 (January-October) from Working Capital and Reserve Fund. Report of TAB.
E/TAC/L.151. Summary statement of 1958 budget estimates and budgetary position at 30 September 1957.
E/TAC/L.153. Programme for 1958. Statement by Executive Chairman of TAB at 150th meeting of Technical Assistance Committee, 25 November 1957.
E/TAC/L.154. Revised text of draft resolution, submitted by TAB in document E/TAC/L.148, adopted unanimously by TAC.
E/3055. Report of TAC.

(See also below, texts of General Assembly resolutions 1214(XII) and 1216(XII).)

CONSIDERATION OF REGULAR UNITED NATIONS PROGRAMME BY ECONOMIC AND SOCIAL COUNCIL

ECONOMIC AND SOCIAL COUNCIL—24TH SESSION
Plenary Meeting 993.
Technical Assistance Committee, meetings 127-149.

E/2966 and Corr.1. Report by Secretary-General.
E/TAC/L.127. Opening statement by Director-General of United Nations TAA on 26 June 1957.
E/TAC/L.132. Czechoslovakia, Egypt, Indonesia, Mexico, Netherlands, Sweden, Yugoslavia draft resolution, adopted unanimously by TAC.
E/3041. Report of TAC (Annex I).
RESOLUTION 657(XXIV), as recommended by Technical Assistance Committee, E/3041, adopted unanimously by Council on 30 July 1957, meeting 993.

"The Economic and Social Council
"1. *Takes note with appreciation* of the report by the Secretary-General on the regular United Nations programme of technical assistance;
"2. *Requests* the Secretary-General to continue his efforts to extend the services of the Technical Assistance Administration to Governments along the lines indicated in his report and in the statement made by the Director-General of the Technical Assistance Administration."

ASSEMBLY CONSIDERATION OF THE TECHNICAL ASSISTANCE PROGRAMMES

GENERAL ASSEMBLY—12TH SESSION
Plenary Meeting 730.
Second Committee, meetings 471, 479-489.

A/3738. Report of Economic and Social Council to General Assembly (Chapter III B).
A/3661. Memorandum by Secretary-General.
A/3738. Estimates of administrative and operational services costs of Expanded Programme of Technical Assistance for 1958. Report of Advisory Committee on Administrative and Budgetary Questions.
A/C.2/L.338. Statement by Executive Chairman of TAB.
A/C.2/L.339. Statement by Director-General of TAB.
A/C.2/196. Outposting of certain programme officers of TAA.
A/C.2/L.347. France, India, Netherlands, Yugoslavia draft resolution on financing of expanded programme of technical assistance, adopted by Second Committee by 59 votes to 0, with 6 abstentions.
A/C.2/L.348 and Rev.1. Canada, Denmark, France, Iraq, Mexico, Netherlands, Peru, Sudan, United Kingdom draft resolution on United Nations Technical Assistance Programme and revision, adopted unanimously by Second Committee, as amended by Romania and the sponsors.
A/3759. Report of Second Committee (draft resolutions I and II).
RESOLUTION 1214(XII), as recommended by Second Committee, A/3759, adopted by Assembly on 14 December 1957, meeting 730, by 75 votes to 0, with 4 abstentions.

"The General Assembly,
"*Noting with concern* that the resources available to the Expanded Programme of Technical Assistance in 1958 might prove to be less than those available in 1957, even though a substantial number of countries have increased their pledges,
"*Recognizing* that the maintenance of the Expanded Programme even at its existing level would require greater resources than those pledged at the Eighth Technical Assistance Conference held on 10 October 1957,
"1. *Appeals* to participating Governments to examine the consequences of the situation mentioned above and to consider, in the light of their economic and other circumstances, the possibility of increasing the financial resources of the Expanded Programme of Technical Assistance;
"2. *Requests* the Secretary-General to call the present resolution to the attention of the Governments participating in the Expanded Programme."

RESOLUTION 1215(XII), as recommended by Second Committee, A/3759, adopted unanimously by Assembly on 14 December 1957, meeting 730.

"The General Assembly,
"*Noting* the achievements of the Expanded Programme of Technical Assistance and of the regular United Nations programme of technical assistance,
"*Noting further* that, for 1958, seventy-five Governments have so far pledged contributions to the Expanded Programme and that, in 1957, the Expanded Programme provided assistance to more than one hundred countries and territories throughout the world,
"*Recognizing* that the Expanded Programme of Technical Assistance is a co-operative programme to the success of which all participating Governments contribute,
"*Further recognizing* that continued efforts should be made to use all the available technical assistance resources as effectively as possible in assisting the less developed countries to further economic progress and achieve higher standards of living,
"1. *Takes note* of chapter III B of the report of the Economic and Social Council,
"2. *Requests* the Economic and Social Council to study the desirability of promoting, with the co-operation of Governments, increased use of such regional and national training facilities as may be made available under the United Nations programme of technical assistance;
"3. *Suggests* that, in the preparation of the report required under section III of Economic and Social Council resolution 659 B (XXIV) of 30 July 1957, account be taken of suggestions put forward by delegations during the twelfth session of the General Assembly for the purpose of assisting in the development of the Expanded Programme of Technical Assistance."

A/C.2/197. Confirmation of allocation of funds for Expanded Programme of Technical Assistance in 1958. Memorandum by Secretary-General containing draft resolution adopted by TAC at its 153rd meeting on 29 November 1957.

A/3769. Report of Second Committee.
RESOLUTION 1216(XII), as recommended by Second Committee, A/3769, adopted by Assembly on 14 December 1957, meeting 730.

RESOLUTION 1216(XII): CONFIRMATION OF THE ALLOCATION OF FUNDS FOR THE EXPANDED PROGRAMME OF TECHNICAL ASSISTANCE IN 1958

"The General Assembly,

"Noting that the Technical Assistance Committee has reviewed and approved the Expanded Programme of Technical Assistance for the year 1958,

"1. *Confirms* the allocation of funds authorized by the Technical Assistance Committee to each of the organizations participating in the Expanded Programme of Technical Assistance as follows:

	Allocation		
Participating organization	*From contributions and general resources*	*From local costs assessments*	*Total*
	(Equivalent of U.S. dollars)		
United Nations Technical Assistance Administration	6,530,000	657,000	7,187,000
International Labour Organisation	3,226,000	290,000	3,516,000
Food and Agriculture Organization of the United Nations	8,085,000	774,000	8,859,000
United Nations Educational, Scientific and Cultural Organization	4,532,000	482,000	5,014,000
International Civil Aviation Organization	1,240,000	149,000	1,389,000
World Health Organization	5,462,000	707,000	6,169,000
International Telecommunication Union	323,000	27,000	350,000
World Meteorological Organization	345,000	32,000	377,000
TOTAL	29,743,000	3,118,000	32,861,000

"2. *Concurs* in the Committee's authorization to the Technical Assistance Board to allocate to the participating organizations an undistributed amount of $180,822 not included in the amounts shown above, and to make such changes in these allocations as may be necessary to provide as far as possible for the full utilization of contributions to the Expanded Programme, provided that such changes shall not in the aggregate exceed 3 per cent of the total amount allocated to the organizations participating in the Expanded Programme."

OTHER DOCUMENTS
International Bibliography of Public Administration (ST/TAA/M/11). U.N.P. Sales No.: 1957.II.H.2.
Housing in Ghana (ST/TAA/K/GHANA/1). U.N.P.

Sales No.: 1957.II.H.3.
ST/TAA/INF/4. Index of unrestricted final reports issued as United Nations Documents or prepared as papers for Governments through 31 December 1957.

PROPOSAL FOR AN INTERNATIONAL ADMINISTRATIVE SERVICE

In May 1956 the Secretary-General suggested that consideration should be given to the establishment of an international administrative service designed to aid Governments of less developed countries—at their request—in meeting their needs for assistance of an operational or executive character.

While it has been possible to respond to some of the requests of this kind, within the present technical assistance programmes, the Secretary-General believes that the United Nations should now make a more systematic and comprehensive effort to meet expressed national needs of this character.

In 1957, in a memorandum submitted to the Economic and Social Council's twenty-fourth session, he proposed that a careful start be made on the development of an internationally recruited reserve of competent and experienced administrators as a step in this direction.

Under this plan, the United Nations would undertake to recruit, upon request, a suitable person to meet the specified need, subject to confirmation of the nomination by the Government. It would assist this Government and the expert to reach agreement in terms of employment, and would share in the costs of the services. During the period of his employment, this expert would be wholly under the direction of the Government he served, would perform exclusively duties assigned to him by that Government, and would not report to or take instructions from the United Nations.

The proposal was discussed both in Technical Assistance Committee and in the Council.

On the recommendation of the Technical Assistance Committee, the Council decided to request the Secretary-General to submit his proposal to Member Governments and to the specialized agencies for their comments. It also

asked him, in the light of such comments and with special attention to the interest in such services indicated by the less developed countries, to prepare a consolidated report for the Council's twenty-sixth session, in 1958. The resolution to this effect (661(XXIV)) was unanimously adopted on 30 July 1957.

A circular letter was addressed to Governments and, in the light of the replies and of consultations held with them, more specific proposals were to be placed before the Council in 1958.

DOCUMENTARY REFERENCES

ECONOMIC AND SOCIAL COUNCIL—24TH SESSION
Plenary Meeting 993.
Technical Assistance Committee, meetings 146, 147.

E/3017. An international administrative service. Memorandum by Secretary-General.
E/3041. Report of Technical Assistance Committee (paragraph 89 and Annex V).

RESOLUTION 661(XXIV), as recommended by Technical Assistance Committee, E/3041, adopted unanimously by Council on 30 July 1957, meeting 993.

"The Economic and Social Council
"1. *Takes note* of the memorandum by the Secretary-General entitled 'An International Administrative Service';
"2. *Requests* the Secretary-General to transmit his proposal to States Members of the United Nations and to the specialized agencies for their comments and, on the basis and in the light of these comments and paying special attention to the demand expressed for such services by the under-developed countries, to prepare a consolidated report for consideration by the Council at its twenty-sixth session."

TECHNICAL ASSISTANCE TO TRUST TERRITORY OF SOMALILAND

The Italian-administered Trust Territory of Somaliland is due to attain its independence in 1960. To this end, the Administering Authority has been making use of the technical assistance facilities of the United Nations and specialized agencies to help in the economic, social and educational development of the Territory, as the Economic and Social Council noted in a unanimous resolution on 30 July 1957.

The Council also asked the Secretary-General, the specialized agencies concerned and the Technical Assistance Board to continue to give sympathetic consideration to requests for technical assistance to the Territory.

The Council's resolution to this effect (660 (XXIV)) was adopted on the recommendation of the Technical Assistance Committee.

DOCUMENTARY REFERENCES

ECONOMIC AND SOCIAL COUNCIL—24TH SESSION
Plenary Meeting 993.
Technical Assistance Committee, meetings 135, 146.

E/TAC/L.130. Egypt, Indonesia, Sudan draft resolution.
E/TAC/L.130/Rev.1. Egypt, Indonesia, Pakistan, Sudan draft resolution, adopted unanimously by Technical Assistance Committee, as amended by Brazil, France, India and Netherlands, E/TAC/L.143.
E/TAC/L.143. Brazil, France, Netherlands amendments to revised joint draft resolution.
E/3041. Report of Technical Assistance Committee (Annex IV).
RESOLUTION 660(XXIV), as recommended by Technical Assistance Committee, E/3041, adopted unanimously by Council on 30 July 1957, meeting 993.

"The Economic and Social Council,
"Recalling the action of the United Nations concerning the achievement of independence by the Trust Territory of Somaliland under Italian administration, pursuant to General Assembly resolution 289 A (IV) of 21 November 1949,
"Recalling that in accordance with that resolution the independence of Somaliland is to become effective by 1960,
"Recalling that the General Assembly in its resolution 755(VIII) of 9 December 1953, and in particular in paragraph 2(e) thereof, recommended to Italy as the Administering Authority of the Trust Territory of Somaliland that use of technical assistance facilities provided by the United Nations and the specialized agencies to assist in economic development and in the improvement of social and educational conditions in the Territory should be encouraged,

"*Noting* that Italy, as the Administering Authority of the Trust Territory of Somaliland, and in accordance with resolution 755(VIII) of the General Assembly and, in particular, paragraph 2(*e*) thereof, is making use of technical assistance facilities provided by the United Nations and the specialized agencies to assist in economic development and in the improvement of social·and educational conditions in the Territory,

"*Noting* the provision of Council resolution 216 (VIII) of 10 February 1949, and *desirous* fully to co-operate with the Trusteeship Council in its efforts to extend to the Trust Territory of Somaliland the help and assistance which it needs in its progress towards independence,

"*Requests* the Secretary-General, the specialized agencies concerned and the Technical Assistance Board to continue to give sympathetic consideration to the requests made on behalf of the Trust Territory of Somaliland for technical assistance, taking into account the needs of Somaliland and the principles of the Expanded Programme of Technical Assistance, and also to consider favourably any request from the Administering Authority that local living costs for experts in connexion with such assistance be waived."

CHAPTER V

ACTIVITIES OF THE REGIONAL ECONOMIC COMMISSIONS

The activities of the Economic Commission for Europe (ECE), the Economic Commission for Asia and the Far East (ECAFE) and the Economic Commission for Latin America (ECLA) were appraised by the Economic and Social Council at its twenty-fourth session, in mid-1957. At that session, the Council also examined the co-ordination of their work programmes and further advances in the ways the commissions worked together, mainly through their secretariats; these matters were also discussed later in the year at the General Assembly's twelfth session.

CONSIDERATION BY ECONOMIC AND SOCIAL COUNCIL

The Council, in giving special attention to the concentration of activities in the economic, social and human rights fields, closely examined the work of the regional economic commissions. (See also below, CHAPTER XV, QUESTIONS OF CO-ORDINATION AND RELATIONS OF UNITED NATIONS WITH SPECIALIZED AGENCIES.) This was done mainly by the Council's Co-ordination Committee, which based its discussions on a report by the Secretary-General on the Council's work programme and on the financial implications of the Council's actions.

One section of this report was devoted to regional economic activities and described in detail how the three commissions had revised their work programmes and their lists of project priorities.

Also before the Council were the annual reports of the three commissions, each containing a section, as requested by the Council by resolution 630 A I (XXII) of 9 August 1956,[1] on the concentration and co-ordination of activities. These reports described the co-operation between the commissions which had been achieved as well as the ways in which the respective secretariats of the regional commissions had sought to maintain the closest co-operation both among themselves and with the units of the Department of Economic and Social Affairs at United Nations Headquarters.

The Co-ordination Committee discussed in detail the changes made by the regional economic commissions in their programmes with a view to achieving greater concentration on major economic problems. Their efforts to co-ordinate their activities and to streamline their work programmes were noted with satisfaction.

In an annex to its report to the Council, the Committee drew the Council's attention to "the desirability of encouraging exchanges of information and experience by the secretariats of the regional commissions on matters of mutual interest". The desirability of such exchanges, particularly in the field of housing and building, was also stressed in that part of the Committee's report dealing with social activities.

The Committee's entire report was annexed to resolution 664(XXIV) which the Council adopted on 1 August 1957. (For text, see DOCUMENTARY REFERENCES to CHAPTER XV below.)

[1]See *Y.U.N., 1956*, p. 273.

Another matter bearing on the activities of the regional economic commissions was also discussed at the Council's twenty-fourth session, in mid-1957. It arose in the course of debate in the Economic Committee on the world economic situation. The USSR submitted a proposal (which was not, however, pressed to a vote) to ask ECE and ECAFE to study, as ECLA had already decided to do, the possible repercussions of the creation of the European Common Market on their respective geographical areas. The USSR also proposed that all three economic commissions be asked to study the possible consequences of plans for setting up a European "free trade" area. (For further details, see above, CHAPTER I, THE WORLD ECONOMIC SITUATION.)

CONSIDERATION BY GENERAL ASSEMBLY

Activities of the regional economic commissions were again discussed at the General Assembly's twelfth session, in the course of debate in the Second Committee on the Economic and Social Council's annual report to the Assembly.

On the recommendation of the Second Committee, the Assembly adopted a resolution expressing appreciation of the valuable services of the regional economic commissions, particularly those rendered in recent years in the realization of projects which depended on co-operation between countries participating in the work of the commissions and which helped to strengthen international economic co-operation and to improve economic conditions, especially in the less developed countries.

The Assembly also noted with satisfaction each regional commission's efforts to co-ordinate its activities further and to streamline its work programme. These efforts, the Assembly believed, would lead to a more effective exchange of information and experience in matters of common interest. It hoped, too, that the Commissions would continue their valuable services and efforts.

Resolution 1158(XII) to this effect was unanimously approved at a plenary meeting of the Assembly on 26 November 1957. It had also been unanimously approved earlier in the Second Committee, on the basis of a proposal by Czechoslovakia revised in the light of amendments by Chile, Tunisia and the United States.

DOCUMENTARY REFERENCES

ECONOMIC AND SOCIAL COUNCIL—24TH SESSION
Plenary Meetings 978, 979, 993, 995, 996.
Economic Committee, meetings 221, 222.
Co-ordination Committee, meetings 152-162, 165.

E/2989. Economic Commission for Europe. Annual report, 22 April 1956-15 May 1957. (Part V and Annex I.)
E/2959. Economic Commission for Asia and the Far East. Annual report, 15 February 1956-28 March 1957. (Part V.)
E/2998. Economic Commission for Latin America, Annual report, 15 May 1956–29 May 1957. (Part VI.)
E/3011 and Corr.1, Add.1 and Add.2. Observations on work programme of Council and on financial implications of actions of Council. Report by Secretary-General.
E/AC.24/L.128 and Add.1. Argentina, Brazil, Dominican Republic and Mexico draft resolution, as orally amended in Co-ordination Committee, adopted unanimously by Co-ordination Committee.
A/3034 and Add.1. Report of Co-ordination Committee (Annex, paragraphs 1-6, 10-16).
E/3039. Co-ordination Committee Report (Annex B).
RESOLUTION 664 B and 665 B (XXIV), as recommended by Co-ordination Committee, E/3034 and Add.1 and E/3039, both adopted unanimously by Council on 1 August 1957, meeting 995. (For text, see DOCUMENTARY REFERENCES to CHAPTER XV.)

Economic Committee, meetings 230-232.

E/AC.6/L.187. USSR draft resolution.
E/3036. Report of Economic Committee (paragraph 4).

GENERAL ASSEMBLY—12TH SESSION
Plenary Meetings 722, 723.
Second Committee, meetings 467, 472, 477-480.

A/3613. Report of Economic and Social Council to General Assembly (Chapter IV).
A/C.2/L.333 and Rev.1, 2. Czechoslovakia draft resolution and revisions, adopted unanimously by Second Committee, as amended by United States.
A/C.2/L.341 and Rev.1, 2. United States amendments and revised amendments to revised draft resolutions of Czechoslovakia, A/C.2/L.333 and Rev. 1 and 2.
A/C.2/L.344. Chile amendment to revised draft resolution of Czechoslovakia, A/C.2/L.333/Rev.1.
A/C.2/L.345. Tunisia amendment to revised draft resolution of Czechoslovakia, A/C.2/L.333/Rev.1.
A/3740. Report of Second Committee (draft resolution IV).
RESOLUTION 1158 (XII), as recommended by Second Committee, A/3740, adopted unanimously by Assembly on 26 November 1957, meeting 723.

"The General Assembly,
"Recalling Economic and Social Council resolutions

579 A (XX) and 579 B (XX) of 4 August 1955 on the expansion of world trade and inter-regional trade consultations, and Council resolution 614 A (XXII) of 9 August 1956 on measures for the development of trade co-operation,

"*Recognizing* the desirability for a more effective international exchange of views within the framework of the United Nations regarding means of improving international economic conditions, as expressed in Economic and Social Council resolutions 654 A (XXIV) and 654 E (XXIV) of 30 July 1957,

"*Considering* that within the scope of their activities the regional economic commission are confronted with similar or related problems,

"1. *Expresses its appreciation* of the valuable services of the regional economic commissions, and in particular those rendered in recent years in the realization of projects depending upon co-operation among countries participating in the work of the commissions and tending, on the one hand, to strengthen international economic co-operation and, on the other, to improve economic conditions, especially in the less developed countries;

"2. *Notes with satisfaction* the efforts being made by each of the regional economic commissions to further co-ordination of its activities and to streamline its work programme, especially in accordance with Economic and Social Council resolution 630 A I (XXII) of 9 August 1956, as referred to in paragraph 10 of the annex to Council resolution 664 (XXIV) of 1 August 1957, and expresses its belief that these efforts will result in a more effective exchange of information and experience in matters of common interest;

"3. *Expresses the hope* that the regional economic commissions will continue, within their respective terms of reference and in conformity with the relevant resolutions of the Economic and Social Council, their valuable services and efforts."

ECONOMIC COMMISSION FOR EUROPE (ECE)

At its twelfth session, held at Geneva between 29 April and 15 May 1957, the Economic Commission for Europe celebrated its tenth anniversary and reviewed the economic situation in Europe. It invited Governments that so wished to submit concrete proposals for promoting economic co-operation among all ECE members. They were to be sent on to the appropriate committees of the Commission. The committees were invited to consider every year the possibilities for further development of contacts between the countries of Eastern and Western Europe. The Commission asked its Executive Secretary to report at its next session about the progress of arrangements between the International Atomic Energy Agency and the United Nations in so far as they were of concern to ECE. Arrangements were made for a study on water pollution control problems in Europe, to be undertaken in collaboration with the Food and Agriculture Organization (FAO) and the World Health Organization (WHO).

Other subjects discussed included the European energy situation and inter-regional trade consultations. Also dealt with was the streamlining of the Commission's programme of work and priorities. The Commission voiced its appreciation of the efforts made in this connexion by Governments and by the ECE secretariat.

During the session stress was placed on the responsibilities of the Commission as an organ for all European co-operation, particularly in the light of the movement towards sub-regional economic integration in various parts of Europe.

AGRICULTURE

In December 1957, the Committee on Agriculture examined the current agricultural situation in all European countries and the market outlook for cereals, meat, livestock, eggs and poultry.

The Committee's Working Party on Mechanization of Agriculture examined such matters as harvesting of grains and root crops, fodder conservation, dairy farm mechanization and fruit and vegetable cultivation.

The Committee's *ad hoc* working parties on the establishment of standard conditions of sale for cereals and citrous fruit had almost completed their work by the end of 1957. A study on general conditions of sale for potatoes was also prepared.

The Working Party on Standardization of Perishable Foodstuffs continued its work on bringing national measures for standardization and quality control into line with the provisions of the protocol (drawn up earlier by the Working Party) applying to all fresh fruit and vegetables traded between one European country and another.

The annual report, entitled *Prices of Agricultural Products and Fertilizers 1956/57*, was published.

FUEL AND ENERGY

COAL AND GAS

The Coal Committee started work on a comprehensive review of fundamental policy questions on the future development of the coal industry and the coal trade in Europe, and the Coal Trade Sub-Committee continued its quarterly studies of the market situation.

A number of reciprocal visits between countries of Eastern and Western Europe to mines for on-the-spot studies of specific problems took place during the year or else were planned.

The Utilization Working Party made progress with its study of low- and medium-temperature carbonization. It also started work on the proper use of low-grade fuels.

The Coal Classification Working Party reached preliminary agreement on an international classification system for brown coals and lignites. This was to be given a one-year trial period. Work began on a suitable classification system for high-temperature hard-coal coke.

The Ad Hoc Working Party on Gas Problems began work on problems in the field of production, transport and use of natural and manufactured gas.

Publications, in addition to regular statistical bulletins, included *Mining and Upgrading of Brown Coal in Europe: Developments and Prospects; Rational Utilization of European Coal Availabilities for Carbonization Purposes,* lists of bibliographical references on selected coal production methods; and *The Position of Natural Gas in the European Economy.*

ELECTRIC POWER

The Electric Power Committee, which celebrated its tenth anniversary during 1957, proceeded with its examination of the economic aspects of mechanization in the construction of hydro-electric plants, undertaking an inquiry into the costs of certain mechanized civil engineering works.

The group of experts for the study of hydro-electric resources in Europe continued its inquiry into methods to determine exploitable hydro-electric resources.

Among the publications issued in 1957 were: *Quarterly Bulletin of Electric Energy Statistics for Europe; Annual Bulletin of Electric Energy Statistics for Europe; Rural Electrification,* Vol-ume II; *Mechanization in Construction of Hydro-Electric Power Plants; Bibliographical Index of Works Published on Hydro-Electric Plant Construction.*

ENERGY PROBLEMS IN EUROPE

A study, entitled *The Energy Situation in Europe,* based on information from Governments was prepared by the ECE secretariat, for consideration by a special meeting of Government experts in 1958.

HOUSING

The Housing Committee examined current building trends and housing progress and, in the light of the observations made in the Committee, the ECE secretariat published a report on *European Housing Trends and Policies in 1956.* This included a discussion of certain long-term problems relating to house-building programmes. The Committee also examined problems of housing finance.

The Working Party on Housing and Building Statistics continued its work on standard definitions of concepts and terms. The *Quarterly Bulletin of Housing and Building Statistics for Europe* was issued for the first time on a subject basis rather than on a country basis, and final arrangements were made for the first issue of an annual bulletin of such statistics.

Work on the housing problems of less industrialized countries covered special questions of practical co-operation between countries of Southern Europe.

INLAND TRANSPORT

The European Agreements concerning the International Carriage of Dangerous Goods by Road (ADR) and on Road Markings were completed and signed during 1957.

Work also continued on: the prevention of road traffic accidents; the adoption of new regulations on night marking of vehicles; arrangements for traffic light signals and braking; and the acceptance of a number of new road symbols; and an agreement on uniform standards of approval of motor vehicle accessories.

The road characteristics defined in the 1950 Declaration on the Construction of Main International Traffic Arteries were revised.

Recommendations on signalling systems for

inland waterways were submitted to Governments for approval. Work continued on conventions on: (1) the contract for the carriage of goods, (2) the unification of certain rules concerning collisions in inland navigation, and (3) the transport of dangerous goods on inland waterways.

A definition of the various types of perishable foodstuffs and the special equipment to be used for transporting them was adopted.

Progress was made in the simplification of frontier formalities for private road vehicles. As a result of studies made by the Inland Transport Committee, several European countries will no longer require customs documents.

STEEL

The Steel Committee examined European steel market conditions in 1956, on the basis of a secretariat report entitled *The European Steel Market in 1956*. A preliminary discussion on the steel market in 1957 was also held.

A report on *Railways and Steel* was revised and published. A comprehensive inquiry into the long-term prospects of the European steel industry was begun.

The Working Party on Steel Statistics revised the regular questionnaires so as to make them simpler and clearer. The *Quarterly Bulletin of Steel Statistics for Europe* continued to be published.

A *Directory of National Organizations in Europe and the U.S.A. and International Organizations Concerned with Iron and Steel* was issued.

Over-all European technical co-operation was intensified, partly by an increased exchange of visits by steel technicians, and partly by participation at congresses and meetings held by technical and scientific institutes in different countries.

TIMBER

The Timber Committee, which also marked its tenth year of existence in 1957, reviewed the European market for sawn softwood, pitprops and pulpwood in 1957 and appraised the prospects for 1958. It also considered a study on the trends on the European market of sawn hardwood and the final version of a study on trends in the utilization of wood and its pro-

ducts in housing construction. It agreed to continue studies in the field of wood utilization.

The Committee also discussed ways of carrying out the recommendations resulting from the joint FAO/ECE meeting, held in January, on fibreboard and particle boards.

The Committee, in addition, took note of the report of the second session of the Joint FAO/ECE Committee on Forest Working Techniques and Training of Forest Workers held in Moscow in September 1957.

INDUSTRY AND MATERIALS

The Ad Hoc Working Party on Contract Practices in Engineering adopted the General Conditions for the Supply and Erection of Plant and Machinery for Import and Export, Numbers 188-A and 574-A, which were published in July 1957.

The Ad Hoc Working Party on Agricultural Machinery agreed to reports being prepared on specific types of agricultural machinery on the basis of inquiries to Governments.

Work on a report on the economic implications of automation proceeded.

ECONOMIC DEVELOPMENT OF SOUTHERN EUROPE

Several questions of special interest to the countries of Southern Europe, in the field of electric power, housing, inland transport, steel and foreign trade, were considered during 1957 by the relevant ECE Committees.

TRADE

The Committee on the Development of Trade reviewed developments in intra-European trade, particularly east-west trade. It also agreed to discuss at its next session the economic consequences of the establishment of the European Common Market. The Committee considered proposals by various delegations to improve intra-European trade techniques, particularly through multiliateral payment arrangements, better facilities for trade fairs and technical shows, and arbitration and standardization of general conditions of sale.

At the fifth annual Consultation of Experts on East-West Trade, over 100 bilateral commercial talks were held between experts of 26 countries.

Procedures for the multilateral compensation of trade balances were put in operation in July 1957; transfers totalling about $19 million were arranged between interested Governments by the end of the year.

OTHER ACTIVITIES

The ECE Secretariat continued its co-operation with the Technical Assistance Administration (TAA). The TAA/ECE in-service training programme for young European economists was continued. The ECE secretariat also collaborated with TAA on specific projects, mostly concerning Southern European countries.

The Conference of European Statisticians considered reports of its working groups dealing with: statistics on distribution of fixed capital formation; higher education and graduate employment; and indicators of short-term economic changes. It also received reports from specialized agencies and other organizations on statistics relating to agriculture, labour and living conditions, and the causes of death. The Conference made specific suggestions about the statistical activities of various ECE Committees.

CONSIDERATION BY ECONOMIC AND SOCIAL COUNCIL

The Council considered the report of ECE at its twenty-fourth session, in mid-1957.

The Council, by resolution 655 A (XXIV) of 30 July 1957, took note of ECE's report and expressed its appreciation of the excellent work done by the retiring Executive Secretary, Gunnar Myrdal, in developing and promoting ESE's work. Mr. Myrdal was succeeded by Sakari Tuomioja.

Several Council members praised the work of ECE during its first 10 years of existence, and stressed its importance as a forum for considering a variety of problems that faced Europe as a whole. Particularly referred to were: the work undertaken by governmental experts acting as rapporteurs to various ECE committees; and the potential importance of the multilateral payments system that had been put into effect.

DOCUMENTARY REFERENCES

ECONOMIC AND SOCIAL COUNCIL—24TH SESSION
Plenary Meetings 973-979, 993.
Economic Committee, meetings 221, 222.

E/2989. Economic Commission for Europe. Annual report, 22 April 1956-15 May 1957.
E/2989, Part IV. Draft resolution submitted by ECE, adopted by Economic Committee, as amended by Pakistan and United States, by 14 votes to 0, with 3 abstentions.
E/AC.6/L.182. Pakistan amendment to draft resolution submitted by ECE.
E/AC.6/L.183. United States amendment to draft resolution submitted by ECE.
E/3029. Report of Economic Committee (draft resolution A).
RESOLUTION 655 A (XXIV), as submitted by Economic Committee, E/3029, adopted by Council on 30 July 1957, meeting 993, by 17 votes to 0, with 1 abstention.

"The Economic and Social Council

"1. Takes note of the annual report of the Economic Commission for Europe for the period 22 April 1956 to 15 May 1957, of the views expressed during the discussion, and the resolutions adopted, during the twelfth session of the Commission;

"2. Endorses the programme of work and priorities contained in the report;

"3. Expresses its appreciation of the excellent work done by the retiring Executive Secretary, Mr. Gunnar Myrdal, in developing and promoting the work of the Economic Commission for Europe."

A/3613. Report of Economic and Social Council to General Assembly (Chapter IV, Section I).

OTHER REPORTS AND STUDIES
Economic Survey of Europe in 1957. U.N.P. Sales No.: 58.II.E.1.
Railways and Steel. U.N.P. Sales No.: 1957.II.E.3.
Trends in Utilization of Wood and Its Products in Housing. U.N.P. Sales No.: 1957.II.E.4.
Mechanization in Construction of Hydro-Electric Power Plants. U.N.P. Sales No.: 1957.II.E/MIM.9.
The Position of Natural Gas in the European Economy. U.N.P. Sales No.: 1957.II.1/MIM.6.
European Housing Trends and Policies in 1956. U.N.P. Sales No.: 1957.II.E/MIM.11.
European Steel Market in 1956. U.N.P. Sales No.: 1957.II.E/MIM.14.
Rational Utilization of European Coal Availabilities for Carbonization Purposes. U.N.P. Sales No.: 1957.II.E/MIM.15.
Table of Bilateral Conventions Relating to the Enforcement of Arbitral Awards and the Organization of Commercial Arbitral Procedure. U.N.P. Sales No.: 1957.II.E/MIM.18.
Mining and Upgrading of Brown Coal in Europe: Developments and Prospects. U.N.P. Sales No.: 1957.II.E/MIM.20.
Methods of Forecasting Gas Demand. U.N.P. Sales No.: 1957.II.E/MIM.22.
Agricultural Mechanization: Harvesting, Transport and Storage of Green Fodder in Mountainous Regions. U.N.P. Sales No.: 1957.II.E/MIM.23.
Bibliographical Index of Works Published on Hydro-Electric Plant Construction. U.N.P. Sales No.: 1957.II.E/MIM.24.

*Prices of Agricultural Products and Fertilizers 1956/
57.* U.N.P. Sales No.: 1957.II.E/MIM.27.
Rural Electrification, Vol. II (E/ECE/260).
Economic Bulletin for Europe. Vol. 9, Nos. 1-3.
*Annual Bulletin of Transport Statistics for Europe,
1956.* U.N.P. Sales No.: 58.II.E.2.
*Annual Bulletin of Electric Energy Statistics for
Europe.*
Quarterly Bulletin of Coal Statistics for Europe.

*Quarterly Bulletin of Electric Energy Statistics for
Europe.*
Quarterly Bulletin of Steel Statistics for Europe.
*Quarterly Bulletin of Housing and Building Statistics
for Europe.*
Timber Bulletin for Europe. Quarterly.
Annual Bulletin of Gas Statistics for Europe. U.N.P.
Sales No.: 1957.II.E/MIM.5.

ECONOMIC COMMISSION FOR ASIA AND THE FAR EAST (ECAFE)

The Economic Commission for Asia and the Far East (ECAFE) celebrated its tenth anniversary in 1957.

At its thirteenth session, held at Bangkok from 18 to 28 March 1957, the Commission adopted resolutions on: regional studies of demographic trends and economic development, the establishment of a Conference of Asian Statisticians, and a land settlement study tour. The committee structure of the Commission was changed by reconstituting the Sub-Committee on Trade into a full committee and changing the name of the Committee on Industry and Trade to Committee on Industry and Natural Resources.

In its decisions, the Commission affirmed the need to concentrate its activities on major economic matters of regional importance.

INDUSTRY AND TRADE

IRON AND STEEL

During 1957, the Sub-Committee on Iron and Steel gave special attention to steel-transforming industries, modernization of rolling mills, the use of processes for manufacturing iron without coking coal, standardization and simplification of specifications, consumption trends and personnel questions.

A study tour to Europe for iron and steel experts from ECAFE countries, co-sponsored by the Commission, took place in October-November 1957.

SMALL-SCALE INDUSTRIES AND HANDICRAFT MARKETING

The Working Party on Small-Scale Industries and Handicraft Marketing examined the technical and economic aspects of the tanning and leather industry, particularly quality improvement, productivity research, increased use of local tanning materials and marketing questions.

ELECTRIC POWER

The Sub-Committee on Electric Power considered, among other things, the problems of rural electrification and standardization. It suggested that members avail themselves of offers made by Japan and the USSR to train personnel in research on hydro-electric potential.

A working party of experts discussed methods of assessing hydro-electric potential and reviewed relevant surveys being made in the region. It recommended the formulation of definite policies for developing water resources, and it stressed the importance of adequate financing of research, especially on hydro-electric power.

MINERAL RESOURCES DEVELOPMENT

The Sub-Committee on Mineral Resources Development discussed mineral legislation, conservation, trade, and aerial surveys and prospecting for radio-active minerals, personnel training problems, and the classification and use of coal (especially low-grade coal).

REGIONAL GEOLOGICAL MAPS

The Working Party on the Preparation of a Regional Geological Map examined a draft map prepared by the Director of the Geological Survey of India, as co-ordinator of the project. It also suggested measures for completion of the work and for the subsequent preparation of regional mineral and tectonic maps. It noted that a joint geological survey of the Malayan-Thai border had yielded significant results.

INLAND TRANSPORT

The Inland Transport Committee gave special attention to: the co-ordination of transport; performance statistics; refrigeration; mechanization of accounts; library services; telecommunications; and the development of international travel and tourism.

INLAND PORTS

The Ad Hoc Working Party on Inland Ports studied port design and construction, and a wide range of operational and development problems. It stressed the need for adequate port facilities to avoid transport-potential losses.

INLAND WATERWAYS

The Inland Waterways Sub-Committee made recommendations on improving government organization, and on the modernization and better use of transport equipment. It asked the ECAFE secretariat for a paper on the work of various international agencies on sea ports and ocean shipping in Asia and the Far East, in order to determine whether ECAFE should undertake any projects in this field.

RAILWAYS

The Railway Sub-Committee considered, in particular, technical and economic aspects of diesel locomotive operation and maintenance, the economic use of rolling stock, workshop productivity, safety, and training facilities for railway officials of the region.

HIGHWAYS

A seminar on highway safety, held in Tokyo in May 1957, considered: problems of administration; traffic and vehicle registration forecasts; accident statistics; traffic design and operation; and training, education and public information on traffic safety. Recommendations covered national highway safety programmes and traffic study weeks.

FLOOD CONTROL AND WATER RESOURCES DEVELOPMENT

The third Regional Technical Conference on Water Resources Development met at Manila in December 1957 and reviewed progress in developing the water resources in the region and made recommendations on the technical and organizational aspects of project planning and construction, and on matters relating to a proposed study tour of water resources development schemes in Europe and North America by experts from the ECAFE region.

The work of the ECAFE Bureau of Flood Control and Water Resources Development during 1957 covered river basin development, as well as analyses of selected multi-purpose projects in the region. The Bureau continued to publish its *Flood Control Series,* in close co-operation with the Food and Agriculture Organization (FAO) and the World Health Organization.

LOWER MEKONG RIVER
DEVELOPMENT PROJECT

Significant progress was made on the Lower Mekong River development project in 1957. A joint meeting of the experts of the four riparian States concerned (Cambodia, Laos, Thailand and Viet-Nam) was held at Bangkok in May 1957. It recommended: (1) that a Committee for Co-ordination of Investigations of the Lower Mekong basin be set up, composed of representatives of the States concerned (2) that these States jointly request United Nations technical assistance; and (3) that the Mekong project be made one of ECAFE's regional projects.

The Committee for Co-ordination held its first session in October-November 1957.

In response to a request to the Technical Assistance Administration (TAA), a United Nations survey mission, under the chairmanship of Lieutenant-General R. A. Wheeler, began work in November on a programme for the development of the Lower Mekong River basin. Its assignment was due to be completed by the end of January 1958.

AGRICULTURE

The ECAFE/FAO Division of Agriculture during 1957 disseminated information on agricultural credit systems and agricultural indebtedness, and continued its study on the relationship between agriculture and industry. Data continued to be collected on the extent to which people in the region increase or decrease their purchases of rice and other cereals according to changes in their income. This work was done in close liaison with FAO, which is preparing a world-wide review of food consumption surveys. Country studies on food and agricultural price policies were prepared for the ECAFE/FAO centre on policies to support and stabilize agriculture prices and incomes in Asia and the Far East. This centre was scheduled to open in New Delhi in March 1958.

Work was begun during 1957 on a joint ECAFE/FAO study of timber trends and prospects.

RESEARCH AND PLANNING

The *Economic Survey of Asia and the Far East* for 1957 surveyed the regional economic situation, and also analysed major economic development problems in selected countries in the region. In appendices, it gave recent Asian economic statistics and a summary of trade agreements concluded in 1957.

ECONOMIC DEVELOPMENT AND PLANNING

The Working Party on Economic Development and Planning considered agricultural development planning and implementation in relation to economic development, particularly to industrialization. It examined a comprehensive document prepared jointly by the secretariats of ECAFE and FAO, and working papers contributed by the Bureau of Economic Affairs of the United Nations, the International Labour Office and participating Governments.

The Working Party emphasized the personnel, co-ordination and statistical aspects of agricultural planning. It recommended measures for greater precision in agricultural planning and drew the attention of the Conference of Asian Statisticians to the subject's statistical aspects.

STATISTICS

The fifth Regional Conference of Statisticians of Asia and the Far East, which reconstituted itself as the first session of the Conference of Asian Statisticians, met in Bangkok in April 1957 under the joint sponsorship of the Statistical Office of the United Nations, FAO and ECAFE. It discussed the FAO draft programme for the proposed 1960 World Census of Agriculture and considered related aspects of the application of sampling methods.

BUDGET RECLASSIFICATION AND MANAGEMENT

The second Workshop on Problems of Budget Reclassification and Management, sponsored by ECAFE jointly with TAA and the Fiscal and Financial Branch of the Bureau of Economic Affairs of the United Nations, was held in Bangkok in August 1957. (For further details, see CHAPTER VI, FISCAL AND FINANCIAL QUESTIONS.)

CONSIDERATION BY ECONOMIC AND SOCIAL COUNCIL

On 30 July 1957, at its twenty-fourth session, the Economic and Social Council approved the annual report of ECAFE. In doing so, it also endorsed the programme of work and priorities contained in the report and approved the changes in ECAFE's committee structure made by the Commission.

DOCUMENTARY REFERENCES

ECONOMIC AND SOCIAL COUNCIL—24TH SESSION
Plenary Meetings 973-979, 993.
Economic Committee, meetings 221, 222.

E/2959. Economic Commission for Asia and the Far East. Annual report, 15 February 1956-28 March 1957.
E/2959, Part IV. Draft resolution submitted by ECAFE, as amended by United States, adopted by Economic Committee, by 14 votes to 0, with 3 abstentions.
E/AC.6/L.180. United States amendment to draft resolution submitted by ECAFE.
E/3029. Report of Economic Committee (draft resolution B).
RESOLUTION 655 B (XXIV), as recommended by Economic Committee, E/3029, adopted unanimously by Council on 30 July 1957, meeting 993.

"The Economic and Social Council
"1. *Takes note with appreciation* of the annual report of the Economic Commission for Asia and the Far East for the period 15 February 1956 to 28 March 1957, and of the recommendations contained in the account of proceedings of the thirteenth session of the Commission;
"2. *Endorses* the programme of work and priorities contained therein;
"3. *Approves* the changes in the committee structure of the Commission referred to in resolution 19 (XIII) of the Commission."

A/3613. Report of Economic and Social Council to General Assembly (Chapter IV, Section II).

OTHER REPORTS AND STUDIES
Economic Survey of Asia and Far East 1957. U.N.P. Sales No.: 58.II.F.1.
Credit Problems of Small Farmers in Asia and Far East. Study prepared by ECAFE/FAO Agriculture Division. U.N.P. Sales No.: 1957.II.F.2.
Mining Developments in Asia and Far East, 1956. U.N.P. Sales No.: 1957.II.F.4.
Survey of Mining Legislation with Special Reference to Asia and the Far East. U.N.P. Sales No.: 1957. II.F.5.
Electric Power in Asia and Far East 1951-1955. U.N.P. Sales No.: 1957.II.F.6.

Uniform System of Buoys and Shore Marks for Inland Waterways in Asia and Far East. U.N.P. Sales No.: 1957.II.F.7.

Development of Water Resources in the Lower Mekong Basin. Flood Control Series, No. 12. U.N.P. Sales No.: 1957.II.F.8.

Convention Regarding Measurement and Registration of Vessels Employed in Inland Navigation. U.N.P. Sales No.: 1957.II.F.9.

Economic Bulletin for Asia and Far East. Three issues and annual survey.

Flood Control Journal (ST/ECAFE/SER.C).

Transport Bulletin (ST/ECAFE/SER.E).

Trade Promotion News (ST/ECAFE/SER.H).

Railway Statistics Bulletin (ST/ECAFE/SER.K).

Electric Power Bulletin (ST/ECAFE/SER.L).

Industrial Development Series (ST/ECAFE/SER.M).

ECONOMIC COMMISSION FOR LATIN AMERICA (ECLA)

At its seventh session, held at La Paz, Bolivia, from 15 to 29 May 1957, the Economic Commission for Latin America (ECLA) adopted resolutions on trade, a Latin American regional market and multilateral payments system, commodity trade, transport, the economic integration of Central America, technical assistance, the steel and pulp and paper industries, nuclear energy, water resources, agricultural productivity, coffee studies, and economic development programming. The Commission also thanked the Government of Chile for its donation of a site for a building for the ECLA secretariat and other United Nations offices in Santiago.

The Commission accepted an invitation from Panama to hold its eighth session at Panama City.

ECONOMIC SURVEY AND BULLETIN

The *Economic Survey of Latin America, 1956,* originally issued in mimeographed form in May 1957, was heavily revised before printing. It consisted of two parts. The first analysed trends of Latin America's economic growth during 1956, with special reference to external factors such as exports and the balance of payments. It also carried a comparative study of import capacities of selected Latin American countries for the period 1946-1955, and dealt with production trends in agriculture, industry, mining and energy. The second part contained a preliminary study on the effects of post-war industrialization programmes on the structure of imports and the vulnerability of Latin American economies to external economic forces, and a special study of productivity in Latin American agriculture.

Volume II, No. 1, of the *Economic Bulletin for Latin America* was published in February 1957. It included articles on: the economic situation in Latin America in 1956; trade between Latin America and Japan; changes in the employment structure in Latin America during the period 1944-1955; and possibilities for the expansion of wheat production in Brazil. Volume II, No. 2, of the *Bulletin,* published in December, carried articles on: the index clause in deferred payments; the economic development of Bolivia; and Latin America's trade in the early months of 1957.

TRADE

The working group of experts from Central Banks, set up by ECLA's Trade Committee, held its first meeting at Montevideo from 29 April to 10 May. It submitted to the Trade Committee a draft standard payments agreement to be used as a model for bilateral trade agreements. This was an important first step towards the elimination of bilateral barriers to intra-regional trade. It was further recommended that ECLA should, on a temporary basis, receive, compile and distribute information on the status of bilateral accounts to Governments maintaining such accounts. The exchange of information began during the second half of the year.

A special report on ECLA's work on inter-Latin American payments and the regional market, was submitted to the International Economic Conference held at Buenos Aires under the auspices of the Organization of American States.

Preparations were made for a meeting of the Working Group of Experts on the Regional Market, to be held from 1 to 10 February 1958.

Work also proceeded on a study of tariff classification and nomenclature for the South American countries.

JOINT ECLA/FAO PROGRAMME

The study of coffee trends and productivity in Latin America was continued. The report on El Salvador was completed and submitted to

ECLA's seventh session. Completed, too, were the field work in Colombia and the first drafts of the report for Colombia. Towards the end of 1957, field work started in Brazil, with the active collaboration of the Instituto Brasileiro do Café (Brazilian Coffee Institute).

ECONOMIC DEVELOPMENT

A study by the ECLA secretariat on the economic development of Bolivia was completed early in 1957, in collaboration with the Food and Agriculture Organization (FAO) and the United Nations Technical Assistance Administration (TAA), followed up by a round-table conference with leading authorities in Bolivia to discuss its findings.

An analysis was made of the influence of unfavourable balances of payment on Latin America's economic development, with specific reference to Mexico.

In response to a long-felt need, a manual of investment projects was completed, intended for students of economic problems, particularly for technicians and officials working in Latin America.

The bulk of the preparatory and drafting work on a report on the economic development of Argentina was also completed. The final report was expected to be issued early in 1958.

ECONOMIC DEVELOPMENT TRAINING PROGRAMME

In addition to the regular annual economic development training programme conducted jointly by ECLA and TAA in Santiago, intensive courses were held in 1957 at Rio de Janeiro and at Caracas.

The 1957 course at Santiago was attended by 14 trainees, from nine Latin American countries. Funds for nine of the trainees were provided by TAA, one trainee held a United Nations fellowship and the participation of the remainder was financed by their respective Governments. The programme of studies covered various economic, social and financial subjects.

The shorter intensive courses at Rio de Janeiro and Caracas were attended by 80 and 82 students, respectively.

Many former trainees now hold important posts in their own countries; among them are a minister of finance, an under-secretary of state, a president of a Central Bank, a director of planning and several university professors.

CENTRAL AMERICAN ECONOMIC INTEGRATION PROGRAMME

At its fourth ordinary session, held at Guatemala City in February 1957, the Central American Economic Co-operation Committee recommended that its member Governments should sign the draft Multilateral Free Trade and Economic Integration Treaty and the draft Agreement on the Integration of Central American Industries. These measures, representing a definite step towards the creation of a free trade zone in Central America, are intended to encourage the establishment of new industries based on the common market constituted by the five countries. Further details of the draft treaty were discussed at a meeting of ECLA's Trade Sub-Committee, held at San Salvador from 23 to 27 September.

At a meeting of representatives of national traffic authorities, held at San Salvador during October, the text of an agreement on highway traffic was approved, together with part of the draft Manual on Specifications, based on the work of two TAA experts. Other meetings under the integration programme were held in November, one on housing, building industries and building materials and one on electric power. Both took place at San José, Costa Rica.

Work proceeded on projects on pulp and paper, livestock and dairy products, fisheries, grain supplies, cotton, preparation of maritime port legislation, and weights and measures.

INDUSTRY

During 1957, first drafts of a detailed study on the motor vehicle industry in Brazil were completed. This study arose out of a recommendation made at the Latin American Meeting of Experts on Steel-Making and Transforming Industries, held at São Paulo in October 1956, under the joint auspices of ECLA, TAA and the Associação Brasileira de Metais (Brazilian Metals Association). The study was prepared in collaboration with the Banco Nacional do Desenvolvimento Economico (National Bank of Economic Development). It analysed industry costs in relation to size of operations by processes, as well as the possible impact of the establishment of the motor vehicle industry on the rest of the economy, with particular reference to the producers of the intermediate products required by the industry. Similar studies have been planned for the motor vehicle industries of Argentina and perhaps Mexico, too.

At the request of the Peruvian Government, ECLA sent a mission to Peru early in 1957 to prepare a study on industrial development, to consist of (*a*) a general economic part, dealing with the whole industrial sector of the economy and its relationship to the economy and (*b*) a technical and industrial part, including analyses and projections of various industries.

Continuing its research on the current situation of the pulp and paper industry in various countries, the members of the ECLA/FAO/ TAA Pulp and Paper Advisory Group visited Peru and Brazil during 1957 to gather data. The Group also revised and brought up to date, prior to final publication, its study *Chile, Potential Pulp and Paper Exporter,* and it prepared a report entitled *Summary of the Pulp and Paper Situation in Argentina: Development Possibilities and Prospects.* Parts of the latter report were adapted to form one of the chapters in the general study on the economic development of Argentina.

ENERGY AND WATER RESOURCES

In 1957, work began on a study of the integrated development of water resources in Latin America, starting with a pilot study on the situation in Chile. The French Government lent the services of a hydrologist for eight months for this study; the World Meteorological Organization has provided an expert on hydropower and hydro-meteorology. Two TAA experts also participated, and help was received from the Chilean Government, including the part-time services of an irrigation expert.

TECHNICAL ASSISTANCE

During 1957, members of the ECLA secretariat spent an increasing amount of time in reviewing job descriptions for TAA experts to be assigned to different countries in the region. This was followed by a briefing of the experts before they started on their assignments, and by comments on and reviews of the reports which they subsequently made. This led to increasingly close co-ordination between the work of the ECLA secretariat and of the experts in the field, particularly in the case of the Central American economic integration programme and the studies on the economic development of selected countries.

CONSIDERATION BY ECONOMIC AND SOCIAL COUNCIL

The annual report of ECLA was considered by the Economic and Social Council at its twenty-fourth session, in mid-1957.

Members of the Council, commending the work of the Commission, referred particularly to the support which member Governments had given to the decisions of ECLA's Trade Committee and to the importance of the plans for the integration of the Latin American economy. Special mention was also made of the introduction of a multilateral payments scheme and the efforts to develop major industries.

On 30 July 1957, by resolution 655 C (XXIV), the Council took note of the Commission's annual report and endorsed ECLA's work programme and the order of priorities set out in it.

DOCUMENTARY REFERENCES

ECONOMIC AND SOCIAL COUNCIL—24TH SESSION
Plenary Meetings 973-979, 993.
Economic Committee, meetings 221, 222.

E/2998. Economic Commission for Latin America. Annual report, 15 May 1956-29 May 1957. (See Annex III of this report for list of Commission documents.)
E/2998, Part V. Draft resolution submitted by ECLA, as amended by United States, adopted by Economic Committee by 14 votes to 0, with 3 abstentions.
E/AC.6/L.181. United States amendment to draft resolution submitted by ECLA.
E/3029. Report of Economic Committee (draft resolution C).

RESOLUTION 655 C (XXIV), as submitted by Economic Committee, E/3029, adopted unanimously by Council on 30 July 1957, meeting 993.
"The Economic and Social Council
"1. *Takes note* of the annual report of the Economic Commission for Latin America for the period 15 May 1956 to 29 May 1957, adopted at its seventh session;
"2. *Endorses* the work programme of the Commission as established by the Commission at its seventh session held at La Paz, Bolivia, from 15 to 29 May 1957, as being of primary importance for the economic development of Latin America;
"3. *Endorses* the order of priorities allocated by the Commission to the individual work projects."

A/3613. Report of Economic and Social Council to General Assembly (Chapter IV, Section III).

OTHER REPORTS AND STUDIES

Economic Survey of Latin America, 1956. U.N.P. Sales No.: 1957.II.G.1.
Economic Integration of Central America, 1956. U.N.P. Sales No.: 1956.II.G.4.
Economic Bulletin for Latin America, Vol. II, Nos. 1 and 2 (February, October 1957).
Energy in Latin America. U.N.P. Sales No.: 1957.II.G.A.
Analyses and Projections of Economic Development: III, Economic Development of Colombia. U.N.P. Sales No.: 1957.II.G.3.
Problems of Steel Making and Transforming Industries in Latin America. Vols. I and II. U.N.P.

Sales Nos.: 1957.II.G.6. Vol. I, Vol. II.
Informe del Comité de Cooperación Económica del Istmo Centroamericano. U.N.P. Sales No.: 1957.II.G.7.
Compendio Estadístico Centroamericano. U.N.P. Sales No.: 1957.II.G.8.
La Política Tributaria y el Desarrollo Económico en Centroamérica. U.N.P. Sales No.: 1957.II.G.9.
E/CN.12/483. ECLA activities relating to payments and regional market in Latin America.
E/CN.12/484. Report submitted to ECLA Trade Committee by Central Banks' Working Group on multilateral payments system.
E/CN.12/485(FAO/ETAP. No. 711). Summary of pulp and paper situation in Argentina: development prospects and economic aspects.

PROPOSED ESTABLISHMENT OF ECONOMIC COMMISSION FOR AFRICA

At its twelfth session, on 26 November 1957, the General Assembly recommended that the Economic and Social Council give prompt and favourable consideration to the establishment of an Economic Commission for Africa. This matter was put on the provisional agenda for the Council's twenty-fifth session, due to be held in April-May 1958.

It may be recalled that when the Council established the Economic Commission for Europe (ECE) and the Economic Commission for Asia and the Far East (ECAFE) in March 1957, no action was taken with regard to Ethiopia and the war-devastated areas in North Africa. On 11 March 1947, the representative of India introduced a draft resolution in the Council for the establishment of a special economic commission for North Africa and Ethiopia. Although this move was limited in geographical scope, it may be considered as the first initiative in the United Nations to set up an economic commission for Africa. The Indian draft resolution, however, was not acted on by the Council.

The question of the establishment of an economic commission for Africa was again raised at the tenth session of the Economic and Social Council in February-March 1950 (at meetings 345, 359-362).[2] Council members, however, generally felt that the immediate creation of a commission at that time would be premature. At the Council's request, a *Review of Economic Conditions in Africa* was prepared by the United Nations Secretariat for the Council's twelfth session in February-March 1951, when

the desirability of creating a regional economic commission for Africa was again discussed (at meetings 453-454, 457-458).[3] But no decision was taken. At its thirteenth session, in mid-1951,[4] the Council had before it a report by a group of experts on *Measures for the Economic Development of the Under-Developed Countries,* which recommended the establishment of an economic commission for Africa. In the course of the Council's discussions (at meetings 483, 492-493, 495, 500-501), the Philippines representative proposed the establishment of an *ad hoc* committee to consider factors bearing upon the creation of an economic commission for Africa, but this was rejected by the Council.

The question was not raised again by the Council Members between 1952 and 1956 (except for a remark by the representative of Yugoslavia at the Council's 940th meeting, in mid-1956, that "the time was fast approaching for the organization of regional co-operation in the Middle East and Africa"). Observers of certain non-governmental organizations, however, continued to propose the establishment of an African commission at the following plenary meetings of the Council: 589, 692, 804, 873, 877, 907, 910, 935, 939.

In 1957, the matter was brought up at the General Assembly's twelfth session, during debate in the Assembly's Second (Economic and Financial) Committee. This was in the course of discussion on the Economic and Social Coun-

[2]See *Y.U.N., 1950,* p. 480.
[3]See *Y.U.N., 1951,* pp. 363, 366, 367.
[4]See *Y.U.N., 1951,* pp. 371-373, 374.

cil's annual report to the Assembly. The representative of Ghana suggested that some thought be given to the possibility of establishing a United Nations economic commission for Africa "in the near future". The suggestion was supported by the representatives of Sudan, India, Brazil, Liberia, Egypt and Czechoslovakia. The discussion resulted in the introduction of a 26-power draft resolution on the subject, to which three additional sponsors were subsequently added. The 29 sponsors were: Afghanistan, Brazil, Burma, Cambodia, Ceylon, Chile, Egypt, Ethiopia, Ghana, Haiti, India, Indonesia, Iran, Iraq, Lebanon, Liberia, Libya, Mexico, Morocco, Nepal, Pakistan, Philippines, Poland, Saudi Arabia, Sudan, Syria, Tunisia, Yemen and Yugoslavia. The operative paragraph of the draft resolution recommended "that, for the purpose of giving effective aid to the countries and territories of Africa, and in accordance with Article 68 of the Charter, the Economic and Social Council should, at its next session, give prompt and favourable consideration to the establishment of an Economic Commission for Africa".

During the debate in the Second Committee, sponsors of the draft resolution repeatedly emphasized the importance of promoting and facilitating concerted action for Africa's economic development and for raising the levels of living in Africa, as well as the need for adequate information about problems facing the under-developed countries in Africa. Hopes were expressed that the proposed commission would make a "continuous appraisal of African problems", define and investigate the special economic development problems of the African territories, and suggest ways and means whereby an effective solution could be attempted. The majority of Committee members were of the opinion that all African countries had a common problem of economic development and that geographic and other differences should not prevent them from joining to form one regional commission. They considered that the purview of the proposed commission should cover the whole of Africa. The representative of Belgium, however, considered that Africa was not a homogeneous region, being separated by natural obstacles into different parts, which differed in their geographical, demographic and economic aspects. He also held that "the economic needs of the northern and southern parts of Africa were completely divergent".

The Second Committee finally approved the draft resolution by a vote of 71 to 0, with 2 abstentions. It was later adopted, on 26 November 1957, at a plenary meeting of the Assembly as resolution 1155(XII), by a roll-call vote of 78 to 0, with 1 abstention (Belgium). Lebanon, Morocco and the Union of South Africa were absent.

The Economic and Social Council, at its resumed twenty-fourth session in December 1957, decided to include "Consideration of the Establishment of an Economic Commission for Africa" in the provisional agenda of its twenty-fifth session.

DOCUMENTARY REFERENCES

GENERAL ASSEMBLY—12TH SESSION
Plenary Meetings 722, 723.
Second Committee, meetings 455, 456, 459, 460, 462, 464, 467-471.

A/C.2/L.334 and Add.1, 2. Afghanistan, Brazil, Burma, Cambodia, Ceylon, Chile, Egypt, Ethiopia, Ghana, Haiti, India, Indonesia, Iran, Iraq, Lebanon, Liberia, Libya, Mexico, Morocco, Nepal, Pakistan, Philippines, Poland, Saudi Arabia, Sudan, Syria, Tunisia, Yemen, Yugoslavia draft resolution, adopted by Second Committee by roll-call vote of 71 to 0, with 2 abstentions, as follows:
In favour: Afghanistan, Albania, Argentina, Australia, Austria, Bolivia, Brazil, Bulgaria, Burma, Byelorussian SSR, Cambodia, Canada, Ceylon, Chile, China, Colombia, Cuba, Czechoslovakia, Denmark, Ecuador, Egypt, Ethiopia, Finland, France, Ghana, Greece, Gutemala, Haiti, Hungary, Iceland, India, Indonesia, Iran, Iraq, Ireland, Israel, Italy, Japan, Laos, Liberia, Libya, Federation of Malaya, Mexico, Morocco, Nepal, Netherlands, New Zealand, Norway, Pakistan, Panama, Paraguay, Peru, Philippines, Poland, Portugal, Romania, Saudi Arabia, Spain, Sudan, Sweden, Syria, Thailand, Tunisia, Turkey, Ukrainian SSR, USSR, United States, Uruguay, Venezuela, Yemen, Yugoslavia.
Against: None.
Abstaining: Belgium, United Kingdom.
A/3740. Report of Second Committee (draft resolution I).
RESOLUTION 1155 (XII), as recommended by Second Committee, A/3740, adopted by Assembly on 26 November 1957, meeting 723, by roll-call vote of 78 to 0, with 1 abstention, as follows:
In favour: Afghanistan, Albania, Argentina, Australia, Austria, Bolivia, Brazil, Bulgaria, Burma, Byelorussian SSR, Cambodia, Canada, Ceylon, Chile,

China, Colombia, Costa Rica, Cuba, Czechoslovakia, Denmark, Dominican Republic, Ecuador, Egypt, El Salvador, Ethiopia, Finland, France, Ghana, Greece, Guatemala, Haiti, Honduras, Hungary, Iceland, India, Indonesia, Iran, Iraq, Ireland, Israel, Italy, Japan, Jordan, Laos, Liberia, Libya, Luxembourg, Federation of Malaya, Mexico, Nepal, Netherlands, New Zealand, Nicaragua, Norway, Pakistan, Panama, Paraguay, Peru, Philippines, Poland, Portugal, Romania, Saudi Arabia, Spain, Sudan, Sweden, Syria, Thailand, Tunisia, Turkey, Ukrainian SSR, USSR, United Kingdom, United States, Uruguay, Venezuela, Yemen, Yugoslavia.
Against: None.
Abstaining: Belgium.

"*The General Assembly,*
"*Recognizing* the urgent need for international co-operation in the economic development of under-developed countries,
"*Reaffirming* its responsibilities and obligations, under Articles 55 and 56 of the Charter of the United Nations, to foster the economic development of all under-developed areas,
"*Recognizing* that the countries and territories of Africa are faced with serious economic problems affecting the welfare and progress of the peoples of that region,
"*Recognizing* that co-operation among the African countries can be of assistance in raising both the level of economic activity and the standards of life in that continent, and that such measures would be facilitated by close co-operation with the United Nations and its subsidiary organs,
"*Considering* that the regional economic commissions of the United Nations have performed valuable functions within their respective areas and that their work is vitally important from the point of view of the United Nations as expressed in General Assembly resolution 627(VII) of 21 December 1952,
"*Noting* that the work of the regional economic commissions has been extremely useful to the economies of under-developed countries in Asia and Latin America, and considering therefore that Africa should benefit from the advantages of such a system,
"*Noting further* that the group of experts appointed by the Secretary-General, at the request of the Economic and Social Council, to study measures for the economic development of under-developed countries, recommended in 1951 that in order to assist the Governments and peoples of Africa to analyse and keep under continuous survey the development problems of that continent, the United Nations should establish an Economic Commission for Africa and provide for it an international secretariat,
"*Recommends* that, for the purpose of giving effective aid to the countries and territories of Africa and in accordance with Article 68 of the Charter of the United Nations, the Economic and Social Council at its next session, give prompt and favourable consideration to the establishment of an Economic Commission for Africa."

ECONOMIC AND SOCIAL COUNCIL—RESUMED 24TH SESSION
Plenary Meeting 998.

CHAPTER VI

FISCAL AND FINANCIAL QUESTIONS

During 1957, the United Nations continued to expand its technical assistance activities as well as its programme of studies and publications in the fiscal and financial fields.

BUDGET CLASSIFICATION

At the request of the Economic Commission for Asia and the Far East (ECAFE), a second regional workshop on problems of budget reclassification and management was held in September 1957. One of its major purposes was to review the progress made and difficulties encountered in applying the simplified scheme of classifications and accounts suggested by the first workshop in September 1955. Working papers submitted by a number of States dealt with national experience in reclassifying budgets along economic and functional lines. A summary account of the experience in these fields of individual countries both within and without the ECAFE region was presented as a Secretariat document entitled *Reclassification of Government Expenditures and Receipts in Selected Countries.* A revised version of a Secretariat document, entitled *A Manual for Economic and Functional Classification of Government Transactions* and intended to serve as a guide in obtaining fiscal data for the formulation of economic and social policies, was used as a basis for discussion at the workshop, which recommended that it be used as a standard reference for guiding future reclassification work.

The workshop was also concerned with the techniques of programme and performance budgeting, i.e., information on the physical results obtained from given budgetary expenditures. It was recommended that a third workshop be held stressing techniques of budget formulation, control and management, with special reference to programme and performance budgeting.

Another budget workshop was scheduled to be held at Santiago, Chile, in the third quarter of 1958, to concentrate mainly on the nature of budget reclassification and budgeting required to form economic and social policies.

TAX PROBLEMS

Work continued on additional volumes in the *International Tax Agreements* series. Volume VII, containing the text of some 70 agreements concluded up to July 1957, went to press late in 1957. Arrangements were completed for placing the series on a current basis from 1958 on, with the use of ring-binders in subsequent volumes, both for the texts of new agreements and the tabular information on the current status of all agreements.

The use of tax measures to promote economic development in under-developed countries continued to receive considerable attention. The Central American Committee for Economic Co-operation considered a United Nations Secretariat study entitled *La Política Tributaria y el Desarrollo Económico en Centroamérica* (Tax Policy and Economic Development in Central America) at its fourth session held at Guatemala City in February 1957. In resolution 50(CCE) on tax policy (adopted on 23 February 1957) the Committee asked its secretariat, in co-operation with the Fiscal and Financial Branch of the Bureau of Economic Affairs of the United Nations Secretariat and the United Nations Technical Assistance Administration (TAA), to continue its tax studies with special reference to problems arising from economic integration, the standardization of legislation on fiscal incentives and the taxation of income, consumption and property.

Preparations were made during the year 1957 to complete a study on taxation of foreign private investments by capital-exporting and capital-importing countries. This was for submission to the Economic and Social Council at its twenty-sixth session in mid-1958. Further country studies were also being prepared for distribution as addenda to the general study.

ECAFE's Working Party on Economic Development and Planning considered the problem of agricultural taxation at its third meeting, at Bangkok in September 1957. The Working Party discussed the subject of agricultural taxation in its report after considering a note, prepared by the Fiscal and Financial Branch of the Bureau of Economic Affairs of the United Nations Secretariat, on *Taxation and Development of Agriculture in Under-Developed Countries with Special Reference to Asia and the Far East.*

The Intergovernmental Copyright Committee, at its second session, in October 1957, at Washington, D.C., continued its consideration of the problem of international double taxation of copyright royalties received by authors and artists. Its discussion was based on a report on the present state of the study on double taxation of authors' royalties. The Secretariat of the United Nations collaborated with that of the United Nations Educational, Scientific and Cultural Organization in the preparation of this study.

The Committee decided, by a resolution (11(II)) adopted on 10 October 1957 on double taxation of copyright royalties, to ask the Secretary-General of the United Nations to undertake an inquiry among Member Governments on measures to reduce international double taxation of such royalties.

FINANCIAL QUESTIONS

The importance of institutional and private financing of economic development has given rise to a continued demand for technical assistance in this field. The Secretariat continued with the work programme in this general area which it had formulated in 1956. A study on the index clause in deferred payments was published in the *Economic Bulletin for Latin America* for October 1957. This paper discussed the implications of tying long-term financial commitments to changes in the price level. Work began, too, during 1957 on the problems of financing industry in under-developed countries. A number of other *ad hoc* projects in the field of financial institutions and policies were undertaken when the operational needs of the technical assistance programme required them.

TECHNICAL ASSISTANCE

Requests from Member Governments for technical assistance continued to increase during the year. Forty fiscal and financial experts from 16 countries undertook missions to 23 countries and assisted four regional projects. Training grants were given to a large number of Government officials from under-developed countries.

Several of them again participated in the special training programmes for tax officials, organized in the United Kingdom by the British Council and in the United States by the Harvard Law School International Program in Taxation.

The Escuela Superior de Administración Pública para América Central (ESAPAC) (Advanced School of Public Administration for Central America) at San José, Cost Rica, which operated with the support of TAA, for the first time included a training course in public finance in its 1957-1958 curriculum. Consultative missions to assist in country programming were undertaken by Secretariat members, and Government officials visited United Nations Headquarters to consult on fiscal and financial issues.

A Manual of Income Tax Administration was being prepared in 1957 in co-operation with the Harvard Law School International Program in Taxation. It is designed for technical assistance experts and fellows in this field, and for Government tax services interested in the improvement of their administrative techniques.

FISCAL INFORMATION SERVICE

As in previous years, data on public debt and on major components of government expenditure and receipts, as well as global data on central government transactions, based on replies to a joint United Nations–International Monetary Fund questionnaire, were published in the United Nations Statistical Yearbook, 1957.

During 1957, the World Tax Series started publication with volumes on Brazil, Mexico and the United Kingdom. The series, published by the International Program in Taxation of the Harvard University Law School in consultation with the United Nations Secretariat, consists of country reports which provide comprehensive and authoritative information on national tax systems under a broadly uniform arrangement intended to make the reports internationally comparable. It is designed to serve as a basis for information and research for the use of government officials, tax specialists and interested investors. The series is expected to cover some 30 countries during an initial three-year period of publication.

Current information on international tax agreements and fiscal statistics was furnished in response to numerous specific requests by Governments, as well as by specialized agencies and non-governmental organizations.

DOCUMENTARY REFERENCES

International Tax Agreements, Vol. VII. U.N.P. Sales No.: 58.XVI.1.

Manual for Economic and Functional Classification of Government Transactions. U.N.P. Sales No.: 58. XVI.2.

"Index Clause in Deferred Payments," Economic Bulletin for Latin America, Vol. II, No. 2, pp. 73-89.

La Política Tributaria y el Desarrollo Económico en Centroamérica. U.N.P. Sales No.: 1957.II.G.9.

"Economic Development and Planning in Asia and the Far East: The Agricultural Section," Economic Bulletin for Asia and the Far East, Vol. VIII, No. 3, pp. 75-76.

International Tax Problems (E/3001). Note by Secretary-General. World Tax Series.

CHAPTER VII

STATISTICAL QUESTIONS

DEVELOPMENT OF STANDARDS FOR STATISTICS

During 1957, the Statistical Office of the United Nations concentrated mostly on carrying out the work programme drawn up by the

Statistical Commission at its ninth session, in 1956, and on preparing reports for the Commission's tenth session, in 1958.

Plans for the 1960 World Census Programme reached their final stages. A revised draft of the principles and recommendations for the 1960 world population census was submitted for review at the ninth session of the Population Commission, held in the first quarter of 1957. These were also to go, for final consideration, to the tenth session of the Statistical Commission in 1958.

Plans were being made in 1957 by the United Nations and the Food and Agriculture Organization (FAO) for joint regional training centres in order to integrate the activities connected with the censuses of population with those of the censuses of agriculture to be taken in or around 1960.

A set of handbooks and methodological studies was prepared for use by countries participating in the 1960 World Census Programme.

A set of general principles for a housing census was circulated to Governments and discussed by regional groups. A revised version incorporating the conclusions of these national and regional consultations was scheduled for review at the Statistical Commission's tenth session in 1958.

Also due to be considered at the Commission's 1958 session was an international programme of social statistics, drawn up with a view to promoting the study of the methodology of the use of statistics in formulating national social policies. This was prepared in collaboration with FAO, the International Labour Organisation (ILO), the United Nations Educational, Scientific and Cultural Organization (UNESCO) and the World Health Organization (WHO). The programme contains a proposal too, for the publication of a compendium of social statistics every four years, beginning in 1963.

Also undertaken in 1957 was a review of the international standards for basic industrial statistics, to take account of national practices and recent developments. The results of this investigation, together with draft proposals for revising the present standards, were to be submitted to the Commission's tenth session in 1958. Similar studies and draft proposals were prepared on changes required in the *International Standard Industrial Classification of All Economic Activities; Concepts and Definitions of Capital Formation;* and *A System of National Accounts and Supporting Tables.*

One paper dealt with the problems of national income accounting confronting countries in a very early stage of economic development. Two other papers prepared for the Statistical Commission reviewed national practices and methodology on price and quantity indexes for national accounts.

Yet another report prepared for the Statistical Commission and based on information received, reviewed country practices in the preparation of basic statistics of income distribution. This study stemmed originally from a General Assembly resolution (403(V)) of 1950 and an Economic and Social Council resolution (369(XIII)) of 1951. Later the need for such data was pointed up in 1952 in the *Preliminary Report on the World Social Situation.*

The fifth regional Conference of Statisticians of Asia and the Far East, which was reconstituted as the first session of the permanent Conference of Asian Statisticians, met in Bangkok from 8 to 17 April 1957. The programme for the 1960 World Census of Agriculture was reviewed and the FAO's assistance to Governments in this connexion was discussed. The Conference also discussed its reorganization as a permanent body, its terms of reference, work programme and methods. The Conference's short-term programme covers the following subjects: statistical training, censuses of population and agriculture and the use of sampling methods. The long-term programme of the Conference and the priorities for its work, it was decided, would be taken up at the next meeting of the Conference, tentatively scheduled for November 1958.

The Conference of European Statisticians held its fifth plenary session in Geneva from 17 to 21 June 1957. A large part of the session was devoted to discussions and plans on activities in the fields of population, housing, agriculture, and general economic censuses. The Conference also considered reports of its Working Parties and a report on the seminar on industrial statistics, held in Greece, as requested at the previous session of the Conference.

In the general field of trade statistics, Governments were asked for data on their free ports and free zones for inclusion in the revised edition of *Customs Areas of the World.* This was in accordance with a request made by the Statistical Commission in 1956.

APPLICATION OF STANDARDS

The United Nations Standard International Trade Classification, recommended in 1950 by the Economic and Social Council, for the compilation of external trade statistics, was used in 1957 by 79 countries and territories, accounting for about 90 per cent of external trade figures.

During 1957, advice was given by 40 statistical consultants to 19 countries under the United Nations technical assistance programme, and nationals of 18 countries were awarded 31 fellowships in statistics. Plans were made for two joint UN/FAO training centres in connexion with the 1960 Census Programme, one to be provided in Latin America, and one in the Far East. A course on the construction of quantum and unit value indices of external trade was given in Mexico City for participants from the five Central American countries. It was arranged in response to a request by the Sub-Committee of Statistical Co-ordination of Central America. Assistance has also been given to the Governments of Costa Rica, El Salvador, Guatemala, Honduras and Nicaragua in the compilation of a preliminary issue of the *Statistical Compendium of Central America*, to be issued triennially.

The permanent Philippine Statistical Centre, set up in 1954 with United Nations aid, opened its 1957-1958 academic year with an enrolment of 103 graduate students. Three students received the degree of Master of Arts in statistics from the Centre at the close of the previous academic year.

COLLECTION AND PUBLICATION OF STATISTICAL DATA

During 1957, the Statistical Office continued to collect and publish economic and social statistics for individual countries on an internationally comparable basis. In addition, the Office compiled global and regional summary figures for the following fields: population, industrial production, production of important raw materials, production of motor vehicles, numbers of motor vehicles in use, traffic by rail and by sea, the value, volume and direction of world external trade, and international price levels in external trade for primary products and for manufactured goods.

The Statistical Office issued the following regular yearbooks:

The Statistical Yearbook, 1957, which is a collection of the more important economic and social series.

The *Demographic Yearbook, 1957,* which contains the principal demographic series, and which features mortality statistics in this issue.

The Yearbook of International Trade Statistics, 1956, in two volumes. The first volume gives detailed data for 115 countries (covering 98 per cent of world trade on imports and exports of merchandise and gold, currency and conversion factors and on indices of quantum and unit value. The second volume shows the flow, between countries and regions, of world trade in each of seven large commodity classes selected for their economic importance.

The following periodicals appeared regularly: *Monthly Bulletin of Statistics; Commodity Trade Statistics* (quarterly); *Direction of International Trade* (monthly, with an annual summary, published jointly by the United Nations, the International Monetary Fund and the International Bank for Reconstruction and Development); *Population and Vital Statistics Reports* (quarterly); *Statistics of National Income and Expenditure* (semi-annual); and *Statistical Notes.*

Also issued in 1957 were: the second study in a series on energy, entitled *World Energy Supplies, 1951-1954; Sample Surveys of Current Interest* (seventh report); *Per Capita National Product of Fifty-Five Countries, 1952-1954;* and *Final Report of the Inter-American Centre of Biostatistics, Santiago, Chile, 1952-1955.*

DOCUMENTARY REFERENCES

APPLICATION OF STANDARDS
Report of the Inter-American Centre of Biostatistics, Santiago, Chile, 1952-1955. Statistical Papers, Series M, No. 25. U.N.P. Sales No.: 1957.XVII.5.
Sample Surveys of Current Interest (Seventh Report). Statistical Papers, Series C, No. 8. U.N.P. Sales No.: 1957.XVII.7.

COLLECTION AND PUBLICATION OF STATISTICAL DATA
Statistical Yearbook, 1957. U.N.P. Sales No.: 1957. XVII.1.
Demographic Yearbook, 1957. U.N.P. Sales No.: 1957.XIII.1.
Yearbook of International Trade Statistics, 1956. U.N.P. Sales No.: 1957.XVII.6. Vols. I and II.

Direction of International Trade. Annual issue. Vol. VIII, No. 7. Annual data for years 1938, 1948, and 1953-1956. U.N.P. Sales No. 1957.XVII.8.

Direction of International Trade. Statistical Papers, Series T, Vol. VIII, Nos. 1-6, 8-12, February-December 1957.

Commodity Trade Statistics. Statistical Papers, Series D, Vol. VI, No. 4, January-December 1956.

Commodity Trade Statistics. Statistical Papers, Series D, Vol. VII, No. 1, January-March 1957; No. 2, January-June 1957.

Monthly Bulletin of Statistics and *Supplement to Monthly Bulletin of Statistics.*

Population and Vital Statistics Reports. Statistical Papers, Series A, Vol. IX, Nos. 1-4.

World Energy Supplies, 1951-1954. U.N.P. Sales No.: 1957.XVII.3.

Statistics of National Income and Expenditure. Statistical Papers, Series H, No. 10. U.N.P. Sales No.: 1957.XVII.4.

Statistical Notes. Statistical Papers, Series B, No. 22.

REPORTS OF CONFERENCES OF STATISTICIANS

E/CN.11/456 (E/CN.11/ASTAT/CONF.1/3). Report of the Conference of Asian Statisticians (first session), Bangkok, 8-17 April 1957.

Conf. Eur. Stats/80. Conference of European Statisticians, report of the fifth plenary session, Geneva, 17-21 June 1957.

CHAPTER VIII

TRANSPORT AND COMMUNICATIONS

THE DEVELOPMENT OF INTERNATIONAL TRAVEL

The development of international travel, its present increasing volume and future prospects were considered at the Economic and Social Council's twenty-third session, held between 16 April and 2 May 1957. Before the Council was a note from the Secretary-General giving the results of a survey which he had undertaken in accordance with a request made by the Council in 1955 by resolution 563(XIX). The Council had before it also the recommendations made by the Transport and Communications Commission at its eighth session, in January 1957.

In the course of the Council's debate, many delegations expressed satisfaction with the Secretary-General's report. It was suggested that the Commission should continue to follow the developments in the field and report to the Council, and that it should also consider specific related problems and maintain close liaison with competent regional organizations, so as to make future reports even broader and more conclusive. The hope was expressed that international assistance in the creation of the necessary facilities for tourism would be made available to countries which were not in a position to undertake alone the work involved.

On 26 April, the Council invited Governments which had not yet done so to submit the desired information to the Secretary-General so that his report on the development of international travel could be completed. It further asked Governments, the appropriate specialized agencies and other inter-governmental and non-governmental organizations in the field to continue their efforts to encourage international travel in view of its economic, social and cultural benefits. The Commission and the Secretary-General were asked to follow developments and to report to the Council any matters making its further action in the field desirable. The Council's resolution to this effect (644(XXIII)) was adopted unanimously.

MARITIME QUESTIONS

The Transport and Communications Commission noted that the International Convention for the Prevention of the Pollution of the Sea by Oil (London, 1954) had been ratified by seven Governments. It also expressed its appreciation of *Pollution of the Sea by Oil,* a publication issued and circulated by the United Nations Secretariat in 1956. During 1957 there were four ratifications to the Convention, raising the total number from six in 1956 to 10. The Convention was to come into force 12 months after the date on which 10 Governments, including those of five countries each with not less than 500,000 gross tons of tanker tonnage, have become parties to it. As these conditions were fulfilled with the tenth ratification on 26 July 1957, the Convention was due to come into force on 26 July 1958.

One additional Government ratified the Convention for a Uniform System of Tonnage Measurement of Ships (Oslo, 1947), which came into force in 1954, bringing the total number of parties to eight.

On the basis of a report and a recommendation made by the Transport and Communications Commission in January 1957, the Economic and Social Council, at its twenty-third session, asked the Secretary-General to establish a group of experts to prepare a report for the Commission's ninth session, expected to take place in 1959, on the differences between the main rules governing tonnage measurement at present in force and their apparent shortcomings. It also asked him to invite interested Governments to make available, at his request and at their own expense, experts to serve on this group. The Council's resolution 645 B (XXIII)) was unanimously adopted on 26 April 1957. Thirty-eight Governments had replied to the Secretary-General's invitation by the end of 1957. Eleven of them had agreed to make experts available.

(For developments regarding the ratification of the Convention on the Inter-Governmental Maritime Consultative Organization, see below, PART TWO, CHAPTER XIV.)

INTERNATIONAL ROAD TRANSPORT
CONVENTION ON ROAD TRAFFIC OF 1949

At the end of 1957, the following 33 States were parties to the Convention on Road Traffic which was concluded in 1949 and came into force in March 1952: Australia, Austria, Belgium, Cambodia, Ceylon, China, Cuba, Czechoslovakia, Denmark, Dominican Republic, Egypt, France, Greece, Israel, Italy, Luxembourg, Monaco, Morocco, Netherlands, Norway, Peru, Philippines, Portugal, Sweden, Syria, Tunisia, Turkey, Union of South Africa, United Kingdom, United States, Vatican City, Viet-Nam and Yugoslavia.

The Transport and Communications Commission, at its eighth session, concluded that further action by the Economic and Social Council was desirable to achieve the adoption of the Convention throughout the world. On 26 April 1957, at its twenty-third session, the Council accordingly recommended that those eligible Governments which had not yet ratified the Convention should do so at an early date.

The resolution to this effect (645 C (XXIII)) was approved by 17 votes to 0, with 1 abstention.

LICENSING OF MOTOR VEHICLE DRIVERS

The Transport and Communications Commission continued its study of the licensing of motor vehicle drivers with a view to achieving a greater degree of international uniformity and to providing guidance to the interested authorities. In a report prepared in accordance with Economic and Social Council resolutions 468 E (XV) and 567 C (XIX), the Secretary-General of the United Nations informed the Commission that the recommendations on minimum uniform regulations, drawn up by a Committee of Experts and submitted to Governments in accordance with these resolutions, had been found to be useful. The Commission noted that the response from Governments to these recommendations continued to be favourable.

On the basis of the Commission's recommendations, the Council, at its twenty-third session, urged Governments to give serious consideration to the contents of the handbook for medical practitioners entitled *Guiding Principles in the Medical Examination of Applicants for Motor Vehicle Driving Permits* and to *Suggestions Concerning Practical Tests to be Carried out by Driving Examiners*, prepared by the World Health Organization (WHO) and already circulated to Governments by the Secretary-General. The resolution to this effect (645 E (XXIII)) was adopted on 26 April 1957 by a vote of 16 to 0, with 2 abstentions.

The Council also recommended that, for international road traffic, Governments recognize any valid domestic driving permit issued by the appropriate authority after proof of the driver's competence.

The Council further recommended that, where language difficulties might prevail and where it was not possible to issue an international driving permit, arrangements should be made to provide either an official translation or a simplified certification of the domestic permit to be attached to such a permit. It invited the Secretary-General to complete, in consultation with WHO, the revision of the provisional recommendations on mental and physical fitness of drivers, and to circulate the revised text to Governments for their comments. He was also invited: to ask Governments what steps they intended to take with a view to implementing the Council's recommendation on the reciprocal recognition of domestic driving permits; and to report at the Commission's ninth session on further progress by Governments in strengthening their licensing standards with regard to the physical and mental fitness of applicants for driving licences.

UNIFORM SYSTEM OF ROAD SIGNS AND SIGNALS

At its 1957 session, the Transport and Communications Commission also examined a progress report by the Secretary-General on the implementation of Council's resolution 567 B (XIX). Adopted on 20 May 1955, this resolution recommended that Governments consider the provisions of the draft Protocol on a Uniform System of Road Signs and Signals as recommended practices when revising their system of road signs and signals either unilaterally or bilaterally, or in regional agreements. This was in order to further the progressive achievement of uniformity in that field.

The Commission noted that the replies so far received to the Secretary-General's inquiries indicated considerable interest in the matter. It noted with satisfaction that there appeared to be widespread agreement on the desirability of eventual unification, although there might still be considerable obstacles in the way of achieving world-wide uniformity.

During discussions at the Council's twenty-third session, the hope was expressed that the Commission would take a definite decision at its next session (the ninth) on the possible preparation of a guide to the implementation of the draft Protocol.

PASSPORTS AND FRONTIER FORMALITIES

In accordance with Economic and Social Council resolution 565 D (XIX) of 20 May 1955, the Secretary-General prepared a report for the Transport and Communications Commission's 1957 session, surveying the progress achieved in the implementation of the recommendations of a meeting of experts on passports and frontier formalities held in 1947. The Commission noted that there was a large measure of agreement on the desirability of further implementation of the recommendations of the meeting of experts.

Acting on the Commission's recommendation, the Council unanimously recommended, by resolution 645 F (XXIII) of 26 April 1957, that Governments continue their efforts to implement the recommendations of the 1947 meeting of experts, particularly by administrative arrangements between neighbouring countries or countries located in the same region.

CUSTOMS FORMALITIES FOR TOURING

The international agreements concluded at the United Nations Conference on Customs Formalities for the Temporary Importation of Private Road Motor Vehicles and for Tourism, held in New York in May and June 1954, have all come into force.

The Convention concerning Customs Facilities for Touring entered into force in September 1957. The 19 States which were parties to it by the end of 1957 were: Austria, Belgium, Cambodia, Canada, Ceylon, Denmark, Egypt, Federal Republic of Germany, Jordan, Israel, Japan, Luxembourg, Mexico, Morocco, Sweden, Switzerland, United Kingdom, United States and Viet-Nam.

By the end of 1957, the following 15 States were parties to the Additional Protocol to the Convention concerning Customs Facilities for Touring, relating to the Importation of Tourist Publicity Documents and Material, which came into force in June 1956: Austria, Belgium, Denmark, Egypt, Federal Republic of Germany, India, Israel, Japan, Jordan, Luxembourg, Mexico, Morocco, Sweden, Switzerland and United Kingdom.

The Customs Convention on the Temporary Importation of Private Road Vehicles entered into force in December 1957. The following 17 States were parties to this Convention by the end of 1957: Austria, Belgium, Canada, Ceylon, Denmark, Egypt, Federal Republic of Germany, Israel, Jordan, Luxembourg, Mexico, Morocco, Sweden, Switzerland, United Kingdom, United States and Viet-Nam.

On 26 April 1957, acting on a recommendation by the Commission, the Economic and Social Council unanimously adopted resolution 645 D (XXIII) recommending that all eligible Governments should ratify the Conventions and the Additional Protocol at an early date so as to facilitate the development of international travel through simplified customs procedures.

TRANSPORT OF DANGEROUS GOODS

At its meeting in January 1957, the Transport and Communications Commission examined and discussed the recommendations made in 1956 at Geneva by a Committee of Experts on the Transport of Dangerous Goods. The Commission pointed out that there was a large and increasing proportion of dangerous goods being transported from one country to another. It also felt that further work was needed to secure more uniformity in regional and national regulations and codes of practice dealing with the transport of dangerous goods. Disharmony in this field, it was noted, hampered the development of this important trade activity.

Acting on the Commission's recommendations, the Economic and Social Council asked the Secretary-General on 26 April 1957 to set up a permanent committee of not more than nine experts and to invite interested Governments, at their own expense, to make available experts to serve on this committee. The duties of this permanent committee were defined as follows: to revise and keep up to date the list of dangerous goods recommended in 1956 by the previous Committee of Experts; to allot to each substance an identification number; to study further the problem of packing; to study related matters; and to report progress to the Commission. The Council's resolution to this effect (645 G (XXIII)) was adopted unanimously.

The Secretary-General was also asked, by this resolution, to arrange for a consultant to make a comparative study of the system of regulations on packing, so as to facilitate the experts' study on packing.

The Council further urged Governments, regional economic commissions and international organizations concerned to take note of the recommendations made by the 1956 Committee of Experts and those to be made by the permanent committee, and to keep the Secretary-General currently informed of the extent to which they could bring their own practices into general conformity with them.

Finally, the Secretary-General was invited to continue consultations with the Director-General of the International Labour Office on the best ways to avoid overlapping of work in this field by the permanent committee and the International Labour Organisation.

DISCRIMINATION IN TRANSPORT INSURANCE

The Transport and Communications Commission at its eighth session in January 1957 noted developments concerning the consideration given to the problem of discrimination in transport insurance by the International Monetary Fund, and also by the Contracting Parties to the General Agreement on Tariffs and Trade (GATT) among whom the problem is known as contractual freedom in transport insurance. The Commission decided to keep the problem under review.

DOCUMENTARY REFERENCES

ECONOMIC AND SOCIAL COUNCIL—23RD SESSION
Plenary Meeting 968.
Economic Committee, meeting 216.

E/2948. Report of eighth session of Transport and Communications Commission, 7-16 January 1957.
E/CN.2/INF.8. Preparatory documentation, eighth session of Commission.

REPORT OF COMMISSION
E/2948, Chapter X. Draft resolution A, recommended by Commission, adopted unanimously by Economic Committee.
E/2979. Report of Economic Committee (draft resolution A).
RESOLUTION 645 A (XXIII), taking note of Transport and Communications Commission report, as recommended by Economic Committee, E/2979, adopted unanimously by Council on 26 April 1957, meeting 968.

DEVELOPMENT OF INTERNATIONAL TRAVEL
E/2933 and Corr.1, Add.1-10, Add.4/Corr.1. Development of international travel, its present increasing volume and future prospects. Note by Secretary-General.
E/2948, Chapter X. Draft resolution F, recommended by Transport and Communications Commission.
RESOLUTION 644 (XXIII), as recommended by Transport and Communications Commission, E/2948, adopted unanimously by Council on 26 April 1957, meeting 968.

"*The Economic and Social Council,*
"*Noting* that many Governments have responded to its resolution 563(XIX) of 31 March 1955 concerning the development of international travel by supplying information relative to their activities in promoting and facilitating international travel,
"*Noting further* that the information supplied shows that Governments recognize the importance of inter-

national travel and the desirability of encouraging its development as set forth in the aforesaid resolution,

"*Noting further* that the existing international organizational machinery for joint action in the field of travel development appears adequate to meet present requirements,

"*Bearing in mind* the recommendations of the Transport and Communications Commission as to further action which might be desirable concerning this question,

"1. *Invites* Governments which have not yet responded to Council resolution 563(XIX) to submit the desired information to the Secretary-General as promptly as possible so that the report can be completed;

"2. *Requests* Governments of States Members of the United Nations or members of the specialized agencies, the organs of the United Nations, the appropriate specialized agencies, and other inter-governmental and non-governmental organizations in this field to continue their efforts to encourage international travel for its economic, social and cultural benefits;

"3. *Further requests* the Transport and Communications Commission and the Secretary-General to follow developments in the field of travel and to report to the Council any matters which would make its further action desirable."

MARITIME QUESTIONS
POLLUTION OF THE SEA BY OIL
E/2948. Report of eighth session of Transport and Communications Commission (paragraphs 30-31).

UNIFICATION OF MARITIME TONNAGE MEASUREMENT
E/2948, Chapter X. Draft resolution B, recommended by Commission, adopted unanimously by Economic Committee.

E/2979. Report of Economic Committee, (draft resolution B).

RESOLUTION 645 B (XXIII), as recommended by Economic Committee, E/2979, adopted unanimously by Council on 26 April 1957, meeting 968.

"*The Economic and Social Council,*

"*Having noted* the opinion of the Transport and Communications Commission that it is necessary to continue the useful work already done in bringing about greater uniformity between the regulations relating to the tonnage measurement of ships,

"*Requests* the Secretary-General:

"(*a*) To establish a group of experts to prepare and present for the consideration of the Transport and Communications Commission, at its ninth session, a report on the differences between the main rules governing tonnage measurement at present in force and their apparent shortcomings;

"(*b*) To invite the Governments of those countries which indicate their interest in the unification of tonnage measurement to make available, at his request and at their own expense, experts to serve on the above group."

INTERNATIONAL ROAD TRANSPORT
CONVENTION OF ROAD TRAFFIC OF 1949

E/2948, Chapter X. Draft resolution C, recommended by Commission, adopted by Economic Committee by 17 votes to 0, with 1 abstention.

E/2979. Report of Economic Committee (draft resolution C).

RESOLUTION 645 C (XXIII), as recommended by Economic Committee, E/2979, adopted by Council on 26 April 1957, meeting 968, by 17 votes to 0, with 1 abstention.

"*The Economic and Social Council,*

"*Recalling* its resolution 603(XXI) of 26 April 1956 relating to the 1949 Convention on Road Traffic adopted at the United Nations Conference on Road and Motor Traffic,

"*Bearing in mind* the consideration of the Transport and Communications Commission that the Convention establishes the main standards for development and safety of international road transport capable of worldwide application,

"*Recommends* those eligible Governments which have not already done so to ratify the 1949 Convention on Road Traffic at an early date."

LICENSING OF MOTOR VEHICLE DRIVERS
E/2948, Chapter X. Draft resolution E, recommended by Commission, adopted by Economic Committee, as amended by E/AC.6/L.174, by 16 votes to 0, with 2 abstentions.

E/AC.6/L.174. Mexico, Netherlands, Pakistan, United States amendment to draft resolution E.

E/2979. Report of Economic Committee (draft resolution E).

RESOLUTION 645 E (XXIII), as recommended by the Economic Committee, E/2979, adopted by Council on 26 April 1957, meeting 968, by 16 votes to 0, with 2 abstentions.

"*The Economic and Social Council,*

"*Having examined* the recommendations of the Transport and Communications Commission concerning both the development of standards of physical and mental fitness of motor vehicle drivers and the broadening of use of valid domestic driving permits in international traffic, in accordance with the requirements of the 1949 Convention on Road Traffic,

"1. *Urges* Governments of all States Members of the United Nations or members of the specialized agencies to give their serious consideration to the contents of the handbook for medical practioners entitled 'Guiding Principles in the Medical Examination of Applicants for Motor Vehicle Driving Permits,' together with certain 'Suggestions concerning Practical Tests to be Carried out by Driving Examiners', already circulated to them by the Secretary-General in accordance with Council resolution 567 C (XIX) of 20 May 1955;

"2. *Recommends* Governments to recognize in international traffic any valid domestic driving permit issued by the competent authority after proof of competence;

"3. *Recommends further* that, where language difficulties may prevail and where the issuance of an international driving permit is not feasible or convenient, arrangements be made to provide for one of the following to be attached to the domestic permit;

"(*a*) A certification of the authenticity and validity of the domestic permit on the lines set forth in the annex hereto;

"(*b*) An official translation of the domestic permit in the languages of the countries in which it is proposed to use the permit, either by the issuing Government or by an automobile association empowered to act for it;

"4. *Invites* the Secretary-General:

"(*a*) To complete, in consultation with the World Health Organization, the revision of the provisional recommendations on the physical and mental fitness of drivers prepared by the Committee of Experts on Licensing of Motor Vehicle Drivers and included in their report to the Transport and Communications Commission;

"(*b*) To circulate the revised text to Governments of States Members of the United Nations or members of the specialized agencies, for their comments, as a supplement to the recommendations on minimum uniform requirements for the licensing of motor vehicle drivers;

"(*c*) To inquire of Governments as to the steps they intend to take with a view to implementing the recommendation of the Council on the reciprocal recognition of domestic driving permits;

"5. *Invites further* the Secretary-General to report to the Commission, at its ninth session, on further progress made by Governments in strengthening their licensing standards relative to the physical and mental fitness of applicants for driving licences."

ANNEX

(The following standard form is to be issued in one or more of the official languages of the United Nations, according to the region in which the domestic driving permit is to be used.)

(Form to be attached to domestic driving permit)

The attached driving permit, No.................

is valid for...

(class(es) of vehicle(s))

....

until.......................*(Strike out whichever*

indefinitely.   *does not apply)*

It was issued in...............................

(Country)   (Subdivision: State or province)

to ....

(Name of holder)

(Place) ....

(Date)........................

Seal or stamp of the competent authority
or of a duly authorized association.

UNIFORM SYSTEM OF ROAD SIGNS AND SIGNALS
E/2948. Report of eighth session of Transport and Communications Commission (paragraphs 24-26).

PASSPORTS AND FRONTIER FORMALITIES
E/2948, Chapter X. Draft resolution G, recommended by Commission, adopted unanimously by Economic Committee.
E/2979. Report of Economic Committee (draft resolution F).
RESOLUTION 645 F (XXIII), as recommended by Economic Committee, E/2979, adopted unanimously by Council on 26 April 1957, meeting 968.

"*The Economic and Social Council,*
"*Noting* the opinion of the Transport and Communications Commission that the international action towards the simplification, reduction and unification of passports and frontier formalities should continue in the direction of implementing the recommendations of the Meeting of Experts on Passports and Frontier Formalities, held at Geneva in 1947,
"*Recommends* to Governments of States Members of the United Nations that they continue their efforts towards the implementation of the recommendations of the 1947 Meeting of Experts, in particular by administrative arrangements between neighbouring countries or countries located in the same region."

CUSTOMS FORMALITIES FOR TOURING
E/2948, Chapter X. Draft resolution D, recommended by Commission, adopted unanimously by Economic Committee.
E/2979. Report of Economic Committee (draft resolution D).
RESOLUTION 645 D (XXIII), as recommended by Economic Committee, E/2979, adopted unanimously by Council on 26 April 1957, meeting 968.

"*The Economic and Social Council,*
"*Taking note* of the considerations and recommendations of the Transport and Communications Commission,
"*Recommends* that all eligible Governments should ratify at an early date the Customs Convention on the Temporary Importation of Private Road Vehicles, the Convention concerning Customs Facilities for Touring and the Additional Protocol thereto (1954), so as to facilitate the development of international travel through simplified customs procedures."

TRANSPORT OF DANGEROUS GOODS
E/2948, Chapter X. Draft resolution H, recommended by Commission, adopted unanimously by Economic Committee, as orally amended by France.
E/2979. Report of Economic Committee (draft resolution G).
RESOLUTION 646 G (XXIII), as recommended by Economic Committee, E/2979, adopted unanimously by Council on 26 April 1957, meeting 968.

"*The Economic and Social Council,*

"*Having noted* the statement of the Transport and Communications Commission that there is a large and increasing proportion of goods in international trade which have inherently dangerous properties, and the opinion of the Commission that the recommendations of the United Nations Committee of Experts on the Transport of Dangerous Goods in the report on its second session and the recommendations of the Committee concerning the classification, listing and labelling of dangerous goods and shipping papers for such goods, form a basis for further work towards overcoming disharmony among regional and national regulations and codes of practice relating to the transport of dangerous goods by individual modes of transport, which at present hampers the development of this important trade,

"1. *Requests* the Secretary-General:

"(*a*) To set up a committee consisting of not more than nine qualified experts from countries interested in the international transport of dangerous goods:

"(i) To revise as may be necessary and keep up to date the list of dangerous goods proposed by the Committee of Experts, taking into account existing practices in the field of transportation and the extent of their usage;

"(ii) To allot to each substance a number for ready identification;

"(iii) To study further the problem of packing;

"(iv) To study related matters;

"(v) To report progress to the Transport and Communications Commission;

"(*b*) To invite Governments of countries interested in the international transport of dangerous goods to make available, at his request and at their own expense, experts to serve on the above committee;

"(*c*) To arrange for a consultant to make a comparative study of the systems of regulations on packing on which the Secretary-General has already received information, so as to make it possible for the Committee of Experts to pursue the study on packing, as provided under (iii) above;

"2. *Urges* the Governments, regional economic commissions and international organizations concerned to take note of the recommendations of the Committee of Experts and of any further recommendations by the committee referred to in paragraph 1(*a*) above, and to keep the Secretary-General currently informed of the extent to which they can bring their own practices into general conformity with them;

"3. *Invites* the Secretary-General to continue his consultations with the Director-General of the International Labour Office on the best means of avoiding any overlapping of the work of the above committee with any work being undertaken in this field by the International Labour Organisation."

DISCRIMINATION IN TRANSPORT INSURANCE

E/2948. Report of eighth session of Transport and Communications Commission (paragraphs 51-56).

WORK PROGRAMME AND PRIORITIES

E/2948, Chapter X. Draft resolution I, recommended by Commission, unanimously adopted by Economic Committee.

E/2979. Report of Economic Committee (draft resolution H).

RESOLUTION 645 H (XXIII), as recommended by Economic Committee, E/2979, adopted unanimously by Council on 26 April 1957, meeting 968.

"*The Economic and Social Council,*

"*Bearing in mind* its resolutions 497 C (XVI) of 29 July 1953, 557 A (XVIII) of 5 August 1954 and 630 A (XXII) of 9 August 1956,

"*Approves* the work programme and priorities for transport and communications projects recommended by the Transport and Communications Commission in resolution 9 adopted at its eighth session."

CHAPTER IX

HUMAN RIGHTS

DRAFT INTERNATIONAL COVENANTS ON HUMAN RIGHTS

During the twelfth session of the General Assembly, the Third (Social, Humanitarian and Cultural) Committee continued the article-by-article consideration of the two draft International Covenants on Human Rights undertaken at the two previous Assembly sessions, in 1955 and 1956. Originally drafted by the Commission on Human Rights, the two draft Covenants contain 83 articles covering virtually every aspect of the individual's life in society.

One text deals with economic, social and cultural rights, and the other deals with civil and political rights.

On 25 September 1957, the Committee decided to devote 38 meetings to the two texts, beginning with three substantive articles of the draft Covenant on Economic, Social and Cultural Rights and continuing with substantive articles of the draft Covenant on Civil and Political Rights.

Between 11 October and 4 November, the Committee discussed and adopted texts for articles 14, 15 and 16 of the draft Covenant on Economic, Social and Cultural Rights. Article 6 of the draft Covenant on Civil and Political Rights was examined and approved, after amendment, between 13 and 25 November. In all, 34 full committee meetings and six meetings or working parties were devoted to the draft Covenants at the Assembly's twelfth session.

DRAFT COVENANT ON ECONOMIC, SOCIAL AND CULTURAL RIGHTS

ARTICLE 14

This article, as submitted to the Committee, recognized the right of everyone to education and set out certain objectives of education. It stated that primary education should be compulsory and free, and that facilities for secondary, higher and fundamental education should be encouraged or made available, subject to certain conditions. It recognized the liberty of parents to choose the type of education for their children.

Most Committee Members felt that the objectives of education should be laid down at the beginning of the article, although the view was expressed that a first declaratory paragraph was out of place in a legal instrument. There was debate on the advisability of retaining a reference to "the suppression of all incitements to racial and other hatreds" as an educational objective. Some representatives felt the phrase was essential in view of the harmful effects of educational discrimination, while others considered that the proper role of education was to encourage positive feelings rather than to suppress incitements to hatred.

The Committee was in agreement that States Parties were obliged to provide free primary education in public schools only, and that a certain latitude should be given to methods for making secondary and higher education available to all. The notion of fundamental education was considered an important factor in raising living standards in under-developed areas. Certain representatives pointed out that fundamental education should not be taken as a substitute for primary education, which remained the basis for eradicating illiteracy.

There was considerable discussion on the right of parents to choose, under certain conditions, the type of education which their children were to receive. Some speakers stressed the need for minimum educational standards to which private schools should conform, but others feared that too large a measure of freedom might lead to teachings contrary to the principles set out in the first paragraph of article 14. It was agreed that references to "religious education" in the article imposed no obligation to provide religious education in public schools. It was also agreed to expand the concept dealt with in the article to cover moral education.

The view was advanced that, although the article acknowledged the existence of private schools, it should explicitly recognize the liberty of individuals and bodies to establish and direct educational institutions. Others felt that such liberty might be abused, particularly through the diffusion of propaganda under the guise of education. Most representatives favoured a formula providing that private institutions should always observe the principles of the article and should conform to minimum teaching standards laid down by the State.

Another proposal discussed by the Committee covered the need to develop a system of schools at all levels, to establish adequate fellowship facilities and to improve the material conditions of teaching staff. In support of this proposal, it was argued that such measures should be specifically mentioned so that the right to education might be given its full practical meaning. Others opposed the proposal on the grounds that it was too detailed for a covenant and that it repeated what was implicit in the remainder of article 14.

The Third Committee decided to establish a working party on article 14, to reconcile the eight amendments to the draft which had been submitted. Composed of representatives of Belgium, Ecuador, Guatemala, Ireland, the Netherlands, Peru, the Philippines and Romania, the working party prepared a consolidated text. This text, with further modifications of a drafting nature, was adopted by a roll-call vote of 71 to 0, with 4 abstentions.

The text of article 14 thus read as follows:

1. The States Parties to the Covenant recognize the right of everyone to education. They agree that education shall be directed to the full development of the human personality and the sense of its dignity,

and shall strengthen the respect for human rights and fundamental freedoms. They further agree that education shall enable all persons to participate effectively in a free society, promote understanding, tolerance and friendship among all nations and all racial, ethnic or religious groups, and further the activities of the United Nations for the maintenance of peace.

2. The States Parties to the Covenant recognize that, with a view to achieving the full realization of this right:

(a) Primary education shall be compulsory and available free to all;

(b) Secondary education, in its different forms, including technical and vocational secondary education, shall be made generally available and accessible to all by every appropriate means, and in particular by the progressive introduction of free education;

(c) Higher education shall be made equally accessible to all, on the basis of capacity, by every appropriate means, and in particular by the progressive introduction of free education;

(d) Fundamental education shall be encouraged or intensified as far as possible for those persons who have not received or completed the whole period of their primary education;

(e) The development of a system of schools at all levels shall be actively pursued, an adequate fellowship system shall be established, and the material conditions of teaching staff shall be continuously improved.

3. The States Parties to the Covenant undertake to have respect for the liberty of parents and, when applicable, legal guardians, to choose for their children schools other than those established by the public authorities which conform to such minimum educational standards as may be laid down or approved by the State and to ensure the religious and moral education of their children in conformity with their own convictions.

4. No part of this article shall be construed so as to interfere with the liberty of individuals and bodies to establish and direct educational institutions, subject always to the observance of the principles set forth in paragraph 1 and to the requirement that the education given in such institutions shall conform to such minimum standards as may be laid down by the State.

ARTICLE 15

Article 15 of the draft Covenant on Economic, Social and Cultural Rights deals with plans for establishing free and compulsory primary education, and required States which are Parties to the Covenant, in cases where such educational facilities were lacking, to work out and adopt detailed plans for the progressive implementation of the principle of such education.

Most representatives agreed that the fundamental character of the right to primary educa-

tion justified the inclusion of a special implementation clause, even though similar provisions were not made with regard to other rights. Extending the scope of the article to cover adult education was, however, considered likely to exceed the resources of many States. Others maintained that the article imposed an immediate obligation upon States Parties, thus conflicting with earlier articles, and that it did not take account of difficulties existing in certain territories. On the other hand, several representatives felt that article 15 merely aimed at securing the progressive implementation of a particular right in an effective and orderly manner.

Reference to non-metropolitan territories in the draft article was opposed by some representatives on the grounds that States Parties could not constitutionally agree to bind the authorities of autonomous territories without their consent. However, the view was expressed that the territorial application clauses of other conventions concluded under United Nations auspices might be examined when the final articles of the draft Covenants were considered.

Further suggestions were made to transfer some provisions of article 14 to article 15, or to combine the two articles without modifying their substance. Others argued that such a rearrangement would not necessarily improve the form of the draft Covenant, and might in fact modify the substance of article 14, already adopted.

Article 15, as submitted by the Commission on Human Rights, was adopted by 60 votes to 3, with 8 abstentions. The text read as follows:

Each State Party to the Covenant which, at the time of becoming a party to this Covenant, has not been able to secure in its metropolitan territory or other territories under its jurisdiction compulsory primary education, free of charge, undertakes, within two years, to work out and adopt a detailed plan of action for the progressive implementation within a reasonable number of years, to be fixed in the plan, of the principle of compulsory primary education free of charge for all.

ARTICLE 16

Article 16 in the text before the Third Committee defined the right of everyone to take part in cultural life and to enjoy the benefits of scientific progress. It provided for the full realization of this right and respect for the freedom indispensable for scientific research and creative activity.

It was generally agreed by Committee Members that the article dealt with important human rights and should be retained in substance.

A proposal was made by Costa Rica and Uruguay to include a reference in the article to the protection of authors' moral and material interests, based on article 27 of the Universal Declaration of Human Rights. It was pointed out that the adoption of such a clause would not only protect authors against improper action by publishers, but would also ensure that the public received authentic versions of artistic works, thus contributing to cultural development throughout the world. Opposing opinions noted that international copyright conventions would be affected, that special conditions in different countries might be disregarded and that the complexities of the matter, linked with the problem of the right to property, called for further consideration.

Much discussion was devoted to a Czechoslovak proposal to state that, while scientific research and cultural activities should remain free, it was the duty of States to promote the development of science and culture in the interests of peace and international co-operation. It was pointed out, however, that the aims of peace would best be served by ensuring the greatest possible freedom for science and culture, and that it was desirable to avoid any pretext for abusive control of such activities by the State.

Also discussed was the reference in the draft to the State's respect for the freedom "indispensable" for scientific research and creative activity. Some found the qualifying word "indispensable" too restrictive. Others maintained that it recognized the right of the State to impose limitations strictly required by national security, public order or morality.

The Committee recognized that one of the best ways to encourage cultural and scientific development was the promotion of international contacts in those fields. It accepted an amended proposal to that effect on the understanding that it did not impose any binding obligation upon States. Some representatives thought the reference superfluous in view of General Assembly resolution 1043(XI) of 21 February 1957, on the promotion of international cultural and scientific co-operation.[1]

Article 16, as amended, was adopted by 71 votes to 0, with 1 abstention. The text as approved read as follows:

1. The States Parties to the Covenant recognize the right of everyone:

(a) To take part in cultural life;

(b) To enjoy the benefits of scientific progress and its applications;

(c) To benefit from the protection of the moral and material interests resulting from any scientific, literary or artistic production of which he is the author.

2. The steps to be taken by the States Parties to the Covenant to achieve the full realization of this right shall include those necessary for the conservation, the development and the diffusion of science and culture.

3. The States Parties to the Covenant undertake to respect the freedom indispensable for scientific research and creative activity.

4. The States Parties to the Covenant recognize the benefits to be derived from the encouragement and development of international contacts and co-operation in the scientific and cultural fields.

DRAFT COVENANT ON CIVIL AND POLITICAL RIGHTS

ARTICLE 6

Article 6 of the draft Covenant on Civil and Political Rights, as presented to the Third Committee, dealt with the individual's right to life, under protection of the law, and stated that sentence of death, in countries where capital punishment exists, might be imposed only as a penalty for the most serious crimes. As drafted by the Commission, anyone sentenced to death would have the right to seek pardon or commutation, and the death sentence should not be carried out on a pregnant woman.

The Third Committee decided to establish a working party on article 6 to harmonize the eleven amendments and other suggestions put forward during the debate. The working party, composed of representatives of 15 Members, prepared an agreed text for certain sections of the article and suggested a voting procedure for the Committee.

A major issue was whether or not Article 6 should provide for the abolition of capital punishment. The question arose from an amend-

[1] See *Y.U.N., 1956*, p. 287.

ment proposed by Colombia and Uruguay suggesting the inclusion of the words "the death penalty shall not be imposed on any person". Supporters of this proposal maintained that an article which guaranteed the right of life should in no way sanction the taking of life, and should prohibit the death penalty. They considered that the existence of capital punishment could not be justified and was contrary to modern theories aiming at rehabilitation of the offender. They felt that an innocent person might be convicted, but the error could not be rectified if the convicted person were executed. They also pointed out that capital punishment had not acted as a real deterrent to crime.

Most representatives, while appreciating the humanitarian motives inspiring the proposal, felt, however, that its adoption would create difficulties for countries where capital punishment existed. The abolition of the death penalty was a highly controversial question and should be left to each State to resolve. However, in order to avoid the impression that the Covenant sanctioned capital punishment, it was agreed to add a clause to the effect that nothing in the article should be invoked to delay or prevent the abolition of capital punishment by any State Party. Specific measures to encourage abolition of the death penalty, such as seminars organized by the United Nations, were suggested.

A majority of the Committee felt that Article 6 should begin with a definite statement on everyone's inherent right to life. It was held that this right was not one conferred on the individual by society, because society in fact owed a duty to the individual in this respect. Those opposing the clause did not disagree in principle, but objected to its inclusion as a declaratory statement and thus out of place in a legal instrument.

An amendment by Belgium, Brazil, El Salvador, Mexico and Morocco led to debate on whether the right to life should be protected by law "from the moment of conception". Some felt that it was only logical to guarantee this right from the moment life began, and pointed out that legislation in many countries accorded protection to the unborn child. This suggestion was opposed by others who said that the State could not determine the moment of conception;

the rights and duties of the medical profession would be involved, and legislation on the subject was based on different principles in different countries.

Some representatives preferred listing the cases in which deprivation of life would be considered lawful, citing precedents to this effect. The majority, however, did not favour such a system, as the list would be incomplete and might underline the exceptions rather than the right itself.

The question whether article 6 should contain a reference to the Convention on the Prevention and Punishment of the Crime of Genocide was also discussed. Some thought it unnecessary to include such a safeguard clause, and cited other articles of the draft Covenants in support of their views. Others argued that a reference to the Genocide Convention was essential, since the individual's right to life could not be adequately protected if the group to which he belonged were threatened with extinction.

Debated, too, was the clause stating that sentence of death should not be carried out on pregnant women. A number of representatives felt that the clause in question sought to prevent the death penalty being executed before a child was born. Others though that the death sentence should not be carried out at all if it concerned a pregnant woman, as the unborn child might be affected by the mother's constant fear of the death penalty.

Another question debated by the Third Committee was whether the death penalty should apply to minors. Those favouring a suggestion that they should be exempt explained that young persons were usually given preferential treatment in most countries, and, with firm guidance, could become useful members of society. Others noted that it was for the legislation of each State to specify the classes of persons not liable to the death penalty, which might be extended to the insane and the aged, for example. Some dissatisfaction was expressed in the Committee over the use of terms such as children and young persons, minors, juveniles or persons below a certain age. The Committee decided to use the words "persons below 18 years of age".

Article 6, as amended, was adopted by a roll-call vote of 55 to 0, with 17 abstentions.

The article read as follows:

1. Every human being has the inherent right to life. This right shall be protected by law. No one shall be arbitrarily deprived of his life.

2. In countries which have not abolished the death penalty, sentence of death may be imposed only for the most serious crimes in accordance with law in force at the time of the commission of the crime and not contrary to the provisions of this Covenant and to the Convention on the Prevention and Punishment of the Crime of Genocide. This penalty can only be carried out pursuant to a final judgment rendered by a competent court.

3. When deprivation of life constitutes the crime of genocide, it is understood that nothing in this article shall authorize any State Party to derogate in any way from any obligation assumed under the provisions of the Convention on the Prevention and Punishment of the Crime of Genocide.

4. Anyone sentenced to death shall have the right to seek pardon or commutation of the sentence. Amnesty, pardon or commutation of the sentence of death may be granted in all cases.

5. Sentence of death shall not be imposed for crimes committed by persons below eighteen years of age and shall not be carried out on pregnant women.

6. Nothing in this article shall be invoked to delay or to prevent the abolition of capital punishment by any State Party to the Covenant.

FUTURE WORK ON THE DRAFT COVENANTS

No recommendation of the Third Committee concerning the future work on the draft Covenant on Human Rights was required at the Assembly's twelfth session because of a resolution adopted at the eleventh session which had asked the Committee to complete its consideration of the Covenants "if possible, by the end of the thirteenth session".

On 10 December 1957, however, at the Third Committee's last meeting of the session, Bolivia, Ceylon, Chile, Colombia, Costa Rica, Ecuador, Egypt, Ghana, Greece, Guatemala, Honduras, Pakistan, Panama and Sudan submitted a draft resolution, by which the Assembly would note that only four articles had been approved at the twelfth session while 62 remained to be considered. It recommended that appropriate steps be taken at the Assembly's thirteenth session to enable the Committee to complete the Covenants by the end of that session, or as reasonably close to that time as possible.

Representatives supporting the motion suggested that the Committee might expedite the work if it met beyond the period of the General Assembly session, devoted more meetings to the draft Covenants or fixed a time-limit for the discussion of each article. Others felt that, in accelerating work on the draft Covenants, other Committee business should not be curtailed and no additional expenditure should be involved.

Because there was little time to debate the proposal, the sponsors withdrew the draft resolution, explaining that its main purpose was to alert Member States to the importance of finding ways and means to speed the work on the draft Covenants.

DOCUMENTARY REFERENCES

GENERAL ASSEMBLY—12TH SESSION
Plenary Meeting 727.
Third Committee, meetings 764, 779-799, 809-821, 834.

A/3588. Note by Secretary-General.

DRAFT COVENANT ON ECONOMIC, SOCIAL AND CULTURAL RIGHTS
ARTICLE 14
A/C.3/L.617. Ireland amendment.
A/C.3/L.618. Netherlands amendment.
A/C.3/L.619 and Corr.1. Chile, Ecuador, Guatemala amendments.
A/C.3/L.620. Romania amendment.
A/C.3/L.621. United Kingdom amendments.
A/C.3/L.622. Philippines amendments.
A/C.3/L.623. Belgium amendments.
A/C.3/L.624. Peru amendments.
A/C.3/L.625. Report of Working Party on Article 14.
A/C.3/L.626. Panama amendments to article 14 as proposed by Working Party.
A/C.3/L.627. Canada amendment to Working Party's text for article 14.
A/C.3/L.628. Costa Rica and Greece amendment to Working Party's text for article 14.
A/C.3/L.629. Bolivia amendment to Working Party's text for article 14.
A/3764 and Corr.1 and Add.1. Report of Third Committee. Article 14 was adopted by Third Committee by roll-call vote of 71 votes to 0, with 4 abstentions, as follows:
In favour: Afghanistan, Albania, Argentina, Austria, Belgium, Bolivia, Brazil, Bulgaria, Burma, Byelorussian SSR, Cambodia, Canada, Ceylon, Chile, China, Colombia, Costa Rica, Cuba, Czechoslovakia, Denmark, Dominican Republic, Ecuador, Egypt, El Salvador, Ethiopia, Finland, France, Ghana, Greece, Guatemala, Haiti, Honduras, Hungary, Iceland, India, Indonesia, Iran, Iraq, Ireland, Israel, Italy, Japan, Jordan, Liberia, Federa-

tion of Malaya, Mexico, Morocco, Nepal, Netherlands, New Zealand, Norway, Pakistan, Panama, Peru, Philippines, Poland, Portugal, Romania, Saudi Arabia, Spain, Sudan, Sweden, Syria, Thailand, Turkey, Ukrainian SSR, USSR, Uruguay, Venezuela, Yemen, Yugoslavia.

Against: None.

Abstaining: Australia, Tunisia, United Kingdom, United States.

ARTICLE 15

A/2910. Draft International Covenants on Human Rights. Observation by Governments. Tenth session of General Assembly.

A/2910/Add.1. United Kingdom amendments.

A/2910/Add.2. Australia amendments.

A/2910/Add.3. Netherlands amendments.

A/C.3/L.630. Bulgaria amendment.

A/C.3/L.631. Peru amendment.

A/C.3/L.632. Ireland amendment.

A/C.3/L.632/Rev.1 and 2. Iraq and Ireland revised amendments.

A/3764 and Corr.1 and Add.1. Report of Third Committee. Article 15, as submitted by Commission on Human Rights, E/2573, was adopted by Third Committee by 60 votes to 3, with 8 abstentions.

ARTICLE 16

A/C.3/L.633. Czechoslovakia amendments.

A/C.3/L.634 and Rev.1. Saudi Arabia amendments and revised amendments to amendments of Czechoslovakia (A/C.3/L.633).

A/C.3/L.635. Greece amendment.

A/C.3/L.636 and Add.1 and Rev.1. Costa Rica and Uruguay amendment and revision.

A/C.3/L.637. Czechoslovakia amendment to amendment of Greece, A/C.3/L.635.

A/3764 and Corr.1 and Add.1. Report of Third Committee. Article 16 was adopted by Third Committee by 71 votes to 0, with 1 abstention.

DRAFT COVENANT ON CIVIL AND POLITICAL RIGHTS

ARTICLE 6

A/C.3/L.644. Colombia and Uruguay amendment.

A/C.3/L.645. France amendments.

A/C.3/L.646. Philippines amendments.

A/C.3/L.647. Guatemala amendment.

A/C.3/L.648. Costa Rica amendment.

A/C.3/L.649 and Add.1. Brazil, Panama, Peru amendment.

A/C.3/L.649/Rev.1. Brazil, Panama, Peru, Poland revised amendment.

A/C.3/L.650. Japan amendments.

A/C.3/L.651. Netherlands amendment.

A/C.3/L.652. Australia amendment.

A/C.3/L.653. Panama amendment.

A/C.3/L.654. Belgium, Brazil, El Salvador, Mexico, Morocco amendment.

A/C.3/L.655 and Corr.1. Report of Working Party on Article 6.

A/C.3/L.656. United Kingdom amendments to amendments proposed in Report of Working Party.

A/C.3/L.657. Brazil, Panama, Peru, Poland amendment to amendments proposed in Report of Working Party.

A/C.3/L.658. Ceylon amendment to amendments proposed in report of Working Party.

A/3764 and Corr.1 and Add.1. Report of Third Committee. Article 6 was adopted by Third Committee, by roll-call vote of 55 votes to 0, with 17 abstentions, as follows:

In favour: Afghanistan, Albania, Argentina, Austria, Brazil, Bulgaria, Burma, Byelorussian SSR, Cambodia, Ceylon, Chile, Cuba, Czechoslovakia, Dominican Republic, Ecuador, Egypt, Ethiopia, Finland, France, Ghana, Greece, Guatemala, Haiti, Hungary, India, Indonesia, Iran, Iraq, Ireland, Israel, Japan, Jordan, Liberia, Mexico, Morocco, Nepal, Nicaragua, Norway, Pakistan, Panama, Peru, Philippines, Poland, Romania, Saudi Arabia, Spain, Sudan, Syria, Thailand, Tunisia, Turkey, Ukrainian SSR, USSR, Yemen, Yugoslavia.

Against: None.

Abstaining: Australia, Belgium, Canada, China, Colombia, Denmark, Italy, Luxembourg, Federation of Malaya, Netherlands, New Zealand, Portugal, Sweden, United Kingdom, United States, Uruguay, Venezuela.

FUTURE WORK ON DRAFT COVENANTS

A/C.3/L.663. Bolivia, Ceylon, Chile, Colombia, Costa Rica, Ecuador, Egypt, Ghana, Greece, Guatemala, Honduras, Pakistan, Panama, Sudan draft resolution.

A/3764/Add.1. Report of Third Committee.

THE RIGHT OF PEOPLES AND NATIONS TO SELF-DETERMINATION

In 1952 and 1953, the General Assembly asked the Commission on Human Rights, through the Economic and Social Council, for recommendations on international respect for the right of peoples and nations to self-determination. After further discussion in the General Assembly, the Council and the Commission on Human Rights, three specific proposals were made.

Two of these were suggested in resolutions adopted by the Commission at its tenth session in 1954 and reaffirmed at its eleventh session in 1955. The first recommended that the General Assembly set up a commission to conduct a survey of the right of peoples and nations to "permanent sovereignty over their natural wealth and resources" and to make recommendations thereon. The second suggested the establishment by the Assembly of a Commission to examine alleged denials or inadequate realization of the right to self-determination, to provide its good offices in such situations and to report the facts to the General Assembly.

At its twentieth session in mid-1955, the Economic and Social Council decided, by resolution 586 D (XX), to transmit the Commission's two proposals to the Assembly as well as a third suggestion of its own which called for the establishment of an *ad hoc* commission to "conduct a thorough study of the concept of self-determination". The General Assembly, decided both in 1955 and in 1956 (at its tenth and eleventh sessions) to postpone consideration of these recommendations to its following session. Because these three proposals were still before the General Assembly, neither the Economic and Social Council nor the Commission on Human Rights discussed self-determination at their 1957 sessions.

The self-determination question was considered at the Assembly's twelfth session, in debates held in its Third Committee between 26 November and 3 December.

Afghanistan, Panama, the Philippines, Saudi Arabia and Uruguay submitted a draft resolution on the subject to the Third Committee. By this text, the Assembly, recalling earlier United Nations action on self-determination, would reaffirm that all States, including those administering Non-Self-Governing Territories should promote the realization of that right. It would also state that "inadequate realization" of the right to self-determination not only undermined friendly relations among nations, but was also contrary to the purposes and principles of the United Nations. The draft resolution expressed the hope that United Nations Members would, in their relations with one another, give due respect to the right of self-determination, and that States administering Non-Self-Governing Territories would promote the realization and facilitate the exercise of this right in accordance with the purposes and principles of the United Nations. It was also proposed that self-determination be further considered at the General Assembly's thirteenth session.

The draft resolution was revised orally by the sponsors during the debate as follows: By one change, the words "inadequate realization" were modified to read "disregard". By another, the Assembly would reaffirm the importance of, rather than express the hope for, due respect for self-determination. The text as thus amended was subsequently adopted by the Third Committee.

Committee Members were generally agreed that no decision could be reached on the three proposals (i.e., those made by the Human Rights Commission in 1954 and that made by the Economic and Social Council in 1957) in view of the lack of available time at the twelfth session. Committee Members also agreed that the discussions should be continued at the next Assembly session. Several representatives regretted the postponement of the debate on self-determination and urged that this question be given priority consideration at the Assembly's thirteenth session.

There was general agreement on the importance of self-determination to the maintenance of international peace and friendly relations between nations, but different opinions were expressed on its legal nature and scope. Some Members of the Third Committee thought that the Charter of the United Nations did not go beyond recognition of the principle of self-determination, and they could not agree that a right was involved. The majority of representatives, however, were opposed to such an interpretation and emphasized that General Assembly resolutions and the draft International Covenants on Human Rights recognized self-determination as a fundamental human right.

Some felt that the right to self-determination should be given universal application, and should not concern the peoples in Non-Self-Governing or Trust Territories alone. They considered that the United Nations should also be concerned with other situations, such as those involving a loss of independence, the position of minority groups within independent States or those people who, although not subject to foreign rule, could not freely participate in the government of their countries. The point was also made that the draft resolution disregarded the principle of universal application by emphasizing the obligations of States administering Non-Self-Governing Territories.

Several representatives held the view that questions of political freedom and claims for secession in independent States were outside the scope of self-determination. The question to be examined was whether a people or nation were under foreign political or economic domination. They thought that independent nations, sooner or later, had the opportunity to regain lost freedom. But liberation from foreign rule was clearly beyond the power of dependent peoples. Helping them to achieve independence should be a primary concern of the United Nations.

Some representatives contended that the right of peoples and nations to permanent sovereignty over their natural wealth and resources, with proper safeguards for foreign investments made for economic development purposes, was a basic constituent of the right to self-determination. It was noted that one proposal submitted by the Commission on Human Rights properly emphasized this factor.

Because of the different opinions in the Third Committee, one suggestion was made for study of the concept and main elements of self-determination, as proposed by the Economic and Social Council. It was felt that this would not necessarily lead to postponement of other prac-

tical measures, but would supplement them.

Several representatives, however, believed that the right to self-determination had already been clearly defined, and that a study of abstract principles, as suggested by the Council, would only serve to confuse the issue or place artificial obstacles in the way of peoples seeking their independence. Enough time had been devoted to the meaning and scope of self-determination, and now measures to carry out the proposals were required. They considered that the suggestion made by the Commission on Human Rights to establish a commission of good offices might lead to fruitful results, providing that all States showed their goodwill by co-operating with such a commission.

After voting on several paragraphs individually, the Third Committee, on 3 December 1957, adopted the five-nation draft resolution, as orally revised by the sponsors, by a roll-call vote of 54 to 0, with 13 abstentions. This resolution was subsequently approved at a plenary meeting of the General Assembly on 11 December by 65 votes to 0, with 13 abstentions, as resolution 1188(XII).

DOCUMENTARY REFERENCES

GENERAL ASSEMBLY—12TH SESSION
Plenary Meeting 727.
Third Committee, meetings 821-827.

A/3587. Note by Secretary-General.
A/C.3/L.659 and Rev.1. Afghanistan, Panama, Philippines, Saudi Arabia, Uruguay draft resolution and revision, adopted by Third Committee, as orally revised by sponsors, by Guatemala and Argentina, by roll-call vote of 54 to 0, with 13 abstentions, as follows:
In favour: Afghanistan, Albania, Argentina, Austria, Bolivia, Brazil, Bulgaria, Burma, Byelorussian SSR, Cambodia, Ceylon, Chile, China, Colombia, Costa Rica, Czechoslovakia, Dominican Republic, Ecuador, Egypt, Ethiopia, Finland, Ghana, Greece, Guatemala, Honduras, Hungary, India, Indonesia, Iran, Iraq, Ireland, Israel, Japan, Liberia, Federation of Malaya, Mexico, Pakistan, Panama, Peru, Philippines, Poland, Romania, Saudi Arabia, Sudan, Syria, Thailand, Turkey, Ukrainian SSR, USSR, United States, Uruguay, Venezuela, Yemen, Yugoslavia.
Against: None.
Abstaining: Australia, Belgium, Canada, Denmark, France, Italy, Netherlands, New Zealand, Norway, Portugal, Spain, Sweden, United Kingdom.
A/3775. Report of Third Committee.
RESOLUTION 1188(XII), as recommended by Third Committee, A/3775, adopted by Assembly on 11

December 1957, meeting 727, by 65 votes to 0, with 13 abstentions.

"*The General Assembly,*
"*Recalling* that one of the purposes and principles of the United Nations is to develop friendly relations among nations based on respect for the principle of equal rights and self-determination of peoples,
"*Recalling further* its resolution 545(VI) of 5 February 1952 in which it decided to include in the International Covenants on Human Rights an article which should provide: 'All peoples shall have the right of self-determination',
"*Reaffirming* the principles embodied in the above-mentioned resolution that all States, including those having responsibility for the administration of Non-Self-Governing Territories, should promote the realization of that right, in conformity with the purposes and principles of the United Nations,
"*Considering* that disregard for the right to self-determination not only undermines the basis of friendly relations among nations as defined in the Charter of the United Nations but also creates conditions which may prevent further realization of the right itself,
"*Believing* that such a situation is contrary to the purposes and principles of the United Nations,
"1. *Reaffirms* that it is of international importance that, in accordance with the purposes and principles of the Charter of the United Nations:

"(*a*) Member States shall, in their relations with one another, give due respect to the right of self-determination;

"(*b*) Member States having responsibility for the administration of Non-Self-Governing Territories shall promote the realization and facilitate the exercise of this right by the peoples of such Territories;

"2. *Decides* to consider further at its thirteenth session the item 'Recommendations concerning international respect for the right of peoples and nations to self-determination', including the proposals contained in Economic and Social Council resolution 586 D (XX) of 29 July 1955."

PERIODIC REPORTS AND SPECIAL STUDIES

PERIODIC REPORTS

On the recommendation of the Commission on Human Rights, the Economic and Social Council by resolution 624 B (XXII) of 1 August 1956, initiated a system of periodic reporting by Governments.

Pursuant to this resolution the Secretary-General requested Members of the United Nations and of the specialized agencies to prepare and transmit reports describing the general developments and the progress achieved in the promotion of human rights during the years 1954, 1955 and 1956. The International Labour Organisation (ILO), the United Nations Educational, Scientific and Cultural Organization (UNESCO), the World Health Organization (WHO), the Food and Agriculture Organization (FAO), the International Telecommunication Union (ITU) and the Universal Postal Union (UPU) were also invited to transmit summaries, in respect of the rights coming within their purview, of the information they had received from their member States for the period under review.

By December 1957, reports had been received from the following Governments as follows: Australia, Austria, Brazil, Cambodia, Cey-lon, Chile, China, Czechoslovakia, Denmark, Dominican Republic, Federal Republic of Germany, Finland, France, Hungary, Israel, Luxembourg, Mexico, Morocco, Nepal, Norway, Pakistan, Panama, the Philippines, Poland, Portugal, Sweden, the Ukrainian SSR, the United Kingdom and the United States. ILO, UNESCO and ITU also sent reports. A brief summary of all these reports was to be submitted by the Secretary-General to the 1958 session of the Commission on Human Rights.

SPECIAL STUDIES

In 1956, the Commission on Human Rights and the Economic and Social Council made arrangements for studies of specific rights or groups of rights to be undertaken with a view to making objective and general recommendations. By resolution 624 B (XXII), the Council approved "the right of everyone to be free from arbitrary arrest, detention and exile" as the first subject for special study. A four-member committee, established by the Human Rights Commission in 1956 to study this subject, reported to the Commission in 1957 with certain preliminary observations on the general approach to the study, of which the Commission took note.

DOCUMENTARY REFERENCES

E/2970. Report of the 13th session of the Commission on Human Rights, 1-26 April 1957 (see Annex II of this report for a list of Commission documents).

ECONOMIC AND SOCIAL COUNCIL—24TH SESSION
Plenary Meeting 989.
Social Committee, meetings 359-364.

E/2970/Rev.1. Report of 13th session of Commission on Human Rights, 1-26 April 1957. (See Annex II of this report for list of Commission documents.)

E/3027 and Corr.2 and Add.1. Report of Social Committee (draft resolution A).

RESOLUTION 651 A (XXIV), taking note of report of 13th session of Commission on Human Rights, as recommended by Social Committee, E/3027, adopted unanimously by Council on 24 July 1957, meeting 989.

ADVISORY SERVICES IN HUMAN RIGHTS

General aspects of the United Nations programme of advisory services in human rights were considered by the Commission on Human Rights in April 1957, at its thirteenth session, and later by the Economic and Social Council, at its twenty-fourth session, in mid-1957.

Before the Commission was a report by the Secretary-General describing activities since the Commission's 1956 session.

When in mid-1957, the Economic and Social Council discussed in general the use of advisory services in human rights, it had before it a report by the Secretary-General on the development of the advisory services programme since its establishment by the General Assembly in December 1955.

Council members voiced general satisfaction at the progress made. However, since it was too early to assess the results achieved, the debate centred on the procedure and methods for organizing seminars. The use of working parties in their preparation was generally approved. It was also maintained that seminars should be organized on a regional rather than on a world-wide basis, and that topics discussed should be related to the work programmes of the Commissions concerned. The point was also made that while seminars were important, scholarships and fellowships should also be granted.

ADVISORY SERVICES FOR
PREVENTION OF DISCRIMINATION
AND PROTECTION OF MINORITIES

Advisory services in human rights were also discussed during 1957 by the Commission on Human Rights in connexion with the report of the ninth session of the Sub-Commission on the Prevention of Discrimination and the Protection of Minorities.

The Commission unanimously approved, with minor amendments, a recommendation by the Sub-Commission on the application of advisory services to the prevention of discrimination and the protection of minorities.

It also recommended that the Economic and Social Council: (1) draw the attention of Governments to the important role which an exchange of views and information through seminars could play in combating discrimination; (2) invite the Secretary-General, on the basis of requests from Governments, to consider the desirability of convening working parties with a view to planning and organizing such seminars; and (3) express the hope that all Governments would co-operate in achieving the purpose of the resolution.

This resolution was subsequently adopted by the Council on 24 July 1957, at its twenty-fourth session, when it was unanimously approved as resolution 651 C (XXIV).

ADVISORY SERVICES AND
FREEDOM OF INFORMATION

Discussed, too, during 1957 was the use of advisory services in developing information media in under-developed countries and in furthering freedom of information. These matters were discussed by the Commission on Human Rights in April, at the Economic and Social Council's twenty-third session, also in April, and later in the year at the General Assembly's twelfth session. (For further details, see section FREEDOM OF INFORMATION, below.)

By a resolution adopted by the General Assembly on 11 December 1957, Member States were urged to consider the possibility of organizing, in co-operation with the Secretary-General, seminars on freedom of information under the United Nations programme of advisory services in human rights. This was approved at a plenary meeting of the Assembly as resolution 1189 C (XII) by 55 votes to 0, with 19 abstentions. It was adopted on the recommendation of the Third Committee, which approved it on 9 December 1957 by 48 votes to 0, with 18 abstentions, on the basis of a proposal by the Philippines.

ADVISORY SERVICES AND
THE STATUS OF WOMEN

Also in 1957, the Commission on the Status of Women discussed the use of advisory services for improving the status of women. So did the Economic and Social Council and the General Assembly. (For details, see CHAPTER X, STATUS OF WOMEN; see also SEMINARS AND EXPERTS below.)

SEMINAR AND EXPERTS

The first seminar convened under the programme of advisory services in human rights, held at Bangkok, Thailand, from 5 to 16 August 1957, was concerned with the civic responsibilities and increased participation of Asian women in public life. The seminar was organized by the United Nations in co-operation with the Government of Thailand. One of its purposes was to enable participants—mainly women responsible for making policies, planning programmes, directing operations and providing leadership in various fields in the countries and territories of Asia—to consider the implications of the responsibilities and increased participation of Asian women in public life.

Participants from 15 countries or territories took part in the proceedings.

The main items discussed were: (1) the meaning of civic rights and responsibilities; (2) participation of women in the process of government at all levels and in all fields; (3) factors, such as educational conditions, economic conditions, health conditions, social and religious attitudes and community development, affecting women's participation in public life; and (4) projects in which participation by women should be developed and increased.

The seminar drew up a tentative list of projects in which the participation of South-East Asian women could be developed and increased. The list was divided into three categories: (a) projects of Governments; (b) projects of intergovernmental organizations; and (c) projects of national and international voluntary organizations.

Early in 1957, the Government of the Philippines asked the Secretary-General to hold a regional seminar in the Philippines in 1958 on the subject of the protection of human rights in criminal law and procedure, or some specific aspects thereof. A working party of experts from Australia, China, India, Indonesia, Japan, the Philippines, Thailand and Viet-Nam met at Manila in May, at the Secretary-General's initiative, to plan a programme of work for the seminar and to discuss other arrangements.

In August 1957, another expert working group met at Santiago, Chile, on the initiative of the Secretary-General, to consider the possibility of organizing a Western Hemisphere seminar on the subject of the protection of human rights in criminal law and procedure. The Chilean Government offered to be host to such a seminar in 1958. The working party drew up a list of topics for discussion, made various arrangements and recommended that all countries in the Western Hemisphere be invited to participate.

In 1957, an expert was sent out, from France, to advise the Haitian Government, at its request, on the development of election procedures and techniques, with particular attention to the problem of identification of voters and candidates.

DOCUMENTARY REFERENCES

ECONOMIC AND SOCIAL COUNCIL—24TH SESSION
Plenary Meeting 989.
Social Committee, meeting 362.

E/2970/Rev.1. Report of 13th session of Commission on Human Rights, Chapter X.
A/3006. Report of Secretary-General on advisory services in the field of human rights, submitted under paragraph 4 of General Assembly resolution 926(X).

PREVENTION OF DISCRIMINATION
AND PROTECTION OF MINORITIES

ECONOMIC AND SOCIAL COUNCIL—24TH SESSION
Plenary Meeting 989.
Social Committee, meetings 359-362.

E/2970/Rev.1. Report of 13th session of Commission on Human Rights, Chapter VI, Section V.
E/2970/Rev.1, Annex I. Draft resolution B submitted by Commission on Human Rights, adopted unanimously by Social Committee.
E/3027 and Corr.2, and Add.1. Report of Social Committee (draft resolution C).
RESOLUTION 651 C (XXIV), as recommended by Social Committee, E/3027, adopted unanimously by Council on 24 July 1957, meeting 989.

"The Economic and Social Council,
"Recalling General Assembly resolution 926(X) of 14 December 1955 on advisory services in the field of human rights,
"Recalling also resolution F adopted by the Sub-Commission on Prevention of Discrimination and Protection of Minorities at its eighth session and the resolution adopted by the Commission on Human Rights at its twelfth session, on the same subject,
"Recalling also its resolution 605(XXI) of 3 May 1956 on this subject,
"1. Draws the attention of Governments to the important role which the exchange of views and information by means of seminars can play in combating discrimination;
"2. Invites the Secretary-General, on the basis of requests received from Governments, to consider the advisability of convening working parties with a view to planning and organizing such seminars;
"3. Expresses the hope that all Governments will co-operate in achieving the purpose of the present resolution."

FREEDOM OF INFORMATION

ECONOMIC AND SOCIAL COUNCIL—24TH SESSION
Plenary Meeting 989.
Social Committee, meeting 362.

E/3002. United Nations news personnel seminar and news personnel fellowships. Report by Secretary-General under Council resolution 605(XXI).

GENERAL ASSEMBLY—12TH SESSION
Plenary Meeting 727.
Third Committee, meetings 828-834.

A/C.3/L.660 and Rev.1. Philippines draft resolution and revision. Part C, as orally amended by Israel, adopted by Third Committee by 48 votes to 0, with 18 abstentions.
A/3778. Report of Third Committee.
RESOLUTION 1189 c (XXII), as recommended by Third Committee, A/3778, adopted by Assembly on 11 December 1957, meeting 727, by 55 votes to 0, with 19 abstentions.

"*The General Assembly,*
"*Recognizing* the desirability of studying all possible means of increasing the free flow of accurate and un-distorted news and information within countries and across national frontiers,
"*Noting* the developing programme of advisory services in the field of human rights authorized by the General Assembly in its resolution 926(X) of 14 December 1955,

"*Considering* that the holding of seminars on freedom of information could contribute to the solution of problems in this field,
"*Urges* Member States to consider the possibility of organizing, in co-operation with the Secretary-General, seminars on freedom of information under the programme of advisory services in the field of human rights."

THE STATUS OF WOMEN
For documentary references and texts of resolutions adopted (Economic and Social Council resolution 652 I (XXIV) and General Assembly resolution 1163 (XXI)) see below, CHAPTER X, THE STATUS OF WOMEN.

SEMINARS AND EXPERTS
E/3006. Report of Secretary-General on advisory services in the field of human rights, submitted under paragraph 4 of General Assembly resolution 926(X).
E/2970/Rev.1. Report of 13th session of Commission on Human Rights, Chapter X.
1957 Seminar on Civic Responsibilities and Increased Participation of Asian Women in Public Life, Bangkok, 5-16 August 1957. U.N.P. Sales No.: 1957.IV.10.

PREVENTION OF DISCRIMINATION AND PROTECTION OF MINORITIES

DISCRIMINATION IN EDUCATION

At its ninth session, held from 18 February to 8 March 1957, the Sub-Commission on Prevention of Discrimination and Protection of Minorities had before it a study on discrimination in education, prepared by Charles D. Ammoun, its Special Rapporteur, and the comments of the United Nations Educational Scientific and Cultural Organization (UNESCO) on an earlier draft of this study.

The study was divided into three main parts. Part I consisted of an analysis of the information which the Special Rapporteur had collected. Part II contained information about action taken on the international, national and local levels to eradicate discrimination in education; it also carried a summary of the general trends revealed by the study. In Part III, the Special Rapporteur submitted general proposals for action to eradicate discrimination in education.

On the basis of the study, the Sub-Commission formulated 10 fundamental principles and proposals for action which, in its opinion, should be applied in order to eliminate discrimination in education on grounds of race, colour, sex, language, religion, political or other opinions, national or social origin, property, birth or other

status. These were submitted to the Commission on Human Rights.

The Sub-Commission also asked the Commission to study three possibilities for attaining the goals set forth in these principles. These concerned: (1) the usefulness and desirability of having the Economic and Social Council prepare an international instrument in which the principles would be set forth; (2) a request that UNESCO consider whether an appropriate international instrument or instruments for the prevention of discrimination in education could be drafted and adopted; and (3) the desirability of drawing the attention of the General Assembly to the necessity of giving these principles due importance in the preparation of the draft international Covenant on Economic, Social and Cultural Rights.

The Sub-Commission also recommended that the Special Rapporteur's study be transmitted to UNESCO for use in that agency's efforts to combat discrimination in education, and proposed that UNESCO be asked to prepare, in collaboration with the Special Rapporteur, a popular summary of the study to be used in universities, schools and other educational institutions.

The matter came before the Commission on Human Rights at its thirteenth session, held between 1 and 26 April 1957. The Commission felt that the Sub-Commission's proposals deserved careful study by Governments. Accordingly, it requested the Secretary-General to ask Members of the United Nations and of specialized agencies for comments and suggestions both on the principles and on the possibility of adopting one or more international instruments in this field. These comments and suggestions were to be submitted before 1 December 1957 so that they might be considered in 1958 at the Sub-Commission's tenth session and at the Commission's fourteenth session.

It asked that the Secretary-General circulate the Special Rapporteur's study widely and that UNESCO prepare a popular summary of it to be used as the Sub-Commission had proposed. The Commission also noted the comments already made by UNESCO on this question as well as UNESCO's decision to continue its consideration of the problem.

The study on discrimination in education was again considered at the Economic and Social Council's twenty-fourth session in mid-1957. In view of the fact that the Sub-Commission had completed its consideration of the study of discrimination in education, and considering that there was little time for the comments of Governments to be circulated and studied at the Sub-Commission's tenth session due to be held early in 1958, the Council unanimously decided to ask the Secretary-General to transmit the comments and suggestions direct to the Commission for consideration at the latter's fourteenth session. The Council's resolution to this effect (651 G (XXIV)) was unanimously adopted on 24 July.

DISCRIMINATION IN FIELD OF EMPLOYMENT AND OCCUPATION

Two reports on discrimination in the field of employment and occupation, prepared by the International Labour Office for the fortieth session of the International Labour Conference (June 1957), were examined by the Sub-Commission on Prevention of Discrimination and Protection of Minorities at its ninth session. The first report analysed the various forms of discrimination in employment and occupation. The second summarized the replies of Governments to the questionnaire contained in the first report, and the proposed conclusions which were intended to serve as a basis for action by the International Labour Conference.

The Sub-Commission recognized in general the validity both of the analysis of the various forms of discrimination in the field of employment and occupation made by the International Labour Organisation (ILO) and of the principles suggested as a guide for the policy of Government authorities. The Sub-Commission asked the Commission on Human Rights: (1) to recommend that the Economic and Social Council inform ILO of the work already accomplished in this field and of its desire that this work should be continued as before; (2) to transmit to ILO, in time for submission to the International Labour Conference in 1957, the records of the exchange of views in the Sub-Commission on the subject; and, (3) recommend that the Council and the Secretary-General authorize suitable arrangements to enable the results of the work of the International Labour Conference to be transmitted directly to the Sub-Commission and to enable the work at the Sub-Commission's 1958 session to be brought to the attention of ILO in time for submission to the International Labour Conference in 1958. The Sub-Commission had further decided to retain the question of discrimination in employment and occupation on the agenda for its tenth session with a view to reaching a conclusion on this problem, in the light, *inter alia,* of the additional work done by ILO in 1957.

The Commission, at its thirteenth session, asked the Secretary-General to transmit to ILO the records of the exchange of views on the reports in the Commission and in the Sub-Commission; and to make suitable arrangements for the results of the work of the International Labour Conference to be transmitted to the Sub-Commission.

DISCRIMINATION IN RELIGIOUS RIGHTS AND PRACTICES

At its ninth session, the Sub-Commission had before it a progress report, prepared by its Special Rapporteur, Arcot Krishnaswami, on discrimination in religious rights and practices. The report was divided into two parts. The first dealt with the collection of material for the study. The second part outlined the views of the Special Rapporteur on the materials to be included and the general approach to be taken to the problem.

Expressing deep appreciation of Mr. Krishnaswami's work, the Sub-Commission requested the Commission on Human Rights again to ask Governments and non-governmental organizations to co-operate in replying as soon as possible to the requests for information already addressed to them. It further asked the Special Rapporteur to prepare, with the assistance of the Secretary-General, a draft report which would be similar in scope to the final report on this subject, for submission to the Sub-Commission's tenth session.

The Commission on Human Rights, at its thirteenth session, asked the Secretary-General to invite Governments, specialized agencies and non-governmental organizations to submit relevant material by 15 August 1957 for use in the preparation of a draft report.

DISCRIMINATION IN POLITICAL RIGHTS

At its ninth session, the Sub-Commission heard an oral report by Hernán Santa Cruz, its Special Rapporteur appointed to study discrimination in the matter of political rights. He advised the Sub-Commission that he had not been able to prepare a preliminary report for submission at the ninth session, the resources of the United Nations Secretariat which could otherwise be used for this having been devoted to the study of discrimination in religion. The Sub-Commission requested the Secretary-General to give the Special Rapporteur all the necessary aid in order to enable him to present an interim report to the Sub-Commission's tenth session.

The Commission on Human Rights, at its thirteenth session, decided that no action on its part was called for in the matter at this stage.

CONFERENCES OF INTERESTED NON-GOVERNMENTAL ORGANIZATIONS

At its ninth session, the Sub-Commission on Prevention of Discrimination and Protection of Minorities also had before it a report by the Secretary-General on the results of his consultations with non-governmental organization on the date, duration and agenda of further conferences of non-governmental organizations interested in the eradication of prejudice and discrimination. (The first conference of this kind had been held in Geneva in 1955.)

The report, prepared in accordance with a request made by the Commission on Human Rights in 1956, indicated that 22 organizations, in addition to the 18 which submitted a joint statement to the Commission's twelfth session favouring a further conference, appeared to express support for a further conference in 1958. Five had expressed the view that there was no urgency about the organization of such a conference, or had suggested that the matter be considered further. One had opposed a further conference in 1958.

The Sub-Commission, after considering the report, unanimously recommended that the Commission on Human Rights ask the Economic and Social Council to make arrangements for convening such a conference, if possible during the last week prior to the Council's mid-1958 session. The Sub-Commission also suggested certain matters which could usefully be taken up by such a conference, and drew attention to the importance of adequate preparation and documentation.

The Secretary-General advised the Commission that he was not convinced of the value of this proposal, as he considered it unlikely that such a conference could go much beyond the achievements of that held in 1955. The Commission, at its thirteenth session, invited the Sub-Commission to consider the matter again at its tenth session, taking into account such additional observations as might be received from the interested non-governmental organizations, particularly from those in Asia, Africa and Latin America, and to report on the question to the Commission.

At its twenty-fourth session in mid-1957, the Economic and Social Council was informed that the Seventh General Conference of Consultative Non-Governmental Organizations had earlier in the year recommended that a second conference on the eradication of prejudice and discrimination should be called. On July 24, by resolution 651 D (XXIV), the Council decided unanimously to ask the Secretary-General to consult non-governmental organizations in consultative status with the Council (especially those in Africa, Asia and Latin America), the Sub-Commission and the Commission on the convening of a second conference of non-governmental organizations. It also asked him to re- port on these consultations to the Council's twenty-sixth session in mid-1958 and to make appropriate recommendations.

(For details about advisory services with regard to the prevention of discrimination and the protection of minorities see above, section on ADVISORY SERVICES IN HUMAN RIGHTS.)

DOCUMENTARY REFERENCES

E/CN.4/740. Report of 9th session of Sub-Commission on Prevention of Discrimination and Protection of Minorities to Commission on Human Rights, 18 February–8 March 1957. (See annex of this report for list of Sub-Commission documents.)

E/2970/Rev.1. Report of 13th session of Commission on Human Rights, 1-26 April 1957. (See Annex II of this report for list of Commission documents.)

ECONOMIC AND SOCIAL COUNCIL—24TH SESSION
Plenary Meeting 989.
Social Committee, meetings 359-364.

DISCRIMINATION IN EDUCATION
Study of Discrimination in Education (E/CN.4/ Sub.2/181/Rev.1). U.N.P. Sales No.: 1957.XIV.3.

E/2970/Rev.1, p. 20. Resolution VIII adopted by Commission on Human Rights.

E/AC.7/L.288 and Rev.1. United Kingdom draft resolution and revision, adopted unanimously by Social Committee.

E/3027 and Corr.2, and Add.1. Report of Social Committee (draft resolution G).

RESOLUTION 651 G (XXIV), as recommended by Social Committee, E/3027, adopted unanimously by Council on 24 July 1957, meeting 989.

"The Economic and Social Council,

"Having considered the resolution adopted by the Commission on Human Rights at its thirteenth session, concerning proposals submitted by the Sub-Commission on the Prevention of Discrimination and Protection of Minorities relating to the study on discriminaton in education prepared by the Special Rapporteur of the Sub-Commission,

"Considering that in submitting these proposals the Sub-Commission has completed its consideration of this study,

"Considering further that, as the Sub-Commission's proposals have been referred to Governments for comments and suggestions before 1 December 1957 and as the Sub-Commission ordinarily meets very early in the year, there is little time for these comments and suggestions to be circulated and considered by the Sub-Commission at its next session,

"Requests the Secretary-General to submit the comments and suggestions of Governments direct to the Commission on Human Rights for consideration by the Commission at its fourteenth session."

CONFERENCES OF INTERESTED NON-GOVERNMENTAL ORGANIZATIONS

E/2970/Rev.1, p.15. Resolution V, adopted by Commission on Human Rights.

E/AC.7/L.286 and Rev.1. France and United States draft resolution and revision as amended by Canada and France, adopted unanimously by Social Committee.

E/3027 and Corr.2 and Add.1. Report of Social Committee (draft resolution D).

RESOLUTION 651 D (XXIV), as recommended by Social Committee, E/3027, adopted unanimously by Council on 24 July 1957, meeting 989.

"The Economic and Social Council,

"Having considered the resolution of the Commission on Human Rights regarding the convening of a second conference of non-governmental organizations interested in the eradication of prejudice and discrimination,

"Having been informed, however, that the Seventh General Conference of Consultative Non-Governmental Organizations at its 1957 session recommend that such a conference be called,

"Noting that the Conference decided to instruct its Bureau to negotiate with the appropriate organ of the United Nations on such procedural matters as the agenda, facilities, working methods, date and duration of such a conference,

"Bearing in mind the desirability of convening such a conference as soon as possible,

"Requests the Secretary-General:

"(a) To consult non-governmental organizations in consultative status concerned, especially those in Africa, Asia and Latin America, the Sub-Commission on the Prevention of Discrimination and the Protection of Minorities, and the Commission on Human Rights regarding the convening of a second conference of non-governmental organizations interested in the eradication of prejudice and discrimination;

"(b) To report to the Council at its twenty-sixth session on these consultations and, in the light of them and having regard to the views expressed in the Council, to make appropriate recommendations."

FREEDOM OF INFORMATION

PROGRESS IN FIELD OF
FREEDOM OF INFORMATION

CONSIDERATION BY COMMISSION

Following an earlier proposal made in 1956, at its twelfth session, the Commission on Human Rights, at its thirteenth session, in April 1957, discussed progress made in the field of freedom of information.

On 18 April 1957, the Commission decided by 15 votes to 0, with 1 abstention, to establish a five-member committee to examine all recommendations, decisions and activities of United Nations organs and specialized agencies in the sphere of freedom of information.

This Committee on Freedom of Information was also asked to report to the Commission on the question of developing information media. (See also INFORMATION MEDIA IN UNDER-DEVELOPED COUNTRIES below.)

Composed of representatives of France, India, Lebanon, Mexico and Poland, the Committee on Freedom of Information met in May and June 1957 to organize its work. Its report was due to be presented to the Human Rights Commission in 1958.

CONSIDERATION BY GENERAL ASSEMBLY

Ways and means of keeping freedom of information problems under constant review were also discussed at the General Assembly's twelfth session in December 1957.

In the course of debate in the Third Committee, the Philippines proposed a draft resolution to ask the Human Rights Commission (1) to consider procedures for ensuring a continuing study of problems of the freedom of information, and (2) to give special consideration, when examining the report of its five-member Committee on Freedom of Information, to the problem of developing media of information in under-developed countries.

The draft also contained provisions under which the Commission would have been asked to give special consideration to problems of censorship and the possibility of preparing a draft declaration on freedom of information based on article 19 of the Universal Declaration of Human Rights. These provisions, however, were rejected in a separate vote on the relevant subparagraphs.

The draft resolution was adopted by the Third Committee in an amended form on 9 December 1957 by 43 votes to 2, with 21 abstentions. On 11 December, it was adopted at a plenary meeting of the Assembly by 50 votes to 0, with 24 abstentions, as resolution 1189 B (XII).

In adopting this resolution, the Assembly also recognized the important role of information media in strengthening friendly relations between peoples. It recognized, too, that a free flow of accurate and undistorted news and information was a powerful factor in maintaining international peace and understanding.

In another resolution (1189 C (XII)), also adopted on 11 December, the Assembly urged Member States to consider organizing seminars on freedom of information under the United Nations programme of advisory services in human rights. Such seminars, it recognized, could help to solve problems in the field of freedom of information. (For further details, see section above on ADVISORY SERVICES IN HUMAN RIGHTS.)

DRAFT CONVENTION

Consideration of the draft Convention on Freedom of Information had been postponed from the ninth session of the General Assembly in 1954 until its twelfth session. Originally prepared by the United Nations Conference on Freedom of Information held at Geneva in 1948,[2] it was revised by an *ad hoc* committee of the General Assembly in 1951.[3]

In the course of debate in the Third Committee at the Assembly's twelfth session, some Members, while recognizing that time for consideration of the draft Convention was limited, stressed the need for further study of both the draft and the general problems of freedom of information. They urged early detailed consideration of the draft Convention by the Committee. Other Committee Members, however, were pessimistic about the possibility of ever drafting an acceptable text and thought that further work on it would serve no useful purpose.

Those in favour of further work on the draft

[2] See *Y.U.N., 1947-1948*, p. 588.
[3] See *Y.U.N., 1951*, pp. 508-13.

pointed out that all Member States should have an opportunity to discuss the formulation of the controversial article 2 of the draft convention, which lists permissible restrictions on the freedom of information. The suggestion was made (though not formally introduced) that an *ad hoc* committee of representatives from 24 States should consider the draft Convention in detail in mid-1958.

On 5 December 1957, the Philippines submitted a draft resolution to the following effect. The Assembly, after noting the need to bring the draft Convention to the attention of the newer Members of the United Nations, would ask the Secretary-General: (*a*) to circulate to Member States the text of the draft Convention, as revised in 1951, and invite them to comment thereon; and (*b*) to report to the thirteenth session of the Assembly, so as to enable it to take appropriate action.

Chile proposed adding a paragraph to ask the Secretary-General to invite Members to provide a statement of the legal provisions "directly or indirectly" relating to freedom of information in force in their countries. This amendment was accepted, except for the words "directly or indirectly" which were rejected by 27 votes to 19, with 19 abstentions.

The draft resolution, as a whole and as amended, was adopted by the Third Committee on 9 December 1957 by 66 votes to 0, with 2 abstentions. On 11 December 1957, it was approved at a plenary meeting of the Assembly by a vote of 75 to 0, with 1 abstention, as resolution 1189 A (XII).

BROADCASTING CONVENTION

The draft Protocol to the International Convention concerning the Use of Broadcasting in the Cause of Peace (Geneva, 1936), contains two new articles to the effect that States parties should refrain from unfair attacks or slander by radio against other peoples and that they should not interfere with the reception within their territories of foreign radio broadcasts. The draft Protocol was prepared by the Secretary-General as a result of a decision taken at the General Assembly's ninth session in 1954 (resolution 841(IX)).

The draft Protocol has been transmitted to the States parties to the Convention with a request that they state whether the functions assigned to the League of Nations under the Convention should be transferred to the United Nations. By 31 December 1957, the following 15 of the 26 States parties to the 1936 Convention had sent replies to the Secretary-General: Burma, Ceylon, Chile, Denmark, Egypt, Finland, India, Ireland, Lebanon, Luxembourg, the Netherlands, Norway, Pakistan, Sweden and Switzerland. All expressed approval of the transfer of functions.

INFORMATION MEDIA IN UNDER-DEVELOPED COUNTRIES

In April 1957, at its twenty-third session, the Economic and Social Council considered a report from the Secretary-General on the development of media of information in under-developed countries, which had been requested by the Council on 26 May 1955.

On 25 April 1957, by 16 votes to 0, with 2 abstentions, the Council adopted a resolution (643(XXIII)) inviting Members of the United Nations or of the specialized agencies, which had not done so, to transmit the information requested in 1955 to the Secretary-General. The Council also invited Governments to take advantage of existing technical assistance programmes and the programme of advisory services in human rights. In addition, it invited the Secretary-General to complete and submit a report to the Council (not later than its twenty-seventh session in 1959) which would enable a concrete programme for the development of information media to be drawn up, taking into consideration recommendations by the Commission on Human Rights.

The resolution to this effect was adopted on the recommendation of the Council's Social Committee, on the basis of a proposal by the United States and Yugoslavia.

There was general agreement at the Council's twenty-third session that Governments should take full advantage of the technical assistance facilities offered by the United Nations and the specialized agencies. These facilities for economic development, it was pointed out, could be used for developing information media, while the programme of advisory services in human rights should promote the freedom of information. The importance of promoting freedom of information, it was also stressed, should not be overlooked in developing information media.

(See also section above on ADVISORY SERVICES IN HUMAN RIGHTS.)

DOCUMENTARY REFERENCES

PROGRESS IN FIELD OF FREEDOM OF INFORMATION

CONSIDERATION BY COMMISSION
E/2970/Rev.1. Report of 13th session of Commission on Human Rights, Chapter VII, resolution IX.

CONSIDERATION BY GENERAL ASSEMBLY

GENERAL ASSEMBLY—12TH SESSION
Plenary Meeting 727.
Third Committee, meetings 828-834.

A/C.3/L.660 and Rev.1. Philippines draft resolution and revision. Part B, adopted by Third Committee by 43 votes to 2, with 21 abstentions.
A/C.3/L.662. United States amendment to Philippines revised draft resolution.
A/3778. Report of Third Committee.
RESOLUTION 1189 B (XII), as recommended by Third Committee, A/3778, adopted by Assembly on 11 December 1957, meeting 727, by 50 votes to 0, with 24 abstentions.

"The General Assembly,
"Recognizing that the media of information have a more important role than ever before in strengthening friendly relations between peoples and that a free flow of accurate and undistorted news and information is a powerful factor in maintaining international peace and understanding,
"Noting that the Commission on Human Rights, at its thirteenth session, appointed a committee of five of its members for the purpose of reviewing the work of the United Nations and the specialized agencies on freedom of information and reporting, with recommendations, to the Commission at its fourteenth session,
"Believing that there is need to ensure that problems of freedom of information shall remain under constant review by the appropriate organs of the United Nations,
"Requests the Economic and Social Council:
"(*a*) To invite the Commission on Human Rights to consider, at its fourteenth session, procedures by which such constant review may be ensured, *inter alia,* by including problems of freedom of information in the agenda of its future sessions and examining means of providing for the continuing study of such problems;
"(*b*) Further to invite the Commission, when examining the report of its committee appointed to review the work of the United Nations and the specialized agencies on freedom of information, to give special consideration to the problem of developing media of information in under-developed countries;
"(*c*) To transmit to the General Assembly at its thirteenth session the report of the Commission on

these matters, together with the Council's recommendation thereon."

See also DOCUMENTARY REFERENCES to section above on ADVISORY SERVICES IN HUMAN RIGHTS.

DRAFT CONVENTION

GENERAL ASSEMBLY—12TH SESSION
Plenary Meeting 727.
Third Committee, meetings 828-834.

A/3589. Note by Secretary-General.
A/C.3/L.660 and Rev.1. Philippines draft resolution and revision, Part A, as amended by Chile, adopted by Third Committee, by 66 votes to 0, with 2 abstentions.
A/3778. Report of Third Committee.
RESOLUTION 1189 A (XII), as recommended by Third Committee, A/3778, adopted by Assembly on 11 December 1957, meeting 727, by 75 votes to 0, with 1 abstention.

"The General Assembly,
"Considering the need to bring the text of the draft Convention on Freedom of Information to the attention of the increased membership of the United Nations,
"Requests the Secretary-General:
"(*a*) To circulate to Member States the text of the preamble and nineteen articles of the draft Convention on Freedom of Information prepared in 1951 by the General Assembly's *Ad Hoc* Committee on the Draft Convention on Freedom of Information, together with a brief history of the development of this project, and to invite them to submit their views and suggestions on the text and on the action which the General Assembly should take thereon;
"(*b*) To invite Member States to provide a statement of the legal provisions relating to freedom of information in their countries;
"(*c*) To report on this consultation to the General Assembly at its thirteenth session to enable the Assembly to give such priority as it may determine to the appropriate consideration of the draft Convention on Freedom of Information."

INFORMATION MEDIA IN UNDER-DEVELOPED COUNTRIES

ECONOMIC AND SOCIAL COUNCIL—23RD SESSION
Plenary Meeting 967.
Social Committee, meetings 355-357.

E/2947 and Add.1. Media of information in under-developed countries. Report by Secretary-General.
E/2972. Note by Secretary-General, circulating text

of resolution adopted by Commission on Human Rights.

E/AC.7/L.284 and Corr.1. United States and Yugoslavia draft resolution, adopted by Social Committee by 14 votes to 0, with 2 abstentions.

E/2978. Report of Social Committee.

RESOLUTION 643(XXIII), as recommended by Social Committee, E/2978, adopted by Council on 25 April 1957, meeting 967, by 16 votes to 0, with 2 abstentions.

"*The Economic and Social Council,*

"*Having considered* the report by the Secretary-General prepared in co-operation with the United Nations Educational, Scientific and Cultural Organization on media of information in under-developed countries,

"*Noting* that a more substantial number of replies by States Members of the United Nations or members of the specialized agencies is necessary to enable the Secretary-General to act on the request addressed to him under paragraph 2 of Council resolution 574 D (XIX) of 26 May 1955,

"*Noting further* the recommendations and suggestions of Governments, contained in the report of the Secretary-General, concerning the development and improvement of media of information.

"1. *Reaffirms* its resolution 574 D (XIX);

"2. *Requests* States Members of the United Nations or members of the specialized agencies which have not done so to transmit to the Secretary-General the information requested in paragraph 1 of resolution 574 D (XIX);

"3. *Invites* the Secretary-General to complete in co-operation with specialized agencies as appropriate and submit to the Council, not later than its twenty-seventh session, the analysis requested in paragraph 2 of resolution 574 D (XIX), taking into account also any recommendations which the Commission on Human Rights may make as a result of its consideration of the problem;

"4. *Invites* Governments in the meanwhile to take advantage of the assistance which is already available from the United Nations and the specialized agencies under the existing programmes of technical assistance, including the possibilities available under Council resolutions 522 F (XVII), 522 J (XVII) and 522 K (XVII) of 29 April 1954, and under the programme of advisory services provided for in General Assembly resolution 926 (X) of 14 December 1955."

See also DOCUMENTARY REFERENCES to section above on ADVISORY SERVICES IN HUMAN RIGHTS.

OTHER QUESTIONS RELATING TO HUMAN RIGHTS

PRISONERS OF WAR

The Ad Hoc Commission on Prisoners of War, which consists of Judge J. G. Guerrero (Chairman), Countess Estelle Bernadotte and Judge Aung Khine, held its seventh session at the European Office of the United Nations between 2 and 11 September 1957.

Representatives of Australia, Belgium, France, the Federal Republic of Germany, Italy, Japan, the Netherlands, the United Kingdom and the United States attended the session in response to the Commission's invitation. The USSR Government had also been invited, but did not reply to the Commission's invitation. The representatives attending were unanimous in their desire to see the work of the Commission continued until the problem of prisoners of the Second World War was completely settled.

In its report, the Commission summarized the progress achieved in the solution of the problem since its establishment in June 1951. The report showed that 33,778 Japanese nationals and 31,623 German nationals had been repatriated since the Commission started its work. The bulk of these repatriates came from the USSR and the People's Republic of China. Other nationals repatriated were: 69 Italians;

147 Austrians; 286 Spaniards. Information submitted by the Governments concerned showed that the number of prisoners who at one time or another were reported to be in the Soviet Union, but whose subsequent fate was unknown, was as follows: 87,353 German prisoners of war and 11,500 German civilians; 933 Italian prisoners of war; and 8,069 Japanese nationals. Information from the Japanese Government also showed that there were some 34,000 Japanese nationals, believed to be on the mainland of China, whose fate was unknown.

Owing to the USSR's refusal to co-operate with it, the Commission said it was unable to negotiate directly with the USSR Government "on whose co-operation the settlement of the problem to a large extent depended". The Commission said it had to request the good offices of several Red Cross societies and to recommend that the Governments concerned initiate direct negotiations with the detaining Governments. It has been largely due to the negotiations conducted by the Governments concerned and by the various national Red Cross societies that the recent progress in repatriation was achieved. The Commission therefore decided to appeal once more to those Governments and to the various interested organizations to continue their efforts as the problem concerning prisoners of war was not yet completely settled.

TRADE UNION RIGHTS

The Secretary-General of the United Nations forwards to the Governing Body of the International Labour Office (ILO)—for reference, if necessary, to the Fact-Finding and Conciliation Commission on Freedom of Association— all allegations from Governments or trade union and employers' organizations relating to States which are members of ILO. Allegations relating to Members of the United Nations which are not members of ILO are brought to the attention of the Economic and Social Council and cannot be forwarded to the Governing Body of ILO without the consent of the Governments concerned. Allegations relating to States which are members neither of the United Nations nor of ILO are also brought to the Council's attention.

At its twenty-third session (16 April–2 May 1957), the Council had before it a reply from the Government of Saudi Arabia (which is not a member of ILO) stating in effect that it did not consent to the forwarding to ILO of two communications alleging infringements of trade union rights by Saudi Arabia, as submitted in 1955 and 1956 by the World Federation of Trade Unions (WFTU) and the International Confederation of Free Trade Unions (ICFTU), respectively. Saudi Arabia pointed out: that the allegations made in 1955 distorted the truth; that the labour decrees referred to in the complaints were measures within the domestic jurisdiction of Saudi-Arabia; and that labour conditions in Saudi Arabia were constantly being improved.

Later, when the matter was discussed in the Council's Social Committee, some representatives, particularly those of France and the United Kingdom, expressed concern over safeguarding the procedure for considering allegations against Members of the United Nations which were not members of ILO. They felt that the Council should note Saudi Arabia's reply "with regret". The representatives of Pakistan and the United States, among others, pointed out that the Saudi Arabian Government had at least sent a reply, which was more than other Governments had done.

The ICFTU representative renewed his request, made at previous sessions, that the Council itself set up a fact-finding committee to investigate allegations against States which were not members of ILO.

The representatives of Egypt and Saudi Arabia questioned the Confederation's motives in submitting the complaint. The Saudi Arabian spokesman pointed out that Saudi Arabia was still a patriarchal, pastoral state, not yet at a level of economic and social development which would permit it to organize its manpower resources. The anti-strike decree which formed the subject of the Confederation's complaint had been issued merely to maintain law and order in the country's only organized essential industry.

The United States proposed that the Council "take note" of the communication received from the Saudi Arabian Government. This should imply neither rejection nor approval of the reply. The United Kingdom suggested adding the words "with regret", and believed that the United States wording though not implying approval, did imply acceptance. The United Kingdom amendment was rejected by 6 votes to 3, with 9 abstentions. The Committee then approved the United States proposal, which the Council subsequently approved, on 1 May, by 14 votes to 0, with 4 abstentions as resolution 648(XXIII).

TENTH ANNIVERSARY OF UNIVERSAL DECLARATION OF HUMAN RIGHTS

In March 1956, the Commission on Human Rights appointed a committee to prepare plans for the widest possible celebration, on 10 December 1958, of the tenth anniversary of the adoption of the Universal Declaration of Human Rights. This committee—composed of Chile, France, Pakistan and the Philippines— reported to the Commission's thirteenth session (2–26 April 1957). On the basis of the committee's suggestions, the Commission presented plans for the celebration of the anniversary to the Economic and Social Council.

At its twenty-fourth session in mid-1957, the Council urged all Members of the United Nations or of the specialized agencies to join in observing the day, making such use of the plans prepared by the Commission as they might consider appropriate. It recommended that they consider the desirability of setting up national committees to prepare for the observance of the anniversary. It also invited the co-operation of the specialized agencies and the non-governmental organizations in consultative status and hoped that regional intergovernmental organizations concerned would join in the observance. The Council also set up a committee, consisting of Chile, Egypt, France, Pakistan, the Philippines and Sweden, to make plans for the celebration. It asked the Secretary-General to make the necessary arrangements, in co-operation with this committee and in consultation with the executive heads of UNESCO and the other specialized agencies, for giving effect to the committee's plans. The resolution to this effect (651 B (XXIV)) was adopted on 24 July 1957, by 14 votes to 0, with 3 abstentions.

The plans approved by the Commission on Human Rights included: a new world-wide distribution of the Universal Declaration of Human Rights and the publication of books, pamphlets and special articles on human rights; conferences of non-governmental organizations; national and regional meetings on human rights; special studies of human rights subjects in schools and universities; establishment of special honours and awards in 1958; art competitions; special radio, television and film programmes; issuance by Governments, as well as by the United Nations, of commemorative postage stamps and use of UNICEF's 1958 greeting cards to illustrate human rights.

The Commission also recommended: that Governments arrange to hold celebrations on 10 December 1958 in their capitals and principal cities; that Parliaments of Member States hold solemn sessions and that the heads of States or of Governments address special messages to their nations on that day; and that appropriate ceremonies be organized at United Nations Headquarters, where the General Assembly would then be in session, as well as at the other offices of the United Nations and at the headquarters of the various specialized agencies.

On 2 August 1957, by a vote of 8 to 6 with 4 abstentions, the Council decided that the 1958 session (the fourteenth) of the Human Rights Commission should be held in Paris to commemorate the tenth anniversary of the General Assembly's adoption of the Universal Declaration in that city on 10 December 1948. This decision, however, was later reversed at the General Assembly's twelfth session, on financial grounds.

DRAFT DECLARATION ON RIGHTS OF THE CHILD

At its thirteenth session (1–26 April 1957) the Commission on Human Rights considered a draft Declaration on the Rights of the Child, originally prepared by the Social Commission. In 1950, the Economic and Social Council had referred the matter to the Commission for consideration in view of the close relationship between that draft and the Universal Declaration of Human Rights.[4]

In its debate during 1957 on the nature and scope of the proposed Declaration, the Commission discussed the following specific points, among others: the desirability of such a document; the question whether it should take the form of a declaration or a treaty; and such questions as equality of rights between legitimate and illegitimate children. Since the Commission felt that it was unable to consider all the aspects of the draft Declaration, it decided to transmit the draft Declaration to Members of the United Nations for comment.

The Economic and Social Council, at its twenty-fourth session, extended the time-limit for submission of Government comments, set by the Commission for 31 December 1957, to 31 December 1958. It did so by resolution 651 E (XXIV), which was adopted on 24 July 1957 by 13 votes to 0, with 4 abstentions.

DRAFT DECLARATION ON THE RIGHT OF ASYLUM

The question of the right of asylum was discussed at the time the Universal Declaration of Human Rights was being prepared. Article 14 of this Declaration proclaims the right to seek and enjoy asylum from persecution except in the case of prosecutions genuinely arising from non-political crimes or from acts contrary to the purposes and principles of the United Nations. It was also discussed in connexion with

[4] For a summary of the draft Declaration and an account of previous action taken on it, see *Y.U.N. 1950*, pp. 597-98.

the draft Covenant on Civil and Political Rights, which does not, however, include any provisions on asylum. The question was briefly discussed, too, by the International Law Commission in 1949 and 1950 in connexion with the selection of topics for codification and preparation of the draft Declaration on the Rights and Duties of States. The Conventions relating to refugees and stateless persons, which were adopted under the auspices of the United Nations, also bear on the right of asylum.

In April 1957, at its thirteenth session, the Commission on Human Rights discussed the question of the right of asylum. France submitted a draft declaration on the right of asylum stating *inter alia,* that: (1) responsibility for granting asylum lay with the international community as represented by the United Nations; (2) a person whose life or liberty was threatened was entitled to seek asylum; (3) States granting asylum incurred no international responsibility; and (4) asylum granted should be respected by other States. Amendments to the draft Declaration were submitted by Israel.

The following were among the questions touched on in the Commission's debate: Would a declaration additional to the Universal Declaration be appropriate? Would a convention be preferable? Should the Commission recommend that the General Assembly include an article on the right of asylum in the draft Covenant on Civil and Political Rights?

The Commission took note of the draft Declaration and asked that it be communicated for comment to all the Members of the United Nations and of the specialized agencies, as well as to the United Nations High Commissioner for Refugees.

The Economic and Social Council, at its twenty-fourth session, extended the time-limit for the submission of comments, set by the Commission for 31 December 1957, to 31 December 1958. It did so by resolution 651 F (XXIV), adopted on 24 July 1957 by 14 votes to 0, with 3 abstentions.

YEARBOOK ON HUMAN RIGHTS

In April 1957, at its thirteenth session, the Commission on Human Rights appointed a committee to consider what measures should be taken to prevent the *Yearbook on Human Rights* from becoming too costly to produce, as well as too bulky and overlapping in content with the two following projects authorized by the Economic and Social Council in 1956: the triennial reporting system of human rights, and the programme of studies of specific rights or groups of rights.

The committee, composed of representatives of France, India, Israel, Mexico and the United Kingdom, met during the last three months of 1957 and prepared its recommendations for submission to the Commission's fourteenth session in 1958.

COMMUNICATIONS ON HUMAN RIGHTS

In accordance with established procedure, the Secretary-General prepared, for the thirteenth session of the Commission on Human Rights (1–26 April 1957), a non-confidential list of communications dealing with principles involved in the promotion of universal respect for and observance of human rights. He also prepared a confidential list containing references to 2,321 other communications about human rights received during 1956, as well as observations by Governments on a number of these communications. At a closed meeting, the Commission decided, by 12 votes to 0, with 4 abstentions, to take note of the distribution of the lists.

Several members of the Commission, however, voiced dissatisfaction with the procedure for dealing with these communications. Various suggestions were advanced for reviewing the procedure but none were pressed since the Commission felt that a more thorough discussion than was possible at its 1957 session was required. It was, however, agreed that the procedure could be studied further at the Commission's fourteenth session.

Lists of communications concerning the status of women and discrimination and minorities were submitted in 1957 to the eleventh session of the Commission on the Status of Women and the ninth session of the Sub-Commission on Prevention of Discrimination and Protection of Minorities, respectively.

DOCUMENTARY REFERENCES

PRISONERS OF WAR
A/AC.46/21. Report of Ad Hoc Commission on Prisoners of War, on work of its 7th session.

TRADE UNION RIGHTS

ECONOMIC AND SOCIAL COUNCIL—23RD SESSION
Plenary Meeting 955, 970.
Social Committee, meeting 358.

E/2587/Add.3. Communication of 20 March 1954 from World Federation of Trade Unions.
E/2951. Communication of 19 September 1956 from International Confederation of Free Trade Unions.
E/2976. Communication of 19 April 1957 from Government of Saudi Arabia.
E/2985. Report of Social Committee, containing draft resolution proposed orally by United States and adopted by Committee by 15 votes to 0, with 3 abstentions.
RESOLUTION 648 (XXIII), as recommended by Social Committee, E/2985, adopted by Council on 1 May 1957, meeting 970, by 14 votes to 0, with 4 abstentions.

"*The Economic and Social Council*
"*Takes note* of the communication dated 19 April 1957 from the Government of Saudi Arabia in reply to the Secretary-General's *notes verbales* of 14 June 1955 and 11 October 1956 regarding alleged violations of trade-union rights in Saudi Arabia."

TENTH ANNIVERSARY OF UNIVERSAL DECLARATION OF HUMAN RIGHTS

ECONOMIC AND SOCIAL COUNCIL—24TH SESSION
Plenary Meetings 989, 996.
Social Committee, meetings 359-364.

E/2970/Rev.1. Report of 13th session of Commission on Human Rights, 1-26 April 1957.
E/2970/Rev.1, Annex I. Draft resolution A as recommended by Commission on Human Rights, and as amended in Committee, adopted by Social Committee by 17 votes to 0, with 1 abstention.
E/AC.7/L.285. United States amendment to draft resolution A.
E/3027 and Add.1, and Corr.1, 2. Report of Social Committee (draft resolution B).
E/L.761. USSR amendment to draft resolution B.
REOLUTION 651 B(XXIV), as recommended by Social Committee, E/3027, adopted by Council on 24 July 1957, meeting 989, by 14 votes to 0, with 3 abstentions.

"*The Economic and Social Council*,
"*Recalling* its resolution 624 C (XXII) of 1 August 1956, in which it noted the resolution of the Commission on Human Rights on plans for the widest possible celebration of the tenth anniversary of the Universal Declaration of Human Rights and invites the collaboration in that undertaking of the United Nations Edu-

cational, Scientific and Cultural Organization and other specialized agencies and non-governmental organizations concerned,
"*Recalling also* General Assembly resolution 423(V) of 4 December 1950 inviting all States to adopt 10 December of each year as Human Rights Day and to celebrate on that day the proclamation of the Universal Declaration of Human Rights by the General Assembly on 10 December 1948, to exert increasing efforts in that field of human progress, and to report annually through the Secretary-General concerning the observance of Human Rights Day,
"*Recognizing* the significance of the Universal Declaration of Human Rights in promoting an understanding of human rights and fundamental freedoms,
"*Deeply convinced* that devotion to the lofty principles set forth in the Universal Declaration of Human Rights would be manifested in the best way by further concrete steps with a view to the protection of human rights and especially by completion of work on the draft International Covenents on Human Rights, including the measures of implementation,
"1. *Urges* all States Members of the United Nations or members of the specialized agencies to join in observing the tenth anniversary of the Universal Declaration of Human Rights, which will fall on 10 December 1958, making such use as they may consider appropriate of the plans annexed to the present resolution, and *invites* them to include information on the observance of this anniversary in the report which they submit regularly under General Assembly resolution 423(V);
"2. *Recommends* all States Members of the United Nations or members of the specialized agencies to consider the desirability of setting up national committees for the purpose of carrying out the objects of the present resolution;
"3. *Invites* the specialized agencies to co-operate in the observance of this anniversary, taking into account the plans annexed to the present resolution, with a view to strengthening support for their objectives through wider understanding of the Universal Declaration of Human Rights and of the relation of the Declaration to their programmes and activities;
"4. *Invites* non-governmental organizations in consultative status to promote the observance of this anniversary in co-operation with their national and local affiliates;
"5. *Expresses the hope* that regional intergovernmental organizations concerned will also join in the observance;
"6. *Requests* the Secretary-General, in co-operation with a committee consisting of representatives of Chile, France, Egypt, Pakistan, the Philippines and Sweden, and in consultation with the Director-General of the United Nations Educational, Scientific and Cultural Organization and the executive heads of the other specialized agencies, to make the necessary arrangements to give effect to the recommendations of the Commission on Human Rights;
"7. *Expresses the desire* that the General Assembly

should take appropriate measures in order that the decision contained in its resolution 1041(XI) of 20 February 1957, concerning the completion of the work on the draft International Covenants on Human Rights, including measures of implementation, may be carried out by 10 December 1958, as the most fitting homage to the Universal Declaration of Human Rights;

"8. *Appeals* to all States Members of the United Nations to co-operate closely to this end."

ANNEX

Plans for the Celebration of the Tenth Anniversary of the Adoption of the Universal Declaration of Human Rights, Approved by the Commission on Human Rights at Its Thirteenth Session

I. GENERAL

"The Commission judged that two main considerations should be borne in mind in planning the celebration of the tenth anniversary of the adoption of the Universal Declaration of Human Rights:

"(*a*) The celebration should demonstrate to the world the great step which the adoption of the Declaration on 10 December 1948 represents, and its unique character as an international document. It would therefore be fitting that the celebration should, wherever possible, serve as a vivid illustration of the work accomplished by the United Nations in defining the rights proclaimed and ensuring respect for them. At the same time, in order to stimulate greater efforts in the field of human rights, the celebration should emphasize the considerable amount of work which yet remains to be done, in particular the importance of the adoption and ratification of the draft covenants on civil and political rights and on economic, social and cultural rights;

"(*b*) The celebration should also afford an opportunity for making better known the rights and freedoms set forth in the Declaration, for awakening renewed interest in, and greater understanding of, these rights and freedoms, and thus encouraging increasing respect for them."

II. RECOMMENDATIONS

"The recommendations submitted by the Commission are as follows:

A. Distribution of the text of the Universal Declaration of Human Rights

"The Commission considers that the Universal Declaration of Human Rights should be widely disseminated, studied and discussed. To this end the Commission recommends that the Secretary-General, with the co-operation of Governments, non-governmental organizations, schools, and local authorities, initiate a new world-wide distribution of the text of the Declaration in 1958 in as many languages as possible and presented in an attractive manner. The Commission hopes that a copy of the Declaration may be made available to the greatest possible number of people in a language they can understand."

B. Publications on human rights

"The Commission considers that as many publications on human rights as possible should be issued during 1958. These should include books, pamphlets, periodicals and special articles. The co-operation of

writers, publishers and non-governmental organizations will be most welcome in this respect.

"The Commission recommends that all specialized agencies should be invited to introduce, in their public information activities in 1957 and 1958, the theme of human rights, particularly when this is appropriate to the work of the agency.

"The Commission considers it important that the work of the United Nations in the field of human rights should be given publicity in 1958. It recommends that the Secretary-General should prepare a commentary on the Universal Declaration of Human Rights, giving its legislative history. Popular essays based on this commentary, and explaining the Declaration to the general public, would also be desirable. The Commission recommends that the Secretary-General issue a new pamphlet on the impact of the Declaration. The work of the Commission on Human Rights and its Sub-commission, and the work of the Commission on the Status of Women, should also be included in publications issued."

C. Conferences of non-governmental organizations on human rights

"The Commission recommends that non-governmental organizations emphasize human rights at their annual conferences in 1958.

"The Commission suggests also that non-governmental organizations, individually or in groups, should draw up and adopt resolutions reaffirming their support for the Universal Declaration of Human Rights."

D. Other conferences and meetings on human rights

"The Commission recommends that Governments encourage national organizations and institutions to hold national, and, whenever possible, regional, conferences and other meetings on human rights in 1958. The organization of these conferences should be left to the initiative of leading civic or social organizations, but the Commission believes that the conferences should be on a large scale and the representatives drawn from as many different walks of life as possible.

"The Commission also recommends that as many societies and other local groups as possible should hold meetings and discussions on human rights during the year."

E. Studies of human rights subjects

"The Commission recommends that schools and universities, wherever possible, should incorporate special studies on human rights in their curricula for 1958.

"The Commission suggests that in the schools, the meaning of the Articles of the Universal Declaration of Human Rights might be taught against the background of the national history of the country concerned and of the country's own efforts in promoting the rights and freedoms which the Declaration proclaims.

"The Committee suggests that universities in various parts of the world should hold seminars on human rights, or meetings timed to coincide with the tenth anniversary of the adoption of the Universal Declaration of Human Rights."

F. Honours and awards

"The Commission suggests that Governments, universities and other institutions might offer special honours or awards in 1958 to persons who have distinguished themselves by their work of studies on human rights."

G. Art competitions

"The Commission submits the following suggestions:

"1. That national competitions in literature, music and the plastic arts might be held. Artists, in whatever forms of art may be most representative of the particular national genius, might well be attracted by the idea of producing a work on the theme of human rights and submitting it to a jury;

"2. That an international competition in children's art might be arranged by the Secretary-General, in co-operation with the Director General of the United Nations Educational, Scientific and Cultural Organization. Children of all countries might be asked to make drawings and paintings illustrating one or more of the rights in the Declaration, which they themselves would choose. Their contributions would first be judged by a national committee. The contributions then submitted should be limited in number and of identical size. The number of awards to be made will have to be decided, but they would be offered by an international jury and the drawings and paintings selected would be exhibited at the United Nations;

"3. That similar national competitions might be held in which children would write essays or short stories with human rights as their theme."

H. Radio, television and film programmes

"The Commission recommends that the Secretary-General, in co-operation with the Director-General of the United Nations Educational, Scientific and Cultural Organization, promote national and international radio, television and film programmes in honour of the tenth anniversary, and that he explore the possibility of arranging an international radio link-up in which outstanding personalities, who have been concerned with human rights at the national or international level, would participate.

"The Commission suggests that the possibility be explored for special awards being made for films connected with human rights at the international film festivals. Similarly, a special television award might be offered for a Human Rights Day programme in 1958."

I. Human rights stamps

"The Commission recommends that every Government issue national human rights stamps, first-day covers, or special cancellations on 10 December 1958.

"The Commission also recommends that United Nations human rights stamps, first-day covers, and special cancellations honouring the tenth anniversary, should be issued."

J. Greeting cards of the United Nations Children's Fund

"The Commission suggests that UNICEF greeting cards might illustrate human rights in 1958. It notes that UNICEF has agreed to a request that it study the possibility of using one or more of the children's drawings or paintings which win the international competition (see G (2) above) on the greeting cards which will be issued in 1959 or 1960."

K. Observances of Human Rights Day 1958

"The Commission considers it important that the widest possible national and international observances of Human Rights Day in 1958 should be held.

"The Commission recommends that all Governments should make arrangements to hold celebrations on 10 December 1958 in their capitals and principal cities.

"The Commission suggests that parliaments of Member States might hold solemn sessions on 10 December 1958 to celebrate the anniversary of the adoption of the Universal Declaration of Human Rights.

"The Commission suggests also that Heads of State or of Governments might, on that day, address special messages to the nation, calling, where appropriate, on government agencies and services, and public and private organizations and enterprises, to make new efforts to achieve fuller enjoyment of the rights and freedoms recognized in the Universal Declaration of Human Rights.

"The Commission recommends that the Secretary-General organize an appropriate ceremony at United Nations Headquarters on 10 December 1958. As the General Assembly will be in session on that date, a special plenary meeting might be held at which the General Assembly would reaffirm its faith in, and pledge its renewed support for, the Universal Declaration of Human Rights in a resolution.

"The Commission recommends also that the Secretary-General organize appropriate observances at the European and other Offices of the United Nations.

"The Commission recommends further that the executive heads of the specialized agencies be asked to organize observances of 10 December 1958 at their respective headquarters. The Commission notes that the eleventh General Conference of the United Nations Educational, Scientific and Cultural Organization will probably be in session on 10 December 1958; arrangements for special sessions of that body might also be made."

E/L.773. Membership of committee on tenth anniversary of Universal Declaration of Human Rights. Note by Secretary-General.

Council Committee on Tenth Anniversary of Universal Declaration of Human Rights, meetings 1, 2.

E/AC.44/1. Observance of tenth anniversary of Universal Declaration of Human Rights. Report by Secretary-General.

E/AC.44/2. Action taken by Conference of Consultative Non-Governmental Organizations on tenth anniversary of Universal Declaration of Human Rights. Note by Secretary-General.

1958 MEETING PLACE FOR
COMMISSION ON HUMAN RIGHTS

ECONOMIC AND SOCIAL COUNCIL—24TH SESSION
Plenary Meeting 989, 996.
Social Committee, meetings 359-364.
Interim Committee on Programme of Conferences, meeting 39.

E/2970/Rev.1. Report of 13th session of Commission on Human Rights, 1-26 April 1957 (resolution VII).

E/3027 and Corr.2 and Add.1. Report of Social Committee (draft resolution H).

E/3040, paragraph 5. Calendar of Conferences for 1958. Report of Secretary-General.

RESOLUTION 651 H (XXIV), as recommended by Social Committee, E/3027, adopted by Council on 2 August 1957, meeting 996, by 8 votes to 6, with 4 abstentions.

"*The Economic and Social Council,*

"*Noting* the resolution contained in the report of the Commission on Human Rights (thirteenth session),

"*Decides* that the fourteenth session of the Commission on Human Rights shall be held at Paris to commemorate the tenth anniversary of the adoption of the Universal Declaration of Human Rights in that city on 10 December 1948."

GENERAL ASSEMBLY—12TH SESSION
Fifth Committee, meeting 636.

A/C.5/710 and Corr.1. Budget estimates for financial year 1958. Report by Secretary-General.

A/3679. Budget estimates for financial year 1958. Sixth report of Advisory Committee on Administrative and Budgetary Questions to 12th Assembly session.

DRAFT DECLARATION ON RIGHTS OF THE CHILD

ECONOMIC AND SOCIAL COUNCIL—24TH SESSION
Plenary Meeting 989.
Social Committee, meetings 359-364.

E/2970/Rev.1. Report of 13th session of Commission on Human Rights, 1-26 April 1957.

E/2970/Rev.1. paragraph 116. Resolution II adopted by Commission on Human Rights.

E/AC.7/L.287 and Rev.1. Indonesia amendments and revised amendments to draft resolution II recommended by Commission.

E/AC.7/L.289. Indonesia draft resolution, as amended, adopted by Social Committee by 10 votes to 0, with 7 abstentions.

E/3027 and Add.1, and Corr.1, 2. Report of Social Committee (draft resolution E).

RESOLUTION 651 E (XXIV), as recommended by Social Committee, E/3027, adopted by Council on 24 July 1957, meeting 989, by 13 votes to 0, with 4 abstentions.

"*The Economic and Social Council,*

"*Having noted* the resolution on the draft Declaration on the Rights of the Child, adopted by the Commission on Human Rights at its thirteenth session,

"*Noting* the Commission's request for comments from Governments on the draft Declaration, on various observations and statements presented to the Commission and on records of discussions held at the eleventh session of the Council, and its request to the Secretary-General to circulate those comments to the members of the Commission by 31 December 1957,

"1. *Considers* that the purposes of the Commission would be fully served if Governments were given more time to prepare their comments;

"2. *Resolves* that the comments of Governments on the draft Declaration, the observations, statements, and records of discussions, referred to in the above-mentioned resolution may be transmitted until 1 December 1958 in order that the Secretary-General may circulate them to the members of the Commission by 31 December 1958 for consideration by the Commission at its next session thereafter."

DRAFT DECLARATION ON THE RIGHT OF ASYLUM

ECONOMIC AND SOCIAL COUNCIL—24TH SESSION
Plenary Meeting 989.
Social Committee, meetings 359-364.

E/2970/Rev.1. Report of 13th session. Commission on Human Rights, 1-26 April 1957.

E/2970/Rev.1, Paragraph 214. Resolution X adopted by Commission on Human Rights.

E/AC.7/L.287 and Rev.1. Indonesia amendments and revised amendments to resolution X, recommended by Commission.

E/AC.7/L.290. Indonesia draft resolution adopted by Social Committee by 13 votes to 0, with 4 abstentions.

E/3027 and Add.1, and Corr.2. Report of Social Committee (draft resolution F).

RESOLUTION 651 F (XXIV), as recommended by Social Committee, E/3027, adopted by Council on 24 July 1957, meeting 989, by 14 votes to 0, with 3 abstentions.

"*The Economic and Social Council,*

"*Having noted* the resolution on the right of asylum adopted by the Commission on Human Rights at its thirteenth session,

"*Noting* the Commission's request to the Secretary-General to communicate the preliminary draft Declaration on the Right of Asylum submitted by France, the proposed amendments thereto, the memoranda by the Secretary-General, and the summary records of the Commission's discussions, to the Governments of States Members of the United Nations or members of the specialized agencies and to the United Nations High Commissioner for Refugees, with the request that they send him their comments thereon by 31 December 1957,

"1. *Considers* that the purpose of the Commission would be fully served if Governments were given more time to prepare their comments;

"2. *Resolves* that the governmental comments and those of the United Nations High Commissioner for Refugees referred to above may be transmitted to the Secretary-General until 31 December 1958 with a view to their consideration by the Human Rights Commission at its next session thereafter."

E/3613. Report of Economic and Social Council to General Assembly. Chapter VII, section VII.

YEARBOOK ON HUMAN RIGHTS

E/2970/Rev.1. Report of 13th session of Commission on Human Rights, paragraph 223, Resolution XI.

E/CN.4/756. Report of Committee on Yearbook on Human Rights.

Yearbook on Human Rights for 1954. U.N.P. Sales No. 1957.XIV.1.

COMMUNICATIONS ON HUMAN RIGHTS

E/2970/Rev.1. Report of 13th session of Commission on Human Rights, paragraphs 230-234, and Annex II.

E/CN.4/CR.26 and Corr.1. Non-confidential list of communications dealing with principles involved in promotion of universal respect for and observance of human rights.

OTHER DOCUMENTS

FORCED LABOUR

A/3621. Resolution adopted by International Labour Conference concerning abolition of concentration camps and deportation of national minorities. Note by Secretary-General.

E/3049. Note by Secretary-General drawing attention to document A/3621.

CHAPTER X

THE STATUS OF WOMEN

The main topics discussed at the eleventh session of the Commission on the Status of Women, held at United Nations Headquarters from 18 March 1957 to 5 April 1957, were: political rights of women, access of women to education, equal pay for equal work, economic opportunities for women, nationality of married women, status of women in private law, tax legislation affecting married women workers, advisory services in human rights, and participation of women in the work of the United Nations and the specialized agencies.

The Commission's report was considered by the Economic and Social Council at its twenty-fourth session, in mid-1957.

At its twelfth session, on 26 November, the General Assembly noted the Commission's work with appreciation, invited it to pursue its efforts for improving the status of women throughout the world, and voiced the hope that seminars on the status of women would be held as often as possible in future under the programme of advisory services in human rights.

POLITICAL RIGHTS OF WOMEN

The Commission had before it the Secretary-General's annual memorandum of 1956 for the General Assembly (A/3145 and Add.1) on the franchise of women and the number of countries which had signed, ratified or acceded to the Convention on the Political Rights of Women. The memorandum included informa-

tion on reservations and objections to the reservations to the Convention as well as tables showing the extent to which women in various countries have the right to be elected to legislative bodies. The Commission also had before it reports by the Secretary-General on the status of women in Trust Territories and Non-Self-Governing Territories.

The Commission reviewed the progress made the past year towards wider recognition of the political rights of women. It noted that, while there were now only 12 countries where women had no political rights, there still remained many other areas where there rights were not fully recognized. Widespread acceptance of the Convention on the Political Rights of Women was considered to be of great importance. The need for assistance from non-governmental organizations in campaigning for acceptance of the Convention was also stressed. By the end of 1957 the Convention had been signed by 41 countries and had been ratified or acceded to by 28 countries. During the year, Haiti signed the Convention, France and the Philippines ratified it, and Canada and Nicaragua acceded to it.

Discussion in the Commission dealt, too, with the need for Governments to recognize the political rights of women and to adhere to the Convention on the Political Rights of Women, and also with the need for a study of these rights in Trust and Non-Self-Governing Territories.

The Commission also asked the Secretary-General to consult with United Nations Member Governments on the possibility of convening an international seminar on civic responsibilities of women and increased participation of women in public life under the United Nations programme for advisory services in human rights and to report to the Commission's twelfth session on the results of this consultation.

On 24 July 1957, the Economic and Social Council adopted resolution 652 B (XXIV), as put forward by the Commission, recommending that Members of the United Nations and of the specialized agencies which had not yet done so, recognize the political rights of women. It also invited non-governmental organizations in consultative status with the Council to continue their activities in support of political rights for women and to apply their efforts towards increasing public support for the adherence to the Convention on Political Rights of Women. The resolution, adopted on 24 July 1957 by 15 votes to 0, with 2 abstentions, further recommended that States invited to sign and ratify or accede to the Convention and which had not already done so, sign and ratify or accede to it.

Also considered by the Council was the Commission's request that the Secretary-General explore the possibility of holding an international seminar on the civic responsibilities of women and the increased role of women in public life. The Council decided, by resolution 652 I (XXIV), that the records of its discussions on the matter be transmitted to the Commission on the Status of Women for further consideration at the latter's 1958 session. This resolution was adopted on 24 July 1957 by 11 votes to 5, with 1 abstention.

ACCESS OF WOMEN TO EDUCATION

The Commission considered a report by the Secretary-General on the access of women to education and two reports by the United Nations Educational, Scientific and Cultural Organization (UNESCO) dealing, respectively, with the access of women to the teaching profession and with UNESCO's activities with regard to access of women to education. In this connexion, the Commission also heard a report of its representative at the ninth session of the Sub-Commission on Prevention of Discrimination and Protection of Minorities.

Discussion in the Commission centred chiefly on the problem of education of girls in the world's under-developed areas. The Commission noted with concern the decline in school attendance by girls starting at the secondary level and increasing progressively at the university level.

Acting on a recommendation by the Commission, the Economic and Social Council adopted a resolution recommending that Members of the United Nations and of the specialized agencies make provision in their programmes of educational advancement for an intensified campaign against illiteracy among women and for increased attendance by girls at primary schools. It also asked UNESCO to continue its study of the access of women to education, indicating the fields of particular interest to the Commission. This resolution (652 C (XXIV)) was adopted on 24 July 1957 by a vote of 16 to 0, with 1 abstention.

EQUAL PAY FOR EQUAL WORK

The Commission discussed a report by the Secretary-General on practical methods for implementing the principle of equal pay for equal work (E/CN.6/296), and a report by the International Labour Organisation on the subject of equal remuneration for men and women workers for work of equal value (E/CN.6/300). The importance of achieving full application of the principle of equal pay for equal work was stressed during the debate, since it was considered to be a fundamental social problem affecting both the human dignity of women and their economic status. In some areas of employment, several Commission members noted, it was difficult to compare the work of women with that of men, because some types of employment were almost exclusively reserved either for women or for men. It was stated, too, that the application of the principle of equal pay in private industry lagged behind that in public services.

Attention was also drawn to the importance of trade unions in furthering the cause of equal pay for equal work in the course of collective bargaining activities. The Commission noted the progress achieved in several countries towards a more general application of the principle. But it also noted that there were still many difficulties to be overcome to achieve full equality of remuneration for men and women. It urged United Nations Members to become parties to ILO Convention No. 100 and recommended that Governments implement the principle of equal pay by legislation, by collective bargaining or by other measures.

A resolution to this effect, submitted by the Commission, was approved by the Economic and Social Council as resolution 652 D (XXIV) on 24 July 1957. The vote in the Council for this was 13 to 0, with 4 abstentions.

ECONOMIC OPPORTUNITIES FOR WOMEN

The Commission considered a draft list of questions prepared by the Secretary-General, on the occupational outlook for women, (E/CN.6/302), and also an ILO memorandum on the same subject (E/CN.6/308). After considerable debate on the scope of the questionnaire and the importance of using the terminology and definitions of occupations included in ILO's International Classification of Occupations, the Commission agreed to the questionnaire as an annex to a draft resolution for adoption by the Economic and Social Council.

This was approved by the Council in a modified form on 24 July 1957 as resolution 652 E (XXIV). The Council thereby decided to undertake a global study of the access of women to training and employment in the principal professional and technical fields. As a first step in this study, it asked the Secretary-General to collect information by circulating the annexed questionnaire to States and non-governmental organizations, together with an extract from the list of professional and technical occupations of jurists, architects and engineers as described and defined in ILO's International Classification of Occupations. The Council's vote for this resolution was 11 to 1, with 4 abstentions.

Also taken up by the Commission were the subjects of part-time work for women, employment for older women workers, and job opportunities for women in handicraft and cottage industries. As background for its discussions, it had reports on these subjects prepared by ILO (E/CN.6/299 and Adds.1 and 2, E/CN.6/298 and Add.1, E/CN.6/303 and Add.1). Debate on older women workers concentrated mostly on problems of the age of retirement and pensionable ages. The Commission invited the Secretary-General to ask non-governmental organizations having consultative status with the Economic and Social Council for their opinions on the retirement age question and right of women workers to pensions, and to report to the Commission.

Also stressed in the Commission's deliberations was the importance of developing cottage industries and handicrafts in easing the transition from agricultural to industrial economies. Particular attention was paid to the danger of exploitation of workers by middle-men and the poor working conditions associated with industrial home-work.

The Commission also considered a joint UNESCO-ILO report on the access of girls to vocational and technical training (E/CN.6/280 and Corr.1). Several speakers stressed the importance of adequate vocational training for raising the economic status of women and for opening up possibilities for their advancement and promotion. The extension of vocational training for girls was considered necessary both for the betterment of the status of women and for the improvement of national economies.

NATIONALITY OF MARRIED WOMEN

The Commission expressed its satisfaction that the General Assembly had, at its eleventh session in January 1957, adopted and opened for signature the Convention of the Nationality of Married Women.

On the Commission's recommendation, the Economic and Social Council urged Members of the United Nations to sign and ratify or accede to the Convention. It further recommended that members of the specialized agencies and parties to the Statute of the International Court of Justice also become parties to the Convention. The Council's resolution to this effect (652 F (XXIV)) was approved on 24 July 1957 by 12 votes to 1, with 5 abstentions.

STATUS OF WOMEN IN PRIVATE LAW

At its 1957 session, the Commission also had before it a report by the Secretary-General on bride-price, polygamy and rights of the mother with respect to her children (E/CN.6/295).

Discussion dealt with the status of women living in less developed countries and territories, and especially with practices of polygamy, bride-price and child marriage.

Particular attention was given, in the debate on polygamy, to transitional measures tending to curtail polygamy and to speed up the natural evolution towards monogamy. Bride-price practices, in so far as they operated against freedom to choose a spouse, were deemed to degrade women to the position of chattels or slaves. It was also thought that they constituted a serious drawback to the recognition of the human dignity of women.

With respect to child marriage, the Commission noted that the 1956 United Nations Conference of Plenipotentiaries on a Supplementary Convention on the Abolition of Slavery, the Slave-Trade and Institutions and Practices Similar to Slavery had recommended initiation of a study of marriage, to draw attention to the desirability of the free consent of both parties to a marriage and the desirability of setting a minimum age for marriage. The Commission asked the Economic and Social Council to entrust this recommended study to the Commission on the Status of Women; consequently, the Commission postponed consideration of the question of child marriage to its twelfth session, to be held in 1958. On 25 April 1957, at its twenty-third session, the Economic and Social Council agreed, by resolution 640(XXIII), that the study be undertaken by the Commission.

At its twenty-fourth session, on 24 July 1957, the Council accepted a further recommendation by the Commission, asking Members of the United Nations and the specialized agencies to encourage a system for compulsory registration of marriage, thereby ensuring that both spouses express their free consent to marriage in the presence of a competent authority, civil or religious. The Council also asked these countries to encourage a system for compulsory registration of divorces. The Council's vote for this resolution (652 G (XXIV)) was 16 to 0, with 1 abstention.

TAX LEGISLATION AFFECTING MARRIED WOMEN WORKERS

Also considered by the Commission and the Council during 1957 was the subject of tax legislation as it affects married women workers. The Commission had before it a preliminary report by the Secretary-General (E/CN.6/297) containing factual information, opinions and proposals submitted by non-governmental organizations in response to a request by the United Nations Secretariat.

The Commission felt that further information should be obtained from United Nations Member Governments and from non-governmental organizations on tax legislation applicable to women and specially to gainfully employed married women. On July 24, acting on a recommendation by the Commission, the Council asked the Secretary-General to obtain this additional information and to prepare a report on the subject for the Commission's thirteenth session. The resolution to this effect (652 H (XXIV)) was approved unanimously.

PARTICIPATION OF WOMEN IN WORK OF UNITED NATIONS AND SPECIALIZED AGENCIES

At its 1957 session, the Commission again displayed considerable interest in the participation of women in the work of the United Nations and the specialized agencies. Several representatives felt that the United Nations should set an example to all Governments by appointing and promoting women to responsible posts in the United Nations career service.

Commission members reiterated their confidence in the Secretary-General in connexion with the implementation of Article 8 of the United Nations Charter but felt that much remained to be done. (Article 8 of the Charter states: "The United Nations shall place no restrictions on the eligibility of men and women to participate in any capacity and under conditions of equality in its principal and subsidiary organs.")

The Commission expressed the hope that the Secretary-General would bear in mind the necessity of avoiding discrimination against women staff members in respect of dependency allowances and other conditions of employment. It also hoped for an increase in the number and proportion of women appointed and promoted to senior and policy-making positions in the Secretariat of the United Nations and the specialized agencies.

TECHNICAL ASSISTANCE IN RELATION TO STATUS OF WOMEN

At its 1957 session, the Commission had before it: a memorandum by the Secretary-General on technical assistance summarizing selected projects affecting the status of women (E/CN.6/289); and a report by him on advisory services in human rights (E/CN.6/294).

During the debate, several members stressed not only the value of technical assistance programmes in furthering international understanding, peace and prosperity but also the importance of the projects undertaken for speeding the emancipation of women. One point made in the discussion was that women should be enabled to play a greater role in technical assistance programmes as experts, fellows and scholars. The Commission asked the Secretary-General to prepare a report for its 1958 session on the proportional number of women who participated in the programmes of technical assistance as experts and as holders of scholarships and fellowships during 1956 and 1957.

In discussing the United Nations programme of advisory services in human rights, Commission members expressed satisfaction with the plans being made for a seminar on civic responsibilities and increased participation of Asian women in public life, which was subsequently held in Bangkok, Thailand, in August 1957. It was also felt that this seminar, and similar ones to be held in the future, would help considerably to improve the status of women. The Commission expressed the hope that meetings of this nature would be organized each year, preferably on a regional, but also on an international basis.

Considered at the Economic and Social Council's twenty-fourth session was the question of holding an international seminar on the civic responsibilities of women and their increased role in public life. (For details, see section above on POLITICAL RIGHTS OF WOMEN.)

The holding of seminars on the status of women was also discussed at the General Assembly's twelfth session, in the Assembly's Third (Social, Humanitarian and Cultural) Committee. The outcome of the debate was a resolution (1163(XII)), whereby the Assembly expressed satisfaction at the success of the Bangkok seminar, and hoped that seminars on the status of women would be held as often as possible in the future under the United Nations programme of advisory services in human rights.

The resolution to this effect was unanimously adopted both by the Third Committee and by a plenary meeting of the Assembly (on 26 November 1957). It was based on a proposal sponsored in the Third Committee by Belgium, Cuba, Ecuador, Ethiopia, Guatemala, Israel, Japan, Pakistan, the Philippines, Tunisia and Yugoslavia.

(See also above, CHAPTER IX, section on ADVISORY SERVICES IN HUMAN RIGHTS.)

DOCUMENTARY REFERENCES

ECONOMIC AND SOCIAL COUNCIL—23RD AND 24TH SESSIONS
Plenary Meetings 966, 989.
Social Committee, meetings 364-367.

E/2968. Report of 11th session of Commission on Status of Women, 18 March—5 April 1957. (Commission documents are cited under subject headings in this report.)
RESOLUTION 652 A (XXIV), taking note of report of 11th session of Commission on Status of Women as recommended by Social Committee, adopted by Council unanimously on 24 July 1957, meeting 989.

POLITICAL RIGHTS OF WOMEN
E/2968, Chapter III and Annex. Draft resolution B recommended by Commission, adopted by Social Committee by 15 votes to 0, with 2 abstentions.
E/3030. Report of Social Committee (draft resolution B).
RESOLUTION 652 B (XXIV), as recommended by Social Committee, E/3030, adopted by Council on 24 July 1957, meeting 989, by 15 votes to 0, with 2 abstentions.

"*The Economic and Social Council,*
"*Considering* the importance of recognizing political rights of women,
"*Believing* it important to increase the participation of women in public life,
"*Observing* the significant role of non-governmental organizations in furthering the political rights of women,
"*Recalling* its resolutions 504 E (XVI) of 23 July 1953 and 547 B (XVIII) of 12 July 1954, in which it appealed to States Members of the United Nations, and recommended to non-member States which had been so invited by the General Assembly, to sign, ratify or accede to the Convention on the Political Rights of Women,
"1. *Recommends* all States Members of the United Nations or members of the specialized agencies which have not yet done so to recognize the political rights of women;
"2. *Invites* non-governmental organizations in consultative status with the Economic and Social Council to continue their activities in support of political rights for women, and to apply their efforts towards increasing public support in the various countries for

the signature and ratification of, or accession to, the Convention on the Political Rights of Women;

"3. *Recommends* those States which have been invited to sign and ratify or accede to the Convention on the Political Rights of Women and which have not already done so, to sign and ratify or accede to this Convention."

See also resolution 652 I (XXIV) and relevant documents cited below under TECHNICAL ASSISTANCE IN RELATION TO STATUS OF WOMEN.

A/3627 and Corr.1. Constitutions, electoral laws and other legal instruments relating to political rights of women. Memorandum by Secretary-General.

ACCESS OF WOMEN TO EDUCATION

E/2968, Chapter IV and Annex. Draft resolution C, recommended by Commission, adopted by Social Committee by 17 votes to 0, with 1 abstention.

E/3030. Report of Social Committee (draft resolution C).

RESOLUTION 652 C (XXIV), as recommended by Social Committee, E/3030, adopted by Council on 24 July 1957, meeting 989, by 16 votes to 0, with 1 abstention.

"*The Economic and Social Council,*

"*Considering* that it appears from the analytical summary of information on discrimination in education based on sex prepared by the Secretary-General and from the documents prepared by the United Nations Educational, Scientific and Cultural Organization for the eleventh session of the Commission on the Status of Women that, in parts of the world where the general development of education has not reached an advanced stage, illiteracy is particularly widespread among women and school attendance by girls falls considerably below that by boys,

"*Recalling* its resolutions 547 K (XVIII) of 12 July 1954 and 587 G (XX) of 3 August 1955 in which it recognized that, in such areas, special measures were needed to encourage increased school attendance by girls and also to provide more extensive opportunities for fundamental education of women, and recommended that Governments take legislative and other measures to improve the position of women in the field of education,

"*Considering* that in its resolution 547 K (XVIII) it recommended, *inter alia,* that Governments take the necessary measures to institute free and compulsory primary education,

"*Considering* that many States are prepared to proceed, in co-operation with the United Nations Educational, Scientific and Cultural Organization, with a programme directly benefiting women and facilitating their access to education and to all levels of the teaching profession without discrimination,

"1. *Recommends* that States Members of the United Nations or members of the specialized agencies should in their programmes of educational advancement:

"(*a*) Make provision for equal participation in

fundamental education programmes by all who have not received primary education, and for an intensified campaign against illiteracy among the female population of areas where the general development of education is not advanced;

"(*b*) Make the necessary provision for increased attendance by girls at primary schools by:

(i) Instituting or extending universal, free and compulsory primary education for all;

(ii) Providing a sufficient number of schools, teachers and general education facilities;

"2. *Requests* the United Nations Educational, Scientific and Cultural Organization to continue its studies concerning the access of women to education and, in particular:

"(*a*) To prepare a report on the access of women to higher education, containing a chapter on the distribution, among students of both sexes, of scholarships and other material aids to higher education;

"(*b*) To bring up to date for the twelfth session of the Commission on the Status of Women statistical data contained in its report on the access of women to secondary education which was prepared for the ninth session;

"(*c*) To supplement, for the Commission at its thirteenth session, the documentation relating to the access of women to the teaching profession."

EQUAL PAY FOR EQUAL WORK

E/2968, Chapter V and Annex. Draft resolution D, recommended by Commission, adopted by Social Committee, as orally amended by United States, by 13 votes to 0, with 5 abstentions.

E/AC.7/L.293. USSR amendment to resolution D, submitted by Commission.

E/3030. Report of Social Committee (draft resolution D).

RESOLUTION 652 D (XXIV), as recommended by Social Committee, E/3030, adopted by Council on 24 July 1957, meeting 989, by 13 votes to 0, with 4 abstentions.

"*The Economic and Social Council,*

"*Considering* that the implementation by legislation, collective bargaining or other measures, of the principle of equal remuneration for workers of both sexes is of primary importance in securing respect for women's rights in the economic field,

"*Considering* that non-governmental organizations expressing the wishes of millions of women have repeatedly called for constructive action in this field, in international conferences as well as in meetings at the national and local levels,

"1. *Urges* all Member States of the United Nations to expedite the signing and ratification of the International Labour Convention (No. 100) on Equal Remuneration for Men and Women Workers for Work of Equal Value, or otherwise to carry our their responsibilities with respect to the Convention;

"2. *Recommends* that Governments of Member States implement the principle of equal pay for men and women for equal work, by legislation, by collective bargaining or by other measures;

"3. *Invites* the International Labour Office to continue to provide current information to the Commission on the results of the efforts undertaken by Member States to eliminate wage discrimination against women and to ensure the practical application of the principle of equal pay for equal work."

ECONOMIC OPPORTUNITIES FOR WOMEN

E/2968, Chapter VI and Annex. Draft resolution E, recommended by Commission.

E/AC.7/L.291. United Kingdom amendments to draft resolution E, submitted by Commission.

E/AC.7/L.294. France, Netherlands, United Kingdom joint amendment to draft resolution E, adopted by Social Committee, as amended in Committee, by 8 votes to 2, with 8 abstentions.

E/3030. Report of Social Committee, (draft resolution E).

RESOLUTION 652 E (XXIV), as recommended by Social Committee, E/3030, adopted by Council on 24 July 1957, meeting 989, by 11 votes to 1, with 5 abstentions.

"*The Economic and Social Council*

"1. *Decides* to undertake a global study of the access of women to training and employment in the principal professional and technical fields;

"2. *Requests* the Secretary-General, as a first step in this study, to collect information and prepare, in collaboration with the specialized agencies concerned, a report on the availability of opportunities for women as jurists, architects and engineers, and to that end:

"(*a*) To circulate, to States Members of the United Nations or members of the specialized agencies and to non-governmental organizations in consultative status, the questionnaire annexed to the present resolution, together with a list of the above-mentioned professional and technical occupations as they are described and defined in the International Classification of Occupations for Migration and Employment Placement (Volume I) published by the International Labour Office, June 1952;

"(*b*) To invite such States and non-governmental organizations to transmit their replies to the Secretary-General, if possible before 1 September 1958, or, if such information has already been transmitted to the United Nations or to a specialized agency, to give a precise reference to the information previously furnished;

"(*c*) To prepare, in collaboration with the specialized agencies concerned, a report on this subject for the Commission on the Status of Women at its thirteenth session, on the basis of information received from Member States, specialized agencies, and non-governmental organizations in consultative status with the Economic and Social Council."

ANNEX
Questionnaire

"NOTE: The International Classification of Occupations for Migration and Employment Placement (Volume I), published by the International Labour Office, June 1952, should be used as a general guide in replying to the following questions. The relevant extracts are given below."

I. LEGAL PROFESSION

"1. State whether women have access to positions in this profession at all levels on equal terms with men:

(i) in law—state restrictions, if any, in recruitment and appointments; salaries at all levels; advancement.

(ii) in fact—differences in attitude, if any, in recruitment and appointments; salaries at all levels; advancement.

—statistics showing proportion of men and women in the profession, and effect of marital and/or maternal status.

"2. State whether women have access to training on equal terms with men

(i) in law—state restrictions, if any.

(ii) in fact—differences in attitude, if any, in vocational guidance.

—statistics

number of schools open to women; enrolment."

II. ARCHITECTURE

"Answer the same questions as in I above."

III. ENGINEERING

"Answer the same questions as in I above."

NATIONALITY OF MARRIED WOMEN

E/2968, Chapter VII and Annex. Draft resolution F, recommended by Commission, approved by Social Committee by 13 votes to 0, with 5 abstentions.

E/3030. Report of Social Committee (draft resolution F).

RESOLUTION 652 F (XXIV), as recommended by Social Committee, E/3030, adopted by Council on 24 July 1957, meeting 989, by 12 votes to 1, with 5 abstentions.

"*The Economic and Social Council,*

"*Noting* that the Convention on the Nationality of Married Women, approved by the General Assembly in its resolution 1040(XI) of 29 January 1957, was opened on 20 February 1957 for signature and ratification, or accession, to States Members of the United Nations and any other State which is or hereafter becomes a member of any specialized agency of the United Nations, or which is or hereafter becomes a Party to the Statute of the International Court of Justice,

"1. *Urges* States Members of the United Nations which have not yet done so to sign and ratify, or accede to, the Convention on the Nationality of Married Women;

"2. *Recommends* that States members of the specialized agencies and States Parties to the Statute of the International Court of Justice which have not yet done so sign and ratify, or accede to, the Convention."

STATUS OF WOMEN IN PRIVATE LAW

E/2934; E/2963. Recommendation addressed to Council by United Nations Conference of Plenipotentiaries on Supplementary Convention on Abolition of Slavery, Slave Trade, and Institutions and Practices Similar to Slavery. Notes by Secretary-General.

RESOLUTION 640(XXIII), as orally proposed by Dominican Republic, and as orally amended by United States and United Kingdom, adopted by Council, as proposed by President, on 25 April 1957, meeting 966.

"The Economic and Social Council,

"*Having noted* the recommendation of the United Nations Conference of Plenipotentiaries on a Supplementary Convention on the Abolition of Slavery, the Slave-Trade, and Institutions and Practices Similar to Slavery, that the Council consider the appropriateness of initiating a study of the question of marriage with the object of drawing attention to the desirability of free consent of both parties to a marriage and of the establishment of a minimum age for marriage, preferably of not less than fourteen years,

"*Decides* that a study of these questions should be undertaken by the Commission on the Status of Women."

E/2968, Chapter VIII and Annex. Draft resolution G, recommended by Commission, amended by United States, adopted by Social Committee by 17 votes to 0, with 1 abstention.
E/AC.7/L.292. United States amendment to draft resolution G submitted by Commission.
E/3030. Report of Social Committee (draft resolution G).
RESOLUTION 652 G (XXIV), as recommended by Social Committee, E/3030, adopted by Council on 24 July 1957, meeting 989, by 16 votes to 0, with 1 abstention.

"The Economic and Social Council,

"*Recalling* General Assembly resolution 843(IX) of 17 December 1954,

"*Observing* that the time is appropriate for the introduction of a system of compulsory registration of marriage as a significant safeguard in achieving the free and full consent of intending spouses to marriage, and *considering* that such registration should also relate to divorce,

"*Recommends* to States Members of the United Nations or members of the specialized agencies that they encourage a system whereby prospective spouses in a marriage themselves express their consent freely in the presence of a competent civil or religious authority, and whereby there is compulsory registration of marriage, and *further* that they encourage a system of compulsory registration of divorce."

Legal Status of Married Women. U.N.P. Sales No.: 1957.IV.8.

TAX LEGISLATION AFFECTING MARRIED WOMEN WORKERS

E/2968, Chapter IX and Annex. Draft resolution H, recommended by Commission, adopted unanimously by Social Committee.
E/3030. Report of Social Committee (draft resolution H).
RESOLUTION 652 H (XXIV), as recommended by Social

Committee, E/3030, adopted unanimously by the Council on 24 July 1957, meeting 989.

"The Economic and Social Council,

"*Noting* the importance of having the Commission on the Status of Women study tax legislation applicable to women,

"*Noting further* the insufficiency of available information on this subject,

"*Requests* the Secretary-General:

"1. To invite Governments of States Members of the United Nations and non-governmental organizations in consultative status with the Economic and Social Council to provide precise information on tax legislation applicable to women and especially to married women employed gainfully;

"2. To prepare for the Commission at its thirteenth session a report on this subject, on the basis of information made available by governments of States Members of the United Nations and of additional information supplied by non-governmental organizations in consultative status."

PARTICIPATION OF WOMEN IN WORK OF UNITED NATIONS AND SPECIALIZED AGENCIES

E/2968. Report of 11th session of Commission on Status of Women, Chapter XI.

TECHNICAL ASSISTANCE IN RELATION TO STATUS OF WOMEN

E/2968, Chapters III and X. Report of 11th session of Commission on Status of Women, resolutions 2(XI) and 10(XI).
E/AC.7/L.295. United Kingdom draft resolution, adopted by Social Committee by 7 votes to 6, with 5 abstentions.
E/3030. Report of Social Committee (draft resolution I).
RESOLUTION 652 I (XXIV), as recommended by Social Committee, E/3030, adopted by Council on 24 July 1957, meeting 989, by 11 votes to 5, with 1 abstention.

"The Economic and Social Council,

"*Having considered* resolution 2(XI) adopted by the Commission on the Status of Women at its eleventh session,

"*Requests* the Secretary-General to transmit to the Commission on the Status of Women the records of the discussion of this resolution at the twenty-fourth session of the Economic and Social Council, in order that the Commission may give further consideration to it at its twelfth session in the light of the discussion in the Council."

GENERAL ASSEMBLY—12TH SESSION
Plenary Meeting 723.
Third Committee, meetings 766-779.

A/3613. Report of Economic and Social Council to General Assembly, Chapter VII, Section XI.
A/C.3/L.609. Seminar on Civic Responsibilities and

Increased Participation of Asian Women in Public Life, Bangkok, Thailand, 5-16 August 1957. Note by Secretary-General.

A/C.3/L.612. Belgium, Ecuador, Ethiopia, Guatemala, Japan, Pakistan, Philippines, Yugoslavia draft resolution.

A/C.3/L.612/Rev.1. Belgium, Cuba, Ecuador, Ethiopia, Guatemala, Israel, Japan, Pakistan, Philippines, Tunisia, Yugoslavia revised draft resolution adopted unanimously by Third Committee.

A/3716. Report of Third Committee (draft resolution IV).

RESOLUTION 1163(XII), as recommended by Third Committee, A/3716, adopted unanimously by Assembly on 26 November 1957, meeting 723.

"The General Assembly,

"Taking note of chapter VII, section XI, of the report of the Economic and Social Council,

"Noting with appreciation the work of the Commission on the Status of Women and the progress achieved in the field of women's rights,

"Noting also with satisfaction the success of the seminar held in August 1957 at Bangkok (Thailand) on the civic responsibilities and increased participation of Asian women in public life,

"1. Invites the Commission on the Status of Women to pursue its efforts aimed at the improvement of the status of women throughout the world, in accordance with its terms of reference,

"2. Expresses the hope that seminars on the status of women will be held as frequently as possible in the future under the programme of advisory services in the field of human rights."

1957 Seminar on Civic Responsibilities and Increased Participation of Asian Women in Public Life, Bangkok, 5–16 August 1957. U.N.P. Sales No.: 1957.IV.10.

SESSIONS AND WORK PROGRAMMES OF COMMISSION ON STATUS OF WOMEN

ECONOMIC AND SOCIAL COUNCIL—24TH SESSION
Plenary Meeting 989.
Social Committee, meetings 364-367.

E/3024/Rev.1. Report of Co-ordination Committee.

E/AC.7/L.296. Pakistan draft resolution, adopted by Social Committee by 9 votes to 6, with 3 abstentions.

E/3030. Report of Social Committee (draft resolution J).

RESOLUTION 652 J (XXIV), as recommended by Social Committee, E/3030, and as amended in plenary, adopted by Council on 24 July 1957, meeting 989, by 9 votes to 5, with 3 abstentions.

"The Economic and Social Council,

"Taking note of the recommendation of the Co-ordination Committee that the Council establish the principle that the Commission on the Status of Women should in future meet biennially,

"Recalling that, by its resolution 445 I (XIV) of 26 May 1952, the Council resolved to continue to convene the Commission for one session every year,

"1. Draws the attention of the Commission on the Status of Women to the recommendation of the Co-ordination Committee;

"2. Invites the Commission to express its views on this recommendation;

"3. Decides not to modify for the present the periodicity of the sessions of the Commission on the Status of Women."

See also below, CHAPTER XV, QUESTIONS OF CO-ORDINATION AND RELATIONS OF THE UNITED NATIONS WITH THE SPECIALIZED AGENCIES.

For information about role of women in community development, see below, CHAPTER XII, section on COMMUNITY DEVELOPMENT.

CHAPTER XI

REFUGEES

In 1957, the Office of the United Nations High Commissioner for Refugees was faced with the considerable Hungarian refugee problem in addition to its tasks of providing international protection for refugees and carrying out the programme of the United Nations Refugee Fund (UNREF). About 200,000 Hungarian refugees came into Austria and Yugoslavia in the course of 1957. By the end of that year, 15,000 had returned to Hungary, and permanent solutions had been found for 164,000 in other countries. By that date, the problem in Yugoslavia had

been nearly solved. But solutions were still required for the majority of the 19,000 refugees remaining in Austria.

The continuing need for international protection for the refugees within the High Commissioner's mandate—there are more than one million such refugees in Europe alone—was recognized by the General Assembly at its twelfth session in 1957, when it decided (by resolution 1165(XII)) to continue the Office of the High Commissioner for a further period of five years from 1 January 1959.

The UNREF programme for permanent solutions and emergency aid to refugees reached its full momentum in 1957. By the end of the third quarter of that year, 16,880 refugees had been firmly settled. It became evident, however, the programme would have to be intensified if permanent solutions were to be found for an estimated 14,000 refugees still likely to be in camps by the end of 1958. An estimated $4,800,000 would be required in addition to the $16,000,000 originally set as a target for governmental contributions for the four-year period 1955-1958. Recognizing the need for further international aid to refugees particularly those in refugee camps, the General Assembly, at its twelfth session, adopted a resolution (1166(XII)) on further international aid for refugees.

HUNGARIAN REFUGEE PROBLEM

The flow of Hungarian refugees into Austria and Yugoslavia stopped almost completely in the early months of 1957, and the extent of the situation then became clearer. There were three over-all problems: (1) to find emigration opportunities for refugees wishing to settle in other countries; (2) to obtain funds to reimburse the Austrian and Yugoslav Governments for the heavy expenditures they had incurred on behalf of Hungarian refugees; and (3) to provide aid for the relatively high number of refugees wishing to make their home in Austria.

No particular difficulties occurred in providing legal protection for the refugees from Hungary, as they were generally recognized as coming within the scope of the 1951 Convention relating to the Status of Refugees. A number of Governments gave facilities to Hungarian refugees going beyond those required by the Convention, particularly in regard to the right to work.

Resettlement from Austria, after proceeding satisfactorily in the first half of the year, later tended to slow down. Out of a total influx of about 180,000 refugees, some 19,000 (including about 8,500 in camps), were still in Austria on 31 December 1957. Approximately 11,000 of the 19,000 either wished to remain in Austria or were considered likely to do so through failing to meet the selection criteria of countries of resettlement. The other 8,000 refugees still awaited emigration.

Resettlement from Yugoslavia, on the other hand, increased in tempo during the second half of 1957. By the end of the year, only about 500 of the 20,000 who had arrived were still waiting to leave the country. About 16,000 had emigrated, 2,800 had returned to Hungary and 600 had settled locally. The rest were all expected to leave Yugoslavia within a few weeks.

Much of the success of the resettlement operation was due to the Intergovernmental Committee for European Migration (ICEM) and to the voluntary agencies which worked in Austria and Yugoslavia.

Expenditures incurred by the Austrian Government by the end of 1957 were expected to amount to over $12,200,000. This sum was fully covered by contributions from other Governments made through the Secretary-General of the United Nations, through the High Commissioner's Office or directly. In Yugoslavia, however, the Government was faced with a deficit of about $6,650,000.

A remarkable contribution was made in both countries by the League of Red Cross Societies, which was awarded the Nansen Medal for 1957 in recognition of services rendered to the cause of refugees. In Austria, it supplied direct care and maintenance in camps. In Yugoslavia, it delivered supplies for distribution by the Yugoslav Red Cross. National Red Cross Societies contributed over $3,000,000 in cash and $9,400,000 in kind for the operation in Austria, and $430,000 in cash and nearly $1,100,000 in kind for Yugoslavia.

The needs of Hungarian refugees wishing to settle in Austria were being met in 1957 by an UNREF permanent solutions programme costing $3,500,000. The major part of this was for housing. The programme also provided for educational and other special facilities for young refugees, aid to students and intellectuals and small loans to help refugees to become integrated into the countries they live in. It was also expected that some further aid might be needed for handicapped refugees.

INTERNATIONAL PROTECTION

1951 CONVENTION RELATING
TO THE STATUS OF REFUGEES

The Government of Liechtenstein ratified the Convention relating to the Status of Refugees on 8 March 1957. Tunisia issued a declaration that it considered France's ratification (made before Tunisia became independent) as binding and was applying the Convention. The number of States parties to the Convention by the end of 1957 thus rose to 22.

ADMISSION AND EXPULSION

During 1957, the Office of the High Commissioner continued to assist the Governments of the main countries of asylum in determining the eligibility of refugees. Arrangements to this effect were made by the High Commissioner in Austria, Belgium, France, the Federal Republic of Germany, Greece, Italy, Morocco and the Netherlands. In most cases, the arrangements made have also enabled the Representatives of the High Commissioner in the countries concerned to state their views in cases where refugees are in danger of expulsion or where there are difficulties with regard to their admission.

RIGHT TO WORK

Permanent solutions for the refugee problem depend considerably on the legal status of refugees in their countries of residence. It is therefore particularly important to help them obtain residence permits and permission to work. Austria, France and Italy were among the countries granting further facilities of this kind in 1957.

The Office of the High Commissioner, in consultation with the Organization for European Economic Co-operation (OEEC), continued to promote the carrying out of a decision by the OEEC's Manpower Committee to enable refugees residing in OEEC member countries to be treated as nationals of these countries when taking up residence and employment in other OEEC member countries.

NATURALIZATION

In the course of 1956 and 1957, there was an increase in the number of refugees naturalized, mainly in Austria where some 60,000 refugees of German ethnic origin had acquired Austrian nationality by 31 December 1956. An estimated 20,000 refugees were naturalized during 1956 in Belgium, France, the Federal Republic of Germany, Greece, Italy, the Netherlands, Sweden, the United Kingdom and other European countries.

TRAVEL FACILITIES

By the end of 1957, travel documents under the 1951 Convention relating to the Status of Refugees were being issued by Austria, Belgium, the Federal Republic of Germany, Ecuador, France, Ireland, Italy, Luxembourg, the Netherlands, Norway, Sweden, Switzerland and the United Kingdom. During the year, Haiti and China agreed to give general recognition to Convention travel documents issued by other States. The number of States formally recognizing Convention travel documents thus rose to 14.

Upon the suggestion of the Office of the High Commissioner, negotiations were arranged between various European countries for the bilateral exemption of refugees from visa requirements.

REFUGEE SEAMEN

The Office took part in three conferences called at The Hague by the Netherlands Government which resulted in an Agreement on 23 November 1957 to regularize the legal status of refugee seamen. The Office of the High Commissioner took steps to implement the Agreement and to encourage other Governments to accede to it.

OTHER PROBLEMS

The Office also continued to promote arrangements for educational, social security and legal aid benefits for refugees and for the indemnification of victims of Nazi persecution.

REPATRIATION AND RESETTLEMENT

VOLUNTARY REPATRIATION

The Office of the High Commissioner continued to apply due safeguards to ensure the protection of those refugees considering repatriation. The countries in which they live inform the High Commissioner's Office of the visit of a repatriation mission and invite it to send a representative to accompany the mission as a neutral observer to ensure that no undue influence is exercised on the refugees from any side.

RESETTLEMENT

About 34,000 refugees other than new Hungarian refugees were resettled in the course of 1957 with the aid of the Intergovernmental Committee for European Migration (ICEM), which arranged for their transport. They included nearly 3,000 European refugees who left China via Hong Kong. Only 1,500 refugees of the approximate total of 34,000 were resettled in European countries, including 127 difficult cases for whom permanent care in institutions or otherwise was ensured.

THE UNREF PROGRAMME

In 1957, the UNREF programme entered its third year of operation. By the end of 1957, a sum of about $10,600,000 had been contributed towards the $16,000,000 target for governmental contributions for the period 1955–1958. This was $2,400,000 less than the sum which had been hoped for by that date.

By 30 September 1957, 16,880 refugees had been firmly settled under the programme, including 5,016 from camps. The majority were in Austria (7,841) and Germany (2,757). In addition, 10,716 other refugees had benefited from projects other than those for emergency assistance but had not yet become firmly settled.

A significant part of the UNREF programme concerns the Far Eastern Operation whereby refugees of European origin on the mainland of China are resettled to overseas countries. Their transport costs are covered by ICEM while costs of their care and maintenance in transit in Hong Kong are met by UNREF. Owing to a sudden increase in the number of exit permits being issued on the mainland of China, the number of refugees of European origin arriving in Hong Kong rose considerably during 1957. The funds for transport proving inadequate, ICEM issued a special appeal which the High Commissioner supported. At the end of 1957, there were nevertheless some 1,140 refugees in transit in Hong Kong for whom it was necessary to provide care and maintenance.

It became evident in 1957 that, despite a focusing of the programme on clearing the refugee camps, the financial resources available or anticipated would not suffice to provide solutions for all refugees living in camps by the end of 1958. The number of refugees in camps in Austria, Germany, Greece and Italy, had been reduced from 84,750 at the beginning of 1955 to 58,300 by mid-1957 (including 16,100 new Hungarian refugees). The High Commissioner's Office estimated that, if permanent solutions were to be found for all those refugees in camps for whom the UNREF programme had been designed, it would be necessary not only to recoup the shortfall in governmental contributions but also to find an additional $4,800,000. This problem was brought up at the UNREF Executive Committee's fifth session and sixth (special) session, at the Economic and Social Council's twenty-fourth session, in mid-1957, and subsequently at the General Assembly's twelfth session. The action taken is described below.

ACTION BY EXECUTIVE COMMITTEE OF UNREF

The UNREF Executive Committee held three sessions in 1957, as follows: its fourth session in January-February, its fifth session in June and its sixth (special) session in July.

At its fourth session, the Committee approved the Revised Plan of Operations for 1957. It agreed on a total combined target of $7,096,303 for governmental contributions for 1957, this sum to include the original $4,400,000 target for 1957 and the $2,696,303 shortfall in governmental contributions for 1956.

The Committee also adopted a resolution declaring that the care of the Hungarian refugees was a burden to be shared by the whole world, and supported the High Commissioner's appeals for financial contributions and offers of resettlement.

The Committee was unable to reach a clear decision on the eligibility of Chinese refugees in Hong Kong for assistance. But, considering that their plight was of international concern, it suggested that the General Assembly examine the question at its twelfth session.

At its fifth session, the Committee approved new and revised projects for the Revised Plan of Operations for 1957, bringing the total value of approved projects up to $6,474,664. In addition, it approved a tentative target of $5.1 million for the Revised Plan of Operations for 1958.

Also at the fifth session, the High Commissioner explained that, upon the termination of the UNREF programme at the end of 1958, permanent solutions would still have to be found for some 14,000 refugees living in camps. To finance these permanent solutions would require an estimated $7.5 million. This sum included an anticipated shortfall of $2.7 million in contributions by Governments to the original $16 million target for governmental contributions for the four-year UNREF programme, plus $4.8 million over and above that target.

It was also understood that even after the camps had been cleared of their present occupants, there would still be many refugees outside camps for whom permanent solutions would still be required. The High Commissioner was asked for a special analysis of the non-settled refugee population in various countries to obtain data on which to base plans for helping these refugees.

At its sixth (special) session, the Executive Committee adopted a resolution in favour of intensifying the programme, most representatives agreeing that this would enable the High Commissioner to provide permanent solutions more rapidly and at less cost. Members agreed, too, that the UNREF programme should continue to concentrate primarily on the clearance of camps. Some representatives pointed out that due account should be taken of the need also to assist the non-settled refugees living outside camps.

CONSIDERATION BY THE ECONOMIC AND SOCIAL COUNCIL

At is twenty-third session, the Economic and Social Council confirmed the membership of the UNREF Executive Committee and endorsed its recommendation that Canada be added, thus raising the Committee's membership to 21. It did so by resolution 639(XXIII), adopted on 24 April 1957 by 16 votes to 0, with 2 abstentions.

At the Council's twenty-fourth session, the High Commissioner, in introducing his annual report, said that the UNREF programme was about a year behind schedule. To clear refugee camps in Europe, he recalled, the UNREF Executive Committee had recommended intensifying the UNREF programme. The Executive Committee had also recommended that his office be prolonged in view of the continuing need for international protection of refugees, roughly a million of whom came within his mandate in Europe alone.

Most representatives agreed with these recommendations, and considered also that the High Commissioner should be supported in his appeal for further financial contributions for this purpose. In this connexion, some representatives hoped that contributions would also be forthcoming from those Governments which had not hitherto contributed to the Fund.

On 24 July 1957, the Council adopted a three-part resolution. By the first part (650 A (XXIV)), adopted unanimously, it transmitted the High Commissioner's report to the twelfth session of the General Assembly. By the second part (650 B (XXIV)), it recognized the need for continued international action for refugees and recommended that the High Commissioner's Office be continued for a period of five years after 1 January 1959. This was adopted by 16 votes to 0, with 2 abstentions. The third part (650 C (XXIV)), adopted unanimously, endorsed the UNREF Executive Committee's request that the High Commissioner intensify his programme and recommended that he be authorized to appeal for the additional funds needed to close the camps.

CONSIDERATION BY GENERAL ASSEMBLY

The work of the Office of the United Nations High Commissioner for Refugees was again considered at the General Assembly's twelfth session.

In an introductory statement in the Assembly's Third Committee, the High Commissioner declared that refugees coming under his mandate should be free to choose between the three main solutions: repatriation, resettlement and integration. The most efficient way of dealing with the refugee problem was to give them the necessary assistance speedily enough to avoid a subsequent need for continued material aid.

He considered that the problem of the refugee for whom the UNREF programme had been established, could be solved by an effort similar to that made for Hungarian refugees. Priority was being given to the achievement of solutions for the 39,000 refugees still living in camps, 80 per cent of whom belonged to family units. Their resettlement would be facilitated if, in accordance with the principle of family unity, liberal criteria were applied whenever the refusal of a visa to one family member might jeopardize the resettlement of the whole family.

For those refugees who could not be resettled or did not wish to be repatriated, the only solution was integration in their countries of residence. Housing was the main requirement for this.

As to non-settled refugees living outside camps, the High Commissioner drew attention to the serious position of refugees of European origin in the Far East, and to the existence of an estimated 15,000 difficult cases.

If permanent solutions were to be achieved for the refugee camp population, he stressed, the UNREF programme would have to be intensified. This objective could be achieved by the end of 1960 if the shortfall of $2.7 million in governmental contributions to UNREF were made up and if an additional amount estimated at $4.8 million were contributed to UNREF.

In the course of the debate three draft resolutions were submitted to the Third Committee.

One, put forward by the Netherlands, proposed that the Office of the High Commissioner be continued for five years from 1 January 1959.

The second, on international assistance to refugees, was sponsored by the following 13 Members: Austria, Canada, Chile, Costa Rica, Denmark, Italy, the Netherlands, Norway, Peru, the Philippines, Sweden, the United Kingdom and the United States.

The third draft resolution dealt with the problem of Chinese refugees in Hong Kong. It was submitted by the Netherlands, Turkey and the United States.

Most representatives supported the Netherlands proposal on prolonging the Office of the High Commissioner, which was adopted by the Third Committee on 12 November 1957 by 63 votes to 0, with 10 abstentions. On 26 November, it was finally approved at a plenary meeting of the Assembly as resolution 1165(XII), by a vote of 66 to 0, with 9 abstentions.

The 13-power draft resolution on international assistance to refugees coming within the High Commissioner's mandate made provision, in a revised form, for the following steps, among others: (a) intensification of the UNREF programme for clearing the refugee camps, but without losing sight of the need to seek solutions for the problems of refugees outside camps; (b) appeals by the High Commissioner for the additional funds required for closing the camps; (c) discontinuance of operations under UNREF

after 31 December 1958 (except for projects started but not completed before then), and liquidation of UNREF; (d) future assistance to refugees; (e) appeals for funds to provide supplemental temporary care and maintenance to refugees and to help finance permanent solutions; (f) the establishment of an emergency fund not to exceed $500,000; and (g) replacement of the UNREF Executive Committee by an "Executive Committee of the High Commissioner's Programme", to consist of representatives from 20 to 25 States elected on the widest possible geographical basis from States with a demonstrated interest in, and a devotion to, the solution of refugee problems.

The revised draft resolution also reaffirmed the basic principle laid down in the statute of the High Commissioner's Office regarding forms of permanent solution of the problems of refugees by actions to "facilitate the voluntary repatriation of such refugees, or their assimilation within new national communities".

In the preamble to this draft, it was stated that if the UNREF programme received the necessary funds, it would be able to reduce the number of unsettled refugees by 31 December 1958 to such a point that most countries would be able to support their refugees without international aid. After that date, there would, however, still remain a residual need for international aid in certain countries, especially among certain groups and categories of these refugees.

In introducing this draft resolution, the United States representative expressed support of the High Commissioner for Refugees and said that the arrangements proposed to replace the UNREF programme were adapted to the continuing but constantly changing nature of the refugee problem. They would make it possible to set up specific programmes for solving specific refugee problems as and when the need arose. Interested Governments would be enabled to earmark their contributions for those programmes which were of special interest to them, so that a large number of contributions might be expected. It would be possible at the same time to continue the aid provided under the UNREF programme and to meet emergency situations that might arise.

Many representatives agreed on the need to

intensify the UNREF programme, and stressed the necessity to solve the problems of those refugees still in camps. Several hoped that Governments which had not yet done so would contribute to UNREF.

The representative of France and others stressed the need to continue aid to those refugees outside camps who were not yet firmly settled.

The French representative also maintained—as did the spokesmen of Denmark and the United Kingdom—that responsibility for aiding refugees should be transferred at an early date to the Governments of the countries where the refugees resided. Others, however, considered this either undesirable or difficult to put into practice.

Representatives of the USSR and of most other countries of origin of refugees considered that repatriation was the best way to solve the refugee problem.

On 12 November 1957, the Third Committee adopted the revised 13-power draft, with some oral amendments, by 59 votes to 0, with 14 abstentions. On 26 November, it was approved at a plenary meeting of the Assembly by a vote of 63 to 0, and 10 abstentions, as resolution 1166(XII). (For text, see DOCUMENTARY REFERENCES, below.)

By a third resolution, approved on 26 November, the Assembly appealed to Members of the United Nations and specialized agencies and non-governmental organizations to give all possible assistance in alleviating the distress of the Chinese refugees in Hong Kong. It authorized the High Commissioner for Refugees to use his good offices to encourage arrangements for contributions.

The resolution to this effect (1167(XII)) was approved by a vote of 50 for, 9 against, and 11 abstentions. It was previously approved in the Third Committee on the basis of a proposal by the Netherlands, Turkey and the United States.

During the discussion of the proposal, the representative of China maintained that the international community could not disclaim responsibility for assistance to this group of refugees. Other representatives, however, could see no possibility of solving the problem without the participation of the People's Republic of China.

The proposal on Chinese refugees in Hong Kong was adopted by the Third Committee on 12 November by 43 votes to 10, with 14 abstentions.

CONTRIBUTION PLEDGES

On 4 October 1957, the Ad Hoc Committee of the General Assembly met for the announcement of pledges of contributions to UNREF. Of the 82 Member States and 5 non-member States invited to attend, approximately 65 were represented. Contributions to UNREF totalling about $3.3 million were pledged by 12 Governments. Other pledges were made later.

DOCUMENTARY REFERENCES

MEMBERSHIP OF UNREF EXECUTIVE COMMITTEE

ECONOMIC AND SOCIAL COUNCIL—23RD SESSION
Plenary Meeting 965.

E/2954. Note by Secretary-General.
E/L.747. Brazil, France, Netherlands, United Kingdom, United States draft resolution.
RESOLUTION 634(XXIII), as submitted in E/L.747, adopted by Council on 24 April 1957, meeting 965, by 16 votes to 0, with 2 abstentions.

"The Economic and Social Council,
"Recalling its resolution 565(XIX) of 31 March 1955 establishing the United Nations Refugee Fund Executive Committee,
"Noting that the Executive Committee has recommended the addition of Canada to the membership of the Committee, that the High Commissioner for Refugees has welcomed the suggestion and that Canada has expressed its willingness to serve,

"Decides:
"1. To confirm the membership of those States at present serving on the United Nations Refugee Fund Executive Committee;
"2. To amend Council resolution 565(XIX) to increase the membership of the Committee to twenty-one;
"3. To add Canada to the membership of the Committee."

ANNUAL REPORT OF HIGH COMMISSIONER FOR REFUGEES; PROPOSAL TO PROLONG OFFICE OF HIGH COMMISSIONER FOR REFUGEES; INTENSIFICATION OF UNREF PROGRAMME

ECONOMIC AND SOCIAL COUNCIL—24TH SESSION
Plenary Meetings 988, 989.

E/3015 and Add.1, 2. Report of United Nations High Commissioner for Refugees, including reports of 4th, 5th and 6th (special) sessions of UNREF Executive Committee.

E/L.760. Brazil, Canada, France, Netherlands, United Kingdom and United States draft resolution.

E/L.762. Greece amendment to joint draft resolution.

RESOLUTION 650 A-C (XXIV), as submitted jointly by six Powers, E/L.760, and as amended by Greece and orally by the Netherlands, adopted by Council on 24 July 1957, meeting 989, as follows: 650 A and C (XXIV), unanimously; 650 B (XXIV), by 16 votes to 0, with 2 abstentions.

A

"The Economic and Social Council,

"Having considered the report of the United Nations High Commissioner for Refugees, with the annexed reports of the United Nations Refugee Fund Executive Committee on its fourth, fifth and sixth (special) sessions,

"Takes note of the report prepared by the High Commissioner for transmission to the twelfth regular session of the General Assembly.

B

"The Economic and Social Council,

"Recalling that the General Assembly, in its resolution 727(VIII) of 23 October 1953, decided to review, not later than at its twelfth regular session, the arrangements for the Office of the High Commissioner for Refugees with a view to determining whether the Office should be continued beyond 31 December 1958,

"Noting that the United Nations Refugee Fund Executive Committee, in paragraph 79 of the report on its fifth session, unanimously decided to recommend that the Office of the High Commissioner be continued for a further period beyond 31 December 1958,

"Recognizing that the need for international action on behalf of refugees will persist after that date,

"Appreciating the valuable work which has been performed by the Office of the High Commissioner in this regard,

"1. *Considers* that the Office of the High Commissioner should be continued for a period of five years from 1 January 1959;

"2. *Recommends* that the General Assembly review, not later than at its seventeenth regular session, the arrangements for the Office of the High Commissioner, with a view to determining whether the Office should be further continued."

C

"The Economic and Social Council,

"Recognizing the value of the United Nations Refugee Fund programme in achieving solutions for the problems of refugees,

"Noting the progress achieved in the implementation of the programme,

"Recognizing the importance of achieving permanent solutions for the refugees in camps as quickly as possible,

"Considering that the closure of the refugee camps will be practicable only to the extent that adequate funds are made available,

"Having considered the report of the United Nations Refugee Fund Executive Committee on its sixth session (special) and in particular resolution No. 6 adopted at that session,

"1. *Endorses* the request made to the High Commissioner in that resolution to the effect that he should intensify his programme to the fullest extent possible in order to achieve permanent solutions for the maximum number of refugees remaining in camps, without losing sight of the need to continue to seek solutions for the problems of refugees outside camps;

"2. *Recommends* that the General Assembly authorize the High Commissioner to make an appeal to States Members of the United Nations or of the specialized agencies for the purpose of raising funds needed for closing the refugee camps."

GENERAL ASSEMBLY—12TH SESSION
Plenary Meeting 723.
General Committee, meeting 111.
Ad Hoc Committee of Whole Assembly, meeting 2.
Third Committee, meetings 800-809.

A/3585/Rev.1. Report of United Nations High Commissioner for Refugees, including reports of 4th, 5th and 6th (special) sessions of UNREF Executive Committee.

A/3585/Rev.1/Add.1. Survey of non-settled refugee population in various countries. Note by High Commissioner.

A/3613. Report of Economic and Social Council to General Assembly, Chapter VI, Section IV.

PROLONGATION OF OFFICE
OF HIGH COMMISSIONER

A/3669. Review of arrangements for Office of United Nations High Commissioner for Refugees. Note by Secretary-General.

A/C.3/L.638. Netherlands draft resolution adopted by Third Committee, meeting 807, by 62 votes to 0, with 10 abstentions.

A/3737 and Add.1/Rev.1. Report of Third Committee, (draft resolution I).

RESOLUTION 1165(XII), as recommended by Third Committee, A/3737, adopted by Assembly on 26 November 1957, meeting 723, by 66 votes to 0, with 9 abstentions.

"The General Assembly,

"Having taken note of the report of the United Nations High Commissioner for Refugees,

"Having regard to its resolution 727(VIII) of 23 October 1953 in which it decided to review, not later than at its twelfth session, the arrangements for the Office of the United Nations High Commissioner for Refugees with a view to determining whether the Office should be continued beyond 31 December 1958,

"Considering the continuing need for international action on behalf of refugees,

"Considering the valuable work which has been performed by the Office of the High Commissioner both in providing international protection for refugees and in promoting permanent solutions for their problems,

"*Noting with appreciation* the effective manner in which the Office of the High Commissioner has been dealing with special emergencies

"*Noting* the recommendation adopted by the Economic and Social Council in its resolution 650 B (XXIV) of 24 July 1957,

"1. *Decides* to continue the Office of the United Nations High Commissioner for Refugees for a period of five years from 1 January 1959 on the basis of the Statute of the Office;

"2. *Decides* that the election of the United Nations High Commissioner for Refugees, for a period of five years from 1 January 1959, shall take place at the thirteenth session of the General Assembly;

"3. *Decides* to review, not later than at its seventeenth session, the arrangements for the Office of the High Commissioner with a view to determining whether the Office should be further continued beyond 31 December 1963."

INTERNATIONAL ASSISTANCE TO REFUGEES

A/C.3/L.639 and Add.1, and Rev.1. Austria, Canada, Chile, Costa Rica, Denmark, Italy, Netherlands, Norway, Peru, Philippines, Sweden, United Kingdom, United States draft resolution and revision, as amended orally by Saudi Arabia, adopted by Third Committee, meeting 808, by 59 votes to 0, with 14 abstentions.

A/C.3/L.640. Venezuela amendment to 13-power draft resolution.

A/C.3/L.641. Egypt, Iraq, Jordan, Saudi Arabia, Sudan, Syria amendment to 13-power draft resolution.

A/C.3/L.642. Saudi Arabia amendments to 13-power draft resolution.

A/3737 and Add.1/Rev.1. Report of Third Committee (draft resolution II).

RESOLUTION 1166(XII), as recommended by Third Committee, A/3737, adopted by Assembly on 26 November 1957, meeting 723, by 63 votes to 0, with 10 abstentions.

"*The General Assembly,*

"*Having considered* the problem of those refugees within the mandate of the United Nations High Commissioner for Refugees who are the concern of the United Nations Refugee Fund (UNREF),

"*Noting with approval* that the United Nations Refugee Fund programme, if it receives the necessary funds, will, by 31 December 1958, have reduced the number of non-settled refugees under the programme to the point where most countries of asylum should be able to support these refugees without international assistance,

"*Recognizing* that, after 31 December 1958, there will be a residual need for international aid in certain countries, and particularly among certain groups and categories of these refugees,

"*Bearing in mind* that new refugee situations requiring international assistance have arisen to augment the problem since the establishment of the Fund, and that other such situations may arise in the future wherein international assistance may be appropriate,

"*Bearing in mind* that, under the Statute of his Office, the High Commissioner is charged with the duty of seeking solutions for the problems of refugees through voluntary repatriation, resettlement and integration,

"*Recalling* its resolution 538 B (VI) of 2 February 1952, in which the General Assembly authorized the High Commissioner to issue an appeal for funds for the purpose of enabling emergency aid to be given to the most needy groups among refugees within his mandate,

"*Recalling* its resolution 832(IX) of 21 October 1954, in which it authorized the High Commissioner to undertake a programme to be devoted principally to the promotion of permanent solutions for certain refugees coming within his mandate and also to permit emergency assistance to the most needy cases among these refugees, and to appeal for voluntary contributions towards a fund set up for the purpose of this programme and incorporating the fund authorized by the General Assembly in resolution 538 B (VI),

"*Further recalling* Economic and Social Council resolution 565(XIX) of 31 March 1955, by which the Council reconstituted the High Commissioner's Advisory Committee on Refugees as an Executive Committee,

"*Having considered* Economic and Social Council resolution 650(XXIV) of 24 July 1957,

"1. *Approves* the recommendations contained in Economic and Social Council resolution 650(XXIV) of 24 July 1957, and accordingly:

"(a) Requests the United Nations High Commissioner for Refugees to intensify the United Nations Refugee Fund programme to the fullest extent possible in order to achieve permanent solutions for the maximum number of refugees remaining in camps, without losing sight of the need to continue to seek solutions for the problems of refugees outside camps;

"(b) Authorizes the High Commissioner to appeal to States Members of the United Nations or members of the specialized agencies for the purpose of raising the additional funds needed for closing the refugee camps;

"2. *Reaffirms* the basic principle laid down in paragraph 1 of the Statute of the High Commissioner's Office regarding forms of permanent solution of the problems of refugees, by actions designed to "facilitate the voluntary repatriation of such refugees, or their assimilation within new national communities";

"3. *Decides* that the operations under the United Nations Refugee Fund shall not be continued after 31 December 1958 except as provided for in paragraph 4 below;

"4. *Requests* the High Commissioner to supervise the orderly completion of projects financed from the United Nations Refugee Fund which were started but not completed before 31 December 1958, and to carry out the liquidation of the Fund in accordance with paragragh 5(a) below;

"5. *Requests* the Economic and Social Council to establish, not later than at its twenty-sixth session, an Executive Committee of the High Commissioner's

Programme to consist of representatives of from twenty to twenty-five States Members of the United Nations or members of any of the specialized agencies, to be elected by the Council on the widest possible geographical basis from those States with a demonstrated interest in, and devotion to, the solution of the refugee problem, this Committee to take the place of the UNREF Executive Committee and to be entrusted with the terms of reference set forth below:

"(*a*) To give directives to the High Commissioner for the liquidation of the United Nations Refugee Fund;

"(*b*) To advise the High Commissioner, at his request, in the exercise of his functions under the Statute of his Office;

"(*c*) To advise the High Commissioner as to whether it is appropriate for international assistance to be provided through his Office in order to help solve specific refugee problems remaining unsolved after 31 December 1958 or arising after that date;

"(*d*) To authorize the High Commissioner to make appeals for funds to enable him to solve the refugee problems referred to in sub-paragraph (*c*) above;

"(*e*) To approve projects for assistance to refugees coming within the scope of sub-paragraph (*c*) above;

"(*f*) To give directives to the High Commissioner for the use of the emergency fund to be established under the terms of paragraph 7 below;

"6. *Authorizes* the High Commissioner, under conditions approved by the Executive Committee of the High Commissioner's Programme, to make appeals for the funds needed to provide supplemental temporary care and maintenance to, and participate in the financing of permanent solutions for, refugees coming within his mandate and otherwise not provided for;

"7. *Further authorizes* the High Commissioner to establish an emergency fund not to exceed $500,000, to be utilized under general directives of the Executive Committee of the High Commissioner's Programme, and to maintain this fund from the repayments of the principal and interest of loans made by the United Nations Refugee Fund and from voluntary contributions made for this purpose;

"8. *Decides* that appropriate financial rules for the use of all funds received by the High Commissioner under the terms of the present resolution shall be established, in consultation with the Executive Committee of the High Commissioner's Programme, and in accordance with the Statute of the Office of the High Commissioner and the Financial Regulations of the United Nations;

"9. *Requests* the UNREF Executive Committee to exercise in 1958 such functions incumbent upon the Executive Committee of the High Commissioner's Programme in conformity with paragraph 5 above as it deems necessary, with a view to assuring the continuity of international assistance to refugees falling within the scope of paragraph 5(*c*) above;

"10. *Requests* the High Commissioner to include in his annual report a statement on the measures which he has taken under the terms of the present resolution."

CHINESE REFUGEES IN HONG KONG

A/C.3/L.643. Netherlands, Turkey, United States, draft resolution, as orally amended by Saudi Arabia, adopted by Third Committee, meeting 808, by 43 votes to 10, with 14 abstentions.

A/3737 and Add.1/Rev.1. Report of Third Committee (draft resolution III).

RESOLUTION 1167(XII), as recommended by Third Committee, A/3737, adopted by Assembly on 26 November 1957, meeting 723, by 50 votes to 9, with 11 abstentions.

"*The General Assembly,*

"*Having considered* the problem of the Chinese refugees in Hong Kong, in accordance with the resolution adopted by the Executive Committee of the United Nations Refugee Fund at its fourth session,

"*Acknowledging* the heavy burden placed upon the Government of Hong Kong in dealing with this problem, and the efforts made to alleviate it,

"*Recognizing however* that the problem is such as to be of concern to the international community,

"*Taking into account* the need for emergency and long-term assistance,

"1. *Appeals* to States Members of the United Nations and members of the specialized agencies and to non-governmental organizations to give all possible assistance with a view to alleviating the distress of the Chinese refugees in Hong Kong;

"2. *Authorizes* the United Nations High Commissioner for Refugees to use his good offices to encourage arrangements for contributions."

OTHER DOCUMENTS

E/AC.79/95. Further report on problem of Hungarian refugees, submitted by High Commissioner to 7th session of UNREF Executive Committee.

CHAPTER XII

SOCIAL AND POPULATION QUESTIONS

THE WORLD SOCIAL SITUATION

REPORT ON WORLD SOCIAL SITUATION

The *Report on the World Social Situation* was discussed in 1957 at the eleventh session of the Social Commission and at the twenty-fourth session of the Economic and Social Council.

It consisted of two parts. The first dealt with population trends, health, food, nutrition and educational conditions, and conditions of work and employment, especially in the economically under-developed areas of the world. The second part dealt particularly with the social problems arising from urbanization in economically under-developed areas, and contained special chapters also on urbanization in Africa south of the Sahara and in Latin America.

The *Report* was prepared by the United Nations Secretariat in collaboration with the International Labour Organisation (ILO), the Food and Agriculture Organization (FAO), the United Nations Educational, Scientific and Cultural Organization (UNESCO) and the World Health Organization (WHO).

The *Report* showed that social conditions had improved significantly in many parts of the world in recent years. The improvements, however, were quite uneven in the different fields of development, in different economic classes within countries, and in the different countries. Measured against the magnitude of the needs in the less developed countries or against the potentialities for progress now offered by modern science and technology, the progress achieved appeared less impressive. In almost all areas, the gap in income per person between the developed and the less developed countries was widening because industry, found mainly in the developed countries, was expanding more rapidly than agriculture, the chief form of economic activity in the under-developed countries. On the other hand, the gap in mortality rates was narrowing because deaths due to communicable diseases, which particularly affected the less developed countries, were everywhere declining much more rapidly than deaths due to degenerative diseases, the main cause of deaths in the developed countries.

The uneven rates of growth of change in different fields had serious social and economic implications. For example, the rapid drop in death rates in less developed countries was causing unparalleled population expansions, and was necessitating exceptional investments in educational and health services and in food production, in order to maintain even the existing standards. Moreover, the uneven increase in productivity in different segments of various economies, such as industry, services and agriculture, could raise prices of certain essential commodities and services, with resulting inflationary tendencies that would adversely affect the levels of living of different occupational groups. (See also below, under heading BALANCED ECONOMIC AND SOCIAL DEVELOPMENT.)

Urbanization was taking place at a very rapid rate in some of the less developed countries. It was, indeed, taking place more rapidly than industrialization, with the result that cities were growing without a proper economic base. There was considerable instability of employment and a shifting of under-employment and poverty from country to city. The *Report* described in some detail the social problems arising from rapid urbanization, with regard to labour, housing, health, nutrition, conditions of family living, changes in social structure and social organization, and crime and delinquency. (See also below, under heading URBANIZATION.)

The *Report* was extensively discussed both in the Social Commission and in the Economic and Social Council. Such reports, it was pointed out, served as a guide for international social policy, and at the same time played an important role in the formulation and development of national social policy.

Members of these bodies expressed gratification at the recent advances in the world social situation. Some representatives, however, deplored the limited nature of these improvements and pointed to a number of unsolved social problems. Some speakers hoped, too, that future *Reports* would give more attention to such subjects as human freedoms, transport, social security, the inter-relationship between economic and social factors, and the effect of international technical assistance programmes. Some Council members also maintained that the information on the People's Republic of China was inadequate. Concern was expressed, too, in the Council at the widening gap in the income between developed and under-developed countries, and at the lack of progress in housing.

The debate in the Council was opened by the Secretary-General. Reviewing some of the *Report*'s conclusions, he expressed qualified optimism regarding current trends in social progress. There was a lack of knowledge, he said, about how to continue the elements of social and economic progress in such a way as to promote optimum development. Questions of balance and integration in development deserved special study. He also stressed the seriousness of the urbanization problem and the need for continuing to give attention to it.

Replying to some of the points made in the Council's debate, a representative of the Secretary-General assured Council members that their suggestions would be given the most serious attention. In a number of cases, however, the appropriate information requested for inclusion in *Report on the World Social Situation* was either unavailable or inadequate or, in some cases, such as social security, available in other United Nations publications.

Among the other matters debated in the Council was a USSR proposal that the Council express the hope that the Governments concerned would conclude an agreement forthwith on discontinuing their nuclear weapon tests. This proposal was put forward in connexion with references in the *Report on the World Social Situation* to some of the effects of radiation. It was, however, rejected on 31 July 1957, one major reason being that it lay outside the Council's competence. The vote, by roll call, was 12 against to 6 in favour, with 1 abstention.

On 31 July, the Council adopted a number of resolutions on matters arising out of the discussion on the world social situation.

By one resolution (663 E (XXIV)), approved by a vote of 16 to 0, with 2 abstentions, the Council asked the Secretary-General, among other things, for: (*a*) a survey of social development programmes to be submitted in 1959; (*b*) a report, to be submitted in 1961, comprising a brief survey of major trends in the social situation and a study of balanced economic and social development; (*c*) a report on the world social situation, to be submitted in 1963, including a comprehensive review of changes in levels of living throughout the world and analyses of such special problems as the situation might demand. At the same time, the Secretary-General was also asked, in collaboration with specialized agencies, to explore ways of improving the quality of information available for an analysis of the world social situation and to undertake various steps and studies in this regard.

This resolution was adopted on the basis of a proposal by the Social Commission.

Another Council resolution (663 I (XXIV)), also adopted on 31 July 1957 on the Commission's proposal, noted that the *Report on the World Social Situation* recommended that Government co-operation in the social field be extended. It particularly recommended that Governments promote and encourage personal contacts and the exchange of experience between experts. The vote for this was 17 to 1. (See also below, under headings URBANIZATION and BALANCED ECONOMIC AND SOCIAL DEVELOPMENT.)

URBANIZATION

During 1957, both the Social Commission and the Economic and Social Council attached special importance to continued examination of the urbanization problem. (See also above, under heading REPORT ON WORLD SOCIAL SITUATION.)

In the Council's debate on the world social situation, for instance, several members stressed the need to view not only the economic and social aspects of development together but also the rural and urban aspects, since the problems of urbanization in less developed countries derived to a large extent from the poverty, backwardness and lack of social services in rural areas from which migrants fled to the cities.

Various specific recommendations were made for action to raise rural levels of living as part of the solution to the social problems of urbanization. Various specific recommendations were made in that connexion. According to some representatives, urbanization should be recognized as inevitable and not necessarily bad. The aim should be to take action against the negative aspects.

In a resolution dealing both with urbanization and the need for balanced economic and social development, the Council urged the Secretary-General and invited the specialized agencies to continue their work on urbanization, looking towards the evolution of integrated policies in this field, with due regard to both the rural and the urban aspects of the question. The resolution on this (663 H (XXIV)) was unanimously adopted on 31 July.

BALANCED ECONOMIC AND SOCIAL DEVELOPMENT

During its debate on the world social situation, the Council also gave special attention to questions of balance in the factors of development and of interactions between social and economic development. Several members observed that progress in one direction could cause difficulties in others. At the same time, it was noted that the difficulties were not easy to anticipate.

By resolution 663 H (XXIV), unanimously adopted on 31 July, the Council expressed concern over the uneven development indicated in the *Report on the World Social Situation*. It considered the problems of balance among the factors of development to be of special importance.

By resolution 663 E (XXIV), as indicated above, the Council asked the Secretary-General to prepare a study of balanced economic and social development.

The importance of balanced and integrated economic and social development was again stressed later in the year at the General Assembly's twelfth session during discussions on the Council's annual report which took place in the Assembly's Third (Social, Humanitarian and Cultural) Committee.

On the basis of a proposal originally introduced in this Committee by Ceylon, Cuba, El Salvador, Guatemala, Pakistan, the Philippines, the United Kingdom and the United States, the Assembly adopted a resolution, recommending that the Economic and Social Council, in co-operation with the specialized agencies, intensify its efforts in the study and recommendation of measures to effect balanced and integrated economic and social progress. The resolution to this effect (1161(XII)) was adopted at a plenary meeting of the Assembly on 26 November 1957 by 67 votes to 0, with 9 abstentions. Prior to that, it was approved in the Third Committee by 45 votes to 0, with 8 abstentions.

DOCUMENTARY REFERENCES

ECONOMIC AND SOCIAL COUNCIL—24TH SESSION
Plenary Meetings 984-987, 994.
Social Committee, meetings 368-371.

REPORT ON WORLD SOCIAL SITUATION
E/3008. Report of 11th session of Social Commission, 6-24 May 1957. (See Annex IV of this report for listing of Commission documents.)
Report on the World Social Situation, including studies of urbanization in under-developed areas. U.N.P. Sales No.: 1957.IV.3.

ORGANIZATION OF REPORTS
E/3008, Annex III. Draft resolution D, recommended by Social Commission, approved unanimously by Social Committee.
E/3035. Report of Social Committee (draft resolution E).
RESOLUTION 663 E (XXIV), as recommended by Social Committee, E/3035, adopted by Council on 31 July 1957, meeting 994, by 16 votes to 0, with 2 abstentions.

"The Economic and Social Council
"1. Requests the Secretary-General to publish, at least four months in advance of each session of the Social Commission, a report under the heading 'World social situation', and specifically:
"(a) To prepare, for the Commission at its twelfth session and for the Council at its twenty-eighth session (1959), a survey of programmes of social development, and to circulate a questionnaire to Governments and to appropriate non-governmental organizations as one means of obtaining information for this report;
"(b) To prepare, for the Social Commission at its thirteenth session and for the Council at its thirty-second session (1961), a report including, in part I, a brief survey of major trends in the social situation and, in part II, a study of balanced economic and social development;
"(c) To prepare, for the Social Commission at its fourteenth session and for the Council at its thirty-sixth session (1963), a report on the world social situation including a comprehensive review of changes

in levels of living throughout the world and analyses of such special problems as the situation demands;

"2. *Further requests* the Secretary-General, in collaboration with the specialized agencies, to explore ways and means of improving the quality of the data available for analysis of the world social situation and, in this connexion:

"(*a*) To establish contacts, through the Governments concerned, with centres engaged in research on social problems of economically under-developed areas, and, through technical assistance and other means, to assist Governments in strengthening research on problems of social policy;

"(*b*) To study the major gaps in the information needed for an evaluation of the world social situation, and the most effective action to improve knowledge in this field;

"(*c*) To undertake a review of the scope and organization of the report on the world social situation, the major types of data and analyses that should be included in successive reports and the possibility of issuing future reports on the world social situation at more frequent intervals, and to present recommendations to the Social Commission at its thirteenth session;

"3. *Invites* the co-operation of the specialized agencies concerned in these efforts."

DEVELOPMENTS OF PERSONAL CONTACTS

E/L.758. USSR draft resolution, as amended by United Kingdom and United States (E/AC.7/ L.299) and by other oral amendments, adopted by Social Committee by 17 votes to 1.

E/AC.7/L.299. United Kingdom and United States amendment to USSR draft resolution, E/L.758.

E/3035. Report of Social Committee (draft resolution I).

RESOLUTION 663 I (XXIV), as recommended by Social Committee, E/3035, adopted by Council on 31 July 1957, meeting 994, by 17 votes to 1.

"*The Economic and Social Council,*

"*Noting* that the *Report on the World Social Situation* contains useful information on the exchange of experience between States in the matter of raising and improving the social conditions of broad sectors of the population in many countries of the world;

"*Considering* that international co-operation and personal contacts in the social field will facilitate the development of mutual understanding between peoples;

"*Recommends* that Governments extend international co-operation in the social field and, in particular, promote and encourage the development of personal contacts and the exchange of experience among experts in the social field."

SUSPENSION OF NUCLEAR TESTS
E/L.759, E/L.766. USSR draft resolution.

URBANIZATION AND BALANCED ECONOMIC AND SOCIAL DEVELOPMENT

E/AC.7/L.301. Brazil, Egypt, Finland draft resolu-

tion, as amended orally by Argentina, Canada, and United Kingdom, adopted unanimously by Social Committee.

E/3035. Report of Social Committee (draft resolution H).

RESOLUTION 663 H (XXIV), as recommended by Social Committee, E/3035, adopted unanimously by Council on 31 July 1957, meeting 994.

"*The Economic and Social Council,*

"*Having examined* the *Report on the World Social Situation,*

"1. *Endorses* the opinion of the Social Commission regarding the importance and value of the reports on the world social situation;

"2. *Commends* the Secretary-General and the specialized agencies concerned on the high quality of the present report;

"3. *Expresses its gratification* with the social progress noted in the present report;

"4. *Expresses concern* over the uneven development in various sectors within countries as well as between different countries;

"5. *Considers of special importance* the problems of balance among the factors of development, having regard especially to the interaction between developments in the economic and in the social fields;

"6. *Attaches special importance also* to the question of urbanization and *urges* the Secretary-General and *invites* the specialized agencies concerned to continue their work in this field, looking towards the evolution of integrated policies in the field of urbanization to be developed with due regard to both rural and urban aspects of the problem."

See also resolution 663 E (XXIV), above.

GENERAL ASSEMBLY—12TH SESSION
Plenary Meeting 723.
Third Committee, meetings 766-779.

A/3713. Report of Economic and Social Council to General Assembly, Chapter VI, Section I, World Social Situation.

A/C.3/L.613. Ceylon, Cuba, El Salvador, Guatemala, Pakistan, Philippines, United Kingdom, United States draft resolution, adopted by Third Committee as amended in Committee, by 45 votes to 0, with 8 abstentions.

A/3716. Report of Third Committee (draft resolution II).

RESOLUTION 1161(XII), as recommended by Third Committee, A/3716, adopted by Assembly on 26 November 1957, meeting 723, by 67 votes to 0, with 9 abstentions.

"*The General Assembly,*

"*Having considered* chapters VI and VII of the report of the Economic and Social Council and Council resolution 663 H (XXIV) of 31 July 1957 on the world social situation,

"*Noting* that in this report it was stated that the elements of economic and social progress were now known but that knowledge was lacking on how to combine them in such a way as to promote optimum development,

"*Considering* that problems of economic and social development interact upon each other,

"*Realizing* that a balanced and integrated economic and social development would contribute towards the promotion and maintenance of peace and security, social progress and better standards of living, and the observance of, and respect for, human rights and fundamental freedom for all,

"1. *Commends* the Economic and Social Council

for the work done during the period under review;

"2. *Notes* the programmes of work approved by the Economic and Social Council for the ensuing two years, particularly the study of balanced economic and social development called for in paragraph 1 (*b*) of Council resolution 663 E (XXIV) of 31 July 1957;

"3. *Recommends* that the Economic and Social Council, in co-operation with the specialized agencies, intensify its efforts in the study and recommendation of measures to effect a balanced and integrated economic and social progress."

OTHER SOCIAL POLICY QUESTIONS

SOCIAL ASPECTS OF INDUSTRIALIZATION

In 1956, at its twenty-second session, the Economic and Social Council adopted a resolution (618(XXII)) calling for a broad programme of action in the field of industrialization. In May 1957, at its eleventh session, the Social Commission recommended that the following projects be carried out under the work programme on industrialization during the period 1957–1959: (1) case studies on the relationship of community development and co-operatives to industrialization; (2) a study on current trends in environmental planning; (3) a seminar on environmental planning and the location of industry for Asia and the Far East; and (4) a study of general social services in relation to industrialization. (See also above, CHAPTER III, section on INDUSTRIALIZATION AND PRODUCTIVITY.)

MEASUREMENT OF LEVELS OF LIVING

In May 1957, the Social Commission adopted a programme of work for 1957–1959[1] which, among other things, called for a continuation of efforts to develop the measurement of levels of living, with further attention to be given to

the measurement of the non-material aspect of levels of living and family living surveys. Preliminary work on this was begun later in 1957.

CONCERTED PRACTICAL ACTION IN SOCIAL FIELD

The programme of work adopted by the Social Commission in 1957 also envisaged continuous review of the co-ordination of the social programmes of the United Nations and the specialized agencies.

On 1 August, by resolution 665 C (XXIV), the Economic and Social Council asked the Secretary-General for an appraisal of the scope, trend and cost of the United Nations programmes in the social field for the period 1959–1964 in order to promote the development of co-ordination between the activities of the United Nations and the specialized agencies. (For further details and text of this resolution see below, CHAPTER XV, under heading DEVELOPMENT AND CO-ORDINATION OF PROGRAMMES AND ACTIVITIES.)

[1] The Commission's future work programme for 1957-1959, which covered all the activities of the United Nations in the social field, was unanimously approved by the Economic and Social Council on 31 July 1957 by resolution 663 A (XXIV).

DOCUMENTARY REFERENCES

E/3008. Report of 11th session of Social Commission, 6-24 May 1957. Chapter VII, and (for list of documents before Commission) Annex IV.

FUTURE WORK PROGRAMME

ECONOMIC AND SOCIAL COUNCIL—24TH SESSION
Plenary Meetings 984-987, 994.
Social Committee, meetings 368-371.

E/3008. Report of 11th session of Social Commission,

6-24 May 1957. Chapter VII, and Annexes II, III and V.

E/AC.7/L.797. Yugoslavia draft resolution, adopted unanimously by Social Committee.

E/1035. Report of Social Committee (draft resolution A).

RESOLUTION 663 A (XXIV), taking note of Social Commissions report and approving Commission's work programme for 1957-1959, unanimously adopted by Council on 31 July 1957, meeting 994.

COMMUNITY DEVELOPMENT

A report by the Secretary-General on the concepts and principles of community development was considered by the Social Commission at its eleventh session in May 1957 and at the Economic and Social Council's twenty-fourth session, in mid-1957. This report also contained proposals for a long-range practical programme for international action in community development.

The programme provided for the following: (1) strengthening of international leadership and co-operation at the national level between international agencies assisting Governments in community development; (2) orientation of existing United Nations operational programmes and non-governmental organizations to help Governments achieve community development objectives; (3) mobilization of national resources for training community development personnel; (4) promotion of community development through regional and national conferences, seminars and study tours; and (5) publications on various aspects of community development.

Among the points made during discussion of the report in the Commission and the Council were the following: More emphasis at the present stage should be given to practical action on community development rather than to concepts and principles. Community development should be aimed mainly at changing the outlook and attitudes of the people rather than at yielding quick material results. National community development programmes should be more related to general economic and social policies.

Some speakers stressed the role,, too, of central governments in planning, administering and financing community development programmes, while others emphasized the importance of self-help efforts in the support of such programmes.

Attention was also drawn by some speakers to the role which community development could play in slowing down the present excessive rate of migration to urban areas, by raising levels of living in rural areas. Others, again, urged special efforts to explore the extent to which community development techniques worked out in a rural setting, especially in cases where cities had grown too rapidly, with resulting social problems.

On the Social Commission's proposal, the Council unanimously adopted a resolution (663 D (XXIV)) on 31 July 1957 commending the community development principles outlined in the Secretary-General's report, and endorsing his proposals for a long-range programme of international action. The Council also recommended various measures which United Nations Members and inter-governmental organizations could take to improve community development work and to strengthen international co-operation to this end. (For details, see text of resolution 663 D (XXIV), quoted in DOCUMENTARY REFERENCES below.)

Community development matters were also discussed at the General Assembly's twelfth session during consideration of the Council's annual report.

The Assembly adopted a resolution which recommended that Member States encourage the full participation of women in the development of their respective communities. It also asked the Secretary-General to include, in future reports to the Economic and Social Council on the progress of community development, a brief description of the methods used, the results obtained and the progress made with regard to participation of women in community development. This resolution (1162(XII)) was unanimously adopted by the Assembly on 26 November 1947, on the recommendation of its Third Committee.

In June 1957, the Working Group on Community Development of the Administrative Committee on Co-ordination (ACC) explored the practical possibilities of collaboration between the United Nations and specialized agencies in implementing the Secretary-General's proposals for the long-range community development programme mentioned above.

An informal regional inter-agency meeting on community development, held in Beirut, Lebanon 14-16 October 1957, reviewed the status of community development programmes in the Middle East region and made suggestions about greater concentration of community development efforts.

The United Nations and the specialized agencies also continued to co-operate in the provision of experts for the three UNESCO regional centres for fundamental education, namely, those in Latin America, the Arab States and South-East Asia, and the ILO project for the Andean Indians in Bolivia and Peru.

Twenty-three experts in community development were assigned during 1957 to Afghanistan, Bolivia, Cambodia, Egypt, Greece, Haiti, Iraq, Mexico, Morocco, Pakistan, the Philippines, Syria, Thailand and Viet-Nam. Fellowships in

community development were also granted.

A joint seminar on training for community development and social work was held in Lahore, Pakistan, in December 1957, attended by representatives from Afghanistan, Burma, Cambodia, Ceylon, China, India, Indonesia, Japan, the Federation of Malaya, Pakistan, the Philippines and Viet-Nam.

DOCUMENTARY REFERENCES

ECONOMIC AND SOCIAL COUNCIL—24TH SESSION
Plenary Meetings 984-987, 994.
Social Committee, meetings 368-371.

E/3008. Report of 11th session of Social Commission, 6-24 May 1957. (For list of documents, see Annex IV of this report.)
E/3008, Annex III. Draft resolution C, recommended by Social Commission, adopted by Social Committee, by 17 votes to 0, with 1 abstention.
E/3035. Report of Social Committee (draft resolution D).
RESOLUTION 663 D (XXIV), as recommended by Social Committee, E/3035, adopted unanimously by Council on 31 July 1957, meeting 994.

"*The Economic and Social Council,*

"*Bearing in mind* General Assembly resolution 1042 (XI) of 21 February 1957 on community development, the report of the Secretary-General entitled 'Concepts and principles of community development and recommendations on further practical measures to be taken by international organizations', the views of different Governments as summarized in that report and the discussion that took place in the Social Commission at its eleventh session,

"1. *Notes with satisfaction* the growing understanding of the basic principles of community development, and the increasing recognition of the community development movement in its different forms as an essential instrument of national and international action, particularly in the under-developed regions, for promoting economic and social progress;

"2. *Commends to the attention* of all Governments and international organizations the latest formulation of the essential character and requirements of the principles and techniques of the community development process embodied in the twentieth report of the Administrative Committee on Co-ordination to the Council and incorporated in the report of the Secretary-General;

"3. *Recognizes* that assistance by international organizations to Governments in the field of community development should be organized on a long-term basis, and endorses the proposals contained in the Secretary-General's report to this end;

"4. *Recommends* to the Governments of States Members of the United Nations and to intergovernmental and non-governmental organizations, so far as may be practicable, the following steps for improving

community development and for strengthening international action for that purpose:

"(*a*) The co-ordinated operation, with special emphasis on their bearing upon community development plans in each country, of the relevant parts of the programmes of the specialized agencies and of the organizations functioning under the guidance of the United Nations, such as the United Nations Children's Fund and other bodies responsible for measures of relief and rehabilitation;

"(*b*) More effective co-ordination, at the country level, of the international agencies assisting Governments in general or particular aspects of their community development programmes, taking into account for this purpose the activities under bilateral assistance programmes and the activities of non-governmental organizations;

"(*c*) Further study of the essential elements of the community development process and of the pre-requisities of a well balanced community development programme, particularly with regard to the training and supervision of personnel;

"(*d*) Further exploration of the possibilities of extending the application of the principles and programmes of community development to urban areas;

"(*e*) Initiation and assistance in the organization of conferences, seminars, workshops and study tours at the international, regional and national levels, for the promotion of better understanding of community development processes and techniques, both in their general and technical aspects, as well as for the establishment and improvement of training facilities for all personnel, both paid and voluntary, concerned with the planning and execution of community development programmes;

"(*f*) Initiation and assistance of programmes of research and publication on particular aspects of community development, as suggested in paragraph 5 of Council resolution 585 C (XX) of 23 July 1955 and in the work programme of the Social Commission for 1957-1959, taking into account the resources of international, regional and national bodies that are available at the present time and utilizing these to the maximum extent for this purpose;

"5. *Requests* the Secretary-General, in co-operation with the specialized agencies concerned, to prepare for the next session of the Social Commission and for the next session thereafter of the Council, a report on the progress of all significant measures in the field of community development, the report to include recommendations for further action as necessary."

See also below, resolution 663 G (XXIV), in DOCUMENTARY REFERENCES to section on SOCIAL SERVICES.

Study Kit on Training for Community Development. U.N.P. Sales No.: 1957.IV.6.

GENERAL ASSEMBLY—12TH SESSION
Plenary Meeting 723.
Third Committee, meetings 766-779.

A/C.3/L.611 and Add.1. Cuba, Ethiopia, Guatemala, Pakistan draft resolution, adopted unanimously by Third Committee, as orally amended by Dominican Republic and United Kingdom.
A/3716. Report of Third Committee (draft resolution III).
RESOLUTION 1162(XII), as recommended by Third Committee, A/3716, adopted unanimously by the Assembly on 26 November 1957, meeting 723.

"*The General Assembly,*
"*Having noted with satisfaction* that community development programmes are being carried out or are being planned on a long-term basis with inter-national collaboration,

"*Recognizing that,* in order to accelerate community development, which depends basically on the human element, women should be encouraged to play an even greater and more effective part in it, both in their own interest and in the interest of the community,

"*Noting* that the reports on this question do not state to what extent women are participating in community development programmes,

"1. *Recommends* to Member States in which community development programmes are being carried out that they should, by every means in their power, encourage the full participation of women in the development of their respective communities;

"2. *Recommends* to the Secretary-General and the specialized agencies concerned that, in giving assistance to Governments, they should collaborate with those Governments in achieving this purpose;

"3. *Requests* the Secretary-General to include, in his future reports to the Economic and Social Council on the progress of community development, a brief description of the methods used to achieve this purpose, the results obtained and the progress made as regards the participation of women in community development."

SOCIAL SERVICES

General social welfare services and particularly the social development problems in under-developed countries continued to receive special attention in the United Nations work programme in social services during 1957.

In May, at its eleventh session, the Social Commission stressed the need for a detailed examination of the objectives and guiding principles of the United Nations social services programme.

On 31 July 1957, at its twenty-fourth session, the Economic and Social Council unanimously adopted a resolution (663 G (XXIV)) asking the Secretary-General to convene a group of experts, to advise on the scope and contents of national social service programmes and the establishment of priorities in the implementation of such programmes, and on the specific contribution of social services, particularly family and child welfare services, to programmes relating to community development, urbanization and the improvement of family levels of living.

It was understood, with reference to the first part of their study, that the experts would not have to enter into a detailed examination of various national programmes, but should only evolve general principles for such programmes in various environments. On the other hand, it was decided that the experts would not be asked to review the objectives of the social service programme of the United Nations and its relationship to other programmes undertaken within the United Nations or by the interested specialized agencies, which matters fell within the direct competence of the Social Commission and such organs as the Administrative Committee on Co-ordination.

The Council also invited the specialized agencies concerned to co-operate in the work of the group of experts and called upon the Social Commission to examine the report of the group, together with the comments of the Secretary-General.

IMPROVEMENT OF FAMILY
LEVELS OF LIVING

In 1957, both the Social Commission and the Economic and Social Council discussed the *Report on a Co-ordinated Policy regarding Family Levels of Living,* prepared the previous year by a group of experts which met in Geneva.

The Commission and the Council both considered that the report of this expert group should be the basis for continuing research and studies for positive national and international action in the field.

On the Commission's recommendation, the Council unanimously adopted a resolution (663 B (XXIV)), on 31 July 1957, asking the Secretary-General to transmit the report to Governments, regional economic commissions and appropriate non-governmental organizations for comment, and to submit an analysis of the replies received to the Social Commission's twelfth session in 1959 so that the Commission could make recommendations on the matter to the Council in 1959.

FAMILY AND CHILD WELFARE

In 1957, the three significant developments in family and child welfare work noted in 1956 continued. These developments were: (1) a trend towards closer working relationships, national and international, between the va ous activities concerned with family and chi' welfare such as social welfare and home ec .omics, or social welfare and health; (2) a g wing interest in stimulating the participatio of women and youth in community development programmes; and (3) a growing concern about the social effects of rapid urbanization on family life.

In May, at the Social Commission's eleventh session, several members of the Commission expressed the opinion that the family and child welfare aspects of the Commission's work programme should be strengthened and should not be limited to co-operation with the United Nations Children's Fund (UNICEF).

Technical assistance in family and child welfare was for the most part provided by the general social welfare advisers. Specialists in family and child welfare were assigned to Afghanistan, Indonesia and Paraguay. A number of fellowships and scholarships were also awarded.

TRAINING OF SOCIAL
WELFARE PERSONNEL

Special attention was given in 1957 to the social welfare training requirements for designing programmes to counter social problems arising in connexion with the economic development of less-developed countries.

As part of the measures taken to obtain substantive material for the third international survey on training for social work, to be issued in 1959, two regional seminars on training for social work were held. One met in Montevideo, Uruguay. The other met in Lahore, Pakistan, in conjunction with a seminar on training for community developmer.t. (See above, under section on COMMUNITY DEVELOPMENT.)

Ten experts were provided during 1957 to give technical assistance in training social welfare personnel to the following countries: Argentina, El Salvador, Honduras, Iran, Pakistan and Uruguay. Fellowships and scholarships were also awarded for the study of social work methods.

REHABILITATION OF THE HANDICAPPED

Technical assistance to Governments continued to occupy a central position in the United Nations programme for the rehabilitation of the handicapped. Special attention was given to the training of personnel and the establishment of pilot centres in economically under-developed countries.

The United Nations co-operated with the Conference of World Organizations Interested in the Handicapped in two meetings which reviewed the progress made in carrying out the concerted international programme and discussed future plans.

United Nations experts undertook survey and advisory missions in Argentina, Austria, Brazil, Egypt, Lebanon, Syria and Uruguay; long-term experts engaged in the training of personnel continued their work at pilot centres in Brazil, Burma, Guatemala, India, Indonesia, Korea, Uganda and Venezuela. A new training project was launched in Viet-Nam.

A regional seminar for participants from Asia and the Far East was held at Solo, Indonesia. The United Nations also participated in a seminar on the rehabilitation of the tuberculous, organized by the World Veterans Federation in France.

Thirteen scholarships and fellowships were awarded to rehabilitation personnel from Europe, Latin America, the Middle East and Asia.

The second issue of the *International Social Service Review,* published in 1957, was devoted to the rehabilitation of the handicapped.

SOCIAL ASPECTS OF MIGRATION

In 1957, as in previous years, the social aspects

of migration were considered mainly within the general framework of United Nations social welfare programmes, particularly in relation to the training of personnel (for example, a European seminar on the application of basic casework principles to work with refugees, held in Bavaria in September 1957) and to family and child welfare programmes (for example, the European Group of Experts on Inter-Country Adoption, which met in Geneva in January 1957).

The United Nations, together with the Inter-national Labour Organisation, continued to sponsor and to co-operate with the Conference of Non-Governmental Organizations Interested in Migration. The sixth Conference, held in August 1957 at Geneva, discussed general principles concerning the protection of migrants, preparation of migration, integration of immigrants, socio-legal assistance to migrants, emigration of physically handicapped migrants, and training and co-operation between social workers.

DOCUMENTARY REFERENCES

ECONOMIC AND SOCIAL COUNCIL—24TH SESSION
Plenary Meetings 984-987, 994.
Social Committee, meetings 368-371.

E/3008. Report of 11th session of Social Commission. Chapters II, VII and Annexes I-IV.
Report on a Co-ordinated Policy regarding Family Levels of Living, U.N.P. Sales No.: 1957.IV.7.

E/AC.7/L.300 and Add.1. Netherlands, Pakistan, United States draft resolution and statement of financial implications submitted by Secretary-General, adopted unanimously by Social Committee as amended in Committee.
E/3035. Report of Social Committee (draft resolution G).
RESOLUTION 663 G (XXIV), as recommended by Social Committee, E/3035, adopted unanimously by Council on 31 July 1957, meeting 994.

"The Economic and Social Council,
"Having considered the part of the report of the Social Commission concerning its work programme for 1957-1959,
"Having noted also the views expressed during the eleventh session of the Social Commission that the 'Report on a Co-ordinated Policy regarding Family Levels of Living' needed to be followed by more detailed examination of the relationship of social services to other services and measures aimed at improving the family levels of living,
"1. *Requests* the Secretary-General to convene, as early as practicable, a group of experts highly qualified in the field of social services and representative of countries at varying stages of economic development, to advise on:
"(*a*) The scope and contents of national social service programmes and the establishment of priorities in the implementation of such programmes, taking into account economic, cultural and other variations;
"(*b*) The specific contribution of social services, particularly family and child welfare services, to programmes relating to community development, urbanization and the improvement of family levels of living;
"2. *Invites* the specialized agencies concerned to co-operate in the work of the group of experts in items of special interest to them;
"3. *Calls upon* the Social Commission to examine the report of the group of experts, together with the comments of the Secretary-General, in connexion with consideration of the work programme of the United Nations in the social field."

IMPROVEMENT OF FAMILY LEVELS OF LIVING
Report on a Co-ordinated Policy regarding Family Levels of Living. U.N.P. Sales No.: 1957.IV.7.
E/3008, Annex III. Draft resolution A, recommended by Social Commission, adopted unanimously by Social Committee.
E/3035. Report of Social Committee (draft resolution B).
RESOLUTION 663 B (XXIV), as recommended by Social Committee, E/3035, adopted unanimously by Council on 31 July 1957, meeting 994.

"The Economic and Social Council
"1. *Expresses appreciation and general approval* of the important work done by the Working Group of Experts and *considers* that its report should be the basis of continuing research and studies for positive action by Governments, the United Nations, and the International Labour Organisation, with the assistance of the other specialized agencies and appropriate non-governmental organizations, with the object of encouraging and helping Governments in the development of a co-ordinated social policy;
"2. *Authorizes* the Secretary-General and *invites* the International Labour Organisation and other specialized agencies to include in their programmes provision for:
"(*a*) Further joint study of the ways and means gradually to achieve, in the countries now entering upon a more rapid economic and social development, a comprehensive system of social security and related social services, taking into account the variety of national problems and resources;
"(*b*) Continuing study of the co-operative arrangements required by intergovernmental and non-governmental agencies to assist countries in achieving co-ordinated social policy;
"3. *Requests* the regional economic commissions to

consider the economic implications of the report within their respective regions;

"4. *Requests* the Secretary-General to transmit the report, his observations and those of the Social Commission, the International Labour Organisation, and the other specialized agencies and non-governmental organizations, to Governments and to appropriate non-governmental organizations for comment, and to prepare an analysis of the replies received in a report to the Social Commission at its twelfth session, so that the Commission may be able to present its recommendations to the Council at its twenty-eighth session."

OTHER DOCUMENTS

International Social Service Review, No. 2 (March 1957). Rehabilitation of the Physically Handicapped. U.N.P. Sales No.: 1957.IV.4.

International Social Service Review, No. 3 (October 1957). Organization and administration of social services. U.N.P. Sales No.: 1957.IV.9.

HOUSING, BUILDING AND PLANNING

The deterioration of housing conditions throughout the world during the past few years was one of the points brought out in the *Report on the World Social Situation* which was presented to the Social Commission and the Economic and Social Council in 1957. The Commission also had before it two reports prepared by the United Nations Secretariat on the subject of financing of housing and community improvement.

One report described the types of problems involved in the financing of housing in Africa, Asia, Europe, Latin America and the Caribbean area, the Middle East, North America and Oceania. In addition, it described the principal ways of meeting these problems.

At its mid-1957 session, the Council agreed that further major efforts should be made to improve housing conditions, especially for the under-developed countries and for low-income groups, through the mobilization of additional resources for self-help housing, slum clearance, housing co-operatives and non-profit housing associations. The Council asked the Secretary-General to prepare a long-range programme of action in the fields of housing, building and planning to be considered in 1959. It did so by resolution 664 B (XXIV), adopted on 1 August 1957, on the recommendation of its Co-ordination Committee. (For details, see annex to this resolution cited in DOCUMENTARY REFERENCES to CHAPTER XV below.)

Various aspects of housing in Europe, particularly the financing problem, were considered at the two 1957 sessions of the Housing Committee of the Economic Commission for Europe.

A regional seminar on the social aspects of housing, sponsored by the United Nations, was held at Sèvres, France, in October 1957. It discussed experiments of social interest relating to housing which might be useful in developing housing programmes.

In November, a meeting on the financing of housing and the integration of the building and building materials industries in Costa Rica, El Salvador, Guatemala, Honduras, Nicaragua and Panama was held in Costa Rica. It ws organized by the Central American Economic Co-operation Committee, with the co-operation of the United Nations, the Organization of American States and the housing agencies of the six countries concerned.

Further assistance was given by the United Nations during 1957 to regional housing centres, established with United Nations encouragement and backing, at Bandung, New Delhi and Bogotá.

A further issue of *Housing, Building and Planning* (No. 10) was published in June 1957.

The 1957 United Nations programme of international action made particular provision for direct aid to Governments: in formulating and carrying out national housing, building and planning policies and programmes; in evolving methods of financing such programmes (especially for low-income groups); in developing research and training institutions so as to increase productivity in the building and building materials industries in order to reduce building costs; and in studies on planning housing and community facilities in urban and regional areas, using natural and man-made resources (i.e., studies on "physical planning").

Technical assistance experts rendered various services in Argentina, Burma, Ceylon, Costa Rica, Ecuador, El Salvador, Greece, Iceland, India, Indonesia, Iran, Jamaica, Jordan, Lebanon, Libya, Nicaragua, Pakistan, Panama, Turkey and Yugoslavia.

In addition, 39 fellowships and scholarships

were awarded in 1957 to nationals from Argentina, Bolivia, Brazil, Colombia, Costa Rica, Ecuador, India, Indonesia, Iran, Japan, the Republic of Korea, Mexico, Pakistan and Yugoslavia.

DOCUMENTARY REFERENCES

E/3008. Report of 11th session of Social Commission, 6-24 May 1957. (See Annex IV of this report for listing of Commission documents.)
Report on the World Social Situation, U.N.P. Sales No.: 1957.IV.3.
Financing of Housing and Community Improvement Programmes. U.N.P. Sales No.: 1957.IV.1.
Trends in Utilization of Wood and Its Products in Housing. U.N.P. Sales No.: 1957.II.E.4.

Housing, Building and Planning, No. 10. U.N.P. Sales No.: 1956.IV.7.
Housing in Ghana (ST/TAA/K/Ghana/1). U.N.P. Sales No.: 1957.II.H.3.

See also text of resolution 664 B (XXIV), paragraphs 5 and 6 of annex to this resolution in DOCUMENTARY REFERENCES to CHAPTER XV below.

PREVENTION OF CRIME AND TREATMENT OF OFFENDERS

On 31 July 1957, on the recommendation of its Social Commission, the Economic and Social Council invited Governments to give the widest publicity to the Standard Minimum Rules for the Treatment of Prisoners (as drawn up in 1955 by the first United Nations Congress on the Prevention of Crime and the Treatment of Offenders). The resolution to this effect (663 C I (XXIV)) also recommended that they report to the Secretary-General every five years on the progress made in the application of these rules. The Secretary-General was authorized to make appropriate arrangements for publishing such information.

By another unanimous resolution of 31 July (663 C II (XXIV)), the Council invited Governments to publicize widely the recommendation made by the 1955 Congress on the selection and training of personnel for penal and correctional institutions, on open penal and correctional institutions, and on the general principles of prison labour. These recommendations should be taken into account as fully as possible in the administration of penal and correctional institutions and in legislative and administrative reforms. At the same time, the Council asked the Secretary-General to arrange for information to be collected and published periodically on the selection and training of personnel for penal and correctional institutions and on open institutions.

By yet another unanimous resolution of 31 July (663 F (XXIV)), adopted on the Social Commission's recommendation, the Council asked the Secretary-General to convene a meeting of the *ad hoc* Advisory Committee of Experts on the Prevention of Crime and the Treatment of Offenders in order to: (*a*) study the difficulties encountered by the Secretary-General in carrying out the work programme in the field of social defence; (*b*) make recommendations on the future programme and policy in this field; and (*c*) advise the Secretary-General on the organization of the second United Nations Congress on the Prevention of Crime and the Treatment of Offenders, to be held in 1960.

STUDIES AND MEETINGS

Being prepared in 1957 were studies, as agreed by the Social Commission, on the following subjects: prevention of juvenile delinquency and criminality resulting from social changes and accompanying economic development in less-developed countries; probation methods, and short-term imprisonment. Also being prepared were: revised editions of the United Nations comparative surveys on juvenile delinquency for North America and Latin America; and a report on a programme of action to combat the traffic in persons and the exploitation of the prostitution of others, and on measures relating to the suppression of the regulation of prostitution.

A working group of the European Consultative Group on the Prevention of Crime and the Treatment of Offenders met at Strasbourg, France, from 9 to 14 September to consider the problems connected with the criminal responsibility of abnormal offenders and the treatment of young adult offenders.

The second Asia and Far East Seminar on the Prevention of Crime and the Treatment of Offenders, held in Tokyo from 25 November to 7 December 1957, dealt with: various aspects of juvenile delinquency; matters concerning probation; the implementation of the recommendation of the first United Nations Congress on the Prevention of Crime and the Treatment of Offenders; ways and means of implementing the Standard Minimum Rules for the Treatment of Prisoners; and questions relating to traffic in persons and the exploitation of the prostitution of others.

A further issue of the *International Review of Criminal Policy*, No. 11, was published during 1957.

Experts were sent in 1957 to Israel, Pakistan and Ecuador to help in the prevention of crime and the treatment of offenders; and 13 fellowships and scholarships were made available to Denmark, India, Japan, Lebanon, Mexico, Syria, Thailand and British Guiana.

DOCUMENTARY REFERENCES

ECONOMIC AND SOCIAL COUNCIL—24TH SESSION
Plenary Meetings 984-987, 994.
Social Committee, meetings 368-371.

E/3008. Report of 11th session of Social Commission, 6-24 May 1957.

RECOMMENDATIONS OF CONGRESS ON PREVENTION OF CRIME AND TREATMENT OF OFFENDERS
E/3008, Annex III. Draft resolution B recommended by Social Commission, approved unanimously by Social Committee.
E/3035. Report of Social Committee (draft resolution C).
RESOLUTION 663 C I and II(XXIV), as recommended by Social Committee, E/3035, adopted unanimously by Council on 31 July 1957, meeting 994.

I

"The Economic and Social Council
"1. *Approves* the *Standard Minimum Rules for the Treatment of Prisoners* adopted by the First United Nations Congress on the Prevention of Crime and the Treatment of Offenders;
"2. *Draws the attention* of Governments to those *Rules* and *recommends*:
"(a) That favourable consideration be given to their adoption and application in the administration of penal and correctional institutions;
"(b) That the Secretary-General be informed every five years of the progress made with regard to their application;
"(c) That Governments arrange for the widest possible publicity to be given to the *Rules*, not only among governmental services concerned but also among non-governmental organizations interested in social defence;
"3. *Authorizes* the Secretary-General to make arrangements for the publication, as appropriate, of the information received in pursuance of sub-paragraph 2(b) above and to ask for supplementary information if necessary."

II

"The Economic and Social Council

"1. *Endorses* the recommendations on the selection and training of personnel for penal and correctional institutions, on open penal and correctional institutions, and on general principles of prison labour, adopted by the first United Nations Congress on the Prevention of Crime and the Treatment of Offenders;
"2. *Draws the attention* of Governments to those recommendations, and *recommends* that they take them as fully as possible into account in their administration of penal and correctional institutions and when considering legislative and administrative reforms;
"3. *Invites* Governments to give the widest publicity to these recommendations;
"4. *Requests* the Secretary-General to arrange for the periodical collection and publication, as appropriate, of information on:
"(a) The selection and training of personnel for penal and correctional institutions;
"(b) Open penal and correctional institutions."

WORK PROGRAMME
E/3008, Annex III. Resolution E, adopted by Social Commission.
E/AC.7/L.298. United Kingdom and United States draft resolution adopted unanimously by Social Committee.
E/3035. Report of Social Committee (draft resolution F).
RESOLUTION 663 F (XXIV), as recommended by Social Committee, E/3035, adopted unanimously by Council on 31 July 1957, meeting 994.
"The Economic and Social Council,
"Having considered resolution E adopted by the Social Commission at its eleventh session, concerning implementation of the work programme of the United Nations in the field of social defence,
"Approves the action called for in that resolution."

OTHER DOCUMENTS
International Review of Criminal Policy, No. 11. U.N.P. Sales No.: 1957.IV.5.

POPULATION QUESTIONS

World population trends during recent years, as described in the *Report on the World Social Situation* (see above), have shown two main characteristics: a steadily declining mortality rate and an almost constant birth rate, far higher than the mortality rate. These trends continued in 1957; as a result, the already high annual rate of population growth again increased slightly.

The publication of recent census results and improved analyses of demographic processes have facilitated the calculation of world population trends by main geographical regions. The calculations have indicated that the present high rate of growth will probably continue for a number of years, for demographic phenomena do not change rapidly. Concurrently with these calculations by main geographical regions, the United Nations Secretariat continued its compilation of detailed country projections and in 1957 concentrated on South-East Asian countries.

The programme of regional population studies in the three areas of the world where the problems raised by population growth are particularly pressing was initiated during 1957. The Regional Demographic Research and Training Centre for Asia and the Far East at Bombay, India, also began operations in 1957. The regional centre at Santiago, Chile, organized along similar lines and to be concerned specifically with Latin America, was to receive its first students early in 1958.

Encouraging progress was made during 1957 in the study being carried out in co-operation with the Philippines Government concerning manpower, unemployment and under-employment.

The Secretariat completed several projects during 1957, too. Thus, publication of the proceedings of the World Population Conference held at Rome in 1954 was completed. A study of the economic and social implications of the aging of populations was also published. Completed, too, was a survey of factors involved in the rise of birth rates which was experienced in many countries after the Second World War. Statistics for selected countries relating to the economic characteristics of international migrants and covering the period 1918-1954 were prepared for publication. So was the text of a demographic dictionary in English, French and Spanish.

POPULATION COMMISSION

The Population Commission held its ninth session at United Nations Headquarters in New York between 25 February and 8 March 1957.

As at previous sessions, it reviewed the work of the Secretariat and discussed the future work programme. Its report to the Economic and Social Council's twenty-third session again emphasized the need for a more intensive study of the important and close relationship between demographic problems and economic and social development. The Commission also hoped that the Secretariat might extend its demographic activities to include Africa.

ACTION BY ECONOMIC
AND SOCIAL COUNCIL

These views were endorsed by the Economic and Social Council. By resolution 642 C (XXIII) of 25 April 1957, the Council urged Governments and invited the specialized agencies to collaborate in providing technical aid in the demographic field. By another resolution of the same date, 642 B (XXIII), the Council asked the Secretary-General "to study the possibilities of encouraging wider co-operation in demographic studies and in the improvement of census and vital statistics in Africa and explore the desirability and feasibility of the early establishment of demographic training and research centres in Africa". In pursuance of the latter resolution, the Secretariat began a study of the possibilities of co-operation with African countries south of the Sahara.

CONSIDERATION BY
GENERAL ASSEMBLY

Later in the year, the General Assembly discussed the relationship between population problems and economic problems.

By resolution 1217(XII), adopted unanimously on 14 December 1957 on the recommendation of its Second Committee, the Assembly invited United Nations Member States (especially those in the process of economic development), to give the closest possible attention to the inter-relationships between economic and population changes. It also invited the Economic and Social Council and the specialized agencies concerned to give attention to the growing importance of this subject. In addition, it asked the Secretary-General to continue to ensure the co-ordination of the demographic and economic work of the United Nations, especially with regard to countries in the process of economic development.

DOCUMENTARY REFERENCES

ECONOMIC AND SOCIAL COUNCIL—23RD SESSION
Plenary Meeting 967.
Social Committee, mettings 353, 354.

E/2957/Rev.1. Report of 9th session of Population Commission, 25 February–8 March 1957. (Commission documents are listed under subject headings in this report.)

E/2957/Rev.1, Annex. Draft resolutions A and B, recommended by Commission, adopted unanimously by Social Committee.

E/2971. Report of Social Committee.

RESOLUTION 642 A-C (XXIII), as recommended by Social Committee, E/2971, adopted unanimously by Council on 25 April 1957, meeting 967.

A

"*The Economic and Social Council*

"*Takes note* of the report of the Population Commission (ninth session).*"

B

"*The Economic and Social Council,*

"*Recognizing* that there is a direct relationship between the problems of population and economic and social development,

"*Considering* that after the establishment of demographic training and research centres in Latin America and in Asia and the Far East, the time has come to focus attention on demographic problems in Africa,

"*Considering* further that the existence of new States in Africa justifies increased attention to these problems,

"*Noting* the useful work done by the African Seminar on Vital and Health Statistics sponsored jointly by the Commission for Technical Co-operation in Africa South of the Sahara and the World Health Organization, held at Brazzaville, French Equatorial Africa, in November 1956,

"*Considering* the desirability of making as much preparation as possible for deriving maximum results from the forthcoming population censuses in Africa,

"*Requests* the Secretary-General, in consultation with the Governments concerned, specialized agencies and other appropriate international agencies, to study the possibilities of encouraging wider co-operation in demographic studies and in the improvement of census and vital statistics in Africa and explore the desirability and feasibility of the early establishment of demographic training and research centres in Africa, and to report as appropriate to the Population Commission at its tenth session."

C

"*The Economic and Social Council,*

"*Recognizing* the importance of technical assistance in the demographic field for the economic and social development of under-developed countries,

"*Recalling* the request made to the Secretary-General, in Council resolution 741 C (XV) of 14 April 1953, to give, within the limits of the resources available and in accordance with the work priorities, appropriate technical assistance to those Governments requesting aid in order to help them carry out analytical studies of their census results,

"*Considering* the small number of experts available in this field in most countries and the difficulties which have been experienced in recruiting qualified experts for demographic missions,

"1. *Recommends* that Governments interested in obtaining technical assistance in the demographic field make their requests as early as possible;

"2. *Urges* Governments to assist the United Nations in its efforts to recruit demographic experts for technical assistance missions by making such experts available to the greatest extent possible;

"3. *Invites* the specialized agencies, particularly the United Nations Educational, Scientific and Cultural Organization, to collaborate with the United Nations in this field, in view of their contacts with non-governmental organizations and institutions which have consultative status or maintain relations with these specialized agencies."

GENERAL ASSEMBLY—12TH SESSION
Plenary Meeting 730.
Second Committee, meetings 492-501.

A/C.2/L.355 and Rev.1, 2. Brazil, Italy, Mexico, Pakistan, Peru draft resolution and revisions, adopted unanimously by Second Committee.

A/3782. Report of Second Committee (draft resolution I).

RESOLUTION 1217(XII), as submitted by Second Committee, A/3782, adopted unanimously by Assembly on 14 December 1957, meeting 730.

"*The General Assembly,*

"*Considering* that there is a close relationship between economic problems and population problems, especially with regard to countries which are in the process of economic development,

"*Bearing in mind* the resolutions of the General Assembly and of the Economic and Social Council which refer to the relations existing between economic development and social change,

"*Recalling* that international co-operation towards economic development will be more effective when more is known about the population changes that accompany such development,

"1. *Invites* States Members, particularly those which are in the process of economic development, to follow as closely as possible the inter-relationships existing between economic and population changes;

"2. *Invites the attention* of the Economic and Social Council and of the specialized agencies concerned to the growing importance of this question;

"3. *Requests* the Secretary-General to continue to ensure the co-ordination of the activities of the United Nations in the demographic and economic fields, particularly with reference to countries which are in the process of economic development;

"4. *Requests* the Eonomic and Social Council to include pertinent information concerning the demographic activities of the Council in the chapter on economic development of its annual report to the General Assembly."

OTHER STUDIES

The Aging of Populations and Its Economic and Social Implications. U.N.P. Sales No.: 1956.XIII.6.

Demographic Yearbook, 1957. U.N.P. Sales No.: 1957.XIII.1.
Recent Trends in Fertility in Industrialized Countries. U.N.P. Sales No.: 1957.XIII.2.

CHAPTER XIII

THE UNITED NATIONS CHILDREN'S FUND (UNICEF)

The Executive Board of the United Nations Children's Fund (UNICEF) held three sessions in 1957: between 8 and 16 April, between 3 and 12 September, and on 12 December. It approved allocations totalling $24,146,761 (in U.S. dollars), as follows:

Total Aid to Programmes	$20,414,791
Operational Services, 1958	1,874,660
Administration, 1958	1,682,310
Administration, 1957 (supplementary allocation)	175,000
Total	$24,146,761

The allocations for assistance in child care, by region, were as follows:

	Long-Range Programmes	Percentage	Emergency Aid
Africa	$ 1,631,500	8.1	—
Asia	7,190,612	35.9	—
Eastern Mediterranean	2,251,954	11.2	$386,404
Europe	972,500	4.9	—
The Americas	7,648,821	38.2	—
Inter-regional	333,000	1.7	—
Totals	$20,028,387	100.0	$386,404

Of the total of $20,414,791 for programme aid, about 47 per cent was for disease control programmes, 31 per cent for basic maternal and child welfare services and training, 20 per cent for child feeding and milk and food conservation, and under 2 per cent for emergency aid.

At the close of 1957, there were 323 programmes being assisted by the Fund in 104 countries and territories. There were 143 disease control programmes; of these, 47 were for malaria eradication and control, 33 for control of yaws and syphilis, 30 for prevention and control of tuberculosis, 13 for control of leprosy, and 10 for control of trachoma and related eye diseases. Almost half of the funds allocated

for long-range child care programmes in 1957 were for disease control.

For each dollar allocated by UNICEF to Governments in 1957, the assisted countries committed an average of $2.80.

At its 1957 sessions, the Board, for the first time approved aid for Argentina and Venezuela. Of the 125 allocations for programme aid, 110 were to continue or expand programmes previously aided, and 15 for programmes not previously aided.

FORECAST OF COMMITMENTS, 1958–1960

The Board again gave its attention to forecasting resources and programme allocations for the years 1958, 1959 and 1960, in order to ensure UNICEF's ability to meet commitments for continuing programmes, especially malaria eradication, and to maintain a balance in aid to other important programmes.

The Board forecast programme allocations totalling $22.2 million in 1958, $23.1 million in 1959 and $24 million in 1960, as against $20.4 million in 1957.

Annual commitments of slightly under $7.6 million for malaria control were envisaged for these three years.

The forecasts of allocations for basic maternal and child welfare services and training involved rises from $5.3 million in 1958 to about $5.7 million in 1960; those for nutrition programmes involved a rise from $4 million in 1958 to $5 million in 1960. The two groups of services would together receive between 40 and 50 per cent of all allocations. The forecast of a 20 per cent rise in nutrition aid between 1958 and 1960 reflected the increasing attention given by the Fund to the developments in that field (for further details, see below, under heading CHILD NUTRITION).

EMERGENCY AID

Of the $386,404 approved in 1957 for emergency aid, $363,727 was for continuation of child feeding in destitute frontier villages of Jordan and $22,677 to Egypt for child feeding among destitute groups in the Gaza Strip.

An amount of $700,000, earmarked by the Board in December 1956 for emergency aid for Hungarian children and mothers in Austria and in Hungary, was used to provide children's clothing, blankets and soap. Distribution was completed by the end of 1957.

BENEFICIARIES

Approximately 48 million children and pregnant and nursing mothers benefited in 1957 from the principal UNICEF-aided health nutrition programmes. Over 50 million were expected to benefit in 1958. Accomplishments in 1957 and targets for 1958 were as follows:

Anti-Malaria Campaigns	1957	1958
Number of children and mothers protected with UNICEF insecticides	24,532,300	30,665,000
BCG Anti-Tuberculosis Vaccination		
Number of children vaccinated	13,255,700	15,280,000
Yaws Control		
Number of children and mothers treated	2,693,500	4,280,000
Control of Trachoma and Related Eye Diseases		
Number of children treated	728,000	1,134,900
Child Feeding through Schools and Maternal and Child Welfare Centres		
Average number of children and mothers receiving daily milk rations	4,007,200	5,537,400

In addition, an estimated 1,793,000 children and mothers received milk through emergency feeding programmes, and large numbers of mothers and children benefited from the health and welfare centres equipped by the Fund. Thousands more benefited from UNICEF's aid to vaccine production plants, milk sterilization, pasteurization or drying plants and from campaigns for the control of diphtheria, whooping cough and leprosy.

BASIC MATERNAL AND CHILD WELFARE SERVICES

Of the 323 programmes aided in 1957 by the Fund, 66 were for basic maternal and child welfare services and training, 18 for improving environmental sanitation, 9 for rehabilitation of handicapped children and 7 for the care of premature infants. Almost one third of the funds allocated for long-range programmes in 1957 were for maternal and child welfare services and training.

During 1957, the Executive Board emphasized qualitative as well as quantitative increase in basic maternal and child welfare services and the integration of these with public health services. The Fund, in close co-operation with the World Health Organization (WHO), the Food and Agriculture Organization (FAO) and the United Nations Bureau of Social Affairs, continued to give more attention to co-ordinating mother and child services with the educational, social welfare, nutrition and agricultural extension programmes of the assisted countries. Increased efforts were also being made through basic maternal and child welfare programmes to consolidate the gains already achieved in disease control campaigns, thus providing further unification of activities affecting the health and welfare of children and the family, and their social environment.

In India, the Philippines, Kenya and Uganda, UNICEF aid for basic maternal and child welfare services has been given as an essential element of community development work. In aid for Kenya and Uganda, homecraft and mothercraft education were stressed, and provided an example of the use of channels other than health departments to reach mothers in the villages.

Additional aid for training staff in child care work went to the two permanent international training centres: the International Children's Centre in Paris and the All-India Institute of Hygiene and Public Health in Calcutta. Further aid was also voted for equipment, transport and, in some cases, stipends for short-term training of traditional village birth attendants and other auxiliary workers and for the professional training of public health nurses, midwives and health visitors. For the first time, the Executive Board approved grants-in-aid to medical and public health schools to help them start or improve the teaching of paediatrics and preventive medicine for senior and supervisory staff in the health services.

On the basis of a WHO report entitled *Review of Maternal and Child Health Activities and Related Training of Professional and Auxiliary Workers,* and of related recommendations of the UNICEF/WHO Joint Health Policy Committee, the Executive Board endorsed the guiding lines for future work in this field covering: (*a*) technical leadership and supervisory services; (*b*) integration of maternal and child health services into general health services, ensuring that special needs of the former are met; (*c*) co-ordination of maternal and child health services with community development and school health services, and with social welfare and other services for mothers and children; (*d*) greater emphasis on pre-natal and child care, especially for the pre-school group; (*e*) extension and improvement of training in paediatrics and child care; (*f*) emphasis on training of all categories and levels of personnel; (*g*) greater emphasis on child nutrition, including nutrition education of mothers and increased milk distribution to priority groups in countries where protein malnutrition is prevalent; (*h*) more effective health education through schools, and related measures; and (*i*) pilot studies on health improvement of children in urban slums.

JOINT HEALTH POLICY COMMITTEE

At its May 1957 session, the UNICEF/WHO Joint Committee on Health Policy (JCHP) considered the possibility of bilharziasis control programmes, but concluded that basic knowledge of the problem and of control methods available were not sufficiently developed to warrant UNICEF support at the present time. It also made other recommendations on UNICEF health programmes noted elsewhere in this chapter.

DISEASE CONTROL PROGRAMMES

UNICEF and WHO, jointly aiding Governments in disease control campaigns, have attached increasing importance to the quality of control campaigns, particularly the strengthening of supervision, the consolidation of gains and the integration of such programmes into the permanent health services of the countries concerned when the mass phase of a particular campaign is completed.

MALARIA ERADICATION

Of $20.4 million voted for long-range child care programmes in 1957, more than $8 million were for malaria control and eradication. The 47 anti-malaria programmes aided by UNICEF at the close of 1957 included 29 focused on eradication, 14 control programmes, one malariometric survey and three DDT-production projects. UNICEF aid for regional eradication efforts was expanded in the Americas (where 20 countries were aided) and in the Eastern Mediterranean area (where seven programmes were aided). About 60 million persons were protected in UNICEF-assisted campaigns during 1957—almost 50 million of them (including 25 million children and mothers) by UNICEF insecticides. In tropical Africa, the techniques of interrupting transmission of malaria have not yet been determined. UNICEF also aided surveys and pilot studies in connexion with a number of technical problems. Efforts have been made to ensure the closest possible co-ordination between all interested international and bilateral aid agencies working in this field.

YAWS CONTROL

Anti-yaws campaigns were aided by the Fund in 26 countries and territories in 1957: 7 in Africa, 11 in Asia, and 8 in the Americas. Of 38 million persons examined in these campaigns during 1957, approximately 5.3 million (including 2.7 million children and mothers) were treated.

TUBERCULOSIS CONTROL

In 1957, UNICEF aided BCG vaccination campaigns in 21 countries. Almost 37 million children were tested and 13.3 million vaccinated.

On the basis of a WHO review of 10 years' experience in BCG vaccination campaigns, the JCHP recommended new emphasis on such campaigns. As a result, BCG vaccinations in areas with a high prevalence of tuberculosis were to be combined with other measures of tuberculosis control, such as treatment of contagious cases and contacts. Preliminary surveys were deemed necessary to determine details of the scope and organization of campaigns.

Since 1955, UNICEF has given aid in the home treatment of tuberculosis involving the use of isoniazid (an anti-TB drug also known as INH) and in pilot projects for the study of simple preventive control measures which could be developed on a large scale and could be used in home care, especially by means of drug treatment.

In September 1957, the Fund's Executive Board adopted a JCHP recommendation for more extensive provision of isoniazid, while maintaining the following criteria approved earlier for aid to tuberculosis centres: the reliable diagnosis of cases; adequate home supervision of patients to ensure correct application of treatment and its continuation for a sufficient period of time. The JCHP did not, however, feel able as yet to recommend the use of the drug on a mass basis.

LEPROSY CONTROL

By the end of 1957, some 642,000 persons in 13 countries had received leprosy treatment under UNICEF-aided programmes.

While cases in the early stages can be controlled fairly rapidly with sulphone drugs, more advanced cases require prolonged treatment which may last six years or more. Experiments on dosage and methods of administration are being carried out, and new groups of drugs are being tested.

TRACHOMA CONTROL

There were 10 UNICEF-aided programmes during 1957 for control of trachoma and related eye diseases. Trials were under way during 1957 in several countries in Asia, the Eastern Mediterranean area and Africa to determine methods of treatment both economical and easy to administer. The Executive Board anticipated allocations of $600,000 in 1958 and in 1959 for such programmes, as against $200,000 in 1957. On the basis of results expected from the present trials, allocation requests would rise still higher in 1960.

CHILD NUTRITION

In 1957, the Board made provision for shipment of about 125 million pounds of dried skim milk during 1957 and 1958. Sixty-nine countries received dried milk during 1957 for distribution to more than 4 million children and pregnant and nursing mothers through schools and maternal and child welfare centres.

The Executive Board stressed the importance of using feeding programmes to spread nutrition education. It drew attention to the special nutritional needs of pregnant and nursing mothers and of children in the crucial post-weaning and pre-school ages. It also called for nutritional surveys as the basis for school feeding programmes.

UNICEF, in collaboration with FAO and WHO, continued to explore local production possibilities for other high-protein foods for children. Projects for the production of fish flour in Chile and soya milk in Indonesia were well advanced in 1957, and substantial progress was made in locating sources of peanut, sesame and cotton-seed flour for laboratory and clinical testing. The aim has been to make such foods available in standardized, reproducible and safe form for use in local diets and feeding programmes in areas of protein deficiency.

The Executive Board urged the study and promotion of the use of other types of foods for infant feeding which can be readily prepared at home or produced at the village level. For this purpose the Fund planned to help Governments develop programmes to teach rural families how to make the best use of available and potential local food resources, reaching people in the villages through various local channels. At its October 1957 session, the Board in principle approved UNICEF aid in the following related fields to help Governments to improve child nutrition: nutrition surveys; professional training in nutrition; nutrition education of the people at the village level; nutritional activities in the villages; and, where appropriate, limited vitamin supplementation.

In 1957, UNICEF was helping to establish facilities in 23 countries for the collection, conservation and distribution of milk from local sources to make free or low-cost milk available to more children. Of 173 plants, for which the Board approved equipment for drying or other processing of milk, 142 were in operation at the close of 1957, providing stable and expanded markets for milk and serving as focal points for the education of farmers in improved milk production practices. When all 173 plants are in operation, they will provide free or low-cost milk for more than 5 million children and mothers and many times this number will benefit from the increased availability of safe milk.

FINANCES AND FUND RAISING

Eighty Governments contributed to UNICEF

in 1957. The figures for 1953-1957 are are follows:

	Amount Contributed	Number of Contributing Governments
1953	$14,267,000	55
1954	13,608,000	61
1955	15,631,000	72
1956	17,505,000	81
1957	17,900,000	80*

* This figure includes the Saar, whose contribution was grouped with that of the Federal Republic of Germany in 1957, but not in 1955 and 1956.

Contributions in 1957 came from: Afghanistan, Antigua, Argentina, Australia, Austria, Belgium, Brazil, Brunei, Burma, Cambodia, Canada, Ceylon, Chile, China (Taiwan), Colombia, Costa Rica, Czechoslovakia, Denmark, Dominican Republic, Ecuador, Egypt, El Salvador, Ethiopia, Finland, France, Federal Republic of Germany, Greece, Grenada, Guatemala, Haiti, Honduras, Hong Kong, Iceland, India, Indonesia, Iran, Iraq, Ireland, Israel, Italy, Jamaica, Japan, Jordan, Republic of Korea, Lebanon, Libya, Liechtenstein, Luxembourg, Federation of Malaya, Mexico, Monaco, Morocco, Netherlands, New Zealand, Nicaragua, North Borneo, Norway, Pakistan, Panama, Paraguay, Peru, Philippines, Poland, Sarawak, Singapore, Spain, Sudan, Sweden, Switzerland, Syria, Thailand, Trinidad and Tobago, Tunisia, Turkey, USSR, United Kingdom, United States, Vatican City, Viet-Nam, and Yugoslavia.

Total income for 1957 from all sources was $20,716,000. Contributions from private sources totalled $1,303,000, a little over 6 per cent of the total income for the year. Of this total, $158,000 came from proceeds of fund-raising campaigns and United Nations Day collections, and $1,145,000 from individuals, private groups and Hallowe'en collections by children in the United States.

UNICEF received $9,000 from UNRRA residual assets in 1957, as compared with $14,000 in 1956. Other income for the year amounted to $1,504,000.

GREETING CARDS

Increase in net income from UNICEF's greeting cards project has risen from $4,200 in 1950, to $340,000 in 1957, when about 7.7 million greeting cards were sold.

NON-GOVERNMENTAL ORGANIZATIONS AND NATIONAL UNICEF COMMITTEES

Membership in the Non-Governmental Organizations Committee on UNICEF rose to 57 by the end of 1957.

The Executive Board again expressed its appreciation to the NGOs for their continued active support. It particularly noted the value of NGOs in promoting the formation of UNICEF national committees. Such committees existed in 14 countries. In 15 others, some of their functions were carried out by United Nations Appeal for Children (UNAC) committees or national UNICEF committees in process of formation.

CONSIDERATION BY ECONOMIC AND SOCIAL COUNCIL

At its twenty-third session, the Economic and Social Council considered reports of the Executive Board of UNICEF covering its sessions in October-November and in December 1956. In the discussion, members generally lauded the work of the Fund and, by resolution 638 (XXIII), of 24 April 1957, the Council took note with satisfaction of the Executive Board's report.

CONSIDERATION BY GENERAL ASSEMBLY

At the Assembly's twelfth session, many representatives praised UNICEF's activities in the course of discussion in the Assembly's Third (Social, Humanitarian and Cultural) Committee. They emphasized the value of the general principles guiding its work. Special mention was made of the Fund's catalytic effect on Government action on behalf of children, the long-range effects of its works, its importance in the whole scheme of international economic and social aid for under-developed countries, its close co-ordination with other United Nations agencies, and its effective and economical administration.

By resolution 1160(XII), of 26 November 1957, adopted unanimously, the Assembly congratulated UNICEF on its outstanding work and expressed the hope that Governments, organizations and individuals would give more support to it.

PROGRAMME ALLOCATIONS BY AREA AND TYPE AS APPROVED IN 1957
(*In U.S. Dollars*)

	Africa	Asia	Eastern Mediterranean	Europe	The Americas	Inter-regional	Total	Per Cent
Maternal and Child Welfare	638,000	4,395,000	460,000	176,000	413,900	333,000	6,415,900	31.43
Disease Control								
Malaria, including DDT production	525,000	908,000	1,045,000	—	5,523,200	—	8,001,200	39.19
BCG vaccination and other TB control	—	605,591	954	30,000	84,119	—	720,664	3.53
Yaws/VD control	124,000	22,000	—	—	240,202	—	386,202	1.89
Trachoma control	100,000	—	44,000	56,500	—	—	200,500	0.98
Leprosy control	82,500	76,000	18,000	—	—	—	176,500	0.86
Penicillin production	—	25,521	—	—	42,900	—	68,421	0.34
	831,500	1,637,112	1,107,954	86,500	5,890,421	—	9,553,487	46.79
Nutrition								
Milk conservation	—	330,000	227,000	710,000	—	—	1,267,000	6.21
Child feeding	162,000	812,000	457,000	—	1,344,500	—	2,775,500	13.60
Goitre control	—	16,500	—	—	—	—	16,500	0.08
	162,000	1,158,500	684,000	710,000	1,344,500	—	4,059,000	19.89
Total, Long-Range Aid	1,631,500	7,190,612	2,251,954	972,500	7,648,821	333,000	20,028,387	98.11
(Per Cent of Total Programme Aid)	(7.99)	(35.22)	(11.03)	(4.77)	(37.47)	(1.63)		
Emergency Aid							386,404	1.89

Grand Total, Programme Aid	20,414,791	100.00
Estimated Operational Services for 1958	1,874,660	
Estimated Administrative Costs for 1958	1,682,310	
Supplementary Allocation for 1957	175,000	
Grand Total, Allocations Approved in 1957	24,146,761	

DOCUMENTARY REFERENCES

ECONOMIC AND SOCIAL COUNCIL—23RD SESSION
Plenary Meetings, 965, 970.

E/2937. United Nations Children's Fund. Report of Executive Board, 22 October–2 November and 11 December 1956.

E/ICEF/366/Add.1. General progress report of Executive Director. Evaluation chapter: An appraisal of major programme trends.

RESOLUTION 638(XXIII), taking note of report of Executive Board of United Nations Children's Fund, as orally proposed by France, adopted by Council on 24 April 1957, meeting 965.

ELECTIONS
E/L.746 and Add.1-4. Election of members of Executive Board of United Nations Children's Fund.

E/ICEF/354. Information note by Executive Director of Executive Board organization.

GENERAL ASSEMBLY—12TH SESSION
Plenary Meeting 723.
Third Committee, meetings 764-766.

A/3613. Report of Economic and Social Council to General Assembly, Chapter VI, Section III.

A/C.3/L.608 and Add.1. Colombia, Costa Rica, Dominican Republic, Ecuador, Egypt, El Salvador, Finland, Panama, Turkey draft resolution adopted unanimously by Third Committee.

A/3716. Report of Third Committee (draft resolution I).

RESOLUTION 1160(XII), as recommended by Third Committee, A/3716, adopted unanimously by Assembly on 26 November 1957, meeting 723.

"*The General Assembly,*

"*Having considered* chapter VI, section III, of the report of the Economic and Social Council, dealing with the United Nations Children's Fund,

"*Impressed* with the practical effectiveness of the Fund in aiding over a hundred countries and territories, particularly in under-developed areas, to establish permanent children's services,

"*Appreciating also* the essential role of the Fund in increasing the capacity of countries for economic and social progress,

"*Aware however* of the many needs which the **Fund** is unable to meet,

"1. *Expresses the hope* that Governments, organizations and individuals will give increased support to the United Nations Children's Fund;

"2. *Congratulates* the Executive Board and the Executive Director of the Fund on their outstanding work."

OTHER DOCUMENTS

E/2977, E/3050. Reports of Executive Board, 8-16 April, 3-12 September 1957, meetings 173-190.

E/ICEF/335, E/ICEF/355. Reports of Executive Board on meetings 172 and 191 held on 30 January and 12 December 1957.

E/ICEF/352. Countries and programmes assisted by UNICEF. A count and listing of countries and territories, and programmes, assisted by UNICEF at time of conclusion of September 1957 session of Executive Board.

E/ICEF/INF.8/Rev.1, E/ICEF/INF.9. Checklist of UNICEF documents issued for April 1957 and September 1957 Executive Board sessions.

For the Children: The Work of UNICEF in the Americas. U.N.P. Sales No.: 1957.I.14.

E/3053. Proceeds of sale of UNRRA supplies. Report by Secretary-General.

CHAPTER XIV

NARCOTIC DRUGS

The control system set up under the international treaties on narcotic drugs to regulate the production, movement and consumption of narcotic drugs for medical and scientific purposes and to combat drug addiction and the illicit traffic continued during 1957. There are five principal international organs for this system: the Economic and Social Council and its Commission on Narcotic Drugs, which are the chief policy-making bodies; and the Permanent Central Opium Board, the Drug Supervisory Body, and the Expert Committee on Addiction-Producing Drugs of the World Health Organization (WHO), which carry out administrative, semi-judicial and technical functions.

REPORT OF COMMISSION ON NARCOTIC DRUGS

At its twelfth session, held at United Nations Headquarters in New York from 29 April to 31 May 1957, the Commission on Narcotic Drugs considered: the implementation of the narcotic treaties; special problems connected with the use of opium, coca leaf, cannabis (Indian hemp, marihuana, hashish), diacetylmorphine (heroin), khat, barbiturates, "tranquilizers" and synthetic narcotics; the illicit traffic in narcotics; and the cure and rehabilitation of drug addicts. It continued its work on the draft of the Single Convention intended to replace all multilateral treaties in the field. The report of the Commission was considered by the Economic and Social Council at its twenty-fourth session; in mid-1957.

IMPLEMENTATION OF TREATIES

STATES BECOMING PARTIES TO TREATIES ON NARCOTIC DRUGS

During 1957, the following States became parties to or declared themselves bound by the following international narcotics treaties: International Opium Convention, 1912, Ceylon; 1925 Narcotic Drugs Convention as amended by the 1946 Protocol, Afghanistan and Ceylon; 1931 Convention (for limiting the manufacture and regulating the distribution of narcotic drugs) as amended by the 1946 Protocol, Ceylon; 1936 Convention (for the suppression of the illicit traffic in dangerous drugs) as amended by the 1946 Protocol, Ceylon; 1948 Protocol (bringing under international control drugs outside the scope of the 1931 Convention), Hungary; 1953 Protocol (for limiting and regulating the cultivation of the poppy plant, production of, international and wholesale trade in, and use of opium), Cambodia, Ceylon, Chile, Indonesia, Israel, and Italy. By the end of 1957 there were 26 States which became parties to the 1953 Protocol.

REPORTS OF GOVERNMENTS

The Commission examined the *Summary of Annual Reports of Governments Relating to Opium and Other Narcotic Drugs, 1955.* Reports for 134 countries and territories (as against 126 in the previous year) had been received by the Secretary-General. The Commission observed that the communication of annual reports was in general satisfactory but, noting that several countries had not sent in reports, appealed to all Governments to do so.

A total of 182 texts of national laws or regulations on the control of narcotic drugs were received by the Secretary-General.

In accordance with Economic and Social Council resolution 626 C III (XXII), of 2 August 1956, the preparation of annual summaries of laws and regulations on the control of narcotic drugs was discontinued in favour of an annual cumulative multi-purpose index to national laws and regulations received from Governments and circulated by the Secretary-General for the period 1947–30 September 1956 inclusive. The Commission considered that the *Cumulative Index 1947–1956* provided comprehensive references to any given aspect of relevant laws and regulations and would be of great practical use nationally and internationally.

PLACING OF NEW DRUGS
UNDER INTERNATIONAL CONTROL

The Commission noted that two additional narcotic drugs produced by synthesis had been added to the list of drugs coming under international control. Having been informed of the dangerous addiction-producing properties of another new synthetic drug, R.875, or dextromoramide (d-3-methyl-2,2-diphenyl-4-morpholinobutyrylpyrrolidine), it took action under the relevant treaty provision to place this drug provisionally under a strict régime of control pending a final decision.

REPORT OF PERMANENT
CENTRAL OPIUM BOARD

In its report to the Economic and Social Council for 1957, the Permanent Central Opium Board gave statistics for 1956 and assessed the application of the narcotics conventions during the past five years. Among its conclusions, the Board stated that, on the whole, there had been a distinct improvement in the operation of the system of control; in particular, statistics had been fuller and more accurate and had been submitted more promptly.

To some extent, however, the work of the Board had continued to be hampered by the fact that the statistical returns of some Governments were incomplete or were delayed in transmission, and by failure to reply to requests for information. In its view, one of the effects of the controls introduced by the various conventions had been to reduce almost to vanishing point the possibility of addicts obtaining narcotic drugs from licit sources; while there were still great numbers of addicts throughout the world, they were now obliged to look to sources which were, in the main, outlawed.

In the Board's opinion, it was clear that the licit manufacture of drugs was limited to medical and scientific requirements and that the purposes of the 1925 and 1931 Conventions had largely been achieved. The Board said that the success thus attained had been due primarily to the high sense of responsibility displayed by most Governments in fulfilling their obligations.

PARTICULAR ASPECTS OF NARCOTIC DRUGS CONTROL

OPIUM

Request by Afghanistan. Under the terms of the 1953 Protocol, only seven countries (not including Afghanistan) were to be permitted to produce opium for export. The Commission, at its twelfth session, again considered a request by Afghanistan to be included among the export producers permitted under international narcotic treaty law. It decided to reconsider the request at its thirteenth session in the light of information then available on such matters as progress towards the abolition of opium cultivation and the eradication of opium addiction in Iran, and the extent of any illicit traffic in opium from Afghanistan to Iran.

Scientific Research on Opium. Under the terms of Economic and Social Council resolution 626 H (XXII), of 2 August 1956, a seminar of not more than nine experts was due to meet in 1958 to review national and international methods for determining the geographical origin of opium seized in the illicit traffic.

In order to facilitate this meeting, the Commission asked the Secretary-General at its 1957 session to carry out as many analyses as possible of authenticated samples of opium. This was to be done as a matter of priority and by means of all the physical and chemical methods which had so far been tried and proved. Governments within whose territories opium was licitly produced were urged to furnish, in sufficient quantity, complete sets of samples of all varieties produced, and, where there was illicit production, to furnish samples from that source also.

On the recommendation of the Commission, the Council asked the Secretary-General (by resolution 667 C (XXIV), adopted on 1 August 1957) to increase the staff and facilities of the United Nations Laboratory in order to permit more analyses of opium samples to be carried out and to expedite research on methods of determination of origin by physical and chemical means.

KHAT

At its 1957 session, the Commission examined the question of khat which had been brought to its attention by the representative of Egypt in 1956 and consideration of which had been deferred. Khat is a shrub whose leaves are used in eastern Africa and the Arabian peninsula in indigenous medicine, in certain religious ceremonies and for pleasure. The Commission was informed that the physical and mental health of habitual users of khat could be seriously impaired and that the habit of chewing khat raised a social problem.

On the Commission's recommendation, the Council, by resolution 667 D (XXIV), of 1 August 1957, invited the World Health Organization (WHO) to study the medical aspects of the problem and to report thereon to the Commission on Narcotic Drugs.

COCA LEAF

The representative of Peru informed the Commission of the progress being made in his country in limiting the production and controlling the exports of coca leaf, in reducing the number of chewers, and in strengthening the relevant administrative machinery. It also heard a statement by the Minister of Public Health of Peru on questions related to the coca leaf and prospects for ameliorating the situation. The Commission discussed the question whether the export of crude cocaine manufactured in Peru rather than of coca leaves would help to tighten international control of that drug.

The Commission also noted that the Government of Chile had recently drafted legislation to prohibit coca leaf chewing and that the Government of Argentina had declared such chewing harmful and had taken action in 1956 regarding the import of coca leaf.

CANNABIS

The Commission had before it surveys on the cannabis problem in a number of countries, including Angola, Brazil, Costa Rica, Egypt, India, Italy, Morocco and Pakistan. Also before it was a general paper summarizing the various aspects of the cannabis problem and the Commission's work in dealing with it. It was informed, too, about the recent progress towards banning the production and use of cannabis in India and Morocco.

The question of the breeding of a narcotic-free strain of the cannabis plant (which is also cultivated for its fibre and seed) was again considered, as was the problem presented by the widespread wild growth of the plant. In the latter connexion, it was suggested that technical assistance might be helpful in eradicating the wild plants.

The preparation of further surveys of the cannabis problem in Lebanon and Nepal, and in any other countries where it was of importance, was requested.

The Commission asked all Governments to abolish the legal use of cannabis, except for the indigenous Ayurvedic, Unani and Tibbi medical systems, and for scientific purposes. It also invited Governments with the necessary facilities to promote research into the active principle or principles of cannabis (the exact nature of which is at present unknown) and to exchange, directly, as well as through the Secretary-General, information on the results obtained from their research.

DIACETYLMORPHINE (HEROIN)

The Commission reviewed the available information on the implementation by Governments of the recommendations made by the Economic and Social Council (by resolution 548 G (XVIII), of 12 July 1954) and by the Commission on Narcotic Drugs on the prohibition of the use of diacetylmorphine. The Commission noted that out of 87 countries considered, including all United Nations Members, 63 had either prohibited the use of diacetylmorphine or had adopted a policy of prohibition, and that 19 had not yet done so either in practice or by a declaration of policy.

SYNTHETIC NARCOTIC DRUGS

The Commission discussed synthetic narcotic drugs on the basis of two studies, one prepared by the secretariat of WHO, in consultation with the United Nations Secretariat, and the other by the Secretary-General of the United Nations. The WHO study dealt both with the therapeutic advantages and with the addiction-producing disadvantages of the various natural and synthetic narcotics used in medicine. The Secretary-General's study was a compilation of information on the licit use and the abuse of the newer narcotics and on related international action.

The Commission gave particular attention to the licit use and the abuse of synthetic and other new narcotics and the measures needed to deal with these matters. Opinion in the Commission as to the desirability of measures for the limitation of the number of new narcotics continued to be divided. The Commission invited all the Members of the United Nations and members of the specialized agencies in whose territories narcotic drugs, natural or synthetic, were manufactured, to take measures to tighten the systems of control and to improve consultations between Governments.

BARBITURATES AND "TRANQUILLIZERS"

The Commission also considered the difficulties which have arisen in various countries as the result of the increasing use of barbiturates and "tranquillizers" and the international action to be taken in this regard.

Barbiturates, when taken in over-doses, can cause mental and neurological impairment in the form of psychoses or convulsions. The WHO Expert Committee on Addiction-Producing Drugs has described them as habit-forming, saying that in certain circumstances they can produce true addiction.

"Tranquillizers", it has been found, produced a calming effect on the central nervous system. Some of them, it has also been found, might produce habituation; their side-effects sometimes produce a greater danger to the user than habituation, and the danger of the abuse of these substances might become very serious.

The Commission recommended that Governments adopt appropriate legislative and administrative measures of control to prevent abuse of barbiturates. By another resolution, it re-

commended that Governments keep a careful watch for any abuse of "tranquillizers" with a view to taking any necessary measures of control.

DRUG ADDICTION

In response to a request by the Commission, the Secretariat prepared an analytical study on drug addiction which, along with a report of a WHO Study Group on Treatment and Care of Drug Addicts, served as a basis for the Commission's examination of the problem of the abuse of drugs.

The Commission noted that, despite ample evidence of a growing awareness of the addiction problem and of increasing efforts to combat it, some countries had reported more addicts for 1955 than for 1954. Close estimates of the extent of addiction could not, however, be made owing to the varying degrees in which addiction was known to the authorities in various countries.

The Commission gave particular attention to questions of the discovery, registration and control of addicts, their treatment and rehabilitation, and preventive measures that might be taken to reduce their number.

The Commission was generally in agreement with the treatment measures proposed by the WHO Study Group and expressed the hope that work on this subject would be continued. The Commission learned from several of its members and observers that their countries were expanding facilities for the treatment of addicts.

ILLICIT TRAFFIC

The basic feature of the illicit traffic remained unchanged during 1957, i.e., the supply still came almost entirely from illicit sources, the illicit traffic being well organized and having wide-spread international ramifications.

The Commission particularly drew the attention of Governments to the conspiratorial nature of this traffic which had added to the several difficulties encountered by enforcement authorities, and it stressed the need for close co-operation between the authorities of all countries.

Opium and opiates were still by far the most important drugs involved in the national and international traffic. Several clandestine factories for the manufacture of crude morphine or diacetylmorphine have been discovered, and there was reason, the Commission felt, to suspect the existence of others. The Commission expressed grave concern at the increasing traffic in cannabis throughout the world. Although the seizures of synthetic drugs reported were not considerable, the matter should be carefully watched. It also noted that traffic in cocaine was at a low level.

With regard to the reporting of the origin of drugs seized in the illicit traffic, the Commission was of the opinion that Governments should give careful attention to the two related aspects of this question and should expand, and, at the same time, arrange more consultations with other countries about these reports on origins.

The Commission also reviewed the obligations of Governments with regard to the reporting of information on seizures, and urged them to carry out their obligations meticulously in order to help in the international struggle against illicit traffic.

CARRIAGE OF NARCOTICS IN
FIRST-AID KITS OF AIRCRAFT

Legal difficulties having been experienced in connexion with the carriage of narcotics in first-aid kits on aircraft flying between one country and another, the Council of the International Civil Aviation Organization decided, on 1 April 1957, to invite the Economic and Social Council and the World Health Organization to study the related legal and medical problems. On 12 December 1957, the Economic and Social Council decided to refer the question to the Commission on Narcotic Drugs for action and report.

MEASURES FOR IMPROVING
THE SYSTEM OF CONTROL

In accordance with Council resolution 246 D (IX) of 6 July 1949, the Commission has been working for several years on a new draft convention (the proposed Single Convention on Narcotic Drugs), intended to codify the existing multilateral treaties governing the control of narcotic drugs, and to simplify and improve the control system, particularly by closing gaps in the existing provisions. The proposed Single Convention would, in general, retain the provisions laid down in the nine existing treaties.[1]

At its 1957 session, the Commission continued its work on the proposed Single Convention, using as a basis for its work the second draft which had been prepared in accordance with

decisions taken by the Commission between 1950 and 1955, and also an analytical compilation of comments on this draft by 24 Governments which were represented on the Council or the Commission or which had been invited to participate as observers in the Commission's work of codification. The Commission considered that the second draft of the Single Convention required a thorough review in order to eliminate the various alternative texts which, in several cases, involved important differences of principle. It prepared revisions of articles 2–20 and 23–27 for the second draft.

The Council, by resolution 667 E (XXIV), of 1 August 1957, reiterated its desire to see the draft Single Convention completed in as short a time as possible, asked the Commission to give priority to this work and authorized it to sit for an additional week at its thirteenth session in 1958 for this purpose.

TECHNICAL ASSISTANCE
FOR NARCOTICS CONTROL

During 1957, the Commission on Narcotic Drugs and the Economic and Social Council continued to follow the new arrangements introduced in 1956 to make technical assistance (in the form of expert advice, fellowships or seminars) more readily available to Governments requiring help in improving the control of narcotics.

The Government of Iran had requested and received technical assistance in carrying out its decision to discontinue opium production as a means of suppressing opium addiction within the country and the illicit traffic in Iranian opium abroad. This decision had far-reaching agricultural, medico-social and administrative consequences. The plight of the farmer, for whom opium was an important cash crop, had been studied by an Exploratory Mission of the Food and Agriculture Organization (FAO), which concluded that while no "complete substitute" for opium could be found, efforts had to be made in many directions to raise the income of the farmers concerned. Experts of FAO had subsequently sought to devise ways and means of doing this.

At the request of Iran, an expert was sent by WHO to advise on methods for treating the

[1] For further details, see *Y.U.N., 1955*, p. 220.

large number of opium addicts in Iran and also on certain other related problems.

In addition, the United Nations Technical Assistance Administration (TAA) sent an administrative expert to Teheran, to meet a request by the Government of Iran, for the services of an expert to help administer and coordinate the anti-opium campaign.

On 1 August 1957, the Economic and Social Council, by resolution 667 G (XXIV), asked the Technical Assistance Board and the appropriate specialized agencies participating in the Expanded Technical Assistance Programme to consider requests for technical aid to Iran in connexion with its effort to suppress the abuse of opium.

The Government of Thailand requested and obtained the short-term services of an expert in connexion with certain provisions in the 1958 national budget touching upon the Government opium monopoly and also in connexion with the Government's policy to suppress the smoking of opium.

The Governments of India and Morocco expressed interest in securing technical assistance in dealing with various aspects of the cannabis problem, which was rather serious in those countries. On 1 August 1957, the Council, by resolution 667 F (XXIV), asked the technical assistance authorities of the United Nations and specialized agencies to give due consideration to any requests for aid which India and Morocco might submit.

A programme for training scientists in methods of determining the geographical origin of opium by means of chemical and physical tests was set up by the Canadian Department of National Health and Welfare and placed without charge at the disposal of requesting Governments and TAA. Two fellowship holders, one from Iran and one from Singapore, participated in the programme. A third, from Turkey, was scheduled to reach Canada early in 1958.

DOCUMENTARY REFERENCES

ECONOMIC AND SOCIAL COUNCIL—24TH AND RESUMED 24TH SESSION
Plenary Meetings 995, 997.
Social Committee, meetings 372-374.

REPORT OF COMMISSION
E/3010/Rev.1. Report on 12th session of Commission on Narcotic Drugs, 29 April–31 May 1957 (see Annex VII of this report for listing of Commission documents).
E/3042. Report of Social Committee (draft resolution A, adopted unanimously by Committee).
RESOLUTION 667 A (XXIV), taking note of report of 12th session of Commission on Narcotic Drugs, as recommended by Social Committee, A/3042, adopted unanimously by Council on 1 August 1957, meeting 995.

IMPLEMENTATION OF TREATIES
E/3010/Rev.1. Report of 12th session of Commission on Narcotic Drugs, Chapter II.
Summary of Annual Reports of Governments Relating to Opium and Other Narcotic Drugs, 1955, and Addendum. U.N.P. Sales No.: 1957.XI.1 and 1957.XI.1/Add.1.
Report of Permanent Central Opium Board to Economic and Social Council on Work of Board in 1957. U.N.P. Sales No.: 1957.XI.3.
Estimated World Requirements of Narcotic Drugs in 1958. Statement issued by Drug Supervisory Body. U.N.P. Sales No.: 1957.XI.4.
Estimated World Requirements of Narcotic Drugs in 1957. Second and Third Supplements. U.N.P. Sales No.: 1956.XI.5/Add.2 and Add.3.

E/NA.1957/1. National authorities empowered to issue certificates and authorizations for the import and export of narcotic drugs.
E/NF.1957/1. List of firms authorized to manufacture drugs.
E/3042. Report of Social Committee (draft resolution B, adopted unanimously by Committee).
RESOLUTION 667 B (XXIV), taking note of report of Permanent Central Opium Board on work of Board in 1956, as recommended by Social Committee, adopted unanimously by Council on 1 August 1957, meeting 995.

PARTICULAR ASPECTS OF NARCOTIC DRUGS CONTROL

ECONOMIC AND SOCIAL COUNCIL—24TH SESSION
Plenary Meeting 995.
Social Committee, meetings 372-374.

OPIUM
Request by Afghanistan
E/3010/Rev.1. Report of 12th session of Commission on Narcotic Drugs, Chapter V and Annex II.
E/L.765. Note from observer of Government of Iran.
E/L.757. Cable from Foreign Office, Government of Afghanistan.
A/3613. Report of Economic and Social Council to General Assembly, Chapter VI, section V.

Scientific Research on Opium
E/3010/Rev.1. Report of 12th session of Commission on Narcotic Drugs, Chapter V and Annex II.

E/3010/Rev.1, Annex I. Draft resolution I, recommended by Commission, adopted by Social Committee by 13 votes to 0, with 5 abstentions.

E/3042. Report of Social Committee (draft resolution C).

RESOLUTION 667 C (XXIV), as recommended by Social Committee, E/3042, adopted by Council on 1 August 1957, meeting 995, by 15 votes to 0, with 3 abstentions.

"*The Economic and Social Council*

"*Requests* the Secretary-General to increase the staff and facilities of the United Nations Laboratory so as to permit an increased number of analyses of opium samples to be carried out and research on methods of determining the geographical origin of opium by physical and chemical means to be expedited."

KHAT

E/3010/Rev.1. Report of 12th session of Commission on Narcotic Drugs, Chapter IX.

E/3010/Rev.1, Annex I. Draft resolution II, recommended by Commission, and amended orally by China, adopted unanimously by Social Committee.

E/3042. Report of Social Committee (draft resolution D).

RESOLUTION 667 D (XXIV), as recommended by Social Committee, E/3042, adopted unanimously by Council on 1 August 1957, meeting 995.

"*The Economic and Social Council,*

"*Having noted* that the habitual chewing of the leaves of khat (*catha edulis*) has become widespread in several countries,

"*Recognizing* that this habit gives rise to a grave social problem in the countries affected,

"*Invites* the World Health Organization to study the medical aspects of the problem and to report thereon to the Commission on Narcotic Drugs."

DRUG ADDICTION, DIACETYLMORPHINE, COCA LEAF, CANNABIS, SYNTHETIC NARCOTIC DRUGS, BARBITURATES AND "TRANQUILLIZERS"

E/3010/Rev.1. Report of 12th session of Commission on Narcotic Drugs, Chapters IV-IX and Annex II.

ILLICIT TRAFFIC

E/3010/Rev.1. Report of 12th session of Commission on Narcotic Drugs, Chapter III and Annex II.

E/NS.1957/Summary 1-12. Summary of reports on illicit transactions and seizures received by Secretary-General between 1 January and 31 December 1957.

CARRIAGE OF NARCOTICS IN
FIRST-AID KITS OF AIRCRAFT

E/3054. Communication from Secretary-General of International Civil Aviation Organization.

*MEASURES FOR IMPROVING
SYSTEM OF CONTROL*

ECONOMIC AND SOCIAL COUNCIL—24TH SESSION
Plenary Meeting, 995.
Social Committee, meetings 372-374.

E/3010/Rev.1. Report of 12th session of Commission on Narcotic Drugs, Chapter XII. Proposed single convention on narcotic drugs.

E/AC.7/L.302. Canada draft resolution, adopted unanimously by Social Committee.

E/3042. Report of Social Committee (draft resolution E).

RESOLUTION 667 E (XXIV), as recommended by Social Committee, E/3042, adopted unanimously by Council on 1 August 1957, meeting 995.

"*The Economic and Social Council,*

"*Having considered* the report of the Commission on Narcotic Drugs on its twelfth session concerning the progress made in codifying the international instruments on narcotic drugs,

"*Recalling* resolution 626 F (XXII) of 2 August 1956, in which it requested the Commission on Narcotic Drugs to devote the maximum time at its twelfth session to the completion of a draft single convention on narcotic drugs,

"*Commending* the Commission on Narcotic Drugs for the progress made in this connexion,

"1. *Reiterates* its desire to see the draft single convention completed in as short a time as possible;

"2. *Requests* the Commission on Narcotic Drugs to give priority to this work;

"3. *Authorizes* the Commission on Narcotic Drugs to sit for an additional week at its thirteenth session for this purpose."

*TECHNICAL ASSISTANCE
FOR NARCOTICS CONTROL*

ECONOMIC AND SOCIAL COUNCIL—24TH SESSION
Plenary Meeting 995.
Social Committee, meetings 372-374.
Technical Assistance Committee, meeting 132.

E/2992 and Add.1-3. Note by Secretary-General.

E/3010/Rev.1. Report of 12th session of Commission on Narcotic Drugs, Chapter XI.

TECHNICAL ASSISTANCE TO IRAN

E/3041. Report of Technical Assistance Committee, paragraphs 34 and 35.

E/AC.7/L.303 and Rev.1. Pakistan draft resolution and revision, adopted unanimously by Social Committee.

E/3042. Report of Social Committee (draft resolution G).

RESOLUTION 667 G (XXIV), as recommended by Social Committee, E/3042, adopted unanimously by Council on 1 August 1957, meeting 995.

"*The Economic and Social Council,*

"*Considering* that, in its resolution 626 E (XXII) of 2 August 1956 concerning technical assistance to Iran, it affirmed that 'Iran is an important opium-producing country and, in order to ensure the execution of the law banning cultivation of the opium poppy, requires increased technical assistance in enabling its cultivators to introduce other agricultural crops to replace opium poppy plantation and also in respect of the treatment of addicts',

"*Recalling* that at its twelfth session the Commission on Narcotic Drugs expressed its appreciation of the considerable progress that had been made in Iran in this regard,

"*Further considering* the importance of the subject and the need for the continuance of technical assistance to Iran by the United Nations and its specialized agencies,

"1. *Requests* the Technical Assistance Board and the participating organizations concerned to continue to give due consideration to requests by the Government of Iran for technical assistance in this field;

"2. *Requests further* that the Secretary-General, after consultation with the participating organizations concerned, report to the Commission on Narcotic Drugs and to the Council on the extent to which it has been possible to meet the request of Iran for technical assistance in this regard."

TECHNICAL ASSISTANCE TO INDIA AND MOROCCO

E/3010/Rev.1, Annex I. Draft resolution III, recommended by Commission on Narcotic Drugs, adopted by Social Committee, by 14 votes to 0, with 4 abstentions.

E/3042. Report of Social Committee (draft resolution F).

RESOLUTION 667 F (XXIV), as recommended by Social Committee, E/3042, adopted by Council on 1 August 1957, meeting 995, by 15 votes to 0, with 3 abstentions.

"*The Economic and Social Council,*

"*Recalling* its resolution 626 D (XXII) of 2 August 1956, by which it invited Governments to consider the possibility of applying, under existing arrangements concerned with technical assistance, for the advisory services of experts, fellowships and scholarships, and seminars, in the field of narcotic control;

"*Recalling also* that under the terms of that resolution the United Nations and the specialized agencies were recommended to give due consideration to any requests which the countries concerned might make for technical assistance in developing appropriate administrative, social or economic measures in order to deal effectively with problems raised by the illicit production of, or traffic in, narcotic drugs or by drug addiction,

"*Noting* that, at the twelfth session of the Commission on Narcotic Drugs, the representative of India drew attention to this country's need for technical assistance on matters connected with the treatment of addicts and also in eradicating the wild growth of cannabis plants, and that the observer of Morocco referred to his country's need for help in carrying out its plan to substitute other crops for the cannabis crop in northern Morocco, and also in the treatment of addicts using cannabis,

"1. *Draws attention* to the importance of the measures being taken, and to be taken, in India and Morocco to deal with the problem of cannabis;

"2. *Invites* the technical assistance authorities of the United Nations and of the specialized agencies to give due consideration to any requests for assistance, within the framework of the existing administrative and financial arrangements, which they may receive from the Governments of those countries in this connexion."

ELECTIONS TO PERMANENT CENTRAL OPIUM BOARD

ECONOMIC AND SOCIAL COUNCIL—23RD AND 24TH SESSIONS
Plenary Meetings 969, 996.

E/2962 and Corr.1, Add.1, Add.1/Corr.1, Add.2-11. Note by Secretary-General.

E/L.749. Canada draft resolution.

RESOLUTION 646(XXIII), as submitted by Canada, E/L.749, adopted by Council on 29 April 1957, meeting 969.

"*The Economic and Social Council,*

"*Noting* that article 19 of the 1925 Convention on Narcotic Drugs and Council resolution 123 D (VI) of 2 March 1948 outline qualifications and criteria for the eligibility of members of the Permanent Central Opium Board,

"*Considering* that further nominations may still be submitted,

"*Decides* to establish a committee of five to review the nominations and inform the Council, at its twenty-fourth session, which candidates possess the necessary technical qualifications in the light of the criteria outlined in the Convention and in Council resolution 123 D (VI)."

E/3028. Report of Committee to Review Candidates for Election to Permanent Central Opium Board.

MEMBERSHIP OF DRUG SUPERVISORY BODY

ECONOMIC AND SOCIAL COUNCIL—24TH SESSION
Plenary Meeting 995.
Social Committee, meetings 372, 373.

E/2962, Annex B. Note by Secretary-General on election of members of Permanent Central Opium Board, containing draft resolution, sponsored formally by Canada, and adopted by Social Committee by 12 votes to 0, with 4 abstentions.

E/3042. Report of Social Committee (draft resolution H).

RESOLUTION 667 H (XXIV), as recommended by Social Committee, E/3042, adopted by Council on 1 August 1957, meeting 995, by 15 votes to 0, with 3 abstentions.

"*The Economic and Social Council,*

"*Recalling* its discussion at its sixth session, the resolution adopted by the Commission on Narcotic Drugs at its third session, and the statement contained in the report of the Permanent Central Opium Board on the work of the Board in 1956, relating to the question of close liaison and the possibility of a personal union between the Permanent Central Opium Board and the Drug Supervisory Body,

"*Taking note with satisfaction* of the results already achieved in these respects,

"*Taking note also with satisfaction* of the willingness of the World Health Organization to co-operate in further steps in this regard,

"*Having regard* to the interlocking character of the functions of the two bodies, and to the provisions contained in the second draft of the single convention on narcotic drugs for the replacement of the two bodies by a single organ,

"*Recalling also* its resolutions 590 A I (XX) of 5 August 1955, and 630 A I (XXII) of 9 August 1956, and the desirability of further streamlining the work of the United Nations in the economic, social and human rights fields,

"1. *Expresses its agreement* with the desirability of ensuring to the greatest possible extent close liaison and a personal union between the two bodies, pending the establishment and coming into effect of a single convention;

"2. *Invites* the World Health Organization, the Commission on Narcotic Drugs, and the Permanent Central Opium Board, in the furtherance of these objects, to consider appointing to the Drug Supervisory Body, for a five-year period corresponding to the term of office of members of the Board provided for in the 1925 Convention, persons who are members of the Board."

OTHER DOCUMENTS

Bulletin on Narcotics. Quarterly.

CHAPTER XV

QUESTIONS OF CO-ORDINATION AND RELATIONS OF THE UNITED NATIONS WITH THE SPECIALIZED AGENCIES

A general review of the development and co-ordination of the economic, social and human rights programmes of the United Nations and the specialized agencies as a whole was undertaken at the Economic and Social Council's twenty-fourth session, in mid-1957. The Council also made a special study of the concentration of activities in those fields.

Discussion was for the most part based on a report by the Secretary-General entitled *Observations on the Work Programme of the Council and on the Financial Implications of the Council's Actions,* on two reports of the Administrative Committee on Co-ordination and on the annual reports of the specialized agencies. The reports to the Council from its regional and functional commissions provided further background material for the debate.

In an introductory statement, the Secretary-General commented on the need to ensure that the best use was made of resources in the execution of given assignments and that efforts were concentrated on matters of first priority. While saying that the primary objective remained that of promoting the economic and social development of the under-developed countries, he suggested the possibility that some new emphases should be introduced or new activities initiated where there was a prospect of particularly productive results. In that connexion, he cited the growing challenge of the needs of Africa and the Middle East.

The fundamental criteria, he said, must be the needs of the under-developed countries and the ability of the United Nations to make a really significant contribution within the limits of the resources available to it. During the past year, certain phases of the work done in three broad fields—transport, natural resources and public administration—had seemed to meet those criteria. In these fields, there were many ways in which the United Nations' assistance might profitably be developed.

With regard to public administration, the Secretary-General said that he had, in response to a request by the Council, submitted specific proposals for the establishment, on an experimental basis, of an international administrative service to help meet the acute shortage of trained administrators in some of the under-developed and particularly in some of the newly independent States (see also above, CHAPTER IV, section on PROPFSAL FOR AN INTERNATIONAL ADMINISTRATIVE SERVICE).

The twentieth report of the Administrative Committee on Co-ordination (ACC) described further practical steps which had been taken to achieve a rational division of functions among the various organizations and agreement on methods of co-operation in various spheres of activity. The report gave details of the understanding reached on the concept and scope of community development, and the action taken by ACC with regard to co-ordination of activities in the peaceful uses of atomic energy. It described relations between the United Nations, the specialized agencies and the proposed International Atomic Energy Agency, and contained statements on existing activities in that field.

Also discussed by ACC were the conditions of effective concerted action by the United Nations and the specialized agencies with regard to broad programmes of economic and social development. It had formulated a series of conclusions and recommendations, the most important of which envisaged the need for special action to ensure that, before final decisions on a broad programme involving a major new initiative were taken by any one organization, the governing bodies of the others directly concerned should be consulted and given an opportunity of expressing their views.

DEVELOPMENT AND CO-ORDINATION OF PROGRAMMES AND ACTIVITIES

On 1 August 1957, the Council unanimously adopted three resolutions on the development and co-ordination of the economic, social and human rights programmes and activities of the United Nations and the specialized agencies as a whole.

By one of them (resolution 665 A (XXIV)), the Council reaffirmed its reliance on ACC to continue to develop and improve arrangements for the fullest consultations between the secretariats concerned in all stages of planning and execution of programmes of common interest. It also recognized the need for establishing regular consultations of the governing bodies of competent organizations in all cases of major programmes calling for the participation of several organizations within the framework of all plans of concerted action. The Council invited ACC: (a) to formulate, for consideration at the Council's twenty-sixth session, in mid-1958, a preliminary list of specific fields of activity requiring concerted action among several organizations; (b) to suggest procedures for the elaboration and execution of plans of

concerted action in such fields, including steps to be taken by the governing bodies of the specialized agencies; and (c) to make proposals about measures to assist the Council in co-ordinating such plans.

By the second resolution (665 B (XXIV)), the Council took note of a report by the Secretary-General on the detailing of certain social affairs personnel from United Nations Headquarters to regional offices. It also took note of a statement in that report to the effect that the extension of the social action of the United Nations Secretariat to the regions had proved itself and that he had therefore included provision for the units at their current level in his budget estimates for 1958. The Council decided to convey to the General Assembly its approval of the action taken by the Secretary-General in the matter.

By the third resolution (665 C (XXIV)), the Council recalled the successive steps taken by it since 1950 to ensure the concentration of efforts and resources of the United Nations and the specialized agencies with respect to their programmes in the economic, social and human rights fields and to bring about a maximum return from international outlays for such programmes. Calling the attention of the General Assembly to its continued interest in the matter, the Council expressed the belief that a general survey of the activities of the United Nations and the specialized agencies in those fields and a forecast of the scope and trend of programmes and expenditures during the next five years would contribute to the increased effectiveness of the work of the United Nations and the specialized agencies, separately and as a whole. They would, it also believed, be of assistance to Governments in formulating policies towards these organizations.

The Council also asked the Secretary-General, in the light of the principles set forth in the annex to its resolution 664 (XXIV) (see below, DOCUMENTARY REFERENCES), to make an appraisal of the scope, trend and cost of the regular United Nations programmes in those fields for the period 1959–1964 for consideration at the Council's twenty-eighth session in mid-1959.

The Council further invited five specialized agencies to consider the most appropriate and practical methods of preparing similar appraisals of their own programmes for the same period equally based on the principles contained in the annex to resolution 664(XXIV). The agencies to which this invitation was addressed were the International Labour Organisation (ILO), the Food and Agriculture Organization (FAO), the United Nations Educational, Scientific and Cultural Organization (UNESCO), the World Health Organization (WHO) and the World Meteorological Organization (WMO).

In addition, the Council asked the Secretary-General and invited the executive heads of the specialized agencies concerned to consult together as soon as possible with a view to having such appraisals prepared by the various organizations concerned in comparable form. The Administrative Committee on Co-ordination was asked to present a special report to the Council's twenty-sixth session, in mid-1958, on the preparation of these appraisals, with particular reference to any major problems which might have been encountered. At its mid-1958 session, it was decided, the Council would also consider the arrangements necessary for preparing, on the basis of the appraisals, a consolidated report with conclusions to be submitted together with the appraisals to the Council's thirtieth session, in mid-1960.

CONCENTRATION OF ACTIVITIES IN ECONOMIC, SOCIAL AND HUMAN RIGHTS FIELDS

In submitting his *Observations on the Work Programme of the Council and on the Financial Implications of the Council's Actions,* the Secretary-General assumed, in accordance with the Council's wishes, that the concentration and co-ordination of the work of the United Nations in the economic, social and human rights fields should be a continuing process. In that sense, his report (which reviewed the United Nations activities in these fields) was to be regarded as a sequel to the review of the organization and work of the Secretariat in the economic and social fields which he had submitted to the Council in 1954.

The Secretary-General's report was considered in detail in the Council's Co-ordination Committee. It recommended that the Council express its appreciation of the report and affirm its general approval of the views and sugges-

tions set forth in it, subject to further detailed comments made by the Committee in its own report (see annex to resolution 664(XXIV) quoted in DOCUMENTARY REFERENCES, below).

The Committee also recommended that the Council reaffirm certain general principles—which the Committee enumerated—as guides to future work in the field of co-ordination. It also gave special attention to problems connected with the preparation and distribution of documents and the frequency of meetings, and it made specific comments on the various proposals of the Secretary-General on the work programme of the Council. Finally, the Committee endorsed the Secretary-General's proposals concerning the procedural aspects of the question of financial implications.

On 1 August 1957, the Council, on the recommendation of the Committee, unanimously adopted resolution 664 A (XXIV) dealing with the concentration of United Nations and specialized agency activities in the economic, social and human rights fields. The Council thereby noted with satisfaction the efforts being made by the specialized agencies to improve the co-ordination of their programmes, both within each agency and in relation to the programmes of other agencies. It invited the agencies to continue to provide the Council with information about the co-ordination of their activities and the concentration of their programmes. The Council also invited the agencies to consider the extent to which they might be able to apply the general guiding principles in the field of co-operation and concentration of activities approved by the Council as guides to the future work of the United Nations and its subsidiary organs in the field of co-ordination (see Annex, sub-paragraph 1(c), to resolution 664(XXIV) in DOCUMENTARY REFERENCES, below).

In another resolution, 664 B (XXIV), also unanimously adopted on 1 August 1957, the Council asked the Secretary-General to submit a further report to its twenty-sixth session, in mid-1958, on the lines of his *Observations on the Work Programme of the Council and on the Financial Implications of the Council's Actions.*

By yet another resolution (665 D (XXIV)), adopted on 2 August 1957, the Council approved the reports of its Co-ordination Committee and the recommendations contained in them with the exception of one about the frequency of sessions of the Commission on Human Rights and the Commission on the Status of Women (see Annex, paragraph 3(e), to resolution 664 (XXIV) in DOCUMENTARY REFERENCES, below). The Council decided not, for the present, to change the frequency of the sessions of these Commissions, but rather to seek their views on the Committee's recommendation that they should in future meet every two years instead of every year. (See also above, CHAPTERS IX, X.)

DOCUMENTARY REFERENCES

ECONOMIC AND SOCIAL COUNCIL—24TH SESSION
Plenary Meetings 980-983, 995, 996.
Co-ordination Committee, meetings 152-166.

E/2931; E/2993. Twentieth and twenty-first reports of Administrative Committee on Co-ordination.
E/3011 and Corr.1, and Add.1, 2. Observations on Work Programme of Council and on Financial Implications of Council's Actions. Report of Secretary-General.

REPORTS OF SPECIALIZED AGENCIES
E/2944 and Add.1. Report of International Bank for fiscal year ended 30 June 1956, and summary of Bank activities, 1 July 1956–31 January 1957.
E/2945 and Add.1. Report of International Monetary Fund for fiscal year ended 30 April 1956, and summary of activities of Fund, 1 May 1956–31 January 1957.
E/2953. Report of UPU for year 1956.
E/2967. Report of WMO.
E/2973 and Add.1, Add.1/Corr.1, and Add.2. Report of FAO, report of 24th and 25th sessions of Council of FAO, and report of FAO on world food and agricultural situation and its implications for work of the Organization.
E/2974 and Add.1. Report of UNESCO for 1956-1957, and resolution of Executive Board of UNESCO on co-ordination between United Nations and specialized agencies with view to concerted action in economic and social field and in field of human rights.
E/2975. Report of ILO for 1956-1957.
E/2980 and Add.1. Report of WHO for 1956, and supplementary report.
E/2994. Report of ITU for year 1956.
E/3007 and Add.1. Report of ICAO for year 1956 and brief summary of major activities of ICAO, January-April 1957.
E/2986; E/3019. Inter-agency agreements and agreements between agencies and other inter-governmental organizations. Letters of 23 April and 27 May 1957 from UNESCO transmitting text of draft agreements between UNESCO and Ibero-American Bureau of Education and between UNESCO and League of Arab States, respectively.

REPORTS OF REGIONAL ECONOMIC COMMISSIONS
E/2959. Economic Commission for Asia and Far East. Annual report.
E/2989. Economic Commission for Europe. Annual report.
E/2998. Economic Commission for Latin America. Annual report.

REPORTS OF FUNCTIONAL COMMISSIONS
E/2948. Transport and Communications Commission. Report of 8th session.
E/2957/Rev.1. Population Commission. Report of 9th session.
E/2968. Commission on Status of Women. Report of 11th session.
E/2970/Rev.1. Commission on Human Rights. Report of 13th session.
E/3003. Third report of Commission on International Commodity Trade.
E/3008. Social Commission. Report of 11th session.
E/3010 and Add.1. Commission on Narcotic Drugs. Report of 12th session.

DEVELOPMENT AND CO-ORDINATION OF PROGRAMMES AND ACTIVITIES
E/3013. Detailing of certain Headquarters personnel to regional offices. Report of Secretary-General.
E/AC.24/L.128 and Add.1. Argentina, Brazil, Dominican Republic, Mexico draft resolution, as orally amended in Committee, adopted unanimously by Co-ordination Committee.
E/AC.24/L.129. Argentina, Canada, United Kingdom draft resolution, as orally amended in Committee, adopted unanimously by Co-ordination Committee.
E/AC.24/L.130. Argentina, France, United States draft resolution, as orally amended in Committee, adopted unanimously by Co-ordination Committee.
E/3039. Report of Co-ordination Committee.
RESOLUTIONS 665 A-C (XXIV), 665 A (XXIV), as recommended by Co-ordination Committee, E/3039, and as amended orally by Pakistan, and 665 B and C (XXIV), as recommended by Committee, adopted unanimously by Council on 1 August 1957, meeting 995.

A
"*The Economic and Social Council,*
"*Having considered* the twentieth and twenty-first reports of the Administrative Committee on Co-ordination and, in particular, paragraphs 27 to 31 of the twentieth report dealing with conditions of effective concerted action, and the corresponding sections of reports of specialized agencies,
"1. *Reaffirms* its reliance on the Administrative Committee on Co-ordination, under the leadership of the Secretary-General, to continue to develop and improve arrangements for the fullest consultations between the secretariats in all stages of planning and execution of programmes of common interest;
"2. *Recognizes* the need for establishing, on a regular basis, consultations of the governing bodies of competent organizations in all cases of major

programmes calling for the participation of several organizations within the framework of a plan of concerted action;

"3. *Invites* the Administrative Committee on Co-ordination, in the light of the opinions expressed in the Council and of the positions taken by the governing bodies of the specialized agencies, to formulate for the consideration of the Council at its twenty-sixth session:

"(*a*) A preliminary list of specific fields of activity requiring concerted action among several organizations;

"(*b*) Suggested procedures for the elaboration and execution of plans of concerted action in such fields, including steps to be taken by the governing bodies of the specialized agencies;

"(*c*) Proposals concerning measures which might be taken to assist the Council in the exercise of its role of co-ordination as regards such plans."

B

"*The Economic and Social Council,*

"*Taking note* of the report by the Secretary-General on the detailing of certain Headquarters social affairs personnel to regional offices, prepared in accordance with its resolution 630 B (XXII) of 9 August 1956 to enable the Council to transmit its views on this experiment to the General Assembly,

"*Taking* note of the statement in paragraph 6 of the report that the Secretary-General believes that this extension of the social action of the United Nations Secretariat to the regions has proved itself, and that he has therefore included provision for the units, at their present level, in his budget estimates for 1958,

"*Decides* to convey to the General Assembly its approval of the above-mentioned action taken by the Secretary-General in this matter."

C

"*The Economic and Social Council,*

"*Noting* General Assembly resolution 1094(XI) of 27 February 1957,

"*Having considered,* as requested in that resolution, paragraphs 6 and 7 of the thirty-seventh report of the Advisory Committee on Administrative and Budgetary Questions,

"*Recalling* the successive steps taken by it year by year since 1950 to ensure the concentration of efforts and resources of the United Nations and the specialized agencies with respect to their programmes in the economic, social and human rights fields, and to bring about a maximum return from international outlays for such programmes,

"1. *Calls the attention* of the General Assembly to the Council's continued interest in co-ordination, concentration and the orderly development of programmes of the United Nations and the specialized agencies in the economic, social and human rights fields, and to its intensified efforts to achieve these ends;

"2. *Expresses* its belief that a general survey of the activities of the United Nations and the specialized agencies in the economic, social and human rights fields, and a forecast of the scope and trend of programmes and expenditures during the next five years, would contribute to the increased effectiveness of the work of the United Nations and the specialized agencies in these fields, separately and as a whole, and be of assistance to Governments in formulating policies towards these organizations;

"3. *Requests* the Secretary-General, in the light of the principles set forth in the annex to its resolution 664(XXIV) of 1 August 1957, to make an appraisal of the scope, trend and cost of the regular United Nations programmes in these fields for the period 1959-1964 for consideration by the Council at its twenty-eighth session;

"4. *Invites* the International Labour Organisation, the Food and Agriculture Organization of the United Nations, the United Nations Educational, Scientific and Cultural Organization, the World Health Organization, and the World Meteorological Organization, to consider the most appropriate and practical methods of preparing similar appraisals of their own programmes for the same period, equally based on the principles contained in the annex;

"5. *Requests* the Secretary-General and *invites* the executive heads of the specialized agencies concerned to consult together, as soon as possible, with a view to the preparation by the various organizations concerned of the appraisals referred to above in comparable form;

"6. *Requests* the Administrative Committee on Co-ordination to present to the Council at its twenty-sixth session a special report regarding the preparation of these appraisals, with particular reference to any major problems that may have been encountered;

"7. *Decides* to consider at its twenty-sixth session the arrangements necessary for preparing on the basis of the above-mentioned appraisals a consolidated report with conclusions, to be submitted together with the appraisals to the Council at its thirtieth session."

CONCENTRATION OF ACTIVITIES IN ECONOMIC, SOCIAL AND HUMAN RIGHTS FIELDS

E/3011 and Corr.1, and Add.1, 2. Observations on Work Programme of Council and on Financial Implications of Council's Actions. Report of Secretary-General.

E/AC.24/L.125. Suggestions regarding work of Co-ordination Committee in pursuance of paragraph 9 of Council resolution 630 A I (XXII). Note by Secretary-General.

E/AC.24/L.126 and Add.1, 2. Note by Secretary-General containing draft texts of Co-ordination Committee's report.

E/3024/Rev.1, and Rev.1/Add.1. Report of Co-ordination Committee, Parts I and II.

E/AC.24/L.127. Proposals made by United Kingdom for draft report of Co-ordination Committee, Part III.

E/AC.24/L.131. United Kingdom draft resolution, adopted unanimously by Co-ordination Committee.

E/3034 and Add.1. Report of Co-ordination Committee, reproducing as Part A of the Annex, documents E/3024/Rev.1, and E/3024/Rev.1/Add.1, and containing two draft resolutions.

RESOLUTION 664 A and B (XXIV), as recommended by Co-ordination Committee, E/3034 and Add.1, adopted unanimously by Council on 1 August 1957, meeting 995.

A

"*The Economic and Social Council,*

"*Having considered* the reports of the specialized agencies presented to the Council, and in particular those sections included in response to paragraph 8 of Council resolution 630 A I (XXII) of 9 August 1956 concerning the co-ordination and concentration of their activities,

"1. *Notes with satisfaction* the efforts being made by the specialized agencies to improve the co-ordination of their programmes, both within each agency and in relation to the programmes of other agencies;

"2. *Invites* the specialized agencies:

"(*a*) To continue to provide information in their annual reports concerning the co-ordination of activities, both within each agency and between the specialized agencies and other international organizations where appropriate;

"(*b*) To include in their reports in 1958 passages dealing specifically with the further concentration of their programmes in the light of the discussions which have taken place in the Council, and to cite examples of concentration achieved during the preceding year;

"(*c*) To consider the extent to which they may be able to apply the general guiding principles in the field of co-operation and concentration of activities, as contained in sub-paragraph 1 (*c*) of the annex to the report of the Co-ordination Committee and approved by the Council at its twenty-fourth session as guides to the future work of the United Nations and its subsidiary organs in the field of co-ordination."

B

"*The Economic and Social Council,*

"*Having noted with appreciation* the report of the Secretary-General entitled 'Observations on the Work Programme of the Council and on the Financial Implications of the Council's Actions',

"*Having noted also* the proposal of the Secretary-General to prepare a further report on similar lines including the subjects not covered in the above-mentioned report,

"*Bearing in mind* that the further measures contemplated by the Council on concentration and co-ordination will require appropriate preparatory work by the Council,

"1. *Requests* the Secretary-General to submit a further report as proposed, for consideration by the Council at its twenty-sixth session;

"2. *Decides* that its Co-ordination Committee shall meet one week before the opening of its twenty-sixth session."

ANNEX

Text of Annex to Report of Co-ordination Committee (E/3034, annex) on Concentration of Activities of United Nations and Specialized Agencies in Economic, Social and Human Rights Fields

A

INTRODUCTION

"1. As a result of its consideration of the observa-

tions made by the Secretary-General in the introduction to his report, the Committee recommends that the Council:

"(*a*) Express its appreciation of the work of the Secretary-General in the preparation of his report;

"(*b*) Affirm its general approval of the views and suggestions set forth therein subject to the further detailed comments of the Committee contained in the present report;

"(*c*) Re-affirm the following general principles as guides to future work in the field of co-ordination:

"(i) All efforts to achieve greater effectiveness in the work of the United Nations in the economic, social and human rights fields should be regarded as a continuing process and to this end programmes of work of the Council and its subsidiary bodies should continue to be reviewed at periodic intervals by the Council on the basis of reports submitted by the Secretary-General;

"(ii) The promotion of economic and social development of under-developed countries should continue to be the overriding objective of all activities in this field as established by the Council at its fourteenth session;

"(iii) The achievement of optimum results, within the limits of whatever resources may be available at any given time, can best be assured by concentration of efforts on a limited number of major areas of activity, by giving preference to those projects which promise practical results, by grouping together and interrelating, where appropriate, individual items of demonstrable urgency or importance, or by eliminating or deferring projects of relatively low priority;

"(iv) Continued attention should be paid to the closer co-ordination of the economic and social aspects of international development work, to the elimination of unrelated and isolated activities which are not of demonstrable urgency or practical value, and to the most effective co-ordination of the work of the Secretariat at Headquarters and in the regional economic commissions.

"2. The Committee devoted special attention to the problems connected with the preparation and distribution of documents and frequency of meetings. In its view, adequate preparation and the distribution of documents in good time are indispensable prerequisites if the discussions are to contribute to the best results. Moreover, the work of the Secretariat can be most fruitful if it is concentrated on a relatively limited number of tasks of major importance, which will also ensure a more effective participation of Governments in the work of the United Nations.

"3. With these considerations in mind, the Committee further recommends that the Council:

"(*a*) Impress on its subsidiary bodies the desirability of limiting their requests for reports to matters of major importance;

"(*b*) Request the regional and functional commissions, whenever they deem it appropriate, to leave to the Secretary-General decisions on the timing of reports requested by them;

"(*c*) Request the Secretary-General to present reports in the briefest and most concise form compatible with the thorough treatment of the subjects under consideration, and to ensure that such reports are distributed in all the working languages as punctually as possible and in accordance with the applicable rules of procedure;

"(d) Request the regional commissions and functional commissions, with a view to obtaining the best possible results, to keep under constant review their calendars of conferences and meetings, particularly those of working parties, *ad hoc* bodies, and subsidiary organs, with the aim of reducing, whenever possible, the number and the length of these meetings;

"(e) Establish the principle that the Commission on Human Rights and the Commission on the Status of Women should in future, in line with the practice of other functional commissions, meet biennially, and request them not later than in the course of their sessions in 1959 to arrange their work programmes accordingly.

I. SOCIAL ACTIVITIES

"4. The Committee noted the great importance attached by many Governments to the reports on the world social situation and the desire expressed in many quarters that they be produced as frequently as practicable. Recognizing the difficulties in producing these reports at very frequent intervals, the Committee concurred in the solution, proposed by the Social Commission and accepted by the Secretary-General in the addendum to his report, concerning the publication of a series of reports on various social questions in 1959, 1961 and 1963. It was understood that the 1959 *International Survey of Programmes of Social Development* would cover international as well as national measures. While the detailed arrangements for the preparation of the report called for in 1961 have yet to be worked out, it was understood that Part I of the 1961 report would consist essentially of a brief survey of trends and would be closely related to the subject of Part II, the study of balanced economic and social developments. The next full report on the world social situation would be scheduled for 1963.

"5. With regard to housing, building and planning, the Committee agreed that the Council should request the Social Commission to concentrate its efforts in this field on work relating to the social aspects of housing, including efforts to mobilize self-help in improving both rural and urban housing.

"6. The Committee also concurred in the desirability of encouraging exchanges of information on housing research, building techniques and related matters between the various regional economic commissions.

II. ACTIVITIES IN THE FIELD OF HUMAN RIGHTS

"7. The Committee endorses the proposals made by the Secretary-General in this section of his report and recommends that the Council decide:

"(a) That the 1955 *Yearbook on Human Rights* be issued without a separate section on arbitrary arrest, detention and exile, and that the inclusion of a section in the *Yearbook* on a specific project be not initiated until the Commission on Human Rights has completed its review of the scope and content of the *Yearbook;*

"(b) That with regard to the programme of studies of discrimination on which the Sub-Commission on the Prevention of Discrimination and the Protection of Minorities is engaged, the country reports utilized in the preparation of these studies be not normally issued as documents;

"(c) That the Commission on the Status of Women be requested to continue the efforts which it has already commenced to: (i) space out the reports called for by its continuing projects and (ii) reduce the number of its *ad hoc* projects;

"(d) That the programme on advisory services in the field of human rights provide the possibility of holding seminars to be arranged on a regional rather than on a world-wide basis and that the topics discussed in the seminars should relate to selected aspects of the work programmes of the commission concerned. The use of working parties in the preparation of such seminars is acceptable although it may not be necessary to utilize this technique for every session.

"8. As regards the questionnaire drawn up by the Commission on the Status of Women as part of the *ad hoc* project on the occupational outlook for women, the Committee, while not competent to deal with the substance of the proposed questionnaire, notes the concern of the Secretary-General regarding its broad and diffuse scope and recommends that this aspect of the problem be given further consideration by the Council or its appropriate substantive committee.

III. ECONOMIC ACTIVITIES

"9. With reference to section III of the Secretary-General's report relating to economic activities, the Committee endorses in general the proposals and suggestions made therein, as supplemented by the additional observations made by the Secretary-General in the course of the debate. The only matter which the Committee considers it necessary to bring to the special attention of the Council concerns the frequency of meetings of the Commission on International Commodity Trade. Here, the Committee notes that the Commission itself has already decided to meet annually, instead of at intervals of six months. After considering the views expressed by the various representatives, the Committee agreed that, for the present at least, the Commission should meet once a year.

IV. REGIONAL ECONOMIC ACTIVITIES

"10. The Committee has noted with satisfaction the efforts made by each of the Regional Economic Commissions for Europe, Latin America, and Asia and the Far East, to co-ordinate its activities and to streamline its work programme in accordance with Council resolution 630 A I (XXII) of 9 August 1956.

"11. The Committee notes the helpful proposals made by the Executive Secretary of the Economic Commission for Europe as contained in the Secretary-

General's report, and the criteria proposed by the Executive Secretaries of the Economic Commission for Asia and the Far East, and the Economic Commission for Latin America for application to the work of their respective Commissions.

"12. The Committee wishes to draw to the Council's attention the desirability of encouraging exchanges of information and experience between the secretariats of the regional commissions on matters of mutual interest.

"13. The Committee devoted a considerable portion of its time during the debate on Section IV of the Secretary-General's report to the three following matters:

"(a) The relationship between the work of the regional economic commissions and the work done under the Technical Assistance Programme;

"(b) The balance between projects which are primarily in the economic field and those which are technological in character:

"(c) The relationship between the work of the regional economic commissions and the United Nations programmes in the social field.

"14. The Committee came to no final or agreed conclusions with regard to these matters, partly because the nature of the documentation available at this session of the Council did not make it possible to enter into a detailed consideration of the problems involved under these headings. The Committee considers that these questions should be the subject of further study at a subsequent session of the Council, and to this end recommends that the Council request the Secretary-General to study and report upon these questions at an appropriate session of the Council.

V. FINAL IMPLICATIONS OF ACTIONS OF THE COUNCIL

"15. The Committee endorses the proposals made by the Secretary-General in Section V of his report and approves his suggestion to present to the Council at the beginning of each summer session a statement showing:

"(a) The financial implications related to decisions taken at the Council's spring session;

"(b) Full particulars, on a provisional basis, of the financial implications related to decisions to be taken on documentation before the Council for the summer session;

"(c) Where appropriate, the extent to which, by the exercise of discretion in the timing of projects, the Secretary-General would expect to undertake the additional work within existing resources.

"16. The Committee considers that the proposals made by the Secretary-General with respect to the summer session should also be made applicable, where possible, to the work of the spring session of the Council.

B

"17. The Committee gave consideration to those sections of the reports of the specialized agencies which were included in response to paragraph 8 of Council resolution 630 A I (XXII) of 9 August 1956 concerning the co-ordination and concentration of their activities.

"18. While noting with satisfaction the efforts being made by the specialized agencies to improve the co-ordination of their programmes both within each agency and in relation to programmes of other agencies, the Committee will welcome more comprehensive information on the subject of concentration of activities undertaken by the specialized agencies to be included in their reports to the twenty-sixth session of the Council.

"19. In the light of the discussion in the Committee, the Committee recommends that the Council should approve the following resolution:— [see resolution 664 A (XXIV)]."

E/L.770 and Corr.1. Argentina, Brazil, Canada, Dominican Republic, Finland, Greece, Mexico, Netherlands, United Kingdom, United States draft resolution.

E/L.772. Pakistan amendment to 10-power joint draft resolution, E/L.770 and Corr.1 and text of draft resolution.

RESOLUTION 665 D (XXIV), as submitted by Pakistan, E/L.772, and as amended by Council, adopted by Council on 2 August 1957, meeting 996, by 8 votes to 0, with 9 abstentions.

"*The Economic and Social Council,*

I

"*Having considered* the reports of the Co-ordination Committee,

"*Approves* the reports and the recommendations contained therein, with the exception of the recommendation contained in sub-paragraph 3(e) of the annex to resolution 664(XXIV) of 1 August 1957 relating to the periodicity of meetings of the Commission on Human Rights and the Commission on the Status of Women;

II

"*Recalling* its resolution 652 J (XXIV) of 24 July 1957 concerning the periodicity of the sessions of the Commission on the Status of Women,

"1. *Invites* the Commission on Human Rights to express its views on the recommendation of the Co-ordination Committee that the Council establish the principle that the Commission on Human Rights should in future meet biennially;

"2. *Decides* not to modify for the present the periodicity of the sessions of the Commission on Human Rights."

FINANCIAL IMPLICATIONS OF ACTIONS OF COUNCIL

ECONOMIC AND SOCIAL COUNCIL—23RD AND 24TH SESSIONS
Plenary Meetings 971, 995.
Co-ordination Committee, meeting 166.

E/2991. Note by Secretary-General.
E/3018/Rev.1. Statement submitted by Secretary-General.
E/3033; E/3044 and Corr.1. Notes by Secretary-General.
E/3045 and Corr.1. Report of Co-ordination Committee.

RESOLUTION 666 (XXIV), as recommended by Co-ordination Committee, E/3045, and as orally amended by United Kingdom, adopted unanimously by Council on 1 August 1957, meeting 995.

"The Economic and Social Council

"1. *Takes note* of the statement on financial implications of actions of the Council,

"2. *Transmits* the estimates contained therein, together with the report of the Co-ordination Committee and the summary records containing the views expressed in the debate on this question to the General Assembly for consideration at its twelfth session."

GENERAL ASSEMBLY—12TH SESSION

Plenary Meeting 730.

Fifth Committee, meeting 645.

A/3613. Report of Economic and Social Council to General Assembly, Chapter X.

A/C.5/710 and Corr.1; A/3769. Revised estimates for sections 6, 7, 8 and 13 of Budget Estimates for 1958 (A/3600). Reports of Secretary-General and of Advisory Committee on Administrative and Budgetary Questions.

A/3792. Report of Fifth Committee.

RESOLUTION 1220(XII), taking note of Chapter X of the Economic and Social Council's report, as recommended by Fifth Committee, A/3792, adopted unanimously by Assembly on 14 December 1957, meeting 730.

CHAPTER XVI

CONSULTATIVE ARRANGEMENTS WITH NON-GOVERNMENTAL ORGANIZATIONS

GRANTING OF CONSULTATIVE STATUS

Eleven applications and re-applications from non-governmental organizations (NGO's) for consultative status with the Economic and Social Council were considered during 1957, at the Council's twenty-third session, held between 16 April and 2 May. On the basis of a report from the Council Committee on Non-Governmental Organizations, the Council decided, on 25 April, to grant category B consultative status to the International Commission of Jurists. It decided not to grant the requests of the following organizations for category B consultative status: International Association of Democratic Lawyers and the International Organization of Journalists. It asked that the following organizations be placed on the Register of NGO's: American Foreign Insurance Association (U.S.A.), Comité d'études économiques de l'industrie du gaz, European Bureau for Youth and Childhood, and the International Federation of Cotton and Allied Textile Industries.

The Council decided not to grant the requests of the following organizations for re-classification from the Register to category B: International Federation of Independent Air Transport and the World Federation of Democratic Youth. It also decided not to place the European Union of Accountants on the Register.

Deferred until 1958 was consideration of the application of the International Confederation of Senior Public Servants for category B consultative status.

OPERATING CONSULTATIVE ARRANGEMENTS

WRITTEN STATEMENTS FROM NGO'S

Sixty-four written statements by 39 NGO's were submitted during 1957 to the Economic and Social Council or to the United Nations Children's Fund (UNICEF), or to the Council's Commissions and their subsidiaries. The Commissions to which statements were directed were: the Transport and Communications Commission, the Population Commission, the Social Commission, the Commission on Human Rights, the Commission on the Status of Women, and the Economic Commission for Asia and the Far East. Written statements were also sent to the Sub-Commission on the Prevention of Discrimination and Protection of Minorities and to UNICEF.

HEARING OF NGO'S

During the Council's twenty-third session, the following NGO's with category A consultative status made statements on various items on the Council's agenda, as indicated.

International Chamber of Commerce, on: the report of the Transport and Communications

Commission; and the development of international travel, its present increasing volume and future prospects.

International Confederation of Free Trade Unions, on: the economic development of under-developed countries; development of international travel, its present increasing volume and future prospects; allegations regarding infringements of trade union rights; and the United Nations Children's Fund.

International Co-operative Alliance, on: the economic development of under-developed countries: co-operatives.

International Federation of Christian Trade Unions, on: the economic development of under-developed countries; and the development of international travel, its present increasing volume and future prospects.

World Federation of Trade Unions, on: the economic development of under-developed countries; and the development of international travel, its present increasing volume and future prospects.

World Federation of United Nations Associations, on: the United Nations Children's Fund.

World Veterans Federation, on: the report of the Population Commission.

No statements on Council agenda items were made to the Council Committee on Non-Governmental Organizations during the Council's twenty-third session by organizations with category B consultative status or by organizations on the Register.

At the Council's twenty-fourth session, held between 2 July and 2 August 1957, statements on agenda items, as indicated below, were made by the following NGO's with category A consultative status:

International Confederation of Free Trade Unions, on: the world economic situation; the world social situation; the financing of economic development; international commodity problems; and the annual report of the United Nations High Commissioner for Refugees.

International Federation of Christian Trade Unions, on: the world economic situation; the world social situation; sources of energy as a means of economic development, the financing of economic development; and the annual report of the United Nations High Commissioner for Refugees.

World Federation of Trade Unions, on: the world economic situation; the world social situation; the financing of economic development; and the report of the Commission on the Status of Women.

World Federation of United Nations Associations, on: human rights; and the annual report of the United Nations High Commissioner for Refugees.

World Veterans Federation, on: the world social situation; human rights; and the annual report of the United Nations High Commissioner for Refugees.

The following NGO's with category B consultative status were also heard during the Council's twenty-fourth session, by the Council Committee on Non-Governmental Organizations:

Anti-Slavery Society (United Kingdom), on: human rights.

Catholic International Union for Social Service, on: the world social situation.

Chamber of Commerce of the United States of America, on: the world social situation; and the financing of economic development.

Co-ordinating Board of Jewish Organizations, on: the annual report of the United Nations High Commissioner for Refugees.

International Association of Penal Law, on: the world social situation.

International Conference of Catholic Charities, on: the annual report of the United Nations High Commissioner for Refugees.

International Council of Women, on: the developemnt and co-ordination of the economic, social and human rights programmes and activities of the United Nations and the specialized agencies as a whole; the report of the Commission on the Status of Women; and the annual report of the United Nations High Commissioner for Refugees.

International Law Association, on: human rights.

International Road Federation, on: technical assistance.

International Society for Criminology, on: the world social situation.

International Society of Social Defence, on: the world social situation.

Society of Comparative Legislation (France), on: the world social situation.

World Union of Catholic Women's Organiza-

tions, on: the report of the Commission on the Status of Women:

The Council Committee on Non-Governmental Organizations also heard brief statements from organizations with category A consultative status on the agenda items on which they were later heard by the Council and/or its Committees. In addition, about 50 Non-Governmental Organizations were heard by the Commissions of the Council, and by the Executive Board of UNICEF.

NON-GOVERNMENTAL ORGANIZATIONS IN CONSULTATIVE STATUS
(As of 31 December 1957)

With the exception of the organizations which are followed by names of countries, all the Non-Governmental Organizations listed below are international.

CATEGORY A
International Chamber of Commerce
International Confederation of Free Trade Unions
International Co-operative Alliance
International Federation of Agricultural Producers
International Federation of Christian Trade Unions
International Organisation of Employers
Inter-Parliamentary Union
World Federation of Trade Unions
World Federation of United Nations Associations
World Veterans Federation

CATEGORY B
Agudas Israel World Organization
All India Women's Conference (India)
All Pakistan Women's Association (Pakistan)
Anti-Slavery Society, The (United Kingdom)
CARE (Cooperative for American Remittances to Everywhere, Inc. (U.S.A.)
Carnegie Endowment for International Peace (U.S.A.)
Catholic International Union for Social Service
Chamber of Commerce of the United States of America (U.S.A.)
Commission of the Churches on International Affairs, The
Confédération internationale du crédit populaire
Consultative Council of Jewish Organizations
Co-ordinating Board of Jewish Organizations
Friends World Committee for Consultation
Howard League for Penal Reform (United Kingdom)
Indian Council of World Affairs (India)
Inter-American Council of Commerce and Production
Inter-American Federation of Automobile Clubs
Inter-American Press Association
Inter-American Statistical Institute
International Abolitionist Federation
International African Institute
International Air Transport Association
International Alliance of Women
International Association of Juvenile Court Judges
International Association of Penal Law
International Association of Schools of Social Work
International Automobile Federation
International Bar Association
International Bureau for the Suppression of Traffic in Persons

International Catholic Child Bureau
International Catholic Migration Commission
International Catholic Press Union
International Commission against Concentration Camp Practices
International Commission of Jurists
International Commission on Irrigation and Drainage
International Committee of Scientific Management
International Committee of the Red Cross
International Conference of Catholic Charities
International Conference of Social Work
International Congresses for Modern Architecture
International Cooperative Women's Guild
International Council for Building Research, Studies and Documentation
International Council of Women
International Criminal Police Organization
International Federation for Housing and Town Planning
International Federation for the Rights of Man
International Federation of "Amies de la jeune fille"
International Federation of Business and Professional Women
International Federation of Journalists
International Federation of Newspaper Publishers (Proprietors) and Editors
International Federation of Settlements
International Federation of University Women
International Federation of Women Lawyers
International Fiscal Association
International Institute of Administrative Sciences
International Institute of Public Finance
International Islamic Economic Organization
International Labour Assistance
Intreanional Law Association
International League for the Rights of Man
International Movement for Fraternal Union among Races and Peoples
International Organization for Standardization
International Road Federation
International Road Transport Union
International Social Service
International Society for Criminology
International Society for the Welfare of Cripples
International Society of Social Defence
International Statistical Institute
International Thrift Institute
International Touring Alliance
International Union for Child Welfare
International Union for Conservation of Nature and Natural Resources
International Union for Inland Navigation

International Union for the Scientific Study of Population
International Union of Architects
International Union of Family Organizations
International Union of Local Authorities
International Union of Marine Insurance
International Union of Official Travel Organizations
International Union of Producers and Distributors of Electric Power
International Union of Public Transport
International Union of Railways
International Union of Socialist Youth
Junior Chamber International
League of Red Cross Societies
Liaison Committee of Women's International Organizations
Lions International—The International Association of Lions Clubs
National Association of Manufacturers (U.S.A.)
Nouvelles Equipes Internationales—Union des democrates chrétiens
Pan Pacific South-East Asia Women's Association
Pax Romana
   International Catholic Movement for Intellectual and Cultural Affairs
   International Movement of Catholic Students
Rotary International
Salvation Army
Société belge d'études et d'expansion (Belgium)
Society of Comparative Legislation (France)
South American Petroleum Institute
Women's International League for Peace and Freedom
World Alliance of Young Men's Christian Associations
World Assembly of Youth
World Confederation of Organizations of the Teaching Profession
World Council for the Welfare of the Blind
World Federation of Catholic Young Women and Girls
World Jewish Congress
World Movement of Mothers
World Power Conference
World Union for Progressive Judaism
World Union of Catholic Women's Organizations
World Young Women's Christian Association
World's Woman's Christian Temperance Union
Young Christian Workers

REGISTER
Aero Medical Association
American Foreign Insurance Association (U.S.A.)
American Jewish Joint Distribution Committee, Inc. (U.S.A.)
Arab Union
Asian Relations Organization
Associated Country Women of the World
Association internationale des intérêts radio-maritimes
Biometric Society
Boy Scouts' International Bureau
Comité d'études économiques de l'industrie du gaz
Committee for Economic Development (U.S.A.)
Conference of Internationally-Minded Schools

Co-ordinating Secretariat of National Unions of Students
Council for International Organizations of Medical Sciences
Dairy Industries Society International
Econometric Society
Engineers Joint Council
European Association of Animal Production
European Broadcasting Union
European Bureau for Youth and Childhood
European Confederation of Agriculture
European Union of Coachbuilders
Fédération internationale libre des déportés et internés de la résistance
Federation of International Furniture Removers
Hansard Society for Parliamentary Government
Institute of International Law
Inter-American Association of Broadcasters
Inter-American Association of Sanitary Engineering
International Academy of Forensic and Social Medicine
International Aeronautical Federation
International Amateur Radio Union
International Association for Liberal Christianity and Religious Freedom
International Association for Research in Income and Wealth
International Association for the Exchange of Students for Technical Experience
International Association for the Prevention of Blindness
International Association for Vocational Guidance
International Association of Art Critics
International Association of Crafts and Small and Medium-sized Enterprises
International Association of Gerontology
International Association of Horticultural Producers
International Association of Legal Science
International Association of Microbiological Societies
International Association of Physical Oceanography
International Association of Universities
International Association of University Professors and Lecturers
International Astronomical Union
International Broadcasting Organization
International Cargo Handling Co-ordination Association
International Catholic Film Office
International Center for Wholesale Trade
International Chamber of Shipping
International Commission on Illumination
International Commission on Radiological Protection
International Commission on Radiological Units
International Committee for Social Sciences Documentation
International Committee of Catholic Nurses
International Committee on Radio Electricity
International Confederation of Midwives
International Confederation of Professional and Intellectual Workers
International Confederation of Societies of Authors and Composers
International Conference on Large Electric Systems

International Container Bureau
International Council for Educational Films
International Council for Philosophy and Humanistic Studies
International Council of Commerce Employers
International Council of Museums
International Council of Nurses
International Council of Scientific Unions
International Council of Social Democratic Women
International Council on Archives
International Dairy Federation
International Dental Federation
International Diabetes Federation
International Economic Association
International Falcon Movement
International Federation for Documentation
International Federation of Air Line Pilots Asssociations
International Federation of Art Film
International Federation of Building and Public Works (Employers' Confederation)
International Federation of Catholic Youth
International Federation of Children Communities
International Federation of Cotton and Allied Textile Industries
International Federation of Film Producers Associations
International Federation of Free Journalists
International Federation of Gynecology and Ostetrics
International Federation of Home Economics
International Federation of Independent Air Transport
International Federation of Library Associations
International Federation of Organisations for School Correspondence and Exchanges
International Federation of Radio Officers
International Federation of Senior Police Officers
International Federation of the Periodical Press
International Federation of the Phonographic Industry
International Federation of Workers' Educational Associations
International Federation of Workers' Travel Associations
International Gas Union
International Geographical Union
International Hospital Federation
International House Association
International Hydatidological Association
International Institute of Differing Civilizations
International Institute of Public Law
International Institution of the Middle Classes
International Landworkers' Federation
International League against Rheumatism
International Leprosy Association
International Literary and Artistic Association
International Music Council
International Olive Growers' Federation

International Organization against Trachoma
International Pediatric Association
International P.E.N. Club—a World Association of Writers
International Permanent Bureau of Automobile Manufacturers
International Pharmaceutical Federation
International Political Science Association
International Radio Maritime Committee
International Rayon and Synthetic Fibres Committee
International Real Estate Federation
International Relief Committee for Intellectual Workers
International Schools Association
International Scientific Radio Union
International Shipping Federation Ltd.
International Social Science Council
International Society for Blood Transfusion
International Society of Soil Science
International Sociological Association
International Special Committee on Radio Interference
International Studies Conference
International Temperance Union
International Theatre Institute
International Union against Cancer
International Union against Tuberculosis
International Union against Venereal Diseases and the Treponematoses
International Union for Health Education of the Public
International Union for Protecting Public Morality
International Union of Aviation Insurers
International Union of Geodesy and Geophysics
International Union of Nutritional Sciences
International Union of Scientific Psychology
International Vegetarian Union
International World Calendar Association
International Youth Hostel Federation
Joint Committee of International Teachers' Federations
Joint International Committee for Tests Relating to the Protection of Telecommunications Lines and Underground Ducts
Liberal International, World Liberal Union
Lutheran World Federation
Medical Women's International Association
New Education Fellowship (The International)
Open Door International
O.R.T. World Union
Pacific Science Association
Permanent Committee for the International Veterinary Congresses
Permanent International Association of Navigation Congresses
Permanent International Committee on Canned Foods
St. Joan's International Social and Political Alliance

DOCUMENTARY REFERENCES

GRANTING OF CONSULTATIVE STATUS

ECONOMIC AND SOCIAL COUNCIL—23RD SESSION
Plenary Meetings 966, 967.
Council Committee on Non-Governmental Organizations, meetings 163-164.

E/2955. Report of Council Committee on NGO's (draft resolutions A and B).
E/L.748. USSR amendments to draft resolution A.
RESOLUTION 641 A and B (XXIII), as recommended by Council Committee on NGO's, E/2955, adopted by Council on 25 April 1957, meeting 967, as follows: 641 A (XXIII), by 12 votes to 2, with 4 abstentions, and 641 B (XXIII), by 16 votes to 1, with 1 abstention.

A

International Non-Governmental Organizations
"The Economic and Social Council,
"Having considered the report of its Committee on Non-Governmental Organizations,
"1. *Decides* not to grant the requests of the following organizations for reclassification from Register to category B:
International Federation of Independent Air Transport;
World Federation of Democratic Youth;
"2. *Decides* not to grant the requests of the following organizations for category B consultative status:
International Association of Democratic Lawyers;
International Organization of Journalists;
"3. *Decides* not to request the Secretary-General to place the following organization on the Register:
European Union of Accountants;
"4. *Decides* to grant the request of the following organization for category B consultative status:
International Commission of Jurists;
"5. *Requests* the Secretary-General to place the following organizations on the Register in accordance with paragraph 17 of Council resolution 288 B (X) of 27 February 1950:
Comité d'études économiques de l'industrie du gaz;
European Bureau for Youth and Childhood;
International Federation of Cotton and Allied Textile Industries;
"6. *Decides* to defer until 1958 consideration of the application of the following organization for category B consultative status:

International Confederation of Senior Public Servants."

B

National Non-Governmental Organizations
"The Economic and Social Council,
"Having considered the report of its Committee on Non-Governmental Organizations and in the light of paragraph 9 of Council resolution 288 B (X) of 27 February 1950, and upon the recommendation of the Government concerned,
"Decides to place the following organization on the Register:
American Foreign Insurance Association (United States of America)."

HEARINGS OF NGO's

ECONOMIC AND SOCIAL COUNCIL—23RD AND 24TH SESSIONS
Plenary Meetings, 958, 960, 962, 965, 968, 975, 976, 986, 987, 989, 991.
Council Committee on Non-Governmental Organizations, meetings 165-169.
Economic Committee, meetings 220, 224, 229, 233.
Social Committee, meetings 354, 358; 360, 361, 366, 369.

E/2969; E/3023; E/3026. Report of Council Committee on NGO's on applications for hearings.
E/3022; E/3025; E/3031. Report of Council Committee on NGO's on hearings.
A/3613. Report of Economic and Social Council covering period 10 August 1956–2 August 1957, Chapter IX.

WRITTEN STATEMENTS FROM NGO's

For written statements submitted to Council or its subsidiary bodies, see E/C.2/476-479, 481-491; E/CN.2/NGO/13; E/CN.4/NGO/69, 70 and Corr.1, 71-76; E/CN.4/Sub.2/NGO/10, 11; E/CN.5/NGO/45-53, 54 and Add.1, 55-60; E/CN.6/NGO/43, 44 and Corr.1, 45-47; E/CN.9/NGO/4; E/CN.11/NGO/16-19; E/ICEF/NGO/40-50.
E/C.2/480. List of written statements submitted to Economic and Social Council and its Commissions by Non-Governmental Organizations in consultative status since publication of previous list (E/C.2/460).

CHAPTER XVII

OTHER ECONOMIC AND SOCIAL QUESTIONS

ESTABLISHMENT OF FOOD RESERVES

The Economic and Social Council, at its twenty-fourth session, in mid-1957, considered the desirability of setting up a working group to examine certain matters in connexion with the establishment of a world food reserve. Before it was a note by the Secretary-General of the

United Nations prepared in accordance with General Assembly resolution 1026(XI), of 20 February 1957. Consultations with the Food and Agriculture Organization (FAO) and the other agencies concerned, he said, had led to the conclusion it would be useful to arrange for a study of a world food reserve without formally establishing a working group at that time. FAO had also agreed to arrange consultations with other interested organizations and to prepare material for a report by the Secretary-General as requested by Council resolution 621(XXII) of 6 August 1956 and General Assembly resolution 1025(XI) of 20 February 1957.

In the course of the discussions in the Council's Economic Committee, several representa-

tives stressed the importance of the subject. Some hoped that the report would deal particularly with the practical possibilities of action. Also referred to was the need for further study on the question of a world food capital fund.

The Council finally agreed, on 30 July 1957, without adopting a resolution, to accept the recommendation in the Secretary-General's note that the question of a world food reserve be studied without the formal establishment of a working group. It also agreed to take up, at its mid-1958 session, the report on the subject being prepared in response to the requests made by the Council in 1956 and the Assembly in February 1957.

DOCUMENTARY REFERENCES

ECONOMIC AND SOCIAL COUNCIL—24TH SESSION
Plenary Meetings 972, 993.
Economic Committee, meeting 232.

E/2996. Note by Secretary-General on establishment

of world food reserve.
E/3003. Commission on International Commodity Trade. Report of 4th and 5th sessions, Chapter IV.
E/3037. Report of Economic Committee.

INTERNATIONAL CO-OPERATION IN SCIENCE, CULTURE AND EDUCATION

On 21 February 1957, the General Assembly asked the Economic and Social Council, by resolution 1043(XI), to give special attention to statements concerning international cultural and scientific co-operation included in the annual reports of the United Nations Educational, Scientific and Cultural Organization (UNESCO) and the other specialized agencies concerned. Such statements in the reports of UNESCO, the Food and Agriculture Organization (FAO) and the World Health Organization (WHO) were considered by the Council and its Co-ordination Committee at the Council's twenty-fourth session, in mid-1957. The Committee took note of the statements and advised the Council that no further action was required at the time. The Council acted on this advice, without adopting a formal resolution on the matter.

At the General Assembly's twelfth session, Czechoslovakia proposed, in the Assembly's Third (Social, Humanitarian and Cultural) Committee, that the Assembly reiterate the view expressed in its resolution 1043(XI) of 21 February 1957 that wider cultural and scientific international co-operation be promoted by mutual agreements or by other means and that no effort

should be spared in trying to achieve the implementation of these peaceful objectives. Czechoslovakia also proposed that the Assembly invite "all States" to consider the possibility and desirability of encouraging the further expansion and development of forms of mutual relationship tested by practice, such as: (a) the exchange of experience among experts competent in this field; (b) the establishment of "broader contacts in greater freedom" between persons engaged in educational, scientific and cultural work; (c) the exchange of books, periodicals and other publications between scientific and research institutions, libraries, scientific and cultural societies and other bodies and private persons; (d) exhibitions illustrating achievements and advances in this field; (e) the exchange of works of art, films, radio and television programmes, musicians and other artists; (f) the mutual exchange of students, scholarship and fellowship grants and contacts between universities and other educational bodies; (g) the reciprocal organization of foreign broadcasting programmes designed to furnish impartial information and to promote mutual understanding among nations as well as the strengthening of peace; exchange of journalists and reporters; and (*h*) the encouragement of international collective and individual tourism and of international activities in the field of psysical education and sports.

The Czechoslovakian proposal would also have the Assembly: (1) invite UNESCO and other specialized agencies concerned to include, in their annual reports to the Economic and Social Council, a statement of their views and activities and any information which they might have on the views and activities of Governments in the field of international educational, scientific and cultural co-operation; and (2) request the Council to consider, at its mid-year session in 1958, ways and means of promoting the further development of co-operation among States in this field, giving special attention to these statements from the specialized agencies, and to report to the General Assembly's thirteenth session in 1958.

The sponsor of the resolution argued that, despite the provisions of General Assembly resolution 1043(XI), the Council had not yet given proper attention to the problem of international cultural and scientific co-operation. Further measures had to be taken as the problem deserved study in all its aspects.

The majority of delegations were in general agreement with the objectives set forth in the Czechoslovakian draft resolution. It was pointed out, however, that it might not be necessary to consider items of that nature every year. Some representatives felt that the form of the draft resolution should be modified. The point was also made that cultural exchange agreements between countries should be on a reciprocal basis, to ensure equal and maximum access to information to their respective citizens in order to promote genuine understanding and friendship between the participating countries and not in order to enhance the domestic authority and international prestige of Governments.

These reservations were reflected in a number of amendments submitted (i) jointly by Brazil, Honduras, Italy, the United Kingdom and the United States; (ii) by the Philippines and (iii) by Chile.

The five-power amendments were intended: (*a*) to have the Assembly invite all Members of the United Nations and specialized agencies, rather than "all States" (as proposed by Czecho-

slovakia) to consider the possibility and desirability of encouraging the further expansion and development of tested forms of mutual relationship; (*b*) to delete the reference in the Czechoslovakian proposal to "international collective and individual tourism"; and (*c*) to amend the request to the Economic and Social Council so that the Council would only consider statements invited from the specialized agencies and report specially on the subject to the 1958 Assembly session.

The Philippine amendment dealt with the reference in the Czechoslovakian draft resolution to radio and television programmes. The wording would thereby have been changed to read as follows: "reciprocal organization of foreign radio and television programmes designed to furnish news and information and to promote mutual understanding among nations as well as the strengthening of peace, thus paving the way for the relaxation or abolition of restrictive practices, including censorship and the jamming of radio broadcasts".

The Chilean proposal was to amend the paragraph on the invitation to States so that the Assembly would "urge" all Members of the United Nations or of the specialized agencies (rather than "all States") to "take more intensive means of every kind to carry out one of the fundamental purposes of the United Nations, namely, exchange and wider co-operation between peoples in science, culture and education". It further called for the deletion of the remainder of the operative part of the Czechoslovakian draft resolution.

The Czechoslovakian representative incorporated most of these amendments in a revised draft resolution, but wanted the Assembly to urge "all States" (rather than all Members of the United Nations or of specialized agencies) to intensify exchange and wider co-operation between peoples in science, culture and education, as proposed in the Chilean amendment.

A UNESCO representative, welcoming the revised text, said UNESCO would carry out the tasks it was invited to undertake.

On 9 October 1957, the Third Committee decided by 40 votes to 26, with 5 abstentions, to accept the wording preferred by Chile. The revised draft resolution, as amended, was then adopted by 67 votes to 0, with 2 abstentions. This resolution was finally approved at a plenary meeting of the Assembly on 26 November 1957 by 75 votes to 0, with 1 abstention, as resolution 1164(XII).

The Assembly thereby reiterated its view that wider international cultural and scientific co-operation should be promoted by mutual agreements or by other means and that no effort should be spared in trying to implement these peaceful objectives. It urged all Members of the United Nations or of the specialized agencies to further develop all measures to encourage exchanges and co-operation among peoples in science, culture and education. It invited

UNESCO and other specialized agencies concerned to include, in their annual reports to the Economic and Social Council, a statement of their views and activities and any information they might have about the views and activities of governments in the fields of international educational, scientific and cultural co-operation. At the same time, the Council was asked to give special attention to these statements from the specialized agencies at its mid-1958 session and to include a section on this subject in its report to the Assembly's thirteenth session later in 1958, for consideration by the Assembly.

DOCUMENTARY REFERENCES

ECONOMIC AND SOCIAL COUNCIL—24TH SESSION
Plenary Meeting 996.
Co-ordination Committee, meeting 164.

E/2973. Annual report of FAO (paragraphs 81-83).
E/2974. Annual report of UNESCO (paragraphs 44-50).
E/2980/Add.1. Supplementary report of WHO (paragraphs 36-39).
E/3039. Report of the Co-ordination Committee (paragraph 7).

GENERAL ASSEMBLY—12TH SESSION
Plenary Meeting 723.
Third Committee, meetings 767, 770, 775-777.

A/3613. Report of Economic and Social Council to General Assembly, Chapter VIII, Section I.
A/C.3/L. 610 and Rev.1, 2. Czechoslovakia draft resolution and revisions, adopted by Third Committee, as amended by Chile, A/C.3/L.616, by 67 votes to 0, with 2 abstentions.
A/C.3/L.614. Brazil, Honduras, Italy, United Kingdom, United States amendments to revised draft resolution, A/C.3/L.610/Rev.1.
A/C.3/L.615. Philippines amendment to revised draft resolution, A/C.3/L.610/Rev.1.
A/C.3/L.616. Chile amendment to revised draft resolution, A/C.3/L.610/Rev.1.
A/3716. Report of Third Committee (draft resolution V).
RESOLUTION 1164(XII), as recommended by Third Committee, A/3716, adopted by Assembly on 26 November 1957, meeting 723, by 75 votes to 0, with 1 abstention.
"*The General Assembly,*
"*Recalling* its resolution 1043(XI) of 21 February 1957 on international cultural and scientific co-operation,
"*Having regard* to Economic and Social Council resolution 663 I (XXIV) of 31 July 1957 urging the extension of international co-operation in the social

field through the development of personal contacts and the exchange of experience among experts,
"*Attaching great importance* to a further development and expansion of relations in the fields of science, including applied science, culture and education, which will assist the promotion of economic and social welfare as well as better mutual understanding among nations and the maintenance of peace,
"*Noting with satisfaction* the results already achieved in the development of such international co-operation and considering it desirable that there should be opportunities for further development in this respect,
"*Recognizing* the positive contribution in this matter by the United Nations Educational, Scientific and Cultural Organization and other specialized agencies and by other international bodies,
"1. *Reiterates* the view expressed in its resolution 1043(XI) of 21 February 1957 that wider international cultural and scientific co-operation should be promoted by mutual agreements or by other means, and that no effort should be spared in trying to achieve the implementation of these peaceful objectives;
"2. *Urges* all States Members of the United Nations or members of the specialized agencies to develop further all measures for the encouragement of exchanges and co-operation among peoples in the fields of science, culture and education, which is one of the basic purposes of the United Nations;
"3. *Invites* the United Nations Educational, Scientific and Cultural Organization and the other specialized agencies concerned to include in their annual reports to the Economic and Social Council a statement of their views and activities and any information which they may have as to the views and activities of Governments in the field of international educational, scientific and cultural co-operation;
"4. *Requests* the Economic and Social Council to give special attention at its twenty-sixth session to the above-mentioned statements of the specialized agencies, and to include, in its report to the General Assembly at its thirteenth session, a section on this subject for consideration by the Assembly."

INTERNATIONAL CO-OPERATION IN CARTOGRAPHY

In 1957 the United Nations continued its efforts to strengthen international co-operation in cartography and to help Governments develop national surveying and mapping for economic and social projects.

A draft geological map was approved for publication and a programme for mineral maps was adopted at the third meeting of the Working Party of Senior Geologists on the Preparation of Regional Geological and Mineral Maps for Asia and the Far East convened in Calcutta, India, by the United Nations Economic Commission for Asia and the Far East, between 5 and 9 November 1957.

Under the joint sponsorship of the United Nations and the Government of Iran, a seminar on topographical mapping as a means of economic development was held in Teheran between 14 and 24 October 1957 to study, with the aid of experts supplied by the United Nations Technical Assistance Administration, modern cartographic development and technical problems of interest to the area. The seminar was attended by officials of cartographic services of the following countries: Afghanistan, Iran, Iraq, Jordan, Pakistan, Saudi Arabia and Turkey.

Consultations with Governments on the preparation of the second United Nations Regional Cartographic Conference for Asia and the Far East were held during 1957, in pursuance of the Economic and Social Council's resolution 600(XXI) of 1956. An agreement was reached with the Government of Japan, the host country, on the meeting date—20 October to 1 November 1958. Suggestions were received from several governments for the agenda of the Conference.

A preliminary survey on world topographical mapping was published in *World Cartography*.

With the information submitted to the United Nations Secretariat by national agencies on their work on the International Map of the World on the Millionth Scale, the current annual report on this project contained a much improved coverage of all sheets published in recent years.

DOCUMENTARY REFERENCES

E/CN.11/1 and NR/4. *Report of the Working Party of the Senior Geologists on the Preparation of Regional Geological and Mineral Maps for Asia and the Far East.*

World Cartography, Vol. V. U.N.P. Sales No.: 1957. I.18.

Report on the International Map of the World on the Millionth Scale, 1956. U.N.P. Sales No.: 58.I.2.

Questions Concerning Non-Self-Governing Territories and the International Trusteeship System

CHAPTER I

INFORMATION FROM NON-SELF-GOVERNING TERRITORIES TRANSMITTED UNDER ARTICLE 73e OF THE CHARTER

TRANSMISSION OF INFORMATION IN 1957

United Nations Members responsible for the administration of Non-Self-Governing Territories whose peoples have not yet attained a full measure of self-government regularly transmit information to the Secretary-General on economic, social and educational conditions in these Territories.

In 1957, information was due from the following Members for the Territories shown below for 1956 or for the administrative year 1956-1957:

Australia: Papua.
Belgium:[1] Belgian Congo.
France: Comoro Archipelago, French Equatorial Africa, French Somaliland, French West Africa, Madagascar, New Hebrides (under Anglo-French Condominium).
Netherlands: Netherlands New Guinea.
New Zealand: Cook Islands, Niue Island, Tokelau Islands.
United Kingdom: Aden, Bahamas, Barbados, Basutoland, Bechuanaland, Bermuda, British Guiana, British Honduras, British Solomon Islands Protectorate, British Somaliland, Brunei, Cyprus, Falkland Islands, Federation of Malaya,[2] Fiji, Gambia, Gibraltar, Gilbert and Ellice Islands, Gold Coast,[3] Hong Kong, Jamaica, Kenya, Leeward Islands, Mauritius, New Hebrides (under Anglo-French Condominium), Nigeria, North Borneo, Northern Rhodesia, Nyasaland, Pitcairn Island, St. Helena, Sarawak, Seychelles, Sierra Leone, Singapore, Swaziland, Trinidad and Tobago, Uganda, Windward Islands, Zanzibar.
United States: Alaska, American Samoa, Guam, Hawaii, Virgin Islands.

Reservations on sovereignty and the transmission of information were made during 1957, either in the General Assembly's Fourth Committee or in the Assembly's Committee on Information from Non-Self-Governing Territories as follows: by Argentina and the United Kingdom in respect of the Falkland Islands (Islas Malvinas) and the Falkland Islands Dependencies; by Guatemala and the United Kingdom in respect of British Honduras (Belize); by Indonesia and the Netherlands in respect of Netherlands New Guinea (West Irian); by Spain and the United Kingdom in respect of Gibraltar; by Yemen and the United Kingdom in respect of Aden. The representative of Mexico stated that, if the status of British Honduras (Belize) were changed, the right of his Government over part of that Territory would have to be taken into account. The representative of Chile stated that his Government regarded its rights over the Antarctic Territory as unquestionable. The representatives of Ceylon, India and Iraq stated

---

[1] See below, under OBLIGATION TO CONTINUE TRANSMITTING INFORMATION.
[2] The United Kingdom ceased to transmit information on the Federation of Malaya when it attained independence in 1957.
[3] The United Kingdom ceased to transmit information on the Gold Coast which, united with the former Trust Territory of British-administered Togoland, attained independence in 1957, to form the new State of Ghana.

the positions of their Governments in respect of sovereignty over Netherlands New Guinea (West Irian). The representative of Guatemala stated that the participation of his delegation in the work of the Committee on Information from Non-Self-Governing Territories did not imply its acceptance of the *de facto* situation regarding Territories the sovereignty over which was in dispute. The representative of Morocco and France reserved the position of their Governments in respect of Mauritania. The representatives of Morocco and Spain reserved the posi-

tion of their Governments in respect of Ifni and Spanish Sahara.

At its eighth session 22 July–15 August 1957), the Committee on Information from Non-Self-Governing Territories[4] gave special attention to economic conditions in Non-Self-Governing Territories. (For details, see section ECONOMIC CONDITIONS IN NON-SELF-GOVERNING TERRITORIES, below. For membership of the Committee, see APPENDIX II.)

[4] For this Committee's terms of reference see *Y.U.N.*, *1956*, p. 290.

DOCUMENTARY REFERENCES

A/3647 and Corr.1. Report of Committee on Information from Non-Self-Governing Territories. (For list of documents before Committee, see Part I, Annex I.)

SUMMARIES OF INFORMATION
TRANSMITTED TO SECRETARY-GENERAL

A/3601 and Corr.1 and Add.1 (ST/TRI/B.1956/1 and Add.1). Central African Territories: French Equatorial Africa, Northern Rhodesia, Nyasaland, Belgian Congo.
A/3602 (ST/TRI/B.1956/2). East African Territories: British Somaliland, French Somaliland, Kenya, Uganda, Zanzibar.
A/3603 (ST/TRI/B.1956/3 and Corr.1). Southern African Territories: Basutoland, Bechuanaland, Swaziland.
A/3604 (ST/TRI/B.1956/4). Indian Ocean Territories: Comoro Archipelago, Madagascar, Mauritius, Seychelles.
A/3605 (ST/TRI/B.1956/5). West African Territories: French West Africa, Gambia, Gold Coast, Nigeria, Sierra Leone.
A/3606/Rev.1 (ST/TRI/B.1956/6 and Add.1).

Caribbean and Western Atlantic Territories: Bahamas, Barbados, Bermuda, British Guiana, British Honduras, Jamaica, Leeward Islands, Trinidad and Tobago, United States Virgin Islands, Windward Islands.
A/3607 (ST/TRI/B.1956/7 and Corr.1). Asian Territories: Brunei, Federation of Malaya, Hong Kong, North Borneo, Sarawak, Singapore.
A/3608 (ST/TRI/B.1956/8). Pacific Territories: Alaska, American Samoa, Cook Islands, Fiji, Gilbert and Ellice Islands, Guam, Hawaii, Netherlands New Guinea, New Hebrides, Niue Islands, Papua, Pitcairn Island, Solomon Islands, Tokelau Islands.
A/3609 (ST/TRI/B.1956/9 and Corr.1). Other Territories: Aden, Cyprus, Falkland Islands, Gibraltar, St. Helena.

RESERVATIONS

GENERAL ASSEMBLY—12TH SESSION
Fourth Committee, meeting 670.

A/3647 and Corr.1. Report of Committee on Information from Non-Self-Governing Territories, Part I, paragraphs 12-14.

QUESTIONS RELATING TO OBLIGATIONS TO TRANSMIT INFORMATION

Three questions relating to the obligation to transmit information were considered at the General Assembly's twelfth session in 1957. These were: the obligation of a United Nations Member to transmit information on a Non-Self-Governing Territory transferred to its administration; the obligation of a Member to continue to transmit information on a Non-Self-Governing Territory; and responsibility of Members.

INFORMATION ON TERRITORY TRANSFERRED TO ANOTHER ADMINISTERING MEMBER

In 1946, eight United Nations Members undertook to transmit information on 74 Terri-

tories administered by them. These included the Cocos Keeling Islands, administered by the United Kingdom as a part of Singapore.

The information transmitted by the United Kingdom on Singapore for the year 1955 stated that, as of 23 November 1955, the administration of the Cocos Keeling Islands had been transferred to Australia. At the 1957 session of the Committee on Information, the representative of India asked the representative of Australia what his Government's intentions were with regard to these islands. The reply was that the Australian Government intended to transmit information under Article 73e of the United Nations Charter on the Cocos Keeling Islands.

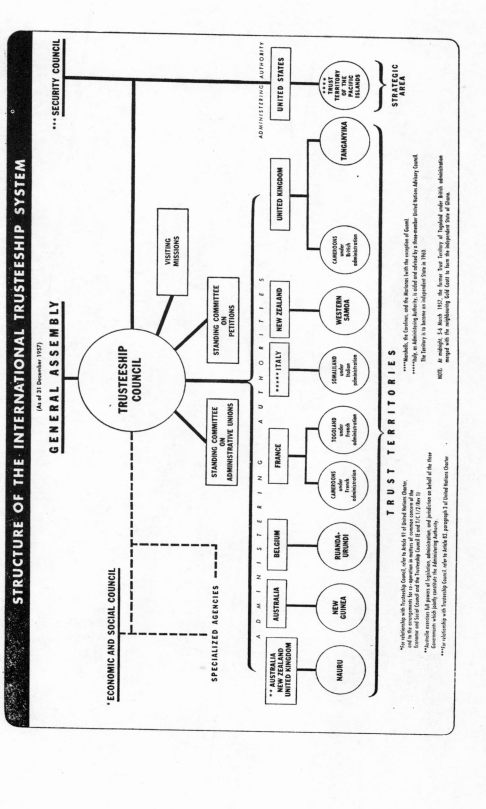

STRUCTURE OF THE INTERNATIONAL TRUSTEESHIP SYSTEM

(As of 31 December 1957)

GENERAL ASSEMBLY

*ECONOMIC AND SOCIAL COUNCIL

***SECURITY COUNCIL

SPECIALIZED AGENCIES

TRUSTEESHIP COUNCIL

STANDING COMMITTEE ON ADMINISTRATIVE UNIONS

STANDING COMMITTEE ON PETITIONS

VISITING MISSIONS

ADMINISTERING AUTHORITIES

ADMINISTERING AUTHORITY

AUSTRALIA — NEW GUINEA

BELGIUM — RUANDA-URUNDI

FRANCE — CAMEROONS under French administration — TOGOLAND under French administration

*****ITALY — SOMALILAND under Italian administration

NEW ZEALAND — WESTERN SAMOA

UNITED KINGDOM — CAMEROONS under British administration — TANGANYIKA

UNITED STATES — ****TRUST TERRITORY OF THE PACIFIC ISLANDS

**AUSTRALIA NEW ZEALAND UNITED KINGDOM — NAURU

STRATEGIC AREA

TRUST TERRITORIES

*For relationship with Trusteeship Council, refer to Article 91 of United Nations Charter, and to the arrangements for co-operation in matters of common concern of the Economic and Social Council and the Trusteeship Council (E and T/C.1/2/Rev.1)

**Australia exercises full powers of legislation, administration, and jurisdiction on behalf of the three Governments which jointly constitute the Administering Authority.

***For relationship with Trusteeship Council, refer to Article 83, paragraph 3 of United Nations Charter

****Marshalls, the Carolines, and the Marianas (with the exception of Guam)

*****Italy, as Administering Authority, is aided and advised by a three-member United Nations Advisory Council. The Territory is to become an independent State in 1960.

NOTE: At midnight, 5-6 March 1957, the former Trust Territory of Togoland under British administration merged with the neighbouring Gold Coast to form the independent State of Ghana.

OBLIGATION TO CONTINUE
TRANSMITTING INFORMATION

DISCUSSION IN COMMITTEE ON INFORMATION

The question of the obligation of a United Nations Member to continue to transmit information under Article 73e of the Charter was raised in the Committee on Information from Non-Self-Governing Territories in July 1957, when the Secretariat was asked about the distribution of the summaries of information on Non-Self-Governing Territories for 1955. These summaries were due in 1956, in accordance with Assembly resolution 218(III), asking Administering Members to transmit regularly to the Secretary-General the most recent information as early as possible and at the latest within six months after the expiration of the administrative year in the Territory concerned.

When the Committee met in July 1957, the summaries of information relating to Belgian and French Territories had not been distributed as information had not been received from the Governments concerned.

The French representative explained that the transmission of information on the French Territories had been delayed because a *loi cadre* and enabling legislation affecting the constitutional position of the French Territories had been adopted in 1956. The work involved had delayed the preparation in the Territories of the reports required under Article 73e

The French Government subsequently transmitted the information to the Secretary-General.

As no explanation was received from the Belgian Government, the Committee asked its Chairman to approach the Belgian authorities informally about the transmission of information under Article 73e. The Chairman later reported to the Committee that the Belgian Permanent Mission to the United Nations had no communication to make. The Committee then asked the Secretary-General to circulate to its members copies of the relevant correspondence exchanged between him and the Belgian authorities.

The Indian representative suggested that the Committee should inform the General Assembly that the Secretary-General had not received the information on the Belgian Congo for the year 1955, which should have been transmitted to him in 1956.

The representative of Iraq drew attention to a Belgian *communiqué* of 2 August 1957 stating that Belgium had always recognized its obligations under the Charter and would continue to conform to its exact terms in transmitting information on the Belgian Congo to the Library of the United Nations. He suggested that the Committee inform the General Assembly of the situation as fully as possible.

The Netherlands representative held, however, that the Committee could do no more than state that no information had been transmitted.

In its report to the Asssembly, the Committee included a full account of this question.

DISCUSSION IN GENERAL ASSEMBLY

When, at the General Assembly's twelfth session, the Fourth Committee considered the report of the Committee on Information, it agreed to a request made by Ceylon on 14 October that the correspondence between the Secretary-General and the Belgian authorities on the transmission of information be circulated. On 17 October, the Belgian representative announced that his Government had transmitted information on the Belgian Congo to the Secretary-General.

On 29 October, the Belgian representative explained that, since the signing of the Charter in 1945, his delegation had maintained the view that the information transmitted under Article 73e was "for information purposes". There had been no change in his delegation's attitude; it had not taken part in the Fourth Committee's general debate on information from Non-Self-Governing Territories or in the work of the Committee on Information as it believed that such discussion constituted improper use of the information. However, in view of some references which had been made to conditions in the Belgian Congo, the Belgian representative furnished additional information to the Fourth Committee on economic, social and educational conditions in the Territory. Some of the information was about developments subsequent to those dealt with in the information for 1955 on economic, social and educational conditions which had been transmitted to the Secretary-General in accordance with Article 73e of the Charter.

Previously, on 11 October, the Belgian Permanent Mission, in transmitting information for 1955, had informed the Secretary-General that the information on the Belgian Congo for 1956 would be transmitted immediately upon publication. The Fourth Committee accepted this as an assurance that the Belgian Government continued to recognize its obligations under Article 73e No further action was taken at the Assembly's twelfth session.

RESPONSIBILITY OF MEMBERS

On their admission to the United Nations in 1957, the Secretary-General invited Ghana, Japan, and the Federation of Malaya to inform him whether they were responsible for the administration of any Territories referred to in Article 73e of the United Nations Charter. At the Assembly's twelfth session, the Fourth Committee had before it the replies of these Members stating that they did not have under their administration any territories referred to in Chapter XI of the United Nations Charter.

It also discussed the question of receiving information from Spain and Portugal.

The Spanish representative informed the Fourth Committee that Spain had terminated its Protectorate in Morocco by recognizing the full sovereignty of that country. This development had affected the administrative structure of Spain, which was the reason for the delay in Spain's reply. He assured the Committee that a reply would be given in due course and that it would be entirely in accordance with the spirit of the Charter.

The representatives of Bulgaria, Guatemala, India, Iraq, Panama, Poland, the USSR and Yugoslavia considered that the Charter was a multilateral treaty and that the obligations under Chapter XI were of the same nature as other obligations assumed by Members on admission to the United Nations. The Assembly was therefore competent to determine the Territories on which information should be transmitted. The Assembly's competence to do so, they maintained, derived from Article 10 of the Charter and had been reasserted by previous Assembly resolutions (222(III), 334(IV) and 742(VIII)).

Also referred to in the Fourth Committee was Portugal's claim that no Territories under its administration came under Chapter XI of the Charter. Portugal had asserted that Mozambique and Angola, under the new Portuguese Constitution, were provinces of Portugal and

that constitutional reasons prevented the transmission of information. The representatives of Poland, the USSR and Yugoslavia held that although Mozambique and Angola were Portuguese colonies with a tradition and culture of their own, Portugal had not fulfilled its obligations under the Charter.

The Portuguese representative maintained that since the entire text of Chapter XI was addressed to Administering Members, they alone could determine any constitutional limitations which might exist in their own fundamental laws. He could not accept the view that the Charter superseded constitutional law; this opinion was tantamount to regarding the United Nations as a world government and contrary to the provisions of Article 2(7). He therefore reaffirmed his Government's position that Article 73 of the Charter did not apply to Portugal.

Burma, Ceylon, Costa Rica, Ghana, Greece, Guatemala, India, Indonesia, Iraq, Liberia, Nepal, Panama, Syria, Tunisia and Yugoslavia proposed a draft resolution whereby the Assembly would take the following measures. (1) It would ask the Secretary-General to prepare a summary of opinions on the transmission of information under Article 73e, based on: the replies of Members to communications of the Secretary-General on the subject of the transmission of information; the statements made during discussions in the Committee concerned; and relevant treatises on the interpretation of the Charter. (2) It would establish an *ad hoc* committee of six members to study the Secretary-General's summary and to report thereon to the Assembly.

The Philippines and Uruguay joined as co-sponsors after the draft had been revised to the following effect: The summaries requested of the Secretary-General should include discussion at plenary meetings of the Assembly; and the terms of reference of the committee of six should be expanded to cover consideration of the question of the transmission of information under Article 73e of the Charter.

In support of the draft, the sponsors explained that past discussion had pointed to the need for an interpretation of Chapter XI of the Charter, particularly with regard to: (1) the meaning and scope of the constitutional limitations referred to in Article 73e; (2) whether Chapter XI applied to Territories which formed an integral part of the metropolitan country; (3) whether the General Assembly had the right to determine the Territories whose peoples had not attained full self-government. They considered that these question could best be resolved after a careful study by the Assembly.

The representatives of Australia, Belgium, Brazil, Canada, Colombia, Cuba, Italy, Spain, Sweden and the United Kingdom criticized the draft resolution on the grounds that it contained contradictions and inaccuracies.

Other reasons adduced against the draft were that the proposed committee could accomplish nothing that the Fourth Committee could not do. The Assembly had carefully studied the factors to be taken into account in determining whether a Territory had achieved full self-government, and it would be better to leave each Government to apply the standards of the Charter accordingly. Moreover, the Assembly was not competent to decide on the transmission of information, and the proposed way to settle the question was unacceptable.

The representative of Peru was against the draft resolution because it would entail the study of the constitutions of Member States and thus infringe upon their domestic jurisdiction.

The representative of the Dominican Republic suggested that the study should be referred to the Committee on Information from Non-Self-Governing Territories. The representative of Venezuela suggested that the proposed *ad hoc* committee should have an equal number of representatives of Administering and Non-Administering Members. Since neither of these proposals were accepted by the sponsors of the draft, they were subsequently withdrawn.

The Fourth Committee approved the draft resolution as a whole by a roll-call vote of 42 to 27, with 8 abstentions.

When it came before a plenary meeting of the Assembly, the Colombian representative, on a point of order, maintained that a two-thirds majority was required for its adoption. He submitted a proposal accordingly. The draft resolution before the Assembly, he said, was for an *ad hoc* committee to study and examine the constitutions of Member States, thus infringing their sovereignty. The work of this committee would thus have even more far-reaching consequences than that of the Committee on Information. As the establishment of the Committee on Information had been approved by a two-thirds majority, he said, the same procedure should be applied to the proposal for an *ad hoc* committee.

The Colombian motion was voted on without debate as it was raised on a point of order, the Assembly deciding by a roll-call vote of 38 to 36, with 7 abstentions, that a two-thirds majority was required. The draft resolution, also voted on by roll-call, received 41 votes in favour, 30 against, with 10 abstentions. It was thus not adopted for lack of the required majority.

After the vote, the representatives of Guatemala, Mexico and Yugoslavia stated that the Colombian motion should have been discussed as it lacked a juridical basis. The draft resolution for setting up an *ad hoc* committee involved a matter not of substance but of procedure, they maintained, and did not therefore require a two-thirds majority vote for approval.

DOCUMENTARY REFERENCES

INFORMATION ON TERRITORY TRANSFERRED TO ANOTHER ADMINISTERING MEMBER

A/3647 and Corr.1. Report of Committee on Information from Non-Self-Governing Territories, Part I, paragraph 101.

OBLIGATION TO CONTINUE TRANSMITTING INFORMATION

GENERAL ASSEMBLY—12TH SESSION
Fourth Committee, meetings 670, 672, 685.

A/3647 and Corr.1. Report of Committee on Information from Non-Self-Governing Territories, Part I, paragraphs 89-100.
A/C.4/359 and Add.1. Exchange of correspondence between Belgian Government and Secretary-General.

RESPONSIBILITY OF MEMBERS

GENERAL ASSEMBLY—12TH SESSION
Plenary Meeting 722.
Fourth Committee, meetings 670-679, 685, 687-694.
Fifth Committee, meeting 624.

A/3647 and Corr.1. Report of Committee on Information from Non-Self-Governing Territories, Part I, Section X(*b*).
A/C.4/357 and Rev.1. General questions relating to transmission and examination of information (communication from Secretary-General to Ghana and Federation of Malaya, and reply from Japan to communication from Secretary-General).
A/C.4/361. Statement by representative of United States at 674th meeting.

A/C.4/363. Statement by representative of United Kingdom at 678th meeting.

A/C.4/365. Statement by representative of USSR at 675th meeting.

A/C.4/366. Statement by representative of Czechoslovakia at 672nd meeting.

A/C.4/368. Statement by representative of Guatemala at 690th meeting.

A/C.4/L.504 and Rev.1. Burma, Ceylon, Costa Rica, Ghana, Greece, Guatemala, India, Indonesia, Iraq, Liberia, Nepal, Panama, Syria, Tunisia, Yugoslavia draft resolution and revision.

A/C.4/L.504/Rev.2. Burma, Ceylon, Costa Rica, Ghana, Greece, Guatemala, India, Indonesia, Iraq, Liberia, Nepal, Panama, Philippines, Syria, Tunisia, Uruguay, Yugoslavia revised draft resolution, adopted by Fourth Committee by roll-call vote of 42 to 27, with 8 abstentions as follows:

In favour: Afghanistan, Albania, Bolivia, Bulgaria, Burma, Byelorussian SSR, Cambodia, Ceylon, Costa Rica, Czechoslovakia, Egypt, El Salvador, Ethiopia, Ghana, Greece, Guatemala, Haiti, Hungary, India, Indonesia, Iran, Iraq, Israel, Jordan, Lebanon, Liberia, Mexico, Morocco, Nepal, Panama, Poland, Romania, Saudi Arabia, Sudan, Syria, Thailand, Tunisia, Ukrainian SSR, USSR, Uruguay, Yemen, Yugoslavia.

Against: Australia, Austria, Belgium, Brazil, Canada, Chile, Colombia, Cuba, Denmark, Finland, France, Honduras, Iceland, Italy, Luxembourg, Netherlands, New Zealand, Norway, Pakistan, Paraguay, Peru, Portugal, Spain, Sweden, Turkey, United Kingdom, United States.

Abstaining: Argentina, China, Dominican Republic, Ecuador, Ireland, Japan, Federation of Malaya, Venezuela.

A/C.4/L.505. Dominican Republic amendment to revised joint draft resolution, A/C.4/L.504/Rev.1.

A/C.4/L.506. Venezuela amendment to revised joint draft resolution, A/C.5/L.504/Rev.2.

A/C.5/729, A/3734, A/3736. Financial implications of draft resolution adopted by Fourth Committee. Note by Secretary-General, report of Advisory Committee on Administrative and Budgetary Questions and report of Fifth Committee.

A/3733. Report of Fourth Committee (draft resolution III [as in A/C.4/L.504/Rev.2]).

Draft resolution III, as recommended by Fourth Committee, A/3733, was not adopted by Assembly, having failed to obtain required two-thirds majority on 26 November 1957, meeting 722. The vote, by roll-call, was 41 in favour, 30 against, with 10 abstentions as follows:

In favour: Afghanistan, Albania, Bulgaria, Burma, Byelorussian SSR, Cambodia, Ceylon, Costa Rica, Czechoslovakia, Egypt, El Salvador, Ethiopia, Ghana, Greece, Guatemala, Haiti, Hungary, India, Indonesia, Iran, Iraq, Israel, Jordan, Liberia, Libya, Federation of Malaya, Mexico, Morocco, Nepal, Panama, Poland, Romania, Saudi Arabia, Sudan, Syria, Tunisia, Ukrainian SSR, USSR, Uruguay, Yemen, Yugoslavia.

Against: Australia, Austria, Belgium, Brazil, Canada, Chile, Colombia, Cuba, Dominican Republic, Finland, France, Honduras, Iceland, Italy, Luxembourg, Netherlands, New Zealand, Nicaragua, Norway, Pakistan, Paraguay, Peru, Portugal, Spain, Sweden, Turkey, Union of South Africa, United Kingdom, United States.

Abstaining: Argentina, China, Ecuador, Ireland, Japan, Laos, Lebanon, Philippines, Thailand, Venezuela.

ECONOMIC CONDITIONS IN NON-SELF-GOVERNING TERRITORIES

REPORT ON ECONOMIC CONDITIONS

In its 1957 report on economic conditions in Non-Self-Governing Territories (drafted by a sub-committee), the Committee on Information from Non-Self-Governing Territories recalled its view that the fundamental aims of economic policy were: to develop the Territories in the interest of all sectors of the population; to raise the standard of living by increasing individual real purchasing power; and to increase the total wealth of each Territory in order to raise standards of social services and administration.

Reviewing broad developments since 1953, it noted that the economies of the territories had generally continued to develop in line with the long-term trends of growth apparent since the end of the Second World War. While there had been no drastic structural change, there had been a further shift towards a momentary economy. Long-term development plans had been

continued and extended in a large number of the Territories. Local public authorities and indigenous inhabitants had participated increasingly in the preparation and execution of development programmes.

In general, the external trade of the Territories had increased over the period 1953-1955. There were, however, no significant changes in the structure of foreign trade of the majority of the Territories whose exports, in most cases, remain limited to one or a few primary commodities.

Growth in industry had occurred mainly in the processing of raw materials and in the production of consumer goods requiring relatively simple processes of manufacture. Industrialization, the Committee considered, should not be regarded as an end in itself, but as a means of raising the income levels of the population. Where favourable conditions existed, Governments should take active measures to encourage the development of industries most suited to the favourable use of the resources of Territories. Since, however, agriculture was the main economic activity of the Non-Self-Governing Territories, the speed of economic development would depend largely on the direction and speed of rural development to which industrial development should be designed to contribute.

Agricultural exports continued to expand. As to output for local consumption, which was less adequate, it seemed that, despite a general rise in the production of starchy staple crops, there were still serious deficiencies in the production of the more nutritious foods and thus in the quality of the diet. Progress towards greater diversification was often slow owing to such factors as the circumstances of the Territory's agricultural development, population pressures, soil conditions and climate which often made it desirable to cultivate crops with high yields. The Committee recognized that the introduction of new crops required a careful assessment of world markets and local conditions. But it noted that the diversification of crops might provide insurance against the risks of over-specialization. To this end, long-term government encouragement and assistance were needed.

As to the use of land, the Committee observed that any modernization programme might fail if attempted as a form of change in land use without full regard to the wider social and political ramifications involved. It was suggested that, to increase productivity, customary forms of land tenure should be modified, and that a lead must be given by Governments.

The Committee once again stressed the importance of integrated economic and social development. Given adequate social programmes, accelerated economic development could assist in overcoming critical phases of social transition.

The Committee recommended that economic progress should be fostered through the fullest use of the elements of the traditional pattern adaptable to new purposes. It noted that where levels of living were low, economic advancement was one of the first necessities of social policy, through which new conditions could be created so that new social institutions would evolve or traditional institutions take on new meaning.

The development of co-operative societies in the Territories, it felt, should be an important factor in social progress and prepare the people for the transition to a modern economy. It considered that there might still be unexplored possibilities for establishing the co-operative movement on a wider and more meaningful basis. By linking the co-operative movement with the basic needs and aspirations of the people, it could be made more effective in assisting economic and social reconstruction.

Community development, the Committee thought, was another promising means of combining economic and social activity.

The Committee maintained, too, that the successful evolution of the society in transition, as was taking place in Non-Self-Governing Territories, depended largely on the co-operation of the Administering Members with the representative elements of the population. One immediate task was training leaders on the widest possible scale and promoting popular leadership.

At the twelfth session of the General Assembly, the report was discussed by the Fourth Committee.

Many representatives, including those of Chile, China, Czechoslovakia, Ecuador, Guatemala, Hungary, India and Venezuela considered that the report and the economic conditions in the Non-Self-Governing Territories should be examined in the light of United Nations Charter principles. The interests of the inhabitants of the Territories were paramount, they stressed, adding that the Administering Members had undertaken the obligation to promote the well-being of the inhabitants.

Some representatives considered that, in the absence of information on political conditions, it was impossible to assess the economic progress in the Territories. Others pointed out that the terms of reference of the Committee on Information prevented it from making recommendations on individual Territories; as a result, the report on economic conditions was too general. The majority of the speakers commended it.

The representatives of Chile, China, Ecuador, India and Pakistan were among those who expressed satisfaction that the objectives of economic development as enumerated in the economic report approved by the General Assembly in 1954 were being pursued by the Administering Members in the Territories. They noted progress in various specific fields.

Nevertheless, they, and other speakers, considered that development was too slow. Much remained to be done in the Territories. Neither industrial nor economic development should be regarded as ends in themselves, but should serve to raise the living levels of all the inhabitants, especially those in rural areas, which accounted for some 90 per cent of the population. It was also urged that more efforts be made to speed up development, and various specific measures to this end were suggested.

The representatives of France and the United Kingdom explained some of the main points of their policies in the Territories and measures taken.

Under the *loi cadre* of 1956, said the French representative, there now existed in the French Territories a political structure based on universal adult franchise; elected assemblies managed all internal affairs, and in each Territory executive power rested with an elected Government Council. The economic development of these Territories would be further stimulated through their association in the European Economic Community (the European Common Market), which, in addition to other features, provided for the establishment of an investment fund.

The representative of the United Kingdom explained that his Government had the fullest sympathy with the representatives who had attached vital importance to the progress of Territories towards nationhood. The presence of Ghana and the Federation of Malaya in the Fourth Committee was eloquent evidence of the successful assistance given by the United Kingdom to countries travelling towards nationhood. In addition to the West Indies Federation, other countries were also steadily moving forward towards this goal. The United Kingdom, he added, regarded economic development not as an end in itself but as a means to progress towards nationhood; its policy was to help the people to take a more responsible share in economic activities in their countries, and to increase national income, ensuring that it was widely spread among the people.

The United Kingdom representative also cited a number of examples of measures taken in the Territories to establish basic economic services, to improve water supplies, to increase production and to associate representatives of the peoples with planning and working out development schemes.

The United States representative stated that the United States was working out new plans for multilateral organizations in the economic field, including new arrangements for capital investments, especially in the African Territories.

On the basis of a recommendation by the Committee on Information from Non-Self-Governing Territories, the Fourth Committee, on 24 October, adopted a draft resolution to approve the new report on economic conditions, communicate it to the Administering Members, to other United Nations organs and to the specialized agencies concerned. This was adopted at a plenary meeting of the Assembly on 26 November, as resolution 1152(XII), by a vote of 62 to 1.

NON-SELF-GOVERNING AREAS AND EUROPEAN ECONOMIC COMMUNITY

The possible effects of association with the European Economic Community (European Common Market) on the economies of Non-Self-Governing Territories was discussed in 1957 both at the eighth session of the Committee on Information from Non-Self-Governing Territories and at the General Assembly's twelfth session. The Rome Treaty of March 1957, establishing the European Economic Community, made provision for associating the following Non-Self-Governing Territory, among others, with the Community: French West Africa, French Equatorial Africa, Comoro Archipelago, Madagascar and dependencies, French Somaliland, the Belgian Congo and Netherlands New Guinea.

Discussion of the matter in the Committee on Information was favoured by the representatives of Guatemala, India and Iraq. The French representative, however, was against a debate and made the following points: The Rome Treaty would not come into effect until 1958. Relevant information would not be transmitted to the United Nations until 1959 and would not be considered by the Committee until 1960.

Representatives of non-administering members feared that association with the European Economic Community would limit the role of Non-Self-Governing Territories to furnishing primary products to Europe and providing markets for manufactured goods. Further, the Rome Treaty contained no provision for the Territories to sever their association with the Community, despite the fact that they were moving towards self-government or independence.

The United States representative thought that the question would be more properly discussed by the Contracting Parties to the General Agreement on Tariffs and Trade (GATT). The Netherlands representative considered discussion premature and maintained that association with the Community would help the economic and political advancement of Territories concerned.

When the matter was discussed in the Fourth Committee at the General Assembly's twelfth session, the French representative, who spoke also on behalf of Belgium, Italy and the Netherlands, and with the consent of the Federal Republic of Germany, reserved the position of the States which had signed the Rome Treaty with regard to the Assembly's debate on the subject.

The French representative later explained that while there was no objection to discussion of the Rome Treaty—which provided for full co-operation with the United Nations—it would, at the present stage be premature, since the full effects of the Treaty would not be felt for 15 years.

The Treaty, he added, provided for the protection of local industries and for benefits through the progressive abolition of customs barriers, opening up to the African Territories a market of 180 million consumers. The representatives of the inhabitants of the French Overseas Territories, he also said, had participated in the discussion of the Treaty and a majority of them had supported its ratification. Further, the Treaty accorded fully with the principles of the United Nations Charter and would help in the economic, political and social emancipation of Africa and its admission to the international community.

Others, however, voiced concern as to the possible economic effects of association with the European Economic Community, and urged a careful study of this. Among those sharing such views were the representatives of Afghanistan, Albania, Bulgaria, Burma, the Byelorussian SSR, China, Czechoslovakia, Ecuador, El Salvador, Guatemala, Haiti, Iraq, Israel, Liberia, Pakistan, Poland, Saudi Arabia, the Ukrainian SSR,

the USSR, Yemen and Yugoslavia.

Argentina, Bolivia, Burma, Ceylon, Costa Rica, Czechoslovakia, Ecuador, Egypt, Ethiopia, Ghana, Guatemala, Haiti, India, Liberia, Pakistan, Panama, Saudi Arabia, Sudan and Uruguay submitted a draft resolution to the following effect. The Assembly would: (1) invite the Administering Members concerned to send information to the Secretary-General on the association with the European Economic Community of the Non-Self-Governing Territories they administered, in conformity with Article 73e of the United Nations Charter; and (2) ask the Secretary-General to prepare a study of the subject for the next Assembly session (in 1958), when the matter would again be discussed.

Opposing this draft resolution, the representatives of Australia, France, the Netherlands and the United Kingdom considered that it would set a dangerous precedent of discussing treaties before they came into effect. The European Economic Community was already being studied by other competent organs of the United Nations, so that there was neither any need nor was it appropriate for the Fourth Committee to do so. The appropriate organ for discussion was that of GATT. Information on the Territories affected would be transmitted to the United Nations in due course, when it could be discussed in the Assembly.

The representative of Canada suggested that instead of adopting a draft resolution, the Fourth Committee could include an account of its discussion in its report to the General Assembly.

Some of the sponsors of the draft resolution and the representatives of Poland, Syria and the USSR maintained, in reply, that it was the function of the Fourth Committee to examine any information concerning Non-Self-Governing Territories. Although the European Economic Community had been discussed in other United Nations organs, none of them had dealt with the specific aspect which would form the subject of the proposed study by the Secretary-General, namely, the economic effects on Non-Self-Governing Territories of association with the European Economic Community. They were against the Canadian suggestion as it would arrogate to the Fourth Committee the function of its Rapporteur and as it would create a precedent for substituting an account for a draft resolution.

The text of the draft resolution was subsequently revised to ask the Secretary-General to prepare a report on the developments connected with the association of the Non-Self-Governing Territories with the European Economic Community, and to authorize him to take into account studies prepared by other organs on this question in so far as these studies might be relevant to the economic development of the Territories.

The draft resolution, as amended, was adopted by the Fourth Committee by a roll-call vote of 51 to 13, with 8 obstentions. On 26 November, it was adopted at a plenary meeting of the Assembly as resolution 1153(XII). The vote was 57 to 12, with 9 abstentions.

DOCUMENTARY REFERENCES

GENERAL ASSEMBLY—12TH SESSION
Plenary Meeting 722.
Fourth Committee, meetings 670-684.

REPORT ON ECONOMIC CONDITIONS
Special Study on Economic Conditions in Non-Self-Governing Territories. U.N.P. Sales No.: 58.VI.B.1.
A/3647 and Corr.1. Report of Committee on Information from Non-Self-Governing Territories, Part II.
A/3647 and Corr.1, Part I, Annex II. Draft resolution A, submitted by Committee on Information from Non-Self-Governing Territories, adopted unanimously by Fourth Committee.
A/3733. Report of Fourth Committee (draft resolution I).
RESOLUTION 1152(XII), as recommended by Fourth Committee, A/3733, adopted by Assembly on 26 November 1957, meeting 722, by 62 votes to 1.

"*The General Assembly,*
"*Considering* that, by resolution 564(VI) of 18 January 1952, it approved the special report drawn up in 1951 as a brief but considered indication of economic conditions in Non-Self-Governing Territories and the problems of economic development,
"*Considering* that, by resolution 846(IX) of 22 November 1954, it approved a further special report on economic conditions as a supplement to the 1951 report,
"*Noting* the 1957 report on economic conditions in Non-Self-Governing Territories, prepared by the Committee on Information from Non-Self-Governing Territories,
"1. *Approves* the 1957 report on economic conditions in Non-Self-Governing Territories and considers that it should be studied in conjunction with the reports approved in 1951 and 1954;
"2. *Invites* the Secretary-General to communicate the 1957 report on economic conditions in Non-Self-Governing Territories to the Members of the United Nations responsible for the administration of Non-Self-Governing Territories, to the Economic and Social Council, to the Trusteeship Council and to the specialized agencies concerned for their consideration."

NON-SELF-GOVERNING AREAS AND EUROPEAN ECONOMIC COMMUNITY
A/3647 and Corr.1. Report of Committee on In-

formation from Non-Self-Governing Territories, Part I, paragraphs 9, 15-36.
A/C.4/360. Treaty establishing European Economic Community.
A/C.4/362. Statement by Under-Secretary at 679th meeting.
A/C.4/364. Statement by representative of France at 678th meeting.
A/C.4/365. Statement by representative of USSR at 675th meeting.
A/C.4/366. Statement by representative of Czechoslovakia at 672nd meeting.
A/C.4/L.498. Argentina, Bolivia, Burma, Ceylon, Czechoslovakia, Ecuador, Egypt, Ethiopia, Ghana, Guatemala, Haiti, India, Liberia, Saudi Arabia, Sudan draft resolution.
A/C.4/L.498/Rev.1. Argentina, Bolivia, Burma, Ceylon, Costa Rica, Czechoslovakia, Ecuador, Egypt, Ethiopia, Ghana, Guatemala, Haiti, India, Liberia, Pakistan, Panama, Saudi Arabia, Sudan, Uruguay revised draft resolution, adopted by Fourth Committee by roll-call vote of 51 to 13, with 8 abstentions, as follows:
In favour: Afghanistan, Albania, Argentina, Bolivia, Brazil, Bulgaria, Burma, Byelorussian SSR, Cambodia, Ceylon, Chile, Colombia, Costa Rica, Czechoslovakia, Egypt, El Salvador, Ethiopia, Ghana, Greece, Guatemala, Haiti, Hungary, India, Indonesia, Iran, Iraq, Japan, Jordan, Lebanon, Liberia, Federation of Malaya, Mexico, Morocco, Nepal, Pakistan, Panama, Peru, Philippines, Poland, Romania, Saudi Arabia, Sudan, Syria, Thailand, Tunisia, Ukrainian SSR, USSR, Uruguay, Venezuela, Yemen, Yugoslavia.
Against: Australia, Belgium, Canada, Denmark, France, Italy, Luxembourg, Netherlands, New Zealand, Norway, Sweden, United Kingdom, United States.
Abstaining: Austria, China, Finland, Ireland, Israel, Nicaragua, Portugal, Spain.
A/C.4/502. Informal working paper by Canada.
A/3733. Report of Fourth Committee (draft resolution II).
RESOLUTION 1153(XII), as recommended by Fourth Committee, A/3733, adopted by Assembly on 26 November 1957, meeting 722, by 57 votes to 12, with 9 abstentions.

"*The General Assembly,*
"*Having examined* the 1957 report on economic

conditions in Non-Self-Governing Territories, prepared by the Committee on Information from Non-Self-Governing Territories,

"*Having noted* that the Treaty establishing the European Economic Community provides for the association with the Community of certain Non-Self-Governing Territories,

"*Believing* that this association may have important effects on the economic development of these Territories,

"1. *Invites* the Administering Members concerned to transmit to the Secretary-General, in conformity with Article 73e of the Charter of the United Nations, information on the association of the Non-Self-Governing Territories under their administration with the European Economic Community;

"2. *Requests* the Secretary-General to prepare for the thirteenth session of the General Assembly a report on the developments connected with the association of Non-Self-Governing Territories with the European Economic Community, taking into account the studies that may be undertaken in this connexion by the Economic and Social Council, the Economic Commission for Europe, the Economic Commission for Asia and the Far East, the Economic Commission for Latin America and other international organs, in so far as these studies may be relevant to the economic development of Non-Self-Governing Territories;

"3. *Decides* to resume consideration of this question at its thirteenth session."

SOCIAL AND EDUCATIONAL CONDITIONS IN NON-SELF-GOVERNING TERRITORIES

As economic conditions in the Non-Self-Governing Territories were the main subject before it in 1957, the Committee on Information dealt only briefly on the social and educational situation in these areas.

SOCIAL CONDITIONS

The Committee's interest centred on social problems in Non-Self-Governing Territories arising from the transition to a money economy, particularly those connected with the impact of industrialization and economic development.

In addition to information prepared by the Secretary-General, the Committee had before it a Secretariat report on the social effects of economic change in peasant societies and a report prepared by the United Nations Educational, Scientific and Cultural Organization (UNESCO) on the social aspects of industrialization in Africa south of the Sahara. The representative of the International Labour Organisation (ILO) informed the Committee about action taken at the 1957 International Labour Conference on conditions of employment adding that Conventions on these subjects were at the drafting stage. ILO, he told the Committee, was also undertaking a broad survey of labour and social conditions in Africa south of the Sahara.

The representatives of China, Guatemala, India and Iraq called for more information to make possible an adequate analysis of social conditions, particularly information on social policy and the problems of cultural adaptation to political and economic changes. They also stressed the need for integrated, balanced development in view of the fact that industrialization, while bringing material improvements to the Territories had often been accompanied by a disruption of rural and urban communities. Indigenous societies were consequently in a state of flux, and Government measures were needed to alleviate the resulting insecurity, which was aggravated by low wages, poor housing and inequality of opportunities. The administering Members, they urged, should adopt a more active policy to improve the social conditions in the territories and give indigenous inhabitants more responsibilities in formulating the policy and in carrying it out.

Owing to the importance of the question of social effect of economic change, the Committee decided that it would again consider the matter at its 1959 session, when social conditions would be the main topic for discussion.

EDUCATIONAL CONDITIONS

The Committee considered educational conditions in the Non-Self-Governing Territories in the light of developments since the adoption in 1956 of its special report on educational conditions. Before the Committee in 1957 was a UNESCO report on the eradication of illiteracy. This included detailed data on the extent and distribution of illiteracy in the world. It also described in outline the assistance given by UNESCO to the Non-Self-Governing Territories through fundamental education projects and in the preparation of reading material for those who had recently become literate.

Some members regretted the lack of enough information on education policies and the progress achieved, including the extent to which the people were being prepared for self-government. Others considered that the problem of education was of great urgency particularly in view of the constant population increases. Of immediate importance were the development of fundamental education and the training for leadership. Stressed, too, was the need for vigorous campaigns to reduce the generally high illiteracy rates in the Territories which had been reported by UNESCO.

DOCUMENTARY REFERENCES

SOCIAL CONDITIONS

A/3647 and Corr.1. Report of Committee on Information from Non-Self-Governing Territories, Part I, sections VIII and XII.

See also summaries of information transmitted to Secretary-General during 1956, as listed in DOCUMENTARY REFERENCES to section above on TRANSMISSION OF INFORMATION IN 1957.

EDUCATIONAL CONDITIONS

A/3647 and Corr.1. Report of Committee on Information from Non-Self-Governing Territories, Part I, section VII.

See also summaries of information transmitted to Secretary-General during 1956, as listed in DOCUMENTARY REFERENCES to section above on TRANSMISSION OF INFORMATION IN 1957.

INTERNATIONAL COLLABORATION ON ECONOMIC, SOCIAL AND EDUCATIONAL MATTERS

INTERNATIONAL COLLABORATION AND TECHNICAL ASSISTANCE

In 1957, the Committee on Information from Non-Self-Governing Territories had before it: a report by the Secretary-General reviewing international collaboration for the economic, social and educational advancement of the Territories; a report on technical assistance to the Territories provided by the United Nations and specialized agencies; and reports on the activities of the United Nations Educational, Scientific and Cultural Organization (UNESCO) and the World Health Organization (WHO). In addition, representatives of the International Labour Organisation (ILO), the Food and Agriculture Organization (FAO) and UNESCO, made statements to the Committee on activities of interest to Non-Self-Governing Territories.

The report on international collaboration summarized decisions of the Economic and Social Council and of the Commissions on Human Rights and on the Status of Women affecting Non-Self-Governing Territories. It also described regional co-operation efforts through the Commission for Technical Co-operation in Africa South of the Sahara, the Caribbean Commission, the Economic Commission for Asia and the Far East, the Colombo Plan and the South Pacific Commission.

The report on technical assistance surveyed the types of aid provided to Non-Self-Governing Territories over the period 1955-1957 by the United Nations Technical Assistance Administration and the specialized agencies, as well as the aid provided by the United Nations Children's Fund (UNICEF) and the International Bank for Reconstruction and Development.

Under the Expanded Technical Assistance Programme, which is operated jointly by the United Nations and specialized agencies, aid to 30 countries at a cost of $983,000 was approved in 1957, as against 23 Territories ($726,000) in 1956 and 26 Territories ($557,000) in 1955.

Aid in public health continued to be provided by UNICEF and WHO, the report added. By 1957, UNICEF had aided 100 projects in 41 Territories, at a total cost of more than $8 million; the 1956-1957 allocation alone was $2,278,600. Under its regular programme, financed from its own budget, WHO continued to co-operate with UNICEF in child-aid programmes and to provide experts and fellowships. Under the Expanded Technical Assistance Programme (which is financed from voluntary contributions by Governments) WHO planned to provide assistance for malaria eradication, tuberculosis control, public health work and training of public health personnel in Non-Self-Governing Territories.

The increase in technical assistance to Non-Self-Governing Territories, was welcomed by the representatives of Ceylon, China, Guatemala and India, who urged that this aid be stepped up. The United Kingdom representative expressed appreciation for the aid given by the specialized agencies to the Territories administered by the United Kingdom.

SCHOLARSHIP OFFERS

The Committee on Information also considered a report by the Secretary-General on offers of study facilities to Non-Self-Governing Territories made by United Nations Member States under General Assembly resolution 845 (IX), of 22 November 1954. Between 20 February 1956 and 28 January 1957, the Secretary-General's report noted, 15 United Nations Member States had offered 247 scholarships, for which 123 applications had been received. These 15 states were: Burma, Czechoslovakia, Greece, India, Iran, Mexico, the Philippines, Poland, Romania, Thailand, Tunisia, Turkey, the USSR, the United States and Yugoslavia. Between 26 July 1956 and 28 June 1957, 12 scholarships had been awarded, the Secretary-General also reported.

The Australian representative asked that the Secretary-General's report include a list of scholarships provided by administering powers to Non-Self-Governing Territories. The French representative supported this suggestion.

The Indian representative noted that, in contrast to the large proportion of the scholarships taken up under an Indian programme, the number of awards as compared with the scholarships offered under Assembly resolution 845(IX) had been very small.

On the basis of a proposal by Ceylon, the Committee adopted a draft resolution by 9 votes to 0, with 4 abstentions, whereby the General Assembly would in effect ask that the procedures for handling applications for scholarships be speeded up. The Assembly would also ask the Secretary-General to give assistance for this. In addition, it would invite States offering scholarships to inform him of the use made by candidates of the scholarships awarded to them. The assembly would also ask the Secretary-General for annual information on the action taken as the result of this resolution.

When this draft resolution came before the Assembly's twelfth session, it was considered in conjunction with the Secretary-General's report to the Committee on Information on the offers of scholarships and the use made of them and a supplementary report which showed that, as at 1 October 1957, 16 Member States (those listed above, plus Ceylon) had offered 250 scholarships, that 140 applications had been received, 19 scholarships granted and 17 refused.

In the course of discussion in the Fourth Committee, the representative of Israel announced that his Government intended to offer scholarships to students from Africa.

On 31 October 1957, the Fourth Committee adopted the draft resolution recommended by the Committee on Information, with some drafting changes, by 61 votes to 0, with 6 abstentions. On 26 November, it was approved at a plenary meeting of the Assembly by 74 votes to 0, with 3 abstentions, as resolution 1154(XII).

DOCUMENTARY REFERENCES

INTERNATIONAL COLLABORATION
AND TECHNICAL ASSISTANCE
A/3647 and Corr.1. Report of Committee on Information from Non-Self-Governing Territories, Part I, section IX(a).

SCHOLARSHIP OFFERS

GENERAL ASSEMBLY—12TH SESSION
Plenary Meeting 722.
Fourth Committee, meetings 670-679, 685-687.

A/3618 and Add.1. Offers of study and training facilities for students from Non-Self-Governing Territories under General Assembly resolution 845(IX) of 22 November 1954. Report of Secretary-General.
A/3647 and Corr.1. Report of Committee on Information from Non-Self-Governing Territories, Part I,

Annex II. Draft resolution B submitted by Committee on Information from Non-Self-Governing Territories, adopted by Fourth Committee, as orally amended by Philippines, Venezuela and Ceylon, by 61 votes to 0, with 6 abstentions.
A/3733. Report of Fourth Committee (draft resolution IV).
RESOLUTION 1154(XII), as recommended by Fourth Committee, A/3733, adopted by Assembly on 26 November 1957, meeting 722, by 74 votes to 0, with 3 abstentions.

"The General Assembly,
"Having taken note of the report presented by the Secretary-General to the General Assembly at its twelfth session in compliance with resolution 931(X) of 8 November 1955,

"*Noting with satisfaction* the further response to resolution 845(IX), of 22 November 1954, inviting Member States to extend offers of facilities for study and training to inhabitants of Non-Self-Governing Territories,

"*Taking into account* the interest in the offers indicated by the steadily increasing number of applications,

"1. *Requests* Members submitting their observations on the qualifications of the candidates, in accordance with paragraph 5 of General Assembly resolution 845 (IX) of 22 November 1954, and Members which offer facilities, to consider the applications with all possible speed;

"2. *Requests* the Secretary-General to give such assistance as is possible and as may be sought by the Members concerned and by the applicants;

"3. *Invites* the offering States to inform the Secretary-General of the use made of the scholarships offered by them;

"4. *Requests* the Secretary-General to include in his annual reports to the General Assembly, prepared in accordance with resolution 931(X) of 8 November 1955, information on the action taken as a result of the present resolution."

QUESTION OF ASSEMBLY VOTING MAJORITY ON MATTERS CONCERNING NON-SELF-GOVERNING TERRITORIES

Early in the course of the general debate on information from Non-Self-Governing Territories which took place in the Fourth Committee at the General Assembly's twelfth session, the question was raised whether Assembly decisions on matters concerning Non-Self-Governing Territories required a two-thirds majority.

Costa Rica, Greece, Iraq, Mexico, Morocco and Yugoslavia proposed a draft resolution with a view to clarifying the application of Article 18, paragraph 2, of the United Nations Charter to questions concerning Non-Self-Governing Territories. (Article 18, paragraph 2, states that Assembly decisions on "important questions" require a two-thirds majority vote, and it lists questions of this category. Paragraph 3 of this Article lays down that decisions on other questions, including the determination of additional questions be decided by a two-thirds majority vote, shall be made by a simple majority.)

The six-power proposal, in effect, was that the Assembly ask the International Court of Justice for an advisory opinion on the following questions: (1) Which voting procedure was applicable to the Assembly's resolutions on matters concerning Non-Self-Governing Territories and falling under Chapter XI of the Charter? (2) Was it in accordance with the United Nations Charter to submit a resolution on Non-Self-Governing Territories to a two-thirds vote if an additional category to that effect had not been established beforehand under Article 18, paragraph 3, of the Charter?

The sponsors of the draft stressed the need for a uniform procedure on resolutions on matters concerning Non-Self-Governing Territories.

They cited instances in which such resolutions had been subject to adoption, on the one hand, by a simple majority and, on the other hand, by a two-thirds majority. It was thus necessary to have an authoritative interpretation of the provisions of Article 18, paragraphs 2 and 3, of the Charter.

The representatives of Belgium, Brazil, the Dominican Republic, Ecuador, Portugal and the United Kingdom thought it inappropriate, however, to seek a ruling on one specific group of questions in relation to Article 18, which concerned voting procedures on broad categories of questions. The decision on the definition of "important questions" (which required a two-thirds majority vote in the Assembly) was political rather than legal and should, in each instance, rest with the Assembly. The Assembly's power of decision might be restricted by the Court's advisory opinion; further, the question was not a legal one, and Article 65 of the International Court's Statute restricted the Court to giving advisory opinions on legal questions only.

In the light of a suggestion by the Colombian representative, the sponsors agreed to amend their draft text and to ask the Sixth Committee for an opinion on the questions.

Brazil, China, the Dominican Republic, Ecuador, Japan, Israel, New Zealand, the Philippines, the United Kingdom and Venezuela opposed the amended text on the ground that the matter concerned the Assembly's plenary meetings and could thus not properly be the subject of questions addressed by one Main Committee of the Assembly to another in whose agenda it was not included.

On 25 October 1957, however, the Fourth

Committee adopted the draft resolution, as amended, by a roll-call vote of 32 votes to 29, with 12 abstentions.

On 21 November, the Sixth Committee took up the questions referred to it by the Fourth Committee. After a brief preliminary discussion, it decided, upon a United Kingdom suggestion, to defer any formal decision on its competence in the matter until after the general debate on the questions referred to the Sixth Committee by the Fourth Committee.

Views on the competence of the Sixth Committee to give an opinion on the questions before it were divided.

The representatives of Brazil, the Dominican Republic, Israel, Portugal and Spain thought there was no basis for considering the questions referred to the Sixth Committee by the Fourth Committee, as these referred neither to any legal aspect of specific questions allocated for consideration by a Main Committee of the Assembly nor to the Assembly's rules of procedure.

The representatives of Peru, Poland, Syria and Romania maintained that the Sixth Committee was competent to discuss questions referred to it by another Main Committee of the Assembly.

The Colombian representative thought that due to its broad scope, question (1), namely, that on which voting procedure was applicable, should be referred to the International Court of Justice. The representative of Portugal stressed the difficulty of adopting what amounted to a decision on the definition of an important question. The Assembly should be left free to decide on the voting majority applicable to each case.

The representative of Cuba pointed out that in the past, the Assembly had not consistently maintained the same voting procedure on matters concerning Non-Self-Governing Territories. However, the great majority of the relevant resolutions had, in fact, been adopted by a majority of two-thirds or more; the Fourth Committee should be told that this was the normal practice and that only the Assembly could answer the second question on which an opinion was sought.

Before the Sixth Committee had completed its debate, the Assembly in plenary meeting adopted resolutions on the agenda item concerning information from Non-Self-Governing Territories from which the question before the Sixth Committee arose. The Sixth Committee's Chairman thought that no further action on the part of the Committee was thus necessary. He added, however, that the general question of the two-thirds majority voting rule might be proposed for the agenda of the Assembly's thirteenth session in 1958.

The Sixth Committee then discussed the form of the reply to the Fourth Committee. Several draft texts and amendments thereto were submitted.

These provided for several alternatives, which included: (1) a suggestion that the Fourth Committee place the request for an opinion on the agenda of the Assembly's thirteenth session; (2) a decision to the effect that since the Assembly had disposed of the agenda item in connexion with which the questions had been raised, the Sixth Committee was not in a position to reply to the request for an opinion; or (3) a decision that it was not appropriate for the Sixth Committee to reply to the request. A draft resolution, incorporating the third alternative reply was adopted by the Sixth Committee by 56 votes to 0, with 1 abstention.

Subsequently, in the Fourth Committee, the representatives of Iraq, Liberia, Mexico and Yugoslavia felt that the discussions on the matter had shown the importance of a clear decision on the question. The Mexican representative said it was a recognized fact that questions concerning Non-Self-Governing Territories were customarily subject to a simple majority vote. The Liberian representative, reserved the right to submit a draft resolution at the Assembly's thirteenth session to refer the question of voting procedure to the International Court of Justice.

DOCUMENTARY REFERENCES

GENERAL ASSEMBLY—12TH SESSION
Fourth Committee, meetings 670, 675, 679-681, 700, 701, 734.

A/C.4/L.497, Add.1, 2, and Rev.1, 2. Costa Rica,

Greece, Iraq, Mexico, Morocco, Yugoslavia draft resolution and revisions, adopted by Fourth Committee, as amended by Czechoslovakia, by roll-call vote of 32 to 29, with 12 abstentions, as follows:
In favour: Albania, Bulgaria, Burma, Byelorussian

SSR, Cambodia, Ceylon, Costa Rica, Czechoslovakia, Egypt, Ghana, Greece, Guatemala, Haiti, Hungary, India, Indonesia, Iraq, Jordan, Lebanon, Liberia, Mexico, Morocco, Nepal, Panama, Poland, Romania, Sudan, Tunisia, Ukrainian SSR, USSR, Yemen, Yugoslavia.

Against: Australia, Austria, Belgium, Brazil, Canada, Chile, China, Colombia, Cuba, Denmark, Dominican Republic, Ecuador, France, Iceland, Italy, Japan, Luxembourg, Netherlands, New Zealand, Norway, Pakistan, Paraguay, Peru, Philippines, Portugal, Spain, Sweden, Turkey, United Kingdom.

Abstaining: Afghanistan, Argentina, El Salvador, Ethiopia, Finland, Ireland, Israel, Federation of Malaya, Thailand, United States, Uruguay, Venezuela.

A/C.4/L.499. Colombia amendments to revised joint draft resolution, A/C.4/L.497/Rev.1.

A/C.4/L.500. Czechoslovakia amendments to revised joint draft resolution, A/C.4/L.497/Rev.2.

A/C.4/L.501. Resolution adopted by Fourth Committee (see text matter above).

A/3733. Report of Fourth Committee.

A/C.4/373. Letter from President of General Assembly transmitting resolution adopted by Sixth Committee on 2 December 1957, A/C.6/L.417.

Sixth Committee, meetings 529, 538-544.

A/C.6/355. Letter of 29 October from President of General Assembly to Chairman of Sixth Committee.

A/C.6/L.408. Working paper prepared by Secretariat at request of Sixth Committee.

A/C.6/L.410. Afghanistan draft resolution.

A/C.6/L.411. Syria amendments to Afghanistan draft resolution.

A/C.6/L.412. Afghanistan and Mexico draft resolution.

A/C.6/L.413. Syria amendments to joint draft resolution, A/C.6/L.412.

A/C.6/L.414. Afghanistan, Mexico, Poland joint draft resolution, adopted by Sixth Committee, as amended by Cuba, Peru and Dominican Republic, and verbally by sponsors, by 56 votes to 0, with 1 abstention.

A/C.6/L.415. Portugal amendments to joint draft resolution, A/C.6/L.414.

A/C.6/L.416. Cuba, Peru, Dominican Republic amendment to joint draft resolution, A/C.6/L.414.

A/C.6/L.417. Text of resolution adopted by Sixth Committee on 2 December 1957 (see text matter above).

OTHER QUESTIONS RELATING TO TRANSMISSION AND EXAMINATION OF INFORMATION

SUMMARIES OF INFORMATION

In 1957, the summaries of information from Non-Self-Governing Territories were presented to the Committee on Information from Non-Self-Governing Territories and to the General Assembly in final form as fascicles, one for each of the following geographical regions: East, Central, West and Southern Africa, Indian Ocean, Caribbean, Pacific, Asian, and Other Territories. These fascicles replaced the mimeographed documents and the single volume of summaries which had been published annually prior to 1957.

The Secretary-General's report stated that the new system, if found satisfactory, would be used in two years of every three, and that the full summaries would still be published every third year. Costs over a three-year period would thus be reduced by $12,000.

Without prejudice to the Assembly's action, the Secretary-General suggested that while the fascicle system for the supplementary summaries facilitated distribution, the new system should be given another year before a final judgement was made.

When, in 1957, the Committee on Information discussed the question of reproducing summaries of information, various representatives considered that, in order to avoid delay in publication, information from United Nations Members administering Non-Self-Governing Territories should be transmitted on time. Further, the fascicles, though not placed on sale, should be publicized and made available for the public.

At the General Assembly's twelfth session, the Fourth Committee accepted the Secretary-General's suggestions and decided to postpone consideration of the question of reproduction and distribution of the summaries, on the understanding that this decision would not in any way prejudice any action by the Assembly at its 1958 session.

REPORT ON THE PROGRESS OF NON-SELF-GOVERNING TERRITORIES

In 1957, the Committee on Information from Non-Self-Governing Territories received an oral report from the Under-Secretary for the Department of Trusteeship and Information from Non-Self-Governing Territories on the preparation of the report on progress of the Non-Self-Governing Territories requested by the Assembly in 1956 by resolution 1053(XI).

The progress report, he said, would consist of three main parts: (1) an introduction reviewing general trends in the Territories; (2) an analysis of economic, social and educational progress; and (3) summaries of information

on conditions in individual Territories, with particular reference to changes occurring, broadly, between 1946 and 1956.

DOCUMENTARY REFERENCES

SUMMARIES OF INFORMATION

GENERAL ASSEMBLY—12TH SESSION
Fourth Committee, meetings 670-679, 685, 687.

A/3619. Methods of reproducing summaries of information concerning Non-Self-Governing Territories. Report of Secretary-General.
A/3647 and Corr.1. Report of Committee on Information from Non-Self-Governing Territories, Part I, Section X(a): Methods of reproducing

information concerning Non-Self-Governing Territories.
A/C.4/361. Statement by representative of United States on 21 October 1957.
A/3733. Report of Fourth Committee.

REPORT ON THE PROGRESS OF
NON-SELF-GOVERNING TERRITORIES
A/3647 and Corr.1. Report of Committee on Information from Non-Self-Governing Territories, Part I, Annex III. Statement by Under-secretary.

CHAPTER II

THE QUESTION OF SOUTH WEST AFRICA

CONSIDERATION BY COMMITTEE ON SOUTH WEST AFRICA

During its fourth session (5 March–2 August 1957) the Committee on South West Africa devoted its attention to the examination of conditions in South West Africa and petitions concerning the Territory. It also studied the question of legal action which might be taken to ensure that the Union of South Africa fulfilled its obligations under the League of Nations Mandate for this Territory.

CONDITIONS IN THE TERRITORY

In its report to the General Assembly, the Committee referred to a "continued trend in the administration of the Territory towards the deliberate subordination and relegation of the vast majority of the population to an inferior status, through the application of such measures as the forced alienation, without proper compensation, of the land which they traditionally occupied" and through "dominatory controls" over their residence and movement, their employment and their ownership of livestock. The majority were thus deprived of opportunities for economic advancement, of education, and of minimum political rights, and were given no opportunity to take part in the various branches of government in the Territory.

The Committee also expressed the opinion

that continued and increasing political, social and economic pressures and restrictions imposed in all walks of life on the vast majority of the inhabitants and especially on the indigenous African population, revealed a policy intended to give paramount importance to the interests of the population of European origin. This policy was also intended to maintain and reinforce the entrenchment of government control in the hands of this minority of European origin, and to secure, as an ultimate goal, the incorporation of the Territory into the Union of South Africa. The international status of the Territory would thus be modified in a way that was contrary to the relevant international agreements, the advisory opinion of the International Court of Justice of 11 July 1950[1] and the interests of the vast majority of the Territory's inhabitants.

After examining the conditions in the Territory, the Committee found no evidence that the Mandatory Power, the Union of South Africa, intended to change the course of the administration to bring it into line with the Mandates System. The Committee therefore felt that the General Assembly should weigh the gravity of the existing situation and consider the need for acting without further delay.

[1] See Y.U.N., 1956, pp. 807-14.

It should do so by such immediate measures as were possible and feasible to ensure and safeguard the well-being and development of the inhabitants of South West Africa and to preserve the Territory's international status until it was placed under the Trusteeship System.

Responsibility for the administration of "Natives", who make up the large majority of the Territory's 457,700 inhabitants, the Committee recalled, had been transferred in 1955 to the Union's Minister of Native Affairs. The Committee indicated that the new developments in "Native" administration subsequent to the transfer of direct control to the Union Government had been the alienation of "Native" land and a more severe application of the *apartheid* policy.

The Committee recommended as a matter of urgency that the Mandatory Power take steps to repeal all racially discriminatory legislation and practices in the Territory and that it take urgent measures to revise the existing policies and practices of "Native" administration so as to ensure the fulfilment of its obligations and responsibilities under the Mandate.

The Committee also recommended that the Mandatory Power undertake a planned programme of economic development designed primarily to assist and equip the "Native" inhabitants to play a greater role in the economy of the Territory. It envisaged the expansion of "Native" production and marketing of dairy products and cattle, the development of suitable land for the settlement of the "Native" farmers engaged in these and other forms of agricultural and pastoral production, including the raising of karakul lambs, and the provision of adequate facilities and assistance for training, instruction and demonstration for these purposes and for the entry of "Natives" into other productive, trading and business enterprises and into skilled employment, particularly in the mining and fishing industries.

The Mandatory Power's practice of allocating progressively increasing areas of land in the Territory to a minority of the population, to the detriment of the "Non-European" majority, was considered inadmissible by the Committee. It urged that no land inhabited by "Non-Europeans" be alienated solely for the benefit of the "European" settler community.

It also urged that immediate steps be initiated to ensure that the "Non-European" majority should not be deprived of the land necessary for their present and future needs; these needs to be assessed on the basis of the natural population growth and the principle of full participation by the "Non-European" population in the Territory's economic development.

The Committee recommended that "Native" workers be given the same legal rights to organize and to participate in conciliation and arbitration preceedings as other workers in the Territory. It deplored the designation, under the principal labour legislation, of the employer and the worker as "master" and "servant". This, it considered, impaired the dignity of the workers and perpetuated a system of racial discrimination which should be abolished. The Committee also deplored the enactment of further discriminatory legislation during 1956 which had the effect of preventing the advancement of "Native" and "Coloured" workers employed in mines. Legislation of this kind, based exclusively on racial differences, was completely contrary to the letter and spirit of the Mandate, it considered. The Committee reiterated its view that improved "Native" labour conditions, including increased wage rates and better living and working conditions, would be more effective in alleviating the shortage of labour than the existing policy of strict labour control.

The Committee again stated its view that the restrictions on freedom of movement in the Territory constituted flagrant disregard of the principles and purposes of the Mandate and of the Universal Declaration of Human Rights.

After noting an increase in the total medical expenditure and in the medical facilities, the Committee drew attention to the disparity between the facilities and expenditure within the Police Zone and outside it, where the majority of the "Native" population lives. It stressed once more the need for giving urgent attention to providing the population of the area with medical services at least comparable with those in the Police Zone.

While welcoming the construction of new houses, the Committee noted with concern the strict *apartheid* policy imposed on housing schemes in urban locations.

The Committee again drew the attention of the General Assembly to the three separate, unequal and racially discriminatory educational systems maintained by the Mandatory Power.

PETITIONS AND COMMUNICATIONS

The Committee examined six petitions and several other communications relating to the Territory. In this connexion, it drew the attention of the General Assembly to the continuing desire of representatives of sections of the indigenous population of South West Africa to appear before appropriate organs of the United Nations and to the expressed willingness of two members of the European community to do so if the occasion arose. It therefore recommended that the General Assembly urge the Mandatory Power to grant petitioners travel documents to enable them to appear before organs of the United Nations when granted hearings and to return thereafter to their places of residence.

The Committee also recommended that the Assembly adopt two resolutions on petitions and related communications.

LEGAL ACTION

As requested by the General Assembly on 25 February 1957 (by resolution 1060(XI)), the Committee made a study of the legal action which might be taken by organs of the United Nations or by United Nations Member States or former members of the League of Nations to ensure that the Union Government fulfilled its obligations under the Mandate. The Committee submitted a special report on this question to the General Assembly (A/3625).

Organs of the United Nations, the Committee's report stated, could request advisory opinions of the International Court of Justice not only on aspects of the supervision procedure as requested in 1954 and 1955 (on voting procedure and admissibility of hearings of petitioners), but also on specific acts of the Mandatory Power. The General Assembly, for example, could request an advisory opinion on whether the status of the Territory had been modified in a manner or to a degree incompatible with the Mandate. The Committee pointed out, however, that the Court might in certain circumstances decline to give its opinion. The Committee also referred to other legal action which might be taken by United Nations organs.

As regards the legal action open to States, either individually or jointly, the Committee reported that disputes between the Mandatory Power and another State or States relating to the Mandate could be brought before the International Court for compulsory jurisdiction in accordance with Article 7 of the Mandate. The Committee also noted, however, that there were doubts as to which categories of States might have the right to take such an action.

CONSIDERATION BY GENERAL ASSEMBLY

During the twelfth session of the General Assembly, the Fourth Committee considered the report and special report of the Committee on South West Africa between 25 September and 11 October 1957.

REQUESTS FOR HEARINGS

The Fourth Committee also considered requests for hearings concerning South West Africa submitted by Mburumba Kerina Getzen and the Reverend Michael Scott. On 24 September, it granted these requests, the first by a vote of 49 to 4, with 14 abstentions, the second by a vote of 50 to 4, with 15 abstentions.

During the general debate on the question of South West Africa, a number of Members—including Guatemala, Indonesia, Liberia and Uruguay—suggested that more time should be allowed for careful study of legal action and its possible consequences. Other members — among whom were Haiti, Iran, Iraq, Israel and Mexico—hoped that further efforts would be made to reach a settlement of the question of South West Africa through persuasion and discussion with the Union of South Africa.

ESTABLISHMENT OF GOOD OFFICES COMMITTEE

On 8 October 1957, the Chairman of the Fourth Committee submitted a draft resolution to establish a Good Offices Committee on South West Africa. Consisting of the United States, the United Kingdom and a third member to be nominated by the President of the twelfth Assembly session, it would discuss with the Government of the Union of South Africa a basis for an agreement which would continue to accord to the Territory an international status. It would report to the Assembly's thirteenth session in 1958.

India submitted amendments, later co-sponsored by Uruguay, to provide for the election of the third member of Good Offices Committee, and to propose that the Committee discuss a basis for "a solution in accordance with the Charter of the United Nations".

The representatives of Canada, Sweden, the United Kingdom and the United States contended, however, that the proposal to amend the terms of reference of the Good Offices Committee would defeat the purpose of the resolution. In any case, they said, the Assembly would have final say on any agreement which might be proposed.

Ecuador and Guatemala later submitted an amendment which, as orally revised, would have the General Assembly request the Good Offices Committee to submit a report to the Assembly's thirteenth session for examination and decision by the Assembly "in accordance with the Charter of the United Nations". Following this, India and Uruguay withdrew their amendments relating to the terms of reference of the proposed Committee. India also withdrew its sponsorship of the amendment to have the third member of Good Offices Committee elected by the General Assembly, thus leaving Uruguay as the sole sponsor of this amendment.

On 11 October 1957, the Fourth Committee adopted two amendments to the preamble of the Chairman's draft resolution. It rejected the Uruguayan amendment calling for the election of the third member of the Committee, rather than for his appointment by the Assembly's President. This was rejected by a roll-call vote of 35 to 28, with 16 abstentions. The revised Ecuadorean and Guatemalan amendment relating to the report of the Good Offices Committee was approved by 67 votes to 0, with 19 abstentions.

The draft resolution as a whole, incorporating various amendments, including a further one by Uruguay, was approved by the Fourth Committee by a roll-call vote of 52 to 10, with 17 abstentions.

On 25 October, it was approved at a plenary meeting of the Assembly by 50 votes to 10, with 20 abstentions, as resolution 1143(XII).

LEGAL ACTION

The Fourth Committee considered a two-part draft resolution on the question of legal action to ensure the fulfilment of the Union Government of its obligations in respect of the Territory of South West Africa. It was submitted by Ceylon, Ecuador, Ethiopia, Ghana, Guatemala, India, Syria and Yugoslavia.

The first part of this draft proposed that the General Assembly draw the attention of Members to the failure of the Union of South Africa to render annual reports to the United Nations and to the legal action provided in Article 7 of the League of Nations Mandate. The Assembly would also decide to resume consideration of the special report of the Committee on South West Africa at its thirteenth session. By the second part of the draft, the Assembly would ask the Committee on South West Africa to consider further the question of securing advisory opinions from the International Court of Justice with regard to the administration of the Territory and to make recommendations concerning acts of the administration on which reference to the Court might usefully be made.

On 11 October 1957, the Committee approved the paragraph calling for consideration of the special report of the Committee on South West Africa at the thirteenth session, by 51 to 1, with 22 abstentions. It then approved the draft resolution as a whole by 55 votes to 4, with 18 abstentions.

On 25 October 1957, at a plenary meeting, the General Assembly adopted the draft resolution as resolution 1142(XII), by 55 votes to 3, with 17 abstentions.

CONDITIONS IN TERRITORY

On 2 October 1957, Liberia submitted a draft resolution, which was later revised to incorporate amendments proposed by Guatemala and Poland. By this text, the General Assembly would note with concern that conditions in the Territory and the trend of its administration represented a situation contrary to the Mandates System, the Charter of the United Nations, the Universal Declaration of Human Rights, the advisory opinion of the International Court of Justice and the resolutions of the General Assembly. The Assembly would, among other things, also call upon the Mandatory Power to give urgent attention to the recommendations and conclusions of the Committee on South West Africa.

Following the introduction by the Chairman of the Fourth Committee of the draft resolution to establish a Good Offices Committee, Liberia submitted a revised draft resolution by which the General Assembly would confine itself to approving the report of the Committee on conditions in the Territory.

An amendment orally proposed by Canada to the effect that the General Assembly should note rather than approve the report was rejected by 40 votes to 20, with 9 abstentions.

The revised draft resolution was approved by the Fourth Committee on 11 October 1957 by 60 votes to 0, with 16 abstentions. On 25 October it was adopted at a plenary meeting of the Assembly as resolution 1140(XII) by a vote of 65 to 0, with 15 abstentions.

STATUS OF TERRITORY

On 2 October 1957, Liberia proposed a draft resolution on the status of the Territory. As later revised, this text would have the General Assembly: (1) reiterate its 10 previous resolutions to the effect that South West Africa be placed under the International Trusteeship System; and (2) assert that, in the present conditions of political and economic development of the Territory, the normal way of modifying its international status was to place it

under the Trusteeship System by means of a trusteeship agreement in accordance with the provisions of the Charter.

The revised draft resolution was approved by the Fourth Committee on 11 October 1957 by 55 votes to 3, with 18 abstentions. On 25 October 1957, it was adopted at a plenary meeting of the Assembly as resolution 1141 (XII) by 60 votes to 3, with 17 abstentions.

PETITIONS AND COMMUNICATIONS

On 11 October 1957, the Fourth Committee, adopted two draft resolutions proposed by the Committee on South West Africa concerning petitions and related communications. The respective votes were 51 to 0, with 16 abstentions, and 60 to 0, with 14 abstentions. On 25 October, they were approved at a plenary meeting of the Assembly as resolution 1138(XII) and 1139(XII), the respective votes being 62 to 0, with 16 abstentions, and 64 to 0, with 15 abstentions.

By the first of these resolutions, the Assembly, among other things, drew the Mandatory Power's attention to a previous resolution (935 (X), of 3 December 1955) on the rights granted to the Rehoboth Community by an agreement of 17 August 1923 between the Union Government and the Rehoboth Community. The second resolution drew the attention of various petitioners to the reports and observations of the Committee on South West Africa on conditions in the Territory. (For details, see texts of resolutions in DOCUMENTARY REFERENCES below.)

DOCUMENTARY REFERENCES

GENERAL ASSEMBLY—12TH SESSION
Plenary Meetings 709, 714, 729.
Fourth Committee, meetings 651-669, 672, 679, 687, 725, 729, 736.
Fifth Committee, meeting 609.

A/3626. Report of Committee on South West Africa.
A/AC.73/L.10. Information and documentation in respect of the Territory of South West Africa.

REQUESTS FOR HEARINGS
Fourth Committee, meetings 651, 653-655, 736.

A/C.4/353. Requests for hearings.

ESTABLISHMENT OF GOOD
OFFICES COMMITTEE
A/C.4/358. Statement by representative of United Kingdom at 666th meeting.
A/C.4/L.492. Draft resolution submitted by Chair-

man of Fourth Committee, and as amended by Uruguay and by Ecuador and Guatemala, adopted by Fourth Committee, on 11 October 1957, meeting 669, by roll-call vote of 52 to 10, with 17 abstentions, as follows:

In favour: Afghanistan, Argentina, Australia, Austria, Belgium, Bolivia, Brazil, Canada, Chile, China, Colombia, Costa Rica, Cuba, Denmark, Dominican Republic, Ecuador, El Salvador, Finland, France, Ghana, Haiti, Honduras, Iceland, Iran, Ireland, Israel, Italy, Japan, Laos, Lebanon, Liberia, Luxembourg, Federation of Malaya, Mexico, Nepal, Netherlands, New Zealand, Norway, Pakistan, Panama, Paraguay, Peru, Philippines, Portugal, Spain, Sweden, Thailand, Tunisia, Turkey, United Kingdom, United States, Venezuela.

Against: Albania, Bulgaria, Burma, Byelorussian SSR, Czechoslovakia, Hungary, Poland, Romania, Ukrainian SSR, USSR.

Abstaining: Cambodia, Ceylon, Egypt, Ethiopia, Greece, Guatemala, India, Indonesia, Iraq, Jordan, Morocco, Saudi Arabia, Sudan, Syria, Uruguay, Yemen, Yugoslavia.

A/C.4/L.493 and Rev.1. India amendment and revised amendments to draft resolution submitted by Chairman.

A/C.4/L.493/Rev.2. India and Uruguay revised amendments to draft resolution submitted by Chairman.

A/C.4/L.494 and Rev.1. Uruguay amendments and revised amendments to draft resolution submitted by Chairman.

A/C.4/L.495. Ecuador and Guatemala amendments to draft resolution submitted by Chairman.

A/C.5/723, A/3706, A/3711. Financial implications of draft resolution submitted by Fourth Committee. Note by Secretary-General, report of Advisory Committee on Administrative and Budgetary Questions, and report of Fifth Committee.

A/3701. Report of Fourth Committee (draft resolution VI).

RESOLUTION 1143(XII), as recommended by Fourth Committee, A/3701, adopted by Assembly on 25 October 1957, meeting 709, by roll-call vote of 50 to 10, with 20 abstentions, as follows:

In favour: Afghanistan, Argentina, Australia, Austria, Belgium, Brazil, Canada, Chile, China, Colombia, Costa Rica, Cuba, Denmark, Dominican Republic, Ecuador, El Salvador, Finland, France, Ghana, Haiti, Honduras, Iceland, Ireland, Israel, Italy, Japan, Laos, Lebanon, Liberia, Luxembourg, Federation of Malaya, Mexico, Netherlands, New Zealand, Nicaragua, Norway, Pakistan, Panama, Paraguay, Peru, Philippines, Portugal, Spain, Sweden, Thailand, Tunisia, Turkey, United Kingdom, United States, Venezuela.

Against: Albania, Bulgaria, Burma, Byelorussian SSR, Czechoslovakia, Hungary, Poland, Romania, Ukrainian SSR, USSR.

Abstaining: Bolivia, Cambodia, Ceylon, Egypt, Ethiopia, Greece, Guatemala, India, Indonesia, Iraq, Jordan, Libya, Morocco, Nepal, Saudi Arabia, Sudan, Syria, Uruguay, Yemen, Yugoslavia.

"*The General Assembly,*

"*Recalling* its previous endeavours to find a settlement with the Union of South Africa regarding the status of South West Africa, particularly under the provisions of resolution 449 A (V) of 13 December 1950 establishing an *ad hoc* committee for the purpose, resolution 570 A (VI) of 19 January 1952 re-establishing the *ad hoc* committee, resolution 749 A (VIII) of 28 November 1953 establishing the Committee on South West Africa, and resolution 1059(XI) of 26 February 1957 requesting the intervention of the Secretary-General to secure, through negotiation with the Union of South Africa, an agreement concerning the Territory of South West Africa based on the international status accorded to it by Mandate of League of Nations dated 17 December 1920,

"*Considering* that the Charter of the United Nations makes it incumbent on each Member State to pursue every available means of negotiation and conciliation for the settlement of international problems on the basis of respect for the purposes and principles of the Charter,

"*Being confident* that the Union of South Africa will wish, in the light of its obligations under the Charter, to co-operate in a further endeavour to arrive at a settlement of the question of South West Africa,

"1. *Decides* to establish a Good Offices Committee on South West Africa, consisting of the United States of America, the United Kingdom of Great Britain and Northern Ireland, and a third member to be nominated by the President of the twelfth session of the General Assembly, to discuss with the Government of the Union of South Africa a basis for an agreement which would continue to accord to the Territory of South West Africa an international status;

"2. *Requests* the Committee to submit to the General Assembly, at its thirteenth session, a report on its activities for examination and decision by the Assembly in accordance with the Charter of the United Nations;

"3. *Requests* the Secretary-General to provide the Committee with all necessary staff and facilities."

LEGAL ACTION

A/3625. Special report of Committee on South West Africa.

A/C.4/L.490. Ceylon, Ecuador, Ethiopia, Ghana, Guatemala, India, Syria, Yugoslavia, draft resolution, adopted by Fourth Committee on 11 October 1957, meeting 669, by 55 votes to 4, with 18 abstentions.

A/3701. Report of Fourth Committee (draft resolution V).

RESOLUTION 1142(XII), as recommended by Fourth Committee, A/3701, adopted by Assembly on 25 October 1957, meeting 709, by 55 votes to 3, with 17 abstentions.

A

"*The General Assembly,*

"*Recalling* its resolution 449 A (V) of 13 December 1950, by which the General Assembly accepted the opinion of 11 July 1950 of the International Court of Justice to the effect that:

"(*a*) South West Africa is a Territory under the international Mandate assumed by the Union of South Africa on 17 December 1920,

"(*b*) The Union of South Africa continues to have the international obligations stated in Article 22 of the Covenant of the League of Nations and in the Mandate for South West Africa, the supervisory functions to be exercised by the United Nations,

"(*c*) The reference to the Permanent Court of International Justice is to be replaced by a reference to the International Court of Justice in accordance with article 7 of the Mandate and Article 37 of the Statute of the International Court of Justice,

"*Recalling also* its resolution 1060(XI) of 26 February 1957, by which it requested the Committee on South West Africa to study what legal action was open to ensure that the Union of South Africa fulfilled the obligations assumed by it under the Mandate for South West Africa,

"*Having received* the Committee's special report on the study referred to in the previous paragraph,

"1. *Commends* the Committee on South West Africa for its useful report;

"2. *Notes with deep concern* that:

"(*a*) The Union of South Africa contends that, the Mandate having 'lapsed', it has no obligations of which the United Nations has cognizance;

"(*b*) The Union of South Africa has not rendered annual reports to the United Nations in accordance with Article 22 of the Covenant of the League of Nations, article 6 of the Mandate, and General Assembly resolution 449 A (V) of 13 December 1950;

"3. *Draws the attention* of Member States to the failure of the Union of South Africa to render annual reports to the United Nations, and to the legal action provided for in article 7 of the Mandate read with Article 37 of the Statute of the International Court of Justice;

"4. *Decides* to resume, at its thirteenth session, consideration of the special report of the Committee on South West Africa."

B

"*The General Assembly,*

"*Noting with concern* the observation in the report of the Committee on South West Africa, that existing conditions in the Territory of South West Africa and the trend of the administration represent a situation contrary to the Mandates System, the Charter of the United Nations, the Universal Declaration of Human Rights, the advisory opinions of the International Court of Justice and the resolutions of the General Assembly,

"*Noting also* that, in its special report, the Committee on South West Africa has stated that questions may be put to the International Court of Justice for its advisory opinion as to whether specific acts of the Mandatory State are in conformity with the obligations assumed by it,

"*Requests* the Committee on South West Africa to consider further the question of securing from the International Court of Justice advisory opinions in regard to the administration of the Territory of South West Africa, and to make recommendations in its next report concerning acts of the administration on which a reference to the Court may usefully be made as to their compatibility or otherwise with Article 22 of the Covenant of the League of Nations, the Mandate for South West Africa and the Charter of the United Nations."

Conditions in Territory

A/C.4/L.487 and Rev.1, 2. Liberia draft resolution and revision, adopted by Fourth Committee, on 11 October 1957, meeting 669, by 60 votes to 0, with 16 abstentions.

A/C.4/L.489. Guatemala amendments to Liberia draft resolution.

A/C.4/L.491. Poland amendment to Liberia draft resolution.

A/3701. Report of Fourth Committee (draft resolution III).

RESOLUTION 1140(XII), as recommended by Fourth

Committee, A/3701, adopted by Assembly on 25 October 1957, meeting 709, by 65 votes to 0, with 15 abstentions.

"*The General Assembly,*

"*Having considered* the fourth report submitted to it, in accordance with resolution 749 A (VIII) of 28 November 1953, by the Committee on South West Africa,

"1. *Expresses its appreciation* of the work of the Committee on South West Africa;

"2. *Approves* the report of of the Committee concerning conditions in the Territory of South West Africa."

Status of Territory

A/C.4/L.488 and Rev.1. Liberia draft resolution and revision, adopted by Fourth Committee, on 11 October, meeting 669, by 55 votes to 3, with 18 abstentions.

A/3701. Report of Fourth Committee (draft resolution IV).

RESOLUTION 1141(XII), as recommended by Fourth Committee, A/3701, adopted by Assembly on 25 October 1957, meeting 709, by 60 votes to 3, with 17 abstentions.

"*The General Assembly,*

"*Having recommended,* by its resolutions 65(I) of 14 December 1946, 141(II) of 1 November 1947, 227(III) of 26 November 1948, 337(IV) of 6 December 1949, 449 B (V) of 13 December 1950, 570 B (VI) of 19 January 1952, 749 B (VIII) of 28 November 1953, 852(IX) of 23 November 1954, 940 (X) of 3 December 1955 and 1055(XI) of 26 February 1957, that the Mandated Territory of South West Africa be placed under the International Trusteeship System, and having repeatedly invited the Government of the Union of South Africa to propose, for the consideration of the General Assembly, a trusteeship agreement for South West Africa,

"*Having accepted,* by its resolution 449 A (V) of 13 December 1950, the advisory opinion of 11 July 1950 of the International Court of Justice on the question of South West Africa,

"*Considering* that, in accordance with Chapter XII of the Charter of the United Nations, all Mandated Territories which have not achieved independence have been brought under the International Trusteeship System with the sole exception of the Territory of South West Africa,

"1. *Reiterates* its resolutions 65(I) of 14 December 1946, 141(II) of 1 November 1947, 227(III) of 26 November 1948, 337(IV) of 6 December 1949, 449 B (V) of 13 December 1950, 570 B (VI) of 19 January 1952, 749 B (VIII) of 28 November 1953, 852(IX) of 23 November 1954, 940(X) of 3 December 1955 and 1055(XI) of 26 February 1957, to the effect that the Territory of South West Africa be placed under the International Trusteeship System;

"2. *Asserts* that, in the present conditions of political and economic development of South West Africa, the normal way of modifying the international status of the Territory is to place it under the International Trusteeship System by means of a trusteeship agreement in accordance with the provisions of Chapter XII of the Charter of the United Nations."

PETITIONS AND COMMUNICATIONS

A/3626, Annex VIII. Draft resolution on petitions and related communications from Mr. Jacobus Beukes of Rehoboth Community, proposed by Committee on South West Africa, adopted by Fourth Committee, on 11 October 1957, meeting 669, by 51 votes to 0, with 16 abstentions.

A/3701. Report of Fourth Committee (draft resolution I).

RESOLUTION 1138(XII), as recommended by Fourth Committee, A/3701, adopted by Assembly on 25 October 1957, meeting 709, by 62 votes to 0, with 16 abstentions.

"*The General Assembly,*

"*Having accepted* the advisory opinion of 11 July 1950 of the International Court of Justice on the question of South West Africa,

"*Having authorized* the Committee on South West Africa by its resolution 749 A (VIII) of 28 November 1953, to examine petitions in accordance with the Mandates procedure of the League of Nations,

"*Having received* a report from the Committee on South West Africa dealing with a petition dated 16 July 1956 and a petition dated 23 January 1957, together with related communications, from Mr. Jacobus Beukes of the Rehoboth Community of South West Africa,

"*Noting* that the petitioner, in his petition dated 16 July 1956, alleges that the 1956 elections to the Advisory Board of the Rehoboth Community were surrounded by confusion and were not conducted in accordance with the patriarchal law of the Community,

"*Noting* that the petitioner, in his petition dated 23 January 1957, raises questions concerning the disposal of Community property and makes allegations concerning the exercise of the functions of the Magistrate of the Rehoboth District and the Advisory Board of the Community,

"1. *Draws the attention* of the Union of South Africa, as the Mandatory Power, to the observations and allegations made by the petitioner and requests it to investigate the matters raised by him;

"2. *Further draws the attention* of the Mandatory Power to General Assembly resolution 935(X) of 3 December 1955 concerning the rights granted to the Rehoboth Community by the Agreement of 17 August 1923 between the Government of the Union of South Africa and the Rehoboth Community, ratified and

confirmed by Proclamation No. 28 of 1923."

A/3626, Annex XIII. Draft resolution on petitions and related communications from Mr. Johanes Dausab and others, proposed by Committee on South West Africa, adopted by Fourth Committee on 11 October 1957, meeting 669, by 60 votes to 0, with 14 abstentions.

A/3701. Report of Fourth Committee (draft resolution II).

RESOLUTION 1139(XII), as recommended by Fourth Committee, A/3701, adopted by Assembly on 25 October 1957, meeting 709, by 64 votes to 0, with 15 abstentions.

"*The General Assembly,*

"*Having accepted* the advisory opinion of 11 July 1950 of the International Court of Justice on the question of South West Africa,

"*Having authorized* the Committee on South West Africa, by resolution 749 A (VIII) of 28 November 1953, to examine petitions in accordance with the Mandates procedure of the League of Nations,

"*Having received* a report from the Committee on South West Africa, arrived at without the assistance of the Mandatory Power, dealing with a petition dated 10 October 1956 from Mr. Johanes Dausab and others in the Hoachanas Native Reserve, a petition dated 30 October 1956 and related communications dated 28 May and 26 June 1957 from Chief Hosea Kutako, a petition dated 3 January 1957 and a related communication dated 16 March 1957 from Mr. Wilhelm Heyn and Dr. Joachim Seegert, and a petition dated 27 March 1957 from Mr. Jacobus Beukes of the Rehoboth Community,

"*Noting* that these petitions and communications raise questions relating to various aspects of the administration of the Territory of South West Africa and of conditions in the Territory upon which the Committee has presented a report,

"*Decides* to draw the attention of the petitioners to the report and observations of the Committee on South West Africa regarding conditions in the Territory, submitted to the General Assembly at its twelfth session, and to the action taken by the Assembly on this report."

ELECTIONS TO COMMITTEE
ON SOUTH WEST AFRICA

GENERAL ASSEMBLY—12TH SESSION
Plenary Meeting 729.
Fourth Committee, meetings 687, 725, 729.

A/3763. Report of Fourth Committee, Part II.

CHAPTER III

OPERATION OF THE INTERNATIONAL TRUSTEESHIP SYSTEM

TERRITORIES UNDER THE SYSTEM

The year 1957 saw the attainment of the objectives of the International Trusteeship System in the Trust Territory of Togoland under British administration when, at midnight, of 5-6 March, it was united with the Gold Coast in the independent State of Ghana and ceased to be a Trust Territory.[1]

A list of the remaining 10 Trust Territories which continued to be administered under the International Trusteeship System is given below together with the Administering Authority of each Territory. Also given are the dates on which the Trusteeship Agreements, placing the Territories under the System, entered into force.

Trust Territory	Administering Authority	Date Agreement Came into Force
IN EAST AFRICA		
Tanganyika	United Kingdom	13 Dec. 1946
Ruanda-Urundi	Belgium	13 Dec. 1946
Somaliland under Italian Administration	Italy	2 Dec. 1950
IN WEST AFRICA		
Cameroons under British administration	United Kingdom	13 Dec. 1946
Cameroons under French administration	France	13 Dec. 1946
Togoland under French administration	France	13 Dec. 1946
IN THE PACIFIC		
Western Samoa	New Zealand	13 Dec. 1946

Trust Territory	Administering Authority	Date Agreement Came into Force
IN THE PACIFIC		
Nauru	Australia, New Zealand and the United Kingdom (administered by Australia)	1 Nov. 1947
New Guinea	Australia	13 Dec. 1946
Trust Territory of the Pacific Islands (strategic area)	United States	18 July 1947

All the Trusteeship Agreements were approved by the General Assembly except that for the Pacific Islands which was approved by the Security Council.

[1] See *Y.U.N., 1956,* pp. 368-71.

EXAMINATION OF THE ANNUAL REPORTS FROM ADMINISTERING AUTHORITIES

In accordance with its supervisory functions over the administration of the Trust Territories on behalf of the United Nations, the Trusteeship Council each year considers the annual reports transmitted by the Administering Authorities.

In examining each report, the Council also takes into consideration any supplementary information which may have been supplied by the Administering Authority on events subsequent to the year covered by the annual report.

Its consideration also covers: petitions raising general questions affecting the Territory; the report of a Visiting Mission to the Territory (if any is pending) and observations thereon by the Administering Authority concerned; any observations which may have been submitted by specialized agencies on conditions in the Territory which are within their sphere of competence; and, for Somaliland under Italian administration, the report of the United Nations Advisory Council. (During its examination of conditions in the Trust Territory of Somaliland at its twentieth session, 20 May–12 July 1957, the Council also considered the report of a mission of the International Bank for Reconstruction and Development.)

Under the procedure followed, the Special

Representative of the Administering Authority makes an opening statement and replies to questions submitted by members of the Council. After a general debate on conditions in the Territory, a draft report (drawn up by a drafting committee) is presented to the Council. The Council then votes on the various recommendations and conclusions of the draft report.

The Trusteeship Council's report to the General Assembly (or the Security Council in case of the Trust Territory of the Pacific Islands— a strategic area) consists of: the Council's conclusions and recommendations on each Territory; an account of conditions in the Territory initially prepared by the Secretariat; and a summary of observations made during the Council's discussion of the Administering Authority's report.

During 1957, the Council considered annual reports on the administration of the 10 Trust Territories.

At its nineteenth session (14 March–15 May), it examined the reports on Ruanda-Urundi, the Cameroons under British administration, the Cameroons under French administration and Togoland under French administration for the year 1955. A report on the Trust Territory of Togoland under British administration was not examined in view of the prior termination of the Trusteeship Agreement for the Territory.[2]

At its twentieth session (20 May–12 July 1957), the Council considered the reports on Tanganyika for the year 1955, Somaliland under Italian administration and Western Samoa for the year 1956 and Nauru, New Guinea and the Trust Territory of the Pacific Islands for the year ending 30 June 1956.

CONSIDERATION BY GENERAL ASSEMBLY

At the General Assembly's twelfth session, the Fourth Committee discussed the Council's report for the period between 15 August 1956 and 12 July 1957. The Committee unanimously adopted a draft resolution submitted by Denmark taking note of the report and recommending that the Council take into account the comments and suggestions made at the Assembly's twelfth session. At a plenary meeting on 13 December 1957, the Assembly adopted it unanimously as resolution 1205(XII).

[2] See Y.U.N., 1956, pp. 368-70.

DOCUMENTARY REFERENCES

GENERAL ASSEMBLY—12TH SESSION
Plenary Meeting 729.
Fourth Committee, meetings 652, 667, 668, 670, 683, 691, 692, 700-702, 714-734, 736.

A/3595 and Corr.1. Report of Trusteeship Council covering period 15 August 1956–12 July 1957.
A/C.4/L.513. Denmark draft resolution adopted unanimously by Fourth Committee.
A/3779. Report of Fourth Committee (draft resolution I).
RESOLUTION 1205(XII), as recommended by Fourth Committee, adopted unanimously by Assembly on 13 December 1957, meeting 729.

"The General Assembly,
"Having examined the report of the Trusteeship Council covering the period from 15 August 1956 to 12 July 1957.
"1. Takes note of the report of the Trusteeship Council;
"2. Recommends that the Trusteeship Council, in its future deliberations, take into account the comments and suggestions made in the course of the discussion of the report at the twelfth session of the General Assembly."

PETITIONS AND ORAL HEARINGS

Petitions concerning the Trust Territories or the operation of the International Trusteeship System are normally examined by the Trusteeship Council.

If the petitions relate to general questions regularly examined by the Council, they are considered during the Council's examination of either the annual report on the Territory concerned or some other appropiate agenda item.

CONSIDERATION BY TRUSTEESHIP COUNCIL

In 1957, the Council dealt with 456 such petitions at its nineteenth session, held from 14 March to 15 May, and eight at its twentieth session, held from 20 May to 12 July.

Petitions containing specific or individual complaints are examined by the Council's Standing Committee on Petitions, which presents its recommendations, in the form of draft resolutions, on the action to be taken in each case. The Council dealt with 62 such petitions at its nineteenth session and 102 at its twentieth session.[3]

In addition, there were 1,097 petitions on the agenda of the Council's twentieth session which could not be dealt with, including five petitions dealt with only in part. Consideration of these was postponed to the twenty-first session.

Under its rules of procedure, the Trusteeship Council may hear oral presentations in support of previously submitted petitions or, in exceptional cases, it may receive oral petitions not previously submitted in writing. In 1957, the Council granted four requests for oral hearings, and heard the petitioners (as set forth below) in connexion with its examination of the annual reports of the Trust Territories concerned.

Nineteenth Session

Cameroons under French administration:
Union des Associations traditionnelles (represented by Kingué Jong, Philippe Mbarga, Anjembé Menye and Gustave Ngomba)
Togoland under French administration:
Comité de l'Unité togolaise (represented by Sylvanus Olympio)

Twentieth Session

Tanganyika:
Tanganyika African National Union (represented by Julius K. Nyerere)
Marealle II, Paramount Chief of the Wachagga

CONSIDERATION BY GENERAL ASSEMBLY

HEARINGS IN CONNEXION WITH REPORT OF THE TRUSTEESHIP COUNCIL

The General Assembly does not usually examine written petitions. But it has been the practice of its Fourth Committee to grant requests for oral hearing to individuals and organizations in Trust Territories if it considers it appropriate to do so.

At the Assembly's twelfth session, the Committee granted a number of requests for oral hearings, listed below, in connexion with its consideration of the sections in the Trusteeship Council's annual report dealing with conditions in individual Trust Territories:

Groupe d'action nationale du Cameroun (represented by Charles Assale, Paul Soppo Priso and Jean Ekwabi Ewane)
One Kamerun (represented by N'deh N'tumazah)
Confédération générale kamerunaise du travail (represented by Jacques N'gom).
Union des Populations du Cameroun (represented by Félix Roland Moumié).
Confédération des Syndicats indépendants du Cameroun (represented by Dika Akwa).

HEARINGS IN CONNEXION WITH FUTURE OF TOGOLAND UNDER FRENCH ADMINISTRATION

The Fourth Committee also granted three requests for oral hearings from organizations in the Trust Territory of Togoland under French administration for oral hearings in connexion with the discussions on the future of the Territory. These organizations were:

All-Ewe Conference (represented by Sylvanus Olympio)
Mouvement de la jeunesse togolaise (JUVENTO) (represented by Anani Ignacio Santos)
Mouvement populaire togolais (represented by Alexandre John Ohin and André Akakpo).
(For further details see CHAPTER IV, below, section on TOGOLAND UNDER FRENCH ADMINISTRATION.)

REVIEW OF PROCEDURES REGARDING PETITIONS

At its nineteenth session, the Council established a committee of four members to study possibilities of improving its procedures in dealing with petitions. After examining the committee's report at its twentieth session, the Council decided, as a temporary measure subject to review at the end of one year, and without prejudice to the existing rules of procedure, to establish a committee of two members to determine, with the assistance of the Secretariat, the provisional classification of all communications received. The resolution to this effect (1713(XX)) was adopted unanimously on 8 July 1957.

[3] For a brief account of the subject matter of petitions considered by the Council and the action taken thereon, see *Report of the Trusteeship Council to the General Assembly for the period 15 August 1956–12 July 1957* (A/3595), pp. 6-19. For a more detailed account, see reports of Standing Committee on Petitions (T/L.739, 742-747, 750-752, 756) and resolutions of Trusteeship Council (T/1319, T/1335).

DOCUMENTARY REFERENCES

CONSIDERATION BY
TRUSTEESHIP COUNCIL

TRUSTEESHIP COUNCIL—19TH AND 20TH SESSIONS
Plenary Meetings 752, 753, 755, 756, 759-770, 777-779, 782, 784-787, 790-792, 795, 801, 809, 813, 817-820, 829, 839.
Standing Committee on Petitions, meetings 403-439, 440-459.

CONSIDERATION BY
GENERAL ASSEMBLY

REPORT OF TRUSTEESHIP COUNCIL

GENERAL ASSEMBLY—12TH SESSION
Fourth Committee, meetings 652, 667, 668, 670, 683, 691, 692, 700-702, 714-720, 727, 728, 736.

A/C.4/355 and Add.1-6. Requests for hearings.

FUTURE OF TOGOLAND
UNDER FRENCH ADMINISTRATION

GENERAL ASSEMBLY—12TH SESSION
Fourth Committee, meetings 651, 652, 655, 672, 695-700.

A/C.4/354 and Add.1-4. Requests for hearings.
A/C.4/367. List of petitions and recommendations concerning future of Togoland under French administration. Note by Secretary-General.

For further details, see also below, CHAPTER IV, sections on TOGOLAND UNDER FRENCH ADMINISTRATION, CAMEROONS UNDER BRITISH ADMINISTRATION, CAMEROONS UNDER FRENCH ADMINISTRATION, SITUATION IN CAMEROONS UNDER BRITISH AND UNDER FRENCH ADMINISTRATION.

REVIEW OF PROCEDURES
REGARDING PETITIONS

TRUSTEESHIP COUNCIL—19TH AND 20TH SESSIONS
Plenary Meetings 752, 761, 770-772, 780, 793, 824, 835, 839.

T/L.777. Report of Committee on Procedures regarding Petitions.
T/L.787. India and Syria draft resolution.
RESOLUTION 1713(xx), as submitted by India and Syria, and as amended orally by Italy, adopted unanimously by Council on 8 July 1957, meeting 835.

"*The Trusteeship Council,*
"*Having examined* the report of the Committee on Procedures regarding Petitions,
"1. *Decides,* as a temporary measure, subject to review at the end of one year and without prejudice to the existing rules of procedure, to establish a Committee of two members to determine, with the assistance of the Secretariat, the provisional classification of all communications received;
"2. *Approves* the procedure set forth in the annex

to the present resolution;
"3. *Decides* that the procedure referred to above shall be applied to the petitions mentioned in paragraph 23 of the report of the Committee on Procedures regarding Petitions."

ANNEX
Membership and Method of Work of the Committee on Classification of Communications
"1. The Council shall appoint at the end of each regular session one member administering Trust Territories and one member having no administering responsibilities to serve on the Committee on Classification of Communications. These two members shall be other than the six appointed to serve on the Standing Committee on Petitions.
"2. The Committee on Classifications of Communications shall meet as often as necessary, depending on the number of incoming communications.
"3. The Committee on Classification of Communications shall examine the contents of each original communication and determine, with the assistance of the Secretariat, its provisional classification in accordance with the rules of procedure. It shall bear in mind the suggestions appearing in the report of the Committee on Procedures regarding Petitions.
"4. When confronted by an unusually large number of petitions concerning general problems of the same Trust Territory, the Committee on Classification of Communications shall, with the assistance of the Secretariat, study their contents and reproduce them in summarized form in one document, setting forth under separate headings the precise subjects raised therein; this document shall be as comprehensive as possible and shall also give the names of the authors, the dates and the places of origin of the petitions.
"5. Similarly, when confronted by an unusually large number of petitions concerning the same specific incident or grievance, the Committee on Classification of Communications shall, with the assistance of the Secretariat, prepare a single document reproducing as fully as possible under appropriate headings the passages setting forth the precise facts contained in the original of each petition and using the exact words of the petitioners. This document shall also give the names of the authors and the date and the place of origin of the petitions. This document, together with three type copies of the full text of each petition, shall be sent to the Administering Authority concerned for its observations.
"6. In the case of a petition which deals primarily with general questions but in which mention is also made of a specific incident adduced by the petitioners to support his broader complaints or requests, the Committee on Classification of Communications shall determine provisionally whether or not the petition should be classified as a general problems petition under rule 85, paragraph 2, of the rules of procedure of the Trusteeship Council. In regard to this matter, the Committee shall consider whether the specific incident mentioned has already been the subject of a petition to which the established procedure has been applied, in which case it shall instruct the Secretariat

to indicate in a footnote the symbol of the document in the T/PET series in which the specific incident mentioned in the otherwise general problems petition was recounted.

"7. The originals of all petitions and communications shall be available for perusal by members of the Standing Committee on Petitions or of the Trustee-ship Council and, if a request for the individual reproduction of any of the petitions or communications is made, a decision shall be taken by the Standing Committee on Petitions or the Trusteeship Council.

"8. The Committee on Classification of Communications shall report on its work to the Standing Committee on Petitions."

VISITING MISSIONS TO TRUST TERRITORIES

At its nineteenth session, held from 14 March to 15 May 1957, the Trusteeship Council made the necessary arrangements for sending a Visiting Mission to Trust Territories in East Africa and decided that this Mission should be composed of four members to be nominated by Australia, Burma, France and Haiti. At the same session, it approved the nominations of Robert Napier Hamilton (Australia), U Tin Maung (Burma), Jean Cédile (France) and Max H. Dorsinville (Haiti) as members of the Mission, and elected Mr. Dorsinville as Chairman of the Mission.

By resolution 1714(XX) of 9 July 1957, the Council defined the terms of reference of the Visiting Mission, which was to depart from Headquarters on 14 July 1957 and visit the Trust Territories of Somaliland under Italian administration, Tanganyika and Ruanda-Urundi, in that order. The Council directed the Mission, first, to report as fully as possible on the steps taken in the three Territories for their progressive development towards self-government or independence, as set forth in Article 76b of the Charter. Secondly, the Mission was to give attention to issues raised in connexion with the annual reports on the administration of the Territories concerned, and to the issues raised in relevant petitions received by the Trusteeship Council, in the reports of the previous periodic visiting missions to Trust Terri-

tories in East Africa, and in the observations of the Administering Authorities on those reports. Thirdly, it was to receive petitions without prejudice to its acting in accordance with the rules of procedure of the Trusteeship Council and it was to investigate on the spot, in consultation with the local representatives of the Administering Authority concerned, any of these petitions which, in its opinion, warranted special investigation. Fourthly, it was to examine, in consultation with the Administering Authorities, the measures taken and to be taken in respect of the provision of information about the United Nations to the peoples of the Trust Territories under the relevant resolutions of the Trusteeship Council and the General Assembly. The Mission was further asked to submit a report on each of the Trust Territories visited to the Council as soon as practicable, together with its findings, and such observations, conclusions and recommendations as it might wish to make.

The Mission visited Somaliland under Italian administration from 18 July to 6 August, Tanganyika from 10 August to 18 September, and Ruanda-Urundi from 18 September to 10 October 1957. Before returning to Headquarters on 23 October 1957, the Mission held discussions with officials of the Italian, Belgian and United Kingdom Governments in Rome, Brussels and London respectively.

DOCUMENTARY REFERENCES

TRUSTEESHIP COUNCIL—19TH AND 20TH SESSIONS Plenary Meetings 786, 787, 809, 815, 836, 840.

T/1322 and Add.1-3. Arrangements for a periodic Visiting Mission to Trust Territories in East Africa in 1957. Note by Secretary-General.
T/L.783. New Zealand draft resolution.
T/L.796. Guatemala amendments to New Zealand draft resolution.
RESOLUTION 1714(xx), as submitted by New Zealand, T/L.783, adopted by Council on 9 July 1957, meeting 836, by 12 votes to 0, with 2 abstentions.

"*The Trusteeship Council,*

"*Having appointed* a fourth periodic Visiting Mission to Trust Territories in East Africa composed of Mr. Max H. Dorsinville (Haiti) as Chairman, Mr. Robert Napier Hamilton (Australia), U Tin Maung (Burma) and Mr. Jean Cédile (France),

"*Noting* that the Visiting Mission will be assisted by members of the Secretariat and also by such members of the local administration as may be appointed by the latter,

"*Having decided* that the Visiting Mission should depart on 14 July 1957 and visit the Trust Territories of Somaliland under Italian administration, Tanganyika and Ruanda-Urundi in that order,

"1. *Directs* the Visiting Mission to investigate and to report as fully as possible on the steps taken in the three above-mentioned Trust Territories towards the realization of the objectives set forth in Article 76b of the Charter of the United Nations, taking into account the terms of General Assembly resolution 321 (IV) of 15 November 1949;

"2. *Directs* the Visiting Mission to give attention, as may be appropriate in the light of discussions in the Trusteeship Council and in the General Assembly and of resolutions adopted by them, to issues raised, in connexion with the annual reports on the administration of the three Trust Territories concerned in petitions received by the Council relating to those Trust Territories, in the reports of the previous periodic Visiting Missions to Trust Territories in East Africa, and in the observations of the Administering Authorities on those reports;

"3. *Directs* the Visiting Mission to receive petitions without prejudice to its acting in accordance with the rules of procedure of the Council and to investigate on the spot, in consultation with the local representative of the Administering Authority concerned, such of the petitions received as, in its opinion, warrant special investigation;

"4. *Directs* the Visiting Mission to examine, in consultation with the Administering Authorities, the measures taken and to be taken in respect of the provision of information about the United Nations to the peoples of the Trust Territories under Council resolution 36(III) of 8 July 1948 and General Assembly resolution 754(VIII) of 9 December 1953, and to undertake the duties enumerated in Council resolution 311(VIII) of 7 February 1951;

"5. *Requests* the Visiting Mission to transmit to the Council as soon as practicable a report on each of the Trust Territories visited containing its findings with such observations, conclusions and recommendations as it may wish to make."

ADMINISTRATIVE UNIONS AFFECTING TRUST TERRITORIES

In 1957 the Standing Committee on Administrative Unions, established by the Trusteeship Council in 1949 to consider the question of administrative unions between certain Trust and neighbouring Non-Self-Governing Territories, consisted of representatives of Guatemala, India, New Zealand and the United States. The Standing Committee submitted two reports to the Council, one dealing with the administrative unions involving Cameroons under British administration and Ruanda-Urundi, respectively, and the other with the administrative unions involving Tanganyika and New Guinea, respectively. (References to these reports are to be found below in CHAPTER IV in the sections dealing with these territories.)

DOCUMENTARY REFERENCES

TRUSTEESHIP COUNCIL—19TH AND 20TH SESSIONS
Plenary Meetings 782, 838, 839.
Standing Committee on Administrative Unions, meetings 94-100.

T/L.741. Report of Standing Committee on Administrative Unions (Cameroons under British administration and Nigeria; Ruanda-Urundi and Belgian Congo).

T/L.786. Report of Standing Committee on Administrative Union (Tanganyika, Kenya and Uganda; New Guinea and Papua).

(See also below, CHAPTER IV, DOCUMENTARY REFERENCES to sections on TANGANYIKA, RUANDA-URUNDI, CAMEROONS UNDER BRITISH ADMINISTRATION, NEW GUINEA.)

ATTAINMENT BY THE TRUST TERRITORIES OF THE OBJECTIVE OF SELF-GOVERNMENT OR INDEPENDENCE

Between January 1952 and December 1955, the General Assembly adopted four resolutions inviting the Administering Authorities of Trust Territories (with the exception of Somaliland under Italian administration, which is to attain independence in 1960) to include information in their annual reports on the following subjects: (1) measures taken or contemplated to lead the Territories towards the objective of self-government or independence in the shortest possible time; (2) the manner in which the particular circumstances of the Territories and their peoples and their freely expressed wishes were being taken into account in these matters; (3) the adequacy of the provisions of the existing Trusteeship Agreement; and (4) estimates of the time needed both to complete one or more of the measures designed to create the pre-conditions for the attainment of self-government or independence and to reach the final objective.

The Assembly further asked the Trusteeship Council to report specially to the General Assembly on the action taken by the Administering Authorities on these matters. Specific mention was to be made of measures for consultations with the inhabitants, the development of representative, executive and legislative organs, universal adult suffrage and direct elections, the training and appointment of indigenous persons for positions of responsibility in the administration, and the development of adequate public revenue. The Council was also asked to note its conclusions and recommendations on these subjects in its reports.

In pursuance of the Assembly's request, the Council decided (by resolutions 1254(XVI) of 19 July 1955 and 1369(XVII) of 16 March 1956) to adopt a special procedure for dealing with the question of attainment of self-government or independence. It subsequently applied that procedure in formulating its report to the General Assembly. As to the establishment of intermediate and final time periods for the development of self-government or independence, the Council has included—in the appropriate chapters of its report on conditions in the Trust Territories concerned—a new section setting out the information available to it and its conclusions thereon.

The information on specific measures asked for by the Assembly has accordingly been included in a readily identifiable form in the political and economic sections of each of the chapters in the Council's report dealing with the individual territories, as are the Council's comments and recommendations on these measures. The Council's report has also included a separate section containing references to the information requested by the Assembly and to the sections of the Council's report in which it might be found.

At its nineteenth session (14 March–15 May 1957), the Council had before it the Assembly's request for a report on the implementation of Assembly resolution of 26 February 1957 (1064 (XI)) on the attainment of self-government or independence by Trust Territories. By that resolution, the Assembly had: (1) recommended that the Administering Authorities concerned take the necessary measures for the early attainment of self-government or independence by Tanganyika, the Cameroons under British administration, the Cameroons under French administration, Togoland under French administration and Ruanda-Urundi; (2) invited the Administering Authorities to estimate the time required for the attainment of self-government or independence by all Trust Territories; and (3) invited the Administering Authorities to submit information on the implementation of the two preceding provisions of this Assembly resolution. This information was to be submitted to the Council's nineteenth and twentieth sessions, in 1957.

On 25 March 1957, the Council, recalling the special procedure adopted at its seventeenth session for dealing with the question, took note of the resolution and instructed its drafting committees to take it into account when they prepared draft reports on conditions in Trust Territories.

The Council again applied the above-mentioned procedure in formulating its report to the Assembly for 1957. (Except for Togoland under French administration, in respect of which the Council decided to postpone consideration of all political questions, the information requested by the Assembly is summarized in Chapter IV below, under the sections dealing with conditions in individual Trust Territories.)

At the Assembly's twelfth session, the representatives of Burma, Guatemala, Haiti, India and Syria proposed a draft resolution whereby the Assembly, reaffirming its resolutions 558(VI) and 1064(XI), would: (1) once again invite the Administering Authorities to implement these resolutions; and (2) request the Trusteeship Council to report to the General Assembly's thirteenth session on the progress made in implementing the proposed resolution. This draft resolution, with two modifications in the preambular paragraph, was approved by the Fourth Committee by 45 votes to 15, with 12 abstentions. On 13 December 1957, it was adopted at a plenary meeting of the Assembly by 51 votes to 15, with 7 abstentions, as resolution 1207(XII).

DOCUMENTARY REFERENCES

TRUSTEESHIP COUNCIL—19TH AND 20TH SESSIONS
Plenary Meetings 753, 759, 794.

GENERAL ASSEMBLY—12TH SESSION
Plenary Meeting 729.
Fourth Committee, meetings 714-734.

A/3595 and Corr.1. Report of Trusteeship Council to General Assembly: Part I, Chapter V(G); Part II, Chapters I, II, IV, V, VII, VIII, IX; and Part III.
A/C.4/L.515 and Rev.1, 2. Burma, Guatemala, Haiti, India, Syria draft resolution and revisions, adopted, as orally revised, by Fourth Committee by 44 votes to 15, with 12 abstentions.
A/3779. Report of Fourth Committee (draft resolution III).
RESOLUTION 1207(XII), as recommended by Fourth Committee, A/3779, adopted by Assembly on 13 December 1957, meeting 729, by 51 votes to 15, with 7 abstentions.

"*The General Assembly,*

"*Considering* that, in accordance with the provisions of Article 76b of the Charter of the United Nations, one of the basic objectives of the International Trusteeship System is the progressive development of the inhabitants of Trust Territories towards self-government or independence,

"*Recalling* that the General Assembly, in its resolution 558(VI) of 18 January 1952, invited the Administering Authority of each Trust Territory, *inter alia,* to estimate the period of time in which the Trust Territories concerned would attain self-government or independence,

"*Recalling also* that the General Assembly, in its resolution 1064(XI) of 26 February 1957, recom-
mended that the Administering Authorities concerned take the necessary measures to ensure that the Trust Territories of Tanganyika, the Cameroons under British administration, the Cameroons under French administration, Togoland under French administration and Ruanda-Urundi achieve self-government or independence at an early date, and further invited the Administering Authorities concerned to estimate the period of time required for the attainment of self-government or independence by all Trust Territories, in conformity with General Assembly resolution 558 (VI),

"*Having examined* part III of the report of the Trusteeship Council,

"*Noting with satisfaction* that the Trusteeship Council has recommended that the Administering Authorities indicate such successive intermediate targets and dates in the political, economic, social and educational development of the Trust Territories as will create the pre-conditions for their attainment of self-government or independence,

"*Noting with disappointment* that the Administering Authorities concerned have not yet submitted the estimates of the periods of time required by the Trust Territories for the attainment of the final objective of trusteeship, namely, self-government or independence,

"*Conscious* of the importance of estimating the time required for the attainment by Trust Territories of self-government or independence,

"1. *Reaffirms* its resolutions 558(VI) of 18 January 1952 and 1064(XI) of 26 February 1957, and once again invites the Administering Authorities to implement the terms of those resolutions;

"2. *Requests* the Trusteeship Council to report to the General Assembly, at its thirteenth session, on the progress made in implementing the present resolution."

OTHER QUESTIONS RELATING TO THE OPERATION OF THE INTERNATIONAL TRUSTEESHIP SYSTEM

RURAL ECONOMIC DEVELOPMENT

The Committee on Rural Economic Development of the Trust Territories was established in 1951 to study the prevailing policies, laws and practices in Trust Territories relating to land, land utilization and the alienation of land. Its seventh progress report was submitted to the Trusteeship Council's twentieth session (held from 20 May to 12 July 1957).

The Committee reported that the heavy schedule of conferences in which its members had participated during the period under review had precluded it from giving detailed consideration to the extensive documentation before it. The Committee planned to meet when circumstances permitted and to submit further progress reports on its conclusions and recommendation.

On 11 July 1957, the Council took note of the Committee's report. It also accepted the resignations of Haiti, India and Syria from the membership of the Committee, and decided to reduce the size of the Committee from six to four members and to appoint Guatemala as a new member. The Committee was then composed of the representatives of China, France, Guatemala and the United Kingdom.

On 13 December 1957, at its twelfth session, the Assembly decided to invite the appropriate specialized agencies to submit their observations and suggestions to the Trusteeship Council on rural economic development problems. It also recommended that the Council take steps, through its Committee on Rural Economic Development or by other appropriate means, to ensure the early submission of the Council's study on the prevailing policies, laws and practices relating to land tenure, land utilization and land alienation in Trust Territories. The study was to take into account the present and future objectives of the International Trusteeship System and the future economic requirements of the Territories, as well as the social and economic consequences of the transfer of land to non-indigenous inhabitants. The Council was asked to include the results of that study in its next report to the General Assembly.

The resolution to this effect (1208(XII)) was unanimously adopted on the recommendation of the Fourth Committee, which approved it, also unanimously, on 5 December 1957, on the basis of a proposal by Burma, Egypt, India, Indonesia, Iraq, Mexico, Panama, Poland and Yugoslavia, as amended in the Committee.

OFFERS OF STUDY AND TRAINING FACILITIES

The programme of scholarships and fellowships for inhabitants of Trust Territories was established by the General Assembly in January 1952. In 1957, as in previous years, the Secretary-General submitted a report to the Council's twentieth session on the progress of that programme, covering the period from 13 July 1956 to 31 May 1957. A total of 109 scholarships or fellowships had been offered, the report noted; 31 had been granted to applicants, and nine students had not used the scholarships granted them.

At its twentieth session, the Council considered this report, together with General Assembly resolution 1063(XI) of 26 February 1957 which asked for reports by the Committee and by the Secretary-General on the use of scholarships and training facilities offered by Member States for inhabitants of Trust Territories.

On 11 June 1957, the Council adopted a resolution (1712(XX)) by which: (1) it invited the Administering Authorities to facilitate to the fullest extent possible the utilization of the educational facilities offered by Members to inhabitants of Trust Territories; (2) it also noted that the Secretary-General would report fully on the matter to the Assembly's twelfth session. The Council's vote on this resolution was 8 to 2, with 4 abstentions.

At the Assembly's twelfth session, the Secretary-General submitted a report on the actual use made of scholarships and other training facilities offered under the programme. This showed that a total of 49 scholarships had been used between 1952 and 1957.

On the recommendation of the Fourth Committee, the Assembly, on 13 December 1957, adopted a resolution to the following effect. It invited the Administering Authorities to take the necessary measures to ensure the use of educational facilities by inhabitants of Trust Territories and to render every assistance to persons having applied for or having been granted such facilities. It asked the Secretary-General to give such assistance as was possible and as might be sought by the Members concerned and by the applicants within the framework of the procedure laid down by the Trusteeship Council and to include in his reports to the Council detailed information about the actual use of the facilities offered. The Assembly also asked the Council to resume consideration of this question at its 1958 sessions and to report thereon to the Assembly's thirteenth session. This resolution (1209(XII)) was adopted by 63 votes to 0, with 7 abstentions.

REVISION OF TRUSTEESHIP COUNCIL'S QUESTIONNAIRE

The Assembly's Sub-Committee on the Questionnaire, consisting in 1957 of the representatives of El Salvador, Haiti, India and Syria, is charged with examining any changes that might be necessary in the Trusteeship Council's questionnaire in order to adapt it to the conditions of each Trust Territory. It submitted its third and fourth progress reports to the Council's twentieth session.

The former report proposed a number of changes in the existing questionnaire in order to adapt it to the special conditions of the Trust Territory of New Guinea. The other report said that the Sub-Committee had asked the United Nations Secretariat to draft a special questionnaire for Nauru. The Sub-Committee, however, had been unable to consider this draft in detail because of the heavy schedule of conferences in which its members had participated.

The Council also had before it a working paper, submitted by Australia, setting forth a number of amendments to the Sub-Committee's proposals for the New Guinea questionnaire.

At its twentieth session, the Council took note of the fourth progress report and decided to refer the third progress report back to the Sub-Committee together with the Australian amendments.

DISSEMINATION OF INFORMATION ON UNITED NATIONS AND TRUSTEESHIP SYSTEM

The Trusteeship Council, by resolution 36 (III), of 8 July 1948, and the General Assembly, by resolution 754(VIII), of 9 December 1953, asked the Secretary-General to submit periodic reports on the steps taken to provide the peoples of the Trust Territories with information concerning the aims and activities of the United Nations.

In his report to the Council in 1957, the Secretary-General stated that there had been an increase in the volume of United Nations information material disseminated, both in terms of the number of titles and quantity. He also reported that the Secretariat had undertaken, in consultation with special representatives from Trust Territories, a review of the available information material and the channels through which it was distributed. Certain basic material on the United Nations had been revised and brought up to date, every effort having been made to meet the special needs of the peoples of the Trust Territories. At its twentieth session, the Council took note of this report.

EFFECTS OF EUROPEAN ECONOMIC COMMUNITY ON DEVELOPMENT OF CERTAIN TRUST TERRITORIES

At its nineteenth session (14 March–15 May 1957), during its consideration of the annual reports on the administration of the Trust Territories of Ruanda-Urundi, the Cameroons under French administration and Togoland under French administration, the Council asked the respective Administering Authorities, if any of these Territories should become associated with the European Economic Community (European Common Market) set up by a Treaty signed at Rome in March 1957, to inform it of the application of the Rome Treaty to the Territories and the effects which it might have on the economies of these Territories.

This question was again discussed at the General Assembly's twelfth session.

On 13 December 1957, it adopted a resolution (1210(XII)), by 50 votes to 13, with 9 abstentions, whereby it invited the Administering Authorities to inform the Trusteeship Council about the association of the Trust Territories under their administration with the European Economic Community and the possible effects of the Treaty establishing that Community on the development of those Territories. It also asked the Trusteeship Council to include in its report to the Assembly's thirteenth session information on that subject in the light of any surveys of this problem carried out by the Secretary-General under Assembly resolution 1153(XII), of 26 November 1957, by the Economic and Social Council and by other United Nations and international bodies, in so far as such surveys were concerned with the development of those Territories.

The Assembly further decided to resume examination of this question at its thirteenth session.

DOCUMENTARY REFERENCES

RURAL ECONOMIC DEVELOPMENT

TRUSTEESHIP COUNCIL—20TH SESSION
Plenary Meeting 893.
Committee on Rural Economic Development of Trust Territories, meetings 20, 21.

T/AC.36/L.59. Legislation on land tenure, forests and mines in French Trust Territories. Summary of provisions of decrees of 20 May 1955.
T/AC.36/L.60. Study of population, land utilization and land system in Ruanda-Urundi.
T/AC.36/L.61. Summary of population, land utilization and land tenure in Cameroons under French administration.

T/AC.36/L.62. Observations on document T/AC.36/L.60 submitted by Administering Authority.
T/1331. Seventh progress report of Committee on Rural Economic Development of Trust Territories.

GENERAL ASSEMBLY—12TH SESSION
Plenary Meeting 729.
Fourth Committee, meetings 728-732.

A/3595. Report of Trusteeship Council to General Assembly, Part I, Chapter V.B.
A/C.4/L.517 and Rev.1 and 2. Burma, Egypt, India, Indonesia, Iraq, Mexico, Panama, Poland and Yugoslavia draft resolution and revisions, adopted unanimously by Fourth Committee.

A/C.4/L.522. United States amendments to revised joint draft resolution, A/C.4/L.517/Rev.1.

A/C.4/L.525. Dominican Republic amendment to revised joint draft resolution, A/C.4/L.517/Rev.1.

A/3779. Report of Fourth Committee (draft resolution IV).

RESOLUTION 1208(XII), as recommended by Fourth Committee, A/3779, adopted unanimously by Assembly on 13 December 1957, meeting 729.

"*The General Assembly,*

"*Recalling* its resolution 438(V) of 2 December 1950, recommending that the Trusteeship Council consider the prevailing policies, laws and practices which, in the Trust Territories, relate to land, land utilization and the alienation of land, taking into account the present and future needs of the indigenous inhabitants from the standpoint of the basic objectives of the International Trusteeship System and the future economic requirements of the Territories, as well as the social and economic consequences of the transfer of land to non-indigenous inhabitants,

"*Having noted* the actions of the Trusteeship Council in this field, both through its regular procedures for the examination of conditions in the Trust Territories and through the establishment of the Committee on Rural Economic Development of the Trust Territories,

"*Bearing in mind* the technical difficulties that the Committee has encountered in the various aspects of the study entrusted to it,

"*Noting with regret* that the Committee has not yet been able to carry out the aforementioned study,

"*Considering* that the questions of land tenure, land utilization and land alienation call for analysis and opinion of a technical and expert nature, and recalling in this connexion General Assembly resolution 561 (VI) or 18 January 1952,

"*Considering* that, in the meantime, it would be appropriate for the Trusteeship Council, with the assistance of the Committee, to continue to devote particular attention to the question of the alienation of land in the Trust Territories,

"1. *Decides,* in order to facilitate the eventual study by the General Assembly of problems of land tenure, land utilization and land alienation in the Trust Territories, to invite the appropriate specialized agencies, particularly the Food and Agriculture Organization of the United Nations and the International Labour Organisation to submit to the Trusteeship Council their observations and suggestions concerning these problems;

"2. *Recommends* to the Trusteeship Council that it ensure, through the Committee on Rural Economic Development of the Trust Territories or by such other means as it deems appropriate, the early submission of its study of the prevailing policies, laws and practices relating to land tenure, land utilization and land alienation in Trust Territories, taking into account the present and future needs of the indigenous inhabitants from the standpoint of the basic objectives of the International Trusteeship System and the future economic requirements of the Territories, as well as the social and economic consequences of the transfer of

land to non-indigenous inhabitants;

"3. *Requests* the Trusteeship Council to include the results of this study in its next report to the General Assembly."

OFFERS OF STUDY AND TRAINING FACILITIES

TRUSTEESHIP COUNCIL—19TH AND 20TH SESSIONS
Plenary Meetings 775, 784, 810.

T/1325. Report of Secretary-General.
T/L.753. Working paper prepared by Secretariat.
T/L.778. India draft resolution.

RESOLUTION 1712(XX), as submitted by India, T/L.778, adopted by Council on 11 June 1957, meeting 810, by 8 votes to 2, with 4 abstentions.

"*The Trusteeship Council,*

"*Having noted* that the General Assembly, in its resolution 1063(XI) of 26 February 1957, had requested the Trusteeship Council to consider, at its sessions in 1957, the question of the way in which the scholarships and training facilities offered by Member States are being utilized by inhabitants of Trust Territories and to report thereon to the General Assembly at its twelfth session,

"*Having received* the report of the Secretary-General on offers by Member States of study and training facilities for inhabitants of Trust Territories,

"*Having noted* that such facilities are not fully utilized by inhabitants of Trust Territories,

"1. *Invites* the Administering Authorities to facilitate to the fullest extent possible the utilization of the educational facilities offered by Member States to inhabitants of Trust Territories;

"2. *Notes* that the Secretary-General will submit to the General Assembly at its twelfth session a detailed report as required by Assembly resolution 1063(XI)."

GENERAL ASSEMBLY—12TH SESSION
Plenary Meeting 729.
Fourth Committee, meetings 721-727, 729-731.

A/3595. Report of Trusteeship Council to General Assembly, Part I, chapter V.D.

A/3718 and Corr.1. Report of Secretary-General.

A/C.4/L.518. Ceylon, Czechoslovakia, Mexico, Pakistan, Panama, Tunisia, Yemen draft resolution.

A/C.4/L.518/Rev.1. Ceylon, Czechoslovakia, Mexico, Pakistan, Panama, Philippines, Tunisia, Yemen revised draft resolution adopted by Fourth Committee by 59 votes to 1, with 6 abstentions.

A/C.4/L.520. Philippines amendment to draft resolution, A/C.4/L.518.

A/3779. Report of Fourth Committee (draft resolution V).

RESOLUTION 1209(XII), as recommended by Fourth Committee, A/3779, adopted by Assembly on 13 December 1957, meeting 729, by 63 votes to 0, with 7 abstentions.

"*The General Assembly,*

"*Having examined* chapter V, section D, of part I of the report of the Trusteeship Council and the report of the Secretary-General on offers by Members States of study and training facilities for inhabitants of Trust Territories,

"*Recalling* that, in its resolutions 753(VIII) of 9 December 1953 and 1063(XI) of 26 February 1957, the General Assembly recommended that the Administering Authorities of the Trust Territories take all such measures as would ensure the greatest possible use by inhabitants of the Trust Territories of the scholarships and training facilities offered by Member States,

"*Noting* that the major part of the scholarships offered by Member States remains unutilized,

"1. *Takes note* of chapter V, section D, of part I of the report of the Trusteeship Council and of the report of the Secretary-General on offers by Member States of study and training facilities for inhabitants of Trust Territories;

"2. *Reaffirms* its resolution 1063(XI) of 26 February 1957 and once again invites the Administering Authorities to take all necessary measures to ensure that scholarships and training facilities offered by Member States may be utilized by inhabitants of the Trust Territories and to render every assistance to those persons who have applied for, or have been granted, scholarships or fellowships;

"3. *Requests* the Secretary-General to give such assistance as is possible, and as may be sought by the Members concerned and by the applicants, within the framework of the procedures laid down by the Trusteeship Council;

"4. *Requests* the Secretary-General to include, in his future reports to the Trusteeship Council, detailed information concerning the actual use of scholarships and training facilities offered by Member States for the education of inhabitants of the Trust Territories;

"5. *Requests* the Trusteeship Council to resume, at its sessions held in 1958, the consideration of this question and to report thereon to the General Assembly at its thirteenth session."

REVISION OF TRUSTEESHIP COUNCIL'S QUESTIONNAIRE

TRUSTEESHIP COUNCIL—19TH AND 20TH SESSIONS
Plenary Meetings 782, 830.

T/1327. Fourth progress report of Sub-Committee on Questionnaire.
T/L.785. Working paper submitted by Australia concerning third progress report of Sub-Committee on Questionnaire, T/1267.

DISSEMINATION OF INFORMATION ON UNITED NATIONS AND TRUSTEESHIP COUNCIL

TRUSTEESHIP COUNCIL—20TH SESSION
Plenary Meeting 832.

T/1328. Report of Secretary-General.

A/3595 and Corr.1. Report of Trusteeship to General Assembly, chapter V.C.

EFFECTS OF EUROPEAN ECONOMIC COMMUNITY ON DEVELOPMENT OF CERTAIN TRUST TERRITORIES

TRUSTEESHIP COUNCIL—19TH SESSION
Plenary Meetings 762, 763, 768-770, 792, 793.

GENERAL ASSEMBLY—12TH SESSION
Plenary Meeting 729.
Fourth Committee, meetings 729-731.

A/3595 and Corr.1. Report of Trusteeship Council to General Assembly covering period 15 August 1956–12 July 1957.
A/C.5/L.519. Argentina, Bolivia, Burma, Ceylon, Costa Rica, Czechoslovakia, Ecuador, Egypt, Ghana, Guatemala, Haiti, India, Liberia, Mexico, Panama, Sudan, Syria, Uruguay draft resolution adopted by Fourth Committee by 43 votes to 14, with 7 abstentions.
A/3779. Report of Fourth Committee (draft resolution VI).
RESOLUTION 1210(XII), as recommended by Fourth Committee, A/3779, adopted by Assembly on 13 December 1957, by 50 votes to 13, with 9 abstentions.

"*The General Assembly*,

"*Having examined* the report of the Trusteeship Council,

"*Having observed* that the Treaty establishing the European Economic Community provides that certain Trust Territories are to be associated with the Community,

"*Believing* that this association may have significant effects on the development of such Territories,

"1. *Invites* the Administering Authorities concerned to submit information to the Trusteeship Council on the association of the Trust Territories under their administration with the European Economic Community and on the possible effects of the Treaty establishing the Community on the development of those Territories;

"2. *Requests* the Trusteeship Council to include in its report to the General Assembly, at its thirteenth session, a separate section dealing with the effects that the association of certain Trust Territories with the Community may have on the development of those Territories, in the light of any surveys of this problem carried out by the Secretary-General in virtue of General Assembly resolution 1153(XII) of 26 November 1957, by the Economic and Social Council, the Economic Commission for Asia and the Far East, the Economic Commission for Latin America, or other international bodies, in so far as such surveys are concerned with the development of those Territories;

"3. *Resolves* to resume examination of this question at its thirteenth session."

CHAPTER IV

CONDITIONS IN TRUST TERRITORIES

TANGANYIKA

Tanganyika, the largest of the Trust Territories, has a population of over 8.2 million Africans, some 77,000 Asians, 20,000 Europeans, 19,000 Arabs and 7,000 others. At its twentieth session (20 May–12 July 1957), the Trusteeship Council was concerned, as in the past, with the problems which it has described as inherent in the presence of the non-African minorities who, for the time being, enjoy a greater degree of advancement than the indigenous majority. In the chief governmental institutions, as the Council has noted, these minorities are given a role more important than might be supported by numerical considerations alone.

The Council also heard the views of African petitioners on the inevitability of a predominantly African government in Tanganyika. It took note of a statement by the representative of the Administering Authority (the United Kingdom) that the latter's whole policy, record and national outlook, as well as the terms of the United Nations Charter and the Trusteeship Agreement, were a full and sufficient guarantee that the progressive development of the inhabitants of Tanganyika towards self-government or independence would be democratic. Furthermore, it was the Administering Authority's policy to provide, in accordance with the Charter and the Agreement, for the full participation of all sections of the population in the progressive development of political institutions. However, as the Africans made up the vast majority of the population, and as their educational, social and economic progress continued, their participation in both the legislative and executive branches of government was bound to increase.

The Council understood this statement to mean that, in the predominantly African society of Tanganyika, the present constitutional arrangements were transitional. It understood further that future development would be along lines leading to the establishment of self-government or independence as appropriate to the particular circumstances of Tanganyika and its peoples and their freely expressed wishes, in accordance with Article 76b of the Charter.

POLITICAL ADVANCEMENT

The Council welcomed the important further steps taken in the constitutional development of the Territory. These included: measures for the introduction of a ministerial system, including the appointment of four African and two non-African assistant-ministers; the introduction of the elective principle for the designation (by direct elections on the basis of a common roll) of the representative members—equal numbers of Africans, Asians and European—of the Legislative Council; and an announced intention to appoint in 1959 a committee of the Legislative Council to consider aspects of further constitutional development.

The Council hoped that the terms of reference of this 1959 committee would be formulated as broadly as possible. Bearing in mind its previously expressed hope that there would be further increases in African representation in the Legislative Council, it particularly hoped that the terms of reference would allow examination of the possibility of modifying the composition of the Legislative Council in that direction. The Council noted in this connexion that the present arrangements envisaged the retention of the parity system of representation until 1962. It recalled its earlier hope that the retention of separate representation on the basis of parity would be transitional. The Council also suggested that the Administering Authority might find it appropriate to review, after the 1959 elections, the present basis of representation in the light of the changed circumstances.

The Council also urged that Administering Authority to continue to foster the growth of effective local government units at the district and lower levels as rapidly as possible. It hoped that this development would be pressed forward on a non-racial basis, and that the progressive introduction of direct elections based on the widest possible suffrage would be continued.

In the elections planned for the Legislative Council, each constituency was to be represented by one member of each of the three main racial communities, with each voter required to cast three votes, except in the case of uncontested seats. The Council was of the opinion that this novel system could only be tested by experience, and awaited with interest the results of its practical operation. It also noted that the qualifications were such as to limit the franchise to a small proportion of the population as a whole. It stressed the desirability of progressively broadening the franchise.

The Council took note of certain restrictive measures which the Administering Authority had recently found necessary to apply in respect of the African political party in the Territory, the Tanganyika African National Union (TANU). It felt confident that, in view of the importance of the forthcoming territorial elections, the Administering Authority would permit the exercise of the maximum freedom compatible with the preservation of public order.

The Council hoped that the present efforts to place Africans in posts of responsibility would be accelerated and that adequate encouragement would be provided to students leaving school or returning from higher studies to enter government service.

ADMINISTRATIVE UNION

After receiving a further report from its Standing Committee on Administrative Unions, the Council adopted a number of conclusions and recommendations relating to various detailed aspects of the inter-territorial arrangements whereby certain government services of Tanganyika, Kenya and Uganda are administered jointly under the East Africa High Commission and Central Legislative Assembly.

ECONOMIC ADVANCEMENT

Recent improvements in the value and diversity of the export trade of the Territory have reflected, in particular, a continuing increase in African agricultural productivity. Noting this trend with interest, the Council had no doubt that the concerted and sustained efforts of the producers and the Administration might soon lead to a general rise in production, and consequently to improvements in standards of living and in public revenues.

Conscious that long-term economic stability must depend primarily on the advancement of the African as a producer of goods and services, the Council was glad to note the emphasis being placed by the Administering Authority on the development of irrigation facilities, the extension of African tenant-farmer schemes, the elimination of surplus cattle, the improvement of cattle, and the growth of secondary industries. The Council urged it to continue these efforts and to seek further ways and means of securing greater African participation in these activities.

Considering that the bulk of the capital needed for further economic development would have to be found overseas, the Council asked the Administering Authority to give the most sympathetic consideration to the claims of the Territory, and to explore all other possible sources of capital, including the International Bank for Reconstruction and Development.

The Council again commended the Administering Authority for the encouragement and assistance which it was providing for co-operative marketing which has had spectacular successes in Tanganyika among African cash-crop producers. It looked forward with interest to the further extension of co-operative principles.

As to land tenure problems, the Council welcomed a statement by the Administering Authority that it intended to modify the tribal system of tenure only with the understanding and support of the African peoples concerned. The Council asked the Administering Authority to include a detailed statement on land alienation in its next annual report, and, meanwhile, to maintain the greatest caution with regard to alienation of land to non-Africans.

SOCIAL ADVANCEMENT

The Council noted with concern that some vestiges of racial discrimination still persisted in Tanganyika in fields outside the direct control of the Administering Authority. Encouraged by the Administering Authority's assurance that it was anxious to eradicate the remaining vestiges of racial discrimination, the Council hoped that this would be accomplished at a very early date.

The Council was pleased to learn of the continuing and gradual improvement in the status of women, and, in particular, of the appointment of women to positions of responsibility.

Noting the formulation and adoption of a further plan for the development of medical and health services, the Council welcomed the emphasis placed upon the preventive aspects of medicine and health, in which the Administering Authority might find it useful to explore the possibilities of securing assistance from the World Health Organization (WHO) and the United Nations Children's Fund (UNICEF). It also noted with interest recent measures to modernize and improve labour legislation and organization in the Territory, and the development of trade union activity and collective bargaining.

EDUCATIONAL ADVANCEMENT

The continued separation of school facilities according to race led the Council to recall its view that it was important to bring children of different races together as soon as the language barrier between them had disappeared. It noted the prospective establishment of two new secondary schools for students of all races who met the standards of the schools, and it again urged the Administering Authority to take steps to unify the educational system as soon as might be practicable.

The Council welcomed the formulation and approval of a new five-year plan for African education which stressed the improvement of primary school education and the expansion of middle and secondary education. It welcomed also the declared objective of the Administering Authority to establish a university college in the Territory.

PROGRESS TOWARDS SELF-GOVERNMENT OR INDEPENDENCE

The Council reconsidered, within the framework of the General Assembly resolutions on the subject, the question of establishing intermediate target dates and final time-limits for the attainment by Tanganyika of self-government or independence. It heard, on the one hand, a reaffirmation of the Administering Authority's views on the difficulties and disadvantages of predicting or determining in advance the pace of political advancement and, on the other hand, the opinions of a prominent African chief and a prominent African political leader in favour of a clearer definition of the road to be taken.

The Council took note of certain economic, social and educational development plans and constitutional reforms, the implementation of which had, in fact, been related to dates in the future. It hoped that other specific aspects of constitutional advance—the broadening of the franchise towards universal suffrage, the further development of the legislature and the extension of the elective principle—would be appropriate intermediate targets.

DOCUMENTARY REFERENCES

TRUSTEESHIP COUNCIL—19TH AND 20TH SESSIONS Plenary Meetings 787, 811-822, 836, 840.

Report by Her Majesty's Government in United Kingdom of Great Britain and Northern Ireland to General Assembly of United Nations on Trust Territory of Tanganyika under United Kingdom Administration for Year 1955. London, H.M.S.O., 1956. Colonial No. 324.

T/1286(A/3636). Note by Secretary-General transmitting report of Government of United Kingdom on administration of Trust Territory of Tanganyika for 1955.

T/1304. Observations by UNESCO concerning annual reports for 1955, Chapter II.

T/1317. Supplementary information submitted by Administering Authority.

T/1318. Special information submitted by Administering Authority concerning action taken on Trusteeship Council resolution 1377(XVII) in respect of petition from representatives of Meru Citizens' Union (T/PET.2/197).

T/L.722 and Add.1, T/L.788, T/L.801. Outline of conditions, report of Drafting Committee, and summary of observations, Chapter as a whole on Tanganyika, T/L.772 and Add.1, T/L.788, as amended, and T/L.801), adopted unanimously by Council, on 12 July 1957, meeting 840.

T/L.797. Haiti and India amendment to report of Drafting Committee, T/L.788.

T/L.786. Report of Standing Committee on Administrative Unions, Part I.

A/3595 and Corr.1. Report of Trusteeship Council to General Assembly, Part II, Chapter I.

See also DOCUMENTARY REFERENCES to CHAPTER III, section on EXAMINATION OF THE ANNUAL REPORTS FROM ADMINISTERING AUTHORITIES.

RUANDA-URUNDI

Over 4,250,000 people live in the two indigenous "states"—united under the Belgian administration—that comprise the central African territory of Ruanda-Urundi. The Trust Territory is, in turn, administratively united in some respects with the Belgian Congo.

At its nineteenth session (14 March–15 May 1957), the Council recommended that the Administering Authority persevere in developing a sense of unity among the inhabitants of the Trust Territory and in strengthening the relationships between Ruanda and Urundi by developing institutions common to both "states" and by other means. It also recommended that the Administering Authority consider the adoption of an official name for the indigenous inhabitants.

POLITICAL ADVANCEMENT

Steps have been taken by the Administering Authority to increase the African membership of the Council of the Vice-Government-General, a territorial advisory body, and to establish a link between that Council and the High Councils of the two "states". Welcoming these moves, the Trusteeship Council expressed the hope that the African membership of the territorial body would be progressively increased so that it might be transformed within a short period into a legislative organ for the Territory.

Another recent political innovation has been the successful introduction, among the indigenous population, of adult male suffrage exercised indirectly for the constitution of the councils of sub-chiefdoms. The Trusteeship Council hoped that direct elections would be undertaken as soon as possible and that this system would be applied progressively to all councils in the Territory, including the Council of the Vice-Government-General.

The Trusteeship Council again expressed its hope that Africans would be trained for, and appointed to high posts within the Belgian administration proper, there still being no Africans in such posts.

ECONOMIC ADVANCEMENT

Ruanda-Urundi faces especially difficult economic problems because its densely settled population is still dependent on agriculture and stock-raising for its subsistence. The Administering Authority has accordingly made special efforts regarding soil conservation, the draining of marsh lands, reafforestation, the abolition of the semi-feudal system of cattle holding, the development of co-operatives and the increased participation of Africans in retail trade as well as in the production of food and commercial crops.

The Trusteeship Council hoped that the advances made in these fields would be followed up by the rational development of livestock and the establishment of an industry for processing livestock products, the resettlement of population from overcrowded areas and increased agricultural development. The Council further hoped that the Administering Authority would devote special care to fostering a more complete participation of the indigenous inhabitants in the major economic activities, including trade, at a higher level. It also asked the Administering Authority to study the possibility of further developing tourism in the Territory, notable with regard to its mountains and bordering lakes.

The Council requested the Administering Authority to continue negotiations with the International Bank for Reconstruction and Development with a view to obtaining development funds in addition to those available under the Administering Authority's 10-Year Plan. It emphasized the need for continued efforts to increase public revenue by making full use of the various resources of all the elements of the population. The Council also hoped that the Administering Authority would make every effort to introduce legislation which would furnish the Africans with credit facilities based on land ownership.

The Council recommended that the Administering Authority explore ways and means of promoting secondary and cottage industries and handicrafts using locally produced raw materials, such as cotton and food products, and of producing consumer goods presently being imported, with increasing participation by the indigenous people. It hoped that the execution of a plan to use the Ruzizi River as a source of hydroelectric power would promote industrial development.

SOCIAL ADVANCEMENT

An appreciable improvement was reported in the relations between the various ethnic groups of the population, which includes a few thousand Europeans and Asians. The Council hoped that the Administering Authority would vigorously pursue its efforts to eliminate all discriminatory practices at an early date.

The curfew and other restrictions on the freedom of movement of Africans have also been relaxed. The Council hoped that all such restrictions would be completely removed as soon as possible.

In the field of labour, the Council hoped that the Administering Authority would take further steps towards making a substantial increase in real wages possible and increasing the employment opportunities of workers in the Territory. The development of trade unions and other bodies with direct representation of African workers should also be facilitated.

EDUCATIONAL ADVANCEMENT

The number of school classes in the Territory, as well as the number of boys and girls attending school, have continued to increase, but the Council hoped that the Administering Authority would find the means to increase school attendance further and to improve the retention rate of pupils in schools, particularly by encouraging them to continue their studies beyond the primary stage.

Noting the slow progress in secondary education and the decrease in the number of students receiving higher education outside the Territory, the Council hoped that the Adminiistering Authority would step up its efforts in these respects. It also recommended the organization of a systematic mass and adult education programme.

PROGRESS TOWARDS SELF-GOVERNMENT OR INDEPENDENCE

The Council had previously recommended that the Administering Authority should indicate such successive intermediate targets and dates in the political, economic, social and educational development of the Territory as would create the pre-conditions for the attainment by the Territory of self-government or independence. At its nineteenth session, it expressed the opinion that the establishment of a central legislative institution and the extension of adult suffrage for elections to all representative bodies would be appropriate targets in that connexion.

DOCUMENTARY REFERENCES

TRUSTEESHIP COUNCIL—19TH SESSION
Plenary Meetings 754-761, 789, 792, 793.

Rapport soumis par le Gouvernement belge à l'Assemblée générale des Nations Unies au sujet de l'administration du Ruanda-Urundi pendant l'année 1955. Bruxelles, Imprimerie Fr. Van Muysewinkel, 23-27 rue d'Anethan, 1956.

T/1282(A/3634). Note by Secretary-General transmitting report of Government of Belgium on administration of Ruanda-Urundi for 1955.

T/1304. Observations by UNESCO concerning annual reports for 1955. Chapter III.

T/L.741. Report of Standing Committee on Administrative Unions, Part II.

T/L.735 and Add.1, T/L.758, T/L.760. Outline of conditions, report of Drafting Committee, and summary of observations by members of Council. Chapter on Ruanda-Urundi as a whole, T/L.735 and Add.1, T/L.758, as amended, and T/L.760, adopted by Council on 15 May 1957, meeting 792, by 6 votes to 0, with 7 abstentions.

T/L.759. India amendment to report of Drafting Committee, T/L.758.

T/L.763. Report of Drafting Committee on Cameroons under French Administration, Annex I, paragraph 13 (on European Economic Community), adopted by Council on 15 May 1957, meeting 793, by 6 votes to 0, with 7 abstentions.

A/3595 and Corr.1. Report of Trusteeship Council to General Assembly, Part II, Chapter II.

See also DOCUMENTARY REFERENCES to CHAPTER III, section on EXAMINATION OF ANNUAL REPORTS.

SOMALILAND UNDER ITALIAN ADMINISTRATION

Somaliland under Italian administration, the only Trust Territory for which a final date for the attainment of independence (1960) has been formally established in advance, has continued to make progress towards that goal. The legislative and executive institutions established in the preceding year continued to function; new elections are envisaged in 1958 for a legislative and constituent assembly leading to the establishment by the end of that year of the four basic institutions of a sovereign State, namely, a Constitution, a Head of State, a Government and a Parliament.

The role to be played in these changing circumstances by the United Nations Advisory Council was discussed at the Trusteeship Council's twentieth session (20 May–12 July 1957). Noting a statement by the Administering Authority that the situation created by the transfer of a substantial measure of responsibility to the Government of Somalia necessitated revision of the procedure for consultation with the Advisory Council, the Trusteeship Council hoped that the Advisory Council and the Administering Authority would be able, through discussion between themselves, to devise suitable procedures which would enable the Advisory Council to continue making useful contributions to the Territory's development.

POLITICAL ADVANCEMENT

Somali Ministers appointed in 1956 have assumed full responsibility for the discharge of their functions. The Legislative Assembly paved the way for the preparation of a number of pieces of basic legislation, including penal and civil codes, a labour code and a maritime code.

Preparations were also made for holding general elections in 1958 to the first Constituent Assembly. In particular, a census of the rural and nomadic populations had been undertaken. In this connexion, the Trusteeship Council expressed the hope that the extension of the suffrage to women would be given urgent consideration by the Somali authorities.

Except for a few foreign experts and advisers at the centre, district and regional administration is now in the hands of the Somalis themselves. The Council was pleased to note that the results have been satisfactory.

ECONOMIC ADVANCEMENT

The report of the survey mission sent to the Territory in 1956 by the International Bank for Reconstruction and Development was examined by the Council in the light of observations made on it by the Administering Authority, the Government of Somalia and the United Nations Advisory Council.

The general picture of the economic future which the Council drew from these discussions was reflected in its formal observation. It noted that continued progress had been achieved under the Administering Authority's existing plans for economic development, and that, in all fields where possibilities of development existed, plans had been made at least until 1960. It became evident, however, that the Territory would continue to require external technical and financial assistance for an indeterminate period after 1960 if, as stated in the report of the Bank mission, Somaliland was to avoid substantial reductions in public services and in economic development plans. While the Council agreed with the Administering Authority that it would be premature to make any specific recommendation on the amount of external aid which might be required after 1960, it noted that the Bank mission had indicated an amount of between $4 and $6 million annually, the Administering Authority an amount between $4 and $5 million (excluding technical assistance), and the representative of the Somali authorities about $4 million.

Italy announced its readiness to continue to make technicians available to Somaliland after 1960, if the Somali authorities should so desire. At the same time, the Government of Somalia pledged that it would give all appropriate encouragement and guarantees to foreign private investment interested in pursuing activities useful for the Territory. The Council welcomed these assurances and drew them to the attention of the General Assembly, to which it also suggested a number of other possibilities that might be explored to meet the situation after 1960.

At the Assembly's twelfth session, the Fourth Committee examined the report of the Trusteeship Council on this question.

Under a draft resolution sponsored by India, the United States and Liberia, the Assembly would: (1) take note from the Trusteeship Council's report that the Administering Authority, in consultation with the Somalia Government, would continue to explore the ways of meeting the requirements of a viable, independent Somalia and report thereon to the Council at its twenty-second session; and (2) ask the Trusteeship Council, in consultation with the Administering Authority and the Somalia Government, to study the question and, in particular, to explore the possibilities suggested by the Council and to report to the Assembly's thirteenth session.

The draft resolution was adopted unanimously by the Assembly in plenary meeting on 13 December 1957 as resolution 1206(XII), on the Fourth Committee's recommendation.

(See also above, ECONOMIC AND SOCIAL QUESTIONS, CHAPTER IV, section on TECHNICAL ASSISTANCE TO TRUST TERRITORY OF SOMALILAND.)

SOCIAL AND EDUCATIONAL ADVANCEMENT

The fact that the population of the Territory is largely nomadic poses special social and educational, as well as economic difficulties. The Council noted the efforts of the Adminitering Authority and the Government of Somalia to raise the standard of living of the nomadic peoples, and hoped that the practical difficulties in the way of their social advancement could be progressively removed by turning their principal assets to greater economic advantage.

Further progress achieved in education, particularly the increased number of pupils attending primary and secondary schools, was also noted with appreciation. The Council hoped, too, that a scholarship scheme which had been introduced by the Administering Authority and the assistance provided by other States would enable an increasing number of Somalis to acquire the skills and knowledge needed by the Territory.

QUESTION OF FRONTIER BETWEEN SOMALILAND AND ETHIOPIA

The Somalia Government has continued to press upon the United Nations the urgency of defining the frontier between Somaliland and Ethiopia, in view of the evident lack of success of negotiations between Ethiopia and Italy on this matter.

At its twentieth session, the Trusteeship Council recalled the opinion which had been expressed by the General Assembly earlier in the year (by resolution 1068(XI) of 26 February 1957) that, if the negotiations (which were about to be resumed) should fail to achieve substantial results by the Assembly's twelfth session, it would be necessary for the Governments of Ethiopia and of Italy to avail themselves of the mediation or arbitration procedures previously laid down.

The situation towards the end of 1957, when the Assembly resumed consideration of the frontier question at its twelfth session, was that, although some progress had been made during the discussions between the two Governments, direct negotiations had not resolved some of the main differences between them.

Three differing approaches towards a procedure other than continued negotiation were proposed under draft resolutions and amendments submitted in the Fourth Committee. A proposal by Ceylon, Greece, Indonesia, Liberia and Sudan envisaged the establishment by the two parties of a tribunal of jurists to decide all points of difference in the interpretation of the Italo-Ethiopian Frontier Convention of 16 May 1908. A proposal by the United Kingdom and the United States envisaged a procedure of arbitration. A proposal by the Philippines envisaged mediation, and if that failed, arbitration.

Consultations among these Members eventually led to a single draft resolution being placed before the Committee—a revised version of the United Kingdom-United States proposal, which was also sponsored by the authors of the five-power draft. This was adopted unanimously by the Assembly in plenary meeting on 14 December 1957 as resolution 1213(XII). The General Assembly thereby expressed the opinion that a final settlement could be achieved most expeditiously by a procedure of arbitration. It recommended that the parties establish, if possible within three months, an arbitration tribunal, to delimit the frontier in accordance with terms of reference to be agreed upon between the two Governments with the assistance of an independent person appointed by agreement between them. The tribunal would consist of three jurists, one appointed by Ethiopia, one by Italy and one by agreement between these two jurists, or failing such agreement, by His Majesty the King of Norway. The Governments of Ethiopia and Italy were asked to report to the Assembly's thirteenth session on the measures taken to give effect to this resolution.

DOCUMENTARY REFERENCES

TRUSTEESHIP COUNCIL—19TH AND 20TH SESSIONS
Plenary Meetings 753, 754, 777, 778, 783, 787, 795-801, 803, 817, 832, 840.

Rapport du Gouvernement italien à l'Assemblée générale des Nations Unies sur l'administration de tutelle de la Somalie, 1956. Ministère des Affaires étrangères. Roma, Istituto Poligrafico dello Stato P.V., 1957.

T/1315(A/3635). Note by Secretary-General transmitting report of Government of Italy on administration of Somaliland under Italian administration for year 1956.

T/1321. Supplementary information submitted by Administering Authority.

T/1311. Report of United Nations Advisory Council for Trust Territory of Somaliland under Italian administration covering period 1 April 1956–31 March 1957.

T/1296. Financing of economic development plans of Trust Territory of Somaliland under Italian administration. Letter of 29 January 1957 from Permanent Representative of Italy transmitting report of International Bank for Reconstruction and Development on "Economy of Trust Territory of Somaliland".

T/1334. Observations of UNESCO.

T/L.765 and Add.1, T/L.779, T/L.784. Working paper by Secretariat, report of Drafting Committee, and summary of observations. Chapter on Somaliland under Italian administration, as a whole, T/L.765 and Add.1, T/L.779, T/L.784, adopted by Council on 3 July 1957, meeting 832, by 13 votes to 0, with 1 abstention.

A/3595 and Corr.1. Report of Trusteeship Council to General Assembly, Part II, Chapter III.

GENERAL ASSEMBLY—12TH SESSION
Plenary Meeting 729.
Fourth Committee, meetings 725, 728-731.

A/C.4/L.514. India and United States draft resolution.

A/C.4/L.514/Rev.1, Rev.1/Corr.1, and Rev.2. India, Liberia, United States revised draft resolution adopted unanimously by Fourth Committee.

A/C.4/L.523. Philippines amendments to revised draft resolution, A/C.4/L.514/Rev.1 and Rev.1/Corr.1.

A/3779. Report of Fourth Committee (draft resolution II).

RESOLUTION 1206(XII), as recommended by Fourth Committee, A/3779, adopted unanimously by Assembly on 13 December 1957, meeting 729.

"The General Assembly,

"Recalling its resolution 855(IX) of 14 December 1954, in which it requested the Trusteeship Council, on the basis of the conclusions of the United Nations Visiting Mission to Trust Territories in East Africa, 1954, and the report of the International Bank for Reconstruction and Development, to endeavour to decide on practical measures for financing the economic development plans for Somaliland under Italian administration,

"Having examined with interest the report of the Mission of the International Bank for Reconstruction and Development, and the observations thereon of the Administering Authority, the Government of Somalia and the United Nations Advisory Council for the Trust Territory of Somaliland under Italian Administration,

"Having taken note of the statement of the Administering Authority that the Territory would require, after 1960, external financial assistance, excluding technical assistance, amounting to about $4 million to $5 million annually,

"Having considered the various possibilities suggested by the Trusteeship Council of furnishing technical and financial assistance to Somaliland under Italian Administration after 1960, and noting the conclusion of the Council, with which the Administering Authority is in agreement, that it is premature to make any specific recommendation as to the amount of external assistance which might be required after 1960,

"1. Notes from the report of the Trusteeship Council that the Administering Authority, in consultation with the Government of Somalia, will continue to assess all requirements for a viable, independent Somalia, explore all possible ways of meeting the requirements indicated by these assessments and submit a report thereon to the Council at its twenty-second session;

"2. Requests the Trusteeship Council to continue its study of this question, in consultation with the Administering Authority and the Government of Somalia, and, in particular, to explore further the possibilities suggested by the Council and to report thereon for the consideration of the General Assembly at its thirteenth session."

QUESTION OF FRONTIER BETWEEN SOMALILAND AND ETHIOPIA

T/1285. Letter of 16 October 1956 from Permanent Representative of Italy transmitting text of speech delivered by Somali Prime Minister to Somali Legislative Assembly.

GENERAL ASSEMBLY—12TH SESSION
Plenary Meeting 730.
Fourth Committee, meetings 734, 735, 737-740.

A/3753 and Corr.1. Report of Ethiopian Government.
A/3754 and Add.1. Report of Italian Government.
A/C.4/L.528 and Rev.1. Ceylon, Greece, Indonesia, Liberia, Sudan draft resolution and revision.
A/C.4/L.529. United Kingdom and United States draft resolution.
A/C.4/L.529/Rev.1. Ceylon, Greece, Indonesia, Liberia, Sudan, United Kingdom, United States revised draft resolution, unanimously adopted by Fourth Committee.
A/C.4/L.530. Philippines amendments to revised joint draft resolution, A/C.4/L.528/Rev.1.
A/3796. Report of Fourth Committee.
RESOLUTION 1213(XII), as recommended by Fourth Committee, A/3796, unanimously adopted by Assembly on 14 December 1957, meeting 730.

"The General Assembly,
"Recalling its resolutions 392(V) of 15 December 1950, 854(IX) of 14 December 1954, 947(X) of 15 December 1955 and 1068(XI) of 26 February 1957,
"Having taken note of the reports transmitted to

the General Assembly by the Governments of Ethiopia and of Italy in accordance with the recommendation contained in resolution 1068(XI),

"*Having heard* the statements made by the delegations of Ethiopia and of Italy, including that of the representative of the Government of. Somalia,

"*Noting* the efforts made by the Governments of Ethiopia and of Italy in negotiations to reach a solution of the question of the frontier between the Trust Territory of Somaliland under Italian administration and Ethiopia,

"*Noting* that, although some progress was made during the discussions, direct negotiations have not resolved some of the main differences between the parties,

"*Considering* that it is in the common interest of Ethiopia and the Trust Territory that there should be a final settlement of the question of the frontier between them before the Territory becomes an independent sovereign State in 1960,

"*Having regard* to the urgency of the matter,

"1. *Expresses the opinion* that a final settlement can be achieved most expeditiously by a procedure of arbitration;

"2. *Recommends* the parties to establish, if possible within three months, an arbitration tribunal—consisting of three jurists, one to be appointed by Ethiopia, one by Italy and one by agreement between the jurists so appointed or, failing agreement between them, by His Majesty the King of Norway—to delimit the frontier in accordance with terms of reference to be agreed upon between the two Governments, with the assistance of an independent person to be appointed by agreement, between them;

"3. *Requests* the Governments of Ethiopia and of Italy to report to the General Assembly at its thirteenth session on the measures taken by them to give effect to the present resolution."

See also DOCUMENTARY REFERENCES to CHAPTER III, section on EXAMINATION OF THE ANNUAL REPORTS FROM.

CAMEROONS UNDER BRITISH ADMINISTRATION

The development of the Cameroons under British administration remains closely linked with that of the Federation of Nigeria, with which the Trust Territory is administratively united in two different ways: the Northern Cameroons, containing some 720,000 people as of mid-1955, is administered as part of the Northern Region of Nigeria, and the Southern Cameroons, with 780,000 people, is administered as a quasi-federal territory possessing some local executive and legislative autonomy.

A representative conference to review the existing constitutional arrangements in Nigeria and the Cameroons as a whole, which had originally been set for September 1956, was postponed until May 1957.

Before that date, at its nineteenth session (14 March–15 May 1957), the Trusteeship Council expressed its confidence that an opportunity would be provided for the views of the inhabitants of the Territory to find free and adequate expression in an atmosphere which would contribute to a spirit of social solidarity among them. In the expectation that the conference would prove to be of utmost significance in the evolution of the Trust Territory towards self-government of independence, the Council looked forward with the greatest interest to receiving information on its outcome.

At the Assembly's twelfth session, the Fourth Committee gave special consideration to the situation in both the Cameroons under British administration and the Cameroons under French administration. The Committee rejected a draft resolution on this subject. Later, however another resolution on this matter (1211 (XII)) was approved at a plenary meeting of the General Assembly on 13 December 1957 by a roll-call vote of 57 to 0, with 17 abstentions. (See below, section on SITUATION IN THE TWO TRUST TERRITORIES OF THE CAMEROONS.)

POLITICAL ADVANCEMENT

For the time being, political progress in the Trust Territory has been primarily a matter of constitutional reforms introduced in 1954 and 1955. The Council observed with satisfaction that the new Constitution was functioning effectively and that the development of political parties and groupings had proceeded in a healthy manner.

The Council also expressed approval of electoral improvements which had been made in both parts of the Territory, and noted with interest the further reforms which had been introduced in the systems of local government.

ECONOMIC ADVANCEMENT

For the second year in succession, the Council formed the opinion that it was in the economic and social fields where advancement was most urgently required. It noted with satisfaction the further economic progress achieved in both parts of the Territory and congratulated the

Government of the Southern Cameroons on the realistic manner in which it had met a period of financial stringency by concentrating its available resources on basic development. The Council was gratified by the initial success of efforts by the Southern Cameroons Government to encourage foreign private investment in the Territory. It was confident that due regard would continue to be paid to the interests of the Cameroons people in the execution of this policy.

Steps taken to develop the production of tea, coffee and cotton attracted the attention of the Council. It also noted the progress made to date with a number of irrigation schemes, and recognized the potential importance of irrigation for agricultural development in areas of the northern part of the Territory. The Council hoped that no effort would be spared to extend these schemes to the fullest extent practicable. It welcomed the attention and assistance given to the co-operative movement in both parts of the Trust Territory.

SOCIAL ADVANCEMENT

The Trusteeship Council noted the evidence of steady social progress in the Territory. In particular, the social and religious cleavage between the different groups in the north was beginning to disappear, village, town and tribal unions were gaining influence and community development was increasing in the south.

Recognizing the need to develop further a sense of unity among the various groups in the northern part of the Territory, the Council recommended that efforts to encourage community development projects there be continued. It hoped, moreover, that the Administering Authority would endeavour to bring the peoples of the north and the south into a closer relationship by promoting other contacts whenever possible.

The Council also noted the gradual emergence of an African middle class in recent years, and expected that this would also help to strengthen social unity and to eliminate those traditional practices and customs which tended

to retard the Territory's social progress.

The Council welcomed the continuing attention being given to improving the status of women and the steady progress being made in this direction, as was indicated by the increasing number of girls attending schools and vocational institutions.

EDUCATIONAL ADVANCEMENT

Increased budgetary appropriations have been made for education in the Southern Cameroons, and there has been an increase in the number of primary schools.

Nonetheless, the Council considered that the situation still called for energetic action. It hoped that the Governments concerned would further hasten the pace of educational advancement, especially in the northern part of the Territory. It also hoped for active participation by the local authorities, particularly through the more extensive introduction of rates (taxes) to be devoted to educational expenditures.

A growing but still relatively small number of students from the Territory are receiving higher education. At the same time the number of enrolments and of scholarship holders in the secondary schools has increased. The Council hoped that this would soon result in more candidates qualified for higher education.

The Administering Authority informed the Council that it would give consideration to the possibility of enlisting the assistance of the United Nations Educational, Scientific and Cultural Organization (UNESCO) in a study of problems relating to the medium of instruction in certain areas of the Northern Cameroons.

PROGRESS TOWARDS SELF-GOVERNMENT OR INDEPENDENCE

In considering the question of the manner and timing of the attainment by the Trust Territory of the final objective of trusteeship, the Council reaffirmed its previously expressed hope that the results of the Constitutional Review Conference would throw light on the matter.

DOCUMENTARY REFERENCES

TRUSTEESHIP COUNCIL—19TH AND 20TH SESSIONS Plenary Meetings 769-778, 788, 805.

Report by Her Majesty's Government in United Kingdom of Great Britain and Northern Ireland to

General Assembly of United Nations on Cameroons under United Kingdom administration for year 1955. London H.M.S.O., 1956. Colonial No. 325 T/1287(A/3637). Note by Secretary-General transmitting report of Government of United Kingdom on administration of Trust Territory of Cameroons under British administration for 1955.

T/1298. Special information submitted by Administering Authority on action taken on recommendations of Trusteeship Council in respect of petitions.

T/1302 and Corr.1. Supplementary information submitted by Administering Authority.

T/1304. Observations by UNESCO concerning annual reports for 1955, Part IV.

T/L.741. Report of Standing Committee on Administrative Unions, Part I.

T/L.737 and Add.1, T/L.757, T/L.773. Outline of conditions, report of Drafting Committee and summary of observations. Chapter as a whole, T/L.737 and Add.1, T/L.757, as amended by Council, and T/L.773, adopted by Council on 4 June 1957, meeting 805, by 12 votes to 0, with 2 abstentions.

A/3595 and Corr.1. Report of Trusteeship Council to General Assembly, Part II, Chapter IV.

See also DOCUMENTARY REFERENCES to section below on SITUATION IN THE TWO TRUST TERRITORIES OF THE CAMEROONS.

CAMEROONS UNDER FRENCH ADMINISTRATION

The Cameroons under French administration, with over three million inhabitants, is the third largest Trust Territory in terms of population. Early in 1957 the Territory took its first major institutional step towards self-government since 1946.

At its nineteenth session 14 March–15 May 1957), the Council was informed of a new statute established by decree on 16 April 1957, after consultation with a territorial assembly which had just been elected by universal suffrage.

There was still some evidence of the tension which had existed in the Territory since the serious disturbances of May 1955; fresh disturbances had occurred during the elections in December 1956 in the Sanaga-Maritime region. The Council hoped that the observance of normal democratic practices by all sections of public opinion in the Territory, as well as the introduction of clemency measures, particularly amnesty legislation envisaged by the Administering Authority, would help to establish in the Territory a climate of complete trust.

At the Assembly's twelfth session, the Fourth Committee gave special consideration to the situation in both the Cameroons under British administration and the Cameroons under French administration. The Committee rejected a draft resolution on this subject. Later, however, another resolution on this matter (1211(XII)) was approved by a plenary meeting of the General Assembly on 13 December 1957 by a roll-call vote of 57 to 0, with 17 abstentions. (See below, section on SITUATION IN THE TWO TRUST TERRITORIES OF THE CAMEROONS).

POLITICAL ADVANCEMENT

The statute of 16 April 1957 establishes a "Trust State of the Cameroons". In the view of the Council, this represented an important step towards the attainment of self-government or independence, since the statute established a Legislative Assembly in the Territory based on universal suffrage and a government responsible to it, since a large measure of internal autonomy was granted to the Territory, and since Cameroons citizenship was established for the indigenous inhabitants.

It was not suggested from any side that the statute represented the attainment of the trusteeship objectives; indeed, the Council noted with interest that, during the electoral campaign, those who were to become the leaders of the majority and of the minority groups in the Cameroons Assembly had expressed themselves in favour of independence as the ultimate goal for the Territory, though some preferred a more complete and rapid evolution than others.

The Council noted with approval that the representatives in the Territorial Assembly had been elected for the first time by direct universal suffrage and that the body thus elected had been consulted by the Administering Authority with regard to the provisions of the new statute. The membership of the Assembly has been expanded from 50 to 70 and, in its new role as a legislative organ, it was entrusted with wider powers and greater responsibilities than before. The Council observed with satisfaction that a ministerial government was responsible to the Legislative Assembly.

An innovation brought about by the new statute—in response to the wish of the majority in the Territorial Assembly—was the establishment of the northern, largely Islamized, region as a province with an assembly and budget of its own. In taking note of this, the Council hoped that the experience gained in the Legislative Assembly in considering common problems would subordinate regional differences to the need for national unity, and thus combat separatist tendencies in the Territory.

The establishment of universal adult suffrage and of a single electoral college was welcomed by the Council, which had made many previous recommendations to that end. At the first elections under the new system (held on 23 December 1956), 55 per cent of the electorate participated and only in one region was the percentage of abstentions very high.

The Council noted with satisfaction that 60 Cameroonians had thus far been appointed to high positions in the administration, including six chiefs of sub-divisions and four regional assistants. The introduction of the new statute has made it possible to expedite the process of Africanization of the civil services so as to keep pace with the Territory's political evolution.

ECONOMIC ADVANCEMENT

A fall in world market prices of cocoa, coffee and cotton, on which the Territory's economy largely depends, led the Administering Authority to take certain measures of financial stringency. The Council felt that, because of the importance of these products to the economy, the situation called for continued vigilance in order to ensure the development of a balanced and diversified economy.

The Council recalled its previous observations on the importance which it also attached to the increasing participation of Africans in the Territory's economy; it commended the Administering Authority for developing the savings habit among the population, providing credit facilities and increasing financial aid to agriculture. The Council noted, however, that African participation in commerce and industry, while increasing, was still relatively small. It hoped that steps taken so far, as well as other measures that the Administering Authority might see fit to take, would further increase and accelerate the participation of Africans in all types of economic activity.

In spite of the need for austerity created by the fall in export crop prices, the current expenditure for public services in the Territory could still be met from local revenue. The Administering Authority continued, however, to grant large subsidies for capital expenditure and the financing of development programmes. The Council noted that the second phase of the economic and social development plan was progressing satisfactorily, and that the Territorial Assembly was fully associated with the preparation and the implementation of such plans.

Prospects for industrial development are emerging in the Territory as a result of the harnessing of hydroelectric power resources, notably for aluminium production at Edéa. The Council recommended that the Administering Authority continue to encourage the technical training of Cameroonians. In particular, it invited the industrial undertakings concerned to set up training programmes which would increase the number of skilled labourers and technicians, as well as of specialists capable of filling managerial posts in the industries.

SOCIAL ADVANCEMENT

Ethnic, tribal and religious differences, separating large groups from one another, are still strong in the Cameroons. The Council noted that the Administering Authority was also very much concerned with this matter. It hoped that the various elements of the population would become more and more aware of the need to develop a homogeneous society.

Special efforts seemed necessary, in particular to improve the conditions of the Kirdi groups, still living outside the currents of modern life in the mountains of the Northern Cameroons. The Administering Authority was asked to draw the attention of the responsible authorities to this problem in order that the necessary steps might be taken to associate these elements with the evolution of the rest of the population through sustained social action.

The Council again stressed the need to continue action to improve the status of women, and to eliminate progressively the "bride-price" system and polygamy. The Administering Authority was commended for introducing a system of family pensions for workers and prenatal, maternity and birth allowances, as well as allowances for children under 14 years of age, and also for its energetic action to improve rural housing.

EDUCATIONAL ADVANCEMENT

Progress in education won praise from the Council. In the north, where educational development is still lagging far behind, conditions are nevertheless improving, and in the south the people are extremely interested in, and favourable to, educational progress. The Council praised the establishment and smooth functioning of schools open to students of all races, without any discrimination.

In the Council's opinion, the balanced development of the Territory and the progressive integration of the indigenous inhabitants in all the fields of economic activity requiring high technical qualifications called for continued efforts to increase technical school attendance. As to higher education, the Council noted that nearly 500 Cameroonian students held scholarships in France. It hoped, however, that the competent authorities would be able to consider the establishment in the relatively near future of a university with a view to satisfying the educational needs of the Territory.

PROGRESS TOWARDS SELF-GOVERNMENT OR INDEPENDENCE

Having previously recommended that the Administering Authority should indicate such successive intermediate targets and dates in the political, economic, social and educational development of the Territory as would create the pre-conditions for the attainment of self-government or independence, the Council reviewed this matter in the light of the introduction of the new statute. It considered that further measures for the development of the executive and legislative organs and the extension of their powers, as well as the training and appointment of indigenous persons for positions of responsibility in the administration, would be suitable targets for which dates might be indicated.

DOCUMENTARY REFERENCES

TRUSTEESHIP COUNCIL—19TH AND 20TH SESSIONS Plenary Meetings 760-770, 777, 784-787, 790-793, 802, 805.

Rapport annuel du Gouvernement Français à l'Assemblée générale des Nations Unies sur l'administration du Cameroun placé sous la tutelle de la France, année 1955. Paris, Imprimerie Chaix, 20 rue Bergère, 1956.

T/1284(A/3638). Note by Secretary-General transmitting report of Government of France on administration of Trust Territory of Cameroons under French administration for 1955.

T/1304. Observations by UNESCO concerning annual reports for 1955, Part V.

T/1314 and Corr.1. Note by Secretary-General (Text of Decree No. 57-501 of 16 April 1957, setting forth Statute of Cameroons, as published in Journal officiel of French Republic of 18 April 1957).

T/L.736 and Add.2, T/L.763, T/L.774. Outline of conditions, report of Drafting Committee, and summary of observations. Chapter as a whole, T/L.736 and Add.2, T/L.763, as amended by Council, and T/L.774, adopted by Council on 4 June 1957, meeting 805, by 10 votes to 0, with 4 abstentions.

A/3595 and Corr.1. Report of Trusteeship Council to General Assembly, Part II, Chapter V.

See also DOCUMENTARY REFERENCES to following section on SITUATION IN THE TWO TRUST TERRITORIES OF THE CAMEROONS.

EXAMINATION OF PETITIONS

T/1303. Note by Secretary-General.

T/L.736/Add.1. General questions raised in communications and petitions circulated to members of Trusteeship Council. Annex to Outline of Conditions.

T/L.742. Report of Committee on Communications concerning Cameroons under French administration.

T/L.748. USSR draft resolution.

SITUATION IN THE TWO TRUST TERRITORIES OF THE CAMEROONS

At the General Assembly's twelfth session, the situation in the Trust Territories of the Cameroons under British administration and the Cameroons under French administration received special consideration in the course of the Fourth Committee's discussion of the Trusteeship Council's annual report. This special consideration was a result both of the recognized importance of the political developments taking place in the two Territories and of the statements made by a number of Cameroons petitioners who had been granted hearings by the Committee.

The petitioners spoke separately on behalf of: one political group composing a minority in the Legislature of the Cameroons under French administration; a trade union organization in the same Territory; a party which had been declared unlawful in both Territories; and a party existing in the Cameroons under British administration but not represented in its institutions.

While taking different views on various aspects of the situation in the Territories, the petitioners indicated that they were in agreement in asking the General Assembly: (1) to recognize and proclaim the right of the Cameroons under French administration to independence; (2) to appoint a commission of inquiry; (3) to call for a general political amnesty; and (4) to recommend that the two Territories should be granted independence simultaneously in order to facilitate their reunification.

The Administering Authorities concerned emphasized the minority nature of the views which had been put forward with regard to the Territories under their respective administrations.

The representative of the United Kingdom explained the most recent constitutional developments affecting the Cameroons under British administration. As a result of the Constitutional Review Conference (see above, section on CAMEROONS UNDER BRITISH ADMINISTRATION), which had now taken place, two regions of Nigeria were already self-governing. In addition, the Northern Region would obtain internal self-government in 1959. Revised constitutional arrangements for the Southern Cameroons, expected to come into force early in 1958, provided for a greatly increased elected element in the legislature and for a Cameroonian majority in the Executive Council, which would become a principal instrument of policy in the Southern Cameroons.

The Secretary of State for the Colonies, the United Kingdom representative added, had stated that the United Kingdom Government fully recognized its obligations under the Trusteeship Agreement, one of which was to administer the Cameroons as an integral part of Nigeria. When Nigeria became an independent country, that arrangement would no longer be possible and the Trusteeship Agreement would have to be reviewed. One possibility would be for the Cameroons to remain part of Nigeria, which would entail the termination, in consultation with the United Nations, of the Trusteeship Agreement. There could, however, be no question of obliging the Cameroons people to remain part of an independent Nigeria contrary to their own wishes.

It was therefore clear, said the United Kingdom representative, that the Cameroons under British administration would not be forced into continued association with Nigeria against the will of the people. Secondly, the Southern Cameroons already had a democratically elected Government while the Northern Cameroons took part in the democratic institutions of Northern Nigeria. Thirdly, the people of the Southern Cameroons and the people of the Northern Cameroons would, in due course, have the opportunity to express their views freely on their future. When the appropriate time came, the United Kingdom would make proposals to the United Nations regarding such consultation.

The representative of France drew attention to the view expressed by the Trusteeship Council that the new statute for the Cameroons under French administration was a significant step towards the attainment of the objectives (see above, section on CAMEROONS UNDER FRENCH ADMINISTRATION). He emphasized the extent to which the elected representatives of the people had been consulted in the formulation of the statute and the fact that more than half of its provisions had been either drafted or radically revised by them. The new Cameroons Government, properly representative of the population, was as anxious as any petitioner to attain the objectives of trusteeship; the Prime Minister, for instance, had only recently reaffirmed that the objective sought was idependence. But it wished to be allowed to proceed to that end by stages. It would be for the people of the Cameroons themselves to decide their own future freely.

Pointing out that the disturbances of May 1955 and December 1956 had taken place in a single and relatively limited area, the representative of France explained that the amnesty bill introduced by the Government in the French National Assembly in August 1956 had had to be reviewed because of the second outbreak of disturbances and also because of the transfer of certain powers to the Cameroons Government. The bill had been resubmitted in amended form, and there was reason to hope that, unless prevented by fresh acts of terrorism, the desired measures could be put into effect in the near future.

The representative of France described the problem of the unification of the two Cameroons as an artificial one. To make unification a prior condition would only place further difficulties in the way of the attainment of the objectives of trusteeship, he said. The petitioners' proposal for a commission of inquiry was unacceptable, since both the United Nations Charter and the Trusteeship Agreement provided that visits should be arranged in agreement with the Administering Authority. A regular visiting mission of the Trusteeship Council was due to go to the Cameroons in 1958.

Under a draft resolution submitted by Ecuador, El Salvador, Haiti, Honduras, Japan, Pakistan and Uruguay, the Assembly would have: (1) transmitted the statements of the petitioners heard to the Trusteeship Council for further study; and (2) recommended that the Council take into account the observations and suggestions made during the current debate, and that it instruct its 1958 Visiting Mission to do likewise. It would also have expressed confidence that the application of appropriate measures (such as an amnesty law) would calm the situation in the disturbed area.

Under several amendments submitted by Afghanistan, Burma, Ceylon, Ghana, India, Indonesia and Nepal, by Syria, and by Guatemala, the draft resolution would also have included references to the questions of the Territories' attainment of independence and of the possible unification of the two Territories.

After some of these amendments had been adopted and others rejected, the seven-power draft resolution, as amended, was rejected by the Committee on a roll-call vote of 23 to 23, with 30 abstentions.

At a plenary meeting of the General Assembly, on 13 December 1957, Ecuador, Peru and Venezuela submitted a modified text of the original seven-power draft resolution, which was adopted by a roll-call vote of 57 to 0, with 17 abstentions, as resolution 1211(XII).

The Assembly thereby hoped that the application of appropriate measures, particularly the early promulgation of the amnesty law by the Administering Authority for the French Cameroons, and the renunciation of the use of violence by all parties would make it possible to achieve conditions in this Territory conducive to the early restoration of a normal situation in the disturbed area and to the furtherance of democratic progress and political activities in the Territory.

The Assembly was confident, too, that the appropriate steps to be taken by the Administering Authorities would further facilitate the realization in both Territories of the final objectives of the Trusteeship System, in accordance with the free expression of the wishes of the populations concerned, taking into account any alternative as to their future status.

The Assembly also transmitted the statements made to it by the petitioners to the Trusteeship Council for further study. It recommended, in addition, that the Council and its 1958 Visiting Mission take into account the observations made at the Assembly's twelfth session when they examined conditions in the two Cameroons Trust Territories.

DOCUMENTARY REFERENCES

GENERAL ASSEMBLY—12TH SESSION
Plenary Meeting 729.
Fourth Committee, meetings 652, 667, 668, 670, 683, 691, 692, 700, 701, 714-734, 736.

A/3595. Report of Trusteeship Council. Part II, Chapter V.
A/C.4/355 and Add.1-6. Requests for hearings.
A/C.4/372 and Add.1. Communications concerning Cameroons under British and Cameroons under French administration. Memorandum by Secretary-General.
A/C.4/L.512 and Corr.1, 2 and Rev.1-3. Ecuador, El Salvador, Haiti, Honduras, Japan, Pakistan, Uruguay draft resolution and revisions, as amended by Syria, Guatemala, and Ecuador, rejected by Fourth Committee by roll-call vote of 23 to 23, with 30 abstentions as follows:
In favour: Burma, Cambodia, Ceylon, Costa Rica, Cuba, Ecuador, El Salvador, Ethiopia, Ghana, Greece, Guatemala, Haiti, India, Federation of Malaya, Mexico, Nepal, Panama, Philippines, Poland, Tunisia, Uruguay, Venezuela, Yugoslavia.
Against: Australia, Austria, Belgium, Canada, Colombia, Denmark, Finland, France, Honduras, Iceland, Ireland, Israel, Italy, Luxembourg, Netherlands, New Zealand, Nicaragua, Norway, Portugal, Sweden, Turkey, United Kingdom, United States.
Abstaining: Afghanistan, Albania, Argentina, Brazil, Bulgaria, Byelorussian SSR, Chile, China, Czechoslovakia, Dominican Republic, Egypt, Hungary, Indonesia, Iran, Iraq, Japan, Lebanon, Liberia, Morocco, Pakistan, Peru, Romania, Saudi Arabia, Spain, Sudan, Syria, Thailand, Ukrainian SSR, USSR, Yemen.
A/C.4/L.516. Burma, Ceylon, Ghana, India, Indonesia, Nepal amendments to 7-power draft resolution, A/C.4/L.512 and Corr.1, 2.
A/C.4/L.516/Rev.1. Afghanistan, Burma, Ceylon, Ghana, India, Indonesia, Nepal revised amendments

to revised 7-power draft resolution, A/C.4/L.512/Rev.1.

A/C.4/L.516/Rev.2. Afghanistan, Burma, Ceylon, Ghana, India, Indonesia, Nepal revised amendments to revised 7-power draft resolution, A/C.4/L.512/Rev.3.

A/C.4/L.521. Syria amendments to revised 7-power draft resolution, A/C.4/L.512/Rev.1.

A/C.4/L.524. Philippines amendments to revised 7-power draft resolution, A/C.4/L.512/Rev.1.

A/C.4/L.526. Guatemala amendment to revised 7-power draft resolution, A/C.4/L.512/Rev.2.

A/3779. Report of Fourth Committee.

A/L.241. Ecuador, Peru, Venezuela draft resolution.

RESOLUTION 1211(XII), as submitted by Ecuador, Peru and Venezuela, A/L.241, adopted by Assembly on 13 December 1957, meeting 729, by roll-call vote of 57 to 0, with 17 abstentions as follows:

In favour: Afghanistan, Argentina, Australia, Austria, Belgium, Bolivia, Brazil, Cambodia, Canada, Ceylon, Chile, China, Colombia, Costa Rica, Cuba, Denmark, Dominican Republic, Ecuador, El Salvador, Finland, France, Greece, Guatemala, Honduras, India, Indonesia, Ireland, Israel, Italy, Japan, Laos, Liberia, Luxembourg, Federation of Malaya, Mexico, Nepal, Netherlands, New Zealand, Nicaragua, Norway, Pakistan, Panama, Paraguay, Peru, Philippines, Portugal, Spain, Sweden, Thailand, Tunisia, Turkey, United Kingdom, United States, Uruguay, Venezuela, Yemen, Yugoslavia.

Against: None.

Abstaining: Albania, Bulgaria, Burma, Byelorussian SSR, Czechoslovakia, Egypt, Ethiopia, Hungary, Iraq, Libya, Morocco, Poland, Romania, Saudi Arabia, Syria, Ukrainian SSR, USSR.

"*The General Assembly,*

"*Having studied* the chapters of the report of the Trusteeship Council which relate to the Trust Territories of the Cameroons under British administration and the Cameroons under French administration,

"*Noting* continued tensions and disturbances in a certain area of the Cameroons under French administration,

"*Noting* the fact that the amnesty law envisaged by the Administering Authority has not yet been promulgated,

"*Taking note* of the progress achieved in both Territories and of the measures to that effect adopted by the Administering Authorities and by the authorities of both Cameroons,

"*Having heard and considered* the statements of the petitioners from these Territories in the course of the hearings granted by the Fourth Committee,

"*Bearing in mind* that the Trusteeship Council will, in the normal course, send a visiting mission to the two Territories in 1958,

"1. *Takes note* of the pertinent chapters of the report of the Trusteeship Council;

"2. *Transmits* the statements of the petitioners to the Trusteeship Council for further study;

"3. *Recommends* that the Trusteeship Council take into account the observations and suggestions made during the debate in the Fourth Committee, when the Council considers conditions in the Trust Territories of the Cameroons under British administration and the Cameroons under French administration at its twenty-first session;

"4. *Expresses the hope* that, as a result of the application of appropriate measures, in particular the early promulgation of the amnesty law by the Administering Authority, and the renunciation of the use of violence by all political parties, it will be possible to achieve, in the Cameroons under French administration, conditions conducive to the early restoration of a normal situation in the disturbed area, and to the furtherance of democratic progress and political activities in the Territory;

"5. *Is confident* that the appropriate steps to be taken by the Administering Authorities will further facilitate the realization in both Territories of the final objectives of the Trusteeship System, in accordance with the free expression of the wishes of the populations concerned, taking into account any alternative relative to their future status;

"6. *Requests* the Trusteeship Council to instruct its next visiting mission, in 1958, to take into account the observations and suggestions made at the twelfth session of the General Assembly during the examination of the situation in the two Territories."

TOGOLAND UNDER FRENCH ADMINISTRATION

The destiny of the slightly more than one million people who inhabit Togoland under French administration was a major preoccupation of the United Nations organs concerned with Trusteeship matters during 1957.

Attention was concentrated principally on political matters, for the question of the termination of the Trusteeship Agreement had been raised by the Administering Authority in 1956. At the same time, the Territory was subject to the regular procedures of supervision by means of the examination in the Trusteeship Council of the annual report and of petitions concerning the Territory.

FUTURE OF THE TERRITORY
REPORT OF THE UNITED NATIONS COMMISSION

In 1956 and early 1957, neither the Trusteeship Council nor the General Assembly had found it possible to accept the Administering Authority's contention that the Trusteeship Agreement for Togoland should be terminated. In support of this contention, the Administering Authority had cited the statute granted to the

Territory under the French Government's decree of 24 August 1956, inaugurating the autonomous Republic of Togoland. It had also cited the results of a referendum held on 28 October 1956, under which the new statute had been endorsed by 71.51 per cent of the voters.

On 23 January 1957, at its eleventh session, the General Assembly decided (by resolution (1046(XI)) to send to the Territory a commission of six members (Canada, Denmark, Guatemala, Liberia, the Philippines and Yugoslavia) to examine the entire situation resulting from a practical application of the statute and the conditions under which it was being applied.

The Commission spent the period between 29 May and 30 June 1957 in Togoland, and held discussions in Paris as well. Its report, submitted to the Trusteeship Council, examined in detail the interpretation and application given to each article of the statute, which had been amended in certain respects by a further decree of 22 March 1957. It also described the prevailing political conditions.

The Commission concluded that, while there were still important restrictions by virtue of the retention of certain specified powers and competences by the Administering Authority, the statute had been broadly interpreted and liberally applied, and Togoland consequently possessed a large measure of internal autonomy or self-government. The Commission had little doubt that a trend of events had been set in motion which made inevitable a further broadening of the degree of autonomy achieved by Togoland towards its full autonomy, by means of the progressive transfer of more of the powers not yet within the competence of the Government of Togoland.

The future political evolution of the status of the Territory and its relationship with France should, in the Commission's opinion, be left open to be decided in accordance with the wishes of the people of Togoland. In the meantime, it might be desirable for Togoland to assume full responsibility for the modification of the statute as it affected the internal organization of the country. It might also be desirable to have the subjects reserved to France form part of a separate agreement between France and Togoland, with a procedure for its modification or termination.

The Commission held that the holding of elections by universal adult suffrage, which had not yet been applied in practice, would represent the implementation of an important democratic principle embodied in the statute and might help to create a more favourable political atmosphere. In addition, a special effort should be made to improve the situation concerning the exercise of political freedom.

Finally, and with specific regard to the termination of trusteeship, the Commission thought that, at an appropriate time, the people of the Territory would need to be consulted by appropriate means on their desires for the future status of the Territory. This consultation should, however, be undertaken in full agreement with the United Nations as one of the two parties to the Trusteeship Agreement.

CONSIDERATION BY TRUSTEESHIP COUNCIL

The Commission's report was discussed by the Trusteeship Council at its seventh special session (12–20 September 1957). By 9 votes to 0, with 5 abstentions, on 19 September 1957, the Council adopted a resolution on the basis of a proposal by the United States. By this resolution (1785(S-VII)), it expressed the opinion that the report, as well as statements which had been made on it by the representative of France and a representative of the Togoland Government, provided a useful and constructive basis for consideration and action by the General Assembly with a view to reaching a mutually satisfactory solution in accordance with the Charter and the Trusteeship Agreement. The Council also transmitted the report, together with the records of its own proceedings, to the Assembly in order to set in motion an appropriate procedure for the early attainment of the final objective of the Trusteeship System.

CONSIDERATION BY GENERAL ASSEMBLY

When the question was discussed by the Fourth Committee at the Assembly's twelfth session, representatives of the Togoland Government and leaders of the opposition parties, as well as the Minister for Overseas France and other representatives of the Administering Authority took part in the discussion.

The position taken at the outset of the debate by the representatives of France and of the Togoland Government was, in effect, as follows. The time was ripe for the emergence of the

Territory from trusteeship. This was so not only because of the extent of autonomy which it was enjoying and which had been confirmed by the Commission. It was also the case because any substantial extension of that autonomy, although intended, could not be carried out as long as the Territory remained under trusteeship and as long as the French Government accordingly remained bound by obligations to the United Nations.

Only three aspects of the situation remained to be settled, these representatives contended.

The first was the question of re-electing the Togoland legislature—in effect, an assembly elected by restricted suffrage in 1955—by means of universal adult suffrage. The Togoland Government was now prepared to agree to such elections in 1958 on the basis of an assurance that trusteeship would then be terminated.

The second question to be settled was the transfer of additional powers to Togoland. The French Government intended, on the termination of trusteeship, to transfer to Togoland the power to legislate in the field of public liberties, the judicial power and the power to modify the internal organization of the country.

The third matter to be settled was the future relationship between Togoland and France: it would be for the Republic of Togoland, once released from trusteeship, to choose, in agreement with the French Republic, the form of the relationship which would, or would not, join it to the French community as a whole.

A programme of action based on these conceptions was proposed. Under this, the existing Togoland legislature would examine and give its agreement to a modified text of the statute embodying the proposed additional transfer of powers. Then the legislature would be re-elected by universal adult suffrage. Thereafter, the modified statute would enter into force. Finally, and simultaneously with the first meeting of the new legislature, the trusteeship system would automatically come to an end.

During the ensuing debate, Canada, Colombia, Denmark, Ireland and Liberia advanced a draft resolution which, in its final form, envisaged the Togoland Legislative Assembly being elected by universal adult suffrage in 1958 and being asked to formulate, in consultation with the Administering Authority, "proposals for the early attainment of the final objective of the Trusteeship System". In view of the responsibilities of the new legislature, the General Assembly would accept an invitation to be made by the Government of Togoland for supervision of the elections by a commissioner to be appointed by the Assembly's President. The Trusteeship Council would then receive a report from the commissioner and information from the Administering Authority on the proposed transfer of powers, the results of the elections, the convening of the new legislature and any wishes which it might have expressed about the new statute and the termination of trusteeship. The Council would report on these matters to the General Assembly's thirteenth session to enable it, if so requested by the new Togoland Legislative Assembly and the Administering Authority, to reach a decision on ending the Trusteeship Agreement for the Territory in accordance with the Charter of the United Nations.

This draft resolution, said its sponsors, was based on the following time-table of events, with which they understood the French and Togoland Governments to be in agreement: (1) All powers now held by France, with the exception of those over defence, diplomacy and currency, would be transferred to Togoland. (2) After that, elections would be held in 1958 under United Nations supervision for a new Togoland Legislative Assembly. (3) The newly elected assembly and the Government would be free to make any proposals they wished as to the further modification of the statute and the termination of trusteeship. (4) Any such proposals would be communicated to the Trusteeship Council, which would report to the General Assembly. The latter would be free to accept or reject, depending on circumstances, any request for the termination of trusteeship.

The sponsors of the five-power draft felt, however, that such a request should not be denied if it were made after an adequate further transfer of powers had taken place and after elections had been satisfactorily carried out under supervision.

The representative of France pointed out that the holding of elections in advance of the normal date (1960) and the presence of international observers could only be justified by an understanding that the elections were a part of a procedure designed to lead to the termination of trusteeship.

In the view of other representatives, however, new elections by universal suffrage were a necessary step in the normal political development of the Territory and, in fact, in the full implementation of the existing statute. Some saw in the proposal for United Nations supervision an implication that the elections would be, in effect, a consultation on the question of terminating trusteeship. Others, however, did not share this view. The proposal for United Nations supervision was also regarded by some speakers as a means of ensuing that the elections in a Territory where prolonged political tensions had existed would be as free and as fair as possible.

These representatives also argued there could be no question of the General Assembly committing itself in any way, in advance, to the termination of trusteeship as a consequence of the steps envisaged. Further steps might still be necessary to bring the Territory to the final objective of trusteeship. Noting the assurances given by the sponsors of the draft resolution on the freedom to be left to the General Assembly in this respect, they considered that the position should be spelled out more clearly in the text.

To meet these points of view in part, Ecuador and Venezuela proposed an amendment to the five-power draft resolution stating that any decision which the General Assembly might be asked to take at its thirteenth session should be made "in the light of the circumstances then prevailing". The sponsors accepted this change.

Eleven Members—Burma, Ceylon, Ghana, Guatemala, Haiti, India, Indonesia, the Philippines, Syria, Uruguay and Yugoslavia—proposed an amendment, along with six other proposed changes—by which the Assembly at its thirteenth session would, without reference to any request from the Administering Authority or the Territory, "examine the entire situation in the light of the circumstances then prevailing". It would then decide on the attainment of the final objective of the International Trusteeship System and the consequent termination of the Trusteeship Agreement, in accordance with the Charter of the United Nations.

The United States orally proposed a sub-amendment whereby the General Assembly would be enabled, at the request of the parties specified in the draft resolution, "to reach a decision, in the light of the circumstances then prevailing, concerning the termination of the Trusteeship Agreement in accordance with Article 76b of the United Nations Charter".

The differences of view on this point were resolved in the Fourth Committee by the adoption of the United States sub-amendment by a roll-call vote of 40 to 9, with 27 abstentions.

Views were also divided on the arrangements for United Nations supervision of the elections to be held in 1958. Some representatives would have preferred a commission of three members to a single commissioner. They, and others, argued that the supervisory authority should, in any case, be elected by the General Assembly rather than appointed by its President.

A further amendment submitted by the 11 Members mentioned above incorporated both of these ideas. An oral sub-amendment by Peru, however, supported the principle of election but envisaged a single commissioner. This compromise was accepted by a roll-call vote of 28 to 15, with 13 abstentions.

Another of the 11-power amendments proposed in effect that, instead of keeping the commissioner "fully informed" of the arrangements for the organization and conduct of the elections, the French and Togoland authorities should make these arrangements "in consultation" with him. The sponsors of the five-power draft resolution accepted this change. A further amendment that the commissioner's report cover the organization, as well as the conduct and results of the election, was adopted by 39 votes to 15, with 16 abstentions.

The draft resolution as a whole, as amended, was approved by the Fourth Committee by a roll-call vote of 50 to 0, with 26 abstentions. It was adopted by the General Assembly at a plenary meeting on 29 November 1957 by a roll-call vote of 50 to 1, with 29 abstentions, as resolution 1182(XII).

On 14 December, the General Assembly, by secret ballot, elected Max H. Dorsinville, of Haiti, as the Commissioner to supervise the elections, in which task, as the resolution provided, he was to be assisted by observers and a staff to be appointed by the Secretary-General in consultation with him.

EXAMINATION OF CONDITIONS

In examining the annual report on conditions in Togoland under French administration at its nineteenth session (14 March–15 May 1957) the

Trusteeship Council did not formulate any conclusions or recommendations on political matters for inclusion in its regular report to the General Assembly. On economic, social and educational matters, however, the Council, in accordance with its usual procedure, made a number of observations and recommendations.

ECONOMIC ADVANCEMENT

The Council was encouraged by the results achieved under the 10-Year Plan for Economic and Social Development which was to end on 30 June 1957, and welcomed the information that a new plan would be put into effect immediately afterwards. While commending the Administering Authority for its continued financial assistance to the Territory, the Council hoped that, in formulating the new plan, it would bear in mind the need to increase productivity by all available means so as to strengthen the economy of the Territory as rapidly as possible. The Adminitering Authority, the Council also recommended, should ensure that representatives of the Territory took an active part in both the formulation and the execution of the new plan.

Although the total volume of Togoland's exports increased in 1955, their value fell substantially as a result of a decline in cocoa and coffee prices. The Council recommended that the Administering Authority intensify its efforts to protect the economy against fluctuations in prices for export crops, particularly by diversifying and improving its agricultural production.

The industrial enterprises of the Territory are still small in size and number, and the Council recommended that the Administering Authority should devote increasing efforts to expanding industrial activity, in particular by encouraging the establishment of processing industries for agricultural products. Noting with interest that the exploitation of the phosphate deposits in the Akoumapé area had begun and that surveys of deposits of chromium, iron and bauxite were being conducted, the Council hoped that the Administering Authority would continue to promote the exploitation of the mineral resources of the Territory. It also felt that the Administer-

ing Authority should take all appropriate measures to encourage and facilitate participation by the indigenous inhabitants in industrial and mining activities, and to ensure that the Territory derived the maximum benefit from the exploitation of its resources.

SOCIAL ADVANCEMENT

The Council recommended that the Administering Authority should intensify its efforts, through educational campaigns and by all other suitable means, to improve the social status of women and to eliminate polygamy and the bride-price system.

Further progress, the Council observed, had been made in the field of public health, but many improvements in the medical services were still needed, especially in the supply of skilled medical personnel and the geographical distribution of hospital services. The Council recommended that the Administering Authority intensify its efforts in this field.

EDUCATIONAL ADVANCEMENT

The number of children attending school showed a further increase, and there had been a relatively more rapid increase than previously in the enrolment of girls and in enrolments generally in the northern part of the Territory. The Council, recommended, however, that the goal of universal and compulsory education at the primary level should be energetically pursued. Efforts should be made to encourage students, particularly girls, who completed the primary stage of education to continue to the secondary stage, progress in which, though steady, had been slow.

The urgent need in the Territory for trained personnel led the Council to recommend that agricultural education, an important factor in the development of the main economic resources, should be encouraged. Further, special attention should be given to the development of vocational training, and, pending the establishment of higher education facilities in the Territory, every effort should be made to increase the number of scholarships for higher education.

DOCUMENTARY REFERENCES

FUTURE OF THE TERRITORY

TRUSTEESHIP COUNCIL—20TH SESSION AND 7TH SPE-
CIAL SESSION
Plenary Meetings 829, 841-847.

T/1336, Corr.1, Add.1, Add.1/Corr.1 and Add.2.
Report of United Nations Commission on Togoland
under French administration.
T/L.808 and Rev.1. United States draft resolution
and revision.
T/L.809. Draft special report of Trusteeship Council.
RESOLUTION 1785(s-VII), as submitted by United
States, T/L.808/Rev.1, and as orally revised by
United States, adopted by Council on 19 September
1957, meeting 846, by 9 votes to 0, with 5
abstentions.

"The Trusteeship Council,
"Having received the report of the United Nations
Commission on Togoland under French Administration, prepared pursuant to General Assembly resolution 1046(XI) of 23 January 1957,
"Having taken note of the presentation of the report
to the Council by the Chairman of the Commission,
"Having taken note of the statement of the representative of the Government of France and that of
the representative of the Government of Togoland,
"1. Expresses its appreciation to the members of
the United Nations Commission on Togoland under
French Administration for the unanimous and comprehensive report which they have submitted on the
situation in the Territory resulting from the practical
application of the new Statute and the conditions
under which it is being applied;
"2. Commends the Administering Authority for
broadly interpreting and liberally applying the Statute
of 24 August 1956, as modified on 22 March 1957;
"3. Notes with satisfaction the exercise by the
Togoland authorities of the powers transferred to
them under the Statute, and the intention of the
Togoland Government to hold new elections before
1960, on the basis of direct universal suffrage for a
new Legislative Assembly;
"4. Considers that the report, as well as the statements made before the Trusteeship Council at its
seventh special session, by the representative of the
Government of France and the representative of the
Government of Togoland, provides a useful and constructive basis for consideration and action by the
General Assembly with a view to reaching a mutually
satisfactory solution in accordance with the Charter
of the United Nations and the Trusteeship Agreement;
"5. Decides to transmit to the General Assembly
the report of the Commission, together with the
proceedings of the Trusteeship Council, in order to
set in motion an appropriate procedure for the early
attainment of the final objective of the Trusteeship
System."

GENERAL ASSEMBLY—12TH SESSION
Plenary Meetings 724, 727, 730.

Fourth Committee, meetings 651, 652, 655, 672, 694-
714, 717.
Fifth Committee, meeting 629.

A/3595 and Corr.1. Report of Trusteeship Council
to General Assembly, Part I, Chapter V.I, Part II,
Chapter VI.
A/3676 and Corr.1. Special report of Trusteeship
Council.
A/3677. Report of United Nations Commission on
Togoland under French administration (previously
distributed under symbol T/1336, Corr.1, Add.1,
Add.1/Corr.1 and Add.2).
A/C.4/354 and Add.1-4. Requests for hearings.
A/C.4/367. List of petitions and recommendations
concerning future of Togoland under French admin-
istration. Note by Secretary-General.
A/C.4/369. Statement by Chairman of United Na-
tions Commission on Togoland under French administration on 7 November 1957.
A/C.4/370. Statement by President of Legislative
Assembly of Togoland, member of French delegation, on 7 November 1957.
A/C.4/371. Statement by representative of France
on 7 November 1957.
A/C.5/L.508 and Rev.1. Canada, Colombia, Den-
mark, Ireland, Liberia draft resolution and revision,
adopted by Fourth Committee, as amended orally
and by 11-power joint amendments, A/C.4/L.510,
by roll-call vote of 50 votes to 0, with 26 absten-
tions, as follows:
In favour: Argentina, Australia, Austria, Belgium,
Brazil, Cambodia, Canada, Ceylon, Chile, China,
Colombia, Costa Rica, Cuba, Denmark, Dominican
Republic, Ecuador, El Salvador, Ethiopia, Finland,
France, Haiti, Honduras, Iceland, Iran, Ireland,
Israel, Italy, Japan, Lebanon, Liberia, Luxembourg,
Federation of Malaya, Mexico, Netherlands, New
Zealand, Nicaragua, Norway, Panama, Peru, Philip-
pines, Portugal, Spain, Sweden, Thailand, Tunisia,
Turkey, United Kingdom, United States, Uruguay,
Venezuela.
Against: None.
Abstaining: Afghanistan, Albania, Bulgaria, Burma,
Byelorussian SSR, Czechoslovakia, Egypt, Ghana,
Greece, Guatemala, Hungary, India, Indonesia,
Iraq, Jordan, Morocco, Nepal, Pakistan, Poland,
Romania, Sudan, Syria, Ukrainian SSR, USSR,
Yemen, Yugoslavia.
A/C.4/L.509. Ecuador and Venezuela amendment to
revised joint draft resolution.
A/C.4/L.510. Burma, Ceylon, Ghana, Guatemala,
Haiti, India, Indonesia, Philippines, Syria, Uruguay,
Yugoslavia amendments to revised joint draft
resolution.
A/3571. Report of Fourth Committee.
A/C.5/730, A/3758. Financial implications of draft
resolution adopted by the Fourth Committee.
Note by Secretary-General and report of Fifth
Committee.
RESOLUTION 1182(XII), as recommended by Fourth
Committee, A/3571, adopted by Assembly on 29

November 1957, meeting 724, by roll-call vote of 50 to 1, with 29 abstentions, as follows:

In favour: Argentina, Australia, Austria, Belgium, Brazil, Cambodia, Canada, Ceylon, Chile, China, Colombia, Costa Rica, Cuba, Denmark, Dominican Republic, Ecuador, El Salvador, Ethiopia, Finland, France, Haiti, Honduras, Iceland, Ireland, Israel, Italy, Japan, Laos, Lebanon, Liberia, Luxembourg, Federation of Malaya, Mexico, Netherlands, New Zealand, Nicaragua, Norway, Panama, Paraguay, Peru, Portugal, Spain, Sweden, Thailand, Tunisia, Turkey, United Kingdom, United States, Uruguay, Venezuela.

Against: Ghana.

Abstaining: Afghanistan, Albania, Bolivia, Bulgaria, Burma, Byelorussian SSR, Czechoslovakia, Egypt, Greece, Guatemala, Hungary, India, Indonesia, Iran, Iraq, Jordan, Libya, Morocco, Nepal, Pakistan, Poland, Romania, Saudi Arabia, Sudan, Syria, Ukrainian SSR, USSR, Yemen, Yugoslavia.

"The General Assembly,

"Bearing in mind the objectives of the International Trusteeship System as set forth in Article 76 of the Charter of the United Nations,

"Recalling its resolution 1046(XI) of 23 January 1957 concerning the future of Togoland under French administration,

"Having received from the Trusteeship Council, in accordance with the above-mentioned resolution, a special report transmitting the report of the United Nations Commission on Togoland under French Administration and the proceedings of the Council on the subject,

"Taking note of Trusteeship Council resolution 1785(S-VII) of 19 September 1957, in which the Council considers that the report, as well as the statements made before the Council at its seventh special session by the representative of the Government of France and the representative of the Government of Togoland, provides a useful and constructive basis for consideration and action by the General Assembly with a view to reaching a mutually satisfactory solution in accordance with the Charter of the United Nations and the Trusteeship Agreement, and decides to transmit to the General Assembly the report of the Commission, together with the proceedings of the Council, in order to set in motion an appropriate procedure for the early attainment of the final objective of the Trusteeship System,

"Taking note of the further statements made in the Fourth Committee on behalf of the Administering Authority and the Government of Togoland concerning, in particular, their proposals for the further political development of the Territory, including the transfer of all powers to the Togoland Government except defence, diplomacy and currency, and the renewal in 1958 by universal adult suffrage of the Legislative Assembly,

"Having heard, during the hearings granted by the Fourth Committee, the points of view expressed by the petitioners,

"1. *Expresses its appreciation* to the United Nations Commission on Togoland under French Administration for its valuable report and draws the attention of the Administering Authority and the Togoland Government to the observations and suggestions contained therein;

"2. *Notes* the statement of the Administering Authority that the Legislative Assembly to be elected by universal adult suffrage in 1958 and the Togoland Government will be asked to formulate, in consultation with the Administering Authority, proposals for the early attainment of the final objective of the Trusteeship System;

"3. *Accepts,* having regard to the responsibilities of the new Legislative Assembly mentioned in the preceding paragraph, the invitation of the Government of Togoland, transmitted by the Administering Authority, to make the necessary arrangements, in consultation with the Administering Authority, for supervision of the elections by the United Nations;

"4. *Decides* to elect a Commissioner who shall supervise the elections to the Legislative Assembly and who shall be assisted by observers and staff to be appointed by the Secretary-General in consultation with him;

"5. *Requests* the Administering Authority and the Government of Togoland to make, in consultation with the United Nations Commissioner, the arrangements for the organization and conduct of the elections to the Legislative Assembly;

"6. *Requests* the Commissioner to submit to the Trusteeship Council, for its consideration, and for transmission to the General Assembly at its thirteenth session, a report on the organization, conduct and results of the elections;

"7. *Invites* the Administering Authority to inform the Trusteeship Council concerning the carrying out of the above-mentioned transfer of powers, the results of the elections, the convening of the new Togoland Legislative Assembly, and regarding any wishes which may have been expressed by the Legislative Assembly concerning the new Statute and the termination of the Trusteeship Agreement for the Territory of Togoland under French Administration;

"8. *Requests* the Trusteeship Council to consider these matters and report thereon on the General Assembly at its thirteenth session, so as to enable it, if so requested by the new Togoland Legislative Assembly and the Administering Authority, to reach a decision, in the light of the circumstances then prevailing, concerning the termination of the Trusteeship Agreement in accordance with Article 76b of the Charter of the United Nations."

EXAMINATION OF CONDITIONS

TRUSTEESHIP COUNCIL—19TH AND 20TH SESSIONS
Plenary Meetings 770, 777-784, 786, 789, 792, 793, 805.

Rapport annuel du Gouvernement français à l'Assemblée générale des Nations Unies sur l'administration du Togo placé sous la tutelle de la France, année 1955. Paris, Imprimerie Chaix, 20, rue Bergère, 1956.

T/1300(A/3639). Note by Secretary-General transmitting report of France on administration of Togoland under French administration for year 1955.

T/1304/Add.1. Observations by UNESCO concerning annual reports for 1955.

T/L.740 and Add.1, T/L.762, T/L.775. Outline of conditions, report of Drafting Committee, and summary of observations. Chapter as a whole, T/L.740 and Add.1, T/L.762, T/L.775, adopted by Council on 4 June 1957, meeting 805, by 11 votes to 0, with 3 abstentions.

T/L.754 and Corr.1. India draft resolution.

T/L.755. India amendments to outline of conditions, T/L.740.

NEW GUINEA

The indigenous population of the Trust Territory of New Guinea, as of 30 June 1956, was estimated at some 1,274,000 persons. The non-indigenous community consisted of 9,827 Europeans, 2,543 Asians and 1,085 others. By 1956, the Administering Authority, Australia, had brought 76,100 of the Territory's total area of 93,000 square miles under administrative control. In the remainder of the Territory, it was continuing its policy of peaceful penetration and of consolidating its control and influence.

At its twentieth session (20 May–12 July 1957), the Trusteeship Council expressed satisfaction with the progress made and the programme drawn up to bring the Territory under full administrative control by 1959. It recommended that continued consideration be given to the question of an official name for the indigenous inhabitants.

POLITICAL ADVANCEMENT

The Trust Territory is administratively united with the adjacent Australian Territory of Papua, and two indigenous inhabitants of the Territory are appointed to the Legislative Council for Papua and New Guinea. The Trusteeship Council hoped that the Administering Authority would introduce more indigenous representation on the Legislative Council in the near future.

No additional local government councils had been established by 30 June 1957, but the number of villages under local government administration had increased.

The Council took note, with satisfaction, of the progress being made in extending local councils, and hoped that the Administering Authority would establish them in other areas. It also noted the substantial contribution which the councils were making towards the provision of their own public services.

Membership in district advisory councils and town advisory councils has been confined to Europeans and Asians, but recently an indigenous member has been appointed to a district advisory council. The Trusteeship Council hoped that similar appointments would be made to other district and town advisory councils.

In addition to continuing its reorganization of the departments of the Administration, the Administering Authority brought into operation an Auxiliary Division of the Public Service. The Council expressed satisfaction with these measures and hoped that vacancies in the Public Service would be filled in a reasonable period of time and that all eligible indigenous employees of the Administration would be absorbed into the Auxiliary Division.

Recalling previous recommendations on the need for granting legal recognition to indigenous tribunals, the Council noted that the Administering Authority's policy was to encourage the people to make more use of the existing judicial system. It requested the Administering Authority to keep it fully informed about the implementation of the policy of increasing indigenous participation in the administration within the present system of justice, and hoped that the Administering Authority would in the near future appoint indigenous persons as assessors to the Courts for Native Affairs.

ECONOMIC ADVANCEMENT

The Council noted with satisfaction the completion of a resources survey in one area in the Territory and hoped that similar surveys elsewhere would assist the Administering Authority in formulating flexible plans for economic development. The Council also noted the economic progress being made by the Territory and the role therein of the indigenous people. It hoped that the Administering Authority would continue to help indigenous commercial and trading activities. It commended the Administering Authority for implementing a plan to develop the fishing industry.

Territorial expenditures have substantially exceeded internal revenues, which are derived principally from import and export tariffs. The budget is balanced through a direct grant by the Administering Authority. A more extensive taxation system, the Council considered, should be found in order to increase local revenues, and it recalled a previous recommendation on the introduction of direct taxation in the Territory, taking into account the taxes paid by indigenous people to Local Government Councils.

The Council commended the Administering Authority for its efforts to develop indigenous agriculture through the introduction of new crops and the improvement of existing ones. It hoped that the Administering Authority would actively pursue its training programme for indigenous agricultural assistances.

The Council noted with satisfaction the continuing expansion of the co-operative movement.

The Council noted that the Administering Authority was making good progress in carrying out its road construction programme, and that it would continue to allocate large sums for road construction and maintenance. It noted with satisfaction the co-operation of the indigenous people, who provided a considerable proportion of labour and material required for the programme.

SOCIAL ADVANCEMENT

Indigenous inhabitants are required to obtain written permission to enter certain towns or be absent from their quarters in those towns between 11:00 P.M. and 5:00 A.M. The Council again recommended that the Administering Authority re-examine the need for maintaining these restrictions. It suggested that they be abolished immediately in a few towns on a trial basis.

The Council noted with satisfaction that substantial expenditures on health services and hospital construction had been made, and also that the Administering Authority had intensified its campaigns for the cure and prevention of malaria, tuberculosis and yaws.

EDUCATIONAL ADVANCEMENT

The great majority of schools in the Territory are conducted by missions. The Council noted with satisfaction that a revised system of grants-in-aid to missions had been established to raise the standards of their indigenous teachers and to ensure a greater concentration on the teaching of English. It expressed the hope that the Administering Authority would consider increasing the number of inspectors in the Department of Education. It suggested that the Administering Authority consider appointing suitable indigenous persons as members of the Education Advisory Board and to district education committees.

The Council noted with satisfaction that the number of Administration primary schools had risen considerably, as had the number of pupils attending these schools and the mission schools. It noted that a new section of the Department of Education was being established for the vocational and educational guidance of students from the Territory studying in secondary schools in Australia. The Council hoped that the Administering Authority would continue to consider the possibility of a full secondary school system in the Territory in the near future.

PROGRESS TOWARDS SELF-GOVERNMENT OR INDEPENDENCE

The Council noted that although the Administering Authority considered rigid targets and dates in all fields of development impracticable, it proposed to bring the Territory under full administrative control by 1959. In addition, plans for the development of cash crops and the fishing industry were being executed, and a resources survey had been completed in one area. The Council also noted certain recent developments (see above). It hoped that the Administering Authority would continue to adopt plans where appropriate, with target dates, wherever it was satisfied that the use of this procedure for any aspect of development would help to promote the objectives of the Trusteeship System.

DOCUMENTARY REFERENCES

TRUSTEESHIP COUNCIL—20TH SESSION
Plenary Meetings 822-829, 831, 838, 840.

Commonwealth of Australia: Report to General

Assembly of United Nations on Administration of Territory of New Guinea from 1st July 1955 to 30th June 1956. A. J. Arthur, Commonwealth Government Printer, Canberra.

T/1326(A/3633). Note by Secretary-General transmitting report of Australia on administration of Trust Territory of New Guinea for period 1 July 1955–30 June 1956.

T/L.776 and Add.1, T/L.799, T/L.803. Outline of conditions, report of Drafting Committee, and summary of observations of Council members. Chapter as a whole on New Guinea, T/L.776 and Add.1, T/L.799, as amended, and T/L.803, adopted unanimously by Council on 12 July 1957, meeting 840.

T/L.786. Report of Standing Committee on Administrative Unions, Part II.

T/L.807. Guatemala, India, Syria amendments to conclusions and recommendations proposed by Drafting Committee.

A/3595 and Corr.1. Report of Trusteeship Council to General Assembly, Part II, Chapter VIII.

See also DOCUMENTARY REFERENCES to CHAPTER III, above, section on EXAMINATION OF THE ANNUAL REPORTS FROM ADMINISTERING AUTHORITIES.

WESTERN SAMOA

The islands forming the Trust Territory of Western Samoa had a total population of 97,327 in 1956. During its twentieth session (20 May–12 July 1957), the Trusteeship Council commended the Administering Authority (New Zealand) and the Samoan people for the harmonious manner in which they were co-operating towards the implementation of the constitutional reforms in the Territory.

POLITICAL ADVANCEMENT

The first of the three distinctive steps towards full cabinet government on which the Administering Authority and the Samoan people had agreed upon was taken in September 1956. In accordance with the Samoa Amendment Act, 1956, the Executive Council was enlarged by the addition of two members.

The Trusteeship Council noted with satisfaction that the elected members of the Executive Council, including the four Samoan members, had been allotted responsibility for particular goverment Departments. A further step in the envisaged constitutional development, the Council noted, would be the elections later in 1957 for a new and enlarged legislature, consisting of 48 members, to replace the present Legislative Assembly and the *Fono of Faipule,* the traditional body of district representatives.

The Council reiterated the hope that the Administering Authority would find it possible progressively to enlarge the competence of the legislature.

In noting with satisfaction that the District and Village Government Board had participated in the work of defining the administrative districts established in 1956 the Council expressed the hope that the findings would soon provide a basis for the early establishment of district councils.

During 1956, the Samoan Status Committee recommended the introduction of legislation concerning Samoan citizenship and domestic status. The Council hoped that the new legislation would provide a solution to the question of the common status of the inhabitants in the near future.

The Council, informed that its views on suffrage had been brought to the attention of the Samoans, reiterated the hope that the Samoans would come to accept adult suffrage for the whole Territory as soon as possible.

The Council noted with satisfaction that Samoan participation in positions of responsibility had increased during 1956 and that the ratio of Samoans in senior positions would increase progressively. It considered, however, that further efforts should be made to accelerate the training of Samoans for senior positions and recommended that the Administering Authority consider sending more Samoans to New Zealand to gain administrative experience.

ECONOMIC ADVANCEMENT

The Council expressed its satisfaction over various measures taken for the economic development of the Territory. It reiterated a previous recommendation that the Administering Authority draw up an over-all, long-term development plan in co-operation with representatives of the Samoans, taking fully into account the outcome of the technical surveys which were being conducted.

Noting that a survey had been conducted on the Territory's banking needs, the Council hoped that the Administering Authority would encourage the development of a suitable banking system.

During 1956 an income tax was introduced. The Council hoped that initial difficulties attending its introduction would soon be overcome, and that it would be possible to find additional ways and means of increasing revenues of the territory.

The Council commended the Administering Authority on its transfer of the New Zealand Reparation Estates to the Western Samoa Trust Estates Corporation.

Co-operative societies increased from seven in 1955 to 29 in 1957. The Council congratulated the Administering Authority and the Samoans for this marked growth and hoped for further progress.

The Land Use Committee made recommendations to the Territorial Government on a policy for the settlement and development of government land, but no substantial change was made in the existing system of land tenure and use. The Council hoped that the Committee would continue its work, and also that the powers of the Legislative Assembly with regard to land legislation would be increased.

SOCIAL ADVANCEMENT

Provisions for the establishment of wages councils and the inauguration of a trade training scheme were noted with satisfaction by the Trusteeship Council. It hoped that these councils would be established in the near future. It also hoped that the Administering Authority would give encouragement to skilled workers to remain in the Territory. It again pointed out the need for labour legislation for the protection of workers and hoped that steps would be taken to encourage the creation of trade unions in the Territory.

The Council expressed satisfaction concerning improvements in public health. It hoped that the progress reported by the Administering Authority would be maintained in acquiring adequate medical personnel and that scholarships, training courses and facilities in the field of health would continue to be made available to Samoans.

It also welcomed statements that the major part of the campaign against yaws, conducted under the auspices of the World Health Organization (WHO) and the United Nations Children's Fund (UNICEF), had been completed and that the Administering Authority was seeking the assistance of WHO for a major campaign against tuberculosis in 1959.

EDUCATIONAL ADVANCEMENT

The Council commended the Administering Authority for the progress made in education. It hoped that the proposed education bill would result in free compulsory primary education in the Territory at an early date. It welcomed the current extension of secondary education facilities and recommended the establishment of a vocational training centre at the earliest possible moment.

The Council noted that while there were no institutions of higher education in the Territory, an increasing number of Samoans were graduating from foreign universities. The Council also noted a statement of the Administering Authority that it would continue to provide adequate funds for scholarships to students at institutions of higher learning abroad. It hoped that the Administering Authority would give due consideration to further extending fellowship and scholarship programmes.

No special institutions exist for the encouragement of indigenous arts and crafts, but these arts and crafts are fostered in Government schools. The Council hoped the Administering Authority would continue its efforts to develop popular arts and culture through the establishment of suitable institutions.

PROGRESS TOWARDS SELF-GOVERNMENT OR INDEPENDENCE

The first of the three steps contemplated for the attainment of full cabinet government in Western Samoa was taken in 1956, when, as has been noted, the member system was introduced. The Administering Authority expected that the second step—the establishment of a ministerial government with a Premier presiding over the Council of Ministers and leading the legislature—would be taken in 1960.

The Council expressed its satisfaction that the first step noted above had been successfully carried out as scheduled and that the second was likely to be taken in accordance with the established time-table. It was confident that the third stage of the plan of constitutional development would be completed according to the schedule. It also noted that the timing of the next significant step—a change in the status of the New Zealand representative and the assumption by the Head of State of the proper functions of that office—would subsequently be discussed between the new Government of Western Samoa and the Government of New Zealand.

The Council hoped that similar developments would take place in other fields.

DOCUMENTARY REFERENCES

TRUSTEESHIP COUNCIL—20TH SESSION
Plenary Meetings 828-835, 839, 840.·

Report by New Zealand Government to General Assembly of United Nations on Administration of Western Samoa for Calendar Year 1956. Wellington, New Zealand, R.E. Owen, Government Printer, 1957.

T/1330 and Add.1 (A/3640). Note by Secretary-General transmitting report of New Zealand on administration of Trust Territory of Western Samoa for year 1956.

T/L.781 and Add.1, T/L.805; T/L.806. Outline of conditions, report of Drafting Committee, and summary of observations. Chapter as a whole, T/L.781 and Add.1, T/L.805, as amended, and T/L.806, adopted unanimously by Council on 12 July 1957, meeting 840.

A/3595 and Corr.1. Report of Trusteeship Council to General Assembly, Part II, Chapter VII.

See also DOCUMENTARY REFERENCES to CHAPTER III, above, section on EXAMINATION OF THE ANNUAL REPORTS FROM ADMINISTERING AUTHORITIES.

NAURU

Nauru, the smallest of the Trust Territories, is an island in the central Pacific with an area of about 8 square miles. Its population in 1956 consisted of 1,976 Nauruans, 286 Europeans, 696 Chinese and 935 other Pacific Islanders.

The entire economy of Nauru is based on its phosphate deposits. Since these will be exhausted in the foreseeable future, attempts have been made to find an area suitable for the resettlement of the Nauruans who have been kept informed of the action taken concerning their future.

At its twentieth session (20 May–12 July 1957), the Council noted the efforts of the Administering Authority to find a solution to the problem of the future of the Nauruan community, particularly the creation of a special committee of the Nauru Local Government Council to consider the question. It recommended that the Administering Authority continue its efforts and that it submit concrete proposals for the solution of the problem in accordance with the wishes of the Nauruans and in conformity with the provisions of the United Nations Charter and the Trusteeship Agreement.

POLITICAL ADVANCEMENT

There is no indigenous representation in the executive organ of government in Nauru. Although the Nauru Local Government Council has full legislative powers concerning local government, its powers in the territorial field are only consultative. The Trusteeship Council reiterated its previous recommendation that the Administering Authority continue to encourage the Local Government Council to exercise its powers increasingly so as to make it possible to grant it additional powers and in order to accelerate the progressive development of a legislative organ with powers in accordance with the provisions of Article 76b of the United Nations Charter.

The Council noted with satisfaction that elections are held by direct, universal adult suffrage with a secret ballot. It considered, however, that the electoral laws could be further improved.

All leading posts except one in the Administration of the Territory—and also in the phosphate-mining industry—still remain in the hands of non-indigenous persons. The Council recommended that the Administering Authority continue its efforts to develop and implement its training programmes now being actively pursued to provide Nauruans with the required technical knowledge, so that more of them could be appointed as soon as possible to responsible posts in the Administration and on the staff of the British Phosphate Commissioners.

The Council expressed its satisfaction that a new Judiciary Ordinance which was under consideration would provide for complete separation between the executive and judiciary.

ECONOMIC ADVANCEMENT

As the economy of the Territory continued to be based entirely on the phosphate industry, the Council hoped that current efforts to develop a fishing industry and to find suitable water supplies with which to increase the limited agricultural potential would be vigorously pursued.

The Council noted that a request by the Nauru Local Government Council for an increase in the royalty rates on phosphate was being considered by the Administering Authority. It considered that full information specifically relating to the operations of the British Phosphate Commissioners in Nauru would be of great assistance in assessing the question, and recommended that the Administering Authority submit such information.

Although the Administering Authority stated that the British Phosphate Commissioners exerted no influence on the budget of the Territory, the Council was concerned lest the present system of direct payments by the Commissioners to cover the expenses of the territorial Administration might lead to the exercise of such influence. It suggested that the Administering Authority review the present arrangements with a view to removing any such possibility.

Nauruans have petitioned for the return to them of an area of land on which a wireless station was formerly located and also the land now used for an airstrip. The Council noted that these matters were being investigated and requested the Administering Authority for information about the air traffic which was expected to use the airstrip.

SOCIAL DEVELOPMENT

The Council hoped that the Administering Authority would increase its efforts to raise the capacity and skill of workers in order to ensure the effective application of the principle of equal pay for equal work and to raise the standard of living still further. It also considered that the Administering Authority should encourage the British Phosphate Commissioners to establish an equal work week for all groups engaged in phosphate extraction.

The Council noted with satisfaction the progress made in providing houses for Nauruans, and the Administering Authority's intention to place housing under the jurisdiction of the local Government Council.

The Trusteeship Council also expressed its satisfaction with the progress which had been achieved, in the field of public health. It noted particularly the completion of the new Administration hospital, the training of Nauruan

medical personnel and the increase in the medical staff. It hoped that the Administering Authority would continue to develop the medical services, taking appropriate measures to train qualified Nauruan personnel and to increase their number holding responsible posts. It further noted the initiation of a campaign against tuberculosis which it hoped would be pursued, particularly by means of health education.

EDUCATIONAL ADVANCEMENT

In commending the Administering Authority for the progress made in education, the Council noted that all children of school age were attending school, and that the recent reorganization of the primary schools was resulting in an improvement of teaching standards and of teacher training. It hoped that the Administering Authority would develop in the Territory a full course of secondary education, and, in view of the fact that up to now no Nauruan had received a higher education, recommended that the Administering Authority would provide Nauruan students with higher education.

The Council endorsed a suggestion by the United Nations Educational, Scientific and Cultural Organization that the Administering Authority include in future annual reports more detailed information on the progress made in the certification of untrained Nauruan teachers. The Council expressed the hope that the Administering Authority would consider providing inducements to encourage qualified teachers to remain in their profession in the Territory.

PROGRESS TOWARDS SELF-GOVERNMENT OR INDEPENDENCE

The Administering Authority informed the Council it was still unable to furnish an estimate of the period required for the attainment by the Territory of self-government or independence. Apart from objections in principle this was due to: (a) difficulties in stimulating the Nauruans to participate in the affairs of the Territory, particularly in the political field; (b) uncertainty about the Territory's economic potential; and (c) the question of the possible resettlement of the Nauruan community.

The Council noted these views. It observed that the phosphate deposits were likely to be exhausted in 40 years, and that the Administing Authority, in continuous consultation with the Nauruans, was considering the possibility of evacuating them to another area. In this connexion, the Council considered that the wishes of the Nauruans regarding their future would have to be ascertained at an appropriate time.

The Council hoped that the Administering Authority would continue to adopt plans, when appropriate with target dates, whenever it was satisfied that this procedure in any aspect of development would help in attaining the objectives of the Trusteeship System.

DOCUMENTARY REFERENCES

TRUSTEESHIP COUNCIL—20TH SESSION
Plenary Meetings 805-810, 813, 837, 838, 840.

Commonwealth of Australia: Report to General Assembly of United Nations on Administration of Territory of Nauru from 1st July 1955 to 30th June 1956. A. J. Arthur, Commonwealth Government Printer, Canberra.

T/1312(A/3622). Note by Secretary-General transmitting report of Australia on administration of Trust Territory of Nauru for period 1 July 1955– 30 June 1956.

T/1324. Observations of UNESCO.

T/L.771 and Add.1, T/L.795, T/L.802. Outline of conditions, report of Drafting Committee, and summary of observations. Chapter as a whole, T/L.771 and Add.1, T/L.795, as amended, and T/L.802, adopted unanimously by Council on 12 July 1957, meeting 840.

T/L.798. Italy amendments to draft conclusions and recommendations prepared by Drafting Committee.

T/L.804. India amendment to draft separate section prepared by Drafting Committee.

A/3595 and Corr.1. Report of Trusteeship Council to General Assembly, Part II, Chapter IX.

See also DOCUMENTARY REFERENCES to CHAPTER III, above, section on EXAMINATION OF ANNUAL REPORTS.

TRUST TERRITORY OF THE PACIFIC ISLANDS

The Trust Territory of the Pacific Islands, covers a total land area of 687 square miles, spread over some 3 million square miles of ocean. Its population in 1956 was reported to total 65,039 persons.

During its twentieth session (20 May–12 July 1957), the Trusteeship Council commended both the Administering Authority (the United States) and the Micronesian people for the general progress which had been achieved in the Trust Territory during the year under review.

The Council noted with satisfaction that the people of Rongelap, who had suffered ill effects from nuclear experiments in 1954, would be returning to their island in the immediate future. It asked the Administering Authority for detailed information on their resettlement in its next annual report. It noted with interest that a settlement had been arrived at to compensate the former residents of Bikini and Eniwetok for having been displaced in 1946–1947 because of nuclear tests and wished to see the full text of this agreement.

POLITICAL ADVANCEMENT

In August 1956, a Micronesian leaders' conference, with participants elected by representative organs in each district of the Territory, was held in Guam; a similar conference was scheduled for 1957. The Council hoped that the Administering Authority's policy of encouraging such conferences would constitute an important step towards the promotion of a territorial consciousness.

The Council commended the Administering Authority for the manner in which it was encouraging the indigenous inhabitants to participate in local government and welcomed the granting of an official charter to a district congress and the Administering Authority's efforts to increase the political activity of the municipalities.

The features of the present organization of the Territory which limit the possibility of a centralized administration are: (a) the location of the headquarters of the Territory on Guam, outside the Trust Territory; (b) the location in different districts of some of the central administrative departments; (c) the fact that the Saipan district is under the immediate authority of the United States Navy. The Council again expressed the opinion that a move of headquarters from Guam to a site within the Territory would make it possible to further centralize the administration of the entire Territory under a single civilian authority, and it recommended that the Administering Authority should continue to examine this question.

The Council noted with interest the completion of the conversion programme of American personnel to the United States Civil Service. It reiterated its approval of the Administering Authority's policy of appointing an increasing number of adequately trained Micronesians to responsible positions in the Administration.

ECONOMIC ADVANCEMENT

The Council noted with interest that a tax study had recently been conducted in the Territory and that the Administering Authority would now find it possible to raise revenues through direct taxation. Recalling a previous observation that in spite of the substantial contribution made by the Administering Authority to the budget of the Territory, even greater subsidies might be needed for speeding up development programmes, the Council urged the Administering Authority to develop the resources of the Territory by all possible means.

The Council noted with satisfaction the efforts made by the Administering Authority to establish agricultural experimental and demonstration stations in the Territory and to recruit additional agricultural specialists. It recommended that vigorous efforts be made to accelerate the homesteading programme with a view to bringing additional land under cultivation.

The Council noted with satisfaction the settlement of all land claims in one district and hoped that all outstanding claims in other districts would be settled as soon as possible.

The Council recalled a previous recommendation for the promotion of industrial development in the Territory.

The Council expressed its satisfaction at the effective functioning of the Copra Stabilization Fund, and at the intention of the Administering Authority to examine the possibility of having Micronesian representatives on the Copra Stabilization Board.

The Council recommended that the Administering Authority continue to devote its closest attention to improving the shipping facilities of the Territory, and hoped that it would train Micronesian personnel to assume more responsibility in the Territory's transport system.

SOCIAL ADVANCEMENT

The Council commended the Administering Authority for its efforts in the field of public health, and particularly for having initiated a Territory-wide BCG vaccination programme, and for having appointed Micronesians to responsible positions.

EDUCATIONAL ADVANCEMENT

The Council noted with satisfaction the progress made in the field of education. It noted that the problem of raising and standardizing elementary school teachers' salaries was receiving the attention of the local legislative bodies. It hoped that teachers' salaries might reach an adequate level in the near future.

PROGRESS TOWARDS SELF-GOVERNMENT OR INDEPENDENCE

At its eighteenth session, the Council had recommended that the Administering Authority continue to keep it informed about successive intermediate targets and dates in the political, economic, social and educational fields, and of the measures taken with a view to creating the conditions necessary for the attainment of self-government or independence. At its twentieth session, the Council noted that the development of representative bodies, local government institutions and the participation of indigenous persons in the administration appeared to be in conformity with this recommendation. It hoped that this method of development would be extended to other fields.

DOCUMENTARY REFERENCES

TRUSTEESHIP COUNCIL—20TH SESSION
Plenary Meetings 801-806, 808, 832, 834, 840.

Ninth Annual Report to United Nations on Administration of Trust Territory of Pacific Islands, 1 July 1955 to 30th June 1956. Transmitted by United States of America to United Nations Pursuant to Article 88 of Charter of United Nations. Department of State Publication 6457. International Organization and Conference Series III, 120. Washington 25, D.C., U.S. Government Printing Office, 1957.

T/1316(S/3828). Note by Secretary-General transmitting report of United States on Trust Territory of Pacific Islands for period 1 July 1955–30 June 1956.

T/1323. Observations of UNESCO.

T/L.769 and Add.1, T/L.780, T/L.800. Outline of conditions, report of Drafting Committee, and summary of observations. Chapter as a whole, T/L.769

and Add.1, T/L.780, as amended, and T/L.800, adopted unanimously by Council on 12 July 1957, meeting 840.

T/L.789. India amendment to report of Drafting Committee.

T/L.790. Draft report of Trusteeship Council to Security Council.

S/3852. Report of Trusteeship Council to Security Council on Trust Territory of Pacific Islands covering period from 2 August 1956 to 12 July 1957.

Legal Questions

CHAPTER I

THE INTERNATIONAL COURT OF JUSTICE

CASE OF CERTAIN NORWEGIAN LOANS (FRANCE *vs.* NORWAY)

On 6 July 1957, the International Court of Justice delivered its judgement in the Norwegian Loans case, brought before the Court in July 1955 by an application of the French Republic against the Kingdom of Norway. Certain preliminary objections by the latter to the jurisdiction of the Court had, at the request of France and with the concurrence of Norway, been joined to the merits by an order of the Court of 28 September 1956.[1]

In its judgement the Court recalled the facts. The loans in question had been floated between 1885 and 1909. The French Government in its application contended that the bonds contained a gold clause which varied in form from bond to bond, but which that Government regarded as sufficient in the case of each bond. This view was disputed by the Norwegian Government. The convertibility into gold of notes of the Bank of Norway had been suspended on various dates since 1914. A Norwegian law of 15 December 1923 provided that:

Where a debtor has lawfully agreed to pay in gold a pecuniary debt in kroner and where the creditor refuses to accept payment in Bank of Norway notes on the basis of their nominal gold value, the debtor may request a postponement of payment for such period as the Bank is exempted from its obligation to redeem its notes in accordance with their nominal value.

Protracted diplomatic correspondence ensued. It lasted from 1925 to 1955. The French Government contended that a unilateral decision could not be relied upon as against foreign creditors and requested the recognition of the rights claimed by the French holders of the bonds involved. The Norwegian Government, not being prepared to agree to the various proposals for international settlement put for-ward by France, maintained that the claims of the bondholders were within the jurisdiction of the Norwegian courts and involved solely the interpretation and application of Norwegian law. The French bondholders refrained from submitting their case to the Norwegian courts. It was in these circumstances that the French Government referred the matter to the Court.

Such being the facts, the Court at the outset directed its attention to the preliminary objections of the Norwegian Government, beginning with the first of these objections which related directly to the jurisdiction of the Court and which had two aspects. In the first place, it was contended that the Court could be seized, by means of a unilateral application, only of legal disputes falling within one of the four categories of disputes enumerated in paragraph 2 of Article 36 of the Statute of the Court and relating to the international law. In the view of the Norwegian Government, the loan contracts were governed by municipal law and not by international law. In the second place, the Norwegian Government declared that, if there should still be some doubt on this point, it would rely upon the reservation made in the following terms by the French Government in its declaration accepting the compulsory jurisdiction of the Court: "This declaration does not apply to differences relating to matters which are essentially within the national jurisdiction as understood by the Government of the French Republic."

[1] See also *Case of Certain Norwegian Loans, Orders of April 24th, May 29th and September 28th, 1956: I.C.J. Reports, 1956*, pp. 18, 20 and 73. See also *Y.U.N. 1956*, p. 378.

The Norwegian Government considered that, by virtue of the clause of reciprocity (embodied in Article 36, paragraph 3, of the Statute and contained in the corresponding Norwegian declaration), Norway had the right to rely upon the restrictions placed by France on its own undertakings. Convinced that the dispute fell within its domestic jurisdiction, the Norwegian Government asked the Court to decline, on grounds that it lacked jurisdiction, the function which the French Government would have it assume.

The Court considered the second ground of this objection and noted that the jurisdiction of the Court in the present case depended upon the declarations made by the parties on condition of reciprocity, and that since two unilateral declarations were involved, such jurisdiction was conferred upon the Court only to the extent to which the declarations coincided in conferring it. Consequently, the common will of the parties which was the basis of the Court's jurisdiction, existed within the narrower limits indicated by the French reservation. In accordance with the condition of reciprocity, Norway, equally with France, was entitled to except from the compulsory jurisdiction of the Court disputes understood by Norway to be essentially within its national jurisdiction.

The French Government argued that there existed between France and Norway a treaty which made the payment of any contractual debt a question of international law, and that, in this connexion, the two States could not therefore speak of domestic jurisdiction. But, in the opinion of the Court, the aim of the treaty referred to, the Second Hague Convention of 1907 respecting the limitation of the employment of force for the recovery of contract debts, was not to introduce compulsory arbitration; the only obligation imposed by the Convention was that an intervening Power should not have the recourse to force before it had tried arbitration. The Court could, therefore, find no reason why the fact that the two parties were signatories to the Second Hague Convention should deprive Norway of the right to invoke the reservation in the French declaration. The French Government also referred to the Franco-Norwegian Arbitration Convention of 1904 and to the General Act of Geneva of 26 September 1928.

Neither of these references, however, was regarded as sufficient by the Court to justify the view that the application of the French Government was based upon the Convention or the General Act. In this respect, the Court considered that it would not be justified in seeking a basis for its jurisdiction different from that which the French Government itself had set out in its application and by reference to which the case had been presented by both parties.

The Court noted that, from one point of view, it might be said that the ground of the first objection which was based on the reservation in the French declaration was solely subsidiary in character. But, in the opinion of the Court, the second ground could not be regarded as subsidiary, in the sense that Norway would invoke the French reservation only in the event of the first ground of this objection being held to be legally unfounded.

The Court's competence was challenged on both grounds and the Court was free to base its decision on the ground which in its judgement was more direct and conclusive. Not only did the Norwegian Government invoke the French reservation, but it maintained the second ground of its first objection throughout. Abandonment could not be presumed or inferred; it had to be declared expressly.

The Court did not consider that it should examine whether the French reservation was consistent with the undertaking of a legal obligation and was compatible with Article 36, paragraph 6, of the Court's Statute. The validity of the reservation had not been questioned by the parties. It was clear that France fully maintained its declaration including the reservation, and that Norway relied upon the reservation. In consequence, the Court had before it a provision which both parties to the dispute regarded as constituting an expression of their common will relating to the competence of the Court. The Court gave effect to the reservation as it stood and as the parties recognized it.

For these reasons, the Court, by 12 votes to 3, found that it was without jurisdiction to adjudicate upon the dispute which had been brought before it by the application of the French Government.

Judge Moreno Quintana appended to the judgement a declaration stating that he considered that the Court was without jurisdiction for a reason different from that given in the judgement. Vice-President Badawi and Judge Sir Hersch Lauterpacht appended statements of their individual opinions. Judges Guerrero, Basdevant and Read appended statements of their dissenting opinions.

DOCUMENTARY REFERENCE

Case of Certain Norwegian Loans, Judgment of July 6th, 1957: I.C.J. Reports 1957, p. 9.

CASE CONCERNING RIGHT OF PASSAGE OVER INDIAN TERRITORY: PRELIMINARY OBJECTIONS (PORTUGAL *vs.* INDIA)[2]

On 26 November 1957, the Court delivered its judgement on the six preliminary objections raised by India to the jurisdiction of the Court in the case concerning right of passage over Indian territory. The case had been commenced by an application filed in the Registry of the Court by Portugal on 22 December 1955.

In its judgement, the Court examined the preliminary objections to its jurisdiction one by one.

FIRST PRELIMINARY OBJECTION

The first of these objections was to the effect that the Portuguese declaration of acceptance of the compulsory jurisdiction of the Court, dated 19 December 1955, was invalid as the third condition attached to it was incompatible with the object and purpose of the optional clause (Article 36, paragraph 2, of the Statute of the Court). This condition provided that:

The Portuguese Government reserves the right to exclude from the scope of the present declaration, at any time during its validity, any given category or categories of disputes, by notifying the Secretary-General of the United Nations and with effect from the moment of such notification.

In the first place, it was contended by India that the condition gave Portugal the right, by making at any time a notification to that effect, to withdraw from the jurisdiction of the Court a dispute which had been submitted to it prior to such notification. India also asserted that such retroactive effect was incompatible with the notion of compulsory jurisdiction under the optional clause. The Court considered that the words "with effect from the moment of such notification" in the Portuguese condition, construed in their ordinary sense, could not be taken to mean that such notification would have a retroactive effect.

In the second place, India claimed that the Portuguese condition was incompatible with the optional clause as it left other signatories in a continuous state of uncertainty as to reciprocal rights and obligations, which might change from day to day. The Court pointed out that, under the Statute, declarations and their alterations had to be deposited with the Secretary-General, and, as a consequence, when a case was submitted to the Court, it was always possible, at that moment, to ascertain the reciprocal obligations of the parties in accordance with their declarations. The Court stated that, while there might be a delay between the date of notification to the Secretary-General and its receipt by the parties to the Statute, which could result in some uncertainty, such uncertainty was inherent in the operation of the system of the optional clause and did not affect the validity of the third condition contained in the Portuguese declaration.

Finally, India argued that the Portuguese condition offended against the basic principle of reciprocity underlying the optional clause inasmuch as it claimed for Portugal a right which was in effect denied to other signatories who had made a declaration without appending any such condition. The Court stated it was not able to accept this contention, as it was clear that any reservation notified by Portugal in pursuance of its third condition became automatically operative against it in relation to other signatories of the optional clause.

For these reasons, by 14 votes to 3, the Court rejected the first preliminary objection.

SECOND PRELIMINARY OBJECTION

On 19 December 1955, the representative of Portugal to the United Nations made the

[2] See also *Y.U.N., 1956,* p. 378.

declaration on behalf of his Government accepting the compulsory jurisdiction of the Court under the optional clause.

On 22 December 1955, the application by Portugal instituting proceedings against India was filed in the Registry of the Court.

On 19 January 1956, the Secretary-General, in compliance with paragraph 4 of Article 36 of the Statute of the Court, officially transmitted to the Government of India a copy of the Portuguese declaration.

India contended' that Portugal had commenced proceedings before the lapse of such brief period as in the normal course of events would have enabled the Secretary-General to transmit copies of the Portuguese declaration accepting compulsory jurisdiction to other parties to the Statute. Therefore, Portugal had violated the equality, mutuality and reciprocity to which India was entitled under the optional clause and under the express condition of reciprocity contained in its declaration of 28 February 1940.

In considering this contention, the Court felt it necessary to examine whether, in filing its application on 22 December 1955, Portugal had acted in a manner contrary to any provision of the Statute, and whether it had violated any right of India under the Statute or its declaration. The Court was unable to accept that Portugal had violated the Statute by filing its application on 22 December 1955. In this respect, the Court declared that, by the deposit of its declaration of acceptance with the Secretary-General, the accepting State became a party to the system of the optional clause in relation to other declarant States, with all the rights and obligations deriving from Article 36 of the Statute. The consensual bond, the basis of the optional clause, came into existence from the day of deposit, and it was not suspended until the Secretary-General had transmitted copies of the declaration to the parties to the Statute. The Court further stated that India had not specified what actual right had been adversely affected by the manner of the filing of the Portuguese application, and the Court had been unable to discover what right had, in fact, been violated.

For these reasons, by 14 votes to 3, the Court rejected the second preliminary objection.

FOURTH PRELIMINARY OBJECTION

As the fourth preliminary objection was closely connected with the second, the Court dealt with it before considering the third objection (details about the third objection follow below).

In this fourth objection, India contended that, since it had had no knowledge of the Portuguese declaration before Portugal filed its application, it had been unable to avail itself, on the basis of reciprocity, of the third Portuguese condition and to exclude from the jurisdiction of the Court the dispute which was the subject-matter of the Portuguese application.

The Court considered that this argument had, in effect, already been dismissed by the Court in its consideration of the second preliminary objection. It reiterated that the Statute did not prescribe any interval between the deposit by a State of its declaration of acceptance and the filing of an application by that State, and that the principle of reciprocity was not affected by any delay in the receipt of copies of the declaration by the parties to the Court's Statute.

For these reasons, by 15 votes to 2, the Court rejected the fourth preliminary objection.

THIRD PRELIMINARY OBJECTION

In its third preliminary objection, India contended that, as the Portuguese application of 22 December 1955 had been filed before the Portuguese claim had been effectively made the subject-matter of diplomatic negotiations, the subject-matter of the claim had not yet been determined. Therefore, there was no legal and justiciable dispute between the parties which could be referred to the Court under the optional clause.

The Court, in examining this objection, considered the question of the extent to which, prior to the filing of the application by Portugal, negotiations had taken place between the parties in the matter of the right of passage. The Court stated that the diplomatic correspondence before it revealed that Portugal had repeatedly complained of denial of facilities for transit across Indian territory, and, while the exchanges between the parties had not assumed the character of a controversy as to the nature and extent of the legal right of passage, Portugal had described the denial of passage requested by it as inconsistent with established custom and international law in general. The correspondence also showed that negotiations had reached a deadlock. The Court considered that, even assuming there was substance in the contention that Article 36, paragraph 2, of the Court's Statute established, as a condition of the jurisdiction of the Court, a requisite definition of the dispute through negotiations, that condition had been complied with to the extent permitted by the circumstances of the case.

For these reasons, by 16 votes to 7, the Court rejected the third preliminary objection.

FIFTH PRELIMINARY OBJECTION

The declaration of acceptance of the compulsory jurisdiction of the Court made by India on 28 February 1940 contained a reservation excluding from that jurisdiction disputes regarding questions which by international law fell exclusively within the jurisdiction of the Government of India. In its fifth preliminary objection, India relied upon this reservation to argue that the facts and the legal considerations adduced before the Court did not permit the conclusion that there was a reasonably arguable case for the contention that the dispute was outside the exclusive jurisdiction of India and therefore the Court had no jurisdiction to entertain it.

The Court stated that the consideration of this objection would require an elucidation of the facts of the case and their legal consequences, hence it would not be possible to pronounce upon this objection without prejudging the merits of the case.

Accordingly, by 13 votes to 4, the Court joined the fifth preliminary objection to the merits.

SIXTH PRELIMINARY OBJECTION

The Indian declaration of acceptance of the compulsory jurisdiction of the Court contained a further reservation, whereby it limited that jurisdiction to disputes arising after 5 February 1930 with regard to situations or facts subsequent to the same date.

In its sixth preliminary objection, India invoked this reservation and contended that the dispute in question did not arise after 5

February 1930, and that in any case it was a dispute with regard to situations and facts prior to that date as the conflicts of views dated as far back as 1818.

Portugal, on the contrary, argued that the dispute submitted to the Court had arisen after 1953, when the Government of India adopted certain measures relating to passage and transit between the Portuguese littoral territory of Daman and the enclaves of Dandra and Nagar-Aveli. Portugal also contended that the dispute before the Court had arisen after 1930, as prior to that date the question of the existence or non-existence of a legal right of passage had not been in controversy between the parties, which had managed to settle, without raising or resolving the question of legal rights, the practical problems arising in this connexion.

The Court considered that it did not possess sufficient evidence at this time to pronounce on these questions. To do so would necessitate the examination and clarification of complicated questions of fact bearing on the practice of the authorities concerned for a period of considerable duration. Any evaluation of these facts at this stage would entail the risk of prejudging some of the issues closely connected with the merits.

Accordingly, by 15 votes to 2, the Court joined the sixth preliminary objection to the merits.

OTHER MATTERS

In its submissions, the Government of Portugal, while expressly disclaiming any intention of invoking Article 41 of the Court's Statute concerning the indication of interim measures, had requested the Court to recall to the parties the universally admitted principle that they should facilitate the accomplishment of the task of the Court by abstaining from any measure capable of exercising a prejudicial effect with regard to the execution of its decisions or which might bring about either an aggravation or an extension of the dispute. The Court did not consider that, in the circumstances of the case, it should comply with this request.

Finally, the Court resumed the proceedings on the merits and fixed time-limits for the rest of the procedure as follows: for the filing of the counter-memorial of the Government of India, 25 February 1958; for the filing of the reply of the Government of Portugal, 25 May 1958; and for the filing of the rejoinder of the Government of India, 25 July 1958.

Dissenting opinions were appended by Judges Badawi and Klaestad and Mahommed Ali Currim Chagla, Judge *ad hoc*. Mr. Manuel Fernandes, Judge *ad hoc*, concurred with the dissenting opinion of Judge Klaestad. Judge Kojevnikov stated that he could concur neither in the operative clause nor in the reasoning of the judgement because, in his opinion, the Court should have held that it was without jurisdiction on one or more of the preliminary objections raised by the Government of India.

DOCUMENTARY REFERENCE

Case concerning Right of Passage over Indian Territory (Preliminary Objections), Judgment of November 26th, 1957: I.C.J. Reports 1957, p. 125.

CASE CONCERNING THE GUARDIANSHIP OF AN INFANT (NETHERLANDS *vs.* SWEDEN)

On 10 July 1957, the Kingdom of the Netherlands filed in the Registry of the Court an application instituting proceedings against the Kingdom of Sweden in respect of the terms of a Convention of 1902 governing the guardianship of infants. The Netherlands contended that the Swedish authorities had not acted in conformity with the provisions of this Convention in instituting and maintaining a *skyddsuppfostran*, or form of guardianship, in respect of a child, Maria Elisabeth Boll, who was claimed to be of Netherlands nationality.

By an order of 19 August 1957, the Court fixed the time-limits for the filing of the pleadings as follows: for the memorial of the Government of the Kingdom of the Netherlands, 30 November 1957; for the counter-memorial of the Government of the Kingdom of Sweden, 31 March 1958.

DOCUMENTARY REFERENCE

Case concerning the Guardianship of an Infant, Order of August 19th, 1957: I.C.J. Reports 1957, p. 102.

INTERHANDEL CASE (SWITZERLAND *vs.* UNITED STATES)

APPLICATION BY SWITZERLAND

On 2 October 1957 the Swiss Confederation filed in the Registry of the Court an application instituting proceedings against the United States in a dispute which had arisen between Switzerland and the United States relating to the restitution by the latter of the assets of the *Société internationale pour participations industrielles et commerciales S. A.* (Interhandel), a limited company, registered in Switzerland in 1928 on the initiative of I. G. Farbenindustrie of Frankfort, Germany.

The most important assets of Interhandel were stated in the application to be represented by its ownership and control of 90 to 95 per cent of the issued shares of the General Aniline and Film Corporation (G.A.F.), an enterprise established in the United States of America. By decisions dated 16 February and 24 April 1942, and others, the Government of the United States, in applying its municipal laws on enemy property, had ordered the vesting of the above-mentioned shares in the Office of Alien Property. These measures were justified by the United States authorities on the ground that the shares were, in fact, the property of an enemy alien, I. G. Farbenindustrie, or were owned by or held for the latter.

Contesting this view, the Swiss Government claimed in its application that Interhandel's links with I. G. Farben had been severed in June 1940 and that from that moment German control of the Company had ceased.

The application thereafter stated that the Swiss Government had been seeking the release of Interhandel's assets in the United States since 1948, on the basis of the Washington Accord of 25 May 1946. Concluded between Switzerland and Allied Governments, this Accord provided, *inter alia,* for the release of

Swiss assets in the United States. The application alleged that the United States Government had refused to accede to several Swiss requests for negotiations between the two Governments to settle the question, and also that it had refused to submit it to arbitration or conciliation, pursuant to the provisions of either the Washington Accord or of the Treaty of Arbitration and Conciliation of 16 February 1931 between Switzerland and the United States.

The application founded the jurisdiction of the Court on the acceptance by both Switzerland and the United States of compulsory jurisdiction under Article 36, paragraph 2, of the Statute. The application asked the Court to adjudge and declare that the United States Government was under an obligation to restore the assets of Interhandel to that company, or, alternatively, that the dispute was one which was fit for submission for judicial settlement, arbitration or conciliation under conditions to be determined by the Court.

THE QUESTION OF INTERIM MEASURES

On 3 October 1957, the Agent for the Swiss Government filed a request in the Registry of the Court for the indication of interim measures of protection. The request referred to the application in the Interhandel case filed the previous day. It stated that, unless the Court indicated certain measures of interim protection, the Swiss Government had serious grounds for believing that the property of Interhandel in the United States, for which restitution was claimed, might be transferred by the United States Alien Property Custodian to third parties, before the Court could adjudicate upon the claim.

The request then enumerated the grounds for such a belief. It asked the Court, with reference to Article 41 of the Statute and Article 61 of the Rules of Court, to indicate the following measures:

(a) The United States Government should take no legislative, judicial, administrative or executive step to part with the property claimed to be Swiss property in the Swiss application, so long as the case was pending before the Court.

(b) In particular, the United States Government should not sell the shares of G.A.F., claimed by the Swiss Government as the property of its nationals, so long as the proceedings in the dispute were pending.

(c) In general, the United States Government should so act that no measure whatever would be taken which would prejudice the right of Switzerland to execution of the judgement which the Court would deliver, either on the merits or on the alternative submission.

On 10 October 1957, the United States Ambassador to the Netherlands informed the Registrar of the Court by letter of a preliminary objection to the jurisdiction raised by his Government. One ground for objection was that the United States Government had determined that the sale or disposition of the shares of G.A.F., title to which was held by the United States Government in the exercise of its sovereign authority, was a matter essentially within its domestic jurisdiction. Accordingly, pursuant to paragraph (b) of the conditions attached to the United States acceptance of the Court's compulsory jurisdiction, dated 14 August 1946, the United States declined, without prejudice to other and further preliminary objections which it might file, to submit the matter of the sale or disposition of such shares to the jurisdiction of the Court.

On 12 and 14 October 1957, the Court heard the observations of the Agents of the parties on the request for the indication of interim measures.

By communications dated 16 and 19 October 1957, the United States Ambassador to the Netherlands informed the Court that, on 14 October 1957, after the conclusion of the oral hearings by the International Court at The Hague, the Supreme Court of the United States had granted Interhandel a writ of *certiorari*, and would hear its appeal against an earlier judgement of the United States Court of Appeals. In this judgement, the Court of Appeals had confirmed an order of the District Court which had, in turn, dismissed Interhandel's suit for the return of the shares on the basis of its failure to produce certain documents relevant to the case within the time-limits determined and several times extended by the Court.

In a letter dated 19 October 1957, the United States Ambassador further declared that his Government was not taking action at that time to fix a time-schedule for the sale of the G.A.F. shares.

By letters dated 18 and 19 October 1957, the Swiss Ambassador to the Netherlands transmitted the views of his Government to the Court on the above communications from the United States Ambassador. In the letter of 19 October, the Swiss Government pointed out that the United States had not indicated how long the sale of the shares would be suspended, or whether such suspension would be maintained as long as the dispute was pending before the Court. The letter also drew attention to the fact that the Swiss request for interim measures was designed in general to ensure the execution of the subsequent decision of the Court, should that decision be in favour of Switzerland.

On 24 October 1957, the Court made an Order in which it found that there was no need to indicate interim measures of protection.

The Court, in its Order, made the following observations on the reasons for its adoption:

(1) The procedure applicable to requests for the indication of interim measures of protection was dealt with in article 61 of the Rules of Court.

(2) The examination of the preliminary objection of the Government of the United States required the application of a different procedure, namely, the procedure contained in article 62 of the Rules of Court, and, if the United States preliminary objection was maintained, it would fall to be dealt with by the Court in due accordance with that procedure.

(3) The request for the indication of interim measures must be examined in conformity with the procedure laid down in article 61.

(4) A decision given under the procedure laid down in article 61 in no way prejudged the question of the jurisdiction of the Court to deal with the merits of the case and left unaffected the right of the respondent to submit arguments against such jurisdiction.

(5) The Court, in order to decide what action should be taken in pursuance of the Swiss request for the indication of interim measures, had, in accordance with article 41 of the Statute, to ascertain what was required by the circumstances to preserve the respective rights of the parties pending the decision of the Court.

(6) Of the three points set forth in the submissions of Switzerland with regard to its request, only the second was formulated in terms which fulfilled the requirement laid down in article 61, paragraph 1, of the Rules and which related to the concern of the Court to preserve the rights which might be subsequently adjudged by the Court to belong either to the applicant or to the respondent.

(7) The Court must direct its attention to the second point raised by the Swiss Government, namely, that the Government of the United States should be requested not to sell the shares of G.A.F. claimed by the Swiss Government as the property of its nationals, as long as the proceedings in the dispute were pending.

(8) In the light of the information furnished to the Court it appeared that, according to the law of the United States, the sale of the shares could only be effected after the unfavourable termination, from the point of view of Interhandel, of a judicial proceeding then pending in the United States, and in respect of which there was no indication of a speedy conclusion.

(9) In transmitting its views to the Court, the United States Government, on 19 October 1957, had declared that it was not taking action at that time to fix a time-schedule for the sale of the shares.

(10) It did not therefore appear to the Court that the circumstances required the indication of the provisional measures envisaged in the request of the Swiss Government.

Separate opinions were appended to the Order by Judges Klaestad and Sir Hersch Lauterpacht. President Hackworth and Judge Read concurred in Judge Klaestad's separate opinion. Judge Wellington Koo, while supporting the decision of the Court not to indicate interim measures, appended a declaration containing his reasons therefor, and Judge Kojevnikov declared that he was unable to agree with the Order.

TIME-LIMITS FOR PROCEEDINGS

The Court made a further Order on 24 October 1957, in which it fixed 31 January 1958 as the time-limit for the memorial of the Swiss Government and 3 March 1958 as the time-limit for the countermemorial or any preliminary objections of the United States.

DOCUMENTARY REFERENCE
*Interhandel Case (interim measures of protection),
Order of October 24th, 1957: I.C.J. Reports 1957,*
pp. 105, 122.

CASES CONCERNING AERIAL INCIDENT OF 27 JULY 1955 (ISRAEL *vs.* BULGARIA; UNITED STATES *vs.* BULGARIA; UNITED KINGDOM *vs.* BULGARIA)

APPLICATION BY ISRAEL

On 16 October 1957, the State of Israel filed in the Registry of the Court an application instituting proceedings against the People's Republic of Bulgaria in respect of an aerial incident of 27 July 1955.

The application stated that units of the Bulgarian Security Forces had on 27 July 1955 shot down, over their own territory, a civilian aircraft of Israel nationality owned by an Israel corporation. Seven crew members and all 51 passengers of various nationalities were killed. The aircraft had been on a scheduled flight from Vienna to Lydda (Lod) and, from correspondence annexed to the application, it appeared that it was driven off its course through Yugoslavia and over Bulgarian territory by strong winds, the crew being unaware of their exact location because of meteorological conditions.

According to the application, diplomatic correspondence between the two Governments regarding the incident had failed to result in a mutually satisfactory solution concerning claims for compensation. The Government of Israel therefore felt constrained to commence proceedings before the International Court of Justice.

The application stated that the Court had jurisdiction to determine the dispute, as both Israel and Bulgaria had submitted declarations, under paragraph 2 of Article 36 of the Court's Statute, accepting the compulsory jurisdiction of the Court. Israel's declaration was dated 3 October 1956, replacing a declaration of 4 September 1950, and covered disputes after 25 October 1951. The declaration of Bulgaria, according to the application, was made on 29 July 1921, on the occasion of Bulgaria's deposit of its instrument of ratification of the Protocol of Signature of the Statute of the Permanent Court of International Justice, and was unconditional.

The application concluded by asking the Court to adjudge and declare that Bulgaria was responsible under international law for the destruction of the Israel aircraft and for the loss of life and property and all other damage that resulted therefrom. The Court was also asked to determine the amount of compensation due from Bulgaria to Israel, and to decide that all costs and expenses incurred by the Government of Israel should be borne by the Bulgarian Government.

APPLICATIONS BY UNITED STATES AND UNITED KINGDOM

On 28 October and 22 November 1957 respectively, the United States and the United Kingdom filed separate applications in the Registry of the Court commencing proceedings against Bulgaria in respect of the above aerial incident. Both States claimed damages for the death of their nationals and the destruction of their property, and founded the jurisdiction of the Court on the acceptance of the compulsory jurisdiction of the Court by the States concerned.

TIME-LIMITS FOR PROCEEDINGS

By three Orders of 26 November 1957 the Court fixed 2 June 1958 as the time-limit for the filing of the memorials of the Government of Israel, United States and the United Kingdom. In each case the Court reserved for a subsequent Order the fixing of the time-limit for the filing of counter-memorials by the Government of Bulgaria.

DOCUMENTARY REFERENCES

*Case concerning Aerial Incident of July 27th 1955
(Israel v. Bulgaria), Order of November 26th, 1957:
I.C.J. Reports 1957,* p. 182.
*Case ocncerning Aerial Incident of July 27th, 1955
(United States of America v. Bulgaria) Order of*
November 26th, 1957. I.C.J. Reports 1957,
p. 186.
*Case concerning Aerial Incident of July 27th, 1955
(United Kingdom v. Bulgaria) Order of November
26th, 1957: I.C.J. Reports 1957,* p. 190.

CASE CONCERNING SOVEREIGNTY OVER CERTAIN FRONTIER LAND
(BELGIUM/NETHERLANDS)

On 27 November 1957, a Special Agreement between the Netherlands and Belgium was filed in the Registry of the Court by the Netherlands Minister for Foreign Affairs. The Agreement related to a difference between the two Governments concerning sovereignty over certain parcels of land situated at the Belgium-Netherlands frontier, and the Court was asked to determine whether the sovereignty over this land belonged to Belgium or to the Netherlands.

The Agreement further provided that written proceedings should consist of: a memorial of Belgium to be submitted within three months of the notification of the Agreement to the Court; a counter-memorial by the Netherlands to be submitted within three months of the above memorial; and a reply of Belgium followed by a rejoinder of the Netherlands to be delivered within such times as the Court might order.

By an Order of 12 December 1957, the Court confirmed the above time-limits in respect of the memorial and counter-memorial.

DOCUMENTARY REFERENCE

Case concerning Sovereignty over Certain Frontier Land, Order of December 12th, 1957: I.C.J. Reports 1957, p. 194.

CHAPTER II

THE INTERNATIONAL LAW COMMISSION

DIPLOMATIC INTERCOURSE AND IMMUNITIES

The International Law Commission was asked by the General Assembly on 5 December 1952, by resolution 685(VII), to codify the rules of international law governing diplomatic intercourse and immunities.

In 1954, at its sixth session, the Commission decided to initiate work on the subject, and appointed Mr. A. E. F. Sandström as Special Rapporteur to report on the matter. At the following session, in 1955, he submitted a report containing a draft for the codification of the law relating to the subject. Because of lack of time, the Commission did not consider it until its ninth session, when it adopted a provisional draft of 37 articles, on the provisional assumption that it would form the basis for a convention. The draft was referred to the General Assembly and transmitted to Governments for comments.

In 1957, at the twelfth session of the General Assembly, the draft was considered by the Assembly's Sixth (Legal) Committee. As this was a provisional draft and as a final text was to be prepared at the Commission's tenth session in 1958 in the light of comments by Governments, most representatives taking the floor made only a few general comments and reserved their right to submit more detailed observations when the final draft was submitted to the Assembly.

The draft dealt only with permanent diplomatic missions. The Commission had also asked its Special Rapporteur to make a study of "*ad hoc* diplomacy", which would cover roving envoys, diplomatic conferences and special missions, and to submit his report at its 1958 session. Some representatives therefore thought that it would perhaps be desirable to await the completion of final reports on both permanent and *ad hoc* missions so that the whole subject of diplomatic immunities would be dealt with at the same time, possibly in 1959, at the fourteenth session of the General Assembly.

Another problem referred to, but not studied, in the Commission's report to the Assembly was that of the relations between States and international organizations, and the privileges and immunities of such organizations.

At the Assembly's twelfth session, some Members of the Assembly's Sixth Committee considered that this problem would some day have to be studied in its entirety and that the principles developed through experience would have to be translated into explicit rules. In particular, the status of representatives to the United Nations could be usefully examined by the International Law Commission. On the other hand, other representatives saw no practical reason for the Commission to make a special study of the question because the matter was already governed by multilateral conventions.

Several representatives stressed the relationship between the rules governing diplomatic intercourse and immunities and those relating to consular intercourse and immunities, a topic also being studied by the Commission. They thought it desirable to study both subjects simultaneously, especially since diplomatic agents often performed both diplomatic and consular functions.

Others, however, maintained that these two issues, though parallel, were not identical and inseparable. In view of the agenda for the Commission's next session, they thought it hardly possible for the Commission to produce a draft on consular immunities. To study both questions at the same time would entail delays.

Some representatives, though not strongly in favour of studying both drafts simultaneously, hoped that the subject of consular intercourse would be given more immediate consideration.

DOCUMENTARY REFERENCES

GENERAL ASSEMBLY—12TH SESSION
Plenary Meeting 727.
Sixth Committee, meetings 509-513, 529, 547.

A/3623. Report of International Law Commission covering work of its ninth session, 23 April–28 June 1957, Chapter II.

Yearbook of International Law Commission, 1957. Vol. I: Summary records of ninth session; Vol. II: Documents of ninth session, including Report of Commission to General Assembly. U.N.P. Sales Nos.: 1957.V.5, Vols. I and II.
A/3768. Report of Sixth Committee.

OTHER MATTERS CONCERNING THE INTERNATIONAL LAW COMMISSION

ARBITRAL PROCEDURE

On 14 December 1955, by resolution 989(X), the General Assembly invited the International Law Commission to consider comments made by Governments and the discussions in the Sixth (Legal) Committee on the draft convention on arbitral procedure prepared by the Commission at its fifth session in 1953. The Commission was asked to report to the Assembly's thirteenth session in 1958.

To carry out the Assembly's request, the Commission appointed a nine-member committee at its ninth session in 1957. After considering the questions involved, the nine-member committee concluded that it would be necessary for the Commission to decide on the ultimate object to be attained in reviewing the draft. The particular point to be determined was whether to draw up a convention or simply a set of rules which might inspire States in the drawing up of provisions for inclusion in international treaties and special arbitration agreements.

In the light of a report submitted to it by its Special Rapporteur on arbitral procedure, Georges Scelle, the Commission decided in favour of the second alternative. After taking provisional decisions on certain points, the Commission adjourned the matter for final consideration and report at its next session.

OTHER STUDIES

LAW OF TREATIES

Another report, on the law of treaties, was submitted at the Commission's ninth session by Sir Gerald Fitzmaurice, the Special Rapporteur on the subject, but was not discussed for want of time. The Special Rapporteur informed the Commission that he would present a report to its next session completing the work, begun in his first two reports, on the validity of treaties.

STATE RESPONSIBILITY

Also submitted to the Commission's ninth session was a second report by F. V. García-Amador, its Special Rapporteur, on the subject of international responsibility. This report dealt with the particular topic of "Responsibility of the State for injuries caused in its territory to the persons or property of aliens—Part I: Acts and Omissions". The Commission, after a general discussion of this report, asked Mr. García-Amador to continue his work.

CONSULAR INTERCOURSE AND IMMUNITIES

Yet another report, on consular intercourse and immunities, was submitted by Mr. Jaroslav Zourek, Special Rapporteur for this subject. This, too, was not discussed by the Commission for want of time. It was agreed to consider it at the Commission's 1958 session.

CO-OPERATION WITH OTHER BODIES

Contacts were established in 1956 between the Commission and the Inter-American Council of Jurists for their respective secretaries to be observers at the sessions of these bodies. In 1957, the Commission was informed that the fourth meeting of the Inter-American Council, originally scheduled for 1958, would be held at Santiago (Chile) in 1959.

Arrangements for co-operation with the Asian Legal Consultative Committee were decided upon at the Commission's ninth session. (The Committee is an inter-governmental body of legal experts set up in November 1956 for an initial period of five years by the Governments of Burma, Ceylon, India, Indonesia, Iraq, Japan and Syria.) At the General Assembly's twelfth session, several Members of its Sixth Committee noted the development of the co-operation between the Commission and other bodies and hoped that it would be extended further.

REPORT OF COMMISSION

On 11 December 1957, the General Assembly unanimously adopted a resolution (1185 (XII)), as recommended by the Sixth Committee, expressing appreciation of the work of the International Law Commission and asked that the records of the discussions in the Assembly's Sixth Committee on the report of the Commission be forwarded to the latter body.

DOCUMENTARY REFERENCES

Yearbook of International Law Commission, 1957. Vol. I: Summary records of ninth session, 23 April–28 June 1957; Vol. II: Documents of ninth session, including Report of Commission to General Assembly. U.N.P. Sales No.: 1957.V.5, Vols. I and II.

ARBITRAL PROCEDURE
A/CN.4/109. Report concerning draft convention on arbitral procedure adopted by Commission at its fifth session (with amended "model draft" attached). Report by Special Rapporteur.
A/3623. Report of International Law Commission, Chapter III, Section II.
Reports of International Arbitral Awards, Vol. VII: Decisions of Mixed Claims Commission. United States–Germany, Part I. U.N.P. Sales No.: 1956. V.5, and Corrigendum.

STATE RESPONSIBILITY
A/C.4/106. International responsibility. Responsibility of State for injuries caused in its territory to persons or property of aliens. Part I: Acts and Omissions. Report of Special Rapporteur.
A/3623. Report of International Law Commission. Chapter III, Section I.

REPORT OF COMMISSION
GENERAL ASSEMBLY—12TH SESSION
Plenary Meeting 727.
Sixth Committee, meetings 509-513, 528, 529, 547.

A/3623. Report of International Law Commission covering work of its ninth session, 23 April–28 June 1957.

A/C.6/L.400. Brazil, Chile, Cuba, Peru, Philippines, Spain draft resolution, as amended by Ceylon, adopted unanimously by Sixth Committee.
A/C.6/L.405. Ceylon amendments to joint draft resolution.
A/3768. Report of Sixth Committee.
RESOLUTION 1185(XII), as recommended by Sixth Committee, A/3768, adopted unanimously by Assembly on 11 December 1957, meeting 727.

"The General Assembly,
"Having considered the report of the International Law Commission on the work of its ninth session,
"1. *Notes* the said report;
"2. *Expresses its appreciation* of the work done by the International Law Commission;
"3. *Requests* the Secretary-General to forward to the International Law Commission the summary records of the discussions of the Sixth Committee on the report of the Commission."

OTHER DOCUMENTS
Yearbook of International Law Commission, 1949. Summary records and report of first session of Commission, 12 April–9 June 1949. U.N.P. Sales No.: 1957.V.1.
Yearbook of International Law Commission, 1950. Vols. I and II: Summary records of second session, 5 June–29 July 1950 and documents of second session. U.N.P. Sales No.: 1957.V.3, Vols. I and II.
Yearbook of International Law Commission, 1951. Vol. II: Documents and report of third session of Commission, 16 May–27 July 1951. U.N.P. Sales No.: 1957.V.6, Vol. II.

CHAPTER III

OTHER LEGAL QUESTIONS

THE QUESTION OF DEFINING AGGRESSION

The question of defining aggression, consideration of which was deferred from the General Assembly's eleventh session, was discussed during the twelfth session at 24 meetings of the Assembly's Sixth (Legal) Committee. Before the Committee was a report prepared, between 8 October and 9 November 1956, by the Special Committee on the Question of Defining Agression.

The debate in the Sixth Committee showed a division of opinion on the desirability of having a definition of aggression and on the nature of the definition, if any, to be adopted.

Some representatives maintained that the adoption of a definition of aggression was increasingly important in view of existing international tension and the gathering pace of the armaments race. Thus, the USSR representative contended that such a definition should take its place among the measures designed to eliminate the threat of a new war. The representatives of Ceylon and Ecuador thought a definition would serve as a warning to aggressors and would make it harder to justify aggression, and Afghanistan's spokesman contended that a definition of aggression would reduce international tension.

Australia, Canada, China, India, Japan, Pakistan, the United Kingdom and the United States were among the Members who did not consider it propitious or feasible at this stage to work out a definition. One point made was that it would not serve to promote peace.

According to other Members, the practical aim of a definition was to provide guidance for the competent United Nations organs responsible for maintaining peace and security. These Members included Ceylon and El Salvador. El Salvador's representative, however, warned that use of a definition involving premature censure of a State for aggression would be liable to increase international tension.

The representatives of Brazil, Japan and other Members considered that a definition of aggression would hardly facilitate the task of the Security Council or of the General Assembly since it would restrict the flexibility which these organs possessed under the United Nations Charter. Moreover—as the spokesmen for China, Japan, Sweden, the United Kingdom and the United States pointed out—the practical importance of a definition was very limited because past experience had shown that such definitions in various treaties had not always succeeded in offering any real protection against aggression. The United States representative further cited past experience to show that the United Nations had not suffered from the absence of a definition. Adoption of a definition, he also warned, could give rise to a false sense of security.

Another argument against having a definition of aggression to serve as guidance for the competent United Nations organs was that developments in international affairs had shown that the United Nations functions of conciliation and mediation had frequently come to receive more emphasis than the coercive functions of the Organization.

Another point made—by the representatives of Chile, France and the Netherlands, for instance—was that a definition of aggression, to be really useful, would have to be accepted by an overwhelming majority of United Nations Members. This majority, Uruguay's spokesman stressed, should include the permanent members of the Security Council.

As to the type of definition to be adopted, various delegations in favour of defining aggression, including those of Iran and Panama, preferred a "mixed type" of definition in which a general description would precede and govern a list of definite acts of aggression. This list of acts would be included merely to illustrate and not to restrict the general description.

Others, again, thought it a mistake to have a "mixed definition". They preferred a definition enumerating various acts to be defined as acts of aggression, but, as the Syrian representative indicated, the list of acts enumerated should not be regarded as a complete and exhaustive one.

Still others preferred a general definition.

As to the substance of the definition, several Members said it was not necessary to define aggression within the meaning of Article 39 of the United Nations Charter.[1] They felt rather that the definition should be confined to the notion of armed attack, in the sense of Article 51 of the Charter.[2]

The representatives of Japan, Mexico, Sweden and the United Kingdom, among others, were against a definition which departed from the idea that the use of force was the essential ingredient of aggression in that it included economic and ideological aggression and indirect acts of aggression under the definition. These actions, they thought, could conceivably be declared illegal in a separate international convention. Including them in a definition of aggression, however, would only lead to confusion.

The Netherlands and Norwegian representatives maintained that there was a difference between "armed attack" and "aggression".

The Norwegian representative, in addition, thought that the only way to get a useful and binding definition of aggression was to amend the Charter. The Danish and Pakistan spokesmen agreed with him. But the representatives of Egypt, Iraq, and Mexico, among others, did not.

A number of Members contended that, under the Charter, aggression was not confined to the use of armed force. In their view, the notion of "armed attack" mentioned in Article 51 of the Charter was but a special case of armed aggression in the sense of Article 39. The latter Article, they said, authorized the Security Council to take measures in the event of a threat to peace, and in modern times certain economic or ideological measures might well constitute such a threat. Attempts to deprive a State of economic resources or to endanger its trade or trade routes should, in their opinion, be regarded as acts of aggression.

Other delegations, while agreeing that economic and ideological aggression could under the Charter be included in the definition, thought it better for the time being to confine the definition to armed attack, without prejudice to the recognition of other forms of aggression.

Some representatives considered that a chronological order of events was a decisive criterion in determining who was responsible for aggression. In preparing any definition of aggression, they maintained, it would be necessary to include an explanation that an aggressor State was one which first committed any of the acts enumerated in the definition. Without that principle, the definition would not only be ambiguous. It might also be used to justify preventive war.

Other delegations thought a definition based on the chronological order of events would have dangerous consequences. The State first committing an act considered as an act of aggression would not necessarily be the aggressor. Whether it was or was not the aggressor would depend on the circumstances peculiar to each case.

The USSR, in addition to proposing a definition enumerating various actions to be regarded as acts of aggression, also proposed that the definition include references to a number of circumstances and situations in a particular State which should in no case serve as a justification for aggression against that State. Criticizing this part of the USSR proposal, some delegations thought it was likely to give the impression that other circumstances and situations, not included in the definition, might justify aggression. The proposal was also criticized on the ground that it would be illogical to list various circumstances and situations which could not serve as justification for aggression when the basic principle was that nothing justified aggression.

Two draft resolutions containing definitions of aggression were submitted to the Sixth Committee. One, by the USSR, contained a definition enumerating various acts of aggression. The other, submitted by Iran and Panama, contained a definition of the "mixed" type, i.e., one with a general description preceding and governing

---

[1] This Article provides that the Security Council shall determine the existence of any threat to the peace, breach of the peace, or acts of aggression, and shall make recommendations or decide what measures shall be taken to maintain or restore international peace and security (i.e., measures which do not involve the use of armed forces and those which do, as specified by Articles 41 and 42).

[2] This Article deals with the inherent right of United Nations Members to take individual or collective defence measures in the event of an armed attack against them until the Security Council has taken the necessary steps to maintain international peace and security.

a list of acts of aggression, the list being intended merely to illustrate the general description and not to restrict the description to these acts. In addition, Belgium submitted a working paper with a general definition of aggression.

The debate showed that most Members favoured postponing consideration of the question. Some wanted it postponed indefinitely, and the United States proposed a draft resolution to this effect.

Other Members wanted consideration of the matter put off until the Assembly's fourteenth session (in 1959). Many of those holding this view argued that the 22 Members admitted to the United Nations since 14 December 1955 should be given the opportunity to comment on previous definitions of aggression as contained in a study prepared by the first Special Committee on the Question of Defining Aggression which the Assembly had set up in 1952. They also suggested that other Members which had not yet submitted the comments requested in 1952 should be given the chance to do so now. The Secretary-General, they further suggested, should report to the General Assembly's fourteenth session on the replies received. These ideas were embodied in a draft resolution submitted by the following seven Members: Chile, Colombia, Cuba, Ecuador, El Salvador, the Philippines and Venezuela.

Egypt and Poland proposed an amendment to this draft resolution which involved simply placing the question of defining aggression on the agenda of the Assembly's fourteenth session.

Another amendment to the seven-power draft came from Afghanistan, Bolivia, Guatemala, Haiti, Mexico and Peru. The aim of this was to re-establish the Special Committee on the Question of Defining Aggression and to increase its membership, particularly by adding some of the newer Member States. The Special Committee would report to the Assembly's fourteenth session.

As a compromise solution, the United States presented a further amendment, and, at the same time, withdrew its own draft resolution. The United States amendment would have the Secretary-General refer the replies of Member States to a committee composed of Member States whose representatives served on the Assembly's General Committee at the most recent regular session of the Assembly. This committee would study the replies in order to determine when it would be appropriate for the Assembly to consider again the question of defining aggression.

There was considerable support in the Sixth Committee for this United States amendment. Some Members, however, were strongly against it. They did not consider it a compromise solution. They thought it tantamount to postponing consideration of the question indefinitely. Further, the United States amendment meant that it would be left to a small political body to decide the appropriate time for considering the matter.

Those for the amendment said that their support did not mean they were against a definition of aggression. To postpone consideration of the matter until circumstances were more favourable, it was argued, would in fact enhance the possibilities of arriving at a definition.

The Sixth Committee finally agreed to the procedural seven-power draft resolution as amended by the United States. It did so by a roll-call vote of 41 to 21, with 11 abstentions. In view of this decision, the draft resolutions relating to the substance of the question (i.e., that proposed by the USSR and that submitted jointly by Iran and Panama) were not put to the vote. The Sixth Committee's decision was endorsed at a plenary meeting of the Assembly on 29 November 1957 by 42 votes to 24, with 15 abstentions, as resolution 1181(XII).

The Assembly thereby took note of the report of the 1956 Special Committee on the Question of Defining Aggression and expressed appreciation for its valuable work. It requested the Secretary-General to ask the 22 new Member States admitted since 14 December 1955 for their views on the question, and to renew the request for comments from Member States which had not yet sent in their comments in pursuance with Assembly resolution 688(VII) of 20 December 1952.

The Secretary-General was also asked to refer the replies of the Members to a committee composed of the Member States on the General Committee of the Assembly's most recent regular session. The new committee was to study the replies to determine when it would be appropriate for the Assembly to reconsider the question of defining aggression. It was to report to him when it had determined that the time was appropriate, setting forth the consideration leading to its decisions. The Assembly also asked that the question of defining aggression be put on the provisional agenda of the Assembly, not earlier than its fourteenth session, when the Committee had advised him that it deemed the time appropriate. The first meeting of the Committee was to be held prior to that session.

Before the Assembly adopted this resolution, it rejected amendments to it, put forward by Ceylon, Egypt, Guatemala, Indonesia, Mexico, Poland and Syria. By these amendments, the Assembly would decide to place the question of defining aggression on the provisional agenda of the Assembly's fourteenth session without deciding to set up a committee on the matter.

DOCUMENTARY REFERENCES

GENERAL ASSEMBLY—12TH SESSION
Plenary Meeting 724.
Sixth Committee, meetings 508, 514-528, 530-538.

A/3574. Report of 1956 Special Committee on Question of Defining Aggression, 8 October–9 November 1956.
A/C.6/L.399. USSR draft resolution.
A/C.6/L.401. Iran and Panama draft resolution.
A/C.6/L.402. United States draft resolution.
A/C.3/L.403 and Corr.1. Chile, Colombia, Cuba, Ecuador, El Salvador, Philippines, Venezuela draft resolution.
A/C.3/L.403/Rev.1. Chile, Colombia, Cuba, Ecuador, El Salvador, Philippines, Venezuela revised draft resolution adopted by Sixth Committee by roll-call vote of 41 to 21, with 11 abstentions as follows:
In favour: Argentina, Australia, Belgium, Brazil, Canada, Chile, China, Colombia, Costa Rica, Cuba, Denmark, Dominican Republic, Ecuador, El Salvador, Ethiopia, Finland, France, Honduras, Iceland, Israel, Italy, Japan, Liberia, Luxembourg, Nepal, Netherlands, New Zealand, Nicaragua, Norway, Pakistan, Paraguay, Philippines, Portugal, Spain, Sweden, Thailand, Turkey, United Kingdom, United States, Uruguay, Venezuela.
Against: Afghanistan, Albania, Bulgaria, Byelorussian SSR, Ceylon, Czechoslovakia, Egypt, Guatemala, Haiti, Hungary, Indonesia, Mexico, Poland, Romania, Saudi Arabia, Syria, Tunisia, Ukrainian SSR, USSR, Yemen, Yugoslavia.
Abstaining: Austria, Bolivia, Burma, Cambodia, Greece, India, Iran, Iraq, Federation of Malaya, Panama, Peru.
A/C.6/L.404. Afghanistan, Bolivia, Guatemala, Haiti, Mexico, Peru amendments to 7-power draft resolution, A/C.6/L.403 and Corr.1.
A/C.6/L.406. Ceylon, Egypt, Indonesia sub-amendments to 6-power amendments, A/C.6/L.404.
A/C.6/L.407. United States amendments to 7-power draft resolution, A/C.6/L.403 and Corr.1.
A/C.6/L.409. Egypt and Poland amendments to 7-power draft resolution, A/C.6/L.403 and Corr.1.
A/3756. Report of Sixth Committee.
A/L.237 and Add.1. Ceylon, Egypt, Guatemala, Indonesia, Mexico, Poland, Syria amendments to draft resolution recommended by Sixth Committee, A/3756.
RESOLUTION 1181(XII), as recommended by Sixth Committee, A/3756, adopted by Assembly on 29 November 1957, meeting 724, by roll-call vote of 42 to 24, with 15 abstentions, as follows:

In favour: Argentina, Australia, Belgium, Brazil, Canada, Chile, China, Colombia, Costa Rica, Cuba, Denmark, Dominican Republic, Ecuador, El Salvador, Ethiopia, Finland, France, Honduras, Iceland, Israel, Italy, Japan, Laos, Liberia, Luxembourg, Federation of Malaya, Netherlands, New Zealand, Nicaragua, Norway, Pakistan, Paraguay, Philippines, Portugal, Spain, Sweden, Thailand, Turkey, United Kingdom, United States, Uruguay, Venezuela.
Against: Afghanistan, Albania, Bulgaria, Byelorussian SSR, Czechoslovakia, Egypt, Guatemala, Haiti, Hungary, Indonesia, Iraq, Jordan, Libya, Mexico, Morocco, Poland, Romania, Saudi Arabia, Syria, Tunisia, Ukrainian SSR, USSR, Yemen, Yugoslavia.
Abstaining: Austria, Bolivia, Burma, Cambodia, Ceylon, Ghana, Greece, India, Iran, Ireland, Lebanon, Nepal, Panama, Peru, Sudan.

"The General Assembly,

"Recalling its resolutions 599(VI) of 31 January 1952, 688(VII) of 20 December 1952 and 895(IX) of 4 December 1954, all referring to a definition of aggression,

"Considering that, in spite of the progress made in the study of the question, the discussion at the present session shows the needs for the elucidation of other aspects of a definition of aggression,

"Considering that the report presented by the 1956 Special Committee on the Question of Defining Aggression is an important study based on the views expressed by States Members of the United Nations up to the date of the preparation of the report,

"Considering that twenty-two additional States have recently joined the Organization and that it would be useful to know their views on the matter,

"Resolves:

"1. To take note of the report of the 1956 Special Committee on the Question of Defining Aggression and to express appreciation for the valuable work done;

"2. To ask the Secretary-General to request the views of the new Member States on the question, and to renew the request to Member States to submit comments as provided in General Assembly resolution 688(VII) of 20 December 1952, furnishing them with the documentation produced after the adoption of that resolution;

"3. To ask the Secretary-General to refer the replies of Member States to a committee composed of the Member States whose representatives have served on the General Committee at the most recent regular session of the General Assembly, which committee shall study the replies for the purpose of determining when it shall be appropriate for the General Assembly to consider again the question of defining aggression, and shall report to the Secretary-General when it has determined that the time is appropriate, setting forth the considerations which led to its decision;

"4. To request the Secretary-General to place the question of defining aggression on the provisional agenda of the General Assembly, not earlier than at its fourteenth session, when the committee has advised him that it considers the time appropriate;

"5. To request the Secretary-General to convene the first meeting of the committee prior to the fourteenth session of the General Assembly."

DRAFT CODE OF OFFENCES AGAINST THE PEACE AND SECURITY OF MANKIND

The draft Code of Offences against the Peace and Security of Mankind, drawn up by the International Law Commission in 1951, was revised by the Commission at its sixth session, in 1954, and submitted to the General Assembly that same year. On 4 December 1954, the Assembly decided to postpone further consideration of the draft Code until its Special Committee on the Question of Defining Aggression (set up in 1954) had submitted its report to the Assembly's eleventh session.

The Assembly took that decision because it considered that the draft Code raised problems closely linked to those involved in working out a definition of aggression. (See QUESTION OF DEFINING AGGRESSION above.)

At its twelfth session the Assembly referred the question of the draft Code, to its Sixth (Legal) Committee. At the outset of its debate, the Sixth Committee agreed not to discuss the draft Code article by article but rather to limit the debate to procedural questions and to general remarks.

The majority of representatives taking part in the debate agreed that the problems raised by the draft Code were closely linked to those raised by the question of defining aggression. For that reason, they were in favour of postponing consideration of the draft Code until the special committee set up by the Assembly on 29 November 1957 by resolution 1181(XII) determined that it was appropriate again to consider the question of defining aggression.

The representative of Colombia suggested that a committee should be set up to determine when it would be appropriate to take up the draft Code again.

Other representatives felt that consideration of the draft Code should simply be postponed until the Assembly again took up the question of defining aggression.

Some representatives, however, thought such procedures insufficient and suggested various ways of keeping the question under study. Thus, the Netherlands representative thought that a small working group, similar to the 1956 Special Committee on the Question of Defining Aggression, should be set up to examine the draft Code, to indicate the problems involved and to offer solutions in order to pave the way for future discussion.

Most representatives favoured transmitting the text of the draft Code to Member States for comment.

Some wanted to transmit the text only to those States newly admitted to the Organization; some wanted it sent also to States which had not previously submitted their comments; and some wanted it to be sent to all Member States. One representative pointed out that the revised text of the draft Code had never been transmitted to Member States for comment.

Many representatives favouring postponement of debate on the draft Code said that their attitude did not mean that they were against the adoption of such a Code. Nor did it mean that they minimized its importance. They hoped, on the contrary, that postponing the question until circumstances were more favourable would enhance the possibility of adopting a Code.

The Philippines submitted a draft resolution whereby the General Assembly would decide to defer the question of the draft Code until such time as it should again take up the question of defining aggression.

Colombia and Spain submitted a joint amendment to ask the Secretary-General to transmit the text of the draft Code to all Member States for comment.

These amendments were accepted by the Philippines and the draft resolution (after a further change made on the proposal of Poland) was adopted in the Sixth Committee by 58 votes to 1, with 1 abstention.

On 11 December 1957, the General Assembly, by 74 votes to 1, with 3 abstentions, approved the Sixth Committee's recommendation as resolution 1186(XII).

DOCUMENTARY REFERENCES

GENERAL ASSEMBLY—12TH SESSION
Plenary Meeting 727.
Sixth Committee, meetings 544-546.

A/3650. Note by Secretary-General.
A/C.6/L.418. Philippines draft resolution, as amended by Colombia and Spain and orally by Poland, adopted by Sixth Committee by 58 votes to 1, with 1 abstention.
A/C.6/L.419. Colombia and Spain amendments to Philippines draft resolution.
A/3770. Report of Sixth Committee.

RESOLUTION 1186(XII), as recommended by Sixth Committee, A/3770, adopted by Assembly on 11 December 1957, meeting 727, by 74 votes to 1, with 3 abstentions.

"The General Assembly,
"Considering that the draft Code of Offences against the Peace and Security of Mankind, as formulated in chapter III of the report of the International Law Commission on the work of its sixth session, raises problems related to that of the definition of aggression,
"Recalling General Assembly resolution 987(IX) of 4 December 1954,
"Considering General Assembly resolution 1181 (XII) of 29 November 1957 concerning the definition of aggression,
"1. Decides to defer consideration of the question of the draft Code of Offences against the Peace and Security of Mankind until such time as the General Assembly takes up again the question of defining aggression;
"2. Requests the Secretary-General to transmit the text of the draft Code to Member States for comment, and to submit their replies to the General Assembly at such time as the item may be placed on its provisional agenda."

INTERNATIONAL CRIMINAL JURISDICTION

In 1954, at its ninth session, the General Assembly decided to postpone consideration of the question of international criminal jurisdiction until it again took up the closely related questions of the definition of aggression and the draft Code of Offences against the Peace and Security of Mankind. (It took this decision by resolution 898(IX) of 14 December 1954.) The opportunity for considering it again did not occur until the Assembly's twelfth session, when the question of international criminal jurisdiction was referred to the Assembly's Sixth (Legal) Committee.

The majority of representatives who took part in the Committee's debate reiterated earlier opinions that the question of an international criminal jurisdiction was related both to the question of defining aggression and to the draft Code of Offences against the Peace and Security of Mankind. They felt that consideration of the matter should be postponed in view of the decisions taken by the Assembly on 29 November 1957, again to defer consideration of the definition of aggression and in view of a Sixth Committee recommendation adopted earlier at the twelfth session for postponing consideration of the draft Code of Offences.

The representative of Haiti, however, did not think that the question of an international criminal jurisdiction was related to the question of defining aggression to the same extent as it was to the draft Code of Offences. He also pointed out that the postponement in respect of the question of an international criminal jurisdiction did not take into consideration Assembly resolution 260(III) of 9 December 1948 which envisaged the possibility of establishing an international judicial organ for the trial of persons charged with genocide.

The Netherlands representative was also against postponement, which, in his view, amounted to an act of treason against the principles established by the judgements of the International Military Tribunals of Nürnberg and Tokyo.

Chile, the Philippines and Spain proposed a draft resolution whereby the General Assembly would decide to defer consideration of the question of an international criminal jurisdiction until it again took up the question of defining aggression and the question of a draft Code of Offences against the Peace and Security of Mankind. This was adopted by the Committee by 54 votes to 2, with 2 abstentions.

On 11 December 1957, it was approved at a plenary meeting of the Assembly, by 74 votes to 2, with 4 abstentions, as resolution 1187 (XII).

DOCUMENTARY REFERENCES

GENERAL ASSEMBLY—12TH SESSION
Plenary Meeting 727.
Sixth Committee, meetings 546, 547.

A/3649. Note by Secretary-General.
A/C.6/L.420. Chile, Philippines, Spain draft resolution, as amended orally by Egypt, adopted by Sixth Committee by 54 votes to 2, with 2 abstentions.
A/3771. Report of Sixth Committee.
RESOLUTION 1187(XII), as recommended by Sixth Committee, A/3771, adopted by Assembly on 11 December 1957, meeting 727, by 74 votes to 2,

with 4 abstentions.
"*The General Assembly,*
"*Considering* its resolution 898(IX) of 14 December 1954,
"*Considering* its resolution 1181(XII) of 29 November 1957 concerning the definition of aggression,
"*Decides* to defer consideration of the question of an international criminal jurisdiction until such time as the General Assembly takes up again the question of defining aggression and the question of a draft Code of Offences against the Peace and Security of Mankind."

THE LAW OF THE SEA

Following the recommendation of the International Law Commission as contained in the report covering the work of its eighth session, the General Assembly decided, by resolution 1105(XI) of 21 February 1957,
that an international conference of plenipotentiaries should be convoked to examine the law of the sea, taking account not only of the legal but also of the technical, biological, economic and political aspects of the problem, and to embody the results of its work in one or more international conventions or such other instruments as it may deem appropriate.

On 25 March 1957, notification of the conference was sent to all Members of the United Nations and to the following members of specialized agencies: Federal Republic of Germany, Republic of Korea, San Marino, Monaco, Switzerland, Viet-Nam and Vatican City. All the specialized agencies and various other intergovernmental organizations were similarly notified. On 26 August the Secretary-General informed the invited bodies of his decision to call the conference in Geneva on 24 February 1958.

The months following the General Assembly's resolution on summoning the conference saw the beginning of preparatory work which was to continue until the conference itself assembled. In accordance with the Assembly's decision of 21 February 1957, 10 experts from 10 different countries were invited to advise and assist the Secretariat in the preparations for the conference. Two series of meetings were held: one from 25 February to 6 March 1957 and the other from 7 to 16 October 1957.

As a result of these meetings, various steps were taken to prepare for the conference. A letter was sent to Governments on 25 March 1957, asking them to send any further provisional comments they might have on the International Law Commission's report. These were then reproduced as a conference document. Also issued were: a provisional agenda for the conference; the provisional rules of procedure; and a memorandum on the method of work and procedures of the conference (A/CONF.13/11). Arrangements were made, too, for the preparation of a number of papers to assist the conference, some of a legal nature and others concerning the scientific and technical aspects of the matters to be dealt with by the conference.

DOCUMENTARY REFERENCES

A/CONF.13/33. Initial list of documents for the United Nations Conference on the Law of the Sea.
Yearbook of the International Law Commission, 1956. Vol. II: Documents of eighth session, including

Report of Commission to General Assembly. U.N.P. Sales No.: 1956.V.3, Vol. II.
Laws and Regulations on the Régime of the Territorial Sea. U.N.P. Sales No.: 1957.V.2.

MULTILATERAL CONVENTIONS

NEW CONVENTIONS CONCLUDED
UNDER UNITED NATIONS AUSPICES

The following conventions, protocols, agreements or other instruments of which the Secretary-General is the depositary were drawn up under the auspices of the United Nations during 1957:

Protocol for extending the period of validity

of the Convention on Declaration of Death of Missing Persons, done at New York on 16 January 1957.

Convention on the Nationality of Married Women, done at New York on 20 February 1957.

European Agreement concerning the International Carriage of Dangerous Goods by Road (ADR) and Protocol of Signature, done at Geneva on 30 September 1957.

STATUS OF INTERNATIONAL AGREEMENTS

The number of international agreements for which the Secretary-General exercises depositary functions rose to 139 by 31 December 1957.

During 1957, a total of 39 signatures was affixed to international agreements for which the Secretary-General exercises depositary functions, and 191 instruments of ratification and

accession or notifications were transmitted to the Secretary-General.

The following multilateral conventions came into force during 1957:

Protocol of 16 January 1957 for extending the period of validity of the Convention on Declaration of Death of Missing Persons. This came into force on 22 January 1957.

Supplementary Convention of 7 September 1956 on the Abolition of Slavery, the Slave Trade and Institutions and Practices similar to Slavery. This came into force on 30 April 1957.

Convention of 20 June 1956 on Recovery Abroad of Maintenance. This came into force on 25 May 1957.

Customs Convention of 4 June 1954 on the Temporary Importation of Private Road Vehicles. This came into force on 15 December 1957.

DOCUMENTARY REFERENCES

Status of Multilateral Conventions of Which Secretary-General Acts as Depositary (ST/LEG/3). Supplements Nos. 16-20, June, September, December 1957. U.N.P. Sales Nos.: 1952.V.2. Supplements 16-18; 1952.V.2. Supplements 19; 1952.V.2. Supplements 20.

ST/LEG/6. Handbook of final clauses.

REGISTRATION AND PUBLICATION OF TREATIES

During 1957, a total of 749 treaties and agreements were registered with the Secretariat; 49 *ex officio*, 658 by 29 Governments, and 42 by six specialized agencies. Three treaties and agreements were filed and recorded, two by the Secretariat and one at the request of a Government.

This brought the total of treaties and agreements registered or filed and recorded to 6,269. In addition, 267 certified statements relating to these treaties and agreements were registered during 1957, and four certified statements were

filed and recorded, bringing the total of certified statements registered or filed and recorded by the end of 1957 to 1,388.

The texts of treaties and agreements registered or filed and recorded are published by the Secretariat in the United Nations *Treaty Series* in the original languages, followed by translations in English and French. Thirty-nine volumes (178-216) of the *Treaty Series* were published in the course of 1957, as well as *Cumulative Index No. 1,* covering Volumes 1 to 100, and an *Interim Index,* covering Volumes 101 to 175.

DOCUMENTARY REFERENCES

United Nations Treaty Series, Vols. 178-216.
Cumulative Index No. 1 (Vols. 1–100).
Interim Index (Vols. 101–175).

PRIVILEGES AND IMMUNITIES

During 1957, four instruments of accession to the Convention on the Privileges and Immunities of the United Nations were deposited with the Secretary-General by the following Member States: Morocco, on 18 March; Tunisia, on 7 May; Austria, on 10 May and Albania, on 2

July (with a reservation). In addition, the Federation of Malaya notified the Secretary-General that it considered itself bound by the Convention, to which the United Kingdom had acceded on 17 September 1946, and that the Diplomatic Privileges (United Nations and International Court of Justice) Order in Council which formed part of the law of the Federation had, pursuant to Article 162 of the Federation's Constitution, been continued in force after 31 August 1957 (*Merdeka Day*), when the Federation attained independence. At the end of 1957, there were therefore 56 States parties to the Convention.

Two more States became parties to the Convention on the Privileges and Immunities of the Specialized Agencies in 1957. The Federal Republic of Germany, which had previously submitted to the Secretary-General an instrument of accession subject to a reservation, withdrew the reservation by a communication received by the Secretary-General on 10 October 1957, thus becoming a party as of that date to this Convention. Tunisia deposited its instrument

of accession on 3 December 1957. There were thus 23 States which had acceded to the Convention by the end of 1957. This number was in addition to the two States (Belgium and Italy) which had previously submitted to the Secretary-General instruments of accession subject to reservations.

Two notifications were received during the year extending application of the Convention to additional specialized agencies.

A revised text of Annex 7 to the Convention was adopted by the Tenth World Health Assembly and, on 1 July 1957, was deposited with the Secretary-General. By the end of the year, four States had accepted this revised text, namely, Denmark, Norway, Sweden and the United Kingdom.

RULES OF PROCEDURE OF UNITED NATIONS ORGANS

GENERAL ASSEMBLY

VICE-PRESIDENCIES AND COMPOSITION OF THE GENERAL COMMITTEE

On 7 October 1957, at its twelfth session, the General Assembly agreed to establish a ninth Vice-Presidency on an *ad hoc* basis for the twelfth session. Spain was elected as Vice-President. As the establishment of this ninth Vice-Presidency was on an *ad hoc* basis, the Assembly did not consider it necessary to change its rules of procedure.

On 12 December, acting on a recommendation of its Special Political Committee, the Assembly amended its rules of procedure so that at future sessions 13 (instead of eight) Vice-Presidents would be elected to serve on the Assembly's General Committee. An annex to this resolution laid down the pattern of geographical distribution to be followed in electing the Vice-Presidents.

(For further details about these decisions, see above, POLITICAL AND SECURITY QUESTIONS, CHAPTER XV, section on QUESTIONS RELATING TO SIZE AND COMPOSITION OF ASSEMBLY'S GENERAL COMMITTEE.)

VOTING MAJORITY IN ASSEMBLY ON MATTERS CONCERNING NON-SELF-GOVERNING AREAS

Also considered at the Assembly's twelfth session was the question of the voting majority required in the Assembly on matters concerning Non-Self-Governing Territories. This question

was considered by the assembly's Fourth Committee (which deals with matters concerning the International Trusteeship System and Non-Self-Governing Territories) and by its Sixth (Legal) Committee. No final decision on the matter, however, was taken by the Assembly.

(For further details, see above, QUESTIONS CONCERNING NON-SELF-GOVERNING TERRITORIES AND THE INTERNATIONAL TRUSTEESHIP SYSTEM, CHAPTER I.)

TRUSTEESHIP COUNCIL

REVIEW OF PROCEDURES ON PETITIONS

On 10 April 1957, at its nineteenth session, the Trusteeship Council set up a four-member committee to study the Council's procedures regarding petitions with a view to suggesting improvements and to report to the next session.

On 8 July 1957, at its twentieth session, the Council set up a two-member committee to determine, with the assistance of the United Nations Secretariat, the provisional classification of all communications received from Trust Territories. This was a temporary measure, approved subject to review after a year and without prejudice to existing rules of procedure for handling communications and petitions.

(For further details, see above, QUESTIONS CONCERNING THE INTERNATIONAL TRUSTEESHIP SYSTEM AND NON-SELF-GOVERNING TERRITORIES, CHAPTER III, section on PETITIONS AND ORAL HEARINGS.)

ELECTION OF OFFICERS

On 11 July 1957, at its twentieth session, the Trusteeship Council amended rule 19 of its rules of procedure so that its President and Vice-President would in future be elected at the beginning of its January session each year instead of at the beginning of its June session. This resolution (1715(XX)), was adopted on the proposal of Burma. The Burmese proposal had previously been submitted at the Council's nineteenth session, when the Council, however, decided to defer consideration of the matter.

DOCUMENTARY REFERENCES

REVISION OF TRUSTEESHIP
COUNCIL'S RULES OF PROCEDURE

TRUSTEESHIP COUNCIL—19TH AND 20TH SESSIONS
Plenary Meetings 791, 793, 794, 838.

T/L.761. Burma draft resolution.
RESOLUTION 1715(XX), as proposed by Burma, T/L.761, adopted unanimously by Council on 11 July 1957, meeting 838.

"*The Trusteeship Council,*

"*Decides* to amend the text of rule 19 of its rules of procedure by substituting the word 'January' for the word 'June'."

T/1/Rev.4/Corr.1. Rules of procedure of Trusteeship Council. Amendment approved by Trusteeship Council at its twentieth session.

(For documentary references on other matters concerning rules of procedure of United Nations organs, see relevant chapters and sections as indicated in text matter above.)

Administrative and Budgetary Questions

CHAPTER I

ADMINISTRATIVE ARRANGEMENTS

UNITED NATIONS SALARY, ALLOWANCE AND BENEFITS SYSTEM

At its twelfth session in 1957, the General Assembly considered a number of administrative matters. Among them were various aspects of the United Nations salary, allowance and benefits system which had been referred from the Assembly's eleventh session, at which a report by a Salary Review Committee (A/3209) had been discussed. These questions included: the extension of the general service category; additional salary increment for long service; the definitions of dependency for use in deciding the entitlements payable to staff members with dependents; dental costs insurance; and machinery for dealing with certain pay and personnel questions.

EXTENSION OF GENERAL SERVICE CATEGORY

In its report to the Assembly's eleventh session, the Salary Review Committee had recommended that the general service category of United Nations staff members be extended to take in certain posts in the first three levels of the professional category which were primarily of a servicing character and which might be appropriately filled by local rather than by international recruitment.

At the twelfth session, the Assembly's Fifth (Administrative and Budgetary) Committee examined an alternative proposal by the Secretary-General whereby he would study the practicability of introducing a separate and limited category to accommodate technical, trades and related personnel.

The Fifth Committee finally agreed that he should proceed with such a study, in consultation with the executive heads of the specialized agencies. The study was to cover all types of posts that had caused difficulty, including a re-examination of the original recommendations of the Salary Review Committee. The Secretary-General was asked to submit a report to the General Assembly on this subject in due course, it being understood that he would re-examine the original recommendations by the Salary Review Committee.

ADDITIONAL SALARY INCREMENTS FOR LONG SERVICE

In 1956, the Salary Review Committee had suggested additional salary increments for certain salary levels to ameliorate the situation of staff members who were qualified for promotion to a higher level but who could not be promoted because of the basic structure of the Secretariat. At its eleventh session, the Assembly referred this matter back to the Advisory Committee on Administrative and Budgetary Questions for further examination.

At the Assembly's twelfth session, the Advisory Committee recommended that two steps be added to the third level in the professional category (P-3, Second Officer) where the immediate problem in the United Nations Secretariat was most acute. The longevity increments, it proposed, should be available at intervals of two years and should not be paid until a staff member had remained at the level for at least five years.

In approving this recommendation on 14 December 1957, on the proposal of its Fifth Committee, the Assembly also agreed that to be eligible for such increments a staff member must be qualified for promotion to the next higher level should a suitable vacancy occur. The resolution providing for this (1225(XII)) was approved by 73 votes to 0.

DEFINITION OF DEPENDENCY

The Salary Review Committee had recommended that the definitions of dependency be improved as a necessary prerequisite for the successful operation of the system of salary adjustment, allowances and benefits which it had proposed in its report, the main features of which had been approved by the Assembly by resolution 1095(XI) on 27 February 1957.

The Secretary-General submitted definitions of dependency arrived at in discussions with the executive heads of specialized agencies. These were designed (a) to obviate duplication of payments; (b) to remove, where practicable, distinctions causing differentiations in administrative treatment between the sexes; (c) to obviate payments in cases where dependency clearly did not exist; (d) to reconcile, as far as possible, the differing practices of the international organizations concerned. The Secretary-General proposed to introduce these definitions at an early date, using reasonable discretion in their application and recognizing that they were subject to review in the light of a full year's working experience. He also proposed an addition to Staff Regulation 3.4.

The Assembly's Fifth Committee agreed to these proposals by a vote of 51 to 0, with 9 abstentions. Its decision was given final approval at a plenary meeting of the Assembly on 14 December 1957, with the adoption, by a vote of 73 to 0, of resolution 1225(XII).

DENTAL COSTS INSURANCE

In 1956, the Salary Review Committee had favoured the provision of some kind of scheme to mitigate the heavy dental expenses which staff members might incur in certain areas. At its eleventh session, the Assembly invited the Secretary-General to examine all practical possibilities in the Headquarters area and to report on this matter during the twelfth session.

The Secretary-General's report, which examined five alternatives, reaffirmed his earlier view that the Group Health Dental Insurance Plan of New York was likely to prove the most effective and most economical arrangement.

The Fifth Committee approved the participation of the United Nations in the Group Health Dental Insurance Plan on an experimental basis, providing that one third of costs of this participation should be borne by the Organization and two thirds by the participating staff members.

The Fifth Committee agreed to participation in the plan by 58 votes to 0, with 1 abstention, and to the cost-sharing arrangements, by 45 votes to 1, with 10 abstentions.

MACHINERY FOR CERTAIN PAY AND PERSONNEL PROBLEMS

The Salary Review Committee had suggested that certain advantages might be gained if an advisory body external to the secretariats of the international organizations, such as the International Civil Service Advisory Board (ICSAB), were invited to review and make recommendations on such subjects as the system of classification of staff, post adjustments and related questions of statistical methodology, and any divergencies in conditions of service in organizations following the common system of salaries, allowances and benefits adopted for the secretariats of six of the major international organizations in 1951. The Board, it felt, should be able to call on experts as the necessity arose and should be provided with an adequate secretariat.

At the General Assembly's twelfth session, the Fifth Committee noted that certain important questions had already been referred to ICSAB but that constitutional and other questions remained to be solved before substantial changes could be made in the status of that body. It also took note of reports on this matter submitted by the Secretary-General and by the Advisory Committee on Administrative and Budgetary Questions.

POST ADJUSTMENTS FOR GENEVA

At its eleventh session, the General Assembly adopted a system of post adjustments, for application to the salary scales of staff members in the Principal Officer and Director category and in the Professional category. This replaced the previous system of differentials and cost-of-living allowances. At the same time, the General Assembly: decided that United Nations Headquarters staff should be placed in Class 5 within this post adjustment system; recommended that Geneva be placed in Class 1; and asked the Secretary-General to place United Nations staff serving in the headquarters area of a specialized agency, which has adopted the system, in the post adjustment class set by that agency for its headquarters area.

At the General Assembly's twelfth session, the Secretary-General reported to the Fifth Committee that the Tenth World Health Assembly of the World Health Organization (WHO), in May 1957, and the Governing Body of the International Labour Organisation (ILO), in June 1957, had approved Class 2, with effect from 1 June 1957, for the staffs of their respective organizations stationed at Geneva.

He pointed out that the two legislative organs of these agencies had also indicated the date 1 January 1957, instead of 1 January 1956 (the base date of the system), as the date from which future cost-of-living adjustments would be measured.

In the light of these developments, the Secretary-General also felt obliged to recommend, on grounds of equity and in the interest of preserving the common system, that United Nations staff in Geneva should be placed on the same footing.

Upon the recommendation of the Fifth Committee, and on the basis of certain comments by the Advisory Committee on Administrative and Budgetary Questions, the General Assembly took the following steps. It decided to place United Nations staff stationed at Geneva in post adjustment Class 5, as of 1 August 1957. It also decided to maintain 1 January 1956 as the date from which changes in the cost of living at Geneva should be measured in determining the post adjustment for United Nations staff members. It hoped, too, that the appropriate legislative authorities of ILO and WHO would reconsider the date from which changes in the cost of living in Geneva should be measured for purposes of post adjustment.

The resolution to this effect (1221(XII)) was approved at a plenary meeting of the Assembly on 14 December 1957, by 60 votes to 9, with 4 abstentions. The vote for it in the Fifth Committee was 49 to 7, with 4 abstentions.

DOCUMENTARY REFERENCES

GENERAL ASSEMBLY—12TH SESSION
Plenary Meeting 731.
Fifth Committee, meetings 626-628.

A/3656. Report of Secretary-General.
A/3681. Report of Advisory Committee on Administrative and Budgetary Questions.
A/C.5/719. Dental costs plan. Report of Secretary-General.
A/3723. Dental costs insurance. Report of Advisory Committee on Administrative and Budgetary Questions.
A/3797. Report of Fifth Committee (Draft resolution A).
RESOLUTION 1225(XII), as recommended by Fifth Committee, A/3797, adopted by Assembly on 14 December 1957, meeting 731, by 73 votes to 0.

"The General Assembly,
"Having considered the reports of the Secretary-General and the Advisory Committee on Administrative and Budgetary Questions on certain outstanding questions relating to the United Nations salary, allowance and benefits system,
"Resolves that the Staff Regulations of the United Nations shall be modified by the amendments annexed to the present resolution, with effect from 1 January 1958."

ANNEX
Regulation 3.4 (Dependency benefits)
"Add a new paragraph (c), to read:
" '(i) With a view to avoiding duplication of benefits and in order to achieve equality between staff members who receive dependency benefits under applicable laws in the form of governmental grants or income tax exemption and staff members who do

not receive such dependency benefits, the Secretary-General shall prescribe conditions under which the dependency allowance for a child specified in (a) (i) above shall be payable to the extent that the dependency benefits enjoyed by the staff member or his spouse under applicable laws amount to less than such a dependency allowance. Where any income tax exemption in respect of the child of a staff member accrues to the benefit of the United Nations under arrangements for reimbursement of income tax, the staff member shall receive the full amount of the dependency allowance for such child.
" '(ii) The Secretary-General may determine the amount of the dependency benefits referred to in (c) (i) above on the basis of categories established by him in the interest of administrative convenience and simplicity provided that the benefit actually received plus the dependency allowance shall be no less than $300 in respect of a child.'
"As a result, the present paragraphs (c) and (d) become paragraphs (d) and (e).
Annex I, paragraph 5
"Add the following new text:
" 'The Secretary-General may provide two further increments at $10,540 and $10,920, at two-yearly intervals, to staff in the Second Officer level who have remained in that level for at least five years and are, in his opinion, qualified for promotion.' "

POST ADJUSTMENTS FOR GENEVA

Plenary Meeting 731.
Fifth Committee, meetings 608, 611, 624, 625, 645, 646.

A/C.5/711. Report of Secretary-General.

A/3721. Report of Advisory Committee on Administrative and Budgetary Questions.

A/3793. Report of Fifth Committee, containing draft resolution, adopted by Committee, by 49 votes to 7, with 4 abstentions.

RESOLUTION 1221(XII), as recommended by Fifth Committee, A/3793, adopted by Assembly on 14 December 1957, meeting 731, by 60 votes to 9, with 4 abstentions.

"*The General Assembly,*

"*Recalling* its resolution 1095(XI) of 27 February 1957 relating to the United Nations salary, allowance and benefits system,

"*Having considered* the reports of the Secretary-General and of the Advisory Committee on Administrative and Budgetary Questions on the question of the classification of Geneva in the schedule of post adjustments established under that resolution.

"*Noting* the action taken by the World Health Assembly and the Governing Body of the International Labour Office in approving Class 2 in the schedule of post adjustments to be applied to the staff of those agencies serving at Geneva,

"1. *Decides* to apply, as of 1 August 1957, Class 2 in the schedule of post adjustments to United Nations staff members at Geneva;

"2. *Decides* to maintain 1 January 1956 as the date from which changes in the cost of living at Geneva should be measured in determining the post adjustment for United Nations staff members;

"3. *Expresses the hope* that the appropriate legislative authorities of the International Labour Organisation and the World Health Organization will reconsider, in the light of paragraph 2 above, the date from which changes in the cost of living at Geneva should be measured in determining the post adjustment for the staff members of those agencies."

QUESTION OF GEOGRAPHICAL DISTRIBUTION OF THE STAFF

The General Assembly returned at its twelfth session to the question of the geographical distribution of the staff in accordance with resolution 1097(XI), of 27 February 1957. Before it was a report submitted by the Secretary-General as called for by that resolution.

While there was some divergence of opinion in the Assembly's Fifth Committee about adequacy of progress achieved in this matter, it was generally agreed that the principle of geographical distribution itself was not at issue, and also that it could not in equity be invoked as a barrier to promotion. Ceylon submitted a draft resolution proposing in effect (*a*) that the United Nations staff be divided into different groups by salary level and (*b*) that quotas of representation, rather than desirable ranges of representation, be sought for each Member State in accordance with the principles approved for the assessment of contributions.

After discussion in the Committee, it was decided not to recommend this approach. Instead, the Committee approved an amended version of Ceylon's draft resolution, from which the reference to the possible use of a quota system was deleted. The Committee adopted the draft reso-

lution as amended by a vote of 43 to 0, with 15 abstentions.

This was given final approval at a plenary meeting of the Assembly on 14 December 1957, in the form of resolution 1226 (XII), adopted by roll-call, by 74 votes to 0, with 5 abstentions. The Assembly thereby expressed appreciation of the action already taken by the Secretary-General in giving appropriate preference, in making new appointments at all levels, to nationalities forming a disproportionately small part of the United Nations Secretariat. It also asked him to continue his efforts in this direction and to report to the Assembly in 1958 on the results.

Before taking its decision on these lines, the Assembly rejected a Bulgarian amendment. This, in effect, asked the Secretary-General in particular: to increase, wherever opportunity offered, the representation of nationalities with a disproportionately low representation; to achieve a more equitable and wider geographical distribution of the more senior posts; and to try to set aside at least three posts for Member States making the minimum contributions to the United Nations budget.

DOCUMENTARY REFERENCES

GENERAL ASSEMBLY—12TH SESSION
Plenary Meeting 731.
Fifth Committee, meetings 629, 630, 632, 633.

A/C.5/718/Rev.1. Changes in geographical distribution. Report of Secretary-General.
A/C.5/L.483. Ceylon draft resolution, as amended

by Ceylon and United States, adopted by Fifth Committee by 43 votes to 0, with 15 abstentions.
A/3797. Report of Fifth Committee (draft resolution B).
A/L.244. Bulgaria amendment to Fifth Committee's draft resolution B, A/3797.
RESOLUTION 1226(XII), as recommended by Fifth

Committee, A/3797, adopted by Assembly on 14 December 1957, meeting 731, by roll-call vote of 74 to 0, with 5 abstentions, as follows:

In favour: Afghanistan, Albania, Argentina, Australia, Austria, Belgium, Bolivia, Brazil, Bulgaria, Burma, Byelorussian SSR, Canada, Ceylon, Chile, China, Colombia, Costa Rica, Cuba, Czechoslovakia, Denmark, Dominican Republic, Ecuador, Egypt, El Salvador, Ethiopia, Finland, France, Ghana, Greece, Haiti, Hungary, Iceland, India, Iraq, Ireland, Israel, Italy, Japan, Laos, Liberia, Libya, Luxembourg, Federation of Malaya, Mexico, Morocco, Nepal, Netherlands, New Zealand, Nicaragua, Norway, Pakistan, Panama, Paraguay, Philippines, Poland, Portugal, Romania, Saudi Arabia, Spain, Sudan, Sweden, Syria, Thailand, Tunisia, Turkey, Ukrainian SSR, Union of South Africa, USSR, United Kingdom, United States, Uruguay, Venezuela, Yemen, Yugoslavia.

Against: None.

Abstaining: Cambodia, Guatemala, Indonesia, Iran, Jordan.

"The General Assembly,

"Having considered the report of the Secretary-General regarding changes in the geographical distribution of the staff of the Secretariat of the United Nations during the year ended 31 August 1957, submitted to the General Assembly at its twelfth session,

"Recalling its recommendation in paragraph 1 of resolution 1097(XI) of 27 February 1957 that, in future appointments to the staff of the Secretariat of the United Nations, at all levels, appropriate preference be given to nationalities which form a disproportionately small part of the Secretariat, subject to the provisions of Article 101, paragraph 3, of the Charter of the United Nations,

"Noting that the appointments listed in the report of the Secretary-General mark a step towards the objectives of that recommendation,

"Expressing appreciation of the action already taken by the Secretary-General pursuant to that recommendation,

"Requests the Secretary-General:

"(*a*) In making future appointments to the staff of the Secretariat of the United Nations, at all levels, to continue his efforts to ensure the fullest possible conformity with the recommendation in paragraph 1 of resolution 1097(XI) of 27 February 1957;

"(*b*) To report to the General Assembly at its thirteenth session the results of his efforts in that direction."

REVIEW OF STAFF REGULATIONS

At its eighth session, the General Assembly had adopted certain amendments to Staff Regulations 9.1(*a*) and 9.3(*b*) to regulate the review of appointments of permanent staff members of the Secretariat whose conduct or integrity had been called in question. It was decided at that time that a review of the principles and standards progressively developed and applied by the Secretary-General should be undertaken at a later date.

At its twelfth session, in 1957, the General Assembly considered a report by the Secretary-General which set out developments which had taken place in implementing the Staff Regulations referred to above. The report also referred to a report on *Standards of Conduct in the International Civil Service* which had been prepared by the International Civil Service Advisory Board in 1954. The Secretary-General concluded with a recommendation that no change be made at the present time in the Staff Regulations.

The General Assembly took note of the Secretary-General's report by resolution 1227(XII), which was adopted without objection on 14 December 1957, on the recommendation of its Fifth Committee.

DOCUMENTARY REFERENCES

GENERAL ASSEMBLY—12TH SESSION
Plenary Meeting 731.
Fifth Committee, meeting 628.

A/C.5/726. Review of Staff Regulations and of principles and standards progressively applied thereto. Report of Secretary-General.

A/C.5/L.465. Staff rules of United Nations. Report of Secretary-General.

A/3797. Report of Fifth Committee (draft resolution C).

RESOLUTION 1227(XII), as recommended by Fifth Committee, A/3797, adopted by Assembly on 14 December 1957, meeting 731, without objection.

"The General Assembly

"Takes note of the report of the Secretary-General on the review of the Staff Regulations and of the principles and standards progressively applied thereto."

PROPORTION OF FIXED-TERM STAFF

The question of the proportion of posts in the United Nations Secretariat to be filled by staff appointed for fixed terms was considered at the General Assembly's twelfth session on conjunction with the question of the geographical distribution of the staff. It had been agreed at the previous session that there should be an annual review of the proportion of staff employed in the Secretariat on fixed-term appointments.

A report by the Secretary-General on the matter pointed out the impracticability of drawing a distinction between posts which the Salary Review Committee had defined in 1956 as "suitable for filling on a secondment basis" and other

professional posts. As of 31 August 1957, there were 960 internationally recruited staff members in the Director, Principal Officer and Professional categories who held appointments on a career basis; the number of staff members with appointments on a fixed-term basis was 153.

The Assembly's Fifth Committee took note of the Secretary-General's report and invited him to report again in a year's time on the further progress made by then.

DOCUMENTARY REFERENCES

GENERAL ASSEMBLY—12TH SESSION
Plenary Meeting 731.
Fifth Committee, meetings 629, 630, 632, 633.

A/C.5/724. Proportion of fixed-term staff. Report of Secretary-General.
A/3797. Report of Fifth Committee.

ORGANIZATION OF SECRETARIAT AT THE SENIOR LEVEL

Changes in the salaries and emoluments of Under-Secretaries (including reimbursement of representation expenses) and consequent amendments to the Staff Regulations were approved at the General Assembly's twelfth session after consideration of a report by the Secretary-General on the organization of the Secretariat at the senior level.

This report suggested a redeployment of officers at this level, affecting the number of such officers and their assignments.

After discussing the Secretary-General's report, the Fifth Committee agreed, by a vote of 45 to 2, with 16 abstentions, to defer consideration of the merging of the Technical Assistance Administration with the Department of Economic and Social Affairs to a later session when fuller and more detailed information on the amalgamation question would be available.

The Secretary-General's report further recommended that the annual base salary of Under-Secretaries be raised from $12,500 net ($18,000 gross under the staff assessment plan)—the rate approved for Directors by the General Assembly at its eleventh session—to $15,000 net ($23,000 gross). Under-Secretaries would become subject to the system of post adjustments and such other allowances and benefits as were available to staff generally, but the basic allowance of $3,500 provided for under paragraph 1 of Annex I of the Staff Regulations would be eliminated.

The Secretary-General also recommended the maintenance of existing arrangements for "additional payments to Under-Secretaries to compensate for such special costs as may be reasonably incurred in the interests of the Organization in the performance of duties assigned to them by the Secretary-General", the authority for such payments to be broadened to include officials away from United Nations Headquarters within the previous budgetary maximum applicable to such officers at Headquarters.

By 50 votes to 7, with 4 abstentions, the Fifth Committee approved the Secretary-General's proposals, as endorsed by the Advisory Committee on Administrative and Budgetary Questions. It did so after rejecting, by 41 votes to 8, with 12 abstentions, a USSR proposal that an Under-Secretary be paid $14,000 a year, in accordance with the recommendations of the Salary Review Committee.

The Fifth Committee's resolution on the matter was later adopted as resolution 1234(XII) at a plenary meeting of the Assembly on 14 December 1957 by 66 votes to 9.

Approved, too, by the Fifth Committee was the retention of the sum of $50,000, proposed by the Secretary-General as the total amount of the additional payments for 1958 to be made in reimbursement of representational and related expenses to Under-Secretaries at United Nations Headquarters and elsewhere. The Committee approved a recommendation to this effect by 36 votes to 21, with 4 abstentions, after rejecting a USSR proposal that the payments in question be limited to $1,500 for any eligible official.

DOCUMENTARY REFERENCES

GENERAL ASSEMBLY—12TH SESSION
Plenary Meeting 731.
Fifth Committee, meetings 607-610, 641-643.

A/C.5/728. Report of Secretary-General.
A/3762. Report of Advisory Committee on Administrative and Budgetary Questions.
A/3800. Report of Fifth Committee (draft resolution E).
RESOLUTION 1234(XII), as recommended by Fifth Committee, A/3800, adopted by Assembly on 14 December 1957, meeting 731, by 66 votes to 9.

"*The General Assembly,*

"*Having considered* the report of the Secretary-General on the organization of the Secretariat at the senior level and the comments thereon of the Advisory Committee on Administrative and Budgetary Questions,

"*Resolves* that the Staff Regulations of the United Nations shall be modified by the amendments annexed to the present resolution, with effect from 1 January 1958."

ANNEX

Annex I, paragraph 1

"Replace the present text by the following:

" 'An Under-Secretary shall receive a salary of $US23,000 (subject to the Staff Assessment Plan provided in staff regulation 3.3 and to post adjustments wherever applied) and, if otherwise eligible, shall receive the allowances which are available to staff members generally.' "

Annex I, paragraph 2

"In the first sentence delete the words 'and officials of equivalent rank at Headquarters.' "

Annex I, paragraph 9 (Post adjustments)

"In the first sentence replace the words 'may adjust the basic salaries set forth in paragraph 3 and 4 of this annex' by the words 'may adjust the basic salaries set forth in paragraphs 1, 3 and 4 of this annex.' "

Regulations 3.4 (Dependency benefits)

"In paragraph (*a*) amend the beginning of the first sentence to read: 'Under-Secretaries and staff members in the Principal Officer and Director category.' "

Regulations 1.10 and 4.5 (*a*)

"Delete the references to 'officials of equivalent rank.' "

JOINT STAFF PENSION FUND

At its twelfth session, the General Assembly took note of: (*a*) the annual report of the United Nations Joint Staff Pension Board and (*b*) the Board's report on the fourth actuarial valuation of the Pension Fund as of 30 September 1956 and the second review of the basic tables of the Fund. The Assembly did so by resolutions 1199(XII) and 1200 (XII), both of which were adopted without objection on 13 December 1957.

On the same day, by resolution 1201(XII), the Assembly unanimously approved several amendments to the regulations of the United Nations Joint Staff Pension Fund, on the basis of recommendations by the Pension Board.

The effect of these amendments may be summarized as follows:

(i) The definition of "final average remuneration" was amended to mean, for a participant who entered the Fund before 3 November 1955, the average pensionable remuneration of the participant during the last 10 years of his contributory service whenever this average is higher than the last five years of his contributory service, which would otherwise apply.

(ii) The rate of interest was changed from 2½ per cent to 3 per cent per annum for all transactions of the Fund after 31 December 1957.

(iii) The formula for calculating benefits payable upon the retirement, disability or death of a participant was increased from 1/60 to 1/55 of the final average remuneration.

(iv) The minimum disability benefit provided under article V(a) of the Pension Fund Regulations was raised from 3/10 to 1/3 of the final average remuneration.

(v) The minimum for a widow's benefit, under article VII(i), was raised. It was set at whichever of the following was the less: (*a*) $750 per annum or (*b*) twice the original amount determined under article VII.

(vi) Provision was made for associate participation in the Fund for staff holding fixed-term appointments for at least one year but less than five years. The scheme provided for benefits in the event of the death or disability of the participant.

(vii) Provision was made for treating the International Atomic Energy Agency as if it were a specialized agency for the purposes of the Pension Fund Regulations.

(For further details, see text of resolution 1201(XII), under DOCUMENTARY REFERENCES below.)

All three resolutions on Pension Fund matters were approved on the recommendation of the Assembly's Fifth Committee.

DOCUMENTARY REFERENCES

GENERAL ASSEMBLY—12TH SESSION
Plenary Meeting 729.
Fifth Committee, meetings 634, 635.

A/3611 and Corr.1, 2. Annual report of United Nations Joint Staff Pension Board.

A/3642. Report of United Nations Joint Staff Pension Board on fourth actuarial valuation of Fund as of 30 September 1956 and second review of basic tables of Fund.

A/3690. Amendment to regulations of United Nations Joint Staff Pension Fund: further actuarial valuation. Note by Chairman of United Nations Joint Staff Pension Board.

A/3749. Report of Advisory Committee on Administrative and Budgetary Questions.

A/C.5/714. Amendment to Regulations of United Nations Joint Staff Pension Fund: admission of International Atomic Energy Agency to Fund. Note by Secretary-General.

A/3788. Report of Fifth Committee.

RESOLUTIONS 1199(XII)–1201(XII), as recommended by Fifth Committee, A/3788, adopted by Assembly on 13 December 1957, meeting 729, as follows: 1199(XII) and 1200(XII), without objection; 1201(XII), unanimously.

RESOLUTION 1199(XII). ANNUAL REPORT OF THE UNITED NATIONS JOINT STAFF PENSION BOARD

"*The General Assembly*

"*Takes note* of the annual report of the United Nations Joint Staff Pension Board."

RESOLUTION 1200(XII). REPORT OF THE UNITED NATIONS JOINT STAFF PENSION BOARD ON THE FOURTH ACTUARIAL VALUATION OF THE UNITED NATIONS JOINT STAFF PENSION FUND AS OF 30 SEPTEMBER 1956 AND SECOND REVIEW OF THE BASIC TABLES OF THE FUND

"*The General Assembly*

"1. *Takes note* of the report of the United Nations Joint Staff Pension Board on the fourth actuarial valuation of the Fund as of 30 September 1956 and the second review of the basic tables of the Fund;

"2. *Takes note* of the observations thereon of the Advisory Committee on Administrative and Budgetary Questions as set forth in its twenty-third report to the twelfth session of the General Assembly."

RESOLUTION 1201(XII). AMENDMENTS TO THE REGULATIONS OF THE UNITED NATIONS JOINT STAFF PENSION FUND

"*The General Assembly*

"*Adopts* the texts annexed to the present resolution as amendments to the Regulations of the United Nations Joint Staff Pension Fund. These amendments shall come into force on 1 January 1958."

ANNEX

Article I, paragraph 4 (amended text)

" 'Final average remuneration' means the average annual pensionable remuneration of the participant during the last five years of his contributory service,

on the understanding that, in the case of participants who have entered the Fund prior to 3 November 1955, it means the average pensionable remuneration of the participant during the last ten years of his contributory service whenever this average is higher. When the participant has less than five years of contributory service, the final average remuneration shall mean the average annual pensionable remuneration during the actual period of contributory service."

Article II, paragraph I (amended text)

"Every full-time member of the staff of each member organization shall become a participant in the United Nations Joint Staff Pension Fund:

"(*a*) If he enters employment under a contract without a time-limit;

"(*b*) If he enters employment under a fixed-term contract for five years or more;

"(*c*) If he has completed five years of employment and remains on a contract providing for further service of at least one year, or remains in employment for more than one year thereafter;

"(*d*) If the member organization certifies that the particular fixed-term contract is considered to cover a probationary period and is designed to lead to employment for an indefinite period,

provided that he is under sixty years of age at the time of entry into the Fund and that his participation is not excluded by his contract of employment."

Article IV, paragraph 1 (amended text)

"A participant who reaches the age of sixty shall, upon retirement, be entitled during the remainder of his life to an annual retirement benefit, payable monthly, equal to one-fifty-fifth of his final average remuneration multiplied by the number of years of his contributory service not exceeding thirty years."

Article V (amended text)

"Subject to the provisions of articles X.1 (*b*) and XVI, a participant who, before reaching the age of sixty, has, in the opinion of the Joint Staff Pension Board, become unable to perform his duties owing to serious physical or mental impairment, shall be entitled, subject to article IX, while such disability continues, to a disability benefit payable in the same manner as a retirement benefit and equal to nine-tenths of one-fifty-fifth of his final average remuneration multiplied by the number of years of his contributory service not exceeding thirty years. This disability benefit shall not be less than the smaller of:

"(*a*) One-third of the final average remuneration;

"(*b*) Nine-tenths of the retirement benefit to which he would have been entitled if he had remained in service until he had reached the age of sixty and his final average remuneration had remained unchanged."

Article VII, paragraph 1 (amended text)

"Subject to the provisions of article XVI, if a married male participant dies, his widow shall be entitled, subject to article IX, to a widow's benefit amounting, except as provided in paragraph 3 below, to half of the benefit which would have been paid to the participant had he qualified for a disability benefit at the time of his death or, if such deceased participant had attained the age of sixty, to one-half of the benefit which would have been paid to the participant had he retired under the provisions of article IV at the time of his death. Whenever the amount of the widow's benefit so determined shall be less than $750 per annum, it shall be increased to the smaller of: (*a*) $750 per annum, or (*b*) twice the original amount determined. This benefit shall cease on the widow's remarriage."

Article XXIX (amended text)

"The Joint Staff Pension Board, upon the advice of a qualified actuary or actuaries, shall adopt from time to time service and mortality tables and the rate of regular interest which shall be used in all actuarial calculations required in connexion with the Pension Fund. The rate of regular interest applicable shall be 2½ per cent per annum through 31 December 1957 and 3 per cent per annum thereafter unless and until changed by the Joint Staff Pension Board. At least once in each six years following the establishment of the Pension Fund, the Board shall have an actuarial investigation made into the mortality, service and compensation experience of the participants and beneficiaries of the Pension Fund; and taking into account the results of such investigation, the Board shall adopt such mortality, service and other tables as it shall deem appropriate.

"(*The change in the rate of regular interest specified in article XXIX entails consequential changes in articles III.1, VII.5, X.1 and 3, XI, XII.1 and 2, and XVI.6. In each case the phrase* 'at the rate of 2½ per cent per annum' *is replaced by the phrase* 'at the rate designated in article XXIX'.)"

Supplementary article B (new text)

"1. Every full-time member of the staff of each member organization shall become an associate participant in the United Nations Joint Staff Pension Fund:

"(*a*) If he enters employment under a fixed-term contract for at least one year but less than five years;

"(*b*) If he has completed one year of continuous employment, provided that he is not eligible under article II.1 to become a participant, provided that he is under sixty years of age, and provided further that his associate participation is not excluded by his contract of employment. For the purposes of this article, intervals of not more than thirty calendar days in the period of employment shall not be considered as breaking the continuity of employment.

"2. The participation of an associate participant shall cease when he reaches the age of sixty.

"3. An associate participant shall be eligible for a disability benefit under article V and his survivors to a death benefit under article VII.1, 2, 3, 4, 6 and 7, and to a child's benefit under article VIII. He shall not be entitled to a retirement benefit under article IV nor to a withdrawal benefit under article X, and his survivors shall not be entitled to a death benefit under article VII.5.

"4. Each member organization shall pay monthly into the Pension Fund, in respect of each associate participant, a contribution equal to 4½ per cent of his pensionable remuneration, or such percentage contribution, not to exceed 6 per cent, as shall be determined from time to time by the Joint Staff Pension Board on the basis of actuarial valuations of the Fund.

"5. Whenever an associate participant is entitled under article II to become a participant, he may elect during the first year of his participation to have the period performed as an associate participant included in his contributory service to the extent to which he pays into the Pension Fund a sum or sums equal to the contributions he would have paid as a participant, plus interest, at the rate designated in article XXIX. Payment into the Pension Fund of amounts sufficient to meet the Fund's obligations, resulting from the inclusion of such additional contributory service, which are not met by payments made by the participants shall be made by the member organization designated for that purpose in accordance with arrangements concluded by the member organizations, provided that payment has not already been made by a member organization for the period concerned.

"6. All other provisions of these regulations consistent with the present article shall be applicable to associate participants, *mutatis mutandis*, in the same manner as to a participant. Such administrative rules as shall be considered necessary for the implementation of this article shall be established by the Joint Staff Pension Board."

Supplementary article C (new text)

"For the purposes of these regulations, the International Atomic Energy Agency shall be treated as if it were a specialized agency."

PROPOSAL TO AMEND ADMINISTRATIVE TRIBUNAL STATUTE

In 1955, at the General Assembly's tenth session, the Fifth Committee decided that an Australian proposal for amending article 9 of the Statute of the Administrative Tribunal be referred to the Secretary-General and the Advisory Committee on Administrative and Budgetary Questions. Article 9 deals with the amount of compensation which the Tribunal may award. The Secretary-General and the Advisory Committee were asked to report to the Assembly on the matter.

Both the Secretary-General and the Advisory Committee recommended at the twelfth session of the Assembly that no change be made at the present time in the Tribunal's Statute.

In the course of the Fifth Committee's discussions, the Australian representative pointed out that experience since the Assembly's tenth session seemed to indicate that the difficulty which the Australian proposal of 1955 sought to remove had been overcome.

Without objection, the Fifth Committee

agreed to his proposal that action in the matter be deferred until such time as further experience showed the need for reviewing the Tribunal's Statute.

DOCUMENTARY REFERENCES

GENERAL ASSEMBLY—12TH SESSION
Fifth Committee, meeting 628.

A/3629. Report of Secretary-General.

A/3684. Report of Advisory Committee on Administrative and Budgetary Questions.
A/3797. Report of Fifth Committee (paragraphs 52, 53).

CHAPTER II

BUDGETARY ARRANGEMENTS

BUDGET OF THE UNITED NATIONS

The General Assembly, at its twelfth session, approved a total appropriation of $55,062,850 to meet United Nations expenses for the year 1958. It did so on 14 December 1957 by resolution 1230(XII), which was adopted by 68 votes to 9, with 2 abstentions. (For text of resolution, see DOCUMENTARY REFERENCES below.)

The Secretary-General had originally submitted to the Assembly an estimated budget of $54,782,500; miscellaneous income was estimated at $3,050,000, thus leaving a net budget of $51,732,500. The Advisory Committee on Administrative and Budgetary Questions, after considering the Secretary-General's estimates, proposed a reduction of $1,052,800, bringing the gross appropriation down to $53,729,700. It estimated miscellaneous income at $3,250,000, or $200,000 more than the figure submitted by the Secretary-General.

As a result of decisions taken at the Assembly's twelfth session, the Secretary-General requested additional appropriations. On 12 December 1957, the Assembly's Fifth (Administrative and Budgetary) Committee recommended by 45 votes to 9, with 3 abstentions, a total appropriation of $55,062,850 for the financial year 1958. This was given final approval two days later at a plenary meeting of the Assembly, by resolution 1230(XII).

BUDGET PRESENTATION

The budget estimates for 1958 were submitted in the revised form which the Assembly had approved in February 1957. The Fifth Committee

gave much attention to this new form of budget presentation. During its discussion, most delegations agreed with the Secretary-General that the revised form, offered scope for budgetary and administrative improvements in three directions. First, it would facilitate the practical application of the order of priorities established by the Assembly because the allocation of funds would be based primarily on the work programmes and activities which the Assembly and the Councils had fixed. Second, the Secretary-General would be able to use staff resources and credits more flexibly than before. Third, it would allow of improved procedures for administrative and financial control of the global credits voted for like or related objects of expenditure.

UNFORESEEN AND EXTRAORDINARY EXPENSES FOR 1958

In considering the budget estimates, the General Assembly, acting on the unanimous recommendation of its Fifth Committee, authorized the Secretary-General to enter into commitments to meet unforeseen and extraordinary expenses in 1958 with the prior concurrence of the Advisory Committee on Administrative and Budgetary Questions. The Advisory Committee's concurrence, however, would not be required for: (1) commitments up to $2 million for maintenance of peace and security or for urgent economic rehabilitation, as certified by the Secretary-General; (2) commitments not exceeding $195,000 relating to the work of the

International Court of Justice, as certified by the President of the Court; and (3) commitments up to $25,000 for any body or *ad hoc* conference not covered in the basic annual conference programme. The resolution to this effect (1231(XII)) was adopted without objection at a plenary meeting of the Assembly on 14 December 1957.

WORKING CAPITAL FUND FOR 1958

On the same day, the Assembly also agreed, without objection, to maintain the Working Capital Fund for 1958 at the 1957 level, namely, $22 million. This it did by resolution 1232 (XII), which had previously been approved unanimously in the Fifth Committee. (For details about the source of the moneys and the use of the Fund, see text of resolution in DOCUMENTARY REFERENCES below. See also CHAPTER III, OTHER ADMINISTRATIVE AND BUDGETARY QUESTIONS, section on REPAYMENT OF HEADQUARTERS LOAN.

DOCUMENTARY REFERENCES

GENERAL ASSEMBLY—12TH SESSION
Plenary Meeting 731.
Fifth Committee, meetings 606-626, 635-638, 640-643, 645-648.

A/3600 and Add.1. Budget estimates for financial year 1958 and information annexes.
A/3624. Report of Advisory Committee on Administrative and Budgetary Questions.
A/C.5/720. Statement by Secretary-General on 15 October 1957.
A/C.5/721. Statement by Chairman of Advisory Committee on Administrative and Budgetary Questions on 15 October 1957.

BUDGET APPROPRIATIONS FOR 1958
A/3624, page 9. Draft appropriation resolution submitted by Advisory Committee, approved by Fifth Committee by 43 votes to 8, following adjustments reflecting decisions of Fifth Committee.
A/C.5/L.470. Summary of proposals made by representatives of Member States during general discussion of budget. Note by Secretariat.
A/C.5/L.486 and Corr.1. Estimates for Sections 6 to 9a and Section 13. Note by Secretariat.
A/C.5/L.503. Note by Secretariat (on manning table).

A/C.5/736. Second reading of budget estimates. Note by Secretariat.

OTHER REPORTS OF SECRETARY-GENERAL AND ADVISORY COMMITTEE ON ADMINISTRATIVE AND BUDGETARY QUESTIONS
A/C.5/710 and Corr.1; A/3679. Revised estimates for sections 6, 7, 8 and 13.
A/C.5/715; A/3752. Methods of implementing by means of budget General Assembly resolutions recommending establishment of system of priorities.
A/C.5/725; A/3744. Revised estimates for sections 6, 7 and 8. Provision of secretariat to serve Committee for Co-ordination of Investigations of Lower Mekong Basin.
A/C.5/727; A/3743. Revised estimates for sections 7 and 13. Study and interne programmes.
A/C.5/733; A/3777. Revised estimates for section 2. Second International Conference on Peaceful Uses of Atomic Energy.
A/3800. Report of Fifth Committee (Annex A).

RESOLUTION 1230(XII), as recommended by Fifth Committee, A/3800, adopted by Assembly on 14 December 1957, meeting 731, by 68 votes to 9, with 2 abstentions.

RESOLUTION 1230 (XII): BUDGET APPROPRIATIONS FOR THE FINANCIAL YEAR 1958

"*The General Assembly*
"*Resolves* that for the financial year 1958:
"1. Appropriations totalling $US55,062,850 are hereby voted for the following purposes:

A. UNITED NATIONS

Section		US dollars	
	Part I. Sessions of the General Assembly, the Councils, commissions and committees: special meetings and conferences		
1.	Travel of representatives, members of commissions and committees	638,800	
2.	Special meetings and conferences	2,250,000	
3.	Board of Auditors	53,000	
	Total, Part I		2,941,800
	Part II. Special missions and related activities		
4.	Special missions and related activities	2,082,900	
5.	United Nations Field Service	893,600	
	Total, Part II		2,976,500

Section		US dollars	
	Part III. The Secretariat		
6.	Salaries and wages	27,685,250	
7.	Common staff costs	5,830,000	
8.	Travel of staff	1,422,200	
9.	Hospitality	20,000	
9a.	Payments under annex I, paragraphs 2 and 3, of the Staff Regulations	65,000	
	Total, Part III		35,022,450
	Part IV. Special offices		
10.	Office of the United Nations High Commissioner for Refugees	739,700	
11.	Permanent Central Opium Board and Drug Supervisory Body	99,200	
12.	Joint Staff Pension Board and United Nations Staff Pension Committee	134,600	
	Total, Part IV		973,500
	Part V. Common services and equipment		
13.	General expenses	5,026,100	
14.	Printing, stationery and library supplies	2,169,900	
15.	Permanent equipment	507,000	
	Total, Part V		7,703,000
	Part VI. Technical programmes		
16.	Technical Assistance Administration	386,700	
17.	Economic development	479,400	
18.	Social activities	925,000	
18a.	Human rights activities	55,000	
19.	Public administration	300,000	
	Total, Part VI		2,146,100
	Part VII. Special expenses		
20.	Special expenses	2,649,500	
	Total, Part VII		2,649,500

B. THE INTERNATIONAL COURT OF JUSTICE

Section		US dollars	
	Part VIII. The International Court of Justice		
21.	The International Court of Justice	650,000	
	Total, Part VIII		650,000
	Grand Total		55,062,850

"2. The appropriations voted by paragraph 1 above shall be financed by contributions from Member States after adjustment as provided by the Financial Regulations of the United Nations, subject to the provision of paragraph 1 of General Assembly resolution 1232(XII) of 14 December 1957 relating to the Working Capital Fund; for this purpose, miscellaneous income for the financial year 1958 is estimated at $US3,250,000;

"3. With the prior concurrence of the Advisory Committee on Administrative and Budgetary Questions, the Secretary-General may transfer credits between sections of the budget;

"4. In addition to the appropriations voted by paragraph 1 above, an amount of $US13,000 is hereby appropriated from the income of the Library Endowment Fund for the purchase of books, periodicals, maps and library equipment and for such other expenses as are in accordance with the objects and provisions of the endowment;

"5. The Secretary-General is authorized, in accordance with the Financial Regulations, to charge against the income derived from the United Nations Postal Administration, the Visitors' Service, the sale of publications, the catering and related services, and the Gift Centre, the direct expenses of those activities; income in excess of those expenses shall be treated as miscellaneous income under the terms of financial regulation 7, and of paragraph 2 above."

UNFORESEEN AND EXTRAORDINARY EXPENSES FOR 1958

A/3624, page 10. Draft resolution submitted by Advisory Committee on Administrative and Budgetary Questions, approved unanimously by Fifth Committee as amended.

A/C.5/L.502. Note by Secretariat on paragraph 4 of draft resolution on pattern of conferences (A/C.5/L.492), suggesting amendment to draft resolution submitted by Advisory Committee on Administrative and Budgetary Questions.

A/3800. Report of Fifth Committee (Annex B).

RESOLUTION 1231(XII), as recommended by Fifth Committee, A/3800, adopted unanimously by Assembly on 14 December 1957, meeting 731.

"The General Assembly

"Resolves that, for the financial year 1958:

"1. The Secretary-General, with the prior concurrence of the Advisory Committee on Administrative and Budgetary Questions and subject to the Financial Regulations of the United Nations, is authorized to enter into commitments to meet unforeseen and extraordinary expenses, provided that the concurrence of the Advisory Committee shall not be necessary for:

"(*a*) Such commitments, not exceeding a total of $US2 million, as the Secretary-General certifies relate to the maintenance of peace and security or to urgent economic rehabilitations;

"(*b*) Such commitments as the President of the International Court of Justice certifies relate to expenses occasioned by:

"(i) The designation of *ad hoc* judges (Statute, Article 31), not exceeding a total of $24,000;

"(ii) The appointment of assessors (Statute, Article 30), or the calling of witnesses and the appointment of experts (Statute, Article 50), not exceeding a total of $25,000;

"(iii) The maintenance in office of judges who have not been re-elected (Statute, Article 13, paragraph 3), not exceeding a total of $40,000;

"(iv) The holding of sessions of the Court away from The Hague (Statute, Article 22), not exceeding a total of $75,000;

"(v) The payment of pensions and travel and removal expenses of judges not re-elected, and travel and removal expenses of new members of the Court, not exceeding a total of $31,000;

"(*c*) Such commitments not exceeding a total of $25,000 as may be authorized by the Secretary-General in accordance with paragraph 4 of General Assembly resolution 1202(XII) of 13 December 1957 relating to the pattern of conferences:

"2. The Secretary-General shall report to the Advisory Committee on Administrative and Budgetary Questions and to the General Assembly, at its thirteenth session, all commitments made under the provisions of the present resolution, together with the circumstances relating thereto, and shall submit supplementary estimates to the General Assembly in respect of such commitments."

WORKING CAPITAL FUND FOR 1958

A/3624, page 11. Draft resolution submitted by Advisory Committee on Administrative and Budgetary Questions, approved unanimously by Fifth Committee.

A/3800. Report of Fifth Committee (Annex C).

RESOLUTION 1232(XII), as recommended by Fifth Committee, A/3800, adopted unanimously by Assembly on 14 December 1957, meeting 731.

"The General Assembly
"Resolves that:

"1. The Working Capital Fund shall be established for the year ending 31 December 1958 at an amount of $US22 million to be derived from cash advances by Members in accordance with the provisions of paragraphs 2 and 3 of the present resolution;

"2. Members shall make cash advances to the Working Capital Fund as required under paragraph 1 above in accordance with the scale adopted by the General Assembly for contributions of Members to the thirteenth annual budget;

"3. There shall be set off against this new allocation of advances the amounts paid by Members to the Working Capital Fund for the financial year 1957, under General Assembly resolution 1085(XI) of 21 December 1956, provided that, should such advance paid by any Member to the Working Capital Fund for the financial year 1957 exceed the amount of that Member's advance under the provision of paragraph 2 above, the excess shall be set off against the amount of contributions payable by that Member in respect of the thirteenth annual budget, or any previous budget;

"4. The Secretary-General is authorized to advance from the Working Capital Fund:

"(*a*) Such sums as may be necessary to finance budgetary appropriations pending receipt of contributions; sums so advanced shall be reimbursed as soon as receipts from contributions are available for the purpose;

"(*b*) Such sums as may be necessary to finance commitments which may be duly authorized under the provisions of General Assembly resolution 1231(XII) of 14 December 1957, relating to unforeseen and extraordinary expenses; the Secretary-General shall make provision in the budget estimates for reimbursing the Working Capital Fund;

"(*c*) Such sums as, together with net sums outstanding for the same purposes, do not exceed $125,-000, to continue the revolving fund to finance miscellaneous self-liquidating purchases and activities; advances in excess of the total of $125,000 may be made with the prior concurrence of the Advisory Committee on Administrative and Budgetary Questions; the Secretary-General shall submit, with the annual accounts, an explanation of the outstanding balance of the revolving fund at the end of each year;

"(*d*) Loans to specialized agencies and preparatory commissions of agencies to be established by intergovernmental agreement under the auspices of the

United Nations to finance their work, pending receipt by the agencies concerned of sufficient contributions under their own budgets; in making such loans, which shall normally be repayable within two years, the Secretary-General shall have regard to the proposed financial resources of the agency concerned, and shall obtain the prior concurrence of the Advisory Committee on Administrative and Budgetary Questions for any cash issues which would increase the aggregate balance outstanding (including amounts previously advanced and outstanding) at any one time to an amount in excess of $1,500,000 and for any issue which would increase the balance outstanding (including amounts previously advanced and outstanding) in respect of any one agency to an amount in excess of $500,000;

"(e) Such sums not exceeding $35,000 as may be required to finance payments of advance insurance premiums where the period of insurance extends beyond the end of the financial year in which payment is made; this amount may be increased with the prior concurrence of the Advisory Committee on Administrative and Budgetary Questions; the Secretary-General shall make provision in the budget estimates of each year, during the life of the related policies, to cover the charges applicable to each such year;

"(f) Such sums as may be necessary to enable the Tax Equalization Fund to meet current commitments pending accumulation of credits; such advances shall be repaid as soon as credits are available in the Tax Equalization Fund."

SUPPLEMENTARY ESTIMATES FOR THE FINANCIAL YEAR 1957

On 14 December 1957, the General Assembly, acting on the recommendation of its Fifth Committee and the Advisory Committee on Administrative and Budgetary Questions, approved supplementary estimates for the financial year 1957 in the amount of $2,359,000. This figure was $107,200 less than the supplementary provision requested by the Secretary-General. The reduction, to be achieved by means of savings or by deferring some expenditures to 1958, was proposed by the Advisory Committee on Administrative and Budgetary Questions and was approved by the Fifth Committee by 51 votes to 8, with no abstentions. The Assembly endorsed this decision at a plenary meeting by 62 votes to 9, with no abstentions, in the form of resolution 1222(XII). (For details, see text of resolution in DOCUMENTARY REFERENCES below.)

DOCUMENTARY REFERENCES

GENERAL ASSEMBLY—12TH SESSION
Plenary Meeting 731.
Fifth Committee, meetings 633, 645.

A/3720. Report of Secretary-General, containing draft resolution.
A/3750 and Add.1. Report of Advisory Committee on Administrative and Budgetary Questions, containing revision of draft resolution submitted by Secretary-General, adopted by Fifth Committee by 51 votes to 8, with 0 abstentions. The resolution was later adjusted to provide for requirements arising from decisions on post adjustments in Geneva.

A/3795. Report of Fifth Committee.
RESOLUTION 1222(XII), as recommended by Fifth Committee, A/3795, adopted by Assembly on 14 December 1957, meeting 731, by 62 votes to 9, with 0 abstentions.

RESOLUTION 1222(XII): SUPPLEMENTARY ESTIMATES FOR THE FINANCIAL YEAR 1957 [IN US DOLLARS]

"The General Assembly,

"Having examined the supplementary estimates for the financial year 1957,

"1. Requests the Secretary-General, by means of savings where possible and by deferring expenditure where saving cannot be realized, to achieve a reduction of $107,200 in the supplementary estimates;

"2. Approves the general recommendations of the Advisory Committee on Administrative and Budgetary Questions as set out in its twenty-fourth report to the General Assembly at its twelfth session, concerning the supplementary estimates for the financial year 1957;

"3. Resolves that for the financial year 1957 the amount of $50,815,700 appropriated by its resolutions 1083(XI) of 21 December 1956 and 1100(XI) of 27 February 1957 be increased by $2,359,000 to a total of $53,174,700;

"4. Considers that the estimate for miscellaneous income for 1957 previously set at $2,531,010 by General Assembly resolutions 1083(XI) should be increased by $625,000 to $3,156,010;

"5. Resolves that, subject to the provisions of paragraphs 3 and 4 above, the revised appropriation for the financial year 1957 shall be as follows:

	Amount appropriated (adjusted where necessary under paragraph 2 of resolution 1100(XI))	Supplementary appropriation, increase or decrease	Revised amounts of appropriation

A. UNITED NATIONS

Section [*In US dollars*]

Part I. Sessions of the General Assembly, the Councils, commissions and committees

1.	The General Assembly, commissions and committees	628,900	109,300	738,200
2.	The Security Council, commissions and committees	—	215,500	215,500
3.	The Economic and Social Council, commissions and committees	144,600	(4,100)	140,500
3a.	Permanent Central Opium Board and Drug Supervisory Body	29,400	—	29,400
3b.	Regional economic commissions	77,500	—	77,500
4.	The Trusteeship Council, commissions and committees	50,000	—	50,000
	Total, Part I	930,400	320,700	1,251,100

Part II. Special missions and related activities

5.	Special missions and related activities	1,852,000	195,200	2,047,200
5a.	United Nations Field Service	780,700	—	780,700
	Total, Part II	2,632,700	195,200	2,827,900

Part III. Headquarters, New York

6.	Offices of the Secretary-General	2,226,400	81,800	2,308,200
6a.	Office of Under-Secretaries without Department	218,900	15,500	234,400
7.	Department of Political and Security Council Affairs	601,000	18,800	619,800
7a.	Secretariat of the Military Staff Committee	113,000	(5,500)	107,500
8.	Department of Economic and Social Affairs	3,608,000	(14,400)	3,593,600
9.	Department of Trusteeship and Information from Non-Self-Governing Territories	822,500	—	822,500
10.	Department of Public Information	2,398,400	86,100	2,484,500
11.	Department of Conference Services	6,873,000	71,000	6,944,000
11a.	Library	534,400	—	534,400
12.	Office of General Services	3,074,500	189,500	3,264,000
13.	Temporary assistance and consultants	527,500	202,500	730,000
14.	Travel of Staff	1,070,500	119,500	1,190,000
15.	Common staff costs	4,050,800	157,700	4,208,500
16.	Common services	3,819,800	348,700	4,168,500
17.	Permanent equipment	250,000	22,600	272,600
	Total, Part III	30,188,700	1,293,800	31,482,500

Part IV. European Office of the United Nations

18.	United Nations Office at Geneva (excluding direct costs, chapter III, joint secretariat of the Permanent Central Opium Board and Drug Supervisory Body	5,209,600	325,100	5,534,700
	Chapter III, joint secretariat of the Permanent Central Opium Board and Drug Supervisory Body	68,700	1,500	70,200
19.	Office of the United Nations High Commissioner for Refugees	772,500	90,300	862,800
	Total, Part IV	6,050,800	416,900	6,467,700

Section		Amount appropriated (adjusted where necessary under paragraph 2 of resolution 1100(XI))	Supplementary appropriation, increase or decrease	Revised amounts of appropriation
		[In US dollars]		
	Part V. Information centres			
20.	Information centres (exclusive of the Geneva Information Centre)	1,206,500	—	1,206,500
	Total, Part V	1,206,500	—	1,206,500
	Part VI. Secretariats of the regional economic commissions (other than the Economic Commission for Europe)			
21.	Secretariat of the Economic Commission for Asia and the Far East	1,525,300	(72,500)	1,452,800
22.	Secretariat of the Economic Commission for Latin America	1,250,700	248,600	1,499,300
	Total, Part VI	2,776,000	176,100	2,952,100
	Part VII. Representation and hospitality expenses			
23.	Special payments under annex I, paragraph 2, of the Staff Regulations	50,000	—	50,000
24.	Hospitality	20,000	—	20,000
	Total, Part VII	70,000	—	70,000
	Part VIII. Contractual printing			
25.	Contractual printing (excluding chapter I, article (v), Permanent Central Opium Board and Drug Supervisory Body)	1,383,925	39,700	1,423,625
	Chapter I, article (v), Permanent Central Opium Board and Drug Supervisory Body	9,975	—	9,975
	Total, Part VIII	1,393,900	39,700	1,433,600
	Part IX. Technical programmes			
26.	Technical Assistance Administration	386.700	—	386,700
27.	Economic development	479,400	—	479,400
28.	Social activities	925,000	—	925,000
28a.	Human rights activities	55,000	—	55,000
29.	Public administration	300,000	—	300,000
	Total, Part IX	2,146,100	—	2,146,100
	Part X. Special expenses			
30.	Transfer of the assets of the League of Nations to the United Nations	649,500	—	649,500
31.	Amortization of the Headquarters construction loan	2,000,000	—	2,000,000
	Total, Part X	2,649,500	—	2,649,500
	Part XI. Joint Staff Pension Board and United Nations Staff Pension Committee			
32.	Joint Staff Pension Board and United Nations Staff Pension Committee	136,100	6,100	142,200
	Total, Part XI	136,100	6,100	142,200

B. INTERNATIONAL COURT OF JUSTICE

Section		Amount appropriated (adjusted where necessary under paragraph 2 of resolution 1100(XI))	Supplementary appropriation, increase or decrease	Revised amounts of appropriation
			[In US dollars]	
	Part XII. International Court of Justice			
33.	International Court of Justice	635,000	17,700	652,700
	Total, Part XII	635,000	17,700	652,700
	General Reduction	—	(107,200)	(107,200)
	Grand Total	50,815,700	2,359,000	53,174,700

SCALE OF ASSESSMENTS FOR THE APPORTIONMENT OF UNITED NATIONS EXPENSES

At the General Assembly's eleventh session it was decided to defer consideration of the two following questions to its twelfth session: (1) the assessment of the States admitted to United Nations membership at the eleventh session of the General Assembly and (2) the scale of assessments for 1958. The Fifth Committee was to consider these questions at the beginning of the twelfth session and decide upon the directives to be given to the Assembly's Committee on Contributions, which would then meet and submit its recommendations to the General Assembly in the course of the twelfth session.

The Fifth Committee's discussions at the beginning of the session were mainly confined to the principles of assessment, including the assessment principle for the highest contributor.[1] In view of the increase in United Nations membership from 60 (in November 1955) to 82 (in September 1957), the United States representative stressed the need for a reduction in the percentage contribution of the largest contributor and submitted a formal proposal to that effect. The majority of Members favoured this proposal on the understanding that the proposed reduction would be progressively achieved and would be consequent upon the admission of other Members or increases in the national income of existing Members. The proposal, as amended in the course of the discussion, was adopted by the Fifth Committee by 43 votes to 17, with 17 abstentions, and later at a plenary meeting of the Assembly on 14 October 1957, by 39 votes to 16, with 13 abstentions as resolution 1137(XII).

The Assembly thereby decided that in principle the maximum contribution of any one Member State to the ordinary expenses of the United Nations should not exceed 30 per cent of the total. (This paragraph was the subject of a separate roll-call vote in the Fifth Committee, where it was approved by 41 votes to 20, with 16 abstentions.) By the final resolution, the Assembly also decided that the percentage contributions for the new Member States—Ghana, Japan, the Federation of Malaya, Morocco, Sudan and Tunisia—should for the years 1956 and 1957 constitute miscellaneous income to the United Nations, while for 1958 they should be incorporated in the scale of assessments. Further, the Assembly gave certain specific directives to the Committee on Contributions about the incorporation of the percentage contribution for these six new Members in the 1958 scale and about steps to be taken in preparing the scales of assessments for subsequent years.

[1] In 1948 the General Assembly recognized, by resolution 238A(III), that in normal times (a) no one Member State should contribute more than one third of the ordinary expenses of the United Nations for any one year and (b) the per capita contribution of any Member should not exceed the per capita contribution of the Member bearing the highest assessments. In 1952, by resolution 665(VII), the Assembly decided to give full effect to principle (a) from 1 January 1954. But it deferred further action on the per capita ceiling principle until the admission of new Members or until there was a substantial improvement in the economic capacity of existing Members. On the admission of 16 new Members in 1955, the per capita ceiling principle was given full effect in the 1956 scale of assessments.

In the light of these directives, the Committee on Contribution, in October 1957, submitted the following scale of assessments for 1958, which was subsequently approved by the General Assembly, by resolution 1223(XII):

Member State	Per cent	Member State	Per cent
Afghanistan	0.06	Ireland	0.18
Albania	0.04	Israel	0.16
Argentina	1.14	Italy	2.03
Australia	1.61	Japan	1.92
Austria	0.35	Jordan	0.04
Belgium	1.24	Laos	0.04
Bolivia	0.05	Lebanon	0.05
Brazil	1.06	Liberia	0.04
Bulgaria	0.14	Libya	0.04
Burma	0.10	Luxembourg	0.06
Byelorussian SSR	0.47	Malaya, Fed. of	0.22
Cambodia	0.04	Mexico	0.68
Canada	3.09	Morocco	0.12
Ceylon	0.11	Nepal	0.04
Chile	0.29	Netherlands	1.12
China	5.01	New Zealand	0.42
Colombia	0.36	Nicaragua	0.04
Costa Rica	0.04	Norway	0.48
Cuba	0.26	Pakistan	0.54
Czechoslovakia	0.82	Panama	0.05
Denmark	0.64	Paraguay	0.04
Dominican Republic	0.05	Peru	0.15
Ecuador	0.05	Philippines	0.40
Egypt	0.35	Poland	1.52
El Salvador	0.06	Portugal	0.24
Ethiopia	0.11	Romania	0.49
Finland	0.36	Saudi Arabia	0.07
France	5.56	Spain	1.11
Ghana	0.07	Sudan	0.11
Greece	0.19	Sweden	1.43
Guatemala	0.07	Syria	0.08
Haiti	0.04	Thailand	0.16
Honduras	0.04	Tunisia	0.05
Hungary	0.39	Turkey	0.61
Iceland	0.04	Ukrainian SSR	1.80
India	2.90	Union of S. Africa	0.67
Indonesia	0.50	USSR	13.62
Iran	0.26	United Kingdom	7.62
Iraq	0.12	United States	32.51

Member State	Per cent	Member State	Per cent
Uruguay	0.16	Yugoslavia	0.35
Venezuela	0.42		
Yemen	0.04		100.00

For 1957, the rates of contributions recommended by the Committee on Contributions, and approved by the Assembly, for the four States admitted to United Nations membership in 1957 were as follows: Morocco, 0.12 per cent; Sudan, 0.11 per cent; Tunisia, 0.05 per cent; Japan, 1.97 per cent.

For the year of their admission, new Member States are required, under General Assembly resolution 69(I) of 1946, to contribute at least one-third of their percentage assessment for the year following their admission. In the course of debate in the Fifth Committee, reductions were proposed in the rates which the Committee on Contributions had suggested would be applicable for the year of admission of the new Member States in the light of the 1946 resolution. The proposed rates—one-ninth instead of one-third for Morocco, Sudan, Tunisia and Japan, one-third instead of two-thirds for Ghana, and one-sixth instead of one-third for the Federation of Malaya—were approved by the Fifth Committee by 62 votes to 0, with 1 abstention. It was emphasized, however, that these reductions were made for special reasons pertaining in each case and should not be considered as precedents.

The scale of assessments submitted by the Committee on Contributions was approved unanimously by the Fifth Committee and subsequently by the Assembly on 14 December 1957, also unanimously, as resolution 1223 (XII).

DOCUMENTARY REFERENCES

GENERAL ASSEMBLY—12TH SESSION
Plenary Meetings 705, 731.
Fifth Committee, meetings 599-605, 631, 632, 646.

A/3714. Report of Committee on Contributions.
A/C.5/708. Note by Secretary-General.
A/C.5/L.458. United States draft resolution.
A/C.5/L.459. United States amendment to United States draft resolution.
A/C.5/L.460. Spain amendment to United States draft resolution.
A/C.5/L.461. United States revised draft resolution.
A/C.5/L.462. Canada, Denmark, Finland, Norway, Sweden amendment to revised United States draft resolutions, A/C.5/L.461.
A/C.5/L.463. United States revised draft resolution, as orally amended by Portugal and Italy, adopted by Fifth Committee by 43 votes to 17, with 17 abstentions.
A/3698. Report of Fifth Committee.
RESOLUTION 1137(XII), as recommended by Fifth Committee, A/3698, adopted by Assembly on 14 October 1957, meeting 705, by 39 votes to 16, with 13 abstentions.

"The General Assembly,

"Recalling its resolutions 14(I) of 13 February 1946, 238(III) of 18 November 1948 and 665(VII) of 5 December 1952, regarding the apportionment of the expenses of the United Nations among its Members and the fixing of the maximum contribution of any one Member State,

"Noting that, when the maximum contribution of any one Member State was fixed at 33.33 per cent effective 1 January 1954, the United Nations consisted of sixty Member States,

"*Noting further* that, since 1 January 1954, twenty-two States have been admitted to membership in the United Nations,

"*Recalling* its resolution 1087(XI) of 21 December 1956, whereby the percentage contributions of the first sixteen new Member States admitted since 1 January 1954 were incorporated into the regular scale of assessments for 1956 and 1957 and were applied to reduce the percentage contributions of all Member States except that of the highest contributor and those of the Member States paying minimum assessments,

"*Noting* that there are now six new Member States—Ghana, Japan, Malaya (Federation of), Morocco, Sudan and Tunisia—whose percentage contributions have not yet been fixed by the Committee on Contributions or incorporated into the 100 per cent scale of assessments,

"*Decides* that:

"1. In principle, the maximum contribution of any one Member State to the ordinary expenses of the United Nations shall not exceed 30 per cent of the total;

"2. The percentage contributions fixed by the Committee on Contributions for Japan, Morocco, Sudan and Tunisia for 1956 and 1957, and for Ghana and Malaya (Federation of) for 1957, shall constitute miscellaneous income of the United Nations;

"3. The Committee on Contributions shall take the following steps in preparing scales of assessment for 1958 and subsequent years;

"(*a*) The percentage contributions fixed by the Committee on Contributions for Ghana, Japan, Malaya (Federation of), Morocco, Sudan and Tunisia for 1958 shall be incorporated into the 100 per cent scale for 1958; this incorporation shall be accomplished by applying the total amount of the percentage contributions of the six Member States named above to a *pro rata* reduction of the percentage contributions of all Members except those assessed at the minimum rate, taking into account the *per capita* ceiling principle and any reductions which may be required as a result of a review by the Committee on Contributions, at its session commencing 15 October 1957, of appeals from recommendations made previously by that Committee;

"(*b*) During the three-year period of the next scale of assessments (1959-1961), further steps to reduce the share of the largest contributor shall be recommended by the Committee on Contributions when new Member States are admitted;

"(*c*) The Committee on Contributions shall thereafter recommend such additional steps as may be necessary and appropriate to complete the reduction;

"(*d*) The percentage contribution of Member States shall not in any case be increased as a consequence of the present resolution."

A/C.5/732. Statement of advances to Working Capital Fund and contributions to budgets for financial years 1955, 1956 and 1957 as at 25 November 1957. Report by Secretary-General.

A/C.5/735. Statement of advances to Working Capital Fund, contributions to budgets for financial years 1955, 1956 and 1957 and initial assessments for 1957 to UNEF Special Account as at 10 December 1957. Report by Secretary-General.

A/C.5/L.481. Japan draft proposal.

A/C.5/L.482. Note by Secretariat, presenting recommendations of Committee on Contributions as draft resolution. Draft resolution, as amended orally by United States, Haiti and Federation of Malaya, adopted unanimously by Fifth Committee.

A/3798. Report of Fifth Committee.

RESOLUTION 1223(XII), as recommended by Fifth Committee, A/3798, adopted unanimously by Assembly on 14 December 1957, meeting 731.

"*The General Assembly*

"1. *Resolves* that the scale of assessments for Members' contributions to the United Nations budget for the financial year 1959 shall be as follows: [The scale is given above as text matter.]

"2. *Resolves* that the scale of assessments given in paragraph 1 shall be reviewed by the Committee on Contributions in 1958, when a report shall be submitted for the consideration of the General Assembly at its thirteenth session;

"3. *Resolves* that for the year 1957 the rates of contributions for Japan, Morocco, Sudan and Tunisia shall be as follows:

Member States	Per cent
Japan	1.97
Morocco	0.12
Sudan	0.11
Tunisia	0.05

These rates shall be in addition to the 1957 scale of assessments of 100 per cent contained in paragraph 2 of General Assembly resolution 1087(XI) of 21 December 1956, and shall be applied to the budget for 1957;

"4. *Resolves* that, in view of the fact that Morocco, Sudan and Tunisia became Members of the United Nations on 12 November 1956, and Japan on 18 December 1956, these States shall contribute for the year of admission to membership an amount equal to one-ninth of their percentage assessment for 1957 applied to the budget for 1956;

"5. *Resolves* that Ghana and Federation of Malaya, which States became Members of the United Nations on 8 March and 17 September 1957 respectively, shall contribute for the year of admission to membership amounts equal to one-third of 0.07 per cent for Ghana, one-sixth of 0.22 per cent for the Federation of Malaya; these amounts will be applied to the budget for 1957;

"6. *Resolves* that, notwithstanding the provisions of paragraph 4 of General Assembly resolution 970 (X) of 15 December 1955, States which are not Members of the United Nations but which participate in certain of its activities shall be called upon to contribute towards the 1958 expenses of such activities on the basis of the following rates:

States	Per cent
Germany, Federal Republic of	4.15
Korea, Republic of	0.13

States	Per cent
Liechtenstein	0.04
Monaco	0.04
San Marino	0.04
Switzerland	0.98
Viet-Nam	0.16

"The following countries being called upon to contribute:

"(a) To the International Court of Justice: Liechtenstein, San Marino and Switzerland;

"(b) To the International Control of Narcotic Drugs: Germany (Federal Republic of), Liechtenstein, Monaco, San Marino, Switzerland and Viet-Nam;

"(c) To the Economic Commission for Asia and the Far East: Korea (Republic of), and Viet-Nam;

"(d) To the Economic Commission for Europe: Germany (Federal Republic of);

"7. *Resolves* that Japan, which participated in certain United Nations activities before admission to membership, shall not be required to contribute separately towards the annual expenses of such activities for the year 1957 onwards, and that for the year 1956 the amounts that Japan is called upon to contribute

under paragraph 4 of resolution 970(X) shall be reduced by one-ninth;

"8. *Resolves* that the Federal Republic of Germany, which acceded to the Convention on the Declaration of Death of Missing Persons on 30 January 1956, shall be called upon to contribute towards the expenses of the International Bureau for Declarations of Death for the years 1956 and 1957 at the rate of 4.61 per cent pursuant to paragraph 4 of resolution 970(X) and for 1958 at the rate of. 4.15 per cent, pursuant to paragraph 6 of the present resolution;

"9. *Urges* Member States, within the limits of their constitutional processes, to seek appropriate measures which would ensure the payment of their annual contributions to the United Nations as early as possible in the financial year;

"10. *Requests* the Secretary-General, under the authority given to him by paragraph 3 of resolution 970(X), to continue in 1958 to make arrangements for the payment of part of Members' contributions in currencies other than United States dollars as comprehensive as practicable."

CHAPTER III

OTHER ADMINISTRATIVE AND BUDGETARY QUESTIONS

THE UNITED NATIONS
POSTAL ADMINISTRATION

During 1957, the total gross revenue of the United Nations Postal Administration was approximately $1,900,000. In accordance with the agreement between the United Nations and the United States, this revenue was derived solely from the sale of stamps for philatelic purposes, revenue from stamps used for postage from United Nations Headquarters being retained by the United States Post Office.

Four new commemoratives and one airmail stamp and postal card were issued during the year.

On 28 January, a stamp honouring the work of the World Meteorological Organization (WMO) was issued in both 3-cent (blue) and 8-cent (red) denominations. The design depicts a weather balloon symbolizing the globe and the world-wide range of WMO's activities.

On 8 April, stamps honouring the United Nations Emergency Force (UNEF) were issued in 3-cent (blue) and 8-cent (red) denominations. Their design depicts the circular badge worn on the armbands and headgear by the United Nations Emergency Force.

On 27 May, a 4-cent (maroon) airmail stamp

and a 4-cent airmail postal card were issued. Their design depicts the concept of flight, through the medium of a globe, set within an aeroplane wing upon part of which appears the United Nations emblem.

On 24 October, two stamps in the 3-cent (tan) and 8-cent (green) denominations were issued to commemorate United Nations Day. Honouring the UN Security Council, the design shows the United Nations emblem shedding light on the globe.

On 10 December, stamps commemorating Human Rights Day were issued in 3-cent (dark red) and 8-cent (dark grey) denominations. The design of the stamp depicts a flaming torch, symbolic of Human Rights and the endeavour to implement the Universal Declaration of Human Rights.

The number of First Day Covers serviced for these issues were respectively as follows:

WMO stamp	376,110
4¢ Airmail stamp and 4¢ Postal Card	542,938
UNEF stamp	461,772
United Nations Day stamp	460,627
Human Rights Day stamp	550,561
Total	2,392,008

UNITED NATIONS PUBLIC INFORMATION ACTIVITIES

The public information activities of the United Nations were considered in two stages by the Assembly's Fifth Committee at the Assembly's twelfth session. The first stage of the discussions, which formed part of the general debate on the 1958 budget estimates as a whole, was devoted to the problem of setting an optimum ceiling figure for expenditure on public information. The second stage involved a study of specific proposals for an inquiry into the working and effectiveness of the United Nations information services.

On the basis of a draft resolution submitted by 13 Member States, and a number of amendments to that text, the Fifth Committee recommended by 66 votes to 0, with 1 abstention, the establishment of a committee of experts composed of six individuals with practical administrative and financial experience in the various fields of information broadly representative of all regions of the world. The experts were to review and appraise the work, methods used and the effectiveness of the results achieved by the public information services of the United Nations (including the information centres), with a view to recommending possible modifications to ensure "a maximum effectiveness at the lowest possible cost." The committee of experts, to be appointed by the Secretary-General from nominees put forward by Egypt, India, the United Kingdom, the United States, the USSR and Uruguay, was to report before the Assembly thirteenth session opened in 1958. The Secretary-General was invited to present their report to that session, together with his comments and recommendations on the report.

The Fifth Committee's recommendations on these lines were approved at a plenary meeting of the Assembly, by resolution 1177(XII), adopted on 26 November by 77 votes to 0.

In taking this decision, the Assembly recalled its resolution 595(VI) of 4 February 1952 approving the principles governing the dissemination of information. It also recalled its recommendation of 21 December 1956[1] that funds be set aside for the progressive establishment of information centres, by means of savings achieved elsewhere in the budget and by other administrative means. Recalled, too, was a recommendation by the Fifth Committee at the Assembly's eleventh session that the over-all expenditure on United Nations public information activities (excluding the Visitors' Service and the Sales and Circulation Service) should be limited within a three-year period to a maximum annual figure of $4.5 million. The Assembly also bore in mind the difficulties which the Secretary-General had experienced in moving towards this maximum.

The 13 sponsors of the original draft resolution in the Fifth Committee were Australia, Canada, Ceylon, Denmark, France, India, Israel, the Netherlands, New Zealand, Norway, Sweden, the United Kingdom and the United States. It was approved as amended by Greece, by Japan and jointly by the following 14 Members: Afghanistan, Egypt, Ethiopia, Iran, Iraq, Jordan, Lebanon, Libya, Morocco, Saudi Arabia, Sudan, Syria, Tunisia and Yemen, with a sub-amendment by the United States.

FINANCIAL REPORTS AND ACCOUNTS AND REPORTS OF THE BOARD OF AUDITORS

Separate financial statements and reports of the Board of Auditors for the year ending 31 December 1956 were submitted to the General Assembly's twelfth session for the United Nations, the United Nations Children's Fund (UNICEF) and the United Nations Refugee Fund (UNREF). A similar report for the United Nations Korean Reconstruction Agency (UNKRA) was submitted for the financial year ended 30 June 1957. All these reports were considered by the Fifth Committee together with the relevant reports of the Advisory Committee on Administrative and Budgetary Questions.

The Fifth Committee, in each case, recommended acceptance of the financial reports and certificates of the Board of Auditors.

The General Assembly, on 26 November 1957, accepted the reports and took note of the observations on them made by the Advisory Committee. It did so in the form of four resolutions (1169(XII), for the United Nations; 1170 (XII) for UNICEF; 1171 (XII), for UNKRA; 1172(XII), for UNREF).

[1] See *Y.U.N., 1956*, pp. 414, 417.

AUDIT REPORTS ON EXPENDITURE OF TECHNICAL ASSISTANCE FUNDS BY SPECIAL AGENCIES

On 26 November 1957 the General Assembly, on the recommendation of its Fifth Committee, unanimously adopted resolution 1168(XII), taking note of the audit reports on expenditure by specialized agencies of technical assistance funds made available under the Expanded Programme of Technical Assistance for the financial year 1956. Also noted were observations on these reports made by the Advisory Committee on Administrative and Budgetary Questions.

REVIEW OF AUDIT PROCEDURES OF UNITED NATIONS AND SPECIALIZED AGENCIES

During its tenth session, in 1955, the General Assembly asked the Secretary-General to review the existing audit procedures of the United Nations and the specialized agencies, in consultation with the Board of Auditors and the specialized agencies, with a view to recommending a common course of action.

In a report on this matter to the Assembly's twelfth session, the Secretary-General stated that the executive heads of the specialized agencies and the Board of Auditors had expressed satisfaction with the existing audit arrangements. Accordingly, the Secretary-General recommended that unless circumstances necessitated a different course, the United Nations should continue to maintain the present system of external audit. The Advisory Committee concurred in this view.

On 26 November 1957, the General Assembly, without objection, accepted this recommendation which had previously been approved by the Assembly's Fifth Committee. It did so without adopting a formal resolution.

ADMINISTRATIVE AND BUDGETARY CO-ORDINATION BETWEEN UNITED NATIONS AND SPECIALIZED AGENCIES

During the General Assembly's twelfth session, the Assembly's Fifth Committee considered the reports of the Advisory Committee on Administrative and Budgetary Questions on the administrative budgets of the specialized agencies for 1958 and also the Advisory Committee's special reports on the Food and Agricultural Organization (FAO), the World Health Organization (WHO) and the World Meteorological Organization (WMO) with particular reference to the working of the Expanded Programme of Technical Assistance.

In introducing the reports, the Chairman of the Advisory Committee stated that upon completion of two remaining special reports, for the International Civil Aviation Organization and the International Telecommunication Union, the Advisory Committee would submit a consolidated report embodying its recommendations and conclusions on administrative and budgetary co-ordination between the United Nations and specialized agencies, with special reference to the working of the Expanded Programme of Technical Assistance.

On the unanimous recommendation of the Fifth Committee, the General Assembly invited FAO, UNESCO, WHO and WMO to give attention to the comments and suggestions contained in the reports of the Advisory Committee. It did so by resolution 1198(XII), which was unanimously adopted at a plenary meeting of the Assembly on 13 December 1957.

NEGOTIATING COMMITTEE FOR EXTRA-BUDGETARY FUNDS

In accordance with resolution 1091(XI) adopted at the General Assembly's eleventh session on 27 February 1957, the Negotiating Committee for Extra-Budgetary Funds, at the Assembly's twelfth session, submitted a report on the results of the meetings of an *ad hoc* committee of the whole Assembly held on 4 October 1957 to enable Governments to announce pledges of contributions to the United Nations Relief Works Agency for Palestine Refugees (UNRWA) and the United Nations Refugee Fund (UNREF).

In this report, the Committee pointed out that the procedure approved at the Assembly's eleventh session had resulted in a marked improvement in attendance by representatives of Governments at the general meetings. It expressed the view that it would be of value to convene a special pledging conference again during 1958 for the two United Nations refugee programmes along the same lines as for 1957.

The Fifth Committee, by 50 votes to 0, with 8 abstentions, endorsed the recommendations of the Negotiating Committee. It also recommended that a new Negotiating Committee should be appointed to serve during 1958.

These recommendations were later endorsed at a plenary meeting of the Assembly, on 13 December 1957 by resolution 1197(XII), which consisted of two parts.

By the first part, approved by 52 votes to 0, with 6 abstentions, the Assembly decided to convene an *ad hoc* committee of the whole Assembly at its thirteenth session at which pledges of voluntary contributions would be announced for each of the two refugee programmes for the following financial year. States which were members of a specialized agency but not Members of the United Nations would also be invited to attend these meetings. By the second part of the resolution, approved by 54 votes to 0, with 7 abstentions, the President of the General Assembly appointed a Negotiating Committee for Extra-Budgetary Funds to serve until the close of the thirteenth session of the Assembly with the same terms of reference as in previous years. The members so appointed were Argentina, Brazil, Canada, France, Lebanon, New Zealand, Pakistan, the United Kingdom and the United States.

UNITED NATIONS INTERNATIONAL SCHOOL AND DELEGATION FACILITIES

The question of securing permanent premises for the United Nations International School in New York was considered at the General Assembly's twelfth session by the Fifth Committee. Noted in the discussions was the urgent need for such premises, which was all the more urgent because the school had to vacate its present temporary premises in June 1959. In order to meet the needs of the greatest possible number of children of the United Nations staff members, delegates and others associated with the United Nations, it was agreed that the permanent premises for the International School should be located in Manhattan, New York.

With these points in mind, the Committee recommended that the Secretary-General should consult the appropriate authorities on the possibility of constructing permanent premises on the United Nations Headquarters site in New York City, and to use his good offices to help the International School's Board of Trustees in finding a site for the school in Manhattan, including the "Headquarters district".

The Committee also suggested that the Secretary-General use his good offices in investigating practical possibilities for providing delegation office facilities in the area close to the United Nations Headquarters.

The Fifth Committee made these recommendations in a two-part resolution. The first part, on the International School, was adopted by 55 votes to 0, with 5 abstentions, and the second, on delegation office facilities, by 43 votes to 6, with 13 abstentions.

On 14 December, the Assembly endorsed these two recommendations by resolution 1228 A and B (XII), the first by a vote of 69 to 0, with 7 abstentions, and the second by a vote of 60 to 8, with 8 abstentions.

OFFER FOR UNITED NATIONS OFFICE SITE IN SANTIAGO DE CHILE

On the recommendation of its Fifth Committee, the General Assembly, on 14 December 1957, accepted with thanks an offer of land in Santiago that had been generously made by the Government of Chile as a site for a building to house the United Nations and specialized agency offices located there. The resolution to this effect (1224(XII)), which was adopted by 64 votes to 0, with 10 abstentions, further asked the Secretary-General to present detailed plans to the Assembly's thirteenth session in 1958 for the construction of the building, together with final financial arrangements.

SECRETARIAT OF MILITARY STAFF COMMITTEE

Two reports on the question of integrating the secretariat of the Military Staff Committee with the United Nations Secretariat were submitted to the General Assembly's twelfth session by the Secretary-General and by the Advisory Committee on Administrative and Budgetary Questions. They were prepared in accordance with resolution 1098(XI) adopted at the Assembly's eleventh session on 27 February 1957.

The Advisory Committee's report, confined to the administrative and budgetary aspects of the matter, agreed with the Secretary-General that considerations of economy, efficiency and sound administration clearly argued in favour of integration.

A draft resolution approved by the Fifth Committee, by 47 votes to 9, with 5 abstentions, recommended that the Secretary-General be asked, subject to any objections from the Security Council, to take appropriate steps to integrate the civilian staff of the Military Staff Committee with the Secretariat of the United Nations. This recommendation was adopted by the General Assembly on 14 December 1957, by 64 votes to 9, with 1 abstention, as resolution 1235(XII).

CONTROL AND LIMITATION OF UNITED NATIONS DOCUMENTATION

On 13 December 1957, by resolution 1203 (XII), the General Assembly asked the Secretary-General to continue his efforts in co-operation with Member States to reduce the length and amount of United Nations documentation during 1958. It suggested a target figure of 25 per cent below the 1957 level of the over-all output of such documentation. The Secretary-General was to report to the General Assembly before the opening of its thirteenth session on the steps he had taken and on the nature and extent of the reductions achieved.

By the same resolution, the General Assembly established a nine-member committee (composed of representatives of Argentina, Canada, China, France, Iraq, Mexico, Pakistan, the USSR and the United Kingdom to consult with and advise the Secretary-General on the most effective ways of making the reductions and to make suggestions to the Assembly's thirteenth session on ways to reduce the over-all output of United Nations documentation.

The General Assembly adopted this resolution by 62 votes to 0, with 4 abstentions. It did so on the recommendation of its Fifth Committee, which had approved it by a vote of 63 to 0, with 2 abstentions, on the basis of a proposal by the United Kingdom.

PATTERN OF UNITED NATIONS CONFERENCES

At its seventh session, by resolution 694(VII), the General Assembly approved a system for a regular pattern of conferences to be held either at United Nations Headquarters in New York or at Geneva to cover the period 1953–1957.

At the Assembly's twelfth session, the Fifth Committee set up a nine-member sub-committee to make recommendations for a further long-term conference pattern. The sub-committee's tasks were to examine and recommend methods whereby United Nations conferences might be so planned and financed as to ensure the most rational use of the budgetary and staffing resources of the Organization. The sub-committee, which was presided over by the Chairman of the Fifth Committee, was composed of the following Member States: Argentina, Chile, China, France, India, Italy, Poland, Tunisia, USSR, United Kingdom and the United States.

The conclusions reached by the sub-committee were unanimously endorsed by the Fifth Committee, subject to an amendment which would permit the expert subsidiary bodies of the Economic Commissions for Asia and the Far East and for Latin America to hold their meetings where they believed it would be most appropriate to do so for technical or substantive reasons.

The Fifth Committee's recommendations were unanimously adopted at a plenary meeting of the Assembly on 13 December 1957, as resolution 1202(XII). By this resolution, the Assembly decided on a fixed pattern of conferences to govern the dates and meeting places of United Nations organs for the period from 1 January 1958 to 31 December 1962. (For details, see text of resolution below, under DOCU-MENTARY REFERENCES.)

REPAYMENT OF HEADQUARTERS LOAN

On 14 December 1957, the General Assembly authorized the Secretary-General to conclude an agreement with the United States modifying the existing Headquarters Loan Agreement of 23 March 1948 whereby the United States gave the United Nations an interest-free loan of $65 million to be repaid annually in varying amounts until it was paid off in 1982. By this decision of the Assembly, the date of annual repayment made to the United States under the Agreement would be changed from 1 July to 1 September for the years 1958–1982 inclusive.

A draft resolution to this effect was introduced in the Assembly's Fifth Committee by the representative of Canada so as to help ease the very difficult cash position of the Organization that arose during the first half of a financial year, because of the pattern of payment of Members' contributions towards a current budget. The Fifth Committee approved the resolution by 46 votes to 0, with 4 abstentions. The Assembly later adopted it as resolution 1233(XII) by a vote of 76 to 0.

*SPECIAL ALLOWANCES AND
HONORARIA FOR MEMBERS OF
UNITED NATIONS SUBSIDIARY ORGANS*

At its eleventh session, by resolution 1075 (XI) of 7 December 1956, the General Assembly established the principles to govern the payment of travel and subsistence expenses to representatives of Members of the General Assembly and other organs of the United Nations.

At its twelfth session the Assembly gave further consideration to the question of any payments to individual members of subsidiary organs in addition to subsistence allowances.

The Fifth Committee made several recommendations on this subject, for final approval at a plenary meeting of the Assembly, as follows: (*a*) by 39 votes to 6, with 10 abstentions, it recommended that the currently authorized exceptional payments should be continued; (*b*) by 42 votes to 5, with 9 abstentions, it recommended that all exceptional payments should be regarded as honoraria and should be fixed in an appropriate lump sum; (*c*) without objection, it recommended that the special allowances being paid at present at a *per diem* rate should be translated into an annual lump sum amount, calculated on the basis of the normal duration of the meetings of the body concerned, and should be considered to be in the nature of honoraria. In the light of these decisions, the Fifth Committee subsequently approved the sums which would be payable in particular instances, so that the approval of these amounts by the General Assembly would give the Secretary-General the authority to include in future budget estimates those monetary provisions corresponding to the needs foreseen by the Fifth Committee in its examination of the question.

The recommendations of the Fifth Committee were approved at a plenary meeting of the Assembly on 13 December 1957 by 48 votes to 0, with 7 abstentions, without a formal resolution on the subject being adopted.

DOCUMENTARY REFERENCES

*THE UNITED NATIONS
POSTAL ADMINISTRATION*

United Nations Postage Stamps. U.N.P. Sales No.: 1957.I.22.

*UNITED NATIONS PUBLIC
INFORMATION ACTIVITIES*

GENERAL ASSEMBLY—12TH SESSION
Plenary Meeting 723.
Fifth Committee, meetings 607-612, 614, 619, 622.

A/C.5/L.468 and Add.1 and Rev.1. Australia, Canada, Ceylon, Denmark, France, India, Israel, Netherlands, New Zealand, Norway, Sweden, United Kingdom, United States draft resolution and revision, adopted by Fifth Committee, as amended in Committee, by 66 votes to 0, with 1 abstention.
A/C.5/L.469. Greece amendment to revised joint draft resolution.
A/C.5/L.472. Afghanistan, Egypt, Ethiopia, Iran, Iraq, Jordan, Lebanon, Libya, Morocco, Saudi Arabia, Sudan, Syria, Tunisia, Yemen amendments to revised joint draft resolution.
A/C.5/L.477. Draft report of Fifth Committee. Note by Rapporteur.
A/3741. Report of Fifth Committee.
RESOLUTION 1177(XII), as recommended by Fifth Committee, A/3741, adopted by Assembly on 26 November 1957, meeting 723, by 70 votes to 0.

"*The General Assembly,*

"*Recalling* its resolution 13(I) of February 1946 approving the recommendations of the Technical Advisory Committee on Information concerning the policies, functions and organizations of the Department of Public Information,

"*Recalling* its resolution 595(VI) of 4 February 1952 approving the principles governing the dissemination of information recommended by Sub-Committee 8 of the Fifth Committee,

"*Recalling* its resolution 1086(XI) of 21 December 1956 recommending the setting aside of funds for the progressive establishment of information centres in new Member States, through savings elsewhere in the budget and by other administrative means,

"*Recalling* the recommendation approved by the Fifth Committee and embodied in its report to the eleventh session of the General Assembly, that the over-all expenditure for the public information activities of the United Nations (excluding the Visitors' Service and the Sales and Circulation Service) should be limited within a period of three years to a maximum annual figure of $4.5 million,

"*Taking note* of the observations of the Advisory Committee on Administrative and Budgetary Questions in paragraphs 26 to 39 of its fifth report to the twelfth session of the General Assembly,

"*Bearing in mind* the difficulties, which the Secretary-General has represented, in moving towards the approved maximum annual expenditure of $4.5 million,

"1. *Requests* the Secretary-General to appoint an expert committee of six individuals with practical, administrative and financial experience in the various fields of information—press, broadcasting, etc.—to be nominated by the Governments of Egypt, India, the Union of Soviet Socialist Republics, the United Kingdom of Great Britain and Northern Ireland, the

United States of America and Uruguay, and with instructions to undertake, in the light of the opinions expressed by delegations during the twelfth session of the General Assembly, a review and appraisal of the work, the methods used and the effectiveness of the results achieved by the public information services of the United Nations (including the information centres), with a view to recommending possible modifications to ensure a maximum of effectiveness at the lowest possible cost, and to report before the opening of the thirteenth session of the Assembly;

"2. *Invites* the Secretary-General to present to the General Assembly at its thirteenth session the report of the Committee of experts, together with his comments and recommendations thereon;

"3. *Authorizes* the Secretary-General to pay the travel and subsistence expenses of the members of the Committee of experts and to provide the necessary servicing facilities."

FINANCIAL REPORTS AND ACCOUNTS AND REPORTS OF BOARD OF AUDITORS

GENERAL ASSEMBLY—12TH SESSION
Plenary Meeting 723.
Fifth Committee, meetings 618, 622.

UNITED NATIONS
A/3590. Financial reports and accounts for year ended 31 December 1956 and report of Board of Auditors.
A/3707. Financial reports and accounts and reports of Board of Auditors: United Nations, United Nations participation in Expanded Programme of Technical Assistance, and Tehnical Assistance Board Secretariat (for year ended 31 December 1956). Report of Advisory Committee on Administrative and Budgetary Questions.
A/3728. Report of Fifth Committee, containing draft resolution adopted by Committee by 49 votes to 0, with 6 abstentions.
RESOLUTION 1169(XII), as recommended by Fifth Committee, A/3728, adopted by Assembly on 26 November 1957, meeting 723, by 72 votes to 0, with 8 abstentions.

"The General Assembly
"1. *Accepts* the financial reports and accounts of the United Nations for the financial year ended 31 December 1956 and the certificates of the Board of Auditors;
"2. *Concurs* in the observations of the Advisory Committee on Administrative and Budgetary Questions as set forth in its twelfth report to the twelfth session of the General Assembly."

UNITED NATIONS CHILDREN'S FUND (UNICEF)
A/3591. Financial reports and accounts for year ended 31 December 1956 and report of Board of Auditors.
A/3709. Report of Advisory Committee on Administrative and Budgetary Questions.

A/3728. Report of Fifth Committee, containing draft resolution adopted unanimously by Committee.
RESOLUTION 1170(XII), as recommended by Fifth Committee, A/3728, adopted unanimously by Assembly on 26 November 1957, meeting 723.

"The General Assembly
"1. *Accepts* the financial report and accounts of the United Nations Children's Fund for the financial year ended 31 December 1956 and the certificate of the Board of Auditors;
"2. *Takes note* of the observations of the Advisory Committee on Administrative and Budgetary Questions as set forth in its fourteenth report to the twelfth session of the General Assembly."

UNITED NATIONS KOREAN RECONSTRUCTION AGENCY
A/3696. Financial report and accounts for year ended 30 June 1957 and report of Board of Auditors.
A/3715. Report of Advisory Committee on Administrative and Budgetary Questions.
A/3728. Report of Fifth Committee, containing draft resolution adopted by Committee by 53 votes to 0, with 10 abstentions.
RESOLUTION 1171(XII), as recommended by Fifth Committee, A/3728, adopted by Assembly on 26 November 1957, meeting 723, by 59 votes to 0, with 11 abstentions.

"The General Assembly
"1. *Accepts* the financial report and accounts of the United Nations Korean Reconstruction Agency for the financial year ended 30 June 1957 and the certificate of the Board of Auditors;
"2. *Takes note* of the observations of the Advisory Committee on Administrative and Budgetary Questions as set forth in its sixteenth report to the twelfth session of the General Assembly."

UNITED NATIONS REFUGEE FUND
A/3622. Accounts for year ended 31 December 1956 and Report of Board of Auditors.
A/3708. Report of Advisory Committee on Administrative and Budgetary Questions.
A/3728. Report of Fifth Committee, containing draft resolution adopted by Committee by 56 votes to 0, with 9 abstentions.
RESOLUTION 1172(XII), as recommended by Fifth Committee, A/3728, adopted by Assembly on 26 November 1957, meeting 723, by 63 votes to 0, with 9 abstentions.

"The General Assembly
"1. *Accepts* the financial report and accounts of the United Nations Refugee Fund for the financial year ended 31 December 1956 and the certificate of the Board of Auditors;
"2. *Takes note* of the observations of the Advisory Committee on Administrative and Budgetary Questions as set forth in its thirteenth report to the twelfth session of the General Assembly."

AUDIT REPORTS ON EXPENDITURE OF TECHNICAL ASSISTANCE FUNDS BY SPECIALIZED AGENCIES

GENERAL ASSEMBLY—12TH SESSION
Plenary Meeting 723.
Fifth Committee, meetings 618, 622.

A/3599. Audit reports for year ended 31 December 1956 relating to expenditure by specialized agencies of technical assistance funds allocated from Special Account. Note by Secretary-General.
A/3710. Report of Advisory Committee on Administrative and Budgetary Questions.
A/3727. Report of Fifth Committee, containing draft resolution adopted by Committee by 64 votes to 0, with 1 abstention.
RESOLUTION 1168(XII), as recommended by Fifth Committee, A/3727, adopted by Assembly on 26 November 1957, meeting 723, by 76 votes to 0.

"The General Assembly
"Takes note of the audit reports relating to expenditure by specialized agencies of technical assistance funds allocated from the Special Account for the financial year ended 31 December 1956, and of the observations thereon of the Advisory Committee on Administrative and Budgetary Questions, as set forth in its fifteenth report to the twelfth session of the General Assembly."

REVIEW OF AUDIT PROCEDURES OF UNITED NATIONS AND SPECIALIZED AGENCIES

GENERAL ASSEMBLY—12TH SESSION
Plenary Meeting 723.
Fifth Committee, meetings 618, 622.

A/3584. Report of Secretary-General.
A/3615. Report of Advisory Committee on Administrative and Budgetary Questions.
A/3726. Report of Fifth Committee, containing recommendation of Committee, accepted by Assembly on 26 November 1957, meeting 723.

ADMINISTRATIVE AND BUDGETARY CO-ORDINATION BETWEEN UNITED NATIONS AND SPECIALIZED AGENCIES

GENERAL ASSEMBLY—12TH SESSION
Plenary Meeting 729.
Fifth Committee, meetings 643, 646.

A/3596, A/3597, A/3598. Administrative and budgetary co-ordination between United Nations and WHO, between United Nations and WMO, and between United Nations and FAO, respectively, with particular reference to working of Expanded Programme of Technical Assistance. Reports of Advisory Committee on Administrative and Budgetary Questions.
A/3767. Administrative budgets of specialized agencies for 1958. Report of Advisory Committee on Administrative and Budgetary Questions.

A/3791. Report of Fifth Committee, containing draft resolution adopted unanimously by Committee.
RESOLUTION 1198(XII), as recommended by Fifth Committee, A/3791, adopted unanimously by Assembly on 13 December 1957, meeting 729.

"The General Assembly
"1. *Takes note* of the report of the Advisory Committee on Administrative and Budgetary Questions on the administrative budgets of the specialized agencies for 1958, and of its special reports relating to the Food and Agriculture Organization of the United Nations, the World Health Organization, and the World Meteorological Organization;
"2. *Invites the attention* of the specialized agencies to the comments and observations made in the Advisory Committee's report on the budgets of the agencies and to the views expressed in the Fifth Committee at the twelfth session of the General Assembly;
"3. *Invites the attention* of the Food and Agriculture Organization of the United Nations, the World Health Organization and the World Meteorological Organization to the observations and suggestions contained in the Advisory Committee's special reports relating to those organizations."

NEGOTIATING COMMITTEE FOR EXTRA-BUDGETARY FUNDS

GENERAL ASSEMBLY—12TH SESSION
Plenary Meeting 729.
Fifth Committee, meetings 638, 645.

A/3668 and Add.1. Report of Negotiating Committee for Extra-Budgetary Funds.
A/3783. Report of Fifth Committee, containing draft resolutions A and B, both adopted by Committee by 50 votes to 0, with 8 abstentions.
RESOLUTION 1197 A and B (XII) as recommended by Fifth Committee, A/3783, adopted by Assembly on 13 December 1957, meeting 729, as follows: 1197 A (XII), by 52 votes to 0, with 6 abstentions; 1197 B (XII), by 54 votes to 0, with 7 abstentions.

A
"The General Assembly,
"Having considered the report of the Negotiating Committee for Extra-Budgetary Funds appointed at the eleventh session of the General Assembly,
"Recognizing the importance of determining the financial resources for activities and programmes to be financed by voluntary contributions before the reports on such activities and programmes are considered and acted upon by the General Assembly,
"Decides that:
"1. During its thirteenth session, the General Assembly shall convene an *ad hoc* committee of the whole Assembly, under the chairmanship of the President of the session, where pledges of voluntary contributions for the two refugee programmes for the following financial year would be announced, with separate meetings dedicated to each programme;
"2. States not Members of the United Nations, but members of one or more of the specialized agencies,

shall be invited to attend meetings of the *ad hoc* committee for the purpose of announcing their pledges to the two refugee programmes;

"3. In order to ensure maximum attendance at the meetings, as great advance publicity as possible shall be given to the meetings of the *ad hoc* committee and the meetings shall be so scheduled that no other meetings are held at the same time."

B

"The General Assembly,

"1. *Requests* the President of the General Assembly to appoint a Negotiating Committee for Extra-Budgetary Funds consisting of not more than ten members, with the same terms of reference as those laid down in Assembly resolution 693(VII) of 25 October 1952, to serve from the close of the twelfth session to the close of the thirteenth session of the Assembly;

"2. *Decides* to include in the provisional agenda of the thirteenth session of the General Assembly the item entitled 'Report of the Negotiating Committee for Extra-Budgetary Funds'."

UNITED NATIONS INTERNATIONAL SCHOOL AND DELEGATION FACILITIES

GENERAL ASSEMBLY—12TH SESSION
Plenary Meeting 731.
Fifth Committee, meetings 636, 644, 645, 648.

A/3688. Report of Secretary-General.
A/C.5/L.497. Brazil, France, India, Poland draft resolution, as amended by sponsors, adopted by Fifth Committee, part A by 55 votes to 0, with 5 abstentions, and part B by 43 votes to 6, with 13 abstentions.
A/C.5/L.498. United States amendment to joint draft resolution.
A/C.5/L.500. Chile amendment to joint draft resolution.
A/3801. Report of Fifth Committee.
RESOLUTION 1228 A and B (XII), as recommended by Fifth Committee, A/3801, adopted by Assembly on 14 December 1957, meeting 731, as follows: 1228 A (XII) by 69 votes to 0, with 7 abstentions; 1228 B (XII) by 60 votes to 8, with 8 abstentions.

A

"The General Assembly,

"Having considered the report of the Secretary-General on the United Nations International School,

"Noting that the School is in urgent need of permanent premises, and that it is under notice to vacate its present temporary premises in June 1959,

"Noting that, in order to meet the needs of the greatest possible number of children of United Nations staff members, delegates and others associated with the United Nations, such permanent premises should be located in Manhattan,

"Noting further that, in the view of the Secretary-General, the provision of truly adequate accommodation for the School is in the best interest of the Organization,

"Recalling its resolution 1102(XI) of 27 February

1957 on this subject and, in particular, the recognition contained therein of the continued functioning of the School as one of the important non-financial factors contributing to the recruitment and retention of international staff,

"1. *Requests* the Secretary-General to consult with the appropriate authorities on the possibility of constructing permanent premises for the United Nations International School on the Headquarters site;

"2. *Requests* the Secretary-General to use his good offices to assist the Board of Trustees of the School in finding a site for the School in Manhattan, including the 'Headquarters District', in developing plans for the building, and in pursuing their efforts to raise funds from private sources for the construction of the School and, if necessary, for the acquisition of a site therefor;

"3. *Requests* the Secretary-General to use his good offices to assist the School in finding suitable accommodation pending completion of the permanent premises;

"4. *Requests* the Secretary-General to present to the General Assembly at its thirteenth session a progress report, together with the comments, if necessary, of the Advisory Committee on Administrative and Budgetary Questions."

B

"The General Assembly,

"Bearing in mind the discussions at previous sessions concerning a delegation building to be constructed in the area close to the United Nations Headquarters, and the increasing interest expressed by many delegations in having such facilities,

"1. *Requests* the Secretary-General to use his good offices to investigate practical possibilities for the provision of delegation office facilities in the area close to United Nations Headquarters;

"2. *Requests* the Secretary-General to make a progress report to the General Assembly at its thirteenth session."

OFFER FOR UNITED NATIONS OFFICE SITE IN SANTIAGO DE CHILE

GENERAL ASSEMBLY—12TH SESSION
Plenary Meeting 731.
Fifth Committee, meetings 639, 640, 648.

A/3461 and Add.1. Offer by Government of Chile of land in Santiago to be used as office site for United Nations and other international organizations. Explanatory memorandum by Secretary-General, and note transmitting letter of 9 September 1957 from Permanent Representative of Chile.
A/C.5/712. Report of Secretary-General.
A/C.5/L.487. Argentina, Bolivia, Brazil, Colombia, Costa Rica, Cuba, Dominican Republic, Ecuador, El Salvador, Guatemala, Haiti, Honduras, Mexico, Nicaragua, Panama, Paraguay, Peru, Uruguay draft resolution, adopted by Fifth Committee, as orally amended by France and United Kingdom, by 53 votes to 0, with 7 abstentions.
A/3799. Report of Fifth Committee.

RESOLUTION 1224(XII), as recommended by Fifth Committee, A/3799, adopted by Assembly on 14 December 1957, meeting 731, by 64 votes to 0, with 10 abstentions.

"The General Assembly,

"Having regard to the reports of the Secretary-General concerning the offer by the Government of Chile to transfer to the United Nations, free of charge, a plot of land in Santiago for the construction of a building to house United Nations and specialized agency offices located in Chile,

"Taking note of resolution 138(VII) of the Economic Commission for Latin America, of 28 May 1957, which was transmitted to the Secretary-General for consideration by the General Assembly at its twelfth session, and the report of the *ad hoc* committee on a building for the Economic Commission for Latin America established within that Commission pursuant to the said resolution,

"Considering, in the light of the details given in the Secretary-General's report, the indubitable advantages presented by the offer of the Government of Chile for improved conduct of the work of the United Nations in Latin America,

"Considering that the construction of such a building will make possible the establishment of common services for the United Nations and the specialized agencies having offices at Santiago, which has been repeatedly requested at various meetings of United Nations organs concerned with administrative matters,

"Considering the need for effective measures to ensure that this plan is executed in the most satisfactory manner possible,

"1. *Requests* the Secretary-General to accept with thanks the generous offer of the Government of Chile;

"2. *Authorizes* the Secretary-General to open with Governments of States members of the Economic Commission for Latin America such negotiations as may be necessary with regard to the financing of the construction of the United Nations building at Santiago, and to convene such meetings with representatives of those Governments as he may deem desirable;

"3. *Requests* the Secretary-General to present to the General Assembly at its thirteenth session, in accordance with the proposals he has made, detailed plans for the construction of the building, together with final financial arrangements and such observations thereon as may be made by the Advisory Committee on Administrative and Budgetary Questions."

SECRETARIAT OF THE MILITARY STAFF COMMITTEE

GENERAL ASSEMBLY—12TH SESSION
Plenary Meeting 731.
Fifth Committee, meetings 626, 648.

A/C.5/709 and Corr.1. Report by Secretary-General.
A/3691. Report of Advisory Committee on Administrative and Budgetary Questions.
A/3800. Report of Fifth Committee (Annex F).
RESOLUTION 1235(XII), as recommended by Fifth Committee, A/3800, adopted by Assembly on 14 December 1957, meeting 731, by 64 votes to 9, with 1 abstention.

"The General Assembly

"Requests the Secretary-General, subject to any objection which may be received from the Security Council, to take appropriate steps to effect the integration of the civilian staff of the Military Staff Committee with the Secretariat of the United Nations."

CONTROL AND LIMITATION OF UNITED NATIONS DOCUMENTATION

GENERAL ASSEMBLY—12TH SESSION
Plenary Meeting 729.
Fifth Committee, meetings 607-609, 616, 617, 622-624, 640, 645, 646.
Fourth Committee, meeting 691.

A/3600. Budget estimates for 1958, p. XI.
A/C.5/L.473. United Kingdom draft resolution as amended by India, Canada and Chairman of Advisory Committee, adopted by Fifth Committee by 63 votes to 0, with 2 abstentions.
A/3789. Report of Fifth Committee.
RESOLUTION 1203(XII), as recommended by Fifth Committee, A/3789, adopted by Assembly on 13 December 1957, meeting 729, by 62 votes to 0, with 4 abstentions.

"The General Assembly,

"Bearing in mind the present very considerable output of United Nations documents,

"Noting paragraph 57 of the Secretary-General's foreword to the budget estimates for 1958,

"Commending the Secretary-General for his efforts to present Secretariat documents as concisely as possible, and in setting, as a target figure, a reduction in length of 25 per cent,

"1. *Requests* the Secretary-General to continue his efforts, in co-operation with Member States, to reduce the length and amount of documentation produced during 1958;

"2. *Suggests* for this purpose the target figure of 25 per cent below the 1957 level for the over-all output of such documentation;

"3. *Decides* to establish a Committee composed of representatives—serving at Headquarters, New York —of the following Member States: Argentina, Canada, China, France, Iraq, Mexico, Pakistan, the United Kingdom of Great Britain and Northern Ireland and the Union of Soviet Socialist Republics; the function of the Committee shall be to consult with and advise the Secretary-General on the most effective means of implementing the present resolution, and to report and make recommendations to the General Assembly at its thirteenth session concerning methods of achieving reductions in the over-all output of documentation;

"4. *Invites* the Secretary-General to report to the General Assembly before the opening of its thirteenth session on the steps taken and on the nature and extent of the reductions achieved."

PATTERN OF UNITED NATIONS CONFERENCES

GENERAL ASSEMBLY—12TH SESSION
Plenary Meeting 729.
Fifth Committee, meetings 607-612, 615, 635, 636.

A/C.5/722. Programme of conferences. Report of Secretary-General.
A/C.5/L.471. United Kingdom draft resolution.
A/C.5/731. Report of Sub-Committee 9 on Pattern of Conferences, containing draft resolution, adopted unanimously by Fifth Committee, as amended by 15 powers, A/C.5/L.484 and Add.1, and by Chairman of Advisory Committee.
A/C.5/L.484 and Add.1 Brazil, Ceylon, Colombia, Cuba, Ecuador, El Salvador, Guatemala, Haiti, Honduras, Mexico, Panama, Paraguay, Peru, Uruguay, Venezuela amendment to draft resolution recommended by Sub-Committee 9, A/C.5/731.
A/3787. Report of Fifth Committee.
A/C.5/737. Basic programme of meetings for 1958.
RESOLUTION 1202(XII), as recommended by Fifth Committee, A/3787, adopted unanimously by Assembly on 13 December 1957, meeting 729.

"*The General Assembly,*
"*Recalling* its resolution 694(VII) of 20 December 1952,
"*Recognizing* the need to establish further clear procedures for the planning and financing of meetings and conferences of the United Nations in order that the most rational and economical use may be made of the resources of the Organization,
"1. *Decides* that a fixed pattern of conferences to govern the places and dates of the meetings of United Nations bodies shall come into force on 1 January 1958 for a period of five years;
"2. *Decides further* that, as a general principle, meetings of United Nations bodies shall be held at the established headquarters of the bodies concerned, with the following exceptions:
"(*a*)   The regular summer session of the Economic and Social Council may be held each year at Geneva, during which period no other United Nations body shall meet there;
"(*b*)   Not more than one functional commission of the Economic and Social Council, to be determined by that Council, in addition to the Commission on Narcotic Drugs, may meet annually in Geneva; a session of the Commission on Narcotic Drugs may, in exceptional circumstances, and by decision of the Economic and Social Council in consultation with the Secretary-General, be held in New York; in such years one other functional commission may meet in Geneva in its place without overlap;
"(*c*)   The regular sessions of the Economic Commission for Asia and the Far East and of the Economic Commission for Latin America as well as meetings of their subsidiary bodies may be held away from their headquarters when the commission concerned so decides, subject, in the case of regular ses-

sions of the commissions, to the approval of the Economic and Social Council and the General Assembly;
"(*d*)   The annual session of the International Law Commission would be held in Geneva without overlapping with the summer session of the Economic and Social Council;
"(*e*)   Meetings may be held away from the established headquarters of any body in other cases where a Government issuing an invitation for a meeting to be held within its territory has agreed to defray, after consultation with the Secretary-General as to their nature and possible extent, the additional costs involved;
"3. *Requests* the Secretary-General to submit to the General Assembly every year a basic programme of conferences for the following year established in conformity with the present pattern and after consultation, as appropriate, with the organs concerned;
"4. *Decides* that as a general rule any meeting, other than an emergency meeting, not covered by the basic programme for a given year shall not be held during that year; the General Assembly nevertheless authorizes the Secretary-General, within a financial limit to be set annually in the resolution relating to unforeseen and extraordinary expenses, to decide when and where any body or *ad hoc* conference not covered by the basic annual programme shall meet; in the event that the decision of the Secretary-General is not accepted, the final decision in the matter shall be taken by the Assembly at its next regular session;
"5. *Invites* all organs of the United Nations as well as the specialized agencies to review their working methods and the frequency and length of sessions in the light of the present resolution and of the growing volume of meetings, the resulting strain on available resources, and the difficulty of effective participation of members."

REPAYMENT OF HEADQUARTERS LOAN

GENERAL ASSEMBLY—12TH SESSION
Plenary Meeting 731.
Fifth Committee, meeting 647.

A/C.5/L.505. Canada draft resolution, adopted by Fifth Committee by 46 votes to 0, with 4 abstentions.
A/3800. Report of Fifth Committee (Annex D).
RESOLUTION 1233(XII), as recommended by Fifth Committee, A/3800, adopted by Assembly on 14 December 1957, meeting 731, by 76 votes to 0.

"*The General Assembly,*
"*Having considered* the need for financing budgetary appropriations pending the receipt of contributions, and taking into account the pattern of payments of contributions,
"*Believing* that the financial situation in this respect would be alleviated by changing the date of the annual repayment made to the United States of America under the Headquarters Loan Agreement of 23

March 1948 between the United States and the United Nations,

"*Authorizes* the Secretary-General to conclude an agreement with the United States of America modifying paragraph 4 of the above-mentioned Agreement so that the date of 1 September is substituted for 1 July for the years 1958 to 1982 inclusive."

SPECIAL ALLOWANCES AND HONORARIA FOR MEMBERS OF UNITED NATIONS SUBSIDIARY BODIES

GENERAL ASSEMBLY—12TH SESSION
Plenary Meeting 729.

Fifth Committee, meetings 613, 615.

A/C.5/713. System of honoraria and special allowances to members of commissions, committees and other subsidiary bodies of General Assembly or other organs of United Nations. Report of Secretary-General.

A/3705. Report of Advisory Committee on Administrative and Budgetary Questions.

A/3766. Report of Fifth Committee, containing recommendations, adopted by Assembly on 13 December 1957, meeting 729, by 48 votes to 0, with 7 abstentions.

PART TWO

*The Inter-Governmental Organizations
Related to the United Nations*

CHAPTER I

THE INTERNATIONAL ATOMIC ENERGY AGENCY (IAEA)

The International Atomic Energy Agency (IAEA)[1] came into being on 29 July 1957, the necessary instruments of ratification of the Agency's Statute having been deposited in Washington. (For text of Statute, see ANNEX I below.) The Agency's main objectives are: to accelerate and enlarge the contribution of atomic energy to peace, health and prosperity throughout the world; and to ensure that assistance provided by it or under its aegis is not used in such a way as to further any military purpose.

In carrying out its functions, IAEA is authorized: to encourage and assist research on, and the development and practical application of, atomic energy; to act, if requested to do so, as an intermediary for securing the performance of services or the supplying of materials, equipment or facilities by one member of the Agency for another; and to perform any operation or service likely to contribute to the peaceful application of atomic energy.

The Agency is also authorized to make provision for the materials, services, equipment and facilities necessary for the production of nuclear power and for research in that field, with due consideration for the needs of the under-equipped areas of the world.

A further aim of IAEA is to foster the exchange of scientific and technical information and encourage the exchange and training of scientists and experts concerned with the peaceful uses of atomic energy. It will ensure, so far as it is able, that assistance provided by it or at its request or under its supervision or control is not used in such a way as to further any military purpose.

The Agency will establish or adopt standards of safety for protection of health and minimization of danger to life and property from radiation. It will do so in consultation and, where appropriate, in collaboration with the competent organs of the United Nations and with the specialized agencies concerned.

The Agency is under an obligation to conduct its activities in accordance with the purposes and principles of the United Nations designed to promote world peace and in conformity with policies of the United Nations furthering the establishment of safeguarded world-wide disarmament and with any international agreements entered into pursuant to such policies.

MEMBERSHIP AND STRUCTURE

Membership of IAEA is open to all States which have signed its Statute within the prescribed period and to any other State, whether or not a Member of the United Nations or of any of the specialized agencies, which deposits an instrument of acceptance of the Statute after its membership has been approved by the General Conference of the Agency upon the recommendation of the Board of Governors. The Agency had 60 members as of 31 December 1957. (For list of members see ANNEX II below.)

The two main organs of IAEA are the General Conference, consisting of all member States and meeting normally in annual session, and the Board of Governors, consisting at present of 23 members, which meets at such times as it may determine.

STATUTE AND PREPARATORY COMMISSION

A first decisive step towards the creation of IAEA was the proposal made by the President of the United States on 8 December 1953 to the United Nations General Assembly for the establishment, under the aegis of the United Nations, of an international agency which would devote its activities exclusively to the peaceful uses of

[1] For further information, particularly about the origins of the International Atomic Energy Agency, see *Y.U.N. 1953*, p. 268; *1954*, p. 3; *1955*, p. 13; *1956*, p. 104. See also report of International Atomic Energy Agency to the twelfth session of the United Nations General Assembly (A/3747).

atomic energy. On 4 December 1954, during its ninth session, the General Assembly unanimously endorsed this proposal. In the meantime, the drafting of the Statute of the Agency had been undertaken in Washington by a group of eight States, subsequently expanded to 12.

On 23 September 1956, an international conference was convened at the United Nations Headquarters to consider the draft Statute which, after a final revision, was unanimously approved on 26 October 1956. During the following three months, it was signed by the representatives of 80 States.

The Statute Conference appointed a Preparatory Commission of 18 States to make arrangements for the first session of the General Conference of the Agency and for the first meetings of the Board of Governors to carry out the preliminary work needed to bring the Agency into operation, and to designate 13 members of the Board of Governors. The members of the Preparatory Commission were: Argentina, Australia, Belgium, Brazil, Canada, Czechoslovakia, Egypt, France, India, Indonesia, Japan, Pakistan, Peru, Portugal, Union of South Africa, the USSR, the United Kingdom and the United States. Dr. Carlos A. Bernardes, of Brazil, was elected as Chairman. Dr. Paul R. Jolles, of Switzerland, was appointed Executive Secretary of the Commission, which met at United Nations Headquarters in New York until 20 August 1957, when it transferred its seat to Vienna.

GENERAL CONFERENCE

The first session of the General Conference of IAEA met in Vienna from 1 to 23 October 1957. Its first task was to complete the constitution of the Board of Governors (see below, ANNEX III). On the Board's recommendation, the General Conference unanimously approved the programme and budget for the first year's activities proposed by the Preparatory Commission. It was recommended that high priority should be given to activities which would be of the greatest benefit in raising the standards of living of peoples in the under-developed areas of the world.

On the recommendation of the Board of Governors, the General Conference unanimously approved the draft agreement governing the relationship between the Agency and the United Nations. This had been negotiated by the Preparatory Commission and the United Nations Advisory Committee on Atomic Energy. (For further details about this agreement, see above, PART ONE, POLITICAL AND SECURITY QUESTIONS, CHAPTER II).

On the recommendation of the Board it was also decided unanimously that the permanent Headquarters of the Agency should be established in Vienna.

The General Conference approved the appointment by the Board of Governors of Mr. Sterling Cole as Director-General of the Agency for a four-year term beginning 1 December 1957.

In the course of the discussions at the first session of the General Conference, several member States made offers of assistance to the Agency. This included specific offers to make available fissionable materials totalling 5,140 kilogrammes, together with some 200 tons of source materials and fellowships for 110 students.

It was decided that the opening date for the second regular session of the General Conference would be 22 September 1958.

The Agency's Board of Governors (under the Chairmanship of Dr. Pavel Winkler of Czechoslovakia), held two series of meetings before the end of 1957, the first series lasting from 4 October to 1 November and the second from 16 to 20 December 1957. The Board considered and approved, before submission to the General Conference, the recommendations of the Preparatory Commission for the Agency's first programme and budget, the draft agreement on the relationship between the Agency and the United Nations, and various other matters of importance, including the appointment of the Director-General. After the close of the first session of the General Conference the Board's work was concerned mainly with the organizational framework and staffing of the Agency and with preparation for the implementation of the Agency's initial programme.

FINANCIAL ARRANGEMENTS

The General Conference fixed a provisional scale of contributions to meet the administrative expenses of the Agency in 1957-58 on the basis of the scale of contributions adopted by the United Nations General Assembly for the financial year 1957. This provisional scale was to be reviewed by the General Conference at its second regular session in the light, *inter alia*, of the expected increase in membership of the Agency between the two sessions.

The Agency's first budget, covering the period to 31 December 1958, amounted to $4,089,000. The General Conference also established a Working Capital Fund of $2 million. In addition, member States were invited to make voluntary contributions to finance an Agency fellowship programme to a total amount of $250,000 for 1958. A loan equivalent to $1 million (made by the Austrian Government to meet the initial expenses of the Agency) was accepted with appreciation by the Board of Governors. The budget and Working Capital Fund related only to the administrative expenses of the Agency; means of financing its operational expenditure were still to be explored.

ANNEX I. STATUTE OF INTERNATIONAL ATOMIC ENERGY AGENCY

ARTICLE I. ESTABLISHMENT OF THE AGENCY

The Parties hereto establish an International Atomic Energy Agency (hereinafter referred to as "the Agency") upon the terms and conditions hereinafter set forth.

ARTICLE II. OBJECTIVES

The Agency shall seek to accelerate and enlarge the contribution of atomic energy to peace, health and prosperity throughout the world. It shall ensure, so far as it is able, that assistance provided by it or at its request or under its supervision or control is not used in such a way as to further any military purpose.

ARTICLE III. FUNCTIONS

A. The Agency is authorized:

1. To encourage and assist research on, and development and practical application of, atomic energy for peaceful uses throughout the world; and, if requested to do so, to act as an intermediary for the purposes of securing the performance of services or the supplying of materials, equipment, or facilities by one member of the Agency for another; and to perform any operation or service useful in research on, or development or practical application of, atomic energy for peaceful purposes;

2. To make provision, in accordance with this Statute, for materials, services, equipment, and facilities to meet the needs of research on, and development and practical application of, atomic energy for peaceful purposes, including the production of electric power, with due consideration for the needs of the under-developed areas of the world;

3. To foster the exchange of scientific and technical information on peaceful uses of atomic energy;

4. To encourage the exchange and training of scientists and experts in the field of peaceful uses of atomic energy;

5. To establish and administer safeguards designed to ensure that special fissionable and other materials, services, equipment, facilities, and information made available by the Agency or at its request or under its supervision or control are not used in such a way as to further any military purpose; and to apply safeguards, at the request of the parties, to any bilateral or multilateral arrangement, or, at the request of a State, to any of that State's activities in the field of atomic energy;

6. To establish or adopt, in consultation and, where appropriate, in collaboration with the competent organs of the United Nations and with the specialized agencies concerned, standards of safety for protection of health and minimization of danger to life and property (including such standards for labour conditions), and to provide for the application of these standards to its own operations as well as to the operations making use of materials, services, equipment, facilities, and information made available by the Agency or at its request or under its control or supervision; and to provide for the application of these standards, at the request of the parties, to operations under any bilateral or multilateral arrangement, or, at the request of a State, to any of that State's activities in the field of atomic energy;

7. To acquire or establish any facilities, plant and equipment useful in carrying out its authorized functions, whenever the facilities, plant, and equipment otherwise available to it in the area concerned are inadequate or available only on terms it deems unsatisfactory.

B. In carrying out its functions, the Agency shall:

1. Conduct its activities in accordance with the purposes and principles of the United Nations to promote peace and international co-operation, and in conformity with policies of the United Nations furthering the establishment of safeguarded world-wide disarmament and in conformity with any international agreements entered into pursuant to such policies;

2. Establish control over the use of special fissionable materials received by the Agency, in order to ensure that these materials are used only for peaceful purposes;

3. Allocate its resources in such a manner as to secure efficient utilization and the greatest possible general benefit in all areas of the world, bearing in mind the special needs of the under-developed areas of the world;

4. Submit reports on its activities annually to the General Assembly of the United Nations and, when appropriate, to the Security Council: if in connexion with the activities of the Agency there should arise questions that are within the competence of the

Security Council, the Agency shall notify the Security Council, as the organ bearing the main responsibility for the maintenance of international peace and security, and may also take the measures open to it under this Statute, including those provided in paragraph C of article XII;

5. Submit reports to the Economic and Social Council and other organs of the United Nations on matters within the competence of these organs.

C. In carrying out its functions, the Agency shall not make assistance to members subject to any political, economic, military, or other conditions incompatible with the provisions of this Statute.

D. Subject to the provisions of this Statute and to the terms of agreements concluded between a State or a group of States and the Agency which shall be in accordance with the provisions of the Statute, the activities of the Agency shall be carried out with due observance of the sovereign rights of States.

ARTICLE IV. MEMBERSHIP

A. The initial members of the Agency shall be those States Members of the United Nations or of any of the specialized agencies which shall have signed this Statute within ninety days after it is opened for signature and shall have deposited an instrument of ratification.

B. Other members of the Agency shall be those States, whether or not Members of the United Nations or of any of the specialized agencies, which deposit an instrument of acceptance of this Statute after their membership has been approved by the General Conference upon the recommendation of the Board of Governors. In recommending and approving a State for membership, the Board of Governors and the General Conference shall determine that the State is able and willing to carry out the obligations of membership in the Agency, giving due consideration to its ability and willingness to act in accordance with the purposes and principles of the Charter of the United Nations.

C. The Agency is based on the principle of the sovereign equality of all its members, and all members, in order to ensure to all of them the rights and benefits resulting from membership, shall fulfil in good faith the obligations assumed by them in accordance with this Statute.

ARTICLE V. GENERAL CONFERENCE

A. A General Conference consisting of representatives of all members shall meet in regular annual session and in such special sessions as shall be convened by the Director-General at the request of the Board of Governors or of a majority of members. The sessions shall take place at the headquarters of the Agency unless otherwise determined by the General Conference.

B. At such sessions, each member shall be represented by one delegate who may be accompanied by alternates and by advisers. The cost of attendance of any delegation shall be borne by the member concerned.

C. The General Conference shall elect a President and such other officers as may be required at the beginning of each session. They shall hold office for the duration of the session. The General Conference, subject to the provisions of this Statute, shall adopt its own rules of procedure. Each member shall have one vote. Decisions pursuant to paragraph H of article XIV, paragraph C of article XVIII and paragraph B of article XIX shall be made by a two-thirds majority of the members present and voting. Decisions on other questions, including the determination of additional questions or categories of questions to be decided by a two-thirds majority, shall be made by a majority of the members present and voting. A majority of members shall constitute a quorum.

D. The General Conference may discuss any questions or any matters within the scope of this Statute or relating to the powers and functions of any origins provided for in this Statute, and may make recommendations to the membership of the Agency or to the Board of Governors or to both on any such questions or matters.

E. The General Conference shall:

1. Elect members of the Board of Governors in accordance with article VI;

2. Approve States for membership in accordance with article IV;

3. Suspend a member from the privileges and rights of membership in accordance with article XIX;

4. Consider the annual report of the Board;

5. In accordance with article XIV, approve the budget of the Agency recommended by the Board or return it with recommendations as to its entirety or parts to the Board, for resubmission to the General Conference;

6. Approve reports to be submitted to the United Nations as required by the relationship agreement between the Agency and the United Nations, except reports referred to in paragraph C of article XII, or return them to the Board with its recommendations;

7. Approve any agreement or agreements between the Agency and the United Nations and other organizations as provided in article XVI or return such agreements with its recommendations to the Board, for resubmission to the General Conference;

8. Approve rules and limitations regarding the exercise of borrowing powers by the Board, in accordance with paragraph G of article XIV; approve rules regarding the acceptance of voluntary contributions to the Agency; and approve, in accordance with paragraph F of article XIV, the manner in which the general fund referred to in that paragraph may be used;

9. Approve amendments to this Statute in accordance with paragraph C of article XVIII;

10. Approve the appointment of the Director-General in accordance with paragraph A of article VII.

F. The General Conference shall have the authority:

1. To take decisions on any matter specifically referred to the General Conference for this purpose by the Board;

2. To propose matters for consideration by the Board and request from the Board reports on any matter relating to the functions of the Agency.

ARTICLE VI. BOARD OF GOVERNORS

A. The Board of Governors shall be composed as follows:

1. The outgoing Board of Governors (or in the case of the first Board, the Preparatory Commission referred to in Annex I)[2] shall designate for membership on the Board the five members most advanced in the technology of atomic energy including the production of source materials and the member most advanced in the technology of atomic energy including the production of source materials in each of the following areas not represented by the aforesaid five: (1) North America (2) Latin America (3) Western Europe (4) Eastern Europe (5) Africa and the Middle East (6) South Asia (7) South East Asia and the Pacific (8) Far East.

2. The outgoing Board of Governors (or in the case of the first Board, the Preparatory Commission referred to in Annex I) shall designate for membership on the Board two members from among the following other producers of source materials: Belgium, Czechoslovakia, Poland, and Portugal; and shall also designate for membership on the Board one other member as a supplier of technical assistance. No member in this category in any one year will be eligible for redesignation in the same category for the following year.

3. The General Conference shall elect ten members to membership on the Board of Governors, with due regard to equitable representation on the Board as a whole of the members in the areas listed in sub-paragraph A-1 of this article, so that the Board shall at all times include in this category a representative of each of those areas except North America. Except for the five members chosen for a term of one year in accordance with paragraph D of this article, no member in this category in any one term of office will be eligible for re-election in the same category for the following term of office.

B. The designations provided for in sub-paragraphs A-1 and A-2 of this article shall take place not less than sixty days before each regular annual session of the General Conference. The elections provided for in sub-paragraph A-3 of this article shall take place at regular annual sessions of the General Conference.

C. Members represented on the Board of Governors in accordance with sub-paragraphs A-1 and A-2 of this article shall hold office from the end of the next regular annual session of the General Conference after their designation until the end of the following regular annual session of the General Conference.

D. Members represented on the Board of Governors in accordance with sub-paragraph A-3 of this article shall hold office from the end of the regular annual session of the General Conference at which they are elected until the end of the second regular annual session of the General Conference thereafter. In the election of these members for the first Board, however, five shall be chosen for a term of one year.

E. Each member of the Board of Governors shall have one vote. Decisions on the amount of the Agency's budget shall be made by a two-thirds majority of those present and voting, as provided in paragraph H of article XIV. Decisions on other questions, including the determination of additional questions or categories of questions to be decided by a two-thirds majority, shall be made by a majority of those present and voting. Two-thirds of all members of the Board shall constitute a quorum.

F. The Board of Governors shall have authority to carry out the functions of the Agency in accordance with this Statute, subject to its responsibilities to the General Conference as provided in this Statute.

G. The Board of Governors shall meet at such times as it may determine. The meetings shall take place at the headquarters of the Agency unless otherwise determined by the Board.

H. The Board of Governors shall elect a Chairman and other officers from among its members and, subject to the provisions of this Statute, shall adopt its own rules of procedure.

I. The Board of Governors may establish such committees as it deems advisable. The Board may appoint persons to represent it in its relations with other organizations.

J. The Board of Governors shall prepare an annual report to the General Conference concerning the affairs of the Agency and any projects approved by the Agency. The Board shall also prepare for submission to the General Conference such reports as the Agency is or may be required to make to the United Nations or to any other organization the work of which is related to that of the Agency. These reports, along with the annual reports, shall be submitted to members of the Agency at least one month before the regular session of the General Conference.

ARTICLE VII. STAFF

A. The staff of the Agency shall be headed by a Director-General. The Director-General shall be appointed by the Board of Governors with the approval of the General Conference for a term of four years. He shall be the chief administrative officer of the Agency.

B. The Director-General shall be responsible for the appointment, organization, and functioning of the staff and shall be under the authority of and subject to the control of the Board of Governors. He shall perform his duties in accordance with regulations adopted by the Board.

C. The staff shall include such qualified scientific and technical and other personnel as may be required to fulfil the objectives and functions of the Agency. The Agency shall be guided by the principle that its permanent staff shall be kept to a minimum.

D. The paramount consideration in the recruitment and employment of the staff and in the determination of the conditions of service shall be to secure employees of the highest standards of efficiency, technical competence, and integrity. Subject to this consideration, due regard shall be paid to the contributions of

[2] Annex I of the Statute, not quoted here, describes the composition and functions of the Preparatory Commission, for further details about which see text matter above and also *Y.U.N., 1956,* p. 107.

members to the Agency and to the importance of recruiting the staff on as wide a geographical basis as possible.

E. The terms and conditions on which the staff shall be appointed, remunerated, and dismissed shall be in accordance with regulations made by the Board of Governors, subject to the provisions of this Statute and to general rules approved by the General Conference on the recommendation of the Board.

F. In the performance of their duties, the Director-General and the staff shall not seek or receive instructions from any source external to the Agency. They shall refrain from any action which might reflect on their position as officials of the Agency; subject to their responsibilities to the Agency, they shall not disclose any industrial secret or other confidential information coming to their knowledge by reason of their official duties for the Agency. Each member undertakes to respect the international character of the responsibilities of the Director-General and the staff and shall not seek to influence them in the discharge of their duties.

G. In this article the term "staff" includes guards.

ARTICLE VIII. EXCHANGE OF INFORMATION

A. Each member should make available such information as would, in the judgement of the member, be helpful to the Agency.

B. Each member shall make available to the Agency all scientific information developed as a result of assistance extended by the Agency pursuant to article XI.

C. The Agency shall assemble and make available in an accessible form the information made available to it under paragraphs A and B of this article. It shall take positive steps to encourage the exchange among its members of information relating to the nature and peaceful uses of atomic energy and shall serve as an intermediary among its members for this purpose.

ARTICLE IX. SUPPLYING OF MATERIALS

A. Members may make available to the Agency such quantities of special fissionable materials as they deem advisable and on such terms as shall be agreed with the Agency. The materials made available to the Agency may, at the discretion of the member making them available, be stored either by the member concerned or, with the agreement of the Agency, in the Agency's depots.

B. Members may also make available to the Agency source materials as defined in article XX and other materials. The Board of Governors shall determine the quantities of such materials which the Agency will accept under agreements provided for in article XIII.

C. Each member shall notify the Agency of the quantities, form, and composition of special fissionable materials, source material, and other material which that member is prepared, in conformity with its laws, to make available immediately or during a period specified by the Board of Governors.

D. On request of the Agency a member shall, from the materials which it has made available, without delay deliver to another member or group of members such quantities of such materials as the Agency may specify, and shall without delay deliver to the Agency itself such quantities of such materials as are really necessary for operations and scientific research in the facilities of the Agency.

E. The quantities, form and composition of materials made available by any member may be changed at any time by the member with the approval of the Board of Governors.

F. An initial notification in accordance with paragraph C of this article shall be made within three months of the entry into force of this Statute with respect to the member concerned. In the absence of a contrary decision of the Board of Governors, the materials initially made available shall be for the period of the calendar year succeeding the year when this Statute takes effect with respect to the member concerned. Subsequent notifications shall likewise, in the absence of a contrary action by the Board, relate to the period of the calendar year following the notification and shall be made no later than the first day of November of each year.

G. The Agency shall specify the place and method of delivery and, where appropriate, the form and composition, of materials which it has requested a member to deliver from the amounts which that member has notified the Agency it is prepared to make available. The Agency shall also verify the quantities of materials delivered and shall report those quantities periodically to the members.

H. The Agency shall be responsible for storing and protecting materials in its possession. The Agency shall ensure that these materials shall be safeguarded against (1) hazards of the weather, (2) unauthorized removal or diversion, (3) damage or destruction, including sabotage, and (4) forcible seizure. In storing special fissionable materials in its possession, the Agency shall ensure the geographical distribution of these materials in such a way as not to allow concentration of large amounts of such materials in any one country or region of the world.

I. The Agency shall as soon as practicable establish or acquire such of the following as may be necessary:

1. Plant, equipment, and facilities for the receipt, storage, and issue of materials;

2. Physical safeguards;

3. Adequate health and safety measures;

4. Control laboratories for the analysis and verification of materials received;

5. Housing and administrative facilities for any staff required for the foregoing.

J. The materials made available pursuant to this article shall be used as determined by the Board of Governors in accordance with the provisions of this Statute. No member shall have the right to require that the materials it makes available to the Agency be kept separately by the Agency or to designate the specific project in which they must be used.

ARTICLE X. SERVICES, EQUIPMENT, AND FACILITIES

Members may make available to the Agency services, equipment, and facilities which may be of assistance in fulfilling the Agency's objectives and functions.

ARTICLE XI. AGENCY PROJECTS

A. Any member or group of members of the Agency desiring to set up any project for research on, or development or practical application of, atomic energy for peaceful purposes may request the assistance of the Agency in securing special fissionable and other materials, services, equipment, and facilities necessary for this purpose. Any such request shall be accompanied by an explanation of the purpose and extent of the project and shall be considered by the Board of Governors.

B. Upon request, the Agency may also assist any member or group of members to make arrangements to secure necessary financing from outside sources to carry out such projects. In extending this assistance, the Agency will not be required to provide any guarantees or to assume any financial responsibility for the project.

C. The Agency may arrange for the supplying of any materials, services, equipment, and facilities necessary for the project by one or more members or may itself undertake to provide any or all of these directly, taking into consideration the wishes of the member or members making the request.

D. For the purpose of considering the request, the Agency may send into the territory of the member or group of members making the request a person or persons qualified to examine the project. For this purpose the Agency may, with the approval of the member or group of members making the request, use members of its own staff or employ suitably qualified nationals of any member.

E. Before approving a project under this article, the Board of Governors shall give due consideration to:

1. The usefulness of the project, including its scientific and technical feasibility;

2. The adequacy of plans, funds, and technical personnel to assure the effective execution of the project;

3. The adequacy of proposed health and safety standards for handling and storing materials and for operating facilities;

4. The inability of the member or group of members making the request to secure the necessary finances, materials, facilities, equipment, and services;

5. The equitable distribution of materials and other resources available to the Agency;

6. The special needs of the under-developed areas of the world; and

7. Such other matters as may be relevant.

F. Upon approving a project, the Agency shall enter into an agreement with the member or group of members submitting the project, which agreement shall:

1. Provide for allocation to the project of any required special fissionable or other materials;

2. Provide for transfer of special fissionable materials from their then place of custody, whether the materials be in the custody of the Agency or of the member making them available for use in Agency projects, to the member or group of members submitting the project, under conditions which ensure the safety of any shipment required and meet applicable health and safety standards;

3. Set forth the terms and conditions, including charges, on which any materials, services, equipment, and facilities are to be provided by the Agency itself, and, if any such materials, services, equipment, and facilities are to be provided by a member, the terms and conditions as arranged for by the member or group of members submitting the project and the supplying member;

4. Include undertakings by the member or group of members submitting the project: (a) that the assistance provided shall not be used in such a way as to further any military purpose; and (b) that the project shall be subject to the safeguards provided for in article XII, the relevant safeguards being specified in the agreement;

5. Make appropriate provision regarding the rights and interests of the Agency and the member or members concerned in any inventions or discoveries, or any patents therein, arising from the project;

6. Make appropriate provision regarding settlement of disputes;

7. Include such other provisions as may be appropriate.

G. The provisions of this article shall also apply where appropriate to a request for materials, services, facilities, or equipment in connexion with an existing project.

ARTICLE XII. AGENCY SAFEGUARDS

A. With respect to any Agency project, or other arrangement where the Agency is requested by the parties concerned to apply safeguards, the Agency shall have the following rights and responsibilities to the extent relevant to the project or arrangement:

1. To examine the design of specialized equipment and facilities, including nuclear reactors, and to approve it only from the viewpoint of assuring that it will not further any military purpose, that it complies with applicable health and safety standards, and that it will permit effective application of the safeguards provided for in this article;

2. To require the observance of any health and safety measures prescribed by the Agency;

3. To require the maintenance and production of operating records to assist in ensuring accountability for source and special fissionable materials used or produced in the project or arrangement;

4. To call for and receive progress reports;

5. To approve the means to be used for the chemical processing of irradiated materials solely to ensure that this chemical processing will not lend itself to diversion of materials for military purposes and will comply with applicable health and safety standards; to require that special fissionable materials recovered or produced as a by-product be used for peaceful purposes under continuing Agency safeguards for research or in reactors, existing or under construction, specified by the member or members concerned; and to require deposit with the Agency of any excess of any special fissionable materials recovered or produced as a by-

product over what is needed for the above-stated uses in order to prevent stockpiling of these materials, provided that thereafter at the request of the member or members concerned special fissionable materials so deposited with the Agency shall be returned promptly to the member or members concerned for use under the same provisions as stated above;

6. To send into the territory of the recipient State or States inspectors, designated by the Agency after consultation with the State or States concerned, who shall have access at all times to all places and data and to any person who by reason of his occupation deals with materials, equipment, or facilities which are required by this Statute to be safeguarded, as necessary to account for source and special fissionable materials supplied and fissionable products and to determine whether there is compliance with the undertaking against use in furtherance of any military purpose referred to in sub-paragraph F-4 of article XI, with the health and safety measures referred to in sub-paragraph A-2 of this article, and with any other conditions prescribed in the agreement between the Agency and the State or States concerned. Inspectors designated by the Agency shall be accompanied by representatives of the authorities of the State concerned, if that State so requests, provided that the inspectors shall not thereby be delayed or otherwise impeded in the exercise of their functions;

7. In the event of non-compliance and failure by the recipient State or States to take requested corrective steps within a reasonable time, to suspend or terminate assistance and withdraw any materials and equipment made available by the Agency or a member in furtherance of the project.

B. The Agency shall, as necessary, establish a staff of inspectors. The staff of inspectors shall have the responsibility of examining all operations conducted by the Agency itself to determine whether the Agency is complying with the health and safety measures prescribed by it for application to projects subject to its approval, supervision or control, and whether the Agency is taking adequate measures to prevent the source and special fissionable materials in its custody or used or produced in it own operations from being used in furtherance of any military purpose. The Agency shall take remedial action forthwith to correct any non-compliance or failure to take adequate measures.

C. The staff of inspectors shall also have the responsibility of obtaining and verifying the accounting referred to in sub-paragraph A-6 of this article and of determining whether there is compliance with the undertaking referred to in sub-paragraph F-4 of article XI, with the measures referred to in sub-paragraph A-2 of this article, and with all other conditions of the project prescribed in the agreement between the Agency and the State or States concerned. The inspectors shall report any non-compliance to the Director-General who shall thereupon transmit the report to the Board of Governors. The Board shall call upon the recipient State or States to remedy forthwith any non-compliance which it finds to have occurred. The Board shall report the non-compliance to all members

and to the Security Council and General Assembly of the United Nations. In the event of failure of the recipient State or States to take fully corrective action within a reasonable time, the Board may take one or both of the following measures: direct curtailment or suspension of assistance being provided by the Agency or by a member, and call for the return of materials and equipment made available to the recipient member or group of members. The Agency may also, in accordance with article XIX, suspend any non-complying member from the exercise of the privileges and rights of membership.

ARTICLE XIII. REIMBURSEMENT OF MEMBERS

Unless otherwise agreed upon between the Board of Governors and the member furnishing to the Agency materials, services, equipment, or facilities, the Board shall enter into an agreement with such member providing for reimbursement for the items furnished.

ARTICLE XIV. FINANCE

A. The Board of Governors shall submit to the General Conference the annual budget estimates for the expenses of the Agency. To facilitate the work of the Board in this regard, the Director-General shall initially prepare the budget estimates. If the General Conference does not approve the estimates, it shall return them together with its recommendations to the Board. The Board shall then submit further estimates to the General Conference for its approval.

B. Expenditures of the Agency shall be classified under the following categories:

1. Administrative expenses: these shall include:

(a) Costs of the staff of the Agency other than the staff employed in connexion with materials, services, equipment, and facilities referred to in sub-paragraph B-2 below; costs of meetings; and expenditures required for the preparation of Agency projects and for the distribution of information;

(b) Costs of implementing the safeguards referred to in article XII in relation to Agency projects or, under sub-paragraph A-5 of article III, in relation to any bilateral or multilateral arrangement, together with the costs of handling and storage of special fissionable material by the Agency other than the storage and handling charges referred to in paragraph E below;

2. Expenses, other than those included in sub-paragraph 1 of this paragraph in connexion with any materials, facilities, plant, and equipment acquired or established by the Agency in carrying out its authorized functions, and the costs of materials, services, equipment, and facilities provided by it under agreements with one or more members.

C. In fixing the expenditures under sub-paragraph B-1 (b) above, the Board of Governors shall deduct such amounts as are recoverable under agreements regarding the application of safeguards between the Agency and parties to bilateral or multilateral arrangements.

D. The Board of Governors shall apportion the expenses referred to in sub-paragraph B-1 above, among members in accordance with a scale to be fixed by the General Conference. In fixing the scale the General Conference shall be guided by the principles adopted by the United Nations in assessing contributions of Member States to the regular budget of the United Nations.

E. The Board of Governors shall establish periodically a scale of charges, including reasonable uniform storage and handling charges, for materials, services, equipment, and facilities furnished to members by the Agency. The scale shall be designed to produce revenues for the Agency adequate to meet the expenses and costs referred to in sub-paragraph B-2 above, less any voluntary contributions which the Board of Governors may, in accordance with paragraph F, apply for this purpose. The proceeds of such charges shall be placed in a separate fund which shall be used to pay members for any materials, services, equipment, or facilities furnished by them and to meet other expenses referred to in sub-paragraph B-2 above which may be incurred by the Agency itself.

F. Any excess of revenues referred to in paragraph E over the expenses and costs there referred to, and any voluntary contributions to the Agency, shall be placed in a general fund which may be used as the Board of Governors, with the approval of the General Conference, may determine.

G. Subject to rules and limitations approved by the General Conference, the Board of Governors shall have the authority to exercise borrowing powers on behalf of the Agency without, however, imposing on members of the Agency any liability in respect of loans entered into pursuant to this authority, and to accept voluntary contributions made to the Agency.

H. Decisions of the General Conference on financial questions and of the Board of Governors on the amount of the Agency's budget shall require a two-thirds majority of those present and voting.

ARTICLE XV. PRIVILEGES AND IMMUNITIES

A. The Agency shall enjoy in the territory of each member such legal capacity and such privileges and immunities as are necessary for the exercise of its functions.

B. Delegates of members together with their alternates and advisers, Governors appointed to the Board together with their alternates and advisers, and the Director-General and the staff of the Agency, shall enjoy such privileges and immunities as are necessary in the independent exercise of their functions in connexion with the Agency.

C. The legal capacity, privileges, and immunities referred to in this article shall be defined in a separate agreement or agreements between the Agency, represented for this purpose by the Director-General acting under instructions of the Board of Governors, and the members.

ARTICLE XVI. RELATIONSHIP WITH OTHER ORGANIZATIONS

A. The Board of Governors, with the approval of the General Conference, is authorized to enter into an agreement or agreements establishing an appropriate relationship between the Agency and the United Nations and any other organizations the work of which is related to that of the Agency.

B. The agreement or agreements establishing the relationship of the Agency and the United Nations shall provide for:

1. Submission by the Agency of reports as provided for in sub-paragraphs B-4 and B-5 of article III;

2. Consideration by the Agency of resolutions relating to it adopted by the General Assembly or any of the Councils of the United Nations and the submission of reports, when requested, to the appropriate organ of the United Nations on the action taken by the Agency or by its members in accordance with this Statute as a result of such consideration.

ARTICLE XVII. SETTLEMENT OF DISPUTES

A. Any question or dispute concerning the interpretation or application of this Statute which is not settled by negotiation shall be referred to the International Court of Justice in conformity with the Statute of the Court, unless the parties concerned agree on another mode of settlement.

B. The General Conference and the Board of Governors are separately empowered, subject to authorization from the General Assembly of the United Nations, to request the International Court of Justice to give an advisory opinion on any legal question arising within the scope of the Agency's activities.

ARTICLE XVIII. AMENDMENTS AND WITHDRAWALS

A. Amendments to this Statute may be proposed by any member. Certified copies of the text of any amendment proposed shall be prepared by the Director-General and communicated by him to all members at least ninety days in advance of its consideration by the General Conference.

B. At the fifth annual session of the General Conference following the coming into force of this Statute, the question of a general review of the provisions of this Statute shall be placed on the agenda of that session. On approval by a majority of the members present and voting, the review will take place at the following General Conference. Thereafter, proposals on the question of a general review of this Statute may be submitted for decision by the General Conference under the same procedure.

C. Amendments shall come into force for all members when:

(i) Approved by the General Conference by a two-thirds majority of those present and voting after consideration of observations submitted by the Board of Governors on each proposed amendment, and

(ii) Accepted by two-thirds of all the members in accordance with their respective constitutional processes. Acceptance by a member shall be effected by the deposit of an instrument of acceptance with the depositary Government referred to in paragraph C of article XXI.

D. At any time after five years from the date when this Statute shall take effect in accordance with paragraph E of article XXI or whenever a member is unwilling to accept an amendment to this Statute, it may withdraw from the Agency by notice in writing to that effect given to the depositary Government referred to in paragraph C of article XXI, which shall promptly inform the Board of Governors and all members.

E. Withdrawal by a member from the Agency shall not affect its contractual obligations entered into pursuant to article XI or its budgetary obligations for the year in which it withdraws.

ARTICLE XIX. SUSPENSION OF PRIVILEGES

A. A member of the Agency which is in arrears in the payment of its financial contributions to the Agency shall have no vote in the Agency if the amount of its arrears equals or exceeds the amount of the contributions due from it for the preceding two years. The General Conference may, nevertheless, permit such a member to vote if it is satisfied that the failure to pay is due to conditions beyond the control of the member.

B. A member which has persistently violated the provisions of this Statute or of any agreement entered into by it pursuant to this Statute may be suspended from the exercise of the privileges and rights of membership by the General Conference acting by a two-thirds majority of the members present and voting upon recommendation by the Board of Governors.

ARTICLE XX. DEFINITIONS

As used in this Statute:

1. The term "special fissionable material" means plutonium-239; uranium-233; uranium enriched in the isotopes 235 or 233; any material containing one or more of the foregoing; and such other fissionable material as the Board of Governors shall from time to time determine; but the term "special fissionable material" does not include source material.

2. The term "uranium enriched in the isotopes 235 or 233" means uranium containing the isotopes 235 or 233 or both in an amount such that the abundance ratio of the sum of these isotopes to the isotope 238 is greater than the ratio of the isotope 235 to the isotope 238 occurring in nature.

3. The term "source material" means uranium containing the mixture of isotopes occurring in nature; uranium depleted in the isotope 235; thorium; any of the foregoing in the form of metal, alloy, chemical compound, or concentrate; any other material containing one or more of the foregoing in such concentration as the Board of Governors shall from time to time determine; and such other material as the Board of Governors shall from time to time determine.

ARTICLE XXI. SIGNATURE, ASSEPTANCE, AND ENTRY INTO FORCE

A. This Statute shall be open for signature on 26 October 1956 by all States Members of the United Nations or of any of the specialized agencies and shall remain open for signature by those States for a period of ninety days.

B. The signatory States shall become parties to this Statute by deposit of an instrument of ratification.

C. Instruments of ratification by signatory States and instruments of acceptance by States whose membership has been approved under paragraph B of article IV of this Statute shall be deposited with the Government of the United States of America, hereby designated as depositary Government.

D. Ratification or acceptance of this Statute shall be effected by States in accordance with their respective constitutional processes.

E. This Statute, apart from the Annex, shall come into force when eighteen States have deposited instruments of ratification in accordance with paragraph B of this article, provided that such eighteen States shall include at least three of the following States: Canada, France, the Union of Soviet Socialist Republics, the United Kingdom of Great Britain and Northern Ireland, and the United States of America. Instruments of ratification and instruments of acceptance deposited thereafter shall take effect on the date of their receipt.

F. The depositary Government shall promptly inform all States signatory to this Statute of the date of each deposit of ratification and the date of entry into force of the Statute. The depositary Government shall promptly inform all signatories and members of the dates on which States subsequently become parties thereto.

G. The Annex to this Statute shall come into force on the first day this Statute is open for signature.

ARTICLE XXII. REGISTRATION WITH THE UNITED NATIONS

A. This Statute shall be registered by the depositary Government pursuant to Article 102 of the Charter of the United Nations.

B. Agreements between the Agency and any member or members, agreements between the Agency and any other organization or organizations, and agreements between members subject to approval of the Agency, shall be registered with the Agency. Such agreements shall be registered by the Agency with the United Nations if registration is required under Article 102 of the Charter of the United Nations.

ARTICLE XXIII. AUTHENTIC TEXTS AND CERTIFIED COPIES

This Statute, done in the Chinese, English, French, Russian and Spanish languages, each being equally authentic, shall be deposited in the archives of the depositary Government. Duly certified copies of this Statute shall be transmitted by the depositary Government to the Governments of the other signatory States and to the Governments of States admitted to membership under paragraph B of article IV.

In witness whereof the undersigned, duly authorized, have signed this Statute.

DONE at the Headquarters of the United Nations, this twenty-sixth day of October, one thousand nine hundred and fifty-six.

ANNEX II. MEMBERS AND PROVISIONAL SCALE OF CONTRIBUTIONS

(Membership as of 31 December 1957; contribution percentages as set for 1958)*

Member	Contribution Percentage	Member	Contribution Percentage	Member	Contribution Percentage
Afghanistan	.06	Germany, Fed. Rep. of,	4.08	Paraguay	.04
Albania	.04	Greece	.19	Peru	.14
Argentina	1.12	Guatemala	.07	Poland	1.50
Australia	1.58	Haiti	.04	Portugal	.24
Austria	.35	Honduras	.04	Romania	.48
Brazil	1.05	Hungary	.44	Spain	1.09
Bulgaria	.13	Iceland	.04	Sweden	1.40
Burma	†	India	2.85	Switzerland	1.00
Byelorussian SSR	.46	Indonesia	.49	Thailand	.15
Canada	3.02	Israel	.15	Tunisia	.05
Ceylon	.11	Italy	2.00	Turkey	.61
China	4.93	Japan	1.89	Ukrainian SSR	1.78
Cuba	.26	Korea, Rep. of,	.13	Union of South Africa	.68
Czechoslovakia	.81	Monaco	.04	USSR	13.40
Denmark	.63	Morocco	.13	United Kingdom	7.50
Dominican Republic	.05	Netherlands	1.10	United States	33.33
Egypt	.35	New Zealand	.41	Vatican City	.04
El Salvador	†	Nicaragua	.04	Venezuela	.41
Ethiopia	.11	Norway	.47	Viet-Nam	.15
France	5.47	Pakistan	.53	Yugoslavia	.35

* This scale of contributions was to be reviewed at the second regular session of the General Conference in the light of the then existing membership.

† To be assessed at the second regular session of the General Conference.

ANNEX III. OFFICERS AND OFFICES

(As of 31 December 1957)

BOARD OF GOVERNORS

Member	Governor	Member	Governor
Argentina†	O. A. Quihillalt	Korea, Rep. of,	W. Y. Sohn
Australia*	O. O. Pulley	Pakistan†	N. Ahmad
Brazil*	C. A. Bernardes	Peru†	J. Sarmiento
Canada*	M. H. Wershof, *Vice-Chairman*	Portugal*	M. de Fontes Pereira de Mello Fonseca
Czechoslovakia*	Pavel Winkler, *Chairman*	Romania†	V. Novacu
Egypt†	I. Fahmy	Sweden*	H. W. A. de Besche
France*	B. Goldschmidt	Turkey†	S. Yemiscibasi
Guatemala†	J. Beltranena	Union of South Africa*	D. B. Sole
India*	H. J. Bhabha	USSR*	V. S. Emelyanov
Indonesia†	S. Sudjarwo	United Kingdom*	M. I. Michaels
Italy†	A. Corrias	United States*	R. M. McKinney
Japan*	H. Furuuchi, *Vice-Chairman*		

* Designated by Preparatory Commission on 31 July 1957 as members of the First Board of Governors.

† Elected at the Agency's first General Conference on 3 October 1957.

SENIOR OFFICERS OF THE AGENCY'S STAFF

Director-General: W. Sterling Cole.
Deputy Director-General for Administration, Secretariat and External Liaison: Paul R. Jolles.
Deputy Director-General for Technical Operations: Hubert de Laboulaye.

Deputy Director-General for Training and Information: Vladimir V. Migulin.
Deputy Director-General for Research and Isotopes: Henry Seligman.

International Atomic Energy Agency
Musikakademie
Lothringerstrasse 18
Vienna 3, Austria
Cable Address: INTATOM VIENNA

CHAPTER II

THE INTERNATIONAL LABOUR ORGANISATION (ILO)

During 1957 membership of the International Labour Organisation (ILO)[1] increased from 77 to 79. Venezuela withdrew in the course of the year, Nicaragua was re-admitted on 9 April, and Ghana and the Federation of Malaya became members on 20 May and 12 November respectively.

During the course of the year, 115 ratifications of International Labour Conventions were registered.[2] These included the first ratification (by the United Kingdom) of the Abolition of Forced Labour Convention (adopted at the fortieth session of the International Labour Conference held in Geneva between 5 and 27 June 1957).

Four other new international labour instruments were adopted at the Conference: a Convention and a Recommendation on the protection and integration of indigenous populations in independent countries, and a Convention and a Recommendation on weekly rest in commerce and offices. This action brought the total of such instruments adopted since 1919 to 107 Conventions and 104 Recommendations, which had received nearly 1,800 ratifications by the end of 1957.

The triennial elections of the Governing Body also took place at the General Conference. Ten of the regular 20 government members, the 10 regular employers' and the 10 workers' regular representatives were elected or re-elected. There were also elections or re-elections for deputy members (for the 10 government deputy members, the 10 employers' and the 10 workers' deputy members). Permanent government members (states of major industrial importance) are: Canada, China, France, the Federal Republic of Germany, India, Italy, Japan, USSR, United Kingdom and United States.

The Conference unseated the employers' and workers' delegates from Hungary after their credentials had been challenged.

The Governing Body, at a meeting prior to the Conference, unanimously re-elected the Director-General, David A. Morse, to a new five-year term, to begin at the expiration of his previous term in September 1958.

TECHNICAL AID ACTIVITIES[3]

The activities of ILO under the Expanded Technical Assistance Programme of the United Nations and specialized agencies showed some increase in 1957, the estimated expenditure on field projects rising to $2.85 million as compared with $2.67 million in 1956.

Fifty-six countries received technical assistance, five more than in the previous year. Two of them, Morocco and Tunisia, were new beneficiaries under the programme.

A total of 279 experts were on assignment; 136 of these were newly recruited, whilst a record number of 210 were in the field. These figures compared with 289, 128, and 185, respectively, in 1956.

Awards of fellowships in 1957 totalled 258,

---

[1] For further information, in particular concerning the functions and organization of ILO and its activities before 1957, see previous volumes of the *Yearbook*, reports of the Director-General to the General Conference and proceedings of the Conference.

[2] For detailed information, see charts of ratifications of International Labour Conventions which are usually appended each year to the issues of *Industry and Labour* for 15 January and 15 June.

[3] Figures given in this section are provisional.

as compared with 224 in 1956. The number of awards for individual study abroad nearly doubled; the majority of awards were for studying vocational training methods, various aspects of manpower organization, labour legislation and administration, and co-operation.

Facilities under the worker-trainee programme were offered to 210 foremen and skilled workers for training in advanced techniques in modern European plants; 136 such trainees completed their training during the year. This programme has proved highly successful in meeting immediate training needs in specific fields, pending development of adequate national vocational programmes on a permanent basis.

Expenditure on equipment amounted to $239,200, as compared with $240,665 in 1956. In addition, orders totalling over $350,000 were placed in the USSR against rouble allocations for 1956 and 1957.

Calculated on the basis of funds expended, the Latin American region received 34 per cent of the over-all assistance provided, followed by Asia with 27 per cent, the Near and Middle East with 16 per cent, Europe with 11 per cent, and Africa with 9 per cent. The remaining 3 per cent was disbursed on inter-regional projects. Field expenditure in all regions, with the exception of Latin America, was more than that for 1956.

The widespread interest in projects aimed at raising levels of productivity is not adequately reflected by the percentage of expenditure in this sphere, despite the fact that fairly large-scale and continuing projects have been operating in Egypt, India and Israel; productivity engineers were also assigned to Ceylon (in the field of cargo-handling), Pakistan (in the field of textiles), Hong Kong, Argentina and Colombia. Reports received from ILO representatives in the field, however, revealed that Governments were becoming increasingly concerned with production problems, especially with those methods of raising productivity which do not involve large capital expenditure.

More than half the experts in co-operation and handicrafts who have been provided have devoted their attention to the development of specific handicrafts training projects and the organization of better marketing facilities. Other experts in this category were engaged in co-operative education, legislation and banking; in the organization of agricultural, wholesale and consumer co-operatives; and in the general development of national co-operative movements, including the training of personnel.

In the wide field of operations immediately influencing social development, such as conditions of work, safety and health in industry, and the expansion of social security systems, the total expenditure involved has remained, since 1951/52, at about 30 per cent of that for the over-all programme.

Under the ILO regular assistance programme for 1957, $85,000 was allocated to advisory services of an operational character financed from ILO's regular budget for 1957. In addition, $50,000 was devoted to workers' education; $12,000 to the internship programme; and $3,000 for participation in the United Nations European social welfare exchange programme.

The workers' education programme was designed to provide opportunities for workers to acquire greater knowledge of social conditions and problems confronting them, so that they might be better equipped to play an effective and responsible role in the economic and social life of a modern society. Workers' education courses have been, or were being, prepared and published on the co-operative movement, on labour legislation, on social security, and on labour-management relations.

The internship programme provides opportunities for study of the structure, purposes and activities of ILO. It was first introduced in 1950, and enables 12 internes from selected countries (four designated by Governments, four by employers' organizations, and four by workers' organizations), to attend a special two-month course of study each year at ILO Headquarters in Geneva.

The financial allocations for operational activities under ILO's regular assistance programme have been small. But they have made it possible to provide some aid to countries not eligible for help under the Expanded Technical Assistance Programme. They have also made it possible promptly to provide urgent advisory and follow-up missions.

LABOUR AND SOCIAL STANDARDS

The International Labour Conference, at its

fortieth session, adopted a Convention on the Abolition of Forced Labour and Conventions and supplementary Recommendations[4] dealing with the protection and integration of indigenous and tribal populations in independent countries, and with weekly rest in commerce and offices. Preliminary action with a view to final discussion in 1958 was taken on four other instruments, a Convention and a Recommendation concerning discrimination in the field of employment and occupations and a Convention and a Recommendation concerning conditions of employment of plantation workers.

The Conference also adopted resolutions calling for the abolition of anti-trade-union legislation, and of concentration camps and the deportation of national minorities. It asked member States to consider the ratification of the ILO Protection of Wages Convention and of the supplementary Convention on Abolition of Slavery adopted by the United Nations. Other resolutions dealt with safety in mines, workers' education, housing construction, the application of International Labour Conventions in non-metropolitan territories, and disarmament.

As is its usual practice, the Conference set up a special tripartite committee to review the information and reports received from Governments on the application of International Labour Conventions and Recommendations.

The Governing Body decided on the broad lines of future ILO action in the field of labour-management relations. The programme covered research studies and reports to be undertaken by the ILO Secretariat, as well as direct ILO technical assistance in the field to be given to countries requesting it.

Later in the year, the Governing Body adopted the conclusions of its Freedom of Association Committee in 16 cases of alleged violations of trade-union rights. It also decided to create a new committee on forced labour. It added three new items to the agenda for the 1959 session of the International Labour Conference: the protection of workers against radiations; collaboration between public authorities and employers' and workers' organizations at the industrial and national level; and problems of non-manual workers, including technicians, supervisory staff, etc.

The fourth Asian Regional Conference of ILO met in New Delhi in mid-November 1957,

and was attended by 187 Government, employer and worker delegates and observers and their advisers from 21 countries. At the opening session, the Conference was addressed by Prime Minister Jawaharlal Nehru, of India. Among the subjects discussed were labour-management relations, small-scale industry, and agriculture.

For the first time, ILO studied labour and social problems in mines other than coal mines at a technical tripartite meeting at ILO Headquarters. Conclusions were adopted on safety, wages and industrial relations, including the employment of young people underground, and the future work of ILO in this field.

Resolutions dealing with methods of improving the organization of work and output in ports and with safety in road transport were adopted at the sixth session of ILO's Inland Transport Committee, held in Hamburg in the latter half of March at the invitation of the Federal Republic of Germany.

The Advisory Committee on Salaried Employees and Professional Workers, meeting in Geneva in April, adopted a resolution stressing the rights of non-manual workers in both public and private sectors of the economy to benefit from the guarantees laid down in the International Labour Convention concerning freedom of association and protection of the right to organize. It drew the attention of all Governments to the various instruments adopted by the Conference concerning freedom of association, collective agreements and voluntary conciliation and arbitration.

The sixth session of ILO's Metal Trades Committee, held in Geneva in May, adopted a report containing a memorandum presented by the employers' group and a statement presented by the workers' group. The Committee also approved a resolution, with an annex, giving a series of general considerations on automation to be communicated to ILO member States with the request that they be transmitted to the em-

[4] The Constitution of ILO requires member states to bring the Conventions and Recommendations adopted by the Conference before the national authorities competent to legislate on the matters dealt with in these instruments, as a rule, their parliaments; members may also be asked by the ILO Governing Body to report from time to time on the position of their laws and practices in relation to certain Conventions they have not ratified and in relation to certain Recommendations.

ployers' and workers' organizations of the metal trades and to other bodies concerned.

At a meeting in November and December, eight experts considered practical international standards that would help to solve the safety problems posed by radiation, especially in non-atomic plants. The experts stressed the imperative need for adequate education of the workers in the field of protection against radiation. The experts devoted considerable attention to revising the chapter on dangerous radiations in the *Model Code of Safety Regulations for Industrial Establishments for the Guidance of Governments and Industries,* issued by ILO in 1949.

Experts on workers' education, meeting at ILO Headquarters in December, expressed the view that the spread of industrialization, the widening role and responsibilities of workers, the growth of their trade unions, the impact of technological and other social and economic developments had created real educational needs.

During 1957, ILO began a study on the conditions of work and employment for nurses. This enquiry, the first of its kind to be undertaken on the international level, was intended to be as complete as possible and to be a study of all aspects of employment and working conditions for nurses.

RESEARCH AND PUBLICATIONS

The research and publications programme of the International Labour Office for 1957 included reports on all the agenda items of the fortieth, forty-first (Maritime) and forty-second sessions of the International Labour Conference. The *Report of the Director-General* to the Conference was divided in 1957 into two parts, the first dealing with automation and the second describing the activities of ILO during the preceding year; the second part constituted at the same time the eleventh report of the International Labour Organisation to the United Nations.

Other publications which appeared during 1957 included: *Systems of Social Security: Great Britain; National Employment Services: Belgium; Proposed International Convention* concerning the Protection of Performers, Manufacturers of Phonographic Records and Broadcasting Organisations; The Landless Farmer in Latin America; and An Introduction to Work Study.

ILO's regular periodicals in English, French and Spanish continued to be issued, as follows: the monthly *International Labour Review* (with statistical supplements), the semi-monthly *Industry and Labour,* the bi-monthly *Legislative Series,* the quarterly *Occupational Safety and Health,* the *Official Bulletin* (published irregularly) and the *Year Book of Labour Statistics, 1957.*

The *ILO News,* a bulletin, was issued monthly in English, French and Spanish, every two months in German and at varying intervals in Arabic, Dutch, Hindi, Japanese, Norwegian and Urdu.

BUDGET

The fortieth session of the International Labour Conference approved a budget totalling $7,972,901 to cover expenses of ILO during 1958. The main details of the expenditure covered by this budget (in U.S. dollars) are as follows:

Ordinary Budget:	
Sessions of the Conference and the Governing Body and other Conferences	$ 401,129
General services of the International Labour Office	6,436,612
Profit and loss on exchange	—
Permanent equipment, library, etc.	124,300
Capital expenditure	100
Unforeseen expenditure	—
Total	$6,962,141
Staff Pension Funds and Related Provisions	644,294
Working Capital Fund	—
Building Fund—Annuity	59,961
Facilities in Additional Languages	243,505
Supplementary Operational Activities	164,000
Total Gross Expenditure Budget	$8,073,901
Deduct: Miscellaneous Income	101,000
Total Net Expenditure Budget	$7,972,901

(For details of contributions due from member States for 1958, see ANNEX I below.)

ANNEX I. MEMBERSHIP AND CONTRIBUTIONS

(Membership as of 31 December 1957; contributions as due for 1958)

Member	Percentage	Gross Contribution (in U.S. dollars)	Member	Percentage	Gross Contribution
Afghanistan	0.12	$ 9,568	Jordan	0.12	9,568
Albania	0.12	9,568	Lebanon	0.12	9,568
Argentina	1.58	125,972	Liberia	0.12	9,568
Australia	1.90	151,485	Libya	0.12	9,568
Austria	0.35	27,905	Luxembourg	0.12	9,568
Belgium	1.41	112,418	Malaya, Federation of*	*	*
Bolivia	0.12	9,568	Mexico	0.78	62,188
Brazil	1.57	125,174	Morocco	0.14	11,162
Bulgaria	0.20	15,946	Netherlands	1.23	98,066
Burma	0.16	12,756	New Zealand	0.50	39,864
Byelorussian SSR	0.45	35,878	Nicaragua	0.12	9,568
Canada	3.56	283,835	Norway	0.53	42,256
Ceylon	0.13	10,364	Pakistan	0.72	57,405
Chile	0.36	28,702	Panama	0.12	9,568
China	2.04	162,647	Paraguay	0.12	9,568
Colombia	0.41	32,689	Peru	0.21	16,743
Costa Rica	0.12	9,568	Philippines	0.37	29,499
Cuba	0.32	25,513	Poland	1.24	98,864
Czechoslovakia	0.94	74,945	Portugal	0.32	25,513
Denmark	0.79	62,986	Romania	0.50	39,864
Dominican Republic	0.12	9,568	Spain	1.14	90,891
Ecuador	0.12	9,568	Sudan	0.12	9,568
Egypt	0.48	38,270	Sweden	1.75	139,526
El Salvador	0.12	9,568	Switzerland	1.47	117,201
Ethiopia	0.12	9,568	Syria	0.12	9,568
Finland	0.30	23,918	Thailand	0.21	16,743
France	6.14	489,536	Tunisia	0.12	9,568
Germany, Fed. Rep. of	4.35	346,821	Turkey	0.78	62,188
Ghana	0.12	9,568	Ukrainian SSR	1.00	79,729
Greece	0.21	16,743	Union of South Africa	0.93	74,148
Guatemala	0.12	9,568	USSR	10.00	797,290
Haiti	0.12	9,568	United Kingdom	10.24	816,425
Honduras	0.12	9,568	United States	25.00	1,993,225
Hungary	0.50	39,864	Uruguay	0.19	15,148
Iceland	0.12	9,568	Viet-Nam	0.21	16,743
India	3.38	267,092	Yugoslavia	0.43	34,283
Indonesia	0.43	34,283			
Iran	0.31	24,716	Total	100.00	$7,972,901
Iraq	0.13	10,364			
Ireland	0.29	23,121			
Israel	0.12	9,568			
Italy	2.45	195,336			
Japan	2.00	159,458			

NOTE: Venezuela withdrew from membership in ILO on 3 May 1957.

* The contribution from the Federation of Malaya had not yet been assessed at the end of 1957.

ANNEX II. OFFICERS AND OFFICES

(As of 31 December 1957)

MEMBERSHIP OF THE GOVERNING BODY OF ILO

Chairman: Emilio Calderón Puig.
Vice-Chairmen: Pierre Waline, Sir Alfred Roberts.

REGULAR MEMBERS

GOVERNMENT GROUP
Belgium *
Brazil — J. A. Barboza-Carneiro
Canada — George V. Haythorne

Chile — Fernando Donoso Silva
China — Yu Tsune-chi
Czechoslovakia *
France — Paul Ramadier
Germany, Fed. Rep. of — Maximilian Sauerborn
India — S. T. Merani
Iraq — Hashim Jawad
Italy — Roberto Ago

Japan   Shingo Kaite

Mexico   Emilio Calderón Puig

Pakistan*

Peru   Max de la Fuente Locker

Philippines   Jorge Bocobo

Sweden   Ernst Michanek

USSR   A. A. Arutiunian

United Kingdom   Sir Guildhaume
                  Myrddin-Evans

United States   J. Ernest Wilkins

* No permanent representative had been appointed by the end of 1957.

EMPLOYERS' GROUP
Gullmar Bergenström (Swedish), L. C. Burne (Australian), Pietro Campanella (Italian), J. Díaz Salas (Chilean), Massoud Ghayour (Iranian), Cola G. Parker (United States), Sir Richard Snedden (United Kingdom), N. H. Tata (Indian), Pierre Waline (French), Fernando Yllanes Ramos (Mexican).

WORKERS' GROUP
Faiz Ahmad (Pakistani), Gangadhar D. Ambekar (Indian), Robert Bothereau (French), George P. Delaney (United States), Albert E. Monk (Australian), Einar Nielsen (Danish), S. de Azevedo Pequeno (Brazilian), Willi Richter (German), Sir Alfred Roberts (United Kingdom), Alfonso Sánchez Madariaga (Mexican).

DEPUTY MEMBERS
GOVERNMENT GROUP

Argentina   Raúl C. Migone

Australia   G. A. Jockel

Cuba   Guillermo de Blanck

Denmark*

Morocco*

Portugal   Manuel A. Fernandes

Switzerland   Max Kaufmann

Syria*

Thailand   Malai Huvanandana

Uruguay   Victor Pomes

* No permanent representative had been appointed by the end of 1957.

EMPLOYERS' GROUP
W. A. Campbell (Canadian), Akio Mishiro (Japanese), Ernst-Gerhard Erdmann (German), Antonio Pinilla (Peruvian), A. G. Fennema (Netherlands), H. Dündar (Turkish), Charles Kuntschen (Swiss), Brasilio Machado Neto (Brazilian), John O'Brien (Irish), M. Aye (Burmese).

WORKERS' GROUP
Mahjoub ben Seddik (Moroccan), Nathalis de Bock (Belgian), Claude Jodoin (Canadian), Yukitaka Haraguchi (Japanese), Aron Becker (Israeli), Jean Möri (Swiss), Giulio Pastore (Italian), Martin Ruppert (Netherlands), Andreas Kyriakopoulos (Greek), Ignacio González Tellechea (Cuban).

OFFICIALS OF THE INTERNATIONAL LABOUR OFFICE

Director-General: David A. Morse (United States).
Deputy Director-General: Jef Rens (Belgium).
Assistant Directors-General: Raghunath Rao (India), C. W. Jenks (United Kingdom), Luis Alvarado (Peru), William Yalden-Thomson (Canada), Abbas Ammar (Egypt), Francis C. Blanchard (France).
Treasurer: Frederick H. Wheeler (Australia).

HEADQUARTERS, LIAISON, BRANCH AND FIELD OFFICES

HEADQUARTERS
International Labour Office
Geneva, Switzerland
   Cable Address: INTERLAB GENEVE

LIAISON OFFICE WITH THE UNITED NATIONS
International Labour Office
345 East 46th Street
New York 17, N. Y., U. S. A.
   Cable Address: INTERLABOR NEWYORKNY

BRANCH OFFICES
International Labour Office
Edificio do Ministério do Trabalho
2° Andar, Sala 216 a 220
Avenida Presidente Antonio Carlos
Rio de Janeiro, Brazil
   Cable Address: INTERLAB RIODEJANEIRO

International Labour Office
Room 307, 202 Queen Street
Ottawa 4, Ontario, Canada
   Cable Address: INTERLAB OTTAWA

International Labour Office
205 Boulevard St. Germain
Paris 7°, France
   Cable Address: INTERLAB PARIS

International Labour Office
Kölner Strasse 64a
Bad Godesberg, Fed. Rep. of Germany
   Cable Address: INTERLAB BONN

International Labour Office
1—Mandi House
New Delhi, India
   Cable Address: INTERLAB NEWDELHI

International Labour Office
Villa Aldobrandini
Via Panisperna 28
Rome, Italy
   Cable Address: INTERLAB ROMA

International Labour Office
c/o Chuo Rodo Kaikan
6-gochi, Shiba-Koen
Minato-ku
Tokyo, Japan
    Cable Address: INTERLAB TOKYO

International Labour Office
38 Parliament Street
London, S.W.1., England
    Cable Address: INTERLAB LONDON

International Labour Office
917 Fifteenth Street N.W.
Washington 5, D. C., U. S. A.
    Cable Address: INTERLAB WASHINGTON

FIELD OFFICES

ASIA
International Labour Office
P. O. Box 4
Bangalore, Mysore State, India
    Cable Address: INTERLAB BANGALORE

CENTRAL AMERICA AND THE CARIBBEAN
International Labour Office
Edificio "América" "B" 10° Piso
Avenida Juárez No. 42
Mexico 1, D. F., Mexico
    Cable Address: CEDEAC MEXICO

LATIN AMERICA
International Labour Office
Avenida Arequipa 173
Lima, Peru
    Cable Address: CENTRAC LIMA

NEAR AND MIDDLE EAST
International Labour Office
Luleciler caddesi No. 26
Tophane
Istanbul, Turkey
    Cable Address: INTERLAB ISTANBUL

CHAPTER III

THE FOOD AND AGRICULTURE ORGANIZATION OF THE UNITED NATIONS (FAO)

The year 1957 was characterized by considerable progress in a number of general projects undertaken by the Food and Agriculture Organization of the United Nations (FAO).[1] It also saw a considered reappraisal within the Agency of its field programmes and of its structure as a whole. Particular attention was given, in the course of the reappraisal, to the further strengthening of the regional offices, especially on the technical side, the aim being to maintain closer contact with individual member Governments. As a result, technical staffs at the regional offices were gradually strengthened. Another objective, achieved to some extent by the same means, was the even closer integration of the Agency's regular programme (financed from its normal budget) with its work financed with funds made available under the Expanded Technical Assistance Programme of the United Nations and specialized agencies.

One of the general projects on which progress was made was the world resources survey, now recognized as an even longer-term project than had originally been thought. It was continued, with the preliminary reports on two pilot areas covering the Ganges-Bramha-Putra basin and the Tigris-Euphrates basin. Useful conclusions, especially on the methodology for a survey of this nature, were drawn from this work. They were especially valuable in connexion with another very large-scale project added to FAO's programme during the year. This was the Mediterranean Development Project, on which a group of economists, and specialist advisers from the technical divisions, worked to produce a preliminary report. The basic idea underlying this scheme was the agricultural rehabilitation of the Mediterranean region, based on the premise that it would first be necessary to re-establish much of the forest cover lost to the region through centuries of overgrazing and bad use of land.

[1] For further information, particularly about FAO's functions and organization, and activities prior to 1957, see previous volumes of the *Yearbook;* FAO reports to the United Nations; reports of the Director-General to the FAO Conference; reports of the Conference; and FAO *Catalogue of Publications.*

These and other developments were fully discussed, and the Director-General's programme approved, at the ninth session of the FAO Conference, held in Rome during November. It was foreshadowed at the Conference that more attention would be given to the uses of atomic energy within FAO's fields of operation. Also approved were plans for strengthening the work in community development and allied activities involving the work of several of FAO's technical divisions. The continued seriousness of the agricultural surplus situation was considered at length, and requests were made for strengthening of work in this field, both on the part of the Committee on Commodity Problems, and, more particularly, through its permanent Consultative Sub-Committee on Surplus Disposal, which met several times during the year in Washington.

FAO had 77 members at the end of 1957.

ACTIVITIES UNDER EXPANDED TECHNICAL ASSISTANCE PROGRAMME

About $9 million were available for technical assistance in 1957, the highest annual sum so far available for FAO operations in this respect. As a result, almost 500 experts were in the field for the greater part of the year, and some 520 by the end of December. Completed assignments totalled about 1,600, and the number of fellowships awarded passed the 1,250 mark.

Significant developments were to be observed in the increased demand for groups of experts working as teams on large-scale development projects, as in Iran, East Pakistan, Tanganyika and Sudan.

Extended, in view of the promising results obtained, was the system of appointing senior experts as "country representatives", with special responsibility for co-ordinating, wherever possible, FAO's technical assistance activities and activities under its regular programme.

The year 1957 also showed a trend towards more requests for expert advice in fundamental problems (such as the making of resource surveys of one sort or another) and in basic-development planning. This was in preference to requests for assistance in solving more specific problems.

A major evaluation project was put in hand with questionnaires being sent to some 700 former holders of FAO fellowships, in an effort to find out if the work done and experience gained during the fellowship period was being put to good use. Replies not only showed that the fellowships had in general been successful from the technical point of view. They also showed that former fellowship holders frequently returned to their homelands to take up higher posts with increased responsibility. No less than seven former fellows were present as members of national delegations at the November Conference.

AGRICULTURE

Significant progress was made during the year in work relating to fertility and soil improvement. A meeting of the International Rice Commission's Working Party on Fertilizers provided an opportunity for bringing together many workers to consider various findings and views on the response of the rice crop to fertilizers. To promote a better understanding of complex soil-water-plant relationships involved in rice culture, another working group was set up under the Commission. There are now several such groups studying various aspects of rice and its culture.

The European Commission on Agriculture also met during the year. So did its Sub-Commission on Land and Water Use, first at Lisbon, and later at Vienna. At Lisbon, it discussed problems of co-ordination in the administration of land and water development schemes. Examined, too, were questions of urban encroachment on good agricultural land, the financing and administration of development schemes, soil conservation and watershed management with particular reference to southern Europe. At its second 1957 meeting, held in Vienna in October, the Sub-Commission continued these discussions and, in addition, considered problems of the consolidation of fragmented holdings.

FAO also collaborated with the United Nations and with the International Labour Organisation on a second report on progress in land reform submitted during the year to the United Nations Economic and Social Council.

Work in plant breeding and seed production continued, especially with regard to hybrid maize (in Europe), rice (in the Far East) and wheat and barley (in the Near East). The standard FAO catalogues of genetic stocks of the major cereals were revised. Preliminary details were worked out for a large-scale campaign for improving seeds in agriculture generally, in the form of an "international seed year". At the same time, increased attention was given to the production and certification of seed for forage crops, since the use of improved and certified seed is less advanced than that of grain crops, even in many countries where agriculture is highly developed. FAO distribution of seed for experimental purposes also continued to increase. More than 20,000 individual seed samples were sent out during the year.

Integration of livestock and crop husbandry was studied at a meeting in Israel of the Working Party on Mediterranean Pasture and Fodder Development. Technical discussions at the meeting also dealt with the results of the co-operative research programme which has been in progress in the region for some years. Work on a world grassland survey continued, and a draft map of the grasslands of Africa was prepared.

Member Governments showed renewed interest in the world reporting service on plant diseases and pests, which also proved of value to individual research workers in many fields. A questionnaire worked out in co-operation with the International Office of Epizootics and sent to members of that organization as well as to FAO member Governments, dealt with proposals for a similar reporting service for pests and diseases of livestock. This was well received, a very large number of Governments indicating their wish to co-operate in such a service.

Field operations in pest and disease control continued.

In the Arabian Peninsula, nine Governments, co-ordinated from an FAO centre at Jeddah, undertook locust control operations, and seven others contributed to this and other anti-desert-locust campaigns. A new co-ordinating centre for anti-locust operations at Addis Ababa came into operation to serve Ethiopia and neighbouring territories, and FAO's role expanded to include parts of north-west Africa.

Foot-and-mouth disease also came in for a great deal of attention during the year. In the control of other livestock diseases, such as haemorrhagic septicaemia, activities under FAO's regular programme and its technical assistance programme were closely co-ordinated.

In co-operation with the United Nations Children's Fund (UNICEF) and, where necessary, with the World Health Organization (WHO), FAO continued the programme of dairy surveys, covering territories in the Far East, Africa and South America. Regional dairy training centres were used to prepare nationals of many countries for future expansion in this field.

Towards the end of the year, there was increasing evidence of the need of many Governments for assistance in agricultural administration, especially for making effective use of expert advice under the Expanded Technical Assistance Programme of the United Nations and specialized agencies.

Co-ordination of research programmes within regions, the organization of co-operative research programmes, and better exchange of information in this field were other aspects of a more fundamental approach to the institutional side of FAO's work in agriculture.

To promote more work among member countries in the uses of atomic energy within FAO's fields of competence, a new atomic energy branch was formed within the agency. There was close co-operation with the United Nations Educational, Scientific and Cultural Organization in preparing for a meeting arranged by the latter on the uses of isotopes in research. First steps were taken to insure that no overlapping of programmes occurred with the newly formed International Atomic Energy Agency.

ECONOMICS

Work on surplus disposal problems continued to expand. New groups were established for the study of the situation as regards grains, coconuts and coconut products. Studies of national price-support programmes were put in hand, and the November Conference of FAO called for an intensification of this work.

The basic work of reporting on world production, trade, prices and consumption of agricultural products was continued. Work on the latter matter was given special emphasis during the year.

Important steps were taken to improve the comparability of data on world production and trade, through the compilation of a World Crop Harvest Calendar, and other basic information.

Preparations for the 1960 world agricultural census continued, and the draft programme for this was completed. Analysis of the results of the 1950 census also continued. To enable countries to provide more accurate and reliable data than hitherto, a number of experts were assigned to many countries in connexion with the 1960 census, to train local personnel in census techniques; there were training centres in Cairo (for Arab countries) and Abidjan (for African territories south of the Sahara).

Among many meetings held during the year was that of the Working Party on Agricultural Development and Planning, convened jointly at Bangkok in September with the United Nations Economic Commission for Asia and the Far East. A number of expert advisers sent out under the Expanded Technical Assistance Programme were concerned with marketing and distribution problems. A new publication, *Marketing Problems and Improvement Programmes,* was issued as the first of an important series of handbooks in this field. The annual report on *The State of Food and Agriculture,* organized on a somewhat broader base than hitherto, included, in addition to the usual statistical material, a review of factors influencing consumption and a study of the impact of institutional changes (i.e., in land tenure, farm credit, etc.) on agricultural development.

FISHERIES

Work on various aspects of a world fisheries resources survey was continued, and synopses of information on several commercially important species were made available to member Governments during the year. In the third quarter of 1957, the first World Fishing Gear Conference was held in Hamburg, attended by a very large number of delegates from every part of the world. One result of this very successful meeting was an increased exchange between the developed and less developed countries of knowledge and experience of new and improved types of gear.

Arrangements were made during the year for co-operative research programmes for the members of the Indo-Pacific Fisheries Council and also for members of the General Council for Fisheries in the Mediterranean. A new departure was the establishment of a European Inland Fisheries Advisory Commission.

Technical assistance projects in the field were devoted not only to helping countries with the development, especially the mechanization, of their fishing fleets, but also to problems of internal distribution of catches, with the aim of increasing the intake of animal protein by inland and urban populations. Good progress was made in a number of countries in surveying inland and marine fishery possibilities; two fisheries technicians were included in the large mission operating in the Amazon region of Brazil under the Expanded Technical Assistance Programme.

Training centres included one at Nouméa, New Caledonia, in conjunction with the South Pacific Commission, for training fisheries officers in new techniques. This was in operation between November 1956 and February 1957. Later in 1957, it was already apparent to technical officers visiting the region that much of what had been taught and demonstrated was already being put into operation by the trainees. At the end of the year, another important course was held in this region, on training in fisheries co-operatives and administration.

FORESTRY

The main aim of FAO work in forestry continued to be encouraging member Governments in the development of sound basic forest policies corresponding to the physical, economic and social needs of their countries. As a result of requests from the regions concerned, plans were made for studies of development trends and future needs for Latin America and the Far East, on lines similar to those of the *European Timber Trends Study* previously published. The general review of the pulp and paper requirements and development possibilities of various countries was continued with assignments under the Expanded Technical Assistance Programme. Renewed emphasis was given to the importance of proper development of tropical forests, and the newly formed Teak Sub-Commission of the Asian-Pacific Forestry Commission met during the year.

With the co-operation of the United Nations Economic Commission for Europe, FAO convened a meeting in Geneva of independent pulp and paper technicians, similar to one held several years ago, to discuss and review developments in the production of hardboard and fibre-board. The report of this meeting was a basic publication in this increasingly important field.

Another important meeting was that of the International Poplar Congress, held in Paris in the first quarter of 1957.

Maintaining the contact set up last year with the USSR in the forestry field, the FAO/ECE Committee on Forestry Working Techniques and the Training of Forest Workers met in Moscow in September. Delegates later took part in a 10-day study tour of research institutes and timber production units.

At Santarem, Brazil, the Director-General of FAO opened the Training Centre in Logging and Sawmilling, on which several experts, sent out under the Expanded Technical Assistance Programme, have been at work for some years. It provides an important part of the forestry activity which forms the core of the Amazon region development scheme.

On the research side, the work of the Latin American Forest Research Institute at Merida, Venezuela, established with the assistance of FAO, was pushed ahead. Plans were also well advanced, and work commenced, on establishing a similar centre for the Near East by the Syrian Government with FAO aid.

NUTRITION

Much of the important nutrition work during the year was carried out in collaboration with WHO, for example, at the fourth Latin American Nutrition Conference, held in Guatemala, and the meetings of the joint FAO/WHO Expert Committee on Nutrition, and the specialized committees on calorie and protein requirements. In Rome, the newly formed Home Economics Advisory Committee met for the first time, stressing the continued increase of interest in this subject among FAO's member Governments. A training centre for the development of practical nutrition workers in the English-speaking territories south of the Sahara was also conducted; this followed a similar course, already completed, for French-speaking workers.

At FAO Headquarters, new emphasis was given to food technology, particularly to work (again carried out in collaboration with WHO) on food additives. In many tropical countries,

studies were made or advice given, on protein-rich foods other than milk. The FAO Nutrition Division was also concerned in the milk surveys made in other regions.

Noticeable in many field projects were an increase in nutrition education work and a growing appreciation of the important role of women in community development schemes. There was also very close liaison with UNICEF.

INFORMATION ACTIVITIES

During the year, a new display kit, suitable for use in many countries, was put out, and the visual aids side of information work expanded. Other innovations included: the development of a system of recording returning holders of FAO fellowships in their mother tongue; and the substitution of a new periodical, the *FAO Bulletin,* for the former monthly *Memo.* Two important general publications were: *Food and Hunger,* a general education pamphlet prepared in collaboration with UNESCO; and *Millions Still Go Hungry,* the first critical appraisal of a non-technical nature of FAO's work, especially under the Expanded Technical Assistance Programme.

BUDGET

The expenses of the Agency are met by contributions from member nations in proportions determined by the Conference. Prior to 1958, the budget was voted on an annual basis, but the FAO Conference in November 1957 agreed to biennial budgeting, and voted a total of $17 million for the period 1958-59. The contributions of member Governments for this two-year period are given in Annex I below.

Of the $17 million budget approved for 1958-59, $16,645,000 consists of contributions from member Governments, the remainder ($355,000) being met from miscellaneous income. The budget for 1958-59 provides for the following expenses (in U.S. dollars):

Conference and Council	$ 432,200
Office of the Director-General	884,850
Information[a]	1,447,850
Administration and Finance	1,074,350
Common Services	1,450,900
Technical Divisions	
Agriculture	3,063,850
Economics	3,091,730
Fisheries	1,398,570

Forestry	1,439,740	Contingencies	200,000
Nutrition	986,780		
Fellowships	110,000	Total	$ 1,619,180
Total	$15,380,820	Grand Total	$17,000,000

| Regional Offices | 1,338,180 |
| Miscellaneous Expenditure | 81,000 |

* Includes Library, Legislative, Headquarters and regional information services.

ANNEX I. MEMBERSHIP AND CONTRIBUTIONS
(Membership as of 31 December 1957; contributions as assessed for 1958-59)

Member	CONTRIBUTION Percentage Scale	CONTRIBUTION In U.S. Dollars	Member	CONTRIBUTION Percentage Scale	CONTRIBUTION In U.S. Dollars
Afghanistan	0.08	13,316.00	Laos	0.04	6,658.00
Argentina*	1.54	256,333.00	Lebanon	0.07	11,651.50
Australia	2.17	361,196.50	Liberia	0.04	6,658.00
Austria	0.47	78,231.50	Libya	0.04	6,658.00
Belgium*	1.67	277,971.50	Luxembourg	0.08	13,316.00
Bolivia	0.07	11,651.50	Malaya, Federation of	0.30	49,935.00
Brazil*	1.43	238,023.50	Mexico*	0.92	153,134.00
Burma	0.14	23,303.00	Morocco	0.16	26,632.00
Cambodia	0.04	6,658.00	Nepal	0.04	6,658.00
Canada*	4.17	694,096.50	Netherlands	1.51	251,339.50
Ceylon	0.15	24,967.50	New Zealand*	0.57	94,876.50
Chile	0.39	64,915.50	Nicaragua	0.04	6,658.00
Colombia*	0.49	81,560.50	Norway*	0.65	108,192.50
Costa Rica	0.04	6,658.00	Pakistan*	0.73	121,508.50
Cuba*	0.35	58,257.50	Panama	0.07	11,651.50
Denmark	0.86	143,147.00	Paraguay	0.04	6,658.00
Dominican Republic	0.07	11,651.50	Peru	0.20	33,290.00
Ecuador	0.07	11,651.50	Philippines*	0.54	89,883.00
Egypt*	0.47	78,231.50	Poland	2.05	341,222.50
El Salvador	0.08	13,316.00	Portugal	0.32	53,264.00
Ethiopia	0.15	24,967.50	Saudi Arabia	0.09	14,980.50
Finland	0.49	81,560.50	Spain*	1.50	249,675.00
France*	7.51	1,250,039.50	Sudan	0.15	24,967.50
Germany, Fed. Rep. of	5.60	932,120.00	Sweden	1.93	321,248.50
Ghana	0.09	14,980.50	Switzerland	1.32	219,714.00
Greece	0.26	43,277.00	Syria*	0.11	18,309.50
Guatemala	0.09	14,980.50	Thailand	0.22	36,619.00
Haiti	0.04	6,658.00	Tunisia	0.07	11,651.50
Honduras	0.04	6,658.00	Turkey*	0.82	136,489.00
Iceland	0.04	6,658.00	Union of South Africa*	0.90	149,805.00
India*	3.91	650,819.50	United Kingdom*	10.29	1,712,770.50
Indonesia*	0.67	111,521.50	United States*	32.51	5,411,289.50
Iran*	0.35	58,257.50	Uruguay	0.22	36,619.00
Iraq	0.16	26,632.00	Venezuela	0.57	94,876.50
Ireland	0.24	39,948.00	Viet-Nam	0.22	36,619.00
Israel	0.22	36,619.00	Yemen	0.04	6,658.00
Italy*	2.74	456,073.00	Yugoslavia	0.47	78,231.50
Japan*	2.59	431,105.50			
Jordan	0.04	6,658.00	Total	100.00	16,645,000.00
Korea, Rep. of	0.18	29,961.00			

* Members of FAO Council for 1958.

ANNEX II. OFFICERS AND OFFICES
(As of 31 December 1957)

OFFICERS OF THE STAFF

OFFICE OF THE DIRECTOR-GENERAL
Director-General: B. R. Sen (India).
Deputy Director-General: Sir Herbert Broadley
(United Kingdom).
Secretary-General: Marc Veillet-Lavallée (France).
Special Assistant to Director-General:
Sushil K. Dey (India).

REGIONAL REPRESENTATIVES
*Regional Representative of the Director-General for
North America:* Harold Vogel (United States).
Regional Officer for Latin America: W. G. Casseres
(Costa Rica).
*Regional Representative of the Director-General for
the Near East:* A. R. Sidky (Egypt).

*Regional Representative of the Director-General for
Asia and the Far East:* W. H. Cummings
(United States).
Director, FAO Liaison Office with United Nations:
Joseph L. Orr (United States).

DIVISION DIRECTORS
Administration and Finance: Frank Weisl
(United States).
Agriculture: F. T. Wahlen (Switzerland).
Economics: A. H. Boerma (Netherlands).
Fisheries: D. B. Finn (Canada).
Forestry: Marcel Leloup (France).
Information: Duncan Wall (United States).
Nutrition: W. R. Aykroyd (United Kingdom).

HEADQUARTERS AND REGIONAL OFFICES

FAO HEADQUARTERS
Viale delle Terme di Caracalla
Rome, Italy
    Cable Address: FOODAGRI ROME

REGIONAL OFFICE FOR ASIA AND THE FAR EAST
Maliwan Mansion
Phra Atit Road
Bangkok, Thailand

REGIONAL INFORMATION CENTRE AND OFFICE OF THE
FAO REPRESENTATIVE IN INDIA
21 Curzon Road
New Delhi, India

REGIONAL OFFICES FOR LATIN AMERICA
Escritorio Regional de la FAO
Rua Jardim Botanico, 1008
Rio de Janeiro, Brazil

Oficina Regional de la FAO
(Apartado Postal 10778)
Namburgo 63-202
Mexico 1, D.F., Mexico

Oficina Regional de la FAO
(Casilla 10095)
Cano y Aponte 995
Santiago de Chile

REGIONAL OFFICE FOR THE NEAR EAST
(Box 2223)
Isis Building, 7 Sharia Lazoghli, Garden City
Cairo, Egypt

REGIONAL OFFICE FOR NORTH AMERICA
1325 C Street S.W.
Washington 25, D.C., U. S. A.

FAO GENEVA OFFICE
Palais des Nations
Geneva, Switzerland

FAO LIAISON OFFICE WITH UNITED NATIONS
United Nations, Room 2245
42nd Street and First Avenue
New York 17, N. Y., U. S. A.

CHAPTER IV

THE UNITED NATIONS EDUCATIONAL, SCIENTIFIC AND CULTURAL ORGANIZATION (UNESCO)

The year 1957 saw the United Nations Educational, Scientific and Cultural Organization (UNESCO)[1] take steps to give concrete

shape to the three new "major projects" in its programme that were decided on in 1956. These deal with: scientific research for the benefit of

[1] For further information, particularly about the functions and organization of UNESCO and its activities prior to 1957, see previous volumes of the *Year-* *book,* reports of UNESCO to the United Nations and annual reports of the Director-General to the General Conference.

arid lands; the extension of primary education in Latin America; and better mutual appreciation of Eastern and Western cultural values. In a year which saw new emphasis placed on scientific research, UNESCO organized in Paris the International Conference on Radio-Isotopes in Scientific Research, the largest conference ever held by this specialized agency.

This expansion of UNESCO's activities followed the agency's ninth General Conference, held in New Delhi from 5 November to 5 December 1956, which had voted a total of $22,679,638 to finance UNESCO's activities in 1957 and 1958. This was the highest budget in UNESCO's history. The agency was enabled to start its "major projects" without reducing its regular activities in education, the natural sciences, social sciences, cultural activities, mass communication and exchange of persons through fellowships, scholarships and travel grants.

The agency had 79 member States at the end of 1957.

Perhaps the biggest single activity of the year was the International Conference on Radio-Isotopes in Scientific Research. Organized by UNESCO's Department of Natural Sciences, it drew 1,200 scientists from 62 countries and 25 international organizations to Paris from September 9 to September 20. The Conference, at which over 200 papers were presented and discussed, focused attention on the tremendous economic and scientific role now being played by radio-isotopes throughout the world—a role so great that, in the opinion of the Chairman of the Conference, they may soon rival atomic power in the benefits they can offer to humanity.

THE MAJOR PROJECTS

From a long-term viewpoint, the launching of UNESCO's three major projects in 1957 was even more important in terms of future benefits to the agency's member States.

The major project on the extension of primary education in Latin America covers a region in which nearly 180 million people live. Nearly every country in this region has laws on its books establishing free and compulsory primary education. But a tremendous number of new schools and adequately trained teachers are required to translate these laws into pupils and classrooms. The project got under way in February 1957 when an inter-governmental advisory committee composed of representatives of 12 countries met in Havana, Cuba, to approve ways and means of carrying it out.

Despite the large amount of planning required to set machinery in motion over such a wide area, certain steps forward were taken later in the year 1957. Plans were made for the organization of a course for educational statisticians at Santiago de Chile in 1958 and a specialist in educational statistics was sent by UNESCO to consult with and gather data from the education ministries in the region. The establishment of two "associated normal schools" (i.e., teacher-training institutions which will benefit from UNESCO aid) at Pamplona, Colombia, and at San Pablo del Lago, Ecuador, was approved. The National University of Chile at Santiago and the University of São Paulo in Brazil were approved as Latin American universities to be associated with the project. UNESCO technical assistance missions working in the field of primary education in Bolivia, Colombia, Ecuador, Haiti, Honduras, Nicaragua and Paraguay were co-ordinated into the over-all project.

The major project on scientific research for arid lands affects 16 member States in the dry belt running from North Africa through the Middle East to South Asia.

UNESCO's Advisory Committee on Arid Zone Research, composed of scientists from 10 different countries, was entrusted by the General Conference with organizing the activities under this project. It held two meetings in 1957—one in Paris in April and a second in November at Karachi. As its first step in carrying out the project, the Committee recommended financial aid to institutions in three countries: the Desert Research Institute at Cairo, Egypt; the Desert Research Institute at Beersheba, Israel; and the Meteorological Service of Pakistan.

Twenty-five soil research workers from nine countries in the Middle East attended a course in soil science at Rayak in Lebanon from 17 September to 6 October.

The third major project, the promotion of mutual appreciation of Eastern and Western cultural values, stirred much interest on the part of UNESCO's member States. During 1957, special committees for this project were set up or planned by UNESCO National Commissions in 18 countries.

One example of this interest was to be found in the United States where the sixth National Conference of the United States National Commission for UNESCO, which met in San Francisco from 6 to 9 November, was devoted to the theme "Asia and the United States: What the American Citizen can do to promote mutual understanding and co-operation".

Among other activities carried out to implement this project were: the organization of a travelling exhibition of Indian frescoes sponsored by the French National Commission for UNESCO; and the first meeting of the Advisory Committee on the Mutual Appreciation of Eastern and Western Cultural Values, held in April at UNESCO House in Paris.

All three major projects involve long-term planning. The project on arid lands research is to last six years and the other two 10 years each.

In addition to these major projects, UNESCO's programme in its normal fields of activity made good progress in 1957. A summary of the agency's work in these spheres follows.

UNESCO'S WORK IN THE FIELD

Under the United Nations Expanded Programme of Technical Assistance for economic development and under its own programme of participation in the activities of member States, UNESCO was able to send out more than 300 experts in 1957 on missions varying from the teaching of reading to the development of nuclear research. To an ever-growing extent, these field missions were co-ordinated with the permanent targets of UNESCO's programme, particularly as far as the major projects were concerned.

In 1951, UNESCO sent out its first mission under the Expanded Technical Assistance Programme. By the end of 1957, 180 requests for technical assistance had been received from 63 countries. UNESCO had 122 technical assistance projects operating in 53 countries in addition to nine regional projects. There were 246 experts on mission at the end of the year and 85 more who had completed their assignments.

UNESCO also provided more than $500,000 worth of equipment in 1957 and awarded nearly 100 fellowships under the Expanded Technical Assistance Programme.

By 30 November 1957, a total of $5,570,052 had been obligated by UNESCO to finance its technical assistance operations.

The programme of participation in the activities of member States, started in 1955, was designed mainly to meet requests not capable of being met under UNESCO's share of the funds for the Expanded Technical Assistance Programme (a specific example: the restoration of art treasures). By 30 November 1957, 229 requests had been received from 78 countries and 47 experts were on mission to 37 countries. Ninety-three fellowships were awarded under this programme, budget obligations for which amounted in 1957 to $644,000 by 30 November.

EDUCATION

Dovetailing into the campaign for the extension of primary education in Latin America, the International Conference on Public Education, organized jointly by UNESCO and the International Bureau of Education, took up the problems of school buildings and the training of primary school teachers at its sessions in Geneva from 8 to 17 July. Attended by 174 delegates (including 10 Ministers of Education), representing 72 States, the Conference strongly recommended the establishment of an international school building centre and suggested that the International Bank for Reconstruction and Development "consider the possibility of making long-term loans for school buildings to countries which request them".

Educators from 13 countries attended a meeting in March at the UNESCO Institute for Education at Hamburg to take up the problem of examinations and other means of evaluation in school education. At Ubol, in northern Thailand, 200 young men and women were attending a two-year course at a rural-teacher training centre organized jointly by the Government of Thailand and UNESCO.

A second major international conference, held in Cairo from 22 November to 5 December, brought 143 representatives from 18 countries together to discuss technical and vocational education in the Arab countries of the Middle East. Convened upon the invitation of Egypt and with the collaboration of UNESCO, the

Food and Agriculture Organization, the International Labour Organisation and the Arab League, the conference made recommendations about the organization, administration and financing of vocational education, the selection of pupils, the training of teachers and the pedagogical methods to be used.

Missions in school education were sent to nine countries under UNESCO's programme of participation in the activities of member States. They covered such fields as rural-teacher training, school inspection and educational research.

As to fundamental education, national fundamental education centres had been established by the end of 1957 in Ethiopia, Cambodia, Indonesia, Jordan, Korea, Liberia, Sudan and Thailand, and 73 experts were at work in 27 countries on technical assistance missions in this field.

The year 1957 also saw the continuation of UNESCO's two regional fundamental education centres, one at Patzcuaro, Mexico, to serve Latin America, and the other at Sirs-el-Layyan, Egypt, to meet the needs of the Arabic-speaking countries. In September 1957, the Patzcuaro centre graduated its sixth class, numbering 63 students from 12 countries, following the entrance of a seventh class in April.

Those enrolled at the Arab States Fundamental Education Centre at Sirs-el-Layyan, in 1957, included 184 students (among them 25 women) from nine member States and the Palestine refugee camps. A class of 58 students was graduated in June, and in October 17 students from seven countries attended another short course on the production of visual aids to education.

In the field of emergency educational assistance, UNESCO continued to supply staff for the project of the United Nations Relief and Works Agency for operating schools for Palestine refugee children. Latest available figures show that 372 such primary schools were open in 1957, with an enrolment of 104,013 pupils and a staff of 3,055 teachers. Secondary school enrolment reached 24,213. Two vocational training schools were also operated.

Emergency educational assistance to the value of $200,000 had been voted by the ninth UNESCO General Conference in 1956 following events in Hungary and Egypt and, by this decision, educational equipment was thereby supplied for the benefit of children and young people of both countries.

NATURAL SCIENCES

The International Conference on Radio-Isotopes in Scientific Research is only one example of the ways in which UNESCO was able to contribute to scientific knowledge in 1957.

UNESCO's concern with the encouragement of basic scientific research was also reflected in the granting of $277,250 to eight scientific unions. Of this sum, $175,000 went to the International Council of Scientific Unions and its 13 national scientific unions. Also assisted were the Special Committee for the International Geophysical Year and the Federation of Astronomical and Geophysical Services. International co-operation in scientific research received further encouragement in September 1957, with the signing of an agreement between UNESCO and the Italian Institute of Higher Mathematics to establish a provisional international computation centre in Rome as of 1 January 1958.

Among UNESCO's activities during 1957 in the field of science-teaching was the preparation of a new edition of its *Source Book for Science Teaching*. This describes how apparatus can be constructed for schools using only locally available and low-cost materials. UNESCO's travelling science exhibitions—science-teaching media outside the classroom—were seen during 1957 by visitors in an area ranging from Antofagasta, Chile, to Ahmedabad, India. Eight exhibitions were on display in Chile, France, India, Malaya and Poland, including a new exhibition on "The Earth as a Planet" which was prepared for the International Geophysical Year and inaugurated in December at the Musée Pédagogique in Paris.

In addition to scientific research for arid lands, work continued on other scientific problems of world or regional importance.

The first session of UNESCO's Advisory Committee for Humid Tropics Research, held in July at Manaos, Brazil, selected research projects in Belgium, Brazil, France, Hawaii, India, Indonesia, the Ivory Coast, Madagascar, the Netherlands, Réunion Island and the West

Indies for financial assistance. An international symposium on curare was held in August at Rio de Janeiro in collaboration with the National Research Council of Brazil. Financial assistance was also given to the Pacific Science Council to hold a symposium on climate, vegetation and rational land utilization in the humid tropics at the ninth Pacific Science Congress, which met in November and December at Bangkok. In the field of marine sciences, UNESCO aided two symposia in September, one at Toronto, Canada, on the general circulation of the ocean (this subject had a bearing on the oceanic disposal of radio-active wastes), and the other at Bergen, Norway, on primary production in the sea.

UNESCO's regional science co-operation offices in Montevideo, Cairo, Jakarta and New Delhi also continued to operate in 1957.

CULTURAL ACTIVITIES

Concentration upon the major project for mutual understanding of Eastern and Western cultural values did not prevent UNESCO's Department of Cultural Activities from continuing its other cultural activities.

The year 1957 saw a marked increase in the number of nations ratifying or adhering to the Universal Copyright Convention and the Convention for the Protection of Cultural Property in the Event of Armed Conflict. By the end of the year, 29 states were parties to the Universal Copyright Convention and 19 states had joined UNESCO's "cultural Red Cross convention", the International Convention on the Protection of Cultural Property in the Event of Armed Conflict.

UNESCO continued its aid to organizations working toward its own goals in the cultural field. An amount of $113,000 was granted to the International Council for Philosophy and Humanistic Studies. Another $111,000 was awarded to six other organizations: the International Theatre Institute (which helped open the Théâtre des Nations in Paris in March 1957), the International Music Council, the International Plastic Arts Association, the International Council of Museums, the International Union of Architects and the International PEN Club.

UNESCO approved requests from Afghanistan, Burma, Ceylon, Ecuador, Egypt, Libya,

Peru and Syria for assistance under its scheme for preserving mankind's cultural heritage. This was under its programme of participation in the activities of member States. In April, an agreement was signed for the establishment in Rome of an International Centre for the Study of the Preservation a ⌐ Restoration of Cultural Property.

UNESCO's activities in the production of reading materials for people who have just learned to read led to contracts for more than 40 books in five of the main languages of South Asia—Burmese, Sinhalese, Tamil, Hindi and Urdu. These will be published under four series: international understanding, simple science, economic and social development, and translations of world classics. UNESCO's Executive Board also approved a proposal for 24 prizes amounting to $11,000 for the best books in these fields.

The Delhi Public Library is now a going concern and completely in the hands of Indian authorities. UNESCO continued to work with the Government of Colombia on a similar pilot project in Latin America, the Medellin Public Library.

In August 1957, the fourth edition of UNESCO's catalogue of colour reproductions of modern paintings was published, covering works from 1860 to 1957. The manuscript of the ninth edition of *Index Translationum,* listing 27,616 translations in 52 countries was prepared for publication in 1958.

The 300th anniversary of the publication of the *Opera Didactica Omnia* by the great Czech humanist, John Amos Comenius, was commemorated by UNESCO in 1957.

SOCIAL SCIENCES

An important event in the social science field was the Inter-Governmental Conference on University Social Science Teaching in Latin America, held in Rio de Janeiro in April with the participation of 18 South American countries. It approved the creation of a Latin American Social Science Faculty, at Santiago de Chile, and a Latin American Social Science Research Institute, at Rio de Janeiro, with assistance under UNESCO's programme of participation in the activities of member States. The Institute's research programme provides for studies in such fields as the status of the social sciences in Latin America, social stratification in Latin America and the social consequences of industrialization. In addition, missions of experts in social science teaching were sent by UNESCO in 1957 to Indonesia, Pakistan, Afghanistan, Chile, Italy, Iran and Greece.

The Research Centre on the Social Implications of Industrialization in Southern Asia, at Calcutta, undertook a major study of the social and cultural factors affecting productivity in Bombay and Calcutta. The Government of Burma invited the centre to plan a research project on the social consequences of electrification in Burma. Also planned was a study of the social implications of the development of small-scale industries in the Philippines and other South Asian countries.

Considerable interest was aroused with the publication in 1957 of the study *World Illiteracy in Mid-Century,* prepared by the statistical division of UNESCO's Department of Social Sciences. The division also prepared the second *World Survey of Education* for publication in 1958, covering some 200 countries and territories.

Grants totalling $115,500 were awarded to nine international social science organizations.

MASS COMMUNICATION

The first regional centre for the training of journalism teachers—the International Centre for Higher Education in Journalism—was opened in 1957 at the University of Strasbourg with the assistance of UNESCO and the French Government. This Centre is intended to train teachers for existing and planned schools of journalism in Europe and adjoining regions of Africa and Asia. Its first session, held from 15 October to 1 December 1957, took up problems concerning radio and television as well as the press, with classes conducted by professors and lecturers from France, the United States, the USSR, Poland, Italy, Switzerland, the United Kingdom, Czechoslovakia, Belgium, the Federal Republic of Germany, Morocco and Israel.

In pursuance of its task of facilitating the flow of information, UNESCO submitted 18 proposals to the XIVth Congress of the Universal Postal Union which met at Ottawa from 14 August to 3 October.[2] As a result of decisions taken by the Congress, weight limits for the dispatch of books will be liberalized, airmail rates for books reduced and customs clearance charges on publications eliminated as far as possible. In addition, 26 states were parties, by the end of 1957, to the UNESCO-sponsored Agreement on the Importation of Educational, Scientific and Cultural Materials which has been in operation for five years.

The UNESCO Coupon Scheme, which enables people in soft-currency countries to purchase books, films and scientific apparatus in hard-currency countries, issued more than $4 million worth of coupons in 1957. This brought the total value of coupons issued since the scheme started in 1948 to $17.8 million. More than $75,000 was collected from donors in 16 countries through the Scheme.

EXCHANGE OF PERSONS

UNESCO is to make 847 fellowships available over the two-year period 1957-58. In 1957, more than 1,100 European workers benefited from UNESCO travel grants.

Publications issued by the Exchange of Persons Service included *Study Abroad, Vacations Abroad, Travel Abroad* and *Workers Abroad.*

BUDGET

UNESCO's budget for 1957, as voted by the ninth session of the General Conference in November-December 1956, was as follows (in U.S. dollars):

Part I. General Policy	$167,386
Part II. Programme Operations and Services:	
1. Education	1,609,571
Major Project on Extension of Primary Education in Latin America	300,778
2. Natural Sciences	967,919
Major Project on Scientific Research on Arid Lands	252,952
3. Social Sciences	750,763
4. Cultural Activities	1,141,882
Major Project on Mutual Appreciation of Eastern and Western Cultural Values	369,999
5. Mass Communication	1,202,787
6. Exchange of Persons	590,973
7. General Resolutions	163,670

[2] See Chapter X, below.

8. Documents and Publications Services	1,180,187
Total, Part II	8,531,481
Part III. General Administration	1,554,059
Part IV. Common Service Costs	889,289
Total, Parts I, II, III, IV	11,142,215

Part V. Undistributed Appropriations	582,531
Total Appropriation	11,724,746

The scale of contributions for 1957-58, as approved for the 79 member States of UNESCO by the ninth session of the General Conference, is given in Annex I, below.

ANNEX I. MEMBERSHIP AND SCALE OF CONTRIBUTIONS

(Membership as of 31 December 1957; contribution percentages as set for 1957-58)

Member	Contribution Percentage	Member	Contribution Percentage	Member	Contribution Percentage	Member	Contribution Percentage
Afghanistan	0.06	Dominican		Italy	1.95	Peru	0.14
Argentina	1.10	Republic	0.05	Japan	1.84	Philippines	0.38
Australia	1.55	Ecuador	0.05	Jordan	0.04	Poland	1.46
Austria	0.34	Egypt	0.34	Korea, Rep. of	0.12	Romania	0.47
Belgium	1.19	El Salvador	0.06	Laos	0.04	Saudi Arabia	0.07
Bolivia	0.05	Ethiopia	0.10	Lebanon	0.05	Spain	1.07
Brazil	1.02	Finland	0.35	Liberia	0.04	Sudan	0.10
Bulgaria	0.13	France	5.35	Libya	0.04	Sweden	1.37
Burma	0.09	Germany,		Luxembourg	0.06	Switzerland	0.95
Byelorussian SSR	0.45	Fed. Rep. of	3.94	Mexico	0.66	Syria	0.07
Cambodia	0.04	Greece	0.19	Monaco	0.04	Thailand	0.15
Canada	2.93	Guatemala	0.07	Morocco	0.11	Tunisia	0.05
Ceylon	0.10	Haiti	0.04	Nepal	0.04	Turkey	0.59
Chile	0.28	Honduras	0.04	Netherlands	1.08	Ukrainian SSR	1.74
China	4.83	Hungary	0.43	New Zealand	0.40	USSR	13.11
Colombia	0.35	India	2.79	Nicaragua	0.04	United Kingdom	7.33
Costa Rica	0.04	Indonesia	0.48	Norway	0.46	United States	31.30
Cuba	0.25	Iran	0.25	Pakistan	0.52	Uruguay	0.15
Czechoslovakia	0.79	Iraq	0.11	Panama	0.05	Venezuela	0.40
Denmark	0.62	Israel	0.15	Paraguay	0.04	Viet-Nam	0.14
						Yugoslavia	0.34

ANNEX II. OFFICERS AND OFFICES

(As of 31 December 1957)

MEMBERS OF EXECUTIVE BOARD*

Chairman: Dr. Vittorino Veronese (Italy).
Vice Chairmen: Oscar Secco Ellauri (Uruguay), G. A. Raadi (Iran).
Members: Itrat Husain Zuberi (Pakistan), Georges Averoff (Greece), Mohammed Awad (Egypt), Rodolfo Baron Castro (El Salvador), Paulo E. de Berredo Carneiro (Brazil), Gardner Davies (Australia), Juan Estelrich y Artigues (Spain), Zakir Husain (India), R. Soebroto (Indonesia), Vladimir Kemenov (USSR), Julien Kuypers (Belgium), Henri Laugier (France), Jean Maroun (Lebanon),

José R. Martínez Cobo (Ecuador), Akira Matsui (Japan), Jacob Nielsen (Denmark), Dr. C. Parra-Pèrez (Venezuela), Maria Schlueter-Hermkes (Fed. Rep. of Germany), Athelstan F. Spilhaus (United States), Sir Ben Bowen Thomas (United Kingdom), Stefan Wierblowski (Poland).

* As constituted by the ninth session of the General Conference for 1957 and 1958, and with changes which have taken place in 1957.

PRINCIPAL OFFICERS OF THE SECRETARIAT

Director-General: Luther H. Evans (United States).
Assistant Directors-General: Jean Thomas (France); Malcolm Adiseshiah (India).

Special Representative to the United Nations: René Maheu (France).

HEADQUARTERS AND OTHER OFFICES

UNESCO House
19, avenue Kléber,
Paris 16°, France
Cable Address: UNESCO PARIS

UNESCO
c/o United Nations Headquarters,
Room 2201,
New York 17, N. Y.
Cable Address: UNESCORG NEW YORK

Centro Regional de la UNESCO en el
Hemisferio Occidental
Calle 5a No. 306, Vedado
La Habana, Cuba

Bulevar Artigas 1320,
Apartado de Correos No. 859
Montevideo, Uruguay

8 Sh.El Salamik
Garden City
Cairo, Egypt

C.S.I.R. Building
21 Curzon Road
New Delhi 2, India

Djalan Diponegoro, 76
Djakarta, Indonesia

CHAPTER V

THE WORLD HEALTH ORGANIZATION (WHO)

In 1957 the World Health Organization (WHO)[1] had 85 full members and three associate members, and operated on an effective working budget of $10,700,000.

In addition to providing Central Technical Services at Headquarters (in Geneva), it assisted its members directly by field demonstration projects to deal with specific diseases and health problems.

Efforts at world-wide malaria eradication, one of the specialized agency's major objectives, received considerable impetus during 1957 through the generosity of the United States Government. When accepting a $5 million cheque from Mr. John Foster Dulles, United States Secretary of State, as a voluntary contribution to WHO's Malaria Eradication Special Account, Dr. M. G. Candau, the agency's Director-General, emphasized that malaria was still one of the world's greatest public health problems. A further contribution of $2 million was made by the United States Government to the Pan American Sanitary Bureau, which is also the Regional Office of WHO for the Americas, for malaria eradication in that region.

Another important event in 1957 was the return to the World Health Assembly, after an eight-year absence, of delegations from the USSR and from Albania, Bulgaria and Poland. The Assembly, which met in May, and which adopted a budget of $13,500,000 for 1958 to cover, *inter alia,* 700 health projects in 112 countries and territories, was also informed that Romania was resuming active participation in the work of WHO.

The World Health Assembly asked Dr. M. G. Candau to continue in office as Director-General after 21 July 1958 when his contract was due to expire. Subsequently, Dr. Candau informed the President of the Assembly that he would remain in office until 21 July 1960.

As the year 1957 closed, preparations for celebrating WHO's tenth anniversary in 1958 were well advanced. It was decided that World Health Day 1958 would be devoted to the theme: "Ten Years of Health Progress". In addition, the World Health Assembly decided that its 1958 session, to take place in May in Minneapolis, Minnesota, at the invitation of the United States Government and the City of Minneapolis, would be preceded by a two-day special session to observe the tenth anniversary.

[1] For further information, in particular concerning WHO's functions and organization, and activities prior to 1957, see previous volumes of the *Yearbook,* also the *Official Records of the World Health Organization,* containing reports, with relevant documents, of the agency and its governing bodies.

COMMUNICABLE DISEASES

MALARIA

Since the Eighth World Health Assembly took its historic resolution in 1955 on malaria eradication, more and more countries and territories have accepted the objective of malaria eradication as the goal of their anti-malaria activities. At the end of the year, 76 countries and territories were either implementing or planning malaria eradication programmes. In the region of the Americas, the impressive progress of such programmes has in large measure been due to the high priority given by Governments to eradication.

The agency has intensified its provision of technical advice. The technical services of WHO at Headquarters were strengthened by the creation of the new post of Director, Malaria Eradication. A Regional Malaria Adviser was appointed for the African Region and another for the European Region, and a Sanitary Engineer was appointed for inter-regional assistance. The three advisory teams for malaria eradication have carried out assignments in Burma, Ceylon, Iraq, the Philippines and Taiwan.

The agency sponsored a number of conferences and technical meetings, including the second conferences on malaria for the countries of South-Eastern Europe, the fourth and fifth Borneo inter-territorial conferences, the second meeting of the Anti-Malaria Co-ordination Board for Viet-Nam, Laos, Cambodia, Thailand, Burma and Malaya, the Malaria Symposium for the South-East Asia and Western Pacific Regions, as well as technical meetings of chiefs of malaria services in the Americas and in the Eastern Mediterranean and African Regions.

In the last quarter of the year, both in the Americas and in Europe, the first two projects of training personnel for international service in malaria eradication were initiated. Planned to last about five months, the training projects were to include at least three months of field work in existing eradication programmes.

The role played by WHO in stimulating, co-ordinating and sponsoring research in malaria-eradication problems was greater in 1957 than in preceding years. Its special *Anopheles gambiae* research and advisory team has carried out work in the Belgian Congo, Dahomey, Liberia and Uganda, and in the third quarter of 1957 moved to Accra, Ghana, where it established its central laboratory.

TREPONEMATOSES AND VENEREAL INFECTIONS

Now that there is promise of controlling endemic treponematoses to an increasing extent so that it ultimately may be eradicated in the rural areas of many countries, it is important that measures to combat venereal syphilis in the cities of these countries be planned and executed. One of the first steps is to obtain accurate data on the prevalence of venereal syphilis. WHO has suggested that a start be made in Africa by recommending that Governments collect data on the frequency of seroreactors in tests for syphilis in random samples of pregnant women.

Under its programme for co-ordinating research, WHO continued to co-operate with the International Treponematoses Laboratory Center at Baltimore (United States), and with the WHO Serological Reference Laboratories at Copenhagen (Denmark) and Chamblee, Georgia (United States). A meeting to assist in the co-ordination of yaws campaigns in certain areas of central African territories was held in Brazzaville.

WHO co-operated with the eleventh International Congress of Dermatology, held in Stockholm, especially in relation to the epidemiology of the treponematoses, the long-term results of penicillin therapy, and the laboratory aspects of these diseases.

TUBERCULOSIS

The two African tuberculosis survey teams, staffed by WHO and equipped by the United Nations Children's Fund (UNICEF), covered five countries and territories during 1957. Striking differences between East and West Africa in the prevalence of infectious cases are appearing. These have important repercussions on subsequent planning and execution of control programmes. Several other regions made plans to start surveys in 1958. A Technical Guide for tuberculosis survey teams, giving detailed instructions for the planning and execution of tuberculosis surveys, was issued during 1957.

BCG vaccination is an already established effective control measure. In most of the countries where anti-tuberculosis work has a public health priority, this control measure has now been applied with the organization methods and techniques recommended by WHO. The possibility of raising community resistance has been clearly demonstrated. During 1957, five laboratories co-operated in a study co-ordinated by WHO to develop laboratory methods that will give reliable indices of the potency of the vaccines.

Chemotherapy and chemoprophylaxis both have highly important places in community control of tuberculosis, but, as was agreed by a WHO study group in September 1957, the role of each needs better definition through reliable information obtained in public health field research projects.

In the joint project between WHO and the Indian Council for Medical Research in Madras, no significant differences have been found between the effects of institutional and domiciliary chemotherapy. In Tunisia, a WHO/UNICEF-assisted pilot project has started work, to provide information on the prophylactic value of INH (isoniazid). Another pilot project was started in Kenya, primarily designed to develop methods for long-term community administration of drugs.

Meanwhile, the WHO/UNICEF Joint Committee on Health Policy recommended an active attitude towards the epidemiological potentialities of chemotherapy and chemoprophylaxis.

ZOONOSES AND VETERINARY
PUBLIC HEALTH

Co-ordinated research, in collaboration with the Food and Agriculture Organization (FAO), on several brucellosis problems (including those of diagnosis in man and animals, bacteriology of *Brucella,* therapy in humans, and vaccines in sheep and goats) was carried out during 1957 in preparation for the third meeting of the Joint FAO/WHO Expert Committee on Brucellosis, held in Lima.

During the year, an FAO/WHO Brucellosis Centre was designated at the Institute of Animal Health in Tokyo. The Expert Committee strongly recommended continued support by FAO and WHO of the 15 FAO/WHO Brucellosis Centres.

Co-ordinated research in rabies was undertaken with respect to continued studies recommended by the Expert Committee on Rabies concerning the effect of serum on vaccine inoculations. Surveys of bat rabies were encouraged in several countries. A small grant was made to the laboratories of the Alabama State Department of Health for research work on anti-rabies serum of human origin. A Rabies Training Course for Central and South American countries, similar to previous ones held in India in 1952 and in Kenya in 1955, was held in Caracas in late March.

The preparation of reference antisera for 18 major types of *Leptospira* was completed in several of the WHO/FAO Leptospirosis Reference Laboratories. In addition to the Reference Laboratories in Australia, Japan, the Netherlands, the United Kingdom and the United States, a Reference Laboratory was designated in Italy.

Because of the uncertain status of domestic animals in the epidemiology of human influenza, steps were taken early in the 1957 pandemic to have serum specimens collected from swine and horses in 25 countries before and after the human epidemic struck. These specimens were to be examined at certain WHO Influenza Centres, and it was hoped valuable information would be gained about the epidemiology of human influenza.

Also started were studies aimed at assessing the significance of the discovery of apparently specific antibodies to human poliomyelitis viruses in cattle and swine sera and of numerous viral agents being isolated from domestic animals analogous to the "oyshan" viruses in human beings. Other zoonoses dealt with during the year included anthrax, bovine tuberculosis, psittacosis, Q-fever, tick-borne encephalitis, and dermatophytosis. WHO continued its collaboration with FAO on milk and meat hygiene work.

A seminar on Veterinary Public Health for European countries was held in Warsaw in late November 1957. The promotion of veterinary public health training in schools of public health was assisted in Europe and South America. The inclusion of public health subjects in undergraduate veterinary curriculums was also encouraged in these areas, as well as in the Middle East.

VIRUS DISEASES AND
VACCINE STUDIES

The most important event of 1957 in the field of virus diseases and vaccine studies was the occurrence of the influenza pandemic which subjected the WHO Influenza Programme to its most serious test since its inception in 1947. The WHO Programme successfully performed the functions for which it was developed. In just under three weeks after WHO received the first news that a significant epidemic was occurring, the agency was able to inform health authorities and vaccine-producing laboratories that the responsible virus was unrelated to all previously isolated strains and that existing vaccines were unlikely to give protection. The warning was given in time for many countries to prepare their health services to face the impending epidemic. In a number of countries significant quantities of vaccine were produced in time for use before the epidemic struck. Fortunately, the disease remained mild up to the time of writing. A close watch for any sign of increasing virulence was maintained.

A second meeting of the Expert Committee on Poliomyelitis was held in July. Particularly important was the recommendation by the Committee that live attenuated poliovirus vaccines should be subjected to more extensive and carefully designed trials. Its report also contained extensive annexes giving guidance on the latest laboratory techniques.

Initial steps were taken for the development of a programme of co-ordinated research on arthropod-borne virus diseases (i.e., those carried by various insects) particularly the group B encephalitis viruses, which include yellow fever and the Russian-spring-summer-like viruses.

Details of the method of preparation of a highly stable dried smallpox vaccine were distributed during the year and assistance was given to a number of countries wishing to initiate production of the vaccine. Arrangements were made for the preparation of large batches of stable dried typhoid vaccines for use in further field trials and eventually for consideration as reference standards.

OTHER COMMUNICABLE DISEASES

Acute diarrhoeal diseases are the greatest single cause of infant mortality on a world-wide basis.

In recent years, activities against these diseases have been intensified in the various WHO regions, and the Americas Region particularly gave high priority to the problem of controlling diarrhoeal diseases by organizing a seminar, by improving sanitation methods and by preventing the death of children in its child-care programme.

Following the African Conference on Bilharziasis, held late in 1956, the interest of some countries in the African Region has been stimulated to undertake pilot control projects. Large collections of different species of the vector snails have been sent to the three WHO Snail Identification Centres.

In the field of the control of communicable eye diseases, satisfactory progress has been achieved towards integrating the internationally assisted control campaigns in Morocco and Tunisia with the national public health services. Pilot trials have been completed in Taiwan and started in Spain, India and Indonesia.

More leprosy projects were undertaken, most of them in co-operation with UNICEF. With the increase in non-infectious cases, more attention had to be paid to physical and social rehabilitation.

The first WHO-assisted onchocerciasis project was started in 1957 in the Sudan. (Onchocerciasis is an insect-borne disease, an important cause of blindness in some countries.) Two training courses in onchocerciasis-control techniques have been started in Africa, the courses being combined with a course of training in countering malaria.

Field projects on sylvatic plague (i.e., plague spread by wild rodents) have been continued in India and Indonesia and encouraged in other countries.

NURSING

The Manual on Nursing Service Administration was completed in 1957, and it is expected that it will be widely used to help strengthen the administrative aspects of nursing service. Being planned during the year was a *Guide for Planning Basic Nursing Education Programmes*; a consultant prepared a draft which was discussed by a group of nurses meeting in Tokyo.

The bibliography of text and reference books suggested for basic and post-basic nursing education programmes was revised and widely distributed. As a supplement to this, a bibliography on auxiliary nursing was prepared.

Seventeen nurses were newly recruited by WHO during 1957, and 14 staff members reassigned.

SOCIAL AND OCCUPATIONAL HEALTH

The role of the hospital in public health programmes was further explored at the technical discussions at the Tenth World Health Assembly.

The study on costs and means of financing medical care services was continued by the appointment of two short-term consultants, one experienced in administrative medicine and the other in social sciences. A hospital adviser was appointed to the Americas Region, and in the European Region a post was created for a social health and medical care adviser in addition to the occupational health adviser.

WHO assisted the International Hospital Federation and the International Union of Architects in the organization of the First International Seminar on Hospital Architecture, held in Geneva in September and attended by 62 participants from countries in Asia, America, Africa and Europe.

A meeting of the Joint Committee of the International Labour Organisation (ILO) and WHO on Occupational Health was held in March. Its report dealt with the training of physicians in occupational health and the organization of occupational health institutes. The Institute of Occupational Health in Alexandria, Egypt, was staffed during the year.

In collaboration with the United Nations, ILO and non-governmental organizations, as well as the Government of Indonesia, WHO co-sponsored a rehabilitation seminar held in Solo, Indonesia, and attended by 31 participants from 13 countries in Asia and the Far East.

HEALTH EDUCATION OF THE PUBLIC

An Expert Committee on Training of Health Personnel in Health Education of the Public met in Geneva during 1957. Assistance was provided in the planning and conduct of three regional seminars and conferences on health education of the public. In March, the WHO Regional Office for Africa sponsored the first African Regional Seminar on Health Education,

held in Dakar, French West Africa, in collaboration with the French Government. In May, an Inter-American Seminar on Health Education was held in Huampani, Peru, under the auspices of the United States International Co-operation Administration, in collaboration with the WHO Regional Office for the Americas. During the last part of June and early July the second European Conference in this field was held in Wiesbaden, Germany.

WHO helped in planning and running an intensive eight-week training course in health education in Nouméa, New Caledonia, sponsored by the WHO Regional Office for the Western Pacific and the South Pacific Commission. This course was attended by 40 trainees from various islands in the Pacific Region.

In co-operation with the United Nations Educational, Scientific and Cultural Organization, WHO completed the drafting of a *Study Guide on Teacher Preparation for Health Education and for Promotion of School Health.*

MATERNAL AND CHILD HEALTH

New field operations in 1957 included the provision of aid to the Government of Pakistan in establishing a new children's hospital in Karachi; a paediatrician and a paediatric nurse were appointed to the project, with other personnel to be assigned later. Another WHO paediatrician was assigned to Kabul, Afghanistan.

Short-term consultants visited a number of countries to give advice on various phases of maternal and child health work. Among the countries visited were Japan, Korea and Austria, by consultants in rehabilitation; China (Taiwan) and Poland, by paediatric consultants; and Turkey by an expert in maternal and child health administration. A maternal and child health consultant was also temporarily assigned to the University of the Philippines.

MENTAL HEALTH

A study group on schizophrenia, which brought together 12 specialists, representing several scientific disciplines, was convened in September to prepare a statement on present knowledge as to the causes, forms and treatment of schizophrenia, the frequency of which makes it probably the most important mental health problem.

In order to consider the extent and type of mental health problems likely to arise from the peaceful uses of atomic energy, another study group was convened in October, while a study group on ataraxics and hallucinogenics met in November.

A short-term consultant started the preparation of a study group to be convened in 1958 on the mental health implications of the introduction of automation.

Three consultants met at WHO Headquarters to carry out a study on the techniques of occupational therapy and the rehabilitation of mental patients in relation to the architectural possibilities of psychiatric hospitals.

NUTRITION

Considerable advances have been made in the joint FAO/WHO/UNICEF programme for the development of protein-rich foods. The sum of $250,000, made available by the Rockefeller Foundation to further the necessary research, has now been almost completely allocated. Some 15 research units in different parts of the world received grants.

The joint FAO/WHO Expert Committee on Nutrition met in Rome during the year. An FAO/WHO Regional Conference on Nutrition for Latin America was held in Guatemala City. Of particular importance was that part of the report dealing with the progress achieved in developing from locally produced vegetable foods a protein-rich food suitable for the weaning child. This was developed with the aid of a WHO grant and as part of a world-wide programme assisted by FAO, WHO and UNICEF.

A training course for medical and other personnel concerned with nutritional problems took place in Kampala in Uganda, East Africa.

DENTAL HEALTH

An Expert Committee on Water Fluoridation expressed the opinion that the effectiveness, safety and practicability of fluoridation as a means of preventing dental caries have now been established.

Another operation during 1957 was a joint project on the epidemiology of periodontal diseases, conducted by the WHO Regional Office for South-East Asia, the India Council of Medical Research and the United States Public Health Service. The major activity was the convening of a workshop in Bombay, India, attended by selected dental research workers of India, a WHO dental consultant and a member of the United States Public Health Service.

A dental consultant was also sent to Thailand.

ENVIRONMENTAL SANITATION

An Expert Committee on Air Pollution was convened in November to review and discuss what is presently known about the effects upon human health of air pollutants and to identify areas of knowledge in which the subject needs further study. A regional conference on air pollution was held in Milan, Italy, and was attended by key officials of most European countries.

A study of food sanitation problems was undertaken by WHO in co-operation with certain countries of Europe and the Eastern Mediterranean Region.

Work was begun in 1957 on an active programme of co-ordinating research on standards of drinking water quality and on methods of water examination.

In the field of the resistance of insects to insecticides, considerable progress was made in establishing WHO as the co-ordinating agency for research. Seven new research projects were set up with grants in aid from WHO. Standard methods for determining insecticide-resistance levels in larval and adult mosquitoes had been established, and work proceeded during 1957 on tests for bedbugs, ticks, fleas, flies, simulium and sandflies. A new survey of lice resistance was started. Testing of new insecticides was proceeding with some very promising materials. Five consultants employed by WHO visited laboratories in 26 countries, and members of the WHO staff paid visits to 43 laboratories to stimulate research. A technical conference on resistance, attended by the directors of 11 laboratories, was held in July, and an Expert Committee on Insect Resistance and Vector Control met in November 1957.

A special effort was made to bring into operation improved methods for removing insects from aircraft in view of the importance of preventing resistant insects being carried from one country to another by air.

EDUCATION AND TRAINING

A study group made detailed recommendations on how the re-orientated teaching of psychology could help develop a proper understanding by medical students of the preventive aspects of medicine. The report of the Study Group on the Training of General Practitioners in Preventive Medicine was published, and a regional meeting on the teaching of preventive medicine was held in the Western Pacific Region. The first year of an experiment at the Harvard School of Public Health in advanced training of teachers of preventive medicine for countries in South-East Asia gave generally encouraging results.

From 1 December 1956 to 30 November 1957, there were 1,106 fellowships awarded to personnel of 112 countries and territories to study in 84 other countries and territories. In addition, assistance was provided to enable persons to attend educational meetings (seminars, etc.) organized by WHO, which were primarily aimed at the exchange of information among participants.

A study on paediatric education was completed in Latin America with the co-operation of the International Paediatric Association and the American Academy of Paediatrics.

The second edition of the *World Directory of Medical Schools* was published in 1957, together with a brief description of the medical education systems in 84 countries. The annotated *Bibliography on Medical Education for 1946-1955,* containing almost 3,000 items, was in print.

WHO teaching personnel assigned in 1957 to educational institutions numbered 27 in medical and public health schools and 11 in other schools.

EPIDEMIOLOGY AND HEALTH STATISTICS

An important development in international health statistics during 1957 was the issue, in English, French and Spanish, of the revised edition of the *Manual of the International Classification of Diseases.*

The monthly issues of the *Epidemiological and Vital Statistics Report* contained special collections of data on mortality from chronic degenerative diseases, nephritis and nephrosis, anaemias, hyperplasia of the prostate, acute infectious encephalitis, maternal mortality, accidents to pedestrians, and cancer of the breast and female genital organs.

The Sub-Committee on Cancer Statistics met in December and made a series of technical recommendations on methods for ascertaining cancer morbidity.

The first of October 1957, marked the completion of five years' existence of the International Sanitary Regulations. About 170 States and territories are bound by the Regulations.

Yellow fever in monkeys spread northwards through the forests of Central America to Guatemala and British Honduras during 1957, but did not result in any human case in the cities, ports or airports, where *Aëdes ægypti* eradication has long been systematically practised.

The year 1957 was an unusual one in the case of smallpox because some 20 countries reported that the disease had been brought in by international traffic.

BIOLOGICAL STANDARDIZATION

During 1957, the Expert Committee on Biological Standardization approved the establishment in the near future of international standards for the following substances: vitamin B_{12}, pyrogen, syphilitic human serum, antistreptolysin O, anti-R_0 (anti-D) blood-typing serum, and poliomyelitis sera of types 1, 2 and 3.

On the basis of 1957 sales, it would seem that increased use is being made of the *Pharmacopoeia Internationalis* throughout the world. Volume II of the *Pharmacopoeia* was issued by WHO in Spanish. It also appeared, at no expense to the agency, in German and Japanese editions.

WHO continued its programme for the selections of recommended international non-proprietary names for pharmaceutical preparations. In accordance with an agreement between WHO and the Swedish Apotekarsocietet, a Centre for Authentic Chemical Substances was set up in the Apotekens Kontrollaboratorium in Stockholm.

On the basis of the recommendation of the Expert Committee on Addiction-Producing Drugs, decisions on the addiction liability of seven drugs—dextramethadone, racemoramide (as well as dextromoramide and levomoramide), etoxeridine, morpheridine, propoxyphene, trimeperidine and a normethadone preparation—were transmitted to the Secretary-General of the United Nations.

A Study Group on Histological Definitions of Cancer Types met in Oslo in June. The Group agreed that tumours should be classified according to (*a*) anatomical site of origin and (*b*) histological characteristics. The Group recommended the initiation of reference work on tumours of the oro-pharynx, lung, soft tissue and breast.

The Joint FAO/WHO Expert Committee on Food Additives, which met in June, made recommendations on uniform methods for evaluating the safety of food additives.

ATOMIC ENERGY AND HEALTH

Two expert committees met in 1957 with the general purpose of providing more detailed recommendations on the type of training which doctors and other health workers would require in a world in which the peaceful uses of atomic energy are likely to become progressively more important. The first of these committees dealt with post-graduate training in public health aspects of atomic energy. The other dealt with the introduction of radiation medicine into the undergraduate curriculum.

During the year, the report of a previous study group on the effects of radiation on human heredity was published in booklet form, together with the working papers submitted by participants.

An international health physics training course was given at the Centre d'Etudes Nucléaires, Mol, Belgium, in association with the United States Atomic Energy Commission and the Belgian Government.

Work was begun on the formation of an Expert Advisory Panel on Radiation, from which would be drawn the members of expert committees on the health aspects of the peaceful use of atomic energy or on health problems of X-radiation.

PUBLICATIONS

In addition to the technical publications, the *Bulletin of the World Health Organization* and the *Chronicle of the World Health Organization,* monographs were issued, in English, on meat hygiene, the teaching of hygiene and public health in Europe, and biology of the treponematoses. Other monographs were published, in French, on infant nutrition in the tropics and sub-tropics, and on dried BCG vaccine. Thirty reports of expert committees, study groups and advisory groups were published in the *Technical Report Series*. Sales of publications continued to develop satisfactorily.

BUDGET

The Ninth World Health Assembly set the 1957 budget at $13,265,420 giving an effective working budget of $10,700,000, plus a supplemental amount not exceeding $1,525,000. The Tenth World Health Assembly appropriated a further amount of $325,000 for 1957 for the purpose of reimbursing the Working Capital Fund in respect of unforeseen expenses resulting from the amendments to the Staff Rules.

The Tenth World Health Assembly appropriated $14,769,160 for 1958 for organizational meetings, operating programmes and administrative services as follows (in U.S. dollars) :

Organizational Meetings	
World Health Assembly	$ 203,240
Executive Board and its Committees	115,260
Regional Committees	86,300
Total	$ 404,800
Operating Programme	
Central Technical Services	$ 1,826,118
Advisory Services	8,111,662
Regional Offices	1,750,182
Expert Committees and Conferences	196,200
Total	$11,884,162
Administrative Services	$ 1,177,168
Other Purposes—Reimbursement of Working Capital Fund	100,000
Undistributed Reserve	1,203,030
Grand Total	$14,769,160

Assessed membership contributions for 1958, after deduction of available amounts of Casual Income, are shown in Annex I below.

ANNEX I. MEMBERS AND CONTRIBUTION ASSESSMENTS

(Members as of 31 December 1957; contributions as assessed for 1958)

Member	Contribution (in U.S. dollars)	Member	Contribution (in U.S. dollars)	Member	Contribution (in U.S. dollars)
Afghanistan	$ 7,760	Greece	25,520	Panama	5,760
Albania	5,760	Guatemala	8,880	Paraguay	5,760
Argentina	177,570	Haiti	5,760	Peru	21,090
Australia	228,620	Honduras	5,760	Philippines	51,050
Austria	41,060	Hungary	52,160	Poland	186,450
Belgium	169,800	Iceland	5,760	Portugal	37,730
Bolivia	6,660	India	402,860	Romania	62,150
Brazil	170,910	Indonesia	62,150	Saudi Arabia	8,880
Bulgaria	18,870	Iran	39,950	Sierra Leone*	3,330
Burma	12,210	Iraq	16,650	Spain	149,820
Byelorussian SSR	55,490	Ireland	29,970	Sudan	14,430
Cambodia	5,760	Israel	19,980	Sweden	206,750
Canada	425,060	Italy	275,230	Switzerland	137,620
Ceylon	12,210	Japan	253,040	Syria	11,100
Chile	44,390	Jordan	5,760	Thailand	24,410
China	709,180	Korea, Rep. of	5,760	Tunisia	5,760
Costa Rica	5,760	Laos	5,760	Turkey	91,000
Cuba	35,520	Lebanon	5,760	Ukrainian SSR	210,850
Czechoslovakia	113,200	Liberia	5,760	Union of South Africa	106,540
Denmark	91,000	Libya	5,760	USSR	1,593,700
Dominican Republic	5,760	Luxembourg	7,760	United Kingdom	1,159,750
Ecuador	5,760	Mexico	91,000	United States	4,666,480
Egypt	62,150	Monaco	5,760	Uruguay	21,090
El Salvador	7,760	Morocco	17,760	Venezuela	52,160
Ethiopia	14,430	Nepal	5,760	Viet-Nam	21,090
Federation of Rhodesia and Nyasaland*	3,330	Netherlands	159,820	Yemen	5,760
Finland	42,170	New Zealand	58,820	Yugoslavia	47,730
France	760,220	Nicaragua	5,760		
Germany, Fed. Rep. of	522,730	Nigeria*	3,330	Total	$14,411,160
Ghana	5,760	Norway	64,370		
		Pakistan	77,690	* Associate Members.	

ANNEX II. OFFICERS AND OFFICES

(As of 31 December 1957)

EXECUTIVE BOARD

Member	Designated by	Member	Designated by
Sir John Charles (Chairman)	United Kingdom	Dr. H. van Zile Hyde	United States
		Dr. M. Jafar	Pakistan
Dr. Dia E. El-Chatti (Vice-Chairman)	Syria	Dr. F. Koch	Federal Republic of Germany
Dr. P. E. Moore (Vice-Chairman)	Canada	Dr. C. K. Lakshmanan	India
		Dr. A. J. Metcalfe	Australia
Dr. Hafez Amin	Egypt	Professor N. N. Pesonen	Finland
Dr. A. Da Silva Travassos	Portugal	Dr. A. C. Regala	Philippines
Dr. L. Baquerizo Amador	Ecuador	Dr. L. Siri	Argentina
Professor G. A. Canaperia	Italy	Dr. J. N. Togba	Liberia
Dr. J. Zozaya*	Mexico		
Dr. M. A. Faquiri	Afghanistan		

* Replaced by his alternate, Dr. C. Díaz-Coller, at the twentieth session.

SENIOR OFFICERS OF THE SECRETARIAT

Director-General: Dr. M. G. Candau (Brazil).
Deputy Director-General: Dr. Pierre Dorolle.
Assistant Director-General, Department of Advisory Services: Dr. P. M. Kaul.

Assistant Director-General, Department of Central Technical Services: Dr. W. Timmerman.
Assistant Director-General, Department of Administration and Finance: M. P. Siegel.

Director, Regional Office for Africa: F. J. C. Cambournac.

Director, Regional Office for the Americas (Pan American Sanitary Bureau): F. L. Soper.

Director, Regional Office for South-East Asia: C. Mani.

Director, Regional Office for Europe: P. J. J. van de Calseyde.

Director, Regional Office for the Eastern Mediterranean: A. H. Taba.

Director, Regional Office for the Western Pacific: I. C. Fang.

HEADQUARTERS AND REGIONAL OFFICES

World Health Organization
Palais des Nations
Geneva, Switzerland
    Cable Address: UNISANTE GENEVA

World Health Organization
Liaison Office with United Nations
New York
    Cable Address: UNSANTE NEW YORK

REGIONAL OFFICES

World Health Organization
Regional Office for Africa
P. O. Box 6
Brazzaville, French Equatorial Africa
    Cable Address: UNISANTE BRAZZAVILLE

Pan American Sanitary Bureau
World Health Organization
Regional Office for the Americas
1501 New Hampshire Avenue, N.W.
Washington 6, D.C.
    Cable Address: OFSANPAN WASHINGTON

World Health Organization
Regional Office for South-East Asia
Patiala House, Princes Park
New Delhi, India
    Cable Address: WORLDHELTH NEW DELHI

World Health Organization
Regional Office for Europe
Scherfigsvej 8
Copenhagen, Denmark
    Cable Address: UNISANTE COPENHAGEN

World Health Organization
Regional Office for the Eastern Mediterranean
P. O. Box 1517
Alexandria, Egypt
    Cable Address: UNISANTE ALEXANDRIA

World Health Organization
Regional Office for the Western Pacific
25th Street, Port Area
(Post Box 2932)
Manila, Philippines
    Cable Address: UNISANTE MANILA

Epidemiological Intelligence Station
World Health Organization
8, Oxley Rise
Singapore 9
    Cable Address: EPIDNATION SINGAPORE

World Health Organization
Tuberculosis Research Office
Scherfigsvej 8
Copenhagen, Denmark
    Cable Address: UNIRESEARCH COPENHAGEN

CHAPTER VI

THE INTERNATIONAL BANK FOR RECONSTRUCTION AND DEVELOPMENT

The Board of Governors of the International Bank for Reconstruction and Development (World Bank)[1] held its twelfth annual meeting in Washington, D.C., from 23 to 27 September 1957.

Ghana, Ireland, Saudi Arabia and Sudan joined the Bank during the year, bringing the total membership to 64 countries. The total subscribed capital on 31 December 1957 was $9,333,400,000.

LENDING OPERATIONS

Twenty-six loans totalling $502.4 million were made in 1957 in 16 different countries. This brought the gross total of Bank loans granted to $3,480 million. The year saw a marked increase

[1] For further information, particularly on the Bank's functions and organization, and activities prior to 1957, see previous volumes of the *Yearbook,* annual reports of the Bank and supplementary reports for the United Nations Economic and Social Council.

in lending in Asia, which accounted for half the number of loans. It received $342 million, compared with $150 million in 1956. More funds were lent for transportation projects—railways, roads, aircraft and ports—than for any other category, the total of transport loans in 1957 reaching $236.5 million. Over $105 million was lent for electric power development and the remainder was lent for industry, agriculture and general development.

A loan equivalent to $3.6 million was made to Austria to help complete the Lunersee 190,000-kilowatt hydro-electric project being built in western Austria. Most of the power from Lunersee will be exported to the Ruhr and south-west Germany, and the remainder will be consumed in the Austrian provinces of Vorarlberg and Tyrol.

A loan of $40 million was made to the Belgian Congo for a road construction and improvement programme which forms part of the 10-Year Plan for the Development of the Belgian Congo. The loan was to cover the cost of imported equipment, materials and services required for work on the highways system during the four years 1957-60.

A loan of $10 million to Belgium was part of a joint operation in which the Bank loan coincided with a public offering of $30 million of Belgian bonds by an underwriting group of 63 investment banking firms in the United States. The funds received from the World Bank were to help finance the improvement of the Charleroi-Clabecq canal, which links the great coal and steel industries in southern Belgium with Brussels and Antwerp.

Chile received two loans, totalling $21.8 million, to modernize and expand the mining operations of two private Chilean companies, which produce about three quarters of the coal consumed in Chile. The modernization and expansion of their operations is essential if Chile is to continue to meet most of its own coal requirements. The projects being carried out with Bank assistance will enable the companies to increase production from the present 1.65 million tons to 2.2 million tons by 1964.

Ecuador received three loans totalling $20.1 million. A loan of $14.5 million was to finance the construction of four new important roads and a four-year road maintenance programme.

The four new roads, having a total length of 330 miles, will open up large fertile but unexploited coastal areas, and one of them will make possible all-weather motor transport between the Quito area and the Pacific coastal region. Another loan, of $5 million, was to assist in the execution of a project for expanding power supplies to Quito and its suburban area, one of Ecuador's main industrial regions. An earlier loan of $5 million was made for the same purpose in 1956. The project, now redesigned, consists of a hydro-electric plant to be located at a new site to develop 20,000 kilowatts of power, a 6,000-kilowatt diesel plant, transmission lines of greater capacity than in the original project and expansion of the distribution system to accommodate the increased generating power. The third loan in Ecuador was one of $600,000. Most of it was to be used to finance imports of spare parts, tools and materials, and eight petroleum tank cars. It was also to pay for the services of experts to assist in improving administrative procedures of the State Railway.

Ethiopia received a loan of $15 million to help carry out three more years of work on a highway programme which was begun in 1950 with the help of an earlier Bank loan. The all-weather road network is now being extended from 2,900 to about 3,400 miles. Parts of the existing network will be further improved, and 500 miles of new "penetration" roads will be constructed. The Bank funds were also to finance the surveying and designing of a further 625 miles of new roads and a training programme for Ethiopian highway personnel.

Seven loans were made in India, bringing the total lent there to $372.6 million, the largest amount lent to any single country. A loan of $5.6 million was part of a joint operation—which included the first direct Indian borrowing in the New York market—whereby Air-India International borrowed a total of $16.8 million for the purchase of three jet passenger aircraft. Five United States commercial banks together provided $11.2 million of the total under a credit agreement with Air-India International. Another loan of $9.8 million was made to the Tata group of power companies to assist in adding 62,500 kilowatts of new capacity to a thermal electric power plant at Trombay, near Bombay. Four other loans, totalling the equivalent of $90 million, were to support a programme for the further improvement and extension of the Indian railway system which, with nearly 36,000 route miles, is the fourth largest in the world. A five-year programme is now under way to increase freight capacity by 40 per cent and passenger capacity by about 15 per cent. The seventh loan in India, amounting to $32.5 million, was made to the Tata Iron and Steel Company, Ltd., in participation with 10 United States and Canadian commercial banks. The latter provided $15 million of the loan—the largest participation yet taken in a World Bank loan. The loan was to help complete an expansion programme aimed at doubling the company's steel ingot-producing capacity.

The year's largest loan was one of $75 million for the Second Seven-Year Plan in Iran. Its purpose was to provide interim financing to help in carrying the Plan Organization of Iran through the early years of a seven-year investment programme which will involve expenditures equivalent to more than $1,000 million.

A loan of $7 million went to Japan to help to finance a multi-purpose programme for irrigation, water supply and power in the Aichi region of central Japan. The programme will make it possible to increase the production of food crops by about 200,000 tons annually, and will also increase water supplies for industry in three cities and in numerous towns and villages. The most important feature of the project will be the perennial irrigation of 42,000 acres of land already under paddy and of 40,000 acres of upland areas never before irrigated.

A sum of $15 million was lent in the Netherlands to enable the Herstelbank, a development bank established jointly in 1954 by the Government and private investors in the Netherlands, to maintain its lending to Netherlands industry.

In Pakistan, the Bank made two loans totalling $35.2 million. One, for $31 million, was to meet part of the foreign exchange cost of a programme of replacement, improvement and expansion on the two railway systems of Pakistan. About half of the loan was to be spent on freight cars. Most of the balance was for cross-ties (sleepers) and rails; a small sum was also to be used for the rebuilding of the Landsdowne bridge, which spans the Indus

River about 250 miles upstream from Karachi. The second loan, of $4.2 million, was made to the Pakistan Industrial Credit and Investment Corporation, Ltd., a development bank formed by private Pakistani, British, United States and Japanese investors. The new Corporation, set up with the assistance of the World Bank, will provide funds to expand or modernize small- and medium-sized industries and to help bring new enterprises into being.

In Peru, following an earlier loan for the same amount, $5 million was lent to the Banco de Fomento Agropecuario to help finance a programme of long-term lending for the development of agriculture. The proceeds of the new loan were to pay for importing agricultural machinery, irrigation equipment, livestock, and some equipment for fisheries.

The Bank's first loan to the Philippines provided $21 million to be used for the Binga hydro-electric project on the island of Luzon. The borrower was the National Power Corporation and the funds were to assist in financing the construction of a dam, a power house with an installed capacity of 100,000 kilowatts, and transmission lines to Manila, about 120 miles to the south, and to various provincial areas.

Ruanda-Urundi, a United Nations Trust Territory in Central Africa administered by Belgium, received its first Bank loan, amounting to $4:8 million for improvement of transport. The loan was to help finance the construction of a modern port on Lake Tanganyika at Usumbura, the administrative capital, and the building of a 25-mile paved highway from Usumbura up 4,500 feet to the central plateau where most of the population and economic activities are concentrated.

In Thailand, the Yanhee Electricity Authority borrowed $66 million to help finance the Yanhee multi-purpose project for the development of electric power, irrigation, flood control and navigation. When its full power potential is realized, installed generating capacity at Yanhee will be 560,000 kilowatts and a national power-grid will bring power to 33 of Thailand's 71 provinces. The loan was to help finance the first stage of the project which consists of the construction of a 500-foot dam and the installation of 140,000 kilowatts of generating capacity to supply Bangkok and 11 other communities with electricity. The dam will help control floods and, by providing water for irrigation, will make it possible to increase the annual value of agricultural production to about $15 million.

The Union of South Africa received a loan of $25 million, concurrently with a $20 million revolving credit from a group of United States commercial banks. The loan was to assist in financing the import of equipment and materials required for the expansion of railway capacity. The most important item in the programme is a further increase in line and yard capacity. Some 160 miles of line will be double-tracked, 140 miles regraded, 450 miles electrified and five marshalling yards enlarged or constructed. About 80 miles of new suburban or branch lines will be built.

ADVISORY ASSISTANCE

Apart from loans, the Bank continued to give assistance on other development problems at the request of its member countries, the type of aid in each case being worked out to meet the special needs of the country concerned. During the year 1957, the Bank continued to post resident representatives in member countries to assist governments on economic development matters. Two staff members were assigned to Peru and one to Haiti, and the Bank continued to have representatives in Ecuador, Honduras and Panama. In Colombia, a staff member was assigned to help the Government to implement a long-term agricultural programme proposed by the Bank early in 1956. In July 1957, a small resident mission was stationed in Thailand to work in close co-operation with Thai experts on drawing up an economic development plan.

As in past years, the Bank helped member countries in recruiting experts required for their economic development. They included economic and financial advisers and experts on banking legislation, development banking, railway and port administration, coal production and other specialized subjects. In certain cases, the Bank also provided members of its regular staff to perform important services for member Governments. Thus, in Ecuador a staff member was assigned as assistant to the economic and financial adviser engaged by the Government with the help of the Bank. In Ceylon, the Bank continued to co-operate with the United Nations Technical Assistance Administration in pro-

viding the Institute of Scientific and Industrial Research with the services of the Director and a senior assistant. In Iran, a staff member remained on leave of absence as chief of a bureau responsible for technical services in the Plan Organization, while another left early in October, on leave of absence, to serve as an economic adviser to the Development Board of Iraq. In Japan, the Bank agreed to finance a quarter of the cost of a survey of the Japanese coal industry to increase productivity.

Other forms of advisory assistance included discussions with various member Governments on ways of stimulating productive private investment in less developed countries. Contact was also maintained with a number of development banks in whose establishment the Bank had participated, and advice was given to several countries on proposals for organizing new institutions of this kind.

Discussions on the Indus Waters question continued in Washington throughout the year between representatives of the Governments of India and Pakistan and with the participation of the Bank. At the end of 1957, discussions on an over-all plan for the use of the Indus Basin Waters were proceeding, and the co-operative work is continuing in an effort to arrive at an agreed solution.

The Economic Development Institute, a staff college operated by the Bank for the study of economic development problems, began its third course on 1 October 1957, in Washington, D.C., with 22 senior officials from 18 countries.

FINANCIAL ACTIVITIES
AND RESOURCES

All interest and principal repayments have been made on the Bank's loans, and its operating income has fully covered costs and also yielded surpluses which have been added to the reserves. During the calendar year 1957, the Bank's net income was $39 million. Reserves, derived both from the Bank's operating income and from a commission charged on all loans, amounted to $319 million. Cumulative disbursements at the end of the year amounted to $2,547 million, and the Bank had received principal repayments totalling $205 million.

Funds for the Bank's operations are obtained, apart from the income on operations, from capital paid in by member countries and from the sale of bonds and other obligations. Funds available from capital subscriptions by 31 December 1957 totalled $1,320 million, and funds from sales of bonds amounted to $1,269 million.

Six issues of bonds and notes aggregating $496.5 million were sold during the year—three of them by means of public offerings in the United States investment market, and three of them by means of private placements outside the United States. The Bank's marketing operations in 1957 were as follows:

Publicly Offered on United States Market

Jan. 1957—4½% 20-year bonds	$100,000,000
Apr. 1957—4¼% 21-year bonds	100,000,000
Oct. 1957—4¾% 23-year bonds	75,000,000
	$275,000,000

Placements Outside United States

Jan. 1957—200 million Sw. fr. Loan from Swiss Government	$ 46,500,000
July 1957—4¼% notes to Deutsche Bundesbank	100,000,000
Oct. 1957—4⅜% notes to Deutsche Bundesbank	75,000,000
	$221,500,000
Total sales World Bank bonds and notes in 1957	$496,500,000

Private investors continued to participate in Bank lending both by taking up parts of new loans as they were made and through the purchase of parts of earlier loans. At the end of the year, sales of principal amounts of loans totalled $371 million, of which $302 million was without the Bank's guarantee.

FUNDED DEBT OF THE BANK
(As of 31 December 1957)

In U.S. Dollars	Equivalent in U.S. Dollars
2% serial bonds of 1950, due 1958-62	$ 50,000,000
4¼% notes of 1957, due 1958-60	100,000,000
4⅜% notes of 1957, due 1959-61	75,000,000
3½% 2-year bonds of 1956, due 1958	75,000,000
2½% 5-year bonds of 1954, due 1959	50,000,000
3½% 15-year bonds of 1954, due 1969	93,383,000
3½% 19-year bonds of 1952, due 1971	57,163,000
3% 25-year bonds of 1947, due 1972	147,885,000
3⅜% 23-year bonds of 1952, due 1975	49,125,000
3% 25-year bonds of 1951, due 1976	50,000,000
4½% 20-year bonds of 1957, due 1977	73,741,000
4¼% 21-year bonds of 1957, due 1978	93,959,000
4¾% 23-year bonds of 1957, due 1980	53,700,000
3¼% 30-year bonds of 1951, due 1981	100,000,000
	$1,068,956,000

In Canadian Dollars

3¼% 10-year bonds of 1955, due 1965 (Can. $14,500,000)	$13,181,818
3½% 15-year bonds of 1954, due 1969 (Can. $25,000,000)	22,727,273
	$35,909,091

In Netherlands Guilders

3½% 15-year bonds of 1954, due 1969 (fl. 40,000,000)	$10,526,316
3½% 20-year bonds of 1955, due 1975 (fl. 40,000,000)	10,526,316
	$21,052,632

In Pounds Sterling

3½% 20-year stock of 1951, due 1971 (£4,594,283)	$12,863,992
3½% 20-year stock of 1954, due 1974 (£5,000,000)	14,000,000
	$26,863,992

In Swiss Francs

3⅜% Swiss franc loan of 1957, due 1960-65 (Sw. fr. 200,000,000)	$46,538,685
3½% 10-year bonds of 1952, due 1962 (Sw. fr. 50,000,000)	11,634,673
3½% 12-year bonds of 1951, due 1963 (Sw. fr. 50,000,000)	11,634,671
3½% 15-year bonds of 1953, due 1968 (Sw. fr. 50,000,000)	11,634,671
3½% 15-year bonds of 1953 (Nov. issue) due 1968 (Sw. fr. 50,000,000)	11,634,671
3½% 18-year bonds of 1954, due 1972 (Sw. fr. 50,000,000)	11,634,671
3½% 20-year bonds of 1955, due 1976 (Sw. fr. 50,000,000)	11,634,671
	$ 116,346,713
Gross total	$1,269,128,428

CAPITAL STRUCTURE AND FUNDS AVAILABLE ON 31 DECEMBER 1957
(In U.S. dollars)

Capital Stock	
Authorized (100,000 shares)	$10,000,000,000
Subscribed (93,334 shares)	9,333,400,000
Paid in:	
2% in gold or U.S. dollars	184,088,000
18% in the currencies of the respective members	1,680,012,000
Total paid in	$1,864,100,000
Payment deferred	2,580,000
Subject to call only to meet obligations of the Bank (80%)	7,466,720,000
	$9,333,400,000

SUMMARY OF LENDABLE FUNDS
(Cumulative Totals, in U.S. dollars)

2% paid-in portion of subscription of all members	$ 184,088,000
18% portion of subscription of the United States	571,500,000
18% portion of subscription made available by other members	564,912,000
Total available capital subscription	**$1,320,500,000**
Funds available from operations and exchange adjustments	$ 214,500,000
Funds available from outstanding debt	1,269,100,000
Funds available from principal repayments	203,454,000
Funds available from loans sold or agreed to be sold:	
Effective loans 343,135,000*	
Non-effective loans 24,419,000	367,554,000
Gross total available funds	**$3,375,108,000**
Disbursed on loans	2,546,980,000
Excess of available funds over loan disbursements	**$ 828,128,000**

STATEMENT OF INCOME AND EXPENSES FOR FISCAL YEAR ENDING 30 JUNE 1957
(In U.S. dollars)

Income

Income from investments	$10,679,446
Income from loans:	
Interest	57,630,772
Commitment charges	4,924,332
Commissions	16,728,564
Service charges	246,166
Other income	434,616
Gross income	**$90,643,896**
Deduct: amount equivalent to commissions appropriated to Special Reserve	16,728,564
Gross income less reserve deduction	**$73,915,332**

Expenses

Administrative expenses:	
Personal services	$ 4,098,912
Contributions to staff benefits	625,963
Fees and compensation	533,572
Representation	87,091
Travel	1,075,548
Supplies and material	73,005
Rents and utility services	595,498
Communication services	189,422
Furniture and equipment	95,126
Books and library services	74,509
Printing	82,307
Insurance	27,151
Other expenses	9,245
Total administrative expenses	**$ 7,567,349**
Interest on bonds	29,561,802
Bond issuance and other financial expenses	848,572
Gross expenses	**$37,977,723**
Net Income. Appropriated to Supplemental Reserve against losses on loans and guarantees	$35,937,609

ADMINISTRATIVE BUDGET

Outlined below is the Administrative Budget (in U.S. dollars) for the fiscal year ending 30 June 1958.

Board of Governors		$200,000
Executive Directors		480,000
Staff		
Personal services	$3,901,800	
Staff benefits	460,500	
Travel	705,000	
Consultants	240,000	
Representation	63,000	5,370,300
Other administrative expenses:		
Fees and compensation	$76,000	
Supplies and materials	68,000	
Rents and maintenance	633,000	
Communications	186,000	
Furniture and equipment	70,000	
Printing	65,500	
Books and library service	87,000	
Insurance	49,500	
Other	10,000	1,245,000
Contingency		100,000
Total		**$7,395,300**
Services to member countries:		
General survey missions	$200,000	
Resident representatives	91,100	
Economic Development Institute	115,400	
Training programmes	50,500	
Indus Basin discussions	45,000	
Other advisory services	53,500	555,500
Grand total		**$7,950,800**

* Of this amount, $146,108,000 has been repaid to purchasers of loans.

ANNEX I. MEMBERS OF THE BANK, THEIR SUBSCRIPTIONS AND VOTING POWER

(As of 31 December 1957)

MEMBER	SUBSCRIPTION Amount (in millions of U.S. dollars)	VOTING POWER Number of Votes	Per cent of Total	MEMBER	SUBSCRIPTION Amount (in millions of U.S. dollars)	VOTING POWER Number of Votes	Per cent of Total
Afghanistan	10.0	350	.32	Iraq	6.0	310	.28
Argentina	150.0	1,750	1.60	Ireland	30.0	550	.50
Australia	200.0	2,250	2.06	Israel	7.5	325	.30
Austria	50.0	750	.69	Italy	180.0	2,050	1.87
Belgium	225.0	2,500	2.29	Japan	250.0	2,750	2.52
Bolivia	7.0	320	.29	Jordan	3.0	280	.26
Brazil	150.0	1,750	1.60	Korea, Rep. of	12.5	375	.34
Burma	15.0	400	.36	Lebanon	4.5	295	.27
Canada	325.0	3,500	3.20	Luxembourg	10.0	350	.32
Ceylon	15.0	400	.36	Mexico	65.0	900	.82
Chile	35.0	600	.55	Netherlands	275.0	3,000	2.74
China	600.0	6,250	5.72	Nicaragua	3.0	280	.26
Colombia	35.0	600	.55	Norway	50.0	750	.69
Costa Rica	2.0	270	.25	Pakistan	100.0	1,250	1.14
Cuba	35.0	600	.55	Panama	.2	252	.23
Denmark	68.0	930	.85	Paraguay	1.4	264	.24
Dominican Republic	4.0	290	.27	Peru	17.5	425	.39
Ecuador	6.4	314	.29	Philippines	15.0	400	.36
Egypt	53.3	783	.72	Saudi Arabia	10.0	350	.32
El Salvador	1.0	260	.24	Sudan	10.0	350	.32
Ethiopia	3.0	280	.26	Sweden	100.0	1,250	1.14
Finland	38.0	630	.58	Syria	6.5	315	.29
France	525.0	5,500	5.03	Thailand	12.5	375	.34
Germany, Fed. Rep. of	330.0	3,550	3.25	Turkey	43.0	680	.62
Ghana	15.0	400	.36	Union of South Africa	100.0	1,250	1.14
Greece	25.0	500	.46	United Kingdom	1,300.0	13,250	12.12
Guatemala	2.0	270	.25	United States	3,175.0	32,000	29.27
Haiti	2.0	270	.25	Uruguay	10.5	355	.32
Honduras	1.0	260	.24	Venezuela	10.5	355	.32
Iceland	1.0	260	.24	Viet-Nam	12.5	375	.34
India	400.0	4,250	3.89	Yugoslavia	40.0	650	.59
Indonesia	110.0	1,350	1.23				
Iran	33.6	586	.54	Totals	9,333.4	109,334	100.00

ANNEX II. BOARD OF GOVERNORS

(As of 31 December 1957)

MEMBER	GOVERNOR	ALTERNATE
Afghanistan	Abdullah Malikyar*	Abdul Karim Hakimi
Argentina	Eduardo Laurencena	Mauricio L. Yadarola*
Australia	Sir Arthur Fadden*	Sir Roland Wilson
Austria	Reinhard Kamitz	Wilhelm Teufenstein
Belgium	Henri Liebaert	Jean Van Nieuwenhuyse
Bolivia	Miguel Gisbert N.	Fernando Pou Munt
Brazil	José María Alkmim*	Eurico de Aguiar Salles
Burma	Boh Khin Maung Gale	U Kyaw Nyun
Canada	Donald M. Fleming*	A. F. W. Plumptre
Ceylon	Stanley de Zoysa*	Rajendra Coomaraswamy
Chile		Felipe Herrera*
China	Peh-Yuan Hsu*	Tse-kai Chang
Colombia	Ignacio Copete-Lizarralde	Eduardo Arias Robledo
Costa Rica	Angel Coronas*	Mario Fernández*
Cuba		Joaquín E. Meyer
Denmark	Svend Nielsen*	Hakon Jespersen

MEMBER	GOVERNOR	ALTERNATE
Dominican Republic	Arturo Despradel*	Oscar G. Ginebra Henríquez*
Ecuador	Federico Intriago	José R. Chiriboga V.
Egypt	Ahmed Zaki Saad	Albert Mansour
El Salvador	Carlos J. Canessa*	Luis Escalante-Arce
Ethiopia	Menasse Lemma	George Peters Rea
Finland	Klaus Waris	Ralf Torngren
France	Minister of Finance	Pierre Mendès-France†
Germany, Fed. Rep. of	Ludwig Erhard	Fritz Schaeffer
Ghana	K. A. Gbedemah*	A. Eggleston*
Greece	Gregory Cassimatis	Ioannis Paraskevopoulos
Guatemala	Edgar Alvarado Pinetta	Mario Asturias-Arévalo
Haiti	Fritz Saint Firmin Thebaud	Silvere Piliet†
Honduras	Jorge Bueso-Arias	Guillermo López Rodezno
Iceland	Petur Benediktsson	Vilhjalmur Thor
India	T. T. Krishnamachari*	H. M. Patel
Indonesia	Soetikno Slamet	Loekman Hakim
Iran	Ali Asghar Nasser	Djalaledin Aghili
Iraq	Ali Mumtaz Al-Daftari	Mudhafar H. Jamil
Ireland	Seamas O Riain*	T. K. Whitaker
Israel	David Horowitz*	Martin Rosenbluth*
Italy	Donato Menichella	Giorgio Cigliana-Piazza
Japan	Hisato Ichimada*	Masamichi Yamagiwa*
Jordan	Anastas Hanania	Mohammad Ali Rida
Korea, Rep. of	Chin Hyung Kim	Byung Kyu Chun
Lebanon	Andre Tueni	Raja Himadeh
Luxembourg	Pierre Werner*	René Franck
Mexico	Antonio Carrillo Flores*	José Hernández Delgado
Netherlands	H. J. Hofstra	A. M. de Jong
Nicaragua	Guillermo Sevilla Sacasa*	Enrique Delgado
Norway	Arne Skaug	Carsten Nielsen
Pakistan	Syed Amjad Ali	M. A. Mozaffar
Panama	Ricardo M. Arias Espinosa	Julio E. Heurtematte
Paraguay	Osvaldo Chaves	Federico Mandelburger
Peru	Fernando Berckemeyer	Emilio Foley
Philippines	Miguel Cuaderno, Sr.*	Eduardo Z. Romuáldez*
Saudi Arabia	Rasem Al-Khalidi*	Saleh Al-Shalfan*
Sudan	Ibrahim Ahmed*	Sayed Hamza Mirghani
Sweden	G. E. Straeng	N. G. Lange
Syria	Husni A. Sawwaf	Sadek Ayoubi
Thailand	Serm Vinicchayakul	Puey Ungphakorn*
Turkey	Hasan Polatkan*	Sait Naci Ergin
Union of South Africa	Jozua Francois Naude*	M. H. de Kock
United Kingdom	Peter Thorneycroft*	Sir Leslie Rowan
United States	Robert B. Anderson*	C. Douglas Dillon*
Uruguay	Nilo Berchesi	Roberto Ferber
Venezuela	José Joaquín González-Gorrondona, Jr.*	Alejandro J. Huizi-Aguiar
Viet-Nam	Tran Huu Phuong*	Vu Quoc Thuc*
Yugoslavia	Avdo Humo	Augustin Papic

* Denotes similar position in International Monetary Fund.   † Denotes Governor of International Monetary Fund.

ANNEX III. EXECUTIVE DIRECTORS AND ALTERNATES
(As of 31 December 1957)

Executive Director	Alternate	Member Government(s)
Tom B. Coughran	John S. Hooker	United States
G. F. Thorold	David B. Pitblado	United Kingdom
Kan Lee	———	China
René Larre	Jean-Maxime Levèque	France
V. Narahari Rao	P. J. J. Pinto	India

Executive Director	Alternate	Member Government(s)
Thomas Basyn (Belgium)	Max Thurn (Austria)	Belgium, Austria, Turkey, Republic of Korea, Luxembourg
Soetikno Slamet (Indonesia)	Carlo Gragnani (Italy)	Italy, Indonesia, Greece, Afghanistan
Mohammad Shoaib (Pakistan)	Ali Akbar Khosropur (Iran)	Pakistan, Egypt, Iran, Syria, Iraq, Lebanon, Ethiopia, Jordan
P. Lieftinck (Netherlands)	J. Smole (Yugoslavia)	Netherlands, Yugoslavia, Israel
Takeshi Watanabe (Japan)	D. C. Gunesekera (Ceylon)	Japan, Burma, Ceylon, Thailand
B. B. Callaghan (Australia)	B. E. Fleming (Australia)	Australia, Union of South Africa, Viet-Nam
Luis Machado (Cuba)	Jorge A. Montealegre (Nicaragua)	Mexico, Cuba, Peru, Venezuela, Costa Rica, Guatemala, El Salvador, Honduras, Nicaragua, Panama
Sven Viig (Norway)	Bjorn Tryggvason (Iceland)	Sweden, Denmark, Norway, Finland, Iceland
Jorge Mejía-Palacio (Colombia)	———	Brazil, Colombia, Philippines, Ecuador, Dominican Republic, Haiti
Otto Donner (Federal Republic of Germany)	Karl-Heinz Drechsler (Federal Republic of Germany)	Federal Republic of Germany
Louis Rasminsky (Canada)	Alan B. Hockin (Canada)	Canada
Victor A. Pane (Paraguay)	Persio da Silva (Paraguay)	Argentina, Chile, Uruguay, Bolivia, Paraguay

NOTE: Ghana, Ireland, Saudi-Arabia and Sudan were not members of the Bank at the time of the election of these Executive Directors and Alternates.

ANNEX IV. PRINCIPAL OFFICERS AND OFFICES
(As of 31 December 1957)
OFFICERS

President: Eugene R. Black.
Vice-President: W. A. B. Iliff.
Vice-President: J. Burke Knapp.
Vice-President and General Counsel: Davidson Sommers.
Director, Economic Staff: Leonard B. Rist.
Director, Technical Assistance and Liaison Staff: Richard H. Demuth.
Director of Operations—Europe, Africa and Australasia: S. R. Cope.
Director of Operations—South Africa and Middle East: Joseph Rucinski.

Director of Operations—Western Hemisphere: Orvis A. Schmidt.
Director of Operations—Far East: Martin M. Rosen.
Director of Technical Operations: Simon Aldewereld.
Director of Marketing: George L. Martin.
Treasurer: Henry W. Riley.
Secretary: M. M. Mendels.
Director, Legal Department: A. Broches.
Director of Administration: William F. Howell.
Director of Information: Harold N. Graves, Jr.
Director, Economic Development Institute: Michael L. Hoffman.

HEADQUARTERS AND REGIONAL OFFICES

HEADQUARTERS
International Bank for Reconstruction and Development
1818 H Street, N.W.
Washington 25, D.C.
Cable Address: INTBAFRAD WASHINGTON

OTHER OFFICES

International Bank for Reconstruction and Development
Marketing Department
33 Liberty Street
New York 5, N.Y.

International Bank for Reconstruction and Development
European Office
67 rue de Lille
Paris 7°, France

CHAPTER VII

THE INTERNATIONAL FINANCE CORPORATION (IFC)

The International Finance Corporation (IFC)[1] is an international financial institution closely affiliated with the International Bank for Reconstruction and Development. Its purpose is to further economic development by encouraging the growth of productive private enterprise in the less developed areas of the world. Membership in IFC is open to countries which are members of the International Bank. The Corporation began operations on 24 July 1956, with 31 members subscribing $78,366,000 of the authorized capital of $100 million. Twenty-two additional countries had joined IFC by 31 December 1957, bringing the total subscribed capital to almost $93 million and its total membership to 53 countries. An agreement on the relationship between the United Nations and IFC was approved by the United Nations General Assembly on 20 February 1957.[2]

IFC hopes to achieve its purpose of furthering economic development in its less developed member countries by investing—without government guarantee—in productive private enterprises in association with private investors who can provide competent management, in cases where sufficient private capital is not available on reasonable terms. IFC is an investing rather than a lending institution.

IFC will invest only in private enterprises; it will not invest in enterprises which are government owned and operated. In its early years, IFC will normally invest in industrial enterprises and will deal with companies whose assets, after financing, are at least $500,000. Its investments will not cover more than half the cost of an enterprise and will range in size from about $100,000 to $2 million in its first years. IFC investments will not be conventional, fixed-interest loans; they will be loans carrying some interest and some right to participate in the growth of the business.

IFC will make investments which will encourage participation by private investors either in the initial stages of an enterprise or subsequently through the purchase of IFC's investment. IFC intends to revolve its portfolio by selling its investments as soon as they prove sufficiently successful to attract private investors. IFC is prepared to give its private partners the right of first refusal to purchase its investments.

Since its capital is in United States dollars, IFC will, in its early years, generally make investments expressed in United States dollars. But it will invest, at least in part, in other currencies if justified by the stability of such currencies and by the participation rights of the investment.

Governors of the International Bank from countries which are also members of IFC are Governors of IFC. The inaugural meeting of the Board of Governors was held in Washington, D.C., in September 1956; the first annual meeting was held in conjunction with the annual meeting of the International Bank in Washington, D.C., on 27 September 1957. The Board of Governors is required to meet once each year, and it has become the practice to hold this annual meeting in September.

The Corporation's Board of Directors is composed of those Executive Directors of the International Bank who represent at least one Government which is also a member of the Corporation.

Between July and December 1956, the Corporation established a working organization, adopted operating policies for the initial stage of its activities, developed working procedures and recruited a staff. At the end of December 1957, the Corporation had made five commitments totalling the equivalent of nearly $6 million, as follows: $660,000 investment in Duncan's Holdings Ltd., in Australia; $2 million in Siemens do Brasil Companhia de Electricidade, in Brazil; $2.2 million in Empresa Minera de Mantos Blancos, S.A., in Chile; and, in Mexico, the equivalent of $600,000 in Engranes y Productos Industriales, S.A., and

[1] For further information, particularly about the origins of the International Finance Corporation, see previous volumes of the *Yearbook*. See also the *First Annual Report of the (IFC) Board of Directors to the Board of Governors, 1956-1957*, and *Summary Proceedings of the First Annual Meeting of the Board of Governors, 1957*.

[2] See *Y.U.N., 1956*, pp. 272, 274-76.

the equivalent of $500,000 in Bristol de Mexico, S.A.

FINANCIAL ACTIVITIES AND RESOURCES

As received, the Coroporation's subscribed capital has been invested in United States Government obligations with maturities up to five years. Gross income from these investments to 30 June 1957 was $2,408,048, and after deduction of operating expenses of $732,666 net income for the year was $1,675,382.

STATEMENT OF INCOME AND EXPENSES
(24 July 1956–30 June 1957)

Income

Income from investments	$2,408,048

Expenses

Administrative expenses:

Personal services	$ 424,905
Contributions to staff benefits	38,294
Fees and compensation	42,123
Representation	13,004
Travel	69,395
Supplies	13,611
Rents and utility services	51,729
Communication services	15,826
Furniture and equipment	33,743
Books and library services	8,834
Printing	13,858
Insurance	1,981
Other expenses	5,363
	$ 732,666
Net income	$1,675,382

ANNEX I. MEMBERS OF INTERNATIONAL FINANCE CORPORATION, THEIR SUBSCRIPTIONS AND VOTING POWER
(As of 31 December 1957)

MEMBER	SUBSCRIPTION Amount (in thousands of U.S. dollars)	VOTING POWER Number of Votes	Per cent of Total	MEMBER	SUBSCRIPTION Amount (in thousands of U.S. dollars)	VOTING POWER Number of Votes	Per cent of Total
Afghanistan	111	361	.34	India	4,431	4,681	4.41
Australia	2,215	2,465	2.32	Indonesia	1,218	1,468	1.38
Austria	554	804	.76	Iran	372	622	.59
Belgium	2,492	2,742	2.58	Iraq	67	317	.30
Bolivia	78	328	.31	Israel	50	300	.28
Brazil	1,163	1,413	1.33	Italy	1,994	2,244	2.11
Burma	166	416	.39	Japan	2,769	3,019	2.84
Canada	3,600	3,850	3.63	Jordan	33	283	.27
Ceylon	166	416	.39	Lebanon	50	300	.28
Chile	388	638	.60	Luxembourg	111	361	.34
Colombia	388	638	.60	Mexico	720	970	.91
Costa Rica	22	272	.26	Netherlands	3,046	3,296	3.11
Cuba	388	638	.60	Nicaragua	9	259	.24
Denmark	753	1,003	.94	Norway	554	804	.76
Dominican Republic	22	272	.26	Pakistan	1,108	1,358	1.28
Ecuador	35	285	.27	Panama	2	252	.24
Egypt	590	840	.79	Paraguay	16	266	.25
El Salvador	11	261	.25	Peru	194	444	.42
Ethiopia	33	283	.27	Philippines	166	416	.39
Finland	421	671	.63	Sweden	1,108	1,358	1.28
France	5,815	6,065	5.72	Thailand	139	389	.37
Germany	3,655	3,905	3.68	Turkey	476	726	.68
Greece	277	527	.50	Union of South Africa	1,108	1,358	1.28
Guatemala	22	272	.26	United Kingdom	14,400	14,650	13.81
Haiti	22	272	.26	United States	35,168	35,418	33.39
Honduras	11	261	.25	Venezuela	116	366	.35
Iceland	11	261	.25	Totals	$92,834	106,084	100.00

ANNEX II. BOARD OF GOVERNORS
(As of 31 December 1957)

MEMBER	GOVERNOR	ALTERNATE
Afghanistan	Abdullah Malikyar	Abdul Karim Hakimi
Australia	Sir Arthur Fadden	Sir Roland Wilson

MEMBER	GOVERNOR	ALTERNATE
Austria	Reinhard Kamitz	Wilhelm Teufenstein
Belgium	Henri Liebaert	Jean Van Nieuwenhuyse
Bolivia	Miguel Gisbert N.	Fernando Pou Munt
Brazil	José María Alkmim	Eurico de Aguiar Salles
Burma	Boh Khin Maung Gale	U Kyaw Nyun
Canada	Donald M. Fleming	A. F. W. Plumptre
Ceylon	Stanley de Zoysa	Rajendra Coomaraswamy
Chile	———	Felipe Herrera
Colombia	Ignacio Copete-Lizarralde	Eduardo Arias Robledo
Costa Rica	Angel Coronas	Mario Fernández
Cuba	———	Joaquín E. Meyer
Denmark	Svend Nielsen	Hakon Jespersen
Dominican Republic	Arturo Despradel	Oscar G. Ginebra Henríquez
Ecuador	Federico Intriago	José R. Chiriboga V.
Egypt	Ahmed Zaki Saad	Albert Mansour
El Salvador	Carlos J. Canessa	Luis Escalante-Arce
Ethiopia	Menasse Lemma	George Peters Rea
Finland	Klaus Waris	Ralf Torngren
France	Minister of Finance	Pierre Mendès-France
Germany, Fed. Rep. of	Ludwig Erhard	Fritz Schaeffer
Greece	Gregory Cassimatis	Ioannis Paraskevopoulos
Guatemala	Edgar Alvarado Pinetta	Mario Asturias-Arévalo
Haiti	Fritz Saint Firmin Thebaud	Silvere Pilie
Honduras	Jorge Bueso-Arias	Guillermo López Rodezno
Iceland	Petur Benediktsson	Vilhjalmur Thor
India	T. T. Krishnamachari	H. M. Patel
Indonesia	Soetikno Slamet	Loekman Hakim
Iran	Ali Asghar Nasser	Djalaledin Aghili
Iraq	Ali Mumtaz Al-Daftari	Mudhafar H. Jamil
Israel	David Horowitz	Martin Rosenbluth
Italy	Donato Menichella	Giorgio Cigliana-Piazza
Japan	Hisato Ichimada	Masamichi Yamagiwa
Jordan	Anastas Hanania	Mohammad Ali Rida
Lebanon	Andre Tueni	Raja Himadeh
Luxembourg	Pierre Werner	René Franck
Mexico	Antonio Carrillo Flores	José Hernández Delgado
Netherlands	H. J. Hofstra	A. M. de Jong
Nicaragua	Guillermo Sevilla Sacasa	Enrique Delgado
Norway	Arne Skaug	Carsten Nielsen
Pakistan	Syed Amjad Ali	M. A. Mozaffar
Panama	Ricardo M. Arias Espinosa	Julio E. Heurtematte
Paraguay	Osvaldo Chaves	Federico Mandelburger
Peru	Fernando Berckemeyer	Emilio Foley
Philippines	Miguel Cuaderno, Sr.	Eduardo Z. Romuáldez
Sweden	G. E. Straeng	N. G. Lange
Thailand	Serm Vinicchayakul	Puey Ungphakorn
Turkey	Hasan Polatkan	Sait Naci Ergin
Union of South Africa	Jozua Francois Naude	M. H. de Kock
United Kingdom	Peter Thorneycroft	Sir Leslie Rowan
United States	Robert B. Anderson	C. Douglas Dillon
Venezuela	José Joaquín González-Gorrondona, Jr.	Alejandro J. Huizi-Aguiar

ANNEX III. EXECUTIVE DIRECTORS AND ALTERNATES
(As of 31 December 1957)

Director	Alternate(s)	Member Government(s)
Tom B. Coughran	John S. Hooker	United States
G. F. Thorold	David B. Pitblado	United Kingdom
René Larre	Jean-Maxime Levèque	France
V. Narahari Rao	P. J. J. Pinto	India

Director	Alternate(s)	Member Government(s)
Thomas Basyn (Belgium)	Max Thurn (Austria)	Belgium, Austria, Turkey, Luxembourg
Takeshi Watanabe (Japan)	D. C. Gunesekera (Ceylon)	Japan, Burma, Ceylon, Thailand
Soetikno Slamet (Indonesia)	Carlo Gragnani (Italy)	Italy, Indonesia, Greece, Afghanistan
Sven Viig (Norway)	Bjorn Tryggvason (Iceland)	Sweden, Denmark, Norway, Finland, Iceland
Mohammad Shoaib (Pakistan)	Ali Akbar Khosropur (Iran)	Pakistan, Egypt, Iran, Iraq, Lebanon, Ethiopia, Jordan
Luis Machado (Cuba)	Jorge A. Montealegre (Nicaragua)	Mexico, Cuba, Peru, Venezuela, Costa Rica, Guatemala, El Salvador, Honduras, Nicaragua, Panama
Otto Donner	Karl-Heinz Drechsler	Federal Republic of Germany
Louis Rasminsky	Alan B. Hockin	Canada
B. B. Callaghan (Australia)	B. E. Fleming (Australia)	Australia, Union of South Africa
P. Lieftinck (Netherlands)	J. Smole (Yugoslavia) L. R. W. Soutendijk* (Netherlands)	Netherlands, Israel
Jorge Mejía-Palacio (Colombia)	———	Brazil, Colombia, Philippines, Ecuador, Dominican Republic, Haiti
Victor A. Pane (Paraguay)	Persio da Silva (Paraguay)	Chile, Bolivia, Paraguay

* Temporary.

ANNEX IV. OFFICERS AND OFFICES
(As of 31 December 1957)
PRINCIPAL OFFICERS

President: Robert L. Garner
Vice-President: John G. Beevor.
Director of Investments: Broderick Haskell.
Engineering Adviser: William J. Jenkins.
Assistant to the President: Richard H. Demuth.

General Counsel: Davidson Sommers.
NOTE: The offices of Treasurer, Secretary, Director of Administration and Director of Information are held by the corresponding officers of the International Bank for Reconstruction and Development.

HEADQUARTERS AND REGIONAL OFFICES

HEADQUARTERS
International Finance Corporation
1818 H Street, N.W.
Washington 25, D.C.
Cable Address: CORINTFIN WASHINGTON

OTHER OFFICES

International Finance Corporation
Paris Office
67 rue de Lille
Paris 7*, France

International Finance Corporation
London Office
27/32 Old Jewry
London, E.C.2, England.

CHAPTER VIII

THE INTERNATIONAL MONETARY FUND

For the International Monetary Fund,[1] the calendar year 1957 was a record year of financial activity. The Fund extended $1,000 million in new credits to member countries, bringing its total transactions in 11 years of operation to $3,000 million. Repayments had reduced the amount outstanding to $1,700 million by the end of the year.

Up to this time, the Fund's largest financial arrangement was a $1,300 million agreement concluded at the end of 1956 by the United Kingdom. This provided for an immediate drawing of $561.5 million from the Fund and a stand-by arrangement authorizing the United Kingdom to draw an additional $738.5 million within the next 12 months. The arrangement was not used during that period, but was extended to run another year from 22 December 1957.

The United Kingdom arrangement was succeeded in 1957 by a series of large drawings on the Fund, including those of France ($262.5 million), India ($200 million), Japan ($125 million), Argentina ($75 million), Denmark ($34 million), Belgium ($50 million), the Netherlands ($68 million) and Brazil ($37.5 million). The Fund also provided a number of smaller credits. Undrawn balances of stand-by arrangements still in effect at the end of the year amounted to $870 million. These arrangements were maintained by Bolivia, Chile, Colombia, the Netherlands, Nicaragua, Paraguay and Peru, in addition to the United Kingdom.

The admission during 1957 of four new members, Ghana, Ireland, Saudi Arabia and Sudan, brought the Fund's membership up to 64 countries and total quotas to $9,000 million. On 31 December 1957, the Fund's resources included $1,379.5 million in gold, $799.2 million in United States dollars and $210 million in Canadian dollars. Earlier during the year, the Fund sold a total of $600 million in gold to the United States Treasury to replenish its holdings of United States dollars.

The Fund reported to its Board of Governors in September 1957 that the payments problems of its members, in most cases, had their roots in the inflationary pressures associated with widespread industrial expansion and national development programmes. The difficulties of many countries had been aggravated by the Suez shipping crisis and by a variety of special circumstances.

During 1957 the Fund conducted a sixth annual round of consultations with individual members which continued to employ exchange controls and discrimination. These consultations afforded an opportunity for countries maintaining restrictions to explain the need for them against the background of balance-of-payments problems and other considerations. At the same time, they presented an opportunity for examination of the role of fiscal and monetary policy in the exchange problems of members and for inquiry as to the plans of their governments looking towards the reduction of restrictive practices. The consultations, and the Executive Board's decisions in individual cases, were confidential. The Fund, however, summarized recent developments in that field and described the restrictive systems in its *Eighth Annual Report on Exchange Restrictions,* published in June 1957.

Technical co-operation was again extended by the Fund, through the activity of missions and other advisory efforts, and the collection and analysis of statistical information was continued. Training programmes on the work of the Fund and in balance-of-payments techniques and economic problems were conducted for staff members of central banks and ministries of finance.

The Fund has published 12 annual reports (1945-57) and eight annual reports on exchange restrictions (1950-57). Other publications include: *International Financial Statistics,* a

---

[1] For further information, particularly about the Fund's functions and organization, and activities prior to 1957, see previous volumes of the *Yearbook,* annual reports of the Executive Directors, summary proceedings of the annual meetings of the Board of Governors, schedules of par values, and quarterly financial statements.

monthly statistical bulletin; *International Financial News Survey*, distributed weekly; *Staff Papers* (published two or three times a year), and a *Balance-of-Payments Yearbook. Direction of International Trade,* a monthly, is compiled by the Fund and published jointly by the Fund, the International Bank for Reconstruction and Development and the United Nations.

The twelfth annual meeting of the Fund's Board of Governors was convened in Washington, D.C., on 23 September 1957, under the chairmanship of Miguel Cuaderno, of the Philippines. It was agreed to hold the next annual meeting of the Governors in New Delhi during October 1958.

ADMINISTRATIVE BUDGET

The Fund's Administrative Budget for the fiscal year ending 30 April 1958, as approved by the Executive Board, is as follows:

	U.S. Dollars
Board of Governors	$ 206,000
Office of Executive Directors	
Salaries	613,000
Other compensations and benefits	91,000
Travel	126,000
	$ 830,000
Staff	
Salaries	$2,768,000
Other compensations and benefits	715,500
Travel	395,000
	$3,878,500
Other Administrative Expenses	
Communications	$ 132,000
Office occupancy expenses	406,500
Books and printing	118,000
Supplies and equipment	97,000
Miscellaneous	57,000
	$ 810,500
Grand total	$5,725,000

CURRENCY TRANSACTIONS: PURCHASES AND REPURCHASES

(For calendar year 1957)

PURCHASES

Member	U.S. Dollars	Member	U.S. Dollars
Argentina	$ 75,000,000.00	Haiti	1,000,000.00
Belgium	50,000,000.00	Honduras	6,250,000.00
Bolivia	1,000,000.00	India	200,000,000.00
Brazil	37,500,000.00	Israel	3,750,000.00
Chile	31,081,620.70	Japan	125,000,000.00
Colombia	5,000,000.00	Netherlands	68,750,000.00
Cuba	35,000,000.00	Nicaragua	3,750,000.00
Denmark	34,000,000.00	Paraguay	4,000,000.00
Ecuador	5,000,000.00	Turkey	13,500,000.00
Egypt	15,000,000.00		
France	262,500,000.00	Total	$977,081,620.70

REPURCHASES

Member	Total (in U.S. dollars)	Gold (in fine ozs.)	Gold (equivalent in U.S. dollars)	In U.S. dollars
Ceylon	$ 1,987,434.18	—	—	$ 1,987,434.18
Chile	12,331,620.70	—	—	12,331,620.70
Colombia	5,000,000.00	—	—	5,000,000.00
Cuba	22,488,171.47	142,857.143	$ 5,000,000.00	17,488,717.47
Denmark	1,844,210.65	52,691.733	1,844,210.65	—
El Salvador	2,495,507.95	—	—	2,495,507.95
Finland	3,343,832.34	95,538.067	3,343,832.34	—
Honduras	2,498,412.29	416.741	14,585.95	2,483,826.34
Iraq	1,996,653.73	56,838.852	1,989,359.83	7,293.90
Nicaragua	1,874,951.66	—	—	1,874,951.66
Paraguay	500,000.00	—	—	500,000.00
Turkey	7,000,000.00	199,692.804	6,989,248.15	10,751.85
Yugoslavia	9,000,000.00	165,714.286	5,800,000.00	3,200,000.00
	$72,360,794.97	713,749.626	$24.981,236.92	$47,379,558.05

NOTE: In addition, Brazil and France, in discharge of repurchase obligations, substituted gold for $27,987,654.91 and $7,849,781.30, respectively, for the same amount previously paid in U.S. dollars.

ANNEX I. MEMBERS OF THE FUND, THEIR QUOTAS, BOARD OF GOVERNORS, AND VOTING POWER

(As of 31 December 1957)

MEMBER	QUOTA Amount (in millions of U.S. dollars)	Per cent of Total‡	GOVERNOR	ALTERNATE	VOTING POWER Number of Votes†	Per cent of Total‡
Afghanistan	$10.0	0.11	Abdullah Malikyar*	Mohammad Sarwar	350	0.34
Argentina	150.0	1.66	Adalberto Krieger Vasena	Mauricio L. Yadarola*	1,750	1.65
Australia	200.0	2.22	Sir Arthur Fadden*	Sir Percy Claude Spender	2,250	2.12
Austria	50.0	0.55	Eugen Margaretha	Franz Stoeger-Marenpach	750	0.71
Belgium	225.0	2.50	Maurice Frère	Maurice Williot	2,500	2.35
Bolivia	10.0	0.11	Franklin Antezana Paz	Santiago Sologuren	350	0.33
Brazil	150.0	1.66	José María Alkmim*	Octavio Paranagua	1,750	1.65
Burma	15.0	0.17	Kyaw Nyein	San Lin	400	0.38
Canada	300.0	3.33	Donald M. Fleming*	James Elliott Coyne	3,250	3.06
Ceylon	15.0	0.17	Stanley de Zoysa*	Sir Arthur Ranasinha	400	0.38
Chile	50.0	0.55	———	Felipe Herrera*	750	0.71
China	550.0	6.10	Peh-Yuan Hsu*	Pao-hsu Ho	5,750	5.42
Colombia	50.0	0.55	Antonio Alvarez Restrepo	Emilio Toro	750	0.71
Costa Rica	5.0	0.06	Angel Coronas*	Mario Fernández*	300	0.28
Cuba	50.0	0.55	Joaquín Martínez Sáenz	Bernardo Figueredo Antúnez	750	0.71
Denmark	68.0	0.75	Svend Nielsen*	Einar Dige	930	0.88
Dominican Republic	10.0	0.11	Arturo Despradel*	Oscar Guaroa Ginebra Henríquez*	350	0.33
Ecuador	10.0	0.11	Guillermo Pérez-Chiriboga	Clemente Vallejo	350	0.33
Egypt	60.0	0.67	Abdel Moneim El Kaissouni	Mohamed Loutfy El-Banna	850	0.80
El Salvador	7.5	0.08	Carlos J. Canessa*	Manuel Meléndez-Valle	325	0.31
Ethiopia	6.0	0.07	Makonnen Habte Wolde	Stanislaw Kirkor	310	0.29
Finland	38.0	0.42	R. V. Fieandt	Eero Asp	630	0.59
France	525.0	5.82	Pierre Mendès-France	Wilfrid Baumgartner	5,500	5.18
Germany Fed. Rep. of	330.0	3.66	Wilhelm Vocke	Hans Karl von Mangoldt-Reiboldt	3,550	3.34
Ghana	15.0	0.17	K. A. Gbedemah*	A. Eggleston*	400	0.38
Greece	40.0	0.44	Zenophon Zolotas	John S. Pesmazoglu	650	0.61
Guatemala	5.0	0.06	Gabriel Orellana	Gustavo Mirón	300	0.28
Haiti	7.5	0.08	Silvere Pilie	Maurice Telemaque	325	0.31
Honduras	7.5	0.08	Gabriel A. Mejía	Roberto Ramírez	325	0.31
Iceland	1.0	0.01	Gylfi Gislason	Thor Thors	260	0.24
India	400.0	4.44	T. T. Krishnamachari*	H. V. R. Iengar	4,250	4.00
Indonesia	110.0	1.22	Sjafruddin Prawiranegara	R. Soegiarto	1,350	1.27
Iran	35.0	0.39	Ebrahim Kashani	Ahmad Majidian	600	0.57
Iraq	8.0	0.09	Abdulilah Hafidh	Saleh Kubba	330	0.31
Ireland	30.0	0.33	Seamas O Riain*	J. J. McElligott	550	0.52
Israel	7.5	0.08	David Horowitz*	Martin Rosenbluth*	325	0.31
Italy	180.0	2.00	Giuseppe Medici	Ugo La Malfa	2,050	1.93
Japan	250.0	2.77	Hisato Ichimada*	Masamichi Yamagiwa*	2,750	2.59
Jordan	3.0	0.03	Izzeddin Mufti	Abdul Karim Humud	280	0.26
Korea, Rep. of	12.5	0.14	Hyun Chul Kim	Yong Chan Kim	375	0.35
Lebanon	4.5	0.05	Nasr Harfouche	Farid Solh	295	0.28
Luxembourg	10.0	0.11	Pierre Werner*	Hugues Le Gallais	350	0.33
Mexico	90.0	1.00	Antonio Carrillo Flores*	Rodrigo Gómez	1,150	1.08
Netherlands	275.0	3.05	M. W. Holtrop	E. van Lennep	3,000	2.83
Nicaragua	7.5	0.08	Guillermo Sevilla-Sacasa*	León DeBayle	325	0.31
Norway	50.0	0.55	Erik Brofoss	Christian Brinch	750	0.71

MEMBER	Amount (in millions of U.S. dollars)	Per cent of Total‡	GOVERNOR	ALTERNATE	Number of Votes†	Per cent of Total‡
Pakistan	100.0	1.11	Abdul Qadir	Vaqar Ahmad	1,250	1.18
Panama	0.5	0.01	Roberto M. Heurtematte	Henrique Obarrio	255	0.24
Paraguay	7.5	0.08	Gustavo F. A. Storm	Pedro R. Chamorro	325	0.31
Peru	25.0	0.28	Andrés F. Dasso	Emilio G. Barreto	500	0.47
Philippines	15.0	0.17	Miguel Cuaderno, Sr.*	Eduardo Z. Romualdez*	400	0.38
Saudi Arabia	10.0	0.11	Rasem Al-Khalidi*	Saleh-Al-Shalfan*	350	0.33
Sudan	10.0	0.11	Ibrahim Ahmed*	Mamoun Beheiry	350	0.33
Sweden	100.0	1.11	Per V. Asbrink	T. L. Hammarskiold	1,250	1.18
Syria	6.5	0.07	Izzat Traboulsi	Rafic Sioufi	315	0.30
Thailand	12.5	0.14	Prince Viwat	Puey Ungphakorn*	375	0.35
Turkey	43.0	0.48	Hasan Polatkan*	Memduh Aytur	680	0.64
Union of South Africa	100.0	1.11	Jozua Francois Naude*	Daniel Hendrik Steyn	1,250	1.18
United Kingdom	1,300.0	14.42	Peter Thorneycroft*	M. H. Parsons	13,250	12.48
United States	2,750.0	30.50	Robert B. Anderson*	C. Douglas Dillon*	27,750	26.14
Uruguay	15.0	0.17	Carlos Sapelli	Carlos Sanguinetti	400	0.38
Venezuela	15.0	0.17	José Joaquín González Gorrondona, Jr.*	Francisco Alfonso Ravard	400	0.38
Viet-Nam	12.5	0.14	Tran Huu Phuong*	Vu Quoc Thuc*	375	0.35
Yugoslavia	60.0	0.67	Nenad Popovic	Nikola Miljanic	850	0.80
	$9,016.0	100.00			106,160	100.00

* Denotes similar position in International Bank for Reconstruction and Development.

† Voting power varies on certain matters with use by members of the Fund's resources.

‡ These figures do not add up to 100 per cent because of rounding.

ANNEX II. EXECUTIVE BOARD
(As of 31 December 1957)

Appointed Director	Alternate	Casting Votes of
Frank A. Southard, Jr. (United States)	John S. Hooker (United States)	United States
G. F. Thorold (United Kingdom)	R. E. Heasman (United Kingdom)	United Kingdom
Beue Tann (China)	Ching-Yao Hsieh (China)	China
Jean de Largentaye (France)	Jean-Maxime Levèque (France)	France
B. N. Adarkar (India)	P. J. J. Pinto (India)	India

Elected Director		
Ahmed Zaki Saad (Egypt)	Albert Mansour (Egypt)	Afghanistan, Egypt, Ethiopia, Iran, Iraq, Jordan, Lebanon, Pakistan, Philippines, Syria
Andre van Campenhout (Belgium)	Maurice Toussaint (Belgium)	Austria, Belgium, Republic of Korea, Luxembourg, Turkey
Pieter Lieftinck (Netherlands)	H. M. H. A. van der Valk (Netherlands)	Israel, Netherlands, Yugoslavia
Carlo Gragnani (Italy)	Costa P. Caranicas (Greece)	Greece, Indonesia, Italy
Octavio Paranagua (Brazil)	Helvecio Xavier Lopes (Brazil)	Brazil, Colombia, Dominican Republic, Haiti, Panama, Peru
Rodolfo Corominas-Segura (Argentina)	Carlos Luzzetti (Argentina)	Argentina, Bolivia, Chile, Ecuador, Paraguay, Uruguay
Takeshi Watanabe (Japan)	Tun Thin (Burma)	Burma, Ceylon, Japan, Thailand
B. B. Callaghan (Australia)	Brian Emmott Fleming (Australia)	Australia, Union of South Africa, Viet-Nam
Jorge Sol (El Salvador)	Jorge Hazera (Costa Rica)	Costa Rica, Cuba, El Salvador, Guatemala, Honduras, Mexico, Nicaragua, Venezuela

Elected Director	Alternate	Casting Votes of
Torben Friis (Denmark)	Jouko J. Voutilainen (Finland)	Denmark, Finland, Iceland, Norway, Sweden
Otmar Emminger (Federal Republic of Germany)	Wilhelm Hanemann (Federal Republic of Germany)	Federal Republic of Germany
Louis Rasminsky (Canada)	Alan B. Hockin (Canada)	Canada

NOTE: Ghana, Ireland, Saudi Arabia and Sudan were not members of the Fund at the time of the sixth regular election of Executive Directors.

ANNEX III. OFFICERS AND OFFICES
(As of 31 December 1957)

OFFICERS

Managing Director: Per Jacobsson.
Deputy Managing Director: H. Merle Cochran.
Director, Asian Department: James Samuel Raj.
Director, European Department: Gabriel Ferras.
Director, Exchange Restrictions Department: Irving S. Friedman.
General Counsel: James E. S. Fawcett.
Director, Middle Eastern Department: Anwar Ali.
Director, Research and Statistics Department: E. M. Bernstein.

Acting Director, Western Hemisphere Department: Jorge Del Canto.
Director, Office of Administration: Phillip Thorson.
Secretary: Roman L. Horne.
Treasurer: Y. C. Koo.
Chief Editor: A. G. B. Fisher.
Information Officer: Jay Reid.
Internal Auditor: A. G. P. Dewing.
Special Representative to the United Nations: Gordon Williams.
Director, European Office, Paris: J. V. Mladek.

HEADQUARTERS AND REGIONAL OFFICE

HEADQUARTERS
International Monetary Fund
1818 H Street, N.W.
Washington 25, D.C.
Cable Address: INTERFUND WASHINGTON

REGIONAL OFFICE
International Monetary Fund
European Office
67 rue de Lille,
Paris 7ᵉ, France

CHAPTER IX

THE INTERNATIONAL CIVIL AVIATION ORGANIZATION (ICAO)

As in 1956, the pending introduction of jet-propelled aircraft on the world's airways was of extreme importance to the International Civil Aviation Organization (ICAO)[1] in 1957—the first appearance in regular airline service of very large jet aircraft is scheduled for early in 1959. Much of the agency's work during the year was devoted to solving problems that must be faced before these aircraft can operate efficiently and economically.

As a result of a resolution of the ICAO's Tenth Assembly in 1956 and subsequent action by the ICAO Council, a special implementation

panel, composed of six members "of high qualifications and wide competence in aviation matters", under the chairmanship of the President of the ICAO Council, made a general survey of the world's flying regions. This panel identified the most critical problems, and then members of the panel met with high governmental offi-

[1] For further information, particularly about ICAO's functions, organization and activities prior to 1957, see previous volumes of the *Yearbook*. See also *Memorandum on ICAO*; reports of the Council to the Assembly on the activities of the organization; ICAO budget estimates; and *ICAO Bulletin*, July 1947, *et seq.*

cials in more than 20 States to see how these problems could best be solved.

Where necessary and possible, the direct help of ICAO in such areas as technical assistance and joint financing is offered.

In April 1957, Dr. Edward Warner, of the United States, retired as President of the ICAO Council, being succeeded by Walter Binaghi, of Argentina. Dr. Warner had been President since the agency began work.

During the year, ICAO's membership rose to 72 with the adherence by Ghana and Tunisia to the Convention on International Civil Aviation.

AIR NAVIGATION

One of the initial steps taken in 1957 towards international preparation for the introduction of new turbine-engined aircraft onto the world's air routes was reflected in an increase of meetings an air navigation matters. Thirteen formal Air Navigation Meetings and three sessions of the Air Navigation Commission were held. There were two Divisional Meetings, on Aerodromes/Ground Aids and Communications; one full-scale Regional Air Navigation Meeting in the South American/South Atlantic Region; two Special Regional Meetings, one a North Atlantic Fixed Services Meeting, and the other a Special Air Traffic Services Meeting in preparation for the fourth European Mediterranean Regional Air Navigation Meeting; two meetings of the Jet Operations Requirements Panel, two of the Teletypewriter Panel, one of the Panel on Visual Aids to Approach and Landing, one of the Panel on Vertical Separation of Aircraft, one of the Panel on Radiotelephony Phraseologies and one of the Airworthiness Committee.

To complete the task called for by ICAO's Assembly at its tenth session, in 1956, before the expected large-scale introduction of new aircraft in 1960, it has also been necessary to plan an unusually heavy programme of meetings on air navigation and other matters in 1958 and 1959.

Fourteen international standards and recommended practices on the technical aspects of international civil aviation were due to come into effect at the beginning of 1958 as annexes to the Convention on International Civil Aviation. Some of these standards were amended during the year to keep abreast of technological developments, amendments being made to Annex 1 (Personnel Licensing), Annex 3 (Meteorology), Annex 4 (Aeronautical Charts), Annex 6 (Operation of Aircraft), Annex 8 (Airworthiness of Aircraft).

The sixth session of the Communications Division, held in Montreal in September-October 1957, was attended by more than 100 specialists from 34 countries and four international organizations. The meeting made recommendations for substantial additions and amendments to International Standards and Recommended Practices concerning VHF radio frequencies and radio navigation systems, including specifications for secondary surveillance radar, together with additional procedures for radiotelephony operations. It also developed a large amount of guidance material to facilitate application of Annex 10 (Communications) both by states and by regional meetings.

In 1957, the Jet Operations Requirements Panel met for a second and a third time, the report of the third meeting consolidating all the work of the Panel. The conclusions reached were in the form of requirements and recommendations. They covered the subjects of aerodromes, air traffic services, meteorology and communications (including aids to navigation). The report was reviewed by the Air Navigation Commission and distributed to contracting States for information. Some of the stated requirements were recognized as tentative, in the light of present-day knowledge in a field which is subject to rapid evolution.

More than 150 representatives from 15 contracting States and three international organizations attended the second South American/South Atlantic Regional Meeting, held in São Paulo, Brazil. The Meeting made a realistic technical re-assessment of the operational requirements of the regions, taking into account the new types of turbine-propeller and turbine-jet-powered aircraft which will shortly be introduced into service. It was also concerned in expediting an increasing orderly flow of air traffic. The major task of the Meeting was to undertake a review of the Regional Plan for Aerodromes, Communications and Radio Aids, Meteorological Services, Air Traffic Services and Search and Rescue, and a review of any regional procedures necessary to supplement the world-wide procedures contained in the relevant Annexes and Procedures for Air Navigation Services.

Details of the Special North Atlantic Fixed Services Meeting are given in the following section.

JOINT FINANCING

The new Agreements with Denmark and Iceland on the joint financing of meteorological, air traffic control, communications and navigational aid services for aircraft flying across the North Atlantic, as developed by the 1956 Joint Financing Conference in Geneva, were implemented as from 1 January 1957 pending their formal coming into force.

A Special ICAO North Atlantic Fixed Services Meeting, held in Montreal in January 1957, recommended a new North Atlantic point-to-point communications system, making use of a new communications technique known as "forward propagation by ionospheric scatter" for more effective control of air traffic in this region. In June 1957, the Council approved the project, which combines three forward scatter radio stations and a new Atlantic cable to provide one direct voice and four teletype communications channels between Gander in Newfoundland, Narssarssuaq in Greenland, Reykjavik in Iceland and Prestwick/Shannon, under the terms of Article VI of the Danish and Icelandic Joint Financing Agreements and after consultation with the interested States.

The Gander installation was to be financed and operated by the Government of Canada. Half the cost of rental of the Scotland-Iceland cable was to be paid by the Government of the United Kingdom. The radio stations in Greenland and Iceland and the second half of the cost of rental of the cable were to be jointly financed through ICAO by those nations which participate in the Danish and Icelandic Agreements.

The North Atlantic Ocean Stations Agreement, under which nine floating weather stations are maintained between Europe and North America, continued in effect during 1957.

AIR TRANSPORT

The report of the Conference on Airport Charges, held in Montreal in November 1956, was reviewed by the Air Transport Committee early in 1957. On the basis of this report, which constituted the first outline of the uniform policy with respect to airport charges envisaged by ICAO Assembly Resolution A2-14, the Committee suggested to the Council the adoption of certain specific resolutions. Following a careful examination of the recommendations and conclusions of the Conference, the Council issued, for the guidance of contracting States, a statement covering the essential aspects of the economics of international airports.

In 1955, the Legal Committee asked the Council for advice on the method and extent of limitation of liability deemed appropriate for embodiment in the draft of the proposed Convention on Aerial Collisions. The Council referred the matter to the Air Transport Committee for consideration. The Committee's studies of these questions during subsequent sessions of the Council culminated, in February 1957, in a report containing the Committee's recommendations and the considerations leading up to them. The report recommended the establishment of different limits for the different types of liability of aircraft operators. It concluded that there was no evident need to determine an over-all limit on the operator's total liability under the proposed convention, as such a limit would, in application, inevitably raise complexities that would more than offset whatever advantages that might be claimed in its favour. The Council accepted this report and referred it to the Legal Committee in response to the latter's request.

As in 1955, ICAO provided the technical secretariat for the 1957 meeting of the European Civil Aviation Conference (ECAC), which met in Madrid from 25 April to 10 May. The major results of the Conference included many recommendations in the field of facilitation, involving such items as the progressive abolition of visas, the elimination of passenger manifests, etc. The Conference also devoted considerable attention to the subject of multilateral agreements of various types among its members.

The Multilateral Agreement on Commercial Rights of Non-Scheduled Air Services in Europe, developed at the first session of ECAC in December 1955 and signed in Paris on 30 April 1956, entered into force between Switzerland and Austria on 21 August 1957, three months after the date of deposit of the second instrument of ratification by Austria, in accordance with Article 6 of the Agreement. Ratification by other European States followed. As of 31 December 1957, the Agreement was in force between Austria, Denmark, France, Norway, Spain, Sweden and Switzerland. Finland deposited her instrument of ratification on 6 November 1957. The Agreement was therefore to come into force for Finland on 6 February 1958.

LEGAL QUESTIONS

During 1957, four States—Hungary, Luxembourg, Mexico and the USSR—ratified the Protocol Amending the Convention for the Unification of Certain Rules Relating to International Carriage by Air (Warsaw Convention of 1929), opened for signature at The Hague on 28 September 1955. Twenty-two more ratifications are necessary to bring the Protocol into force. The number of States party to the Convention on the International Recognition of Rights in Aircraft, opened for signature at Geneva on 19 June 1948, remained unchanged at eight at the end of 1957. With ratification by three more States (Luxembourg, Pakistan, Spain), the Convention on Damage Caused by Foreign Aircraft to Third Parties on the Surface, opened for signature at Rome on 7 October 1952, will enter into force on 4 February 1958 among the five States which have now ratified it.

Four more States—Finland, Morocco, Ireland, and Ceylon—became parties during 1957 to the International Air Services Transit Agreement, bringing the number of States which have accepted this Agreement to 48. Ten States remained parties to the International Air Transport Agreement.

At its twelfth session in Tokyo in September, the Legal Committee drew up a Draft Convention for the Unification of Certain Rules Relating to International Carriage by Air Performed by a Person Other Than the Contracting Carrier, on the basis of a text prepared by its Sub-Committee on the Hire, Charter and Interchange of Aircraft. The ICAO Council decided to circulate this draft to Governments for comment.

TECHNICAL ASSISTANCE

During 1957, the emphasis in technical assistance continued to be on the improvement of ground facilities and services required for air transport. There was clear recognition that preparation for the jet age is the most urgent problem before ICAO, and the technical assistance programme is helping to prepare the way for the operation of turbine-engined aircraft.

Assistance was given to 32 countries. Experts were sent to 19 of them. Assistance in the establishment or operation of air navigation services was given to 30 countries, either by sending experts or by granting fellowships or by both means. There were two regional projects, one in Latin America and one in the Middle East. Training programmes were maintained in 1957, and advice of various kinds was given to Governments to strengthen the various aspects of their civil aviation departments. The number of fellowships granted during the year (19) was less than in recent years because Governments showed a preference for experts and for more on-the-site training.

ICAO received $1,391,000 in 1957 as its share of the funds available under the Expanded Technical Assistance Programme of the United Nations and specialized agencies, the largest amount the agency has had since the Expanded Programme was launched. Of this amount, $129,400 came from the Contingency Fund of the Executive Chairman of the Technical Assistance Board.

PUBLICATIONS

ICAO publishes complete documentation on its work. Public information material on ICAO available in English, French and Spanish includes: *Memorandum on ICAO,* a complete summary of the aims, history and work of the organization; *Winged World,* a detailed report of the ICAO technical assistance programme; and the *ICAO Bulletin,* a precise account of the activities of the organization and information of general interest to contracting States and the aeronautical world.

BUDGET

In 1956, the tenth session of the ICAO Assembly approved a net budget of $2,987,901

(Canadian) for the calendar year 1958, as follows (in Canadian dollars):

Meetings	$ 140,001
The Secretariat	2,819,900
General Services	490,400
Equipment	37,000
Other budgetary provisions	5,600
	$3,492,901
Less miscellaneous income	505,000
Net Budget	$2,987,901

In apportioning the expenses of ICAO among member States, the Assembly takes into consideration their relative capacity to pay, relative interest in international civil aviation and war damage suffered. It follows the principle that in no case should contributions fall below a minimum or exceed a maximum percentage of the total budget. Between sessions of the Assembly, the Council, on the recommendation of its Finance Committee, fixes the amount of contribution of any member brought into the organization during that period, and the Council may increase the budget to the extent of that contribution.

The scale of contributions, by units, as fixed for the 1958 budget in 1956 by the tenth session of the Assembly is given in the Annex I below.

ANNEX I. MEMBERS AND SCALE OF CONTRIBUTIONS
(As of 31 December 1957)

Member	Units	Member	Units	Member	Units	Member	Units
Afghanistan	2	Ecuador	2	Italy*	38	Poland	25
Argentina*	21	Egypt*	6	Japan*	35	Portugal*	4
Australia*	36	El Salvador	2	Jordan	2	Spain*	20
Austria	4	Ethiopia	2	Korea, Rep. of	2	Sudan	2
Belgium*	23	Finland	7	Laos	2	Sweden*	25
Bolivia	2	France*	111	Lebanon*	2	Switzerland	20
Brazil*	29	Germany, Fed. Rep. of	68	Liberia	2	Syria	2
Burma	2	Ghana	2	Libya	2	Thailand	3
Cambodia	2	Greece	4	Luxembourg	2	Tunisia	2
Canada*	63	Guatemala	2	Mexico*	23	Turkey	9
Ceylon	2	Haiti	2	Morocco	2	Union of South	
Chile	6	Honduras	2	Netherlands*	40	Africa*	12
China	10	Iceland	2	New Zealand	7	United Kingdom*	145
Colombia	13	India*	43	Nicaragua	2	United States*	500
Cuba	6	Indonesia	11	Norway	11	Uruguay	3
Czechoslovakia	13	Iran	3	Pakistan	9	Venezuela*	11
Denmark	14	Iraq	2	Paraguay	2	Viet-Nam	2
Dominican Republic	2	Ireland*	5	Peru	2		
		Israel	4	Philippines	8	Total Units	1,508

* Members of the ICAO Council. *Council President:* Dr. Edward Warner, until 18 April 1957, when he was succeeded by Walter Binaghi.

ANNEX II. OFFICERS OF THE SECRETARIAT AND OFFICES
OFFICERS

Secretary-General: Carl Ljungberg.
Assistant Secretary-General for Air Navigation: T. S. Banes.
Assistant Secretary-General for Air Transport: E. M. Weld.

Director, Legal Bureau: P. K. Roy.
Director, Administration and Services Bureau: J. F. Berrier.
Director, Technical Assistance Bureau: E. R. Marlin.

HEADQUARTERS AND REGIONAL OFFICES

HEADQUARTERS
International Civil Aviation Organization
International Aviation Building
Montreal, Canada
   Cable Address: ICAO MONTREAL

REGIONAL OFFICES
North American and Caribbean Office*
42 Ejército Nacional
(Apartado Postal 32346)
México 7, D. F., México.
   Cable Address: ICAOREP MEXICO

Far East and Pacific Office
Sala Santitham
Rajadamnoen Avenue
Bangkok, Thailand
    Cable Address: ICAOREP BANGKOK

Middle East Office
Wadie Saad Building
Sharia Salah El Dine
Zamalek
Cairo, Egypt
    Cable Address: ICAOREP CAIRO

South American Office
Apartado 680
Lima, Peru
    Cable Address: ICAOREP LIMA

European and African Office
60 bis, avenue d'Iéna
Paris 16e, France
    Cable Address: ICAOREP PARIS

* Transferred from Montreal Headquarters to Mexico in April 1957.

CHAPTER X

THE UNIVERSAL POSTAL UNION (UPU)

The main event for the Universal Postal Union (UPU)[1] during the year 1957 was the meeting of its Fourteenth Universal Postal Congress, held in Ottawa, Canada, between 14 August and 3 October. The Congress revised the Universal Postal Convention (previously amended at Brussels in 1952[2]) which governs the functions and operations of the Union. The revised Convention is to enter into force on 1 April 1959. In amending the Convention, the Congress also set up a new permanent body within the Union, the Consultative Commission on Postal Studies, which was authorized to start work immediately (for details, see CONSULTATIVE COMMISSION ON POSTAL STUDIES below). Some changes were made too in the functions assigned to UPU's Executive and Liaison Committee (for details, see EXECUTIVE AND LIAISON COMMITTEE below).

Membership of UPU rose during 1957 to 97 countries with the admission of Ghana.

RELATIONS WITH OTHER INTERNATIONAL BODIES

UPU continued its efforts during the year to co-ordinate its activities with those of other major international organizations and to co-operate more closely with them.

Its relations with the United Nations bore primarily upon technical assistance to under-developed countries—the nomination of postal experts—and upon the international control of narcotic drugs, the transport of dangerous goods and UPU participation in the Brussels Universal and International Exhibition of 1958. In addi-

tion, the two organizations exchanged a large volume of documentation, provided the customary information to each other and arranged to be represented at meetings at which matters of common interest were discussed.

The International Civil Aviation Organization (ICAO) continued to make an effective contribution to the study of various questions concerning air-mail services, particularly with respect to variations in basic rates for conveyance by air. It did so by providing the Executive and Liaison Committee of UPU with statistical data and its views and comments on the Union's suggestions with respect to conveyance charges for air mail. It sent an observer to the meetings of the Executive and Liaison Committee and its various organs and also to the Universal Postal Congress held at Ottawa.

The International Air Transport Association (IATA) agreed, at the meeting of the IATA/UPU Contact Committee on 15 and 16 March, to maintain the regulations concerning the rounding out, up and down, of air-mail weights. An agreement was also reached between the two organizations on the new bases laid down for calculating air-mail distances. IATA also presented its views on the proposed scheme for calculating remunerations, time-table changes

[1] For further information about UPU, see *L'Union postale universelle: Sa fondation et son développement, 1874-1949; Mémoire* (Berne, Bureau international de l'Union 1950); annual reports of UPU and previous volumes of the *Yearbook*.

[2] For text of Universal Postal Convention as revised at Brussels in 1952, see *Y.U.N., 1953*, pp. 798-814.

and the proposal for remunerating air transport carriers. All these problems were also dealt with by the Air Mail Sub-Committee (Expanded).

The observer of the World Health Organization (WHO) to the Executive and Liaison Committee, in the light of the replies received from Postal Administrations to WHO's proposals, agreed that the conveyance of perishable biological materials should be limited to those exchanged between qualified and officially recognized laboratories. He expressed satisfaction, too, with the possibility of sending such materials as registered items and was prepared, in co-operation with the International Bureau of UPU, to provide detailed instructions on the packing and make-up of such items. Proposals in this connexion were submitted to the Ottawa Congress.

The Congress, to which an observer from WHO had been invited, decided upon the optional acceptance, at the general rate for letters, of perishable biological materials packed in accordance with detailed regulations and exchanged under the conditions specified above.

Representatives of the International Labour Office (ILO), WHO and the International Bureau of UPU noted the results of the inquiry into occupational diseases of postal workers; the technical services of ILO and WHO stated that they were ready, if required, to continue their co-operation with UPU in this field.

The United Nations Educational, Scientific and Cultural Organization (UNESCO) submitted proposals to its member States, which had previously been examined by UPU's Executive and Liaison Committee, with the suggestion that they be submitted to the Ottawa Congress on UNESCO's behalf. Some of them were adopted by the Congress; facilities will thereby be given to persons using the mails with regard to the forwarding of books, newspapers and other publications, from the date the new revised Universal Postal Convention enters into force (1 April 1959).

FOURTEENTH UNIVERSAL POSTAL CONGRESS

The Universal Postal Congress held in Ottawa between 14 August and 3 October 1957 was the fourteenth of its kind, the previous one meeting in Brussels in 1952. The Congress meets once every five years, each time in a different capital city. Ninety-five of the 96 countries which were UPU members at the time were represented at Ottawa. Ghana became a member on 10 October, after the Congress had ended.

About 1,300 proposals were submitted to the Congress by UPU member countries. It is not possible here to list in detail all the decisions taken and all the amendments to the Acts of the Union. Reference should, however, be made to the establishment of a new permanent body, the Consultative Commission on Postal Studies.

All UPU members are full members of this Commission. It was authorized to start work immediately, that is, before 1 April 1959, the date on which the Acts as revised and signed at the Ottawa Congress and other decisions taken at the Congress were to enter into force.

The new Consultative Commission is charged with carrying out studies and issuing advice on technical, operational and economic questions of concern to postal services. It elects a Steering Committee consisting of 20 members who choose a Chairman and three Vice-Chairmen from among themselves. The Steering Committee reports annually to UPU's Executive and Liaison Committee.

The Consultative Commission meets in plenary session on the decision of the Chairman of its Steering Committee, after agreement with the Chairman of UPU's Executive and Liaison Committee and the Director of the International Bureau of UPU.

Among the technical decisions adopted by the Congress for the purpose of improving the quality of postal services for the user are the following:

The establishment of a maximum weight of 5 kilogrammes for sending books at the tariff for printed papers, with the possibility of raising this maximum to 10 kilogrammes upon agreement between the Postal Administrations of the countries of origin and destination;

The acceptance for postal transport of perishable biological materials exchanged between officially recognized laboratories, subject to certain conditions for packing and labelling;

The conclusion of an international post office savings bank agreement;

The extension to foreign countries which agree of facilities already offered by internal postal cheque services.

The Congress approved the preparation of a

multilingual vocabulary of postal terms so that words or expressions relating to postal questions would have the same specific meaning for postal workers throughout the world.

It also adopted a humanitarian measure for the benefit of the blind; henceforth, letters for the blind will be exempt from postal charges, an exemption previously limited to literature for the blind. In both cases, the exemptions from postal charges will be extended to registration fees, advices of delivery, special delivery items, enquiries and reimbursements.

In order to bring international postal rates into line with operating costs, the Congress authorized the Postal Administrations, if they deemed it necessary, to increase basic charges for items of correspondence by 25 per cent.

The Congress further decided to raise the credit limit for UPU's ordinary expenditure, including the working expenses of the Executive and Liaison Committee and the Consultative Commission on Postal Studies, from 1,300,000 gold francs to 1,750,000 gold francs.

EXECUTIVE AND LIAISON COMMITTEE

In 1957, the Executive and Liaison Committee met at Lausanne, Switzerland, from 1 to 12 April. Its discussions bore primarily upon relations with the United Nations, the specialized agencies and other international organizations, the proposals it intended to submit on its own behalf to the Ottawa Congress, questions concerning air mail and, lastly, the work of its various sub-committees.

The constituent meeting of the new Executive and Liaison Committee, appointed by the Congress at Ottawa, was held in that city on 26 September 1957. The Congress entrusted to it a number of studies, the most important of which is perhaps the revision of the Universal Postal Convention.

As a result of the Ottawa Congress, the Executive and Liaison Committee was empowered to transmit questions for consideration by the Consultative Commission on Postal Studies on which the latter shall undertake studies and give advice. This is in addition to the other main functions of the Executive and Liaison Committee, which, as in earlier years, are: (1) to maintain close relations with the Postal Administration of UPU members, with a view to improving international postal service; (2) to

study administrative, legislative and juridical questions affecting that service, and to transmit the results of such studies to Postal Administrations; (3) to establish and maintain working relations with the United Nations, other specialized agencies and other international organizations; and (4) to control the activities of the International Bureau of UPU.

WORK OF SUB-COMMITTEES

During 1957, all the UPU Sub-Committees of the Executive and Liaison Committee met at Lausanne in conjunction with the session of the main Committee.

The Sub-Committee on the Film Library took note of the current production programme of films and slides serving as visual counterparts of certain brochures in the Postal Studies Series. In its programme of future work, the Sub-Committee included, in particular, the problem of postal mechanization considered from the point of view of development through films.

The Universal Decimal Classification Sub-Committee completed: the second reading of its draft extension of the postal section of the Universal Decimal Classification system (UDC); its study of the extract from the UDC[3] covering material affecting activities related to Postal Administrations; and the examination of analytical tables which serve to classify material by various categories. The draft extension was to be submitted to the International Federation of Documentation (IFD) for approval and review and was to be made available at the same time to Postal Administrations interested in the UDC for any proposals they might wish to make before final publication.

In pursuance of its terms of reference, the Sub-Committee on Technical Studies submitted proposals to the Executive and Liaison Committee for the establishment of a Consultative Commission on Postal Studies and drew up a list of subjects which the Committee might study. After approving the work of the Sub-Committee, the Executive and Liaison Committee decided to discontinue this body.

The Sub-Committee on Costs of Postal

---

[3] Intended as a consolidated excerpt of the many scattered references in the UDC to various postal matters, to be appended as an annex to the draft extension of the postal part proper of the UDC which the Sub-Committee had previously prepared.

Operations completed the final draft of a brochure entitled *The Calculation of Costs in Postal Administrations*. The brochure was accompanied by a draft recommendation, for eventual submission to the Ottawa Congress, that the work on costs should be continued. The study in question, after being approved by the Executive and Liaison Committee, was published in the Postal Studies Series and distributed to the Administrations.

The Sub-Committee on the Organization of the Rural Postal Service also prepared a draft brochure, on rural postal service, for publication in the Postal Studies Series. The draft was submitted to the Executive and Liaison Committee and approved. Published under the title *The Organization of the Rural Postal Service*, the study was distributed to all the Administrations. The Executive and Liaison Committee decided to discontinue this Sub-Committee.

The Sub-Committee on the Multilingual Vocabulary of Postal Terms met in order to put the finishing touches to a draft second edition of the multilingual vocabulary, which includes a selection of approximately 1,300 French words and phrases translated into different languages by various working groups. It also prepared, for submission to the Ottawa Congress, a draft recommendation and a draft resolution providing, on the one hand, for continuation of the work on the vocabulary and, on the other, for the inclusion of technical terms in the vocabulary in collaboration with the Consultative Commission on Postal Studies. After approving the Sub-Committee's work and the drafts, the Executive and Liaison Committee decided to discontinue this body.

The Air-Mail Sub-Committee (Expanded) continued to study a large number of air-mail problems, particularly those dealing with the weight of air mail, methods of calculating remuneration, the payment of remuneration to carriers, the list of postal distances by air, timetables and forms. It made its customary annual report on its work to the Executive and Liaison Committee.

As a result of the Executive and Liaison Committee's recommendation in 1956 that the study of rates for conveyance by air should be continued so as to keep the problem under review, the Sub-Committee on Variations in Basic Rates for Conveyance by Air was reconvened for the purpose of examining additional statistical data, furnished by ICAO, on the financial year of airline companies and supplementary information supplied by countries which are members of the Committee. All this information was brought together in a special fascicle, which was distributed to UPU members.

CONSULTATIVE COMMISSION ON POSTAL STUDIES

The Consultative Commission on Postal Studies held its constituent meeting on 13 September 1957, during the Ottawa Congress, and appointed 20 of its members to its Steering Executive Committee to initiate and co-ordinate the Commission's work.

The Steering Committee elected the United States as its Chairman and the Netherlands, France and the USSR as its three Vice-Chairmen, each of whom is to direct one of the three sections established. The Technical Section was to be directed by the Netherlands, the Operations Section by France, and the Economic Section by the USSR.

The programme adopted by the Steering Committee includes, in particular, the following studies:

By the Technical Section: mechanization and automation of letter sorting, mechanization of the sorting of parcels, packages, etc.; standardization of the format and colour of letter envelopes and the wording of addresses of postal items; mechanical equipment for post offices, conveyors, etc.

By the Operations Section: Functional architecture of buildings to meet the needs of the postal service; organization of work in the the postal services; conditions and methods of work in handling air mail; motorization of urban and rural delivery; health conditions, etc.

By the Economic Section: Methods of determining, and the economic basis for, rates applicable to different categories of postal items; determination of postal operating costs and output; elaboration of work standards, methods of determining the economic efficiency of the mechanization and automation of post offices.

Member countries of UPU were invited by circular letter to state whether they wished to associate themselves with the work of the Steering Committee or to propose the study of specific questions.

INTERNATIONAL BUREAU OF UPU

In the course of 1957, the International Bureau of UPU issued 217 circulars, including about 100 dealing with the execution, suspension, restoration or abolition of various services provided for by the Convention and Agreements of the Union, 75 bulletins and 86 circular letters. To the Postal Administrations, it issued 6,302,800 international reply coupons and 1,137,098 postal identity cards, and it distributed, in 11 different consignments, 2,738 kinds of postage stamps and sample cancellations, comprising 1,792 ordinary stamps of all kinds, 11 blocks or miniature sheets, 928 entires and 7 sample cancellations.

The International Bureau also issued or re-issued certain publications, including the report on the work of the Union for 1956, the list of publications of the International Bureau, the list of the heads and senior officials of Postal Administrations, the list of kilometric distances and two compendiums of statistics.

BUDGET

Expenses of the International Bureau of UPU are met in common by all UPU members. For this purpose, members are divided into seven classes, each of which contributes to the Agency's expenditures in the following proportions:

CLASS OF CONTRIBUTION		CONTRIBUTORY SHARES	
Class	Units	Gold Francs	Swiss Francs
First	25	33,442.50	47,775.00
Second	20	26,754.00	38,220.00
Third	15	20,065.50	28,665.00
Fourth	10	13,337.00	19,110.00
Fifth	5	6,688.50	9,555.00
Sixth	3	4,013.10	5,733.00
Seventh	1	1,337.70	1,911.00

(See Annex, below, for classification of UPU members for apportionment of contributions as of 31 December 1957.)

In case of a new accession to the Convention, the Government of the Swiss Confederation determines, in agreement with the Government of the member concerned, the contribution class to which it will belong.

The financial ceiling of 1,300,000 gold francs (1,857,143 Swiss francs) for the ordinary expenses of the Union is fixed by article 110, paragraph 1, of the Regulation of the Brussels Convention of 1952.

The Swiss Government supervises the expenses of the International Bureau and advances the necessary funds. These sums must be repaid by the debtor Governments as quickly as possible and, at the latest, before the end of the year in which the account is rendered. If this time limit is not met, the sums due are charged interest at the rate of 5 per cent per year, from the date of expiration of the period.

Receipts and expenditures for the year 1957 may be summarized as follows:

RECEIPTS	
Ordinary	Swiss Francs
Contributions from members	1,767,675.00
Sale of documents and other receipts	111,943.98
Extraordinary	
Sale of documents and other receipts	357,980.03
Total Receipts	2,237,599.01

EXPENDITURE	
Ordinary	
Personnel	878,615.00
Premises	102,479.85
Supplies	265,368.80
Miscellaneous	212,342.46
Total Ordinary Expenditure	1,458,806.11
Extraordinary	
Special work	77,092.20
Congress and Conferences	701,700.70
Total Extraordinary Expenditure	778,792.90
Total of Ordinary and Extraordinary Expenditure	2,237,599.01

ANNEX. MEMBERS, CLASS OF CONTRIBUTION, OFFICERS AND HEADQUARTERS
(As of 31 December 1957)

MEMBERS OF UPU AND CLASS OF CONTRIBUTION

Member	Class of Contribution	Member	Class of Contribution	Member	Class of Contribution	Member	Class of Contribution
Afghanistan	6	Australia*	1	Bolivia	6	Byelorussian	
Albania*	6	Austria*	5	Brazil	1	SSR*	5
Algeria*	3	Belgium*	3	Bulgaria*	5	Cambodia*	7
Argentina*	1	Belgian Congo*	6	Burma*	6	Canada*	1

Member	Class of Contribution	Member	Class of Contribution	Member	Class of Contribution	Member	Class of Contribution
Ceylon*	5	Honduras*	6	Nicaragua*	6	Syria*	7
Chile*	5	Hungary*	4	Norway*	4	Thailand*	6
China*	1	Iceland*	7	Pakistan*	1	Tunisia*	5
Colombia	5	India*	1	Panama	6	Turkey*	3
Costa Rica	6	Indonesia*	3	Paraguay*	6	Ukrainian	
Cuba*	6	Iran	5	Peru*	5	SSR*	3
Czechoslovakia*	3	Iraq	7	Philippines*	7	Union of South	
Denmark*	4	Ireland*	4	Poland*	3	Africa*	1
Dominican		Israel*	6	Portugal*	4	USSR*	1
Republic*	6	Italy*	1	Portuguese		United Kingdom*	1
Ecuador	6	Japan*	1	Provinces of		United Kingdom	
Egypt*	3	Jordan†	7	West Africa*	4	Overseas	
El Salvador*	6	Korea, Rep. of*	4	Portuguese		Colonies,	
Ethiopia*	6	Laos*	7	Provinces of		Protectorates	
Finland*	4	Lebanon*	7	East Africa,		and Territories	
France*	1	Liberia	7	Asia and		under Trustee-	
French Overseas		Libya†	7	Oceania*	4	ship*	3
Territories and		Luxembourg*	6	Romania*	3	United States*	1
Territories ad-		Mexico*	3	San Marino*	7	United States	
ministered as		Monaco†	7	Saudi Arabia†	7	Territories*	3
such*	3	Morocco*	4	Spain*	1	Uruguay	6
Germany,		Nepal†	6	Spanish		Vatican City*	7
Fed. Rep. of†	1	Netherlands*	3	Colonies*	7	Venezuela*	6
Ghana†	6	Netherlands		Sudan†	7	Viet-Nam*	6
Greece*	5	Antilles and		Sweden*	3	Yemen	7
Guatemala*	6	Surinam*	6	Switzerland*	3	Yugoslavia*	3
Haiti*	6	New Zealand*	1				

NOTE: The UPU official nomenclature differs from that of the United Nations.

* Members who had deposited their instruments of ratification of the Universal Postal Convention of Brussels, 1952, by 31 December 1957.

† Countries which acceded to the Convention after the Congress of Brussels, by 31 December 1957.

MEMBERS OF EXECUTIVE AND LIAISON COMMITTEE

President: United Kingdom.

Vice-Presidents: (1) Canada, (2) Union of South Africa, (3) Japan, (4) Yugoslavia.

Secretary-General: Dr. Fritz Hess (Switzerland), Director of the International Bureau.

Members: Argentina, Belgium, Canada, Chile, Federal Republic of Germany, Indonesia, Italy, Japan, Lebanon, Libya, Mexico, New Zealand, Norway, Pakistan, Poland, Turkey, Union of South Africa, United Kingdom, Venezuela, Yugoslavia.

MEMBERS OF STEERING COMMITTEE OF CONSULTATIVE COMMISSION ON POSTAL STUDIES

President: United States.

First Vice-President: USSR.

Vice-Presidents: France, Netherlands.

Members: Australia, Belgium, Bulgaria, China, Co-lombia, Czechoslovakia, Egypt, France, Federal Republic of Germany, Italy, Japan, Netherlands, Paraguay, Romania, Sweden, Switzerland, Tunisia, USSR, United Kingdom, United States.

OFFICERS OF INTERNATIONAL BUREAU OF UPU

Director: Dr. Fritz Hess (Switzerland).

Deputy Director: Fulke Radice (United Kingdom).

Senior Counsellor: F. Deprez (Switzerland).

Counsellors: E. Kern (Switzerland), M. Parra (Chile), A. Boënnec (France), A. Vuilleumier (Switzerland), M. Rahi (Egypt).

First Secretaries: W. Schlaefli (Switzerland), P. Piguet (Switzerland), M. Froidevaux (Switzerland), Z. Caha (Czechoslovakia).

HEADQUARTERS

Bureau international de l'Union postale universelle
Schosshaldenstrasse 46
Berne, Suisse

Postal Address: U.P.U., Case postale, Berne 15, Suisse

Cable Address: UPU BERNE

CHAPTER XI

THE INTERNATIONAL TELECOMMUNICATION UNION (ITU)

At the end of 1957, the International Tele-communication Union (ITU)[1] had 94 members and five associate members.

During the year, seven signatories to the International Telecommunication Convention (signed at Buenos Aires on 22 December 1952) ratified that Convention and four countries acceded to it.

ADMINISTRATIVE COUNCIL

The Administrative Council held its twelfth session from 29 April to 25 May 1957. It confirmed the programme of conferences proposed in 1956. As a result of the Council's decisions, it was arranged that the next ordinary Administrative Telegraph and Telephone Conference should open on 29 September 1958, the next ordinary Administrative Radio Conference on 1 July 1959 and the next Plenipotentiary Conference on 1 October 1959. The Council further agreed that the International Telegraph and Telephone Consultative Committee (CCITT) should hold a special meeting one week before the Administrative Telegraph and Telephone Conference, to consider tariff and operating questions. The Council also decided that the next Plenary Assembly of the International Radio Consultative Committee (CCIR), to be held in the United States, should open on 1 April 1959.

The Council paid special attention to technical assistance. It was noted that the ITU technical aid programme for 1956 had been put into effect very satisfactorily and that the 1957 programme was even more comprehensive.

The Council reviewed the question of concluding an agreement with the Council of the International Civil Aviation Organization (ICAO) on the subject of telegraph traffic to be routed over the aeronautical fixed telecommunication network. In the light of the views expressed by ICAO members, the ICAO Council felt that the conclusion of an agreement could not be recommended at the moment. The Council of the Union took note of the ICAO Council's view and recognized that the question

of an agreement could not be pursued at present. It was decided to present a comprehensive report (including a review of the working of bilateral and multilateral arrangements) to the Administrative Telegraph and Telephone Conference in 1958.

Also considered was the question of revising the basic salary scales for the ITU staff, a matter which has been on the Council's agenda for several years. In 1957, the Council decided in principle that the remuneration conditions of the ITU staff would, in due course, be brought into alignment with those of the common system of the United Nations and the other specialized agencies. For this purpose, reports were to be prepared for the Council on the effects of full assimilation, including the system of pensions and allowances, so that proposals could be submitted to the next Plenipotentiary Conference. After consulting the members and associate members of the Union, the Council adopted a proposal of the Secretary-General of ITU based on the United Nations common system, but with substantially lower salaries in the top half of the scale. His proposal involved the maintenance of the 7 per cent cost-of-living allowance granted in 1956. The Council, however, decided to withdraw this allowance. The new scales, to come into force on 1 January 1958, were to involve an additional expenditure of about 950,000 Swiss francs in 1958, and 235,000 Swiss francs in 1959 (these sums include payments by the Union into the Staff Superannuation and Benevolent Fund).

The Council again gave particular consideration to financial matters. It was noted that the original 1957 budget as drawn up in 1956 gave rise to special difficulties because of certain ex-

[1] For further information about ITU, in particular about its functions and organization, see previous volumes of the *Yearbook;* reports of ITU to the United Nations; annual and financial reports by the Secretary-General of ITU; Final Acts of the International Telecommunication and Radio Conferences, Atlantic City, 1947, and of the Plenipotentiary Conference of Buenos Aires, 1952; and the *Telecommunication Journal.*

ceptional expenses. The 1957 budget was therefore revised. The revision, carried out within the limits of the credits allocated, did not, however, affect the amount of the contributions unit (8,800 Swiss francs) for 1957. The 1958 budget was balanced by a withdrawal from the Reserve Fund, with the result that the contributory unit was kept at the same level as in previous years. The Council noted the soundness of ITU's financial position.

INTERNATIONAL CONSULTATIVE COMMITTEES

INTERNATIONAL TELEGRAPH AND TELEPHONE CONSULTATIVE COMMITTEE

The International Telegraph and Telephone Consultative Committee (CCITT), a new body, is the result of a merger of the International Telegraph Consultative Committee (CCIT) and of the International Telephone Consultative Committee (CCIF). It began work in 1957 under its Director, J. Rouvière, who was elected at this Committee's first Plenary Assembly, held in Geneva, in December 1956.

The study groups and sub-study groups decided on by that Assembly were set up early in 1957, and held several meetings in the course of the year.

In the course of these meetings, rules were drawn up for assessing charges in fully automatic international telephony. The ground was prepared for a standardization of national tones and of abnormal terminal conditions (absent subscribers, etc.). A special study was also made of the conditions governing stability in the international network.

There was considerable activity in connexion with telegraph operating and tariff questions, in preparation for the Administrative Telegraph Conference in 1958 and the special CCITT Plenary Assembly preceding that Conference. This activity was also due, to some extent, to the development of what is known as "Gentex", i.e., automatic switching in the routing of telegrams.

Work on the First Part of the Glossary of Essential Telecommunication Terms (General Terms–Telephony–Telegraphy) was completed. (The Second Part will be devoted to radio terminology.)

INTERNATIONAL RADIO CONSULTATIVE COMMITTEE

During 1957, the International Radio Consultative Committee (CCIR) held a joint meeting with representatives of CCITT to discuss means of extending the role of the International Consultative Committees in the Union's technical assistance activities.

A further joint meeting was held during the year in order to discuss the standardization of circuits for the international transmission of television programmes, for the present, in black and white—and, in the future, in colour.

In addition, the findings of the eighth Plenary Assembly (held in Warsaw in 1956) were published. Work was initiated on a second volume on ground-wave propagation curves, covering the same frequency range of 30–300 Mc/s as the first volume (published in 1956), but for greater antenna heights and distances.

INTERNATIONAL FREQUENCY REGISTRATION BOARD

The International Frequency Registration Board (IFRB) is responsible for compiling and maintaining the Master Radio Frequency Record (MRFR) and the Supplementary Information to the Record, which together form a compendium of world radio communications. The year 1957 saw the introduction, on 1 June, of the final adjustment period established (by the Agreement of the Extraordinary Administrative Radio Conference [EARC], held in Geneva in 1951) for the transfer of the remaining high frequency (short-wave) operations into their appropriate bands, so as to conform to the Table of Frequency Allocations adopted at Atlantic City in 1947. This adjustment period was scheduled to extend from 1 June 1957 to 31 March 1958. The final adjustments, the expansion of existing services and the accommodation of new services resulted in an increase in the activities of Administrations, and of the International Frequency Registration Board.[2]

The Board studied the question of assignments of radio frequencies in cases where mutual interference to the radio operations resulted. When possible, ways to eliminate such interference were recommended. However, in certain instances, in which the matter was still

[2] For further details about IFRB, see previous volumes of the *Yearbook*.

being studied by the Administrations concerned, it was still not possible to find ways or proposals to improve services.

Developments since 1954 in the use of radio frequencies and progress in the implementation of plans adopted by members of the Union have necessitated additions and changes in the frequency assignments of Administrations. This resulted in nearly 90,000 frequency assignment notices being handled during 1957. Although the number of changes in frequency usage during 1957 was not as great as the volume handled in 1956, the problems of frequency assignments and of frequency adjustments became more complicated and, in some respects, difficult for such reasons as the increased congestion in the use of the frequency spectrum resulting from expanding radio communications. In addition, there was a comparatively greater increase in the use of very high frequencies for radio services.

The Board continued to co-ordinate activities relating to the implementation and operation of plans established by ITU conferences to ensure the effectiveness of aeronautical and maritime radio-communications and the effective use of exclusive bands for the many radio services.

In preparation for the International Radio Conference, to be held during the latter half of 1959, IFRB was engaged in preparing draft frequency allocation plans for the high frequency broadcasting service. Early in 1957, the Board completed a Draft Reference Plan for Phase June Sunspot No. 70, to be used for the preparation of draft plans for the other seasons and phases of the solar cycles. Draft plans for Equinox and December 70 were completed, and draft plans for the phases of low and high solar activity were under study. The purpose of the continuing efforts is to find a technical solution to the allocation problems of high frequency broadcasting service, so as to improve the quality of the service.

Summaries of monitoring information compiled by the Board from reports received from International Frequency Monitoring Centres in different parts of the world were published for the information of Administrations and other frequency users. Hitherto, these summaries had been published quarterly. In the future, however, they are to be issued monthly in order to make the information available more quickly to the user. The more frequent publications of this information, it was considered, would enhance the value of data recorded by the International Monitoring System. The remaining problem is to fill the gaps in the global coverage of the monitoring system.

PUBLICATIONS

In 1957, the General Secretariat issued a large number of publications, generally in separate English, French and Spanish editions. Among them were:

The Financial Operating Report, 1956.
Annual Report on the Activities of the International Telecommunication Union, 1956.
General Telegraph Statistics, 1956.
General Telephone Statistics, 1956.
General Radio Statistics, 1956.
List of Coast and Ship Stations, 29th edition.
Analytical Table of Subjects Dealt With in the Documents of the Plenipotentiary Conference of ITU, Buenos Aires, 1952.
List of Aeronautical and Aircraft Stations, 26th edition.
List of Fixed Stations, 15th edition, Volumes I and II.
Radio Frequency Record, 4th edition, Volumes I, II, III, and Prefaces.
CCIF Green Book, Annexes to Volume IV, Seventeenth Plenary Assembly, Geneva, 1954.
CCIT Documents of the Eighth Plenary Assembly, Geneva, 1956.
CCITT Red Book, Volume I, First Plenary Assembly, Geneva, 1956.
CCIR Documents of the Eighth Plenary Assembly, Warsaw, 1956, Volumes I, II and III.
Summary of International Monitoring Information, Booklets 14, 15 and 16.
IFRB Technical Standards, Groups A, B, C, B.1, B.2.
International Maritime VHF Radiotelephone Conference, Final Acts, The Hague, 1957.
ITU Information Folders.

Also published was ITU's trilingual monthly *Telecommunication Journal,* which provides general information and bibliographical data about telecommunication matters.

BUDGET

The ordinary expenses of the Union, borne by all members and associate members, include the expenses pertaining to: the meetings of the Administrative Council; staff salaries; and other ordinary expenses of the General Secretariat, the International Frequency Registration Board, the international consultative committees, and the laboratories and technical installations set up by the Union.

The extraordinary expenses include all those pertaining to: plenipotentiary conferences, administrative conferences, and meetings of the international consultative committees. These are borne by the members and associate members of ITU which have agreed to participate in them. Private operating agencies and international organizations make contributions for the extraordinary expenses of the administrative conferences and the meetings of the international consultative committees in which they participate, in proportion to the number of units corresponding to the class chosen by them. The Administrative Council may, nevertheless, excuse certain international organizations from making contributions for these expenses.

The Buenos Aires Conference (in 1952) authorized the Administrative Council to approve up to 6,477,550 Swiss francs for ordinary expenses for 1957. The following revised budget for 1957 was adopted at the Council's eleventh and twelfth sessions:

Ordinary Budget	Swiss Francs
Administrative Council	189,600
General Secretariat	2,263,550
IFRB	2,068,200
CCITT	581,500
CCIR	546,200
Common Services and Miscellaneous	815,700
Total	6,464,750

Extraordinary Budget	
CCITT Study Groups	196,500
CCIR Study Groups	78,000
International Telegraph and Telephone Conference (Preliminary work)	13,000
International Administrative Radio Conference (Preliminary work)	120,000
Total	407,500

Each member or associate member of ITU chooses the class of contribution in which it wishes to be included and pays in advance its annual contributory share to the ordinary budget calculated on the basis of the budgetary provisions. The classes of contributions for the various members and associate members are listed in the Annex below. As of the end of 1957, the total number of units was 616, excluding the unit for Nepal, the contributions class of which was not known at that time. The amount of the contributions unit is 8,800 Swiss francs.

ANNEX: MEMBERSHIP, OFFICERS AND HEADQUARTERS
(As of 31 December 1957)

MEMBERS OF ITU

Member	Contribution (unit class)	Member	Contribution (unit class)	Member	Contribution (unit class)	Member	Contribution (unit class)
Afghanistan	1	Denmark	5	Hungary	1	Antilles,	
Albania	½	Dominican		Iceland	½	New Guinea	10
Argentina	25	Republic	3	India	20	New Zealand	5
Australia	20	Ecuador	1	Indonesia*	10	Nicaragua*	3
Austria	½	Egypt	5	Iran	1	Norway	5
Belgium	8	El Salvador	3	Iraq	1	Pakistan	15
Belgian Congo		Ethiopia	1	Ireland	3	Panama	3
and Territory		Finland	3	Israel	1	Paraguay*	1
of Ruanda-		France	30	Italy	20	Peru	2
Urundi	2	Group of the dif-		Japan	25	Philippines	1
Bolivia	3	ferent territor-		Jordan	1	Poland	10
Brazil*	25	ries represented		Korea, Rep. of	1	Portugal	8
Bulgaria	1	by the French		Laos	½	Portuguese	
Burma	3	Overseas Postal		Lebanon	½	Overseas	
Byelorussian SSR	3	and Telecom-		Liberia	3	Provinces	8
Cambodia	1	munication		Libya	½	Rhodesia and	
Canada	20	Agency	20	Luxembourg	½	Nyasaland,	
Ceylon	1	Germany,		Mexico	8	Fed. of	½
Chile*	3	Fed. Rep. of	20	Monaco	½	Romania	1
China	15	Ghana†	½	Morocco	1	Saudi Arabia	1
Colombia	3	Greece	3	Nepal†	‡	Spain	3
Costa Rica	3	Guatemala*	1	Netherlands,		Spanish Provinces	
Cuba	2	Haiti†	1	Surinam,		in Africa	1
Czechoslovakia	8	Honduras	2	Netherlands		Sudan, Rep. of†	1

Member	Contribution (unit class)	Member	Contribution (unit class)	Member	Contribution (unit class)	Member	Contribution (unit class)
Sweden	10	Union of South		torates, Over-		Territories of	
Switzerland	10	Africa and Ter-		seas Territories		United States	25
Syria*	1	ritory of South		and Territories		Uruguay	3
Thailand	5	West Africa	13	under Mandate		Vatican City	½
Tunisia	1	USSR	30	or Trusteeship		Venezuela	10
Turkey	5	United Kingdom	30	of the United		Viet-Nam	1
Ukrainian SSR	5	Colonies, Protec-		Kingdom	8	Yemen	1
				United States	30	Yugoslavia	1

ASSOCIATE MEMBERS OF ITU

Associate Member	Contribution (unit class)	Associate Member	Contribution (unit class)
British West Africa	½	Malaya-British Borneo Group	½
British East Africa	½	Somaliland under Italian Administration,	
Bermuda-British Caribbean Group	½	Trust Territory of	½

NOTE: The ITU official nomenclature differs from that of the United Nations. For ratifications and accessions before 1957, see previous volumes of the *Yearbook*.

* Ratified in 1957.
† Acceded in 1957.
‡ Not known as of 31 December 1957.

MEMBERS OF THE ADMINISTRATIVE COUNCIL

Chairman: Mexico.
Vice-Chairman: India.
Members: Argentina, Brazil, Canada, China, Czecho- slovakia, Egypt, France, India, Italy, Mexico, Pakistan, Spain, Switzerland, Turkey, USSR, United Kingdom, United States, Yugoslavia.

MEMBERS OF INTERNATIONAL FREQUENCY REGISTRATION BOARD (IFRB)

Chairman: John H. Gayer.
Vice-Chairman: Boris A. Iastrebov.
Members: Alfonso Hernández Catá y Galt (Cuba), Fioravanti Dellamula (Argentina), John H. Gayer (United States), John A. Gracie (United Kingdom), Boris A. Iastrebov (USSR), René Petit (France), P.S.M. Sundaram (India), Noel Hamilton Roberts (Union of South Africa), J. J. Svoboda (Czechoslovakia), T. K. Wang (China), Sidney H. Witt (Australia), Ralf Eric Page (Australia) (from 10 April 1957).

OFFICERS OF GENERAL SECRETARIAT

Secretary-General: Dr. Marco Aurelio Andrada (Argentina).

Assistant Secretaries-General: Gerald C. Gross (United States), Hugh Townshend (United Kingdom).

OFFICERS OF INTERNATIONAL CONSULTATIVE COMMITTEES

Director of CCITT: Jean Rouvière (France).
Director of CCIR: Dr. Ernst Metzler (Switzerland).

Vice-Director of the CCIR: L. W. Hayes (United Kingdom).

HEADQUARTERS

General Secretariat of the International Telecommunication Union
Palais Wilson
Geneva, Switzerland
Cable Address: BURINTERNA GENEVA.

CHAPTER XII

THE WORLD METEOROLOGICAL ORGANIZATION (WMO)

In 1957, the membership of the World Meteorological Organization (WMO)[1] rose to 97 with the admission of Albania, Chile and Ghana. Morocco and Tunisia changed their status from that of member Territories to that of member States.

INTERNATIONAL EXCHANGE OF WEATHER REPORTS

One of WMO's most essential and permanent tasks is to arrange for an international exchange of weather reports. At regular intervals, both by day and by night, observers at weather stations throughout the world make meteorological observations at exactly the same times. The methods and practices followed (and even the order in which readings are made) are based on internationally agreed decisions and are practically uniform everywhere.

Every day, about 7,800 stations, 3,000 transport and reconnaissance aircraft and 3,000 ships transmit 100,000 weather observations for the surface of the earth and 10,000 observations relating to the upper air. The volume of this information is increasing from year to year as new stations are brought into service.

The Technical Regulations containing the international rules which govern this work were adopted by WMO in 1955 and have been kept up to date. A series of handbooks and schedules of the international weather codes and lists of weather stations of the world, including the ships aboard which weather observations are made, are kept up to date by a regular and frequent service of supplements. They are used not only by meteorological services but also by airlines, shipping interests, fishing vessels, whaling companies, etc.

INTERNATIONAL GEOPHYSICAL YEAR

The International Geophysical Year (IGY), which has generally been recognized as the most important international project of its kind ever undertaken, opened on 1 July 1957, to continue until 31 December 1958. In the preparatory stages, the primary role of WMO was to co-ordinate the meteorological pro-

gramme and to ensure the collaboration of all the meteorological services of the world. The next vital task of the agency was to make arrangements for collecting and publishing the principal meteorological observations made during the IGY, for which purpose the IGY Meteorological Data Centre was established in the WMO secretariat in October 1956.

The preparatory stages included the organization of an IGY trial period, from 6 to 10 January 1957, for which meteorological services entered their observations on WMO standard forms which were then sent to the IGY Meteorological Data Centre, where a selection from them were transferred to microcards. This provided a valuable try-out of the whole machinery from which many valuable lessons were learnt.

The information to be collected and published by the Centre was at first limited to the principal meteorological observations and a selection of the radiation and ozone observations. This programme was later expanded to include observations in atmospheric chemistry and atmospherics. Assistance was also given by WMO in the auroral programme; meteorological services were invited to make auroral observations; a list of auroral stations was prepared; and standard WMO forms were drawn up and distributed.

Since the IGY began, forms have arrived at the Centre in increasing numbers; plans for filing and cataloguing them and for reproducing them on microcards were further advanced. The Microcard Corporation set up a special photographic workshop in Geneva in September 1957 for preparing the negatives of the microcards.

The need for uniform procedures in making the IGY observations and in entering them on standard forms has involved the Centre in considerable correspondence with meteorological services. This work was greatly facilitated by preparing and distributing a series of IGY

[1] For further information, particularly about the functions, organization and activities of WMO prior to 1957, see previous volumes of the *Yearbook*.

Meteorological Data Centre Reports, 10 of which were issued during 1957.

In all the IGY work, WMO maintained close liaison with the Special Committee for the IGY (CSAGI) and with the CSAGI Bureau. At its ninth session, held in 1957, the Executive Committee of WMO adopted an important resolution on the relationship between the IGY Meteorological Data Centre and the two main IGY World Data Centres in the United States and the USSR. This was to ensure that all three centres would be able to obtain complete sets of the IGY meteorological data.

TECHNICAL ASSISTANCE IN METEOROLOGY AND HYDROLOGY

WMO gave aid to 26 countries in 1957 under the United Nations Expanded Programme of Technical Assistance. Assistance ranged, as in previous years, from that of a highly technical nature to advice on the establishment and organization of national meteorological services.

Twenty-one fellowships or scholarships were granted in the field of meteorology and hydrology, and there were 23 experts in the field.

Regional projects in 1957 included:

1. An Inter-regional Seminar on Hydrologic Forecasting and the Water Balance, held in September 1957 in Belgrade, with 40 participants from 17 different countries in south-east Europe, Africa and the Middle East. Five top-level consultants from the United States and the USSR lectured at the seminar on methods currently used in their countries for forecasting river flow and for determining precipitation, evaporation and run-off, which are the main factors in the water balance.

2. The appointment of a hydrometeorologist to work with a survey team attached to the United Nations Economic Commission for Latin America on water resource problems in Latin America.

3. The appointment of a consultant to edit the material arising from the Caribbean Hurricane Seminar held in 1956.

DEVELOPMENT OF WATER RESOURCES

A report on major deficiencies in hydrologic data was prepared jointly by the secretariats of WMO and the United Nations Economic Commission for Asia and the Far East (ECAFE). This was submitted to the third ECAFE Regional Technical Conference on Water Resources Development, held in Manila from 4 to 10 December 1957. The report highlighted the inadequacy of the existing networks of hydrologic stations in the region and called attention to certain basic considerations which should be borne in mind when planning to extend the networks.

A draft report on the National Hydrologic Services of the World was prepared by WMO in consultation with the United Nations for presentation by the Secretary-General of the United Nations to the April 1958 session of the Economic and Social Council.

During 1957, there were also developments with regard to possible future activities of WMO in the field of hydrology. At present, WMO activities are confined to the common ground between meteorology and hydrology in accordance with a decision of the second WMO Congress. At its ninth session, held in 1957, the Executive Committee of WMO considered the recommendation of WMO's Panel on Water Resources Development that WMO should extend its activities to include the whole field of hydrology. The Executive Committee strongly supported the recommendation, but as the final decision on this matter could only be made by a Congress, the Secretary-General of WMO was asked, as a first step, to seek the views of the agency's members by correspondence.

METEOROLOGY AND ATOMIC ENERGY

WMO activities in the field of meteorology and atomic energy during 1957 followed the policy established by the Executive Committee in 1956 and reaffirmed in 1957. The panel of experts set up in 1956 continued its work in 1957. It was re-established by the Executive Committee, which supported the panel's views that there was a need for keeping WMO members currently informed on papers dealing with the meteorological aspects of atomic energy. A resolution requesting the co-operation of the panel in providing bibliographical information on this subject for distribution to member States was adopted by the Executive Committee.

In another resolution adopted at its ninth session, the Executive Committee emphasized the importance of close international collaboration in this field. It directed the Secretary-General of WMO, assisted as required by the

Panel of Experts on Atomic Energy, to approach the International Atomic Energy Agency (IAEA) in order to negotiate an agreement and to invite IAEA to assist WMO and its members in matters of mutual interest.

WMO participated in the meetings of the United Nations Scientific Committee on the Effects of Atomic Radiation. At the request of this Committee, it gave advice on suitable standards applicable to the collection of monthly precipitation samples for the measurement of radioactivity.

The possibility of using radioactive tracers in meteorology was further studied. It was suggested that, for various technical reasons, it would be premature to begin planning their use at the present stage for meteorological purposes. Several attempts are, however, being made to derive interesting results about the general circulation of the atmosphere from observations of radioactivity already present in the atmosphere.

Progress was made by the panel in preparing a WMO technical note on the application of meteorology to the siting and operation of atomic energy reactor plants.

REGIONAL NETWORK CHARTS

Complete sets of network charts of surface and upper-air observation stations were prepared and issued for South America, Europe and for North and Central America. Charts for the southern part of Asia were distributed to WMO members of that area for completion. Charts for Africa, modified as decided by the Regional Association for Africa, were distributed to all WMO members.

INTERNATIONAL CLOUD ATLAS

The following volumes of the *International Cloud Atlas*[2] were published at the beginning of 1957: (*a*) the first volume of the *Complete Atlas* (text), English and French versions; (*b*) *Abridged Atlas*, French version (the English version was available in 1956); (*c*) *Cloud Album for Observers in Aircraft* (English and French versions).

The publication of these volumes completed one of the most important publications ever undertaken by WMO. The other parts were completed in 1956.

The demand for most parts of the *Atlas* greatly exceeded previous indications of require-ments. A reprint of the bare plates of the *Album* was made in the third quarter of 1957 to cover orders received; by the end of 1957 the English versions of the *Abridged Atlas* and the *Album* were exhausted.

Several requests were received for reproduction of cloud photographs in handbooks, for use in television programmes, at exhibitions, etc.

CLIMATIC ATLASES

The Working Group on Climatic Atlases, established by the Executive Committee, held its second session in Centerton, New Jersey (United States) in January 1957. Its task was to prepare definite proposals for the specifications of requirements to be met by national, sub-regional and regional climatic atlases and of guidance material on how these requirements can be met.

The recommendations of the Working Group were considered at the second session of the Commission for Climatology, which was held immediately after the Working Group's meeting. They were subsequently approved at the Executive Committee's ninth session.

The detailed WMO specifications will enable WMO members and regional Associations of WMO to prepare national and regional atlases. Such an atlas is under preparation for Africa and working groups have started on a study of this problem in Europe and South America.

Geographical societies and commercial publishers are being informed of the WMO specifications to promote uniformity in the preparation of all climatic maps.

ARID ZONE AND HUMID TROPICS RESEARCH

Throughout 1957, WMO continued its collaboration with the United Nations Educational, Scientific and Cultural Organization (UNESCO) in the field of arid zone and humid tropics research.

The Panel of Meteorological Experts on Arid Zone Research, established by resolution 8 (EC-VIII) of WMO's Executive Committee has studied: (*a*) climatological observational requirements in arid zones; and (*b*) the evolution and trends in recent years of the arid and semi-arid areas from a climatic viewpoint.

[2] For a detailed description of this publication, *see Y.U.N., 1956*, p. 478.

WMO participated in the first session of the UNESCO Advisory Committee on Humid Tropics Research, held in Manaus, Brazil, in July 1957. One of the recommendations made at this meeting was that WMO's attention be drawn to the great and urgent interest of the Committee in having a special study made of rainfall and run-off, and their correlation, in humid regions, and in establishing a method of long-range forecasts of droughts and floods. It also recommended that networks of meteorological stations, particularly in mountainous and forested areas, be augmented and that a survey be made of available literature on bioclimatology, with particular reference to the effects of climatic extremes of high temperature and high humidity on man and animals.

In accordance with resolution 29 (II-RA III) of the WMO Regional Association for South America, a regional working group to promote and co-ordinate the activities of WMO member countries in arid zone research was established.

METEOROLOGICAL SERVICE FOR JET AVIATION

In view of the forthcoming general introduction of jet aircraft on international commercial airlines, the Executive Committee decided at its ninth session to set up a panel of experts to study the new meteorological problems involved and evaluate the present degree of precision of the instruments and systems of weather-forecasting. The panel was to present its first report in the early part of 1958 at the Executive Committee's tenth session. The Executive Committee also decided to establish a special unit within the WMO Secretariat in Geneva to keep the required meteorological installations (observational networks, telecommunications, etc.) and their state of implementation under constant review.

METEOROLOGICAL SERVICE FOR FISHERIES

Also during its ninth session, the Executive Committee called the attention of WMO members to the need for special efforts to meet the meteorological needs of fishermen, in view of the valuable experience obtained in certain countries. The following paragraphs explain some of the meteorological needs of the fisheries industry.

When fishing operations are to be undertaken in new areas, information is required on the prevailing average meteorological conditions from one month to the next and their variability.

Recent marked changes in the reappearance and abundance of various species of sea life in different seas of the world appear to be linked with meteorological factors, including climatic tendencies.

Weather forecasts and climatic data are important factors in the preparation and carrying out of fishing operations, in the use of fishing equipment and in the stocking of fish.

Fishing is carried out mainly from small boats and in the sea areas where storms are the most frequent.

At the present time, there are a large number of people and concerns engaged in sea fishing, who may need meteorological and climatic data even more than the operators of merchant fleets.

TIDAL WAVE INVESTIGATIONS AND WARNINGS

As tidal waves caused by underwater earth tremors, tropical storms and other geophysical phenomena may cause enormous destruction and loss of life in coastal areas, the Executive Committee decided at its ninth session that WMO should initiate an international programme for the study of tidal waves with a view to developing international warning services on the formation and movement of such waves.

Following on the Executive Committee's directive on this matter, an enquiry was begun among WMO members, and the collaboration of the International Union of Geodesy and Geophysics has been sought.

TECHNICAL METEOROLOGICAL ACTIVITIES

Four Technical Commissions of WMO held their second sessions in 1957. A brief summary of their work at these meetings is given below.

COMMISSION FOR CLIMATOLOGY

In connexion with the exchange of past weather data, the Commission for Climatology stressed the need for setting up and maintaining a single national unit for the collection, cataloguing and dissemination of reliable and useful observational weather data. The study of this question was entrusted to a working group. The existing arrangements for broadcasting certain monthly mean values of climatic elements in the form of CLIMAT messages were reviewed. Present Technical Regulations in climatology were examined, and the preparation of an international guide to climatological practices recommended. Eight working groups were established to deal with specific problems up to the Commission's third session.

COMMISSION FOR AEROLOGY

The Commision for Aerology examined the problem of artificial precipitation and, in view of rapid developments in this feld, considered that the WMO Technical Note issued in 1955 on the subject should be revised. This task was entrusted to working group. Also considered was a draft monograph on the jet stream; it was recommended that this monograph be published as soon as possible. The terms "jet stream" and "tropopause" were given new scientific definitions. Also examined were the setting up of networks to locate "atmospherics" (electric discharges in the atmosphere) and the techniques used in this field. The working group studying this subject was re-established. The Commission further recommended that responsibility for international ozone observations be partly transferred from the International Union of Geodesy and Geophysics to WMO. A working group was established to examine current experimental methods of long-range weather forecasting. The publication of a monograph on mountain waves was recommended.

COMMISSION FOR INSTRUMENTS AND METHODS OF OBSERVATION

Minimum acceptable standards of accuracy for weather observations for inclusion in the WMO Technical Regulations were recommended by this Commission. It was considered that information on hydro-meteorological instruments should be included in the *Guide to International Meteorological Instrument and Observing Practice,* and a working group set up to draft a chapter for inclusion in this *Guide.* In view of the desirability of having a common international standard for the preparation of international precipitation charts, it was recommended that WMO adopt an interim international reference precipitation gauge. A working group was set up to study the results of international comparisons of precipitation gauges. Another working group was established to study automatic weather stations for recording and transmitting meteorological data. The Commission also examined a new measure of the optical state of the atmosphere and the present state of hydrometrical, evaporation, radiation and upper-air measurements.

COMMISSION FOR BIBLIOGRAPHY AND PUBLICATIONS

The Commission for Bibliography and Publications made several recommendations which were submitted by correspondence to the WMO members not represented at the session, the attendance at which was limited. One of the recommendations was that all meteorological services should adopt the system of transliteration of cyrillic characters introduced by the International Standardization Organization. The publication of a provisional world meteorological bibliography was also recommended. The Commission further dealt with the meteorological section of the Universal Decimal Classification system. It also examined a draft meteorological lexicon and polyglot vocabulary. Prepared by a working group, this draft vocabulary included definitions of meteorological terms and equivalents of these terms in the four official languages of WMO. It was to be submitted to the Executive Committee as soon as possible.

DEVELOPMENTS IN OTHER FIELDS

AERONAUTICAL METEOROLOGY

WMO continued its close collaboration in the field of aeronautical meteorology with the International Civil Aviation Organization (ICAO), in accordance with the working arrangements between the two agencies approved in 1954. Chapter 12 of the Technical Regulations of WMO, which deals with aeronautical meteorology, was kept up to date.

To meet the desire of airline operators to participate directly in the action taken to ensure the security, regularity, efficiency and economy of air transport and, thus, to complement the services provided by national governmental exchanges, a new concept known as "operational control" was being developed.

WMO collaborated with ICAO on a study of the important meteorological factors involved.

The problem of weather observations from aircraft in flight was also kept under review.

MARITIME METEOROLOGY

Most of the meteorological information obtained from sea areas is provided by voluntary observers aboard merchant ships under a world-wide plan of WMO. Ships are supplied with instruments, and they report regularly by radio to the nearest coastal station. In 1957, there were about 3,000 such ships. A number of different codes were developed to facilitate the reporting of these observations. For the duration of the IGY, a special scheme was adopted to obtain weather information from areas where observations are sparse.

Notes on the Problem of Cargo Ventilation was published in 1957 as WMO Technical Note 17.

SYNOPTIC METEOROLOGY

The density of meteorological observing networks and the frequency of observations were studied by a working group which met in De Bilt, Netherlands, in March 1957. The working group established criteria for the distribution of stations and the definition of a basic network. A *Guide of Synoptic Meteorological Practices* was prepared for submission to the Commission's second session, in 1958, and the codes used for the transmission of meteorological information were reviewed.

METEOROLOGICAL TELECOMMUNICATIONS

Owing to the increasing demand for a wider and faster exchange of meteorological data, telecommunications have become progressively more and more important to meteorological services. Collaboration with the International Telecommunication Union increased in 1957. The Working Group on Telecommunications of the Commission for Synoptic Meteorology met in October 1957 to deal with various technical problems. It stressed the importance of handling these problems more actively than in the past.

REGIONAL ACTIVITIES

Regional Association I (for Africa). This Association held its second session in Las Palmas, Canary Islands, in January 1957. It defined a recommended basic network of meteorological observation including the possibility of the establishment of additional observations. The Association approved an absolute standard barometer for the region, that is, a standard reference instrument with which all instruments in the region, particularly national standard instruments, are to be compared. The Association also drew up plans for a network of meteorological ground radar stations, to be set up in 1958. Also examined were several problems relating to tropical meteorology, solar radiation observations, agrometeorology, hydrology and telecommunications in the region. Work on the climatic atlas for Africa continued in 1957; several maps have already been issued.

Regional Association II (for Asia). Progress was achieved in the comparison of standard barometers of various countries in the region. Charts of the networks of the meteorological observations in Southern Asia, distributed by the WMO secretariat, were considered by the members concerned so as to enable the secretariat to bring them up to date.

Regional Association III (for South America). This Association met for its second session in Caracas, Venezuela, in December 1957. By arrangement with ICAO, the meeting was held shortly after the South American/South Atlantic Regional Meeting of ICAO, so that the ICAO recommendations on meteorology could be considered promptly. The decisions of the Association dealt with: the definition of a new basic network of observations and the elimination of deficiencies; regional meteorological telecommunications; maritime meteorology problems; climatology and hydrology; the need to intensify training of meteorological personnel; co-operation among meteorological services with regard to agriculture and the study of tropical agriculture.

Regional Association IV (North and Central America). This Association dealt with the establishment of ozone and solar radiation stations, Arctic observation stations and meteorological observations by rockets. Meteorological telecommunications in the Caribbean area were reviewed, and hurricane and tornado research continued.

Regional Association V (for the South-West Pacific). Activities in this region during 1957 dealt with arid zone research, meteorological telecommunications, barometer, comparisons and the establishment of new upper-air observation stations on islands.

Regional Association VI (for Europe). On 1 June 1957, the meteorological teleprinter networks of Western Europe were connected with those of Central and Eastern Europe. The Working Group on Telecommunications of the European Region and the Working Group on Climatic Atlases of the Region met during the year.

BUDGET

The financial year 1957 was the second year of WMO's second financial period (1 January 1956-31 December 1959). A maximum expenditure of $1.7 million was set for this period by the Second World Meteorological Congress. The 1957 budget amounted to $438,401. This figure included the original budget of $425,013 and supplementary estimates for $13,388. A budget of $462,751 for 1958 was adopted by the WMO Executive Committee in October 1957 as follows (in United States dollars):

REVENUE	
Contributions	$434,929
Sale of publications	12,500
Advertising in *WMO Bulletin*	1,000
Per General Fund	14,322
Total	$462,751

EXPENDITURE	
Meetings	$ 59,080
Personal services	309,851
General services	43,225
Regular programme	44,035
Other budgetary provisions	6,560
Total	$462,751

At the same time, the Executive Committee decided to submit to WMO member States and Territories supplementary estimates for the second financial period for an amount of $70,008. Of this, $19,336 is intended to supplement the 1958 budget and $50,672 is intended for the 1959 budget. The consultations with members had not yet been concluded by 31 December 1957.

The proportional scale of contributions for 1958 is to be found in the Annex below.

ANNEX. MEMBERS, CONTRIBUTION UNITS, OFFICERS AND HEADQUARTERS

(As of 31 December 1957; contribution units as set for 1958)

MEMBERS OF WMO

STATES

State	Contribution Units	State	Contribution Units	State	Contribution Units	State	Contribution Units
Afghanistan	2	Dominican		Israel	5	Romania	8
Albania	2	Republic	2	Italy	28	Spain	16
Argentina	22	Ecuador	2	Japan	29	Sudan	4
Australia	23	Egypt	12	Jordan	2	Sweden	19
Austria	8	El Salvador	2	Korea, Rep. of	2	Switzerland	18
Belgium	17	Ethiopia	3	Laos	1	Syria	3
Bolivia	5	Finland	8	Lebanon	2	Thailand	6
Brazil	22	France	46	Libya	1	Tunisia	3
Bulgaria	6	Germany,		Luxembourg	2	Turkey	13
Burma	5	Fed. Rep. of	48	Mexico	13	Ukrainian SSR	17
Byelorussian SSR	8	Ghana	3	Morocco	7	Union of South	
Cambodia	2	Greece	5	Netherlands	17	Africa	17
Canada	27	Guatemala	1	New Zealand	10	USSR	68
Ceylon	5	Haiti	2	Norway	9	United Kingdom	64
Chile	8	Hungary	6	Pakistan	14	United States	171
China	32	Iceland	2	Paraguay	2	Uruguay	8
Cuba	5	India	32	Peru	8	Venezuela	7
Czechoslovakia	10	Indonesia	13	Philippines	10	Viet-Nam	3
Denmark	11	Iraq	3	Poland	13	Yugoslavia	8
		Ireland	6	Portugal	11		

TERRITORIES

Territory	Contribution Units	Territory	Contribution Units	Territory	Contribution Units	Territory	Contribution Units
Belgian Congo	9	Borneo Territories	8	French Polynesia	1	Netherlands New Guinea	1
Bermuda	1	British West African Territories	4	French Somaliland	1	New Caledonia	1
British Caribbean Territories	4	Rhodesia and Nyasaland, Fed. of	6	French Togoland	1	Portuguese East Africa	4
British East African Territories and Indian Ocean Islands	7	French Cameroons	2	French West Africa	7	Portuguese West Africa	2
British Malaya-		French Equatorial Africa	4	Hong Kong	2	Spanish Territories of Guinea	1
				Madagascar	3	Surinam	1
				Netherlands Antilles	1		

NOTE: The WMO official nomenclature differs in some cases from that of the United Nations.

MEMBERS OF THE EXECUTIVE COMMITTEE

A. Viaut   A. Nyberg   M. F. Taha   A. Thomson

M. A. F. Barnett   F. W. Reichelderfer   J. Ravet   C. Del Rosario

H. Amorim Ferreira   A. A. Solotoukhine   S. Basu   J. Lugeon

L. de Azcárraga   Sir Graham Sutton   J. L. Maldonado

OFFICIALS OF WMO

President: A. Viaut.   *Deputy Secretary-General:* J. R. Rivet.
First Vice-President: M. A. F. Barnett.   *Chief of Technical Division:* K. Langlo.
Second Vice-President: H. Amorim Ferreira.   *Chief of Administrative Division:* J. Rubiato.
Secretary-General: D. A. Davies.

PRESIDENTS OF REGIONAL ASSOCIATIONS AND TECHNICAL COMMISSIONS

REGIONAL ASSOCIATIONS		TECHNICAL COMMISSIONS	
I. Africa	J. Ravet	Aerology	R. C. Sutcliffe
II. Asia	S. Basu	Aeronautical Meteorology	A. H. Nagle
III. South America	J. L. Maldonado	Agricultural Meteorology	J. J. Burgos
IV. North and Central		Bibliography and Publications	M. Mézin (acting)
America	A. Thomson	Climatology	R. G. Veryard
V. South-West Pacific	C. Del Rosario	Instruments and Methods	
VI. Europe	A. Nyberg	of Observation	A. Perlat
		Maritime Meteorology	H. Thomsen
		Synoptic Meteorology	W. Bleeker

HEADQUARTERS

World Meteorological Organization
Avenue de la Paix
Campagne Rigot
Geneva, Switzerland
Cable Address: METEOMOND GENEVE

CHAPTER XIII

THE INTERNATIONAL TRADE ORGANIZATION AND THE GENERAL AGREEMENT ON TARIFFS AND TRADE

THE INTERNATIONAL TRADE ORGANIZATION (ITO)
(Not yet established)

The United Nations Conference on Trade and Employment, held in Havana from 21 November 1947, to 24 March 1948, drew up a Charter, known as the Havana Charter, for an International Trade Organization (ITO)[1] and established an Interim Commission for the International Trade Organization (ICITO).

The main task of the Interim Commission was to prepare for the first session of ITO, including a plan of work for the first year of the proposed organization. This task, so far as events could be foreseen, was completed in 1949. Since that time, the secretariat of ICITO has been occupied with the performance of duties for the Contracting Parties to the General Agreement on Tariffs and Trade (GATT).

As a result of the lack of acceptances of the Havana Charter, it became evident that the establishment of ITO would be indefinitely postponed. In view of the decision of the Contracting Parties to GATT to provide for the establishment of an organization to administer GATT, there is tacit recognition that the proposal to establish ITO has been abandoned.

THE GENERAL AGREEMENT ON TARIFFS AND TRADE (GATT)

While the Charter for ITO was in course of preparation, the members of the Preparatory Committee decided to proceed forthwith with tariff negotiations among themselves, and also held discussions leading to the formulation of the General Agreement on Tariffs and Trade (GATT).[2] On 30 October 1947, the 23 participating countries signed a Final Act which authenticated the text of GATT.

GATT is an international contract which contains provisions to protect the tariff concessions resulting from the 1947 and subsequent tariff conferences. These concessions are incorporated in the schedules of GATT. The agreement also contains a set of rules to govern the commercial relations of the Contracting Parties. It provides that representatives of the Contracting Parties should meet from time to time to give effect to those provisions which require joint action. Up to the end of 1957, the Contracting Parties had held twelve regular sessions. At the end of that year, there were 37 contracting parties.

As of 31 December 1957, the Contracting Parties had held four major negotiations conferences for the reduction of tariffs. As a result, tariffs are now stabilized over a very wide area of world trade. The trade of the 37 contracting parties represents over 80 per cent of the total volume of world trade.

CONSULTATIONS ON IMPORT RESTRICTIONS

In accordance with a decision of the eleventh session of the Contracting Parties, held in November 1956, a series of consultations on import restrictions took place during 1957. Contracting parties restricting imports for balance-of-payments reasons were invited to enter into consultations, under the terms of article XII:4(b) of GATT. The general purpose of these consultations was to consider whether these restrictions were being applied in ways which were least harmful to the flow of international trade or whether they could produce less injurious effects if applied in alternative ways.

The following countries entered into consultations: Australia, Austria, Brazil, Ceylon, Denmark, Finland, France, Federal Republic

[1] For further information, see previous volumes of the *Yearbook*.

[2] For a fuller description of the structure and functions of GATT, see *Y.U.N., 1953*, pp. 836-37.

of Germany, Greece, India, Italy, Japan, Netherlands, New Zealand, Norway, Pakistan, Federation of Rhodesia and Nyasaland, Sweden, Turkey, Union of South Africa, United Kingdom. These consultations were opened in June and were completed during the twelfth session of the Contracting Parties to GATT, held between 17 October and 30 November 1957. During the consultations, a number of participating countries announced that measures had been taken, or would shortly be taken, to reduce these restrictions and to minimize the discriminatory element in them.

The consultations themselves were the first full-scale discussions of the nature and effects of import restrictions since a review undertaken in 1951. They constituted one of the most important GATT activities of 1957 and were of considerable significance both for international trade co-operation and for the future operation of the General Agreement. They were of mutual benefit to all contracting parties concerned, and were expected to influence the commercial policies of those contracting parties still applying restrictions.

TWELFTH SESSION OF THE CONTRACTING PARTIES

The twelfth session of the Contracting Parties to GATT was held at Geneva from 17 October to 30 November 1957. Main developments included the following:

(1) The most important task undertaken was the consideration of the Treaty establishing the European Economic Community (EEC). This Treaty, known as the "Rome Treaty", was signed on 25 March 1957 by Belgium, France, the Federal Republic of Germany, Luxembourg, the Netherlands and Italy and was due to enter into force on 1 January 1958. (The Treaty provides for the creation, at the end of a transitional period of 12 to 15 years, of a single customs territory among the six countries. This implies the elimination of customs duties between the six member States and the creation of a common customs tariff. The Treaty provides for the elimination of quantitative restrictions on imports between the member States; there are also special provisions regarding trade in agricultural products. Part of the Treaty deals with the association of certain overseas countries and territories with the Community.)

Following the signature of the Rome Treaty, it was submitted to the Contracting Parties for consideration in accordance with the terms of article XXIV, paragraph 7, of GATT. At this session, it was decided, at a Ministerial Meeting (28-30 October), to create a Committee on the Treaty of Rome to examine the relevant provisions of the Rome Treaty and of the General Agreement on Tariffs and Trade and to consider the most effective methods of implementing the inter-related obligations which Governments have assumed in the two instruments.

The Committee on the Treaty of Rome created four sub-groups to examine the arrangements provided for in the EEC Treaty with respect to tariffs, the use of quantitative restrictions for balance-of-payments reasons, trade in agricultural products and the association of certain overseas countries and territories with the Community. These sub-groups held extensive discussions during the twelfth session of the Contracting Parties and progress was made in clarifying the issues which might arise both during and after the transitional period.

At the end of the session, the Contracting Parties decided that the GATT Inter-sessional Committee should continue the work started at the session. Because of the importance of the issues, all of the contracting parties will be represented on the Inter-sessional Committee between the twelfth and thirteenth sessions. (Normally, this Committee is composed of about half the member countries.) The Inter-sessional Committee is scheduled to meet on 14 April 1958. The Committee made arrangements for the sub-group dealing with the association of the overseas territories to continue its work in February and March 1958.

(2) Discussions also took place on the trade aspects of the Treaty establishing the European Atomic Energy Community (EURATOM). (The EURATOM Treaty, drafted and signed in conjunction with the EEC Treaty by the same six nations party to the latter, provides for accelerated establishment of a common market with respect to materials and equipment for the production and use of nuclear energy.) Only the trade provisions were considered, and it was decided that further consideration could take place along with the provisions of the EEC Treaty.

(3) The completion of a series of consultations

with 21 countries concerning the quantitative restrictions on imports which they maintain in order to protect their foreign exchange reserves is referred to above, under the heading "Consultations on Import Restrictions".

(4) Following discussions in ministerial meetings on certain significant trends in international trade, the Contracting Parties instructed the Executive Secretary to appoint a panel of three or four non-governmental experts of international repute to examine these trends and their implications and, in particular, to assess the medium-term prospects for international trade. The panel was to hold its first meeting in February 1958, reporting to the thirteenth session of the Contracting Parties.

(5) The United States delegation reported, as at the previous two sessions, on the United States disposal programme for surplus agricultural products, under the terms of Public Law 480 and other legislation. It did so in connexion with the resolution on the disposal of surpluses of 4 March 1955 (as it dealt with: liquidation of agricultural surpluses in such a way as to avoid provoking disturbances in world markets; consultations with principal suppliers so as to achieve orderly liquidation). A number of countries, while expressing appreciation of the efforts made by the United States to solve the problem, stated that the consultation procedures had not been entirely effective.

(6) The Contracting Parties examined reports on waivers of GATT obligations granted at previous sessions, in particular from the following countries: (a) the six countries which form the European Coal and Steel Community, on developments in the last stages of the transitional period, which will end on 10 February 1958; (b) the United States, on action to restrict imports of agricultural products under Section 22 of the Agricultural Adjustment Act (as in earlier years, the Netherlands formally complained that action by the United States had impaired concessions granted by the United States to the Netherlands); the Netherlands was authorized to take equivalent action against the United States by limiting imports of wheat flour from the United States to a maximum of 60,000 tons; (c) Belgium, on action to eliminate quantitative controls on its imports, in accordance with the decision of 1955, known as the "hardcore" waiver, which permits a country whose

balance-of-payments situation has improved to such an extent that it is no longer justified in retaining quantitative controls on imports, to maintain some of these import controls on a decreasing basis and for a limited time; the Contracting Parties urged Belgium to hasten the process of eliminating the restrictions.

(7) France and Germany requested a waiver in connexion with certain provisions of the Franco-German Treaty on the Saar, which are not in conformity with article I of the General Agreement. The Contracting Parties took a decision permitting the two countries to give special tariff treatment to their trade with the Saar. The decision called for an annual report.

(8) In the sphere of customs tariffs, the following arrangements were made: (a) Finland was given authority to raise the specific duties in its Schedule by an amount necessary to compensate for the devaluation of the Finnish Mark which took place earlier in 1957. (b) Following the entry into force of the new Brazilian Customs Tariff on 14 August 1957, arrangements were made for Brazil to conduct negotiations with other contracting parties on the basis of the new tariff. The negotiations were to open at Geneva in February 1958. (c) Following the introduction of a revised Cuban Customs Tariff, interested contracting parties agreed to take account of Cuba's special problems in the negotiations which will be held in 1958. The Contracting Parties also authorized Cuba to impose limited restrictions on imports, if this should become necessary in order to forestall an abnormal flood of imports in anticipation of higher rates of duty. (d) New Zealand proposed to make certain adjustments in her tariff in order to modernize it. Where such adjustments resulted in increases of bound duties, New Zealand would be prepared to enter into negotiations for offering equivalent tariff concessions. (e) Arrangements were made for Switzerland to conduct tariff negotiations with a view to becoming a contracting party. These were to open in Geneva in May 1958. (f) The year 1957 marked the end of a period of about three years during which contracting parties agreed not to withdraw tariff concessions. Several countries therefore initiated negotiations to permit them to modify certain rates of duty which they had previously bound. These negotiations were held in part concurrently with the

twelfth session. A new period of three years during which concessions may not normally be withdrawn began on 1 January 1958. (g) Two territories which attained independence in 1957, Ghana and Malaya, became the thirty-sixth and thirty-seventh contracting parties to the General Agreement. Both countries were sponsored by the United Kingdom under a provision of GATT by which a dependent territory to which GATT has applied may automatically become a contracting party in its own right when it achieves autonomy in trade matters, if it is sponsored by the former metropolitan territory.

(10) Under article XVIII (by which a contracting party in the early stages of development may obtain authority to impose non-discriminatory protective measures to assist the establishment of new industries), Ceylon obtained authority to enable it to regulate the import of a short list of products in order to protect new domestic industries.

(11) By the end of the session, practically all complaints of breaches of GATT obligations had been settled. Three recent complaints were left over for bilateral talks and, if necessary, reference to the Inter-sessional Committee.

(12) Shortly before the opening of the session, important amendments to the Preamble and Parts II and III of the General Agreement, which had been negotiated in 1955, became effective for those countries which had accepted them. The Contracting Parties took a number of actions required by the fact of the amendments entering into force; they also recom-mended that certain other protocols and the Agreement on the Organization for Trade Co-operation be accepted and brought into force at an early date.

TRAINING PROGRAMME

During 1957, the training programme for Government officials holding fellowships granted by the United Nations Technical Assistance Administration was continued. By the end of the year, 21 officials from 17 countries had taken part in the course comprising an intensive study of GATT and active participation in the work of the GATT secretariat.

PUBLICATIONS

In 1957, the GATT secretariat published *International Trade 1956*, which presented the work of GATT against a comprehensive account of the main developments in international trade in 1955, with extensive statistical material. The Secretariat also published the *Fifth Supplement to Basic Instruments* which contained the Decisions and Resolutions and other documentation of the eleventh session of the Contracting Parties.

FINANCIAL ARRANGEMENTS

The Governments which are party to GATT participate financially in accordance with a scale of contributions which is assessed on their share of foreign trade. The scale of contributions representing the assessments for 1958 is given in Annex I below.

ANNEX I. CONTRACTING PARTIES TO GATT AND SCALE OF CONTRIBUTIONS
(As of 31 December 1957)

Contracting Party	Contributions (in U.S. dollars)	Contracting Party	Contributions (in U.S. dollars)	Contracting Party	Contributions (in U.S. dollars)
Australia	$ 10,500	France	$33,250	Norway	$4,970
Austria	4,350	Germany, Fed. Rep. of	33,330	Pakistan	2,150
Belgium	16,440	Ghana	2,150	Peru	2,150
Brazil	8,060	Greece	2,150	Rhodesia and Nyasaland, Fed. of	2,560
Burma	2,150	Haiti	2,150		
Canada	28,360	India	7,610	Sweden	10,460
Ceylon	2,150	Indonesia	4,440	Turkey	2,160
Chile	2,320	Italy	13,020	Union of South Africa	7,200
Cuba	3,540	Japan	13,270	United Kingdom	73,980
Czechoslovakia	6,310	Luxembourg	2,150	United States	81,020
Denmark	6,350	Malaya	3,340	Uruguay	2,150
Dominican Republic	2,150	Netherlands	21,770		
Finland	4,230	New Zealand	4,110	Total	$430,600
		Nicaragua	2,150		

ANNEX II. OFFICERS AND HEADQUARTERS

OFFICERS

Chairman: L. K. Jha, I.C.S. (India).
Vice-Chairmen: Fernando García-Oldini (Chile),

Heinz Standenat (Austria).
Alternate: Emmanuel Treu (Austria).

OFFICERS OF THE SECRETARIAT

Executive Secretary: Eric Wyndham White.
Deputy Executive Secretary: J. Royer.
Special Assistant, Office of Executive Secretary: F. A. Haight.
Head, Trade Intelligence Division: H. Staehle.
Head, Commodity Section of Trade Intelligence Division: G. Hortling.
Head, Country and Area Section of Trade Intelligence Division: P. Carré.
Head, Trade Policy Division: ———.

Head, General Section of Trade Policy Division: G. Maggio.
Head, Tariff Section of Trade Policy Division: F. Liebich.
Head, Quantitative Restrictions Section of Trade Policy Division: C. Shih.
Head, Library and Information Unit: R. Ford.
Head, Languages Unit: R. Glémet.
Administrative Officer: Mrs. I. Tissot.

HEADQUARTERS

GATT Secretariat
Villa le Bocage
Palais des Nations
Geneva, Switzerland
Cable Address: ICITO GENEVA

CHAPTER XIV

THE INTER-GOVERNMENTAL MARITIME CONSULTATIVE ORGANIZATION (IMCO)
(Not established as of 31 December 1957)

The United Nations Maritime Conference, called at the request of the Economic and Social Council, met in Geneva from 19 February to 6 March 1948. On the latter day, it opened for signature and acceptance the Convention on the Inter-Governmental Maritime Consultative Organization (IMCO).[1]

IMCO was to come into being when 21 States, of which seven had a total tonnage of at least one million gross tons of shipping, each, became parties to the Convention.

The purpose and functions of IMCO, as laid down in the Convention, are: (1) to provide machinery for co-operation among Governments in the field of governmental regulation and practices relating to technical matters, including those concerning safety at sea; (2) to encourage the removal of discriminatory action and of unnecessary restrictions by Governments; (3) to consider matters concerning unfair restrictive

practices by shipping concerns; (4) to consider any matters concerning shipping that might be referred to it by any organ or specialized agency of the United Nations; (5) to provide for the exchange of information among Governments on matters under consideration by the organization.

IMCO is also to provide for the drafting of conventions and agreements, to recommend these to Governments and to inter-governmental organizations and to convene such conferences as may be necessary. The organization is to function in a consultative and advisory capacity.

To make the necessary preparations for the

[1] For further information, see *Final Act and Related Documents of the United Nations Maritime Conference* (U.N.P., Sales No.: 1948.VIII.2), and the following documents which were before the Conference: E/CONF.4/1, 4. See also IMCO/PC/3, and previous volumes of the *Yearbook*.

first session of the Assembly of IMCO, the Conference established a Preparatory Committee, which will cease to exist upon resolution of the first session of that Assembly.

The following States had accepted the Convention by the end of 1957: Argentina, Australia, Belgium, Burma, Canada, Dominican Republic, Ecuador (with a declaration), Egypt, France, Haiti, Honduras, Ireland, Israel, Italy, Mexico, Netherlands, Switzerland, United Kingdom, United States.

ANNEX. MEMBERS AND OFFICERS

MEMBERS OF THE PREPARATORY COMMITTEE

Argentina	France	Norway
Australia	Greece	Sweden
Belgium	India	United Kingdom
Canada	Netherlands	United States

OFFICERS OF THE PREPARATORY COMMITTEE

Chairman: Canada.

Secretary: M. H. Higgins, Division of Transport and Communications, United Nations Secretariat, United Nations, New York.

Appendices

MEMBERSHIP OF THE UNITED NATIONS, THE INTERNATIONAL ATOMIC ENERGY AGENCY AND THE SPECIALIZED AGENCIES

(As of 31 December 1957)

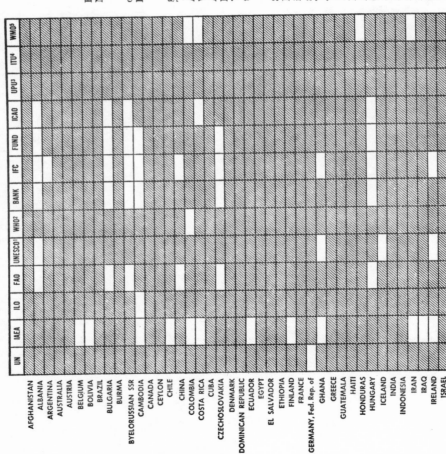

[1] UNESCO also has four associate members: British Borneo Group; British Caribbean Group; Nigeria; Sierra Leone.

[2] WHO also has three associate members: Federation of Rhodesia and Nyasaland; Nigeria; Sierra Leone.

[3] UPU membership also includes: Algeria; Belgian Congo; French Overseas Territories and Territories administered as such; Netherlands Antilles and Surinam; Portuguese Provinces of West Africa; Portuguese Provinces of East Africa, Asia and Oceania; Spanish Colonies; United Kingdom Overseas Colonies, Protectorates and Territories under Trusteeship; United States Territories.

[4] In ITU, Netherlands membership includes Surinam, Netherlands Antilles and Netherlands New Guinea; Union of South Africa's membership includes Territory of South West Africa. ITU membership also includes: Belgian Congo and Territory of Ruanda-Urundi; French Overseas Territories and Territories administered as such; Potuguese Overseas Provinces; Federation of Rhodesia and Nyasaland; Spanish Provinces in Africa; United Kingdom Colonies, Protectorates, Overseas Territories and Territories under Mandate or Trusteeship; United States Territories. In addition, ITU has five associate members: Bermuda-British Caribbean Group; British East Africa; British West Africa; Malaya-British Borneo Group; Trust Territory of Somaliland under Italian Administration.

[5] WMO membership also includes: Belgian Congo; Bermuda; British Caribbean Territories; British East African Territories and Indian Ocean Islands; British Malaya-Borneo Territories; British West African Territories; Federation of Rhodesia and Nyasaland; French Cameroons; French Equatorial Africa; French Polynesia; French Somaliland; French Togoland; French West Africa; Hong Kong; Madagascar; Netherlands Antilles; Netherlands New Guinea; New Caledonia; Portuguese East Africa; Portuguese West Africa; Spanish Guinea Territories; Surinam.

	UN	IAEA	ILO	FAO	UNESCO[1]	WHO[2]	BANK	IFC	FUND	ICAO	UPU[3]	ITU[4]	WMO[5]
ITALY													
JAPAN													
JORDAN													
KOREA, Rep. of													
LAOS													
LEBANON													
LIBERIA													
LIBYA													
LUXEMBOURG													
MALAYA, Federation of													
MEXICO													
MONACO													
MOROCCO													
NEPAL													
NETHERLANDS												4	
NEW ZEALAND													
NICARAGUA													
NORWAY													
PAKISTAN													
PANAMA													
PARAGUAY													
PERU													
PHILIPPINES													
POLAND													
PORTUGAL													
ROMANIA													
SAN MARINO													
SAUDI ARABIA													
SPAIN													
SUDAN													
SWEDEN													
SWITZERLAND													
SYRIA													
THAILAND													
TUNISIA													
TURKEY													
UKRAINIAN SSR													
UNION OF SOUTH AFRICA													
USSR												4	
UNITED KINGDOM													
UNITED STATES													
URUGUAY													
VATICAN CITY													
VENEZUELA													
VIET-NAM													
YEMEN													
YUGOSLAVIA													
TOTAL MEMBERS	82	60	79	77	79[1]	85[2]	64	53	64	72	97[3]	94[4]	97[5]

APPENDIX I

ROSTER OF THE UNITED NATIONS
(As of 31 December 1957)

MEMBER	TOTAL AREA (Square kilometres)	ESTIMATED POPULATION (IN THOUSANDS) Date	Total	DATE OF U.N. MEMBERSHIP
Afghanistan	650,000	1 July 1956	12,000	19 Nov. 1946
Albania	28,748	30 June 1956	1,421	14 Dec. 1955
Argentina	2,778,412	1 July 1957	19,858	24 Oct. 1945
Australia	7,704,159	31 Dec. 1956	9,533	1 Nov. 1945
Austria	83,849	31 Dec. 1956	6,985	14 Dec. 1955
Belgium	30,507	31 Dec. 1956	8,951	27 Dec. 1945
Bolivia	1,098,581	5 Sep. 1957	3,273	14 Nov. 1945
Brazil	8,513,844	31 Dec. 1957	61,993	24 Oct. 1945
Bulgaria	111,493	1 Dec. 1956	7,601	14 Dec. 1955
Burma	677,950	1 July 1957	20,054	19 Apr. 1948
Byelorussian SSR	207,600	1 Apr. 1956	8,000	24 Oct. 1945
Cambodia	175,000	1 July 1955	4,358	14 Dec. 1955
Canada	9,974,375	1 Sep. 1957	16,745	9 Nov. 1945
Ceylon	65,610	1 July 1956	8,929	14 Dec. 1955
Chile	741,767	30 Apr. 1957	7,093	24 Oct. 1945
China	9,796,973	31 Dec. 1956	637,190[1]	24 Oct. 1945
Colombia	1,138,355	5 July 1957	13,227	5 Nov. 1945
Costa Rica	50,900	31 Dec. 1957	1,055	2 Nov. 1945
Cuba	114,524	1 July 1957	6,410	24 Oct. 1945
Czechoslovakia	127,859	1 July 1957	13,353	24 Oct. 1945
Denmark	43,042	31 Dec. 1956	4,479	24 Oct. 1945
Dominican Republic	48,734	1 July 1957	2,698	24 Oct. 1945
Ecuador	270,670	30 June 1957	3,890	21 Dec. 1945
Egypt	1,000,000	1 July 1957	23,884	24 Oct. 1945
El Salvador	20,000	1 July 1957	2,348	24 Oct. 1945
Ethiopia	1,184,320	1956	20,000	13 Nov. 1945
Finland	337,009	31 Oct. 1957	4,347	14 Dec. 1955
France	551,208	1 July 1957	44,000	24 Oct. 1945
Ghana	237,873	1 July 1957	4,763	8 Mar. 1957
Greece	132,562	31 Dec. 1956	8,062	25 Oct. 1945
Guatemala	108,889	31 Dec. 1956	3,400	21 Nov. 1945
Haiti	27,750	1 July 1957	3,384	24 Oct. 1945
Honduras	112,088	1 July 1956	1,711	17 Dec. 1945
Hungary	93,030	30 Sep. 1957	9,831	14 Dec. 1955
Iceland	103,000	1 July 1957	164	19 Nov. 1946
India	3,288,876	1 July 1957	392,440	30 Oct. 1945
Indonesia	1,491,562	1 July 1957	85,500	2b Sep. 1950
Iran	1,630,000	1-15 Nov. 1957	18,945	24 Oct. 1945
Iraq	444,442	12 Oct.-15 Dec. 1957	6,538	21 Dec. 1945
Ireland	70,283	1 July 1957	2,885	14 Dec. 1955
Israel	20,700	1 July 1957	1,924	11 May 1949
Italy	301,226	1 July 1957	48,353	14 Dec. 1955

[1] Based on information contained in the United Nations *Demographic Yearbook, 1957.*

MEMBER	TOTAL AREA (Square kilometres)	ESTIMATED POPULATION (IN THOUSANDS) Date	Total	DATE OF U.N. MEMBERSHIP
Japan	369,766	1 July 1957	90,900	18 Dec. 1956
Jordan	96,610	31 Dec. 1956	1,500	14 Dec. 1955
Laos	237,000	6 June 1956	1,450	14 Dec. 1955
Lebanon	10,400	1 July 1957	1,525	24 Oct. 1945
Liberia	111,370	1 July 1956	1,250	2 Nov. 1945
Libya	1,759,540	1 July 1956	1,118	14 Dec. 1955
Luxembourg	2,586	31 Dec. 1956	314	24 Oct. 1945
Malaya, Federation of	131,287	17 June 1957	6,277	17 Sep. 1957
Mexico	1,969,269	1 July 1957	31,426	7 Nov. 1945
Morocco	410,805	1 July 1956	9,823	12 Nov. 1956
Nepal	140,753	15 July 1952-15 July 1954	8,432	14 Dec. 1955
Netherlands	40,893	31 Oct. 1957	11,058	10 Dec. 1945
New Zealand	267,995	30 Sep. 1957	2,244	24 Oct. 1945
Nicaragua	148,000	1 July 1957	1,331	24 Oct. 1945
Norway	323,917	1 Jan. 1957	3,478	27 Nov. 1945
Pakistan	944,824	1 July 1957	84,777	30 Sep. 1947
Panama	74,470	1 July 1957	960	13 Nov. 1945
Paraguay	406,752	1 July 1957	1,638	24 Oct. 1945
Peru	1,249,049	1 July 1957	9,923	31 Oct. 1945
Philippines	299,404	1 July 1957	22,690	24 Oct. 1945
Poland	311,730	31 Mar. 1957	28,180	24 Oct. 1945
Portugal	92,200	1 Dec. 1957	8,939	14 Dec. 1955
Romania	327,500	31 Dec. 1956	17,708	14 Dec. 1955
Saudi Arabia	1,600,000	1 Jan. 1956	6,036	24 Oct. 1945
Spain	503,486	1 July 1957	29,431	14 Dec. 1955
Sudan	2,505,823	17 Jan. 1956	10,226	12 Nov. 1956
Sweden	449,682	1 Jan. 1957	7,341	19 Nov. 1946
Syria	184,479	31 Dec. 1956	4,025	24 Oct. 1945
Thailand	514,000	1 July 1957	21,076	16 Dec. 1946
Tunisia	125,180	1 July 1957	3,800	12 Nov. 1956
Turkey	776,980	1 Oct. 1956	24,797	24 Oct. 1945
Ukrainian SSR	576,600	1 Apr. 1956	40,600	24 Oct. 1945
Union of South Africa	1,223,409	1 July 1957	14,167	7 Nov. 1945
Union of Soviet Socialist Republics	22,403,000	1 Apr. 1956	200,200	24 Oct. 1945
United Kingdom	244,016	30 June 1956	51,208	24 Oct. 1945
United States	7,827,976	1 Nov. 1957	172,327	24 Oct. 1945
Uruguay	186,926	31 Dec. 1956	2,668	18 Dec. 1945
Venezuela	912,050	31 Dec. 1957	6,224	15 Nov. 1945
Yemen	195,000	1 July 1949	4,500	30 Sep. 1947
Yugoslavia	255,804	31 Dec. 1956	18,011	24 Oct. 1945

STRUCTURE OF THE UNITED NATIONS

THE GENERAL ASSEMBLY

The General Assembly is composed of all the Members of the United Nations. (For delegations to the twelfth regular session, see APPENDIX IV.)

President, twelfth regular session: Sir Leslie Knox Munro (New Zealand).

Vice-Presidents, twelfth regular session: Ceylon, China, France, Paraguay, Spain, Tunisia, USSR, United Kingdom, United States. Spain was elected on 8 October 1957, to serve on an *ad hoc* basis as the ninth Vice-President for the duration of the twelfth regular session of the General Assembly.[1]

The Assembly has four types of committees: (1) Main Committees; (2) procedural committees; (3) standing committees; (4) subsidiary and *ad hoc* bodies.

MAIN COMMITTEES

Seven Main Committees have been established under the rules of procedure of the General Assembly, as follows:

Political and Security Committee (including the regulation of armaments) (First Committee)

Special Political Committee

Economic and Financial Committee (Second Committee)

Social, Humanitarian and Cultural Committee (Third Committee)

Trusteeship Committee (including Non-Self-Governing Territories) (Fourth Committee)

Administrative and Budgetary Committee (Fifth Committee)

Legal Committee (Sixth Committee)

In addition to these seven Main Committees, the General Assembly may constitute other committees, on which all Members have the right to be represented.

At the Assembly's twelfth session the officers of the Main Committees were as follows:

FIRST COMMITTEE

Chairman: Djalal Abdoh (Iran).
Vice-Chairman: Jayme de Barros (Brazil).
Rapporteur: Franz Matsch (Austria).

SPECIAL POLITICAL COMMITTEE

Chairman: Emilio Arenales Catalán (Guatemala).

Vice-Chairman: Ato Gabre-Meskal Kifle-Egzy (Ethiopia).
Rapporteur: Mihai Magheru (Romania).

SECOND COMMITTEE

Chairman: Jiri Nosek (Czechoslovakia).
Vice-Chairman: Toru Hagiwara (Japan).
Rapporteur: J. G. Hadwen (Canada).

THIRD COMMITTEE

Chairman: Mrs. Aase Lionaes (Norway).
Vice-Chairman: Salvador López (Philippines).
Rapporteur: Carlos Manuel Cox (Peru).

FOURTH COMMITTEE

Chairman: Thanat Khoman (Thailand).
Vice-Chairman: Aleksandar Bozovic (Yugoslavia).
Rapporteur: Mrs. Brita Skottsberg-Ahman (Sweden).

FIFTH COMMITTEE

Chairman: W. H. J. Van Wyck (Netherlands).
Vice-Chairman: Ahmed M. el-Messir (Egypt).
Rapporteur: Jaime de Pinies (Spain).

SIXTH COMMITTEE

Chairman: Santiago Pérez Pérez (Venezuela).
Vice-Chairman: Assen Georgiev (Bulgaria).
Rapporteur: Abdul Hakim Tabibi (Afghanistan).

PROCEDURAL COMMITTEES

There are two procedural committees: the General Committee and the Credentials Committee.

GENERAL COMMITTEE

The General Committee at the Assembly's twelfth session consisted of the President of the Assembly, the nine Vice-Presidents (Ceylon, China, France, Paraguay, Spain, Tunisia, USSR, United Kingdom, United States) and the Chairmen of the seven Main Committees of the Assembly.

At future Assembly sessions, the membership of the General Committee will be increased to 21, because of

[1] On 12 December 1957, at its twelfth session, the General Assembly decided to increase the number of its Vice-Presidents at future sessions to 13. It did so by resolution 1192(XII) by which the membership of the General Committee was enlarged.

the decision taken on 12 December 1957 by resolution 1192(XII) to increase the number of Vice-Presidents to 13.

CREDENTIALS COMMITTEE

The Credentials Committee consists of nine Members appointed by the Assembly on the proposal of the President. Its members at the twelfth session consisted of Burma, Canada, Iceland, Liberia, Nicaragua, Panama, USSR, United Kingdom, United States.

STANDING COMMITTEES

Two standing committees have been established by the General Assembly's rules of procedure: the Advisory Committee on Administrative and Budgetary Questions and the Committee on Contributions. Each consists of experts appointed in their individual capacities.

ADVISORY COMMITTEE ON ADMINISTRATIVE AND BUDGETARY QUESTIONS

Serving until 31 December 1957: Thanassis Aghnides (Greece), *Chairman;* Eduardo Carrizosa, (Colombia); Igor V. Chechetkin (USSR).

To serve until 31 December 1958: Carlos Blanco (Cuba); Arthur H. Clough (United Kingdom); John E. Fobes (United States).

To serve until 31 December 1959: André Ganem (France); Kadhim Khalaf (Iraq); T. J. Natarajan (India).

On 26 November 1957, the General Assembly reappointed Thanassis Aghnides and Eduardo Carrizosa for three-year terms commencing 1 January 1958 and appointed Alexey Fedorovich Sokirkin (USSR) for the same three-year period, replacing Igor V. Chechetkin (USSR).

COMMITTEE ON CONTRIBUTIONS

Serving until 31 December 1957: René Charron (France); Arthur S. Lall (India); Josué Sáenz (Mexico); G. F. Saksin (USSR).

To serve until 31 December 1958: Robert E. Merriam (United States); Jiri Nosek (Czechoslovakia); Agha Shahi (Pakistan).

To serve until 31 December 1959: Fernando A. Galvão (Brazil); A. H. M. Hillis (United Kingdom); Sidney D. Pollock (Canada).

On 13 December 1957, the General Assembly reappointed René Charron and Arthur S. Lall for three-year terms commencing 1 January 1958, and, for the same three-year period, appointed Georgy Petrovitch Arkadev (USSR) and José Pareja (Peru) to replace G. F. Saksin (USSR) and Josué Sáenz (Mexico). A. H. M. Hillis (United Kingdom) was elected on 13 December 1957 to serve for two years commencing 1 January 1958 to replace Arthur H. Clough who had resigned.

SUBSIDIARY AND AD HOC BODIES

The following subsidiary and *ad hoc* bodies were in existence or were created during 1957. Those marked † were created and those marked * were discontinued during this period.

Interim Committee of the General Assembly
Disarmament Commission
 Sub-Committee on Disarmament
United Nations Emergency Force (UNEF)
Advisory Committee on the United Nations Emergency Force
Committee on the Financing of the United Nations Emergency Force (appointed under General Assembly resolution 1089(XI))
United Nations Conciliation Commission for Palestine
United Nations Relief and Works Agency for Palestine Refugees in the Near East (UNRWA)
 UNRWA Advisory Commission
Panel for Inquiry and Conciliation
Advisory Committee on the Peaceful Uses of Atomic Energy
Scientific Committee on the Effects of Atomic Radiation
Peace Observation Commission
 Balkan Sub-Commission
Collective Measures Committee
 Panel of Military Experts
Special Committee on the Problem of Hungary†
General Assembly's Special Representative on the Hungarian Problem†
United Nations Commission for the Unification and Rehabilitation of Korea (UNCURK)
 Committee on UNCURK
United Nations Korean Reconstruction Agency (UNKRA)
 UNKRA Advisory Committee
United Nations Commission to Investigate Conditions for Free Elections in Germany
United Nations Children's Fund (UNICEF)
Office of the United Nations High Commissioner for Refugees
 United Nations Refugee Fund Executive Committee
Ad Hoc Committee on a Special Fund for Economic Development*
Preparatory Committee for the Special Fund†
Ad Hoc Commission on Prisoners of War
United Nations Advisory Council for Somaliland
United Nations Commission on Togoland under French Administration†*
United Nations Commissioner for Supervision of Elections in Togoland under French Administration†
Sub-Committee on the Revision of the Questionnaire (relating to Trust Territories)
Committee on South West Africa
Good Offices Committee on South West Africa†
Committee on Information from Non-Self-Governing Territories
 Sub-Committee on Economic Conditions†*
Advisory Committee for the United Nations Memorial Cemetery in Korea
Negotiating Committee for Extra-Budgetary Funds
United Nations Staff Pension Committee
Investments Committee
Board of Auditors
Committee on the Control and Limitation of Documentation†
Expert Committee on United Nations Public Information†

United Nations Administrative Tribunal
Committee on Applications for Review of Administrative Tribunal Judgements
International Law Commission
Committee on Arrangements for a Conference for the Purpose of Reviewing the Charter
Special Committee on Defining Aggression*
Committee on Government Replies on the Question of Defining Aggression†

INTERIM COMMITTEE OF THE GENERAL ASSEMBLY

Each Member of the United Nations has the right to be represented on the Interim Committee.
Chairman: Oscar Thorsing (Sweden).
Vice-Chairman: Tiburcio Carías, Jr. (Honduras).
Rapporteur: Mahmood Shafqat (Pakistan).
These officers were elected on 1 January 1956 but continued their terms of office through 1957 as there was no interim period between the eleventh and twelfth regular sessions of the General Assembly.

DISARMAMENT COMMISSION

The members of the Disarmament Commission for 1957 comprised the members of the Security Council and Canada, represented as follows:
Australia. *Representantive:* E. Ronald Walker. *Alternate:* Brian C. Hill.
Canada. *Representative:* R. A. MacKay. *Alternate:* M. A. Crowe.
China. *Representative:* Tingfu F. Tsiang. *Alternate:* K. W. Yu.
Colombia. *Representative:* Alfonso Araujo. *Alternate:* Alberto Zuleta Angel.
Cuba. *Representative:* Emilio Núñez Portuondo. *Alternate:* Carlos Blanco.
France. *Representative:* Jules Moch. *Alternate:* Guillaume Georges-Picot.
Iraq. *Representative:* Hashim Jawad. *Alternate:* Hadhim Khalaf.
Philippines. *Representative:* Carlos P. Romulo. *Alternate:* José D. Inglés.
Sweden. *Representative:* Gunnar V. Jarring. *Alternate:* Claes Carbonnier.
USSR. *Representative:* Arkady A. Sobolev. *Alternate:* Georgy P. Arkadev.
United Kingdom. *Representative:* Sir Pierson Dixon. *Alternate:* P. M. Crosthwaite.
United States. *Representative:* Henry Cabot Lodge. *Deputy Representatives:* James J. Wadsworth, James W. Barco.
On 19 November 1957, the General Assembly decided, by resolution 1150(XII), to enlarge the Disarmament Commission by the addition of 14 members. As a result, the Commission will consist of 25 members, plus Canada when Canada is not a member of the Security Council.
The membership of the Disarmament Commission for 1958 will be made up as follows:
Members of the Security Council: Canada, China, Colombia, France, Iraq, Japan, Panama, Sweden, USSR, United Kingdom, United States.
Appointed by the Assembly on 19 November 1957: Argentina, Australia, Belgium, Brazil, Burma,

Czechoslovakia, Egypt, India, Italy, Mexico, Norway, Poland, Tunisia, Yugoslavia.

SUB-COMMITTEE ON DISARMAMENT

The members of the Sub-Committee on Disarmament in 1957 and their representatives were:
Canada. *Representative:* David M. Johnson.
France. *Representative:* Jules Moch.
USSR. *Representative:* Valentin A. Zorin.
United Kingdom. *Representative:* Selwyn Lloyd.
United States. *Representative:* Harold E. Stassen.

UNITED NATIONS EMERGENCY FORCE (UNEF)

On 4 November 1956, the General Assembly, by resolution 998(ES-I), asked the Secretary-General for a plan for establishing, with the consent of the nations concerned, an emergency international force to secure and supervise the cessation of hostilities resulting from the penetration of Israel armed forces into Egyptian territory and the military operations conducted by France and the United Kingdom against Egyptian territory. On 5 November 1956, by resolution 1000(ES-I), the Assembly established a United Nations Command for the United Nations Emergency Force (UNEF) to secure and supervise the cessation of hostilities. It was to act in accordance with all the terms of General Assembly resolution 997(ES-I) of 2 November 1956 which, *inter alia*, called for: a cease-fire and the halting of the movement of military forces and arms into the area; the withdrawal of all forces behind the armistice lines and the observance of the armistice agreements; and, upon a cease-fire being effective, the reopening of the Suez Canal and the restoration of secure freedom of navigation.

In accordance with the Assembly's resolution 1125 (XI) of 2 February 1957, following the withdrawal of forces, UNEF was stationed on the Egyptian-Israel Armistice Demarcation Line.

On 5 November 1956, the General Assembly appointed Major-General E. L. M. Burns as the Chief of the Command.

As of 31 December 1957, the Force was composed of units voluntarily contributed by the following United Nations Member States: Brazil, Canada, Colombia, Denmark, India, Norway, Sweden and Yugoslavia. A contingent from Indonesia was withdrawn in September 1957 and a contingent from Finland in December 1957.

ADVISORY COMMITTEE ON THE UNITED NATIONS EMERGENCY FORCE

The Advisory Committee on the United Nations Emergency Force, established by the General Assembly on 7 November 1956 (by resolution 1001 (ES-I)), was to develop those aspects of the planning of the Force and its operation not already dealt with by the Assembly and not falling within the area of the direct responsibility of the Chief of the Command. It was empowered to request the convening of the Assembly and to report to the Assembly whenever matters arose which, in its opinion, were of such urgency and importance as to require Assembly consideration.
Members: Brazil, Canada, Ceylon, Colombia, India,

Norway, Pakistan, serving under the chairmanship of the Secretary-General.

COMMITTEE ON THE FINANCING OF THE UNITED NATIONS EMERGENCY FORCE
(as appointed under General Assembly resolution 1089(XI))

Members: Canada, Ceylon, Chile, El Salvador, India, Liberia, Sweden, USSR, United States.

UNITED NATIONS CONCILIATION COMMISSION FOR PALESTINE
France: Pierre Ordonneau.
Turkey: Adil Derinsu.
United States: James W. Barco.

UNITED NATIONS RELIEF AND WORKS AGENCY FOR PALESTINE REFUGEES IN THE NEAR EAST (UNRWA)
Director: Henry R. Labouisse.

UNRWA ADVISORY COMMISSION
Belgium: F. Seynaeve.
Egypt: General Salah Gohar.
France: A. M. Radenac.
Jordan: Abdel Mini'm Rifai.
Lebanon: Georges Haimari.
Syria: Asaad Talas.
Turkey: General Refet Bele.
United Kingdom: G. H. Middleton.
United States: Henry N. Howard.

SPECIAL COMMITTEE ON THE PROBLEM OF HUNGARY
Members: Australia (K. C. O. Shann, *Rapporteur*); Ceylon (R. S. S. Gunewardene); Denmark (Alsing Andersen, *Chairman*); Tunisia (Mongi Slim); Uruguay (Enrique Rodríguez Fabregat).

GENERAL ASSEMBLY'S SPECIAL REPRESENTATIVE ON THE HUNGARIAN PROBLEM
On 14 September 1957, by resolution 1133(XI), the General Assembly asked the President of its eleventh session, Prince Wan Waithayakon, as its special representative on the Hungarian question, to take such steps as he deemed appropriate to achieve the objectives of the United Nations in accordance with the General Assembly's resolutions on the Hungarian question (resolutions 1004(ES-II), of 4 November 1956; 1005(ES-II), of 9 November 1956; 1127(XI), of 21 November 1956; 1131(XI), of 12 December 1956; 1132(XI), of 10 January 1957. It also asked him to consult with the Special Committee on Hungary and to report and make recommendations to the General Assembly.

PANEL FOR INQUIRY AND CONCILIATION
The Panel, established by the General Assembly in 1949, by resolution 268 D (III), consists of qualified persons, designated by their States to serve a term of five years, who are readily available to assist the United Nations organs or States parties to a controversy in the settlement of disputes and situations by serving on commissions of inquiry or of conciliation.
The following persons have been designated to be on the panel:

Afghanistan. *Designated 7 November 1955:* Sardar Mohammed Naim, Mohammed Kabir Ludin, Dr. Najibullah, Mohammed Naorouz, Abdul Majid Zabouli.

Australia. *Designated 7 March 1955:* Sir Owen Dixon, Sir Raymond Kelly, Sir John Latham, Sir Charles Lowe.

Bolivia. *Designated 25 March 1955:* Alberto Mendoza López, Santiago Jordán Sandoval, Carlos Morales Guillén.

Brazil. *Designated 22 December 1954:* Braz Arruda, Levi Carneiro, Santiago Dantas, Linneu de Albuquerque Mello, Francisco Pontes de Miranda.

Burma. *Designated 4 June 1955:* U Lun Baw, U Myint Thein, U Ba Nyunt.

Canada. *Designated 22 September 1955:* L. M. Gouin, Norman P. Lambert, Sir Albert Walsh, R. M. Fowler, Sherwood Lett.

China. *Designated 13 July 1955:* F. T. Cheng, Hsieh Kun-Sheng, Shuhsi Hsu, Ching-Hsiung Wu.

Colombia. *Designated 28 January 1955:* Alberto Lleras Camargo, Eliseo Arango, Alberto Zuleta Angel, José Gabriel de la Vega, Antonio Rocha.

Cuba. *Designated 24 March 1955:* Miguel Angel Campa, Ernesto Dihigo, Alberto Blanco, Enrique Guiral.

Denmark. *Designated 19 March 1957:* Erik Vetli, Hans Topsoe-Jensen, Erik Andreas Abitz, Max Sorensen, Alf Ross.

Dominican Republic. *Designated 13 October 1954:* Themistocles Messina Pimentel, Tulio Franco y Franco, Carlos Sanchez y Sanchez.

Ecuador. *Designated 12 October 1954:* Carlos Salazar Flor, José Vicente Trujillo, Antonio J. Quevedo.

Egypt. *Designated 2 March 1957:* Wadih Farag, Sami Guenena, Ahmed Hassan, Abdel Khalik Hassouna.

El Salvador. *Designated 28 September 1954:* Ernesto A. Núñez, Reynaldo Galindo Pohl, Ramón González Montalvo.

Greece. *Designated 13 October 1954:* Constantin Psaroudas, Jean Spiropoulos, Pierre C. Stathatos, Michel N. Tsouderos, Pierre G. Vallindas.

Haiti. *Designated 30 October 1954:* Max H. Dorsinville, Ernest G. Chauvet, Dantes Bellegarde, Timoleon Paret.

India. *Designated 26 November 1954:* Sardar Teja Singh, Zakir Husain, Shri Kavalam Madhava Panikkar.

Israel. *Designated 3 October 1954:* Leo Kohn.

Netherlands. *Designated 19 October 1954:* Roslov Kranenburg, Maximilian Paul Leon Steenberghe, Willem Jan Mari van Eysinga.

Pakistan. *Designated 23 October 1956:* S. M. A. Faruqi, Ibrahim Khan, Mohammad Ibrahim, Muhammad Asir, Ghulam Nabi M. Memon.

Sweden. *Designated 28 September 1954:* Baron C. F. H. Hamilton.

Syria. *Designated 21 December 1954:* Adnan Atassi, Naim Antaki, Sami Midani, Salah Eddine Tarazi, Jaoudat Mufti.

United Kingdom. *Designated 9 December 1954:* Sir Hughe Montgomery Knatchbull-Hugessen, Sir Horace Seymour.

United States. *Designated 1 June 1955:* James F.
Byrnes, Roger D. Lapham, Charles H. Mahoney,
Walter Bedell Smith, Charles A. Sprague.

ADVISORY COMMITTEE ON THE PEACEFUL
USES OF ATOMIC ENERGY

Members: Brazil, Canada, France, India, USSR,
United Kingdom, United States.

SCIENTIFIC COMMITTEE ON THE EFFECTS
OF ATOMIC RADIATION

Members: Argentina, Australia, Belgium, Brazil,
Canada, Czechoslovakia, Egypt, France, India,
Japan, Mexico, Sweden, USSR, United Kingdom,
United States.

PEACE OBSERVATION COMMISSION

On 21 December 1956, the General Assembly
decided by resolution 1114(XI), to reappoint the
1956 members of the Peace Observation Commission
for the calendar years 1957 and 1958.

Members: China, Czechoslovakia, France, Honduras,
India, Iraq, Israel, New Zealand, Pakistan, Sweden,
USSR, United Kingdom, United States, Uruguay.

Officers: Enrique Rodríguez Fabregat (Uruguay),
Chairman; Sir Leslie Knox Munro (New Zealand),
Vice-Chairman; Hashim Jawad (Iraq), *Rapporteur.*

BALKAN SUB-COMMISSION

Members: Colombia, France, Pakistan, Sweden,
United States.

COLLECTIVE MEASURES COMMITTEE

Australia. *Representative:* E. Ronald Walker.
Belgium. *Representative:* Joseph Nisot.
Brazil. *Representative:* Cyro de Freitas-Valle.
Burma. *Representative:* U Thant.
Canada. *Representative:* R. A. MacKay.
Egypt. *Representative:* Omar Loutfi.
France. *Representative:* Guillaume Georges-Picot.
Mexico. *Representative:* Rafael de la Colina.
Philippines. *Representative:* Felixberto Serrano.
Turkey. *Representative:* Seyfullah Esin.
United Kingdom. *Representative:* Sir Pierson Dixon
United States. *Representative:* James J. Wadsworth.
Venezuela. *Representative:* Santiago Pérez-Pérez.
Yugoslavia. *Representative:* Dimce Belovski.

PANEL OF MILITARY EXPERTS

The experts, appointed by the Secretary-General
with the approval of the Collective Measures Committee, under the General Assembly's "Uniting for
Peace" resolution (377(V)), are to be available, on
request, to Member States wishing to obtain technical
advice on the organization, training and equipment
of elements within their national armed forces which
could be made available in accordance with national
constitutional processes, for service as a unit or units
of the United Nations upon the recommendation of
the Security Council or the Assembly.

UNITED NATIONS COMMISSION FOR THE UNIFICATION
AND REHABILITATION OF KOREA (UNCURK)

Members: Australia, Chile, Netherlands, Pakistan,
Philippines, Thailand, Turkey.

COMMITTEE OF UNCURK

Members: Australia, Philippines, Thailand, Turkey.

UNITED NATIONS KOREAN RECONSTRUCTION AGENCY
(UNKRA)

Agent-General: Lieutenant-General John B. Coulter
(United States).

On 26 November 1957, by resolution 1159(XII),
the General Assembly approved a recommendation
by the Agent-General that the Agency cease as an
operational organization on 30 June 1958.

UNKRA ADVISORY COMMITTEE

Canada: R. A. MacKay, *Chairman.*
India: Arthur S. Lall.
United Kingdom: Arthur H. Clough.
United States: Henry Cabot Lodge.
Uruguay: Enrique Rodríguez Fabregat.

UNITED NATIONS COMMISSION TO INVESTIGATE
CONDITIONS FOR FREE ELECTIONS IN GERMANY[a]

Members: Brazil, Iceland, Netherlands, Pakistan,
Poland.

UNITED NATIONS CHILDREN'S FUND (UNICEF)

UNICEF, established by the General Assembly,
also reports to the Economic and Social Council (see
below under ECONOMIC AND SOCIAL COUNCIL).

OFFICE OF THE UNITED NATIONS HIGH COMMISSIONER
FOR REFUGEES

High Commissioner: Auguste Lindt.
Deputy High Commissioner: James M. Read.
Director: Marcel Pagès.

On 26 November 1957, the General Assembly decided to continue the Office of the High Commissioner for five years beginning 1 January 1959.

UNITED NATIONS REFUGEE FUND (UNREF)
EXECUTIVE COMMITTEE

Members: Australia, Austria, Belgium, Brazil, Canada,
Colombia, Denmark, France, Federal Republic of
Germany, Greece, Iran, Israel, Italy, Netherlands,
Norway, Switzerland, Turkey, United Kingdom,
United States, Vatican City, Venezuela.

Officers:
  Fourth Session: N. Tuncel (Turkey), *Chairman;*
    J. Cappelen (Norway), *Vice-Chairman;* N.
    Currie (Australia), *Rapporteur.*
  Fifth Session: J. Cappelen (Norway), *Chairman;*
    A. Valladão (Brazil), *Vice-Chairman;* N. Currie
    (Australia), *Rapporteur.*
  Sixth (Special) Session: J. Cappelen (Norway),
    Chairman; A. Patriota (Brazil), *Vice-Chairman;*
    N. Currie (Australia), *Rapporteur.*

On 26 November 1957, by resolution 1166(XII),
the General Assembly decided that operations under
UNREF should be discontinued after 31 December
1958 except for the orderly completion of those
projects started but not completed before that date.
It also asked the Economic and Social Council to
set up, not later than its twenty-sixth session, in
mid-1958, an Executive Committee of the High

[a] Adjourned *sine die* on 5 August 1952.

Commissioner's Programme to replace the UNREF Executive Committee. This new body was to consist of representatives of between 20 and 25 Members of the United Nations or members of any of the specialized agencies, elected by the Council. Its tasks, briefly, were set forth as follows: to give directives to the High Commissioner for liquidating UNREF; to advise him, at his request, on the exercise of his functions and on the appropriateness of international aid through his office to help solve specific refugee problems unsolved or arising after 31 December 1958; to authorize him to appeal for funds for solving these problems and approve assistance projects in this regard; to give him directives on the use of an emergency fund not exceeding $500,000.

AD HOC COMMITTEE ON A SPECIAL UNITED NATIONS FUND FOR ECONOMIC DEVELOPMENT

This Committee, set up by General Assembly resolution 923(X), ceased to exist after submitting its final report to the twelfth session of the General Assembly and so completing the task assigned to it (resolution 1219(XII), of 14 December 1957).

PREPARATORY COMMITTEE FOR THE SPECIAL FUND

On 14 December 1957, by resolution 1219(XII), the General Assembly decided that a Special Fund be established as an expansion of existing technical assistance and development activities of the United Nations and the specialized agencies so as to provide systematic and sustained assistance essential for the integrated technical, economic and social development of the less developed countries. The operations of the Fund were to be directed towards enlarging the scope of United Nations technical aid programmes so as to include special projects in certain basic fields.

Looking forward to the Fund's establishment as of 1 January 1959, the Assembly set up a Preparatory Committee with the following functions: to define the basic fields for assistance which the Special Fund should encompass, and, within these fields, the types of projects eligible for assistance; to define the administrative and operational machinery to be recommended for the Fund, including any changes required in the legislation and procedures of the Expanded Technical Assistance Programme; to ascertain the extent to which Governments would be willing to contribute to the Fund. It was to undertake these tasks, taking into account the various principles laid down by the Assembly for the Special Fund and the views and suggestions put forward by Governments. The result of the Preparatory Committee's work were to be reported together with recommendations to the mid-1958 session of the Economic and Social Council, which would transmit the report with its own comments to the Assembly later in 1958 for final action.

Members of the Preparatory Committee: Canada, Chile, Denmark, Egypt, France, Ghana, India, Japan, Mexico, Netherlands, Pakistan, Peru, USSR, United Kingdom, United States, Yugoslavia.

AD HOC COMMISSION ON PRISONERS OF WAR

Members: Countess Bernadotte (Sweden); José Gustavo Guerrero (El Salvador); Judge of the International Court of Justice, *Chairman;* Aung Khine (Burma), Judge of the High Court of Burma.

UNITED NATIONS ADVISORY COUNCIL FOR SOMALILAND

Colombia: Edmundo de Holte Castello.

Egypt: Mohamed Kamal Eddine Salah (until his death on 16 April 1957), succeeded by Mohamed Hassan el-Zayyat.

Philippines: Mauro Baradi.

UNITED NATIONS COMMISSION ON TOGOLAND UNDER FRENCH ADMINISTRATION

The Commission was established by the General Assembly on 23 January 1957 (by resolution 1046 (XI)). Its purposes were to examine in the light of discussions in the Assembly's Fourth Committee, the entire situation in the Trust Territory of Togoland under French administration resulting from the practical application of a new Statute and the conditions under which the Statute is being applied, and to submit a report, with its observations and suggestions, to the Trusteeship Council for its consideration. The Commission reported to the Trusteeship Council's seventh special session in September 1957, after which it ceased to exist.

The membership of the Commission was as follows:

Canada. *Representative:* Jean-Louis Delisle.

Denmark. *Representative:* Hermod Lannung (later replaced by Lars Tillitse).

Guatemala. *Representative:* José Rolz-Bennett.

Liberia. *Representative:* Charles T. O. King, *Chairman.*

Philippines. *Representative:* Victorio D. Carpio.

Yugoslavia. *Representative:* Aleksander Bozovic.

UNITED NATIONS COMMISSIONER FOR SUPERVISION OF ELECTIONS IN TOGOLAND UNDER FRENCH ADMINISTRATION

The General Assembly, on 29 November 1957, by resolution 1182(XII), decided to elect a United Nations Commissioner to supervise the elections to the Legislative Assembly of the French-administered Trust Territory of Togoland to be held in 1958. Assisted by observers and staff appointed by the Secretary-General in consultation with him, the Commissioner was directed to report the results of the elections to the Trusteeship Council for transmission to the General Assembly's thirteenth session. On 14 December 1957, the General Assembly elected Max H. Dorsinville (Haiti) to this position.

SUB-COMMITTEE ON THE REVISION OF THE QUESTIONNAIRE (relating to Trust Territories)

El Salvador. *Representative:* Miguel Rafael Urquía.

Haiti. *Representative:* Max H. Dorsinville, *Chairman.*

India. *Representative:* Rikhi Jaipal.

Syria. *Representative:* Rafik Asha.

COMMITTEE ON SOUTH WEST AFRICA

Brazil: Donatello Grieco, *Rapporteur.*

Ethiopia: Haddis Alemayehou.
Finland: G. A. Gripenberg.
Mexico: Eduardo Espinosa y Prieto.
Pakistan: R. S. Chhatari, S. A. Karim.
Syria: Najmuddine Rifai.
Thailand: Thanat Khoman, *Chairman.*
United States: Benjamin Gerig.
Uruguay: Enrique Rodríguez Fabregat, *Vice-Chairman.*

On 13 December 1957, the General Assembly, acting on the recommendation of its Fourth Committee, approved the election of Egypt and Indonesia (to replace Syria and Thailand) and the re-election of Uruguay, each for a three-year term beginning 1 January 1958.

The membership of the Committee on South West Africa for 1958 is thus: **Brazil, Egypt, Ethiopia, Finland, Indonesia, Mexico, Pakistan, United States and Uruguay.**

GOOD OFFICES COMMITTEE ON SOUTH WEST AFRICA

On 25 October 1957, by resolution 1143(XII), the General Assembly decided to set up a three-member Good Offices Committee on South West Africa to discuss with the Government of the Union of South Africa a basis for an agreement which would continue to accord an international status to the Territory of South West Africa. The resolution named the United States and the United Kingdom to the Committee and specified that a third member be nominated by the President of the twelfth session of the Assembly. On 1 November 1957, the President nominated Brazil as the third member.

Members: Vasco T. Leitao da Cunha (Brazil), Sir Charles Noble Arden-Clarke (United Kingdom), Walter N. Walmsley (United States).

COMMITTEE ON INFORMATION FROM
NON-SELF-GOVERNING TERRITORIES

The Committee consists of United Nations Members transmitting information and an equal number of Members elected for three-year terms by the Fourth Committee on behalf of the General Assembly.

Administering Members: Australia, Belgium, France, Netherlands, New Zealand, United Kingdom, United States.

Non-Administering Members: Ceylon, China, Guatemala, India, Iraq, Peru, Venezuela.

On 13 December 1957, the Fourth Committee, acting for the Assembly, elected Brazil for a three-year period to replace Peru, whose term had expired.

The representatives serving on the Committee during 1957 were as follows:

Australia. *Representative:* John Ryan.
Belgium. (Not represented.)
Ceylon. *Representative:* A. Basnayake. *Alternate:* Y. Duraiswamy.
China. *Representative:* Liu Yu-wan. *Alternate:* Hsi-kun Yang.
France. *Representative:* R. Bargues. *Alternate:* Michel de Camaret.
Guatemala. *Representative:* Emilio Arenales Catalán. *Alternate:* I. L. Dimas.

India. *Representative:* Arthur S. Lall. *Alternate:* R. Jaipal.
Iraq. *Representative:* Adnan Pachachi, *Vice-Chairman.*
Netherlands. *Representative:* J. Vixseboxse, *Chairman.* *Alternate:* J. P. A. Idenburg.
New Zealand. *Representative:* W. G. Thorp, *Rapporteur.*
Peru. *Representative:* Jorge Velando. *Alternate:* Andrés Aramburu.
United Kingdom. *Representative:* B. O. B. Gidden. *Alternate:* P. Selwyn.
United States. *Representative:* Mason Sears. *Alternate:* James A. Lynn.
Venezuela. *Representative:* F. Alfonzo-Ravard. *Alternate:* R. A. Rojas.

SUB-COMMITTEE ON ECONOMIC CONDITIONS

The Committee on Information from Non-Self-Governing Territories appointed a Sub-Committee in 1957 to prepare a special report for it on economic conditions in Non-Self-Governing Territories. The members of the Sub-Committee were as follows:

Ceylon: Y. Duraiswamy.
China: Hsi-kun Yang.
France: Michel de Camaret.
Guatemala: Ramiro Aragón.
India: Rikhi Jaipal, *Chairman.*
Netherlands: Ch. J. Grader.
United Kingdom: B. O. B. Gidden, P. Selwyn.
United States: James A. Lynn.

ADVISORY COMMITTEE FOR THE UNITED NATIONS
MEMORIAL CEMETERY IN KOREA

Members: Australia, Canada, France, Netherlands, New Zealand, Norway, Turkey, Union of South Africa, United Kingdom.

NEGOTIATING COMMITTEE FOR EXTRA-BUDGETARY FUNDS

Members: Argentina, Brazil, Canada, France, Lebanon, New Zealand, Pakistan, United Kingdom, United States.

The same Members of the United Nations were appointed by the President of the General Assembly on 13 December 1957 to serve on the Negotiating Committee from the close of the Assembly's twelfth session (14 December 1957) to the close of the following session.

UNITED NATIONS STAFF PENSION COMMITTEE

Elected by the General Assembly to serve until 31 December 1958:

Members: Rigoberto Torres Astorga (Chile); Albert S. Watson (United States); Arthur H. Clough (United Kingdom), who resigned during 1957 and was replaced, by resolution 1196(XII) of 13 December 1957, by A. H. M. Hillis (United Kingdom). Mr. Hillis was appointed for one year beginning 1 January 1958.

Alternates: Johan Kaufmann (Netherlands); Fazlollah Nouredin Kia (Iran); Arthur C. Liveran (Israel).

Appointed by the Secretary-General:
 Members: J. A. C. Robertson, Bruce R. Turner, David B. Vaughan.
 Alternates: John McDiarmid, William McCaw, Syed H. Ahmed.
 Elected by participants to serve until 31 December 1958:
 Members: Michael H. Higgins, Carey Seward, Marc Schreiber.
 Alternates: Preston W. Cox, Charles Hogan, Robert Harpignies.

INVESTMENTS COMMITTEE

Serving until 31 December 1957: Leslie R. Rounds, former Senior Vice-President of the Federal Reserve Bank of New York.
To serve until 31 December 1958: Ivar Rooth, former Governor of the Bank of Sweden, Managing Director of the International Monetary Fund.
To serve until 31 December 1959: Jacques Rueff, Honorary Governor of the Bank of France.

On 26 November 1957, by resolution 1175(XII), the General Assembly confirmed the reappointment by the Secretary-General of Mr. Rounds for a three-year term to begin 1 January 1958.

BOARD OF AUDITORS

Elected to serve until 30 June 1957: Auditor-General of Colombia.
Elected to serve until 30 June 1958: Auditor-General of Norway.
Elected to serve until 30 June 1959: Auditor-General of the Netherlands.

On 27 February 1957, by resolution 1093(XI), the General Assembly reappointed the Auditor-General of Colombia for a further three years beginning 1 July 1957. On 26 November 1957 by resolution 1174(XII), the Assembly reappointed the Auditor-General of Norway for another three years to commence 1 July 1958.

COMMITTEE ON CONTROL AND LIMITATION OF DOCUMENTATION

This Committee was set up by the General Assembly on 13 December 1957 to consult with and advise the Secretary-General on the most effective ways of reducing the amount and length of United Nations documentation produced during 1958. Consisting of representatives, serving at United Nations Headquarters, from nine Member States, it was also to make recommendations for the Assembly's thirteenth session on ways to reduce the over-all output of documentation.
Members: Argentina, Canada, China, France, Iraq, Mexico, Pakistan, United Kingdom, USSR.

EXPERT COMMITTEE ON UNITED NATIONS PUBLIC INFORMATION

On 26 November 1957, by resolution 1177(XII), the General Assembly asked the Secretary-General to appoint an expert committee of six individuals with practical, administrative and financial experience in the various fields of information, to be nominated by the Governments of Egypt, India, the USSR, the United Kingdom, the United States and Uruguay.

Its task was to undertake, in the light of the opinions expressed by delegations during the Assembly's twelfth session, a review and appraisal of the work, the methods used, and the effectiveness of the results achieved by the public information services of the United Nations (including the information centres) with a view to recommending possible modifications to ensure a maximum of effectiveness at the lowest possible cost. The Expert Committee was to report before the Assembly's thirteenth session, to which the Secretary-General was invited to present their report with his comments and recommendations.

UNITED NATIONS ADMINISTRATIVE TRIBUNAL

Elected to serve until 31 December 1957: Bror Arvid Sture Petren (Sweden), *Second Vice-President;* Francisco A. Forteza (Uruguay).
Elected to serve until 31 December 1958: Mme Paul Bastid (France), *President;* Omar Loutfi (Egypt); R. Venkataraman (India).
Elected to serve until 31 December 1959: Lord Crook (United Kingdom); Jacob Mark Lashly (United States), *First Vice-President.*

On 26 November, the General Assembly reappointed Mr. Petren and Mr. Forteza, each for three years commencing 1 January 1958.

COMMITTEE ON APPLICATIONS FOR REVIEW OF ADMINISTRATIVE TRIBUNAL JUDGEMENTS

The Committee is composed of the representatives of Member States which have served on the General Committee of the most recent regular session of the General Assembly. The following Members served on the Committee in 1957, until the election of the General Committee at the twelfth Assembly session: China, Czechoslovakia, Denmark, Dominican Republic, Egypt, El Salvador, France, India, Italy, Pakistan, Peru, Turkey, Thailand, USSR, United Kingdom, United States.

The membership of the Committee on Applications for Review of Administrative Tribunal Judgements which will serve until the Assembly's thirteenth session is as follows: Ceylon, China, Czechoslovakia, France, Guatemala, Iran, Netherlands, New Zealand, Norway, Paraguay, Spain, Thailand, Tunisia, USSR, United Kingdom, United States, Venezuela.

The General Assembly's resolution 1192(XII), increasing the size of the General Committee to 21, also means an increase in the size of the Committee on Applications for Review of Administrative Tribunal Judgements from the Assembly's thirteenth session onwards.

INTERNATIONAL LAW COMMISSION

Members for 1957: Roberto Ago (Italy); Gilberto Amado (Brazil); Milan Bartos (Yugoslavia); Douglas L. Edmonds (United States); Abdullah El-Erian (Egypt); Sir Gerald Fitzmaurice (United Kingdom), *Rapporteur;* J. P. A. Francois (Netherlands); F. V. García-Amador (Cuba); Shuhsi Hsu (China); Thanat Khoman (Thailand); Faris El-Khouri (Syria); Ahmed Matine Daftary (Iran); Luis Padilla Nervo (Mexico), *Second Vice-Chair-*

man; Radhabinod Pal (India), *First Vice-Chairman*; A. E. F. Sandstrom (Sweden); Georges Scelle (France); Jean Spiropoulos (Greece); Grigory I. Tunkin (USSR); Alfred Verdross (Austria); Kisaburo Yokota (Japan); Jaroslav Zourek (Czechoslovakia), *Chairman*.

COMMITTEE ON ARRANGEMENTS FOR A CONFERENCE FOR THE PURPOSE OF REVIEWING THE CHARTER
All Members of the United Nations are members of this committee.

SPECIAL COMMITTEE ON DEFINING AGGRESSION
Members in 1957: China, Czechoslovakia, Dominican Republic, France, Iran, Iraq, Israel, Mexico, Netherlands, Norway, Panama, Paraguay, Peru, Philippines, Poland, Syria, USSR, United Kingdom, United States, Yugoslavia.
This Committee ceased to exist as a result of General Assembly resolution 1181(XII) of 29 Novem-

ber, by which a new committee (see below) was set up.

COMMITTEE ON GOVERNMENT REPLIES ON THE QUESTION OF DEFINING AGGRESSION
Arrangements to set up this Committee were made on 29 November 1957, by General Assembly resolution 1181(XII), (*a*) to study the comments sent by Member States on the question of defining aggression in order to determine when it was appropriate for the Assembly to consider the question again; and (*b*) to report to the Secretary-General when it considered the time appropriate. The Secretary-General was asked to place the question on the provisional agenda of the Assembly when the Committee had reported that it considered the time appropriate, but not earlier than at the Assembly's fourteenth session.
The Committee was to consist of the Member States represented on the General Committee at the most recent regular session of the Assembly.

THE SECURITY COUNCIL

The Security Council consists of 11 Members of the United Nations. Five are permanent members of the Council. The remaining six and non-permanent members are elected for two-year terms by the General Assembly. (For representatives to the Council, see APPENDIX IV.) The members of the Security Council for 1957 were as follows:

PERMANENT MEMBERS
China, France, USSR, United Kingdom, United States.

NON-PERMANENT MEMBERS
Australia, Colombia, Cuba, Iraq, Philippines, Sweden.
Elected to serve for one year, beginning 1 January 1957, to fill vacancy created by withdrawal of Yugoslavia: Philippines.
Elected for two-year terms ending 31 December 1957: Australia, Cuba.
Elected for two-year terms ending 31 December 1958: Colombia, Iraq, Sweden.
On 1 October 1957, the General Assembly elected Canada, Japan and Panama, each for two years beginning 1 January 1958, in the place of Australia, Cuba and the Philippines.
The Presidency of the Council is held in turn by Member States in the English alphabetical order of their names. The following served as Presidents during 1957:

Month	Country	Representative
January	Philippines	Carlos P. Romulo
February	Sweden	Gunnar V. Jarring
March	USSR	Arkady A. Sobolev
April	United Kingdom	Sir Pierson Dixon
May	United States	Henry Cabot Lodge
June	Australia	E. Ronald Walker
July	China	Tingfu F. Tsiang
August	Colombia	Francisco Urrutía
September	Cuba	Emilio Núñez Portuondo
October	France	Guillaume Georges-Picot
November	Iraq	Hashim Jawad
December	Philippines	Carlos P. Romulo

MILITARY STAFF COMMITTEE

The Military Staff Committee held bi-monthly meetings throughout 1957. The first meeting during 1957 was held on 3 January and the last on 19 December.
China. *Army Representative:* Lieutenant-General Ho Shai-lai. *Navy Representative:* Captain Wu Chia-hsun.
France. *Army Representative:* Général de Brigade M. Pénette (up to 19 December 1957), Général de Brigade J. Brice de Bary (from 20 December 1957). *Navy Representative:* Capitaine de Vaisseau E. Cagne.
USSR. *Army Representative:* Major-General I. M. Saraev. *Navy Representative:* Lieutenant-Commander Y. D. Kvashnin. *Air Force Representative:* Colonel A. M. Kuchumov.
United Kingdom. *Army Representative:* Major-General V. Boucher. *Navy Representative:* Vice-Admiral R. F. Elkins. *Air Force Representative:* Air Vice-Marshal A. D. Selway.
United States. *Army Representative:* Lieutenant-General T. W. Herren (up to 31 July 1957), Lieutenant-General B. M. Bryan (from 1 August 1957). *Navy Representative:* Vice-Admiral F. W. McMahon. *Air Force Representative:* Lieutenant-General W. E. Hall.

DISARMAMENT COMMISSION

The Commission reports to both the General Assembly and the Security Council (see above, under GENERAL ASSEMBLY.)

SUB-COMMITTEE ON DISARMAMENT
(See above, under GENERAL ASSEMBLY.)

COLLECTIVE MEASURES COMMITTEE

The Committee reports to both the General Assembly and the Security Council (see above, under GENERAL ASSEMBLY.)

STANDING COMMITTEES

The Committee of Experts and the Committee on the Admission of New Members are each composed of representatives of all Security Council members.

AD HOC COMMITTEES AND COMMISSIONS

UNITED NATIONS COMMISSION FOR INDONESIA[a]
Members: Australia, Belgium, United States.

UNITED NATIONS TRUCE SUPERVISION ORGANIZATION IN PALESTINE (UNTSO)
Chief of Staff: Major-General E. L. M. Burns.

General Burns was appointed Commander of The United Nations Emergency Force (UNEF) in November 1956, and Colonel Byron V. Leary, Deputy Chief of Staff of UNTSO, became the Acting Chief and remained so during all of 1957. General Burns, however, retained his duties as Chief of Staff in relation to the Demarcation Lines between Israel and Egypt.

UNITED NATIONS REPRESENTATIVE FOR INDIA AND PAKISTAN
Frank P. Graham.

UNITED NATIONS MILITARY OBSERVER GROUP FOR INDIA AND PAKISTAN
Chief Observer: Lieutenant-General Robert H. Nimmo.

THE ECONOMIC AND SOCIAL COUNCIL

The Economic and Social Council consists of 18 Members of the United Nations elected by the General Assembly, each for a three-year term of office. The members of the Council during 1957 were as follow:

Serving until 31 December 1957: Argentina, China, Dominican Republic, Egypt, France, Netherlands.

To serve until 31 December 1958: Brazil, Canada, Greece, Indonesia, United States, Yugoslavia.

To serve until 31 December 1959: Finland, Mexico, Pakistan, Poland, USSR, United Kingdom.

The officers of the Council during 1957 were as follows:

President: Mohammad Mir Khan (Pakistan).

First Vice-President: Minerva Bernardino (Dominican Republic).

Second Vice-President: Jerzy Michalowski (Poland).

(For representatives to the Council, see APPENDIX IV.)

On 1 October 1957, the General Assembly re-elected China, France and the Netherlands and elected Chile, Costa Rica and Sudan to fill the six vacancies on the Council created by the expiration of the terms of office of Argentina, China, the Dominican Republic, Egypt, France and the Netherlands. It elected them for three years, to commence on 1 January 1958.

Members of the Council for 1958: Brazil, Canada, Chile, China, Costa Rica, Finland, France, Greece, Indonesia, Mexico, Netherlands, Pakistan, Poland, Sudan, USSR, United Kingdom, United States, Yugoslavia.

Subsidiary organs reporting to the Economic and Social Council are of five types: functional commissions and one sub-commission; regional economic commissions; standing committees; special bodies and ad hoc committees.

The Council has in addition, various sessional committees such as its Economic, Social, and Co-ordination Committees.

FUNCTIONAL COMMISSIONS AND SUB-COMMISSION

The Council had eight functional commissions and one sub-commission during 1957:

Transport and Communications Commission
Statistical Commission
Population Commission
Social Commission
Commission on Human Rights
  Sub-Commission on Prevention of Discrimination and Protection of Minorities
Commission on the Status of Women
Commission on Narcotic Drugs
Commission on International Commodity Trade

The Transport and Communications, Statistical, Population and Social Commissions meet once every two years. (The Statistical Commission did not meet during 1957.)

The members of the commissions during 1957, and the representatives serving on those commissions which met in 1957, are listed below:

TRANSPORT AND COMMUNICATIONS COMMISSION

The Transport and Communications Commission consists of 15 members, each elected by the Council for a four-year term.

Elected to serve until 31 December 1957: Chile, India, Netherlands, Poland, United Kingdom.

Elected to serve until 31 December 1959: Burma, China, Ecuador, France, Norway.

Elected to serve until 31 December 1960: Bulgaria, Lebanon, USSR, United States, Venezuela.

On 1 May 1957, the Economic and Social Council elected the following to serve from 1 January 1958 to 31 December 1961: Austria, Indonesia, Mexico, Romania and the United Kingdom.

The following represented the members of the Commission at its eighth session, held at United Nations Headquarters, New York, from 7 to 16 January 1957:

Bulgaria: Nacho Petkov Simeonov.
Burma: Shwe Shane.
Chile: Octavio Echegoyen.
China: C. Y. Hsiao.
Ecuador: Alberto Barriga (alternate).

[a] On 1 April 1951, the Commission adjourned sine die while continuing to hold itself at the disposal of the parties.

France: Henri Barbier.
India: S. K. Ghosh, *Vice-Chairman*.
Lebanon: Assad Kotaite.
Netherlands: W. L. de Vries, *Chairman*.
Norway: Erling Foien.
Poland: Kazimierz Pierzyński.
USSR: M. P. Voronichev.
United Kingdom: R. R. Bullmore.
United States: John C. Baker.
Venezuela: Ignacio Silva Sucre.

STATISTICAL COMMISSION

The Statistical Commission consists of 15 members, each elected by the Council for a four-year term. The Commission did not meet in 1957.
Elected to serve until 31 December 1959: Canada, Dominican Republic, India, New Zealand, Ukrainian SSR.
Elected to serve until 31 December 1960: Cuba, Denmark, France, Romania, United Kingdom.
Elected to serve until 31 December 1961: China, Ireland, Netherlands, USSR, United States.
The members of the Commission in 1957 were Australia, Canada, China, Cuba, Denmark, Dominican Republic, France, India, Netherlands, New Zealand, Romania, Ukrainian SSR, USSR, United Kingdom, United States.

POPULATION COMMISSION

The Population Commission consists of 15 members, each elected by the Council for four years.
Elected to serve until 31 December 1957: Costa Rica, India, USSR, United Kingdom, United States.
Elected to serve until 31 December 1959: China, France, Israel, Norway, Ukrainian SSR.
Elected to serve until 31 December 1960: Argentina, Belgium, Brazil, Canada, Egypt.
On 1 May 1957, the Council elected the following to serve from 1 January 1958 to 31 December 1961: El Salvador, Japan, USSR, United Kingdom, United States.
The representatives to the ninth session of the Commission, held at United Nations Headquarters, New York, from 25 February to 8 March 1957, were as follows:
Argentina: Juan Antonio Rodal.
Belgium: J. Mertens de Wilmars, *Vice-Chairman*.
Brazil: Germano Jardim.
Canada: J. T. Marshall, *Chairman*.
China: Choh-Ming Li.
Costa Rica: Ricardo Jímenez.
Egypt: Salah El-Dine Abou-Gabal.
France: Alfred Sauvy.
India: P. N. Kaul.
Israel: Roberto Bachi.
Norway: Bjornulf Bendiksen.
Ukrainian SSR: L. M. Koretzky.
USSR: T. V. Ryabushkin.
United Kingdom: Bernard Benjamin, *Rapporteur*.
United States: Kingsley Davis.

SOCIAL COMMISSION

The Social Commission consists of 18 members, each elected by the Council for four years.

Elected to serve until 31 December 1957: France, Greece, India, Philippines, USSR, United States.
Elected to serve until 31 December 1959: Colombia, Czechoslovakia, Dominican Republic, Egypt, Sweden, United Kingdom.
Elected to serve until 31 December 1960: Byelorussian SSR, China, Ecuador, Netherlands, New Zealand, Spain.
On 2 May 1957, the Council elected the following to serve from 1 January 1961: Australia, France, Indonesia, Italy, USSR, United States.
The following were the representatives to the eleventh session of the Commission, which met at United Nations Headquarters in New York from 6 to 24 May 1957:
Byelorussian SSR: Anatoly E. Gurinovich.
China: Hua-Kuo Pao.
Colombia: Jesús Zárate Moreno.
Czechoslovakia: Jaroslav Pscolka, *Second Vice-Chairman*.
Dominican Republic: Miss Minerva Bernardino.
Ecuador: Luis Coloma.
Egypt: Abdel Hamid Abdel-Ghani, *Chairman*.
France: Henry Hauck.
Greece: Anreas Psarras.
India: Sushila Nayar, *First Vice-Chairman*.
Netherlands: J. F. de Jongh.
New Zealand: Arthur B. Thompson, *Rapporteur*.
Philippines: Octavio L. Maloles.
Spain: José Félix de Lequerica.
Sweden: Rolf Broberg.
USSR: Andrei A. Fomin.
United Kingdom: Sir Oswald Allen.
United States: Althea K. Hottel.

COMMISSION ON HUMAN RIGHTS

The Commission consists of 18 members, each elected by the Council for three years.
Elected to serve until 31 December 1957: China, Lebanon, Mexico, Norway, Poland, United Kingdom.
Elected to serve until 31 December 1958: France, India, Iraq, Philippines, Ukrainian SSR, USSR.
Elected to serve until 31 December 1959: Argentina, Ceylon, Iran, Israel, Italy, United States.
On 1 May 1957, the Council elected the following to serve from 1 January 1958 to 31 December 1960: Belgium, China, Lebanon, Mexico, Poland, United Kingdom.
The representatives to the thirteenth session of the Commission, held at the European Office of the United Nations, Geneva, from 1 to 26 April 1957, were:
Argentina: Carlos A. Bertomeu.
Ceylon: Ratnakirti S. S. Gunawardene, *Second Vice-Chairman*.
China: Cheng Paonan.
France: René Cassin.
India: Rajeshwar Dayal.
Iran: Fereydoun Adamiyat.
Iraq: Saadi Ibrahim.
Israel: Haim Herman Cohn.
Italy: Francisco Maria Dominedo.

Lebanon: Edward Rizk.
Mexico: Emilio Calderón Puig, *Rapporteur.*
Norway: Erik Colban, *First Vice-Chairman.*
Philippines: F. M. Serrano, *Chairman.*
Poland: Zofia Wasilkowska.
Ukrainian SSR: Peter P. Mikhailenko.
USSR: P. D. Morosov.
United Kingdom: Sir Samuel Hoare.
United States: Mrs. Oswald B. Lord.

SUB-COMMISSION ON PREVENTION OF DISCRIMINATION AND PROTECTION OF MINORITIES

The Sub-Commission on Prevention of Discrimination and Protection of Minorities consists of 12 persons, elected by the Commission on Human Rights (in consultation with the Secretary-General), subject to consent of their Governments. On 9 March 1956, at its twelfth session, the Commission on Human Rights decided to extend the term of office of the members of the Sub-Commission to 31 December 1959.

The members, or their alternates, serving in their individual capacities, at the Sub-Commission's ninth session, held at United Nations Headquarters, New York, from 18 February to 8 March 1957, were as follows:
Charles D. Ammoun (Lebanon).
Mohammed Awad (Egypt), *Chairman.*
Pierre Chatenet (France), *Vice-Chairman.*
Wojciech Ketrzynski (Poland) (*alternate*).
A. A. Fomin (USSR) (*alternate*).
Philip Halpern (United States).
C. Richard Hiscocks (United Kingdom).
José D. Inglés (Philippines), *Rapporteur.*
Gérard Roy (Haiti).
Hernán Santa Cruz (Chile).
Voitto Saario (Finland).

Arcot Krishnaswami (India) was unable to attend the session.

COMMISSION ON THE STATUS OF WOMEN

The Commission on the Status of Women consists of 18 members, each elected by the Council for three years.
Elected to serve until 31 December 1957: Argentina, Australia, Byelorussian SSR, China, Indonesia, Pakistan.
Elected to serve until 31 December 1958: Belgium, Israel, USSR, United Kingdom, United States, Venezuela.
Elected to serve until 31 December 1959: Cuba, Dominican Republic, France, Mexico, Poland, Sweden.

On 2 May 1957, the Economic and Social Council elected the following to serve from 1 January 1958 to 31 December 1960: Argentina, Canada, China, Czechoslovakia, Japan, Pakistan.

The representatives to the eleventh session of the Commission, held at United Nations Headquarters, New York, from 18 March to 5 April 1957, were as follows:
Argentina: Mrs. C. Cristina Correa Morales de Aparicio.
Australia: Miss Ruth Gibson, *Rapporteur.*

Belgium: Mrs. Georgette Ciselet.
Byelorussian SSR: Mrs. Faina Novikova.
China: Miss Pao Swen Tseng.
Cuba: Miss Uldarica Nañas, *First Vice-Chairman.*
Dominican Republic: Miss Minerva Bernardino.
France: Mrs. Marie-Hélène Lefaucheux.
Indonesia: Mrs. Rusiah Sardjono.
Israel: Mrs. Mina Ben-Zvi.
Mexico: Miss Maria Lavalle Urbina.
Pakistan: Begum Anwar Ahmed.
Poland: Mrs. Zofia Dembinska, *Second Vice-Chairman.*
Sweden: Mrs. Agda Rossel, *Chairman.*
USSR: Mrs. N. S. Spiridonova.
United Kingdom: Dame Lucile Sayers.
United States: Mrs. Lorena Hahn.
Venezuela: Mrs. Isabel Sánchez de Urdaneta.

COMMISSION ON NARCOTIC DRUGS

The Commission on Narcotic Drugs consists of 15 Members of the United Nations which are important producing or manufacturing countries, or countries in which illicit traffic in narcotic drugs constitutes a serious problem. Ten Members of primary importance in these fields are appointed for an indefinite period until such time as they may be replaced by decision of the Council; the remaining five are appointed for three years.
Elected for an indefinite period: Canada, China, France, India, Peru, Turkey, USSR, United Kingdom, United States, Yugoslavia.
Elected for three-year term ending on eve of the opening of the Commission's fifteenth session (1960): Austria, Egypt, Hungary, Iran, Mexico.

The following were the representatives to the twelfth session of the Commission, held at United Nations Headquarters, New York, from 29 April to 31 May 1957:
Austria: Friedrich Obermayer.
Canada: Kenneth C. Hossick.
China: H. R. Wei.
Egypt: Amin Ismail.
France: Charles Vaille.
Hungary: Zoltan Foldi.
India: S. Kampani.
Iran: A. G. Ardalan, *Rapporteur.*
Mexico: Luciano Joublanc Rivas.
Peru: D. B. Caravedo.
Turkey: Mazhar Ozkol.
USSR: Mrs. Valentina Vasilyeva.
United Kingdom: T. C. Green.
United States: Harry J. Anslinger, *Chairman.*
Yugoslavia: Dragan Nikolic, *Vice-Chairman.*

COMMISSION ON INTERNATIONAL COMMODITY TRADE

The Commission on International Commodity Trade consists of 18 members, each elected for three years.
Elected to serve until 31 December 1957: Egypt, France, India, Pakistan, Turkey, USSR.
Elected to serve until 31 December 1958: Argentina, Australia, Belgium, Chile, China, Denmark.
Elected to serve until 31 December 1959: Brazil, Canada, Greece, Indonesia, Poland, Uruguay.

On 2 August 1957, the Council elected the following to serve from 1 January 1958 to 31 December 1960: Austria, Egypt, France, India, Pakistan, USSR.

The representatives to the fifth session, held at United Nations Headquarters, New York, from 6 to 17 May 1957, were as follows:

Argentina: Eduardo Bradley.
Australia: J. Bevan Todd.
Belgium: Jules Woulbroun.
Brazil: Eurico Penteado, *Chairman.*
Canada: John R. Downs.
Chile: Alfonso Grez.
China: Kan Lee.
Denmark: Mrs. N. Wright.
Egypt: M. A. Anis.
France: Georges Henri Janton.
Greece: Costa Caranicas, *Vice-Chairman.*
India: Balachandra Rajan.
Indonesia: Mr. Nuradi.
Pakistan: Ahmed Zahiruddin.
Poland: Lychowski Taseusz.
Turkey: T. Menemencioglu.
USSR: E. C. Shershnev.
Uruguay: Enrique Rodríguez Fabregat.

REGIONAL ECONOMIC COMMISSIONS

There are three regional economic commissions:
Economic Commission for Europe (ECE)
Economic Commission for Asia and the Far East (ECAFE)
Economic Commission for Latin America (ECLA)

At its twelfth session the General Assembly recommended, by resolution 1155(XII), that the Economic and Social Council at its twenty-fifth session (15 April 1958) give prompt and favourable consideration to the establishment of an Economic Commission for Africa.

The membership, principal subsidiary bodies and chief representatives attending sessions of ECE, ECAFE, and ECLA during 1957 were as follows:

ECONOMIC COMMISSION FOR EUROPE

Members: Albania, Austria, Belgium, Bulgaria, Byelorussian SSR, Czechoslovakia, Denmark, Finland, France, Federal Republic of Germany, Greece, Hungary, Iceland, Ireland, Italy, Luxembourg, Netherlands, Norway, Poland, Portugal, Romania, Spain, Sweden, Turkey, Ukrainian SSR, USSR, United Kingdom, United States, Yugoslavia.

Switzerland, not a Member of the United Nations, participates in a consultative capacity.

The Commission has established the following subsidiary organs, among others:
Committee on Agricultural Problems
Coal Committee
Committee on Electric Power
Housing Committee
Industry and Materials Committee.
Inland Transport Committee
Committee on Manpower
Steel Committee
Timber Committee
Committee on the Development of Trade

Some of these Committees have established subsidiary bodies, including standing sub-committees and working parties. The Coal Committee, for example, has the Coal Trade Sub-Committee, and the Transport Committee has the Sub-Committees on Rail Transport and Road Transport. There is also the Joint FAO/ECE Committee on Forest Working Techniques and the Training of Forest Workers, a subsidiary of the Timber Committee.

The principal representatives to the twelfth session of the Commission, held at Geneva from 29 April to 16 May 1957, were as follows:

Albania: Mufit Sejko.
Austria: Bruno Kreisky.
Belgium: Pierre A. Forthomme.
Bulgaria: Eugene G. Kamenov.
Byelorussian SSR: F. L. Kokhonov.
Czechoslovakia: Karel Kurka.
Denmark: Jens Otto Krag.
Finland: Veikko Makkonen.
France: André Philip.
Germany, Federal Republic of: Alfred Muller-Armack.
Greece: G. Coustas.
Hungary: Jeno Baczoni.
Ireland: H. J. McCann.
Italy: Tommaso Notarangeli, *Vice-Chairman.*
Luxembourg: Michel Rasquin.
Netherlands: J. Linthorst Homan.
Norway: Arne Skaug.
Poland: Oskar Lange, *Chairman.*
Portugal: Ruy Teixeira Guerra.
Romania: Valentin Steriopol.
Spain: Don José Antonio de Sangróniz.
Sweden: Mrs. Karin Kock.
Switzerland: Friedrich Bauer.
Turkey: T. Carim.
Ukrainian SSR: G. L. Sakhnovsky.
USSR: A. V. Zakharov.
United Kingdom: The Earl of Gosford.
United States: Stanley C. Allyn.
Yugoslavia: Vladimir Velebit.

ECONOMIC COMMISSION FOR ASIA AND THE FAR EAST

Members: Afghanistan, Australia, Burma, Cambodia, Ceylon, China, France, India, Indonesia, Japan, Republic of Korea, Laos, Federation of Malaya (on its admission to the United Nations on 17 September 1957), Nepal, Netherlands, New Zealand, Pakistan, Philippines, Thailand, USSR, United Kingdom, United States, Viet-Nam.

Associate Members: Hong Kong and (upon the admission of the Federation of Malaya to the United Nations) Singapore and British Borneo.

The Commission has established the following subsidiary organs, among others:
Committee on Industry and Natural Resources
Committee on Trade
Inland Transport Committee
Working Party on Economic Planning and Developments

Some of these bodies have set up subsidiary bodies,

including standing sub-committees and working parties. For example, the Committee on Industry and Natural Resources has sub-committees on iron and steel, on electric power and on mineral resources development; and the Inland Transport Committee has inland waterway and railway sub-committees.

The principal representatives to the thirteenth session of the Commission held at Bangkok from 18 to 28 March 1957, were as follows:

Members:
Afghanistan: Abdul Hai Aziz.
Australia: T. K. Critchley.
Burma: Thiri Pyanchi U Pa Aung.
Cambodia: Ty Kim Sour.
Ceylon: P. H. William de Silva.
China: C. T. Chien.
France: Pierre Abelin.
India: D. P. Karmarkar.
Indonesia: Mr. Siddik, *Second Vice-Chairman.*
Japan: Koichiro Asakai.
Korea, Republic of: Pyo Wook Han.
Laos: Phagna Nith Singharaj.
Nepal: Ram Chandra Malhotra.
Netherlands: H. Jonker.
New Zealand: R. L. G. Challis.
Pakistan: G. A. Faruqi.
Philippines: Perfecto E. Laguio, *First Vice-Chairman.*
Thailand: Rak Panyarachun, *Chairman.*
USSR: P. A. Maletin.
United Kingdom: Sir Berkeley E. F. Gage.
United States: Walter M. Kotschnig.
Viet-Nam: Tran-Le-Quang.

Associate Members:
Hong Kong: E. S. Kirby.
Malaya and British Borneo: Ismail bin Dato Abdul Rahman.

ECONOMIC COMMISSION FOR LATIN AMERICA

Members: Argentina, Bolivia, Brazil, Chile, Colombia, Costa Rica, Cuba, Dominican Republic, Ecuador, El Salvador, France, Guatemala, Haiti, Honduras, Mexico, Netherlands, Nicaragua, Panama, Paraguay, Peru, United Kingdom, United States, Uruguay, Venezuela.

The Economic Commission for Latin America (ECLA) meets once every two years. In the years in which it does not meet, the ECLA Committee of the Whole meets.

The Commission has established the following subsidiary organs:

Committee on Trade
Central American Economic Co-operation Committee
These Committees have established subsidiary bodies, including standing sub-committees and *ad hoc* working parties. Thus, the Central American Economic Co-operation Committee has the Statistical Co-ordination Sub-Committee, the Central American Trade Sub-Committee and the Industrial Initiatives Committee.

The principal representatives to the Commission's seventh session, held at La Paz, Bolivia, from 15 to 29 May, were as follows:

Argentina: Isidoro Martínez.
Bolivia: Hugo Moreno Córdova, *Chairman.*
Brazil: Roberto Oliveira Campos, *Rapporteur.*
Chile: Alejandro Hales.
Costa Rica: Porfirio Morera Batre.
Cuba: Fausto Gamboa.
Dominican Republic: Oscar Guaroa Ginebra.
Ecuador: José María Ponce, *First Vice-Chairman.*
El Salvador: Rolando Duarte.
France: Robert Buron.
Guatemala: Luis Melgar Larrieu, *Second Vice-Chairman.*
Honduras: Rubén Mondragón.
Mexico: Ricardo Torres Gaitán.
Netherlands: P. H. Zijderveld.
Nicaragua: José María Castillo.
Panama: Luis Felipe Clement.
Paraguay: Hermógenes Gonzáles Maya.
Peru: Augusto Morelli.
United Kingdom: James Thyne Henderson.
United States: Harold M. Randall.
Uruguay: Ariosto D. González.
Venezuela: León Alfonso Pino.

STANDING COMMITTEES

The Economic and Social Council has four standing committees:
Technical Assistance Committee
Committee on Negotiations with Inter-Governmental Organizations (has not met since 1951)
Council Committee on Non-Governmental Organizations
Interim Committee on Programme of Conferences.

TECHNICAL ASSISTANCE COMMITTEE

On 1 May 1957, at its twenty-third session, the Economic and Social Council, in accordance with General Assembly resolution 1036(XI), expanded the membership of the Technical Assistance Committee (TAC) as of 1 June 1957 so it would henceforth consist of: the 18 members of the Council (as formerly) plus six additional members elected by the Council from among other United Nations Members or members of the specialized agencies.

The membership of the Technical Assistance Committee for 1957 was as follows:

Members from Council: Argentina, Brazil, Canada, China, Dominican Republic, Egypt, Finland, France, Greece, Indonesia, Mexico, Netherlands, Pakistan, Poland, USSR, United Kingdom, United States, Yugoslavia.

Other members:
To serve until 31 December 1958: Czechoslovakia, Sudan,[4] Switzerland.
To serve until 31 December 1959: India, Sweden, Venezuela.

[4] On 10 December 1957, the Council elected Morocco to the Committee, to serve from 1 January to 31 December 1958 in place of Sudan, as Sudan had been elected to serve on Economic and Social Council as of 1 January 1958.

ADMINISTRATIVE REVIEW GROUP OF TAC
Members: Brazil, Egypt, France, Netherlands, Pakistan, USSR, United Kingdom, United States.

COUNCIL COMMITTEE ON NON-GOVERNMENTAL
ORGANIZATIONS

The members serving on this Committee in 1957 (Brazil, China, France, Netherlands, USSR, United Kingdom, United States) were all re-elected by the Economic and Social Council, on 10 December 1957, to serve in 1958.

INTERIM COMMITTEE ON PROGRAMME
OF CONFERENCES

Members: China, France, USSR, United Kingdom, United States.

SPECIAL BODIES

Under this heading may be placed the following:
Permanent Central Opium Board
Drug Supervisory Body
United Nations Children's Fund (UNICEF)
United Nations Refugee Fund (UNREF) Executive
Committee[5]
Technical Assistance Board
Administrative Committee on Co-ordination
Interim Co-ordinating Committee for International
Commodity Arrangements

PERMANENT CENTRAL OPIUM BOARD

The Permanent Central Opium Board consists of eight persons appointed in an individual capacity for five years by the Economic and Social Council. *Members in 1957:* Ramón Sánchez Cornejo (Chile); Chi-Kwei Liang (China); Paul Reuter (France), *Vice-President;* Mohamed E. Rahman (India); Fouad Abou Zahr (Lebanon); Hans Fischer (Switzerland); Sir Harry Greenfield (United Kingdom), *President;* Herbert L. May (United States).

The terms of office of all of these members were due to expire on 2 March 1958, when they were to be succeeded by new board members elected by the Economic and Social Council on 2 August 1957, as follows: Ibrahim El Tersawi (Egypt), Sir Harry Greenfield (United Kingdom), George Joachimoglu (Greece), Vladimir Kusevic (Yugoslavia), Estefanus Looho (Indonesia), Herbert L. May (United States), Decio Parreiras (Brazil), Paul Reuter (France).

DRUGS SUPERVISORY BODY

The Supervisory Body consists of four members (until June 1958), as follows:
Appointed by the Commission on Narcotic Drugs: Colonel C. H. L. Sharman (Canada), *President.*
Appointed by Permanent Central Opium Board: Herbert L. May (United States).
Appointed by the World Health Organization (WHO): Hans Fischer (Switzerland), *Vice-President;* Sedat Tavat (Turkey).

UNITED NATIONS CHILDREN'S FUND

Executive Director: Maurice Pate.
Executive Board Members for 1957: Australia, Austria, Belgium, Brazil, Canada, Colombia, Czecho-

slovakia, Dominican Republic, Ecuador, Egypt, El Salvador, France, Federal Republic of Germany, Greece, India, Indonesia, Iran, Israel, Italy, Japan, Pakistan, Philippines, Poland, Sweden, Switzerland, USSR, United Kingdom, United States, Venezuela, Yugoslavia.
Officers for 1957:
Chairman: M. Shafqat (Pakistan).
First Vice-Chairman: Mrs. Zena Harman (Israel); *Second Vice-Chairman:* Miss Lily Tongson (Philippines); *Third Vice-Chairman:* Dr. Ludwik Rajchman (Poland); *Fourth Vice-Chairman:* Mrs. María Elvira López (Colombia).
All these officers were re-elected on 12 December 1957 to serve for 1958.
Executive Board Members for 1958:
To serve until 31 December 1958: Australia, Belgium, Canada, El Salvador, Federal Republic of Germany, Italy, Pakistan, Poland, Venezuela, Yugoslavia.
To serve until 31 December 1959: Austria, Colombia, Czechoslovakia, Dominican Republic, Ecuador, Egypt, Indonesia, Iran, Israel, Sweden, Switzerland, United Kingdom.
Elected in 1957 to serve until 31 December 1960: Brazil, China, France, India, Philippines, Tunisia, USSR, United States.
The Executive Board has established the following subsidiary organs:
Programme Committee
Sub-Committee on Public Relations and Fund Raising
Committee on Administrative Budget.
In addition there is a UNICEF/WHO Joint Committee on Health Policy (JCHP).

UNITED NATIONS REFUGEES FUND
EXECUTIVE COMMITTEE
(See above, under GENERAL ASSEMBLY.)

ADMINISTRATIVE COMMITTEE
ON CO-ORDINATION

The Administrative Committee on Co-ordination (ACC) consists of the Secretary-General of the United Nations, as Chairman, and the executive heads of the following specialized agencies: International Labour Organisation (ILO), Food and Agriculture Organization (FAO), United Nations Educational, Scientific and Cultural Organization (UNESCO), World Health Organization (WHO), International Bank for Reconstruction and Development (BANK), International Monetary Fund (FUND), International Civil Aviation Organization (ICAO), Universal Postal Union (UPU), International Telecommunication Union (ITU), World Meteorological Organization (WMO).

Arrangements have been made, too, for the International Atomic Energy Agency (IAEA) to take part in the work of ACC.

In 1957, the Bank's representative also participated

[5] Until 31 December 1958, when it will be replaced by the Executive Committee of the Programme of the United Nations High Commissioner for Refugees.

in the work of the Committee on behalf of the President of the International Finance Corporation (IFC). Representatives of the United Nations Korean Relief Agency (UNKRA), the United Nations Children's Fund (UNICEF), the United Nations High Commissioner for Refugees, and the secretariat of the Contracting Parties to the General Agreement on Tariffs and Trade (GATT), and the Executive Chairman of the Technical Assistance Board have also attended ACC meetings.

TECHNICAL ASSISTANCE BOARD

The Technical Assistance Board (TAB) consists of an Executive Chairman and the executive heads, or their representatives, of the organizations sharing in the funds for the Expanded Programme of Technical Assistance (United Nations, ILO, FAO, UNESCO, WHO, ICAO, ITU, WMO). Although the International Bank and the International Monetary Fund do not share in the funds for the Expanded Pro-

gramme and are not titular members of the Board, they are invited to participate in the meetings of the Board and to co-operate fully in promoting the objectives of the Programme.
Executive Chairman: David Owen.

INTERIM-CO-ORDINATING COMMITTEE FOR INTERNATIONAL COMMODITY ARRANGEMENTS

Edwin McCarthy, *Chairman* (nominated by the contracting parties to GATT) .
Georges Peter (appointed by the Secretary-General for his experience with non-agricultural primary commodities)
Walter Miller (appointed by the Secretary-General for his experience in problems of less developed countries whose economies depend on production and international marketing of primary commodities)
R. H. Roberts and T. C. Robinson (*alternate*) (nominated by FAO)

THE TRUSTEESHIP COUNCIL

The Trusteeship Council consists of the following:
Members of the United Nations administering Trust Territories.
Permanent members of the Security Council which do not administer Trust Territories.
As many other members elected for a three-year term by the General Assembly as will ensure that the membership of the Council is equally divided between United Nations Members which administer Trust Territories and Members which do not.

The following were the members of the Council during 1957:
Members administering Trust Territories: Australia, Belgium, France, Italy, New Zealand, United Kingdom, United States.
Permanent members of the Security Council not administering Trust Territories: China, USSR.
Elected to serve until 31 December 1958: Burma, Guatemala, Syria.
Elected to serve until 31 December 1959: Haiti, India.
(For list of representatives, see APPENDIX IV.)

The officers of the Council during 1957 were:

NINETEENTH SESSION
President: Rafik Asha (Syria).
Vice-President: Remigio Danilo Grillo (Italy).

TWENTIETH SESSION AND
SEVENTH SPECIAL SESSION
President: John Douglas Lloyd Hood (Australia).
Vice-President: Emilio Arenales Catalán (Guatemala).
Subsidiary organs reporting to the Trusteeship Council are standing committees, *ad hoc* committees and visiting missions.

VISITING MISSION

UNITED NATIONS VISITING MISSION TO EAST AFRICAN TRUST TERRITORIES IN 1957
Members: Max H. Dorsinville (Haiti); Robert Na-

pier Hamilton (Australia); U Tin Maung (Burma); Jean Cédile (France).

STANDING COMMITTEES

The Trusteeship Council has two standing committees, as follows:

STANDING COMMITTEE ON
ADMINISTRATIVE UNIONS
Chairman: Rikhi Jaipal (India).
Members: Guatemala, India, New Zealand, United States.
On 10 July 1957, India resigned, being replaced by Burma.

STANDING COMMITTEE ON PETITIONS
Elected at end of 18th session, to serve until end of 19th session: Belgium, Burma, China, France, USSR, United States.
Elected at end of 19th session, to serve until end of 20th session: Belgium, China, France, Guatemala, USSR, United Kingdom.
Elected at end of 20th session, to serve until end of 21st session: China, France, India, Italy, USSR, United Kingdom.

AD HOC COMMITTEES

In addition to drafting committees, the following *ad hoc* committees either met or were established during 1957:

COMMITTEE ON RURAL ECONOMIC DEVELOPMENT
OF THE TRUST TERRITORIES
Chairman: Max H. Dorsinville (Haiti).
Members: China, France, Haiti, India, United Kingdom, United States.
On 11 July 1957, Haiti, India and the United States resigned, whereupon the Trusteeship Council decided to reduce the size of the Committee to four members, China, France, Guatemala and the United Kingdom.

COMMITTEE ON COMMUNICATIONS FROM THE
CAMEROONS UNDER FRENCH ADMINISTRATION
Members: India, United States.

COMMITTEE ON PROCEDURES REGARDING PETITIONS
On 10 April 1957, at its nineteenth session, the Trusteeship Council established a four-member committee, to be nominated by the Council's President, to study the Council's procedures with regard to petitions, to suggest possible improvements and to report to the twentieth session.
Members: Belgium, Guatemala, Haiti, Italy.

COMMITTEE ON CLASSIFICATION
OF COMMUNICATIONS
This Committee was set up on 8 July 1957, at the Trusteeship Council's twentieth session, to determine, with the aid of the United Nations Secretariat, the provisional classification of communications received from Trust Territories. It was set up as a temporary measure, subject to review after a year and without prejudice to existing rules of procedure, for handling communications and petitions.
Members (serving until end of 21st session): Belgium, Syria.

THE INTERNATIONAL COURT OF JUSTICE

The Court consists of 15 judges elected for nine-year terms by the General Assembly and the Security Council, voting independently.

The judges of the Court serving from 15 July 1956, in order of precedence, with the year their term of office ends, are as follows:

Judge.	End of Term	Nationality
Green Hackworth, *President*	1961	American
Abdel Hamid Badawi, *Vice-President*	1958	Egyptian
José Gustavo Guerrero	1964	Salvadorian
Jules Basdevant	1964	French
Bohdan Winiarski	1958	Polish
Milovan Zoricic	1958	Yugoslav
Helge Klaestad	1961	Norwegian
John E. Read	1958	Canadian
Enrique C. Armand-Ugon	1961	Uruguayan
Feodor Ivanovich Kojevnikov	1961	Russian
Sir Muhammad Zafrulla Khan	1961	Pakistani
Sir Hersch Lauterpacht	1964	British
Lucio M. Moreno Quintana	1964	Argentinian
Roberto Córdova	1964	Mexican
V. K. Wellington Koo	1958	Chinese

Registrar. Julio López Oliván.
Deputy-Registrar. Jean Garnier-Coignet.

On 1 October 1957, the General Assembly and the Security Council, voting independently, re-elected Judges Abdel Hamid Badawi, V. K. Wellington Koo and Bohdan Winiarski, each for nine years beginning 6 February 1958, to fill the vacancies occurring on the expiration of their terms of office. At the same time, two new judges were elected for the same period, Sir Percy Spender (Australian) and Jean Spiropoulos (Greek), to fill vacancies occurring on the expiration of the terms of office of Judges Read and Zoricic.

CHAMBER OF SUMMARY PROCEDURE
(as elected by the Court on 6 May 1957)
Members:
President Green Hackworth.
Vice-President Abdel Hamid Badawi.
Judges José Gustavo Guerrero, Jules Basdevant and Bohdan Winiarski.
Substitutes:
Judges Helge Klaestad and Enrique C. Armand-Ugon.

PARTIES TO THE COURT'S STATUTE
All Members of the United Nations are *ipso facto* parties to the Statute of the International Court of Justice. The following non-member States have also become parties to the Court's Statute: Liechtenstein, San Marino and Switzerland.

STATES ACCEPTING COMPULSORY
JURISDICTION OF THE COURT
Declarations made by the following States accepting the Court's compulsory jurisdiction[6] (or made under the Statute of the Permanent Court of International Justice and deemed to be an acceptance of the jurisdiction of the International Court for the period for which they still have to run) were in force at the end of 1957: Australia, Cambodia, Canada, China, Colombia, Denmark, Dominican Republic, Egypt, El Salvador, France, Haiti, Honduras, Israel, Liberia, Liechtenstein, Luxembourg, Mexico, Netherlands, New Zealand, Nicaragua, Norway, Pakistan, Panama, Paraguay,[7] Philippines, Portugal, Sweden, Switzerland, Thailand, Union of South Africa, United Kingdom, United States, Uruguay.

ORGANS AUTHORIZED TO REQUEST ADVISORY
OPINIONS FROM THE COURT
Authorized in the Charter to request opinions on any legal questions: General Assembly, Security Council.
Authorized by the General Assembly in accordance with the Charter to request opinions on legal questions arising within the scope of their activities: Economic and Social Council; Trusteeship Council; Interim Committee of the General Assembly; Inter-

[6] In 1957 Israel, the United Kingdom, and the United States instituted proceedings before the Court against Bulgaria in connexion with an aerial incident of 27 July 1955. The applicants in these three cases relied on a declaration made by Bulgaria in 1921 accepting the compulsory jurisdiction of the Permanent Court of International Justice and contended that that declaration became effective as an acceptance of the compulsory jurisdiction of the International Court of Justice upon Bulgaria's admission to United Nations membership in December 1955.

[7] Paraguay's declaration, made without limitation, was withdrawn by Paraguay on 26 April 1938.

national Atomic Energy Agency; International Labour Organisation; Food and Agriculture Organization of the United Nations; United Nations Educational, Scientific, and Cultural Organization; World Health Organization; International Bank for Reconstruction and Development; International Finance Corporation; International Monetary Fund; International Civil Aviation Organization; International Telecommunication Union; World Meteorological Organization.

PRINCIPAL MEMBERS OF THE UNITED NATIONS SECRETARIAT
(As of 31 December 1957)

Secretary-General: Dag Hammarskjold.

EXECUTIVE OFFICE OF THE SECRETARY-GENERAL

Executive Assistant to the Secretary-General: Andrew W. Cordier.
Special Assistant in Charge of Special Unit: Alfred G. Katzin.
Chief Editor: Meurig Evans.
Special Assistant to the Executive Assistant: Leo Malania.
Chief, General Assembly Section and Personal Assistant to the Secretary-General: Lennart Finnmark.
Personal Assistant to the Secretary-General: Claude de Kemoularia.
Personal Assistant to the Secretary-General: Hernando Samper.
Personal Assistant to the Secretary-General: Shiv K. Shastri.
Chief, Protocol and Liaison Section: Jehan de Noue.

INDEPENDENT UNITS
(reporting to the Executive Office of the Secretary-General)
Health Service. *Medical Director:* Dr. Szeming Sze.
Internal Audit Service. *Director:* Frode Hansen.

OFFICE OF LEGAL AFFAIRS

The Legal Counsel: Constantin A. Stavropoulos.
Deputy Director of the Office of the Legal Counsel: W. W. Cox.
Director, General Legal Division: Oscar Schachter.
Deputy Director, General Legal Division: Marc Schreiber
Director, Codification Division: Yuen-li Liang.

OFFICE OF THE CONTROLLER

Controller: Bruce R. Turner.
Deputy Controller: William McCaw.
Chief, Budget Division: A. E. Lethbridge.
Chief, Accounts Division: Pieter C. J. Kien.
Treasurer: Noel Monod.

OFFICE OF PERSONNEL

Director of Personnel: J. A. C. Robertson (until 23 December 1957).
Acting Director of Personnel: John McDiarmid.
Chief, Rules and Procedures Section: Charles P. Holmes.
Chief, Departmental and Staff Services: F. P. E. Green.
Acting Chief, Placement Services: A. D. Vieira.

Chief, Technical Assistance Recruitment Services: W. P. Barrett.

OFFICE OF THE UNDER-SECRETARIES WITHOUT DEPARTMENT

Under-Secretaries: Ralph J. Bunche, Anatoly F. Dobrynin.

DEPARTMENT OF POLITICAL AND SECURITY COUNCIL AFFAIRS

Under-Secretary: Dragoslav Protitch.
Director, Political Affairs Division: Alfonso García Robles (until 2 April 1957; position vacant as of 31 December 1957).
Chief, General Problems and Procedures of Pacific Settlements Section: Sanford Schwarz.
Assistant Director, Chief, Regional Affairs and Services to Commissions Section: William M. Jordan.
Director, Council and Committee Services Division: T. G. Narayanan.
Chief, Section for Security Council Affairs: Lev Emelianov.
Assistant Director, Chief, Section for Political Committees: Feng Yang Chai.
Chief, Atomic Energy Section: Otto Frey.
Chief, Conventional Armaments and Enforcement Measures Section: William Epstein.

DEPARTMENT OF ECONOMIC AND SOCIAL AFFAIRS

Under-Secretary: Philippe de Seynes.
Deputy Under-Secretary: W. Martin Hill.
Director, Bureau of Economic Affairs: Sune L. Carlson.
Assistant Director in Charge of Fiscal and Financial Branch: Henry S. Bloch.
Assistant Director in Charge of Resources and Industry Branch: John N. Reedman.
Assistant Director in Charge of Economic Survey Branch: Jacob L. Mosak.
Director, Statistical Office: William R. Leonard.
Deputy Director, Statistical Office: P. J. Loftus.
Director, Bureau of Social Affairs: Miss Julia Henderson.
Assistant Director in Charge of Housing, Building and Planning Branch: Ernest Weissmann.
Assistant Director in Charge of Population Branch: John Durand.
Assistant Director in Charge of Community Development and Social Welfare Groups: Zahir Ahmed.
Director, Division of Human Rights: John P. Humphrey.

Deputy Director, Division of Human Rights: Egon Schwelb.

Chief, Status of Women Section: Mrs. Mary Tenison-Woods.

Deputy Director, Transport and Communications Division: M. H. Higgins.

Director, Division of Narcotic Drugs: Gilbert Yates.

Secretary, Economic and Social Council: Mehdi Vakil.

ECONOMIC COMMISSION FOR EUROPE

Executive Secretary: Sakari Tuomioja.

Deputy Executive Secretary: A. G. Stetsenko.

Director, Research and Planning Division: Frederick Strauss.

Director, Steel, Engineering and Housing Division: A. F. Ewing.

Director, Energy Division: P. Sevette.

Director, Transport Division: P. Le Vert.

Director, ECE/FAO Agriculture Division: P. Sinard.

Director, ECE/FAO Timber Division: E. Glesinger.

ECONOMIC COMMISSION FOR ASIA AND THE FAR EAST

Executive Secretary: C. V. Narasimhan.

Deputy Executive Secretary: U Nyun.

Chief, Research and Planning Division: John H. G. Pierson.

Chief, Bureau of Flood Control and Water Resources Development: Shen-Yi.

Chief, Industry and Trade Division: (vacant).

Chief, Transport Division: M. S. Ahmad.

Chief, ECAFE/FAO Agriculture Division: E. M. Ojala.

Chief, Social Affairs Division: M. Raja-Nayagam.

ECONOMIC COMMISSION FOR LATIN AMERICA

Executive Secretary: Raúl Prebisch.

Deputy Executive Secretary: Louis Swenson.

Director, Office in Mexico: Victor L. Urquidi.

Chief, Economic Development Division: Jorge Ahumada.

Chief, Industrial Development Division: Carlos Quintana.

Chief, Social Affairs Division: Gustavo Duran.

Chief, ECLA/FAO Joint Programme: Alfredo Saco.

Chief, Programme of Energy and Water Resources: Adolfo Dorfman.

Chief, Transport Programme: Jules De Kock.

TECHNICAL ASSISTANCE ADMINISTRATION

Director-General: Hugh L. Keenleyside.

Deputy Director-General: Gustavo Martínez Cabañas.

Acting Director, Programme Division: Myer Cohen.

Acting Director, Public Administration Division: Frederick J. Tickner.

DEPARTMENT OF TRUSTEESHIP AND INFORMATION FROM NON-SELF-GOVERNING TERRITORIES

Under-Secretary: Benjamin A. Cohen.

Director, Division of Trusteeship: H. A. Wieschhoff.

Acting Deputy Director, Division of Trusteeship: José A. Correa.

Deputy Director, Division of Information from Non-Self-Governing Territories: Arnold V. Kunst.

Principal Secretary, United Nations Advisory Council for the Trust Territory of Somaliland under Italian Administration: Taylor C. Shore.

DEPARTMENT OF PUBLIC INFORMATION

Under-Secretary: Ahmed S. Bokhari.

Director, External and Specialized Agencies Service: V. J. G. Stavridi.

Director, Press and Publications Division: Wilder Foote.

Chief, Press Services: Matthew Gordon.

Director, Radio and Visual Services Division: Peter Aylen.

Deputy Director, Radio and Visual Services Division: Franco Passigli.

Director, Public Liaison and Distribution Division: G. J. Janecek.

UNITED NATIONS INFORMATION CENTRES AND OFFICES

Athens. *Director:* James B. Orrick.

Bangkok. *Information Officer:* César Ortiz-Tinoco.

Belgrade. *Director:* Milan Hofman

Bogota. *Director:* Jorge Viteri de la Huerta.

Buenos Aires. *Director:* L. Bertrand Ges.

Cairo. *Director:* John King Gordon.

Copenhagen. *Director:* Jan Gunnar Lindstrom.

Djakarta. *Information Officer:* Nazri M. Rashed.

Geneva. *Director:* W. Gibson-Parker.

Karachi. *Director:* A. Faryar.

London. *Director:* George Ivan Smith.

The Hague. *Information Officer:* Erwin Baumgarten.

Manila. *Information Officer:* Martin A. Arostegui.

Mexico. *Director:* Miguel A. Marin.

Monrovia. *Director:* B. Leitgeber.

Moscow. *Acting Director:* Sergey G. Bratchikov.

New Delhi. *Director:* Eugenio Soler-Alonso.

Paris. *Director:* David Blickenstaff.

Prague. *Director:* Arnost Bares.

Rio de Janeiro. *Director:* Georges S. Rabinovitch.

Santiago. *Information Officer:* Antonio Ramos Oliveira.

Sydney. *Director:* A. H. W. Williams.

Teheran. *Director:* Olav Rytter.

Washington. *Director:* Brian Meredith.

DEPARTMENT OF CONFERENCE SERVICES

Under-Secretary: Victor Hoo.

Director, Language and Meetings Service: Georges Peissel.

Director, Library: R. Borba de Moraes.

Chief, Editorial Control: Romain Godet.

OFFICE OF GENERAL SERVICES

Director: David B. Vaughan.

Director, Communications and Records Service: Byron F. Wood.

Chief, Purchase and Transportation Service: Carey Seward.

Chief, Buildings Management Service: Frank M. Begley.

Chief, Field Operations Service: George Lansky.

EUROPEAN OFFICE OF THE UNITED NATIONS, GENEVA

Director Representing the Secretary-General: Adrian Pelt.
Deputy Director: Georges M. Palthey.
Chief, Administrative and Financial Services: Paul Coidan.

UNITED NATIONS CHILDREN'S FUND

HEADQUARTERS
Executive Director: Maurice Pate.
Deputy Executive Director (Operations): Eric J. R. Heyward.
Deputy Executive Director (Programmes): Mrs. A. Sinclair.
Deputy Executive Director (Planning): Dr. Georges Sicault.
Chief, Administrative Division: John T. Birckhead.
Comptroller: Stanley Sroka.
Chief, Supply Division: E. T. Bridgwater.
Chief, Public Information Division: Mrs. P. L. Hartwell.
Chief Reports Officer: John J. Charnow.
Chief Medical Advisor: Dr. I. C. Yuan.
Food Conservation Co-ordinator: Donald R. Sabin.
FAO Advisor: Dr. J. M. Hundley.

UNICEF REGIONAL OFFICES
Asia. *Regional Director:* S. M. Keeny.
Africa and Europe. *Regional Director:* Charles A. Egger.
The Americas. *Regional Director:* Robert L. Davée.

TECHNICAL ASSISTANCE BOARD

Executive Chairman: David Owen.
Senior Director: Laurence Michelmore.
Director, Programme Division: Sudhir Sen.
Acting Director, Administration Division: R. B. Stedman.

FIELD PERSONNEL
Afghanistan. *Resident Representative:* D. Hopkinson.
Argentina. *Officer-in-Charge:* John Foster.
Bolivia. *Resident Representative:* A. Oropeza-Castillo.
Brazil. *Resident Representative:* H. Laurentie.
Burma. *Resident Representative:* D. Masuric.
Ceylon. *Resident Representative:* J. N. Corry.
Chile. *Resident Representative:* B. F. Osorio-Tafall.
Colombia. *Resident Representative:* Warren Cornwell.
Ecuador. *Resident Representative:* A. Balinski.
Egypt. *Resident Representative:* Taghi Nasr.
Ethiopia. *Resident Representative:* T. Lilliefelt.
Europe (Geneva). *Liaison Office of TAB:* Branko Lukac.
Ghana. *Resident Representative:* Wilfrid Benson.
Haiti. *Resident Representative:* Albert Le Bel.
India. *Resident Representative:* James Keen.
Indonesia. *Resident Representative:* A. Rosenborg.
Iran. *Resident Representative:* Thomas F. Power.
Iraq. *Resident Representative:* Arnljot Engh.
Israel. *Resident Representative:* Eric Ward.

Jordan. *Resident Representative:* N. G. Abhyankar.
Lebanon. *Officer-in-Charge; Liaison Office of TAB:* George Berouti.
Liberia. *TAB Correspondent:* H. H. Grantham.
Libya. *Resident Representative:* H. L. Spence.
Mexico, Central America and Panama. *Regional Representative:* R. Etchats.
Morocco. *Special Representative of the Executive Chairman:* M. Perez-Guerrero.
Nepal. *TAB Correspondent:* W. G. Schulthess.
Pakistan. *Acting Resident Representative:* Jean Taupin.
Paraguay. *Resident Representative:* M. Albornoz.
Peru. *Acting Resident Representative:* E. Albertal.
Philippines. *Resident Representative:* C. Hart Schaaf.
Somaliland, Trust Territory of. *TAB Correspondent:* Taylor C. Shore.
Sudan. *Resident Representative:* Rahat Bokari.
Thailand. *Regional Representative:* Sir Alexander MacFarquhar.
Tunisia. *Special Representative of the Executive Chairman:* M. Perez-Guerrero.
Turkey. *Resident Representative:* Charles Weitz.
Uruguay. *Officer-in-Charge:* Joan Anstee.
Venezuela. *TAB Correspondent:* J. J. Gallagher.
Yugoslavia. *Representative:* J. R. Symonds.

JOINT SECRETARIAT OF THE PERMANENT CENTRAL OPIUM BOARD AND DRUGS SUPERVISORY BODY

Secretary, Permanent Central Opium Board: Louis Atzenwiler.

JOINT STAFF PENSION BOARD AND UNITED NATIONS STAFF PENSION COMMITTEE

Secretary, Joint Staff Pension Board: J. Isaac-Georges.

UNITED NATIONS KOREAN RECONSTRUCTION AGENCY

KOREAN HEADQUARTERS
Agent-General: Lieutenant-General John B. Coulter, USA (Retired).
Deputy Agent-General: Brigadier-General Harold E. Eastwood, USA (Retired).
Executive Officer, Office of the Agent-General: Cyril H. Perry.
Chief, Operations Division: Brigadier-General Harold E. Eastwood, USA (Retired).
Chief, Supply Division: Cyril H. Perry.
Chief, Budget and Finance Division (and Deputy Comptroller): Verda Welch.
Chief, Public Information Division: Elma Ferguson.

HEADQUARTERS DETACHMENT, NEW YORK
Comptroller: James McLean.

AMERICAN REGIONAL OFFICE
Chief of Office: John L. Thurston.
Chief, Division of Procurement: Brigadier-General Andrew C. Tychsen, USA (Retired).

TOKYO LIAISON AND PROCUREMENT OFFICE
Officer in Charge: Wesley C. Phipps.

UNITED NATIONS RELIEF AND WORKS
AGENCY FOR PALESTINE REFUGEES
IN THE NEAR EAST

Director: Henry R. Labouisse.
Deputy Director: Leslie J. Carver.
General Counsel: Jean-Flavien Lalive.

Assistant Director, Department of Administration and Services: Bernardus T. Twigt.
Assistant Director, Department of Operations: Thomas Jamieson.
Comptroller: Lloyd Callow.
Executive Assistant to the Director: Sherwood G. Moe.

MATTERS CONSIDERED BY THE PRINCIPAL ORGANS

MATTERS CONSIDERED BY THE GENERAL ASSEMBLY AT ITS RESUMED ELEVENTH SESSION AND TWELFTH REGULAR SESSION

RESUMED ELEVENTH SESSION, 10–14 SEPTEMBER 1957

Agenda Item	*Consideration and Action Taken*
67. Question considered by the second emergency special session of the General Assembly from 4 to 10 November 1956.	Plenary meetings, 669-677. *Resolution 1133(XI).*
2. Minute of silent prayer or meditation.	Plenary meeting, 677.

TWELFTH REGULAR SESSION, 18 SEPTEMBER—14 DECEMBER 1957

1. Opening of the session by the Chairman of the delegation of Thailand.	Plenary meeting, 678.
2. Minute of silent prayer or meditation.	Plenary meetings, 678, 731.
3. Credentials of representatives to the twelfth session of the General Assembly: (a) Appointment of the Credentials Committee; (b) Report of the Credentials Committee.	Plenary meetings 678, 726. *Resolution 1183(XII).*
4. Election of the President.	Plenary meeting 678.
5. Constitution of the Main Committees and election of officers.	First Committee meetings 864, 865. Special Political Committee meetings 42, 43. Second Committee meetings, 452, 453. Third Committee meetings 762, 763. Fourth Committee meetings 650, 651. Fifth Committee meetings 597, 598. Sixth Committee meetings 507, 508. Plenary meeting 679.
6. Election of vice-presidents.[1]	Plenary meeting 679.
7. Notification by the Secretary-General under Article 12, paragraph 2, of the Charter.	Plenary meeting 682.
8. Adoption of the agenda.	General Committee meetings 111-116. Plenary meetings 682, 684, 686, 688, 696, 702, 705, 706.
9. Opening of General Debate.	Plenary meetings 680-683, 685-694, 697-703.
10. Report of the Secretary-General on the work of the Organization.	
11. Report of the Security Council.	Plenary meeting 728. *Resolution 1193 (XII).*
12. Report of the Economic and Social Council.	Second Committee meetings 454-480, 490, 491. Third Committee meetings 764-779. Fifth Committee meeting 645. Plenary meetings 722, 723, 730. *Resolutions 1155-1158(XII), 1160-1164(XII), 1220(XII).*
13. Report of the Trusteeship Council.	Fourth Committee meetings 652, 667, 668, 670, 683, 691, 692, 700, 701, 714-734, 736. Plenary meeting 729. *Resolutions 1205-1211(XII).*
14. Election of three non-permanent members of the Security Council.	Plenary meeting 695.

[1]See also under Item 67, below.

Agenda Item	*Consideration and Action Taken*

15. Election of six members of the Economic and Social Council.

Plenary meeting 695.

16. Election of five members of the International Court of Justice.

Plenary meetings 695, 696.

17. Appointment of the Secretary-General of the United Nations.

Plenary meetings 690, 731. *Resolution 1229(XII).*

18. Draft relationship agreement between the United Nations and the International Atomic Energy Agency: report of the Advisory Committee on the Peaceful Uses of Atomic Energy.

Plenary meeting 715. *Resolutions 1145(XII), 1146 (XII).*

19. Question of amending the United Nations Charter in accordance with the procedure laid down in Article 108 of the Charter, to increase the number of non-permanent members of the Security Council and the number of votes required for decisions of the Council.

Special Political Committee meetings 74, 75. Plenary meeting 728. *Resolution 1190(XII).*

20. Question of amending the United Nations Charter in accordance with the procedure laid down in Article 108 of the Charter, to increase the membership of the Economic and Social Council.

Special Political Committee meetings 74, 75. Plenary meeting 728. *Resolution 1190(XII).*

21. Question of amending the Statute of the International Court of Justice, in accordance with the procedure laid down in Article 108 of the Charter of the United Nations and Article 69 of the Statute of the Court with respect to an increase in the number of judges of the International Court of Justice.

Special Political Committee meetings 74, 75. Plenary meeting 728. *Resolution 1190(XII).*

22. Report of the Committee on Arrangements for a Conference for the Purpose of Reviewing the Charter.

Plenary meeting 705. *Resolution 1136(XII).*

23. The Korean question: report of the United Nations Commission on the Unification and Rehabilitation of Korea.

First Committee meetings 894, 899-904. Plenary meeting 724. *Resolution 1180(XII).*

24. Regulation, limitation and balanced reduction of all armed forces and all armaments; conclusion of an international convention (treaty) on the reduction of armaments and the prohibition of atomic, hydrogen and other weapons of mass destruction:
    (*a*) Report of the Disarmament Commission;
    (*b*) Expansion of the membership of the Disarmament Commission and of its Sub-Committee;
    (*c*) Collective action to inform and enlighten the peoples of the world as to the dangers of the armaments race, and particularly as to the destructive effects of modern weapons;
    (*d*) Discontinuance under international control of tests of atomic and hydrogen weapons.

General Committee meetings 111, 113. First Committee meetings 865-893. Plenary meetings 696, 715-719. *Resolutions 1148-1150(XII).*

25. Admission of new Members to the United Nations.

Special Political Committee meetings 44-49. Plenary meetings 678, 709. *Resolutions 1134(XII), 1144 (XII).*

26. Report of the Director of the United Nations Relief and Works Agency for Palestine Refugees in the Near East.

Special Political Committee meetings 64-73, 75-79. Plenary meeting 728. *Resolution 1191(XII).*

27. Report of the Agent General of the United Nations Korean Reconstruction Agency.

Second Committee meetings 490, 491, 494. Plenary meeting 723. *Resolution 1159(XII).*

28. Economic development of under-developed countries. Question of the establishment of a Special United Nations Fund for Economic Development: final and supplementary reports of the

Second Committee meetings 492-510. Plenary meeting 730. *Resolutions 1217-1219(XII).*

Agenda Item	*Consideration and Action Taken*

Ad Hoc Committee, and recommendations of the Economic and Social Council.

29. Programmes of technical assistance:
    (*a*) Report of the Economic and Social Council;
    (*b*) Confirmation of allocation of funds under the Expanded Programme of Technical Assistance.

Second Committee meetings 471, 479-489, 497, 502. Plenary meeting 730. *Resolutions 1214-1216(XII).*

30. Report of the United Nations High Commissioner for Refugees.

Third Committee meetings 800-809, 816. Plenary meeting 723. *Resolutions 1166(XII), 1167(XII).*

31. Review of the arrangements for the Office of the United Nations High Commissioner for Refugees.

Third Committee meetings 800-809, 816. Plenary meeting 723. *Resolution 1165(XII).*

32. Recommendations concerning international respect for the right of peoples and nations to self-determination.

Third Committee meetings 821-827. Plenary meeting 727. *Resolution 1188(XII).*

33. Draft International Covenants on Human Rights.

Third Committee meetings 779-799, 809-821, 834. Plenary meeting 727.

34. Draft Convention on Freedom of Information: report of the Economic and Social Council.

Third Committee meetings 828-834. Plenary meeting 727. *Resolution 1189(XII).*

35. Information from Non-Self-Governing Territories transmitted under Article 73e of the Charter: reports of the Secretary-General and of the Committee on Information from Non-Self-Governing Territories:
    (*a*) Information on economic conditions;
    (*b*) Information on other conditions;
    (*c*) General questions relating to the transmission and examination of information;
    (*d*) Offers of study and training facilities under resolutions 845(IX), of 22 November 1954, and 931(X), of 8 November 1955;
    (*e*) Methods of reproducing summaries of information concerning Non-Self-Governing Territories: report of the Secretary-General.

Fourth Committee meetings 670-694, 700, 701, 712, 734. Fifth Committee meeting 624. Sixth Committee meetings 529, 538-544. Plenary meeting 722. *Resolutions 1152-1154(XII).*

36. Election to fill vacancies in the membership of the Committee on Information from Non-Self-Governing Territories.

Fourth Committee meetings 687, 724, 725. Plenary meeting 729.

37. The future of Togoland under French administration: report of the Trusteeship Council.

Fourth Committee meetings 651, 652, 655, 659, 672, 694-714, 717. Fifth Committee meeting 629. Plenary meetings 724, 727, 730. *Resolution 1182(XII).*

38. Question of South West Africa:
    (*a*) Report of the Committee on South West Africa;
    (*b*) Study of legal action to ensure the fulfilment of the obligations assumed by the Mandatory Power under the Mandate for South West Africa: special report of the Committee on South West Africa;
    (*c*) Election of three members of the Committee on South West Africa.

Fourth Committee meetings 651-669, 672, 679, 736. Fifth Committee meeting 609. Plenary meetings 709, 714. *Resolutions 1138-1143(XII).*

Fourth Committee meetings 687, 725, 729. Plenary meeting 729.

39. Question of the frontier between the Trust Territory of Somaliland under Italian administration and Ethiopia: reports of the Governments of Ethiopia and of Italy.

Fourth Committee meetings 734, 735, 737-740. Plenary meeting 730. *Resolution 1213(XII).*

40. Supplementary estimates for the financial year 1957.

Fifth Committee meeting 633, 645. Plenary meeting 731. *Resolution 1222(XII).*

41. Budget estimates for the financial year 1958.

Fifth Committee meetings 606-626, 635-638, 640-643, 645-648. Plenary meetings 723, 729, 731. *Resolutions 1177(XII), 1202(XII), 1203(XII), 1221(XII), 1230-1235(XII).*

42. Appointments to fill vacancies in the membership of subsidiary bodies of the General Assembly.

Agenda Item	*Consideration and Action Taken*
(a) Advisory Committee on Administrative and Budgetary Questions;	Fifth Committee meetings 608, 640, 645. Plenary meetings 723, 729. *Resolutions 1173(XII), 1194 (XII).*
(b) Committee on Contributions;	Fifth Committee meetings 628, 640, 645. Plenary meeting 729. *Resolution 1195(XII).*
(c) Board of Auditors;	Fifth Committee meeting 622. Plenary meeting 723. *Resolution 1174(XII).*
(d) Investments Committee: confirmation of the appointment made by the Secretary-General;	Fifth Committee meeting 608. Plenary meeting 723. *Resolution 1175(XII).*
(e) United Nations Administrative Tribunal	Fifth Committee meeting 622. Plenary meeting 723. *Resolution 1176(XII).*
(f) United Nations Staff Pension Committee	General Committee meeting 111. Fifth Committee meetings 640, 645. Plenary meeting 729. *Resolution 1196(XII).*
43. Report of the Negotiating Committee for Extra-Budgetary Funds.	Fifth Committee meetings 638, 645. Plenary meeting 729. *Resolution 1197(XII).*
44. Scale of assessments for the apportionment of the expenses of the United Nations: report of the Committee on Contributions.	Fifth Committee meetings 599-605, 631, 632, 646. Plenary meetings 705, 731. *Resolutions 1137(XII), 1223(XII).*
45. United Nations Joint Staff Pension Fund: (a) Annual report of the United Nations Staff Pension Board; (b) Report of the United Nations Joint Staff Pension Board on the fourth actuarial valuation of the United Nations Joint Staff Pension Fund as of 30 September 1956, and second review of the basic tables of the Fund.	Fifth Committee meetings 634, 635, 645. Plenary meeting 729. *Resolutions 1199-1201(XII).*
46. Audit reports relating to expenditure by specialized agencies of technical assistance funds allocated from the Special Account.	Fifth Committee meetings 618, 622. Plenary meeting 723. *Resolution 1168(XII).*
47. Review of audit procedures of the United Nations and the specialized agencies.	Fifth Committee meetings 618, 622. Plenary meeting 723.
48. Administrative and budgetary co-ordination between the United Nations and the specialized agencies: reports of the Secretary-General and of the Advisory Committee on Administrative and Budgetary Questions.	Fifth Committee meetings 643, 646. Plenary meeting 729. *Resolution 1198(XII).*
49. Financial reports and accounts and reports of the Board of Auditors: (a) United Nations (for the financial year ended 31 December 1956); (b) United Nations Children's Fund (for the financial year ended 31 December 1957); (c) United Nations Korean Reconstruction Agency (for the financial year ended 30 June 1957); (d) United Nations Refugee Fund (for the financial year ended 31 December 1956).	Fifth Committee meetings 618, 622. Plenary meeting 723. *Resolution 1169-1172(XII).*
50. Offer by the Government of Chile of land in Santiago to be used as office site for the United Nations and other international organizations.	Fifth Committee meetings 639, 640, 648. Plenary meeting 731. *Resolution 1224(XII).*
51. Personnel questions: (a) United Nations salary, allowance and benefits system: outstanding questions from the eleventh session;	Fifth Committee meetings 626-628, 646. Plenary meeting 731. *Resolution 1225(XII).*
(b) Question of the geographical distribution of the staff of the Secretariat of the United Nations: report of the Secretary-General;	Fifth Committee meetings 629, 630, 632, 633, 646. Plenary meeting 731. *Resolution 1226(XII).*
(c) Question of the proportion of fixed-term staff: report of the Secretary-General;	Fifth Committee meetings 629, 630, 632, 633, 646. Plenary meeting 731.

Agenda Item	*Consideration and Action Taken*
(d) Review of the staff regulations and the principles and standards progressively applied thereto: report of the Secretary-General;	Fifth Committee meetings 628, 646. Plenary meeting 731. *Resolution 1227(XII).*
(e) Proposal to amend article 9 of the Statute of the United Nations Administrative Tribunal: report of the Secretary-General.	Fifth Committee meetings 628, 646. Plenary meeting 731.
52. United Nations International School: report of the Secretary-General.	Fifth Committee meetings 636, 644, 645, 648. Plenary meeting 731. *Resolution 1228(XII).*
53. Report of the International Law Commission on the work of its ninth session.	Sixth Committee meetings 509-513, 528, 529, 547. Plenary meeting 727. *Resolution 1185(XII).*
54. Question of defining aggression: report of the 1956 Special Committee.	Sixth Committee meetings 514-528, 530-538. Plenary meeting 724. *Resolution 1181(XII).*
55. Draft Code of Offences against the Peace and Security of Mankind.	Sixth Committee meetings 544-547. Plenary meeting 727. *Resolution 1186(XII).*
56. International criminal jurisdiction.	Sixth Committee meetings 546, 547. Plenary meeting 727. *Resolution 1187(XII).*
57. Effects of atomic radiation.	First Committee meetings 894-898. Plenary meeting 715. *Resolution 1147(XII).*
58. The Cyprus question.	General Committee meeting 111. First Committee meetings 927-934. Plenary meetings 682, 731.
59. The question of Algeria.	General Committee meeting 111. First Committee meetings 913-926. Plenary meeting 726. *Resolution 1184(XII).*
60. The question of race conflict in South Africa resulting from the policies of *apartheid* of the Government of the Union of South Africa.	General Committee meeting 111. Special Political Committee meetings 50-57. Plenary meetings 682, 723. *Resolution 1178(XII).*
61. Treatment of people of Indian origin in the Union of South Africa: reports of the Governments of India and of Pakistan.	General Committee meeting 111. Special Political Committee meetings 58-63. Plenary meetings 682, 723. *Resolution 1179(XII).*
62. The question of West Irian (West New Guinea).	General Committee meeting 111. First Committee meetings 905-912. Plenary meetings 682, 724.
63. The question of Hungary.	General Committee meeting 112. Plenary meetings 684, 726, 731.
64. Clearance of the Suez Canal: report of the Secretary-General.	General Committee meeting 112. Plenary meetings 686, 696, 730. *Resolution 1212(XII).*
65. United Nations Emergency Force: report of the Secretary-General.	General Committee meeting 112. Fifth Committee meetings 639, 646. Plenary meetings 686, 696, 720, 721, 729. *Resolutions 1151(XII), 1204(XII).*
66. Declaration concerning the peaceful co-existence of States.	General Committee meeting 113. First Committee meetings 894, 935-940. Plenary meeting 731. *Resolution 1236(XII).*
67. Question of the establishment on an *ad hoc* basis of a ninth Vice-Presidency for the twelfth session of the General Assembly.	General Committee meetings 113, 114. Plenary meetings 702. 704.
68. Question of the composition of the General Committee of the General Assembly.	General Committee meeting 115. Special Political Committee meetings 49, 75, 79-83. Plenary meeting 728. *Resolution 1192(XII).*
69. Complaint about threats to the security of Syria and to international peace.	General Committee meeting 116. Plenary meetings 706, 708, 710-714.

Other Matters Discussed

Organization and closing date of the twelfth session of the General Assembly.	General Committee meeting 111. Plenary meeting 682.
The question of the representation of China.	General Committee meeting 112. Plenary meetings 684, 686, 726. *Resolution 1135(XII).*
The question of granting requests for hearings from petitioners.	Fourth Committee meeting 702.
The question of circulation of statements.	Fourth Committee meeting 691.

GENERAL DEBATE

The General Debate at the opening of the Assembly's twelfth session began at the 680th plenary meeting, on 19 September 1957, and finished at the 703rd plenary meeting, on 8 October. Representatives of the following 71 countries took part, speaking at the meetings listed:[2]

Country	Meeting	Date
Afghanistan	688	25 Sep.
Albania	691	27 Sep.
Argentina	693	30 Sep.
Australia	687	25 Sep.
Austria	687	25 Sep.
Belgium	685	24 Sep.
Bolivia	690	26 Sep.
Brazil	780	19 Sep.
Bulgaria	701	7 Oct.
Burma	691	27 Sep.
Byelorussian SSR	693	30 Sep.
Cambodia	689	26 Sep.
Canada	683	23 Sep.
Ceylon	698	2 Oct.
Chile	687	25 Sep.
China	689	26 Sep.
Colombia	683	23 Sep.
Costa Rica	692	27 Sep.
Cuba	697	2 Oct.
Czechoslovakia	686, 698	24 Sep., 2 Oct.
Dominican Republic	686	24 Sep.
Ecuador	691	27 Sep.
Egypt	699	3 Oct.
El Salvador	690	26 Sep.
Ethiopia	693	30 Sep.
France	700	3 Oct.
Ghana	680	19 Sep.
Greece	689	26 Sep.
Guatemala	702	7 Oct.
Honduras	700	3 Oct.
Hungary	688	25 Sep.
India	703	8 Oct.
Indonesia	700	3 Oct.
Iran	687	25 Sep.
Iraq	700	3 Oct.
Ireland	682	20 Sep.
Israel	701	7 Oct.
Italy	681	20 Sep.
Japan	680	19 Sep.
Jordan	701	7 Oct.
Laos	698	2 Oct.
Lebanon	703	8 Oct.

Country	Meeting	Date
Liberia	685	24 Sep.
Libya	698	2 Oct.
Malaya, Federation of	688	25 Sep.
Mexico	699	3 Oct.
Morocco	694	30 Sep.
Nepal	698	2 Oct.
Netherlands	689	26 Sep.
New Zealand	683	23 Sep.
Pakistan	694	30 Sep.
Panama	697	2 Oct.
Paraguay	681	20 Sep.
Peru	683	23 Sep.
Philippines	691	27 Sep.
Poland	697	2 Oct.
Romania	689	26 Sep.
Saudi Arabia	697	2 Oct.
Spain	699	3 Oct.
Sudan	690	26 Sep.
Syria	702	7 Oct.
Tunisia	702	7 Oct.
Turkey	692	27 Sep.
Ukrainian SSR	700	3 Oct.
USSR	681	20 Sep.
United Kingdom	685	24 Sep.
United States	680	19 Sep.
Uruguay	685	24 Sep.
Venezuela	693	30 Sep.
Yemen	692	27 Sep.
Yugoslavia	688	25 Sep.

The General Assembly was also addressed by the following distinguished guests:

H. M. Queen Elizabeth II, at the 707th plenary meeting on 21 October 1957.

H. M. King Mohamed V of Morocco, at the 725th plenary meeting on 9 December 1957.

At its 678th plenary meeting, the Assembly was also addressed by Prince Wan Waithayakon (President of the eleventh session of the General Assembly), Temporary President and Chairman of the Delegation of Thailand, and by Sir Leslie Munro, of New Zealand, after his election as President of the twelfth session.

[2] The representatives of the following countries spoke in reply to certain statements made during the General Debate at the following plenary meetings indicated in parentheses: Nicaragua (700th meeting) India and Portugal (703rd meeting).

MEETINGS OF SECURITY COUNCIL AND MATTERS DISCUSSED IN 1957

Meeting	Subject	Date
760	Election of a member of the International Court of Justice to fill the vacancy caused by the death of Judge Hsu Mo.	11 Jan.
761	The India-Pakistan question.	16 Jan.
762	Same.	23 Jan.
763	Same.	23 Jan.
764	Same.	24 Jan.
765	Same.	24 Jan.

Meeting	Subject	Date
766	Same.	30 Jan.
767	Same.	8 Feb
768	Same.	15 Feb
769	Same.	15 Feb
770	Same.	18 Feb
771	Same.	18 Feb
772	Same.	20 Feb.
773	Same.	20 Feb.
774	Same.	21 Feb.

Meeting	Subject	Date	Meeting	Subject	Date
775	Admission of new Members.	7 Mar.	(private)	Security Council to the General Assembly.	
776	Letter dated 24 April 1957 from the representative of the United States of America to the President of the Security Council, relating to the Suez Canal (item 28 of the list of matters of which the Security Council is seized).	26 Apr.	786	Admission of new Members.	5 Sep.
			787	The Palestine question.	6 Sep.
			788	Same.	6 Sep.
			789	Admission of new Members.	9 Sep.
			790	Same.	9 Sep.
			791	The India-Pakistan question.	24 Sep.
777	Same.	26 Apr.	792	Question of the recommendation for the appointment of the Secretary-General of the United Nations.	26 Sep.
778	Letter dated 15 May 1957 from the representative of France addressed to the President of the Security Council, relating to the Suez Canal (item 28 of the list of matters of which the Security Council is seized).	20 May	(private)		
			793	Election of five members of the International Court of Justice.	1 Oct.
			794	Election of one member of the International Court of Justice.	1 Oct.
			795	The India-Pakistan question.	9 Oct.
779	Same.	21 May	796	Same.	9 Oct.
780	The Palestine question.	23 May	797	Same.	25 Oct.
781	Same.	28 May	798	Same.	29 Oct.
782	Same.	28 May	799	Same.	5 Nov.
783	Letter dated 13 August 1957 from the permanent representatives of Egypt, Iraq, Jordan, Lebanon, Libya, Morocco, Saudi Arabia, Sudan, Syria and Yemen addressed to the President of the Security Council.	20 Aug.	800	Same.	11 Nov.
			801	Same.	13 Nov.
			802	Same.	15 Nov.
			803	Same.	18 Nov.
			804	Same.	20 Nov.
			805	Same.	21 Nov.
			806	The Palestine question.	22 Nov.
784	Same.	20 Aug.	807	The India-Pakistan question.	28 Nov.
785	Consideration of the Report of the	21 Aug.	808	Same.	2 Dec.

MATTERS CONSIDERED BY THE ECONOMIC AND SOCIAL COUNCIL AT ITS TWENTY-THIRD AND TWENTY-FOURTH SESSIONS

TWENTY-THIRD SESSION, 16 APRIL—2 MAY 1957

Agenda Item	Consideration and Action Taken
1. Election of the President and Vice-Presidents for 1957.	Plenary meeting 955.
2. Adoption of the sessional agenda.	Plenary meeting 955.
3. Report of the International Monetary Fund.	Plenary meetings, 956, 957. *Resolution 636(XXIII)*.
4. Report of the International Bank for Reconstruction and Development.	Plenary meetings, 958, 959. *Resolution 637(XXIII)*.
5. Economic development of under-developed countries.[a]	Economic Committee meetings 217-220. Plenary meetings 960-964, 971. *Resolution 649(XXIII)*.
6. Financing of economic development.	Plenary meeting 955.
7. Report of the Transport and Communications Commission (eighth session).	Economic Committee meeting 216. Plenary meeting 968. *Resolution 645(XXIII)*.
8. Development of international travel, its present increasing volume and future prospects.	Plenary meeting 968. *Resolution 644(XXIII)*.
9. Report of the Population Commission (ninth session).	Social Committee meetings 353, 354. Plenary meeting 967. *Resolution 642(XXIII)*.
10. Recommendation addressed to the Council by the United Nations Conference of Plenipotentiaries on a Supplementary Convention on the Abolition of Slavery, the Slave Trade and Institutions and Practices Similar to Slavery.	Plenary meeting 966. *Resolution 640(XXIII)*.
11. Allegations regarding infringements of trade union rights.	Social Committee meeting 358. Plenary meeting 970. *Resolution 648(XXIII)*.
12. Freedom of information.	Social Committee meetings 355-357. Plenary meeting 967. *Resolution 643(XXIII)*.
13. United Nations Children's Fund.	Plenary meeting 965. *Resolution 638(XXIII)*.

[a] The Council decided, at its 955th plenary meeting, to consider General Assembly resolution 1033 A (XI), on industrialization of under-developed countries, in connexion with item 5.

Agenda Item	*Consideration and Action Taken*
14. Review of the membership of the United Nations Refugee Fund Executive Committee.	Plenary meeting 965. *Resolution 639(XXIII)*.
15. Non-governmental organizations.	Council Committee on Non-Governmental Organizations meetings 163-165. Plenary meetings 958, 966, 967. *Resolution 641(XXIII)*.
16. Elections.	Plenary meetings 969-971: *Resolution 646(XXIII)*.
17. Confirmation of members of functional commissions of the Council.	Plenary meeting 971.
18. Financial implications of actions of the Council.	Plenary meeting 971.
19. Consideration of the provisional agenda for the twenty-fourth session and establishment of dates for opening debate on items.	Plenary meeting 971.
20. International commodity problems: General Assembly resolution 1029(XI).	Plenary meeting 959.
21. Question of the membership of the Technical Assistance Committee.[4]	Plenary meeting 970, 971. *Resolution 647(XXIII)*.

Other Matters Discussed

Report of the President and the Vice-Presidents on the credentials of representatives to the twenty-third session of the Council.	Plenary meeting 971.
Date of meeting of the Technical Assistance Committee.	Plenary meetings 967, 969.
Question of the representation of China.	Council Committee on Non-Governmental Organizations meeting 163. Plenary meeting 955.

TWENTY-FOURTH SESSION, 2 JULY—2 AUGUST 1957

Agenda Item	
1. Adoption of the agenda.	Plenary meeting 972.
2. World economic situation:	
(a) Survey of the world economic situation;	Economic Committee meetings 227-232. Plenary meetings 973-979, 993. *Resolution 654(XXIV)*.
(b) Consideration of the reports of the regional economic commissions.	Economic Committee meetings 221, 222. Plenary meetings 973, 978, 979, 993. *Resolution 665(XXIV)*.
3. World social situation.	Social Committee meetings 368-371. Plenary meetings 984-987, 994. *Resolution 663(XXIV)*.
4. Development and co-ordination of the economic, social and human rights programmes and activities of the United Nations and the specialized agencies as a whole.	Co-ordination Committee meetings 152-165. Plenary meetings 980-983, 995, 996. *Resolutions 661(XXIV), 664(XXIV), 665(XXIV)*.
(a) General review	
(b) Consideration of statements by specialized agencies of their views and activities in the field of international cultural and scientific co-operation.	
5. Sources of energy as a means of economic development.	Economic Committee meetings 223-226. Plenary meetings 972, 990. *Resolution 653(XXIV)*.
6. Financing of economic development.	Plenary meetings 990-994. *Resolution 662(XXIV)*.
7. International commodity problems.	Economic Committee meetings 232, 233. Plenary meeting 993. *Resolution 656(XXIV)*.
8. Establishment of a world food reserve.	Economic Committee meeting 232. Plenary meeting 993.
9. Technical assistance.	Technical Assistance Committee meetings 127-149. Plenary meeting 993. *Resolutions 657-660(XXIV)*.
10. Human rights.	Social committee meetings 359-364. Plenary meeting 989. *Resolution 651(XXIV)*.
11. Report of the Commission on the Status of Women.	Social Committee meetings 364-367. Plenary meeting 989. *Resolution 652(XXIV)*.
12. International control of narcotic drugs.	Social Committee meetings 372-374. Plenary meeting 995. *Resolution 667(XXIV)*.

Supplementary item.

Agenda Item	*Consideration and Action Taken*
13. Annual report of the United Nations High Commissioner for Refugees.	Plenary meetings 988, 989. *Resolution 650(XXIV)*.
14. Non-governmental organizations.	Council Committee on Non-Governmental Organizations meetings 165-169. Plenary meeting 974.
15. Calendar of conferences for 1958.	Interim Committee on Programme of Conferences meeting 39. Plenary meeting 996.
16. Financial implications of actions of the Council.	Co-ordination Committee meeting 166. Plenary meetings 972, 995. *Resolution 666(XXIV)*.
17. Arrangements regarding the report of the Council to the General Assembly.	Plenary meeting 996.
18. Elections.	Plenary meeting 996.
19. Confirmation of members of functional commissions of the Council.	Considered at resumed twenty-fourth session.
20. Work of the Council in 1958.	Considered at resumed twenty-fourth session.

Other Matters Discussed

Question of the representation of China.	Plenary meeting 972.

RESUMED TWENTY-FOURTH SESSION, 10—13 DECEMBER 1957

Agenda Item	
18. Elections.	Plenary meeting 997.
19. Confirmation of members of functional commissions of the Council.	Plenary meetings 997, 998.
20. Work of the Council in 1958.	Plenary meeting 998.
21. Carriage of narcotic drugs in first-aid kits of aircraft engaged in international flight.	Plenary meeting 997.

Other Matters Discussed

Opening date of the mid-year session of the Technical Assistance Committee.	Plenary meeting 998.

MATTERS CONSIDERED BY THE TRUSTEESHIP COUNCIL AT ITS NINETEENTH, TWENTIETH AND SEVENTH SPECIAL SESSIONS

NINETEENTH SESSION, 14 MARCH—15 MAY 1957

Agenda Item	*Consideration and Action Taken*
1. Adoption of the agenda.	Plenary meeting 752.
2. Report of the Secretary-General on credentials.	Plenary meeting 784.
3. Examination of annual reports of Administering Authorities on the administration of Trust Territories:	
(*a*) Ruanda-Urundi, 1955;	Plenary meetings 754-761, 789, 792, 793.
(*b*) Cameroons under British administration, 1955;	Plenary meetings 769-778, 788.
(*c*) Cameroons under French administration, 1955;	Plenary meetings 760-770, 777, 784-786, 790-792.
(*d*) Togoland under British administration, 1955;	Plenary meeting 753.
(*e*) Togoland under French administration, 1955.	Plenary meetings 777-784, 786, 789, 792, 793.
4. Examination of the petitions listed in the annex to the agenda.	Standing Committee on Petitions meetings 403-439. Plenary meetings 753, 755, 756, 759-770, 777-779, 782, 784-787, 790-792. *Resolutions 1656-1711(XIX)*.
5. Arrangements for a periodic visiting mission to Trust Territories in East Africa in 1957.	Plenary meetings 786, 787.
6. Administrative unions affecting Trust Territories: reports of the Standing Committee on Administrative Unions.	Standing Committee on Administrative Unions meetings 94, 95. Plenary meeting 782.
7. Financing of the economic development plans of the Trust Territory of Somaliland under Italian administration: report of the Mission of the International Bank for Reconstruction and Develop-	Plenary meetings 753, 754.

Agenda Item	*Consideration and Action Taken*

ment to the Trust Territory of Somaliland under Italian administration (Trusteeship Council resolution 1255(XVI)).

8. Revision of the Questionnaire relating to Trust Territories: third progress report of the Sub-Committee on the Questionnaire (General Assembly resolution 751(VIII)).

Plenary meeting 782.

9. The future of Togoland under British administration (General Assembly resolution 1044(XI)).

Plenary meeting 753.

10. Offers by States Members of the United Nations of study and training facilities for inhabitants of Trust Territories (General Assembly resolution 1063(XI)).

Plenary meetings 775, 784.

11. Attainment of self-government or independence by Trust Territories (General Assembly resolution 1064(XI)).

Plenary meetings 753, 759.

12. The future of the Trust Territory of Tanganyika (General Assembly resolution 1065(XI)).

Plenary meeting 787.

13. Report of the Trusteeship Council covering the period from 23 July 1955 to 14 August 1956 (General Assembly resolution 1066(XI)).

Plenary meeting 753.

14. Hearings of petitioners from the Trust Territory of the Cameroons under French administration (General Assembly resolution 1067(XI)).

Plenary meetings 760-770, 777, 784-786, 790-792.

15. Review of the procedures regarding petitions.

Plenary meetings 761, 770-772, 780, 793.

16. Appointment of the members of the Standing Committee on Petitions.

Plenary meeting 787.

17. Revision of the rules of procedure of the Trusteeship Council.

Plenary meetings 791, 793.

Other Matters Discussed

Question of the representation of China.

Plenary meeting 784.

Organization of work for the twentieth session of the Trusteeship Council.

Plenary meeting 787.

Telegram to the Legislative Assembly of the Cameroons under French administration.

Plenary meeting 793.

TWENTIETH SESSION, 20 MAY—12 JULY 1957

Agenda Item

1. Adoption of the agenda.

Plenary meeting 794.

2. Report of the Secretary-General on credentials.

Plenary meeting 836.

3. Election of the President and the Vice-President.

Plenary meeting 794.

4. Examination of annual reports of Administering Authorities on the administration of Trust Territories:

(a) Tanganyika, 1955;

Plenary meetings 811-822, 836, 840.

(b) New Guinea, year ended 30 June 1956;

Plenary meetings 822-829, 831, 838, 840.

(c) Nauru, year ended 30 June 1956;

Plenary meetings 805-810, 813, 837, 838, 840.

(d) Trust Territory of the Pacific Islands, year ended 30 June 1956;

Plenary meetings 801-806, 808, 832, 834, 840.

(e) Somaliland under Italian administration, 1956;

Plenary meetings 795-801, 803, 817, 832.

(f) Western Samoa, 1956.

Plenary meetings 828-835, 839, 840.

5. Examination of the petitions listed in the annex to the agenda.

Standing Committee on Petitions meetings 440-459. Plenary meetings 795, 801, 809, 813, 817-820, 829, 839. *Resolutions 1716-1784(XX)*.

6. Arrangements for a periodic visiting mission to Trust Territories in East Africa in 1957.

Plenary meetings 809, 836. *Resolution 1714(XX)*.

7. Administrative unions affecting Trust Territories: reports of the Standing Committee on Administrative Unions.

Standing Committee on Administrative Unions meetings 96-100. Plenary meetings 838, 839.

Agenda Item	*Consideration and Action Taken*
8. Report of the Committee on Rural Economic Development of the Trust Territories.	Committee on Rural Economic Development of Trust Territories meetings 20, 21. Plenary meeting 838.
9. Report of the Committee on Procedures regarding Petitions.	Plenary meetings 824, 835, 839. *Resolution 1713 (XX)*.
10. Dissemination of Information on the United Nations and the International Trusteeship System in Trust Territories: report of the Secretary-General (Trusteeship Council resolution 36(III) and General Assembly resolution 754(VIII)).	Plenary meeting 832.
11. Financing of the economic development plans of the Trust Territory of Somaliland under Italian administration: report of the Mission of the International Bank for Reconstruction and Development to the Trust Territory of Somaliland under Italian administration (Trusteeship Council resolution 1255(XVI)).	Plenary meetings 795-801, 803, 817, 832.
12. Revision of the Questionnaire Relating to Trust Territories: third progress report of the Sub-Committee on the Questionnaire (General Assembly resolution 751(VIII).	Plenary meeting 830.
13. The future of Togoland under French administration (General Assembly resolution 1046(XI)).	Plenary meeting 829.
14. Offers by States Members of the United Nations of study and training facilities for inhabitants of Trust Territories (General Assembly resolution 1063(XI)).	Plenary meeting 810. *Resolution 1712(XX)*.
15. The future of the Trust Territory of Tanganyika (General Assembly resolution 1065(XI)).	Plenary meeting 811.
16. Report of the United Nations Advisory Council for the Trust Territory of Somaliland under Italian administration.	Plenary meetings 795-801, 803, 817, 832.
17. Adoption of the report of the Trusteeship Council to the Security Council.	Plenary meeting 840.
18. Adoption of the report of the Trusteeship Council to the General Assembly.	Plenary meetings 805, 840.
19. Appointment of the members of the Standing Committee on Petitions.	Plenary meeting 839.
20. Revision of the rules of procedure of the Trusteeship Council.	Plenary meetings 794, 838. *Resolution 1715(XX)*.

Other Matters Discussed

Communication from the President of the Legislative Assembly of the Trust Territory of the Cameroons under French administration.	Plenary meeting 802.
Appointment of the Committee on Classification of Communications.	Plenary meeting 839.
Question of the representation of China.	Plenary meeting 836.

SEVENTH SPECIAL SESSION, 12–20 SEPTEMBER 1957

Agenda Item

1. Adoption of the agenda.	Plenary meeting 841.
2. The future of Togoland under French administration: report of the United Nations Commission on Togoland under French administration (General Assembly resolution 1046(XI)).	Plenary meetings 841-847. *Resolution 1785(S-VII)*.

MATTERS BEFORE THE INTERNATIONAL COURT OF JUSTICE DURING 1957

CASES BEFORE THE COURT

Case of Certain Norwegian Loans (France *vs.* Norway).

Right of Passage through Indian Territory (Portugal *vs.* India).

Case concerning the Guardianship of an Infant (Netherlands *vs.* Sweden).

Interhandel Case (Switzerland *vs.* United States).

Cases concerning Aerial Incident of 27 July 1955 (Israel *vs.* Bulgaria, United States *vs.* Bulgaria, United Kingdom *vs.* Bulgaria).

Case concerning the Sovereignty over Certain Frontier Lands (Belgium/Netherlands).

OTHER MATTERS

Election of members of the Chamber of Summary Procedure for 1957-1958.

Election of members of the Budgetary and Administrative Committee.

Approval of Closed Accounts for 1956.

Adoption of Budget Estimates for 1958.

Miscellaneous administrative matters.

DELEGATIONS TO THE GENERAL ASSEMBLY AND THE COUNCILS

DELEGATIONS TO THE TWELFTH SESSION OF THE GENERAL ASSEMBLY[1]

Afghanistan. *Representatives:* Dr. Najibullah, Abdul Hamid Aziz, Abdul Hakim Tabibi. *Alternates:* Said M. Kacem, Mohammed Younos Rafik, Faiz Ahmad Zikria, Amanullah Hasrat.

Albania. *Representatives:* Behar Shtylla, Nesti Nase, Reis Malile, Halim Budo, Dimitri Lamani. *Alternates:* Jonus Mersini, Nabi Agolli, Kleanth Andoni.

Argentina. *Representatives:* Mariano José Drago, Felipe Espil, Rodolfo García Arias, Roberto Enrique Guyer, Constantino Ramos. *Alternates:* Eduardo Bradley, Julio Cesar Carasales, Leopoldo Hugo Tettamanti, Raúl Quijano, Ramón A. Salem.

Australia. *Representatives:* R. G. Casey, E. Ronald Walker, P. R. Heydon, William D. Forsyth, K. C. O. Shann. *Alternates:* Brian C. Hill, T. A. Pyman, P. E. Lucock, E. W. Peters, K. T. Kelly.

Austria. *Representatives:* Leopold Figl, Bruno Kreisky, Franz Gschnitzer, Franz Prinke, Franz Olah, Franz Matsch, Kurt Waldheim. *Alternates:* Josef A. Schoener, Heinrich Haymerle, Egon Ranshofen-Wertheimer.

Belgium. *Representatives:* Victor Larock, Joseph Nisot, Henri Rolin, Paul Struye, G. Ciselet, Pierre Ryckmans (in the absence of Victor Larock). *Alternates:* Pierre Ryckmans, J. de Thier, M. Wéry, L. G. Delhaye, Baron P. de Gaiffier d'Hestroy.

Bolivia. *Representatives:* Manuel Barrau Peláez, Germán Quiroga Galdo, Alberto Mendoza López, Marcial Tamayo, Manuel Frontaura Argandoña. *Alternates:* Heberto Añez Añez, Sandoval Moron, Carlos Casap, Jorge Peralta Soruco, Alberto Canedo.

Brazil. *Representatives:* Oswaldo Aranha, Cyro de Freitas-Valle, Gilberto Amado, Augusto Frederico Schmidt, Hermes Lima. *Alternates:* Ranulpho Bocayuva Cunha, J. C. de Ataliba Nogueira, Jayme de Barros, Newton Barbosa Tatsch.

Bulgaria. *Representatives:* Milko Tarabanov, Peter Voutov, Dimiter Bratanov, Evgeni Kamenov, Ivan Daskalov. *Alternates:* Christos Boev, Assen Georgiev, Atanas Belinski.

Burma. *Representatives:* Sithu U Thant, Sithu U Aung Soe, Maha Thiri Thudama Justice Thaung Sein, U Hla Kyaing, U Sein Win. *Alternates:* U Ko Ko Gyi, Thiri Pyanchi U Thet Tin, U Than Hla.

Byelorussian SSR. *Representatives:* K. V. Kiselev, O. A. Zdorovenin, P. F. Glebko, Mrs. O. A. Sysoeva, G. F. Basov. *Alternates:* G. M. Denichenko, G. G. Chernushchenko.

Cambodia. *Representatives:* Penn Nouth, Nong Kimny. *Alternates:* Koun Wick, Ly Chinly, Lert Wongsanith, Phuong Margain, Lamouth Kang, Penn Thol.

Canada. *Representatives:* John G. Diefenbaker, Mrs. Ellen Louk Fairclough, Sidney E. Smith, Wallace Nesbitt, R. A. MacKay, Mrs. Harry S. Quart, Frank Lennard. *Alternates:* Harry O. White, Théogène Ricard, Escott Reid, W. D. Matthews, E. Benjamin Rogers.

Ceylon. *Representatives:* R. S. S. Gunewardene, Nimal Karunatilleke, Badiudin Mahmud, A. B. Perera, D. W. Rajapatirana. *Alternates:* H. S. Amerasinghe, Hevanpola Ratanasara Thera.

Chile. *Representatives:* José Serrano, Raúl Aldunate, Oscar Aguero, Luis Melo Lecaros, Alfonso Grez. *Alternates:* Horacio Suárez, Joaquín Figueroa, Miguel Ignacio Bravo, Luis Humbser, Leonidas Irarrázaval.

China. *Representatives:* George K. C. Yeh, Tingfu F. Tsiang, Wang Yun-Wu, Dr. Hu Shih, Liu Chieh. *Alternates:* Hsueh Yu-Chi, Chiping H. C. Kiang, Cheng Paonan, Hsioh-Ren Wei, Chun-Ming Chang.

Colombia. *Representatives:* Carlos Sanz de Santamaría, Alfonso Araújo, Alberto Zuleta Angel, Antonio Rocha, Alfredo Vasquez Carrizosa. *Alternates:* Germán Zea, Gabriel Carreño Mallarino, Diego Mejía.

Costa Rica. *Representatives:* Alberto F. Cañas, Gonzalo J. Facio, Hernán González, Rogelio Sotela, Raúl F. Trejos. *Alternates:* Mrs. Karen de Figueres, Alvar Antillon, Mrs. Irma Morales, José F. Carballo, Mrs. Emilia C. de Barish.

Cuba. *Representatives:* Emilio Núñez Portuondo, Carlos Blanco, Miss Uldarica Mañas, Miss Silvia Shelton, Manuel Secades y Manrara. *Alternates:* Juan O'Naghten, Miss Josefina García Sierra, Miss Ana María Perera.

Czechoslovakia. *Representatives:* Vaclav David, Jiri

Listings in this appendix are based on information and credentials officially submitted by Member States to the United Nations.

[1] Listing includes names of those representatives and alternates who were only able to attend part of the General Assembly's twelfth session, and also names of those replacing them.

Nosek, Joseph Ullrich, Karel Petrzelka, Mrs. Helena Leflerova. *Alternates:* Jaroslav Pscolka, Zdenek Trhlik, Gejza Mencer, Milos Vejvoda.

Denmark. *Representatives:* Jens Otto Krag, Ernst Christiansen, Alsing Andersen, Henry L. W. Jensen, C. F. Ladefoged, Mrs. M. A. Von Lowzow, P. Veistrup. *Alternates:* Karl I. Eskelund, Alfred Jorgensen, Hessellund Jensen, Ernst Meinstorp, Dr. Esther Ammundsen.

Dominican Republic. *Representatives:* Porfirio Herrera Baez, Enrique de Marchena, Temístocles Messina, Ambrosio Alvarez Aybar, Miss Minerva Bernardino. *Alternates:* Federico Llaverias, Albaro Logrono Battle, Kémil L. Dipp Gómez, Miss Marina Prats Nieto.

Ecuador. *Representatives:* Jose Vicente Trujillo, Augusto Dillon Valdez, Luis Ponce Enriquez, Luis Coloma Silva, Gustavo Larrea. *Alternates:* Alfonso Moscoso, Julio Prado Vallejo.

Egypt. *Representatives:* Mahmoud Fawzi, Omar Loutfi, M. Zaki Kenawi, Abdel Moneim El Banna. *Alternates:* Salah Gohar, Ahmed Talaat, Ahmed El-Messiri, Abdel Hamid Abdel-Ghani, Abdullah El-Erian.

El Salvador. *Representatives:* M. Rafael Urquía, Carlos Adalberto Alfaro, F. Antonio Carrillo, Francisco R. Lima, Roberto E. Quirós. *Alternates:* Miguel A. Magaña, Guillermo Trigueros.

Ethiopia. *Representatives:* Yilma Deressa, Haddis Alemayehou, Gabre-Meskel Kifle-Egzy. *Alternates:* Tesfaye Gabre-Egzy, Addimau Tesemma, Miss Judith Imru, Yawand-Wossen Mangasha.

Finland. *Representatives:* Johannes Virolainen, Ralph Enckell, George de Gripenberg, Reinhold Svento, Mrs. Tyyne Leivo-Larsson. *Alternates:* Helge Miettunen, Miss Kyllikki Pohjala, Unto Miettinen, Erik Castren, Matti Tuovinen.

France. *Representatives:* Christian Pineau, Félix Houphouet-Boigny, Sid Cara, Gérard Jacquet, Jules Moch, Guillaume Georges-Picot. *Alternates:* Louis Jacquinot, Félix Gouin, Pierre Abelin, André Armengaud, Jacques Koscziusko-Morizet.

Ghana. *Representatives:* Ako Djei, F. Y. Asare, Daniel A. Chapman, S. K. Anthony, G. K. Amegbe, I. J. Adomako-Mensah. *Alternates:* Ebenezer Adam, E. A. Mahama, F. S. Arkhupst, R. M. Akwei, Amon Nikoi, Miss Gloria Addae.

Greece. *Representatives:* Evangelos Averoff-Tossizza, Andreas Stratos, George Voyatzis, George V. Melas, Christian X. Palamas. *Alternates:* Savvas Loizides, George Christopoulos, Constantin Triantaphyllakos, Phedon Annino Cavalierato, Zenon Rossides.

Guatemala. *Representatives:* Jorge Skinner-Klee, Emilio Arenales Catalán, Isidro Lemus Dimas, David Vela, José Rölz Bennett. *Alternates:* Gabriel Biguria, Mrs. Graciela Quan, Ramiro Aragón, Maximiliano Kestler, Fernando Juarez Rodas.

Haiti. *Representatives:* Emile Saint-Lot, Max H. Dorsinville, Salnave Zamor, Ernest G. Chauvet, Hérard C. L. Roy. *Alternates:* Rémy Bastien, Georges Salomon, Henry Ch. Rosemond.

Honduras. *Representatives:* Marco Antonio Batres, Raúl Alvarado, Juan J. Funes, Miguel Paz Paredes.

Hungary. *Representatives:* Imre Horvath, Endre Sik, Peter Mod, Janos Peter, Janos Szita. *Alternates:* Mme Marta Kolozs, Endre Ustor, Laszlo Sarkany, Imre Hollai, Janos Szabo.

Iceland. *Representatives:* Thor Thors, Gudmundur I. Gudmundsson, Thorarinn Thorarinsson, Hannes Kjartanson.

India. *Representatives:* V. K. Krishna Menon, Ali Yavar Jung, G. S. Pathak, Arthur S. Lall, J. D'Souza. *Alternates:* Fakhruddin Ali Ahmed, M. Gopala Menon, J. N. Sahni, Mrs. Mona Hensman.

Indonesia. *Representatives:* Dr. Subandrio, Ali Sastroamidjojo, Abu Hanifah, Moekarto Notowidigdo, Zairin Zain. *Alternates:* Miss Laili Roesad, Mr. Nugroho, H. Mohammed Sharif, Basri Haznam, Effendi Nur.

Iran. *Representatives:* Ali Gholi Ardalan, Nasrollah Entezam, Djalal Abdoh, Abbas Gholi Ardalan, Mohammad Ali Massoud-Ansari, Fereydoun Adamiyat. *Alternates:* Amir Rashidi, Aslan Afshar, Ahmad Eghbal, Bahman Ahaneen, Majid Rahnema.

Iraq. *Representatives:* Ali Mumtaz Al-Daftari, Mousa Al-Shabandar, Abdul Ghani Al-Dalli, Hashim Jawad, Tarik Al-Askari. *Alternates:* Mrs. Bedia Afnan, Hashim Khalil, Kadhim M. Khalaf, Usamah Kadry, Ismat Kittani.

Ireland. *Representatives:* Frank Aiken, Frederick H. Boland, Sean Nunan, Conor Cruise O'Brien, Eamonn L. Kennedy. *Alternates:* Miss Maire C. MacEntee, Aedan P. J. O'Beirne, Paul J. G. Keating.

Israel. *Representatives:* Mrs. Golda Meir, Abba Eban, Arthur Lourie, Ishar Harari, Emile Najar, Mordecai R. Kidron. *Alternates:* Joseph Avidar, Daniel Lewin, Tuvia Arazi, Shabtai Rosenne, Arthur C. A. Liveran.

Italy. *Representatives:* Giuseppe Pella, Attilio Piccioni, Emilio Battista, Giuseppe Cerulli Irelli, Leonardo Vitetti. *Alternates:* Edoardo Martino, Nicolo Di Bernardo, Enrico Guastone Belcredi, Mario Toscano, Eugenio Plaja.

Japan. *Representatives:* Aiichiro Fujiyama, Koto Matsudaira, Toru Hagiwara, Koichiro Asakai, Katsushiro Narita. *Alternates:* Akira Miyazaki, Takezo Shimoda, Miss Taki Fujita, Masayoshi Kakitsubo, Mitsuo Tanaka.

Jordan. *Representatives:* Yusuf Haikal, Thabet Khalidi. *Alternate:* Mrs. Denise Haikal.

Laos. *Representatives:* Phoui Sananikone, Ourot R. Souvannavong, Khamphan Panya, Khun One Voravong, Sisouk Na Champassak. *Alternates:* Pan Sisouphanthong, Khamsing Sananikone, Kham King Souvaniasy, Khamchan Pradith.

Lebanon. *Representatives:* Charles Malik, Victor Khouri, Nagib Sadaka, Nadim Dimeshkieh, Mouhieddine Nsouli. *Alternates:* Ghassan Tueni, Karim Azkoul, Edward A. Rizk.

Liberia. *Representatives:* Henry Ford Cooper, Charles T. O. King, George T. Brewer, Roland Cooper, Miss Angie E. Brooks. *Alternates:* J. B. Watson, John G. Howe, Nathaniel Richardson, Daubney B. Cooper.

Libya. *Representatives:* Suleiman Gerbi, Abdurrazzak O. Missallati, Hassan Makhlouf, Omar Muntasser.

Luxembourg. *Representatives:* Joseph Bech, Georges

Heisbourg, Albert Borschette, Paul Reuter. *Alternates:* Charles de Clervaux, Jean Wagner, Guy de Muyser.

Malaya, Federation of. *Representatives:* Ismail bin Dato Abdul Rahman, Ismail bin Mohamed Ali, Too Joon Hing, K. Devasar, Tuan Syed Omar bin Syed Abdullah, Abu Bakar bin Baginda, Tay Hooi Soo, Engku Muhsein bin Abdul Kadir. *Alternates:* Tunku Ja'afar, Lim Taik Choon, Lim Teow Chong, Ramaswamy Iyer, Tuan Syed Adam Hogan Shaidali.

Mexico. *Representatives:* Luis Padilla Nervo, Rafael de la Colina, Alfonso García Robles, Daniel Cosío Villegas, Eduardo Espinosa y Prieto. *Alternates:* Antonio Gómez Robledo, Jorge Castañeda, Julián Sáenz Hinojosa, José Trinidad Delgado.

Morocco. *Representatives:* Ahmed Balafrej, Ahmed Laraki, Abdellatif Filali, Ahmed Osman, M'hamed Elkohen. *Alternates:* Taieb Bouazza, Abdessadak Khattabi.

Nepal. *Representatives:* Rishikesh Shaha, Sardar Prakat Man Singh, Brija Kanta Thakur. *Alternate:* G. R. Pandey.

Netherlands. *Representatives:* J. M. A. H. Luns, C. W. A. Schurmann, L. J. C. Beaufort, G. J. N. M. Ruygers, Jonkheer W. H. J. van Asch van Wijk. *Alternates:* J. Meijer, B. V. A. Roling, J. P. Bannier, H. R. van Houten, A. M. Donner.

New Zealand. *Representatives:* T. L. Macdonald, G. R. Laking, C. Craw, T. C. Larkin, R. Q. Quentin Baxter. *Alternates:* F. A. Small, N. V. Lough, R. M. Miller, William Gray Thorp.

Nicaragua. *Representatives:* Guillermo Sevilla Sacasa, Luis Mena Solórzano, Alejandro Abaunza Marenco, Alfredo Ortega Urbina, Julio C. Morales.

Norway. *Representatives:* Halvard Lange, Arne Skaug, Finn Moe, Alv Kjos, Trond Hegna, Sverre Rostoft, Hans Engen. *Alternates:* Dag Bryn, Paul Ingebretsen, Hans Borgen, Kjell Bondevik, Mrs. Aase Lionaes.

Pakistan. *Representatives:* Malik Firoz Khan Noon, G. Ahmed, Sardar Mumtaz Ali Khan, S. M. Khan, S. K. Sen. *Alternates:* Agha Shahi, Begum Nur Jehan-Murshid, Muzaffar Ahmad Chaudhuri, Zulfiqar Bhutto, Peter Paul Gomez.

Panama. *Representatives:* Aquilino E. Boyd, Alejandro Remón Cantera, Jorge E. Illueca, César A. Quintero, Roberto E. Arias. *Alternates:* Eusebio A. Morales, George Westerman, Samuel Lewis Galindo, Roberto R. Alemán, Ernesto de la Ossa.

Paraguay. *Representatives:* Raúl Sapena Pastor, Pacífico Montero de Vargas, Augusto R. Fuster, Miguel Solano López, Fernando A. Caballero Marsal. *Alternates:* Carlos Augusto Saldivar, Manuel Avila.

Peru. *Representatives:* Manuel Cisneros Sánchez, Víctor Andrés Belaúnde, Fernando Berckemeyer, Carlos Mackehenie, Carlos Manuel Cox. *Alternates:* Manuel Félix Maúrtua, José Pareja Paz Soldan, José Antonio Encinas, Jorge Velando, Andrés A. Aramburú.

Philippines. *Representatives:* Carlos P. Romulo, Emmanuel Pelaez, Feliciano P. Leviste, Salvador P. Lopez, Joaquin Miguel Elizalde. *Alternates:* Octavio

L. Maloles, Victorio D. Carpio, Urbano A. Zafra, Hortencio J. Brillantes, Ernesto L. Calingasan.

Poland. *Representatives:* Adam Rapacki, Jozef Winiewicz, Jerzy Michalowski, Stanislaw Gajewski, Aleksander Krajewski. *Alternates:* Manfred Lachs, Boleslaw Jelen, Tadeusz Lychowski.

Portugal. *Representatives:* Vasco Vieira Garin, Henrique Miranda Martins de Carvalho, Albano Nogueira, Adriano José Alves Moreira, Alberto Franco Nogueira. *Alternates:* José Madeira Rodrigues, Fernando Olavo Gouveia da Veiga, Luis Teixera, Antonio Bandeira Guimararaes, José Manuel Fragoso, Julio Miguel Monteiro, Jr.

Romania. *Representatives:* Ion Gheorghe Maurer, Mihai Magheru, Silviu Brucan, Edouard Mezincescu, Grigore Geamanu. *Alternates:* Bazil Serban, Corneliu Bogdan, George Ivascu, Teodor Marinescu, Mircea Malitza.

Saudi Arabia. *Representatives:* Ahmad Shukairy, Sheikh Abdel Rahman Bassam, Jamil M. Baroody, Aouney W. Dejany, Omar Haliq. *Alternates:* Omar A. Khadra, Mohammad Charara, Ibrahim Bakur, Faisal Hegelan, Mamdouh Adeeb.

Spain. *Representatives:* José Félix de Lequerica, José Fernández Villaverde (Marquess of Santa Cruz), José María de Areilza, Manuel Aznar, Antonio de Luna. *Alternates:* Diego Buigas de Dalmau, José Miguel Ruiz Morales, Ramón Sedó, Jaime de Piniés, Antonio Cacho Zabalza.

Sudan. *Representatives:* Yacoub Osman, Abbas El-Dabi, Mohamed Ahmed Yagi, Mohammed Abdel Maged Ahmed, Hassan Mohamed Hassan. *Alternates:* Abubakr Osman, Muatasim El Berreir.

Sweden. *Representatives:* Osten Unden, Mrs. Ulla Lindstrom, Rickard Sandler, Ake Holmback, Rolf Sohlman, Sten Wahlund, Gunnar V. Jarring, Bror Arvid, Sture Petren, Sverker Astrom. *Alternates:* Rolf Edberg, Elis Hastad, Bertil von Friesen, Torsten Bengtsson, Mrs. Agda Rossel, Otto Westling, Leif Cassel, Karl Kilsmo.

Syria. *Representatives:* Salah Eddine Bitar, Farid Zeineddine, Adib Daoudy, George Tomeh, Jawdat Mufti. *Alternates:* Najmuddine Rifai, Mohammed H. El-Farra, Tarek Jabri.

Thailand. *Representatives:* Prince Wan Waithayakon, Thanat Khoman, Thuaithep Devakul. *Alternates:* Yuad Loesrit, Banthern Amatyakul, Swate Komalabhuti.

Tunisia. *Representatives:* Bahi Ladgham, Sadok Mokkadem, Mongi Slim, Ahmed Tlili, Mahmoud El Messaadi, Moncef Kedadi, Mustapha Abdesselam, Mahmoud Mestiri. *Alternates:* Habib Achour, Habib Bourguiba, Jr., M'hammed Ali Annabi, M'hammed Essafi, Ezzedine Bouhila, Taufik Mazik.

Turkey. *Representatives:* Seyfullah Esin, Selim Sarper, Turgut Menemencioglu, Necdet Kent, C. S. Hayta. *Alternates:* Ismail Soysal, Haluk Kura, Nejat Ertuzun, Vahap Asiroglu, Umit Haluk Bayulken.

Ukrainian SSR. *Representatives:* L. F. Palamarchuk, P. D. Leshchenko, J. V. Kriven, Mrs. V. Y. Bilai, N. G. Maksimovich. *Alternates:* K. S. Zabigailo, V. P. Kozachenko.

Union of South Africa. *Representatives:* J. S. F. Botha, M. I. Botha. *Alternates:* W. Theunissen, D. S. Franklin.

USSR. *Representatives:* A. A. Gromyko, V. V. Kuznetsov, Y. V. Peive, Arkady A. Sobolev, G. N. Zarubin. *Alternates:* Gani Sultanov, Mrs. Z. V. Mironova, B. F. Podtserob, K. B. Novikov, Georgy P. Arkadev.

United Kingdom. *Representatives:* Selwyn Lloyd, Allan Noble, Sir Pierson Dixon, Mrs. Walter Elliot, Gilbert Longden. *Alternates:* William Aitken, Sir Alec Randall, P. M. Crosthwaite, Sir Andrew Cohen, I. T. M. Pink, F. A. Vallat.

United States. *Representatives:* John Foster Dulles, Henry Cabot Lodge, A. S. J. Carnahan, Walter H. Judd, George Meany, Herman Wells. *Alternates:* James J. Wadsworth, Miss Irene Dunne (Mrs. Francis D. Griffin), Philip Klutznick, Mrs. Oswald B. Lord, Genoa S. Washington.

Uruguay. *Representatives:* César Charlone, Enrique Rodríguez Fabregat, Manuel Flores Mora, Alberto M. Rosselli, Adolfo Tejera. *Alternates:* Quintín Alfonsín, César Montero Bustamante, Américo Paz Aguirre, Mateo Marques Seré, Eduardo Acevedo.

Venezuela. *Representatives:* José Loreto Arismendi, Santiago Pérez Pérez, Martín Pérez Matos, Lorenzo Mendoza Fleury, Francisco Manuel Mármol, Francisco López Herrera, Eduardo Plaza, Gabriel Angel Lovera. *Alternates:* Delfín Enrique Páez, Francisco Alfonzo Ravard, Rafael Armando Rojas, Luis Herrera Marcano, Nelson Himiab, Juan Alvarado, Armando Molina.

Yemen. *Representatives:* Prince Sayful Islam Al-Hassan, Mohammed Kamil Abdul Rahim, Ahmad Zabarah, Mohammed Al-Haifi Abdul Haidi Al Hamdani. *Alternates:* Mohammed Abou-Taleb, Tawfik Chamandi.

Yugoslavia. *Representatives:* Koca Popovic, Srdja Prica, Joza Brilej, Sergije Makiedo, Djura Nincic, Janez Stanoynik. *Alternates:* Lazar Lilic, Dimce Belovski, Janvid Flere, Miss Mara Radic, Aleksandar Bozovic.

OBSERVERS OF NON-MEMBER STATES MAINTAINING PERMANENT OBSERVERS' OFFICES AT HEADQUARTERS

Germany, Federal Republic of: Georg von Broich-Oppert, Gerhard Rödel, Ellinor von Puttkamer, Gunther van Well, Carl von Mutius.

Korea, Republic of: You Chan Yang, Ben C. Limb, Pyo Wook Han, Young Choo Kim, Bob Lin Kim, Kwan Sik Min, Helen Kim, Hyong Keun Kim, Suk Hun Yoon.

Monaco: Marcel A. Palmaro, John Dubé.

Switzerland: Agostino J. Soldati, Jurg Iselin, Pierre Keller.

REPRESENTATIVES OF SPECIALIZED AGENCIES

International Labour Organisation (ILO): Emilio Calderón Puig, Sir Guildhaume Myrddin-Evans, G. P. Delaney, N. H. Tata, David A. Morse, C. W. Jenks (alternate to Mr. Morse).

Food and Agriculture Organization (FAO): Sir Herbert Broadley, Frank Weisl, Joseph L. Orr, J. Drake.

United Nations Educational, Scientific and Cultural Organization (UNESCO): René Maheu, Malcolm, S. Adiseshiah, Arthur F. Gagliotti, William Frye, Asdrúbal Salsamendi.

World Health Organization (WHO): Dr. M. G. Candau, M. P. Siegel, Dr. Rodolphe L. Coigney, Dr. V. E. Z. Tabona, Mrs. S. Meagher.

International Bank for Reconstruction and Development: Enrique López Herrarte.

International Monetary Fund: Gordon Williams.

International Civil Aviation Organization (ICAO): Carl Ljunberg, B. J. Kwiecinski.

Universal Postal Union (UPU): Dr. Fritz Hess, F. R. Radice, A. M. Boennec.

International Telecommunication Union (ITU): Marco Aurelio Andrada.

REPRESENTATIVES AND DEPUTY, ALTERNATE AND ACTING REPRESENTATIVES TO THE SECURITY COUNCIL

Australia: E. Ronald Walker, Brian C. Hill.

China: Tingfu F. Tsiang, Chiping H. C. Kiang.

Colombia: Francisco Urrutia, Alfonso Araujo, Carlos Vesga Duarte, Alberto Zuleta Angel.

Cuba: Emilio Núñez Portuondo, Carlos Blanco, Miss Uldarica Mañas.

France: Hervé Alphand, Guillaume Georges-Picot, Louis de Guiringaud, Pierre de Vaucelles.

Iraq: Hashim Jawad, Moussa Al-Shabandar, Khadim M. Khalaf.

Philippines: Carlos P. Romulo, José D. Ingles, Mauro Mendez.

Sweden: Gunnar V. Jarring, Claes Carbonnier.

USSR: Arkady Aleksandrovich Sobolev, Georgy Petrovich Arkadev.

United Kingdom: Sir Pierson Dixon, P. M. Crosthwaite.

United States: Henry Cabot Lodge, James J. Wadsworth, James W. Barco.

DELEGATIONS TO THE ECONOMIC AND SOCIAL COUNCIL

TWENTY-THIRD SESSION

MEMBERS OF THE COUNCIL

Argentina. *Representative:* Mariano José Drago. *Alternates:* Roberto A. Carman, Eduardo Bradley.

Brazil. *Representative:* Cyro de Freitas-Valle. *Alternate:* Eurico Penteado.

Canada. *Representative:* R. A. MacKay. *Alternates:* George F. Davidson, Jean Boucher.

China. *Representative:* Cheng Paonan. *Alternate:* P. Y. Tsao.

Dominican Republic. *Representatives:* Enrique de Marchena, Ambrosio Alvarez Aybar, Miss Minerva Bernardino, Kémil L. Dipp Gómez.

Egypt. *Representative:* Omar Loutfi. *Alternates:* Abdel Hamid Abdel-Ghani, Mahmoud Amin Anis.

Finland. *Representative:* Mrs. Tyyne Leivo-Larsson. *Alternates:* Taru Reino Kai Rossi, Bjorn-Olof Alholm, Ilkka O. Pastinen.

France. *Representatives:* Pierre Abelin, Guillaume Georges-Picot. *Alternates:* Georges Boris, Valéry Giscard d'Estaing, Gilles Gozard.

Greece. *Representative:* Christian X. Palamas. *Alternates:* Costa P. Caranicas, Dennis Carayannis, Theodore P. Pyrlas, John G. Gregoriades.

Indonesia. *Representative:* R. A. Asmaoen. *Alternate:* H. Mohammed Sharif.

Mexico. *Representative:* Daniel Cosío Villegas. *Alternates:* Enrique Pérez López, Enrique Bravo Caro.

Netherlands. *Representative:* J. M. A. H. Luns. *Alternates:* C. W. A. Schurmann, J. Meyer, J. Kaufmann.

Pakistan. *Representative:* Mohammad Mir Khan. *Alternates:* G. A. Faruqui, Zahiruddin Ahmed.

Poland. *Representative:* Jerzy Michalowski. *Alternates:* Tadeusz Lychowski, Jacek Machowski, Antoni Czarkowski.

USSR. *Representative:* G. P. Arkadev. *Alternate:* G. F. Saksin.

United Kingdom. *Representative:* R. D. J. Scott Fox.

United States. *Representative:* John C. Baker. *Alternate:* Walter M. Kotschnig.

Yugoslavia. *Representative:* Joza Brilej. *Alternates:* Janvid Flere, Miss Mara Radic.

OBSERVERS FROM UNITED NATIONS MEMBER STATES NOT MEMBERS OF THE COUNCIL

Albania: Reis Malile, Nabi Agolli.
Belgium: J. Woulbroun, Jacques Raeymaeckers.
Bulgaria: Peter G. Voutov, Bogomil D. Todorov.
Chile: Alfonso Grez, Octavio Allende.
Czechoslovakia: Josef Ullrich, Jaroslav Pscolka, Milos Vejvoda, Dusan Spacil, Zdenek Paukner.
Hungary: Peter Mod, Pal Racz, Janos Szabo.
India: P. N. Kaul.
Ireland: Eamonn L. Kennedy.
Israel: Mrs. Tamar Shoham-Sharon, Zvi Neeman.
Italy: Luciano Giretti.
Japan: Haruki Mori, Motoo Ogiso, Hisahiko Okazaki.
Philippines: Pablo A. Peña, Miss Lirio Tongson.
Romania: Athanase Jopa, Mircea Malitza.
Saudi Arabia: Jamil M. Baroody, Omar Haliq.
Venezuela: Santiago Pérez Pérez, Martín Pérez Matos, Francisco Alfonzo Ravard, Ignacio Silva Sucre.

REPRESENTATIVES AND ALTERNATE REPRESENTATIVES OF SPECIALIZED AGENCIES

International Labour Organisation (ILO): R. A. Métall, R. L. Roux.

Food and Agriculture Organization (FAO): Joseph L. Orr, R. Schickele.

United Nations Educational, Scientific and Cultural Organization (UNESCO): René Maheu, A. F. Gagliotti, A. Salsamendi.

World Health Organization (WHO): Dr. V. E. Z. Tabona, Mrs. Sylvia Meagher.

International Bank for Reconstruction and Development: Eugene R. Black, Enrique López Herrarte.

International Monetary Fund: Per Jacobsson, Gordon Williams.

International Civil Aviation Organization (ICAO): R. J. Moulton, F. X. Byrne.

World Meteorological Organization (WMO): James W. Osmun, E. J. Christie.

Preparatory Committee of the Inter-Governmental Maritime Consultative Organization (IMCO): Branko Lukac.

REPRESENTATIVES OF NON-GOVERNMENTAL ORGANIZATIONS (CATEGORY A)

International Chamber of Commerce: Carl E. McDowell, Mrs. Roberta M. Lusardi, Mrs. Sandra S. Berlstein.

International Confederation of Free Trade Unions: William Kemsley, Ismael Rodríguez.

International Co-operative Alliance: Leslie E. Woodcock, Mrs. Cedric Long.

International Federation of Christian Trade Unions: Gérard Thormann.

World Federation of Trade Unions: Jan Dessau, Miss Elinor Kahn.

World Federation of United Nations Associations: Hilary Barratt-Brown, Mrs. Santha Rama Rau.

World Veterans Federation: Jacques Katel, Mrs. Claire Rogger.

REPRESENTATIVES OF NON-GOVERNMENTAL ORGANIZATIONS (CATEGORY B)

Agudas Israel World Organization: Isaac Lewin.

Chamber of Commerce of the United States of America: Earl F. Cruickshank.

Commission of the Churches on International Affairs: Dominique Micheli.

Consultative Council of Jewish Organizations: Mrs. Carol R. Lubin.

Friends World Committee for Consultation: Grant C. Fraser.

International Air Transport Association: J. A. Paine.

International Catholic Child Bureau: Mrs. Margaret M. Bedard.

International Catholic Press Union: Gay MacEoin.

International Conference of Catholic Charities: Louis C. Longarzo.

International Council of Women: Mrs. Eunice H. Carter.

International Federation for Housing and Town Planning: Charles S. Ascher.

International Federation of Business and Professional Women: Mrs. Esther Hymer.

International Federation of University Women: Mrs. Barbara D. Evans.

International Federation of Women Lawyers: Miss A. Viola Smith, Mrs. Frances Cymberg, Mrs. Rose K. Hirschman, Mrs. Raymonde I. Paul.

International Institute of Administrative Sciences: Charles S. Ascher.
International Law Association: Samuel K. C. Kopper.
International League for the Rights of Man: Mrs. Dora Roitburd.
International Movement for Fraternal Union among Races and Peoples: Miss Marjory Krynen.
International Society for the Welfare of Cripples: Donald V. Wilson, Henk Nieuwenhuize.
International Road Transport Union: Eric Rath.
International Union of Local Authorities: Charles S. Ascher.
Nouvelles Equipes Internationales: Konrad Sieniewicz, Janusz Sleszynski.
Women's International League for Peace and Freedom: Mrs. Adelaide Baker.
World Alliance of Young Men's Christian Associations: Owen E. Pence.
World Assembly of Youth: Robert S. Perlzweig.
World Federation of Catholic Young Women and Girls: Mrs. Frank Berberich, Mrs. Peter Cass.
World Jewish Congress: Gerhard Jacoby.
World Union of Catholic Women's Organizations: Miss Catherine Schaefer, Miss Alba Zizzamia.
Young Christian Workers: Miss Caroline Pezzullo.

REPRESENTATIVES OF NON-GOVERNMENTAL ORGANIZATIONS (REGISTER)

International World Calendar Association: James Avery Joyce.
World Federation for Mental Health: Mrs. Helen S. Ascher.

TWENTY-FOURTH SESSION

MEMBERS OF THE COUNCIL

The following listing includes the names, where available, of those attending also the resumed twenty-fourth session of the Economic and Social Council.
Argentina. *Representative:* Mariano José Drago. *Alternates:* Raúl C. Migone, Andrés M. Lescure, Roberto Potente, Juan Martese.
Brazil. *Representative:* Henrique de Souza Gomes. *Alternate:* Antonio Correa do Lago.
Canada. *Representative:* R. A. MacKay, George F. Davidson. *Alternates:* George F. Davidson, Max Wershof, O. Firestone, Sydney Pollock.
China. *Representative:* Cheng Paonan. *Alternate:* P. Y. Tsao.
Dominican Republic. *Representative:* Salvador Ortiz. *Alternates:* Miss Minerva Bernardino, José Savinon.
Egypt. *Representative:* El Attafi Sinbel. *Alternates:* Abdel Moneim El Banna, Abdel Hamid Abdel-Ghani.
Finland. *Representative:* Mrs. Tyyne Leivo-Larsson. *Alternates:* Eino Saari, Erik Tornqvist, Pentti Suomela, Bjorn-Olof Alholm.
France. *Representative:* Pierre Abelin. *Alternates:* André Armengaud, Valéry Giscard d'Estaing, Gilles Gozard, Henri Longchambon, Jacques Masteau.

Greece. *Representatives:* Georges Bensis, Costa P. Caranicas.
Indonesia. *Representative:* Ismael Thajeb, Ali Sastroamidjojo. *Alternate:* August F. Ompi.
Mexico. *Representative:* Daniel Cosío Villegas. *Alternates:* Francisco Vazquez Treserra, Jorge Castañeda.
Netherlands. *Representative:* J. M. A. H. Luns. *Alternates:* C. W. A. Schurmann, G. J. N. M. Ruygers, Miss J. C. H. H. de Vink, J. Meyer, Baron C. A. Bentinck, J. P. Bannier, Jonkheer W. H. J. van Asch van Wijck.
Pakistan. *Representative:* Mohammad Mir Khan. *Alternates:* G. A. Faruqui, S. M. Raza, S. S. Jafri, N. M. Uquali, Akbar Adil, Zahiruddin Ahmed.
Poland. *Representative:* Jerzy Michalowski. *Alternates:* Adam Meller-Conrad, Tadeusz Lychowski, Mieczyslaw Blusztajn.
USSR. *Representatives:* Aleksey V. Zakharov, G. P. Arkadev. *Alternates:* Pavel M. Chernyshev, Anatoly S. Chistyakov, Mrs. Nonna A. Muravieva, Evgeny S. Shershnev, Yakov M. Lomakin, Aleksandr I. Bechin, Vitaly P. Romadin.
United Kingdom. *Representative:* W. Ormsby-Gore. *Alternates:* Sir Alec Randall, Sir Samuel Hoare, R. D. J. Scott Fox, J. D. Murray.
United States. *Representative:* Neil H. Jacoby. *Alternates:* Walter M. Kotschnig, Franklin C. Gowen.
Yugoslavia. *Representative:* Joza Brilej. *Alternates:* Gustav Vlahov, Jovan Vukmanovic, Janez Stanovnik, Janvid Flere, Stjepan Han.

OBSERVERS FROM UNITED NATIONS MEMBER STATES NOT MEMBERS OF THE COUNCIL

Australia: Miss J. F. Crichton.
Belgium: Jean Etienne.
Bulgaria: Atanas Belinski, Todor Stoyanov, Peter G. Voutov, Bogomil D. Todorov.
Chile: Fernando Donoso-Silva, Miss Leonora Kracht.
Cuba: J. Enrique Camejo-Argudín.
Czechoslovakia: Pribyslav Pavlik, Karel Svec, I. Sronek.
Denmark: Finn Gundelach, Poul Boeg.
Hungary: Janos Szita, Karoly Kapcsos.
India: K. V. Padmanabhan.
Iran: Hossein Davoudi.
Israel: Menahen Kahany.
Italy: Marcello del Drago, Fausto Bacchetti, Lionello Cozzi, Dante Negretti, Reginaldo Munafo.
Japan: Ichiro Kawasaki, Masao Ito, Kazuo Chiba.
Luxembourg: I. Bessling.
Norway: Johan Z. Cappelen.
Portugal: Fernando de Alcambar Pereira.
Romania: Stefan Gal.
Saudi Arabia: Jamil M. Baroody, Omar Haliq.
Spain: Luis García de Llera.
Sudan: Mohammed Khogali, Abdel-Hadi Hamadto.
Sweden: Per Lind, Sixten Heppling, Arne Faeltheim.
Syria: Zoher Kabbani, Atef Danial.
Venezuela: Víctor Manuel Rivas, Ignacio Silva-Sucre, Angel Francisco Lujan.

NON-MEMBERS OF THE UNITED NATIONS REPRESENTED BY OBSERVERS

Germany, Fed. Rep. of: Rudolf Thierfelder, Karl Barte, Jürgen Ruhfus, Walter Goeller, Knud Winter.

Switzerland: Samuel Campiche, A. Kilchmann, C. Wetterwald, Yves Berthoud.

Vatican City: Monseigneur Giovanni Ferrofino, Monseigneur Antonio Innocenti, Father Henri de Riedmatten.

REPRESENTATIVES AND ALTERNATE REPRESENTATIVES OF SPECIALIZED AGENCIES

International Labour Organisation (ILO): D. Morse, C. Jenks, L. Alvarado, F. H. Wheeler.

Food and Agriculture Organization (FAO): B. Sen, Sir Herbert Broadley, A. H. Boerma, P. Terver, Dr. S. K. Dey, Dr. Gerda Blau, A. G. Orbaneja, R. A. Silow.

United Nations Educational, Scientific and Cultural Organization (UNESCO): Luther Evans, René Maheu, Malcolm S. Adiseshiah, Bozidar Aleksander.

World Health Organization (WHO): Dr. M. G. Candau, Dr. P. Dorolle, Dr. P. M. Kaul, Dr. W. Aeg Timmerman, Dr. Rodolphe L. Coigney, P. Bertrand, Dr. H. Hafezi, Dr. O. Leroux, Miss B. Newton, Miss B. Howell.

International Bank for Reconstruction and Development: Enrique López-Herrarte, Michael Hoffman.

International Monetary Fund: Marcus Fleming, J. J. Polak.

International Civil Aviation Organization (ICAO): Air Vice-Marshal Alan Ferrier, E. M. Lewis.

Universal Postal Union (UPU): Fritz Hess, Fulke M. Radice.

International Telecommunication Union (ITU): Hugh Townshend.

World Meteorological Organization (WMO): D. A. Davies, J. R. Rivet, W. R. Dyer, R. Monteanu.

Preparatory Committee of the Inter-Governmental Maritime Consultative Organization (IMCO): Branko Lukac.

Interim Commission for the International Trade Organization—Contracting Parties to the General Agreement on Tariffs and Trade: Eric Wyndham White, Jean Royer.

REPRESENTATIVES OF OTHER INTER-GOVERNMENTAL ORGANIZATIONS

Commission for Technical Co-operation in Africa South of the Sahara: Paul-Marc Henry.

League of Arab States: Zoher Kabbani, Moukhtar El Wakil (alternate).

REPRESENTATIVES OF NON-GOVERNMENTAL ORGANIZATIONS (CATEGORY A)

International Chamber of Commerce: Jacques L'Huillier.

International Confederation of Free Trade Unions: Herman Patteet, Borek Zofka.

International Co-operative Alliance: Marcel Boson.

International Federation of Agricultural Producers: Roger Savary.

International Federation of Christian Trade Unions: Georges Eggermann.

International Organization of Employers: Charles Kuntschen, Josef Vanek.

World Federation of Trade Unions: M. G. Boglietti, T. L. Drinkwater, Jan Kabourek, Mr. N'Gom, F. Runturambi.

World Federation of United Nations Associations: Charles Judd, Anoushiravan Khoshkish, Robert Smith, Mrs. Béatrice Troupin.

World Veterans Federation: Jacques Katel.

REPRESENTATIVES OF NON-GOVERNMENTAL ORGANIZATIONS (CATEGORY B)

Agudas Israel World Organization: H. Goodman, D. Rotschild, Chief Rabbi A. Safran.

All Pakistan Women's Association: Begum T. Faridi, Begum M. Jawad, Begum M. Khan.

Anti-Slavery Society: C. Greenidge.

Catholic International Union for Social Service: Miss Anne-Marie Hertoghe, Miss Pia de Ribeiro.

Chamber of Commerce of the United States of America: Earl Cruickshank.

Commission of the Churches on International Affairs: Elfan Rees.

Consultative Council of Jewish Organizations: Mrs. Carol Lubin.

Co-ordinating Board of Jewish Organizations: G. Warburg.

Friends World Committee for Consultation: Duncan Wood.

Inter-American Council of Commerce and Production: Earl Cruickshank.

International Alliance of Women: Mrs. Nina Spiller, Mrs. Clara Campoamor.

International Association of Penal Law: Paul Cornil.

Interntional Catholic Child Bureau: Miss Renée de Lucy-Fossarieu.

International Catholic Migration Commission: J. Aroca, Miss M. Houser, L. Kampschoer, J. Norris.

International Catholic Press Union: Jacques Allet.

International Committee of the Red Cross: H. Coursier, R. Olgiati.

International Conference of Catholic Charities: Mrs. Henri Beckmans de Westmeerbeck, Father Paul Bouvier, Antoine Pugin, Maurice Pugin.

International Conference of Social Work: Mrs. Sally Smith.

International Council of Women: Mrs. Eunice Carter, Miss Louise van Eeghen, Dr. Renee Girod.

International Federation "Amies de la Jeune Fille": Mrs. E. Berthoud van Werveke.

International Federation for Housing and Town Planning: Charles Ascher.

International Federation of Business and Professional Women: Miss Ruth Tomlinson.

International Federation of Catholic Youth: Bernard Fages.

International Federation of University Women: Miss Renée Dubois, Mrs. Marie Fiechter.

International Federation of Women Lawyers: Lady Gladys Chatterjee.

International Institute of Administrative Sciences: Charles Ascher.

International Law Association: Edmond Martin-Achard, Harvey Moore.

International League for the Rights of Man: André de Maday, Mrs. Hélène Romnicíano.

International Organization for Standardization: Roger Marechal, Henry St. Leger.

International Road Federation: Douglas Clarke.

International Society for Criminology: Paul Cornil, Charles Germain.

International Society of Social Defence: Charles Germain.

International Statistical Institute: J. Nixon.

International Union for Child Welfare: Miss Audrey Moser, Dan Mulock Houwer, Mrs. Jeanne-Marie Small.

International Union for Inland Navigation: Raymond Otten-Sooser.

International Union of Family Organizations: François Delaby.

International Union of Local Authorities: Charles Ascher.

League of Red Cross Societies: F. Daubenton, H. Dunning, B. de Rougé.

Liaison Committee of Women's International Organizations: Mrs. L. de Cazotte, Mrs. M. Fiechter, Mrs. A. Wiblé.

Pan Pacific South-East Asia Women's Association: Mrs. Constance Jones.

Pax Romana: Father Linus Grond.

Société Belge d'Etudes et d'Expansion: Miss Marguerite Crahay, Eugène-Jean Prost.

Society of Comparative Legislation: Charles Germain.

Women's International League for Peace and Freedom: Mrs. Gertrude Baer, Mrs. Ellen Holmgaard.

World Alliance of Young Men's Christian Associations: M. Doss.

World Assembly of Youth: Miss Helen Dale.

World Federation of Catholic Young Women and Girls: Miss Léone Herren.

World Jewish Congress: Gerhart Riegner.

World Movement of Mothers: Mrs. Marthe Jobert.

World Union of Catholic Women's Organizations: Miss Agnès de Kalbermatten, Miss Renée de Lucy-Fossarieu.

World Young Women's Christian Association: Miss Alice Arnold, Mrs. Kitty Strong, Miss Dorothea Woods.

Young Christian Workers: Patrick Keegan, Miss Caroline Pezzullo.

REPRESENTATIVES OF NON-GOVERNMENTAL ORGANIZATIONS (REGISTER)

International Committee of Catholic Nurses: Miss Lucie van Keerberghen.

International Council of Commerce Employers: Alfred Koch, Walter Pfund.

International Federation of Free Journalists (of Central and Eastern Europe and Baltic and Balkan Countries): Boleslaw Wierzbianski.

International Federation of Settlements: Miss Fern Colborn.

Open Door International: Mrs. Gertrude Baer.

O. R. T. World Union: Vladimir Grossman.

World Federation for Mental Health: Mrs. Helen S. Ascher, Dr. Audeoud-Naville, Dr. J. Rees.

World Federation of Democratic Youth: Tamaas Loering.

World Federation of the Deaf: Caesaro Maragotto.

World Union of Catholic Teachers: Paul Roger.

DELEGATIONS TO THE TRUSTEESHIP COUNCIL

NINETEENTH SESSION

MEMBERS OF THE COUNCIL

Australia. *Representative:* John Douglas Lloyd Hood. *Alternate:* Robert Napier Hamilton.

Belgium. *Representative:* Alfred Claeys-Boúúaert. *Alternate:* Luc Smolderen.

Burma. *Representative:* U Pe Kin. *Alternates:* U Than Hla, U Paw Htin.

China. *Representative:* Chiping H. C. Kiang. *Alternate:* Hsi-kun Yang.

France. *Representative:* Robert Bargues.

Guatemala. *Representative:* Emilio Arenales Catalán. *Alternates:* Isidro Lemus Dimas, José Rölz Bennett, Ramiro Aragón, Maximiliano Kestler.

Haiti. *Representative:* Max H. Dorsinville. *Alternate:* Georges Salomon.

India. *Representative:* V. K. Krishna Menon. *Alternate:* Arthur S. Lall.

Italy. *Representative:* Remigio Danilo Grillo. *Alternate:* Vittorio Zadotti.

New Zealand. *Representative:* Sir Leslie Munro. *Alternates:* T. P. Davin, William Gray Thorp.

Syria. *Representative:* Rafik Asha. *Alternates:* Jawdat Mufti, Najmuddine Rifai.

USSR. *Representative:* Ivan Ivanovich Lobanov. *Alternate:* Vladimir Nikolaevich Bendryshev.

United Kingdom. *Representative:* H. T. Bourdillon. *Alternate:* B. O. B. Gidden.

United States. *Representative:* Mason Sears. *Alternate:* Benjamin Gerig.

SPECIAL REPRESENTATIVES OF THE ADMINISTERING AUTHORITIES

Belgium: Pierre Leroy (for questions concerning Ruanda-Urundi).

France: Xavier Deniau (for questions concerning the Cameroons under French administration).

United Kingdom: J. O. Field, R. N. Jacobsen (for questions concerning the Cameroons under British administration).

REPRESENTATIVES OF SPECIALIZED AGENCIES

International Labour Organisation (ILO): R. A. Métall.

Food and Agriculture Organization (FAO): Joseph L. Orr.

United Nations Educational, Scientific and Cultural Organization (UNESCO): René Maheu, Asdrubal Salsamendi.

World Health Organization (WHO): Dr. Rodolphe L. Coigney.

TWENTIETH SESSION

MEMBERS OF THE COUNCIL

Australia. *Representative:* John Douglas Lloyd Hood. *Alternate:* Robert Napier Hamilton.

Belgium. *Representative:* Alfred Claeys-Boúúaert. *Alternate:* Luc Smolderen.

Burma. *Representative:* U Than Hla. *Alternate:* U Paw Htin.

China. *Representative:* Chiping H. C. Kiang. *Alternate:* Hsi-kun Yang.

France. *Representative:* Robert Bargues.

Guatemala. *Representative:* Emilio Arenales Catalán. *Alternates:* Isidro Lemus Dimas, José Rölz Bennett, Ramiro Aragón, Maximiliano Kestler.

Haiti. *Representative:* Max H. Dorsinville. *Alternate:* Georges Salomon.

India. *Representative:* V. K. Krishna Menon. *Alternate:* Arthur S. Lall.

Italy. *Representative:* Remigio Danilo Grillo. *Alternates:* Vittorio Zadotti, Sergio Kociancich.

New Zealand. *Representative:* Sir Leslie Munro. *Alternates:* T. P. Davin, R. M. Miller, William Gray Thorp.

Syria. *Representative:* Rafik Asha. *Alternates:* Jawdat Mufti, Najmuddine Rifai.

USSR. *Representative:* Ivan Ivanovich Lobanov. *Alternates:* Vladimir Nikolaevich Bendryshev, Gennady Stepanovich Stashevsky.

United Kingdom. *Representative:* Sir Andrew Cohen. *Alternate:* B. O. B. Gidden.

United States. *Representative:* Mason Sears. *Alternate:* Benjamin Gerig.

SPECIAL REPRESENTATIVES OF THE ADMINISTERING AUTHORITIES

Australia: John Herbert Jones (for questions concerning Nauru and New Guinea).

Italy: Haji Farah Ali Omar, Mohammed Scek Osman, Luigi Gasbarri, Vittorio Zadotti, Omar Mohallim Mohamed (for questions concerning Somaliland under Italian administration).

New Zealand: T. R. Smith (for questions concerning Western Samoa).

United Kingdom: J. Fletcher-Cooke (for questions concerning Tanganyika).

United States: Delmas H. Nucker (for questions concerning the Trust Territory of the Pacific Islands).

MEMBERS OF THE UNITED NATIONS ADVISORY COUNCIL FOR THE TRUST TERRITORY OF SOMALILAND UNDER ITALIAN ADMINISTRATION

Colombia. *Representative:* Edmundo de Holte Castello.

Egypt. *Representative:* Mohammed Hassan El Zayat.

Philippines. *Representative:* Mauro Baradi.

REPRESENTATIVES OF SPECIALIZED AGENCIES

International Labour Organisation (ILO): R. A. Métall.

Food and Agriculture Organization (FAO): Joseph L. Orr.

United Nations Educational, Scientific and Cultural Organization (UNESCO): A. F. Gagliotti, Asdrubal Salsamendi.

World Health Organization (WHO): Dr. Rodolphe L. Coigney.

International Bank for Reconstruction and Development: J. H. Williams.

SEVENTH SPECIAL SESSION

MEMBERS OF THE COUNCIL

Australia. *Representative:* John Douglas Lloyd Hood. *Alternate:* Kevin T. Kelly.

Belgium. *Representative:* Pierre Ryckmans. *Alternate:* Luc Smolderen.

Burma. *Representative:* U Than Hla. *Alternate:* U Paw Htin.

China. *Representative:* Chiping H. C. Kiang. *Alternate:* Hsi-kun Yang.

France. *Representative:* Jacques Koscziusko-Morizet. *Alternates:* Georges Apedo-Amah, Georges Spenale.

Guatemala. *Representative:* Emilio Arenales Catalán. *Alternates:* Isidro Lemus Dimas, José Rölz Bennett, Ramiro Aragón, Maximiliano Kestler.

Haiti. *Representative:* Georges Salomon.

India. *Representative:* V. K. Krishna Menon. *Alternate:* Arthur S. Lall.

Italy. *Representative:* Leonardo Vitetti. *Alternate:* Vittorio Zadotti.

New Zealand. *Representative:* Sir Leslie Munro. *Alternate:* William Gray Thorp.

Syria. *Representative:* Jawdat Mufti. *Alternate:* Najmuddine Rifai.

USSR. *Representative:* Ivan Ivanovich Lobanov. *Alternate:* Vladimir Nikolaevich Bendryshev.

United Kingdom. *Representative:* Sir Andrew Cohen. *Alternate:* B. O. B. Gidden.

United States. *Representative:* Mason Sears.

REPRESENTATIVES OF SPECIALIZED AGENCIES

International Labour Organisation (ILO): R. A. Métall.

Food and Agriculture Organization (FAO): Joseph L. Orr.

United Nations Educational, Scientific and Cultural Organization (UNESCO): René Maheu, Asdrubal Salsamendi.

World Health Organization (WHO): Dr. Rodolphe L. Coigney.

UNITED NATIONS INFORMATION CENTRES AND OFFICES
(As of 31 December 1957)

ATHENS. United Nations Information Centre
37 Vassilissis Sophias Avenue
Athens, Greece
Area covered: Greece, Israel, Turkey.

BANGKOK. Information Officer, Economic Commission for Asia and the Far East
Sala Santitham
Bangkok, Thailand
Area covered: Cambodia, Laos, Thailand.

BELGRADE. United Nations Information Centre
1, Bulevar Revolucije
(Post Office Box No. 157)
Belgrade, Yugoslavia
Area covered: Albania, Yugoslavia.

BOGOTA. Centro de Información de las Naciones Unidas.
Calle 19, Número 7-30 — Séptimo Piso
(Post Office Box No. 65-67)
Bogotá, Colombia
Area covered: Colombia, Ecuador, Peru, Venezuela.

BUENOS AIRES. Centro de Información de las Naciones Unidas
Charcas 684, 3 F
Buenos Aires, Argentina
Area covered: Argentina, Bolivia, Paraguay, Uruguay.

CAIRO. United Nations Information Centre
Sharia El Shams
Imm. Tagher
Garden City
Cairo, Egypt
Area covered: Egypt, Ethiopia, Iraq, Jordan, Lebanon, Libya, Saudi Arabia, Sudan, Syria, Yemen.

COPENHAGEN. United Nations Information Centre
37 H. C. Andersen's Boulevard
Copenhagen V, Denmark
Area covered: Denmark, Finland, Iceland, Norway, Sweden.

DJAKARTA. Information Officer for Indonesia
76 Kebon Sirih
Djakarta, Indonesia
Area covered: Indonesia.

GENEVA. Information Service of the Geneva Office, United Nations
Palais des Nations
Geneva, Switzerland
Area covered: Austria, Bulgaria, Hungary, Italy, Poland, Romania; also Germany and Switzerland.

HAGUE, THE (see under LONDON)

KARACHI. United Nations Information Centre
Strachen Road
(Post Office Box No. 349 G.P.O.)
Karachi 1, Pakistan
Area covered: Pakistan.

LONDON. United Nations Information Centre
14/15 Stratford Place
London W.1, England
Area covered: Ireland, Netherlands, United Kingdom and British Dependencies (except the British West African territories of the Gambia, Nigeria, Sierra Leone).

THE HAGUE. Information Officer for the Netherlands
21 Bezuidenhoutseweg
The Hague, The Netherlands
Area covered: The Netherlands.

MANILA. Information Officer for the Philippines
United Nations Building, Padre Faura
(Post Office Box No. 2149)
Manila, Philippines
Area covered: Philippines.

MEXICO CITY. Centro de Información de las Naciones Unidas
Génova 34
México 6 D.F., México
Area covered: Costa Rica, Cuba, Dominican Republic, El Salvador, Guatemala, Honduras, Mexico, Nicaragua, Panama.

MONROVIA. United Nations Information Centre
24 Broad Street
(Post Office Box No. 282)
Monrovia, Liberia
Area covered: Ghana, Liberia and the British West African territories of the Gambia, Nigeria, Sierra Leone.

MOSCOW. United Nations Information Centre
15 Hohlovski Pereulok, Apartment 36
Moscow, USSR
Area covered: Byelorussian SSR, Ukrainian SSR,
Union of Soviet Socialist Republics.

NEW DELHI. United Nations Information Centre
21 Curzon Road
New Delhi, India
Area covered: Burma, Ceylon, India, Nepal.

PARIS. Centre d'Information des Nations Unies
36, rue La Pérouse
Paris 16e, France
Area covered: Belgium, France, Luxembourg, Belgian
Congo, French Overseas Dependencies.

PRAGUE. United Nations Information Centre
Panská 5
Prague II, Czechoslovakia
Area covered: Czechoslovakia.

RIO DE JANEIRO. Centro de Informações das
Nações Unidas
Rua Mexico 11, Sala 1502

(Caixa Postal 1750)
Rio de Janeiro, Brazil
Area covered: Brazil.

SANTIAGO. Information Officer, Economic Com-
mission for Latin America
Avenida Providencia 871
Santiago, Chile
Area covered: Chile.

SYDNEY. United Nations Information Centre
44 Martin Place
(Box 4030, General Post Office)
Sydney, Australia
Area covered: Australia, New Zealand.

TEHERAN. United Nations Information Centre
Heshmat Dowleh
Khiaban Keyvan
Teheran, Iran
Area covered: Afghanistan, Iran.

WASHINGTON. United Nations Information Centre
1908 Q Street, N.W.
Washington 9, D.C.

INDEX

ABBREVIATIONS

ACC, Administrative Committee on Co-ordination
act., activities
admin., administration, administrative
adv., advisory
art., article
Bank, International Bank for Reconstruction and Development
Commr., Commissioner
Comm., Commission
conf., conference
consid., consideration
conv., convention
cttee., committee
ECAFE, Economic Commission for Asia and the Far East
ECE, Economic Commission for Europe
ECLA, Economic Commission for Latin America
ESC, Economic and Social Council
exec., executive
estab., established or establishment
FAO, Food and Agriculture Organization of the United Nations
Fund, International Monetary Fund
GA, General Assembly
GATT, General Agreement on Tariffs and Trade
IAEA, International Atomic Energy Agency
ICAO, International Civil Aviation Organization
ICITO, Interim Commission for ITO
ICJ, International Court of Justice

IFC, International Finance Corporation
ILC, International Law Commission
ILO, International Labour Organisation (Office)
IMCO, Inter-Governmental Maritime Consultative Organization
inf., information
int., international
ITO, International Trade Organization
ITU, International Telecommunication Union
NGO, non-governmental organization
NSGT, Non-Self-Governing Territories
org., organization
part., participation
pet., petition
prep., preparatory
prog., programme
provs., provisions
qn., question
recomm., recommendation
rel., relations
resol., resolution
rev., revision
SC, Security Council
SG, Secretary-General
sp., special
SSR, Soviet Socialist Republic
SUNFED, Special United Nations Fund for Economic Development
TA, technical assistance

TAA, Technical Assistance Administration
TAB, Technical Assistance Board
TAC, Technical Assistance Committee
TC, Trusteeship Council
UK, United Kingdom of Great Britain and Northern Ireland
UN, United Nations
UNCURK, United Nations Commission for the Unification and Rehabilitation of Korea
UNEF, United Nations Emergency Force
UNESCO, United Nations Educational, Scientific and Cultural Organization
UNICEF, United Nations Children's Fund
UNKRA, United Nations Korean Reconstruction Agency
UNREF, United Nations Refugee Emergency Fund
UNRWA, United Nations Relief and Works Agency for Palestine Refugees in the Near East
UNTSO, United Nations Truce Supervision Organization
UPU, Universal Postal Union
US, United States of America
USSR, Union of Soviet Socialist Republics
WFTU, World Federation of Trade Unions
WHO, World Health Organization
WMO, World Meteorological Organization

Index

Mejía, Gabriel A., 469
Mejía-Palacio, Jorge, 462, 466
Mekong River, lower, development project, 164, 179
Melas, George V., 540
Meléndez-Valle, Manuel, 469
Melgar Larrieu, Luis, 519
Meller-Conrad, Adam, 544
Mello, Linneu de Albuquerque, 509
Melo Lecaros, Luis, 539
Memon, Ghulam Nabi M., 509
Mena Solórzano, Luis, 541
Mencer, Gejza, 540
Mendels, M. M., 462
Mendès-France, Pierre, 461, 465, 469
Mendez, Mauro, 542
Mendoza Fleury, Lorenzo, 542
Mendoza López Alberto, 509, 539
Menemencioglu, T., 518, 541
Menichella, Donato, 461, 465
Menon, M. Gopala, 540
Menon, V. K. Krishna, 540, 546, 547
Mental health, WHO act., 449-50
Merani, S. T., 430
Meredith, Brian, 524
Merriam, Robert E., 507
Mersini, Jonus, 539
Mertens de Wilmars, J., 516
Messina Pimental, Temistocles, 509, 540
Mestiri, Mahmoud, 541
Métall, R. A., 543, 546, 547
Metcalfe, A. J., 453
Meteorology see World Meteorology Organization
Metzler, Ernst, 486
Mexico:
  admission to UN, date of, area, population, 505
  contribution to: Bank, 460; Expanded Prog. of TA, 163; FAO, 437; Fund, 469; ICAO, 475; IFC, 464; ILO, 430; ITU, 485; UN, 398; UNESCO, 444; UNICEF, 261; UNKRA, 95; UPU, 481; WHO, 453; WMO, 493
  GA General Debate, part. in, 532
  ICJ: acceptance of compulsory jurisdiction of, 522; party to Statute of, 522
  member of: Bank, 460; ECLA, 519; ESC, 515; ESC organs, 515-17, 519; FAO, 437; FAO Council, 437; Fund, 469; GA organs, 508, 510-14; ICAO, 475; ICAO Council, 475; IFC, 464; ILO, 430; ILO Governing Body, 431; ITU, 485; ITU Admin. Council,

486; UNESCO, 444; UPU, 481; WHO, 453; WMO, 493
  qn. of status of British Honduras, 289
  representatives on Bank Board of Governors, 461; ECLA, 519; ESC, 543, 544; ESC organs, 517; Fund Board of Governors, 469; GA organs, 510 512; GA 12th regular session, 541; IFC Board of Governors, 465; ILO Governing Body, 431
Meyer Joaquín E., 460, 465
Mézin, M., 494
Mezincescu, Edouard, 541
Michaels, M. I., 425
Michalowski, Jerzy, 515, 541, 543, 544
Michanek, Ernst, 431
Micheli, Dominique, 543
Michelmore, Laurence, 525
Midani, Sami, 509
Middle East: community development progs., 247; economic developments in, 122; see also Aqaba, Gulf of; Arabian Peninsula, communication on; southern part of; Palestine question; Suez Canal; United Nations Emergency Force; Syria, complaints about threats to security of, and international peace; Oman and Muscat
Middleton, G. H., 509
Miettinen, Unto, 540
Miettunen, Helge, 540
Migone, Raúl C., 431, 544
Migration: Conf. of NGO's Interested in, 251; social aspects of, 250-51; see also Intergovernmental Committee for European Migration
Migulin, Vladimir V., 425
Mikhailenko, Peter P., 517
Military Experts, Panel of: GA subsidiary body, 507; functions of, 510
Military Staff Committee: integration of, with Secretariat, 403-4, 409 (resol.); members and representatives, 514
Miljanic, Nikola, 470
Milk: conservation, UNICEF allocations for, 262; FAO-WHO act., 447; processing, 258; UNICEF act. on nutrition and, 260
Miller, R. M., 541, 547
Miller, Walter, 521
Min, Kwan Sik, 542
Mineral resources: conservation of non-agricultural resources and, 156; ECAFE act., 178; ex-

ploitation of, in Togoland under French administration, 346
Mining development: ILO study, 428; TA in, 156; UNKRA act., 91
Minorities, see Discrimination
Miranda Martins de Carvalho, Henrique, 541
Mirghani, Hamza, 461
Mirón, Gustavo, 469
Mironova, Mrs. Z. V., 542
Mishiro, Akio, 431
Missallati, Abdurrazak O., 540
Missiles, rockets and outer-space weapons, 3-4, 9, 11, 15, 20 (resol.)
Missing Persons, Conv. on Declaration of Death of, 378
Miyazaki, Akira, 540
Mladek, J. V., 471
Mo, Hsu, 532
Moch, Jules, 508, 540
Mod, Peter, 540, 543
Moe, Finn, 541
Moe, Sherwood G., 526
Mohamed V, King of Morocco, 532
Mohamed, Omar Mohallim, 547
Mokkadem, Sadok, 541
Molina, Armando, 542
Monaco:
  contribution to: Expanded Prog. of TA, 163; IAEA, 425; ITU, 485; UN, 400; UNESCO, 444; UNICEF, 261; UNKRA, 95; UNRWA, 43; UPU, 481; WHO, 453
  member of: IAEA, 425; ITU, 485; UNESCO, 444; UPU, 481; WHO, 453
  observer at GA 12th regular session, 542
Mondragón, Rubén, 519
Mongolian People's Republic: application for UN membership, 110; SC consid., 110-11; GA consid., 111-12
Monk, Albert E., 431
Monod, Noel, 523
Montealegre, Jorge A., 462, 466
Monteanu, R., 545
Monteiro, Julio Miguel, Jr., 541
Montero Bustamante, César, 542
Montero de Vargas, Pacífico, 541
Moore, Harvey, 547
Moore, P. E., 453
Moraes, R. Borba de, 524
Morales, Eusebio A., 541
Morales, Miss Irma, 539
Morales, Julio C., 541
Morales Guillén, Carlos, 509
Morelli, Augusto, 519
Moreno Córdova, Hugo, 519

GA General Debate, part. in, 532
GATT, contracting party to, 498
ICJ: acceptance of compulsory
  jurisdiction of, 522; party to
  Statute of, 522
ILO projects in, 427
member of: Bank, 460; ECAFE,
  518; ESC, 515; ESC organs,
  517-20; FAO, 437; Fund,
  470; GA organs, 509-13;
  IAEA, 425; IAEA Board of
  Governors, 425; IAEA Prep.
  Comm., 416; ICAO, 475;
  IFC, 464 ILO, 430; ILO
  Governing Body, 431; ITU,
  485; ITU Admin. Council,
  486; UNESCO, 444; UNI-
  CEF Exec. Board, 520; UPU,
  481; WHO, 453; WMO, 493
Meteorological Service of, 439
representatives on: Bank Board
  of Governors, 461; ECAFE,
  519; ESC, 543, 544; ESC
  organs, 517, 518; Fund Board
  of Governors, 470; GA organs,
  509, 512; GA 12th regular
  session, 541; IAEA Board of
  Governors, 425; IFC Board
  of Governors, 465; ILO Gov-
  erning Body, 431
UN Military Observer Group
  for India and, 515
UN Representative for India and
  Pakistan, 515
Pal, Radhabinod, 514
Palamarchuk, L. F., 541
Palamas, Christian X., 540, 543
Palestine question, 33-39
  Egyptian-Israel Armistice De-
    marcation Line, UNEF respon-
    sibilities re, 49
  General Armistice Agreements,
    complaints of violations of,
    33-39
  Jordan and Israel complaints re
    zone in area of Government
    House, Jerusalem, SC consid.,
    35-38, 38-39 (resol.)
  Mount Scopus, problem of, 38
  refugees, see below, UN Relief
    and Works Agency for Pales-
    tine Refugees in the Near East
  Syrian complaint re bridge in
    Demilitarized Zone, SC con-
    sid., 33-35
  UN Conciliation Comm. for
    Palestine: GA subsidiary
    cttee., 507; members, 509
  UNESCO emergency educational
    assistance for Palestine refugee
    children, 441
  UN Relief and Works Agency,
    for Palestine Refugees in the

Near East (UNRWA): Adv.
  Comm.: GA subsidiary body,
  507, representatives, 509; director, 509; financial situation, 39-41; GA subsidiary
  body, 507; Negotiating Cttee.
  for Extra-Budgetary Funds,
  report re pledges of contribution to, 402-03, 407-08
  (resol.); officers, 526; pledges
  of contributions, 42-43 (list);
  report on assistance to refugees, 39-43, 43-44 (resol.)
UN Truce Supervision Org.
  (UNTSO): Acting Chief of
  Staff: report on Jordan and
  Israel complaints re Zone in
  area of Government House,
  Jerusalem, 36-37, report on
  Syrian complaint re bridge in
  Demilitarized Zone, 33-35;
  Chief of Staff, 515
see also Aqaba, Gulf of; Suez
  Canal; United Nations Emer-
  gency Force
Palmaro, Marcel A., 542
Palthey, Georges M., 525
Panama:
  admission to UN, date of, area,
    population, 505
  contribution to: Bank, 460; Ex-
    panded Prog. of TA, 163;
    FAO, 437; Fund, 470; IFC,
    464; ILO, 430; ITU, 485;
    UN, 398; UNESCO, 444;
    UNICEF, 261; UNKRA, 95;
    UPU, 481; WHO, 453
  GA General Debate, part. in, 532
  ICJ: acceptance of compulsory
    jurisdiction of, 522; party to
    Statute of, 522
  member of: Bank, 460; ECLA,
    519; FAO, 437; Fund, 470;
    GA organs, 507, 514; IFC,
    464; ILO, 430; ITU, 485;
    SC, 514; UNESCO, 444;
    UPU, 481; WHO, 453
  representatives on: Bank Board
    of Governors, 461; ECLA,
    519; Fund Board of Gover-
    nors, 470; GA 12th regular
    session, 541; IFC Board of
    Governors, 465
Pandey, G. R., 541
Pane, Victor A., 462, 466
Panel for Inquiry and Conciliation,
  see Inquiry and Conciliation,
  Panel for
Panel of Military Experts, see
  Military Experts, Panel of
Panikkar, Shri Kavalam Madhava,
  509

Pan Pacific South-East Asia Wo-
  men's Association, 282, 546
Panya, Khamphan, 540
Panyarachun, Rak, 519
Pao, Hua-Kuo, 516
Paonan, Cheng, 516, 543
Paper, research on, in Latin Ameri-
  ca, 183
Papic, Augustin, 461
Papua, inf. transmitted re, 289
Paraguay:
  admission to UN, date of, area,
    population, 505
  contribution to: Bank, 460; Ex-
    panded Prog. of TA, 163;
    FAO, 437; Fund, 470; IAEA,
    425; ICAO, 475; IFC, 464;
    ILO, 430; ITU, 485; UN,
    398; UNESCO, 444; UNI-
    CEF, 261; UNKRA, 95;
    UPU, 481; WHO, 453;
    WMO, 493
  Fund acts., 467
  GA General Debate, part. in, 532
  ICJ: acceptance of compulsory
    jurisdiction, 522; party to
    Statute of, 522
  member of: Bank, 460; ECLA,
    519; FAO, 437; Fund, 470;
    GA organs, 506, 513-14;
    IAEA, 425; ICAO, 475; IFC,
    464; ILO, 430; ITU, 485;
    UNESCO, 444; UPU, 481;
    WHO, 453; WMO 493
  representatives on: Bank Board
    of Governors, 461; ECLA,
    519; Fund Board of Gover-
    nors, 470; GA 12th regular
    session, 541; IFC Board of
    Governors, 465
Paranagua, Octavio, 469, 470
Paraskevopoulos, Ioannis, 461, 465
Pareja Paz Soldan, José, 507, 541
Paret, Timoleon, 509
Parker, Cola G., 431
Parra, M., 481
Parra-Pérez, C., 444
Parreiras, Decio, 520
Parsons, M. H., 470
Passigli, Franco, 524
Passports, 193
Pastinen, Ilkka O., 543
Pastore, Giulio, 431
Pate, Maurice, 520, 525
Patel, H. M., 461, 465
Pathak, G. S., 540
Patriota, A. 510
Patteet, Herman, 545
Paukner, Zdenek, 543
Paul, Mrs. Raymonde I., 543
Pavlik, Pribyslav, 544
Paw Htin, 546, 547
Pax Romana, 282, 546

Staff of the UN (*cont.*)
regulations of Joint Staff Pension Fund, 387, 388-89 (*resols.*); definition of dependency, 382, 383 (*resol.*); dental costs insurance, 382; extension of general service category, 381; geographical distribution of, qn. of, 384, 384-85 (*resol.*); machinery for certain pay and personnel problems, 382; post adjustments for Geneva, 382-83, 383-84 (*resol.*); proportion of fixed-term posts for, 385-86; report on org. of secretariat at senior level, 386, 387 (*resol.*); review of regulations of, 385, 385 (*resol.*); Salary Review Cttee., report by, 381-84

Standard International Trade Classification, 190

Standenat, Heinz, 499

Stanovnik, Janez, 542, 544

Stashevsky, Gennady Stepanovich, 547

Stassen, Harold E., 508

Stathatos, Pierre C., 509

Statistical qns.: collection and dissemination of data, 190; Comm., 515, members, 516; Conf. of Asian Statisticians, 178, 189; Conf. of European Statisticians, 177, 189; ECAFE act., 180; ECLA Sub-Cttee. of Statistical Co-ordination, 190; health, WHO acts. on, 451; Philippine Statistical Centre, 190; publications, 189-90; social statistics, study of, 189; standards, application and development of, 188-90; *see also* Population

Status of Women, *see* Women, status of

Stavridi, V. J. G., 524

Stavropoulos, Constantin A., 523

Stedman, R. B., 525

Steel, *see* Iron and steel

Steenberghe, Maximilian Paul Leon, 509

Steriopol, Valentin, 518

Stetsenko, A. G., 524

Steyn, Daniel Hendrik, 470

Stoeger-Marenpach, Franz, 469

Storm, Gustavo F. A., 470

Stoyanov, Todor, 544

Straeng, G. E., 461, 465

Stratos, Andreas, 540

Strauss, Frederick, 524

Strong, Mrs. Kitty, 546

Strontium-90, 23-28 *passim*

Struye, Paul, 539

Suarez, Horacio, 539

Subandrio, Dr., 540

Sudan:
admission to UN, date of, area, population, 505
contribution to: Bank, 460; Expanded Prog. of TA, 163; FAO, 437; Fund, 470; ICAO, 475; ILO, 430; ITU, 485; UN, 398; UNESCO, 444; UNICEF, 261; UNRWA, 43; UPU, 481; WHO, 453; WMO, 493
FAO act., 433
GA General Debate, part. in, 532
ICJ, party to Statute of, 522
member of: Bank, 460; ESC, 515; FAO, 437; Fund, 470; ICAO, 475; ILO, 430; ITU, 485; TAC, 519; UNESCO, 444; UPU, 481; WHO, 453; WMO, 493
observer at ESC session, 544
representatives on: Bank Board of Governors, 461; Fund Board of Governors, 470; GA 12th regular session, 541

Sudjarwo, S., 425

Suez Canal: qn. of, 44-48, SC consid., 45-47, 48; clearance of, SG report, GA consid., 47, 48 (*resol.*)

Sultanov, Gani, 542

Sundaram, P. S. M., 486

Suomela, Pennti, 544

Surinam: contribution to WMO, 494; member of WMO, 494; *see also* Netherlands Antilles and Surinam

Sutcliffe, R. C., 494

Sutton, Sir Graham, 494

Svec, Karel, 544

Svento, Reinhold, 540

Svoboda, J. J., 486

Swaziland, inf. transmitted *re*, 289

Sweden:
admission to UN, date of, area, population, 505
case concerning guardianship of infant (Netherlands *vs.* Sweden), 364
contribution to: Bank, 460; Expanded Prog. of TA, 163; FAO, 437; Fund, 470; GATT, 498; IAEA, 425; ICAO, 475; IFC, 464; ILO, 430; ITU, 486; UN, 398; UNESCO, 444; UNICEF, 261; UNKRA, 95; UNRWA, 43; UPU, 481; WHO, 453; WMO, 493
GATT, contracting party to, 498
ICJ: acceptance of compulsory

jurisdiction of, 522; party to Statute of, 522
member of: Bank, 460; ECE, 518; ESC organs, 516, 517, 519, 520; FAO, 437; Fund, 470; GA organs, 508-11, 513-14; IAEA, 425; IAEA Board of Governors, 425; ICAO, 475; ICAO Council, 475; IFC, 464; ILO, 430; ILO Governing Body, 431; IMCO Prep. Cttee., 500; ITU, 486; SC, 514; UNESCO, 444; UNICEF Exec. Board, 520; UPU, 481; WHO, 453; WMO, 493
observer at ESC session, 544
representatives on: Bank Board of Governors, 461; ECE, 518; ESC organs, 516, 517; Fund Board of Governors, 470; GA organs, 508, 509; GA 12th regular session, 541; IAEA Board of Governors, 425; IFC Board of Governors, 465; ILO Governing Body, 431; SC, 542
UNEF, part. in, 508

Swenson, Louis, 524

Switzerland:
contribution to: Expanded Prog. of TA, 163; FAO, 437; IAEA, 425; ICAO, 475; ILO, 430; ITU, 486; UN, 400; UNESCO, 444; UNICEF, 261; UNKRA, 95; UNRWA, 43; UPU, 481; WHO, 453; WMO, 493
ICJ: acceptance of compulsory jurisdiction of, 522; party to Statute of, 522
Interhandel case (Switzerland *vs.* United States), 364-66
member of: ECE, 518; FAO, 437; IAEA, 425; ICAO, 475; ILO, 430; ILO Governing Body, 431; ITU, 486; ITU Admin. Council, 486; TAC, 519; UNESCO, 444; UNICEF Exec. Board, 520; UNREF, 510; UPU, 481; WHO, 453; WMO, 493
observer at: ESC session, 545; GA 12th regular session, 542
representatives on: ECE, 518; ESC organs, 518; IAEA Prep. Comm., 416; ILO Governing Body, 431

Symonds, J. R., 525

Syphilis control, UNICEF act., 257

Syria:
admission to UN, date of, area, population, 505

task of, 513; Field Service: budget for, 391, supplementary estimates for 1957, budget for, 395; IAEA, agreement between UN and, 28-29, 29-32 (*text*); IFC, agreement on relationship with, 463; member of TAB, 521; offer of office site in Santiago, Chile, 181, 403, 408-9 (*resol.*); organs of, rules of procedure for, 379-80; pattern of confs. 404, 410 (*resol.*); Postal Administration, 400; qn. relating to organs of, 115-19; roster, 504-5; sessions of, GA, the Councils, commissions and committees, budget, 391, sp. expenses of, 392; sp. meetings and confs., budget, 391; sp. missions and related acts.: budget, 391, supplementary estimates for 1957, budget for, 395; structure, 506-26; transfer of assets of League of Nations to UN, supplementary estimates for 1957, budget for, 396; *see also* Finances of the United Nations; Secretariat; Staff of the United Nations

United Nations Administrative Tribunal: Cttee. on Applications for Review of Admin. Tribunal Judgements: GA subsidiary body, 508, members, 513; GA subsidiary body, 508; members, 513; proposal to amend Statute of, 389-90

United Nations Appeal for Children, 261

United Nations Children's Fund (UNICEF):

acts, 257-63, ESC consid., 261, 262 (*resol.*), GA consid., 261, 262-63 (*resol.*); beneficiaries, 258; child nutrition, 260; dairy surveys prog., 434; disease control progs., 257, 258, 259-60, 352; emergency aid, 258; greeting cards, 261; int. collaboration and aid for NSGT's, 302; joint FAO/WHO/UNICEF prog. for development of protein-rich foods, 450; maternal and child welfare services, 258-59; NGO's, written statements from, 279; NGO's and national UNICEF cttees., 261; tuberculosis control, WHO/UNICEF project, 447; tuberculosis survey teams, staffed by WHO, 446; UNICEF/WHO Joint Committee on

Health Policy (JCHP), 259-60, 447, 520

admin., finances, co-ordination: Admin. and Budgetary Adv. Cttee., report, 401, 406 (*resol.*); Admin. Budget, Cttee. on, 520; allocations in 1957, 257, 262 (*table*); Board of Auditors report, 401, 406 (*resol.*); commitments for 1958-60, 257; emergency aid, 258; Exec. Board: Exec. Director, 520, members, 520; finances and fund raising, 260-61; GA subsidiary body, 507; liaison with FAO, 436; meetings with ACC, 521; officers, 520, 525; Prog. Cttee., 520; Public Relations and Fund Raising, Sub-Cttee. on, 520; subsidiary organs, 520

United Nations Commission for India and Pakistan (UNCIP), 80, 81

United Nations Commission for the Unification and Rehabilitation of Korea, *see under* Korean question

United Nations Educational, Scientific and Cultural Organization (UNESCO), 438-45

acts.: access of women to education, reports on, 225-26; Agreement on Importation of Educational, Scientific and Cultural Materials, 443; arid zone and humid tropics research, 439, 489-90; Arid Zone Research, Adv. Cttee. on, 439; community development progs., UN co-operation in regional centres for fundamental education, 247-48; Conv. for Protection of Cultural Property in Event of Armed Conflict, 442; co-operation with Scientific Cttee. on Effects of Atomic Radiation, 27; copyright royalties, 187; Coupon Scheme, 443; cultural acts., 442; discrimination in education, 209-10; easing of mail facilities, 477; educational act. of, 440-41; emergency educational assistance for UNRWA schools for Palestine refugee children, 441; eradication of illiteracy in NSGT's, report, 301; Expanded Prog. of TA, 170, 440; extension of primary education in Latin America, 439; fellowships prog., 440, 443;

Foreign Language Institute and Fundamental Educational Centre, transferred from UN-KRA, 92; human rights, report on promotion of, 206; Humid Tropics Research, Adv. Cttee. for, 441-42, 490; industrialization, projects on effects of, 443; Institute for Education, 440; isotopes: uses of, 434, Int. Conf. on Radio-Isotopes in Scientific Research, 439; marine sciences, 442; mass communication, 443; Mutual Appreciation of Eastern and Western Cultural Values, Adv. Cttee. on, 440; natural sciences, 441-42; new energy sources for economic development. 157-59, 159-60 (*resol.*); SGT's, assistance to, 302; promotion of int. co-operation in science, culture and education: ESC consid., 285, GA consid., 285-87, 87 (*resol.*); publications, 442, 443; social aspects of industrialization in Africa south of Sahara, report, 301; social sciences, 442-43; social statistics, 189; technical and vocational education conf., 440-41; UNESCO-ILO report on access of girls to vocational and technical training, 226; Universal Declaration of Human Rights, plans for celebration of 10th anniversary of, 218; UNKRA/UNESCO/Republic of Korea Fundamental Education Centre (Suwon), 93; water resources, 4th interagency meeting on, 156; world social situation report, 242

admin., finances, co-ordination: budget, 439, 443-44; co-ordinate prog. appraisals with ACC, 272-73; headquarters and other offices, 445; ICJ, authorized to request adv. opinions of, 523; member of: ACC, 520, TAB, 521; members and contributions, 444; officers and offices, 444; representatives at: ESC sessions, 543, 545, GA 12th regular session, 542, TC session, 546, 547

United Nations Emergency Force (UNEF): act.: SG reports *re*, 48-50, GA consid., 51, 52 (*resol.*); Adv. Cttee. for: GA subsidiary body, 507, members